Batsford Chess Openings 2

GARY KASPAROV
World Chess Champion

RAYMOND KEENE
International Grandmaster

Introductions: **Jonathan Tisdall**
International Master

Adviser: **Eric Schiller**
US Master

B.T. Batsford Ltd, *London*

First published 1982
Second edition 1989

© Gary Kasparov and Raymond Keene 1989

ISBN 0 7134 6099 7

A CIP catalogue record for this book
is available from the British Library

Photoset by Andek Printing, London
and printed in Great Britain by
The Bath Press, Bath
for the publishers
B.T.Batsford Ltd, 4 Fitzhardinge Street,
London W1H 0AH

A BATSFORD CHESS BOOK
Adviser: R.D.Keene GM, OBE
Technical Editor: Ian Kingston

Contents

Symbols

+	Check
± ∓	Slight advantage
± ∓	Clear advantage
+− ∓∓	Winning advantage
∞	With compensation
=	Level position
∞	Unclear position
!	Good move
!!	Outstanding move
!?	Interesting move
?!	Dubious move
?	Weak move
??	Blunder
corr.	Correspondence
Ol	Olympiad
Z	Zonal
IZ	Interzonal
C	Candidates
L	League
Ch	Championship
½f	Semi-final

Acknowledgments

We would like to thank Graham Hillyard, Adam Raoof, Jim Stayt, Ian White and Ian Kingston for their co-operation on this project, and Mark Huba for the cover photograph of Raymond Keene. Our thanks, too, to all those readers whose enthusiasm helped make the first edition of *BCO* such a success. Finally, we are grateful to Daniel Olim and Dennis Monokroussos for their helpful suggestions.

Gary Kasparov, Baku
Raymond Keene, London
February 1989

Opening Preparation at the Highest Level

Raymond Keene

The benefits of deep, precise and original openings research were cogently demonstrated by co-author Kasparov in the following game against his perennial rival, Anatoly Karpov, from their fourth game at the Amsterdam Tournament in 1988. Kasparov employed the new theoretical weapon 5 ♘g5 against Karpov's now favourite Caro-Kann Defence. Kasparov seized the initiative in the opening stages and Karpov was never fully able to recover. Such games, with hyper-accurate exploitation succeeding highly pointed openings preparation, propelled Kasparov to a world record-breaking performance in the Amsterdam event, where he scored six wins and six draws in a tournament whose strength was virtually Category 18!

Kasparov-Karpov
Caro-Kann Defence
Options Exchange Tournament,
Amsterdam 1988

1	e4	c6
2	d4	d5
3	♘d2	de
4	♘xe4	♘d7
5	♘g5!	

The new anti-Caro-Kann weapon, which Kasparov is helping to pioneer.

5	...	♘gf6
6	♗d3	e6
7	♘1f3	♗d6
8	0-0	h6
9	♘e4	♘xe4
10	♗xe4	0-0
11	c3	e5
12	♗c2	♖e8
13	♖e1	ed
14	♖xe8+	♕xe8

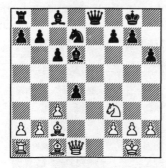

Kasparov is not averse to exchanges and

evidently has no desire to repeat the wild speculations of his win against Karpov in their second game from Amsterdam.

15	♕xd4	♕e7
16	♗f4	♗xf4
17	♕xf4	♘f8
18	♖e1	♗e6
19	♘d4	♖d8
20	h4	♕c5
21	♖e3	♕d6
22	♘xe6	fe

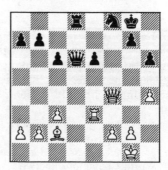

Under severe pressure Karpov commits what, in the highest sense, can be construed as the decisive error. Black should strive at all costs to avoid weaknesses in his pawn structure, and hence 22 ... ♘xe6 is to be preferred.

23	♕g4	♕d2
24	♗b3	♔h8

If Black snaps at the bait with 24 ... ♕xb2 then 25 ♖g3 ♕b1+ 26 ♔h2 ♕h7 27 ♗c2 g6 28 h5 gives White a winning attack.

25	♖e2	♕d6

26	g3	a6
27	♔g2	♖e8
28	♖e3	♖e7
29	♖f3	♖d7
30	♕h5	♕e7
31	♕e5	♖d8
32	a4	b5
33	♕e4	♕c7
34	♖f4	c5
35	♕f3	♕d6
36	ab	ab
37	♖f7	♖b8
38	♖a7	b4

Now that Kasparov has infiltrated Black's lines of defence, Karpov's pawn weaknesses begin to tell against him.

39	♗c2	bc
40	bc	♕e5
41	♖f7	♘h7

42	♕g4	♔g8
43	♖e7	♘f8
44	♕f3	c4
45	♗e4	♔h8
46	♗c6	♘h7
47	♕f7	♘f8
48	♖e8	♖xe8
49	♗xe8	♘h7
50	♗d7	♘f6
51	♗xe6	h5
52	♗xc4	♕e4+

This counter-attack is ultimately proven to be hopeless. If, however, 52 ... ♕xc3 53 ♕f8+ ♔h7 54 ♕c5 dominating the centre and threatening ♗g8+. In this case an endgame remarkably similar to that of game 24 from the 1987 world championship match in Seville would arise. Black's prospects of survival would be minimal.

53	♔h2	♔h7
54	♕e6	♕f3
55	♕e1	♘g4+
56	♔g1	♕c6
57	♗d3+	g6
58	♕e7+	♔h6
59	♗e4	♕b6
60	♕f8+	♔h7
61	♕f7+	♔h6
62	c4	♕a6
63	c5	

Karpov **resigned** and Kasparov rushed back to Moscow to attend a party thrown by President Reagan at the US Ambassador's residence.

The main arena of recent K-K openings conflict has been the "Seville Variation" of the Grünfeld, introduced by Karpov in game 5 of the 1987 world championship match. Neither side has so far renounced its willingness to play the variation, and at the time of writing Karpov leads the 'series' 2-1, with several draws. We are presenting *BCO 2*'s coverage of this fascinating and highly contemporary line by annotating Kasparov's win in game 11 at Seville.

Karpov-Kasparov
Grünfeld Defence, Seville Variation
World Championship 1987

1	d4	♘f6
2	c4	g6
3	♘c3	d5
4	cd	♘xd5
5	e4	♘xc3
6	bc	♗g7
7	♗c4	c5
8	♘e2	♘c6
9	♗e3	0-0
10	0-0	♗g4
11	f3	♘a5

This line of the Exchange Grünfeld had been played for years, yet nobody had taken seriously the fact that White could not only win a pawn but also disrupt Black's kingside by hurling his bishop at f7.

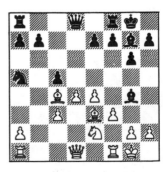

| 12 | ♗xf7+ | ♖xf7 |

13	fg	♖xf1+
14	♔xf1	♕d6

In game 9 Kasparov tried what was, perhaps, his least successful treatment of the whole line. Black exchanged prematurely on d4 and this gave White the chance to exploit the unprotected e6 square, no longer defended by a pawn on f7. That game went 14 ... cd 15 cd ♕b6 16 ♔g1 ♕e6 17 ♕d3! (clinging to the pawn with 17 ♘g3 would transpose to previously known theory and give Black no problems) 17 ... ♕xg4 18 ♖f1 ♖c8 19 h3 ♕d7 20 d5 ♘c4 21 ♗d4 e5 22 de ♕xe6 23 ♗xg7 ♔xg7 24 ♘f4 ♕d6 25 ♕c3+ ♔h6 and now Karpov could have won with 26 ♘d3!! threatening both 27 ♖f7 and the murderous ♘f2-g4. Instead Karpov speedily played the natural, but inferior, 26 ♘d5, after which he could only draw.

Portisch-Korchnoi, Reykjavik 1988, varied with 14 ... ♕c8 15 ♕a4 cd 16 cd ♘c4 17 ♗f4 a6 18 g5 b5 19 ♕b3 e5 20 de ♕c6 21 ♖d1 ♖f8.

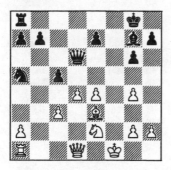

15 ♔g1

The most frequently seen continuation in Karpov-Kasparov games has been 15 e5 ♕d5 16 ♗f2 ♖d8 (16 ... ♖f8 17 ♔g1 ♗h6 18 h4 ♕f7 19 ♗g3 ♗e3+ 20 ♔h2 ♕c4 was the stem game 5 at Seville. Karpov eventually won, but through a time-trouble blunder. 16 ... ♖f8 has not been refuted.) and now:

a) 17 ♕e1 ♕e4 18 g5 ♕f5 19 h4 ♘c4 20 ♔g1 ♕g4 21 a4 h6 was the highly complicated continuation of game 7 at Seville.

b) 17 ♕c2 ♕c4 18 ♕b2 ♗h6 was fine for Black in the third Karpov-Kasparov game at Amsterdam 1988.

c) 17 ♕a4 b6 (17 ... ♘c4 or 17 ... ♖f8 is probably better. After the latter a plausible variation is 18 ♔g1 ♕f7 19 ♗e3 ♘c4 or even 18 ... ♗h6 19 ♕xa5 ♕f7 20 ♖f1 - *not 20 ♗g3 ♗e3+ 21 ♔h1 ♕f1+* - 20 ... ♗e3 21 ♕xc5 ♗xf2+ 22 ♔h1 ♗xd4 23 ♖xf7 ♗xc5 24 ♖xf8+ ♔xf8, when the ending looks like a draw as White's extra pawn is unimpressive) 18 ♕c2 ♖f8 (Rejecting 18 ... ♕c4, which would be exactly the same as 'b' above except that Black has gained the move ... b6. On

the whole this extra move seems to be a disadvantage, since it represents a weakening of Black's entire queenside pawn chain) 19 ♔g1 ♕c4 20 ♕d2 ♕e6 21 h3 ♘c4 22 ♕g5 h6 23 ♕c1 ♕f7 24 ♗g3 with a large advantage to White in Karpov-Kasparov, Belfort 1988 (1-0, 38).

15 ... ♕e6

Not only with the thought of capturing on g4 but with the deeper positional intention of occupying the weak c4 square.

16	♕d3	♕c4!
17	♕xc4+	♘xc4
18	♗f2	

Keeping the bishop in touch with the sensitive d4 pawn. If 18 ♗c1 cd 19 cd e5 20 d5 ♗f8 21 ♗g5 h6 22 ♗f6 ♗c5+ 23 ♔h1 ♖f8 24 g5 ♗e3 25 ♗e7 ♖f7 26 d6 ♗xg5, undermining the support of the passed d-pawn. It is important to note the role of the move ... e5 in Black's counterplay. It cedes White a passed d-pawn and also blocks the a1-h8 diagonal, but it has the virtue of establishing a choice of two other key diagonals for Black's bishop, c1-h6 and a3-f8.

18	...	cd
19	cd	e5

A further plus to ... e5 is the setting up of d6 as a base for the black knight.

20 d5 ♗h6

The bishop promptly seizes the important diagonal and Karpov takes countermeasures to shut it out of play.

21 h4 ♗d2

Necessary, before White shuts the bolt with g5.

22 ♖d1

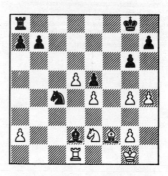

With ♖d1 White is toying with such ideas as ♘c1 and perhaps the tactical shot d6. In fact, neither of these is dangerous and Black should now have played the consistent and strong 22 ... b5!. If 23 ♘c1 then 23 ... a5 24 ♘b3 ♗b4 followed by the advance of Black's queenside majority. In comparison with this asset White's extra pawn, doubled and on the other wing, is irrelevant. Dorfman claimed that Black is at least equal after 22 ... b5!.

Similarly, if 22 ... b5 23 d6 then 23 ... a5 followed by ... ♖d8 and Black will simply round up the white d-pawn, which has wandered too far beyond its own lines of communication.

22	...	♗a5?
23	♖c1	b5
24	♖c2	♘d6
25	♘g3	♘c4
26	♘f1	♘d6
27	♘g3	♘c4
28	g5	

Karpov quite rightly elects to continue the struggle rather than accede to a draw by repetition. The text is an excellent choice that set Kasparov thinking for 38 minutes. The point is that White nails down f6 as a future point for invasion, especially by a knight travelling via f1-h2-g4.

28	...	♔f7

Black's position is exceedingly difficult.

29	♘f1	♘d6
30	♘g3	♘c4
31	♔f1	

Again Karpov rejects the draw and sets off with his king towards d3, its optimum post.

31	...	♔e7
32	♗c5+	♔f7
33	♖f2+	♔g7
34	♖f6	

Georgadze's suggestion 34 h5 may have been stronger.

34	...	♗b6

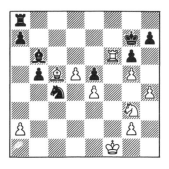

35	♖c6??	

Perhaps the worst move of Karpov's world championship career.

35	...	♘a5
36	♗xb6	♘xc6
37	♗c7	♖f8+
38	♔e2	♖f7
39	♗d6	♖d7
40	♗c5	♘a5
41	♘f1	♖c7
42	♗d6	♖c2+
43	♔d3	♖xa2
44	♘e3	♔f7
45	♘g4	♘c4
46	♘xe5+	♘xe5+
47	♗xe5	b4
48	♗f6	b3
49	e5	♖xg2
50	e6+	♔f8

White resigns

Introduction

This book was conceived to fill a gap in the extensive list of Batsford chess publications. Batsford had already published the five-volume *Encyclopaedia of Chess Openings*, but our feeling was that both the price and the complexity of these highly specialized technical volumes were soaring beyond the reach and the needs of the average player. Accordingly, we attempted to create a single, inexpensive volume, covering all openings to a depth that will be adequate for all social, club, postal and county players, plus competitors in weekend tournaments, especially junior players. The latter may indeed perceive this light-weight compendium as a particular boon when assembling their weekend luggage. The compression required to pack coverage of all openings into some 400 pages may render our book's utility more problematic for masters and grandmasters on the international circuit, but we hope that the new suggestions and our selection of material may be helpful even for this exalted class of player.

The key points of this book are as follows:

● Co-operation by an expert international team from the USSR, England and USA.
● All openings are covered.
● Ease of reference. All notes connected to the rows of main moves appear on one and the same double-spread, thus avoiding all that tedious juggling with separate pages to find the right note which one associates with so many other reference books.
● Strategic introductions, ideas and historical background to each opening.
● The material is very up to date. This second edition has been revised up to January 1989.
● All moves appear in FIDE-approved international figurine algebraic notation.

Our choice of material and methods of presentation have been massively endorsed by the chess public, who have made the first edition of *BCO* a runaway international bestseller. We are confident that the extensive new material and original research in the second edition will maintain the standards of excellence that *BCO I* established.

Gary Kasparov, Ray Keene

Unusual Openings (1 b4; 1 g4; 1 ♘c3; 1 g3)

Under this heading comes a collection of infrequently essayed first moves. In general, they have been shunned because they are more committal and have less central influence than more orthodox debuts.

1 b4 Sokolsky's Opening, or the Orangutan as it was dubbed by Polish GM Tartakower after a visit to the zoo during the New York 1924 international tournament. Too eccentric to achieve popularity, it is restricted to sporadic appearances in the hands of maverick players.

1 g4 Grob's Attack, now championed by England's free spirit Michael Basman, has considerable psychological impact but does little to improve the White position. Black does well to develop sensibly.

1 ♘c3 The Dunst Opening has been employed of late by Mestrović, Sahović and Bellon. It is obscure and unambitious.

1 g3 Benko's Opening is the most reputable of the bunch, and first received attention when Benko used it to defeat Tal and Fischer in succession at the 1962 Candidates tournament in Curaçao. Extremely flexible, it keeps the option of transposing into more common positions or using certain defensive formations with an extra tempo. Larsen and Miles have also unleashed the move at the grandmaster level with considerable success.

Reference: *Unorthodox Openings* (Benjamin and Schiller)

	1	2	3	4	5	6	7	8	9	
1	g4[1]	♗g2	h3[4]	d4[6]	c4	♘c3	g5	h4	♗h3	∓
	d5[2]	c6[3]	e5[5]	e4	♗d6[7]	♘e7	♗e6	♘f5	0-0[8]	

[1] Grob

[2] 1 ... e5 2 d3 (2 ♗g2 h5 3 gh ♕g5 4 ♗f3 ♕h4 5 ♘c3 ♘f6 6 e4 ♗c5 ∓ Skembris-Mariotti, Budva 1981) 2 ... d5 (2 ... h5 3 g5) 3 ♗g2 ♘c6 4 h3 ♘ge7 ∓ Larsen

[3] 2 ... ♗xg4 3 c4 c6 4 cd cd 5 ♕b3 ±
2 ... e5 3 h3 (3 c4!?) 3 ... ♘c6 (3 ... c5 4 e3 ♘c6 5 ♘e2 ♗e6 6 ♘g3 ♗d6 7 d3 ♕d7 8 ♘c3 ♘ge7 9 ♘h5 0-0 ∞ Barua-Hug, Dhaka 1985) 4 c4 dc 5 ♕a4 (5 b3 ♗e6 6 bc ♗c5 7 ♘c3 ♘ge7 8 ♘f3 ♘g6 9 d3 0-0 ∞ Basman-Whitehead, Manchester 1981) 5 ... ♘e7 6 ♘f3 ♘g6 7 ♘c3 ♗e6 8 h4 ♗b4 9 ♘g5 ♗d7 10 ♗d5 0-0 ∞ Basman-Miles, Manchester 1981

[4] 3 g5 h6 4 h4 hg 5 hg ♖xh1 6 ♗xh1 ♕d6 7 ♘f3 ♗g4 ∓
3 e4!? de 4 ♘c3 ♘f6 5 h3 ∞ Skembris

[5] 3 ... h5 4 g5 h4 (4 ... e5 5 d4 e4 6 ♘c3 ∞ Skembris) 5 e4 de 6 ♘c3 ♕a5 7 ♘xe4 ♗f5 8 ♘c3 e6 9 ♗e4 ♘d7 10 ♕e2 ∞ Skembris-Gheorghiu, Skopje 1984

[6] 4 e4 ♘e7 5 d3 (5 d4!?) 5 ... ♘g6 6 ed ♘h4 7 ♔f1 ♘xg2 8 ♔xg2 cd ∓ Grob-Richards, corr. 1965

[7] 5 ... ♘a6 6 ♘c3 ♘c7 7 f3 f5 8 cd cd 9 ♕b3 ♗d6 10 ♔f1 ♘e7 ∓ Basman-King, Brighton 1984

[8] Basman-Keene, Manchester 1981

1

	1	2	3	4	5	6	7	8	9	
2	g3[9]	♗g2[11]	c4[13]	♕a4+	♕xc4	♘f3	0-0	b3	♕c2	=
	e5[10]	d5[12]	dc[14]	♗d7[15]	♗c6	♘d7	♗d6	♘b6	♘f6[16]	
3	♘c3	e4[18]	♘ce2	♗g3[21]	♘f3[22]	♗b5+	♗a4	♗b3	♗xe6	=
	d5[17]	d4[19]	e5[20]	♗e6	f6	c6[23]	♘d7	♘c5	♘xe6[24]	
4	b4[25]	e3[27]	♗b2[29]	♘f3[30]	c4	a3	♗e2	d3	0-0	∞
	c6[26]	d5[28]	♘f6	♘bd7	e6[31]	♗d6	e5	0-0	♕e7[32]	
5	...	♗b2	e3	♘f3[35]	c4[36]	c5	♘d4	♖xb1		=
	d5	♘f6[33]	♗f5[34]	e6	♘bd7[37]	♗e7	♗xb1	c6[38]		
6	...	♗b2[39]	b5[41]	e3	d4[43]	♘d2[45]	a4	c4	♘h3	∞
	e5	f6[40]	d5	♗e6[42]	e4[44]	c6	♗d6	f5	♘f6[46]	
7	...	...	♗xe5	c4[47]	e3[49]	cd[50]	♘f3	♗b2[52]		∞
		♗xb4	♘f6	0-0[48]	d5	♘xd5[51]	♖e8	♗f5[53]		

[9] Benko-Bilek-Barczay Opening

[10] **1 ... d5** 2 ♗g2 c6 (2 ... g6 3 c4 dc 4 ♘a3 ♗g7 5 ♘xc4 ♘d7 6 ♘f3 ♘gf6 7 0-0-0-0 8 d3 ±; 2 ... ♘f6 3 d3 c5 4 ♘d2 ♘c6 5 e3 e5 = Fostel-Pfleger, West Germany 1981) 3 d3 ♘f6 4 ♘d2 e5 5 e4 ♗c5 6 ♘gf3 ♘bd7 7 0-0 0-0 = Bilek-Geller, Havana 1971

1 ... g6 2 ♗g2 ♗g7 3 ♘c3 (3 e4 e5 4 ♘e2 ♘e7 5 0-0 0-0 6 d4 ed 7 ♘xd4 d5 = Forintos-Lengyel, Kecskemet 1972) 3 ... e5 (3 ... c5) 4 d3 ♘e7 (4 ... ♘f6 5 f4 ef 6 ♗xf4 d5 =) 5 f4 ef 6 ♗xf4 d5 7 ♘f3 0-0 8 0-0 d4 9 ♘e4 ♘d5 = Larsen-Sloth, Copenhagen 1965

[11] **2 ♘f3** e4 3 ♘d4 d5 4 d3 ed 5 ♕xd3 ♘f6 6 ♗g2 ♗b4+ 7 ♗d2 = Reti-Alekhine, Baden-Baden 1925

2 d3 d5 3 ♘f3 ♘c6 4 ♗g2 ♘f6 5 0-0 ♗e7 6 c3 0-0 7 ♕c2 (7 ♘bd2 ♖e8 8 ♕c2 ♗e6 9 b4 ♘d7 10 b5 ♘a5 ∞ Dzindzihashvili-Korchnoi, Tilburg 1985) 7 ... ♗f5 8 ♘bd2 ♕d7 (8 ... e4!?) 9 e4 ♗h3 10 ♖e1 ♗xg2 11 ♔xg2 ♖fe8 ∞ Dzindzihashvili-Ljubojević, Tilburg 1985

[12] **2 ... ♘f6** (2 ... f5 3 ♘f3 ♘c6 4 d4 e4 5 ♘g5 d5 6 0-0 h6 7 ♘h3 g5 ∞ Andersson-Tringov, Havana Ol 1966) 3 ♘f3 e4 4 ♘d4 c5 ∞

[13] **3 d3** c6 (3 ... ♘c6 =; 3 ... ♘f6 4 ♗g5 ♗e7 5 ♘c3 d4 6 ♗xf6 ♗xf6 7 ♘e4 ♗e7 = Dorfman-Ubilava, USSR 1981) 4 ♘f3 ♘d7 5 0-0 ♗d6 6 ♘c3 ♘e7 7 e4 d4 8 ♘e2 h6 ∞ Tal-Christiansen, Lone Pine 1981

3 ♘f3 ♘c6 4 0-0 e4! 5 ♘e1 f5 6 d3 ♗e6 7 c4 dc 8 ♘c3 ♘f6 9 ♗g5 cd 10 ed ♗e7! ∓ Hartston-Miles, British Ch 1982

[14] **3 ... c6** – 1 c4

3 ... d4 4 d3 ♘f6 5 ♘f3 ♘c6 – 1 ♘f3 d5 2 c4 d4

[15] **4 ... c6** 5 ♕xc4 ♘f6 6 ♘f3 ♗d6 7 ♘c3 ±

4 ... ♘d7 5 ♕xc4 ♘gf6 6 ♘f3 ♗d6 7 0-0 0-0 8 d3 ♕e7 9 ♘bd2 ♖e8 10 b3 ± Bilek-Andersson, Stockholm 1970-71

[16] **10 ♗b2** ♕e7 11 d3 0-0 12 ♘bd2 ♖fe8 = Barczay-Kluger, Hungarian Ch 1958

[17] **1 ... c5** 2 ♘f3 (2 d4 cd 3 ♕xd4 ♘c6 4 ♕h4 g6 5 ♗d2 ♗g7 ∓) and now:

2 ... d5 3 d4 cd 4 ♕xd4 ♘f6 5 e4 ♘c6 6 ♗b5 ♗d7 7 ♗xc6 ♗xc6 = Ermenkov-Ghinda, Prague 1985

2 ... ♘c6 3 d4 cd 4 ♘xd4 ♘f6 (4 ... g6 5 ♗g5 ♗g7 6 ♘db5 ♘f6 7 ♘d5 ± Welling-Flamion, 1983) 5 ♗g5 e6 6 ♗xf6 gf 7 e3 d5 = van Geet-Balashov, Beverwijk 1965

1 ... e5 2 ♘f3 (2 d4 ed 3 ♕xd4 ♘c6 4 ♕a4 d5 5 e4 de 6 ♗b5 ♗d7 7 ♘d5!? Schlenker-Wenk, 1985) 2 ... ♘c6 3 d4 ed 4 ♘xd4 ♘f6! (4 ... ♘xd4 5 ♕xd4 ♕f6 6 ♕a4 c6 7 h4! ± van Geet-Taksroud, corr. 1984) =

[18] **2 d4** – 1 d4

2 ♘f3 ♘f6 =

[19] **2 ... de** 3 ♘xe4 e5 4 ♘f3 (4 ♗c4!?) 4 ... ♘f6 5 ♘c3 (5 ♘xf6+ ♕xf6 6 d3 ♗d6 =) 5 ... ♗g4 6 ♗e2 ♘c6 7 d3 ♗b4 8 ♗g5 0-0 = Eising-Capelan, Solingen 1968. 3 ... ♗f5!? 4 ♕f3 ♕d5 ∞/=

[20] **3 ... d3?!** 4 cd e5 5 d4 ed 6 d3 ♘c6 7 ♘f3 ♗g4 8 ♘f4 ⊥

[21] **4 ♘f3!?** ♘d7 (4 ... ♗d6 5 ♘g3 ♗e6 =) 5 d3 c5 6 c4 b5!? 7 cb ♕a5+ ∓

4 d3 c5 5 f4 ♘c6 6 ♘f3 ♗d6 =

[22] **5 d3** ♘c6 6 a3 g6 7 f4 ef 8 ♗xf4 ♗d6 9 ♕d2 ♕e7 =

5 c3 c5 6 ♗b5+ ♘d7 7 ♕h5 ♗d6 8 ♘f5 ♗xf5 9 ♕xf5 ♘e7 = van Geet-Pirc, Amsterdam 1964

[23] 6 ... ♘c6 7 c3 dc 8 bc ± Larsen

[24] 10 d3 g6 11 0-0 ♕d7 = Figueroa-Marcussi, Argentina 1963

[25] Sokolsky Opening

[26] 1 ... f5!? 2 ♗b2 ♘f6 3 e3 (3 f4 e6 4 a3 b6 5 ♘f3 ♗b7 6 e3 ♗e7 =; 3 c4 e6 4 a3 ♗e7 5 ♘f3 0-0 6 g3 d5 = Perez-Najdorf, Mar del Plata 1961) 3 ... e6 4 b5 ♗e7 5 c4 0-0 6 ♘f3 d5 7 d4 ♕e8 8 ♗e2 ♘bd7 = Schaufelberger-Bhend, Lugano 1970

1 ... a5 2 b5 ♘f6 (2 ... e5 3 ♗b2 d6 =) 3 ♗b2 d6 4 e3 g6 5 d4 ♗g7 6 ♘f3 0-0 7 c4 c5 8 ♘c3 cd 9 ed ♕c7 = Sokolsky-Luik, USSR 1957

1 ... ♘f6 2 ♗b2 e6 (2 ... g6 3 e3 ♗g7 4 ♘f3 0-0 5 c4 d6 6 d4 e6 7 ♘c3 ♕e7 8 ♗e2 e5 9 0-0 e4 = Sunder-Korchnoi, West Germany 1985) 3 b5 b6 4 e3 ♗b7 5 ♘f3 ♗e7 (5 ... c5!?) 6 ♗e2 0-0 7 0-0 d5! 8 d3 c5 9 ♘bd2 ♘bd7 = Miles-Ribli, London 1984

[27] 2 ♗b2 a5! (2 ... ♕b6 3 a3 a5 4 c4 ab 5 c5 ± Katalimov) 3 a3 ab 4 ab ♖xa1 5 ♗xa1 ♕b6 ∓

2 c4 d5 (2 ... ♕b6 3 ♗b2 ♘f6 4 e3 ♗a6 5 a3 g6 6 ♗g2 ♗g7 7 ♘f3 ± Pecherik-Short, London 1975) 3 e3 e5 4 ♗b2 ♗d6 5 ♘f3 = Hort

[28] 2 ... b5 3 a4 ♗b7 4 ♘f3 a6 5 c4 bc 6 ♗xc4 e6 7 ♕b3 ±

2 ... ♕b6 3 a3 a5 4 b5! cb 5 ♘c3 b4 6 ab ♕xb4 7 ♗a3 ± Rudenkov-Stugach, USSR 1961

[29] 3 a4!? Myers

[30] 4 c4 ♗g4 5 ♕b3 e6 6 h3 ♗h5 7 ♘e2 dc 8 ♕xc4 ♘d5 = Miralles-van der Wiel, Montpellier C 1985

[31] 5 ... dc!? 6 ♗xc4 e6 ∞

[32] Miralles-Urzica, Bucharest 1984

[33] 2 ... ♕d6 (Andersson) 3 a3 (3 b5 ♕b4 4 ♗e5!? Tisdall) 3 ... e5 4 ♘f3 (4 e3 ♘f6 5 d3 ♘bd7 6 ♘f3 c6 = Lalić-Uhlmann, Sarajevo 1980) 4 ... e4 5 ♘d4 ♘c6 6 c4! dc 7 e3 ± Sokolsky

2 ... ♗g4!? 3 c4 e6 4 ♕b3 ♘f6 5 e3 ♘bd7 6 ♘f3 c6 7 d4 a5 = Rubinetti-R.Garcia, Buenos Aires 1973

[34] 3 ... e6 4 b5 (4 a3 ♗d6 5 f4 ♘bd7 6 ♘f3 ∞; 4 ... a5!? 5 b5 c5 =) 4 ... ♗e7 5 ♘f3 0-0 6 c4 c5 7 ♗e2 ♘bd7 8 a4 ♗d6 9 0-0 e5 = Flesch-Lengyel, Budapest 1963

[35] 4 ♗d3 ♗xd3 5 cd ♘bd7 6 g4?! h6 7 h4 e5 ∓ Gutman-Lee, London 1985

4 f4 e6 5 b5 c5 6 ♘f3 ♘bd7 7 ♗e2 ♗d6 8 0-0 0-0 =

[36] 5 a3 ♗d6 6 c4 c6 7 ♗e2 ♘bd7 8 0-0 ♕e7 =

[37] 5 ... a5 6 b5 ♘bd7 7 cd ed 8 ♘d4 ♗g6 9 f4! ∞ Sokolsky

[38] Katalimov-Litvinov, USSR 1971

[39] 2 b5 d5 3 ♗b2 ♗d6 4 ♘f3 ♕e7 5 e3 ♗g4 6 ♗e2 ♘d7 ∞ Whitehead-Temmink, corr.

1984

2 ... a3!? a5 (2 ... d5 3 e3 ♘f6 4 ♗b2 ♗d6 5 c4 c6 6 ♘f3 ♗g4 7 ♕b3 ∞ Basman-Scheffer, Biel 1979) 3 ♗b2 e4 4 c4 ♘f6 5 ♕b3 ♘a6! = Forgac-Forintos, Hungary 1981

[40] 2 ... d5 3 ♗xe5 ♘c6 4 ♗b2 ♘xb4 5 a3 ♘c6 6 e3 ♘f6 7 ♘f3 ♗e7 8 c4 ♗g4! = Yudovich

2 ... d6 3 c4 f5 4 e3 ♘f6 5 ♘f3 a5 6 b5 g6 =

[41] 3 e4!? c6 (3 ... ♗xb4 4 ♗c4 ♘e7 5 ♕h5 ♘g6 6 f4 ef 7 ♘f3!? ± Fischer-Cloger, USA 1964) 4 f4 (4 ♗xe5!? fe 5 ♕h5+ g6 6 ♕xe5 ♕e7 7 ♕xh8 ♘f6 =; 5 ... ♔e7 ∞) 4 ... ef 5 ♘h3 ♕e7 6 ♗d3 d5 7 ♘xf4 de 8 0-0 ♕xb4 9 ♗xe4!? ∞

[42] 4 ... c5 5 d4 ed 6 ed c4 7 ♘c3 ♗e6 8 ♘h3 ♗d6 9 ♕f3 ∞

4 ... ♗d6!? 5 c4 c6 =

[43] 5 c4 dc 6 ♕c2 c6 7 ♗xc4 ♗xc4 8 ♕xc4 cb =

[44] 5 ... ♗d7 6 de fe 7 ♘f3 ♗d6 8 ♘bd2 ♘gf6 9 c4 ± Sokolsky

5 ... ed 6 ♕xd4 ♘e7 7 ♗e2 c5 8 ♕d2 ♘g6 ∞ Balendo-Katayev, USSR 1978

[45] 6 c4 dc 7 ♘d2 ♗b4 8 ♖c1 a6 9 ♗xc4 ♗xc4 10 ♖xc4 ∞ Sokolsky

[46] 10 ♕b3 0-0 11 ♗a3 ∞ Sokolsky

[47] 4 ♘f3 ♘c6 5 ♗b2 d5 6 g3?! 0-0 7 ♗g2 ♖e8 8 0-0 ♗f5 ∓ Dumpov-Ghitescu, Biel 1986

4 e3 0-0 (4 ... ♘c6!? Soltis) 5 a3 (5 ♘f3 ♖e8 6 c3 ♗f8 7 ♕a4 c5 ∞ Klarić-Diždarević, Sarajevo 1981) 5 ... ♗e7! 6 c4 d5 7 ♘c3 ♗e6 8 ♕b3 ♘c6 9 ♗xf6 ♗xf6 ∞/= Diner-Widenmann, corr. 1985

[48] 4 ... ♘c6 5 ♗b2 0-0 6 e3 d5 7 ♘f3 ♖e8 8 cd ♘xd5 (8 ... ♕xd5 9 ♗e2 ♗f5 10 a3 ♗a5 11 0-0 ♖ad8 12 d4 ♘e4 13 ♕c1! ± Miralles-Spiridonov, Bourgas 1985) 9 a3 ♗a5!? 10 ♗e2 ♗g4 11 0-0 ♕e7 =

[49] 5 ♘f3 d5 (5 ... ♘c6 6 ♗b2 d5 7 cd ♘xd5 8 g3 =; 5 ... ♖e8!?) 6 cd (6 e3 ♗e7 7 ♗e2 c5 8 ♗b2 ♘c6 9 cd ♘xd5 10 0-0 ♗f6 ∓ Urzica-Adorjan, Sweden 1970) 6 ... ♘xd5 7 g3 =

[50] 6 ♘f3 ♘c6 (6 ... c5 7 cd ♘xd5 8 ♗e2 ♘c6 9 ♗b2 ♗g4 = Miralles-Gulko, Marseilles 1986) 7 ♗b2 ♖e8 8 cd ♘xd5 9 ♗e2 ♖xe3!? 10 fe ♘xe3 11 ♕b3 ♘xg2+ 12 ♔f2 ♗h3! ∞ Fran-Lefler, corr. 1986

[51] 6 ... ♕xd5 7 ♗xf6 gf 8 ♘e2 ♖d8 9 ♘bc3 ♕e5 10 ♖c1 ♘c6 11 ♘g3 ♗e6 ∞ Teichmann-McKay, London 1985

[52] 8 ♗e2? ♖xe5! 9 ♗xe5 ♕f6 ∓ Groszpeter-Lukacs, Kecskemet 1979

[53] 8 ... ♘f4?! 9 ♘e5! ♘c6 10 ef f6 11 ♗b5! ± Sachler-Beutler, corr. 1981

8 ... ♗g4!?

8 ... ♗f5 9 ♕b3 ∞

Nimzowitsch-Larsen Attack

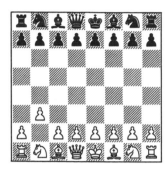

1 b3 was tried by Nimzowitsch in the 1920s but had to wait another 40 years before Bent Larsen made it really respectable. In common with most other flank openings White's idea is to control the centre by indirect means and avoid committing his central pawns too early. White's reticence allows Black to equalize in a number of ways. His most ambitious counter is 1 ... e5, which leads to an unbalanced position with equal chances.

Reference: *The Nimzowitsch/Larsen Attack* (Keene)

	1	2	3	4	5	6	7	8	9	
1	b3	Bb2[2]	e3	Nf3	Be2[4]	0-0	d3	Nbd2	a3[5]	=
	c5[1]	Nc6[3]	Nf6	g6	Bg7	b6	Bb7	e6	Qe7[6]	
2	...	Bb2	e3	Bb5[9]	f4	Bxc6+	Nf3	0-0	d3	∞
	d5	c5[7]	Nc6[8]	Qc7[10]	a6	Qxc6	Nf6	g6	Bg7[11]	
3	...	Bb2	e4[12]	g3[14]	Bg2	Ne2	0-0	Re1	a4	=
	Nf6	g6	d6[13]	Bg7	0-0	e5[15]	Re8[16]	c5	Nc6[17]	
4	...	Bb2	e3[19]	Bb5[21]	f4[23]	g3	Nf3[25]	h3[27]	Qxf3	∞
	e5	Nc6[18]	d5[20]	Bd6[22]	Qh4+[24]	Qe7	Bg4[26]	Bxf3	Nf6[28]	
5	...	...	c4	e3[30]	cd	a3[33]	Qc2	Nf3	Bd3[36]	∞
	...	...	Nf6[29]	d5[31]	Nxd5[32]	Bd6[34]	0-0[35]	Qe7	Kh8[37]	

[1] 1 ... b6 2 ♗b2 ♗b7 3 e3 f5 4 ♗e2 ♘f6 5 ♗xf6 ef 6 ♗f3 ♘c6 7 ♘e2 ± Larsen-Bellon, Palma de Mallorca 1971
1 ... b5 2 e3 ♗b7 3 ♘f3 (3 ♗b2 e6 4 f4 ♘f6 5 ♘f3 b4 6 ♗e2 ♗e7 = Pritchard-Basman, British Ch 1972) 3 ... a6 4 ♗b2 e6 5 c4 b4 6 d4 ♘f6 7 ♘bd2 ♗e7 8 ♗d3 0-0 9 ♕c2 ± Larsen-Menvielle, Las Palmas 1972
1 ... f5 2 ♗b2 ♘f6 3 f4 – 1 f4

[2] 2 c4 b6 3 ♗b2 ♗b7 4 ♘f3 ♘f6 5 e3 e6 = Petrosian-Saidy, San Antonio 1972

[3] 2 ... ♘f6 3 c4 d6 4 g3 ♘c6 5 ♗g2 g6 6 ♗xf6 ef 7 ♘c3 h5! = Keene-Bellon, Montilla 1974

[4] 5 ♗xf6 ef 6 ♗e2 ♗g7 7 0-0 ∞

[5] 9 ♘e4 d5 10 ♘xf6+ ♗xf6 11 ♗xf6 ♕xf6 12 d4 =

[6] Andersson-Keene, Montilla 1974

[7] 2 ... ♘d7 3 e3 e5 4 c4 ± Larsen
2 ... ♘f6 3 e3 (3 d3 c5 4 ♘d2 ♘c6 5 e4 d4 6 h3 e5 7 a4 ♗e7 ∓ Lubislavlević-Boutteville, Val Thorens 1985) 3 ... c6 4 ♘f3 ♗g4 5 ♗e2 ♘bd7 6 0-0 ♗xf3 7 ♗xf3 e5 ∞ B.Stein-Johansen, London 1985
2 ... ♗g4 3 h3 ♗h5 4 ♘f3 (4 d3 e6 5 ♘d2 ♘f6 6 ♘gf3 ♘bd7 7 e3 a5 = Nikolac-Kovačević, Maribor 1980) 4 ... ♘d7 5 e3 c6 6 d3 e6 = Larsen

[8] 3 ... f6 4 e4!? de 5 ♕h5+ g6 6 ♕xe5 Keene

[9] 4 f4 d4 5 ♗b5 ∞; 4 ♘f3 ± – 1 ♘f3

[10] 4 ... a6 5 ♗xc6+ bc 6 d3 ♘h6 7 ♘c3 e5 8 e4 ± Larsen-Dominguez, Las Palmas 1972
4 ... ♗d7 5 f4 ♘f6 6 ♘f3 e6 7 0-0 ♗e7 8 a4 0-0 9 ♗xc6 ♗xc6 10 ♘e5 ± Zaitsev-Klovans, USSR Ch 1967
4 ... ♕b6 5 a4 a6 6 ♗e2 e5!? Bellon

[11] 10 ♘bd2 0-0 11 ♕e1 b5 12 ♕h4 ♘g4 ∞ Spiridonov-Mandov, Bulgaria 1974

[12] 3 g4!? h6 (3 ... ♗g7 4 g5 ♘h5 5 ♗xg7 ♘xg7 6 ♕c1 0-0 7 ♕b2 d6! = Soltis) 4 ♗g2 d5 5 h3 ♗g7 6 d3 c5 7 ♘d2 = Krnić

[13] 3 ... ♗g7 4 e5 ♘d5 5 ♘f3 ±

[14] 4 ♕e2 ♗g7 5 d4 c5 6 dc ♕a5+ Larsen

[15] 6 ... c5 7 d4 (7 0-0 e5! = – 6 ... e5) 7 ... ♘bd7 8 0-0 ♖b8 9 a4 b6 =

[16] 7 ... ♗h5 8 d4 ♘d7 (8 ... ♘c6 9 ♘a3! ±) 9 ♘d2 ♕e7 10 f4 ed 11 ♗xd4 ± Bagirov-K.Grigorian, USSR 1976
7 ... ♘c6 8 d4 (8 c4 ♘d7!?) 8 ... ed 9 ♘xd4 ♖e8 =

[17] 10 ♘a3 ♗e6 (Bellon-Polugayevsky, Palma de Mallorca 1972) 11 d3 = Larsen

[18] 2 ... d6 3 g3 (3 e3!? ♘c6 4 ♗b5 a6 5 ♗xc6+ bc 6 f4 ef 7 ♕f3 d5 8 ♕xf4 ± Schneider-Ghinda, Kiel 1979) 3 ... ♘f6 (3 ... g6 4 d4 ♗g7 5 de ♗xe5 6 ♘c3 ♘c6 7 ♘f3 ♗g7 8 ♗g2 ♘f6 9 ♘d4 ± Larsen-Hort, Monte Carlo 1968) 4 ♗g2 g6 5 c4 (5 d4 e4) 5 ... ♗g7 6 ♘f3 0-0 7 ♘c3 c6 8 0-0 ±

[19] 3 ♘f3 e4 4 ♘d4 ♕f6!? (4 ... ♘xd4 5 ♗xd4 ♘f6 6 e3 d5 7 c4 ∞ Welling-de Roos, Strasbourg 1982) 5 e3 ♗c5 6 ♘b5 ♕xb2 7 ♘1c3 ♘b4 8 ♖b1 ♕xc2 9 ♘xc7+ ♔d8 10 ♕h5! ♘xa2! = Welling-van der Sterren, Hilversum 1985

[20] 3 ... g6 4 d4 ed 5 ♘f3 ♗g7 6 ♘xd4 ♘f6 7 ♘xc6 bc 8 ♗e2 0-0 9 ♘d2 ± Bellon-Ljubojević, Palma de Mallorca 1972
3 ... ♘f6 4 ♗b5 d6 (4 ... ♕e7 5 ♘e2 g6 6 f4 ef 7 ♘xf4 ♘e5 8 0-0 ♗g7 9 ♗a3 ± Chandler-Popović, Groningen 1976-77) 5 ♘e2 ♗d7 6 d4 ed 7 ♘xd4 ♘xd4 8 ♗xd7+ ♕xd7 9 ♕xd4 ♗e7 = Ljubojević-Unzicker, Milan 1975
3 ... d6 4 ♗b5 ♗d7 5 ♘c3 a6 6 ♗xc6 ♗xc6 7 ♘f3 ♗e7 8 ♕e2 ♘g6 ∞ Groszpeter-Portisch, Hungary 1985-86

[21] 4 ♘f3 e4 5 ♘d4 ♘xd4 6 ♗xd4 ♗f5 7 d3 ♘f6 =

[22] 4 ... f6 5 d4 e4 6 ♘e2 a6 7 ♗xc6+ bc 8 c4 f5 9 ♕c2! ± Larsen

[23] 5 ♘c3 ♘f6 6 d4 0-0 7 de ♘xe5 ∓ Chandler-Botterill, Haifa Ol 1976
5 ♘f3 f6 (5 ... ♕e7 6 d4! e4 7 ♘e5 ∞) 6 c4 a6 7 cd ab 8 dc bc 9 ♕c2 ♘e7 = Keene

[24] 5 ... f6 6 ♕h5+ g6 7 ♕h4 ef 8 ♘f3! ♔f7 9 0-0 ♘ce7 10 g4! ∞

[25] 7 ♘c3?! ♘f6 8 ♕f3 0-0 9 ♗xc6+ bc 10 ♘ce2 a5! ∓ Wolf-Hardicsay, Boblingen 1985

[26] 7 ... f6?! 8 ♕e2 ♗g4 9 h3 ♗h5 10 g4 ♗f7 11 ♗xc6+ bc 12 ♕a6 ± Keene-Martin, Alicante 1977

[27] 8 fe ♗xe5 9 ♗xe5 ♗xf3 10 ♕xf3 ♕xe5 11 ♘c3 ♘f6 = Ljubojević-Portisch, Teesside 1972

[28] 10 ♘c3 0-0 11 ♗xc6 bc 12 ♘e2 ∞

[29] 3 ... f5 4 e3 ♘f6 5 ♘f3 d6 6 ♗e2 ♗e7 7 0-0 0-0 8 d4 e4 9 ♘g5 ±
3 ... g6 4 g3 ♗g7 5 ♗g2 d6 6 e3 ♘h6 (6 ... ♘ge7 =) 7 ♘e2 0-0 8 ♘bc3 f5 = Flesch-Suttles, Sombor 1970

[30] 4 ♘f3 e4 5 ♘d4 ♗c5 ∓ Larsen-Spassky, Belgrade 1970
4 ♘c3 d5 5 cd ♘xd5 6 ♘f3 ♘xc3 7 ♗xc3 ♗d6 8 d3 0-0 9 e3 ♕e7 10 ♗e2 ♗d7 ∞ Korchnoi-Gipslis, USSR 1976

[31] 4 ... g6 5 ♘f3 d6 6 d4 ♗g7 7 de ♘d7!? ± Ivkov
4 ... ♗e7 5 a3 0-0 6 ♕c2 ♖e8 7 d3 ♗f8 8 ♘f3 a5 9 ♗e2 ± Fischer-Andersson, Sweden (radio game) 1970

[32] 5 ... ♕xd5?! 6 ♘c3 ♕d7 7 a3 ♗e7 8 ♕c2 0-0 9 ♘f3 ± Smyslov-Grigorian, USSR Ch 1971

[33] 6 ♘f3 ♗d6 7 d3 0-0 8 a3 ♕e7 9 ♕c2 ∓ Larsen
6 ♘c3 ♗b4 7 ♕c2 ∞

[34] 6 ... a5!? 7 ♕c2 ♗d6 8 ♘f3 ♕e7 9 d3 0-0 10 ♘bd2 ♗d7 ∞ B.Stein-Kruszynski, Copenhagen 1986

[35] 7 ... ♗e6!? 8 ♘f3 0-0 9 b4 a6 10 ♗c4 ♗xb4!? 11 ♗xd5 ♕xd5 ∞ B.Stein-Chandler, London 1985

[36] 9 ♘c3 ♘xc3 10 ♕xc3 f5 11 ♗b5 e4 ∞ Larsen-Spassky, Leiden 1970

[37] 10 ♗e4 ♗e6 (10 ... ♘b6?! 11 ♗xc6! bc 12 d3 ± Petrosian-Balashov, USSR 1978) ∞ Larsen

Bird's Opening

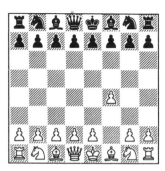

1 f4 was popularized by the English master Henry Bird in the latter half of the last century, but its history goes back a millennium earlier. The strategic ideas of Bird's Opening, in particular control of e5, are similar to those in the more popular Dutch Defence (1 d4 f5). White's extra tempo is not enough to counterbalance the fact that 1 f4 is a basically innocuous move. The From Gambit 1 f4 e5 is periodically 'refuted' but at present looks good enough for dynamic equality. White also has the option of transposing into the King's Gambit by 2 e4.

	Bird's Opening	1 f4							
	1	2	3	4	5	6	7	8	9
1	f4	♘f3[2]	e3[4]	♗e2[5]	0-0[6]	b3[8]	c3	♕e1	d3	∞
	♘f6[1]	g6[3]	♗g7	0-0	d6[7]	♘e4	c5	♘c6	♘f6[9]	
2	...	fe[10]	ed[11]	♘f3[12]	g3[14]	♗g2	d3	♘c3[17]	♗g5	∞/±
	e5	d6	♗xd6	♘f6[13]	♘c6[15]	♗g4	♗c5[16]	a6	h6[18]	
3	...	♘f3[19]	e3[21]	♗e2[23]	0-0	d3[25]	♕e1[27]	♕h4[29]	♘bd2	=
	d5	♘f6[20]	g6[22]	♗g7	0-0[24]	c5[26]	♘c6[28]	b6[30]	♗a6[31]	

[1] 1 ... Nc6 2 g3 g6 3 Bg2 Bg7 4 d3 d6 5 Nf3 e5 6 fe de 7 e4 Nge7 8 0-0 0-0 = Lutikov-Gligorić, Sarajevo 1969
1 ... c5 and now:
2 Nf3 Nc6 3 e3 g6 4 Bb5 Bg7 5 0-0 Nf6 6 d3 0-0 7 Bxc6 bc 8 c4 d6 =
2 b3!? Nf6 3 Bb2 b6 4 Nf3 Bb7 5 e3. e6 6 g3!? (6 Be2 Be7 7 0-0 0-0 8 a4 Nc6 9 Na3 d5 10 Qe1 a6 11 Qg3 ± Pliester-Pik, Deeren 1986) 6 ... Be7 7 Bg2 0-0 8 Qe2 Qc7 9 0-0 a6 10 d3 b5 11 Nbd2 ± Bellin-Ivell, British Ch 1985
1 ... f5 2 Nf3 Nf6 3 b3 b6 4 Bb2 Bb7 5 Bxf6 ef 6 e3 Be7 7 Nc3 g6 = Larsen-M.Colon, San Juan 1969

[2] 2 b3 b6 (2 ... g6 3 Bb2 Bg7 4 Nf3 0-0 5 e3 d6 6 Qc1 Nc6 =) 3 Bb2 Bb7 4 e3 g6 5 Nf3 Bg7 6 Be2 0-0 7 0-0 c5 = Ljubojević-Keene, Orense 1975

[3] 2 ... d6 3 e3 Bg4 4 d4 Nbd7 5 Be2 g6 6 c4 Bg7 7 Nc3 ±

[4] 3 b4 Bg7 4 Bb2 0-0 5 e3 d6 6 Na3 e5 7 fe Ng4 ∞ Ivkov-D.Byrne, Vršac 1969
3 g3 Bg7 4 Bg2 0-0 5 c4 d6 6 Nc3 c6 7 0-0 d5 8 cd cd 9 e3 Nc6 = Basman-Tal, Hastings 1973-74

[5] 4 d4 c5 5 Bd3 0-0 6 c3 d6 7 0-0 b6 ∞

[6] 5 c4 d6 6 Nc3 Nbd7 7 d4 e5 8 fe de 9 0-0 Qe7 ∓ Leow-Grünberg, Groningen 1976-77

[7] 5 ... c5 6 Qe1 Nc6 7 d3 d6 8 Qh4 Bd7 9 Nc3 Re8 ∞

[8] 6 Qe1!? O'Kelly

[9] 10 e4 b5 11 Bb2 a5 12 a4 ba 13 Rxa4 Nd7 ∞ Bisguier-Mednis, USA 1973

[10] 2 d3 Nc6 3 Nf3 ef 4 Bxf4 d5 5 Nbd2 Nf6 6 e4 de 7 Nxe4 Nxe4 8 de Qf6 9 Qc1!? ∞ O'Kelly

[11] 3 Nf3 de (3 ... g5 4 e4 g4 5 Bc4 gf 6 Qxf3 ±) 4 e4 Bc5 (4 ... Nc6 5 Bb5 Bc5 6 Qe2 Nf6 7 Nxe5 0-0 ∞) 5 Bc4 Nf6 6 Qe2 Nc6?! 7 Bxf7+ Kf8 8 Bb3 Nd4 9 Qxd4 Qxd4 ∞ Bellin-Watson, British Ch 1985

[12] 4 g3 h5! 5 Bg2 h4 ∓

[13] 4 ... g5 5 g3 (5 d4 g4 6 Ne5 =) 5 ... g4 6 Nh4 Ne7 7 d4 (7 e4 ∞ Muhana-Estrin, corr. 1985) 7 ... Ng6 8 Nxg6! (8 Ng2 Nc6 9 c3 h5 10 e4 h4 11 e5 Be7 ∞) 8 ... hg 9 Qd3 Nc6 10 c3 Qe7 11 Bg2 Bf5 12 e4 0-0 13 Be3 (13 0-0 Ne5! ∓ Panchenko) ± Pliester

[14] 5 d4 Ng4 6 Qd3 c5 (6 ... 0-0 7 e4 c5 ∞) 7 Nc3 Nc6 8 dc Bxc5 9 Qxd8+ Kxd8 10 Ne4 Bb6 =. 7 Qe4+ Be6 8 Ng5 ∞ O'Kelly

[15] 5 ... h5?! 6 d4! Ne4 (6 ... h4 7 gh Ne4 8 Qd3 Bf5 9 Qh3! ±) 7 Qd3! Qe7 8 Nc3 Bf5 9 Qh3!

[16] 7 ... 0-0 8 0-0 Nh5 9 c3 ±
7 ... Qe7 8 Bg5 0-0-0 9 Nbd2 ±

[17] 8 c3!?

[18] 10 Bxf6 Qxf6 11 Qd2 0-0-0 12 Rf1 Rhe8 13 e4 ∞/±

[19] 2 b3?! Bg4! 3 Bb2 Nc6 4 g3 e5! (4 ... f6 ∓) 5 fe f6 6 Bh3 Bxh3 7 ef Nxf6 8 Nxh3 Bc5 ∓ Kupreichik-Yusupov, Erevan Z 1982
2 g3 h5!? 3 Nf3 h4 4 Nxh4 Rxh4 5 gh e5 6 d3 Bc5 ∞ Rewitz-Bang, Denmark 1986
2 e3 Nf6 3 b3 d4 4 Bc4!? de 5 Nf3 ed+ 6 Nbxd2 e6 7 Qe2 ∞∞

[20] 2 ... Nc6 3 e3 g6 4 Bb5 Bg7 5 0-0 Nh6 ∞
2 ... Bg4 3 Ne5 (3 e3 Nd7 4 Be2 e6 5 0-0 Bd6 6 c4 Nf6! = Parma) 3 ... Bf5 4 c4 dc 5 Na3 Nd7 6 Naxc4 e6 = Henley-Martz, Lone Pine 1977
2 ... g6 3 g3 (3 e3 Bg7 4 Be2 Nd7!? 5 d3 e5) 3 ... Bg7 4 Bg2 c6 5 d3 Nh6 6 e4 de 7 de Qxd1+ 8 Kxd1 Na6 = Hübner-Taimanov, Leningrad IZ 1973

[21] 3 d3 g6 4 Nbd2 d4 5 c3 dc 6 bc Nd5 7 Qa4+ Nc6 8 Ne5 Bg7 ∞ Larsen-Fischer, Copenhagen 1962
3 g3 g6 (3 ... c5 4 Bg2 Nc6 5 d3 g6 6 0-0 Bg7 7 Qe1 0-0 8 e4 d4 9 de ∞ Knežević-Danner, Oberwart 1986) 4 Bg2 Bg7 5 0-0 0-0 6 d3 c5 (6 ... b6 7 Ne5 Bb7 8 c4 e6 8 Nc3 Nbd7 Armas-van Mil, Tatabanja 1985) 7 c3 Nc6 8 Kh1 b6 9 Na3 Bb7 10 Nc2 Qd7 = Volovich-D.Gurevich, Somerset (USA) 1986

[22] 3 ... c5 4 b3 Nc6 5 Bb5 ± Euwe
3 ... Bg4 4 b3 (4 Be2 Nbd7 5 Ne5 Bxe2 6 Qxe2 e6 7 0-0 Bd6 = Parma; 6 ... g6 =) 4 ... Nbd7 5 Bb2 c6 6 Be2 Qc7 7 0-0 Bxf3 8 Bxf3 e5 = Romanishin-Kasparov, USSR 1976

[23] 4 b4 Bg7 5 Bb2 0-0 6 Be2 Bg4 7 0-0 c6 = Larsen-Spassky, Amsterdam IZ 1964
4 b3 Bg7 5 Bb2 0-0 6 Be2 Nbd7 (6 ... c5 7 0-0 Nc6 8 Ne5 Nd7 9 d3 Ne8 = Botvinnik) 7 0-0 b6 8 Qe1 e6 9 d3 Bb7 10 Nbd2 c5 = Sax-Farago, Hungarian Ch 1977

[24] 5 ... c5 6 d3 Nc6 7 Qe1 Qc7 8 Qh4 ∞

[25] 6 d4 c5! 7 c3 b6 8 Qe1 Nc6 9 Kh1 Ne4 10 Nbd2 d6 ∓
6 Ne5 Nbd7 7 Bf3 Nxe5 8 fe Ne4 ∓ Gusev-Geller, USSR 1970

[26] 6 ... b5!? 7 Qe1 Bb7 8 a4 c6 9 Qh4 e6 =
6 ... Nc6 7 Qe1 Re8 8 d4 Bf5 9 c4 e6 10 Ne5 ∞ Pelikan-Shocron, Argentina 1955

[27] 7 Ne5 Nfd7 (7 ... Nbd7) =

[28] 7 ... b6!? 8 Qh4 e6 9 Nbd2 Bb7 =

[29] 8 a4 b6 9 Nbd2 Qc7! 10 Qh4 e5 ∓ A.Zaitsev-Zuchovitsky, USSR 1969

[30] 8 ... Bg4 9 Nc3 Bxf3 10 Bxf3 e5 =

[31] 10 Ne5 Nxe5 11 fe Nd7 12 e6 fe 13 Nf3 e5 14 e4 = Larsen-Benko, Portorož IZ 1958

1 ♘f3; Reti; KI Attack

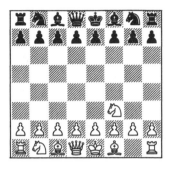 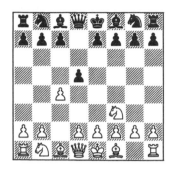 

Brainchild of the hypermodern movement, the Reti attempts to control and influence the centre from a distance. It avoids immediate theoretical debate and postpones the conflict, a slow positional development of the struggle being the customary result. Because of its shy personality the game can tend toward Black systems with an extra move, and the reversed Benoni and King's Indian Attack make up significant portions of the opening's theory. Another frequent choice is the Neo-Catalan, where White delays or omits entirely the advance d4.

Although indirect, this opening still maintains good chances of a small but tangible plus and should appeal to those who prefer a non-theoretical struggle.

The King's Indian Attack is distinguished by White's playing ♘f3, g3 and ♗g2 virtually irrespective of Black's reply. A secondary feature is that White's central build-up tends to be based on pawns at d3 and e4. A significant advantage is flexibility, and it is ideal for players who can vary systems and want to keep their opponents guessing as to middlegame intentions.

	1 ♘f3									
	1	2	3	4	5	6	7	8	9	
1	♘f3	e4[2]	♗xb5	0-0	d4	c4[3]	♘c3	d5	♗a4	±
	b5[1]	♗b7	♗xe4	♘f6	e6	♗e7[4]	♗b7	0-0	♗b4[5]	
2	...	e4[6]	♘g5	d3[8]	♗xe3	g3[10]	♗g2	c4	♕a4	∞
	f5	fe	e5[7]	e3	♘c6[9]	♘f6	d5[11]	dc	♗d7[12]	
3	...	g3[13]	♗g2	d3[16]	0-0	e4[18]	c3[19]	♘bd2[21]	a4	∞
	c5	♘c6[14]	g6[15]	♗g7	e5[17]	♘ge7	d6[20]	0-0	h6[22]	
4	...	...	...	...	...	e4[23]	c3[24]	♘bd2[25]	a4	=
	...	...	...	...	♘f6	d6	0-0	♖b8[26]	a6[27]	

[1] **1 ... d6!?** intending ... ♗g4
  1 ... b6 2 c4 ♗b7 3 ♘c3 e6 4 e4! ♗b4
5 ♕c2 ±
  1 ... g6!? 2 g3 ♗g7 3 ♗g2 e5 4 0-0 (4 d4 e4 =)
4 ... ♘c6 5 e4 ♘ge7 6 d3 0-0 ∞ Pliester-Nunn,
Lugano 1984

[2] **2 g3** e6 3 ♗g2 (3 a4 b4 4 b3 ♗b7 5 ♗g2 ±)
3 ... ♗b7 4 0-0 ♘f6 5 d3 d6 6 e4 ♘bd7 7 ♘bd2 ±
Vladimirov-Novopashin, USSR 1981
  2 e3 a6 3 d4 (3 a4 b4 4 d4 e6 5 ♗d3 c5 6 c3
d5 =) 3 ... ♗b7 4 c4 (4 ♗d3!?) 4 ... bc 5 ♗xc4
♘f6 6 ♘c3 e6 7 0-0 ±
  2 c3!? e6 3 g3 ♗b7 4 ♗g2 ♘f6 5 0-0 ♗e7
6 d3 d6 7 a4! ± Korchnoi-Hodgson, Brussels 1985

[3] 6 ♗e2 ♗e7 7 c4 ♗b7 8 ♘c3 0-0 9 h3 d6
10 ♗e3 ♘bd7 11 b4 ± Szekely-Psakhis, Tallinn
1983

[4] 6 ... c5 7 ♘c3 ♗b7 8 d5 ±

[5] 9 ... ♘a6 10 ♖e1 ♗b4 11 ♗g5 ♘c5 12 ♗c2 ±
Eingorn-Semenyuk, Kiev 1984
  9 ... ♗b4 10 ♗g5 ♗xc3 11 bc h6 12 ♗h4 ±
Speelman-Hodgson, London 1985

[6] **2 d3** d6! 3 e4 e5 4 ♘c3 ♘f6 5 ♗e2 ♗e7
6 0-0 0-0 = Romanishin
  2 g3 ♘f6 (2 ... b6 3 ♗g2 ♗b7 4 0-0 ♘f6
5 d3 e6 6 e4 fe 7 ♘g5 ±) 3 ♗g2 g6 (3 ... e6 4 b3!?
Romanishin) 4 d3 ♗g7 5 ♘bd2 d6 6 0-0 0-0
7 e4 ± Csom-Lukacs, Hungarian Ch 1971

[7] 3 ... ♘f6 4 d3 e3 (4 ... ed?! 5 ♗xd3 g6 6 h4
e6 7 h5 ± Dorfman-Villareal, Mexico 1977;
4 ... e5 5 de ♘c6 5 ♗c4 ♕e7 7 ♗xf7+ Botvinnik;
4 ... d5 5 de h6 6 ♘f3 de 7 ♕xd8+ ♔xd8 8 ♘e5
♗e6 9 ♘c3 ±) 5 ♗xe3 (5 fe e5 6 e4 ♘f6 7 ed
♕xd5 8 ♘c3 ♗b4 ∞ Katayev-Malanyuk, USSR
1984) 5 ... e5 (5 ... e6 6 d4 ♗e7 7 ♗d3 0-0 8 c3
♘c6 9 ♕c2 ±) 6 d4 ♘c6 (6 ... d5 7 de ♘g4
8 ♕e2 ♗e7 9 ♘f3 ♘c6 10 h3 ± Botvinnik) 7 d5
♘e7 8 ♘c3 d6 9 ♗c4 ♗f5 10 f3 ± Romanishin

[8] 7 ♘xe4 ♘c6 (4 ... ♘f6) 5 ♗g5 ♘f6 6 ♘bc3
♗e7 7 ♘xf6+ ♗xf6 8 ♗c4 (Dorfman-Menvielle,
Cienfuegos 1977) 8 ... ♘a5 ∞

[9] 5 ... ♗e7 6 h4 ♘f6 7 d4 ed 8 ♗xd4 ♘c6
9 ♘c3 ±

[10] 6 ♕h5+ g6 7 ♕f3 ♕f6 ∓
  6 ♗e2 d5 7 0-0 ♗e7 8 ♘f3 d4 ∓ Vladimirov-
Mikadze, USSR 1974
  6 c4!? Botvinnik

[11] 7 ... ♗e7 8 0-0 0-0 9 c4 d6 10 ♘c3 ±
Romanishin

[12] 10 ♕xc4 ♕e7 ∞

[13] **2 e3** g6 3 d4 ♗g7 4 dc ♕a5+ 5 ♘bd2 ♕xc5
6 ♗e2 d6 =
  2 b3 ♘c6 (2 ... ♘f6 3 ♗b2 ♘c6 4 e3 e6
5 ♗b5 ±) 3 ♗b2 d6 4 d4 (4 g3 e5 5 ♗g2 f5 6 0-0
♗e7 7 c4 ♘f6 = Simagin-Stein, USSR Ch 1965)
4 ... cd 5 ♘xd4 ♘f6 6 g3 ♘xd4 (6 ... e5 7 ♘xc6

bc 8 ♗g2 ♕c7 9 0-0 ±) 7 ♗xd4 ♗d7 8 ♗g2
♘c6 = Ribli-Csom, Kecskemet 1972

[14] **2 ... b6** 3 ♗g2 ♗b7 4 0-0 ♘f6 5 d3 g6 (5 ... e6
6 e4 d6 7 ♖e1 ♗e7 8 ♘c3 0-0 9 b3 ± Romanishin-
Vogt, Polanica Zdroj 1980) 6 e4 d6 (6 ... ♗g7?!
7 e5! ♘d5 8 ♖e1 0-0 9 d4! ± Vaganian-van der
Wiel, Plovdiv 1983) 7 ♘bd2 ♗g7 8 a4 0-0
9 ♘c4 ±
  2 ... g6 3 ♗g2 ♗g7 and now:
  4 c3 ♘c6 5 d4 cd 6 cd d5 7 ♘c3 e6 8 ♗f4
♘ge7 = Miles-Sosonko, Tilburg 1981
  4 d4 cd 5 ♘xd4 ♘c6 6 c4 ♘f6 7 0-0 0-0
8 e4 ♕c7 ∞
  4 0-0 ♘c6 5 c3 e5 6 d4 cd (6 ... ed 7 cd ♘xd4
8 ♘xd4 cd 9 ♘a3 ∞) 7 cd e4!? 8 ♘e5 d5 9 ♘xc6
bc 10 ♘c3 ♗e7 11 ♘a4 ♘f5 ∞ Cvitan-Lerner,
Polanica Zdroj 1985

[15] 3 ... e5 4 d3 ♘f6 5 e4 d6 6 0-0 ♗e7 =

[16] 4 d4 cd 5 ♘xd4 ♗g7 =

[17] 5 ... e6 6 e4 ♘ge7 7 ♖e1 (7 c3 e5 8 a3 a5 9 a4
0-0 10 ♘a3 d6 ∞ Hort-Knaak, Halle 1978)
7 ... d6 (7 ... 0-0 8 e5 b6 9 ♘bd2 d6 10 ed ♕xd6
11 ♘c4 ♕d8 = Ivkov-Ree, Nice Ol 1974) 8 c3 0-0
9 d4 (9 ♘a3 e5 10 ♗e3 b6 =) 9 ... cd 10 cd ♕b6!
∞ Ljubojević-Hübner, Buenos Aires Ol 1978

[18] 6 c3 ♘ge7 7 a3 a5 = Planinc-Parma,
Yugoslav Ch 1972

[19] 7 ♘c3 – 1 e4 c5 2 ♘c3
  7 h4 d6 8 ♘g5?! h6 9 ♘h3 ♗e6 ∓ Quinteros-
Portisch, Mar del Plata 1982

[20] 7 ... d5 – 1 ♘f3 d5 2 g3 c5

[21] 8 a3 0-0 9 b4 b6 10 ♘bd2 h6 ∞ Toran-
Larsen, Palma de Mallorca 1968
  8 ♘h4 0-0 9 f4 ef 10 gf f5 ∞ Ciocaltea-
Fischer, Varna Ol 1962

[22] 9 ... ♖b8 10 ♖b1 a6 11 b4 cb 12 ab b5 =
Byrne
  9 ... h6 10 ♘c4 ♗e6 11 ♘fd2 d5 12 ed
♗xd5 = Najdorf-Ivkov, Nice Ol 1974

[23] 6 ♘c3 0-0 7 a3 ♖b8!? (7 ... d6 8 ♖b1 b6
9 b4 ♗b7 10 ♗g5 ♕d7 = Larsen-Geller,
Copenhagen 1966) 8 ♖b1 b5 = Hulak-Miles,
Amsterdam 1977

[24] 7 ♘bd2 0-0 8 a4 (8 ♖e1 ♖b8 9 a4 b6 10 ♘c4
♗b7 ∞ Larsen-Gligorić, Vinkovci 1970) 8 ...
♖b8 9 ♘c4 b6 ∞ Hort-Siaperas, Athens 1969

[25] 8 ♗e3 e5 9 h3 h6 10 ♘bd2 b6 =
  8 ♖e1 ♘e8 9 a4 a6 10 ♘bd2 ♖b8 11 ♘f1
b5 = Planinc-Tal, Wijk aan Zee 1973

[26] 8 ... ♗g4 9 h3 ♗xf3 10 ♕xf3 ♘d7 11 ♕e2
♖b8 12 f4 ± Bilek-Kavalek, Salgotarjan 1967
  8 ... e5 9 a4 h6 (9 ... ♘h5) 10 ♘c4 ♗e6
11 ♕e2 ♕c7 ∞ Romanishin

[27] 10 ♕e2 (10 ♖e1 ♘g4 11 ♘b3 e5 =) 10 ...
b5 11 ab ab 12 d4 ♘d7 13 ♘b3 c4 ∞ Barczay-
Forintos, Hungary 1968

	1	2	3	4	5	6	7	8	9	
5	...	g3	♗g2	0-0	d3[30]	♘bd2[32]	c3[33]	♕c2	e4	=
	♘f6	b6[28]	♗b7	e6[29]	d5[31]	♘bd7	♗e7	0-0	de[34]	
6	...	...	♗g2[35]	0-0[37]	d3[39]	e4	♘bd2[42]	♘e1	f4	∞
	...	b5	♗b7[36]	e6[38]	d6[40]	♗e7[41]	0-0[43]	♘fd7[44]	c5[45]	
7	...	...	b4[46]	♗b2	♗g2	0-0	a3	ab	♗xa1	=
	...	g6	♗g7[47]	0-0	c6[48]	a5	ab	♖xa1	♕b6[49]	

[28] 2 ... d6 3 ♗g2 e5 4 d3 ♗e7 5 e4 0-0 6 0-0 ♘c6 (6 ... ♘bd7) =; 3 d4 ± – 1 d4

[29] 4 ... g6 5 d3 d6 (5 ... d5 6 ♘bd2 ♘bd7 7 ♖e1 ♗g7 8 e4 de 9 de e5 10 b4 ± Vaganian-Furman, USSR Ch 1975) 6 e4 e5 (6 ... c5 7 ♘bd2 ♗g7 8 ♘h4 ♘c6 9 f4 ♕c7 10 a4 ± Flesch-Csom, Hungarian Ch 1971) 7 ♘h4 ♗g7 8 f4 ± Timman-Hartston, Nice Ol 1974

4 ... c5 5 d3 e6 6 e4 d6 7 ♖e1 (7 ♘h4 ♘c6 8 f4 ♗g7 9 ♘c3 0-0 10 f5 ♘e5! Hübner-Adorjan, Bad Lauterberg 1980; 7 ♘c3 ♗e7 8 ♘d2 ±) 7 ... ♘bd7 8 ♘c3 ♗e7 9 d4 cd 10 ♘xd4 ± Romanishin-Ermenkov, Riga 1981

[30] 5 b3 ♗e7 6 ♗b2 0-0 7 d3 d5 8 ♘bd2 ♘bd7 = Romanishin

[31] 5 ... ♗e7 6 e4 d6 7 ♘fd2!? (7 ♘c3 0-0 8 ♘e1 ♕c8 9 f4 c5 10 g4 ±) 7 ... d5 (7 ... e5 8 f4 ±) 8 e5 ♘fd7 9 ♖e1 b5 10 a4 a6 11 ♕g4 g6 12 ♘f3 ± Miles-Maninang, Indonesia 1982

[32] 6 e4!? de 7 ♘fd2 ♕c8 8 ♘xe4 ♘bd7 =

[33] 7 ♖e1 ♗c5 8 c3 (8 c4 0-0 9 cd ed 10 ♘b3 ♗b4 11 ♗d2 a5! ∓ Portisch-Karpov, Moscow 1977) 8 ... a5 9 a4 0-0 10 ♕c2 ♖e8 = Planinc-Lombardy, Amsterdam 1974

[34] **9 ... c5** 10 ♖e1 ♕c7 11 b3 (11 c4?! de 12 de ♖ad8 ∓ Olafsson-Karpov, Tilburg 1977) =

9 ... de 10 de ♘c5 11 ♘d4 e5! 12 ♘f5 ♖e8 = Najdorf-Pomar, Nice Ol 1974

[35] 3 c3 ♗b7 4 a4 a6 5 e3 (5 ab ab 6 ♖xa8 ♗xa8 7 ♕b3 c6 8 d4 ∞ Miles-Giardelli, Manila 1974) 5 ... ♘c6 6 d4 e6 7 b4 ♗e7 = Korchnoi-Karpov, USSR Ch 1973

3 ♘a3!? a6 4 c4 c6 5 ♗g2 d5 6 b3 ♘bd7 Quinteros-Miles, Buenos Aires 1979

[36] 3 ... d5!? 4 d4 e6 5 c3 c5 6 ♗g5 ♘bd7 7 a4 ♕b6 = Keene-Romanishin, Amsterdam 1973

[37] 4 ♘a3 a6 5 c4 b4 6 ♘c2 e6 7 0-0 c5 8 b3 ♗e7 9 ♗b2 0-0 = Larsen-Ljubojević, Teesside 1972

[38] **4 ... g6** 5 d3 ♗g7 6 e4 d6 7 ♘bd2 0-0 8 ♘h4 ♘fd7 9 f4 c5 10 ♘df3 ± Gufeld-Bohosian, Tbilisi 1974

4 ... c5 5 d3 d6 (5 ... d5 6 c4 dc 7 dc ♕xd1 8 ♖xd1 Reshevsky-Damjanović, Netanya 1973) 6 e4 e5 7 ♘g5 h6 8 ♘h3 ∞ Bilek-Ljubojević, Palma de Mallorca 1972

[39] 5 c3 c5 6 ♕b3 ♗c6 7 d3 d6 8 ♗g5 ♗e7 9 ♘fd2 ♗xg2 10 ♔xg2 a6 ∞ Gutman-Grünfeld, Beer-Sheva 1985

[40] **5 ... ♗e7** 6 e4 d6 7 ♘a3!? a6 8 c4 c6 9 e5! ± Romanishin-Petrosian, USSR 1980

5 ... d5 6 ♘bd2 ♗e7 7 e4 c5 (7 ... 0-0 8 ♕e2 c5 9 ♖e1 ♘c6 10 c3 a5 =) 8 ♕e2 ♘c6 9 c3 = Romanishin

[41] 6 ... c5 7 a4 a6 8 ab ab 9 ♖xa8 ♗xa8 10 ♘a3 (Vukić-Karpov, Bugojno 1978) 10 ... ♕b6!? ∞

[42] **7 a4** a6 8 ab ab 9 ♖xa8 ♗xa8 10 ♘a3 b4 11 ♘c4 0-0 = Saidy-Karpov, San Antonio 1972

7 ♘d4!? ♕d7 8 f4 ∞

[43] 7 ... c5 8 h3 ♘c6 9 ♘h2 ♕b6 ∞ Csom-Romanishin, Erevan 1976

[44] 8 ... c5?! 9 e5 ♗xg2 10 ef ♗xf1 11 fe ♕xe7 12 ♘xf1 ± Portisch-Panno, Madrid 1973

[45] Ribli-Hecht, Helsinki 1972

[46] 3 ♗g2 ♗g7 4 0-0 0-0 – King's Indian

3 b3 ♗g7 4 ♗b2 b6 5 ♗g2 ♗b7 6 0-0 0-0 7 d3 c5 8 e4 d6 9 ♘bd2 ♘bd7 = Polugayevsky-Vaganian, USSR Ch 1975

[47] 3 ... c6!? 4 a4 (4 ♗b2 a5! 5 a3 ab 6 ab ♖xa1 7 ♗xa1 ♕b6 8 c3 =) 4 ... ♗g7 5 ♘a3 d5 6 ♗g2 0-0 7 0-0 ♕d6 8 c3 e5 = Bronstein-Doroshkevich, USSR Ch 1967

[48] **5 ... a5** 6 b5 d6 (6 ... c5 7 c4 ±) 7 d4 ♘bd7 8 c4 ±

5 ... d6 6 0-0 e5 7 d3 ♘h5 8 e4 ± Sapi-Ribli, Hungarian Ch 1969

[49] 10 c3 d5 (10 ... ♕a6!? Polugayevsky-Korchnoi, Moscow 1966) 11 d3 ♖e8 (11 ... ♘bd7 12 ♘bd2 ♕c7 13 c4 e5 = Petrosian-Najdorf, Santa Monica 1966) 12 ♘bd2 e5 13 e4 ♘bd7 = Rubinetti-Mecking, Palma de Mallorca IZ 1970

1 ♘f3 d5

	2	3	4	5	6	7	8	9	10	
1	b3[1]	♗b2[2]	e3[4]	♗e2[5]	d3	♘bd2	c4	0-0	a3	=
	♗g4	♘d7[3]	e5	♗d6	♘h6	0-0	c6	♖e8	a5[6]	
2	...	e3[7]	♗b2	♗b5+[10]	♗e2[12]	0-0	c4	♘c3	♘b5	=
	c5	♘f6[8]	e6[9]	♗d7[11]	♘c6	♗d6[13]	0-0	♕e7	dc	
3	...	♗b2	e3[16]	h3	♕xf3	g3[19]	♗g2	0-0	d3	=
	♘f6	♗g4[15]	e6[17]	♗xf3[18]	♗e7	c5	♘c6	0-0	♘d7[20]	

[1] **2 d3** ♘f6 3 ♘bd2 (3 ♗f4!?) 3 ... ♗g4 4 h3 ♗h5 5 c4 c6 6 b3 e6 =
2 e3!? Euwe

[2] 3 ♘e5 ♗h5 4 c4 f6 5 ♘f3 d4 = Euwe
3 e3 e6 4 h3 ♗xf3 5 ♕xf3 ♘f6 6 ♗b2 ♗d6 ∞ Gulko

[3] 3 ... ♗xf3!? 4 gf (4 ef e6 5 f4 ♘e7 6 g3 ♘bc6 =) 4 ... e6 5 e3 ♘f6 6 f4 ♗d6 7 c4 ♕e7 8 ♖g1 g6! 9 ♕c2 ♘bd7 ∞ Sunye-Timman, Amsterdam 1983

[4] **4 g3** ♗xf3 5 ef ♘gf6 = 2 ... ♘f6
4 c4!? Euwe

[5] 5 h3 ♗xf3 6 gf ♕h4! Euwe

[6] 11 cd cd 12 e4 ♘b6 = Andersson-Portisch, Teesside 1972

[7] **3 ♗b2?!** f6! 4 e3 e5 ∓
3 c4 d4 4 b4!? ∞

[8] 3 ... a6 4 ♗b2 ♘c6 5 d4 cd 6 ♘xd4 ♘f6 7 ♘d2 e6 8 ♗e2 ♗d6 9 c4 ± Andersson-Spassky, Göteborg 1971
3 ... ♘c6 4 ♗b5 (4 ♗b2 f6 5 d4! ± Korchnoi-Dzenal, Silvaplana 1985; 4 ... ♗g4 5 h3 ♗h5 6 ♗b5 ±) 4 ... ♘f6 5 ♗b2 ♗d7 6 0-0 e6 7 d3 ♗e7 8 ♘bd2 0-0 9 ♗xc6 ♗xc6 10 ♘e5 ± Martin-Chandler, London 1985

[9] 4 ... g6!? 5 ♗b5+ ♗d7 6 ♕e2 ♗g7 7 ♗xd7+ ♘bxd7 8 c4 0-0 9 0-0 ♖c8 = Larsen-Pomar, Palma de Mallorca 1971

[10] **5 ♘e5** ♘bd7 (5 ... ♗e7 6 ♗b5+!?) 6 ♗b5 a6 7 ♗xd7+ ♘xd7 8 ♗xd7 ♗xd7 9 0-0 =
5 c4 dc (5 ... ♗e7; 5 ... ♘c6!?) 6 bc (6 ♗xc4 ♗e7 7 d4 cd 8 ♕xd4 ♕xd4 9 ♘xd4 0-0 10 ♘d2 ♗d7 11 0-0 ♘c6 = Hort-Gheorghiu, Nice Ol 1974) 6 ... ♗e7 7 ♕c2 ♘c6 8 a3 b6 = Keene-Denman, England 1974

[11] 5 ... ♘c6 6 0-0 ♗d7 7 c4 ♗d6 8 cd ♘xd5 (8 ... ed 9 ♗xf6!? ±) 9 d4 cd (9 ... 0-0 10 dc ♗xc5 11 ♘bd2 ±) 10 ♗xc6 ♗xc6 11 ♘xd4 ♕c7 12 ♕h5 ± Gulko-Vulfson, USSR 1981

[12] **6 ♗xd7+** ♘bxd7 (6 ... ♕xd7 7 c4 ♘c6 8 cd ♕xd5 ∞) 7 c4 ♗e7 8 0-0 0-0 9 cd ed 10 d4 ♖c8 11 dc ♘xc5 12 ♘c3 ♘ce4 = Keene-Nunn, Hastings 1975-76
6 ♕e2 ♗e7 7 ♗xd7+ ♘fxd7 8 0-0 ♗f6 = Larsen-Bronstein, Las Palmas 1972

[13] 7 ... ♗e7 8 c4 0-0 =

[14] 11 ♘xd6 ♕xd6 12 bc e5 Korchnoi-Ligterink, Wijk aan Zee 1985

[15] **3 ... g6** 4 e3 ♗g7 5 c4 0-0 6 cd ♘xd5 7 ♗xg7 ♔xg7 =
3 ... ♗f5 4 e3 e6 5 ♗e2 (5 ♘e5 ♗d6 6 f4 ♘bd7 7 ♗e2 c5 =) 5 ... ♗d6 6 0-0 ♘bd7 7 ♘d4 ♗g6 8 f4 c5 9 ♘f3 ♕c7 10 ♘h4 0-0-0 ∞

[16] 4 d3 ♗xf3 5 ef e6 6 f4 ♗e7 7 g3 0-0 8 ♗g2 ♘fd7 9 0-0 ♗f6 = Taimanov-Savon, USSR 1975

[17] **4 ... c6** 5 h3 ♗xf3 (5 ... ♗h5 6 g4 ♗g6 7 d3 ±) 6 ♕xf3 ♘bd7 7 d4 ± Taimanov
4 ... ♘bd7 5 h3 ♗h5 6 d3 e6 7 g4 ♗g6 ∞

[18] 5 ... ♗h5 6 d3 c5 7 g4 ♗g6 8 ♘e5 ♘bd7 9 ♘xg6 hg 10 ♗g2 ♕b6 = Korchnoi-Mecking, match 1974

[19] 7 d4!? Euwe

[20] 11 ♕e2 ♗f6 12 c4 ♗xb2 13 ♕xb2 ♘f6 = Smyslov-Savon, Petropolis IZ 1973

11

1 ♘f3 d5   *continued*

	2	3	4	5	6	7	8	9	10	
4	g3	♗g2	0-0[23]	d3[24]	♘bd2	e4[26]	♕e2[27]	b3[28]	♗b2	=
	c6[21]	♗g4[22]	♘d7	e6[25]	♗d6	♘e7	0-0	♘g6	♘ge5[29]	
5	...	♗g2	0-0[30]	d3	♘bd2[32]	e4	c3	ed	a4	=
	♘f6	g6	♗g7[31]	0-0	♘c6[33]	e5[34]	a5[35]	♘xd5	h6[36]	
6	...	...	d3[38]	0-0[40]	♘bd2[42]	♕e1[44]	e4	♕e2	b3[46]	=
	...	♗f5[37]	e6[39]	h6[41]	♗e7[43]	0-0[45]	♗h7	c5	♘c6[47]	
7	...	...	c4	♕b3	d3[50]	0-0[52]	♘bd2	a3	♕c2	=
	...	...	e6[48]	♘c6[49]	♖b8[51]	h6	♗e7	0-0	a5[53]	
8	...	...	...	cd[54]	♕b3	♕xb6	♘c3	d3	♗d2[59]	=/∞
	...	...	c6	cd[55]	♕b6[56]	ab	♘c6[57]	e5[58]	h6[60]	

[21] 2 ... ♘d7 3 ♗g2 e5 4 c4 dc 5 ♕a4 (5 0-0 ♘gf6 6 ♕a4 ♗d6 7 ♘a3 c6 8 ♘xc4 ♗c7 = Portisch-Smyslov, Las Palmas 1972) 5 ... ♗d6 6 ♘a3 ♘f6 7 ♘xc4 0-0 8 ♘xd6 cd 9 0-0 ±

2 ... ♘c6 3 ♗g2 e5 4 d3 ♘f6 5 0-0 ♗e7 6 a3 0-0 7 b4 e4 8 ♘fd2 ♗f5 (8 ... ed 9 cd ± Day-Timman, Malta Ol 1980) 9 ♘c3 ed 10 cd ± Miles-Sosonko, Reykjavik 1980

2 ... ♗g4 3 ♗g2 ♘d7 4 c4 e6 5 ♕a4! (5 b3 c6 6 ♗b2 ♕b6 7 ♕c2 ♘gf6 8 0-0 ♗e7 9 d3 0-0 ∞ Vukić-Campora, Bor 1985) ±

[22] 3 ... e6 4 0-0 ♗d6 5 d3 ♘e7 6 e4 0-0 7 ♕e2 ±

[23] 4 c4 ♘d7!? (4 ... ♗xf3 5 ♗xf3 ♘f6 6 ♕b3 ♕b6 = Suetin) 5 cd cd 6 ♕a4 ♘f6 7 ♘c3 e6 8 ♘e5 ♗f5 ∞ Littlewood-Kovačević, Hastings 1982-83

4 d3 e6 (4 ... ♘d7 5 h3 ♗h5 =) 5 b3 ♗b4 6 c3 ♗d6 7 ♗b2 ♘f6 8 ♘bd2 ♘bd7 9 c4 e5 = Smejkal-Tal, Sochi 1973

4 h3 ♗xf3 (4 ... ♗h5 5 d3 e6 6 ♘c3!? ± Korchnoi) 5 ♗xf3 ♘d7 6 d3 e6 7 e4 ♗d6 8 ♘d2 ♘e7 = Gufeld-Vasyukov, USSR 1972

[24] 5 c4 ♗xf3 (5 ... e6 6 b3 ± Tischbierek-Hector, Budapest 1986) 6 ♗xf3 ♘e5 7 ♕b3 ♘xf3+ 8 ef ♕d7 =/∓

[25] 5 ... e5 6 e4 de 7 de ♗c5 8 h3 ♗e6!? (8 ... ♗h5 9 ♘bd2 f6 10 c3 ♗f7 11 ♕h4± Dzindzihashvili-Qi, Thessaloniki Ol 1984) 9 ♘g5 ♗c4 10 ♖e1 ♕f6! ∞

[26] 7 b3 ♘e7 8 ♗b2 0-0 9 c4 a5 (9 ... ♕b6 R.Byrne) 10 a3 b5 11 ♕c2 e5 = Keres

[27] 8 b3 0-0 9 h3 ♗h5 10 ♗b2 ♖c8 11 ♕e1 c5 = Portisch-Ivkov, Amsterdam 1969

8 h3 ♗h5 9 ♕e1 0-0 10 b3 a5 11 a3 b5 =

[28] 9 h3 ♗h5 10 ♖e1 ♔h8 11 d4 ♖ac8 12 c4 c5! ∞ D.Byrne-Smyslov, Lugano Ol 1968

[29] 11 ♕e3 ♘xf3+ 12 ♘xf3 ♗xf3 13 ♗xf3 de 14 ♗xe4 ♕a5 = Rajković-Rukavina, Yugoslavia 1976

[30] 4 b4 a5 5 b5 ♗g7 6 ♗b2 0-0 7 0-0 ♘bd7

8 ♘a3 ♖e8 9 c4 e5 ∞ Hébert-Ftacnik, New York 1983

[31] 4 ... c6 5 b3 ♗g7 6 ♗b2 0-0 7 d3 a5 8 a3 ♘bd7 9 ♘bd2 b6 =

[32] 6 c3 ♘c6 7 b4 a6 8 ♘bd2 ♘e8! 9 ♕b3 e5 =∓ Kärner-Arnason, Tallinn 1983

6 a3!? b6 7 b4 ♗b7 8 ♗b2 c5! ∞ Diždarević-Uhlmann, Sarajevo 1981

[33] 6 ... c6 7 e4 ♗g4 (7 ... de 8 de ♘bd7 9 ♕e2 ♘c5 10 e5 ±) 8 h3 ♗xf3 9 ♕xf3 ±

[34] 7 ... de 8 de ♘e5 9 c3 ♗e6 (9 ... h6 10 ♕c2 ♗e6 11 ♖d1 ♕e7 12 b4 ± R.Byrne) 10 ♘g5 ♗g4 11 f3 ♗c8 12 ♖e1 a5 13 a4 ± Petrosian

[35] 8 ... h6 9 ♖e1 ♖e8 10 ♕c2 ♗e6 11 b4 a6 =

[36] 11 ♖e1 ♖e8 12 ♘c4 ♗f5 13 ♘h4 ♗e6 = Keene-Andersson, Palma de Mallorca 1971

11 ♘c4 ♖e8 12 ♕b3 ♘de7 13 ♖e1 = Cvetković-Sveshnikov, 1976

[37] 3 ... e6 4 0-0 ♗e7 5 d3 c5 6 ♘bd2 ♘c6 7 b3 b6 8 ♗b2 ♗b7 9 e4 ♕c7 ∞ Norwood-Przewoznik, Lvov 1986

3 ... ♘c6 4 0-0 e5 5 d3 ♗g4 6 h3 ♗f5 7 ♘c3!? ♕d7 (7 ... d4 8 e4 ±) 8 ♔h2 d4 (8 ... h6 9 e4! ± Tal-Kupreichik, USSR 1981) 9 e4 ♗e6 10 ♘e2 h6 ∞ Tal

[38] 4 0-0 e6 5 d3 – 4 d3

[39] 4 ... h6 5 c4! c6 6 cd cd 7 ♕b3 ± Gutman

[40] 5 ♘h4 ♗g4 (5 ... ♗g6!? 6 c4 c6 7 ♕b3 ♘a6! =) 6 h3 ♗h5 7 c4 c6 8 ♕b3 ♘a6! 9 ♘c3 ♘c5 = Gutman

5 c4 ♘c6 6 ♘h4 ♗g4 7 h3 ♗h5 8 g4 ♗g6 9 g5 ♘g8 10 cd ed 11 ♕b3 ♗b4 ∞ Kurajica-Marjanović, Kavala Z 1985

[41] 5 ... ♗e7 6 c4 c6 7 ♘h4 ♗g4 8 h3 ♗h5 9 g4 ♗g6! (9 ... ♘fd7?! 10 cd cd 11 ♘f5 ± Gutman-Berg, 1984) = Gutman

[42] 6 c4!? c6 7 cd ed 8 ♘c3 ♗e7 8 ♘d4 (9 ♕b3!? ♕b6 10 e4 ∞/± Gutman-Haldarsson, Reykjavik 1984) 9 ... ♗h7 10 e4 0-0 11 ♖e1 ♘a6 12 e5 ♘e8 13 ♗h3! ± Gutman-Chandler, Ostend

1984; 7 ... cd = Suetin

43 6 ... ♗c5 7 ♕e1 (7 e4 de 8 de ♗h7! ∓ Petrosian) 7 ... 0-0 8 e4 de 9 ♘xe4 ♘xe4 10 de ♗h7 11 b4 ± Petrosian-Euwe, Zürich C 1953

6 ... ♘bd7 7 ♕e1 ♗h7 8 e4 de 9 de e5!? =

44 7 b3 0-0 8 ♗b2 c5 9 ♕e1 ♘c6 10 e4 ♗h7 11 ♕e2 c4! ∓ Berkovich-Yusupov, USSR 1975

45 7 ... ♘c6!? 8 a3 0-0 9 b4 ♘d7 10 ♘b3 ♗f6 = R.Garcia-Smyslov, Buenos Aires 1970

46 10 ♘e5!? ♘fd7 = Suetin

47 11 ♗b2 c4!? (11 ... ♕c7 =) 12 bc de 13 de ♕c7 ∞ Plachetka-Yusupov, Lucerne Ol 1982

48 4 c4 dc 5 ♘a3 ♗e6 6 ♘g5!? (6 ♕c2 ♗d5 7 ♘xc4 ♘c6 = Korchnoi) 6 ... ♗d5 7 e4 ♗c6 8 ♘xc4 h6 9 ♗xf7 ♔xf7 10 ♘e5+ ♔g8 11 0-0! ♗e8 12 ♕b3+ ∞ Diždar-Korchnoi, Sarajevo 1984

49 5 ... ♘a6!? 6 cd ed 7 ♘d4 ♗c8! 8 ♘c3 c6 = Romanishin-Polugayevsky, USSR 1980

50 6 ♕xb7 ♘b4 7 ♘d4 ♖b8 8 ♕xa7 ♖a8 =

51 6 ... ♗b4+!?

52 7 ♘h4 ♗g4!

53 Csom-Marjanović, Titograd 1984

54 5 ♕b3 ♕b6 6 cd ♕xb3 7 ab cd 8 ♘c3 ♘c6 9 d3 e6 10 0-0 ♗e7 = Fischer-Polugayevsky, Palma de Mallorca IZ 1970

5 0-0 e6 6 cd ed 7 ♘c3 ♗e7 8 d3 h6 (8 ... 0-0 9 ♘d4 ♗c8 10 e4 ± Dorfman-A.Petrosian, USSR Ch 1976) 9 ♘d4 ♗h7 10 e4 0-0 11 ♗f4 ♘a6 ∞

55 5 ... ♗xb1 6 ♖xb1 cd 7 ♕b3 ♕b6 8 ♕xb6 ab 9 a3 ±

5 ... ♘xd5 6 ♘e5 ♗e6 7 0-0 g6 8 b3 ♗g7 9 ♗b2 0-0 10 ♕c1 ±

56 6 ... ♕c8 7 ♘c3 e6 8 d3 ♘c6 9 ♗f4 ♗e7 10 0-0 (10 ♘b5 ± Botvinnik) 10 ... 0-0 11 ♖ac1 ± Kirov-Agzamov, Potsdam 1985

57 8 ... e6 9 ♘b5 ♗a6 10 a3 ♗e7 11 b4 0-0 12 ♗b2 ±

58 9 ... ♗d7 10 ♗e3 ♖a6 11 0-0 e6 12 ♘b5 ♔d8 13 a3 ±

9 ... e6 10 ♘b5 ♗b4+ 11 ♗d2 ♔e7 12 ♘fd4 ♗xd2+ 13 ♔xd2 ♗g6 14 f4 h6 15 a3 ± Portisch-Smyslov, Wijk aan Zee 1972

59 10 0-0 h6 (10 ... ♗e7 11 ♗g5 ♗e6 12 ♘d2 ± Kirov-Pribyl, Moscow 1977) =

60 11 a3 ♗c5 ∞ Ribli-Seirawan, London 1984

	Reti	1 ♘f3 d5 2 c4[1]							
	2	3	4	5	6	7	8	9	10
1	...	♘a3[3]	♘xc4[5]	b3[6]	♗b2	g3	♗g2	0-0	♘e1	±/=
	dc[2]	c5[4]	♘c6	f6	e5	♘ge7	♘f5[7]	♗e7	♗e6[8]	

1 Reti

2 2 ... ♘f6 3 cd ♘xd5 4 e4 ♘f6 5 ♘c3 c5 6 d4 ±

2 ... c6 and 2 ... e6 – 1 c4

3 3 e4 e5!? 4 ♗xc4 ♘c6 =

3 e3 ♘c6 4 ♘a3 ♘f6 5 ♘xc4 g6 6 b3 ♗g7 7 ♗b2 0-0 8 ♗e2 c5 = Geller-Keres, USSR 1963) 4 ... ♗d5 5 e4 ♗c6 6 ♗xc4 e6 = Taimanov

3 ♕a4+ ♘d7! (3 ... c6 4 ♕xc4 ♘f6 5 g3 ♗g4 6 ♗g2 ♘bd7 7 d4 ♗xf3 8 ♗xf3 e5 9 ♗e3 ± Korchnoi-Garcia Palermo, Brussels 1985) 4 g3 a6 (4 ... ♘f6 5 ♗g2 e6 6 0-0 a6 7 ♕xc4 c5 =) 5 ♕xc4 b5 6 ♕c2 ♗b7 7 ♗g2 c5 8 0-0 ♖c8 =

4 3 ... e5?! 4 ♘xe5 ♗xa3 5 ♕a4+ b5 6 ♕xa3 ± Tartakower-Spielmann, Moscow 1925

3 ... g6 4 g3 ♗g7 5 ♗g2 e5 6 0-0 ♘c6 7 ♘xc4 ♘ge7 8 d3 ±; 4 e3!?

3 ... a6 4 ♘xc4 b5 5 ♘e3 ± Lombard-Knežević, Budapest 1976

3 ... ♘f6 4 ♘xc4 g6 (4 ... e6 5 g3 b6 6 ♗g2 ♗b7 7 0-0 ♗e7 8 d3 ± Andersson-Radulov, 1974) 5 b4 (5 b3 ♗g7 6 ♗b2 0-0 7 g3 b6 8 ♗g2 ♗b7 9 0-0 c5 =) 5 ... ♗g7 6 ♗b2 0-0 7 g3 ♗e6 8 ♕c2 ± Jansa-Estevez, Luhacovice 1973

5 4 g3!? Suetin

6 5 ♘ce5 ♘xe5 6 ♘xe5 g6 (6 ... ♘f6 =) 7 g3 ♗g7 8 ♕a4+ ♔f8 9 ♘f3 ♗d7 10 ♕f4 ♗c6 = Bilek-Keres, Budapest 1955

5 g3 f6 6 ♗g2 e5 7 0-0 ♘ge7 8 d3 ♗e6 9 a3 (9 ♘fd2 ♘d5 10 ♘e4 ♗e7 11 f4 f5! 12 ♘c3 ef 13 gf 0-0 ∓ Vladimirov-Garcia Palermo, Havana 1986) 9 ... ♘d5 10 ♘e3 =

7 Alekhine

8 ... ♘d5 9 0-0 ♗e7 10 ♘h4 0-0 11 ♕b1! ♖f7 12 ♘f5 ± Botvinnik-Fine, Nottingham 1936

8 11 f4 ef 12 ♖xf4 ♕d7 13 ♘d3 0-0 14 ♖c1 ±/= Kengis-Yakovich, USSR 1985

	2	3	4	5	6	7	8	9	10	
2	...	b4[9]	e3[11]	a3[13]	b5	d3	g3	♗g2	0-0	=
	d4	f6[10]	e5[12]	a5[14]	c5	♗d6	♘e7	0-0	♗g4[15]	
3	...	e3	ed[17]	♘xd4	♘c3	d3[19]	♕e2[21]	♗e3	0-0-0	=
	...	♘c6[16]	♘xd4	♕xd4	e5[18]	♘e7[20]	♗d7[22]	♕d6	0-0-0[23]	
4	...	g3	b4[25]	d3[27]	♘bd2	♗g2	0-0	a4	♗a3	±
	...	g6[24]	♗g7[26]	e5[28]	♘e7	0-0	h6	♗e6	♕c8[29]	
5	...	...	e3[30]	ed	♘xd4	d3[32]	f3[33]	g4	♕e2	±
	...	c5	♘c6	♘xd4	♕xd4[31]	♗g4	♗f5	♗d7[34]	e6[35]	

[9] 3 d3 g6 4 e3 de 5 ♗xe3 ♗g7 6 ♕d2 ♘c6 = Reshevsky-Pfleger, Nice Ol 1974

[10] 3 ... a5 4 b5 (4 ♗b2 ab 5 ♘xd4 ±/ ±) 4 ... c5 5 e3 g6 6 ed cd 7 d3 ♗g7 8 g3 ±
3 ... c5 4 bc ±

[11] 4 d3 e5 5 a3 c5 (5 ... a5 6 b5 ♘d7 7 g3 ♘c5 8 ♗g2 = Taimanov) 6 g3 cb! 7 ab (7 ♗g2?! ♘c6 8 0-0 a5 9 e3 ♗g4! ∓ Korchnoi-Seirawan, London 1984) 7 ... ♗xb4+ 8 ♗d2 ∞

[12] 4 ... de 5 fe e5 6 a3 c5 7 bc ♗xc5 8 d4 ± Gufeld

[13] 5 ♗b2 c5 (5 ... de 6 fe ♗b4 7 c5!? ± Vaganian-Mikenas, USSR Ch 1970) 6 ed cd 7 a3 ♘h6 8 ♗d3 a5 = Tartakower

[14] 5 ... c5 6 ♗b2 ∞

[15] 11 h3 ♗h5 12 ed cd 13 ♘bd2 ♘d7 = Hébert-Kir.Georgiev, Monts 1985

[16] 3 ... c5 4 d3 (4 ed cd 5 g3 ♘c6 6 d3 e5 7 ♗g2 ♗d6 8 0-0 ♘ge7 9 ♘a3 ± Szymczak-Szrankowski, Poland 1976) 4 ... ♘c6 5 ed cd 6 g3 e5 7 ♗g2 ♗d6 8 0-0 ♘ge7 9 a3 a5 10 ♘bd2 ± Speelman-Miles, British Ch 1979

[17] 4 b4 de 5 fe ♘xb4 6 d4 e5 (6 ... e6 7 a3 ♘c6 8 ♗d3 ±) 7 a3 ♘c6 (7 ... e4 8 ♘d2 ♘d3 9 ♗xd3 ed 10 0-0 ♘f6 11 ♕b3 ±) 8 ♘c3 (8 d5 e4! ∓ Plachetka-Lukacs, Vrnjačka Banja 1985) 8 ... ♘f6 9 d5 =

[18] 6 ... ♘f6 7 d3 c6 8 ♗e3 ♕d7 9 d4 ± Alekhine-Euwe, match (22) 1937
6 ... ♗g4 7 ♕a4! ± Espig-Knaak, East German Ch 1978

[19] 7 ♘b5 ♕b6 8 ♕e2 ♗e6 9 b3 a6 10 ♘c3 ♘f6 11 ♗b2 ♗d6 ∓ Misuchkov-Zilberstein, USSR 1984

[20] 7 ... ♘f6 8 ♗e2 c6 9 ♗e3 ♕d8 10 d4 ed 11 ♕xd4 ♕xd4 12 ♗xd4 ± Panno-Polugayevsky, Petropolis IZ 1973

[21] 8 ♗e3 ♕d8 9 d4 ed 10 ♕xd4 ♕xd4 11 ♗xd4 ♘c6 = Langeweg-Hort, Amsterdam 1978

[22] 8 ... ♗g4!? 9 f3 ♗d7 10 ♗e3 ♕d6 11 0-0-0 ♘f5 12 f4 ♗e7 = Stean-Hort, Biel 1981

[23] 11 d4?! ed 12 ♗xd4 ♕a6! ∓ Espig-Tal, Erevan Z 1982
11 g3 ♘f5 12 ♗h3 ♘xe3 13 ♗xd7+ ♖xd7 14 fe ♗e7 = Bagirov-A.Mikhalchishin, USSR Ch 1978

[24] 3 ... ♘c6 4 ♗g2 e5 5 0-0 (5 d3 ♗b4+!? 6 ♘fd2 a5 7 ♘a3 ♘f6 7 ♘c2 ♗f5 ∓ Vadasz-Vaganian, Erevan 1980; 6 ♘bd2 =) 5 ... ♘f6 (5 ... g6!? 6 d3 ♗g7 7 ♘bd2 a5 Lobron-Korchnoi, Bad Kissingen 1981) 6 d3 ♘d7 (6 ... ♗d6 7 ♘a3 ♗xa3 8 ba 0-0 9 ♖b1 ± Quinteros-Larsen, Mar del Plata 1981) 7 ♘a3 ♗xa3 8 ba 0-0 9 a4 a5 10 ♖b1 ♘b4 11 a3 ♘a6 12 e3 ± Geller-Kupreichik, USSR Ch 1980-81

[25] 4 ♗g2 ♗g7 5 0-0 ♘c6 6 d3 (6 e3 ♘f6 7 d3 de 8 fe 0-0 = Miles-Murey, London 1981) 6 ... e5 7 e4 de 8 fe e4! ∞ Gavrikov-Malanyuk, USSR 1982

[26] 4 ... b6!? 5 ♗g2 ♗b7 6 a3 ♗g7 7 d3 a5 8 ♗b2 e5 9 0-0 Ermolinsky-Malanyuk, USSR 1981

[27] 5 ♗b2 a5 6 a3 e5 7 d3 ♕e7 8 ♘bd2 ♘f6 9 ♗g2 0-0 10 0-0 ♖d8 ∞ Kuligowski-Hort, 1983

[28] 5 ... b6 6 ♗g2 ♗b7 7 0-0 e5 (7 ... ♘f6 8 ♗b2 c5 9 bc bc 10 ♘bd2 ♕c7 11 ♖b1 ± Savon-Korchnoi, USSR 1972) 8 ♘bd2 ♘e7 9 ♘b3 0-0 10 a4! ± Korchnoi-Timman, Linares 1985

[29] 11 ♖e1 ♗h3 12 ♗h1 ♘f5 13 b5 ± Vaganian-Speelman, Moscow 1985

[30] 4 ♗g2 ♘c6 5 0-0 ♘f6 6 e3 e5 7 ed ed 8 d3 ♗e7 = Kasparov-Pinter, Skara 1980

[31] 6 ... cd 7 ♗g2 ♘f6 8 0-0 e6 9 d3 ♗d6 10 b4 0-0 11 a3 ± Szabo-Flohr, Amsterdam 1966

[32] 7 ♘c3 ♗g4 8 ♗c2 ♗xe2 9 ♕xe2 e6 10 d3 ♕d7 11 ♗e3 ♘f6 12 0-0-0 ♕c6 = Korchnoi-Mecking, match 1974

[33] 8 ♗e2 ♗xe2 9 ♕xe2 0-0-0 = Suetin

[34] 9 ... ♗g6 10 ♕a4+! ♕d7 11 ♕xd7+ ♔xd7 12 ♘c3 e5 13 f4 ± Polugayevsky-Portisch, Petropolis IZ 1973

[35] 11 ♗e3 ♕d6 12 ♘c3 ♗e7 13 ♘e4 ± Bagirov

	3	4	5	6	7	8	9	10	11	
1	...	d4	0-0	c4[4]	♘a3	♘xc4[5]	♗f4	a3	♘ce5	=
	♘c6[1]	e6[2]	♗d7[3]	dc	cd	♗c5[6]	♕e7	b5[7]	♖c8[8]	
2	...	0-0	d3[10]	♘bd2[11]	e4	c3[13]	de	♕e2	♘e1	=
	...	♘f6[9]	g6	♗g7	0-0[12]	de[14]	h6[15]	♗e6	♕b6[16]	
3	...	...	d3	e4	♘bd2[17]	♖e1[18]	ed[20]	♘e4	a3	±/=
	...	e6	♗d6	♘ge7	0-0	♗c7[19]	♘xd5[21]	♗b6[22]	h6[23]	
4	...	...	...	♘bd2	e4	♖e1	c3[26]	♕e2[27]	a3	∞
	...	...	♘f6	♗e7[24]	b6[25]	♗b7	♕c7	0-0-0[28]	h6[29]	
5	...	...	...	♘bd2	e4	♖e1[31]	a4	h4	♔f1	=
	...	...	g6	♗g7	♘ge7[30]	h6[32]	b6	a5	♖a7[33]	

[1] 3 ... e6 4 c4 dc 5 ♘e5 ♘f6 6 0-0 ♗e7 7 ♘a3 0-0 8 ♘axc4 ♘d5 9 d4 cd 10 ♕xd4 ± Vaganian-Sokolov, match 1986
3 ... g6 4 0-0 ♗g7 5 d3 (5 d4 cd 6 ♘xd4 ♘f6 7 ♘c3 e6 8 e4 e5 9 ♘b3 d4 ∞; 7 c4 is a Grünfeld reversed) 5 ... ♘f6 6 ♘bd2 ♘c6 7 e4 0-0 8 ♖e1 h6 (8 ... b6 9 ♖e1 ♗g4 10 ♕e2 ♕c8 11 ♔f1 ♕a6 12 h3 ♗c8 13 e5± Kochiev-Zaitsev, Minsk 1983; 8 ... d4!?) 9 c3 de 10 de ♗e6 11 ♕e2 ♘d7 = Polugayevsky-Vladimirov, Sochi 1966

[2] 4 ... ♘f6 5 0-0 ♗g4 (5 ... ♗f5 6 c4 dc 7 ♕a4± Dzindzihashvili-Ljubojević, Thessaloniki Ol 1984) 6 dc e5 7 c4 ♗xc5 8 cd ♕xd5 9 ♘c3 ♕xd1 10 ♖xd1± Petrosian-Sosonko, Las Palmas 1980

[3] 5 ... cd 6 ♘xd4 ♗c5 7 ♘b3 (7 ♘xc6 bc 8 c4±) 7 ... ♗b6 8 c4 ♘ge7 9 cd ♘xd5 10 ♘c3 ♘xc3 11 ♕xd8+! ♔xd8 12 bc ± Speelman-Mestel, Hastings 1979-80

[4] 6 dc!? ♗xc5 7 c4 d4 8 ♘d2 e5 9 ♘b3 ♗b6 ∞ Osnos

[5] 8 ♘xd4 ♗xa3 9 ♘xc6 ♗xc6 10 ♗xc6+ bc 11 ba ♘f6 ∞

[6] 8 ... ♘f6?! 9 ♘xd4 ♗e7 10 ♘xc6 ♗xc6 11 ♗xc6+ bc 12 ♕a4 ±

[7] 10 ... a5 11 b4! ±

[8] 12 ♘xd7 ♕xd7 13 ♖c1 ♗b6 14 ♕d3 ♘f6! = Gutman-Eng, West Germany 1984-85

[9] 4 ... e5 5 c4 d4 6 d3 f6 7 e3 (7 ♘a3 ♗g4 8 ♘c2 ♕d7 9 a3 ♗h3 10 ♖b1 a5 ∞ Spassov-Djurić, Pamporovo 1981) 7 ... ♗d6 8 ed cd 9 ♘bd2 ♘ge7 10 ♘e4± Ginsburg-Wilder, Toronto 1984

[10] 5 c4 dc 6 ♕a4 (6 ♘a3 ♕d5! = Anikayev-Zaitsev, Minsk 1983) 6 ... ♗d7 7 ♕xc4 e6 8 ♘c3 a6 9 d4 ± Anikayev; 5 ... d4!?

[11] 6 ♘c3 d4 7 ♘a4 ♕d6 8 c4 ♗g7 9 a3 0-0 10 b4 cb 11 ab ♘xb4 12 c5 ♕d8 13 ♘b6 ab 14 ♖xa8 bc ∞ Hoi-Chandler, Reykjavik 1984

[12] 7 ... d4 8 a4 0-0 9 ♘c4 ± Zlotnik-Godes, USSR 1975

[13] 8 ♖e1 d4 (8 ... e5!? 9 ed ♘xd5 10 ♘c4 h6 = Wade-Browne, Hastings 1972-73) 9 e5 ♘d5 10 a4 ♖b8 11 ♘c4 b6 = Planinc-Sosonko, Amsterdam 1974

[14] 8 ... d4 9 cd cd 10 a4 ± Balashov-Pfleger, Tallinn 1973

[15] 9 ... b6 10 ♕e2 ♘e8 11 ♖d1 ♘c7 12 ♘c4 ±

[16] 12 h3 ♖ad8 = Petrosian-Reshevsky, Zürich C 1953

[17] 7 ♕e2 0-0 = Uhlmann

[18] 8 ♘h4 ♕c7 (8 ... f5 9 f4 ♗c7 10 c3 ♔h8 11 ef ef 12 ♘df3 ± Ciocaltea-Liberzon, Netanya 1983) 9 f4 f6 10 c3 ♗d7 = Rigo-Sax, Hungarian Ch 1976

[19] 8 ... ♕c7 9 c3 ♗d7 10 ♕e2 f6 ∞/±

[20] 9 c3 a5 10 a4 b6 (10 ... ♖b8!?) 11 ed (11 e5?! ♗a6 12 d4 cd 13 cd b5! ∓ Yurtayev-Ehlvest, USSR 1983) 11 ... ed 12 ♔b1! ∞/± Vaganian-Sokolov, match 1986
9 ♘h4!?

[21] 9 ... ed 10 d4 c4 11 ♔f1 ±

[22] 10 ... b6!? ±/=

[23] 12 c4 ♘f6 13 ♗f4 ♘xe4 14 de ±/= Hort-Lobron, Dortmund 1983

[24] 6 ... g6 7 e4 ♗g7 8 ed! ♘xd5 (8 ... ed 9 ♖e1 ±) 9 ♘b3 b6 10 c4! ± Csom-Ivkov, Portorož/Ljubljana 1973

[25] 7 ... h6 8 ♖e1 ♕c7 9 c3 b6 10 ed ♘xd5 11 ♘c4 ♗b7 12 a4 ♖d8 ∞ Jansa-Martinović, Bagneux 1983
7 ... 0-0 8 ♖e1 ♕c7 (7 ... b5 9 e5 ♘d7 10 ♘f1 a5 ∞ Fischer-Miagmasuren, Sousse IZ 1967) 9 e5 (9 ♘f1 de 10 de ♖d8 11 ♕e2 ♘d4 ∞) 9 ... ♘d7 10 ♕e2 b5 11 h4 a5 12 ♘f1 ♘d4 13 ♘xd4 cd 14 ♗f4 ♖a6 = Fischer

[26] 9 ♕e2!? ♘b4 10 e5 ♘xc2 11 ef ♗xf6 12 ♖b1 ∞ Tseitlin-Polovodin, USSR 1981

[27] 10 a3 0-0 11 e5 ♗d7 12 d4 g5 ∞ Hort-Lobron, Bad Kissingen 1981

[28] 10 ... h6!? 11 a3 a5 12 e5 ♘d7 13 c4 d4 14 h4 ∞ Dolmatov-Diždar, Graz 1981

[29] 12 b4 g5 13 ♘b3 de 14 de g4 ∞ Osmanović-Martinović, Sarajevo 1981

[30] 7 ... d4 8 ♘b3 ♕e7!? Vasyukov

[31] 8 ed!? ed 9 d4 cd 10 ♘b3 Dvoretsky-Vulfson, USSR 1986

[32] 8 ... b6 9 c3 (9 h4 h6 10 c3 a5 11 a4 ♖a7! ∞ Ljubojević-Kasparov, Nikšić 1983) 9 ... h6 10 e5 ♕d7 11 d4 cd 12 cd ♗a6 13 a3! ± Yurtayev-Dolmatov, USSR 1984

[33] 12 ♘1h2 de 13 ♖xe4 0-0 14 ♖e1 e5 = Ivanović-Petrosian, Nikšić 1983

	KI Attack II		1 ♘f3 d5 2 g3 ♘f6 3 ♗g2 c6						

	4	5	6	7	8	9	10	11	12	
1	0-0[1]	c4[2]	b3	♗b2	d3	♘bd2	a3[5]	♗c3	♘e5	∞
	♗f5	e6	♗e7[3]	0-0	h6	♗h7[4]	a5	♘a6	♗c5[6]	
2	...	d3	c4[8]	♗e3![10]	♕b3	♘c3	♖ac1	cd	♗d4[13]	±
	...	h6[7]	e6[9]	♗e7[11]	♕c8	0-0	♗h7[12]	ed	♘bd7[14]	
3	...	...	♘bd2[15]	♕e1[17]	e4	♕e2[18]	a4	b3[19]	♗b2	∞
	...	e6	h6[16]	♗e7	♗h7	a5	0-0	♘a6	♘b4[20]	
4	...	d3[21]	♘bd2	e4[23]	♕e1	de	h3[26]	♘xf3	♗d2	=
	♗g4	♘bd7	e6[22]	♗e7[24]	de[25]	0-0	♗xf3[27]	e5	♗d6[28]	
5	...	c4	b3	♗b2	d3[32]	♘bd2[33]	cd	h3	♗xf3	=
	...	e6[29]	♘bd7[30]	♗d6[31]	0-0	e5[34]	cd	♗xf3	♖e8[35]	
6	...	...	♘e5[36]	d4	♘c3	♕b3[38]	♘xd7	e4	♗xe4[39]	=
	...	...	♗h5[37]	♘bd7	♗e7	♕b6	♘xd7	de	♘f6[40]	

[1] 4 d3 and now:
4 ... h6 5 b3 ♗f5 6 ♗b2 e6 7 ♘bd2 ♗c5 8 e4!? de 9 ♘xe4 10 ♘xe4 ♕xd1+ 11 ♖xd1 ♗xe4 12 ♗xg7 ♖h7 13 ♗f6 = Hodgson-Agdestein, London 1986
4 ... ♗g4 5 ♘bd2 ♘bd7 6 h3 ♗h5 7 g4 ♗g6 8 ♘h4 e6 9 e3 ♗g8! 10 ♘xg6 hg 11 ♕e2 ♗d6 12 b3 ♕f6 13 d4 g5! ∞ Quinteros-Georgadze, Hanover 1983

[2] 5 b3 e6 6 ♗b2 a5 7 a4 h6 8 d3 ♗e7 = Hansen-Belyavsky, Plovdiv 1983

[3] 6 ... ♘bd7 7 ♗b2 h6 (7 ... ♗d6 8 d3 0-0 9 ♘bd2 e5 10 cd cd 11 ♖c1 ♕e7 = Reti-Lasker, New York 1924) 8 d3 ♗c5 9 ♘c3 0-0 10 ♕c2 ♗h7 11 e4 de 12 de ♕e7 (12 ... ♗b4!? Euwe) 13 ♕e2 e5 14 ♖ad1 ♖ad8 =

[4] 9 ... ♘bd7 10 ♘e5 ♘xe5 11 ♗xe5 ♗d6 12 ♗xe7 ♕xe7 13 ♖c1 e5 = Kavalek-Karpov, Amsterdam 1981

[5] 10 ♕c2 a5 11 a3 ♘bd7 = Psakhis-Ubilava, USSR 1983

[6] 13 ♕c2 ♘e8 ∞ Barlov-Marjanović, Yugoslav Ch 1984

[7] 5 ... ♕c8 6 ♘c3 ♗h7 7 e4 ♗xg2 8 ♔xg2 e6 9 ♗g5 ♘bd7 10 ♕e2 ± Larsen

[8] 6 ♘c3 e6 7 ♕e1 ♗h7 8 e4 de 9 de ♗b4 = Velimirović-Skembris, Kavala Z 1985

[9] 6 ... dc 7 dc ♕xd1 8 ♖xd1 ±

[10] 7 ♘d4!? ♗h7 8 cd ♘xd5 9 ♘b3 ♗e7 10 e4 ♘f6 11 ♘c3 ± Romanishin-Rajković, Plovdiv 1983
7 cd cd 8 ♕b3 ♕b6 9 ♘d4! ♗g6 10 ♕xb6 ab 11 ♘b5 ± Vaganian-Rivas, Linares 1985

[11] 7 ... ♘bd7 8 ♕b3 ♕b8 9 cd ed 10 ♘d4 ♗g6 11 ♗f4 ± Korchnoi-Böhm, San Bernardino 1983

[(7)] 7 ... dc!? 8 dc ♕xd1 9 ♖xd1 ♗c2 10 ♖c1 ♗h7 ± Korchnoi

[12] 10 ... ♘bd7 11 ♘d4 ♗h7 12 cd ♘c5 13 ♕d1 ed 14 ♘xd5 ± Korchnoi

[13] 12 ♘e5 ♗d6! 13 ♗d4 (13 d4 ♘c7!) 13 ... ♘c7 14 e4 de 15 de ± Korchnoi-Polugayevsky, London 1984

[14] 13 ♗h3 ♕b8 14 e4 ± Korchnoi

[15] 6 c4 ♗c5 (6 ... dc!? 7 dc ♕xd1 8 ♖xd1 ♗c2 9 ♖f1 ♘bd7 10 ♘c3 ♗e7 = Inkiov-Smagin, Moscow 1986) 7 ♘c3 (7 ♕b3 ♕b6 8 ♘bd2 ♘bd7 9 ♕xb6 ab 10 b3 dc! = Karlsson-Nikolić, 1985) 7 ... 0-0 8 ♕b3 ♕c8 9 ♗g5 ♘bd7 10 cd ed 11 ♖ac1 ♗b6 ∞ Ree-Nikolić, Wijk aan Zee 1986
6 b3 ♗c5 7 ♗b2 0-0 8 ♘bd2 h6 9 ♕e1 ♗h7 10 e4 a5 11 a3 b5 ∞ Granda-Agdestein, Gausdal 1986

[16] 6 ... ♗e7 7 ♕e1 h6 – 6 ... h6

[17] 7 b3 ♗e7 8 ♗b2 0-0 9 ♘e1 a5 10 e4 ♗h7 11 a4 ♘bd7 (11 ... ♘a6!?) 12 e5 ♘e8 13 ♕e2 ♘c7 ∞ Yudasin-Sveshnikov, USSR 1982

[18] 9 e5!? ♘fd7 10 ♕e2 c5 11 ♖e1 ♘c6 12 ♘f1 g5! 13 h3 ♕c7 14 a3 0-0-0 ∞ Vaganian-Belyavsky, USSR Ch 1983

[19] 11 e5 ♘fd7 12 ♘e1 (12 ♘d4?! c5! ∓ Nikolić-Matulović, Yugoslavia 1984) ∞
11 c3!? Farago

[20] 13 ♘e1 b5! 14 ♔h1!? (14 ed ed 15 ♘df3 ♖e8 16 ♕d2 ♗d6 17 ♘d4 ♕b6 ∓ Miles-Short, London 1985) ∞ Keene

[21] 5 h3 ♗xf3 6 ♗xf3 e6 7 d3 ♘db7 8 ♗g2 ♕c7 = Korchnoi-Petrosian, match 1971
5 d4 ♘bd7 6 ♘bd2 e6 7 ♖e1 ♗e7 8 e4 0-0 9 c3 ∞ Hug-Vaganian, Lucerne 1985

[22] 6 ... e5 7 e4 de 8 de ♗c5!? 9 c3 (9 h3 ♗h5

10 Qe1 0-0 11 Nc4 Bxf3 12 Bxf3 Qe7 ∞ Larsen-Vaganian, Naestved 1985) 9 ... a5 10 Qc2 0-0 11 b3 ± Ivkov-Marović, Yugoslavia 1972

[23] 7 h3 Bh5 (7 ... Bxf3 8 Nxf3 Be7 9 e3 0-0 10 Qe2 a5 = Portisch-Hort, Lugano Ol 1968) 8 Qe1 Be7 9 e4 0-0 10 e5 Ne8 11 Nh2 Nc7 ∞ Dorfman-Georgadze, USSR 1983

[24] 7 ... de 8 de Be7 9 Qe2 Ne5 ∞ Taimanov

[25] 8 ... 0-0 9 h3 Bxf3 10 Nxf3 a5 11 a4 ±

[26] 10 Nc4!? Bxf3 11 Bxf3 a5 = Suetin

[27] 10 ... Bh5 11 g4 Bg6 12 Qe2 Qc7 13 b3 =

[28] 13 Nh4 Re8 14 Nf5 Bf8 = Cuellar-Ivkov, Caracas 1970

[29] 5 ... Nbd7 6 cd cd 7 Qb3 Qb6 8 Qxb6 Nxb6 9 Nc3 Bxf3 10 Bxf3 e6 11 d3 Bc5 12 a4?! ± Vaganian-Flear, London 1986

[30] 6 ... Bxf3 7 Bxf3 dc 8 bc Qd4 9 Qb3!

[31] 7 ... Bc5 8 d4!? Be7 9 Nbd2 0-0 10 Rc1 ± Hort-Malich, Karlovy Vary 1975

7 ... Be7 8 d3 0-0 9 Nbd2 a5 (9 ... Re8 10 h3 Bh5 11 Qc2 Bf8 = Larsen) 10 a3 Qb6 11 Qc2 h6 12 Bc3 Rfc8 = Bilek-Geller, Sousse IZ 1978; 8 d4 - Slav

[32] 8 h3 Bh5 9 d3 0-0 10 Nc3 Bxf3 11 Bxf3 dc 12 dc Qe7 13 Qc2 Ba3 = Hübner-Taimanov, Sukhumi 1972; 8 d4 - Slav

[33] 9 Qc2 Qe7 10 e4 de 11 de Bxf3 12 Bxf3 e5 =

[34] 9 ... a5 10 a3 Qe7 11 h3 Bxf3 12 Nxf3 e5 = Vaganian

9 ... Qe7!? Larsen

[35] 13 Bg2 Qe7 14 a3 a5 = Larsen-Gligorić, Bugojno 1984

[36] 6 cd ed (6 ... cd 7 Ne5 Bf5 8 Qa4+ Nc6 9 Nxc6 Qd7 ∞ Farago) 7 h3 Bf5 8 d3 Bc5! 9 Qc2 Bb6 10 Nc3 h6 11 e4 Bh7 = Kirov-Farago, Rome 1986

6 d3 Be7 7 Be3 Nbd7 8 Qb3 Qc8 9 Nc3 0-0 10 Rac1 dc 11 dc Qc7 12 h3 Bxf3 13 Bxf3 Bc5 = Korchnoi-Spassky, Linares 1985

[37] 6 ... Bf5 7 d4 Nbd7 8 Nc3 Nxe5 9 de ± Kavalek-van der Wiel, Bochum 1981

[38] 9 cd Nxe5 10 de Nxd5 11 Qc2 0-0 12 h3 Qa5! ∓ Romanishin-Karpov, USSR Ch 1983

[39] 12 Nxe4 0-0 = Romanishin-Larsen, Lone Pine 1981

[40] 13 Bg2 0-0 14 Be3 Qxb3 15 ab Rfd8 16 h3 h6 = Sveshnikov-Geller, Moscow 1985

Catalan

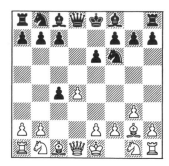
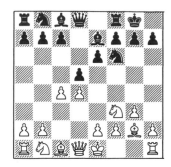

With the early fianchetto of his king's bishop White sidesteps the traditional varieties of the Queen's Gambit in order to follow a more subtle path. By eyeing the long diagonal White's bishop can exert annoying pressure on the Black queenside, hampering the easy development of that flank.

The Open Catalan (with ... dc) has enjoyed tremendous popularity of late due to its straightforward bid for active counterplay. Black can try the risky stratagem of holding on to his extra c-pawn or negotiate its return so as to mobilize his forces quickly and execute the freeing break ... c5. White's hopes for a plus depend on preventing this liberation, and if he is successful the black c-pawn can become a fixed target on the half open c-file, a victim of the line-opening strategy which Black hoped would equalize. At present the well-prepared defender can find his way to comfortable equality but, like all fashionable variations, the body of theory is constantly shifting and developing.

The Closed Catalan is solid but cramped and the task of equalizing is gradual and arduous. By careful play, however, Black may balance the chances.

Reference: *Catalan Opening* (Moiseyev and Ravinsky)

	Catalan I		**1 d4 ♘f6 2 c4 e6 3 g3**							
	3	4	5	6	7	8	9	10	11	
1	...	♗d2[1]	♕xd2	♗g2	♘f3	♘xd4	e3	cd	♕xd4	±
	♗b4+	♗xd2+	c5[2]	cd[3]	♘c6	♕b6	d5	♘xd4	♕xd4[4]	
2	...	♗g2	♘d2	♘f3	0-0[6]	♕xd2	a4	♕c3	♖d1	∞
	d5	♗b4+	♘c6[5]	dc	♗xd2[7]	♖b8	b6	♗a6	0-0[8]	
3	...	...	♗d2	♘f3	0-0	♕c2[11]	♖d1	♗f4[14]	♘c3	∞
	...	...	♗e7[9]	0-0	c6[10]	♘bd7[12]	b6[13]	♗b7	♘h5[15]	
4	...	...	♘f3	♘xd4	♘b3[16]	e3[17]	ed	♘3d2[18]	0-0	=
	...	c5	cd	e5	d4	a5	a4	ed	♗e7[19]	
5	...	...	...	...	♘f3	0-0	e3	♘c3	♘xe5[23]	∞
	...	...	...	...	d4[20]	♘c6	d3[21]	♗b4[22]	♘xe5[24]	
6	...	...	...	...	...	...	...	ed	♘xd4	=
	...	...	...	...	...	...	♗c5	♗xd4[25]	ed[26]	
7	...	...	cd	♘f3	0-0	dc	♕c2	♖d1	a3[29]	±
	...	...	♘xd5[27]	♘c6	♗e7[28]	♗xc5	♗e7	0-0	♗d7[30]	

1   4 ♘d2 c5 5 ♘f3 ♘c6 (5 ... cd!? 6 ♘xd4 ♕b6
Alburt-Adorjan, New York 1985) 6 a3 ♗xd2+
7 ♕xd2 cd 8 ♘xd4 ♘a5 9 e3 d5 10 cd ♕xd5
11 f3 0-0 12 b4 e5 ∞/= Fedorowicz-Short,
Dortmund 1986

2   5 ... d5 6 ♗g2 = 3 ... d5 4 ♗g2 ♗b4+

3   6 ... 0-0 7 dc ♕c7 8 ♕d6 ♕a5 9 ♘c3 ♘a6
10 ♘h3 (10 a3 ♕xc5 11 ♕xc5 ♘xc5 12 0-0-0 ±)
10 ... ♕b4 11 ♕d2 ♘xc5 12 ♖c1 ± Vaganian-
Adorjan, Thessaloniki Ol 1984

4   12 ed ♗xd5 13 ♘c3 ± Nogueiras-Lobron,
Reggio Emilia 1985-86

5   5 ... 0-0 6 ♘f3 dc 7 ♕c2 (7 0-0!? b5 8 a4
Alburt-Christiansen, US Ch 1983) 7 ... ♘c6
8 ♕xc4 ♕d5 9 0-0 ♗xd2 10 ♕xd5 ed 11 ♗xd2
♗g4 12 ♖fc1 ♖ac8 13 e3 ♘e4 14 ♗e1 ± Kuzmin-
Eingorn, Polanica Zdroj 1984

6   7 ♕c2!? ♗xd2+ 8 ♗xd2 ♘xd4 9 ♘xd4
♕xd4 10 ♗e3 ♕g4 11 h3 ♕g6 12 ♕xc4 ♘d5
13 ♗c5 ♗d7 14 0-0 ∞ Birnboim-Korchnoi,
Jerusalem 1986

7   7 ... c3 8 ♘c4 cb 9 ♗xb2 0-0 10 ♕c2 ♗e7
11 ♖ac1 ♘b4 12 ♕b1 ♗d7 13 ♘fe5 ♖b8
14 ♘a5 ∞ Toshkov-Makarichev, Warsaw 1985

8   Alburt-Nogueiras, Taxco IZ 1985

9   5 ... ♗xd2+ 6 ♕xd2 0-0 7 ♘f3 c6 (7 ... ♕e7
8 0-0 dc 9 ♘a3! ± Kasparov-Petrosian, Bugojno
1982) 8 0-0 b6 9 ♖c1 ♘bd7 10 cd cd 11 ♘a3! ±
Nogueiras-Andersson, Sarajevo 1985

10   7 ... dc 8 ♕c2 ± – 4 ... ♗e7 but with ♗d2
played

    7 ... b6 8 cd ed 9 ♕c2 ♗b7 10 ♘c3 c5
11 ♖ad1 ♘a6 12 ♗f4 ♕c8 13 ♗e5 ± Yusupov-
Yudasin, Minsk 1982

11   8 ♕b3 b6! 9 ♗f4 (9 ♘c3 ♗a6 10 cd cd
11 ♘e5 ♗b7! 12 ♖fc1 ♘bd7 = Alburt-Tal,
Taxco IZ 1985) 9 ... ♗a6 10 ♘bd2 ♘db7
11 ♖fd1 ♘h5! ∞ Kasparov-Hübner, match
1985

12   8 ... b6 9 ♘e5 ♗b7 10 cd (10 ♗c3 ♘a6 =
Hübner-Polugayevsky, Linares 1985) 10 ... cd
11 ♖c1 ♗d6 12 ♗g5 h6 13 ♗xf6 ♕xf6 14 f4 ±/∞
Chiburdanidze-Akhmilovskaya, match 1986

13   9 ... ♘e4 10 ♘c3 f5 11 ♘e5 ♘xe5 12 de ♗d7
13 ♗e3 ♔h8 14 ♘xe4 fe 15 cd cd = Schweber-
Larsen, Buenos Aires 1983

14   10 ♗e1 ♗b7 11 ♘bd2 c5 = Andersson-
Polugayevsky, Bugojno 1980

15   12 ♗c1 f5 ∞ Belyavsky-Wirthensohn,
Lucerne 1985

16   7 ♘c2 d4 8 0-0 ♘c6 9 e3 (9 f4 e4 10 f5 ♕b6
11 ♔h1 ∞ Rogers) 9 ... d3 10 ♘e1 e4 11 ♘c3
♗b4! 12 ♗d2 ♗g4 13 f3 ef 14 ♘xf3 0-0 ∞/∓
Uusi-Tal, Tallinn 1981

17   8 0-0 ♘c6 9 e3 ♗g4 10 ♕d3 (10 f3 ♗e6 ∓)
10 ... e4! 11 ♗xe4 ♘b4 12 ♕xd4 ♕xd4 13 ♘xd4
♘xe4 14 f3 ♗h3 ∓ Gheorghiu-Rubinetti,
Buenos Aires 1970

    8 f4 ♘c6! 9 ♗xc6+ bc 10 fe ♗g4 11 ♕xd4
♕xd4 12 ♘xd4 ♘xe5 13 ♘d2 ♗h3! ∓ Böhm-
Langeweg, Dutch Ch 1982

18   10 ♘c5 ed 11 ♕e2+ ♕e7 12 ♘e4 ♘xe4
13 ♗xe4 ♖a6 ∞/∓ Sosonko-H.Olafsson,
Reykjavik 1980

19   12 ♘a3 ♘c6 13 ♘f3 ♗e6 14 ♗f4 0-0 =
Kochiev-Tal, USSR 1981

20   7 ... e4 8 ♘d4 dc 9 0-0 ♗e7 10 ♕a4+ ♘d7
11 ♖d1 0-0 12 ♕xc4 ± Draško-Nogueiras,
Sarajevo 1985

21   9 ... ♗g4 10 h3 ♗xf3 11 ♗xf3 ♗e7 12 ed
ed 13 ♗f4 0-0 14 ♘d2 ± Karpov-Quinteros,
Linares 1981

    9 ... ♗e7 10 ed ed 11 ♗f4 0-0 12 ♘e5 ♘xe5
(12 ... ♕b6 13 ♕b3 ± Alburt-Quinteros, USA
1984) 13 ♗xe5 ♗c5 14 ♘d2 ±

22   10 ... ♗e6 11 ♘g5! ♗g4 12 ♕b3 ♕d7 (12 ...
♕b6 13 ♘b5 ±) 13 ♘d5 ♘xd5 14 ♗xd5 f6
15 f3 ± Khalifman-Oll, USSR 1984

23   11 ♗d2 0-0 12 ♘d5 ♘xd5 13 cd ♕xd5
14 ♘d4 ♕d6 15 ♘xc6 ♗xd2 16 ♕xd2 bc
17 ♖ac1 ♖b8 18 ♖xc6 ♕b4 = Rashkovsky-
Panchenko, Sochi 1980

24   12 ♕a4+ ♘c6 13 ♗xc6+ bc 14 ♕xb4 ♗h3!
(14 ... d2? 15 ♗xd2 ♕xd2 16 ♖ad1 ♕c2 17 ♕d6 ±
Sosonko-Miles, Bad Lauterberg 1977) 15 ♖d1
♗g4 ∞ Mishuchkov-Kopilov, corr. 1981

25   10 ... ed 11 ♖e1+ ♗e6 12 ♘g5 0-0 13 ♘xe6
fe 14 ♘d2! ±/∞ Alburt-Sax and Sosonko-
Hébert, Thessaloniki Ol 1984

26   12 b4 0-0 13 b5 ♘e5 14 ♗b2 ♘xc4 15 ♕xd4
♘xb2 16 ♕xb2 ♕b6 = Nogueiras-Portisch,
Montpellier C 1985

    12 ♖e1+ ♗e6 13 ♗h3 0-0 14 ♗xe6 fe
15 ♖xe6 ♕d7 ∞; 13 ♕b3!? Portisch

27   5 ... ed 6 ♘f3 – Tarrasch

28   7 ... cd!? 8 ♘xd4 ♗d7

29   11 ♘c3 ♘cb4 12 ♕b3 ♕e8 13 ♘xd5 ♘xd5
14 ♘e5 ± Zhidkov-Bernstein, USSR 1978

30   12 e4 ♘b6 13 ♘c3 ♖c8 14 ♗f4 ± Kavalek-
Grünfeld, Thessaloniki Ol 1984

Catalan II   1 d4 ♘f6 2 c4 e6 3 g3 d5 4 ♗g2 dc

	5	6	7	8	9	10	11	12	13	
1	♕a4+	♕xc4	♘f3	♘c3	♕b3	a3	♕c2	bc	0-0	±
	♗d7	♗c6[1]	♘bd7[2]	♘b6	a5	♘e4[3]	♘xc3	♗e7	0-0[4]	
2	...	♕xc4[5]	♘f3	♘c3[6]	0-0	dc	♕h4	♗g5	♖ad1	=
	♘bd7	c5	b6	♗b7	a6[7]	b5	♗xc5	♖c8	♕c7[8]	
3	...	♘f3	♘c3	♕xc4	♕d3	0-0	dc	♗f4	♖ad1	=
	...	a6[9]	♖b8	b5	♗b7	c5	♗xc5	♖c8	0-0[10]	
4	...	...	♕xc4	dc[11]	♕d3	0-0	♘c3	♘g5	♕b1	=
	...	...	c5	♗xc5	0-0	♕e7	b6	♘e5	♗b7[12]	
5	...	...	...	♕c6[13]	♗f4[14]	♗g5	♗xe7	0-0	♕c2	=
	...	...	b5	♖b8	♘d5	♗e7	♕xe7	♗b7	c5[15]	
6	♘f3	0-0	♘a3	♘xc4[18]	♕a4+	♕xc4	♕b3[20]	♕c2	b3[21]	±
	♘bd7[16]	c5[17]	♘b6	♘xc4	♗d7	b5[19]	c4	♗c6		
7	...	a4	♘e5	ab	♘c3	0-0	e4	ed[23]	♗a3	∞
	b5	c6	♘d5	cb	♗b4	♗xc3	♗xb2[22]	♗xa1	a5[24]	
8	...	...	...	0-0	b3	ab[26]	♕xb3	e4	d5	±
	...	...	...	♗b7[25]	cb	cb	a6	♘f6	♗c5[27]	
9	...	♘e5[28]	♘a3[29]	♘axc4	♗d2	0-0[30]	♕b3	♘xd7	♖ac1	∞
	a6	c5	cd	♗c5	♘d5	0-0	♘d7	♗xd7	♕e7[31]	
10	...	0-0	♘e5	b3[33]	♘xc6	♘a5	♘xb3	♗g5[35]	♘1d2	∞
	...	b5[32]	c6	cb	♕b6	♖a7	♖d7[34]	♗e7	h6[36]	
11	...	...	...	a4[37]	e4	ab	♖xa8	♘c3	♗g5	∞
	...	...	♘d5	♗b7	♘f6	ab	♗xa8	c6	♗e7[38]	
12	...	...	...	...	b3	ab	♖xa8	♕xb3	e4	∞
	...	...	...	...	cb[39]	ab	♗xa8	c6	♘f6[40]	

[1] 6 ... ♘c6 7 ♘f3 ♘a5 8 ♕d3 c5 9 0-0 ♖c8 10 ♘c3 ♗c6 11 ♖d1 c4 (11 ... cd 12 ♘xd4 ±) 12 ♕c2 ♗b4 13 d5!? ∞ Ftacnik-Lechtynsky, Czechoslovakia 1979; 13 ♗g5 intending e4 ±

[2] 7 ... ♗d5 8 ♕d3 ♗e4 9 ♕d1 c5 10 ♘c3 ♗c6 11 0-0 cd 12 ♕xd4 ±

[3] 10 ... ♗e7 11 ♕c2 ♘bd5 12 ♘e5 ±

[4] 14 e4 ± Akopov-Borisov, corr. 1985

[5] 6 ♘d2 c6 7 ♕xc4 e5 8 de ♘xe5 9 ♕c3 ♗d6 10 ♘gf3 ♗e7 11 0-0 0-0 12 ♘xe5 ♗xe5 13 ♕c2 ♖e8 = Kogan-Tarjan, US Ch 1981

[6] 8 ♘e5 cd! 9 ♗xa8 ♘xe5 10 ♕b5+ ♗d7 11 ♕xe5 ♕xa8 12 0-0 d3 ∞∞ Kondratiev

[7] 9 ... ♖c8 10 ♖d1 a6 11 dc ♗xc5 = Ivkov-Makarichev, Sochi 1983

[8] ½-½ Karpov-Ljubojević, Tilburg 1983

[9] 6 ... ♗e7 7 ♕xc4 0-0 8 0-0 c5 9 ♖d1 ±
6 ... c5 7 0-0 cd (7 ... a6! - 6 ... a6) 8 ♘xd4 ±

[10] Andersson-Kasparov, match 1985, and Andersson-Inkiov, Rome 1985

[11] 8 a4 b5 9 ♕c2 ♗b7 =
8 ♕c2 b6! 9 ♘e5 ♘d5 10 ♘c3 ♗b7 11 ♘xd5 ed 12 0-0 ♗e7 13 ♖d1 0-0 = Hübner-Smyslov, Tilburg 1982

[12] Szekely-Salov, Leningrad 1984

[13] 8 ♕c2 ♗b7 9 0-0 c5 10 e3 ♖c8 = Quinteros-Portisch, Linares 1981; 10 ♗g5 ♖c8 = Kelečević-Belyavsky, Sarajevo 1982

[14] 9 ♗g5 ♗b7 10 ♕c2 (10 ♗xf6 ♗b4+! 11 ♘bd2 ♕xf6 12 ♕xc7 ♗xf3 ∓) 10 ... c5 11 dc ♗xc5 12 0-0 ♖c8 13 ♕d3 0-0 = Smyslov-Tal, Montpellier C 1985

[15] Portisch-Hübner and Kavalek-Ljubojević, Turin 1982

[16] 5 ... c6 6 ♘e5 ♗b4+ 7 ♗d2! ♗e7! (7 ... ♕xd4 8 ♗xb4 ♕xe5 9 ♘a3! ±) 8 e3 ± Neistadt
5 ... ♗b4+ 6 ♗d2 c5 7 ♗xb4 cb 8 ♘e5 0-0 9 ♘xc4 ± Bareyev, Balashov, USSR Ch 1986
5 ... ♗d7 6 ♕c2 c5 7 ♘e5! (7 0-0 ♘c6 ±/= Kasparov-Korchnoi, match 1983) 7 ... ♘c6 8 ♘xc6 ♗xc6 9 ♗xc6+ bc 10 dc ♗xc5 11 0-0 ± Korchnoi
5 ... ♘c6 6 0-0 ♖b8 7 ♘c3 a6 – 5 ... a6

[17] 6 ... ♖b8 7 a4 b6 8 ♘fd2! ± Kasparov-Korchnoi, match 1983
6 ... a6 7 ♘bd2 b5 8 ♘e5 ♘xe5 9 ♗xa8 ♕xd4 10 ♘e4 ±/∞ Stean-Raičević, Hastings 1979-80

[18] 8 ♘e5!? cd 9 ♘axc4 ∞∞ Alburt-Browne, US Ch 1984, and Smejkal-Pachman, Baden-Baden 1985

[19] 10 ... ♕b6 11 dc ♗xc5 12 b4 ± Korchnoi-Miles, Volmac v Porz 1984
10 ... ♖c8 11 ♘e5 ± Alburt-Browne, Taxco IZ 1985

[20] 11 ♕c2 ♖c8 12 dc ♗xc5 13 ♕b3 0-0 14 ♘e5 ± Kasparov-Korchnoi, match 1983

[21] C.Hansen-Browne, Naestved 1985

[22] 11 ... ♘e7 12 bc ± Gulko-Mikhalchishin, USSR 1981

11 ... ♗xd4 12 ♕xd4 ♕b6 13 ♘f3! ±

[23] 12 ♗xb2 ♘e7 13 d5 0-0 14 ♗a3 f6! 15 d6 ♘ec6 16 ♘xc6 ♘xc6 17 d7 b4! 18 dc♕ ♖xc8 ∞ Oll

[24] Chernin-Yudasin, Sverdlovsk 1984, Glek-Oll, USSR 1986, and Balashov-Belyavsky, USSR Ch 1986

[25] 8 ... a6 – 5 ... a6

[26] 10 ♕xb3 a6 11 ♘c3 ♘d7 12 ab ab 13 ♖xa8 ♗xa8 14 ♘xd5 ed 15 e4! ± Mochalov-Spirin, corr. 1986

[27] 13 ... ed 14 ed ♗xd5 15 ♕e3! ♗e7 16 ♖d1 ±±
13 ... ♕b6 14 ♘c4! ♕c7 15 ♘a5 ± Agzamov-Foisor, Sochi 1985
13 ... ♗c5! 14 de fe 15 ♕xe6+ ♕e7 16 ♕xe7+ ♗xe7 17 ♘c3 ± Agzamov

[28] 6 a4 c5 7 0-0 cd! 8 ♕xd4 ♕xd4 9 ♘xd4 e5 ∓ Rashkovsky-Sveshnikov, USSR Ch 1976

[29] 7 ♗e3 ♗d5 8 dc ♘d7 9 ♗d4 ♘xe5 10 ♗xe5 f6 11 ♗d4 ♗xc5 12 ♗xc5 ♕a5+ 13 ♘c3 ♘xc3 14 ♕d6 ♘d5+! 15 ♔f1 ♕d8 ∞∞ Gleizerov-Panchenko, USSR 1987

[30] 10 ♕d3 ♗a7 11 ♗a5 ♕d7 12 ♘de5 ♕e7 13 ♕b3 ♘c6 14 0-0 0-0 ∓ Alburt-I.Ivanov, New York 1983

[31] 14 ♘e5 ♗b5 15 a4 ♗e8 16 ♗xd5 ed 17 ♕xd5 ½-½ Kochiev-Tunik, USSR 1984

[32] 6 ... ♘c6 7 ♘c3 ♖b8 8 e4 b5 9 ♕e2! ♘xd4 10 ♘xd4 ♕xd4 11 ♗g5 ♕b6 12 e5 ± Khalifman-Ivanchuk, Minsk 1986

[33] 8 ♘xc6 ♕b6 9 ♘e5 ♗b7 10 a4 ♗xg2 11 ♔xg2 ♕b7+ 12 ♔g1 ♘bd7 ∞∞ Razuvayev-Novikov, Volgodonsk 1983, and Cebalo-Sveshnikov, Athens 1983

[34] 11 ... ♗e7 12 e4 0-0 13 ♗e3 ± Razuvayev-M.Gurevich, USSR Ch 1985

[35] 12 ♕c2 ♖c7 13 ♕d3 ♗b7 14 e4 ♘c6 ∞ Kuzmin-Machulsky, Toliatti 1985

[36] 14 ♗xf6 ♗xf6 15 e3 0-0 ∞ Flear-Andersson, Wijk aan Zee 1987

[37] 8 ♘c3 ♗b7 9 ♘xd5 (9 e4 ♘f6 10 d5 ♘bd7! ∞ Speelman-van der Sterren, Baku 1983) 9 ... ed 10 b3 (10 e4 de 11 ♕h5 g6 12 ♘xg6 fg 13 ♕e5+ ♕e7 14 ♕xh8 ♘d7 ∞∞ Sosonko-Korchnoi, Bad Kissingen 1981) 10 ... c3 11 e4 de 12 ♕h5 g6 13 ♘xg6 fg 14 ♕e5+ ♕e7 15 ♕xh8 ♘d7 16 d5! ♕g7! ∞∞ Vainerman-Novikov, Lvov 1986

[38] 13 ... ♗b7 14 ♘xf7 (14 d5 ∞∞ Smejkal-Chandler, West Germany 1985) 14 ... ♔xf7 15 e5 ∞∞ Khalifman-Novikov, USSR 1985
13 ... ♗e7 14 ♕a1 ♗b7 15 ♕a7 ♕c8 16 ♘f3 ∞∞ Dlugy-Flear, London 1986

[39] 9 ... f6 10 bc! fe 11 cd ed 12 e4 ± Sosonko
9 ... c3 10 e4 b4 11 ed ♗xd5 12 ♕h5 g6 13 ♕h3 ♗g7 14 ♘xc3! bc 15 ♗a3 ± Buturin-Novikov, USSR 1986

[40] 13 ... ♘c7 14 ♕f3 ♕f6 15 ♗f4 ♗b4 ∞∞ Bronstein-Sveshnikov, USSR 1983
13 ... ♘f6 14 d5 cd 15 ♕xb5+ ♘bd7 = Popchev-Velikov, Vrnjačka Banja 1985

Catalan III   1 d4 ♘f6 2 c4 e6 3 g3 d5 4 ♗g2 dc 5 ♘f3 c5

	6	7	8	9	10	11	12	13	14	
1	0-0[1]	♕a4+[2]	♕xc4	♕xd4	♘c3	♗e3	♗xd4	♖ac1	♘e5	±
	cd	♗d7	♘a6[3]	♗c6	♘c5[4]	♕xd4	♗e7	0-0	♗xg2[5]	
2	...	♘e5	♘xc6	♗xc6+	♕a4	♕xc6+	♕xc4	♘d2	♘e4[7]	=
	♘c6	♗d7[6]	♗xc6	bc	cd	♘d7	♗c5	0-0	♗b6[8]	
3	...	...	♘a3	♘axc4	♕b3[10]	♗f4	♘d3	♖fc1[11]	♗xd5	∞
	...	...	cd	♗c5[9]	0-0	♕c8	♗e7	♘d5	ed[12]	
4	...	♕a4	♘xd4	♗xc6+	♖d1	♕xd1	♘d2[14]	a4	ab	±
	...	cd	♕xd4	♗d7	♕xd1+[13]	♗xc6	b5[15]	♗e7	♗xb5[16]	
5	...	...	dc	♕c2[18]	♘e5	♘c3[19]	♘xc4	♖d1	♗e3	=
	...	♗d7	♘a5[17]	♗xc5	♖c8	♘c6[20]	0-0	♕e7	♗xe3[21]	
6	...	...	♕xc4	♘xd4	♘c3	♕xd4	♕h4	♖d1[22]	♗xc6+[24]	±
	...	...	cd	♖c8	♘xd4	♗c5	♗c6	♕a5[23]	♖xc6[25]	
7	...	...	...	♕d3	dc[27]	♘c3	♘b5[28]	♘d6[29]	♗f4	∞
	...	...	b5	♖c8[26]	♗xc5	b4	0-0	♘d4	♘d5[30]	

---

[1] 6 ♕a4+ ♗d7 (6 ... ♘bd7! – 5 ♕a4+) 7 ♕xc4 ♗c6 8 dc ♘bd7 9 ♗e3 ± Korchnoi-Kasparov, match 1983

[2] 7 ♕xd4 ♕xd4 8 ♘xd4 a6 9 ♘d2± Balashov-A.Petrosian, Erevan 1986

[3] 8 ... ♗c6 9 ♘xd4 ♗xg2 10 ♔xg2 a6 11 ♖d1 ♕d5+ 12 ♕xd5 ♘xd5 13 e4 ± Palatnik-Kholmov, USSR 1982

[4] 10 ... ♕xd4 11 ♘xd4 ♗xg2 12 ♔xg2 ♗c5 13 ♘db5 0-0 14 a3± Korchnoi-Miles, London 1984

[5] 15 ♔xg2 ♖fc8 16 ♖fd1 ± Rogers-Miles, Reggio Emilia 1984-85

[6] 7 ... ♘xe5 8 de ♕d1 (8 ... ♘d5 9 ♘a3 c3 10 ♘c4 ∞) 9 ♖xd1 ♘d7 10 f4 ♖b8 11 a4 ±

[7] 14 ♘f3 ♖c8 15 ♗d2 ♗b6 16 ♕d3 ♘c5 = Petrosian-Andersson, Moscow 1981

[8] 15 ♗g5 ♕b8? 16 ♖ac1 ± Dorfman-Korzubov, USSR 1983; 15 ... ♖c8! =

[9] 9 ... ♘d5 10 ♘xc6 ♗xc6 11 ♕xd4 ♘b4 12 ♗xc6+ ♘xc6 13 ♕c3! ± Kasparov-Andersson, match 1985

9 ... ♖c8 10 ♕b3 ♘xe5 11 ♘xe5 ♗c6 12 ♘xc6 bc 13 ♖d1 ± Kasparov-Andersson, match 1985

[10] 10 a3!? 0-0 11 b4 ♗e7 12 ♗b2 ∞ Ivanchuk-A.Sokolov, USSR 1986

[11] 13 ♖ac1 ♘d5 14 ♗d6 ♗xd6 15 ♘xd6 ♕c7 16 ♘b5 ♕b6 17 ♘d6 ♕c7 = Nogueiras-A.Sokolov, Montpellier C 1985

[12] 15 ♘ce5 ♖d8 16 ♕xd5 ♗e8 17 ♕b3 ♔f8 18 ♘xc6 bc ∞ Ivanchuk-Dohoyan, Irkutsk 1986

[13] 10 ... ♗xc6 11 ♕xc6+ bc 12 ♖xd4 ±

[14] 12 ♕c2 ♗e7 13 ♕xc4 0-0±/= Polugayevsky-Andersson, Moscow 1981, and Razuvayev-Speelman, Sochi 1982

[15] 12 ... h5 13 h3 h4 14 g4 ♖d8 15 ♕c2 ± Polovodin-Kiselev, USSR 1982

12 ... c3 13 bc 0-0-0 14 ♕b3 ♗c5 15 ♘f3 ± H.Olafsson-Hjartarson, Reykjavik 1984

12 ... ♗e7 13 ♘xc4 0-0 14 b3 ♖fd8 15 ♕e1 ♖ac8 16 ♗a3 ± Gorelov-Salov, USSR 1982

[16] 15 ♘xc4 0-0 16 b3 ± Kasparov-Andersson, Nikšić 1983, Vaganian-Ribli, Montpellier C 1985, and Hjartarson-H.Olafsson, Reykjavik 1986

[17] 8 ... ♗xc5 9 ♕xc4 ♗e7 10 ♘c3 0-0 11 ♖d1 ± Suba-Stefanov, Romanian Ch 1983

8 ... ♘e5 9 ♕c2 ♘xf3+ 10 ♗xf3 ♕c8 11 ♗e3 ♗xc5 12 ♗xb7 ± Rashkovsky-Shminin, Nikolayev 1983

[18] 9 ♕a3 b6 10 b4 cb 11 ab ♗xc5 12 b4 ♗e7 13 ♘e5 ♖c8 ∞ Hulak-Afifi, Budva 1981

[19] 11 ♗g5 h6! 12 ♗xf6 gf 13 ♘xd7 ♕xd7 ∓/∞ Polugayevsky-Kupreichik, USSR 1983

[20] 11 ... b5?! 12 ♗g5

[21] 15 ♘xe3 ♖fd8 = Razuvayev-A.Sokolov, USSR Ch 1985

[22] 13 ♗g5 ♕d4 14 e4 0-0 15 ♖ad1 ♕e5 16 ♔h1 ♘d7 ∞

[23] 13 ... ♕b6 14 ♗xc6+ ♖xc6 15 ♗h6! ± Portisch-Radulov and Ribli-Ljubojević, Buenos Aires Ol 1978

[24] 14 ♗h6 0-0 15 ♗xc6 ♖xc6 16 ♗xg7 ♗xf2+ 17 ♔xf2 ♔xg7 ∞/= Csom-Peters, Hastings 1978-79

14 ♗d2 ♗e7 15 ♘d5 ♘xd5 16 ♕xe7+ ♘xe7 17 ♗xa5 ♗xg2 18 ♔xg2 ♘c6 ±/= Ftacnik-Peters, Hastings 1980-81

[25] 15 ♗g5 ♗e7 16 ♘e4 ± Benko-Peters, USA 1979
[26] 9 ... c4 10 ♕c2 ♖c8 11 e4 ±
[27] 10 ♘c3 cd 11 ♘xd4 ♘e5 12 ♕d1 b4 13 ♘e4 ♘xe4 14 ♗xe4 ♗e7 ∞ Agzamov-Kuzmin, Tashkent 1984
[28] 12 ♘e4 ♘xe4 13 ♕xe4 ♘e7! 14 ♗e3 ♕b6 = Bronstein-A.Sokolov, Moscow Ch 1983
[29] 13 ♗e3 ♗xe3 14 ♕xe3 ♘e7! 15 ♖fd1 ♘ed5 = Yusupov-A.Sokolov, match 1986
[30] Balashov-Ljubojević, Buenos Aires 1980, and Alburt-Andersson, Hastings 1980-81

	Catalan IV	1 d4 ♘f6 2 c4 e6 3 g3 d5 4 ♗g2 dc 5 ♘f3 ♗e7 6 0-0 0-0							
	7	8	9	10	11	12	13	14	15
1	♘a3[1]	ba	♘e5[3]	♘xc6	♗b2	♖c1	e3	♕g4	h4[5]	∞
	♗xa3	♗d7[2]	♗c6	♘xc6	♘d5	♕b6[4]	♕d6	f6		
2	♘e5	♘xc4[7]	♘ba3	♕b3	♖d1	♗d2	♗a5	♖ac1	♗b4[9]	±
	♕d6[6]	♕a6	♖d8	c6[8]	♘bd7	♘b6	♘fd7	♖e8		
3	...	♘xc6[10]	♗xc6[11]	♘c3	♗g2	♕c2	♖d1	e4	bc	=
	♘c6	bc	♖b8	♕d6[12]	♖d8	♕b4	♘d5	♘xc3	♕a5[13]	
4	♕c2	a4[15]	♕xc4[17]	♗g5[18]	♘c3	♖ac1	♘e5	♔xg2		=
	a6[14]	♗d7[16]	♗c6	a5[19]	♘a6	♕d6	♗xg2	♕b4[20]		

[1] 7 **♘bd2** b5 8 a4 c6 9 ♕c2 ♗b7 10 b3 cb 11 ♘xb3 ∞∞

7 ♘c3 ♗c6 8 e3 (8 e4 ♖b8 9 e5 ♘d5 10 ♘e4 ∞) 8 ... ♖b8 9 ♕a4 ♘b4 10 ♕a7 ♗d7 11 ♘e5 ♘fd5 12 ♕xb8 ∞ Sosonko-Dlugy, Tunis IZ 1985

[2] 8 ... **b5** 9 ♘g5 c6 10 e4 ∞
8 ... **♘bd7** 9 a4 a5 10 ♗a3 ♖e8 11 ♖c1 ∞∞ Sveshnikov-Ubilava, USSR 1981

[3] 9 ♗g5 ♗c6 10 ♗xf6 ♕xf6 11 ♕c2 ♘d7 12 ♕xc4 ♖fd8 = Murey-Geller, Moscow IZ 1982

[4] 12 ... c3 13 ♗a1 ∞ Sunye-Rubinetti, Rio de Janeiro 1985

[5] 15 **♖c2** ♘a4 ∓ Romanishin-Razuvayev, USSR Ch 1983

15 **h4** ∞ Razuvayev

[6] 7 ... c5 8 dc ♕c7 9 ♘xc4 ♕xc5 (9 ... ♗xc5 10 ♘c3! ♗xf2+? 11 ♖xf2 ♕xc4 12 ♖xf6! ±) 10 b3 ±

[7] 8 ♘a3 ♖d8 8 ♘axc4 ♕a6! = Palatnik-Kuzmin, USSR 1980

[8] 10 ... ♖xd4 11 ♘b5 ♖d7 12 ♘e5 ±

[9] Ribli-Ivanović, Zagreb/Rijeka 1985

[10] 8 ♗xc6 bc 9 ♘xc6 ♕e8 10 ♘xe7+ ♕xe7 11 ♕a4 c5 12 ♕xc4 cd 13 ♕xd4 e5 14 ♕h4 ♖b8 ∞∞ Chernin-Belyavsky, Sochi 1986

[11] 9 **♘c3** ♖b8 10 e4?! (10 ♗xc6 – 9 ♗xc6) 10 ... c5 11 d5 ed 12 ed ♗f5 ∓

9 **♘a3** ♗xa3 10 ba ♗a6 11 ♗xc6 ♖b8 12 ♕a4 ♖b6 13 ♗f3 ♘d5 14 ♕a5 c3 15 ♖e1 ♕f6 16 ♗xd5 ed 17 ♕xc3 ♖c6 = Belyavsky-Geller, Moscow 1981

[12] 10 ... ♗b7 11 ♗xb7 (11 ♗b5 ♗d5) 11 ... ♖xb7 12 e3 c5 =

[13] 16 ♗f1 ♗a6 17 ♗e3 ♗a3 18 ♖ab1 ♖b6 = Akopov-Govashelishvili, corr. 1981

[14] 7 ... **b5** 8 a4 b4 (8 ... c6? 9 cb cb? 10 ♘g5) 9 ♕xc4 ±

7 ... **c5** 8 dc ♕c7 9 ♕xc4 ♕xc5 10 ♕xc5 ♗xc5 11 a3 ±

[15] 8 **♗g5** b5 9 ♗xf6 ♗xf6 10 ♘g5 ♗xg5 11 ♗xa8 ♕xd4 ∞/∓ Korchnoi-Vaganian, Montpellier C 1985

8 **♘bd2** b5 9 ♘g5 ♖a7 10 b3 cb 11 ♘xb3 ♗b7 12 ♗xb7 ♖xb7 13 e4 ♘fd7! 14 ♘f3 c5 = Shabalov-Ivanchuk, USSR 1986

[16] 8 ... **b6** 9 ♘e5 ♘d5 10 ♕xc4 ♗b7 11 ♖d1 ±

8 ... **♘c6** 9 ♕xc4 ♘d5 10 ♕d3 ♖d8 11 ♘c3 ♕h5 12 ♕xc4 ♗d7 13 ♗g5 ♗e8 14 e3 ♖ac8 ±/∞ Dlugy-Speelman, London 1986

[17] 9 ♘e5 ♗c6 10 ♘xc6 ♘xc6 11 e3 (11 ♗xc6 bc 12 ♘a3 ♕d5 =) 11 ... ♘a5 12 ♕d2 c5 13 dc ♖c8 14 b4 cb 15 ♘xb3 ♘xb3 16 ♕xb3 ♘d7 = Rogers-Browne, London 1983

[18] 10 **♘c3** b5! 11 ♕d3 b4 ∓

10 **♗f4** ♘bd7 11 ♘c3 ♘b6 12 ♕d3 (12 ♕b3 a5 = Petrosian-Ivanović, Vrbas 1980) 12 ... ♘bd5 = Alburt-Prandstetter, Taxco IZ 1985

[19] 10 ... ♗d5 11 ♕d3 c5 12 dc ♘bd7 13 ♘c3 ♘xc5 14 ♕e3! ± Smyslov-Nogueiras, Graz 1984

[20] 14 ... **c6** 15 ♗xf6! ± Kasparov-Karpov, match (22) 1984-85

14 ... **♕b4!** =

	7	8	9	10	11	12	13	14	15	
5	♕c2	a4	♖d1	♘c3	♗xf3	♗xc6	a5	♕a4[23]	♕xc4	=
	a6	♗d7	♗c6	♗xf3[21]	♘c6	bc	♕b8[22]	c5	cd[24]	
6	...	♕xc4	♕c2	♗f4[25]	♖d1	♕c1	♘c3	♘xd5	♗e3	=
	...	b5	♗b7	♘c6[26]	♘b4	♘bd5[27]	♖c8	♗xd5[28]	c6[29]	
7	...	...	...	♗g5	♗xf6[30]	♘bd2	♘b3	dc	♖fd1	=
	...	...	...	♘bd7	♘xf6	♖c8	c5[31]	♗d5	♗xb3[32]	
8	...	...	...	♗d2	♕c1	♗f4[35]	♘c3	♕xf4	dc	±
	...	...	...	♗e4[33]	♗b7[34]	♘d5	♘xf4	c5	♗xc5[36]	
9	...	...	...	...	...	♗e3[37]	♖d1[39]	♘c3	a4	∞
	...	...	...	...	♘c6	♖c8[38]	♘b4	♗b7	♗xf3[40]	

[21] **10 ...** ♘bd7 11 e4 b5 12 d5 ed 13 e5 ±
10 ... ♗b4 11 ♗g5 ♗xc3 (11 ... ♘bd7 12 d5! ±) 12 ♗xf6 ♕xf6 13 bc ♕g6 14 ♕a2 ± Sveshnikov-Georgadze, Erevan Z 1982

[22] 13 ... ♗b4 14 ♗g5 (14 ♖a4!?) 14 ... ♗xc3 15 bc ♖b8 16 ♖a4 ♗b5 17 ♗xf6 ♕xf6 18 ♖xc4 e5 = Timoshchenko-Azmaiparashvili, USSR 1982

[23] 14 ♖a4 ♕b3 (14 ... c5 15 ♖xc4 cd 16 ♖dxd4 ± Khalifman-Spassov, Moscow 1985) 15 ♕xb3 cb 16 ♖c4 ♖fb8 17 ♖xc6 ♗b4 =

[24] 16 ♖xd4 c5 17 ♖d1 ♕b4 = Razuvayev-Geller, Moscow 1982

[25] **10** ♘bd2 ♘bd7 11 e4 c5 =
10 ♘c3 ♘bd7 11 ♖d1 ♕c8 12 ♗e3 c5 =

[26] **10 ...** ♘d5 11 ♘c3 ♘xf4 12 gf ♘d7 13 ♖fd1 ♕c8 14 ♘e4! ± Ribli-Karpov, Amsterdam 1980
10 ... ♗d6 11 ♘bd2 (11 ♗g5!?) 11 ... ♗xf4 12 gf ♘bd7 13 e3 ♖c8 14 b4 (14 ♘b3!?) 14 ... ♘b6 ∞ Seirawan-Karpov, London 1984

[27] 12 ... ♕c8 13 ♗g5! c5 14 ♗xf6 gf 15 ♘c3 ± Agzamov-Karpov, USSR Ch 1983

[28] 14 ... ♘xd5 15 ♗g5 c5 16 dc ♕e8 17 ♗xe7 ♕xe7 18 ♘e5 ♖xc5 19 ♕d2 ±/= Ribli-Gligorić, Novi Sad 1982

[29] 16 ♕c3 ♕b6 17 ♖ac1 ♗b7 = Azmaiparashvili-Geller, USSR 1983

[30] 11 ♘bd2 c5! 12 ♗xf6 gf ∞

[31] 13 ... ♗e4 14 ♕c3 ♘d5 15 ♕d2 c5 16 ♘xc5 ♗xc5 17 dc ♖xc5 18 ♖ac1 ± Larsen-Tal, Naestved 1985

[32] **16** ab ♖xc5 =
16 ♕xb3 ♕c7 = Kasparov-Karpov, match (20) 1986

[33] **10 ...** ♘c6 11 e3 ♘b4 12 ♗xb4 ♗xb4 13 a3

♗d6 14 ♘bd2 ♕e7 15 e4 e5 16 ♘h4 ± Pigusov-Rozentalis, Sevastopol 1986

10 ... ♘bd7 11 ♗a5 ♖c8 12 ♘bd2 ♕e8 (12 ... ♘b8 13 ♖ac1 ♘c6 14 ♘b3 ± Speelman-Taulbut, British Ch 1981) 13 b4 ♗d6 ∞ Hergott-Hartman, Canada 1985

[34] **11 ...** ♘bd7 12 ♗a5 ♖c8 13 ♘bd2 (13 a4 ± Benjamin-Zuckerman, New York 1986) 13 ... ♗a8 14 ♖d1 ± Suba-Morovic, Dubai Ol 1986
11 ... ♕c8 12 ♗e3 ♘d5 13 ♘c3 ♘xe3 14 ♕xe3 ♗b7 15 ♘e4 ± Zlochevsky-Kozunov, USSR 1986
11 ... ♖a7!? 12 ♖d1 ♘bd7 13 ♗a5 ♕a8 Azmaiparashvili-Zaitsev, Moscow 1986

[35] **12** ♖d1 ♕c8 13 ♗a5 c5 (13 ... ♘c6 14 ♗e1 ±) 14 dc ♕xc5 15 ♘bd2 ♘bd7 = Chernin-M.Gurevich, Vilnius 1985
12 ♗e3 ♘d5 13 ♘c3 ♘d7 14 ♖d1 ♖c8 15 ♘xd5 (15 ♘e5!?) 15 ... ♗xd5 16 ♘e1 ±/= Kasparov-Karpov, match (8) 1984-85

[36] 16 ♖fd1 ♕b6 17 ♘e5 ± Vaganian-Andersson, Leningrad 1987

[37] 12 e3 b4! = Sosonko-Gligorić, Lucerne Ol 1982

[38] 12 ... ♘b4 13 ♘bd2 ♗b7 14 ♗g5 ♖c8 15 a3 ± Korchnoi-Kasparov, match 1983, and Sosonko-Zuckerman, New York 1984

[39] 13 ♘bd2 ♗d5 14 ♖d1 ♘g4 15 ♗f4 (15 ♘b3 ♘b4 ∞ Agzamov-Gligorić, Vršac 1983) 15 ... f5 16 h3 ♘f6 17 ♗g5 ♘e4 = Suba-Damljanović, Belgrade 1984

[40] **15 ...** ♘fd5 16 ab ♘xe3 17 fe ab 18 ♘xb5 ♗a6 ∞ Cvetković
15 ... ♗xf3 16 ♗xf3 c6 17 ♕b1 ♕d7 18 ♗f4 ♖fd8 19 e4 ♕e8 20 ♖d2 ½-½ Panno-Lobron, Lucerne 1985

	6	7	8	9	10	11	12	13	14	
1	♕c2[1]	0-0[3]	♘xd4	♘xc6	b3	♗b2	a3	♘c3	♖fd1	=
	c5[2]	cd	♘c6	bc	♗b4[4]	♕e7	♗d6	♗b7	♖ac8[5]	
2	0-0	♘c3	b3[8]	♗b2	♘e5[9]	de	cd	♕d2	♖fc1	=
	♘bd7[6]	c6[7]	b6	♗a6	♘xe5	♘d7	cd	♖c8	♖c7[10]	
3	...	♘bd2	cd	♘e5	♘df3[12]	b3	♗b2	♖c1	♘xd7	=
	...	b6[11]	ed	♗b7	c5	a5	♘e4	♖e8	♕xd7[13]	
4	...	♕c2	b3	♖d1	♘c3	e4	♘xe4	♘xf6+	♗b2[17]	=
	...	c6[14]	b6[15]	♗b7[16]	♖c8	de	c5	♗xf6	cd[18]	
5	...	...	♘bd2	b3	♗b2	e4	ed	♕f5[20]	♕h3	±
	...	...	b6	♗a6[19]	♖c8	c5	ed	g6	♖c7[21]	
6	...	...	...	e4	b3[22]	♗b2	ed	dc	♕f5	±
	...	...	...	♗b7	♖c8	c5[23]	ed	♗xc5[24]	♖e8[25]	

---

[1] 6 ♘c3 dc 7 ♘e5 ♘c6 8 ♗xc6 bc 9 ♘xc6 ♕e8 10 ♘xe7+ ♕xe7 11 ♕a4 c5 12 ♕xc4 cd 13 ♕xd4 e5 14 ♕h4 ♖b8 ∞ Korchnoi-Karpov, match (15) 1978
6 ♕b3 c5 7 0-0 ♘c6 8 cd ed 9 dc ♗xc5 10 ♗g5 d4 =/∓ Sveshnikov-Geller, Sochi 1986

[2] 6 ... dc 7 ♕xc4 a6 8 ♗f4 ♗d6 9 ♘e5 ♘d5 10 ♘c3 ♘xf4 11 gf ± Kasparov-Andersson, match 1985
6 ... ♘c6 7 0-0 ♘b4 8 ♕d1! c5 (8 ... dc 9 ♘a3 ±) 9 a3 ♘a6 10 cd ♘xd5 11 ♘c3 ± Vera-Vilela, Cuban Ch 1985
6 ... a6 7 ♘bd2! ♘c6 8 0-0 dc 9 ♕xc4 ♕d5 10 b3 ± Gulko-Pigusov, Sochi 1985

[3] 7 dc ♕a5+ 8 ♘c3 (8 ♘d2 ♕xc5 9 a3 a5 =; 8 ♕c3 ♕xc5 9 cd ♘xd5 10 ♕xc5 ♗xc5 = Korchnoi-Tal, Moscow 1968) 8 ... ♘c6 9 cd ed 10 ♕a4 ♕xc5 11 ♗e3 ♕b4 12 ♕xb4 ♗xb4 13 ♖c1 ♘e4! 14 0-0 ♗xc3 15 bc ♗e6 16 ♖fd1 ♖ac8 17 ♘d2 ♖fd8!? = Korchnoi-Andersson, Tilburg 1987
7 cd cd! 8 ♘xd4 ♘xd5 = Grigorian-Vizhmanavin, Pinsk 1986

[4] 10 ... a5 11 ♗b2 ♗a6 12 ♘d2 ♘d7 13 ♖fd1 ♗f6 14 ♖ac1 ♖c8 15 ♘f3 ± H.Olafsson-Geller, Reykjavik 1986
10 ... e5!? 11 ♗b2 ♗d6

[5] 15 e4 dc 16 bc e5 = Tukmakov-Belyavsky, USSR Ch 1987

[6] 6 ... b6 – Queen's Indian
6 ... dc – 4 ... dc
6 ... c5 7 cd ♘xd5 8 dc – 4 ... c5
6 ... c6 7 ♘c3 b6 (7 ... dc 8 ♘e5 ±) 8 ♘e5 ♗a6 (8 ... ♗b7 9 e4 ±) 9 cd cd 10 ♗f4 ±

[7] 7 ... dc 8 e4 c6 9 a4 b6 10 ♕e2 ♗a6 11 ♖d1 ∞

[8] 8 ♕d3 b6 9 e4 a5 10 b3 ♗a6 11 ed cd 12 a4 ♘b8 13 ♘e5 ♗b7 14 ♕e2 ♘a6 15 f4 ♘b4 ∞ Romanishin-Dolmatov, Erevan 1982

[9] 10 ♘d2 b5 11 c5 b4 12 ♘a4 ♕c7 13 ♖e1 ♖fb8 14 e4 de 15 ♘xe4 ♘xe4 16 ♗xe4 ♘f6

17 ♗g2 (Pytel-Benko, Skopje Ol 1972) 17 ... ♖d8 =

[10] 15 f4 ♕b8 = Smejkal-Spassky, Baden 1980

[11] 7 ... c6 8 b3 b6 9 ♗b2 ♗a6 10 ♖e1 c5 11 e4 ±/=

[12] 10 ♘dc4 ♘e4 11 ♕c2 ♘xe5 12 ♘xe5 c5 =

[13] 15 ♘e5 ♕e6 16 ♘d3 ♗d6 = Korchnoi-Karpov, match (19) 1978

[14] 7 ... c5 8 cd ♘xd5 9 ♘c3 =
7 ... ♘e4 8 ♘c3 ♘xc3 9 ♕xc3 c6 10 ♗f4 ±

[15] 8 ... b5 9 c5 ♘e4 10 ♗b2 f5 11 ♘e1 a5 (11 ... ♗g5!?) 12 ♘d3 ♗f6 13 f3 ♘g5 14 ♘d2 ± Sosonko-Larsen, Amsterdam 1980

[16] 9 ... ♗a6 10 a4 ♖c8 11 a5 b5 (11 ... c5 12 ab ♕xb6 13 ♕a2 ± Korchnoi-Spraggett, Wijk aan Zee 1985) 12 c5 b4 ∞

[17] 14 ♘g5 ♗xg5 15 ♗xb7 ♖c7 16 dc ♗xc1 17 ♖axc1 ♖xb7 18 c6 ♖c7 = Schmidt-Janošević, Belgrade 1977

[18] 15 ♗xd4 ♕c7 = Dorfman-Lputian, USSR 1982

[19] 9 ... ♗b7 10 ♗b2 ♖c8 11 e4 – 9 e4

[20] 13 ♖fd1 cd 14 ♘xd4 b5 15 ♕f5 bc 16 bc ± Ghitescu-Radulov, Bucharest 1971, and Sosonko-Radulov, Plovdiv 1983

[21] 14 ... cd 15 ♗xd4 ♘c5 16 ♖ad1 ± Razuvayev-Lputian, USSR 1979
14 ... ♖c7 15 dc ♘xc5 16 ♕h6 ± Gelfand-Sorokin, USSR 1986

[22] 10 e5 ♘e8 11 cd ed 12 ♖e1 ♕c7 13 ♕d3 ♖c8 14 ♗f1 ♘b8?! (14 ... f6) 15 ♕b3 ± Alburt-Westerinen, Reykjavik 1982

[23] 11 ... de 12 ♘xe4 c5 13 ♘xf6+ ♗xf6 14 ♘g5 ♗xg5 15 ♗xb7 ♖c7 16 ♗e4 g6 17 d5 ± Padevsky-Janošević, Orense 1982

[24] 13 ... ♘xc5 14 ♘g5 g6 15 ♕c3 ±
13 ... dc 14 ♘xc4 b5 15 ♘ce5 ♖xc5 16 ♕e2 ♘xe5 17 ♗xe5 ±

[25] 15 ♖ae1 ♕c7 16 ♘d4 ± Vukić-Knežević, Yugoslavia 1981

English

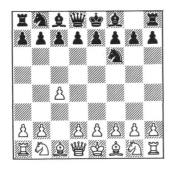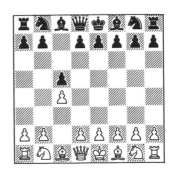

The English has gradually achieved respectability after its original reception as an uninspired and uninspiring opening. As positional understanding has developed, the English has emerged as a viable alternative to classical central action (1 d4, 1 e4) and its less travelled paths hold appeal to those wishing to journey away from the crush of modern opening theory.

With co-author Kasparov giving the English his stamp of approval and promoting it to his main weapon in his title defence against Karpov in Seville 1987, the opening may be on the verge of attaining widespread popularity.

White's first move prepares a grip on the d5 square and much of the strategy will, not surprisingly, correspond to that of the Sicilian. The English can, however, be a real chameleon. Besides its similarity to a Sicilian with colours reversed, it can transpose at a moment's notice into the King's Indian, Grünfeld, Queen's Gambit, Nimzo-Indian or Dutch, as well as following its own unique paths.

Black is not at a loss for playable options:

1 c4 ♞f6 embraces a number of defences akin to the Nimzo-Indian, King's Indian and Grünfeld where White foregoes the move d4, giving these formations an independent turn. 2 ♞c3 e6 3 e4 (the Mikenas Variation) is a sharp attempt to get an edge without allowing Black the opportunity to head for quiet waters.

1 ... e5 is a natural reply and leads to a variety of reversed Sicilian positions, of which the English Four Knights (2 ♞c3 ♞f6 3 ♞f3 ♞c6) is, at present, the most deeply researched.

1 ... c5 is sharper than its reputation and its range includes the "Keres-Parma-Rubinstein" Variation (2 ♞c3 ♞f6 3 g3 d5 4 cd ♞xd5), the 'Asymmetrical" Variation (2 ♞c3 ♞f6 3 ♞f3 d5) and the Hedgehog, all these options demanding serious theoretical preparation due to their complexity and popularity.

References: *How to Play the English Opening* (Povah)
              Symmetrical English 1 ... c5 (J.Watson)
              Closed Openings in Action (Karpov)

1 c4

	1	2	3	4	5	6	7	8	9	
1	...	♘f3[1]	g3[2]	♗g2	0-0	d3[4]	♘c3	♖b1[6]	a3	±
	f5	♘f6	e6	♗e7[3]	0-0	d6	♘c6[5]	a5	♕e8[7]	
2	...	e4	♘f3[9]	d4	♘xd4	♘c3[12]	g3[13]	♗g2	cd	=
	g6[8]	e5	♗g7[10]	ed	♘f6[11]	0-0	♖e8	d5	♘xd5[14]	
3	...	...	d4	de[16]	♗d3[17]	♘f3	♗c2	ed	0-0[20]	∞
	...	...	♘f6[15]	♘xe4	♘c5[18]	d6	♘c6	♗xd6[19]	0-0[21]	

[1] **2 e4** fe 3 ♘c3 ♘f6 4 d3 e5 5 de ♗b4 = Tompa 1972

2 ♘c3 ♘f6 3 g3 e6 4 ♗g2 ♗e7 (4 ... ♗b4 5 ♕b3 a5 6 ♘f3 0-0 7 0-0 ±) 5 d3 0-0 6 e4 fe 7 de e5 8 ♗e3 d6 =

[2] 3 ♘c3 e6 4 b3 b6 5 g3 ♗b7 6 ♗g2 ♗b4 7 ♗b2 0-0 8 0-0 ♗xc3 9 ♗xc3 d6 = Korchnoi-Spassky, match 1977-78

[3] 4 ... d5 5 0-0 c6 6 b3 ♗d6 7 ♗b2 0-0 8 d3 ♘bd7 9 ♘bd2 ± Polugayevsky-Durao, Lugano Ol 1968

[4] 6 ♘c3 d5 (6 ... ♘e4!?) 7 d3 c6 8 cd ed 9 ♗g5 ♘a6 10 a3 ♘c5 11 b4 ♗e6 ∞ Ljubojević-Byrne, Bugojno 1978

[5] **7 ... e5** 8 ♖b1 ♕e8 9 b4 ♘bd7 10 ♕b3 ± Pedersen-Skembris, Groningen 1977-78

7 ... ♕e8 8 e4 fe 9 de e5 10 ♘h4 ♘c6 11 ♘f5 ±

[6] 8 e4 e5 9 h3 ♘h8 10 ef ♗xf5 11 d4 ± Timman-Padevsky, Nice Ol 1974

[7] 10 b4 ab 11 ab ♕h5 12 b5 ♘d8 13 ♗d2 ± Bönsch-Grottke, East German Ch 1977

[8] 1 ... b6 2 ♘c3 (2 d4 – 1 d4 b6) 2 ... ♗b7 3 e4 e6 4 ♘f3 (4 b3 ♘f6 5 e5 ♘e4 6 ♘xe4 ♗xe4 7 ♗b2 ♘c6 ∞ Ljubojević-Miles, Bugojno 1986) 4 ... ♗b4 5 ♕b3 ♗xc3 (5 ... c5 6 ♘b5 d6 7 ♕d3 ± Csom-Keene, Dortmund 1977) 6 ♕xc3 ♗xe4 7 ♕xg7 ♕f6 8 ♕xf6 ♘xf6 9 ♗e2 ± Smejkal-Miles, Reykjavik 1978

[9] 3 ♘e2 d6 4 ♘bc3 f5 5 d4 ♘c6 6 ef ♗xf5 7 d5 ♘ce7 = Csom-Sax, Hungarian Ch 1977

[10] **3 ... ♘c6** 4 d4 ed 5 ♘xd4 ♗g7 6 ♘xc6 bc 7 ♘c3 ± Korchnoi-Bilek, Palma de Mallorca 1972

3 ... d6 4 d4 ♗g4!? Korchnoi

[11] 5 ... ♘e7 6 ♘c3 ♘bc6 7 ♗e3 d6 8 ♗e2 0-0 9 0-0 f5 = Adorjan

[12] 6 ♗d3 0-0 7 0-0 ♖e8 8 ♖e1 d6 9 ♘c3 ♘g4 = Rajković-Hartston, Hastings 1972-73

[13] 7 ♗e3 ♖e8 8 ♗d3 d6 9 h3 c5 10 ♘de2 ♘c6 = Pekarek-Ftacnik, Czechoslovak Ch 1986

7 ♗d3 d5 8 cd c6 9 0-0 cd 10 ed ♘xd5 11 ♗e4 ♘xc3 12 bc ♕a5 = Petrosian-Adorjan, Sochi 1977

[14] 10 ♘de2 ♘xc3 11 ♕xd8 ♖xd8 12 ♘xc3 c6 = Miles-Timman, Bugojno 1986

[15] 3 ... ed 4 ♕xd4 ♘f6 5 ♗g5 ♗e7 6 ♘c3 ♘c6 7 ♕d2 d6 8 0-0-0 ♗e6 9 ♘f3 ± Razuvayev-Gavrikov, USSR 1978

[16] 4 ♘f3 ed 5 e5 ♗b4+ 6 ♗d2 ♕e7 7 ♗xb4 ♕xb4+ 8 ♕d2 ♕xd2+ 9 ♘bxd2 ♘h5 10 ♘d4 ♘c6 11 ♘xc6 dc 12 g3 0-0 ∞ Romanishin-Gulko, Tallinn 1977

[17] **5 ♕d4** ♘c5 6 ♘f3 ♘c6 7 ♕e3 ♘e6 ∓ Ree-Ribli, Wijk aan Zee 1973

5 ♘f3 ♗c5 6 ♕d5 ♗xf2+ 7 ♔e2 f5 8 ef ♗xf6 9 ♕e5+ ♔f7 ∞ Timman-Hartston, Vienna 1972

[18] 5 ... ♗b4+ 6 ♘d2 d5 7 ed ♘xd2 8 ♗xd2 ♗d6 ± Hartoch

[19] 8 ... ♕xd6 9 ♕e2+ ♕e7 10 ♗e3 ♗g4 ∞ Murey-Jansa, Thessaloniki Ol 1984

[20] 9 ♕e2+ ♕e7 10 ♕xe7+ (10 ♗e3?! ♘b4! ∓ Quinteros-Jansa, Biel IZ 1985) =

[21] 10 ♗h6 ♖e8 11 ♘bd2 ∞ Jansa

	3	4	5	6	7	8	9	10	11	
	1 c4 c6 2 ♘f3 d5									
1	b3	♗b2	e3²	♗e2	0-0	d3⁵	♘bd2	♘d4⁷	♕xe2	=
	♘f6	♗g4¹	e6	♘bd7	♗d6⁴	0-0	♕e7⁶	♗xe2	♗a3⁸	
2	g3	♗g2	♘a3	♘g5	e4	ed	dc	♘xc4	0-0	∞
	♘f6	dc⁹	♗e6¹⁰	♗d5¹¹	h6	hg	♘xc6	e6	♘d5¹²	
3	...	...	0-0	♘a3	♕c2	♘h4	e4	b3¹⁴	♗b2	∞∞
	...	...	♘bd7¹³	♘b6	♕d5	♕e6	g6	♗g7	cb¹⁵	

¹ 4 ... g6 5 e3 ♗g7 6 ♗e2 0-0 7 0-0 ♘bd7 (7 ... ♗g4 8 ♘c3 ♘e4 9 ♕c2 ♘d7 10 cd ♘xc3 11 ♗xc3 cd 12 ♗xg7 ♔xg7 13 ♕c3+ ± Panno-Averbakh, Palma de Mallorca 1972) 8 ♘c3 (8 ♕c2 a5 9 a3 ♖e8 =) 8 ... ♖e8 9 ♕c2 dc 10 bc e5 11 d3 ♕c7 =
4 ... ♗f5 5 e3 e6 6 ♗e2 ♘bd7 7 0-0 h6 8 ♘c3 ♗e7 9 d3 ♗h7 10 ♕d2 0-0 = Panno-Addison, Palma de Mallorca IZ 1970

² 5 h3 ♗h5 6 d3 ♘bd7 7 ♘bd2 e6 8 g3 ♗xf3 9 ef dc 10 dc ♕a5 ∞ Szabo-Pomar, Palma de Mallorca 1969

³ 6 h3 ♗xf3 7 ♕xf3 ♘bd7 8 ♘c3 ♗d6 = Taimanov-Vaganian, USSR Ch 1976

⁴ 7 ... ♗e7 8 d3 0-0 9 ♘bd2 ♖e8 10 a3 a5 11 ♖e1 ♗f8 12 ♘f1 ♕b6 13 ♕c2 e5 = Andersson-Petrosian, Manila 1974

⁵ 8 h3 ♗h5 9 d3 ♕e7 10 ♘bd2 0-0 11 ♖c1 ♗a3 = Taimanov-Bagirov, Vrnjačka Banja 1974
8 cd ed = Filip

⁶ 9 ... e5!? Hort

⁷ 10 ♖e1 ♗a3 11 ♕c1 ♗xb2 12 ♕xb2 ♖fd8 = Uhlmann-Hennings, Sarajevo 1969

⁸ 12 ♗xa3 ♕xa3 13 f4 ♕e7 = Andersson-Hort, Gothenburg 1971

⁹ 4 ... ♗f5 and 4 ... ♗g4 – 1 ♘f3

¹⁰ 5 ... ♕d5 6 0-0 e5 7 ♘g5 e4 8 d3! ♗xa3 9 ba cd 10 ed ♕xd3 11 ♘xe4 ♕xd1 12 ♘xf6+ gf 13 ♖xd1 ± Szabo-Short, Hastings 1981-82
5 ... e5 6 ♘xc4 e4 7 ♘g5 ♕e7?! 8 d3 ed 9 ♕xd3 h6 10 ♗f4! ± Vaganian-P.Nikolić, Thessaloniki Ol 1984
5 ... b5 6 ♘e5 (6 b3?! cb 7 ab ♗b7 ∓ Vaganian-Rodriguez, Moscow 1985) 6 ... a6 (6 ... ♘d5 7 d3 ♕a5+ 8 ♕d2! ± Sveshnikov-Tukmakov, USSR 1980) 7 ♘xc6 ♕b6 ∞

¹¹ 6 ... ♗g4 7 ♘xc4 ♘bd7 8 ♕b3 ♘c5 9 ♕e3 e6 10 ♗xf7! ♔xf7 11 ♘e5+ ♔e8 12 b4 ± Dzindzihashvili-Torre, Thessaloniki Ol 1984

¹² 12 d4 ♗e7 13 ♘e3 ♕d7 14 ♘xd5 ½-½ Jansa-Agzamov, Calcutta 1986

¹³ 5 ... b5 6 a4 ♗b7 7 b3 cb 8 ♕xb3 a6 9 ♗a3 ∞∞ Plaskett-I.Ivanov, Brighton 1983

¹⁴ 10 ♖e1 ♘fd7 11 b3 ∞∞ Salov-Torre, Leningrad 1987

¹⁵ 12 ab 0-0 13 d4 ∞∞ Salov-Belyavsky, USSR Ch 1987

	4	5	6	7	8	9	10	11	12	
1	♗g2[1]	b3[2]	♘c3[4]	♘a4	cd	0-0	d3	♕c2	e4[6]	∞/±
	b5	♗b7[3]	b4	d5[5]	♗xd5	♗e7	0-0	♘bd7	♗b7[7]	

[1] **4 ♘c3** d5 and now:
5 d4 dc 6 ♗g2 b5 7 ♘e5 ♖a7! ∞ Nogueiras-Popović, Sarajevo 1985
5 ♗g2 dc 6 ♘e5 ♖a7 7 ♕a4+ ♘bd7 8 f4 c5 9 d3 ∞ Nogueiras-Diždarević, Sarajevo 1985
5 cd ed 6 ♗g2 c6 7 d4 ♗d6 8 0-0 0-0 9 ♗g5 ♘bd7 = Andersson-Dzindzihashvili, Thessaloniki Ol 1984

[2] **5 cb** ab 6 ♘d4 ♖a5! 7 ♘b3 ♖a7 8 d4 ♗b7 ∞ Klauser-Korchnoi, Switzerland 1985
5 ♘d4 c6! 6 cb ab 7 ♘xb5 cb 8 ♗xa8 d5 9 a4 ♕a5 10 ♕c2 ♗d7 ∞ Vaganian
5 ♘e5 ♖a7 6 cb ab 7 ♕b3 ♗b7 8 0-0 ♗xg2 9 ♔xg2 c6 (9 ... ♘a6 10 ♕xb5 ±/± Vaganian-Seirawan, Biel IZ 1985) 10 d4 ♗e7 11 ♗g5 d6 12 ♘f3 ♘bd7 ∞/± Vaganian-Korchnoi, London 1984
5 d3 ♗e7 6 0-0 ♗b7 7 b3 d5 8 ♘bd2 c5 9 e3 0-0 ∞/± I.Ivanov-Alburt, USA 1986

[3] **5 ... c5** 6 ♘c3 (6 ♘a3 ♕a5 7 0-0 ♗b7 8 d3 ♗e7 9 ♕d2 ♕b6 = Skembris-Nikolić, Heraklion 1985) ∞/±

[4] **6 0-0** c5 (6 ... ♗e7 7 ♗b2 0-0 8 ♕c2 ♖a7 9 d3 ± Csom-Plaskett, Esbjerg 1985) 7 d3 (7 ♗b2 ♗e7 8 ♘c3 d5 ∞ Miles-Korchnoi, Biel 1986) 7 ... ♗e7 8 e4 0-0 9 ♗b2 d5 ∞ Pelts-Alburt, USA 1985

[5] **7 ... c5** 8 d4 cd 9 ♕xd4 ± Pigusov

[6] **12 ♘d4!?** ♗xg2 13 ♔xg2 ♘e5 14 ♗b2 c5 15 ♘f3 ∞/±

[7] **13 h3** c5 14 ♗e3 ♖c8 15 ♖ac1 ∞/± Pigusov-Romanishin, Irkutsk 1986

English 1 ... ♘f6 II   1 c4 ♘f6 2 ♘f3 e6 3 g3 d5

	4	5	6	7	8	9	10	11	12	
1	b3	♗g2	0-0	e3	♗b2	ed	♖e1	d3	a3	=
	♗e7[1]	0-0	c5	♘c6[2]	d4	cd	♖e8	♗c5[3]	a5[4]	
2	♗g2	♕a4+[5]	♕xc4	0-0	d4[8]	♘c3	dc	♖d1	♕h4	=
	dc	♘bd7[6]	c5	b6[7]	♗b7	a6	♗xc5	♖c8	b5[9]	
3	...	...	...	♕b3	d3[11]	♘c3[12]	0-0[13]	♘g5	♘ce4	=
	...	...	...	♖b8[10]	♗d6	a6	b5[14]	♕b6	♘xe4[15]	

[1]   4 ... b6 5 ♗g2 ♗b7 6 0-0 ♗d6 7 ♗b2 0-0
8 ♘c3 ♘bd7 9 ♖c1 a6 10 cd ed 11 ♘d4 g6 ∞
A.Sokolov-Sveshnikov, USSR Ch 1985

[2]   7 ... b6 8 ♗b2 ♗b7 9 ♘c3 – 1 c4 c5 2 ♘f3
♘f6 3 g3 b6 4 ♗g2 ♗b7 5 0-0 e6 6 ♘c3 ♗e7 7 b3
0-0 8 ♗b2 d5 9 e3

[3]   11 ... ♗f8 12 a3 a5 13 ♘e5 ♘xe5 14 ♖xe5
♘d7 15 ♖b5! ± Eingorn-Agzamov, USSR 1979

[4]   13 ♘bd2 e5 14 ♘g5 ♗g4 15 ♗f3 ♗d7 (15 ...
♗xf3 16 ♕xf3 ± Miles-Geller, Lone Pine 1980)
16 ♖c1 h6 17 ♘ge4 ♘xe4 18 ♘xe4 ♗f8 19 c5
♗e6 20 ♘d2 ♗d5 = Berkovich-Vizhmanavin,
USSR 1986

[5]   5 ♕c2 ♘bd7 6 0-0 ♘b6 7 ♘a3 ♗xa3 8 ba
♗d7 9 ♘e5 ♗a4 10 ♕c3 ♘fd5 11 ♕d4 ♕f6
12 ♗b2 0-0 ∞ Suba-Nogueiras, Szirak 1986

[6]   5 ... ♗d7 6 ♕xc4 ♗c6 7 0-0 ♘bd7 8 ♕c2
e5 9 ♘c3 ♗c5 10 a3 a5 11 ♖b1 a4 12 ♘g5 ±
Karpov-Sunye, Amsterdam 1985

[7]   7 ... a6 8 ♕b3 ♗e7 (8 ... ♗d6 9 a4 0-0
10 ♘a3! ± Miles-Timman, Tilburg 1985) 9 ♘c3
♖b8 10 d3 b5 11 ♗f4 ♖b6 12 a4 ba 13 ♕a2! ±
Keene-Littlewood, England 1979

[8]   8 ♕d4 ♘e5 9 ♘c6 (9 ♕c2 ♘d5) 9 ... ♘xc4
10 ♘xd8 ♘d5 11 ♘c3 ♔xd8 12 ♘xd5 ♗b7 =
Tal-Polugayevsky, USSR Ch 1977

[9]   8 b4 ♗b7 9 b5 (9 bc ♖c8 10 d4 bc =) 9 ... ♗e7
10 ♗b2 0-0 11 a4 a6 = Kir.Georgiev-Arnason,
Plovdiv 1986

[9]   Ivkov-Makarichev, Sochi 1983

[10]   7 ... ♗e7 8 ♘c3 0-0 9 0-0 ♖b8 (9 ... a6
10 a4 ♘b8 11 ♘e5 ± Chernin-van der Sterren,
Wijk aan Zee 1986) 10 d3 b5 11 ♗f4 ♖b6 12 a4
b4 13 ♘d1 ± Vaganian-Arnason, Dubai Ol
1986

  7 ... ♗d6 8 ♘c3 0-0 9 0-0 a6 10 ♖d1 e5 11 e3
b5 ∞ Diždarević-Ribli, Sarajevo 1985

[11]   8 a4 b6 9 ♘c3 a6 10 0-0 ♗b7 11 ♖d1 ♗d6
12 d4 0-0 = Sunye-Sveshnikov, Rio de Janeiro
1985

[12]   9 ♘fd2 b6 (9 ... b5 10 a4 a6 11 ab ab 12 ♘c3
♕b6 13 ♘de4 ±/∞ M.Gurevich-Sveshnikov,
USSR Ch 1985) 10 ♘c4 ♗c7 11 ♘c3 a6 12 a4
♗b7 = Barlov-Sveshnikov, Sochi 1985

[13]   10 ♘g5 b6 (10 ... 0-0? 11 ♘xe6) 11 ♘ge4
♘xe4 12 ♘xe4 ♗e5! = Stean-Sveshnikov,
Smederevska Palanka 1980

[14]   10 ... 0-0 11 ♘g5 ♗c7 12 ♘ge4 b6 13 ♖d1!
♘xe4 14 ♘xe4 ♗b7 15 d4 ± Diždarević-
A.Petrosian, Sarajevo 1986

[15]   13 ♘xe4 0-0 14 ♗e3 ♗b7 15 ♖fc1 ♖fc8 =
Romanishin-Lputian, Irkutsk 1986

	4	5	6	7	8	9	10	11	12	
1	♕a4+	♕b3	♕xc4	g3	♗g2	d3[2]	♕a4[4]	0-0[5]	♗xf3[6]	∞
	♗d7	dc	♗g7	0-0	♘c6[1]	♗g4[3]	♕d7	♗xf3	♘d4[7]	
2	cd	g3[8]	♗g2	0-0	♘xd5[11]	d3	♗e3[12]	♕a4	♘xd4	=
	♘xd5	♗g7	e5[9]	0-0[10]	♕xd5	♘c6	♕d6[13]	♘d4	ed[14]	
3	...	♕a4+	♕h4[16]	♕d4	e3[18]	♗e2	♕c4	d4	0-0	±
	...	♗d7[15]	♗c6[17]	f6	♗g7	e5[19]	♕d6[20]	♘d7	f5[21]	

[1] **8 ... ♕c8!?** 9 0-0 c6 10 ♕h4 h6 11 d3 g5 12 ♗xg5! ± Tal-Donchev, Erevan 1986

8 ... ♗c6 9 0-0 a6 10 ♖e1! b5 11 ♕b3 ± Ghinda

8 ... ♘e8!? 9 d4 ♘d6 10 ♕d3 ♘a6 11 0-0 c5 12 ♖d1 ♖c8 13 e3 b5 ∞ Gavrikov-Tseshkovsky, USSR Ch 1986

[2] 9 0-0 e5 (9 ... ♗g4 10 ♕a4 ♕d7 11 ♔h1 e5 12 d3 h6 13 ♗e3 ± Andersson-Popović, Sarajevo 1985) 10 d3 h6 11 ♕h4 ♘e8! (11 ... ♘h7 12 ♕xd8 ♖fxd8 13 ♗d2 ♘f8 14 ♖fc1 ±/± Tal-Popović, Titograd 1984) 12 ♕xd8 ♖xd8 13 ♗e3 ∞/=

[3] 9 ... ♘e6 10 ♕h4 ±

[4] 10 ♗f4 ♗e6 11 ♕a4 ♘d5 12 ♗d2 ∞

[5] 11 ♗e3 ♗h3 12 0-0 ♗xg2 13 ♔xg2 ♘d5 =

[6] 12 ef?! ♘d4 13 ♕d1 ♖fd8 ∓ Toshkov-Ghinda, Heraklion 1985

[7] 13 ♕xd7 ♘xf3+ 14 ♔g2 ♘h4+ 15 ♔h3 = Ghinda

[8] **5 e4** ♘xc3 6 dc ♕xd1+ 7 ♔xd1 ♘d7 (7 ... f6 8 ♘d4 e5 9 ♘b5 ♗a6 10 ♗e3 ♗e6 11 b4 ± Cvetković-Simić, Belgrade 1980) 8 ♗f4 (8 ♗e3 e5 9 ♘d2 ♗c5 =) 8 ... c6 10 ♔c2 f6 11 ♘d2 e5 12 ♗e3 ♗c5 =

5 h4 h6 (5 ... ♗g7 6 h5 f5 7 ♕b3 c6 8 d4 ♕d6 9 ♗d2 ± Ftacnik-Kouatly, Thessaloniki Ol 1984) 6 e4 ♘xc3 7 bc ♗g7 8 d4 c5 9 ♖b1 0-0 10 ♗e2 ♘d7 ∞ Ribli-Smejkal, Novi Sad 1982

[9] 6 ... 0-0 7 0-0 ♘c6 8 ♘xd5 (8 ♕b3 ♘b6 9 d3 ♗g4 10 ♗e3 e5 = Miles-Timman, London 1975) 8 ... ♕xd5 9 d3 ♕b5 10 ♖b1 a5 11 b3 (11 a4 ♕a6 12 ♗e3 e5 13 ♕c1 e4 = Portisch) 11 ... a4 12 ♗b2 ♗xb2 13 ♖xb2 ♗e6 = Andersson-Olafsson, Wijk aan Zee 1976

[10] 7 ... ♘e7 8 d3 ♘bc6 9 ♗d2 0-0 10 ♖c1 ♗d4 = Hübner-Korchnoi, Solingen 1973

[11] 8 d4 ed 9 ♘xd4 ♘xc3 10 bc c5 11 ♘b3 ♘a6 ∞ Ribli-Vaganian, London 1984

[12] 10 ♕a4 ♕d6 11 ♗d2 a5 12 ♖ac1 h6 13 ♗e3 ♖d8 = Taimanov-Savon, USSR Ch 1975

[13] 10 ... ♕d8 11 ♕d2 ♖e8 12 ♗h6 (12 ♗g5 ♕d6 13 ♖ac1 ♗e6 14 a3 ♗d5 = Taimanov-Korchnoi, Titograd 1984) 12 ... ♗h8 13 ♗g5 ♕d6 14 ♖ac1 ± Taimanov

[14] Mecking-Korchnoi, match 1974

[15] 5 ... ♘c6 6 ♘e5 ♘b4 7 a3 ♗g7 8 ab ♗xe5 9 b5 ±

5 ... c6 6 ♕d4 ♖g8 (6 ... ♘f6 7 ♕xd8+ ♔xd8 8 ♘e5 ±) 7 e4 ♗g7 8 ♕a4 ♘b6 9 ♕c2 e5 10 b3 ♗g4 11 ♗e2 ± Bagirov-Novak, Stary-Smokovec 1981

[16] 6 ♕c2 ♘b4!? (6 ... ♘b6 7 d4 ♗g7 8 ♗f4 0-0 9 ♖d1 ♘c6 10 ♕c1 ± Azmaiparashvili-Lputian, USSR Ch 1986) 7 ♕e4 c5 8 a3 ♗c6 (8 ... ♗f5!? Makarichev) =

6 ♕b3 ♘b6 7 d4 ♗g7 (7 ... ♗e6 8 ♕b5 ♘8d7 9 e4 c6 10 ♕a5 ± Bukić-Popović, Vrbas 1980) 8 ♗g5 h6 9 ♗h4 ♗e6 10 ♕c2 ♘c6!? 11 ♖d1 0-0 ∞ Bagirov

[17] 6 ... ♘xc3 7 dc ♘c6 8 e4 h6 9 ♗f4! ♗g7 10 ♕g3 ♖c8 11 h4 e6 12 0-0-0 a6 13 ♘e5! ± Barbero-Aguerreberry, Argentina 1985

6 ... ♘f6 7 e4 c5 8 e5 ♘h5 9 ♕c4 ♘c6 10 ♕xc5 e6 11 ♕c4 ♘b4 ∞/± I.Ivanov-Rohde, New York 1983

[18] 8 e4 ♘xc3 9 bc ♘a6 10 ♕e3! e5 11 d4 ed 12 ♘xd4 ∞/± Barbero-Zukerfeld, Argentine Ch 1985

[19] 9 ... a5 10 0-0 ♕d7 11 ♕c4 ♘b6 12 ♕b3 ± Chekhov

[20] 10 ... ♘xc3 11 ♕e6+ ♕e7 12 ♕xe7+ ♔xe7 13 bc ♖d8 14 d4 ± Polugayevsky-Mecking, match 1977

[21] 13 ♕b3! 0-0-0 14 a4 ± Chekhov-Lputian, Kharkov 1985

English 1 ... ♘f6 IV		1 c4 ♘f6 2 ♘c3 d5 3 cd ♘xd5 4 g3 g6 5 ♗g2							

	5	6	7	8	9	10	11	12	13	
1	... ♘xc3	bc ♗g7	♗a3[1] ♘d7[2]	♘f3 ♘b6[3]	0-0 0-0	♕c2 ♖e8[4]	d3 ♗d7	♖ab1 ♗a4	♕c1 ♗c6[5]	=
2	... ...	... ...	♖b1 ♘d7[6]	♘f3[7] 0-0	0-0 ♘b6[8]	♘g5[9] ♕d7[10]	♘e4 ♖d8[11]	♕b3[12] ♕f5[13]	c4 ♗d7[14]	∞/=
3	... ♘b6	d3 ♗g7	♗e3[15] 0-0[16]	♕d2[17] ♘8d7[18]	♘f3 ♖e8[19]	♗h6 e5	♗xg7 ♔xg7	0-0 ♘f6	b4 ♕e7[20]	=
4	... ...	♘f3[21] ♗g7	0-0 0-0	d3[22] ♘c6[23]	♗e3[24] h6[25]	♖c1[26] ♔h7	♘d2 ♘d4	♘de4 c6	♘c5 a5[27]	±

[1] **7 h4** h6 (7 ... ♘d7 8 ♕b3 c5 9 ♗a3 ♕c7 10 h5 ± Suba-Roos, Buenos Aires Ol 1978) 8 ♘h3 ♘d7 9 ♗a3 0-0 =
7 a4 ♘d7 8 a5 ♖b8 9 ♘f3 0-0 10 0-0 ♘f6 11 ♕c2 ♘d5 ∞ Miles-Gutman, London 1984

[2] 7 ... 0-0 8 ♖b1 c6 (8 ... ♖e8 9 ♖xb7 ±) ±

[3] 8 ... c5 9 ♕a4 0-0 10 ♖b1 a6 11 c4 ♖b8 12 0-0 ♕c7 = Botvinnik-Smyslov, match (10) 1958

[4] 10 ... ♗d7 11 ♖ab1 ♘c4 12 ♗c1 ♗c6 13 d3 ♘b6 14 c4 e5 = Gheorghiu-Stupica, Ljubljana 1969

[5] 14 c4 ♘d7! = Petrosian-Popović, Vrbas 1980

[6] 7 ... ♘c6 8 ♕a4 0-0 9 h4 h6 10 ♘f3 ± Cebalo-Nikolić, Yugoslavia 1985

[7] 8 c4 0-0 9 ♗b2 c5 10 ♗xg7 ♔xg7 11 ♘f3 ♕c7 12 0-0 b6 = Popov-Zakhariev, Bulgaria 1984
8 ♕c2 ♘b6 (8 ... ♖b8 9 d3 b6 10 ♘f3 ♗b7 = Korchnoi-D.Byrne, Palma de Mallorca 1968) 9 c4 0-0 10 d3 e5 11 ♘f3 ♗d7 12 ♘d2 ♖b8 ∞ Bischoff-Wittman, 1985

[8] **9 ... ♖b8** 10 d4 b6 11 e4 ♗e6 12 ♕c2 ±/± Averbakh-Gheorghiu, Budapest 1970
9 ... c6 10 ♕c2 ♕c7 (10 ... ♕a5 11 c4 e5 12 d3 ± Matanović) 11 d4 e5 12 ♖d1 ♖e8 13 e4 ± Tal-Mukhin, Sukhumi 1972

[9] 10 ♕c2 ♗d7 10 d3 ♗a4 12 ♕d2 ♗c6 =

[10] 10 ... ♖e8 11 ♘e4 ♗d7 12 ♘c5 ♗c6 13 e4 ± Ftacnik-Gutman, Thessaloniki Ol 1984

[11] 11 ... ♕f5 12 ♗a3! ♖e8 13 d3 ♕h5 14 c4 ♗g4 15 ♖e1 ± Gutman

[12] 12 d3 ♕e8! =

[13] 12 ... ♕e8 13 c4 ±

[14] 14 c5 ♗a4 15 ♕f3 ♗c2 16 ♖b4 a5 = Quinteros-Gutman, Biel IZ 1985

[15] 7 h4 h6 8 ♗e3 ♘8d7 9 ♘f3 ♘f6 10 ♕c1 ♘g4 =

[16] 7 ... h6 8 ♕c1 ♘8d7 9 ♘f3 ♘f6 10 0-0 c6
11 ♖b1 ± Miles-Tisdall, Lone Pine 1976
7 ... ♘c6 8 ♕c1 ♘d4 9 ♘f3 e5 10 0-0 h6 11 ♖e1 c6 12 ♘e4 ± Gheorghiu-London, New York 1984

[17] **8 ♘f3** ♘c6 9 ♕d2 e5 10 ♗h6 ♘d4 = Polugayevsky
8 ♕c1 ♘c6!? (8 ... ♘8d7 9 ♗h6 c6 10 h4 ± Timman-Jansa, Amsterdam 1974) 9 ♗h6 ♗xh6 10 ♕xh6 ♘d4 ∞

[18] 8 ... e5 9 ♗h6 ♘8d7 10 h4 ♘f6 11 ♗xg7 ♔xg7 12 h5 ♘xh5 13 ♗f3 ± Petrosian-Tukmakov, USSR 1973

[19] 9 ... ♘f6 10 ♗h6 a5 11 0-0 c6 12 ♗xg7 ♔xg7 13 ♖ab1 ± Larsen-Hort, Amsterdam 1980

[20] 14 ♕b2 a5 15 a3 a4 16 ♖ac1 c6 = Adorjan-Vaganian, Linares 1985

[21] 6 h4 h6 7 d3 ♗g7 8 ♗e3 ♘8d7 9 a4 ♘f6 10 a5 ♘bd5 11 ♗d4 ♘xf4 12 gf ∞ Seirawan-Korchnoi, Wijk aan Zee 1983

[22] **8 b3** ♘c6 9 ♗b2 e5 10 ♖c1 ♖e8 11 d3 ♘d4 = Taimanov-Vaganian, USSR Ch 1971
8 d4 – Grünfeld

[23] 8 ... ♗d7 9 ♗f4 c5 10 ♘e5 ♗c8 11 h4 h6 12 ♘f3 ♗h7 13 ♖c1 ± Smejkal-Popović, Novi Sad 1984

[24] 9 ♗d2 h6 (9 ... e5 10 ♖c1 a5 11 ♕c2 ± Uhlmann-Tukmakov, Madrid 1973) 10 ♖c1 ♔h7 11 ♕c2 ♗g4 12 ♖b1 ♕d7 13 ♖fe1 ±/= Uhlmann-Vaganian, Skopje 1976

[25] 9 ... e5 10 ♕d2 ♘d4 11 ♗h6 ♖e8 12 ♗xg7 ♔xg7 13 b4 ± Romanishin-Whiteley, Hastings 1976-77

[26] **10 a3** a5 11 ♖c1 ♘d4 12 ♘e4 c6 = Bilek-Smejkal, Kapfenberg 1970
10 ♕c1 ♔h7 11 ♖d1 e5 12 ♗c5 (12 b4!? Pribyl) 12 ... ♖e8 13 e3 f5 (13 ... ♘d7 14 ♗a3 ♘f8 15 d4 ± Gheorghiu-Ogaard, Nice Ol 1974) 14 a4 ♗e6 15 ♕c2 ♘d5 ±/=

[27] 14 ♖e1 e5 15 ♘3a4 ♖e8 16 a3 ± Cebalo-Popović, Novi Sad 1984

	4	5	6	7	8	9	10	11	12	
1	g3[1]	♗g2	a3[4]	d4	0-0	b3[7]	♗b2	♖c1	cd	=
	0-0[2]	d5[3]	♗e7[5]	c6[6]	♘bd7	b6	♗b7	c5[8]	♘xd5[9]	
2	♕c2	a3[11]	g3[13]	♗g2	0-0	d3[16]	e3	b3	♗b2	±
	c5[10]	♗a5[12]	♘c6[14]	0-0	♕e7[15]	h6[17]	d6	♗d7	♖ab8[18]	
3	...	a3[19]	♕xc3	b4[21]	♗b2	g3	♗g2	ab	♗xa1	±
	0-0	♗xc3	b6[20]	♗b7	a5[22]	♕e7	ab	♖xa1+[23]	♘a6[24]	

[1]   4 a3 ♗xc3 5 bc (5 dc d6 6 g3 e5 7 ♗g2 0-0 8 0-0 ♕e7) 5 ... d6 (5 ... c5 6 g3 ♘c6 7 d3 d5 8 cd ed 9 ♗g2 0-0 10 0-0 ♖e8 =) 6 g3 e5 7 ♗g2 ♕e7 8 a4 a5 9 0-0 0-0 10 d3 e4 = Damjanović-Petrosian, Zagreb 1965

  4 ♕b3 c5 (4 ... ♘c6 =) 5 a3 ♗a5 6 g3 ♘c6 7 ♗g2 d5 8 0-0 ♗xc3 9 ♕xc3 d4 = Polugayevsky-Korchnoi, Sochi 1966

[2]   4 ... b6 5 ♗g2 ♗b7 6 d3 0-0 7 e4 ± Olafsson-Timman, Reykjavik 1972; 6 0-0 0-0 7 ♕b3 a5 8 d4 ♖e8 = Hölzl-Karpov, Vienna 1986

[3]   5 ... c5 6 a3 (6 0-0 ♘c6 7 ♘a4 d6 8 a3 ♗a5 = Tukmakov-Grigorian, USSR Ch 1975) 6 ... ♗xc3 7 dc ∞/±

[4]   6 cd ed 7 0-0 = Geller

[5]   6 ... ♗xc3 7 dc (7 bc c5 8 0-0 ♘c6 ∞ Eingorn) 7 ... ♘bd7 8 cd ed 9 0-0 ♖e8 10 ♗f4 c6 11 ♕c2 ♘b6 12 a4 ± Eingorn-P.Popović, Bor 1985

[6]   7 ... ♘c6 8 cd ed 9 ♘e5! ♗e6 10 ♘xc6 bc 11 ♗g5 ± Nogueiras-Romanishin, Taxco IZ 1985

  7 ... dc 8 ♘e5 ♘c6!? Nogueiras

[7]   9 ♕d3!? b6 10 e4 ♗a6 11 b3 c5 (11 ... dc?! 12 bc ♘c5 13 ♕c2 ♘bd7 14 ♖d1 ± Gavrikov-M.Gurevich, Vršac 1985) ∞ Gavrikov

[8]   11 ... ♖c8 12 ♖e1 c5 13 cd ♘xd5 14 ♘xd5 ♗xd5 15 e4 ± Gavrikov-Chernin, Moscow 1985

[9]   13 ♘xd5 ♗xd5 14 ♖e1 f5! = Chernin

[10]   4 ... d5 5 a3 ♗xc3 6 ♕xc3 0-0 – 4 ... 0-0

  4 ... b6 5 g3 ♗b7 6 ♗g2 0-0 7 0-0 ♗xc3 (7 ... c5 8 ♖d1 ♘c6 9 b3! ♗xc3 10 dc ± Suba-Polugayevsky, Buenos Aires Ol 1978) 8 ♕xc3 c5 9 b4 d6 10 d3 ± Geller

[11]   5 e3 ♘c6 6 ♗b3 0-0 7 ♗b2 ♖e8 8 ♗e2 ± Petrosian-Velimirović, Vršac 1981

  5 g3 ♘c6 6 ♗g2 0-0 7 0-0 ♕e7 8 d3 (8 ♖d1 ♗xc3 9 ♕xc3 e5 = Vaganian-Romanishin, USSR Ch 1975) 8 ... h6 9 a3 ♗a5 10 ♖b1 e5 = Hübner-Sosonko, Tilburg 1977

[12]   5 ... ♗xc3 6 ♕xc3 ♘c6 (6 ... b6 7 e3 0-0

8 ♗e2 ♗b7 9 b3 ± Furman-A.Petrosian, USSR Ch 1976) 7 b4 d6 8 e3 ♕e7 9 ♗b2 0-0 10 ♗e2 ± Smejkal-Buljovčić, Novi Sad 1976

[13]   6 e3 0-0 (6 ... ♘c6 7 d4 d6 8 ♗d3 ± Larsen-Gheorghiu, Winnipeg 1967) 7 d4 b6 8 ♗d3 ♗b7 9 0-0 ± Korchnoi-Panno, Wijk aan Zee 1978

[14]   6 ... 0-0 7 ♗g2 d5 8 ♘a4 ♘bd7 9 0-0 ± Razuvayev-G.Garcia, Cienfuegos 1976

[15]   8 ... d6 9 d3 a6 10 ♖b1 ♗d7 11 ♘a2 ± Matanović

[16]   9 ♖d1 d5! = Tal

  9 ♖b1 d6 10 ♘a2 e5 11 b4 cb 12 e3 ±

[17]   9 ... d6 10 ♖b1 (10 e4 Lombardy) 10 ... h6 11 ♘a2 d5 12 b4 ± Tal-Polugayevsky, USSR Ch 1975

[18]   13 d4 ± Lombardy-Polugayevsky, Reykjavik 1978

[19]   5 e3 b6 6 ♗e2 ♗b7 7 0-0 d5 8 a3 ♗d6 =

  5 g3 d5 6 a3 ♗e7 7 cd ed 8 d4 c5 = Vaganian

[20]   6 ... d6 7 b4 (7 g3 b6 8 ♗g2 ♗b7 9 0-0 c5 10 b4 ♘c6 11 d3 ♖e8 12 b5 ± Petrosian-Larsen, Vinkovci 1970) 7 ... e5 8 ♗b2 ♘c6 9 e3 ♘e4 10 ♕c2 f5 11 ♗e2 a5 12 d3 ± Portisch-Larsen, Palma de Mallorca 1971

[21]   7 g3 d5 (7 ... ♗b7 8 ♗g2 d5 9 0-0?! dc 10 ♘e5 ♗xg2 11 ♔xg2 b5 干 Djurić-Plaskett, Hastings 1984-85; 9 cd ♘xd5 10 ♕c2 =) 8 ♗g2 c5 9 0-0 ♘bd7 = Schüssler-Korchnoi, Vienna 1986

  7 e3 ♗b7 8 ♗e2 ♘e4 (8 ... c5?! 9 b4 d6 10 ♗b2 ♘bd7 11 0-0 ±; 8 ... d6 9 b4 ♘e4 10 ♕c2 ♘g5 = Polugayevsky-Larsen, Büsum 1969) 9 ♕c2 f5 = Ree-Korchnoi, Amsterdam 1976

[22]   8 ... d6 9 e3 e5 10 d3 ♘bd7 11 ♗e2 ± Ree-Langeweg, Dutch Ch 1984

  8 ... c5 9 e3 d6 10 ♗e2 ♘bd7 11 0-0 ♖c8 12 d3 ♕e7 13 ♘d2 (13 ♖fe1 ♖fe8 14 ♘d2 e5 = Vaiser-Rozentalis, Sverdlovsk 1984) ± Psakhis

[23]   11 ... ♘a6 12 ♖a4! ± Chernin

[24]   13 b5 ♘c5 14 0-0 ♖a8 15 ♕c2 ± Nikolić-Chernin, Tunis IZ 1985

33

	4	5	6	7	8	9	10	11	12	
1	e4	♗d3[1]	0-0[3]	e5	♗e4	d3[4]	ef	♗f4	♘b5	=
	♗b7	c5[2]	♘c6	♘g4	♕c8	f5[5]	♘xf6	♗e7	0-0[6]	

[1] 5 e5 ♘e4 6 d4 ♗e7 7 ♗d3 ♘xc3 8 bc d6 ∞
5 ♕e2 ♗b4 6 e5 ♘g8 7 g3 (7 d4 ♘e7 =)
7... ♘c6 8 ♗g2 ♘d4 9 ♕d3 ♗xf3 10 ♗xf3 ♘xf3+
11 ♕xf3 ♘e7 = Korchnoi-Portisch, match 1983
5 d3 d6 (5 ... d5!? 6 cd ed 7 e5 ♘fd7 8 d4 ♗e7
9 ♗d3 ♘f8 10 0-0 ♘e6 = Boleslavsky) 6 g3 c5
7 ♗g2 ♗e7 8 0-0 0-0 9 b3 (9 h3 ♘c6 10 d4 cd
11 ♘xd4 ♖c8 12 ♘xc6 ♗xc6 13 ♗f4 a6 14 ♕e2
♕c7 ∞ Romanishin-Ftacnik, Wijk aan Zee
1985) 9 ... a6 10 ♗b2 ♘c6 11 d4 cd 12 ♘xd4
♘xd4 13 ♕xd4 ♖b8 14 ♖fd1 ♕c7 15 a4
♖fd8 ∞/= Smejkal-Gheorghiu, Novi Sad 1982
[2] 5 ... d6 6 ♗e2 c5 7 d4 cd 8 ♘xd4 ♗e7 9 0-0
0-0 10 b3 ♘c6 11 ♗b2 a6 12 ♘xc6! ♗xc6
13 ♕d3 ± Spraggett-I.Ivanov, Montreal 1983
5 ... d5 6 cd ed 7 e5 ♘e4 8 0-0 ♘c5 9 ♗b5+ c6
10 d4 (Chekhov-A.Ivanov, USSR 1978) 10 ... cb

11 dc bc ∞
[3] 6 ♗c2 ♘c6 7 d4 cd 8 ♘xd4 ♕b8 9 ♘de2
(9 0-0 ♘xd4 10 ♕xd4 ♘g4 ∞) 9 ... ♗e7 10 f4
d6 11 0-0 0-0 12 a3 a6 13 ♕d3 b5 ∞ Simić-
Marjanović, Yugoslavia 1983
6 e5 ♘g4 7 0-0 (7 h3 ♗xf3 8 ♕xf3 ♘xe5
9 ♕xa8 ♘xd3+ ∞ Korchnoi-Polugayevsky,
match 1977) 7 ... d6 8 ed ♗xd6 9 ♗e4 ∞ Lerner-
Eingorn, Moscow 1986
[4] 9 ♖e1 d6 10 ed ♗xd6 11 d4 cd (11 ... ♘xd4
12 ♗xb7 ♕xb7 13 ♘xd4 ♗xh2+ 14 ♔f1 cd
15 ♕xg4 dc 16 ♕h5! ± Speelman-Yudasin,
Leningrad 1984) 12 ♘b5 ♗c5 13 ♘fxd4 h5 ∞
Korchnoi-Polugayevsky, match 1980
[5] 9 ... ♘gxe5 10 ♘xe5 ♘xe5 11 f4 ♘c6
12 f5 ± Tal-van der Wiel, Moscow IZ 1982
[6] Stohl-Salov, Leningrad 1984

	3	4	5	6	7	8	9	10	11	
1	...	e5[2]	cd	d4	♘f3	♗b5	♗xc6	0-0	dc	±
	d5[1]	♘fd7	ed[3]	c5	♘c6	a6	bc	♗e7	♘xc5[4]	
2	...	...	♘xe4	♕g4	♕xe4	♘f3	♗e2	0-0		∓
	...	♘e4	de	c5[5]	♘c6	♕d7	b6	♗b7[6]		
3	...	...	♘f3	♗e2[8]	d4[9]	♗e3	♕c2	bc	de	∞
	...	...	♘c6[7]	♗e7	0-0	f6[10]	♘xc3	fe	♕e8[11]	
4	...	...	ef	bc[12]	d4	♘f3	♗g5	cd	♗d2	±
	...	d4	dc	♕xf6	c5[13]	cd[14]	♕f5	♗b4+	♘c6[15]	
5	...	...	...	...	...	♘f3[16]	♗g5[17]	♗e2	♗xe7	∞
	...	...	...	...	e5	ed	♕e6+	♗e7[18]	d3[19]	
6	...	e5	d4	♕xd4	♕e4	♘f3	♘xe5	♘xd7	♗g5	∞
	c5	♘g8	cd	♘c6	d6[20]	de[21]	♗d7[22]	♕xd7	♗b4[23]	

1 c4 ♘f6 2 ♘c3 e6 3 e4 c5 4 e5 ♘g8 5 ♘f3 ♘c6 6 d4 cd 7 ♘xd4 ♘xe5[24]

	8	9	10	11	12	13	14	15	16	
7	♘db5	♗f4[25]	♘d6+[26]	♕xd6	♕a3	♗e2	♖d1	cd	♗f3	∞
	f6	a6	♗xd6	♘f7	♘e7	0-0	d5	♘xd5	♕e8[27]	
8	...	♘d6+	♕xd6	♗e3	♗b6	♗xd8[28]	♗c7	c5	♗b6[29]	∞/=
	a6	♗xd6	f6	♘e7	♘f5	♘xd6	♔e7	♘e8	d5[30]	
9	♕a4	♗g5	♘xe6[32]	♘b5	c5[33]	♘d6+	♗b5	♘e4	♖d1+	$\overline{\infty}$
	♘e7[31]	f6	♕b6	de	♕c6	♔d8	♕xc5[34]	♕c7	♗d7[35]	
10	♗f4	c5	♕b3	♕d2	♗xd6	cd	h4	♕e3	h5	±
	d6[36]	a6	♘f6	♘g6	♗xd6	♗d7	h6	♗c6	♘f8[37]	
11	...	♗g3	♘db5	♘d6+[39]	♕xd6	♘b5	♘xd6+	0-0-0	c5[40]	∞
	♘g6	♘f6[38]	e5	♗xd6	♕e7	♕xd6	♔e7	♘e8		

¹ 3 ... ♘c6 4 ♘f3 (4 d4 d5 ∞) 4 ... d5! 5 e5 ♘e4 – 3 ... d5

² 4 cd ed 5 e5 ♘e4! 6 ♘f3 (6 ♘xe4 de 7 ♕a4+ ♘c6 8 ♕xe4 ♕d4 ∞) 6 ... ♗f5! 7 ♕b3?! ♘c5 8 ♕xd5 ♘c6 9 ♗b5 ♕xd5 10 ♘xd5 0-0-0 11 ♗xc6 bc 12 ♘f4 ♘d3+ 13 ♘xd3 ♗xd3 ∓ Korsh-Markaus, corr. 1981

³ 5 ... ♘xe5 6 d4 ♘g6 7 de ♗xe6 8 d5 ♗d7 9 ♘f3 (9 ♕b3 ♘a6!) 9 ... ♗d6 10 ♗g5 f6 11 ♗e3 ± Seirawan-Handoko, Skien 1979

⁴ 12 ♘d4 ± Smyslov-Farago, Hastings 1976-77

⁵ 6 ... ♘c6 7 ♕xe4 ♕d4 8 ♕xd4 ♘xd4 9 ♔d1! ♗c5 10 d3 ± Dvoretsky-Petrosian, USSR Ch 1975

6 ... ♗d7 7 ♕xe4 ♗c6 8 ♗e3 ♘a6 9 d4 ♘b4 10 ♔d2 a5 ∞ Seirawan-Timman, Wijk aan Zee 1980, and Chandler-Mednis, New York 1980

⁶ 11 ♕f4?! h6 12 b3 g5 13 ♗e3 g4 14 ♘e1 h5 15 f4 ♘d4 ∓ Bezman-Ehlvest, USSR 1980

⁷ 5 ... c5 6 cd ♘xc3 7 dc ed 8 ♗g5 ±

⁸ 6 d4 ♗b4 7 ♗d2 0-0 8 ♗d3 ♘xd2 9 ♕xd2 f6 ∞

⁹ 7 ♕c2 ♘g5 = Seirawan-Christiansen, US Ch 1981

¹⁰ 8 ... b6 9 0-0 ♘xc3 10 bc dc 11 ♗xc4 ♘a5 12 ♗d3 ♗b7 13 ♘d2 c5 14 ♕g4 ± Yusupov-van der Wiel, Lucerne Ol 1982

¹¹ 12 ♖d1 dc 13 ♗xc4 ♖xf3! 14 gf ♘xe5 ∞ Figler-Shakarov, corr. 1986

¹² 6 fg cd+ 7 ♕xd2 ♕xd2+ 8 ♗xd2 ♗xg7 9 0-0-0 ♘c6 10 ♘f3 (10 ♘e2!? ♗d7 11 ♘g3) 10 ... ♗d7 11 ♗d3 0-0-0 =

¹³ 7 ... b6 8 ♘f3 ♗b7 9 ♗d3 ♗d6 (9 ... ♗xf3 10 gf intending ♕e2-e4 ±; 9 ... h6 10 ♕e2 intending ♗e4 ±) 10 ♗g5 ♗xf3 11 ♕d2 ♗f4 12 ♗xf4 ♗xg2 13 ♖g1 ± Miles-Sosonko, Amsterdam 1977

¹⁴ 8 ... h6 9 ♗d3 cd 10 cd ♗b4+ 11 ♔f1 ♘c6 12 ♗b2 ♗c5 13 ♗c2 0-0 14 ♕d3 ± Seirawan-Korchnoi, Wijk aan Zee 1980

¹⁵ 12 ♗xb4 ♘xb4 13 ♖b1 ♘c6 14 ♗d3 ♕a5+ 15 ♕d2 0-0 16 ♗e4 ± Romanishin-Yusupov, Sarajevo 1984

¹⁶ 8 ♕e2 ♗e7! 9 ♕xe5 (9 de ♕g6 10 ♕e3 ♗f5 ∞) 9 ... ♕xe5 10 de ♘c6 11 ♘f3 ♗g4 12 ♗e2 0-0-0 13 ♗f4 ♖he8 ∞ Chekhov-Zaichik, USSR 1980

¹⁷ 9 cd ♗b4+ 10 ♗d2 ♗xd2+ 11 ♕xd2 0-0 ∓

¹⁸ 10 ... d3? 11 0-0! ± Cramling-Ornstein, Gausdal 1980

10 ... h6 11 ♕xd4 ♕e5 12 ♗h4 ♗e7 13 ♗g3 ♕a5 14 0-0 0-0 ∞ Bagirov-Cherepkov, USSR 1982

¹⁹ 12 0-0! ♕xe7 (12 ... ♕xe2? 13 ♕b3) 13 ♗d3 0-0 14 ♕c2 h6 15 ♖ae1 ♕f6 ∞ Adorjan-Speelman, Banja Luka 1983

²⁰ 7 ... f5 8 ♕e2 a6 10 ♗d2 ♕c7 11 f4 d6 11 ♘d5! ± Bagirov-Yudasin, USSR 1982

7 ... ♕a5 8 ♘f3 f5 9 ef ♘xf6 10 ♕c2 ± Christiansen-Kudrin, US Ch 1981

7 ... ♗b4 8 ♗d2 d6 9 ♘g4 de 10 ♕xg7 ♕f6 11 ♕g3 ∞/± Seirawan-Hort, Bad Kissingen 1981

²¹ 8 ... ♕a5 9 ed ♗xd6 10 ♕d3! ♗e7 11 ♗d2 ± Seirawan-Peters, US Ch 1980

²² 9 ... ♗f6 10 ♘xc6 ♕b6 11 ♕f3 ±/= Korchnoi-Karpov, match (29) 1978, and Korchnoi-Andersson, Johannesburg 1981

²³ 12 ♗e2 ♘f6 13 ♕e3 ♕d4 = Seirawan-Andersson, Mar del Plata 1982

12 ♖d1 ♕c7 13 ♗e2 ♘f6 14 ♗xf6 gf ∞

²⁴ 7 ... ♕c7 8 ♗f4 a6 9 ♘xc6 bc 10 ♗d3 ♗b7 11 0-0 c5 12 ♗e4 ± Adorjan-Yap, Szirak 1985

²⁵ 9 ♗e3 a6 10 ♘d6+ – 8 ... a6

9 f4!? ♘f7 10 f5 Keene

²⁶ 10 ♗xe5 ab 11 ♗g3 bc 12 ♗xc4 d5 =

²⁷ 17 ♘xd5 ed+ 18 ♗e3 ♗e6 19 ♘c5 (19 0-0 ♕b5 ∓ Timman-Karpov, Las Palmas 1977) 19 ... ♗g4+ 20 ♕e3? ♗xf3 21 gf ♕d7 ∓∓ Suttles-Timman, Thessaloniki Ol 1984; 20 ♔d2! Timman

²⁸ 13 ♕c5 d6 14 ♕a5 ♕e7 15 0-0-0 0-0 16 f4 ∞ Kasparov-Sokolov, Belfort 1988

²⁹ 16 ♗xe5 fe 17 ♘a4 d5 18 cd+ ♘xd6 19 ♘b6 ♖b8 20 ♖c1 ♖d8 21 ♖c7+ ♔f6 ∓ Belov-Sideif Zade, USSR 1981

³⁰ 17 cd+ ♘xd6 18 ♗c5 ♘f7 19 ♖d1 (19 0-0-0 b5 20 a4 ♗d7 ∞/= Shvedchikov-Yudasin, USSR 1981) 19 ... ♖d8 20 h4 ♗d7 21 ♖h3 ♖ac8 22 ♗b4 ♗c6 23 ♖g3 g6 ∞/= Salov-Siegel, Groningen 1981-82

³¹ 8 ... ♘f6 9 ♘db5 a6 (9 ... ♘g6 10 h4 h5 11 ♗d3 ±) 10 ♗f4 ab 11 ♕xa8 ♗xc4 ∞

³² 10 0-0-0!? fg ∞ J.Watson

³³ 12 ♗e3 ♘c6 13 ♘c7+ ♔d8 14 ♕xc6 ♘7xc6 15 ♘xa8 ♗b4+ ∓ Lipman-Sideif Zade, USSR 1979

³⁴ 14 ... ♕xg2 15 0-0-0! ♕xg5+ 16 f4 ± Bezman-Shnaider, USSR 1986

³⁵ 17 ♗xd7 ♘xd7 18 ♘c5! ♔e8! 19 ♘xd7 ♔f7 20 ♗f4 ♕c6 21 ♕xc6 bc 22 ♗d6 ∞ Bezman/Bangiev

³⁶ 8 ... ♕c7 9 ♗g3 a6 10 ♕a4 ♘f6 11 ♗e2 ∞
8 ... f6 9 ♕a4! ♕b6 10 ♘cb5 a6 11 0-0-0 ∞ Yusupov-Yudasin, USSR Ch 1981

³⁷ 17 ♘d4! ± Vaiser-Lechtynsky, Trnava 1983

³⁸ 9 ... e5 10 ♘db5 (10 ♕e2!? J.Watson) 10 ... a6 11 ♕a4 ∞

³⁹ 11 h4 h5 12 ♘d6+ ♗xd6 13 ♕xd6 ♕e7 14 ♘b5 ♕xd6 15 ♘xd6+ ♔e7 16 0-0-0 ♘e8 17 c5 ∞ Dorfman-Flesch, Lvov 1981

⁴⁰ 16 ... b6 17 f4 ± Spassky-I.Ivanov, Toluca IZ 1982

16 ... ♘xd6 17 cd+ ♔f6 ∞ I.Ivanov

	2	3	4	5	6	7	8	9	10	
1	g3[1]	Bg2	d4	Qxd4	cd[4]	Nf3	Qa4[6]	Bd2	Nc3	=
	Nf6[2]	c6	ed[3]	d5	cd[5]	Nc6	Bb4+[7]	Be7	0-0[8]	
2	Nf3	Nd4	Nxc6[11]	Nc3	e3[13]	d4	Bxd3	Qc2	b3	∞
	e4[9]	Nc6[10]	dc[12]	Nf6	Bd6	ed	Qe7	Be6	0-0-0[14]	
3	Nc3	d4	Qxd4	g3[16]	Qd2	Nd5[17]	b3	Qe3[19]	Qxe4	∞
	d6	ed	Nf6[15]	Nc6	Be6	Ne5	Ne4![18]	c6[20]	cd[21]	
4	...	Nf3	d4	Ng5[23]	Nh3[25]	Bg5[26]	Bxf6	e3[27]	Qh5+[28]	∞
	...	f5[22]	e4	Nf6[24]	c6	h6	Qxf6	g5	Qf7[29]	
5	...	g3	Bg2[31]	d3[33]	Nf3[34]	Bxh3	Nd5	0-0	d4	±
	...	Be6[30]	Nc6[32]	Qd7	Bh3	Qxh3	Qd7[35]	Nd8	e4[36]	
6	...	Nd5[37]	Nf3[39]	Nc3	d3	e3	Be2	0-0	b3[41]	=
	Bb4	Bc5[38]	c6	Qe7	h6[40]	Bb6	Nf6	0-0	d5[42]	
7	...	g3	bc	Bg2	d3[46]	f4	Nf3	Bxf4[47]	gf	±
	...	Bxc3[43]	Nc6[44]	Nge7[45]	d6	Ng6	ef	Nxf4	0-0[48]	

[1]   **2 e3** d6 (2 ... Nc6 3 Nc3 d6 4 d4 g6 5 Nf3 Bg7 6 de Nxe5 7 Be2 Nxf3+ 8 Bxf3 Nf6 ∞ Miles-Kurajica, Reggio Emilia 1984-85) 3 Nc3 g6 4 g3 Bg7 5 Bg2 Ne7 6 d4 0-0 7 Nge2 Nd7 (7 ... Nbc6 =) 8 0-0 f5 = Plaskett-Miles, Lugano 1986

2 Qc2 Nf6 3 e3 Nc6 4 a3 g6 5 b4 Bg7 6 Bb2 d6 7 Nc3 0-0 8 d3 a5 9 b5 Ne7 ∞ Miles-Sosonko, Tilburg 1984

[2]   **2 ... c6** 3 d4 Bb4+ (3 ... e4 4 Nc3 f5 5 h4 Nf6 6 Bg5 ± Suba-Timman, Thessaloniki Ol 1984) 4 Bd2 Bxd2+ 5 Qxd2 d6 6 Nc3 Nf6 7 Bg2 0-0 8 e4 Nbd7 9 Nge2 a6 (9 ... Rb8 10 0-0 b5 11 cb cb 12 de de 13 Rfd1 ± Smejkal-Garcia Palermo, Szirak 1986) 10 0-0 b5 = Suba-Garcia Palermo, Szirak 1986

2 ... Nc6 3 Bg2 f5 4 e3 Nf6 5 Ne2 g6 6 d4 e4 (6 ... d6 7 b4 ± Tal) 7 Nbc3 d5 8 cd ± Tal-Nikolić, Naestved 1985

2 ... f5 3 Bg2 Nf6 4 d4 e4 5 Nc3 Bb4 6 Bg5 0-0 7 e3 Bxc3 8 bc d6 9 Ne2 ± Sunye-Milos, Rio de Janeiro 1985

[3]   **4 ... d6** 5 Nc3 Qa5 6 Nf3 Be7 7 0-0 0-0 8 a3 ± Csom-Barlov, Dubai Ol 1986

4 ... e4 5 Nd4 d5 6 cd Qxd5 7 Nc2 Qh5 8 h3 Bg6 9 Nc3 Bd6 10 b3 0-0 11 Ba3 ± Spraggett-Yrjölä, Dubai Ol 1986

4 ... Bb4+ 5 Bd2 Bxd2+ 6 Qxd2 d6 7 Nc3 0-0 8 Rd1 ± Lobron-Miles, Plovdiv 1983

[4]   **6 Nf3** Bb4+ (6 ... Be7 7 cd cd 8 0-0 Nc6 9 Qa4 0-0 10 Be3 Bd7 = Suba-Hübner, Thessaloniki Ol 1984; 6 ... dc!?) 7 Bd2 Be7 8 cd cd 9 Ne5 0-0 10 Nc3 Nc6 = Pähtz-Chekhov, Rostock 1985

[5]   6 ... Nxd5 7 Nf3 Bb4 8 Qxd8+ Kxd8

[6]   **8 Qd1** Bc5 9 0-0 0-0 10 Bg5 (10 Nc3 d4 11 Na4 ∞ Andersson) 10 ... h6 11 Bxf6 Qxf6 12 Nc3 ∞ Andersson-Portisch, Tilburg 1981

[7]   8 ... Be7 9 0-0 0-0 10 Be3 Bg4 11 Rd1 Qd7 12 Nc3 Rfd8 = Spassky

[8]   11 Be3 Ng4 (11 ... Bd7 =) 12 Bd4 Nxd4 13 Nxd4 Bc5 = Dokholan-Chekhov, Kharkov 1985

[9]   **2 ... Nc6** 3 d4 e4 (3 ... ed 4 Nxd4 Nf6 5 g3 ±) 4 d5 ef 5 dc fg 6 cd+ Qxd7 7 Qxd7+ Bxd7 8 Bxg2 0-0-0 9 Bf4 Be6 = Polugayevsky

[10]   **3 ... d5** 4 cd Qxd5 5 Nc2 Nf6 6 Nc3 Qd8 7 g3 Bc5 8 Bg2 Qe7 =

3 ... Nf6 4 Nc3 Bc5 5 Nb3 Bb4 6 d4 Bxc3 7 bc h6 8 Bf4 d6 ∞ Karoly-Romanishin, Tbilisi 1986

[11]   **4 Nc2** d5 5 cd Qxd5 6 Nc3 Qe5 =

4 e3 Nf6 5 Nc3 Bb4 6 Nxc6 dc 7 Be2 0-0 8 0-0 Bf5 = Polugayevsky

[12]   4 ... bc 5 Nc3 Nf6 6 g3 d5 =

[13]   6 Qc2 Bf5 7 h3 Bc5 8 e3 h5 9 b3 Qc7 Murey-Sax, Bagneux 1984

[14]   11 Bb2 h5 12 0-0-0 ∞ Botvinnik-Kan, USSR Ch 1955

[15]   4 ... Nc6 5 Qd2 g6 6 b3 Bg7 7 Bb2 Nf6 8 g3 0-0 9 Bg2 (9 Nh3 Re8 10 Nf4 Ne5 11 Bg2 ± Ftacnik-Plachetka, Bratislava 1983) 9 ... Re8 10 Nf3 Bc5 11 Nh4 ± Timman-Kuijpers, Dutch Ch 1983

[16]   5 b3 g6 (5 ... Nc6) 6 Bb2 Bg7 7 g3 (7 Nd5 Nbd7 8 Qe3+ Bf8 9 Nc3 Nc5 ∞ Adorjan-Jansa, Prague Z 1985) 7 ... 0-0 8 Bg2 Re8 9 Qd2 Nbd7 10 Nf3 Nc5 11 0-0 a5 ∞ Miles-Smejkal, Bad Wörishofen 1985

17 7 e3 d5! = Uhlmann-Klinger, Szirak 1985
    7 e4 g6 (7 ... ♕e7!? 8 f3 ♖d8 9 ♘d5 ♗xd5
10 cd ♘e5 11 ♗g2 g6 = Martinović-Rukavina,
Vršac 1985) 8 b3 ♗g7 9 ♗g2 (9 ♗b2 0-0 10 ♗g2
a5 11 ♘ge2 a4 = Cebalo-Smejkal, Zagreb 1985)
9 ... 0-0 10 ♘ge2 ♘d7 11 0-0 Dlugy-Hort, Tunis
IZ 1985

18 8 ... ♗e7 9 ♗g2 c6 10 ♘xe7 ♕xe7 11 f4!
(11 ♗a3 ± Ligterink-Timman, Wijk aan Zee
1985) ± Ligterink

19 9 ♕d4 f5 10 ♗g2 g6! ∓ Kristiansen-Reinert,
Denmark 1985

20 9 ... ♘c5!? 10 ♗h3 (10 ♗b2? c6 ∓ Hübner-
Kasparov, match 1985) =

21 11 cd ♕a5+ 12 ♗d2 ♗xd5 (12 ... ♕xd5 =)
13 ♗xa5 ♕xe4 14 f3 ♗c6 ∞ Ftacnik-Timman,
Wijk aan Zee 1985

22 3 ... ♗g4 4 d4 ♘d7 (4 ... ♗xf3 ±) 5 g3 ♘gf6
6 ♗g2 ♗e7 7 0-0 0-0 8 h3 ± Dorfman-Bronstein,
USSR Ch 1975

23 5 ♘d2 ♘f6 6 e3 c6 (6 ... g6 =) 7 b4!? ∞
Polugayevsky
    5 ♗g5 ♘f6 6 ♘d2 ♗e7 =

24 5 ... ♗e7 6 ♘h3 ♘f6 7 e3 (7 ♗g5 c6 8 ♘f4
0-0 9 e3 ∞ Stefanov-Polugayevsky, Sochi 1981)
7 ... c6 8 ♗e2 0-0 9 0-0 ♔h8 10 f3 ∞ Pinter-
Mokry, Dubai Ol 1986

25 6 e3 g6 (6 ... h6 7 ♘h3 g5 ∞) = Browne
    6 f3 ♘c6 7 fe h6 8 ♘h3 fe 9 g3 g5 =
Romanishin-Gulko, Erevan 1976

26 7 e3 d5 8 ♘g4 ♗d6 = Sax

27 9 ♘f4 e3! 10 fe g5 11 ♗d3 ♗g7 ∞

28 10 ♗e2 ♗g7! 11 ♗h5+ ♔e7 Sax

29 11 ♕xf7+ ♔xf7 12 g4 ♘d7! ∞ Uhlmann-
Sax, Szirak 1985

30 3 ... f5 4 d4 ♗e7 (4 ... e4 5 f3 ±) 5 de de
6 ♕xd8 ♗xd8 7 ♗g2 ♘f6 8 b3 ± Taimanov-
Vaganian, Leningrad 1977

31 4 d3 c6 5 e4 ♘f6 6 ♗g2 ♗e7 7 ♘ge2 0-0 ∞
Polugayevsky

32 4 ... c6 5 d3 ♘f6 (5 ... ♗e7 6 ♘f3 ♘d7
7 b3 ±) 6 ♘f3 ♗e7 7 0-0 0-0 8 c5 ± Averbakh-
Balashov, USSR 1973

33 5 b3 g6 6 ♗b2 ♗g7 7 ♘d5 ♘ge7 8 d3 0-0 =
Akesson-Kupreichik, Polanica Zdroj 1981

34 6 e4 g6 7 h4 ♗g7 8 ♘ge2 ♘f6 9 ♘d5 0-0 ∞
Hébert-Kupreichik, Hastings 1984-85
    6 ♘d5 ♘d8 7 e4 g6 8 ♘f3 ♗g7 9 ♘g5 ♗xd5

10 cd c6 = Ree-Bellon, New York 1984
    6 ♖b1!? g6 7 b4 ♗g7 8 b5 ♘d8 9 e3 ±
Seirawan-Suttles, Vancouver 1981

35 8 ... ♖c8 9 ♕a4 ±

36 10 ... c6 11 ♘c3 ±
    10 ... e4 11 ♘d2 ± Hübner-Ljubojević,
Tilburg 1981

37 3 ♕b3 ♘c6 (3 ... ♗a5 4 ♕a3 ♗xc3 5 ♕xc3
♕e7 6 b4 ♘f6 7 ♗b2 d6 8 g3 ± Miles-Timman,
Reggio Emilia 1984-85) 4 e3 ♘f6 5 a3 ♗xc3
6 ♕xc3 d5 7 cd ♕xd5 = Cebalo-Cirić, Pula 1986
    3 ♕c2 ♘f6 (3 ... ♘c6 4 ♘f3 a5!? 5 a3 ♗c5
6 e3 d6 7 ♗e2 f5 8 0-0 ♘f6 = Psakhis-Pribyl,
Sochi 1984) 4 ♘f3 ♕e7 5 d3 0-0 6 ♗d2 c6 7 a3
♗a5 8 e4 d5! = Tal-Yrjölä, Tallinn 1985
    3 e3 ♗xc3 4 bc ♘f6 (4 ... ♘e7 5 ♘e2 0-0
6 ♘g3 d6 7 ♗e2 f5 ∞ Abramović-Groszpeter,
Zenica 1986) 5 d4 e4 6 ♘e2 (6 c5!? 0-0 7 ♘e2
b6 8 cb ab 9 ♘g3 d5 ∓ Cebalo-Barlov, Budva
1986) 6 ... 0-0 7 ♘g3 d6 = Barlov

38 3 ... ♗a5 4 b4 c6 5 ba cd 6 cd (6 e3!? ∞
Smart-Hodgson, England 1984) 6 ... ♕xa5
7 ♕b3 ♘f6 8 ♘f3 (8 ♕g3 0-0 9 ♕xe5 ♘c6 ∓
Zaichik-Malanyuk, USSR 1981) 8 ... d6 9 ♗a3
♘e4 10 e3 0-0 11 ♖c1 ± Smejkal-Dely, Hradec
Kralove 1981

39 4 e3 ♘f6 5 ♘e2 c6 6 ♘xf6+ ♕xf6 7 d4 ed
8 ed ♗b6 9 ♗e3 d5 = Smejkal-Timman, Zagreb/
Rijeka 1985

40 6 ... ♘f6 7 ♗g5 ±

41 10 ♕b3 ♘a6 =

42 11 cd c6 12 ♘b5 ♖d8 13 ♗a3 ♕e6 =
Adorjan-Timman, Linares 1985

43 3 ... ♘e7!?

44 4 ... d6 5 ♗g2 f5 6 d4 ♘c6 7 c5!? (7 ♘f3 e4 =
Uhlmann-Razuvayev, Leipzig 1983) 7 ... e4
8 cd cd 9 ♘h3 ∞/± Uhlmann-Stohl, Potsdam
1985

45 5 ... d6 6 d3 f5 7 f4!? ± Saidy-McCambridge,
New York 1986

46 6 c5 b6 7 ♗a3 (7 d4!? Speelman) 7 ... ♗b7
8 ♘f3 (8 d4?! d5 9 cd cd 10 de de 11 ♕a4 0-0 ∓
Speelman-Timman, Taxco IZ 1985) 8 ... d6 9 cd
cd 10 0-0 ±; 7 ♘f3 g6 8 d4 ± Uhlmann-Stohl,
Stary Smokovec 1985

47 9 gf ♘h4!

48 11 0-0 ♖e8 12 ♕d2 ♗g4 13 ♖ae1 ± Rivas
Pastor-Timman, Linares 1985

	3	4	5	6	7	8	9	10	11	
1	♘f3	♘g5[1]	d3[3]	de	♘xf7!?[6]	e5	ef	e4	♗e3[8]	±
	e4	b5!?[2]	bc[4]	h6[5]	♔xf7	c6![7]	♕xf6	d5	♗b4[9]	
2	e3[10]	♘ge2	a3	d4	♕xd4[14]	b3	♗b2	♘c1	e4[15]	∞
	♗b4[11]	0-0[12]	♗e7	ed[13]	a5!	♘a6	♘c5	c6	♖e8[16]	
3	g3	d4	♕xd4	♗g2[18]	cd	♘f3	0-0	♕a4	♗g5[22]	=
	c6	ed[17]	d5	♗e6[19]	cd[20]	♗e7[21]	♘c6	0-0	h6[23]	
4	...	♗g2	cd[25]	♕b3[26]	♘xd5	♘xf6+	♕d1[29]	♔f1	b3	∞∞
	...	d5[24]	cd	♘c6[27]	♘d4	gf[28]	♕c7	♗e6	♘c2[30]	
5	...	♘f3	♘d4	♘b3	♗g2	cd	0-0	d3	♗g5	=
	...	e4[31]	♗c5[32]	♗b4[33]	d5	cd	0-0	♗f5[34]	♗xc3[35]	
6	...	♗g2[36]	e4[38]	dc[40]	♕e2[42]	♘f3	♘h4	0-0	♗g5	∞
	♗b4	0-0[37]	♗xc3[39]	d6[41]	b6[43]	♗b7	♘bd7	♘c5	h6[44]	
7	...	cd	♗g2	d3[47]	f4	♗xf4	♘f3	0-0	e4	∞
	d5[45]	♘xd5	♘b6[46]	♗e7[48]	ef	0-0	♗e6	c5[49]	♘c6[50]	

---

[1] 4 ♘d4 ♘c6 5 ♘xc6 dc = Polugayevsky

[2] Bellon Gambit
4 ... ♕e7 5 ♕c2 ±

[3] 5 ♘gxe4 ♘xe4 6 ♘xe4 bc 7 ♘c3 d5 =
5 ♘xb5 c6 6 ♘c3 d5 7 cd cd 8 d3 (8 e3 ♗d6
9 ♗b5+ ♔f8 ∞) 8 ... h6 9 ♘h3 ♘c6 10 g3 ♗g4
11 de d4 12 ♘b1 ♕a5 ∞∞ Sznapik-Bellon,
Cienfuegos 1976
5 cb d5 6 d4 ♗d6 (6 ... a6!?) 7 g3 h6 8 ♘h3
g5 9 ♘g1 a6 10 h4 g4 ∞∞ Spassov-Ermenkov,
Bulgarian Ch 1975
5 ♕c2 bc 6 ♘gxe4 ♗b7 7 ♘xf6+ ♕xf6
8 e4 ♗c5 9 d3 ♘a6 10 dc 0-0-0 ∞ Iskov-
Ackermann, Dortmund 1976

[4] **5 ...** ♗b4 6 ♗d2 ed 7 ♘xb5 ♗xd2 8 ♕xd2 ±
van der Sterren-Bellon, Wijk aan Zee 1977
5 ... ♗b7 6 ♘gxe4 bc 7 g3 cd 8 ed ♗b4
9 ♗g2 ± Uhlmann-Bellon, Bucharest 1978
5 ... ed 6 cb h6 7 ♘f3 de 8 ♗xe2 a6 9 0-0
♗c5 10 ♘d4! ± Stean-Regan, New York 1977

[5] 6 ... ♘c6 7 e3 ♗b4 8 ♗xc4 0-0 9 0-0 ♗xc3
10 bc h6 11 f4! ± Keene-Wockenfuss, Bad
Lauterberg 1977

[6] 7 ♘f3 ♗b7 8 e5 ♘e4 9 ♘xe4 ♗xe4
10 ♘d2 ∞/±

[7] 8 ... d5 9 ef ♗e6 10 e4 d4 11 f4 ± Keene

[8] 11 ed ♗b4 12 ♗d2 ♖e8+ 13 ♗e2 ∞

[9] 12 ♗d4 ♕h4 13 ♗e2! (13 ♕f3+ ♔g6 ∞)
13 ... ♖e8 14 0-0 (14 ♗h5+!? g6 15 ♕f3+
Ghitescu) 14 ... ♗xc3 15 ♗xc3 ♖xe4 16 f4! ±
Ghitescu-Kerkhof, Ostend 1985

[10] 3 a3 d6 4 g3 g6 5 ♗g2 ♗g7 6 e3 0-0 7 ♘ge2
♖e8 8 0-0 c6 ∞ Plachetka-Chernin, Stary
Smokovec 1984

[11] 3 ... ♘c6 and now:

4 a3 d5 5 cd ♘xd5 6 ♕c2 ♘xc3 7 dc ♗d6
8 e4 ♗e6 9 ♘f3 f6 ∞ Korchnoi-Chernin,
Montpellier C 1985
4 ♕c2 g6 5 a3 ♗g7 6 b4 0-0 7 ♗b2 (7 ♘f3
e4! 8 ♘g5 ♖e8 9 ♗b2 d6 10 h4 ♗f5 ∞/∞ Sunye-
Karpov, Amsterdam 1985) 7 ... ♖e8 8 ♘f3
(8 b5?! ♘a5 9 ♘f3 c6 10 ♗e2 d5 ∞/∞ Miles-
Ljubojević, Linares 1985) 8 ... e4 9 ♘g5 h6
10 ♘h3 g5 ∞ Ljubojević

[12] 4 ... d5 5 cd ♘xd5 6 ♘xd5 ♕xd5 7 a3 ±

[13] 6 ... d6 7 g3 c6 8 ♗g2 ♕c7 9 0-0 ♖e8 ∞

[14] 7 ♘xd4 d5 8 cd ♘xd5 9 ♘db5 ♘xc3 =
Polugayevsky
7 ed d5 8 c5 b6 9 b4 a5 10 ♗b2 ∞ Kouatly

[15] 11 ♗e2 d5 12 cd cd 13 0-0 ♘e6 =

[16] 12 ♗e2 d6 13 0-0 ♗f8 14 ♗f3 ♕b6 ∞
Quinteros-Kouatly, Lucerne 1985

[17] 4 ... e4 5 ♗g2 d5 6 ♘h3 ♗b4 ∞

[18] 6 ♗g5 ♗e7 7 ♘f3 0-0 8 ♗g2 h6 9 ♗f4 c5
10 ♕d3 d4 = Taimanov
6 ♘f3 ♗e7 7 ♗g2 c5 8 ♕d3 d4 9 ♘e4 ♘c6 =
Pfleger-Keres, Bamberg 1968

[19] 6 ... dc 7 ♕xc4 ♗e6 8 ♕a4 ♘bd7 ∞
Polugayevsky

[20] 7 ... ♘xd5 8 ♘f3 ♕b6 9 0-0 ♕xd4 10 ♘xd4 ±

[21] 8 ... ♘c6 9 ♕a4 ♗c5 = Szabo-Tompa,
Hungary 1978

[22] 11 ♗e3!?

[23] 12 ♗xf6 ♗xf6 13 ♖fd1 ♕b6 = Lehmann-
Ristić, Plovdiv 1985

[24] 4 ... ♗b4 5 ♕b3 ♕e7 6 ♘f3 0-0 7 0-0 ♖e8
8 d3 ±

[25] 5 d4 ed 6 ♕xd4 – 4 d4

[26] 6 d3 ♘c6 (6 ... ♗e7 7 ♕b3 ♘c6) 7 ♘f3
♗e7 8 0-0 0-0 9 d4 e4 = Szabo-Keres, Moscow

1956

27 6 ... e4 7 f3 ef 8 ♗xf3 ± Taimanov

28 8 ... ♕xf6 9 ♕d3 ♗f5 10 ♗e4 ♗d7 (10 ... ♗xe4 11 ♕xe4 ♖c8 ∞ Taimanov) 11 ♗xb7 ♖b8 12 ♘f3 ♖xb7 ∞ Taimanov

29 9 ♕d3 ♗f5 10 ♗e4 ♗xe4 11 ♕xe4 ♕c7 12 ♔f1 ∞

30 12 ♖b1 ♖c8 13 ♗b2 ♗a3 14 ♗h3 ∞ Saines-Kovačević, corr. 1977

31 4 ... d6 5 ♗g2 ♗e7 6 0-0 0-0 7 d4 e4 8 ♘d2 a5 9 f3 ±

32 5 ... ♕b6 6 e3 d5 7 ♕c2 ♗d7 8 a3 ♗e7 9 b4 0-0 10 ♗b2 ± Najdorf-Rossetto, Buenos Aires 1968

5 ... d5 6 cd ♕b6 (6 ... cd 7 d3 ♗c5 8 ♘b3 ± Ivkov) 7 ♘b3 cd (7 ... a5 8 d4 cd 9 ♗g2 ♗e7 10 0-0 0-0 11 ♗g5 ± Botvinnik) 8 ♗g2 ♗f5 (8 ... ♗b4 9 0-0 ♗g4 10 d3 ed 11 ♕xd3 ± Martinovsky-McCambridge, Lone Pine 1977) 9 d3 ♗b4 10 0-0 ♗xc3 11 bc 0-0 12 ♗e3 ±

33 **6 ... ♗b6** 7 c5 ♗c7 8 ♗g2 ±

6 ... d6 7 ♗g2 ♗f5 8 0-0 ♘bd7 9 d3 ed 10 ed 0-0 11 ♗f4 ± Smyslov-Bronstein, Monte Carlo 1969

34 10 ... ♗xc3 11 bc ♘c6 12 de ♘xe4 13 c4 ± Taimanov

35 12 bc ♘bd7 13 ♘d4 ♗g6 = Psakhis-Georgadze, Lvov 1984

36 4 ♘f3 e4 5 ♘d4 ♘c6 6 ♘c2 ♗xc3 7 dc h6 8 ♗e3 ♕e7 = Larsen-Petrosian, Milan 1975

37 4 ... ♘c6 5 ♘d5 ♗c5 6 a3 (6 e3 0-0 7 ♘e2 ♖e8 8 0-0 ♗f8 9 d3 ±) 6 ... ♘xd5 7 cd ♕f6 8 e3 ♘e7 9 b4 ♗b6 10 ♗b2 ± Suba-Kir.Georgiev, Thessaloniki Ol 1984

38 **5 ♕b3** a5 (5 ... ♘c6 6 ♗xc6 ♗xc3 7 ♕xc3

bc 8 ♘f3 d6 9 d3 e4 = Palatnik-Eingorn, USSR 1977) 6 a3 ♗xc3 7 ♕xc3 ♖e8 8 ♘f3 d5 9 d3 ♘c6 10 ♗g5 d4 ∞ Browne-Hort, Boblingen 1985

5 d3 ♖e8 6 ♗d2 c6 7 ♘f3 d5 8 0-0 d4 =

5 ♘f3 ♖e8 6 0-0 e4 7 ♘d4 (7 ♘g5 ♗xc3 8 dc h6 9 ♘h3 d6 ∞ Garcia Padron-Timman, Las Palmas 1977) 7 ... ♗xc3 8 bc ♘c6 9 d3 ed 10 ed h6 = Pfleger-Korchnoi, Hastings 1971-72

39 **5 ... ♘c6** 6 ♘ge2 ♖e8 7 a3 ♗f8 8 d3 a5 ± Korchnoi

5 ... c6 6 ♘ge2 (6 a3 ♗xc3 7 dc Taimanov) 6 ... d5 7 cd cd 8 ♘xd5 ♘xd5 9 ed ♗f5 10 0-0 ♘d7 ∞ Ivkov-Ree, Amsterdam 1968

40 6 bc c6 7 ♘e2 d5 8 cd cd 9 ed ♘xd5 10 0-0 ♘c6 = Stein-Gheorghiu, Las Palmas 1973

41 6 ... a6!? Tal

42 7 ♘e2 ♘bd7 8 0-0 b6 9 f3 a5 10 ♗e3 ♗b7 =

43 **7 ... ♘bd7** 8 ♘f3 ♘c5 9 ♘h4 a6 10 b3 b5 ∞ Korchnoi-Mecking, match 1974

7 ... a6 8 ♘f3 b5 9 c5 ♗b7 10 cd cd 11 ♘h4 d5 ∞ Korchnoi-Kuzmin, USSR Ch 1973

44 Djurić-Tal, Titograd 1984

45 **3 ... d6** 4 ♗g2 ♘bd7 5 ♘f3 c6 6 e4 ♗e7 7 0-0 ±

3 ... ♗c5 4 ♗g2 0-0 5 e3 ♖e8 6 ♘ge2 ± Hort

46 **5 ... c6** 6 ♘f3 ♕c7 7 d4 ±

5 ... ♘xc3 6 bc ♘c6 7 d3 ♗c5 8 ♘f3 0-0 9 0-0 ± Taimanov

47 6 ♘f3 ♘c6 – 3 ♘f3 ♘c6 4 g3 d5

48 6 ♘c6 7 ♘h3 ♗f8 8 f4 ♕d7 9 ♘f2 ef 10 ♗xf4 ♗e7 ∞

49 10 ... ♘c6!?

50 12 ♕d2 ♕d7 13 ♘g5 ♗g4 ∞ Langeweg-Donner, Amsterdam 1961

	3	4	5	6	7	8	9	10	11	
1	♘f3	d4	♘g5[1]	♘h3[3]	e3	♘f4[5]	h4	♗e2[6]	d5	∞
	f5	e4	♘f6[2]	g6[4]	♗g7	d6	0-0	♘e7	c6[7]	
2	g3	♗g2	e3[9]	d4	♘ge2	b3	♗a3	0-0	♕d2[12]	±
	f5[8]	♘f6	d6[10]	♗e7	0-0	♕e8	♗d7[11]	♘d8	♗c6[13]	

1 c4 e5 2 ♘c3 ♘c6 3 g3 g6 4 ♗g2 ♗g7

	5	6	7	8	9	10	11	12	13	
3	e3	♘ge2	0-0[16]	d3	h3[18]	♘d5	♔h2	f4	♗d2	∞
	d6[14]	♘ge7[15]	0-0	♗g4[17]	♗e6	♕d7	f5[19]	♖ae8	♘c8![20]	
4	...	...	h4[21]	d3	b4	♖b1[25]	♕c2[26]	♗d2	0-0	=
	...	h5	♗g4[22]	♘ge7[23]	a6[24]	♖b8	0-0	♖e8[27]	♕d7	
5	♖b1	a3[29]	b4[31]	ab	d3	♕b3[32]	♘f3	♘xe5	b5[34]	∞∞
	a5[28]	♘f6[30]	ab	0-0	♘e7	c6[33]	d5	♗e6	♘e8[35]	
6	d3	e4[36]	♘ge2	0-0[39]	ef[40]	♘d5[41]	cd	d4[43]	♘f4[44]	±
	d6	f5[37]	♘f6[38]	0-0	gf	♘xd5	♘e7[42]	e4		
7	...	...	♘ge2[45]	0-0	f3	♘d5	♗e3	♕d2	♖ae1	∞
	...	♘ge7	0-0[46]	♗g4[47]	♗e6	f5	♕d7	♖f7[48]	♖af8[49]	
8	...	♘f3	0-0	♖b1[50]	a3	♗g5[53]	♗xf6	b4	ab	∞
	...	♘f6	0-0	a5[51]	♘d4[52]	h6	♗xf6	ab	♗g4![54]	

[1] 5 ♘d2 ♘f6 6 e3 g6 (6 ... ♗b4 7 ♘d5 0-0 8 ♘xb4 ♘xb4 9 d5 a5 ∞) 7 ♗e2 ♗g7 8 ♖b1 a5 9 a3 0-0 10 b4 ab 11 ab ♘e7 =
5 ♗g5 ♗e7 6 ♗xe7 ♘cxe7! 7 ♘d2 ♘f6 8 e3 0-0 9 ♗e2 c6! ∓ Sax-Stean, 1979

[2] 5 ... ♗b4 6 ♘h3 ♘f6 7 ♘f4 0-0 8 h4 d6 9 e3 ♗xc3 10 bc ♘e7 (10 ... ♕e8 Smejkal-Kurajica, Sarajevo 1982) 11 ♗a3 ♘g6 12 ♘xg6 (12 g3 ♘xf4 13 gf b6 ∞ Timman-Sax, Linares 1983) 12 ... hg 13 c5 ±
5 ... ♕f6 6 ♘d5 ♗b4+ 7 ♗d2 ♕xg5 8 ♘xb4 f4 9 ♘xc6 bc 10 e3 ± Gheorghiu-Ljubojević, 1979
5 ... h6 6 ♘h3 g5!? (Browne) 7 e3 ♘f6 8 ♗e2 ♗g7 9 ♗h5+ ♔xh5 10 ♕xh5+ ♔f8 ∞ J.Watson

[3] 6 e3 d6 7 d4 h6 8 ♘h3 g5 ∞

[4] 6 ... ♗b4 7 e3 ♘e7 8 ♗d2 ± Kavalek-Ljubojević, 1980

[5] 8 a3 d6 9 b4 ♘e7 10 ♕b3 0-0 ∞

[6] 10 h5 g5 (10 ... ♘e7!? Psakhis) 11 h6 ♗h8 12 ♘h3 g4 13 ♘f4 ∞

[7] 12 ♕b3 h6 13 ♗d2 ♔h7 14 0-0-0 ∞ Psakhis-Kharitonov, Sverdlovsk 1984

[8] 3 ... ♗c5 4 ♗g2 ♘f6 5 e3 0-0 6 a3 ♖e8 7 d3 d6 8 b4 ♗b6 9 ♘ge2 ♗e6 10 0-0 ± Cebalo-Makropoulos, Budva 1981
3 ... ♘f6 4 ♗g2 d6 5 e3 ♗e7 6 ♘ge2 0-0

[9] 5 d3 ♗b4 (5 ... g6 6 e3 ♗g7 7 ♘ge2 d6 8 ♖b1 a5 9 a3 ♘e7 ∞ Campora-Sunye, Deeren 1984) 6 ♘h3 (6 ♗d2 0-0 7 ♘f3 d6 8 a3 ♗xc3 9 ♗xc3 ♕e8 10 0-0 ♕h5 ∞ Bruno-Kurajica, Lugano 1985) 6 ... ♗xc3 7 bc d6 8 ♕b3 ♕e7 9 0-0 h6 10 f4 0-0 11 c5 ♔h7 ∞ Portisch-Kurajica, Thessaloniki Ol 1984

[10] 5 ... ♗e7 6 d4 e4 7 f3 0-0 8 ♘ge2 ± Botvinnik
5 ... ♗b4 6 ♘ge2 0-0 7 0-0 ♗xc3 (7 ... d6 ±) 8 ♘xc3 f4 9 ef! ± Tal-Plaskett, Sochi 1984
5 ... g6 6 ♘ge2 ♗g7 7 d3 0-0 8 ♖b1 a5 9 a3 ♘e7 10 f4 ± Khuzman-Ehlvest, Kuibishev 1986

[11] 9 ... ♖f7 10 ♘d5 ±

[12] 11 ♘d5 ♘xd5 12 ♗xd5 ♔h8 intending ... ♗c6 = Kovačević

[13] 12 d5 ♗d7 13 f4 e4 14 ♘d4 a6 15 ♖ac1 ± Smejkal-Kovačević, Zagreb/Rijeka 1985

[14] 5 ... f5 6 ♘ge2 ♘f6 7 d4 e4 8 f3 ± Hort-Browne, Amsterdam 1978

[15] 6 ... ♗e6 7 d4 ed 8 ♘xd4 ♗d7 9 0-0 ♘ge7 10 ♘de2 0-0 11 b3 ± Mikenas-Podgayets, USSR Ch 1970
6 ... f5 7 d3 (7 d4 e4 8 b4 ♘f6 9 ♖b1 ♘e7 10 f3 ± Spassky-Hort, match 1977) 7 ... ♘f6 8 ♖b1 0-0 9 b4 a6 10 a4 a5 11 b5 ♘e7 12 ♗a3! ± Suba-Korchnoi, Lucerne 1985

¹⁶ 7 ♖b1 ♗e6 8 ♘d5 ♕d7 9 d3 0-0 10 0-0 ♖ab8! Nunn

7 d4 ed 8 ed 0-0 9 0-0 ♗g4 10 h3 (10 f3 ♗f5 11 g4 ♗c8 12 ♗f4 d5 13 c5 b6 = Larsen-Spassky, Belgrade 1964) 10 ... ♗xe2 11 ♘xe2 ♘f5 12 d5 ♘e5 13 ♕c2 ♖e8 14 ♗d2 a5 ∞ Uhlmann-Taimanov, Leningrad 1984

¹⁷ 8 ... ♗e6 9 ♘d5 ♕d7 10 ♗d2 (10 ♗g5 f6 11 ♗e3 f5 12 ♕d2 ♖f7 13 ♖ac1 ♖af8 = Csom-Jansa, Prague Z 1985; 10 ♖b1 ♘c8 11 b3 f5 12 ♗b2 ± Csom-Keene, Esbjerg 1981) 10 ... ♘d8 11 ♕c2 c6 12 ♘xe7+ ♕xe7 13 b4 ± Larsen-Mortensen, Copenhagen 1985

¹⁸ 9 ♖b1 ♕d7 10 b4 ♗h3 ∞

¹⁹ 11 ... ♖ae8 12 ♖b1 ♘c8 13 b4 ♘d8 ∞ Rajković

²⁰ 14 ♖c1 ♘d8 15 b4 ∞ Seirawan-Korchnoi, Montpellier C 1985

²¹ 7 h3 h4 8 g4 f5 9 gf ♗xf5 10 ♘e4 ♘f6 ∞ Suba-Nunn, Lucerne 1985

7 d4 h4 8 d5 ♘ce7 (8 ... ♘b8 9 e4 ♗g4 10 ♕a4+ ♕f8 11 ♘g1 ♘a6 12 f3 ± Portisch-Petrosian, Tilburg 1982) 9 e4 h3!? (9 ... f5 10 ♘g1 ♘f6 11 ♘h3 fe 12 ♘g5 ♗h6! ∞ Hort-Seirawan, Wijk aan Zee 1983) 10 ♗f1 f5 11 ♘g1 fe 12 ♘xe4 ♘f6 13 ♗d3 c6 = Portisch-Yusupov, Indonesia 1983

²² 7 ... ♘ge7 9 d3 ♗g4 – 7 ... ♗g4

²³ 8 ... ♘h6!? Cvetković

²⁴ 9 ... e4 10 d4 ±

²⁵ 10 a4 ♘xb4 11 ♗xb7 ♖b8 ∞

²⁶ 10 a4?! a5! ∓ Pfleger-Nunn, West Germany 1986

²⁷ 12 ... ♕d7 13 ♘d5! b5 14 a4 e4 ∞ Sunye-Nunn, Amsterdam 1985

²⁸ 5 ... ♘f6 6 e3 0-0 7 ♘ge2 d6 8 b4 (8 0-0 ♗e6 9 ♘d5 ♕d7 = Makarichev) 8 ... ♗e6 9 b5 ♘a5 10 d3 a6 11 a4 ab 12 ab ± Karpov-Ljubojević, Bugojno 1986

5 ... d6 and now:

6 b4 f5 7 d3 (7 b5 ♘ce7 8 e3 ♘f6 9 d4 e4 10 ♘ge2 ♗e6 11 d5 ♗f7 = Spassky) 7 ... ♘f6 8 b5 ♘e7 9 ♕b3 h6 10 e3 0-0 ∞ Korchnoi-Seirawan, Lugano 1986

6 d3 ♗d7 (6 ... ♘ge7 7 b4 a6 8 e3 ♗e6 9 ♘d5 ♖b8 10 ♘e2 0-0 ∞ J.Watson-Kavalek, New York 1984) 7 b4 ♘c8 8 b5 ♘d8 9 a4 ♘e7 10 ♗a3 ♘e6 ∞ Suba-Eingorn, Moscow 1986

²⁹ 6 e3 ♘f6 7 ♘ge2 0-0 8 a3 ♖e8 9 d3 d6 10 b4 ab 11 ab ♗f5 = Larsen-Haik, New York 1984

³⁰ 6 ... f5 7 b4 ab 8 ab ♘f6 9 d3 0-0 10 b5 ♘d4 11 e3 ± Polugayevsky

6 ... d6 7 b4 ab 8 ab ♘f6 9 b5 ♘e7 10 ♘f3 0-0 11 0-0 = Taimanov

³¹ 7 e3 0-0 8 ♘ge2 d6 9 d3 ♘e7 10 e4 c6 11 d4 d5 = I.Ivanov-Razuvayev, USSR Ch 1978

³² 10 e4!? Pigusov

³³ 10 ... ♖e8 11 ♘f3 d5 12 cd ♘exd5 13 ♘g5 c6 ∞ Ribli-Balashov, Leipzig 1973

³⁴ 13 0-0 ♘e8 14 ♘f3 dc 15 dc ♘d6 = Pigusov-Balashov, Irkutsk 1986

³⁵ 14 ♘f3 dc 15 dc ♘d6 ∞̅ Pigusov

³⁶ 6 f4 ♘ge7 7 ♘f3 0-0 8 0-0 ♘d4 9 e3 ♘xf3+ 10 ♕xf3 c6 11 e4 ♗e6 =

³⁷ 6 ... h5 7 h4 ♘d4 8 ♘ce2 ♘e6 9 ♘h3 ♘h6 10 0-0 ± Smejkal-Hernandez, Vršac 1977

6 ... ♗e6 7 ♘ge2 ♕d7 8 ♘d5 ♘ce7 9 d4 ± Portisch-Gheorghiu, Nice Ol 1974

³⁸ 7 ... ♘h6 8 h4! (8 0-0 0-0 9 ♘d5 g5 10 ef ♗xf5 11 h3 g4 12 h4 ♗e6 13 b4 ± Smejkal-Kindermann, Thessaloniki Ol 1984) 8 ... 0-0 9 ♗g5 ♕d7 10 ♘d5 ♘f7 11 ♗e3 ♘cd8 12 h5 ± Chernin-Kupreichik, USSR Ch 1985

³⁹ 8 ♘d5 0-0 9 ♗g5 ±

⁴⁰ 9 ♘d5 h6 10 ♖b1 ♘e7 11 ♗xf6+ ♖xf6 12 d4 ± Suba-Sax, Moscow 1977

⁴¹ 10 f4 ♔h8!? (10 ... ♗e6 11 ♘d5 ±) Nunn

⁴² 11 ... ♘d4 12 ♘xd4 ed 13 ♗f4 ±

⁴³ 12 f4? c6! ∓ Sunye-Nunn, Dubai Ol 1986

⁴⁴ Nunn

⁴⁵ 7 f4 ♗e6 8 ♘f3 ef 9 ♗xf4 ♘e5 =

⁴⁶ 7 ... ♘d4 8 ♘xd4 ed 9 ♘e2 c5 10 ♘f4 ♗d7 11 h4 ± Hort-Zinn, Leipzig 1973

⁴⁷ 8 ... ♗e6 9 ♘d5 ♕d7 10 ♗e3 f5 11 ♕d2 ♖f7 12 ♖ac1 ± Csom

8 ... f5 9 ef (9 h3 ♗e6 10 ♘d5 ♕d7 11 ♔h2 ♖f7 12 ♗e3 ♖af8 ∞ Hort-Spassky, match 1977) 9 ... ♘xf5 10 ♖b1 ♘fd4 11 ♘xd4 ♘xd4 12 b4 a6 13 ♗e3 ♖b8 ∞ Spraggett-Kogan, New York 1984

⁴⁸ 12 ... ♖ae8? 13 ♖ae1 ± Sunye-Kindermann, Dubai Ol 1986

⁴⁹ 14 b4 ♘c8 15 b5 ♘d8 = Sunye

⁵⁰ 8 a3 ♘d4 9 ♘d2 c6 10 b4 h5! ∞ Karlsson-Jansa, 1981

8 ♗g5 h6 9 ♗xf6 ♗xf6 10 ♖b1 a5 11 a3 ♗g7 ∞ Sloth-Jansa, Svendborg 1981

⁵¹ 8 ... h6 9 b4 ♗e6 10 b5 ♘e7 11 a4 ♕c8 12 ♗a3 ± Miles-Belyavsky, Hastings 1974-75

⁵² 9 ... ♘h5 10 b4 ab 11 ab f5 12 b5 ♘e7 13 ♕b3 ± Andersson-Smejkal, Amsterdam 1973

9 ... h6 10 b4 ab 11 ab ♗e6 12 b5 ♘e7 13 ♗b2 ♕d7 14 ♘d2 ♖ab8 = Mednis-Zapata, Amsterdam 1986

⁵³ 10 b4 ab 11 ab c6 12 b5 ♘xf3+ (12 ... ♗g4 13 ♗g5 ♗xf3 14 ♗xf3 h6 15 ♗xf6 ± Andersson-Nunn, Johannesburg 1981) 13 ♗xf3 d5 ∞ Andersson

10 ♘d2 c6 11 b4 ab 12 ab d5 13 ♗b2 ♖e8 = Smejkal-Smyslov, Biel IZ 1976

⁵⁴ 14 ♘xd4 ed 15 ♘d5 ♗g7 16 b5 ♖a2 ∞

14 e3 ♖a3 15 ♘d5 ∞ Benjamin-W.Watson, Hastings 1984-85

41

	4	5	6	7	8	9	10	11	12	
1	e3[1] ♗b4[2]	♘d5 e4[3]	♘g1[4] 0-0	a3[5] ♗d6	♕c2[6] ♖e8	♘e2 b6[7]	♘ec3 ♗b7	b4 a5	b5 ♘e5[8]	∞
2	... ...	♕c2 ♗xc3[9]	♕xc3[10] ♕e7	a3[11] d5[12]	d4 ♘xd4	♘xd4 ed	♕xd4 0-0[13]	c5[14] b6	b4 bc[15]	∞
3	g3 ♗b4[16]	♘d5 ♗c5[17]	♗g2[18] 0-0	0-0 d6[19]	e3 a6[20]	d4[21] ♗a7	de ♘xe5[22]	♘xe5		=
4	♗g2 ...	0-0 0-0	0-0[23] ♖e8[24]	♘d5 ♘xd5[25]	cd ♘d4	♘e1 c6[26]	e3 ♘b5	d3 ♘c7	♘c2 ♗f8[27]	∞
5	... ...	... ...	... e4[28]	♘e1[29] ♗xc3[30]	dc[31] h6[32]	♘c2 ♖e8[33]	♘e3 d6[34]	♕c2[35] b6[36]	f4[37] ♗d7[38]	=
6	... d5	cd ♘xd5	♗g2 ♘b6[39]	0-0[40] ♗e7	a3[41] ♗e6	b4 0-0	♖b1[42] a6[43]	d3 ♕c8	♗b2 ♖d8[44]	∞

1 c4 e5 2 ♘c3 ♘c6 3 ♘f3 ♘f6 4 g3 d5 5 cd ♘xd5 6 ♗g2 ♘b6 7 0-0 ♗e7

	8	9	10	11	12	13	14	15	16	
7	d3 0-0[45]	a3 a5[46]	♗e3[47] ♗e6[48]	♖ac1 ♘d5[49]	♘xd5 ♗xd5	♕a4 ♗d6	♗c5 ♘e7	e4 ♗c6	♕c2 b6[50]	±

[1]   **4 a3** g6 (4 ... d5 5 d4 ±) = Bagirov
4 e4 ♗b4 5 d3 d6 =
4 d3 d6 (4 ... g6 5 g3 ♗g7 6 ♗g2 0-0 7 0-0
♖e8 8 ♗g5 h6 = Westerinen-Smyslov, Graz
1984) 5 g3 g6 6 ♗g2 ♗g7 7 0-0 0-0 8 ♖b1 (8 ♗g5
h6 9 ♗xf6 ♕xf6 10 ♖b1 a5 ∞ Suba-Farago,
Prague Z 1985) 8 ... a5 9 a3 ♖e8 10 ♗g5 h6 =
Miles-Littlewood, England 1984
4 d4 ed 5 ♘xd4 ♗b4 6 ♗g5 (6 g3 ♘e4 7 ♕d3
♘c5 8 ♕e3+ ♘e6 9 ♘c2 d5 ∞ Chekhov-
Kosikov, USSR 1978) 6 ... h6 7 ♗h4 ♗xc3 (7 ...
♘e5 8 ♕b3! ± Hernandez-Vaiser, Havana 1985)
8 bc d6 9 f3 (9 e3 ♘e5 10 ♕c2 0-0) 9 ... ♘e5 10 e4
♘g6 11 ♗f2 0-0 = Tal-Dvoretsky, Wijk aan Zee
1976
[2]   **4 ... ♗e7** and now:
5 a3 d5 6 cd ♘xd5 7 ♗b5 0-0 8 ♗xc6 bc
9 ♘e5 ∞ Lerner-Aseyev, USSR 1983
5 d4 ed 6 ♘xd4 0-0 7 ♗e2 (7 ♘de2 ♖e8
8 ♘f4 ♘e5 9 ♗e2 c6 = Timman-Miles, Bugojno
1984) 7 ... ♘xd4 8 ♕xd4 c6 9 e4 d5 10 cd b5 ∞∞
Suba-M.Braun, Baden-Baden 1986
5 ♗e2 0-0 6 0-0 d5 7 cd ♘xd5 8 d3 ♗c6 =
Dobosz-Ermenkov, 1986
[3]   5 ... ♗e7!? 6 d3 0-0 7 ♗e2 ♘xd5 8 cd ♗b4+
9 ♗d2 ♗xd2+ 10 ♕xd2 ♘e7 = Hübner-
Makarichev, Oslo 1984
[4]   6 ♘xb4 ♘xb4 7 ♘d4 (7 ♘g5 h6 8 ♘h3
d5 =/∓ Sunye-Hansen, Thessaloniki Ol 1984)
7 ... c5 8 ♘b5 d5 9 cd 0-0 ∓ Möhring-Knaak,

East German Ch 1973
[5]   7 ♘e2 ♘xd5 8 cd ♘e5 9 ♘g3 f5 10 a3
♗d6 ∞ Seirawan-Sosonko, Tilburg 1983
[6]   8 d3 ed 9 ♗xd3 ∞
[7]   9 ... ♘xd5 10 cd ♘b8 11 ♘c3 f5 12 d3 ±
Stean
    9 ... ♗e5 10 ♘g3 ♗xg3 11 hg d6 12 ♖h4!?
(12 ♗e2 ±) 12 ... ♘xd5 13 cd ♘e5 14 d3! ± Miles-
Kindermann, Biel 1983
    9 ... b5!? 10 ♘xf6+ ♕xf6 11 cb ♘e5 ∞
[8]   Miles-Kindermann, Bath 1983
[9]   5 ... d6 6 ♘d5 ♗c5 7 a3 a5 8 b3 ± Vilela-
Stohl, Stary Smokovec 1984
    5 ... 0-0 6 ♘d5 ♖e8 7 ♕f5 d6 7 ♘xf6+ gf
9 ♕h5 d5 ∞ J.Watson-Shirazi, Lone Pine 1980
[10]   6 bc e4 7 ♘g5 d5 8 f3 ef 9 ♘xf3 ♗g4 ∞
Suba-Liberzon, Beer-Sheva 1984
[11]   7 ♗e2 0-0 8 d4 ed 9 ♘xd4 ♘xd4 10 ♕xd4
c5 =/± Korchnoi-Timman, Hilversum 1982
[12]   7 ... 0-0 8 d3 d5 9 cd ♘xd5 10 ♕c2 ±
Ermenkov-Bisguier, Lone Pine 1980
    7 ... a5 8 b4 (8 b3 d5 9 cd ♘xd5 10 ♕b2
0-0 ∓ Grooten-Timman, Leeuwarden 1981)
8 ... ab 9 ab ♖xa1 10 ♕xa1 e4 11 b5 ef 12 bc fg
13 cd ♕xd7 14 ♗xg2 ± Rodgaard-Hjartarson,
Esbjerg 1985
[13]   10 ... c5 11 ♕fc4 dc 12 ♗xc4 0-0 13 0-0 ♗e6
14 ♗d3 (14 ♗e2 ♗b3 = Seirawan-Timman,
Linares 1983) 14 ... ♖fd8 15 ♗c2 ± Timman-
Balashov, Wijk aan Zee 1982

[14] 11 cd?! ♖d8 12 ♕h4 ♖xd5 13 ♗e2 ♗f5 $\overline{\mp}$ Pereira-Bang, corr. 1985

[15] 13 bc ♗f5 14 ♗b2 ♖ab8 15 ♗e2 = Hébert-Bang, corr. 1983

[16] **4 ... ♘d4** 5 ♗g2 ♘xf3+ 6 ♗xf3 ♗b4 (6 ... ♗e7 7 d4 d6 8 ♗g2 0-0 9 0-0 c6 10 b3 ± Gheorghiu-Portisch, Skopje Ol 1972) 7 ♕b3 ♗a5 8 0-0 0-0 9 d3 d6 10 ♕a3 ± Timman-Campora, Amsterdam 1984

4 ... ♗c5 5 ♗g2 (5 ♘xe5?!) 5 ... d6 6 d3 0-0 7 0-0 a5 (7 ... h6 8 ♘a4 ♕e7 9 e3 ±/=) ∞

[17] 5 ... ♘xd5 6 cd ♘d4 7 ♘xd4 ed 8 ♕c2 ♕e7 9 ♗g2 ♗a5 (9 ... ♗c5 10 0-0-0 11 e3± Adorjan-Miles, Oslo 1984) 10 ♕c4 (10 0-0 0-0 11 e3 c5! 12 ed cd 13 d3 = Adorjan-Hübner, Wijk aan Zee 1984) 10 ... ♗b6 11 b4 a5!? 12 ba ♖xa5 13 0-0 d6 14 e4 =/± Miles-Hübner, Tilburg 1984

[18] 6 d3 h6 7 ♗g2 d6 8 0-0 0-0 9 e3 a5 = Korchnoi-Petrosian, match 1977

[19] 7 ... ♘xd5 8 cd ♘d4 9 ♘e1 d6 10 e3 ± Eingorn-Tseshkovsky, Moscow 1985

[20] **8 ...** ♖e8 9 d4 ♗b6 10 b3 ♘xd5 11 cd ± Miles-Smyslov, Tilburg 1984

8 ... ♗g4 9 h3 ♗xf3 (9 ... ♗h5!?) 10 ♗xf3 ♘xd5 11 cd ♘e7 12 b3 ± Korchnoi-Karpov, match (15) 1981

[21] d3 ♗a7 10 ♘c3 ♗f5 11 h3 h6 ∞ Hansen-Miles, Esbjerg 1984

[22] 10 ... de 11 b3 ♗g4 12 h3 ♗h5 13 ♗b2 ♖e8 14 g4 ♗g6 15 g5 ±

[23] 6 ♘d5 ♘xd5 7 cd ♘d4 8 ♘xd4 ed 9 b3 ♗e7 10 ♗b2 c5 = Gheorghiu-Savon, Petropolis IZ 1973

[24] **6 ... d6** and now:

7 ♘d5 ♗c5 8 d4?! ♘xd4 9 ♗g5 c6 $\overline{\mp}$ Adorjan-Miles, Linares 1985

7 d3 ♗xc3 8 bc e4 9 ♘g5 ed 10 ed ♗g4 ∞ Bartes-Miles, London 1984

7 ♕c2 ♗g4 8 d3 ♗xf3 (8 ... ♕d7?! 9 ♗g5 ♘h5 10 ♘d5 ± Karlsson-Miles, Esbjerg 1984) 9 ef ♗c5 = Miles

6 ... ♗xc3!? 7 dc d6 8 ♗g5 h6 9 ♗xf6 ♕xf6 10 ♘e1 ♕g6 11 ♘c2 f5 ∞ Adorjan-Spassky, Linares 1985

[25] **7 ...** ♗c5 8 d3 ♘xd5 9 cd ♘d4 10 ♘d2 d6 11 e3 ± Botvinnik

7 ... ♗f8 8 d3 h6 9 ♗d2 ±

[26] 9 ... d6 10 e3 ♘f5 11 ♘c2 ♗c5 12 b4 ± Smyslov-Lein, USSR 1973

[27] 13 dc dc 14 ♕e2 ∞ Petrosian-Kuzmin, USSR Ch 1974

[28] Mecking

[29] 7 ♗g5 ♗xc3 8 dc ♖e8 9 ♕c2 ♕e7 10 ♘h3 h6 11 ♘f4 ♕e5 = Adorjan-Garcia Palermo, Reggio Emilia 1984-85; 8 bc ♖e8 9 f3 ef (9 ... e3!? 10 d3!) 10 ♘xf3 d5 11 d4! ♘e4 (11 ... dc 12 ♗g5 $\overline{oo}$) 12 ♕c2 dc 13 ♖b1 f5 14 g4! ∞ Kasparov-Ivanchuk, USSR Ch 1988

[30] 7 ... ♖e8 8 ♘d5 ± Uhlmann

[31] 8 bc ♖e8 9 ♘c2 d6 10 ♘e3 ♘e5 = Tal-Kholmov, Tbilisi 1969

[32] 8 ... ♖e8 9 ♘c2 (9 ♗g5 ±) 9 ... ♘e5 10 ♘e3 d6 11 f4 ef 12 ef ♗e6 13 b3 ± Psakhis-Dvoiris, Kharkov 1985

[33] 9 ... b6 10 ♘e3 ♗b7 11 f4 (11 ♕c2 ♘e5 12 h3 ♖e8 = Vasyukov-Gipslis, USSR 1981) 11 ... ef 12 ef ♘e7 13 ♕c2 ♖e8 = Adorjan-Gipslis, Riga 1981

[34] 10 ... b6 11 ♘d5 = Bagirov

[35] 11 b3 a5 12 a4 b6 =

[36] 11 ... a5 12 a4 ♕e7 13 ♘d5 ♘xd5 14 cd ♘b8 15 ♗e3 ♗f5 = Karpov-Korchnoi, match (6) 1978

[37] **12 ♖d1** a5 13 b3 ♖b8 14 a4 ♘e5 = Korchnoi-Mecking, match 1974

12 ♗d2 ♘e5 13 ♖ad1 ♘eg4 14 h3 ♘xe3 15 ♗xe3 ♕e7 = Petrosian-Rogoff, Biel IZ 1976

[38] **13 h3** ♘h5 14 ♔h2 f5 $\overline{\mp}$

13 ♗d2 ♘e7 14 h3 ♘f5 15 ♘xf5 ♗xf5 = Uhlmann-Tan, Manila IZ 1976

[39] **6 ... ♘de7** 7 0-0 ♘f5 8 b4 a6 9 a3 ♗e7 10 ♗b2 0-0 11 ♖c1 ♖e8 12 d3 ± Uhlmann-Taimanov, Budapest 1982

6 ... ♗e6 7 d3 (7 0-0 ♗e7 8 d4 ed 9 ♘b5 ± Bisguier-Martinović, Las Vegas 1974) 7 ... ♗e7 8 0-0 0-0 9 ♗d2 ± Polugayevsky-Romanishin, USSR Ch 1976

6 ... ♘xc3 7 bc e4 8 ♘g1 f5 9 ♘h3 g5 10 0-0 ♗g7 ± Adorjan-Timman, Reggio Emilia 1984-85

[40] 7 d3 ♗e7 8 a3 ♗e6 9 b4 a6 10 ♗b2 ♕d7 = Portisch-Karpov, Linares 1981

[41] 8 b3 0-0 9 ♗b2 ♗g4 10 ♖c1 f5 =

[42] 10 d3 ♘d4 11 ♖b1 f6 (11 ... ♘d5 12 ♗b2 ♘xc3 13 ♗xc3 ± Sunye-Timman, Amsterdam 1985) 12 ♘d2 ♘d5 13 ♗b2 c6 = Miles-Hübner, Linares 1985

[43] 10 ... f6 11 ♘e4 ♗a2 12 ♖b2 ♗d5 13 ♘c5 ♘c4 14 ♖b1 b6 ∞ Adorjan-Hübner, Linares 1985

[44] 13 ♕c1 ♗h3 14 ♘e4 ♗xg2 15 ♔xg2 ♕e6 ∞ Hübner-Vaganian, Linares 1985

[45] 8 ... ♗e6 9 a3 f5 10 b4 ± Adorjan-Fedorowicz, New York 1981

[46] 9 ... ♗g4 10 b4 a6 11 ♗b2 ♘h8 12 ♘e4 ± Timman-Sax, Wijk aan Zee 1981

9 ... f5 10 b4 ♗f6 11 ♗b2 ♘h8 12 ♖c1 ± Chernin-Rantanen, Järvenpää 1985

[47] 10 b3 f5 11 ♗b2 ♗f6 12 ♘d2 ♘d4 13 ♘c4 c6 14 e3 ♘e6 ∞

[48] **10 ...** ♖a6 11 ♖c1 ♗e6 12 ♘e4 f6 13 ♗c5 ± Korchnoi-Hübner, Lucerne Ol 1982

10 ... ♗g4 11 ♖c1 ♖e8 12 ♘d2! (12 ♘e4 ♘d4! = Suba-Timman, Las Palmas IZ 1982) 12 ... ♕d7 13 ♖e1 ♖a6 14 ♗xb6 cb 15 ♕a4 ± Petrosian-Psakhis, USSR 1983

[49] 11 ... ♕d7 Taimanov

[50] 17 d4 ± Polugayevsky-Hübner, Bugojno 1982

43

1 c4 e5 2 Nc3 Nc6 3 Nf3 Nf6 4 g3 d5 5 cd Nxd5 6 Bg2 Nb6 7 0-0 Be7 *continued*

	8	9	10	11	12	13	14	15	16	
8	d3	Be3	Qc1[52]	Nd2	Nb3[53]	Qxe3	Na4	ab	Bxb7	∞
	0-0	Be6[51]	f6	Nd5	Nxe3	Qd7	Bxb3	Nd4	Rab8[54]	
9	...	a3	b4	b5	Bb2[56]	Rb1	Nd2	a4[59]	Ra1	∞
	...	Be6	a5[55]	Nd4	Nb3[57]	f6	Nc5[58]	Rf7	Rc8[60]	

[51] 9 ... f5 10 Qc1 (10 Rc1 Kh8 11 a3 Be6 12 Na4 ∞/± Cebalo-Romanishin, Taxco IZ 1985) 10 ... h6 11 Rd1 Nf6 12 Bc5 Rf7 13 e3 Be6 14 d4 ± Korchnoi-Toth, Rome 1981
9 ... Bg4 10 a4 a5 11 Rc1 Kh8 (11 ... Re8!? Suba) 12 Nb5 Nd5 13 Bc5 Ndb4 14 Qb3 Be6 ∞ Alburt-Fedorowicz, US Ch 1981; 12 h3!?

[52] 10 Na4 Bd5! 11 a3 Nd4 12 Bxd4 ed 13 Rc1 Nxa4 14 Qxa4 = Uhlmann-Ghinda, Potsdam 1985
10 Ne4 Nd5 11 Bc5 f6 12 Rc1 Bf7 ∞ Belyavsky-Psakhis, USSR 1982
10 Rc1 f6 11 a3 Qd7 12 Ne4 Rfd8 13 Bc5 Bd5 ∞ Suba-F.Garcia, Dubai Ol 1986
10 Qd2 Nd5 11 Rfc1 f6 12 a3 ±/= Ljubojević-Chernin, Wijk aan Zee 1986

[53] 12 Nxd5 Bxd5 = Miles

[54] Suba-Miles, Tunis IZ 1985

[55] 10 ... f6 11 Ne4 (11 Be3!? Qe8 12 Bxb6 ab 13 d4 ∞/± Vaganian-Psakhis, Erevan 1982) 11 ... Qd7 12 Bb2 a6 13 Qc2 ± Miles-Timman, Tilburg 1984
10 ... f5 11 Bb2 Bf6 12 Nd2 Nd5 (12 ... Rb8 Sosonko) 13 Rc1 ± Taimanov
10 ... Nd4 11 Bb2 f6 (11 ... Nb3 12 Rb1 f6 13 Ne4 a5 14 Bxe5! Adorjan-Romanishin, Szirak 1986) ∞ Ftacnik

[56] 12 Nd2 c6! 13 bc Nxc6 ∞ Portisch-Romanishin, Reggio Emilia 1985-86
12 Be3 Nd5 13 Bxd4 ed 14 Na4 Bf6 =

[57] 12 ... Bb3!? 13 Qc1 Nd5 ∞ Miles-Steinbacher, West Germany 1983-84

[58] 14 ... Nxd2 15 Qxd2 Nc4 16 Qc1 Nxb2 17 Qxb2 Rb8 18 a4 ± Mednis-I.Ivanov, Brighton 1983

[59] 15 Nde4 Nb3

[60] Cvetković-Cebalo, Yugoslavia 1986

1 c4 c5 2 Nc3 Nc6 3 g3 g6 4 Bg2 Bg7

	5	6	7	8	9	10	11	12	13	
1	b3	Bb2	Qc1[2]	Nd5[3]	d3	h4	h5	f4	e4	∞
	e6[1]	Nge7	d6	e5	0-0	h6	g5	f6	ef[4]	
2	a3	Nf3	0-0	Rb1[5]	d3	Bd2	Qa4[6]	Rfc1	Qd1	±
	d6	e5	Nge7	a5	0-0	Rb8	Bd7	Nd4	Bc6[7]	
3	...	Rb1	b4[8]	ab	cb[9]	Nf3	d4	Nxd4	Ne4	∞
	a6	Rb8	cb	b5	ab	e5	Nxd4	ed	d5[10]	
4	...	Rb1[11]	Nh3[12]	Nf4	0-0[13]	d3	Bd2	Na2	b4	=
	e6	a5	Nge7	0-0	d6	b6	Rb8	Bb7	ab[14]	
5	e4	Nge2	0-0	d3	Rb1	a3	Be3	b3	d4[19]	=
	e6[15]	Nge7	0-0	d6[16]	b6[17]	a5[18]	Ba6	Rb8	e5[20]	
6	e3	Nge2	0-0	d4[22]	Nxd4	cd	ed	Qb3[25]	Bg5	=
	e6[21]	Nge7	0-0	cd	d5	Nxd4[23]	Nxd5[24]	Ne7[26]	h6[27]	
7	Nf3	0-0	b3[28]	Bb2	d3[29]	Nd2	a3[31]	Nd5		=
	e5	d6	Nf6	0-0	Ne8[30]	Nc7	Be6	Qd7		
8	...	0-0	d4	Nxd4	Qxd4	Qd3[33]	Bd2[34]	Rac1	b3	=
	Nf6	0-0	cd	Nxd4[32]	d6	a6	Rb8	Nd7	Nc5[35]	
9	...	0-0	d3[37]	Rb1	Bg5	cd[39]	Bxe7	d4	Nxd4	=
	e6	Nge7	0-0	d5[38]	h6	ed	Nxe7	cd	Nc6[40]	

[1] 5 ... ♘f6 6 ♗b2 0-0 7 ♘h3 d6 8 0-0 ♗d7 9 e3 ♘e4 10 ♕c1 ♘xc3 11 ♗xc3 e5 12 f4 ♖b8 = Larsen-Polugayevsky, Bugojno 1980

[2] 7 ♘a4 ♗xb2 8 ♘xb2 0-0 9 e3 d5 ∓ Smyslov-Fischer, Palma de Mallorca IZ 1970

7 h4 h6 8 ♕b1 d6 9 ♘e4 e5 10 ♕d3 ♘f5 11 e3 0-0 12 a3 ♗e6 13 h5 g5 ∞ J.Watson-Keene, New York 1981

[3] 8 f4 0-0 9 ♘e4 e5 10 fe ♘xe5 11 ♘f3 f5 12 ♘f2 ♘7c6 ∞ Hort-Gulko, Nikšić 1978

[4] 14 gf ♘xd5 15 cd ♘b4 16 ♕d2 ♕a5 ∞/∓ Donchev-Adorjan, Prague Z 1985

[5] 8 b4 e4 9 ♘e1 f5 10 ♗b2 ♗e6 11 d3 0-0 (11 ... ed 12 ♘xd3 ♗xc4 13 ♘a4! ∞ Romanishin-Short, Lvov 1984) 11 de fe 12 ♗xe4 ♗xc4 ∞ Romanishin-Agzamov, Sochi 1984

[6] 11 ♘e1 ♗e6 12 ♘c2 d5 = Ribli-Cebalo, Reggio Emilia 1985-86

[7] 14 e3 ♘e6 15 b4 ± Ribli-Hellers, Amsterdam 1986

[8] 7 ♕a4 d6! 8 b4 ♗f5 9 ♗xc6 bc 10 ♕xc6+ ♗d7 11 ♕xa6 ♗xc3 12 dc ♘f6 ∞/∓ Seirawan-Timman, Montpellier C 1985

[9] 9 c5 a5 10 ♗a3 ab 11 ♗xb4 ♘xb4 12 ♖xb4 ♗xc3 13 dc ♕c7 14 ♕d4 ♘f6 = Tarjan-Gheorghiu, Riga IZ 1979

[10] **13 ... d6** 14 ♗f4 ♖b6 (14 ... ♗e5!?) 15 ♖c1 ♗f5 ∞ Velimirović

13 ... d5 14 ♗f4 de 15 ♗xb8 ♗f5 16 ♗a7 ♘e7 ∞ Despotović-Velimirović, Yugoslavia 1984

[11] 6 b4 ♘xb4! 7 ab cb 8 d4 (8 ♘b5 ♗xa1 ∓ Lobron-Kavalek, Bochum 1981) 8 ... bc 9 e3 ♘e7 ∓ Smyslov-Hartston, Hastings 1972-73

[12] 7 e4 – 5 e4

[13] 9 b3 b6 10 ♗b2 ♗b7 11 ♘e4 ♗xb2 12 ♖xb2 d5 13 ♘f6+ ♔g7 14 cd ♔xf6 15 dc ♗xc6 ∞

[14] 14 ab ♕d7 = Romanishin-van der Wiel, Wijk aan Zee 1985

[15] 5 ... ♘f6 6 ♘ge2 0-0 7 0-0 d6 8 d3 a6 9 h3 ♖b8 10 a4 ♘e8 11 ♗e3 ♘c7 12 d4 cd 13 ♘xd4 ♗d7 14 a5 ♘e6 = Romanishin-P.Popović, Sarajevo 1984

[16] 8 ... b6 9 a3 ♗b7 10 ♗g5 h6 11 ♗e3 ♘d4 12 ♖b1 d6 13 b4 ♕d7 14 a4 ± Wedberg-Ligterink, Amsterdam 1984

[17] 9 ... a6 10 a3 b5!? 11 cb ab 12 b4 (12 ♘xb5 ♗a6 13 ♘bc3 ♘e5 14 ♘f4 ♖b8 ∞) 12 ... cb 13 ab e5 = Makarichev-Kasparov, USSR Ch

1978

[18] 10 ... ♗b7 11 b4 ♕d7 12 ♗e3 ♘d4 13 ♕d2 ♖fd8 = Barbero-Panno, Argentina 1984

[19] 13 ♕d2 ♘e5! = Osmanović-Psakhis, Sarajevo 1981

[20] Martinović-Psakhis, Sarajevo 1981

[21] 5 ... ♘f6 6 ♘ge2 e6 7 0-0 0-0 8 ♘f4 b6 9 b3 (9 d4!?) 9 ... ♗a6 10 ♗b2 d5 = Larsen-Tal, Bugojno 1984

[22] 8 ♘f4 d6 9 b3 a6 intending ... b5 =

[23] 10 ... ed 11 ♕b3 ±

[24] 11 ... ed 12 ♗g5 ♗e6 13 ♕b3 ± Hort-Spassky, Montreal 1979

[25] **12 ♘xd5** ed =

12 ♖e1 ♕b6! = Keene-Hecht, Dortmund 1973

[26] 12 ... ♗xd4 13 ♘xd5 ed 14 ♗h6 ♗g7 15 ♗xg7 ♔xg7 16 ♗xd5 ± Andersson-Gheorghiu, Moscow 1981

[27] 14 ♗xe7 ♕xe7 15 ♖ad1 ♖d8 16 d5 ♕f8 17 ♖d2 ed 18 ♘xd5 ♖b8 = Gheorghiu-Jansa, Prague Z 1985

[28] 7 a3! – 5 a3

[29] 9 e3 ♗f5 = Webb-Kasparov, Skara 1980

[30] 9 ... ♘g4 10 a3 a5 11 ♖b1 f5 12 ♘d5 ♗e6 13 ♗c3 ±/∞ Cebalo-Velimirović, Vinkovci 1982

[31] 11 e3?! ♗e6 12 ♖c1 (12 ♘d5? ♗xd5 13 cd ♘b4) 12 ... ♕d7 13 ♖e1 ♖ad8 ∓ Tempone-Kasparov, Dortmund 1980

[32] 8 ... d6!? 9 ♘xc6 bc 10 ♗xc6 ♖b8 11 ♗g2 ♕a5 12 ♘b5 ♗b7 13 ♗xb7 ♖xb7 14 ♕d3 d5 ∞ Savon-Ermolinsky, USSR 1985

[33] 10 ♕h4 ♗e6 11 ♗xb7 ♖b8 12 ♗f3 ♕a5 ∞ Mikhalchishin-Gulko, USSR Ch 1978

[34] 11 ♗e3 ♘g4 12 ♗d4 ♘e5 13 ♕d1 ♖b8 14 ♖c1 ♗e6 15 ♘d5 b5 = Tal-Torre, Leningrad IZ 1973

[35] 14 ♕b1 b5 = Uhlmann-Smejkal, Arandjelovac 1976

[36] 6 d4 cd 7 ♘b5 d5 8 cd ♕a5+ 9 ♕d2 ♕xb5 10 dc e5! ∓ Chernin-Aseyev, USSR 1978

[37] 7 e3 0-0 8 d4 cd (8 ... d6!? 9 d5 ♘a5) 9 ♘xd4 – 5 e3

[38] 8 ... b6 9 ♗f4 d5 = Larsen-Portisch, Tilburg 1982

[39] 10 ♗d2 b6 11 a3 ♗b7 12 b4 cb 13 ab dc 14 dc ♖c8 15 c5 ∞ Diždarević-Cebalo, Sarajevo 1986

[40] Larsen-Tukmakov, Las Palmas IZ 1982

45

English 1 ... c5 II

1 c4 c5 2 ♘c3 ♘f6 3 g3 d5[1] 4 cd ♘xd5

	5	6	7	8	9	10	11	12	13	
1	♗g2	bc	♕a4+[4]	♘f3	0-0	d4[5]	♕a3	cd	♗g5	±
	♘xc3[2]	g6[3]	♘d7	♗g7	0-0	♘b6[6]	cd	♗f5	♘c4[7]	
2	...	d3[8]	f4[10]	♗xf4	♕a4+[12]	♘f3	0-0	♕c2	a3	∞/=
	♘c7	e5[9]	ef[11]	♗e7	♘d7	0-0	♘b6	♘cd5	♘xf4[13]	

1 c4 c5 2 ♘c3 ♘f6 3 g3 d5 4 cd ♘xd5 5 ♗g2 ♘c7 6 ♘f3 ♘c6

	7	8	9	10	11	12	13	14	15	
3	♕a4[14]	♕e4[16]	♘e5	♘xd7	0-0	a3[19]	♖b1	b4	♘d5	=
	♗d7[15]	g6[17]	♗g7[18]	♕xd7	0-0	♖ac8	♘e6	b6	♘ed4[20]	
4	0-0	d3[22]	♘d2[24]	♘c4	f4	♘e3	a4[29]	♘e4	♘f2[31]	∞
	e5[21]	♗e7[23]	♗d7[25]	f6[26]	b5[27]	♖c8[28]	b4	f5[30]	0-0[32]	

---

[1] 3 ... e6 4 ♘f3 ♘c6 5 ♗g2 ♗e7 6 0-0 d5 7 cd ed – Tarrasch; 7 ... ♘xd5 – Semi-Tarrasch

[2] **5 ... e6** 6 ♘xd5 ed 7 ♕b3 ±
5 ... ♘b4 6 f4 g6 7 ♘f3 ♗g7 8 0-0 0-0 9 b3 ±

[3] **6 ... e5** 7 ♘f3 ♘c6 8 0-0 ♗e7 9 d3 0-0 10 ♘d2 ±
6 ... ♘c6 7 ♖b1 e5 8 ♕a4 ±

[4] 7 ♖b1 ♘c6 (7 ... ♕c7 8 ♕a4+ ♘d7 9 d4 ± Euwe) 8 ♘f3 ♗g7 9 0-0 0-0 10 ♕a4 ♘a5 11 d3 b6 = Karpov-Korchnoi, match (30) 1978

[5] 10 ♖b1!? ♘b6 11 ♕a5 ±

[6] 10 ... cd 11 cd e5 12 de ♘xe5 13 ♘xe5 ♗xe5 14 ♗h6! ±

[7] 14 ♕b3 ♘d6 15 ♖ac1 ♗e4 16 ♖fd1 ± S.Garcia-Boudy, Pinar del Rio 1980

[8] 6 ♕a4+ ♗d7 7 ♕c4 (7 ♕b3 ♗c6!) 7 ... ♘c6 8 ♕xc5 ♘e6 9 ♕e3 ♘ed4 10 ♗e4 e5 ∞ Hanken-Peters, Los Angeles 1979
6 ♕b3 ♘c6 7 ♗xc6+ bc 8 ♘f3 f6 9 ♕a4 ♗d7 10 d3 e5 11 ♗e3 ♖b8 12 0-0 d5 13 ♖fc1 a5 ∞ Quinteros-A.Sokolov, Biel IZ 1985
6 a3!? e5 7 b4 ♘c6 8 ♘f3 f6 9 bc ♗xc5 10 0-0 0-0 ∞ Seirawan-Sax, Amsterdam 1983

[9] 6 ... ♘c6 7 ♗xc6+! bc 8 ♕a4 ♕d7 9 ♘f3 f6 10 ♗e3 e5 11 ♘e4 ± Taimanov
6 ... ♕d7 7 ♘f3 ♘c6 8 0-0 e5 9 ♘d2 (9 a3 ♗e7 10 ♖b1 f6 11 ♗d2 ♖b8! = J.Watson) 9 ... ♗e7 10 ♘c4 0-0 11 ♗xc6 ♕xc6 12 ♘xe5 ♕e6 ∞∞ J.Watson

[10] **7 ♕b3** ♘d7 8 ♘f3 ♗e7 9 ♘d5 ♘xd5 10 ♕xd5 ♕c7 11 ♗e3 ♖b8! = J.Watson
7 ♗e3 ♗e7 8 ♖c1 ♘e6 9 ♘f3 ♘c6 10 ♘a4 ♕a5 11 ♘d2 ♘ed4 = Karpov-A.Sokolov, Bugojno 1986

[11] 7 ... ♘d7 8 ♕a4! ef 9 ♗xf4 ♘e6 10 ♘h3 ± J.Watson

[12] 9 ♘f3 ♘c6 10 0-0 0-0-0 11 ♖c1 ♘e6 12 ♗e3 ♖e8 ∞ Evans-H.Olafsson, Lone Pine 1977

[13] J.Watson

[14] **7 a3 and now:**
7 ... e6 8 0-0 ♗e7 9 d3 0-0 10 ♗e3 ♘d5 11 ♖c1 ♘xe3 12 fe ± Vaganian-Ljubojević, Tilburg 1983
7 ... e5 8 b4 f6 9 bc ♗xc5 10 0-0 0-0 11 ♖b1 ♖b8 12 d3 ♗e6 13 ♘e4 ± Plachetka-Horvath, Malmö 1985-86
7 ... g6 8 0-0 (8 b4 ♗g7! 9 bc ♘e6 10 0-0 ∞) 8 ... ♗g7 9 d3 0-0 10 ♗d2 ♘e6 11 ♖b1 a5 12 ♘e4 ♗d7 ∞ Vaganian-Korchnoi, Linares 1985
7 b3 e5 8 ♗b2 ♗e7 9 ♖c1 ♘e6 10 0-0 0-0 11 ♘e1 ♗d7 = Speelman-Sax, Plovdiv 1983

[15] 7 ... ♕d7 8 0-0 e5 (8 ... g6 9 ♘c4 b6 10 b4 ±) 9 e3! ♗e7 10 ♖d1 0-0 11 d4 ± Uhlmann-Ivanović, Plovdiv 1986

[16] 8 ♕h4 e5 9 ♕xd8+ ♖xd8 10 0-0 ♗e7 11 d3 0-0 12 ♘d2 f6 = Uhlmann-Grünberg, Potsdam 1985

[17] 8 ... ♘e6 9 e3 g6 10 d4 cd 11 ed ♗g7 12 ♗e3 f5 13 ♕d5 ♘c7 14 ♕b3 ♘a5 15 ♕d1 ± Romanishin-Tal, USSR Ch 1976

[18] 9 ... f5?! 10 ♕f4 ♘e6 11 ♗xc6+ bc ♕c4 ± Pytel-Andre, Dortmund 1977

[19] 12 d3 ♘e6 13 ♕d5 ♕c7 14 ♕c4 ♖ab8 Vaganian-Polugayevsky, USSR Ch 1971

[20] Smejkal-A.Sokolov, Novi Sad 1984

[21] 7 ... g6 8 ♘a4 b6 (8 ... ♘e6!? Taimanov) 9 d4 cd 10 ♗f4 ♗g7 11 ♘xd4 ♘xd4 12 ♗xc7 ♕xc7 13 ♗xa8 0-0 14 ♗g2 ± Razuvayev-Kirov, Bulgaria 1981

[22] **8 a3** ♕d7 9 ♖b1 f6 10 d3 ♗e7 11 ♗d2 ♖b8 12 ♕c2 ∞ Smyslov-Korchnoi, USSR Ch 1967
8 b3 ♗e7 9 ♗b2 0-0 10 ♖c1 f6 12 ♘a4 b6 12 ♘h4 ♘d5 = Taimanov-Korchnoi, USSR Ch 1954

8 ♘e1 ♗e6 9 ♘d3 f6 10 f4 e4 11 ♘f2 ef 12 gf ♕d7 = Smyslov-Hübner, match 1983

[23] 8 ... ♗d7 9 e3 ♗e7 10 d4 ±

[24] 9 ♗e3 0-0 10 ♖c1 ♗d7 11 ♘d2 b6 12 ♘c4 f6 13 f4 ef 14 gf f5 ∞ Vukić-Bašagić, Sarajevo 1972

[25] 9 ... 0-0 10 ♗xc6+ bc 11 ♘c4 f6 12 b3 ♗h3 13 ♖e1 ♘e6 14 ♗b2± Dzindzihashvili-Timman, Tilburg 1985

[26] 10 ... 0-0 11 ♗xc6 ♗xc6 12 ♘xe5 ♗e8 13 ♗e3 (13 e4 ♗f6 14 ♘g4 ♗d4 15 ♘e3 ♗c6 ∞ Schüssler-Donaldson, Malmö 1985-86) 13 ... ♗f6 14 ♘f3 ♘e6 15 ♘e4! ± Kir.Georgiev-Chandler, Sarajevo 1985

[27] 11 ... ef 12 gf ♖b8 13 e4 ♗e6 14 ♘e3 ± Shamkovich-Alburt, New York 1983

[28] 12 ... ef 13 gf ♖b8 14 ♗d2 0-0 15 f5± Vilela-Lukacs, Albena 1985

[29] 13 ♘ed5 ♘xd5 14 ♗xd5 0-0 15 fe ♘xe5 16 ♗f4 ♘c6 17 a4 b4 = Smyslov-Hübner, match 1983

[30] 14 ... 0-0 15 f5! ±

[31] 15 ♘d2 0-0 16 ♘ec4 ef 17 gf ♔h8 ∞ Korchnoi-Portisch, Lucerne 1985

[32] 16 ♘c4 ef 17 ♗xf4 ♘e6 18 ♗d6 ♗e8 ∞ Portisch-A.Sokolov, Bugojno 1986

English 1 ... c5 III   1 c4 c5 2 ♘f3 ♘f6 3 d4 cd 4 ♘xd4

	4	5	6	7	8	9	10	11	12	
1	...	♘c3[1]	f3[2]	e4	♗e2[5]	♗e3	0-0	♕d2[8]	♖fd1	±
	b6	♗b7	d6[3]	e6[4]	♗e7[6]	0-0	♘bd7[7]	a6	♕c7[9]	
2	...	♘b5[10]	cd	♘5c3[13]	e3[14]	a3[16]	♘d2	♕c2[18]	h3[19]	±
	e5	d5[11]	♗c5[12]	0-0	e4[15]	a5[17]	♕e7	♗f5	♖d8[20]	

[1] 5 f3 ♗b7 6 e4 d6 7 ♗e2 e6 8 0-0 a6 9 ♗e3 ♘bd7 10 ♘c3 ♗e7 11 a4± Grünfeld-Fedorowicz, Hastings 1985-86

[2] 6 ♗g5 a6 (6 ... e6) 7 ♗xf6 (7 ♕c2 h6 8 ♗h4 ♕c7 9 e3 e6 10 0-0-0!? Ivkov) 7 ... gf 8 e3 (8 e4 e6 9 ♗e2 ♕c7 10 0-0 h5 ∓ Hansen-Plaskett, Copenhagen 1985) 8 ... e6 9 ♕h5 ♕c7 10 ♘f3 ♕c5 11 ♕h4 f5 ∞ Lerner-Psakhis, USSR Ch 1985

[3] 6 ... ♘c6 7 e4 e6 (7 ... ♘xd4 8 ♕xd4 e6 9 ♗f4 ± Spraggett) 8 ♗e3 ♗c5 9 ♕d2 0-0 10 0-0-0 ♕e7 11 ♗e2 ± Spraggett-Spassky, Montpellier C 1985

[4] 7 ... ♘bd7 8 ♗e3 e6 9 ♗e2 ♗e7 10 0-0 0-0 11 ♖c1 a6 12 ♕e1 ± Strauss-D.Gurevich, USA 1985

[5] 8 ♗g5 ♘bd7 9 ♕d2 a6 10 ♗e2 ♗e7 = Botvinnik-Smyslov, USSR 1967

[6] 8 ... ♘bd7 9 0-0 a6 10 ♗e3 ♗e7 11 b4 ± Nikolić-Veličković, Vršac 1981

[7] 10 ... a6 11 ♕e1! ♘bd7 12 ♕f2 ♖c8 13 ♖ac1 ± Seirawan-Benjamin, US Ch 1981

[8] 11 ♖c1 a6 12 ♕e1 ♖e8 13 ♕f2 ♖c8 14 ♖fd1 ♗f8 = Hort-Minić, Vinkovci 1970

[9] 13 ♖ac1 ± Gheorghiu-Popov, Berlin 1985

[10] 5 ♘f3 ♘c6 6 ♘c3 ♗b4 7 ♗d2 0-0 8 e3 e4 = Novikov-Bukhman, Leningrad 1975

[11] 5 ... ♗c5 6 ♘d6+ ♔e7 7 ♘xc8+ ♕xc8 8 e3 ♖d8 9 ♘c3 ±

[12] 6 ... ♕a5+ 7 ♘5c3 b5 8 ♘d2 b4 9 ♘b3 ♕d8 10 ♘a4 ± Kurajica-Rajković, Yugoslavia 1983

6 ... ♗b4+ 7 ♗d2 ♗c5 8 ♕c2 (8 d6 ♘a6 9 e3 0-0 10 ♗c3 ♖e8 =) 8 ... ♘a6 9 b4 ♗b6 10 ♘1c3 0-0 11 ♕b3 ♗f5 12 e3 ♗e4 ∞ Palatnik-Agzamov, USSR 1977

[13] 7 d6 0-0 8 ♘c7 ♘e4 9 e3 ♗b4+ 10 ♘d2 ♕d6 11 ♘xa8 ♖d8 ∓

7 d6 0-0 8 a3 ♘xd5 9 ♗c4 ♗e6 10 ♗xd5 ♗xd5 ∞ Ubilava-Tseitlin, USSR 1981

[14] 8 g3 ♘g4 (8 ... ♕b6 9 e3 ♗g4 ∞) 9 e3 f5 10 ♗e2 ♘f6 11 a3 ♘bd7 12 b4 ♗d6 ∞ Peshina-Vaganian, Moscow 1979

[15] 8 ... ♗f5 9 ♗c4 a6 10 a3 ♘bd7 11 ♘d2 ± Donchenko-Sher, Odessa 1978

[16] 9 ♘d2 ♗f5 10 g3 ♘bd7 11 ♗g2 ♖e8 ∞ Kogan-Benjamin, USA 1981

9 ♗e2 ♕e7 10 ♘d2 ♖d8 11 a3 ♘xd5 12 ♘xd5 (12 ♘ce4 ♘xe3! ∓) 12 ... ♖xd5 13 ♕c2 ♗f5 ∞ Mikhalchishin-Kasparov, Frunze 1981

[17] 9 ... ♗f5 10 b4 ♗d6 11 ♘d2 ♘bd7 (11 ... ♕e7 12 ♗e2 ♖d8 13 ♘c4 ± Hansen-Grünfeld, Copenhagen 1981) 12 ♗e2 a6 ±

[18] 11 ♗e2 ♖d8 12 0-0 ♗f5 13 ♘b3 ♗d6 ∓ Nenashev-Gorelov, Moscow 1984

11 d6!? ♗xd6 12 ♘dxe4 ♘xe4 13 ♘xe4 ♖d8 14 ♘xd6 (14 ♕c2 ♗f5 15 ♗d3 ♘c6 ∓) 14 ... ♖xd6 15 ♕c2 ♘c6 ∞ Palatnik-Kasparov, Frunze 1981

11 b3 ♖d8 12 ♗c4 ♗f5 ∞ Kiss-Honfi, Budapest 1986

[19] 12 ♗e2 ♖d8 13 g4 ♗g6 14 h4 h6 15 h5 ♗h7 ∞ Modr-Tseitlin, Prague 1983

[20] 13 g4 ♗g6 14 ♗g2 ♘xd5! ∞ Hansen-Reinert, Danish Ch 1985

English 1 ... c5 IV **1 c4 c5 2 ♘f3 ♘f6 3 d4 cd 4 ♘xd4 e6**

	5	6	7	8	9	10	11	12	13	
1	g3	♘c3[1]	♗d2	♕xd2	♗g2	♘b3	c5	♖c1	♘a4	±
	♕a5+	♘e4	♘xd2	a6	♗e7	♕c7	0-0	♘c6	♖b8[2]	
2	...	♘c3[3]	♗g5[5]	♖c1	♗g2	0-0	♗e3	h3	f4	∞
	♕c7	a6[4]	♗e7	d6	♘bd7	h6	0-0	♖e8	♘f8[6]	
3	...	♗g2	b3	♗d2	0-0	♘c2	♘c3	♖c1	f4	±
	...	a6[7]	♗b4+	♗e7[8]	♘c6	0-0[9]	d6	♘e5	♘ed7[10]	
4	...	♗g2	e3	0-0[12]	ed	♘c3	♘b5	♘xd4	b3	=
	♕b6	♗c5[11]	♘c6	♘xd4[13]	♗xd4	e5	0-0[14]	ed	d5[15]	
5	...	♗d2[16]	♕xd2[17]	♕e3	♘d2	♕xd2	♔xd2	♗g2	♔c3	=
	♗b4+	♗xd2+	♘e4	♕a5+	♘xd2	♕xd2+	♔e7	♘c6	♘xd4[18]	
6	♘c3	♗g5[19]	♘b3[20]	♘d5	♘xe7	e3	ed[21]	♗e2	♗h4[22]	±
	d5	e5	d4	♗e7	♕xe7	♘c6	ed+	h6		
7	...	♘b5[23]	a3[24]	♘xc3	♗g5	♗xf6	cd	♕xd5	e3	±
	♗b4	0-0	♗xc3+	d5	h6	♕xf6	ed	♘c6	♗g4[25]	
8	...	g3	♘b3	cd	♘xd5[28]	♗g2	♗d2	0-0	♕xd2	∞/=
	♘c6	♕b6[26]	d5[27]	♘xd5	ed	♗b4+	a5[29]	♗xd2	a4[30]	
9	...	♘db5	♗f4	♗c7[31]	♗d6	♕xd6	e4[32]	♕d2	♘d6	∞
	...	♗b4	0-0	♕e7	♗xd6	♕d8	♕a5[33]	a6	♘e8[34]	
10	...	...	♗f4[35]	cd	dc	♕xd8+	♖d1+[36]	♘d6	♖xd6	=
	...	d5	e5	ef	bc	♔xd8	♗d7	♗xd6[37]	♖b8[38]	
11	...	...	...	...	...	...	♘d4	g3	hg	=
							♗d7[39]	fg	♗b4[40]	

---

[1] 6 ♗d2 ♕b6 7 ♗c3 e5 8 ♘b3 ♕c6 ∞ Pribyl-Razuvayev, Helsinki 1984

[2] 14 0-0 ♖fd8 15 ♕e3 ♗f6 16 ♖fd1 h6 17 ♕d2 ♗g5 18 f4 ♗e7 19 ♕d6!! ± Ivanchuk-Chekhov, USSR 1987

[3] **6 ♕a4** a6 7 ♗g2 ♘c6 8 ♘b5 ♕b8 9 ♘5c3 ♗e7 = G.Garcia-Kavalek, Bochum 1981
6 ♘d2 b6 7 ♗g2 ♗b7 8 ♘b5 ♕c8 9 ♗xb7 ♕xb7 10 ♘f3 ♘e4 = Nogueiras-Ljubojević, Dubai Ol 1986

[4] 6 ... ♕xc4 7 e4 ∞

[5] **7 ♗g2** ♕xc4 (7 ... ♗b4 8 0-0 ♗xc3 9 bc d6 10 ♕a4 ± Flear-Ilić, Lugano 1986) 8 ♗f4 ♘c6 9 ♘xc6 bc 10 ♖c1 ♕b4 11 a3 ♕b7 12 ♗d6 ♗xd6 13 ♕xd6 ♕b8 14 ♕c5 ♕a7 = Sosonko-Kavalek, Wijk aan Zee 1978
7 ♕d3 b6 8 ♗g2 ♗b7 9 ♗xb7 ♕xb7 10 0-0 d6! (10 ... ♗e7 11 ♗g5 0-0 12 ♗xf6! ♗xf6 13 ♘e4 ± Adianto-Bischoff, Dubai Ol 1986) 11 ♗g5 ♘bd7 =

[6] Yusupov-Psakhis, Erevan Z 1982

[7] 6 ... ♕xc4 7 0-0 ♘c6 8 ♘xc6 dc 9 ♗g5 ♗c7 10 ♘c3 0-0 11 ♘e4 ∞ Djurić-Antonov, Pernik 1981

[8] 8 ... ♗c5 9 ♗c3 d5 10 cd ♘xd5 11 ♗b2 ♕a5+ 12 ♘d2 ♘c3 13 ♕c2! ♗xd4 14 ♘c4 ♕c7 15 ♗xc3 ± Rajković-Petkovski, Yugoslavia 1984

[9] **10 ... d5** 11 cd ♘xd5 12 ♘c3 ♘xc3 13 ♗xc3 0-0 14 ♕c1 intending ♕b2 ±
10 ... b5 11 cb ab 12 ♘c3 ♖b8 13 ♖c1 d5 14 e4 ± Kupreichik

[10] 14 ♘d4 ± Kupreichik-Martinović, Zenica 1985

[11] 6 ... ♘c6 7 ♘c2 d5 8 0-0 dc 9 ♘ca3 ♕a6 10 b3 ∞ Alburt-de Firmian, New York 1985

[12] 8 ♘b3 ♗b4+ 9 ♗d2 ♘e5 10 ♕e2 (10 ♕c2 d5 11 cd ♕a6! ∓ Sosonko-Suba, Tunis IZ 1985) 10 ... d5 11 cd ed = Flear-Ionescu, Lucerne 1985

[13] 8 ... ♗xd4 9 ed ♕xd4 10 ♕xd4 ♘xd4 11 ♘c3 ± Nogueiras-Rodriguez, Havana 1986

[14] 11 ... ♗c5 12 ♗g5 0-0 13 ♕d2 ∞ Rogers-Suba, Szirak 1986

[15] **14 cd** ♗f5 15 ♗b2 d3 ∓ Nogueiras
14 ♗b2 dc 15 ♕xd4 cb 16 ♕xb6 ab 17 ab ♗e6 = Nogueiras-Psakhis, Szirak 1986

[16] 6 ♘c3! – Nimzo-Indian (4 g3 c5)

[17] 7 ♘xd2 ♕b6 =

[18] 14 ♔xd4 d6 = Rashkovsky-Sideif Zade, Baku 1983

[19] 6 cd ♘xd5 7 ♗d2 ♗e7 8 e4 ♘b4 9 ♗b5+

(9 ♗e3 0-0 10 ♗e2 ♘8c6 = Quinteros-Kasparov, Moscow IZ 1982) 9 ... ♗d7 10 0-0 0-0 11 a3 ♘4c6 = Skembris-Tseshkovsky, Vrnjačka Banja 1982
[20] 7 ♘db5 a6 8 ♕a4 (8 ♘xd5? ab 9 ♘xf6+ ♕xf6! ∓∓) 8 ... ♗d7 9 cd ♕b6 10 ♗e3 ♗xb5 11 ♗xb6 ♗xa4 = Mikhalchishin
[21] 11 ♗e2 h6! 12 ♗xf6 ♕xf6 = Ortega-Tal, Erevan 1986
[22] Tal
[23] 6 g3 – Nimzo-Indian
   6 ♗d2 0-0 7 a3 ♗e7 8 ♗f4 (8 e4 d5 9 cd ♘xe4! 10 ♘xe4 ♕xd5 ⯝ Hess-Hardicsay, Budapest 1986) 8 ... d5 =
[24] 7 ♗f4 d5 8 e3 ♘c6 9 a3 ♗xc3+ 10 ♘xc3 ♕e7 11 ♗d3 ♖d8 12 ♕c2 dc 13 ♗xc4 ♘h5 14 ♗g3 ± P.Nikolić-Chandler, Vršac 1981
[25] 14 ♕b3 ♕g6 15 f3 ♗e6 16 ♕xb7 ♖fc8 ∓ Murey-West, Biel 1985
   14 ♗b5 ♖ad8 15 ♕e4! ± Murey
[26] 6 ... ♗c5 7 ♘b3 ♗e7 8 ♗g2 b6 9 0-0 ♗b7 10 ♘d5 0-0 11 ♗f4 ed 12 cd ♘b4 13 d6 ♗xg2 14 de ♕xe7 15 ♔xg2 ♘bd5 16 ♗g5 ♕e5 = Portisch-Velimirović, Sarajevo 1986
[27] 7 ... ♗b4 8 ♗g2 ♕a6 9 c5 b6 10 0-0! bc 11 ♗e3 ± Eingorn-Georgiev, Lvov 1984
   7 ... ♘e5 8 e4 d6 (8 ... ♗b4 9 ♕e2 0-0 10 f4 ♘c6 11 e5 ± Dvoiris-Tal, USSR 1985) 9 f4 ♘g6 10 ♕e2 ♗e7 11 ♗e3 ♕c7 12 ♗g2 ± Polugayevsky-Ljubojević, Tilburg 1985
[28] 9 ♗g2 ♘xc3 10 bc ♗e7 11 0-0 e5 =

Kasparov-Karpov, match (26) 1984-85
[29] 11 ... ♗g4 12 ♗xb4 ♕xb4+ 13 ♕d2 ♕xd2+ 14 ♔xd2 ± Smyslov-H.Olafsson, Copenhagen 1985
[30] 14 ♘c1 0-0 15 ♘d3 ♖d8 16 ♘f4 d4 17 ♖ac1 h6 18 ♘d5 ♕a7 19 ♖fd1 ♗d7 20 ♕f4 ♕a5 = Eingorn-Gligorić, Sochi 1986
[31] 8 ♗d6 ♗xd6 9 ♘xd6 ♕b6 10 ♕d2 ♘d4 11 0-0-0 ♕xd6 12 ♕xd4 ♕xd4 13 ♖xd4 b6 14 e4 ♖d8 = Rubinetti-Hulak, Toluca IZ 1982
[32] 11 0-0-0 a6 12 ♘d4 ♘e8 13 ♘xc6 bc 14 ♕d4 d6 ∞ Korchnoi-Polugayevsky, match 1970
[33] 11 ... a6 12 ♘c7 ♘e8 13 ♘xe8 ♖xe8 14 ♗e2 ± Korchnoi-Grünfeld, Lucerne Ol 1982
[34] 14 ♗e2 ♘xd6 15 ♕xd6 b5 ∞ Kishnev-Dvoiris, USSR 1984
[35] 7 cd ♘xd5 8 ♘xd5 ed 9 ♕xd5 ♗b4+ 10 ♗d2 ♕e7 ∞∞ Suba-Portisch, Thessaloniki Ol 1984
[36] 11 0-0-0+ ♗d7 12 ♘d6 ♔c7 (12 ... ♗xd6!? 13 ♖xd6 ♘g4) 13 ♘xf7 ♖g8 14 ♘e5 ♗f5 ∞∞ Trois-Rogulj, Virovitica 1980
[37] 12 ... ♔c7 13 ♘xf7 ♖g8 14 ♘e5 (14 g3 ♖b8 ∞∞ Andersson-Tal, match 1983) 14 ... ♖b8 ∞∞ Adorjan-Cebalo, Vršac 1983
[38] Korchnoi-Portisch, match 1983, and Karpov-Polugayevsky, London 1984
[39] 11 ... ♔c7 12 g3 ♗c5 13 ♖c1! ± Korchnoi-Portisch, match 1983
[40] 14 ♖c1 c5 15 ♘f3 ♖b8 16 ♘e5 ♔e7 =
   14 ♗g2 ♗xc3+ 15 bc ♔c7 16 0-0 ♖ab8 = Timman-Gligorić, Volmac v Partizan 1984

	5	6	7	8	9	10	11	12	13
1	d4[1]	bc	e3[3]	♗b5+[4]	0-0	♕e2[6]	♗d3	♖b1	♕c2	∞
	♘xc3[2]	g6	♗g7	♘d7[5]	0-0	a6	e5	♕a5	b5[7]	

English 1 ... c5 V   1 c4 c5 2 ♘f3 ♘f6 3 ♘c3 d5 4 cd ♘xd5

[1] 5 e3 ♘c6 6 ♗b5 ♘xc3 7 bc ♗d7 8 0-0 a6 9 ♗e2 e5 ∞
[2] 5 ... cd 6 ♕xd4 ♘xc3 7 ♕xc3 ♘c6 and now:
   8 e3 ♗g4 9 ♗d2 ♗xf3 10 gf ♕d5! ⯝ Ribli-Ljubojević, Tilburg 1978
   8 e4 ♗g4 (8 ... a6 9 ♗c4 ♕a5 10 ♗d2 ♕xc3 11 ♗xc3 e6 12 0-0 ± Korchnoi-Karpov, USSR Ch 1970) 9 ♗b5 ♖c8 10 0-0 a6 11 ♗xc6 ♖xc6 12 ♕e3 ∞/± Korchnoi-Ljubojević, 1978
[3] 7 ♗f4 ♗g7 8 e3 ♕a5 9 ♕d2 0-0 10 ♗e2 ♘c6 = Korchnoi
   7 ♕a4+ ♘c6 8 dc ♗g7 9 ♗b2 0-0 10 e3 ♗d7 ∞∞ Korchnoi-Furman, USSR 1973
[4] 8 ♗e2 0-0 9 0-0 ♕c7 (9 ... b6 10 a4 ♘d7 11 a5 ± Ivkov-Miles, Bugojno 1978) 10 ♕b3 b6 11 ♖d1 e6 = Larsen

   8 ♗d3 0-0 9 0-0 ♕c7 10 ♖b1 (10 ♗a3 ♘d7 11 ♕e2 b6 12 e4 ♗b7 13 ♖fd1 ♖fd8 = Portisch-Tal, Milan 1975) 10 ... ♘d7 11 e4 e5 12 ♗a3 ♖d8 13 ♕b3 ed 14 cd cd 15 ♖fc1 ∞∞ Karpov-Timman, Amsterdam 1985
[5] 8 ... ♗d7 9 a4 ♕a5 10 ♗xd7 (10 ♕b3!? Makarichev) 10 ... ♘xd7 11 ♗d2 0-0 12 0-0 e5 = Polugayevsky-Vaganian, USSR Ch 1983
[6] 10 a4 ♘f6!? (10 ... a6?! 11 ♗d3 b6 12 ♖b1 ♗b7 13 e4 ± Karpov-Korchnoi, match (12) 1981 11 ♗d3 ♗f5 12 ♗xf5 (12 ♖e1 ♗xd3 13 ♕xd3 ♖c8 14 e4 e6 15 ♗f4 ♕a5! ⯝ Spraggett-Shamkovich, New York 1983) 12 ... gf 13 ♘d2 ♖c8 13 ♗a3 b6 = Shamkovich
[7] 14 a4 ♖b8 15 ab ab 16 ♗d2 c4 ∞ Portisch-Miles, Bugojno 1986

49

	5	6	7	8	9	10	11	12	13	
2	g3	♗g2[9]	0-0[10]	♘g5[11]	♘ge4	d3[13]	♗g5	♘xd5	♘c3[14]	∞
	g6[8]	♘c6	♗g7	e6[12]	b6	0-0	f6	ed		
3	...	...	0-0	♘xd5[15]	d3	♗e3[16]	♘d4[18]	♘xc6[19]	♗xc6	=
	...	♗g7	0-0	♕xd5	♘c6	♗d7[17]	♕d6	♗xc6	♕xc6[20]	

[8] 5 ... ♘xc3 6 bc g6 7 ♕a4+ ♘d7 8 h4! h6 9 ♖b1 ±

[9] 6 d3 ♗g7 7 ♗d2 ♘c6 8 ♗g2 0-0 9 0-0 b6 10 ♕a4 (10 ♖b1 ♗b7 11 a3 e6 12 ♕h4 ♘d4 = Georgadze) 10 ... ♗b7 ∞ Spiridonov-Bukić, Bajmok 1980

 6 ♕a4+ ♘c6 7 ♘e5 ♘xc3 8 dc ♕d5 9 ♘xc6 ♗d7 = Gheorghiu-G.Garcia, Orense 1975

[10] 7 ♕b3 e6 8 0-0 ♗g7 9 d3 0-0 = Uhlmann-Skrobek, 1981

 7 h4 h6 8 d3 ♗g7 9 ♗d2 ♗e6! 10 ♖c1 ♖c8 = Larsen-Sosonko, 1979

 7 ♕a4 ♗g7 (7 ... ♘b6 8 ♕h4 ♗g7 9 d3 ±) 8 ♕c4 (8 ♘g5 e6 9 ♘ge4 ♘b6 10 ♕b5 c4 11 ♘a4 0-0 ∞ Tatai-Karpov, Las Palmas 1977) 8 ... ♘db4 9 0-0 ♕a5 10 d3 ♘c2! (10 ... ♗e6 11 ♕h4 h6 12 ♗d2 ± Cebalo-Bukić, Banja Luka 1981) 11 ♖b1 h6 ∞ Bukić

[11] 8 ♕b3 ♘c7 9 d3 0-0 10 ♗e3 b6 11 ♖ac1 ♘e6 ∓ Reshevsky-Kirov, Nice Ol 1974

[12] 8 ... ♘b6 9 ♗xc6 bc ∞ Gipslis

[13] 10 ♕a4 ♗d7! (10 ... ♗b7 11 ♘xd5 ed 12 ♘c3 ♕d7 13 ♘xd5 0-0-0 ∞ Romanishin-Ligterink, Wijk aan Zee 1985) 11 ♘xd5 ed 12 ♘c3 ♘e7 ∓ Browne-Miles, Lanzarote 1977

[14] Miles

[15] 8 ♘g5?! e6 9 ♘ge4 b6 10 d3 ♗b7 11 ♗g5 f6 12 ♗d2 ♕d7 ∓ Sokolov-Miles, Bugojno 1986

 8 d4 cd 9 ♘xd4 ♘xc3 10 bc a6 11 ♕b3 ♕c7 12 ♖b1 ♘d7 ∞ Petrosian-Draško, Sarajevo 1986

[16] 10 ♘g5 ♕d7 11 ♖b1 b6 12 a3 ♗b7 =

 10 a3 ♕d6 (10 ... b6 11 ♖b1 ♗b7 = Ribli-Miles, Amsterdam 1978) 11 ♖b1 c4 = Taimanov

 10 ♕a4 ♕d7 (10 ... ♕h5 11 ♗e3 ♗d7 12 ♖ac1 b6 = Lanka) 11 ♖b1 b6 12 a3 ♘d4 13 ♕d1 ♗b7 = Angantysson-Gislason, Reykjavik 1986

[17] 10 ... ♕d6 11 ♖c1 ♘d4 12 ♘d2 f5 13 ♘c4 ♕a6 14 a3 ± Schmidt-Dieks, Wijk aan Zee II 1975

 10 ... ♗xb2 11 ♘d4 ♕d7 12 ♘xc6 ♗xa1 13 ♕xa1 bc = Vilela-Campo, Mexico 1978

[18] 11 ♕d2 ♕d6 12 ♖fc1 b6 = Bönsch-Chekhov, 1981

 11 ♕c1 b6 12 d4 cd 13 ♘xd4 ♘xd4 14 ♗xd5 ♘xe2+ 15 ♔g2 ♘xc1 = Bagirov-Tukmakov, USSR Ch 1978

 11 d4 cd 12 ♘xd4 ♕c4 13 ♘xc6 ♗xc6 14 ♗xc6 bc 15 b3 ♕a6 = Kochiev-Smejkal, Leningrad 1977

[19] 12 ♘b5 ♕e5 13 ♖b1 ♖ac8 14 ♕d2 b6 = Mikhalchishin-Platonov, USSR 1980

[20] 14 ♖c1 ♕e6 15 ♖xc5 (15 ♗xc5 ♗xb2 16 ♖b1 ♗f6 =; 15 ... ♕xa2!?) 15 ... ♕xa2 16 ♖b5 b6 (16 ... ♕a6!? 17 ♖b4 b6 18 ♕b3 ♖fb8 ∞/= Ribli-Timman, Tilburg 1980) 17 ♕a1 ♕e6 (17 ... ♕xa1 18 ♖xa1 ♖fb8 19 ♖a6 ± Karpov-Ribli, Amsterdam 1980) 18 ♕a6 ♕d7 19 ♖a1 h5 20 ♖b4 ♖fc8 = I.Ivanov-Timman, Lucerne Ol 1982

English 1 ... c5 VI			**1 c4 c5 2 ♘f3 ♘f6 3 ♘c3 d5 4 cd ♘xd5 5 e4**						
	5	6	7	8	9	10	11	12	13
1	...	dc	♔xd1	♗f4[2]	♔c2	♖d1	♗c4	♗f7+	♖xd7[4]	±
	♘xc3[1]	♕xd1+	♘c6	g6	♗g7	♗d7[3]	f6	♔xf7		
2	...	♗c4	♔e2	♔f1	b4[6]	♘e2[7]	d4	♗b2	h4	∞∞/±
	♘b4	♘d3+[5]	♘f4+	♘e6	cb	♘c7[8]	e6	♘d7	♘f6[9]	
3	...	...	...	...	...	bc	♗xe6	d4	♗e3	∞
	...	...	...	...	g6	♗g7	♗xe6	♘c6	♕a5[10]	
4	...	♗b5+	d4[11]	a3	♕xd8+	ab	♗xb2	0-0	♗c4	∞/=
	...	♘8c6	cd	dc[12]	♔xd8	cb[13]	♗d7[14]	f6	♘xb4[15]	

[1]   5... ♘c7 6 d4 cd 7 ♘xd4 e5 8 ♘db5 ♕xd1+ 9 ♔xd1 ♘xb5 10 ♘xb5 ♘a6 11 ♗e3± Timman-Miles, Nikšić 1983

[2]   8 ♗e3 b6 9 ♘d2 ♗b7 10 f3 g6 11 ♔c2 h5 12 a4 ± Vaganian-Mikhalchishin, Lvov 1984

[3]   10 ... 0-0 11 ♗b5 ± Miles

[4]   Miles-Vaganian, London 1984

[5]   6... ♗e6 7 ♗xe6 ♘d3+ 8 ♔f1 fe 9 ♘g5 ♕b6 (9 ... ♕d7 10 ♕f3 ♘e5 11 ♕h3 ♕d3+ 12 ♕xd3 ♘xd3 13 ♔e2 ♘f4+ 14 ♔f3 e5 15 d4 ±) 10 ♕f3 c4 11 b3 ± Tukmakov-Peshina, USSR 1980, and Levin-Zilberstein, USSR 1983

[6]   9 ♘e5 ♕d4! 10 ♕a4+ ♘d7 11 f4 ♘xf4! 12 ♘xf7 ♘d3 ∓ Klinger-Reichmann, Austria 1984

[7]   10 ♘d5 g6 11 ♗b2 ♗g7 12 ♗xg7 ♘xg7 13 ♘xb4 0-0 14 h3 (14 d4 ♗g4 = Hübner-Portisch, match 1980) 14 ... e5 15 g3 ♗e6 ±/∞ Seirawan-Sax, Linares 1983

[8]   10 ... ♕c7 11 ♗b2! ± Loginov-Sideif Zade, USSR 1983

10 ... g6 11 ♗b2 ♗g7 12 ♗xe6 ♗xb2 13 ♗xf7+ ± Kavalek-Zimmermann, West Germany 1983

10 ...♘c5 11 ♕c2 e6 12 d4 ± Miles-Hort, match 1983

10 ... ♘d7 11 ♗xe6 fe 12 d4 e5 13 ♕b3! ed 14 ♘g5 ± Dzindzihashvili-Peters, US Ch 1984

[9]   13 ... ♗e7 14 ♖c1 ♘f6 15 ♗d3 ♗d7 16 ♘e5 0-0 17 g3 ∞∞/± Sideif Zade-Mikhalchishin, Baku 1983

13 ... ♘f6 14 ♗d3 ♗d7 15 h5 h6 16 ♘f4 ♗e7 17 ♕e2 ∞∞/± Psakhis-Vaganian, Lvov 1984

[10]   13 ... ♗g4 14 ♘e2 f5 15 h3 fe 16 hg ef 17 gf ± Seirawan-Miles, London 1982

13 ... ♕a5 14 ♖c1 (14 ♕d2 0-0-0 15 ♖c1 f5 ∓ Ftacnik-Pinter, Prague Z 1985) 14 ... ♗c4+ 15 ♔g1 0-0-0 ∞

[11]   7 a3 ♘d3+ 8 ♗e2 ♘f4+ 9 ♔f1 ♘e6 ∞

[12]   8 ... ♕b6 9 ♗xc6+ bc 10 ab dc 11 bc ± Ribli-Ftacnik, Baile Herculane Z 1982

8 ... ♗d7 9 ♗xd4 ♘xd4 10 ♗xd7+ ♕xd7 11 ab ± Uhlmann-Lukacs, Berlin 1982

[13]   10 ... c2 11 ♗xc6 bc 12 ♘e5 ♗e8 13 ♔d2 ± D.Gurevich-Tseshkovsky, Somerset (USA) 1986

[14]   11 ... e5 12 ♗xc6 bc 13 ♘xe5 ♗xb4+ 14 ♔e2 ± Szabo-Horvath, Hungary 1979

11 ... e6 12 0-0 f6 13 e5 ± Pishkin-Strautins, corr. 1983, and Hübner-Timman, West Germany 1985

[15]   14 e5 ♖c8 15 ♗f7 ♖c2 ∞/= Tal-Timman, match 1985

	3	4	5	6	7	8	9	10	11	
1	...	cd	♗g2	d4[2]	♘xd4	♘xc6	♔xd1	♘c3[4]	♗e3	=
	d5[1]	♘xd5	♘c6	cd[3]	♘db4	♕xd1+	♘xc6	♗d7	e5[5]	
2	...	♗g2	♘c3	d4	♕xd4	0-0[6]	e4[7]	♕e3	♘d4	±/=
	b6	♗b7	e6	cd	d6	a6	♘bd7	♗e7	♕c7[8]	

[1] 3 ... ♘c6 4 ♗g2 ♕b6 5 ♘c3 e6 6 0-0 ♗e7 = Vukić-S.Garcia, Novi Sad 1975
3 ... g6 4 b3 ♗g7 5 ♗b2 0-0 6 ♗g2 ♘c6 7 0-0 b6 8 d3 ♗b7 9 ♘bd2 d5 = Gipslis

[2] 6 0-0 e5 7 ♘c3 ♗e6 8 ♘g5 ♕xg5 9 ♘xd5 ♕d8 10 ♘e3 ♖c8 = Timman-Portisch, Nikšić 1978

[3] 6 ... ♘f6 7 ♕a4 ♗d7 8 dc e5 9 0-0 ♗xc5 10 ♘c3 h6 11 ♘d2 ± Andersson-Portisch, Reggio Emilia 1985-86
6 ... ♘c7!? 7 e3 ♗g4 8 ♘c3 cd 9 ed e6 10 ♕a4 ♕d7 = Miles-Ljubojević, Bugojno 1986

[4] 10 ♗xc6+ bc 11 ♘c3 g6 12 ♗e3 ♗g7 13 ♖c1 ♗e6 = Smyslov-Hübner, match 1983

[5] 11 ... ♖c8 12 ♖c1 g6 13 f4 ♗g7 ∞ Andersson-Farago, Rome 1986
11 ... e5 = Speelman-Alburt, London 1986

[6] 8 ♗g5 ♘bd7 9 ♘b5 e5 (9 ... h6 10 ♗xf6 ♘xf6 11 ♖d1 ♘xe4 12 ♘h4 ♘c5 13 0-0! ± Suba-Kindermann, Dortmund 1985; 9 ... ♕b8 10 ♖d1 e5 11 ♕e3 a6 12 ♘c3 ♗e7 13 ♗h3 ± Grünfeld-Suba, Thessaloniki Ol 1984) 10 ♘xd6 ♗xd6 11 ♕xd6 ♘xe4 = Suba

[7] 9 ♖d1 ♘bd7 10 ♘g5 ♗xg2 11 ♔xg2 ♖c8 12 ♘ge4 ♖c6 13 ♗f4 ♘xe4 14 ♕xe4 ½-½ Adorjan-Suba, Prague Z 1985

[8] 12 b3 0-0 13 ♗b2 ♖fe8 14 ♖fe1 (14 h3 ♗f8 15 ♖fe1 ♖ad8 16 ♖e2 g6 17 ♖ae1 ♕b8 = Hübner-Kasparov, Tilburg 1981) 14 ... ♗f8 15 ♖e2 ♖ac8 16 ♖d1 ♕b8 17 ♕d2 ♘c5 18 ♗a1 (18 ♕e1 ♖ed8 = Uhlmann-Adorjan, Szirak 1985) 18 ... ♕a8 19 f3 ♖ed8 20 ♔h1 ±/= Uhlmann-Grünberg, Dresden 1985

	6	7	8	9	10	11	12	13	14	
1	d4	♕xd4[1]	♕f4	♘e5[3]	♔xg2	♘xg6	♘c3	b3	♖d1	=
	cd	♘c6	♘e7[2]	♗xg2	♘g6	hg	♖c8	d5	♗b4[4]	
2	♘c3	b3	♗b2	e3[7]	bc	♕e2	♖fd1	♖ab1	d3[9]	=
	♗e7[5]	0-0	d5[6]	dc	♘c6	♖c8[8]	♘a5	♘d7	a6[10]	
3	...	d4	♘xe4[11]	♗f4[12]	♕d2	dc	♖fd1	♗g5	♗xe7	=
	...	♘e4	♗xe4	0-0[13]	♘c6	bc	♕b6	♖ad8	♘xe7[14]	

[1] 7 ♘xd4 ♗xg2 8 ♔xg2 ♕c8 =

[2] 8 ... d5 9 ♖d1 ♗d6 10 ♕h4 0-0 11 ♘c3 ♗e7 12 ♗g5! h6 13 cd ed 14 ♗e3 ± Shtukaturkin-Shakarov, USSR 1981
8 ... ♗c5 9 ♘c3 0-0 10 ♖d1 ♘e7! 11 g4 ♘g6 12 ♕g3 ♘e4 = Dziuban-Petrosian, USSR 1979

[3] 9 ♖d1 ♘g6 10 ♕d2 ♖c8 11 b3 d5 =

[4] 15 ♗a1 ♗e7 = Rashkovsky-Kharitonov, Sverdlovsk 1984

[5] 6 ... ♘c6 7 e4 ♕b8 8 ♖e1 d6 9 d4 cd 10 ♘xd4 ♘xd4 11 ♕xd4 ♗e7 12 b3 0-0 13 ♗b2 ♖d8 14 ♖ad1 ± Romanishin-Vaiser, Sochi 1984

[6] 8 ... d6 9 e3 a6 10 d4 ♕c7 (10 ... ♘bd7 11 d5! ed 12 ♘h4 ± Andersson-Browne, Wijk aan Zee 1983) 11 ♕e2 ♘e4 12 ♖fd1 ♘d7 = Vukić-Sunye, Tuzla 1983

[7] 9 cd ♘xd5 10 ♘xd5 ♗xd5 11 d4 ♗f6 =

[8] 11 ... ♕c7 12 ♖fd1 ♖fd8 13 ♖ab1 a6 14 ♗a1 ♖ab8 15 d3 ♘a7 16 d4! ± A.Sokolov-Li Zunian, Biel IZ 1985, and Korchnoi-Kir.Georgiev, Lugano 1986

[9] 14 ♗a1 ♗xf3 =

[10] 15 ♗a1 ♕c7 16 ♘e1 (16 ♗h3 ♕c6 = Csom-Petrosian, Biel IZ 1976) 16 ... ♗xg2 17 ♔xg2 ♗f6 18 f4 ♖b8 ∞/= Vukić-Jelen, Yugoslavia 1977

[11] 8 ♕d3 ♘xc3 9 ♕xc3 0-0 – Queen's Indian

[12] 9 d5 0-0 10 ♘h4 ed 11 cd ♗xg2 12 ♘xg2 d6 13 ♗f4 ♗g5 14 ♕d2 ♗xf4 15 ♕xf4 ♘d7 16 ♕xd6 ♘f6 = Sahović-Adamski, Valjevo 1984

[13] 9 ... ♘c6 10 d5 ♘a5 11 ♘d2 ♗xg2 12 ♔xg2 0-0 13 e4 ♗g5 14 ♗xg5 ♕xg5 15 f4 ± Uhlmann-Bischoff, Budapest 1985

[14] Smyslov-Hübner, match 1983

English 1 ... c5 IX   **1 c4 c5 2 ♘f3 ♘f6 3 g3 b6 4 ♗g2 ♗b7 5 0-0 e6 6 ♘c3 ♗e7 7 d4 cd 8 ♕xd4 d6**

	9	10	11	12	13	14	15	16	17	
1	♗g5	♗xf6	♕d3[1]	♖ad1	♘d4[3]	♔xg2	f4	f5	e4	∞
	a6	♗xf6	♖a7[2]	♗e7	♗xg2	♕c8	g6	gf	fe[4]	
2	♖d1	b3	e4	♗b2[7]	♘d2	♖ac1	h3	a3	b4	=
	a6[5]	♘bd7	♕c8[6]	0-0	♕c7	♖ac8	♖fe8	♕b8	♖ed8[8]	
3	...	♘g5[9]	♔xg2	♕f4	♘ce4[11]	♘xf6+	♘xh7	♕e4	♕xc6	∞
	...	♗xg2	♘c6	♖a7[10]	♖d7[12]	♗xf6	♖xh7	♖h5	♖c5[13]	

[1] 11 ♕f4 0-0 (11 ... ♗xf3 12 ♕xf3 ♖a7 13 ♖ad1 0-0 14 b3 ♘d7 15 ♘e4 ♗e7 16 ♕f4 ± Hébert-Grünfeld, Thessaloniki Ol 1984) 12 ♖fd1 ♗e7 13 ♘e4 ♗xe4 14 ♕xe4 ♖a7 15 ♘d4 ♗c7 16 b3 ♖c5 ∞ Pigusov-Aseyev, USSR 1984

[2] 11 ... ♕c7 and now:
12 ♖ad1 ♗e7 13 ♘d4 ♗xg2 14 ♔xg2 ♘c6 15 f4 0-0!? (15 ... ♘xd4 16 ♕xd4 0-0 17 f5 ♖ac8 18 fe fe = Ftacnik-Browne, Naestved 1985) 16 ♘xc6 ♕xc6 17 ♖f3 b5 ∞ Welin-Browne, Reykjavik 1986
12 ♖fd1! ♗e7 13 ♘e4 0-0 14 ♘fg5 g6 15 ♕d4 h6! 16 ♘f3 ♗xe4 17 ♕xe4 ♘c6 ∞ Tal-Browne, Taxco IZ 1985

[3] 13 ♘e4 0-0 14 ♖d2 (14 ♖ac1 ♗a8 15 ♕e3 ♘c6 16 ♘c3 ♕b8 = Grigorian-Karpov, USSR 1975) 14 ... ♕c7 15 ♘eg5 g6 16 h4 ♘d7 17 b3 ♘f6 = Smyslov-Short, Montpellier C 1985

[4] 18 ♖xe4 f5 19 ♘g5!? (19 ♘c3 ♘c6! 20 ♕e2 ♘xd4 21 ♕h5+ ♔d7 22 ♖xd4 ∞ Tal-Gavrikov, Tallinn 1985) 19 ... ♗xg5 20 ♘xe6 ♕xe6 21 ♖de1 ∞ Tal-Short, Naestved 1985

[5] 9 ... 0-0 10 ♗g5 h6 (10 ... ♘bd7 11 ♘b5 d5 12 cd ♗xd5 13 ♘c3 ♗c6 ± Korchnoi-Ftacnik, Biel 1984) 11 ♗xf6 ♗xf6 12 ♕xd6 ♕xd6 13 ♖xd6 ♘a6! 14 ♖c1 ♖fd8 = Kengis-Shabalov, USSR 1986

[6] **11 ... 0-0** 12 ♗a3! ± de Firmian
11 ... ♕c7 12 ♗a3 ♘c5 13 e5 de 14 ♕xe5 ♖c8 (14 ... ♕c8 15 ♕e3 ♘fd7!? Ftacnik) 15 ♕xc7 (15 ♗b2 h5! Ivanka-Browne, Las Vegas 1986) 15 ... ♖xc7 16 ♗c1! ♘fxe4 17 ♘xe4 ♗xe4 18 ♗f4 ♖c8 19 ♗d6! ± Andersson-Browne, Naestved 1985, and Gutman-Ljubojević,

Biel IZ 1985
11 ... ♕b8 12 ♗a3 ♘c5 13 e5 (13 ♘d2 0-0 14 ♗b2 ♖d8 15 b4 ♘cd7 16 a3 ♕c7 = Hulak-Ribli, Zagreb/Rijeka 1985) 13 ... de 14 ♕xe5 ♘cd7 (14 ... ♕a7 15 ♘a4! ♖c8 16 ♘xc5 bc 17 ♗b2 ± Ribli-A.Sokolov, Lugano 1985) 15 ♕xb8 ♖xb8 16 ♗c1 ♖c8 17 ♗b2 ♖g8 ∞ Pelts-Browne, New York 1986

[7] 12 ♗a3 ♘c5 13 e5 de 14 ♘xe5 ♗xg2 15 ♔xg2 ♕b7 = Ribli

[8] 18 ♕e3 ♗a8 19 ♕e2 ♘e8 = Karpov-Ribli, Dubai Ol 1986

[9] 10 ♗g5 ♘bd7 11 ♘d2 ♗xg2 12 ♔xg2 0-0 13 ♘de4 ♕c7 14 ♖ac1 (14 ♖d2 ♖fd8 15 ♖ad1 h6 16 ♗e3 ♘c5 = Draško-Grünberg, Polanica Zdroj 1985) 14 ... ♖fd8 15 ♔g1 h6 16 ♘xf6+ ♗xf6 17 ♗xf6 ♘xf6 18 b3 ♖ac8 = Korchnoi-Adorjan, Cannes 1986

[10] 12 ... 0-0 13 b3 (13 ♘ge4 ♘xe4 14 ♘xe4 ♖a7 15 b3 ± Csom-Kindermann, Biel 1986) 13 ... ♖a7 14 ♗b2 ♖d7 15 ♘ce4 ♘e8 16 ♘f3! b5 (16 ... ♕a8 17 ♔g1 ♖d8 18 ♕e3 ± Adorjan-Schneider, Hungarian Ch 1984) 17 ♔g1 ± Adorjan-Rohde, New York 1985

[11] 13 ♘ge4 ♖d7 14 ♗e3 ♘e5 (14 ... ♘b4 15 ♖d2! ±) 15 ♘xf6+ ♗xf6 16 ♘a4 ♕a8! = Horvath-Schneider, Hungarian Ch 1984

[12] 13 ... ♘e5 14 ♘xf6+ ♗xf6 15 ♘e4 ♗e7 16 b3 0-0 17 ♗b2 ♕b8 ∞ Hansen-Gheorghiu, Reykjavik 1986

[13] 18 ♕e4 ♕c8! (18 ... ♕c7 19 ♗e3 ♖xc4 20 ♕a8+ ♕c8 21 ♕xc8+ ♖xc8 22 ♖ac1 ± Csom-Diždarević, Sarajevo 1981) 19 ♗e3 ♖xc4 20 ♖ac1 ♖dc7 = Adorjan-Bischoff, New York 1986

English 1 ... c5 X		1 c4 c5 2 ♘f3 ♘f6 3 g3 b6 4 ♗g2 ♗b7 5 0-0 g6						
	6	7	8	9	10	11	12	13	14
1	b3[1]	♗b2	♘c3	d4	♕xd4[3]	♕d2	♖fd1	♘d4	♔xg2	=
	♗g7	0-0	d6[2]	cd	♘bd7[4]	♖c8	a6	♗xg2	♕c7[5]	
2	...	...	...	d4[6]	♘e5[7]	dc	cd	♘f3[8]	♖c1	=
	...	...	♘a6	d5	e6	♘xc5	ed	♕d7	♖fe8[9]	
3	...	...	...	♖c1	d4	cd[11]	dc	♘b5	♘bd4	=
	...	...	...	e6[10]	d5	ed	♘xc5[12]	♕d7	♘fe4[13]	
4	♘c3	d4	♘xd4	♔xg2	e4	b3[16]	♘xe4	♕f3	♗a3[17]	=
	♗g7	cd[14]	♗xg2	0-0[15]	♕c7	♘xe4	♕e5	♕xd4	♘c6[18]	
5	...	...	♕xd4	♕f4[19]	♖d1	♗d2[21]	♖ac1	b3	♘d5[22]	±
	...	...	♘c6	♖c8[20]	d6	0-0	h6	♕d7		
6	...	...	...	♖d1[23]	b3	♗b2	♕e3[24]	♖ac1	♗a1	∞
	...	...	d6	♘bd7	♖c8	0-0	♖e8	a6	♖c5[25]	

[1]   6 d3 ♗g7 7 e4 0-0 8 ♘c3 d6 9 ♘h4 ♘c6 10 f4 a6 11 a4 ♖b8 ∞/∓ Romanishin-Rodriguez, Moscow 1985, and Lerner-Tseshkovsky, USSR Ch 1986

[2]   **8 ... d5** 9 ♘xd5 ♘xd5 10 ♗xg7 ♔xg7 11 cd ♕xd5 12 d4 cd 13 ♕xd4+ ♕xd4 14 ♘xd4 ♗xg2 15 ♔xg2 ♖c8 16 ♖ac1 ♘a6 ±/= Speelman-Dvoiris, Sochi 1982, and Csom-Short, Hastings 1983-84
    8 ... e6 9 d4 cd 10 ♕xd4 d5 11 cd ♘xd5 12 ♕xg7+! ♔xg7 13 ♘xd5+ e5! 14 ♗xe5+ f6 ∞ Schneider-Ftacnik, Stary Smokovec 1983

[3]   10 ♘xd4 ♗xg2 11 ♔xg2 d5 12 cd ♘xd5 13 ♘db5 ♘xc3 14 ♗xc3 ♗xc3 15 ♘xc3 ♘c6 = Szekely-Lau, Pernik 1984

[4]   10 ... ♘e4 11 ♕e3 ♘d7 12 ♖ac1 ♘dc5 13 ♖fd1 f5 14 b4 ♘e6 15 ♘xe4! ± Andersson-Kurajica, Sarajevo 1985

[5]   Korchnoi-Adorjan, Wijk aan Zee 1984

[6]   9 e3 ♘a6 10 d4 d5 11 ♘e5 ♕e7 12 ♕e2 dc 13 bc ♖ac8 = Andersson-Polugayevsky, Biel IZ 1985

[7]   10 cd ♘xd5 = Andersson-Kasparov, match 1985

[8]   13 ♖c1 d4! ∓ Andersson-Littlewood, Hastings 1981-82

[9]   Ftacnik-Speelman, Thessaloniki Ol 1984

[10]   9 ... d5 10 ♘xd5 ♘xd5 11 ♗xg7 ♔xg7 12 cd ♕xd5 13 d4 ♖fd8!? (13 ... cd – 8 ... d5) 14 e4 ♕h5 15 d5 e6 ∞

[11]   11 e3 ♕e7 12 ♕e2 ♖fd8 13 ♖fd1 ♘e4 = Andersson-Vaganian, Biel IZ 1985

[12]   12 ... bc 13 ♘a4 ♕e7 14 ♗a3 ♖ac8 15 ♘e1! ± Taimanov-Tal, USSR 1983, and Andersson-Vaganian, Tilburg 1983

[13]   **14 ... ♖fe8** 15 ♖c2 a5 = Taimanov-Kudrin, Titograd 1984

[14]   ... ♘fe4 15 ♖c2 a5 = Csom-Stempin, Prague Z 1985

[14]   7 ... ♘e4 8 ♘xe4 ♗xe4 9 d5 ± Korchnoi-Panno, Lucerne 1985, and Karpov-Timman, Brussels 1986

[15]   9 ... ♕c8 10 b3 ♗b7+ 11 f3 d5 12 cd ♘xd5 13 ♘xd5 ♕xd5 14 ♗e3! ♘c6 15 ♘xc6 ♗xc6 16 ♖c1 ♕e6 17 ♕d3 0-0 18 ♖fd1 ± Tal-Polugayevsky, USSR Ch 1976, and Poluagevsky-Smyslov, USSR Ch 1976

[16]   11 ♕e2 ♘c6 12 ♕c2 a6 13 ♗g5 (13 ♖d1 e6 14 b3 ♗b7 15 ♗b2 ♖fd8 16 f3 d6 ∞ Hansen-Adorjan, Gladsaxe 1983) 13 ... e6 14 ♖ac1 ♖fc8 15 b3 ♘e8 ∞ Vukić-Psakhis, Bor 1985

[17]   14 ♖b1!? ♕e5 15 ♗f4 ♕e6 16 ♘f6+ ♗xf6 17 ♕xa8 ♘c6 18 ♕b7 g5 19 ♖be1 ♕f5 20 ♗c1 ∞

[18]   15 ♖ad1 ♕e5 16 ♖xd7 ♕a5! 17 ♗xe7 ♘e5 18 ♕d1! ♖xd7 19 ♕xd7 ♕xa2! 20 ♗xf8 ♖xf8 = Karpov-Kasparov, match (13) 1984-85

[19]   9 ♕h4 h6 10 ♗d4 g5! 11 ♘xc6 dc 12 ♕h3 ♕d7 = Kirov-Garcia Gonzalez, Potsdam 1985

[20]   9 ... 0-0 10 ♕h4 ♘a5 11 ♗g5 ♖c8 12 b3 ♖c5 13 ♖ac1 h6 14 ♗xf6 ♗xf6 15 ♕f4 ♗g7 16 ♖fd1 d6 17 ♕e3 ♕d7 18 ♘e4 ♗xe4 19 ♕xe4 ± Kengis-Makarichev, Moscow 1986

[21]   11 b3 ♘e4? 12 ♗xe4! ♖xa1 13 ♗a3 ♗g7 14 ♘fg5 0-0 15 ♘xh7! ±± Ribli-Kouatly, Lucerne 1985; 11 ... 0-0 12 ♕h4 ±

[22]   Ribli-Spassky, Montpellier C 1985

[23]   9 ♗e3 ♘bd7 10 ♕d2 ♖c8 11 b3 a6 12 ♖ac1 0-0 13 ♗h6 ♖c5 14 ♗xg7 ♔xg7 15 ♖fd1 ♕a8 = Korchnoi-D.Gurevich, Jerusalem 1986

[24]   12 ♘d5 ♗xd5?! 13 cd ♖c2 14 ♖d2 ♘e8 15 ♖xc2 ♗xd4 16 ♘xd4 ∞; 12 ... a6! intending ... b5

[25]   Karpov-Kasparov, match (23) 1986

Dutch

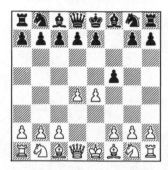 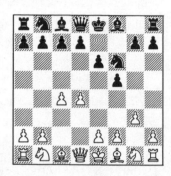 

The Dutch has always been a black sheep of a defence, despite successful results by Morphy, Alekhine, Botvinnik and Larsen. Black's early claim to the e4 square weakens his kingside (particularly the square e6) and often leads to a certain congestion and slow development. The second player hopes that his f-pawn will secure a grip on the centre and facilitate a kingside attack. White's trump is the advance e4 which, when successfully executed, allows him a tangible advantage in space and activity as well as highlighting the weaknesses in the Black camp.

Despite these handicaps, the Dutch has recently gained in acceptance as enterprising young GMs like Short, Yusupov, Agdestein and Malanyuk labour to revamp this maligned defence.

The greatest advances have been made in the **Stonewall Variation**. Black balances potentially fatal dark-squared weaknesses against his grip on the e4 square and a certain amount of kingside space. Recent plans involving unravelling his queenside tangle with ... b6, ... ♗b7 and ... c5 offer interesting counterchances. It is this idea, replacing crude kingside attacks, which has revitalized the variation.

The **Leningrad** is more of a chameleon. Black hopes to advance on the queenside or neutralize White's central ambitions, depending on circumstances. White's success still hinges on the prospect of implementing e4. The Leningrad remains less explored than the Stonewall.

While both variations have overcome their previous stigma as inferior defences, they have yet to earn total acceptance.

The **Staunton Gambit** (2 e4 fe 3 ♘c3) is a dangerous attempt to expose Black's position to an early assault. It is certainly sound, but Black's defensive resources are sufficient to hold the balance.

Reference: *Winning with the Dutch* (Bellin)

	2	3	4	5	6	7	8	9	10	
1	g4[1]	e4[2]	h3	♘c3[4]	d5[5]	hg	f3	♗e3	♕d2	∞
	fg	d6[3]	♘f6	e5	♗e7	♗xg4	♗c8	♘bd7	c5[6]	
2	♘c3	♘f3[7]	♗f4[8]	e3	♘b5[10]	c4	a3	♗d3	♖c1	∞
	d5	e6	♘f6	♗e7[9]	♘a6	0-0	♘e4	♗d7	c6[11]	
3	...	♗g5	♗xf6[12]	e3	♗d3	♕f3	h3[15]	♘ge2	h4	±
	...	♘f6	ef	c6[13]	♗d6[14]	g6	♕e7	0-0	h5[16]	
4	♗g5	♗h4	e3	♗g3	♗d3[20]	♘e2	f3	c4	♘bc3	∞
	h6[17]	g5[18]	♗g7	♘f6[19]	e6	d6	♕e7	e5	0-0[21]	
5	...	h4[22]	♘c3[23]	e3[24]	♕f3[26]	♗d3	♘ge2	h5	hg	∞
	g6	♗g7	d5	c6[25]	♗e6	♘f6	♘bd7	♖g8	hg[27]	

1 d4 f5 2 e4[28] fe

	3	4	5	6	7	8	9	10	11	
6	♘c3	f3[30]	fe	♗g5[32]	♗c4[33]	♘ge2[35]	0-0	d5	♗b5	∞
	♘f6[29]	d5[31]	de	♗f5	♘c6[34]	♕d7	0-0-0[36]	♘e5	c6[37]	
7	...	♗g5	♘xe4	♗xf6[39]	♕h5+[40]	♕h6	♘f3	♗d3	0-0-0	∞/±
	...	e6[38]	♗e7	♗xf6	g6	b6[41]	♗b7	♕e7	♘a6[42]	
8	...	...	d5[43]	♕d4[44]	♗xf6[45]	♘xe4[46]	♘g3	0-0-0[48]	f4	=
	...	♘c6	♘e5	♘f7	ef	f5[47]	g6	♗h6+	0-0[49]	

[1]   2 ♕d3 d5 3 g3 (3 ♗f4 e6 4 ♕g3 ♘a6 5 e3 c6 ∓ Ivkov) 3 ... ♘f6 4 ♗g2 e6 5 c4 ♗d6 6 ♘f3 0-0 7 0-0 c6 ∞ Gavrikov-Psakhis, Tallinn 1983

[2]   3 ♗f4 ♘f6 4 h3 d5 5 ♘c3 ♗f5 ∞ Utasi-M.Gurevich, Jurmala 1985

[3]   3 ... d5 4 e5 ♗f5 5 h3 ∞

[4]   5 hg ♗xg4 6 f3 ♗c8 7 ♘c3 e5 8 ♗e3 ♘c6 ∞

[5]   6 hg ed 7 ♕xd4 ♘c6 8 ♗b5 ∞

[6]   11 dc bc 12 ♗c4 ♘b6 13 ♗b3 ♗a6 ∞ Piket-Weemaes, Amsterdam 1986

[7]   3 g4 fg 4 e4 c6 5 ♗g2 de 6 ♗e3 ♘f6 7 ♘ge2 ♗f5 8 ♘g3 e6 ∓
3 f3 c5! 4 e4 e5 = Pomar-Larsen, Spain 1975
3 ♗f4 ♘f6 4 e3 e6 5 ♘b5 ♘a6 6 a4 ♗e7 7 c3 0-0 8 ♗d3 c6 9 ♘a3 ♘b8 ∞ Raičević-Psakhis, Troon 1984

[8]   4 ♗g5 ♘f6 5 g3 ♗e7 6 ♗g2 0-0 7 0-0 b6 = Mestrović-Minev, Sarajevo 1971

[9]   5 ... a6!? 6 ♘e2 c5 7 c3 ♗d7 ∞

[10]   6 ♗d3 a5 7 0-0 0-0 8 ♘e5 b6 9 ♘e2 ♘fd7 =

[11]   11 ♘c3 ♗e8 12 cd ed 13 b4 ♘xc3 14 ♖xc3 ♘c7 ∞ Dobosz-Panbukchian, Varna 1985

[12]   4 e3 e6 5 ♘f3 ♗e7 6 ♗d3 0-0 7 0-0 ♘e4 = Smyslov-Guimard, Havana 1962

[13]   5 ... ♗b4 6 ♘e2 c6 7 a3 ♗d6 8 g3 ±
5 ... ♗e6 6 ♗d3 ♘c6 7 ♕f3 ♕d7 8 ♘ge2 ♗d6 9 ♘f4 ±

[14]   6 ... g6 7 ♕f3 ♗e6 8 h3 ♗g7 9 ♘ge2 ♘d7 10 g4 ± Korchnoi
6 ... ♕b6 7 ♖b1 ♘a6 8 a3! ± Taimanov-Larsen, Copenhagen 1966

[15]   8 h4 h5 9 ♘ge2 ♗e6 10 ♘f4 ♗f7 11 g3 ♘d7 12 0-0-0 ∞/± Gipslis-Luik, USSR 1965
8 ♘ge2 ♘d7 9 h3 ♘e5!? 10 de fe 11 e4 ∞ Keene-Bellin, Hastings 1975-76

[16]   Christiansen-Gurevich, Somerset (USA) 1986

[17]   2 ... ♘f6 3 ♗xf6 (3 ♘d2 d5 4 ♗xf6 ef 5 e3 ♗e6 6 ♕e2 ♗d6 7 c4 dc 8 ♘c3 ∞/± Hort-Hartoch, Amsterdam 1982) 3 ... ef 4 e3 d5 5 ♘e2 ♗d6 6 ♘d2 ♘a6 7 c4 c6 8 ♕b3 ♕b6 9 c5 ± Kozlov-Gleizerov, USSR 1984
2 ... c5 3 dc ♘a6 4 e4 fe 5 ♘c3 ♘xc5 6 ♗c4 ♕a5 7 ♗d2 ± Benjamin-de Fotis, New York 1985
2 ... c6 3 c4 (3 e3 g6 4 c4 ♗g7 5 ♘c3 d6 6 ♗d3 ♕a5 = Chernin-Yusupov, Montpellier C 1985) 3 ... ♕b6 4 ♕d2 d6 5 ♘c3 h6 6 ♗e3 ♘f6 7 f3 ♕a6 8 b3 e5 ∞ Cebalo-Kovačević, Yugoslav

Ch 1984

18 3 ... **g6** 4 e4! ± Bagirov

3 ... **c5** 4 e4 (4 e3 ♕b6 5 ♘f3 cd 6 ♕xd4 ♕xd4 7 ♘xd4 g5 8 ♗g3 ♗g7 = Arkell-Becx, Guernsey 1985) 4 ... ♕b6 5 ♘d2 cd 6 ef ♘f6 7 ♗d3 ± Skembris

19 5 ... **d6** 6 h4! g4 (6 ... ♘f6 7 hg hg 8 ♖xh8+ ♗xh8 9 ♘h3 g4 10 ♘f4 ±) 7 ♘c3 e5 8 de de 9 ♕xd8+ ♔xd8 10 0-0-0+ ♗d7 11 ♗c4 ± Lputian-Tseitlin, Sochi 1985

20 6 ♘c3 d6 7 ♗d3 ♘c6 8 ♘f3 e6 9 ♗b5 ♗d7 ∞ Arkhipov-Tseitlin, USSR 1985

21 11 de de 12 e4 ∞ Damljanović-M.Gurevich, Baku 1986

22 3 ♘**d2** ♗g7 4 c3 h6 5 ♗f4 f6 6 e3 e5 =

3 ♘c3 ♗g7 (3 ... d5 4 e3 c6 5 h4 ♘h6 6 h5 ± Szymczak-Halasz, Budapest 1986) 4 e4 fe 5 ♘xe4 d5! 6 ♘g3 ♘c6 7 c3 ♕d6 ∞ Marchader-P.Garcia, Barcelona 1979

23 4 **h5** h6 5 ♗c1 g5 6 ♗d3 e6 7 e4 d6 =

4 e3 h6 5 ♗f4 d6 6 ♗c4 ♘c6 7 c3 e5 8 ♗g3 ♕e7 9 ♘e2 ♘f6 ∞ Kouatly-Kovačević, Thessaloniki Ol 1984

24 5 ♕d2 c6 6 ♘f3 and now:

6 ... ♘**d7** 7 h5 h6 8 hg! hg 9 ♖h7! ± Vaganian-Knežević, Dubna 1973

6 ... ♗**e6** 7 ♗e3 ♗f7 8 h5 ♘d7 9 h6!? Shereshevsky-Malanyuk, Minsk 1985

6 ... **h6** 7 ♗f4 ♘d7 8 e3 ♘f6 =

25 5 ... ♘f6 6 h5! (6 ♘h3 ♗e6 7 ♘f4 ♗f7 8 ♗xf6 ef 9 ♗d3 c6 10 g4 ∞/± Raynes-Smith, Torquay 1983) 6 ... ♘xh5 7 ♖xh5 gh 8 ♕xh5+ ♔f8 9 ♘f3 c6 (9 ... ♗e6 10 ♗h6 ± Vaiser-Knežević, Havana 1985) 10 ♗d3 ♕e8 11 ♕h2 ± Bareyev-Dreyev, USSR 1984

26 6 ♗d3 ♗e6 7 ♘f3 ♘d7 8 h5 ♘gf6 9 hg hg 10 ♖xh8+ ♗xh8 = Kovačević-Kristiansen, Plovdiv 1983

27 11 0-0-0 ♕a5 ∞ Kochiev-Malanyuk, USSR 1984

28 Staunton Gambit

29 3 ... **g6** 4 ♗c4 ♘f6 5 ♗g5 ±

30 4 g4 h6! 5 f3 (5 f4 d5 6 ♗e2 g6! ∓) 5 ... d5 6 g5 hg 7 ♗xg5 ♗f5 8 ♗g2 e3! ∓

31 4 ... **e3** 5 ♗xe3 d5 6 ♕d2 ♘bd7 7 ♘h3 ♘b6 8 ♘f4 ± Gulko-Knežević, 1973

4 ... ♘**c6** 5 fe e5 6 de ♘xe5 7 ♘f3 ♗d6 (7 ... d6 8 ♗f4 ♘g6 9 ♗g3 ± Furman) 8 ♗g5 h6 9 ♗h4 ♘g6 10 ♗g3! ± Grigorian-Tal, USSR

1972

4 ... **ef** 5 ♘xf3 g6 (5 ... e6 6 ♗d3 ♗e7 7 ♕e2 c5 8 dc ♗xc5 9 ♗g5 ±) 6 ♗f4 ♗g7 7 ♕d2 0-0 8 ♗h6 d5 9 ♗xg7 ♔xg7 10 ♗d3 ∞ Bronstein

32 6 ♗c4 e5 7 de ♕xd1+ 8 ♔xd1 ♘g4 =

33 7 ♕**d2** e6 8 h3 ♗d6 9 0-0-0 h6 ∓ Arbakov-Gleizerov, Saratov 1984

7 ♘ge2 e6 8 ♘g3 ♗e7 9 ♕d2 h6 10 ♗e3 ♘bd7 ∓ Gulko-M.Gurevich, USSR Ch 1985

34 7 ... **e6** 8 ♘ge2 ♗b4 9 0-0 c6 =

7 ... ♘**bd7** 8 ♘ge2 ♘b6 9 ♗b3 ♕d7 =

35 8 ♗b5 ♗d7 ∞ Milić

36 9 ... e6 10 ♕e1 ♘a5!? Taimanov

37 Burger-Hempel, West Germany 1975

38 4 ... **b6** 5 f3 e3 6 ♗xe3 e6 7 ♘h3 ♗b7 8 ♗e2 ±

4 ... **g6** 5 f3 (5 ♗xf6 ef 6 ♘xe4 d5 7 ♘g3 ♗d6 =) 5 ... d5 (5 ... ef 6 ♘xf3 d5 7 ♗d3 ♗g7 8 ♕e2) 6 ♕d2 ♗f5 7 0-0-0 ♘bd7 (7 ... ♗g7 8 g4 ♗e6 9 ♖e1 ♗f7 10 h4! ±) 8 g4 ♗e6 9 ♖e1 h6 10 ♗f4 c6 11 ♔b1 ♗g7 12 h4 ± Nikolić-Stojanovski, Bela Crkva 1984

4 ... **c6** 5 f3 ef (5 ... ♕a5 6 ♗d2 e3 7 ♗xe3 e5 8 ♕d2 ♗b4 9 ♘ge2 ±) 6 ♘xf3 d5 7 ♗c4!? ♗g4 8 h3 ♗xf3 9 ♕xf3 ♘bd7 10 0-0-0 ∞ Byrne, Mednis

39 6 ♘xf6+ ♗xf6 7 h4!? Pachman

40 7 ♘f3 ♕e7 8 ♗d3 ♘c6 9 c3 b6 10 ♕e2 ♗b7 11 0-0-0 0-0-0 =

41 8 ... ♗**xd4** 9 0-0-0 ♗f6 10 h4 ±

8 ... ♘**c6** 9 0-0-0 (9 ♘f3 ± Knaak-Ftacnik, Trnava 1980) 9 ... b6 10 ♘e2 ♕e7 11 ♕e3 ♗g7 12 ♘2c3 ± Fedorowicz-Leow, Philadelphia 1986

42 12 c3 ♗g7 13 ♕e3 ∞/± Ash-Yusupov, Winnipeg 1986

43 5 ♗**xf6** ef 6 d5 ♘e5 7 ♗xe4 f5! ∓

5 ♗**b5** a6 6 ♗xc6 bc 7 ♕e2 e6 8 ♘xe4 ♗e7 =

5 f3 e5 (5 ... d5 Taimanov) 6 d5 ♘d4 7 ♘xe4 ♗e7 8 ♗xf6 ♗xf6 = Larsen

44 6 f3 ♘f7 7 ♗xf6 ef 8 ♘xe4 ∞

45 7 ♗**h4** g5 8 ♗g3 ♗g7 9 0-0-0 c6! ∓

7 **h4** c6 (7 ... e5!?) 8 0-0-0 ♕b6 9 ♗xf6 gf ∓

46 8 0-0-0 f5! 9 f3 ♗d6 10 fe ♗e5 ∓

47 8 ... ♗e7 9 0-0-0 0-0 10 ♘f3 (10 f4 f5 11 ♘g3 ♗f6 = Taimanov) 10 ... d6 11 ♔b1 c5 =

48 10 h4 ♗h6 11 d6 0-0 12 ♗c4 ♗g7 ∓

49 12 ♘f3 ♗g7 13 ♕d2 b5 14 ♘d4 ♘d6 =

	2	3	4	5	6	7	8	9	10	
1	g3	♗g2	♘f3[2]	0-0	b3[4]	♗b2	a4[7]	♘bd2	e3	±
	♘f6	e6[1]	♗e7[3]	0-0	d6[5]	a5[6]	♕e8	♕h5	g5[8]	
2	c4	♘c3[9]	♕c2[11]	e3[12]	♗d3	♘e2	a3	♕xc3[13]	0-0	±
	e6	♗b4[10]	♘f6	0-0	d6	c5	♗xc3+	♘c6	a5[14]	
3	...	g3	♗g2	♗d2[15]	♕b3[17]	d5	cd	♘c3	♘f3	∞/±
	...	♘f6	♗b4+	♗e7[16]	c6[18]	cd[19]	e5[20]	d6	♘bd7[21]	

1 d4 f5 2 c4 ♘f6 3 g3 e6 4 ♗g2 d5 5 ♘f3

	5	6	7	8	9	10	11	12	13	
4	...	0-0[22]	b3[23]	♘e5[25]	♗b2[26]	♕c1!	♗a3	♘d3	♗xd6	±
	c6	♗d6	♕e7[24]	0-0	♗d7	♗e8	♘bd7	♗f7	♕xd6[27]	
5	...	0-0	b3[28]	♗a3[30]	♗xe7[32]	♘bd2[33]	♘e5	♘d3[34]	♘f3	∞
	♗e7	0-0	c6[29]	♗d7[31]	♕xe7	♗e8	♘bd7	♘e4	g5[35]	
6	...	...	♘bd2	♘e5[37]	♘d3	♕c2!	♘f3	b3	♗a3	±
	...	...	c6[36]	♘bd7[38]	♘e4[39]	♗f6[40]	♔h8	♕e8	♖g8[41]	
7	...	...	♘c3	♕c2[42]	♗g5[44]	e3	♘e2	♘f4	♗xf6	±
	...	...	c6	♕e8[43]	♕h5[45]	♘bd7[46]	h6	♕f7	♕xf6[47]	

1 d4 f5 2 c4 ♘f6 3 g3 e6 4 ♗g2 ♗e7 5 ♘f3 0-0 6 0-0 d6

	7	8	9	10	11	12	13	14	15	
8	♘c3[48]	♕c2[50]	♗g5[52]	♖ad1	♗xf6	d5	♕b3	de	♕c2[55]	±
	♕e8[49]	♕h5[51]	♘c6[53]	h6[54]	♗xf6	♘b4	♘a6	♘c5		
9	...	b3	♗b2[57]	♖e1[59]	e3[60]	a3	♕c2	♖ac1	♗xc3	±
	...	a5[56]	♘a6[58]	♕g6	♖b8	♗d7	♘e4	♘xc3	b6[61]	

[1] 3 ... d6 4 ♘f3 c6 5 0-0 ♕c7 6 c4 e5 7 ♘c3 e4 8 ♘g5 h6 9 ♘h3 ♕f7 10 d5 ± Gavrikov-Psakhis, USSR Ch 1985

[2] 4 ♗g5 ♗e7 5 ♗xf6 ♗xf6 6 e4 0-0 7 f4 fe 8 ♗xe4 d5 ∞ Cobo-Pritchett, Siegen Ol 1970
   4 ♘h3 d5 (4 ... ♗e7 5 0-0 0-0 6 c3 d6 7 ♘d2 c6 8 ♕b3± Rogers-Böhm, Wijk aan Zee II 1985) 5 0-0 ♗e7 =

[3] 4 ... b5 5 ♘e5 c6 6 a4 b4 7 0-0 ♗e7 8 c4 ±
   4 ... c5 5 0-0 ♘c6 6 c4 cd 7 ♘xd4 ♗c5 8 e3 0-0 9 ♘c3 ±

[4] 6 ♕d3 d6 7 ♘bd2 ♘c6 8 e4 fe 9 ♘xe4 e5 = Spiridonov-Sax, 1969

[5] 6 ... b6 7 ♘e5 c6 8 c4 ♗b7 9 ♗b2 d6 10 ♘d3 ± Ivkov

[6] 7 ... ♗e8 8 ♘bd2 ♘c6 9 ♖e1 ±

[7] 8 a3 ♕e8 9 ♘e1 ♕h5 10 ♘d3 ♕h6 11 ♘d2 g5 12 e4 ±

[8] 11 ♘e1 ♕g6 12 ♘d3 ♘c6 13 ♖e1 ± Udovčić-Stanciu, Hamburg 1965

[9] 3 e4 fe 4 ♘c3 ♘f6 5 f3 ♗b4 6 ♗g5 c5 ∓

[10] 3 ... ♗e7 4 e3 d6 5 f4 ±

[11] 4 ♗d2 b6 5 e3 ♗b7 6 f3 ♕h4+ 7 g3 ♕e7 8 ♗g2 ♘f6 9 ♘ge2 ± Ivkov

[12] 5 a3!? ♗xc3+ 6 ♕xc3 0-0 7 g3 d6 8 ♗g2 ±

[13] 9 ♘xc3 ♘c6 10 dc dc 11 b3 ♗d7 12 ♗b2 ♘e5 13 0-0-0! ± Botvinnik

[14] 11 b3 ♕e7 12 ♗b2 ± Taimanov

[15] 5 ♘d2 0-0 6 ♘f3 a5 (6 ... d6 7 0-0 ♗xd2 8 ♕xd2 ♕e7 9 b3 ♘e4 10 ♕c2 ± Murey-Eslon, Amsterdam 1986) 7 0-0 ♔h8 8 b3 (8 c5 ♗xd2 9 ♗xd2 d6 10 cd cd 11 ♗g5 ± Lerner) 8 ... ♗c3 9 ♖b1 ♘c6 10 e3 (10 ♗b2 ♗xb2 11 ♖xb2 d6 12 ♘b1 e5 ∞ Lerner-Eingorn, Kiev 1984) 10 ... d6 11 ♕c2 ± Lerner

[16] 5 ... a5 6 ♗g2 b6 7 ♘e5 ± Grooten-Hodgson, Wijk aan Zee II 1985
   5 ... ♗e7 6 ♕b3!? (6 ♘f3 0-0 7 0-0 ±) 6 ... ♗xd2+ 7 ♘xd2 0-0 8 ♘gf3 d6 9 0-0 e5 10 c5! ± Hébert-Spraggett, Toronto 1985

[17] 6 ♘c3 0-0 7 ♘f3 ♘e4 8 0-0 ♗f6 9 ♕c2 ±

[18] 6 ... 0-0 7 ♘c3 (7 ♗xb7 ∞) 7 ... c5 8 d5

(8 ♘f3!?) 8 ... e5 9 e4 d6 10 ef ♗xf5 11 ♕xb7! ± Chernenko-Maslovsky, corr. 1984

19 7 ... ♘a6 8 ♘c3 ♘c5 9 ♕c2 ± Petrosian

20 8 ... ♘xd5 9 ♗xd5 ed 10 ♘c3 ±

21 11 0-0 0-0 12 ♘g5 ♘c5 13 ♕c4 ± Sosonko-Abramović, New York 1986

22 6 ♕c2 ♗d6 7 ♗f4 0-0 8 ♘bd2 ♗xf4 9 gf ♘bd7 = Rashkovsky-Bareyev, USSR Ch 1986

23 7 ♘c3 0-0 and now:
8 c5 ♗c7 9 ♗f4 ♘e4 (9 ... ♗xf4 10 gf ♘e4 11 ♕c2 ± Ogaard-Ostenstad, Oslo 1986) 10 ♗xc7 ♕xc7 11 ♘d2 ♘xd2 12 ♕xd2 e5 =
8 ♕c2 ♕e8 9 c5 ♗c7 10 ♗f4 ♗xf4 11 gf ±
7 ♘bd2 ♘bd7 8 ♕c2 0-0 9 cd cd 10 b3 ♕e7 11 ♗b2 b6 12 e3 ♗a6 ∞ Gheorghiu-Yusupov, Lucerne 1985

24 7 ... ♘bd7 8 ♗a3 ±

25 8 a4 0-0 9 ♗a3 ♗xa3 10 ♘xa3 ♗d7 11 ♘c2 ♗e8 12 ♘e5 ♘bd7 13 ♘xd7 ♘xd7 ∓ Danner-Vaiser, Vrnjačka Banja 1986
8 ♗f4 ♗xf4 9 gf 0-0 10 ♘e5 ♘bd7 11 e3 ♔h8 = Yrjölä-Yusupov, Mendoza 1985
8 ♗b2 0-0 9 ♘bd2 ♗d7 10 ♘e5 ♗e8 11 ♘df3 ♗h5 12 ♘d3 ♘bd7 13 ♕c2 ♖ac8 14 ♘fe5 ♖fd8 = Martinović-Ivanović, Budva 1986
8 ♘c3 0-0 9 ♗f4 ♗xf4 10 gf b6 11 ♘e5 ♗b7 12 cd! ed 13 ♕c2 ± Plaskett-Karlsson, Copenhagen 1985

26 9 ♘d3 b6 10 ♗f4 ♗xf4 11 gf ♗b7 = Zaichik-Psakhis, Kharkov 1985

27 14 ♕a3 ♕xa3 15 ♘xa3 ♖fe8 16 f4 ± Timman-Short, Brussels 1987

28 7 ♕c2 ♘e4 8 ♘bd2 c6 ± - 7 ♘bd2

29 7 ... a5 8 a3 c6 9 ♗b2 ♘e4 10 ♘bd2 ♘bd7 11 ♕c2 ± Remon-Spraggett, Havana 1986
7 ... ♘c6 8 ♗b2 ♘e4! 9 ♘c3 ♘f6 10 e3 ♘e7 11 ♕e2 ♗d7 12 ♘e5 ♗xe5 13 de ♗c6 = Mikhalchishin-Eingorn, USSR Ch 1985

30 8 ♘c3 ♘e4! 9 ♗b2 ♘d7 10 e3 ♗f6 11 ♖c1 b6 = Seirawan-Spraggett, Montpellier C 1985
8 ♗b2 b6 9 ♘e5 ♗b7 10 ♘d2 ♘bd7 11 ♘d3 ♗d6 = H.Olafsson-Kristiansen, Esbjerg 1985
8 ♕c2 ♗d7 9 ♗b2 ♗e8 10 ♘e5 ♘bd7 11 ♘d3 ♗h5 12 ♘c3 ♗d6 13 f3 ♗g6 ∞ Kasparov-Petrosian, Nikšić 1983

31 8 ... ♗xa3 9 ♘xa3 ♕e7 10 ♘c2 ♗d7 11 ♘ce1 ♗e8 12 ♘d3 ♘bd7 13 cd! ± van der Sterren-Enklaar, Amsterdam 1985
8 ... ♘e4 9 ♗xe7 ♕xe7 10 ♘bd2 ♕f6 11 e3 ♘d7 12 ♖c1 ± Hort-Bertok, Vinkovci 1970
8 ... ♘bd7 9 ♕c1 ♘e4 10 ♗xe7 ♕xe7 11 e3 ♘df6 12 ♘e5 ∞/±

32 9 ♕c1 ♗e8 10 ♘g5 ♗f7 11 ♘d2 ♘bd7 12 ♘xf7 ♖xf7 13 ♗xe7 ♕xe7 ∞

33 10 ♕d3 ♗e8 11 ♘bd2 ♘e4 12 ♘e5 ♘xd2 13 ♕xd2 ♘d7 =

34 12 ♘df3 ♖d8 = Taimanov

35 14 ♘fe5 ♗xe5 15 ♘xe5 ♘d6 ∞ Sosonko-Salazar, New York 1986

36 7 ... ♕e8 8 ♕c2 c6 - 7 ... c6

37 8 ♕c2 and now:
8 ... ♕e8 9 ♘e5 ♘bd7 (9 ... ♕h5 10 ♘df3 ♘e4 11 ♘d3 g5 12 ♘fe5 ♘d7 13 f3 ±) 10 ♘d3 ♘e4 11 ♘f3 ♘d6 12 b3 b6 13 ♘fe5 ±
8 ... b6 9 ♘e5 ♗b7 10 ♘df3 ♘e4 11 ♘d3 (11 b3 ♗d6 12 ♘d3 ♘bd7 13 ♗b2 ♕e7 11 ♖fe5 ± Gorelov-Gulko, Minsk 1985) 11 ... ♘f6 12 ♗f4 ♘d7 13 cd ed 14 ♘fe5 ± Farago-Abramović, Brussels II 1986

38 8 ... b6 9 ♘df3 ♘e4 10 cd ed 11 ♘d3 ± Botvinnik

39 9 ... ♕e8 10 e3 ♕h5 11 b3 ♕xd1 12 ♖xd1 ±
9 ... ♗d6 10 c5 ♗c7 11 ♘f3 b6 12 ♕c2 ±

40 10 ... b6? 11 cd ±

41 14 ♖ac1 ± Kasparov-Short, Brussels 1987

42 8 ♗g5 ♘bd7 9 e3 h6 10 ♗xf6 ♗xf6 11 cd ed 12 ♘e2 a5 ∞ Eingorn-Abramović, Bor 1986

43 8 ... ♘e4 9 ♘e5 ♘d7 10 ♘xe4 fe 11 ♗f4 ♗f6 12 ♘xd7! ♕xd7 13 ♖ad1 ± Larsen

44 9 ♗f4 ♕h5 10 ♖ad1 ♘bd7 11 b3 ♘e4 12 ♘e5 ♘d6 ∞ Taimanov

45 9 ... ♔h8 10 e3 ♘bd7 11 ♘e2 h6 12 ♗xf6 ♗xf6 13 ♘f4 ±

46 10 ... h6 11 ♗xf6 ♗xf6 12 ♘e2 ♘d7 13 ♘f4 ±

47 14 ♖ab1 ♗d6 15 b4 ±

48 7 b3 ♕e8 8 ♗b2 a5 9 ♘c3! ±

49 7 ... ♘c6 8 d5 ed 9 cd ♘e5 10 ♘d4 ♗d7 11 ♕c2 ±

50 8 ♖e1 ♕g6 9 e4 fe 10 ♘xe4 ♘xe4 11 ♖xe4 ♘c6 12 ♕e2 ♗f6 13 ♗d2 e5 = Matulović-Milić, Yugoslav Ch 1959

51 8 ... ♘bd7 9 e4 fe 10 ♘xe4 ♘xe4 11 ♕xe4 ♘f6 12 ♕d3 ♕h5 13 ♗f4 ±

52 9 b3 a5 10 ♗b2 (10 e4!? Gligorić) 10 ... ♘a6 (10 ... ♘c6 11 a3 e5 12 de de 13 ♘d5 ± Lobo-Rumens, England 1976) 11 ♖fe1 c6 12 ♖ad1 ♗d8 =

53 9 ... h6 10 ♗xf6 ♗xf6 11 e4 ♘c6 12 ♘b5 ♕f7 13 ♖ad1 ±

54 10 ... e5 11 de ♘xe5 12 ♗xf6 ♗xf6 13 c5 dc 14 ♘d5 ±

55 Stahlberg-Holm, Copenhagen 1960

56 8 ... ♕h5 9 ♗a3 g5 (9 ... a5 10 d5! ± Portisch) 10 e3 ♖f7 11 c5 ♗c7 12 ♘d2 ♕xd1 13 ♖axd1 ±

57 9 ♗a3 ♘a6 10 ♖c1 ♗d7 11 e3 ♖b8 ∞
9 ♖e1!? ♕g6 10 e4 fe 11 ♘xe4 ♘xe4 12 ♖xe4 ♘c6 13 ♕e2 ± Csom

58 9 ... c6 10 ♖e1 b5 11 cb cb 12 d5 ±
9 ... ♕h5 10 e3 c6 (10 ... ♔h8 11 ♘e1 ±) 11 ♘d2 ♕h6 12 ♕e2 ±

59 10 e3 c6 11 ♕e2 ♗d7 12 e4 fe 13 ♘xe4 ♕h5 14 ♖fe1 ♘e4 ∞ Miniböck-Dückstein, Wolfsberg 1985

60 11 e4 f4 ∞
11 a3!? Tisdall

61 16 b4 ab 17 ab ± Thorsteins-Lombardy, Westmann Islands (Iceland) 1985

	2	3	4	5	6	7	8	9	10	
1	...	♗g2	♘f3²	0-0³	b3⁴	♗b2	♘bd2	♘c4⁷	♘fd2	=
	♘f6¹	g6	♗g7	0-0	d6⁵	♘e4⁶	♘c6	e6	d5⁸	
2	...	...	c4	♘h3⁹	♘c3	d5	0-0¹³	de	b3	=
	...	...	♗g7	0-0¹⁰	d6¹¹	c6¹²	e5¹⁴	♗xe6	♘a6¹⁵	

1 d4 f5 2 c4 ♘f6 3 g3 g6 4 ♗g2 ♗g7 5 ♘f3 0-0 6 0-0 d6

	7	8	9	10	11	12	13	14	15	
3	d5¹⁶	♘d4	cd	♘c3	b3¹⁹	♗b2	♖c1	♗a1	♕d2	=
	c6¹⁷	cd¹⁸	♘a6	♘c5	♗d7	♕b6	a5	♖fc8	♕b4²⁰	
4	♘c3	d5²¹	♘xe5²²	e4²³	b4²⁵	♖e1	♗b2	c5²⁶	c6!²⁷	±
	♘c6	♘e5	de	f4²⁴	g5	a6	♕e8	♗d7	bc²⁸	
5	...	...	♕d3²⁹	b3³¹	♗b2	♖ae1³³	♗a1	bc	♘d2	±
	...	♘a5	c5³⁰	a6³²	♖b8	b5	bc	♖b4	♘g4³⁴	
6	...	b3³⁵	♗b2	♕c2	♖ad1	d5	♘d4	e3	♕b1	=
	c6	a5³⁶	♘a6³⁷	♕c7	♔h8³⁸	♘c5	♗d7	♖ac8	♕b6³⁹	
7	...	d5	de⁴¹	♕d3⁴²	♗f4⁴⁴	♘xe4	♕xe4	♕e3	♖ad1	±
	...	e5⁴⁰	♗xe6	♘a6⁴³	♘e4⁴⁵	fe	♘c5	♗xc4	♖e8⁴⁶	
8	...	♘d5	cd	♘e1⁴⁹	e3	♘d3	dc	♗xc6	♕b3+	=
	♕e8	♘xd5⁴⁷	♕b5⁴⁸	♘a6⁵⁰	♗d7	c5	♗xc6	bc	♖f7⁵¹	

---

¹ 2 ... g6 3 ♗g2 (3 ♘d2 ♗g7 4 e4 fe 5 ♘xe4 d5 6 ♘g5 ♘h6 7 ♗h3 ♘f5 = Bilek-Barcza, Balatonfured 1958) 3 ... ♗g7 4 ♘f3 c6 5 0-0 ♘h6 (Basman) 6 c4 d6 7 ♘c3 0-0 8 ♕c2 (8 ♖b1 a5 9 b3 ♘f7 10 e4 fe 11 ♘xe4 d5! ∓ Rellstab-Basman, Hastings 1973-74) 8 ... ♘a6 9 ♖d1 ♗d7 10 b3 (Keene-Basman, Hastings 1973-74) 10 ... ♘f7 =

² 4 ♘d2 ♘c6 5 d5 ♗b4 6 c4 a5 7 a3 ♘a6 = Gheorghiu
  4 ♘c3 ♗g7 5 e4 (5 ♗g5 ♘c6 6 ♕d2 d5 = Ivkov) 5 ... fe 6 ♘xe4 ♘xe4 7 ♗xe4 d5 8 ♗g2 ♘c6 9 c3 e5 (9 ... ♗e6 10 ♘f3 ♗f6 11 h4 ± Pähtz-Jablonicky, Vysledok 1985) 10 de ♘xe5 =
  4 ♘h3 ♗g7 5 0-0 0-0 6 ♘c3 d6 7 d5 c6 =

³ 5 b3 0-0 6 ♗b2 d5! 7 c4 c6 8 0-0 ♗e6 = Portisch-Smyslov, match 1971

⁴ 6 ♖e1 d6 7 ♘bd2 ♘c6 8 e4 fe 9 ♘xe4 ♘xe4 10 ♖xe4 ♗f5 11 ♖h4 e5 12 ♗g5 ♗f6 ∞ Djurić-Kovačević, Novi Sad 1985
  6 ♘bd2 d6 (6 ... c5 7 dc ♘a6 8 ♘b3 ♘e4 9 c3 ♘axc5 10 ♘xc5 ♘xc5 11 ♕d5+ ♘e6 12 e4 ± Neckar-Skoko, Stara Pazova 1985) =

⁵ 6 ... ♘e4 7 ♗b2 ♘c6 8 ♘bd2 d5 9 e3 e6 10 ♘e1 ±

  6 ... c5 7 ♗b2 cd 8 ♘xd4 d5 9 ♘f3 (9 e3 ♖e8 10 ♘a3 e5 = Karolyi-Dolmatov, Tallinn 1985) 9 ... ♘c6 10 c4 dc 11 ♘bd2 ∞ Dolmatov

⁶ 7 ... c6 8 a4 a5 9 ♘bd2 ♘a6 10 ♘e1 ♘g4 11 h3 ♘h6 12 ♘d3 ± Suba-Yilmaz, Heraklion 1985
  7 ... ♘c6 8 d5 ♘a5 9 ♘fd2 c5 10 a4 ♗d7 11 c3 ♘e8!? Taimanov
  7 ... ♘a6!? 8 c4 ♕e8 9 ♘bd2 e5 10 de ♘g4 ∞ Ionescu-Grigorov, Albena 1984

⁷ 9 c4 e6 10 ♕c2 ♘xd2 11 ♕xd2 ♕e7

⁸ 11 ♘xe4 dc (11 ... fe 12 ♘e3 ±) 12 ♘c5 ♗xd4 13 ♘xb7 ♗xb7 14 ♗xd4 ♕xd4 = Hausner-Mikh.Tseitlin, Kecskemet 1985

⁹ 5 e3 0-0 6 ♘c3 d6 7 ♘ge2 ♘c6 8 b3 ♗d7 = D.Byrne-Larsen, Palma de Mallorca 1968

¹⁰ 5 ... c5 6 d5 ♕a5+ 7 ♗d2 ♕b6 8 ♘c3 ± Polugayevsky-Gurgenidze, USSR 1972

¹¹ 6 ... e6 7 0-0 d6 8 b3 c6 9 ♗a3 ♕a5 10 ♕c1 ± Ree-Hübner, Wijk aan Zee 1975
  6 ... ♘c6 7 ♖b1 d6 8 d5 ♘e5 9 b3 c5 10 0-0 ♗d7 11 ♕c2 ± Suba-Ermenkov, Tunis IZ 1985

¹² 7 ... c5 8 ♘f4 ♘a6 9 0-0 ♘c7 10 a4 ± Shamkovich-Alburt, Reykjavik 1984
  7 ... ♘bd7 8 0-0 ♘c5 9 ♕c2 e5 10 de ♗xe6

11 ♘f4 ± Botvinnik
   7 ... ♘a6!? 8 0-0 ♗d7 Dolmatov
[13] 8 ♘f4 ♛e8 9 ♛b3 e5 10 de ♘a6 =
[14] **8 ...** ♗d7 9 ♖e1 (9 ♛b3 ♛b6 10 ♗e3 ♛xb3 11 ab c5 ∞ Zaichik-Dolmatov, Kharkov 1985) 9 ... ♘a6 10 e4 fe 11 ♘xe4 ♘xe4 12 ♖xe4 ♘c5 13 ♖e1 ± Dolmatov
   8 ... cd 9 cd ♘bd7 10 ♗e3 ♘g4 11 ♗d4 ± Suba-Afifi, Tunis IZ 1985
[15] 11 ♘g5 ♛e7 (11 ... ♗c8 12 ♗b2 ♛e7 13 ♘a4 ♗d7 14 e3 ±) 12 ♘xe6 ♛xe6 13 ♗b2 ♘e4 14 ♛c1 d5 = Taimanov-Kholmov, USSR Ch 1975
[16] 7 b3 c6 (7 ... e5 8 de ♘g4 ∞ Wexler-Uhlmann, Buenos Aires 1960) 8 ♗b2 ♛c7 (8 ... a5 9 ♘bd2 ♘a6 =) 9 ♘bd2 a5 10 a3 ♘a6 11 ♛d2 ♗d7 12 c5 ♔h8 = Portisch-Uhlmann, Stockholm IZ 1962
[17] 7 ... c5 8 ♘c3 ♘a6 9 ♖b1 (9 ♘e1 ♖b8 10 ♘c2 ± Botvinnik) 9 ... ♗d7 (9 ... ♖b8 10 b3 ♘c7 11 ♗b2 a6 12 e3 b5 13 ♘e2 ± Keene-Ree, Paignton 1970) 10 b3 ♖b8 11 ♗b2 ♘c7 12 a4 a6 13 a5 ± H.Olafsson-Larsen, Reykjavik 1985
[18] **8 ...** c5 9 ♘f3 ♘a6 10 ♘c3 ♛c7 11 a4 ♔h8 12 ♖b1 ± Kochiev-Tal, USSR 1978
   8 ... ♛b6 9 ♘c3 (9 ♘b3 e5!? 10 dc ♘xc6 11 ♛xd6 ♖d8 Harding) 9 ... ♘e4 10 ♘xe4 ♛xd4 11 ♛xd4 ♗xd4 12 ♘g5 c5 = Taimanov
[19] 11 ♛c2 ♗d7 12 ♘b3 ♘a4 13 ♖xa4 ♗xa4 14 ♛c4 ♗xb3 15 ♛xb3 ♛b6! ⹀ Bany-Pytel, Poland 1985
[20] Schmidt-Pytel, Poland 1975
[21] **8** ♛c2 e5 9 de de 10 ♖d1 ♗d7 11 ♗e3 e4 12 ♘d4 ♘g4 =
   8 b3 e4 9 ♗b2 e5 10 de ♘xc3 11 ♗xc3 de 12 ♛d5+ ♔h8 13 ♛xd8 ♖xd8 14 ♘g5 ± Pomar-Peredes, Barcelona 1977
[22] 9 ♛b3!? ♘fd7 10 ♘xe5 ♘xe5 11 ♖d1 ♔h8 12 f4 ± Mortazavi-Flear, London 1985
[23] 10 ♛b3 e6 (10 ... ♘h5 11 ♖d1 ♔h8 12 a4 a5 13 c5 ± Andersson-Mascarenhas, Rio de Janeiro 1985) 11 ♖d1 ed 12 ♘xd5 c6 13 ♗g5!? ∞ Ribli-Barbero, Lugano 1985
[24] 10 ... e6 11 ef ef (11 ... gf!? Botvinnik) 12 ♗e3 e4 13 ♗d4 ±
[25] **11 c5** g5 12 ♛b3 ♔h8 ⹀ Wells-Hansen, Kiljava 1984
   11 ♘f3 c6 12 dc ♛b6+ 13 ♔h1 bc 14 b3 g5 ∞ Hjartarson-Plaskett, Hastings 1985-86
[26] 14 ♖c1 ♘g4 15 f3 ♘e3 16 ♖xe3 fe 17 g4 ⹀⹀ Florian
[27] 15 ♖c1 ♖d8 16 a4 ♛f7! ∞ Hansen-Kristiansen, Esbjerg 1984
[28] 16 dc ♗xc6 17 ♘d5 ± Kristiansen
[29] **9** ♛a4 c5 10 dc ♗xc6 11 ♖d1 ♛a5 =
   9 ♛d2 c5 10 a3 ♗d7 11 ♛c2 ♛c7 12 b3 a6 13 ♗b2 b5 14 ♘d1! ± Botvinnik-Matulović,

Belgrade 1970
[30] 9 ... e5 10 de ♗xe6 11 b3 ± Botvinnik
[31] **10** ♘g5 a6 11 ♘e6!? ♗xe6 12 de ♘c6 ∞ Euwe
   10 ♗d2 a6 11 ♖ac1 ♗d7 12 b3 ♖b8 13 e4 ±
[32] 10 ... ♘e4 11 ♗b2 a6 12 ♖ac1 b5 13 ♗a1 ± Botvinnik
[33] 12 ♘d2!? Vukić
[34] 16 a3 ♖b8 17 ♛c2 ♗d7 18 e3 ♘e5 19 ♘e2 ± Nikolac-Bertok, Yugoslavia 1969
[35] **8** ♛c2 ♛c7 (8 ... ♘a6 9 ♖d1 ♛e8 =) 9 e4 (9 b4 e5 10 de de ⹀ Bonaldi-San Filippo, Buenos Aires 1983) 9 ... fe 10 ♘xe4 ♘xe4 11 ♛xe4 ♗f5 12 ♛h4 e5 = Gofstein-Bikhovsky, USSR 1977
[36] ... ♘a6 9 ♗b2 ♛c7 10 ♛c2 ♖b8! 11 a4 a5 = Smyslov-Lutikov, USSR 1976
[37] 9 ... ♛c7 10 d5 ♘a6 11 ♘d4 ♗d7 12 ♖b1 ♘c5 = Averkin-Knežević, Dubna 1976
[38] 11 ... ♗d7 12 a3 ♖ae8 13 d5 e5 =
[39] Kovacs-Knaak, Polanica Zdroj 1975
[40] 8 ... ♛a5 9 ♗e3 ♛b4 10 ♛d3 (10 ♛b3 ♛xb3 11 ab ∞ Goodman-Harding, England 1975) ±
   8 ... ♗d7 9 ♖b1! ♘a6 10 b3 ♘c5 11 ♗b2 a5 12 ♛d2 ± Ribli-Mestel, London 1986
[41] 9 dc!? Tukmakov
[42] 10 b3 ♘a6 and now:
   11 ♘g5 ♗c8 12 ♖b1 ♘g4 13 ♘a4 ♛e7 = Adorjan-Vaiser, Szirak 1985
   11 ♗b2 ♛e7 12 ♛c2 d5 13 cd ♘b4 (13 ... ♘xd5 14 ♘a4 ♘f6 15 ♖ad1 ± Kir.Georgiev-Ivkov, Sarajevo 1986) 14 ♛c1 ♘fxd5 ∞ Scheeren-Kovačević, Thessaloniki Ol 1984
[43] **10 ...** h6 11 ♗f4 d5 12 ♖ad1 ♘a6 13 cd ± Amado-Tempone, Buenos Aires 1983
   10 ... ♘bd7 11 ♗f4 ♘b6 12 b3 ♘e4 13 ♘d4 ±
[44] 11 ♘g5 ♛e7 (11 ... ♘c5 12 ♘xe6 ♘xe6 13 b3 ♛e7 14 ♗a3 ± Kozul-Kovačević, Novi Sad 1985) 12 ♗f4 ♖ad8 13 ♖ad1 ♘g4 = Ubilava-Knežević, Trencianske Teplice 1985
[45] **11 ...** ♘e8 12 ♘g5 ♛d7 13 b3 ± Yusupov
   11 ... ♛b6 12 ♘g5 ♘c5 (12 ... ♖fe8? 13 ♗xd6! ± Hulak-Gazik, Montpellier 1985) ± Hulak
[46] 16 ♛c1 ♗xe2 17 ♖xd6 ♛a5 18 ♗d2 ± Yusupov-Barbero, Mendoza 1985
[47] 8 ... ♘a6 9 ♘xf6+ ♗xf6 10 ♗h6 ♗g7 11 ♛d2 c6 12 b4 ± Uhlmann-Banas, Stary Smokovec 1985
[48] 9 ... c6 10 ♛b3 ♔h8 11 ♘g5 ♘a6 12 dc bc 13 ♛a4 ± Uhlmann-Grünberg, Kecskemet 1984
[49] 10 ♛b3 ♛xb3 11 ab cb 12 ♗g5 ♖e8 ∞ Zhukovitsky-M.Tseitlin, USSR 1986
[50] 10 ... ♛b6 11 e3 c6 12 ♘d3 cd 13 ♗xd5 e6 14 ♗b3 ± Dautov-Ragozin, USSR 1986
[51] 16 ♛xb5 cb 17 ♗d2 e5 = Balashov-Malanyuk, USSR Ch 1986

61

1 d4 f5 2 c4 ♘f6 3 g3 g6 4 ♗g2 ♗g7 5 ♘f3 0-0 6 0-0 d6 *continued*

	7	8	9	10	11	12	13	14	15	
9	♘c3	♕b3[52]	♗g5	♗xf6[55]	♖ad1	♕c2	e4	♕xe4[57]	♘d5	=
	♕e8	♘a6[53]	c5[54]	♗xf6	♔h8[56]	♖b8	fe	♗d7	♗c6[58]	
10	...	♖e1	♘g5[60]	♗f1	a3	e4	♗c4+	♘f7+	♗xf7	∞∞
	...	♕f7[59]	♕xc4	♕b4[61]	♕b6[62]	fe	♔h8	♖xf7	♗g4[63]	
11	...	d5[64]	♘d4[66]	e4[67]	♘xe4	♗xe4	♗g2	♗e3	♕d2	∞/±
	...	♘a6[65]	♗d7	fe[68]	♘xe4[69]	♘c5	♕f7	a5	a4[70]	

[52] 8 ♕c2 e5 9 de de 10 e4 ♘c6 ∓ Fatzer-van Parreren, San Bernardino 1985

[53] 8 ... ♘e4 9 ♘xe4 fe 10 ♘g5 ♗xd4 11 ♘xe4 ± Lerner

[54] 9 ... ♘h5 10 ♘d5 ♖f7 11 c5 e6 12 ♘f4 ♘f6! = Vizhmanavin-Malanyuk, USSR 1986

 9 ... ♔h8 10 ♗xf6 ♗xf6 11 e4 e5 12 ♖fe1 ed 13 ef ♕d8 14 ♘b5 ♘c5 = Lputian-Vizhmanavin, Irkutsk 1986

[55] 10 d5!? Lerner

[56] 11 ... ♗g7 and now:

 12 ♘d5 ♔h8 (12 ... e5?! 13 de de 14 e4! ± Lputian-Malanyuk, USSR 1986) ∞

 12 e3 h6 13 dc ♘xc5 14 ♕c2 ♗e6 15 b3 ± Lerner-Malanyuk, USSR Ch 1986

[57] 14 ♘xe4 ♗g7 =

[58] 16 ♕e2 ♗xd5 17 cd ♕a4! = Tukmakov-Malanyuk, USSR 1986

[59] 8 ... ♘c6 9 d5 ♘a5!? (9 ... ♘e5 10 ♘xe5 de 11 c5 ± Ricardi-Remon, Granma 1986) 10 b3 c5 11 ♗d2 ± Petran-Grigorov, Tbilisi 1986

 8 ... c6 9 e4 ♘xe4 10 ♘xe4 fe 11 ♖xe4 ♗f5 12 ♖e3 ♘d7 13 b3 ± Gheorghiu-Grigorov, Prague 1985

[60] 9 b3 ♘e4 10 ♗b2 ♘c6 11 ♖c1 h6 12 ♖f1 ♘xc3 13 ♗xc3 e5 = Gavrikov-Malanyuk, USSR Ch 1986

[61] 10 ... ♕c6 11 e4 fe 12 ♗b5 ♕b6 13 ♗c4+ ♔h8 14 ♘f7+ ♖xf7 15 ♗xf7 ♗f5 16 ♗e3 ± Neverov-M.Gurevich, Baku 1986

[62] 11 ... ♕a5 12 b4 ♕b6 13 ♕b3+ d5 14 e4! ± Khuzman-Vizhmanavin, USSR 1986

[63] Vizhmanavin, Kharitonov

[64] 8 b3 e5 9 de de 10 e4 ♘c6 11 ♗a3 ♖f7 12 ♖e1 (12 h3 f4 13 ♕d3 ♗e6 14 ♖ad1 h6 = Casafus-Lin Ta, Dubai Ol 1986) 12 ... f4!? 13 gf ♘h5 14 f5 gf ∞ Meduna-Belyavsky, Sochi 1986

[65] 8 ... c6 9 ♘d4 ♗d7 10 ♕b3 ± Welling

 8 ... ♗d7 9 ♕b3 ♕c8 10 e4 fe 11 ♘g5 ∞/± Vokacs-Armas, Bucharest 1985

[66] 9 ♖b1 c5 (9 ... ♗b7 10 b4! ± Rukavina-Cvitan, Yugoslav Ch 1986) 10 b3 ♘c7 11 a4 ♗d7 12 ♗b2 b6 13 ♕d2 ± Garcia Martinez-Lin Ta, Dubai Ol 1986; 10 ... h6 11 ♗b2 g5 ∞

[67] 10 e4?! fe 11 ♘xe4 ♘xe4 12 ♗xe4 c6! 13 ♗e3 ♘c7 ∓ Hernandez-Chernin, Cienfuegos 1981

 10 ♖e1 ♘c5 ∞ Cramling-Bücker, Biel II 1984

 10 b3 c6 11 ♗b2 ♘c7 12 ♖c1 ♖b8 = Lengyel-Kremenetsky, Satu Mare 1983

 10 ♖b1 c6 11 b3 ♘c7 (11 ... ♖b8 12 ♗b2 ♘c7 13 b4 e5! ∞ Cebalo-Jasimović, Pula 1985) 12 e3 c5 13 ♘de2 b5 ∞ Adorjan-Grigorov, Prague Z 1985

[68] 10 ... ♘xe4 11 ♘xe4 fe 12 ♗xe4 c5 ± Schmidt-Grigorov, Prague Z 1985

[69] 11 ... c5 12 ♘e6! ± Ivkov-Bischoff, Thessaloniki Ol 1984

[70] Gheorghiu-Cosma, Timisoara 1985

1 d4: Early Divergences

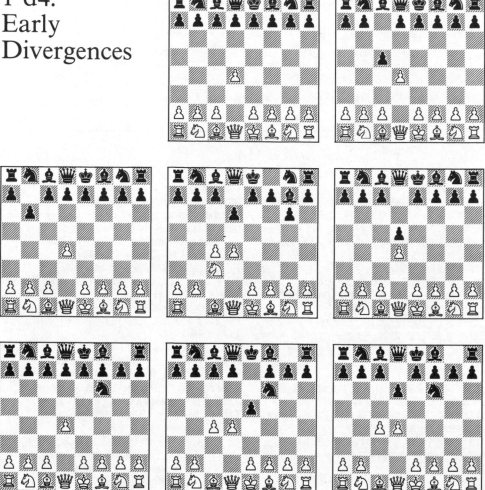

These less usual systems offer rich scope for the adventurous spirit, with either White or Black. In the **Modern Defence**, transpositions between pages 67 and 220 should be noted. The **English Defence** has recently attracted much interest, while the inventive Jon Speelman has sought to revive one discredited line of the **Old Indian** against co-author Kasparov.

References: *Trompowsky Opening and Torre Attack* (Bellin)
                       Budapest Gambit (Borik)
                       The English Defence: ... e6, ... b6, ... ♗b7 (Keene, Plaskett and Tisdall)
                       An Opening Repertoire for White (Keene)

	1	2	3	4	5	6	7	8	9	
1	...	Nf3[2]	e3[4]	a4[5]	c4	Bd3	Nbd2	b3	Bb2	±
	b5[1]	Nf6[3]	a6	b4	e6[6]	Bb7	c5	d6	Nbd7[7]	
2	...	c4	Bd2	e4!	e5	Nf3	Qxd2	Nc3	Bxc4[11]	±
	e6	Bb4+[8]	Qe7[9]	d5[10]	Nc6	Bxd2+	dc	Nh6	0-0[12]	
3	...	c4[13]	Nf3[14]	Nc3	d5	c5![16]	Qb3	Qxb7[17]	e4	±
	d6	e5	Nc6[15]	Bg4	Nce7	Nf6	Ng6	dc	Bd6[18]	
4	...	c4[19]	Nf3[20]	e4	dc[22]	Nfd2[23]	Be2[24]	0-0	Bd3	±
	g6	Bg7	c5	Nc6[21]	Qa5+	Qxc5	d6[25]	Nd4	Nf6[26]	

[1] 1 ... Nc6 and now:
2 d5 Ne5 3 f4 Ng6 4 e4 e6 5 Nf3 ed 6 ed Bc5 7 Qd3 d6 ∞ Gerusel-Miles, Porz 1981
2 Nf3 f5!? (2 ... d6 3 e4 Nf6 4 Nc3 Bg4 5 Bb5 ± Hulak-Miles, Indonesia 1982) 3 d5 Nb4 4 a3 Na6 5 b4 c5! 6 dc bc 7 c4 Nc7 ∞ Bisguier-Shirazi, Pasadena 1983
2 c4 e5 3 d5 Nce7 4 Nc3 Ng6 5 g3 Bb4 6 Qc2 a5 7 a3 Be7 8 h4 d6 9 e4 ± Barlov-Z.Nikolić, Novi Sad 1985

[2] 2 e4 Bb7 3 Bd3 c5 4 c3 Nf6 5 Nd2 e6 6 Ngf3 Qb6 7 Qe2 cd 8 cd Nc6 9 d5 Nb4 10 Bb1 ± van der Sterren-Hodgson, Wijk aan Zee II 1985

[3] Polish Defence

[4] 3 g3 e6 4 Bg2 Bb7 5 0-0 Be7 6 Bg5 a6 7 Nbd2 ± Timman-Miles, London 1982

[5] 4 c4 bc 5 Bxc4 e6 6 Nc3 ± Kurajica-Skalkotas, Kavala Z 1985

[6] 5 ... bc 6 bc e6 7 Nbd2 Nf6 8 Qb3 ±

[7] 10 0-0 Be7 11 Qe2 ± P.Garcia-Gelpke, Holland 1983

[8] Keres
2 ... b6 – 1 d4 b6

[9] 3 ... a5 4 e4 d6 (4 ... d5 5 a3! Bxd2+ 6 Qxd2 Nc6 7 Ngf3 Nge7 8 Qc2 ± Eingorn) 5 a3 Bxd2+ 6 Qxd2 e5 7 Ne2 Nf6 8 Nbc3 0-0 9 f3 Nc6 10 d5 ± Sahović-Eingorn, Lvov 1984

[10] 4 ... Nf6 5 e5 Ne4 6 Nf3 ±

[11] 9 d5 Nxe5 10 Nxe5 ed 11 Qe2 Be6 12 0-0-0 c6 ∞ Timman-Spraggett, Montpellier C 1985

[12] Spraggett

[13] 2 Nf3 Bg4 3 e4 Nf6 4 Nc3 (4 Nbd2 e6 5 c3 Be7 6 Bd3 d5 7 0-0 de 8 Nxe4 Nbd7 =

Langeweg-Timman, Holland 1984-85) 4 ... e6 5 Be2 Be7 6 0-0 0-0 7 Bf4 ±

[14] 3 d5 f5 4 Nc3 Nf6 5 g3 g6 6 Bg2 Bg7 7 Nf3 0-0 8 0-0 h6 9 e4 f4 ∞
3 de de 4 Qxd8+ Kxd8 5 Nc3 c6 6 Nf3 f6 7 g3 Be6 8 b3 Nd7 =

[15] 3 ... Nd7 4 Nc3 g6 5 e4 ±

[16] 6 e4 g6 7 Be2 Bxf3 8 Bxf3 Bh6 9 Bxh6 Nxh6 10 Qd2 ∞/±

[17] 8 cd Bxd6 9 Qxb7 0-0 ∞∞

[18] 10 Bb5+ Nd7 11 Nd2 ± Kouatly-Georgiev, Dubai Ol 1986

[19] 2 Nf3 c5 3 dc Qa5+ 4 Qd2! Qxc5 5 b4 Qc6 6 Bb2 ± Keres-Adorjan, Amsterdam 1971

[20] 3 Nc3 c5 4 d5 Bxc3+ (4 ... f5?! 5 e4! Bxc3 6 bc fe 7 h4! ± Farago-Davies, Balatonbereny 1985) 5 bc f5 6 e3 (6 g4?! fg 7 h3 g3 ∓ D.Gurevich-Dzindzihashvili, US Ch 1984) 6 ... Nf6 7 Bd3 e5 8 f3 ± Gurevich
3 e4 Nc6 4 d5 (4 Nf3 e5 5 Bg5 f6 6 Be3 d6 7 d5 Nce7 = Gligorić-Keene, Teesside 1972) 4 ... Nd4 5 Nc3 e5 6 Nge2 d6 7 Nxd4 ed 8 Nb5 ± A.Rodriguez

[21] 4 ... Qa5+ 5 Bd2 Qb6 6 Bc3 ±

[22] 5 d5 Nd4 6 Nxd4 Bxd4 7 Bd3 d6 8 Nd2 a6 9 0-0 ± Browne-Bellon, Nice Ol 1974

[23] 6 Bd2 Qxc5 7 Nc3 Nf6 8 Be2 Qb6 9 0-0 0-0 ±

[24] 7 Qb3 Qb6 8 Be2 d6 9 0-0 Nf6 (9 ... Qc7 10 Kh1 Be6 11 f4 ± Keene-Timman, Hastings 1973-74) 10 Nc3 0-0 11 Be3 Qd8 12 Rc1 ± Petrosian-Fischer, Rovinj/Zagreb 1970

[25] 7 ... Nd4 8 0-0 b5 9 Na3 b4 10 Nb5 ±

[26] 10 Nb3 Nxb3 11 ab Ng4 12 h3 h5 13 Qd2! ± Miles-Ljubojević, Tilburg 1986

1 d4 c5

	2	3	4	5	6	7	8	9	10	
1	d5[1]	e4[3]	ed	♘f3[4]	♘c3	♗e2[5]	0-0	h3[7]	a4	±
	e6[2]	ed	d6	♘f6	♗e7	0-0[6]	♘a6	♘c7	b6[8]	
2	...	e4[9]	♘c3[10]	♘f3[12]	h3[14]	♕xf3	♗xg5[15]	♘b5	♕g4	±
	e5	d6	♗e7[11]	♗g4[13]	♗xf3	♗g5	♕xg5	♕d8	♔f8[16]	
3	...	♘c3	e4	♘f3[17]	♗e2[18]	0-0[20]	h3[22]	a4[23]	♖e1	±
	♘f6	d6	g6	♗g7	0-0[19]	♘a6[21]	♘c7	a6	♖b8[24]	

[1] 2 dc ♘a6 (2 ... e6 3 ♘c3 ♗xc5 4 ♘e4 ±) 3 ♘f3 ♗xc5 4 e3 ♘f6 5 c4 g6 6 b3 ♗g7 7 ♗b2 0-0 8 ♗e2 d6 9 0-0 b6 = Muco-Velimirović, Kavala Z 1985

[2] 2 ... d6 3 c4 g6 4 e4 ♗g7 5 ♗d3 b5 6 cb a6 7 ♘c3 ab 8 ♗xb5+ ♗d7 9 ♗e2 ± Seirawan-Shirazi, US Ch 1984
2 ... ♘f6 3 ♘c3 ♕a5 4 e4!? ♕xe4 5 ♕f3 ♕xc3 (5 ... ♘f6?! 6 ♗g5 d6 7 ♗xf6 ef 8 0-0-0 ± Pomez-Bellon, Benidorm 1985) 6 ♗d2 d6 7 ♗xc3 ♕c7 8 0-0-0 e5 ∞ Bellon

[3] 3 ♘c3!? ed 4 ♘xd5 ♘e7 5 ♗g5 ♕a5+ 6 ♗d2 ♕d8 7 ♗c3 ♘xd5 8 ♕xd5 ± Vaganian-Quinteros, Biel IZ 1985

[4] 5 ♗b5+ ♗d7 6 ♘f3 ♘f6 7 0-0 ♗e7 8 ♖e1 a6 9 ♗f1 0-0 10 a4 b6 11 c4 ± Böhm-Johansen, Amsterdam 1983
5 ♘c3 ♘f6 6 ♗b5+ ♘bd7 7 a4 g6 8 ♕e2+ ♕e7 9 ♗g5 ♗g7 10 ♕xe7+ ♔xe7 11 0-0-0 a6 ∞ Kärner-Suba, Tallinn 1983

[5] 7 ♗b5+ ♗d7 8 a4 0-0 9 0-0 ♘a6 10 ♗xa6 ba 11 b3 ± Vaganian-Agzamov, USSR Ch 1983

[6] 7 ... ♗g4 8 0-0 ♗xf3 9 ♗xf3 0-0 10 ♗f4 ±

[7] 9 ♖e1 ♘c7 10 a4 b6 11 ♖b1 ♖e8 12 h3 ± Vaganian-L.Bronstein, Sao Paulo 1977

[8] 11 ♖e1 ♗b7 12 ♗c4 a6 13 ♘h4 ♖e8 14 ♘f5 ± D.Gurevich-Kavalek, US Ch 1984

[9] 3 de fe 4 ♘c6 5 ♘c3 ♘f6 6 f4 d6 7 ♘f3 ♗e7 8 ♗d3 0-0 9 0-0 a6 ∞ Nikolić-Ivanović, Yugoslav Ch 1984
3 c4 d6 4 e4 ♗e7 5 ♘c3 (5 ♘f3 ♗g4 6 ♗e2 ♗xf3 7 ♗xf3 ♗g5 8 ♗xg5 ♕xg5 9 ♘c3 ♘h6 ∞) 5 ... ♗g5 6 ♗xg5 ♕xg5 7 ♘f3 ♕e7 8 g3 ♘f6 9 ♘h4 ♘a6 10 a3 ♘c7 11 b4 ± Hébert-Ivanović, Toronto 1984

[10] 4 f4 ef 5 ♗xf4 ♕e7 (5 ... ♘e7 6 ♗b5+ ♗d7 7 ♗xd7+ ♘xd7 8 ♗xd6 ♕b6 9 ♗g3 ♕xb2 10 ♘d2 ± D.Gurevich-Short, Hastings 1982-83) 6 ♘c3 a6 7 a4 g5 8 ♗g3 ♘d7 9 ♘f3 ♗g7 ∞

[11] 4 ... ♘e7 5 ♘f3 (5 a4 a6 6 a5 ♘d7 7 ♘f3 ♗g6 8 ♘d2 b5!? ∞ Cebalo-Ivanović, Zagreb 1985) 5 ... ♘g6 6 h4 h5 7 g3 ♗e7 8 ♗e2 ♘d7 9 a4 ± Filip

[12] 5 f4 a6 6 fe de 7 a4 ♘f6 8 ♘f3 ♗g4 9 ♗e2 ♗xf3 10 ♗xf3 0-0 11 0-0 ♘e8 ∞ Lobron-Ivanović, Reggio Emilia 1984-85

[13] 5 ... ♘f6 – Czech Benoni

[14] 6 ♗e2 ♗xf3 7 ♗xf3 ♗g5 8 ♗xg5 ♕xg5 9 a4 ∞/±

[15] 8 ♗b5+ ♔f8 9 ♗xg5 ♕xg5 10 h4 ♕e7 11 ♗e2 h5 ∞

[16] 10 ... ♘f6 11 ♕xg7 ♖g8 12 ♕h6 ± Vaganian-Hug, Caracas 1976
10 ... ♔f8 11 ♘xd6 ♘f6 12 ♕c8 ♗xc8 13 ♘xc8 ♘xe4 14 ♗d3 ± Miles-Gheorghiu, Ostend 1986

[17] 5 ♗b5+ ♗d7 6 ♗xd7+ (6 a4 Larsen) 6 ... ♘bxd7 7 a4 ♗g7 8 f4 ♕a5 9 ♗d2 0-0 = Larsen

[18] 6 ♗b5+ and now:
6 ... ♘fd7 7 a4 ♘a6 8 0-0 ♘c7 9 ♗f4 0-0 10 ♕d2 ± Kharitonov-Tseshkovsky, USSR 1985
6 ... ♘bd7 7 a4 0-0 8 0-0 a6 9 ♗e2 ♖b8 10 ♖e1 ± Adorjan-Horvath, Hungarian Ch 1984
6 ... ♗d7 7 a4 ♗xb5 (7 ... 0-0 8 0-0 ♘a6 9 ♖e1 ± Kasparov-Belyavsky, match 1983) 8 ab 0-0 9 0-0 ♘bd7 10 h3 ♘e8 11 ♗g5 ♘c7 ∞ Browne-Alburt, New York 1984

[19] 6 ... ♘a6 7 0-0 ♘c7 8 a4 a6 9 ♘d2 ♗d7 10 ♘c4 b5 11 e5! ± Botvinnik-Schmid, Leipzig Ol 1960

[20] 7 ♘d2 b6 8 a4 ♘a6 9 0-0 ♘c7 10 ♘c4 ♗a6 11 ♗f4 ♖b8 ∞ Inkiov-Gheorghiu, Thessaloniki Ol 1984

[21] 7 ... ♗g4 8 ♗f4 (8 ♘d2!? ♗xe2 9 ♕xe2 ♘bd7 10 ♘c4 ♘b6 11 ♘e3 ∞/±) 8 ... ♘bd7 9 a4 ♗xf3 10 ♗xf3 ♘e8 11 ♕d2 a6 12 ♗e2 ± Ribli-Karlsson, Portorož/Ljubljana 1985
7 ... e6 8 ♗d2 ed 9 ed ♘a6 10 ♘c4 (10 ♗xa6!? Eingorn) 10 ... ♘c7 11 ♗f4!? b5 12 ♘xd6 b4 13 ♘a4 ± Eingorn-Velimirović, Bor 1986

[22] 8 ♗f4 ♘c7 9 a4 ♗g4 (9 ... b6 10 ♖e1 ♗b7 11 ♗c4 ♕d7 12 ♕d3 a6 13 h3 ♖ad8 14 ♖ad1 ± Speelman-Plaskett, British Ch 1986; 9 ... ♗d7!? 10 ♕d2 a6 11 e5 de 12 ♘xe5 ♗f5 13 ♗f3 ♘ce8 ∞ Smyslov-Seret, Lucerne 1985) 10 h3 ♗xf3 11 ♗xf3 ♘d7 12 ♕d2 a6 13 ♗e2 ♖b8 14 ♗h6 b5 = Benjamin-de Firmian, New York 1986
8 ♖e1 ♘c7 9 a4 b6 10 ♗f4! a6 11 h3 ♘d7 12 ♕d2 ± Belyavsky-Stoica, Lucerne 1985

[23] 9 ♖e1 b6 (9 ... b5 10 ♗xb5 ♘xe4 11 ♖xe4 ♗xc3 12 ♗c6 ± Speelman) 10 ♗f4 ♗b7 11 a4 (11 ♗f1?! ♕d7 12 ♕d2 b5 13 a3 ♖fe8 ∞ Speelman-Plaskett, London 1986) 11 ... ♕d7 12 ♗c4 ± Speelman

[24] 11 a5 b5 12 ab ♖xb6 13 ♗f1 ± Nikolić-Danner, Vrnjačka Banja 1986

1 d4 b6

	2	3	4	5	6	7	8	9	10	
1	c4[1]	e4[3]	Nc3	Qc2[4]	Bd3	Nf3[5]	Qxc3	0-0	Ne5[6]	∞
	e6[2]	Bb7	Bb4	Qh4	f5	Bxc3+	Qg4	fe		
2	...	...	Bd3	ef[8]	Qh5+	fg	gh+	Ne2	Qh4	±
	...	...	f5[7]	Bxg2[9]	g6	Bg7	Kf8	Nf6	Bxh1[10]	
3	...	...	Qc2	Nd2	Bd3	Nf3	Bxd2[12]	Ne5	0-0-0	±
	...	...	Qh4	Bb4	f5	Bxd2+[11]	Qg4	Qxg2	fe[13]	

[1] 2 e4 – 1 e4

[2] 2 ... Bb7 3 Bg5 (3 d5 e6 4 a3 Nf6 5 Nc3 Bd6!?; 5 ... b5!?) 3 ... f6 4 Bd2 e6 5 Nc3 f5 6 Nf3 Nf6 7 g3 Nc6 8 e3 Bb4 9 Bg2 ± Smejkal-Miles, Baden 1980

[3] 3 Nc3 Bb4 (3 ... Bb7 4 Nf3 Bb4 5 Qb3 a5 6 a3 a4 7 Qxb4 Nc6 8 Qb5 Ra5 9 d5! ± Ghitescu-Forintos, Metz 1984) 4 e3 Bb7 5 a3 Bxc3+ 6 bc f5! Polgar-Rogers, Amsterdam 1985
3 d5 Qh4 4 Nc3 Bb4 5 Bd2 Nf6 6 e3 Bxc3 7 Bxc3 Ne4 8 Qc2 ± Karpov-Miles, Bugojno 1978

[4] 5 f3 f5 (5 ... Qh4+ 6 g3 Bxc3+ 7 bc Qh5 8 Nh3 f5 9 Nf4 Qf7 ∞ Donner-Miles, England 1978) 6 ef Nh6! 7 fe Nf5 8 Ne2 de 9 Nf4 0-0 10 Qd2 Qh4+ 11 Ng3 Bd6 ∞ Panno-Miles, Buenos Aires 1979

[5] 7 g3 Qh5 8 Be2 Qf7 ∓ Farago-Miles, Hastings 1976-77

[6] 10 ... Qh5 11 Bc2 Nf6? 12 Bd1 Qh4 13 Be3 Nc6 14 d5 ± Garcia Gonzales-Forintos, Montpellier C 1985; 11 ... Ne7
10 ... Qh4 11 Bc2 d6 12 Ba4+ c6 13 d5! ∞ Garcia Gonzalez

[7] 4 ... Bb4+ 5 Bd2 Bxd2+ 6 Nxd2 Qg5 (6 ... c5 7 d5 e5 8 f4! ± Pytel-Schüssler, Trstenik 1979) 7 Ngf3! Qh6 8 Qa4 ± Bagirov-Ermenkov, Riga 1981
4 ... Nc6!? 5 Nf3 Bb4 Sosonko-Miles, Tunis IZ 1985

[8] 5 Qh5+ g6 6 Qe2 Nf6 =

[9] 5 ... Bb4+ 6 Kf1 ef 7 c5! bc 8 a3 c4 9 Bxc4 Bd6 10 Nc3 Nf6 11 Nf3 ± Seirawan-Schüssler, Malmö 1979

[10] 11 Bg5 Nc6 and now:
12 Nf4 e5! 13 Ng6+ Kf7 14 de (14 Nxe5+ Nxe5 15 de Re8) 14 ... Rxh7 15 Qf4 Rh3 16 ef Bxf6 ∓
12 Nd2 e5 13 0-0-0 (13 Ng3 e4 ⩲ Akesson-Short, Dortmund 1980) 13 ... e4 14 Bxe4 Bxe4 15 Nxe4 Rxh7 16 Qf4 Kf7 17 N2c3 ± Magerramov-Psakhis, USSR 1980 (17 ... Nb4 18 a3 d5 19 Nxf6 Bxf6 20 ab g6? 21 Bxf6 Qxf6 22 Rg1+ Kf7 23 Qxc7+ Qe7 24 Qc6! ±)

[11] 7 ... Qg4 8 0-0 Bxd2 9 Nxd2 ±

[12] 8 Kf1? Qh5 9 Bxd2 Nf6 ∓ Polugayevsky-Korchnoi, match 1977

[13] 11 Be2 ± Remlinger-Rogers, USA 1986

1 d4 d6 2 c4 g6 3 Nc3 Bg7

	4	5	6	7	8	9	10	11	12	
1	Nf3	g3	Bg2	0-0[3]	e4[4]	Nxd4	Nde2	b3	f4	∞
	Nd7[1]	e5	Ne7[2]	0-0	ed[5]	Nc6	Nde5	f5	Ng4[6]	
2	e4	Nf3[8]	Be2[9]	0-0[11]	Be3[12]	Qc2	de	Rad1	Bc5	±
	Nd7[7]	e5	Ne7[10]	0-0	h6	f5	de[13]	f4	Rf7[14]	

[1] 4 ... Bg4 5 e3 (5 g3 Bxf3 6 ef c6 7 Be3 Nf6 8 f4 0-0 9 Bg2 ∞/± Bagirov-Arapović, Trud v Bosna 1985) 5 ... Nc6 (5 ... c5 6 Be2 cd 7 ed Nh6 8 d5 ± Enklaar-van Wijgerden, Holland 1984-85) 6 Be2 e5 7 d5 Nce7 8 e4 Bxf3 9 Bxf3 f5 10 h4 ± Blees-van Putten, Dieren 1986
4 ... e5 5 de (5 g3 Nc6 6 d5 Nce7 7 e4 h6 8 h4 f5 9 h5 g5 10 Bd3 Nf6 ∞ Djurić-Rukavina, Budva 1986) 5 ... de 6 Qxd8+ Kxd8 7 Bg5+ f6 8 0-0-0+ Nd7 9 Bd2 ± Portisch-Keene, Teesside 1972

[2] 6 ... Nh6 7 h4 f6 8 h5 Nf7 9 e4 c6 10 Be3 ed ∞ Kristinsson-Cramling, Reykjavik 1984

[3] 7 h4 h6 8 e4 ed 9 Nxd4 Ne5 10 0-0-0 0-0 11 b3 N7c6 = Bareyev-Azmaiparashvili, USSR Ch 1986

[4] 8 e3 ed! 9 Nxd4 Nb6 10 b3 c5 11 Nde2 d5 12 Ba3 dc = Basin-Azmaiparashvili, Minsk 1985

[5] 8 ... h6 9 h3 f5 10 de de 11 Nh4 c6 12 Qe2 ± Csom-Ljubojević, Nice Ol 1974

[6] 13 ef Bxf5 14 h3 Nf6 ∞ Tomaszewski-Azmaiparashvili, Moscow II 1986

[7] 4 ... Nc6 5 d5 (5 Be3 e5 6 d5 Nce7 7 g4 ±)
5 ... Nd4 6 Be3 c5 7 dc (7 Nge2 Qb6 8 Nxd4
cd 9 Na4 de!? 10 Nxb6 ef+ 11 Kxf2 ab ∞
Agdestein-Keene, Gausdal 1983) 7 ... Nxc6
8 Rc1 Nf6 9 f3 0-0 10 Nge2 a6 11 Bf4 ± Suba-
Mestel, Las Palmas IZ 1982
    4 ... e5 and now:
    5 d5 f5 6 h4 Nf6 7 Bd3 f4 8 Nf3 0-0 9 Bd2
h6 10 b4 a5 11 a3 Bg4 ∞ Martinović-Todorčević,
Cuprija 1986
    5 de de 6 Qxd8+ Kxd8 7 f4 Nc6 8 Nf3
(8 fe!?) 8 ... Nd4 (8 ... Bg4 9 fe Bxf3 10 gf Bxe5
11 Bg5+ Ke8 12 0-0-0 ± Tarjan-Matulović,
Novi Sad 1975) 9 Bd3 Nxf3+ 10 gf Ne7 11 fe
Bxe5 12 Be3 ± Tukmakov-Mestel, Hastings
1982-83

[8] 5 Be3 e5 6 Nge2 Nh6 7 f3 f5 8 Qd2 Nf7
9 0-0-0 0-0 =
    5 Nge2 e5 6 Be3 Nh6 7 f3 f5 8 Qd2 fe
9 Nxe4 Nf7 (9 ... Nf5?! 10 Bg5 Bh6 11 h4!
Bxg5 12 hg ± Spassov-Ermenkov, Bulgarian
Ch 1984) ∞/± Spassov

[9] 6 g3 Ne7 7 Bg2 0-0 8 0-0 Nc6 9 d5 Nd4
10 Be3 Nxf3+ 11 Bxf3 f5 ∞ Velimirović

[10] 6 ... c6 7 0-0 Nh6 8 de de 9 b4 0-0 10 Rb1
Qe7 (10 ... f5 11 Ng5 Qe7 12 c5 ±) 11 c5 a5
12 a3 ab 13 ab f6 14 Nd2 Nf7 15 Nc4 ± Cebalo-
Kovačević, Yugoslav Ch 1985

[11] 7 d5 0-0 8 h4 f5 9 Ng5 Nc5 10 Be3 h6 ∞

[12] 8 Re1 f5 9 ef gf 10 de de 11 Bg5 ±

[13] 10 ... f4 11 Bc1 de 12 b3 ±

[14] 13 Ba3 ± Cebalo-Minić, Yugoslavia 1986

1 d4 d5

	2	3	4	5	6	7	8	9	10	
1	Bg5[1]	Bxf6[3]	e3[5]	c3	Qb3	Nd2	Ngf3	Be2	Qc2	=
	Nf6[2]	gf[4]	c5	Qb6	e6[6]	Nc6	Bd7	Na5	cd[7]	
2	Nc3	Bg5[8]	Bxf6[10]	e3	Rb1	Qd2	Bd3	a3	Nf3	=
	Nf6	c6[9]	ef	Qb6[11]	Bb4	f5	Be6	Bd6	Nd7[12]	

[1] 2 e4 de 3 Nc3 e5! ∞/∓
    2 Bf4 c5! 3 e3 cd 4 ed Nc6 5 c3 g6 6 Nd2
Bg7 7 Ngf3 Nh6 ∞ Hulak-Garcia Palermo,
Wijk aan Zee II 1986

[2] 2 ... c6 3 Nf3 Qb6 4 b3 Bf5 5 e3 e6 6 Bd3
Bxd3 7 Qxd3 Nd7 8 Nbd2 h6 = Hodgson-
Belyavsky, Sochi 1986
    2 ... h6 3 Bh4 c5 4 c3 ∞

[3] 3 Nd2 g6 (3 ... c5 4 dc Qa5 5 Bxf6 gf 6 g3! ±
Ermenkov-W.Schmidt, Prague Z 1985) 4 Bxf6
ef 5 c3 Bg7 6 e3 0-0 7 Bd3 f5 8 Ne2 Nd7 9 0-0
Nf6 = Kovačević-Hulak, Rovinj/Zagreb 1975

[4] 3 ... ef 4 e3 c6 (4 ... Bd6 5 Qd2 0-0 6 Ne2
c6 7 c4 ± Mikh.Tseitlin-Gulko, Sochi 1985)
5 Bd3 Bd6 6 Qf3 0-0 7 Ne2 (7 Qd2!? Na6 8 a3
Nc7 9 Ne2 ∞/± Hodgson-Taimanov, Erevan
1986) 7 ... Qb6 8 b3 a5 9 c3 ± Hort-Tukmakov,
Madrid 1973

[5] 4 c4 dc 5 e3 c5 6 Bxc4 cd 7 ed Bg7 8 Ne2
0-0 9 Nbc3 Nc6 ∞ Romero Holmes-Sunye,
Benasgue 1985

[6] 6 ... c4?! 7 Qxb6 ab 8 e4 e6 8 Nd2 ± Pribyl-
Sax, Skara 1980

[7] 11 ed Bb5 = Fernandez-Tatai, Barcelona
1985

[8] 3 e4 de 4 f3 ef 5 Nxf3 Bg4 6 h3 Bxf3 (6 ...
Bh5) 7 Qxf3 c6 8 Be3 e6 9 Bd3 Nbd7 ∞/∓
Callaghan-Bisguier, Washington 1986
    3 Bf4 Bf5 4 e3 c6 5 Nf3 e6 6 Bd3 Nbd7
7 0-0 Be7 8 h3 0-0 9 Qe2 Re8 = S.Nikolić-
Martinović, Smederevo 1981

    3 Nf3 g6 4 Bf4 Bg7 and now:
    5 Qd2 0-0 (5 ... Ne4!? 6 Nxe4 de 7 Ng5
h6 8 Nxe4 g5 9 Be5 f6 ∞ Dolmatov-Gavrikov,
USSR 1984) 6 Bh6 Bxh6 7 Qxh6 c5 =
Gurgenidze-Azmaiparashvili, Tbilisi 1986
    5 e3 0-0 (5 ... b6 6 Bb5+! c6 7 Bxb8 cb
9 Be5 ± Wiedenkeller-Mestel, Esbjerg 1984)
6 Be2 Nbd7 (6 ... c5 7 Ne5 Nc6 8 h4!? cd 9 ed
Qb6 10 Nxc6 bc = Pribyl-Vigh, Tapolca 1986)
7 Ne5 c6 8 h4 h5 9 Bxd7 Bxd7 10 Be5 b5 ∞
Kozul-Vogt, Budapest 1986

[9] 3 ... h6 4 Bxf6 ef (4 ... gf 5 e3 e6 6 Qh5!
Spassky-Uusi, USSR 1960) 5 e3 c6 6 Bd3 Bd6
7 Qf3 0-0 8 Nge2 ±
    3 ... g6 4 Qd2 Bg7 5 0-0-0 c6 6 Bh6 Bxh6
7 Qxh6 Nbd7 ∞
    3 ... c5 4 Bxf6 (4 e3 cd 5 ed Bg4 6 Be2 Bxe2
7 Qxe2 e6 8 Bxf6 gf 9 0-0-0 Nc6 ∞ Arkhipov-
Cserna, Kecskemet 1985) 4 ... gf 5 e3 cd 6 ed h5
7 Be2 h4 8 Bf3 e6 9 Nge2 Bh6 = Maksimović-
Tatai, Vrnjačka Banja 1979

[10] 4 e3 Qb6 5 Rb1 g6 6 Bd3 Bg7 7 Nf3 Bg4 =
    4 Qd3 Nbd7 5 e4 de 6 Nxe4 Nxe4 7 Qxe4
h6 8 Bd2 Nf6 =

[11] 5 ... Bd6 6 Bd3 0-0 7 Qf3 Re8 8 Nge2 ±
Miles-Tisdall, England 1982
    5 ... f5 6 Bd3 g6 7 Nce2 Nd7 8 Nf3 Bd6
9 c4 dc 10 Bxc4 Qe7 = Burger-Henley, New
York 1983

[12] 11 0-0 Qc7 = van der Vliet-Ligterink,
Amsterdam 1982

	2	3	4	5	6	7	8	9	10	
3	♘c3	♗g5	f3[13]	♘xd5	e4	♗h4	♕d3[15]	ef	♕c3	=
	♘f6	♗f5	♘bd7[14]	♘xd5	h6	♘e3	♘xf1	♘c5	♘a4[16]	
4	...	...	♘f3[17]	♗h4	e4	♘xe4	♘xf6+	♗xf6	♕d2	=
	...	♘bd7	h6[18]	e6[19]	de[20]	♗e7	♗xf6	♕xf6	0-0[21]	
5	♘f3	♗f4[23]	e3	♘bd2	c3	h3[28]	♗d3	0-0	♘e5	=
	♘f6[22]	c5[24]	e6[25]	♘c6[26]	♗e7[27]	0-0	b6	♗b7	♘xe5[29]	
6	...	♗g5	e3	♘bd2[32]	c3	♗d3	0-0	a4[37]	♕b1	=
	...	e6[30]	c5[31]	♗e7[33]	♘bd7[34]	b6[35]	♗b7[36]	a6	h6[38]	
7	...	...	e3[39]	♘bd2	♗d3[40]	c3	♖b1	0-0	♘xe5	∞
	...	g6	♗g7	0-0	c5[41]	♕b6[42]	♘c6	e5	♘xe5[43]	
8	...	e3	♗d3[45]	b3[47]	♗b2	0-0	♘bd2[50]	♘e5	ed	∞
	...	e6[44]	c5[46]	♘c6[48]	♗d6[49]	0-0	♕e7[51]	cd	♗a3[52]	

[13] **4 ♗xf6** ef (4 ... gf!?) 5 e3 c6 6 ♗d3 ♗xd3 7 ♕xd3 ♗b4 =
  4 e3 e6 5 ♗d3 ♗xd3 6 ♕xd3 ♘db7 7 e4 de 8 ♘xe4 ♗e7 =

[14] **4 ...** ♗g6 5 ♘h3 e6 6 ♘f4 ♗d6 7 ♕d2 c6 8 ♘xg6 hg = Garwell-Cramling, Thessaloniki Ol 1984

[15] 8 ♕e2 ♘xf1 9 ef ♘b6 10 0-0-0 ♕d6 11 g4 ∞

[16] 11 ♕b3 ♘b6 12 ♘e2 ♕d5 13 ♖xf1 ♕xf5 = Dolmatov, Smagin

[17] **4 ♕d3** h6 5 ♗h4 e6 6 e4 de 7 ♘xe4 ♗e7 = Lalev-Espig, Varna 1983
  4 e3 e6 5 ♗d3 c5 6 ♘f3 c4 7 ♗e2 ♗b4 8 0-0 ♗xc3 9 bc ♕a5 = Hoi-Lein, Copenhagen 1984
  4 f3 c5 5 e4 cd 6 ♗xf6 ♘xf6 7 ♕xd4 de =;
  4 ... e6!? 5 e4 h6 6 ♗h4 de 7 fe ♗b4 ∞

[18] **4 ...** c6 5 e3 ♕a5 6 ♗d3 ♘e4 7 0-0 ♘xg5 8 ♘xg5 g6 9 e4 de 10 ♘cxe4 ♗g7 11 ♖e1 0-0 = Hoi-Tukmakov, Jurmala 1985
  4 ... g6 5 e3 ♗g7 6 ♗d3 0-0 7 0-0 h6 8 ♗f4 c5 9 ♖e1 b6 10 ♘e5 ♗b7 11 ♕f3 ♘h5 = Miles-Portisch, London 1982

[19] 5 ... c6 6 e3 (6 ♕d3 ♕a5 7 ♘d2 e5 8 ♘b3 ♕b6 ∞ Hoi-Gutman, Cap d'Agde 1986) 6 ... e6 7 ♗d3 ♗e7 8 0-0 0-0 9 ♖e1 c5 10 ♗g3 ♘h5 = Veresov-Boleslavsky, USSR 1971

[20] **6 ...** g5 7 ♗g3 ♘xe4 8 ♘xe4 de 9 ♘e5 (9 ♘d2 f5 10 ♗c4 f4! ∓) 9 ... ♗g7 10 h4 ♘xe5 11 ♗xe5 ∞
  6 ... ♗b4 7 e5 g5 8 ♗xg5 hg 9 ♗xg5 ♖g8 10 ♗xf6 ♘xf6 11 ef ♕xf6 = Hoi-Smyslov, Copenhagen 1985

[21] 11 0-0-0 e5 = Hoi-Larsen, Copenhagen 1985

[22] **2 ...** ♗f5 3 ♗f4 e6 4 e3 ♗d6 5 ♗xd6 c6 6 ♗d3 ♘e7 = Kurajica-Kovačević, Sarajevo 1983
  2 ... e6 3 ♗f4 ♗d6 4 e3 ♗xf4 5 ef ♕d6 6 ♕d2 ♘f6 = Kovačević-Vaganian, Hastings 1982-83
  2 ... c5 3 c4! – Queen's Gambit

[23] 3 g3 c6 (3 ... g6 =; 3 ... c5 4 ♗g2 e6 5 0-0 ♘c6 6 c3 ♕b6 7 e3 ♗d6 = Ardiansyah-Farago, Polanica Zdroj 1983) 4 ♗g2 ♗f5 5 ♘bd2 (5 0-0 ♘bd7 6 ♘bd2 e6 7 b3 ♗e7 8 ♗b2 a5 =) 5 ... e6 6 ♘h4 ♗g4 7 c3 ♗e7 8 h3 ♗h5 9 g4 ♘fd7 ∞ Sygulski-Sydor, Warsaw 1983

[24] 3 ... c6 4 e3 ♗b6 5 b3 ♗g4 6 ♗e2 ♘bd7 7 0-0 e6 8 c4 ♗e7 9 h3 ♗h5 = Z.Nikolić-Kirov, Smederevo 1984
  3 ... ♗f5 4 e3 e6 5 ♗d3 ♗g6 6 0-0 ♗d6 7 ♗xd6 ♕xd6 8 ♘e5 ♗xd3 9 ♕xd3 0-0 = Bukić-Kurajica, Banja Luka 1983
  3 ... e6 4 e3 ♗d6 5 ♗g3 c5 6 c3 ♘e4 7 ♗xd6 ♕xd6 8 ♘bd2 ♘xd2 9 ♕xd2 ♘c6 = Osmanović-Lputian, Sarajevo 1983

[25] 4 ... ♘c6 5 c3 ♕b6 6 ♕b3 c4 7 ♕c2 ♗f5 8 ♕c1 e6 9 ♘bd2 ♕a5 10 ♗e2 b5 = Plaskett-Pinter, Copenhagen 1985
  4 ... cd!? 5 ed ♘c6 6 c3 a6 7 ♗d3 ♗g4 8 ♘bd2 e6 9 0-0 ♗d6 10 ♗xd6 ♕xd6 11 ♕e1 ♘d7 = Rakić-Bagirov, Frunze 1983

[26] 5 ... ♗e7 6 c3 ♘bd7 (6 ... 0-0?! 7 ♗d3 b6 8 ♘e5! ±) 7 ♗d3 b6 8 0-0 ♗b7 9 ♘e5 ♘xe5 10 ♗xe5 0-0 11 ♕f3 ♘d7 = Glienke-Yusupov, Plovdiv 1983

[27] 6 ... ♗d6 7 ♗g3 0-0 8 ♗d3 b6 (8 ... ♖e8!?) 9 ♘e5 ♗b7 10 f4 ♘e7 11 ♕f3 ♘f5 = Rakić-Makarichev, Novi Sad 1983

[28] 7 ♗d3 ♘h5 8 ♗e5 f6 9 ♗g3 g6 10 ♕e2 0-0 += Eslon-Cramling, Biel 1984; 8 ♗g3!?

[29] 11 ♗xe5 c4 12 ♗c2 b5 13 a3 ♘d7 = Remon-Agzamov, Cienfuegos 1984

[30] 3 ... c6 4 e3 ♗f5 5 ♗d3 ♗xd3 6 cd e6 7 0-0 ♗e7 8 ♘c3 0-0 9 ♕b3 ♕b6 = Grünfeld-Stean,

Beer-Sheva 1982

3 ... ♘e4 4 ♗h4 c5 5 e3 ♕b6 6 ♕c1 ♘c6 7 ♗e2 cd 8 ♘xd4 ∞; 7 ... ♗g4!? =

[31] 4 ... ♗e7 5 ♘bd2 ♘bd7 (5 ... 0-0?! 6 ♗d3 b6 7 ♘e5 ♗b7 8 ♗xf6! ♗xf6 9 f4 ± Timman-Geller, Linares 1983) 6 ♗d3 b6 7 0-0 ♗b7 8 ♘e5 (8 c3 0-0 9 ♕a4 ♘e4 10 ♗xe7 ♕xe7 11 ♖ad1 ♖fd8 = Hug-Tatai, Thessaloniki Ol 1984) 8 ... ♘xe5 9 de ♘d7 10 ♗xe7 ♕xe7 11 f4 0-0-0 ∞ Spassky-Tatai, Reggio Emilia 1983-84

[32] 5 c3 ♗e7 (5 ... ♕b6 6 ♕c1 ♘e4 7 ♗h4 ♘c6 8 ♘bd2 f5 ∞) 6 ♗d3 ♘bd7 7 0-0 b6 8 ♘e5 ♘xe5 9 de ♘d7 = Vaganian-Timman, Tilburg 1983

[33] 5 ... ♘c6 6 c3 ♗e7 7 ♗d3 ♘d7 (7 ... b6!?) 8 ♗xe7 ♕xe7 9 0-0 0-0 10 ♖e1 ± Timman-Belyavsky, Wijk aan Zee 1985

5 ... ♕b6 6 ♗xf6 gf 7 c4 cd 8 ed dc 9 ♗xc4 ♘c6 10 0-0 ♗d7 11 d5 ± Spassky-A.Zaitsev, USSR 1963

[34] 6 ... 0-0 7 ♗d3 b6 8 ♘e5 ♗b7 9 ♕f3 ±

[35] 7 ... 0-0 8 ♘e5 ♘xe5 9 de ♘d7 10 ♗f4 ±

7 ... a6 8 0-0 b5 9 ♘e5 ♗b7 10 f4 ± Seirawan-Larsen, Linares 1983

7 ... ♕c7 8 0-0 0-0 9 ♕e2 b6 10 e4 ±

[36] 8 ... 0-0 9 ♘e5 ♗b7 10 ♕f3! h6 11 ♗f4 ♘xe5 12 de ♘h7 13 ♕g4 ±

[37] 9 ♘e5 ♘xe5 10 de ♘d7 11 ♗xe7 ♕xe7 12 f4 ∞ Spassky-A.Sokolov, Bugojno 1986

9 ♕c2 0-0 10 ♖ae1 c4 11 ♗e2 b5! ∞ Torre-A.Sokolov, Biel 1985

[38] 11 ♗f4 ♘h5 12 ♗e5 0-0 13 h3 c4 = Hort-Kir.Georgiev, Thessaloniki Ol 1984

[39] 4 c3 ♘e4 5 ♗f4 c5 6 e3 ♘c6 7 ♘bd2 cd 8 ♘xe4 de 9 ♘xd4 ♕b6 10 ♘xc6 bc = Vaganian

[40] 6 ♗e2 c5 7 c3 ♕b6 8 ♕b3 ♘c6 9 0-0 ♗f5 10 ♗xf6 ♗xf6 = Vaganian-Ftacnik, Hastings 1982-83

6 c3 ♘bd7 (6 ... b6 7 b4 c5!? 8 ♗e2 a5 9 bc bc 10 0-0 a4 ∞ Lputian-Dvoiris, USSR Ch 1986) 7 ♗e2 ♖e8 8 ♕b3 c6 9 0-0 ♗e5 10 de ♘xe5 11 ♘xe5 ♖xe5 = Kochiev-Gavrikov, Minsk 1983

[41] 6 ... ♘bd7 7 0-0 ♖e8 8 c4! c5 9 ♕b3 ± Plachetka-Hausner, Trnava 1985

[42] 7 ... b6 8 0-0 ♗b7 9 ♕b1! ♘c6 10 b4 cd 11 cd ♕d6 12 a3 ± Agzamov-Loginov, USSR 1983

7 ... ♘bd7 8 0-0 b6 9 ♕b1 ♗b7 10 b4 ± Malanyuk-Loginov, Tallinn 1982

7 ... cd 8 ed ♘c6 9 0-0 ♕c7 (9 ... h6 10 ♗h4

♘h5 11 ♖e1 ♕d6 12 ♗b5± Schüssler-Vaganian, Tallinn 1983) 10 ♖e1 ♘h5 11 ♘f1 ♘f4 12 ♗b5 ±

[43] 11 de ♘g4 12 ♕f3 ♘xe5 13 ♘xe5 ♗xe5 14 f4 ♗f6 15 ♗xf6 ♕xf6 16 f5 ♕e5 ∞ Neverov-Glek, USSR 1985

[44] 3 ... ♗g4 4 ♘bd2 ♘bd7 5 h3 ♗h5 6 c4 e6 7 ♕b3 ♖b8 ∞/= Kovačević-Timman, Bugojno 1984

3 ... c5 4 b3 ♗g4 (4 ... cd =) 5 ♗e2 e6 6 0-0 ♘c6 7 ♗b2 ♗e7 8 ♘bd2 0-0 9 c4 ♖c8 10 dc ♗xc5 = Jakobsen-Petrosian, Plovdiv 1983

[45] 4 ♘bd2 c5 5 c3 ♘c6 6 ♗b5 ♕c7 7 ♘e5 ♗d6 8 f4 0-0 ∞; 6 ... ♕b6 =

[46] 4 ... g6 5 b3 ♗g7 6 ♗a3 ♘bd7 7 ♘bd2 c5 8 0-0 0-0 9 c4 ± Yusupov-Sosonko, Tunis IZ 1985

4 ... b6 5 0-0 (5 ♘bd2 ♗b7 6 ♕e2 ♗e7 7 e4 de 8 ♘xe4 ♘bd7 9 0-0 ∞/±) 5 ... ♗b7 6 ♘e5 (6 b3 ♘bd7 7 ♗b2 ♘e4 8 ♘e5 ♗d6 9 f4 0-0 10 ♗xe4 de = Petrosian-Miles, Nikšić 1983) 6 ... ♗d6 7 f4 0-0 8 ♘d2 ♘e4 9 c4 ∞ Yusupov-Draško, Sarajevo 1984

[47] 5 0-0 c4 6 ♗e2 b5 7 b3 ♗b7 8 bc bc 9 ♘c3 ♘bd7 ∞ Diždar-Chandler, Jurmala 1983

5 c3 ♘bd7 6 ♘bd2 ♗d6 7 0-0-0-0 8 e4 (8 ♖e1 ♕b6 9 b3 e5 =) 8 ... cd 9 cd de 10 ♘xe4 ♘xe4 11 ♗xe4 h6 12 ♗c2 b6 13 ♕d3 ♘f6 = Smyslov-Romanishin, USSR 1976

[48] 5 ... ♕a5+ and now:

6 ♘bd2 cd 7 ed ♗b4 8 0-0 ♗c3 ∞ Yusupov-Miles, London 1984

6 c3 ♘c6 7 0-0 ♕c7 8 c4 dc 9 bc ♗e7 10 ♗b2 ± Kovačević-Popović, Zagreb/Rijeka 1985

5 ... ♘bd7 6 ♗b2 ♗e7 7 0-0-0-0 8 ♘bd2 ♕c7 9 ♘e5 b6 10 f4 ±

[49] 6 ... cd 7 ed g6!? (7 ... ♗b4+ 8 c3 ♗d6 9 0-0 0-0 10 c4 ±) 8 0-0 ♗g7 9 ♗a3 ♘e4 10 c3 f5 ∞ Petrosian-Sunye, Las Palmas IZ 1982; 9 ♘bd2!?

6 ... ♗e7 7 0-0 0-0 8 ♘bd2 b6 9 ♘e5 ♘b4 10 ♗e2 ♗b7 11 f4 ± Yusupov-Spiridonov, Plovdiv 1983

[50] 8 ♘e5 ♕c7 9 f4 cd 10 ed ♘b4 11 ♘c3 ♘xd3 12 ♕xd3 ♗d7 = Rabinovich-Bogoljubow, Moscow 1924

[51] 8 ... b6 9 ♘e5 ♗b7 10 a3 ♕c7 11 f4 ± Kovačević-Diždar, Sarajevo 1983

[52] 11 ♕c1 ♗xb2 12 ♕xb2 ♗d7 13 a3 ♕d6 14 ♖ae1 a6 15 f4 ♘e7 ∞ Lobron-Kir.Georgiev, Wijk aan Zee 1985

1 d4 ♘f6

	2	3	4	5	6	7	8	9	10	
1	♗g5	♗xf6²	d5	♕c1⁵	g3⁷	c3	♘d2	♕c2	♗h3!?⁹	∞
	c5¹	gf³	♕b6⁴	f5⁶	♗g7⁸	d6	♕c7	e6	0-0¹⁰	
2	...	♗f4¹¹	d5¹²	♗c1¹³	f3	c3	e4	♗d2¹⁶	c4	∞
	♘e4	c5	♕b6	e6¹⁴	♕a5+¹⁵	♘f6	d6	♕b6	♕xb2¹⁷	
3	...	...	f3¹⁸	♘c3	♕d2	0-0-0	e4	d5	♕e1	∞
	...	d5	♘d6¹⁹	♘f5	♘c6	e6	de	e3	ed²⁰	
4	...	♗h4	f3²¹	♘c3	dc²³	♗f2	♘e4	g4	♗xe3	∞
	...	d5	♘d6	c5²²	♘f5	d4	♘c6	♘e3	de²⁴	
5	...	...	f3²⁵	fe	e3	♔f2	ed	♘c3	♘f3	∞
	...	c5	g5²⁶	gh	♗h6²⁷	cd	♕b6²⁸	e6	♘c6²⁹	
6	♘f3	d5³¹	♗g5	♘c3³³	e4	♘a4	♗xf6	b3	♗d3	±
	c5³⁰	b5	♕b6³²	♗b7³⁴	b4	♕a5	ef	d6	g6³⁵	
7	...	g3³⁶	♗g2³⁸	0-0³⁹	c3⁴⁰	♗g5	♘bd2	e3⁴²	♗xf6	=
	e6	b5³⁷	♗b7	c5	♘a6⁴¹	♗e7	0-0	h6	♗xf6⁴³	
8	...	e3	♗d3	0-0⁴⁴	♘bd2⁴⁶	b3⁴⁸	♗b2⁴⁹	ed	a3	∞
	...	b6	♗b7	c5⁴⁵	♗e7⁴⁷	♘c6	cd	0-0	♖c8⁵⁰	

---

¹ **2 ... e6** 3 c3 b6 4 e4 h6 5 ♗xf6 ♕xf6 6 e5 ♕e7 7 ♕f3 ♘c6 ∞ Qi Jingxuan-Karpov, Lucerne 1985
2 ... g6 3 ♗xf6 ef 4 e3 ♗g7 5 ♘e2! b6 6 ♘f4 d5 7 h4 h5 8 c4 ∞/± Vaganian-Botterill, Hastings 1974-75

² **3 ♘c3** cd 4 ♕xd4 ♘c6 5 ♕h4 e6 6 e4 ♗e7 7 f4 b5! ∞ Nei-Taimanov, USSR 1981
3 d5 ♕b6 4 ♘c3!? ♕xb2 5 ♗d2 ♕b6 6 e4 e5 (6 ... d6 7 f4 e6 ∞/± Hort) 7 f4 d6 8 fe de 9 ♘f3 ♗d6 10 ♗c4 ∞̄ Pribyl-Hazai, Varna 1978

³ 3 ... ef 4 c3 ♕b6 5 ♕d2 ±

⁴ 4 ... d6!? 5 ♘d2 ♗g7 6 e3 f5 7 c3 0-0 ∞

⁵ 5 ♘d2 ♕xb2 6 e3 f5 7 ♖b1 (7 ♗h3!? Jansa) 7 ... ♕f6 8 ♗d3 ♗h6 9 ♘e2 d6 10 ♘g3 f4 ∞ Hort-Hartston, Hastings 1972-73

⁶ 5 ... ♗h6 6 e3 d6 7 c4 ♘d7 8 ♘c3 f5 9 ♕d2 ♘f6 10 ♘ge2 ♗d7 11 g3 ± Zaichik-Maliskauskas, USSR 1985
5 ... e6 6 ♘c3 f5 7 e3 d6 8 g3 ♘d7 9 ♗g2 ♘f6 10 ♘ge2 ♗h6 11 0-0 0-0 ∞ Ermenkov-de Firmian, Tunis IZ 1985

⁷ 6 e3 ♗g7 7 c3 c6 8 ♗h3 ∞ Hort

⁸ 6 ... ♗h6 7 ♗g2 ♗g7 8 c3 d6 (8 ... ♕d6!?) 9 ♘a3 ♘d7 10 ♘c4 ♕c7 11 a4 ♘f6 12 ♕d1 0-0 13 ♘e2 ± Ermenkov-Kruszynski, Albena 1983
6 ... d6 7 ♗g2 ♘d7 8 ♘d2 ♘f6 9 c4 ♗g7 10 ♕c2 ♘e4 11 ♗xe4 fe 12 ♖b1 f5 ∞ Kuporosov-Oll, Kostroma 1985

⁹ 10 ♗g2 ♘d7 11 ♘h3 ♘f6 ∞ Kogan

¹⁰ 11 ♘gf3 ♘d7 12 0-0 ♘f6 13 c4 ♗d7 14 ♖fe1 ∞ Kogan-Browne, US Ch 1985

¹¹ 3 h4!? d5 4 ♘d2 ♘xg5 5 hg ♗f5 6 e3 e6 (6 ... c5? 7 g4 ♗d7 8 g6! fg 9 ♗d3 ♕b6 10 dc ± Depasquale-Kudrin, London 1986) 7 g4 ♗g6 8 f4 ∞

¹² 4 f3 ♕a5+ (4 ... ♘f6 5 dc ♘a6?! 6 e4 ♘xc5 7 ♘c3 d6 8 ♕d2 ± M.Gurevich-Yap, Jurmala 1985; 5 ... ♕a5+!?) 5 c3 ♘f6 6 d5 e6! 7 e4 ed 8 ed d6 ∞ Kogan-Wilder, US Ch 1986

¹³ 5 ♘d2 ♘xd2 6 ♗xd2 ♕xb2 7 e4 g6 (7 ... e6 8 ♘f3 ♗e7 9 ♖b1 ♕a3 10 ♗d3 ∞ Buckmire-Lawton, Edinburgh 1985) 8 ♖b1 ∞̄ Piket-Ivanchuk, Paris 1984
5 ♕c1 e6 6 de fe 7 ♘f3 ♘c6 8 e3 ♗e7 9 ♗d3 ♘f6 =

¹⁴ 5 ... g6 6 f3 ♘f6 7 c4 ♗g7 8 ♘c3 0-0 9 ♘h3! ± Ermolinsky-Uhlmann, Leningrad 1984

¹⁵ 6 ... ♘f6 7 c4 ♕b4+!? (7 ... ed 8 cd c4 9 e4 ♗c5 10 ♘h3 d6 11 ♗c4 ±) 8 ♘c3 ♕xc4 9 e4 ♕b4 ∞ van der Wiel

¹⁶ 9 ♘a3 ed 10 ed ♗c7 11 ♘c4 ♕d8 12 ♘e3 0-0 = van der Wiel-Kasparov, Moscow IZ 1982

¹⁷ 11 ♕xc4 ♕b6 12 f4!? ∞ Vaganian-Ehlvest, USSR Ch 1984

¹⁸ 4 e3 ♗f5 5 f3 ♘d6 = Efimov-Kuzmin, USSR 1986

¹⁹ 4 ... ♘f6 5 ♘c3 e6 6 e4 c5 7 ♘b5 ♘a6 8 e5 ♘d7 9 c3 ♗e7 ∞ Yudasin-Uhlmann, Leipzig 1986

²⁰ 11 ♘xd5 ♗d6 12 ♗xd6 cd 13 g4 ♘fe7 ∞
Huerta-Garcia Gonzalez, Havana 1985
²¹ 4 ♘d2 c5 5 ♘xe4 de 6 dc ♕a5+ 7 ♕d2 ♕xc5
8 0-0-0 ♘c6 =
²² 5 ... c6 6 e4 ♕b6 7 ♖b1 g6 8 ♗f2 ♗h6
9 ♗d3 ± Shereshevsky-Kupreichik, USSR 1979
²³ 6 ♘xd5 ♘f5 7 ♗f2 cd 8 e4 de =
²⁴ 11 ♕xd8+ ♘xd8 ∞ Shereshevsky-Tukmakov,
USSR 1981
²⁵ 4 d5 ♕b6 =
    4 ♘d2 ♕a5 =
²⁶ 4 ... ♘f6 5 d5 ♕b6 6 e4 ♕xb2 7 ♘d2 g6
8 ♖b1 ♕c3 9 ♗d3 ∞ Shereshevsky-Kärner,
USSR 1979
    4 ... ♕a5+!? 5 c3 ♘f6 6 d5 ♕b6 (6 ... d6
7 e4 g6 8 ♗xf6!? ef 9 ♗d3 ♗h6 10 ♘e2 ∞/±
Romero-Howell, Groningen 1984-85) 7 e4
♕xb2 8 ♘d2 ♕c3 9 ♗c4 d6 10 ♘e2 ∞ Hodgson-
Nunn, Brussels 1986
²⁷ 6 ... ♕b6!? 7 ♘c3 ♕xb2 8 ♘d5 ♗d8 9 ♗c4
e6 10 ♖b1 ±/ ± Romero-Agdestein, Groningen
1984-85
²⁸ 8 ... d5 9 ed ♕xd5 10 ♘f3 ♘c6 11 ♘c3 ♕a5
12 ♗b5 ♗d7 13 ♖e1 0-0-0 ∞ Bellon-Hjartarson,
Hastings 1985-86
²⁹ 11 ♗b5!? (11 ♘b5?! 0-0 12 c4 d6 13 b4
♕d8 ∓ Bellon-W.Watson, Hastings 1985-86) ∞
³⁰ 2 ... d6 3 ♘c3 (3 g3 ♗g4 4 ♗g2 ♕c8 =) 3 ...
♗f5 4 ♘h4 (4 g3 c6 5 ♗g2 h6 6 0-0 ♗h7 7 b3
♘bd7 8 ♖e1 d5! = Plachetka-Spraggett, Vienna
1986) 4 ... ♗d7 5 g3 (5 e4 e5 6 ♘f3 ♘c6 =
Spraggett) 5 ... d5 6 ♗g2 e6 7 0-0 c5 8 dc ♗xc5
9 e4 ± Spassky-Shirazi, Somerset (USA) 1986
³¹ 3 dc e6 4 a3 ♗xc5 5 b4 ♗e7 6 ♗b2 a5 =
³² 4 ... ♘e4?! 5 ♗h4 (5 ♕d3 ♘xg5 6 ♘xg5 h6
7 ♘h7 ♕a5+ 8 c3 d6 9 ♘xf8 ♗xf8 10 e4 ± Wells-
Buckmire, Oakham 1986) 5 ... ♕a5+ 6 ♘bd2
♗b7 7 a4! ♗xd5 8 ab ♕c7! 9 ♖a4! ± Kasparov-
Miles, match 1986
    4 ... g6 5 ♘bd2 ♗g7 6 e4 0-0 7 a4 b4 ±
Ingbrandt-Tisdall, Oslo 1986
    4 ... d6 5 ♗xf6 ef 6 e4 a6 7 a4 b4 8 ♗d3 ±
Yusupov-Miles, Bugojno 1986
³³ 5 a4 b4 ∞
    5 c3 ♗e4 (5 ... d6 6 ♗xf6 ef 7 a4 ba 8 ♕xa4+
♗d7 9 ♕c2 ± Barlov-Forintos, Bela Crkva
1986) 6 ♗h4 e6 7 e3 c4 8 a4 ♗b7 9 de fe 10 ab
♕xb5 11 ♘bd2 ± De Boer-Weemaes, Amsterdam
1986
³⁴ 5 ... b4 6 ♘a4 ♕c7 7 ♗xf6 gf 8 b3 ± Smyslov-
Szmetan, Buenos Aires Ol 1978
³⁵ 11 h4 ± Dreyev-Glek, Tallinn 1986
³⁶ 3 ♘c3 d5 4 ♗g5 ♗e7 (4 ... h6 5 ♗xf6 gf
6 e4 ± Kavalek-Quinteros, Hanover 1983) =
³⁷ 3 ... c5!? 4 ♗g2 cd (4 ... ♘c6 5 0-0 cd 6 ♘xd4
♕b6 7 ♘b3 = Sosonko-Nikolić, Wijk aan Zee

1986) 5 0-0 (5 ♘xd4 ♘c6 6 0-0 ♗c5 7 ♘xc6 bc
8 c4 0-0 9 ♕c2 ♗e7 ∞ Kogan-Fedorowicz, New
York 1984) 5 ... a6 6 ♘xd4 ♕c7 7 b3 d5 (7 ...
♗e7 8 c4 0-0 9 ♗b2 d6 10 ♘c3 ♘bd7 11 ♖c1
♖e8 12 e3! ± Speelman-Csom, Hastings 1983-
84) 8 c4!? dc 9 bc ♕xc4 10 ♘a3 ♕c3 11 ♖b1
♗xa3 12 ♕a4+ ∞∞
³⁸ 4 ♕d3 b4 5 ♗g2 ♗a6 6 ♕d1 ♗b7 (6 ... c5
7 ♘e5 d5 8 c4 ± Dorfman-Skrobek, Warsaw
1983) ∞ Dorfman
³⁹ 5 ♗g5 c5 6 c3 cd 7 ♗xf6 ♕xf6 (7 ... gf 8 cd
d5 9 0-0 ♘d7 10 ♕d3 ♕b6 11 ♘bd2 ♗e7 ∞
Speelman-Karpov, London 1984) 8 cd ♗b4+
9 ♘c3 0-0 10 0-0 a6 11 ♖c1 ♕d8 12 e3 ♘c6
(12 ... ♕b6 13 ♘e5 ± Speelman-H.Olafsson,
Wijk aan Zee 1983) 13 ♘e5 ♖c8 14 ♘d3 ♗xc3
15 ♖xc3 ♘a5 = Speelman-Andersson, Wijk aan
Zee 1983
    5 ♕d3 a6 (5 ... b4 6 c4 ♗e7 7 0-0 c5 8 ♘bd2 ±
Vera-Vaiser, Sochi 1985) 6 0-0 c5 7 dc ♗xc5
8 ♗g5 ♗e7 9 ♘bd2 d5 10 ♗xf6 ♗xf6 11 c3
♘bd7 = Kir.Georgiev-Adorjan, Szirak 1985
⁴⁰ 6 ♗g5 ♕b6 7 c3 d5 8 ♘bd2 ♘bd7 9 a4 ±
Kaidanov-Yudasin, USSR 1986; 6 ... ♗e7 =
⁴¹ 6 ... ♘c6 7 ♗g5 d5 8 ♘bd2 ♗e7 9 ♗xf6! gf
10 e4 ± Plachetka-Plaskett, Trnava 1984
    6 ... cd 7 cd ♗e7 8 ♗g5 0-0 9 ♘c3 0-0 10 ♕d3
d5 11 ♘e5 ♘c6 12 f4 ± Li Zunian-Polugayevsky,
Biel IZ 1985
⁴² 9 ♕b1 d5 10 a3 cd 11 cd ∞ Li Zunian-Short,
Biel IZ 1985
⁴³ 11 ♕e2 ♖b8 = Plachetka-Suba, Belgrade
1984
⁴⁴ 5 ♘bd2 c5 6 b3 ♘c6 7 ♗b2 cd 8 ed ♘b4 =
⁴⁵ 5 ... ♗e7 6 b3 0-0 7 ♗b2 ♘e4 (7 ... c5 8 c4
cd 9 ed d5 10 ♕e2 ♘c6 11 ♘bd2 ♖ac8 = Bellon-
Browne, New York 1984) 8 c4 d5 9 ♘bd2 ♘d7 =
Nei-Gurevich, Tbilisi 1985
⁴⁶ 6 b3 and now:
    6 ... ♗e7 7 ♗b2 0-0 8 ♘bd2 ♖e8 9 a3 cd
10 ed d6 11 c4 ♘bd7 12 ♘g5 h6 13 f4 e5! ∞
Razuvayev-Lerner, USSR Ch 1985
    6 ... g6!? 7 ♗b2 ♗g7 8 ♘bd2 0-0 Diždar-
Timman, Sarajevo 1984
⁴⁷ 6 ... cd 7 ed ♗e7 8 ♖e1 0-0 9 a4 a6 10 ♘f1
d6 = Kovačević-Hulak, Zagreb 1985
⁴⁸ 7 ♖e1 d6 (7 ... cd 8 ed 0-0 9 c3 d6 10 a4 a6
11 ♕e2 ± Kovačević-Marjanović, Yugoslavia
1985) 8 c3 0-0 9 dc bc 10 e4 ♘c6 11 ♘f1 ♕c7
12 ♘g3 ♖fd8 ∞ Kovačević-Adorjan, Thessaloniki Ol 1984
    7 e4!? d5 8 e5 ♘fd7 9 ♖e1 ♘c6 Yusupov-
Timman, match 1986
⁴⁹ 8 a3 cd 9 ed 0-0 10 ♗b2 ♖c8 11 ♖e1 ♕c7 =
⁵⁰ 11 ♖c1 ♖e8 12 ♖e1 d5 13 ♘e5 ♘xe5 14 de
♘e4! = Yusupov-Gentes, Winnipeg 1986

71

	2	3	4	5	6	7	8	9	10	
9	♘f3	♗g5[51]	♗xf6[52]	e4[53]	♘bd2[55]	c3	♘c4	♗d3	♕e2	∞
	e6	h6	♕xf6	d6[54]	g5!?	♘d7	♗g7	♕e7	b6[56]	
10	...	...	e3	d5![57]	♗xf6	♘c3	e4	e5!	♘xd5	±
	...	c5	b6	h6[58]	♕xf6	♗b7[59]	♕d8	ed	♘c6[60]	
11	...	...	...	♘bd2[62]	♗d3[64]	c3[66]	♗h4	ed	0-0	∞
	...	...	♗e7[61]	b6[63]	♗b7[65]	h6[67]	cd	0-0	d6[68]	
12	...	...	...	♘bd2[69]	♗d3[71]	♗xf6[73]	c4!	♗e2	0-0	∞∞
	...	...	♕b6	♕xb2[70]	d5[72]	gf	♕c3	dc	♕a5[74]	
13	...	g3	♗g2	0-0	b3[77]	de	♗b2	e4	♘c3	=
	g6	♗g7	0-0[75]	d6[76]	e5[78]	♘fd7	♘c6[79]	de	b6[80]	
14	...	♗f4	e3[82]	♗e2[83]	h3	c3	dc	♕xd8	♘a3	∞
	...	♗g7[81]	0-0	d6[84]	c5[85]	♗e6	dc	♖xd8	♘c6[86]	
15	...	♗g5	♘bd2	e4[89]	c3	dc	♗e2[92]	h3	0-0	∞
	...	♗g7[87]	d6[88]	0-0[90]	c5[91]	dc	♘c6	♕c7	h6[93]	

[51]   3 ♗f4 c5 4 c3 cd 5 cd b5 6 e3 a6 = Knežević-Velimirović, Yugoslav Ch 1978

[52]   4 ♗h4 g5 (4 ... b6!?) 5 ♗g3 ♘e4 6 ♘bd2 ♘xg3 7 hg ♗g7 = Hort-Browne, 1979

[53]   5 ♘bd2 c5 6 ♘e4 ♕f5 7 ♘g3 ♕f6 8 e3 cd 9 ed b6 10 ♗e2 ♗b7 11 0-0 h5 ∞ Vaganian-Taimanov, USSR 1983

[54]   5 ... ♘c6 6 c3 d5 7 ♘bd2 ♗d7 8 ♗d3 0-0 9 e5 ♕e7 10 b4! ± Vaganian-Psakhis, USSR Ch 1983

5 ... b6 6 ♘c3 ♗b7 7 ♗d3 ♕d8 (7 ... d6 8 ♕e2 ♕d8 9 0-0 ♘d7 10 d5 e5 11 ♗a6 ± Schmidt-Miles, Porz 1981-82) 8 0-0 ♗e7 9 e5 d6 10 ♕e2 ± Bisguier-Kudrin, Philadelphia 1985

[55]   6 ♗d3 g6 7 0-0 ♗g7 8 e5 ♕e7 9 ♕e2 ♘d7 10 c4 c5 ∞ Sideif Zade-A.Ivanov, USSR 1985

6 ♘c3 a6 7 e5 ♕d8 (7 ... de 8 de ♕f4 9 a3! ±) 8 ♗d3 d5 9 ♘e2 c5 10 c3 ♕b6 = Yap-Sax, Szirak 1985; 6 ... ♘d7 7 ♕d2 a6 ∞ And.Martin-Hébert, Hastings 1984-85

[56]   Yusupov-Gurgenidze, USSR 1981

[57]   5 ♘bd2 cd 6 ed ♗b7 7 ♗d3 ♗e7 8 0-0 0-0 9 ♖e1 d6 10 a4 ♘c6 11 c3 ∞/± Spassky-Belyavsky, Montpellier C 1985

[58]   5 ... b5 6 de fe 7 ♗xb5 ♕a5+ 8 ♘c3 ♘e4 9 ♕d3 ± Kavalek

5 ... ed 6 ♘c3 and now:

6 ... ♗b7 7 ♘xd5 ♗xd5 (7 ... ♗e7 8 ♗xf6 ♗xf6 9 c3 ♘c6 10 ♕c2! ± Barlov-Ostermeyer, Biel 1985) 8 ♗xf6 ♕xf6 9 ♕xd5 ♘c6 10 0-0-0 ♖d8 11 ♗b5 ± Barlov-Grünfeld, Biel 1985

6 ... ♗e7 7 ♘xd5 0-0 8 ♗f4 ♘xd5 9 ♕xd5 ♘c6 10 ♖d1 b5 11 ♗d3 ± Welling-Roose,

[59]   7 ... d6 8 ♘d2 e5 9 ♗b5+ ♗d7 10 0-0 ♗xb5 11 ♘xb5 ♕d8 12 f4! a6 13 ♘c3 ± Chernin-Kudrin, Mendoza 1985

[60]   11 ♗c4 ♘a5 12 ♕d3 ♘xc4 13 ♕xc4 ♗e7 14 0-0-0 ± Kavalek-Brunner, Solingen 1986

[61]   4 ... cd 5 ed ♗e7 6 ♘bd2 0-0 7 ♗d3 b6 8 0-0 ♗b7 9 ♖e1 d6 10 ♘f1 ∞/± Palatnik-Przewoznik, Lvov 1986

4 ... h6 5 ♗h4 b6 6 ♘bd2 ♗b7 7 ♗d3 ♗e7 8 c3 cd 9 ed d6 = Nikolić-Spiridonov, Bela Crkva 1986

[62]   5 dc ♗xc5 6 ♗e2 ♗e7 7 c4 b6 8 ♘c3 ♗b7 = Hort-Adorjan, Reggio Emilia 1984-85

5 c3 b6 6 ♗d3 ♗b7 7 0-0 ♘c6 8 ♘bd2 0-0 = Barlov-Adorjan, New York 1985

5 ♗e2 b6 6 0-0 ♗b7 7 c3 ♘c6 8 ♘bd2 0-0 = Pribyl-Tal, Tallinn 1985

[63]   5 ... cd 6 ed b6 7 ♗d3 ♗b7 8 0-0 0-0 9 ♖e1 d6 10 ♖c1 ♘bd7 11 c4 ♖e8 ∞ Bisguier-Wedberg, New York 1986

[64]   6 c3 0-0 7 ♗d3 ♗a6?! 8 ♗xa6 ♘xa6 9 ♕e2 ± Spassky-Alburt, Hollywood 1985

6 dc bc 7 e4 ♘c6 8 ♗b5 ♗b7 9 0-0 0-0 ∞ Utasi-Adorjan, Hungarian Ch 1984

[65]   6 ... cd 7 ed ♘a6 8 ♗xf6 ♗xf6 9 ♘e4 ♗e7 10 d5 ed 11 ♗xa6 ♘xa6 12 ♕xd5 ± Salov-Cebalo, Leningrad 1984

6 ... ♗a6 7 c4 cd 8 ♘xd4 ♗b7 9 0-0 0-0 10 ♕e2 d6! = Belyavsky-Dolmatov, USSR Ch 1986

[66]   7 0-0 cd 8 ed 0-0 9 ♖e1 ♘c6 10 c3 h6 11 ♗h4 ♘d5 = Z.Nikolić-Plachetka, Vrnjačka Banja

1985

67 **7 ...** Nc6 8 0-0-0 9 e4 cd 10 Nxd4 ± Yusupov-Hmadi, Tunis IZ 1985

7 ... cd 8 ed d6 9 0-0 Nbd7 10 Re1 0-0 11 a4 Qc7 ∞ Remon-Utasi, Granma 1986

68 11 Re1 Nbd7 12 a4 a6 13 Nc4 Re8 ∞ Piket-Rogers, Wijk aan Zee II 1985

69 5 Qc1 Ne4 6 Bh4 (6 Bf4!? Hort) 6 ... Nc6 7 Bd3 d5 8 c3 Bd7 9 Nbd2 f5 ∞ Lobron-Korchnoi, Biel 1984

70 5 ... cd 6 Nxd4 a6 7 Be2 Be7 8 Nc4 Qc7 ∞

71 **6 Bxf6** gf 7 Be2 Nc6 8 0-0 cd 9 Nc4 Qb4 10 Rb1 Qe7 11 ed ∞ Hug-Hort, Zürich 1984

6 Rb1!? Qc3 7 Rb3 Qa5 8 Rb5 Qd8 (8 ... Qxa2 9 Bxf6 gf 10 Ne4 a6 11 Rxc5! ± Kopec-de Firmian, USA 1985-86) 9 c4 ∞∞

72 6 ... cd 7 ed Nc6 8 Nc4 Qb4 9 Bd2 = Parma

73 7 c4 Qc3 8 Ke2!? (8 Qe5?! Nc6 9 Rc1 Qa3 10 Nxc6 bc 11 Qc2 Rb8 ∓ Spassky-Miles, Tilburg 1978) 8 ... Nbd7 9 Qa4 ∞ *ECO*

74 Vaganian-Razuvayev, USSR 1983

75 4 ... c5 5 0-0 cd 6 Nxd4 d5 7 Nc3 e6 8 e4! ±

76 5 ... c5 6 dc Na6 7 Be3! Ne4 8 Bd4 Bh6 9 Ne5 ± Geller

77 6 Nbd2 Nc6 7 c3 e5 8 de de 9 Nb3 Qe7 =

78 6 ... c5 7 Bb2 Ne4 8 Nbd2 f5 ∞

79 8 ... de 9 e4 Nc6 10 Nbd2 b6 11 Qe2 Qe7 12 Rfd1 ± Polugayevsky

80 Polugayevsky-Stein, USSR Ch 1969

81 3 ... c5 4 c3 b6 5 dc!? bc 6 e4 Bb7 7 Bc4 e6 8 Nbd2 ∞ Plaskett-Razuvayev, Manchester 1983

82 4 Nc3 Nh5 5 Be5 f6 6 g4 fe 7 gh ed ∓ Morgado-Estrin, corr. 1983

4 Nbd2 0-0 5 e4 d6 6 Bd3 Nc6 7 d5 e5! Herzog-Hort, Zürich 1984

83 5 h3 c5 6 c3 Qb6 7 Qb3 Nc6! =

84 5 ... d5 6 h3 c5 7 c3 Nc6 8 0-0 Nd7 9 Nbd2 b6 10 Qa4 ± Langeweg-Kouatly, Montpellier Z 1985

85 6 ... Nbd7 7 Bh2 (7 0-0 Qe8 8 Bh2 e5 9 c3 Qe7 10 a4 Re8 11 a5 ± J.Garcia-Vaganian, Dubai Ol 1986; 7 ... Ne4 =) 7 ... Qe8 8 c4 Ne4! =

86 Bellon-Timman, Thessaloniki Ol 1984

87 3 ... Ne4 4 Bh4 c5 5 c3 Bg7 6 Nbd2 Nxd2 7 Qxd2 cd 8 Nxd4! 0-0 9 e4 ± Bellon-Fraguela, Lanzarote 1975

88 4 ... c5 and now:
5 b6 6 c3 Bb7 7 Qa4 0-0 8 Be2 d6 9 0-0 Nbd7 10 b4 Qc7 ∞ Kovačević-Larsen, Bugojno 1984

5 Bxf6 Bxf6 6 Ne4 Bxd4 (6 ... Qb6 7 Nxf6+ Qxf6 8 c3 cd 9 Qxd4 Qxd4 10 Nxd4 = Torre-Timman, London 1984) 7 Nxd4 cd 8 Qxd4 0-0-0 9 0-0-0 Nc6 10 Qd2 d5!? ∞ Agzamov-Loginov, USSR 1986

89 5 e3 0-0 6 Bd3 Nbd7 7 0-0 h6 8 Be3 e5 9 de Nxe5 =

90 5 ... h6 6 Bh4 g5 7 Bg3 Nh5 8 c3 Nd7 9 Nc4 Nxg3 10 hg e6 11 Bd3 Qe7 12 Qa4 a6 13 Ne3 c6 ∞ Chernin-Short, Wijk aan Zee 1986

91 **6 ... Nbd7** 7 Nc4 e5 8 0-0 Qe7 9 Re1 Re8 10 Qb3 h6 11 Bh4 ± Kuijf-Scheeren, Hilversum 1984

6 ... h6 7 Bh4 Qe8 8 Bd3 e5 9 de de 10 0-0 Nbd7 11 Re1 Nc5 12 Bf1 Bg4 13 Qe2 ± Torre-Gutman, Biel IZ 1985

92 8 Bc4 Nc6 9 0-0 Qc7 10 Qe2 Na5! 11 Bd3 h6 =

93 11 Be3 b6 12 Qc2 Bb7 ∞ Khalifman-Howell, Groningen 1985-86

Budapest Gambit 1 d4 Nf6 2 c4 e5[1] 3 de

	3	4	5	6	7	8	9	10	11	
1	...	Nf3[2]	a3![4]	ed[6]	Nbd2	Nxe4[7]	e3![8]	Bd3[9]		±/±
	Ne4	Nc6[3]	d6[5]	Bxd6	Bf5	Bxe4	Qf6			

1 d4 Nf6 2 c4 e5 3 de Ng4

	4	5	6	7	8	9	10	11	12	
2	Nf3[10]	Bg5!?[11]	Bxe7	Nc3	Nd5	e3	Nxe5	Be2	0-0[13]	±
	Nc6	Be7	Qxe7	0-0[12]	Qd8	Ngxe5	Nxe5	d6		
3	...	e3	Be2[14]	0-0[16]	Nc3	Nxe5[17]	b3	Bb2[19]	Qd5![20]	±
	Bc5	Nc6	0-0[15]	Re8	Ngxe5	Nxe5	a5[18]	Ra6	Ba7[21]	
4	Bf4	Nf3	Nc3	bc	Qd5	ef	Qd3[25]	Bg5[26]	e3	∞
	Nc6[22]	Bb4+[23]	Bxc3+	Qe7	f6[24]	Nxf6	d6	0-0[27]	Bg4[28]	
5	...	...	Nbd2	e3![29]	Nxe5	Be2	0-0	Qxd2	Rfd1	±
	...	...	Qe7	Ngxe5	Nxe5	0-0	Bxd2	d6	b6[30]	

[1] 2 ... b6 3 Nc3 Bb7 4 Qc2! d5 5 cd Nxd5 6 Nf3 (6 e4 ±) ± ECO

[2] 4 Qc2 d5 5 ed Bf5 6 Nc3 Nxd6 7 e4 ∞

[3] 4 ... Bb4+ 5 Nbd2 (5 Bd2 Bc5 6 e3 Nc6 7 Nc3 Nxd2 8 Qxd2 0-0 9 Nd5 ± ECO) 5 ... Nc6 6 a3 Nxd2 7 Bxd2 Bxd2+ 8 Qxd2 Qe7 9 Qc3 b6!? (9 ... 0-0 10 Rd1 Re8 11 Rd5 ± Smyslov-Steiner, Groningen 1946) 10 e3 Bb7 11 Be2 0-0-0 12 0-0-0 Rhe8 13 Rd5! ± Zsinka-Kamp, Dortmund 1986

[4] 5 Nbd2 Bc5 6 e3!? (6 a3 Qe7 7 e3 ± ECO) 6 ... g5 7 h3 Bg7 8 Be2 Qe7 9 a3 Nxe5 10 Nxe5 Bxe5 11 Nf3 Bf6 12 Qc2 ± Johansson-Nielsen, Randaberg 1985-86

[5] 5 ... a5 6 b3 d6 7 Bb2 Be7 8 Nbd2 ±

[6] 6 Qc2 d5 (6 ... Bf5 7 Nc3! Nxf2 8 Qxf5 Nxh1 9 e6 ± Reshevsky-Bisguier, New York 1954-55) 7 e3 Bg4 8 cd Qxd5 9 Bc4 ± Bisguier-Ljubojević, Malaga 1971

[7] 8 e3 Qf6 9 Be2 0-0-0 10 Nxe4 Bxe4 11 Qa4 Rhe8 ∞∞

[8] 9 Bg5 f6 10 Be3 Qe7 11 Qa4 0-0-0 12 Nd2 Bg6 ∞∞

[9] Dlugy-Aristizabal, Montpellier 1985

[10] 4 e4 Nxe5 5 f4 Nec6 6 Nf3 (6 Be3 Bb4+ 7 Nd2 Qe7 ∞ N.Nikolić-Lev, Groningen 1985-86) 6 ... Bc5 7 Nc3 d6 8 Bd3 Bg4 (8 ... 0-0 9 Bd2 Re8 10 Qe2 Bg4 11 0-0-0 ± Šahović-Haik, Panchevo 1986) 9 h3 Bxf3 10 Qxf3 Nd4 11 Qg4 ∞

4 e3!? Nxe5 5 Nc3 Nbc6 6 Nh3!? Bb4 7 Bd2 0-0 8 Nf4 Re8 9 Be2 Bf8 10 0-0 d6 11 Nfd5 ± Ubilava-Toshkov, Varna 1986

[11] 5 Nc3 Ngxe5 6 Nxe5 Nxe5 7 Qc2 Bb4 = Hebden-Hodgson, Guernsey 1985

5 e3 Ngxe5 6 Be2 g6 7 Nc3 Nxf3+ 8 Bxf3 Bg7 9 Qd2 d6 10 b3 Ne5 ∞ Sosonko-Ree, Amsterdam 1982

5 a3 Ngxe5 6 Nxe5 Nxe5 7 e4 Be7 8 Be2 ± ECO

[12] 7 ... Ncxe5 8 Nd5 Nd6 9 e3 c6 10 Nxe5 Nxe5 11 Nc3 ± Polugayevsky

[13] Polugayevsky-Nunn, Biel 1986

[14] 6 Bd2 0-0 7 Bc3 Qe7 (7 ... Re8 8 Nbd2 a5 9 Bd3 Bb4 10 Qc2 g6 11 e6! ± Ftacnik-Blatny, Czechoslovak Ch 1986) 8 Be2 Ngxe5 9 Nxe5 Nxe5 10 0-0 a5 11 Nd2 Bb4 =

6 Nc3 Ngxe5 (6 ... Ncxe5 7 h3 Nxf3+ 8 Qxf3 Ne5 9 Qg3 Ng6 10 h4! ± Hort-Novoselsky, Böblingen 1986) 7 Be2 Nxf3+ 8 Bxf3 0-0 9 0-0 d6 10 Be2 d6 11 Na4 Bb6 12 b3 ∞ Karolyi-Rogers, Tallinn 1985

6 a3 a5 7 b3 0-0 8 Bb2 (8 Nc3 Re8 9 Be2 ± ECO) 8 ... Re8 9 Bd3 Ra6 10 e6! ± Schneider-Moroz, USSR 1986

[15] 6 ... Ngxe5 7 0-0 0-0 8 Nc3 Re8 – 7 ... Re8

[16] 7 Nc3!? Re8 8 b3 Ncxe5 9 Nxe5 Nxe5 10 Bb2 ± Banas-Kouatly, Trnava 1986

[17] 9 b3 a5 10 Bb2 Nxf3+ 11 Bxf3 Ne5 12 Be2 Ra6 13 Qd5! (13 Ne4 Ba7 14 Qd5 Rae6 15 Qa5 ∞ Oll-Romero, Groningen 1984-85) 13 ... Ba7 (13 ... Qe7 14 Ne4 Ba7 15 c5! ± Akesson-Tagnon, Berlin 1984) 14 c5!? ±

[18] 10 ... d6 11 Bb2 Re6 12 g3 ± Gheorghiu-Terreaux, Mendisio 1985

[19] 11 a3!? d6 (11 ... Ra6 12 Nd5! ±) 12 Bb2 ±

[20] 12 ♘e4 ♗a7 13 ♕d5 ♖ae6 14 ♕xa5 ♗b6 15 ♕c3 ♕h4 ∞ Vainerman-Legky, USSR 1986

[21] 13 c5 ♖h6 14 f4 ♕h4 15 h3 ±

[22] 4 ... g5?! 5 ♗g3 (5 ♗d2 ♘xe5 6 ♘c3 ♘bc6 7 e3 ♗b4 8 ♘f3 ±) 5 ... ♗g7 6 ♘f3 ♘c6 7 ♘c3 ♘gxe5 8 ♘xe5 ♘xe5 9 e3 d6 10 h4! h6 11 c5! ±/± Schüssler-Herrera Perez, Havana 1985

[23] 5 ... ♗c5?! 6 e3 ♕e7 7 ♘c3 ♗b4 8 ♖c1 0-0 9 ♗e2 ± Barigov-Shabalov, Jurmala 1985

[24] 8 ... ♕a3 9 ♖c1 ♘e7 10 ♕d2 ♘g6 11 ♗g3 h5 12 h3 h4 13 ♗f4 ± Gheorghiu-Shipman, USA 1979

[25] 10 ♕d1 d6 11 e3 0-0 12 ♗e2 ♘e4 13 ♖c1 ♔h8 14 0-0 g5 ∓ Inkiov-Djukić, Bor 1983

[26] 11 e3 0-0 12 ♗e2 (12 ♕c2 ♘c5 13 ♗e2 0-0 14 ♘d4 ♘e5 = Dolmatov-Malanyuk, USSR Ch 1986) 12 ... ♘e4 (12 ... g5 13 ♗g3 h5 14 h4 g4 ∞ Nunn) 13 ♘d4 ♘xf2!? (13 ... ♘c5?! 14 ♕c2 ±

Cvitan-Djukić, Medulin 1983) 14 ♔xf2 g5 15 g3 ♗h3 ∞ Djukić

[27] 11 ... ♗g4 12 ♗xf6 ♕xf6 13 ♕e4+ ♘e7 ∞ Nunn

[28] 12 ... h6 13 ♗h4 ♗g4 14 ♗e2 ± Dlugy-McCambridge, US Ch 1985

12 ... ♗g4 13 ♗e2 ♘e5 (13 ... ♕f7 14 ♗xf6 ♕xf6 15 0-0 ♔h8 16 ♘d4 ± Dlugy-Horvath, Sharjan 1985) 14 ♘xe5 ♗xe2 15 ♕xe2 ♕xe5 16 ♗xf6 ♖xf6 ∞ Schmidt-Klarić, Vinkovci 1986

[29] 7 a3 ♘gxe5 8 ♘xe5 ♘xe5 9 e3 ♗xd2+ 10 ♕xd2 d6 11 ♗e2 (11 ♕c3 0-0 ∞) 11 ... b6 (11 ... a5 12 ♖c1 0-0 13 b3 b6 14 0-0 ♗b7 15 ♗g3 ± Korchnoi-Kaposztas, Berlin 1985) 12 e4 ♗b7 13 f3 0-0-0 14 0-0-0 f6 15 h4 h5 ∞ Browne-Speelman, Taxco IZ 1985

[30] 13 b4 ± Garcia Palermo-Rogers, Reggio Emilia 1984-85

		Old Indian		1 d4 ♘f6 2 c4 d6				

	3	4	5	6	7	8	9	10	11	
1	♘f3	♕b3[2]	h3	♕xf3	♘c3[5]	g3	e3	♗g2	♕d1!	±
	♗g4[1]	♕c8	♗xf3[3]	g6[4]	♗g7	♘c6	0-0	♖e8	e6[6]	
2	♘c3	de[7]	♕xd8+	♘f3[8]	♗d2[10]	g4	g5	h4	♗e3	±
	e5	de	♔xd8	♘fd7[9]	c6	a5	♘a6	♘ac5	f5[11]	

[1] 3 ... ♗f5 4 ♘c3 ♘bd7 5 g3 e5 6 ♗g2 c6 7 0-0 (7 ♘h4 ed 8 ♘xf5 dc 9 b3 ♕c7! ∓ D.Gurevich-Gheorghiu, New York 1986) 7 ... h6 8 ♘h4 ♗h7 9 e4 ♕b6 10 d5 ♕a6 11 b3 ♘c5 12 ♖e1 ± Andersson-Westerinen, Stockholm 1972

[2] 4 ♘c3 ♘bd7 5 e4 e5 6 ♗e2 (6 ♗e3 ed 7 ♗xd4 g6 8 ♗e2 Sosonko-Kavalek, Hanover 1983) 6 ... ed!? 7 ♕xd4 ♗xe2 8 ♕xe2 g6 9 0-0 ♗g7 10 ♗f4 0-0 11 ♖ad1 h6 12 ♗e3 ♖e8 = Andersson-Spassky, Bugojno 1982

[3] 5 ... ♗h5 6 g4 ♗g6 7 ♗g2 ♘bd7 8 ♗f4 c6 9 ♘c3 e6 10 0-0 ♗e7 11 ♖ac1 ± Sosonko-Kovačević, Amsterdam 1973

[4] 6 ... e5 7 d5 ♘a6 8 e4 ♘b4 9 ♘a3 ♗e7 10 ♗e2 ±

[5] 7 g3 ♗g7 8 ♗g2 ♘c6 9 e3 0-0 10 ♘c3 e5 11 de de 12 ♘d5 ♘d7 ∞ Keene-Larsen, Orense 1975

[6] 12 0-0 d5 13 b3! ± Portisch-Larsen, Tilburg 1979

[7] 4 d5 ♗e7 5 e4 0-0 6 ♗d3 ♘bd7 7 e3 c6 8 h3 a6 9 ♘ge2 cd 10 cd b5 = Tal
4 e3 ♘bd7 5 ♗d3 g6 6 ♘ge2 ♗g7 7 a4 a5! = Foisor-Gheorghiu, Romania 1986

[8] 6 ♗g5 c6 7 0-0-0 ♔c7 8 ♘f3 ♘bd7 =

[9] 6 ... ♘bd7 7 ♖g1 c6 8 g4 h6 9 h4 e4 10 ♘d4 ±

[10] 7 ♗e3!? c6 8 g4 ♗b4 9 ♗d2 ♘a6 10 ♖d1 ± Hort-Ciocaltea, Skopje 1969

[11] 12 gf gf 13 0-0-0 ± Spassky-Gheorghiu, Siegen Ol 1970

	3	4	5	6	7	8	9	10	11	
3	♘c3 / e5	♘f3 / e4[12]	♗g5[13] / ♗f5[14]	g4! / ♗xg4[15]	♘gxe4[16] / ♘xe4[17]	♘xe4 / ♗e7[18]	♗g2![19] / ♕d7	♕b3 / c6	♘g3 / ♕c7[20]	±
4	... / ♘bd7	♘f3[21] / e5[22]	g3 / ♗e7[23]	♗g2 / 0-0	0-0[24] / c6	e4[25] / ♕c7[26]	b3[27] / a6	♗b2 / b5	♕e2! / bc[28]	∞/±
5	... / ...	... / ...	♗g5 / ♗e7[29]	e3 / 0-0[30]	♕c2[31] / c6[32]	♗d3[33] / h6[34]	h4[35] / ♖e8[36]	de[37] / de	♗xf6 / ♘xf6[38]	∞/±
6	... / ...	... / ...	e4 / c6	♗e2 / ♗e7[39]	0-0 / 0-0[40]	h3[41] / ♖e8[42]	♗e3 / a6	♖e1[43] / ♕c7	♗f1 / h6[44]	∞/±
7	...	...	...	...	...	♖b1 / ♖e8[45]	♕c2 / a6[46]	b4 / ♕c7	h3! / ed[47]	±
8	...	...	...	...	...	♖e1 / a6[48]	♗f1[49] / b5[50]	a3[51] / ♖e8	h3[52] / ♗b7[53]	±
9	...	...	...	...	...	♕c2 / a6[54]	♖d1[55] / ♕c7	♗g5[56] / h6[57]	♗h4 / ♖e8[58]	±

[12] 4 ... ♘c6 5 g3 ♗e7 6 ♗g2 0-0 7 0-0 ♗g4 8 d5 ♘b8 9 h3 ± Uhlmann.

[13] 5 ♘d2 ♗f5 (5 ... ♕e7 6 ♕c2 ♗f5 7 f3 ♘c6 8 fe ♗g6 9 e3 0-0-0 10 a3 ± Donner-Vasyukov, Wijk aan Zee 1983) 6 e3 c6 7 ♗e2 d5 8 ♕b3 ♕d7 9 cd cd 10 f4 ∞/±

[14] 5 ... ♕e7!? 6 ♕c2 (6 h4 c6 7 ♘h3 h6 8 ♗f4 ♘h5 9 e3 g6 ∞ Douven-Gheorghiu, Amsterdam 1986) 6 ... ♗f5 7 g4 ♗g6 8 ♗g2 ♘c6 9 ♘gxe4 ♘xe4 10 ♗xe4 ♘xd4 11 ♕d3 ♘e6 12 ♗e3 ± Farago-Gheorghiu, Baile Herculane Z 1982

[15] 6 ... ♗g6 7 ♗g2 ♕e7 8 ♕c2 ± Milić

[16] 7 ♗g2 ♘c6 (7 ... ♗e7!? ∞ Kasparov-Speelman, Belfort 1988) 8 ♘gxe4 ♘xe4 9 ♗xe4 g6!? 10 ♕d3 f5 11 ♕e3 ♗e7 ∞

[17] 7 ... ♘bd7 8 ♕d3 ♗e7 9 ♕g3 ♗f5 10 ♗g2 ± Alburt-Ginsburg, Lone Pine 1980

[18] 8 ... d5 9 ♘c3 dc 10 ♕a4+ ♕d7 11 ♕xc4 ♕c6 12 ♕b5 ±

[19] 9 b3 ♘c6 10 ♗g2 0-0 11 ♗b2 a5 12 ♘g3 ♖e8 = Portisch-Schmid, Oberhausen 1961

[20] 12 0-0 0-0 13 ♗f4 ± Pinter-McNab, Malta Ol 1980

[21] 4 e4 e5 5 d5 (5 ♘ge2 ♗e7 6 f3 c6 7 ♗e3 0-0 = Novikov-Dorfman, USSR Ch 1984) 5 ... ♘c5 (5 ... ♗e7 6 ♘ge2 0-0 7 ♘g3 c6 8 ♗e3 a6 9 ♘f5 ± Miles-Stein, Ostend 1986) 6 f3 a5 7 ♗e3 ♗e7 8 ♕d2 h6 9 0-0-0 ♗d7 10 g3 ∞/± Miles-Mestel, Esbjerg 1984

[22] 4 ... c6 5 g3 ♘b6 6 b3 ♗g4 7 ♗g2 e6 8 0-0 d5 9 ♘e5 ± A.Petrosian-Lputian, USSR 1984

[23] 5 ... c6 6 e4 ♗e7 7 ♗g2 0-0 8 0-0 a6 (8 ... ♖e8 9 b3 ♗f8 10 ♗b2 a6 11 ♕c2 b5 12 cb ab 13 ♖fd1 ± Kurtenkov-Gligorić, Plovdiv 1986) 9 a4 a5 10 h3 ♖e8 11 ♗e3 ed 12 ♗xd4 ± Bareyev-Malanyuk, USSR 1986

[24] 7 e4 a6! 8 0-0 b5 9 ♕e2 c6 10 c5 ♖e8! = Polugayevsky-Larsen, Mar del Plata 1982

[25] 8 ♖b1 ed 9 ♕xd4 a5 10 b3 ♘c5 11 ♗b2 ♖e8 12 ♖bd1 ♗f8 = Donchev-Ermenkov, Prague Z 1985
   8 ♕c2 and now:
   8 ... ♕c7 9 b3 ♖e8 10 e3 ♘f8 11 ♗b2 ♘g6 12 h3 ♗d7 ∞ Korchnoi-Ivanović, Titograd 1984
   8 ... ♖e8 9 b3 ♘f8 10 e4 (10 ♗b2 a6 11 e4 ♕c7 12 ♖ac1 b6 13 ♖fd1 ♗b7 14 ♖d2 ed 15 ♘xd4 b5 16 cb c5 ∞ Portisch-Vaganian, Montpellier C 1985) 10 ... a6 11 ♖d1 b5 12 c5 ♕c7 13 cd ♗xd6 14 ♗b2 ♗b7 15 ∞ Timman-Tal, Montpellier C 1985

[26] 8 ... a6 9 d5 cd 10 cd b5 11 ♘e1 ♘b6 12 ♘d3 ♗d7 13 b3 ± Dlugy-Day, Toronto 1985; 9 h3 ♖e8 10 ♗e3 ♘f8 11 d5 ± A.Petrosian-Gulko, USSR 1984

[27] 9 ♕c2 a6 10 ♗g5 h6 11 ♗xf6 ♘xf6 12 h3 ♗e6! ∓ Kirov-Tal, Albena 1984

[28] 12 ♕xc4 a5 13 de de 14 ♖fc1 ± Polugayevsky-Espig, Budapest 1975

[29] 5 ... c6 6 ♕c2! (6 a3!? ♗e7 7 ♕c2 0-0 8 e3 ♖e8 9 ♗d3 ed 10 ed ± Burger-Lein, New York 1984) ± Adorjan

[30] 6 ... c6 7 ♕c2 ♕a5 8 ♗d3 a6 9 0-0 h6 10 ♗h4 0-0 11 a4 ♖e8 12 b4 ± Grivas-Burgess, Sharjan 1985

[31] 7 ♗e2 c6 8 0-0 ♘e8 9 ♗xe7 ♕xe7 10 ♕c2 ± Wallinger-Werner, Hamburg 1984

32 7 ... ♘e8 8 ♗xe7 ♕xe7 9 0-0-0 ♘ef6 10 ♖g1! ± Christiansen-Frias, New York 1985

7 ... h6 8 ♗h4 ed 9 ♘xd4 ♘e5 10 ♗e2 ♖e8 11 0-0 ± Ogaard-Moen, Gausdal 1985

33 8 ♗e2 h6!? 9 ♗h4 ♘h5 10 ♗xe7 ♕xe7 ∞

34 8 ... ♖e8 9 0-0 ♕c7 10 h3 ♘f8 11 ♖ad1 ± Polugayevsky-Mochalov, USSR 1978

35 9 ♗h4 ♘h5 10 ♗xe7 ♕xe7 11 0-0 g6 12 ♘d2 ∞/± Ree-Hug, Las Palmas 1973

36 9 ... b5 10 de ♘xe5 11 ♘xe5 de 12 0-0-0 ♕a5 13 ♔b1 ± Kasparov-Larsen, Tilburg 1981

37 10 ♗xf6 ♗xf6 11 0-0-0 ed 12 ♘xd4 ♘e5 13 ♗e2 ♘g4 14 ♗xg4 ♗xg4 15 f3 ♗d7 ∞ Alburt-Morovic, Santiago 1981

38 12 ♘xe5 ♕a5 13 ♘f3 ∞/± Glek-Podgayets, USSR 1984

39 6 ... a6 7 d5 ♗e7 8 0-0 0-0 9 ♗e3 cd 10 cd b5 11 ♘d2 ♘b6 12 a4 ± Rukavina-Kovačević, Yugoslavia 1984

40 **7 ... a6** 8 ♘h4! g6 9 ♗h6 ± Miles-Larsen, London 1980

7 ... ♕c7 8 ♖e1 ♘f8 9 c5 dc 10 de ♘g4 11 ♘d5! ± Bareyev-Serper, USSR 1985

41 **8 ♗e3** ♖e8 9 d5 a6 10 ♘d2 ♕c7 11 b4 ♕b8 12 ♘b3 cd 13 cd ♗d8 ∞ Rukavina-Ivanović, Budva 1986

8 d5 ♘c5 (8 ... a6 9 ♗e3 cd 10 cd b5 11 ♘d2 ♘xe4!? 12 ♘cxe4 f5 13 a4 ba 14 ♕xa4 fe 15 ♘xe4 ± Kasparov-Stein, West Germany 1986) 9 ♕c2 cd 10 cd ♕c7! 11 ♘d2 ♗d7 12 a4 ♖ac8 = Kasparov-Larsen, Bugojno 1982

42 8 ... a6 9 ♕c2 ♕c7 10 ♖e1 ♖e8 11 ♗g5 h6 12 ♗e3 ♕b8 13 a3 ♗f8 14 d5 ± Rogers-Ivanović, Reggio Emilia 1984-85

43 10 ♕c2 b5 11 b4 ♗b7 12 ♖fd1 ♕c7 13 ♖ac1 ed 14 ♘xd4 ♗f8 15 ♕b3 ± Murei-Dzindzihashvili, New York 1983

44 12 ♖c1 ♕b8 13 b4 ed 14 ♘xd4 ♗f8 15 ♗f4 ∞/± Pinter-Ivanović, Thessaloniki Ol 1984

45 **8 ... ed** 9 ♘xd4 d5!? 10 ed cd 11 cd ♘b6 12 ♕b3 ± Conquest-Dunnington, Oakham 1986

8 ... a6 9 b4 b5 10 c5 ♕c7 11 de! de 12 ♕c2 ♖d8 13 ♗b2 h6 14 ♘d1 ♘h7 15 ♘e3 ± Gligorić-Rasmussen, Plovdiv 1986

46 9 ... ♗f8 10 ♖d1 a6 11 b4 ♕c7 12 ♗e3 ± Sosonko-Larsen, Tilburg 1981

47 12 ♘xd4 ♗f8 13 ♗f4 b5 14 ♘f3! ± Gligorić-Vaganian, Sochi 1986

48 8 ... h6 9 ♕c2 ♘h7 10 ♗e3 ♘g5 11 ♖ad1 ± Spassov-Lukov, Primorsko 1985

49 **9 a4** a5 10 h3 ♘e8!? 11 ♕c2 ♘c7 12 ♗e3 ♘a6 ∞ Yusupov-Kovačević, Indonesia 1983

9 d5 ♘c5 10 ♘d2 a5 11 b3 ♗d7 12 a3 ♕b6 13 ♖b1 ♖fc8 = Short-Spiridonov, Plovdiv 1983

50 9 ... ♖e8 10 ♖b1 (10 h3 ♕c7 11 ♖b1 b5 12 a3 ♗b7 13 b4 ± Cebalo-Ivanović, Novi Sad 1984) 10 ... ♕c7 11 ♗g5 h6 12 ♗h4 b5 13 b4 ± Panchenko-Zaid, Kiev 1986

51 10 b3 ♗b7 11 ♗b2 ♖e8 12 d5 b4 = Schmidt-Rajković, Smederevo 1981

52 11 ♗g5!? ♗b7 12 ♖c1 h6 13 ♗xf6 ♗xf6 14 d5 cd 15 ♘xd5 ♗xd5 16 ♕xd5 ♘b6 ∞ Nikitin-Podgayets, USSR 1985

53 **12 ♕c2** ♖c8 13 ♗e3 ♕c7 14 ♖ad1 ± Razuvayev-Malanyuk, Minsk 1985

12 ♗g5!? h6 13 ♗h4 ♕b8 14 ♗g3 ♗f8 15 b4 ♕a7 16 ♖a2 g6 17 ♖d2 ± Balashov-Tukmakov, USSR 1984

54 **8 ... ♖e8** 9 de de 10 ♖d1 ♕c7 11 a3 ♘f8 12 h3 ♘e6 13 ♗e3 h6 14 ♖ac1 ±

8 ... ♕c7 9 ♗g5 ♖e8 10 h3 (10 d5 h6 11 ♗e3 ♘f8 12 ♖ac1 ♘g6 13 b4 ♘g4 = Braga-Douven, Amsterdam 1986) 10 ... h6 11 ♗h4 ♘h5 12 ♗xe7 ♖xe7 13 ♖fd1 ♘f4 14 ♗f1 ± Kouatly-Vaganian, Lucerne 1985

55 **9 ♗e3** ♖e8 10 ♖ad1 ♕c7 11 h3 ♗f8 12 a3 b5 13 cb cb 14 d5 ♘b6 = Dolmatov-Malanyuk, Kostroma 1985

9 h3 b5 10 c5 ♗b7 11 cd ♗xd6 12 ♗g5 h6 13 ♗h4 ed ∞ Rogers-Lobron, Biel 1986

56 **10 ♗d2** b5 11 cb cb 12 ♖ac1 ♕b8 13 a4 b4 ∞ Eingorn-Malanyuk, Kiev 1986

10 h3 b5 11 a3 ♗b7 12 ♗e3 ♖fe8! (12 ... ♖ac8 13 ♖ac1 ♕b8 14 ♕b1 ed 15 ♘xd4 g6 16 ♘b3 ± Short-Hort-Arnhem/Amsterdam 1983) 13 cb cb 14 d5 ♖ec8 = F.Garcia-Christiansen, Dubai Ol 1986

57 10 ... ♖e8 11 ♖ac1 b6 12 b4 ♗b7 13 d5! (13 b5 ∞ Anand-Lobron, Philadelphia 1986) 13 ... c5 14 a3 ±

58 **12 h3** b6 13 ♗g3 ♗b7 14 c5! ± Yusupov-Vaganian, Montpellier C 1985

12 c5!? ∞/± Belyavsky-Malanyuk, USSR Ch 1986

Queen's Gambit

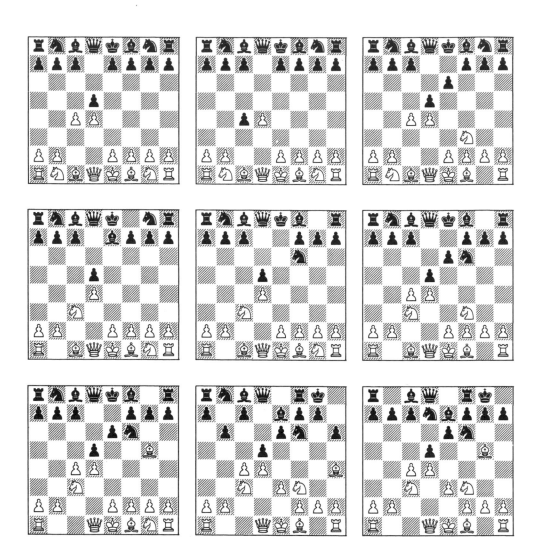

Miscellaneous

Of Black's various ways of refusing rather than declining the Queen's Gambit, the most dynamic are the **Albin Countergambit** (2 ... e5) and the **Chigorin Defence** (2 ... ♘c6). The Albin is an infrequent choice that has probably been underestimated. White is well advised to spurn the prospect of a material plus in return for the bishop pair and a small but tangible edge. The Chigorin has been attracting more followers of late but cannot be said to have gained full respectability. White seems able to wend his way through to a slight superiority in most cases but the complexion of the defence is unusual and consequently it is hard to handle.

Queen's Gambit Accepted *(2 ... dc)*

Black's temporary loss of central control does not seem to handicap him, but his subsequent hopes of keeping the balance must be based on undermining White's d4 pawn with either ... e5 or ... c5. In the latter case he should familiarize himself with the standard isolated queen's pawn positions that can also arise from the Nimzo-Indian, Semi-Tarrasch and Panov Caro-Kann.

The QGA has had a dependable reputation for over sixty years now. Marshall, Capablanca, Rubinstein, Bogoljubow, Bronstein, Smyslov, Petrosian, Portisch, Korchnoi and Tal have all played both sides of the position – a sure sign of its vitality.

Queen's Gambit Declined *(2 ... e6)*

Not the most enterprising choice of defence, the Queen's Gambit Declined sets out to neutralize White's opening advantage. The Black position requires accuracy in order to avoid permanent congestion but if it is well handled Black can achieve level prospects.

The **Exchange Variation** (3 ♘c3 ♘f6 4 cd ed) leads to a formation well studied and well mapped and it is a handy position to know. White strives to fracture the Black queenside with the 'minority attack' (b4-b5) in order to create and fix a pawn weakness on c6 or d5. In the meantime Black balances kingside counterplay with keeping a watchful eye on his queen's wing. A rarer treatment involves White castling long and launching a full-scale kingside attack. This policy entails considerable risk but White may have a minuscule plus.

The **Ragozin** (3 ♘c3 ♘f6 4 ♘f3 ♗b4) is a hybrid system which often transposes into the Nimzo-Indian. The **Vienna Variation** (5 ♗g5 dc) has risen from the junkheap to enjoy fashionability. An intricate tactical line, White appears slightly better *at the moment*, but in such sharp variations . . .

The **Orthodox Variation** (3 ♘c3 ♘f6 4 ♗g5 ♗e7 5 e3 0-0 6 ♘f3 ♘bd7) is the classical answer to the Queen's Gambit. Black methodically seeks equality by negotiating exchanges and achieving either ... e5 or ... c5. White can preserve some semblance of an advantage but the sterile nature of the line makes it hard to realize.

The **Lasker Defence** (3 ♘c3 ♘f6 4 ♗g5 ♗e7 5 e3 0-0 6 ♘f3 h6 7 ♗h4 ♘e4) aims at a quick balance by a rapid exchange of material. Like other variations in this section it is not clear whether Black equalizes or still labours under a microscopic disadvantage. In either case he should be able to keep matters under control.

The **Tartakower (Makagonov-Bondarevsky) System** (3 ♘c3 ♘f6 4 ♗g5 ♗e7 5 e3 0-0 6 ♘f3 h6 7 ♗h4 b6) has been a favourite of Soviet world champions, figuring prominently in the repertoires of Petrosian, Spassky and Karpov. It is more complex strategically than the Orthodox. White can maintain a structural advantage but Black gains compensatory piece activity.

5 ... h6 6 ♗xf6 / 6 ... h6 7 ♗xf6 was the topic of years of constant debate after Kasparov and Karpov battered each other with it during their long-running title dispute. Unsurprisingly, such scrupulous attention unearthed defensive resources and the line currently rests in approximate equilibrium.

This line and the Tartakower System have proved their durability at the highest level.

References: *Queen's Gambit Accepted* (Gufeld)
Queen's Gambit: Orthodox Defence (Polugayevsky)
The Closed Openings in Action (Karpov)

1 d4 d5 2 c4

	2	3	4	5	6	7	8	9	10	
1	...	cd	e4[2]	dc	♘c3[3]	b4!	♕c2	a3	♘xd5	±
	c5[1]	♘f6	♘xe4	♘xc5	e6	♕f6	♘ca6	ed	♕e5+[4]	
2	...	♘f3[5]	♕b3[6]	c5[7]	♗f4[8]	e3	a3	♗g3	♗e2	±
	♗f5	e6	♘c6	♖b8	♘ge7[9]	a6	♘g6	♗e7	0-0[10]	
3	...	♘f3[12]	cd[13]	dc[14]	♘c3	e4	f3	g3	♗e3	∞
	♘c6[11]	♗g4	♗xf3	♗xc6	e6[15]	♗b4	♕h4+[16]	♕f6	0-0-0[17]	
4	...	♘c3	♘f3[19]	cd	e4	bc	d5	♕a4+	♘xe5	±
	...	♘f6[18]	♗g4	♘xd5	♘xc3[20]	e5	♘b8	♘d7	♕f6[21]	
5	...	de	♘f3	♘bd2[23]	a3[24]	h3	♘xf3	g3	♗g2	±/±
	e5[22]	d4	♘c6	♗g4	a5[25]	♗xf3[26]	♗c5	♘ge7	0-0[27]	
6	...	...	...	g3	♘bd2	a3[30]	b4[31]	♗g2[32]	e6[33]	±/±
	...	...	...	♗e6[28]	♕d7[29]	♘ge7	♘g6	♗h3		
7	...	...	...	...	♗g2[34]	0-0	♕b3[36]	♖d1	♕xf3	±/±
	...	...	...	♗g4	♕d7	0-0-0[35]	♘ge7	♗xf3	♘g6[37]	

---

[1] 2 ... ♘f6 3 cd ♘xd5 4 ♘f3! ♗f5 5 ♕b3 ±

[2] 4 ♘f3 cd 5 ♘xd4 ♘xd5 6 e4 ♘c7 (6 ... ♘b4 7 ♕a4+ ♘4c6 8 ♘xc6 ♘xc6 9 ♗e3 ±) 7 ♘c3 e5 8 ♘db5 ± Timman-Miles, Nikšić 1983
4 dc ♕xd5 5 ♗d2 ♘e4 6 ♘f3 e5 7 ♘c3 ♘xc3 8 ♗xc3 ♕xd1+ 9 ♖xd1 ±/±

[3] 6 ♘f3 e6 7 ♘c3 ed 8 ♕xd5 ± Portisch-Bronstein, Monte Carlo 1969

[4] 11 ♘e3 ♗e6 12 ♗b2 ± Bondarevsky

[5] 3 cd ♗xb1 4 ♕a4+ (4 ♖xb1 ♕xd5 5 a3 ♘c6 6 ♘f3 0-0-0 7 ♕c2!? Khuzman-Fadeyev, USSR 1985) 4 ... c6 5 ♖xb1 ♕xd5 6 e3 ♘d7 7 b4 ♘gf6 8 ♘gf3 ± Gofstein-Fadeyev, USSR 1984
3 ♕b3 e5 4 cd (4 ♕xb7 ♘d7 5 ♘c3 ed 6 ♘xd5 ♗d6 7 e4! ∞ Miles-Gobet, Geneva 1986) 4 ... ed 5 ♘f3 ♗e4 6 ♘xd4 ♗xd5 7 ♕e3+ ♕e7 8 ♘c3 ± Gligorić-Schiffer, Berlin 1981

[6] **4 cd** ed 5 ♕b3 ♘c6 6 ♘c3 ♗b4 7 a3 ♗xc3+ 8 ♕xc3 ♘f6 9 ♗g5 ± Ree-Sahović, Amsterdam 1979
4 ♘c3 ♘f6 5 ♕b3 ♘c6 6 c5 ±

[7] **5 ♕xb7** ♘b4 6 ♘e5 ♖b8 7 ♕xa7 ♕c2+ 8 ♔d1 ♘f6 9 g4 ∞ Goldberg-Hayamy, USA 1986
5 ♗d2 ♖b8 6 cd ed 7 ♘c3 ♘f6 8 ♗g5 ♗e6 9 e3 ♗e7 10 ♗b5! ± Dorfman-Knežević, Polanica Zdroj 1978

[8] 6 ♘c3 ♘f6 7 ♗f4 a6 8 e3 ♗e7 9 ♗e2 ♘e4 10 ♘xe4 ♗xe4 11 0-0 ± H.Olafsson-Knežević, 1984

[9] 6 ... h6 7 e3 g5 8 ♗g3 ♗g7 9 ♘c3 a6 10 h4 g4 11 ♘e5 ± Portisch-Larsen, Montreal 1979

[10] 11 0-0 ± Polugayevsky-Vaganian, USSR 1981

[11] Chigorin

[12] 3 cd ♕xd5 4 ♘f3 e5 5 ♘c3 ♗b4 6 e3 ♗g4 7 ♗e2 ∞/± Quinteros-Kavalek, Lanzarote 1974

[13] 4 ♕a4 ♗xf3 5 ef 5 gf e6 6 e3 ♘e7 7 ♘c3 g6 8 ♗g2 ♗g7 9 f4 ♕d7 = Flear-Watson, Geneva 1984) 5 ... e6 6 ♘c3 ♘e7 7 cd (7 ♗g5 ♕d7 8 ♖d1 h6 9 ♗f4 g5 10 ♗e3 ♗g7 11 cd ed 12 h4 0-0-0 ∞ I.Ivanov-Watson, New York 1984) 7 ... ed 8 ♗d3 g6! 9 ♗g5 ♗g7 ∞; 8 ♗e3 g6! 9 ♗d3 ♗g7 10 0-0 0-0 11 ♘e2 a6 ∞ Davies-Flear, British Ch 1984

[14] 5 gf ♕xd5 6 e3 e5 7 ♘c3 ♗b4 8 ♗d2 ♗xc3 9 bc ♕d6 (9 ... ed 10 cd ♘ge7 ∞) 10 ♖b1 ♖b8 (10 ... b6 11 f4 ef 12 e4 ♘ge7 13 ♕f3 0-0 14 ♗f4 ± Kasparov-Smyslov, match 1984, and Lukacs-Pinal, Havana 1986) 11 f4 ef 12 e4 ♘ge7 13 ♕f3 ♘g6 14 h4 ♕a3! ∞ Lin-Ye, Chinese Ch 1986; 6 ... e6 7 ♘c3 ♘h5 8 f4 ♕xd1+ 9 ♔xd1 0-0-0 10 ♗d2 ♘f6 11 ♗b5 ± Karpov-Miles, Bugojno 1986

[15] 6 ... ♘f6 7 ♗g5 e6 (7 ... ♕d6 8 ♕d2! 0-0-0 9 ♖d1 ± Watson) 8 ♕d3 ♗e7 9 ♖d1 0-0 10 e4 ±

[16] 8 ... f5 9 ♗c4 ♕h4+ 10 g3 ♕h3 11 ♕b3! ±/±

[17] 11 ♗d3 ♗a5 12 0-0 ♗b6 13 e5 ♕e7 ∞ Bass-Chow, Chicago 1983

[18] 3 ... e6 4 ♘f3 ♘f6 5 ♗g5 ♗e7 6 e3 0-0 7 ♖c1 a6 8 a3 b6 9 cd ed 10 ♗d3 ± Psakhis-Sahović, Lvov 1984
3 ... dc and now:
4 e3 e5 5 d5 ♘a5 6 ♕a4+ c6 7 b4 cb 8 ab ♕b6 9 ♗d2 ♘b3 ∞ Kogan-Rizzitano, New York 1983

4 d5 ♘e5 5 f4 ♘g4 (5 ... ♘g6 6 e4 e6 7 de ♕xd1+ 8 ♔xd1 fe 9 ♗c4 ± Gunawan-Keene, Indonesia 1982) 6 h3 ♘4h6 7 e4 e6 8 ♗c4 ± Meyer-Martz, USA 1982

4 ♘f3 ♘f6 (4 ... ♗g4 5 d5 ♗xf3 6 ef ♘e5 7 ♗f4 ♘d7 8 ♗c4 ± Donner-Keene, London 1971) 5 e4 (5 ♗g5 h6 6 ♗xf6 ef 7 e3 ♗e7 8 ♗c4 0-0 9 a3 ± Tisdall-Cox, Gausdal 1983) 5 ... ♗g4 6 ♗e3 ♗xf3 7 gf e5 8 d5 ♘e7 9 ♕a4! ♘d7 10 d6 cd 11 ♗c4 ± Ligterink-Haldarsson, Reykjavik 1986

[19] 4 cd ♘xd5 5 e4 ♘xc3 6 bc e5 7 d5 ♘b8 8 ♘f3 ♘d7 ∞

[20] 6 ... ♗xf3 7 gf ♘xc3 8 bc e5 9 ♖b1 ± Ribli-Wittmann, Dubai Ol 1986

[21] **11 f4** ♗d6 12 ♗b5 c6! ∞ Palmo-Boey, corr. 1985

11 ♘g4 ♕c3+ 12 ♔d1 ♕xa1 13 ♗b5! ± Pein-Geenen, Brussels II 1986

[22] Albin

[23] 5 a3 ♗g4 6 b4 ♕e7 7 ♕a4 ♗xf3 8 gf ♕e5 ∞

[24] 6 g3! – 5 g3

[25] 6 ... ♕e7 7 h3 ♗h5 8 ♕a4 0-0 9 b4 ♔b8 10 g4 ♗g6 11 ♗g2 ± Suetin

[26] 7 ... ♗e6 8 g3 ♕d7 9 ♗g2 ♗c5 10 ♘g5! ± Pachman-Plachetka, Czechoslovakia 1968

[27] 11 0-0 ♘g6 12 ♕a4 ±/± Collins-Santasiere, USA 1952

[28] 5 ... ♗f5 6 a3 a5 7 ♗g2 ♘ge7 (7 ... ♗c5 8 0-0

♕d7 9 b4 ab 10 ♗b2 ba 11 ♘xa3 ♘ge7 12 ♘b5 ± Botterill-Povah, London 1980) 8 0-0 ♕d7 9 ♕a4 ± Hawksworth-Povah, England 1985

[29] 6 ... ♗b4 7 ♕c2 ♘ge7 8 ♗g2 ♘g6 9 0-0 ♕d7 10 ♘b3 0-0-0 11 ♗g5 ± Hough-Tapper, USA 1984

[30] 7 ♗g2 ♘ge7 8 0-0 ♘g6 9 ♕a4 ♗e7 10 ♘b3 11 ♖d1 ±/± Meduna-M.Mikhalchishin, Prague 1980

[31] 8 ♗g2 ♘g6 9 ♕a4 ♗e7 10 b4 ♖d8 11 ♗b2 0-0 ∞

[32] 9 ♗b2!? ± Inkiov-Peyev, Plovdiv 1984

[33] Fedorowicz-Jokšić, New York 1982

[34] 6 ♘bd2 ♕d7 7 ♗g2 0-0-0 (7 ... ♗h3 8 0-0 0-0-0 9 ♘b3 ♗xg2 10 ♔xg2 ♕e6 11 ♕d3 ± Korchnoi) 8 0-0 h5 9 b4! ♗xb4 10 ♕a4 ± de Boer-Crawley, Ramsgate 1984

[35] 7 ... ♗h3 8 e6 ♗xe6 9 ♕a4 0-0-0 10 ♖d1 a6 11 ♘c3 ±

[36] 8 ♖e1 ♘ge7 (8 ... ♔b8 ± Shipov-Shatskes, Moscow 1965; 8 ... h5 9 h4 f6 10 ef ♘xf6 11 ♗f4 ♗d6 12 ♗xd6 ♕xd6 13 ♘bd2 ♖he8 14 a3 ± Barendregt-Cortlever, Holland 1974) 9 ♗g5 h6 10 ♗xe7 ♗xe7 11 ♘bd2 ♖he8 12 a3 ♗f8 13 ♕b3 a6 14 ♖ac1 ♘a5 15 ♕a2 ♘c6 16 b4 ♘xe5 17 ♘xe5 ♖xe5 18 ♘f3 ♗xf3 19 ♗xf3 ± Minev

[37] 11 ♕h5 ♔b8 12 ♗f4 ±/± Korchnoi-Weinger, Beer-Sheva 1978

	3	4	5	6	7	8	9	10	11	
1	e3[1]	♘c3	ed	♗xc4	♘f3	h3[3]	0-0	♗b3	♖e1	±
	e5	ed[2]	♘f6	♗e7	0-0	♘bd7	♘b6	c6[4]	♘fd5[5]	
2	...	♗xc4	ed	♘c3	♘f3[7]	0-0	a3[8]	bc	h3	±
	...	ed	♗b4+[6]	♘f6	0-0	♗g4	♗xc3	c5	♗h5[9]	
3	...	♗xc4	♘c3	♕f3[10]	a3	♘ge2	h3	d5	e4	∞
	♘f6	e6	a6	♘c6	♗d6	0-0[11]	e5	♘e7	♘e8[12]	
4	e4	♘f3[13]	♗xc4	♗e3	gf	♗b5[16]	♘d2	♘b3[17]		±
	♘c6	♗g4	e6[14]	♗xf3[15]	♕f6	♘e7	0-0-0			
5	...	e5[18]	♗xc4	♗b3[20]	♘f3	♗xf7+	♘g5+	♕xg4	♕e2[21]	±
	♘f6	♘d5	♘b6[19]	♘c6	♗g4	♔xf7	♔e8	♕xd4	♕xe5[22]	
6	...	d5[23]	♗xc4	♘c3	ed[25]	a4	♕e2+	♕xe7+	♗f4	±
	c5	e6[24]	♘f6	ed	a6	♗d6	♕e7	♗xe7		
7	...	♘f3	♗xc4[26]	♘bd2	0-0	e5	♘b3	♗b5	♘bxd4	±
	e5	ed	♗b4+[27]	♘c6	♘f6	♘d5	♘b6[28]	♗d7[29]	♘xd4[30]	
8	...	...	♗d2[31]	♘bxd2	♗xc4	0-0[33]	e5	h3	♘b3	±
	...	♗b4+	♗xd2+	ed	♘c6[32]	♘f6[34]	♘g4	♘h6	0-0[35]	
9	♘f3	d5[37]	♘c3	♕xd5	♘xd5	e4	♗xc4	ed	0-0[39]	±
	c5[36]	e6	ed	♕xd5	♘a6[38]	♘e7	♘xd5	♗d6	0-0[40]	
10	...	e4[41]	a4	ab[42]	♖xa8	♘c3	♗g5	e5	♕a1[45]	∞∞
	a6	b5	♗b7	ab	♗xa8	c6[43]	♘f6[44]	♘d5		
11	...	e3	♗xc4[47]	♕b3[48]	gf	♗e2	a4	♘d2[51]	♘e4	±
	...	♗g4[46]	e6	♗xf3	b5[49]	♘d7[50]	b4	♘gf6	c5[52]	
12	...	...	...	h3	♘c3[54]	g4	h4[55]	h5	g5	±
	...	...	...	♗h5[53]	♘f6	♗g6	♗b4	♗e4	♘d5[56]	
13	...	...	...	...	...	0-0	♗e2	b3[58]	♗b2	±
	...	...	...	...	...	♘c6[57]	♗d6	0-0[59]	♕e7[60]	

---

[1] 3 ♘c3 a6 (3 ... e5 4 e3 – 3 e3) 4 e4 b5 5 a4 b4 6 ♘a2 e6 7 ♗xc4 ♗b7 8 f3 c5 ∞ Browne-Dlugy, US Ch 1985

[2] 4 ... ♘c6 5 ♘f3 ed 6 ed ♗g4 7 ♗xc4 ♕e7 8 ♗e3 ± Browne-Shirazi, US Ch 1984

[3] 8 0-0 ♘c6 (8 ... ♘bd7 9 ♖e1 ♘b6 10 ♗b3 c6 11 ♗g5 ± Vaganian-Hübner, Tilburg 1983) 9 ♖e1 ♗g4 10 ♗g5 ∞/= Hübner-P.Nikolić, Wijk aan Zee 1984

[4] 10 ... ♘bd5 11 ♖e1 ♗e6 12 ♘g5 ♘xc3 13 bc ♗xb3 14 ♕xb3 ± Vaganian-Tal, Moscow 1982

[5] 12 ♘e4 ♖e8 13 ♗d2 ± Timman-Panno, Mar del Plata 1982

[6] 5 ... ♗d6 6 ♘f3 ♘f6 7 0-0 0-0 8 ♘c3 ♗g4 9 h3 ♗h5 10 g4 ♗g6 11 ♘e5 ± Gavrikov-Vorotnikov, Leningrad 1984
   5 ... ♘f6 6 ♕b3 ♕e7 7 ♗e3 g6 8 ♘f3 ♗g7

9 0-0 0-0 10 ♖e1 ♘c6 11 ♗d2 ± Plaskett-Lukin, Plovdiv 1984

[7] 7 ♕b3!? ♕e7 8 ♘e2 ± Wilder-Rohde, US Ch 1986, and Plachetka-Pekarek, Czechoslovak Ch 1986

[8] 9 h3 ♗h5 10 g4 ♗g6 11 ♘e5 ± Malanyuk-Pekarek, Tbilisi 1986

[9] 12 ♗g5 ♕d6 13 ♖e1 ♘c6 14 d5 ± Eingorn-Paunović, Belgrade 1986

[10] 6 ♘ge2 c5 7 0-0 b5 8 ♗b3 ∞/=

[11] 8 ... e5!? 9 ♘d5 ♘xd5 10 ♗xd5 0-0 11 ♗xc6 bc ∞

[12] 12 g4 b5 ∞ Groszpeter-Szymczak, Prague 1985

[13] 4 ♗e3 ♘f6 5 ♘c3 e5 6 d5 ♘e7 7 f3 ∞/± Redzepagić-Marjanović, Yugoslavia 1985

[14] 5 ... ♗xf3 6 ♕xf3 e6 7 d5 ♘e5 8 ♕e2 ♘xc4 9 ♕xc4 ± Inkiov-Kupreichik, USSR 1982

82

15 6 ... ♘f6 7 ♘c3 ♗b4 8 ♕c2 0-0 9 ♖d1 ±
16 8 e5 ♕h4 9 ♗b5 ∞ Alburt-Speelman, match 1986
17 Taimanov
18 4 ♘c3 e5 5 ♘f3 ed 6 ♕xd4 ♗d6 7 ♗g5 ♘c6 8 ♕xc4 h6 = Goldin-Balashov, Irkutsk 1986
19 5 ... ♘c6 6 ♘c3 ♘b6 7 ♗b5 ♗d7 8 ♘f3 a6 9 ♗d3 ♗g4 10 ♗e4 ± Kir.Georgiev-Draško, Sarajevo 1985
20 6 ♗d3 ♘c6 7 ♗e3 g6 (7 ... ♘b4 8 ♗e4 c6 9 ♘c3 ♗e6 10 ♘ge2 ♘4d5, Timman-Spraggett, Wijk aan Zee 1985) 8 ♘c3 ♗g7 9 ♘ge2 0-0 ∞/± Portisch-Spraggett, Wijk aan Zee 1985
21 11 ♕xd4 ♘xd4 12 ♘a3 e6 13 ♗e3 = Ftacnik-Spraggett, Wijk aan Zee 1985
22 12 ♗e3 ♘d5 13 ♘f3 ± Alburt-Gulko, Somerset (USA) 1986
23 4 ♘f3 cd 5 ♕xd4 ♕xd4 6 ♘xd4 ♗d7 (6 ... a6 7 ♗xc4 e6 8 ♗e3 ♘f6 9 f3 ♗e7 10 ♘d2 0-0 11 ♔f2 ± Hübner-P.Nikolić, Wijk aan Zee) 7 ♗xc4 ♘c6 8 ♘xc6 ♗xc6 9 ♘c3 e6 10 f3 ♗c5 = Dolmatov-Yakovich, USSR Ch 1986
24 4 ... ♘f6 5 ♘c3 b5 6 e5 b4 7 ef bc 8 bc ♘d7 9 ♕a4 ±
25 7 ♘xd5 ♕xd5 8 ♗xd5 ♗e7 9 ♘f3 0-0 10 0-0 ♕b6 11 ♗e3 ♘c6 12 ♖c1 ♗g4 = Bukić-Kovačević, Tuzla 1981
26 5 ♕xd4 ♕xd4 6 ♘xd4 ♘f6 7 ♘c3 ♗c5 8 ♗e3 ♗g4 ∞ Mikhalchishin-Gulko, USSR Ch 1985
27 5 ... ♘c6 6 0-0 ♗e6 7 ♗xe6 fe 8 ♕b3 ±
28 9 ... 0-0 10 ♘bxd4 ± Dorfman-Barua, Delhi 1982
29 10 ... ♕d5 11 ♘bxd4 ± P.Nikolić-Matulović, Yugoslavia 1984
30 12 ♘xd4 ♗c5 13 e6 ± Yusupov-Rüfenacht, Mexico 1980
31 5 ♘c3 ed 6 ♕xd4 ♕xd4 7 ♘xd4 ♘f6 8 f3 a6 9 ♗c4 b5 10 ♗e2 c5 11 ♘c2 ♗a5 12 ♗d2 (12 0-0 ±) 12 ... ♗e6 13 e5 ± Rashkovsky-Lerner, Lvov 1981
32 7 ... ♘h6 8 0-0 c5 9 ♘b3 ♕e7 10 ♖c1 ± Partos-Miles, Biel 1977
33 8 b4 a6 9 h3 ♕f6 10 0-0 ♘ge7 11 e5 ♕g6 12 ♕b3 0-0 13 ♗d3 ♕h6 ∓ Arbakov-Chekhov, Irkutsk 1983
34 8 ... ♕f6 9 e5 ♕g6 10 ♗b5 ♘e7 11 ♘xd4 ± Miles-Dlugy, Tunis IZ 1985
35 12 ♘bxd4 ♘xd4 13 ♕xd4 ♕e7 14 ♖fd1 ± Bukić-Matulović, Vršac 1975
36 3 ... ♗g4 4 ♘e5 ♗h5 5 ♘c3 ♘d7 6 ♘xc4 ♘gf6 7 f3 ♘b6 8 ♘a5 ± Andersson-Kavalek, Bugojno 1982
3 ... e6 4 e4 b5 5 a4 c6 6 ♗g5 ♗b4+ 7 ♘c3 ♘e7 8 ♗e2 ♗b7 9 0-0 ± Lputian-Kupreichik, Erevan 1984
3 ... ♘d7 4 e4 ♘b6 5 ♗xc4 (5 a4 ±) 5 ... ♘xc4 6 ♕a4+ c6 7 ♕xc4 ♘f6 8 ♘c3 ♗e6 9 ♕d3 g6 10 0-0 ♗g7 11 h3 ± Petursson-Bellon,

Hastings 1985-86
37 4 e3 cd 5 ♗xc4 ♕c7 6 ♕b3 e6 7 ed ♘f6 8 ♘c3 ♘c6 9 0-0 ♗d7 = Dorfman-Lukin, USSR 1984
4 ♘c3!? e6 5 e4 cd 6 ♕xd4 ♗d7 7 ♘e5 ± Miles-Korchnoi, Tilburg 1985
38 7 ... ♗d6 8 ♘d2 ♗e7 9 ♗xc4 ♘xd5 10 ♘xd6+ ♔e7 11 ♘xc8+ ♖xc8 12 ♗g5+ f6 13 0-0-0 ± Ribli-Seirawan, Montpellier C 1985
39 11 ♗b5+ ♗d7 12 ♗xa6 ba 13 ♗e3 ♗b5 ∞ Bareyev-N.Nikolić, Gausdal 1986
40 12 ♗xa6 ba 13 ♘d2 ± Ludvigsen-N.Nikolić, Oakham 1986
41 4 ♘c3 b5 5 a4 b4 6 ♘e4 ♘d7 ∞ Karpov-Portisch, Tilburg 1983
4 a4 ♘f6 5 e3 ♘c6 6 ♗xc4 ♗g4 7 0-0 e6 8 h3 ♗h5 9 ♗e2 ♗d6 10 b3 ♕e7 = Mikhalchishin-Donchev, Lvov 1983
42 6 b3 ♗xe4 7 ♘c3 ♗b7 8 ab ab 9 ♖xa8 ♗xa8 10 bc e6 = Vaiser-Chekhov, USSR 1983
43 8 ... e6 9 ♗xb5 ♗xe4 10 ♗xc4 ± Lputian-Kaidanov, Irkutsk 1983
44 9 ... h6 10 ♗h4 ♕b6 11 ♗e2 e6 12 0-0 ♗e7 13 b3 ∞ Knaak-Chekhov, Leipzig 1986
45 Lputian
46 4 ... b5 5 a4 ♗b7 6 b3 e6 7 bc bc 8 ♗xc4 ±
47 5 h3 ♗h5 6 g4 ♗g6 7 ♘e5 ∞/±
48 6 0-0 ♘f6 7 b3 ♗d6 8 ♗b2 0-0 9 ♘bd2 ♘c6 = Rukavina-Hulak, Budva 1981
6 ♗e2 ♘f6 7 0-0 c5 8 b3 ♘c6 9 ♗b2 ♖c8 (9 ... ♗e7 10 ♘bd2 0-0 11 ♖c1 ± Speelman-Timman, London 1984) 10 ♘bd2 ♗e7 11 dc ♗xc5 = Speelman
6 ♘c3 ♘f6 7 0-0 ♘c6 8 ♗e2 ♗d6 9 b3 ♕e7 ∞/=
49 7 ... ♖a7 8 ♗d2 ♘f6 9 ♘c3 ♘bd7 10 ♗e2 c5 11 d5 ±
50 8 ... c5 9 dc ♗xc5 10 a4 b4 11 ♘d2 ±/±
51 10 f4 ♘gf6 11 ♗f3 c5 12 ♖xa8 ♕xa8 ∞
52 12 ♘xc5 ♘xc5 13 dc ♗xc5 14 ♗d2 ±
53 6 ... ♗xf3 7 ♕xf3 ♘c6 8 0-0 ♘f6 9 ♘c3 ♗d6 10 ♖d1 ± Farago-Kierzek, Dortmund 1978
54 7 ♕b3 ♗xf3 8 gf b5 9 ♗e2 ♘d7 10 ♘c3 ♘gf6 11 a4 ±
55 9 ♘e5 ♘bd7 10 ♘xg6 hg 11 ♗f1 c6 12 ♗g2 ♕c7 13 0-0 ♗e7 14 f4 ± Kasparov-Petrosian, Tilburg 1981
56 12 ♗d2 ♗xc3 13 bc ± Balashov-Kupreichik, USSR 1967
57 8 ... c5 9 dc ♕xd1 10 ♖xd1 ♗f3 11 gf ♗c5 12 b3 ♘bd7 13 f4 ± Belyavsky-Romanishin, USSR Ch 1978
58 10 a3 0-0 11 b4 ♘d5 11 ♗b2 ∞ Hjartarson-Vorotnikov, Leningrad 1984
59 10 ... ♗g6 11 ♗b2 ♘d5 12 ♘a4 b6 13 ♖c1 ± Rivas Pastor-Vorotnikov, Leningrad 1984
60 12 ♘d2 ♗xe2 13 ♕xe2 ♘d5 = Tal-Hort, Porz 1982
12 ♖c1 ♖fd8 13 ♘e5 ±

83

QGA II   1 d4 d5 2 c4 dc 3 ♘f3 ♘f6

	4	5	6	7	8	9	10	11	12	
1	♕a4+	♕xc4	♘c3[3]	g3	♗g2	0-0	♖e1[4]	e3	♕e2	=
	c6[1]	♗f5[2]	e6	♘bd7	♗e7	0-0	♘e4	♕b6	♖ad8[5]	
2	♘c3	d5[7]	e4	e5	♗g5[10]	♗xe7	♘xd5	♗xc4[11]	♕c2	±
	c5[6]	e6[8]	ed[9]	♘fd7	♗e7	♕xe7	♕d8	0-0[12]	b5[13]	
3	...	e4[14]	e5	a4[15]	bc	g3	♗g2	♗a3[19]	♗xf8	±
	a6	b5	♘d5	♘xc3[16]	♕d5[17]	♗b7[18]	♕d7	e6[20]	♔xf8[21]	
4	...	...	...	...	♗e2	0-0	♖a2[22]	♖a3	♘h4	±
	...	...	...	♘b4	♗f5	♘c2	♘b4	♘c2	♗d3[23]	
5	e3	♗xc4	♕b3[25]	gf	♕xb7[26]	dc[27]	♘c3	f4	♗e2	∞∞
	♗g4[24]	e6	♗xf3	♘bd7	c5	♗xc5	0-0	♘b6	♘fd5[28]	
6	...	...	h3	♘c3[29]	0-0[30]	e4[32]	g4[33]	de	♘xe5	=
	...	...	♗h5	♘bd7	♗d6[31]	e5	♗g6	♘xe5	♗xe5[34]	
7	...	...	...	...	...	...	♗e2	de[36]	♘d4[37]	±
	...	...	...	...	...	...	0-0[35]	♘xe5	♗c5[38]	

[1] **4 ... ♕d7** 5 ♕xc4 ♕c6 6 ♘a3 ♕xc4 7 ♘xc4 e6 8 a3 c5 9 ♗f4 ± Alekhine-Fine, Kemeri 1937
4 ... ♘bd7 5 ♘c3 e6 6 e4 c5 7 ♗xc4 cd 8 ♘xd4 ♗c5 9 ♘b3 0-0 10 ♗e2 ♕c7 11 ♗g5 h6 12 ♗h4 ± Quinteros-Braga, Mar del Plata 1982
4 ... ♗c6 5 ♘c3 ♘d5 6 e4 ♘b6 7 ♕d1 ♗g4 8 d5 ♗e5 9 ♗f4 ♘g6 10 ♗g3 ± Alburt-Dlugy, US Ch 1984

[2] **5 ... g6** 6 ♘bd2 ♕d5 7 e3 ♗g7 8 b3 0-0 9 ♗b2 ♗f5 10 ♖c1 ± Gheorghiu-Bastian, Baden-Baden 1981
5 ... ♗g4 6 ♘c3 ♘bd7 7 e4 ♗xf3 8 gf e5 9 ♗e3 ± Andersson-Christiansen, London 1982

[3] 6 g3 e6 7 ♗g2 ♘bd7 8 0-0 ♗e7 9 ♗g5 0-0 10 ♘bd2 a5 = Kurajica-Seirawan, Indonesia 1983

[4] 10 e3 ♘e4 (10 ... ♖c8 11 ♕e2 c5 12 e4 ± Tal-Shabalov, Jurmala 1985) 11 ♕e2 ♕a5 12 ♗d2 ♕b6 13 ♘xe4 ♗xe4 = Csom-Tal, Titograd 1984

[5] 13 ♘d2 ♘xd2 14 ♕xd2 ♗g6 = Andersson-Hübner, Tilburg 1983

[6] **4 ... ♘bd7** 5 e4 ♘b6 6 ♘e5 g6 7 ♘xc4 ♗g7 8 ♘e5 0-0 9 ♗e2 ± Farago-Donchev, Prague 1985
4 ... e6 5 e4 c5 6 d5 ± – 4 ... c5; 6 ♗xc4 cd 7 ♘xd4 ±
4 ... ♗f5 5 ♗e5 e6 6 f3 ♘fd7 7 ♘xc4 ♘c6 8 e4 ♗g6 9 ♗f4 ±/± Sosonko-Hort, Tilburg 1980

[7] 5 e4 cd 6 ♕xd4 ♕xd4 7 ♘xd4 e5 8 ♘db5 ♔d8! 9 ♗e3 ♗e6 = Alburt-Seirawan, Hollywood 1985

[8] 5 ... ♗f5 6 ♘e5 a6 7 g3 ♗e4 8 ♘xe4 ♘xe4 9 ♗xc4 ± Gorelov-Lukin, USSR 1985

[9] 6 ... ♘xe4 7 ♘xe4 ed 8 ♗g5 ♕a5+ 9 ♘c3 ♗e6 10 ♗d2 ♕d8 11 ♘g5 ± Tal-Karolyi, Tbilisi 1986

[10] 8 ♕xd5 ♘b6 (8 ... ♘c6 9 ♕e4 ♘b6 10 ♗g5 ♗e7 11 ♖d1 ± Ubilava-Zaichik, Tbilisi 1986) 9 ♕xd8+ ♔xd8 10 ♗g5+ ♗e7 11 0-0-0+ ♔e8 12 ♘b5 ♘a6 = Torre-Seirawan, London 1984

[11] 11 ♕c2 ♘b6 12 0-0-0! ± Lukacs-Polgar, Budapest 1986

[12] 11 ... ♘c6 12 ♕a4 (12 ♕c2 ♕a5+ 13 ♕c3 ♖b8 14 ♕xa5 ♘xa5 15 ♗b5 a6 16 ♗d3 c4 = Boersma-Marjanović, Amsterdam II 1986) 12 ... 0-0 13 0-0-0 ± Flear-Garcia Palermo, Szirak 1986

[13] 13 0-0-0 ♘c6 (13 ... ♘xe5?! 14 ♖he1 ♘bc6 15 ♘xe5 ♘xe5 16 ♗b5 ±± Belyavsky-Seirawan, USSR v World 1984) 14 ♖he1 ±

[14] 5 e3 b5 6 a4 b4 7 ♘b1 e6 8 ♗xc4 ♗b7 9 0-0 ♘bd7 10 ♘bd2 c5 ∞ Pigusov-P.Nikolić, Sochi 1982
5 a4 ♘c6 6 e4 ♗g4 7 ♗e3 ∞; 7 ♗xc4 =

[15] 7 ♘g5 e6 8 ♕h5 ♕d7 9 a3 ♘c6 10 ♗e3 ∞ Rogers-Littlewood, British Ch 1983

[16] **7 ... ♗f5** 8 ♗h4 ♘xc3 9 bc ♗e4 10 e6 ± Miles-Heinbuch, Ostend 1985
7 ... c6 8 ab ♘xc3 9 bc cb 10 ♘g5 f6 11 ♕f3 ♖a7 12 e6 ± Vaiser-Vera, Berlin 1982

[17] 8 ... ♗b7 9 e6 f6 (9 ... fe 10 ♗e2 ♕d5 11 ♘g5 ♕xg2 12 ♖f1 ±/±) 10 ♗e2 ♕d5 11 0-0 ♕xe6 12 ♖e1 ♕d7 13 ♘h4 ±/± Belyavsky-

Dlugy, Tunis IZ 1985

[18] 9 ... ♗e6 10 ♗g2 ♕b7 11 0-0 ♗d5 12 e6 ♗xe6 13 ab ab 14 ♘e5 ±/± Vaganian-P.Nikolić, Naestved 1985

[19] 11 0-0 e6 12 ♘h4 ♗xg2 13 ♘xg2 b4 14 ♘f4 ♘c6 ∞ Nemet-Hort, Lugano 1983

[20] 11 ... ♗d5 12 0-0 ♘c6 13 ♖e1 ± Ehlvest-Chekhov, USSR Ch 1984

[21] 13 0-0 ♗d5 14 ♘h4 ± Inkiov-Bellon, Rome 1985

[22] 10 ♖b1 e6 11 ab ab 12 ♘xb5 ♘b4 13 ♗g5 ♕d7 ∞ Knaak-Donchev, Bratislava 1983

[23] 13 ♗xd3 cd 14 e6 ± Petursson-Thorsteins, Reykjavik 1985

[24] 4 ... ♗e6 5 ♘c3 c6 6 a4 g6 7 e4 ±/±

4 ... g6 5 ♗xc4 ♗g7 6 0-0 0-0 7 ♘c3 c6 8 h3 ♗f5 9 ♘g5 b5 10 ♗b3 ± Suba-Negulescu, Romanian Ch 1981

[25] 6 0-0 ♘bd7 7 ♗e2 ♗d6 8 ♘bd2 0-0 9 ♘c4 ♗e7 10 b3 c5 = Kavalek-Miles, Tilburg 1977

6 ♘c3 ♘bd7 7 ♗e2 ♗d6 8 e4 ♗b4 = Gligorić-Miles, Bugojno 1978

[26] 8 ♘c3 ♘b6 9 ♗e2 ♗e7 10 ♗d2 0-0 11 ♖d1 c5 12 dc ♗xc5 = Gligorić-Smyslov, Hastings 1962-63

[27] 9 ♘c3 cd 10 ed ♗d6 11 f4 0-0 12 ♗b3 ♘h5 ∞

[28] 13 0-0 ♕h4 ∞ Quinteros-Miles, Amsterdam 1977

[29] 7 0-0 ♘bd7 8 ♗e2 ♗d6 9 ♘bd2 0-0 10 b3 e5 11 de ♘xe5 12 ♗b2 ♖e8 = Donner-Matulović, Wijk aan Zee 1974

[30] 8 e4 ♘b6 9 ♗d3 (9 ♗b3!?) 9 ... ♗xf3 10 gf c5 11 ♗g5 ∞/± Kozma-Smejkal, Czechoslovak Ch 1964

[31] 8 ... ♗e7 9 e4 (9 ♗e2 0-0 10 e4 ♘b6 11 ♗e3 ± Razuvayev-Mestrović, Keszthely 1981) 9 ... 0-0 10 ♗e3 ♗g6 11 ♗d3 c6 12 a3 ♖c8 13 ♖e1 ± Larsen-Spassky, Santa Monica 1966

[32] 9 ♗e2 0-0 10 b3 c5 (10 ... a6 11 ♗b2 ♕e7 12 ♘d2 ♗xe2 13 ♘xe2 ± Skembris-Flear, Paris 1983) 11 ♗b2 cd 12 ♘xd4 ♗xe2 13 ♕xe2 a6 = Tukmakov-Smyslov, Hastings 1972-73

[33] 10 de ♘xe5 11 ♗e2 0-0 - 10 ♗e2

[34] Ftacnik-Matulović, Vršac 1981

[35] 10 ... ♗g6 11 de ♘xe5 12 ♗e3 ♘xf3+ 13 ♗xf3 0-0 14 ♕b3 ±

[36] 11 ♗e3 ♖e8 12 d5 ♗g6 13 ♘d2 = Unzicker-Miles, South Africa 1979

[37] 12 ♘xe5 ♗xe2 13 ♕xe2 ♗xe5 14 ♗g5 ♕e8 = Balashov-Miles, Tilburg 1977

[38] 13 ♘b3 ♗xd1 14 ♗xd1 ± Farago-Nogueiras, Kecskemet 1979

	7	8	9	10	11	12	13	14	15	
	QGA III			**1 d4 d5 2 c4 dc 3 ♘f3 ♘f6 4 e3 e6 5 ♗xc4 c5 6 0-0 a6[1]**						
1	♗b3[2]	♕e2	♘c3	♗d2	♖ac1	dc	♘a4	♗c3	♘c5	∞
	♘c6	♕c7[3]	♗d6	0-0	b6[4]	♗xc5	♗e7	b5	♗xc5[5]	
2	a4	ed	♘c3	♗e3[7]	♕e2	♖ad1	♘e5	f4	f5	±
	cd[6]	♘c6	♗e7	0-0	b6	♘b4	♗b7[8]	♘bd5	♕d6[9]	
3	...	♕e2[10]	♘c3	♖d1[12]	h3	♘g5[14]	♘ge4	♘xe4	ed	=
	♘c6	♕c7[11]	♗d6	0-0	♖e8[13]	♗e7	♘xe4	cd	♘a5[15]	
4	...	...	♖d1	ed	♘c3	♕e4[18]	♘e5	♕g4[20]	♕e2	∞
	...	cd	♗e7[16]	0-0	♘d5[17]	♘cb4	♕d6[19]	f5	b6[21]	
5	♕e2	♘c3[23]	♗d3	dc	♘e4	b3	♗xe4	♗b2	♕xb2[25]	±/±
	♘c6[22]	♕c7	♗e7	♗xc5	♗e7	♘xe4	♗f6[24]	♗xb2		
6	...	♗d3	ed	a4	♖xa4	♗c4[28]	♗g5	♗b5+	♘e5	∞
	b5	cd[26]	♘c6[27]	ba	♘b4	♗e7	a5	♗d7	0-0[29]	
7	...	♗b3	dc[30]	e4	♗e3[31]	♘c3	fe	♘d5	ed	±/±
	...	♘c6	♗xc5	e5	♕b6	♗xe3	0-0	♘xd5	♘a5[32]	
8	...	...	a4	ab	♖xa8	♘c3	♘b5	gf	♗d2[35]	∞
	...	♗b7	♘bd7[33]	ab	♕xa8	b4	♗xf3[34]	♕b8		
9	...	...	♖d1	♘c3[37]	d5[39]	e4[41]	♗c2	♘xe4	♗xe4	±
	...	...	♘bd7[36]	♕b8[38]	ed[40]	de	♗e7	♘xe4	♘f6[42]	
10	...	...	...	...	d5[43]	♗xd5	♘xd5	♖xd5	e4	∞/±
	...	...	...	♕b6	♘xd5	♗xd5	ed	♗e7[44]	♖d8[45]	

1 **6 ... cd** 7 ed ♘c6 (7 ...♗e7 8 ♕e2 0-0 9 ♘c3 b6 10 ♗g5 ♗b7 11 ♖ad1 ±/± Rogers-V.Zivković, Valjevo 1984) 8 ♘c3 ♗e7 9 ♗e3 0-0 10 ♘e5 ±

6 ... ♘c6 7 ♕e2 cd 8 ♖d1 ♗e7 9 ed 0-0 10 ♘c3 ♘a5 (10 ... ♘b4 11 ♗g5 ♘bd5 12 ♖ac1 ±) 11 ♗d3 b6 12 ♗g5 ♗b7 13 ♖ac1 ± Djurić-Mascarinas, Subotica 1984

2 **7 a3** b5 8 ♗a2 ♗b7 9 ♘c3 ♗e7 10 dc ♕xd1 11 ♖xd1 ♗xc5 = Frias-Skembris, Thessaloniki Ol 1984

7 ♘c3 b5 8 ♗e2 ♗b7 9 b3 ♘bd7 10 ♗b2 ♗d6 11 dc ♗xc5 12 ♖c1 0-0 = Andersson-Tarjan, Indonesia 1983

7 e4 b5 8 ♗d3 ♗b7 9 ♖e1 (9 ♗g5 cd ∞ Kasparov-Gulko, USSR 1982) 9 ... cd 10 a4 ba 11 ♖xa4 ♘fd7 12 ♘d4 ♗e7 = Portisch-Petrosian, Stockholm IZ 1962

3 **8 ... cd** 9 ♖d1 ♗e7 10 ed ♘a5 11 ♗c2 b5 12 ♘c3 ♗b7 13 ♗g5 0-0 ∞ Vaganian-Seirawan, Montpellier C 1985

4 **11 ... cd** 12 ed ♗f4 13 ♖fd1 ♗d7 14 ♘e4 ± A.Petrosian-Gulko, Tashkent 1984

5 A.Rodriguez-Vera, Cuba 1986

6 **7 ... ♘bd7** 8 ♕e2 cd 9 ed ♘b6 10 ♗b3 ♗e7

11 ♘c3 ♘bd5 12 ♗g5 0-0 13 ♖ad1 ±/± Taimanov

7 **10 d5** ed 11 ♘xd5 ♘xd5 12 ♗xd5 0-0 13 ♗xc6 bc = Gheorghiu-Karpov, Dubai Ol 1986

10 ♖e1 0-0 11 ♗g5 ♕a5 12 d5 ed 13 ♗xf6 ♗xf6 14 ♘xd5 ♕d8 = Osnos-Anikayev, USSR 1983

8 13 ... ♘fd5 14 f4 (14 ♗c1 ♗b7 15 f4 g6 = Rivas Pastor-Pliester, Amsterdam 1986) 14 ... g6 ±

9 16 ♗g5 ♘xc3 17 bc ± Lerner-Kharitonov, USSR Ch 1984

10 8 ♘c3 ♗e7 9 ♕e2 cd 10 ♖d1 e5 11 ed ed 12 ♘xd4 ♘xd4 = Tukmakov-Gulko, USSR Ch 1985

11 8 ... ♗e7 9 ♖d1 ♕c7 10 ♘c3 0-0 and now:

11 ♗d2 ♖d8 12 ♗e1 cd 13 ed ♗d7 14 ♖ac1 ♗e8 ∞ Vizhmanavin-Chekhov, USSR 1986

11 h3 ♖d8 12 d5 ed 13 ♗xd5 ♘b4 14 ♗c4 ♖xd1 15 ♘xd1 ♗f5 = P.Nikolić-Dlugy, Tunis IZ 1985

12 10 d5 ed 11 ♗xd5 0-0 12 h3 h6 13 e4 ♖e8 = Hulak-Radulov, Indonesia 1982

13 11 ... e5!? 12 d5 ♘e7 13 e4 ♘g6 14 ♗e3

♘h5 15 g3 ± Pinter-Kallai, Hungary 1985

[14] 12 dc ♗xc5 13 e4 ♘d7 14 ♗e3 b6 = Eingorn-Gulko, USSR Ch 1985

[15] 16 ♗a2 ♗d7 = Ostermeyer-Balashov, Reykjavik 1984

[16] 9 ... d3 10 ♗xd3 ♕c7 11 ♘c3 ♗e7 12 b3 0-0 13 ♗b2 ♖d8 14 ♖ac1 ± Rivas Pastor-Smyslov, Hastings 1981-82

[17] 11 ... ♘b4 12 ♗g5 ♘fd5 13 ♘xd5 ♘xd5 14 ♗xd5 ♗xg5 15 ♗e4 ♗f6 = Tukmakov-Balashov, USSR Ch 1985

[18] **12 ♗e3** ♘cb4 13 ♘e5 ♗d7 14 ♗b3 ♗c6 15 ♘xc6 bc ∞ Ftacnik-P.Nikolić, Novi Sad 1984

12 ♗d3 ♘cb4 13 ♗b1 b6 14 ♕e4 g6 15 ♗h6 ♖e8 ∞/=

[19] 13 ... ♖a7 14 ♕g4 ± Vegh-Kallai, Budapest 1984

[20] 14 ♗d2 b6 15 ♘d5 ♘xd5 16 ♗d3 f5 = Vera-Garcia Palermo, Bayamo 1983

[21] 16 ♘xd5 ♘xd5 ∞ Meister-Kallai, Liechtenstein 1986

[22] **7 ...** ♗e7 8 ♘c3 0-0 9 dc ±/±

7 ... cd 8 ed ♗e7 9 ♘c3 b5 10 ♗b3 ♗b7 11 ♗g5 ±/± Shamkovich-Dlugy, USA 1983

[23] **8 dc** ♗xc5 9 e4 ♕c7 10 e5 ♘g4 11 ♗f4 f6 12 ♘bd2 ± Nogueiras-Seirawan, Montpellier C 1985

8 a3!? b5 9 ♗a2 ♗b7 10 ♖d1 ±

[24] 13 ... ♗d7 14 ♗b2 0-0 15 ♖ac1 ± Timman-Miles, Tilburg 1986

[25] Timman

[26] 8 ... ♘c6 9 dc ♗xc5 10 a3 ♕c7! 11 b4 ♗d6 ∞ Henley

[27] 9 ... ♗e7 10 ♘c3 ♘c6 11 ♖d1 ♘b4 12 ♗b1 ♗b7 13 ♘e5 ♖c8 14 ♗g5 0-0 15 a3 ♘bd5 ∞ Georgadze-Kupreichik, Erevan 1982

[28] 12 ♗b5+ ♗d7 13 ♗xd7+ ♕xd7 14 ♘c3 ♗e7 15 ♗g5 ♕b7 ∞/= Pergericht-Garcia Palermo, Brussels 1985

[29] 16 ♖xb4 ab 17 ♗xd7 ♘xd7 ∞ Portisch-Seirawan, Dubai Ol 1986

[30] 9 ♘c3 ♗b7 10 ♖d1 ♘a5 11 ♗c2 ♕b6 12 dc (12 e4 cd 13 ♘xd4 ♗c5 14 ♗e3 0-0 ∞) 12 ... ♗xc5 13 a3 ♗e7 14 e4 ♖c8 ∞ Tatai-Velikov, Rome 1983

[31] 11 ♗g5 ♘d4 12 ♘xd4 ♗xd4 13 ♘c3 h6 14 ♗e3 ♗g4 15 f3 ♗e6 = Nogueiras-Garcia Palermo, Cuba 1986

[32] Nogueiras-Spraggett, Szirak 1986

[33] 9 ... b4!? 10 ♖d1 ♘bd7 11 ♘bd2 ♕c7 ∞ Kallai-Lanc, Tbilisi 1985

[34] 13 ... ♕a5 14 e4 ♗e7 15 e5 ♘e4 16 ♖d1 ±/± Farago-Dory, Hungary 1972

[35] Miles-Seirawan, Dubai Ol 1986

[36] 9 ... ♗e7 10 ♘c3 0-0 11 e4 b4 12 d5 bc 13 de ♕c7 14 ef+ ♔h8 15 e5 ±/± Vaiser-Donchev, Vrnjačka Banja 1984

[37] 10 e4 cd 11 e5 ♗xf3 12 gf ♘h5 13 f4 g6 ∞ Timman-Seirawan, Indonesia 1983

[38] **10 ...** ♗d6 11 e4 cd 12 ♖xd4 ♗c5 13 ♖d3 ♕b8 14 ♗g5 ± Ortega-Garcia Palermo, Cuba 1985

10 ... ♕c7 11 e4 cd 12 ♘xd4 ♘c5 13 e5 ♘fd7 14 ♗f4 ± Farago-Dobosz, Lodz 1980

[39] 11 ♘e5 ♘xe5 12 de ♘d7 13 f4 ♗c6! ∞ Barczay-Brilla Banfalvi, corr. 1983

[40] 11 ... ♘xd5 12 ♘xd5 ♗xd5 13 ♗xd5 ed 14 a4 ba = Geller-Korchnoi, Curaçao C 1962

[41] 12 ♘xd5 ♘xd5 13 ♗xd5 ♗xd5 14 ♖xd5 ♗e7 =

[42] 16 ♗f4 ± Ribli-Marjanović, Reggio Emilia 1985

[43] 11 e4 cd 12 ♘xd4 ♗c5 13 ♗e3 0-0 14 a4 ♖ad8 = Haik-Pliester, Holland 1984

[44] 14 ... ♕b7 15 e4 ♘b6 16 ♗g5 ♗e7 17 ♖d2 0-0 18 ♖ad1 ±

[45] Ree-Portisch, Wijk aan Zee 1985

QGD I   1 d4 d5 2 c4 e6 3 ♘f3

	3	4	5	6	7	8	9	10	11	
1	...	cd	♗g5	♗xe7	dc	♘c3[3]	e3[4]	♗e2	a3	=
	c5	ed	♗e7	♕xe7[1]	♘f6[2]	♕xc5	0-0	♕b6	♗d7[5]	
2	...	...	g3	♗g2	0-0[7]	dc[8]	♘bd2[9]	♘b3	♘fd4	∞
	...	...	♘c6	♘f6[6]	♗e7	♗xc5	0-0	♘b6	♖e8[10]	
3	...	♕c2	g3	c5!	♗g2	♘c3	bc	a4	ab	∞
	c6	♘f6	b5[11]	♘bd7	♘e4[12]	♘xc3	f5	♗a6	♗xb5[13]	

1 d4 d5 2 c4 e6 3 ♘f3 ♘f6

	4	5	6	7	8	9	10	11	12	
4	e3	♗d3[14]	0-0[15]	♘e5	de	♘c3	♗c2	cd	f4[17]	±
	c6	♘bd7	♘e4[16]	♘xe5	♘c5	♗e7	♕c7	cd		
5	...	cd[18]	♗b5+[19]	0-0	♘xd4	b3	♗e2	♗b2	♘xc6	=
	c5	ed	♘c6[20]	cd[21]	♗d7	a6	♗d6	0-0	bc[22]	
6	♗g5	e3	♗h4	cd	♗xe7	e4	♘c3	e5	♖c1[26]	=
	♗e7[23]	h6[24]	0-0[25]	♘xd5	♕xe7	♘f6	c5	♘d5	♖d8[27]	
7	...	♕a4[28]	♕xc4[29]	♘bd2[30]	dc	b4	♕b3	e4	♗d3	=
	dc	♘bd7	a6	c5	♗xc5	b5	♗e7	♗b7	h6[31]	

[1]   6... ♘xe7 7 dc ♘a6 8 e3 ♘xc5 9 ♘c3 0-0 = Rashkovsky-Lputian, Erevan 1984

[2]   7... ♕xc5 8 ♘bd2 ♘c6 9 ♘b3 ± Seirawan-Ekström, Zürich 1984

[3]   8 e3 ♕xc5 9 ♘bd2 ♘c6 10 ♖c1 ♕a5 11 a3 0-0 12 ♗e2 ♗g4 = Smyslov-Barle, Portorož/Ljubljana 1985

[4]   9 ♕d4 ♕e7 10 ♘xd5 ♘xd5 11 ♕xd5 ♘c6 12 e3 0-0 ∞ Korchnoi-Marjanović, Titograd 1984

[5]   12 b4 a5 13 b5 ♗e6 14 ♕d4 ♘bd7 = Pytel-Lputian, Erevan 1984

[6]   6... c4 7 0-0 ♗b4 8 b3 cb 9 ♕xb3 ♘ge7 ∞/± Korchnoi-Mikenas, USSR Ch 1970

[7]   7 b3 ♗e7 8 ♗b2 ♘e4 9 dc ♗f6 ∞ R.Rodriguez-Geller, Moscow IZ 1982

[8]   8 ♗e3 c4 9 ♘e5 0-0 10 b3 cb 11 ♕xb3 ♕b6 12 ♖c1 ♕xb3 13 ab ♘b4 = Korchnoi-Kasparov, match 1983

[9]   9 ♕c2 ♗b6!? (9... ♗e7 10 ♖d1 0-0 11 ♘c3 ♕a5 12 ♗e3 ♗e6 13 a3 ± Ribli-Lalić, Sarajevo 1985) ∞ Larsen

[10]   12 ♗f4 ♗g4 13 h3 ♗h5 14 ♖c1 ♖c8 ∞ Romanishin-Lobron, Wijk aan Zee 1985

[11]   5... ♘bd7 6 ♗g2 ♘e4 7 ♘c3 ♗b4 8 0-0 ♗xc3 9 bc ♕a5 10 cd ed 11 c4 ± Kochiev-Kupreichik, USSR 1981

[12]   7... e5?! 8 ♘xe5 ♘xc5 9 de ♘d7 10 e4 d4

[11] 0-0 ♘xe5 12 ♘d2 ♗g4 13 f4 ± Velikov-Vera, Thessaloniki Ol 1984

[13]   12 ♘d2 ♕f6 13 ♗b2 e5 14 de ♕e6 ∞ Smejkal-Vera, Bratislava 1983

[14]   5 ♘bd2 ♗d6 6 ♗e2 0-0 7 0-0 ♘bd7 8 b3 ♖e8 9 ♗b2 ♕e7 10 ♘e5 ♗a3 = Larsen-Bellon, Las Palmas 1981

[15]   6 ♘bd2 ♗d6 7 0-0 0-0 8 e4 e5 9 cd cd 10 ed ed 11 ♘c4 ♘b6 12 ♘d4 ♘xc4 15 ♗xc4 ♕c7 ∞ Ftacnik-Nikolić, Vršac 1981

[16]   6... dc 7 ♗xc4 b5 8 ♗d3 a6 9 a4 ♗b7 10 e4 ♗e7 11 ♘bd2 ±

[17]   Vaganian-Belyavsky, USSR 1978

[18]   5 dc ♗xc5 6 a3 0-0 7 b4 ♗e7 8 ♗b2 dc = Gurgenidze-Spassky, USSR 1975

[19]   6 ♗e2 ♘c6 7 0-0 cd 8 ♘xd4 ♗d6 9 b3 0-0 10 ♗b2 a6 11 ♘d2 ♕e7 ∞/= Christiansen-D.Gurevich, US Ch 1984

[20]   6... ♗d7 7 ♗xd7+ ♘bxd7 8 dc ♘xc5 9 0-0 ♗d6 10 ♘c3 ± Eingorn-Agzamov, USSR 1983

[21]   7... ♗d6 8 dc ♗xc5 9 ♗xc6+ bc 10 ♕c2 ∞ Eingorn-Kindermann, Polanica Zdroj 1984

[22]   Seirawan-Andersson, London 1984

[23]   4... h6 5 ♗xf6 ♕xf6 6 ♘c3 ♕d8 7 a3 ♗e7 8 e4 de 9 ♘xe4 ♘d7 10 ♗d3 ± Christiansen-Lombardy, Grindavik 1984

    4... c6!? 5 e3 ♘bd7 6 ♘bd2 h6 7 ♗h4 ♗d6 8 ♗d3 0-0 9 0-0 e5 10 ♗g3 ♕e7 = Rivas Pastor-

Yusupov, Minsk 1982

24 5 ... c6 6 Nbd2 0-0 7 Bd3 b6 8 0-0 Bb7 9 cd ed 10 Ne5 Nfd7 11 Qh5 g6 12 Nxg6 = Belyavsky-Sveshnikov, USSR 1978

25 6 ... c6 7 Nbd2 Nbd7 8 Bd3 0-0 9 0-0 b6 10 Rc1 c5 11 Qe2 Bb7 12 Rfd1 a6! = Larsen

26 12 Nxd5 ed 13 dc Bg4 ∞ Korchnoi-Hort, Wijk aan Zee 1983

27 13 Nxd5 Rxd5 14 Bd3 Nc6 = Petrosian-Karpov, Moscow 1981

28 5 Nc3 a6 6 e4 b5 7 e5 h6 8 Bh4 g5 9 Nxg5 hg 10 Bxg5 Nbd7 11 Be2 ∞ Razuvayev-Sveshnikov, USSR Ch 1979

29 6 e3 c5 7 Bxc4 cd 8 ed Be7 9 Nc3 0-0 = Andersson-Ribli, Tilburg 1984

6 e4!? Be7 7 Nbd2 0-0 8 Bxc4 ∞ Mikhalchishin-Lukacs, Lvov 1984

30 7 Nc3 Be7 8 Rd1 b5 9 Qb3 0-0 10 e3 Bb7 ∞/=+ Rivas Pastor-Pinter, Rome 1984

31 Dolmatov-Sveshnikov, Manila 1982

QGD II	1 d4 d5 2 c4 e6 3 Nc3 Be7 4 cd ed 5 Bf4 c6							
6	7	8	9	10	11	12	13	14
e3	Nge2[2]	Ng3	Be2[4]	h4	Bg5[5]	Rh3	Qd2	Kf1	∞
Bf5[1]	Nd7	Bg6[3]	Ngf6	h5	Bd6	Qb6	0-0	Rfe8[6]	
...	g4	h3[8]	Bd3[10]	g5	h4	Kf1	Nge2	Rc1	∞/=
...	Be6[7]	Nf6[9]	0-0[11]	Nfd7	c5	Nc6	Re8	a6[12]	
...	...	h4	h5	Be2	Rc1	Bxc4	Bxh6	∞
...	...	Nd7[13]	Nh6[14]	Nb6	Nc4[15]	dc	gh	
Qc2	e3[16]	Qd2!	f3	Bb5+[19]	dc	Na4	Bh6	Ne2[20]	∞/±
g6	Bf5	Nf6[17]	c5[18]	Nc6	Bxc5	Be7	Bd7	a6[21]	

[1] 6 ... Bd6 7 Bg3 Ne7 8 Bd3 Bf5 9 Nf3 Bxg3 10 hg Nd7 11 Qc2 Bxd3 12 Qxd3 h6 13 0-0-0 ± Cebalo-Abramović, Yugoslav Ch 1985; 8 Nf3 ±

[2] 7 Bd3 Bg6 8 Nf3 Nd7 9 0-0 Ngf6 10 Rb1 a5 11 Bxg6 hg = Larsen-Najdorf, Bugojno 1982

[3] 8 ... Be6 9 Nh5! ± Portisch

[4] 9 Rc1 h5 10 Bd3 h4 11 Bxg6 hg 12 Bd3 gf+ 13 Kxf2 Bg5 = Speelman-Geller, Skara 1980

[5] 11 Bf3 Qb6 12 Qe2 a5 13 Bg5 Qa6 = Bagirov-Lerner, USSR 1979

[6] Portisch-Geller, Portorož 1973

[7] 7 ... Bg6 8 h4 h5 9 g5 Bd6 (Miles-Portisch, Reggio Emilia 1984-85) 10 Nge2 Ne7 11 Bxd6 Qxd6 12 Nf4 ± Miles

[8] 8 Bd3 Nd7 9 h3 h5 10 gh Ndf6 11 h6 Nxh6 12 Qc2 Qd7 13 Nf3 Bf5 = Lputian-Geller, USSR Ch 1985

[9] 8 ... Bd6!? 9 Qb3 (9 Nge2 Ne7 10 Qb3 Bc8 11 Bg2 h5!? 12 0-0-0 Ng6 Korchnoi) 9 ... Bxf4 10 ef Bc8 11 0-0-0 Qd6 12 Kb1 ∞ Littlewood-Chandler, Hastings 1981-82

[10] 9 Nf3 0-0 10 Qc2 c5 11 0-0-0 Nc6 =

[11] 9 ... c5 10 Nf3 Nc6 11 Kf1 0-0 12 Kg2 Rc8 = Korchnoi-Karpov, match (13) 1981

[12] 15 Bb1 Nf8 ∞/= Donner-Enklaar, Wijk aan Zee 1974

[13] 8 ... Bxh4 9 Qb3 g5 10 Bh2 Qb6 11 Nf3 Qxb3 12 ab Bxg4 13 Nh4 ± Psakhis, Vaiser

8 ... Nf6 9 f3 c5 10 Bd3 Nc6 11 Nge2 a6 12 Rc1 ± Chernin-Pigusov, Copenhagen 1986

[14] 9 ... Qb6 10 Rb1 Ngf6 11 f3 0-0 (11 ... h6 12 Bd3 0-0 13 Nge2 c5 14 Kf1 ± Knaak-Geller, Moscow 1982) 12 Bd3 c5 13 Nge2 Rac8 14 Kf1 cd 15 ed ∞/± Belyavsky-Geller, USSR Ch 1983

[15] 11 ... Bd6 12 Nh3 Bxf4 13 Nxf4 Bd7 14 Rg1! ± Kasparov-Karpov, match (21) 1985

[16] 7 e4 Be6! 8 e5 Bf5 9 Qd2 Nd7 10 Be2 h5 11 Nf3 Nf8 12 0-0 Ne6 = Garcia Palermo-Portisch, Reggio Emilia 1984-85

[17] 8 ... Nd7 9 f3 Nb6 10 e4 Be6 11 e5! ± Karpov-Kasparov, match (7) 1986

[18] 9 ... h5 10 Bd3 Bxd3 11 Qxd3 Nbd7 12 Nge2 0-0 13 0-0 ± Ionescu-Geller, Sochi 1986

[19] 10 h6! cd?! (10 ... Bf8 ±) 11 ed a6 12 g4 ± Kasparov-Short, Thessaloniki Ol 1988

[20] 14 Bxc6 Bxc6 15 Nc3 Bc5 = Petrosian-Belyavsky, USSR 1982

[21] 15 Bxc6 Bxc6 16 Nac3 ∞/±

QGD III   1 d4 d5 2 c4 e6 3 ♘c3 ♘f6 4 cd ed

	5	6	7	8	9	10	11	12	13	
1	♗f4	e3[2]	♗d3[4]	♘f3	0-0	♗e2	♗e5	♗g3	hg	=
	♗e7[1]	0-0[3]	c5	♘c6	c4[5]	♘h5	f6	♘xg3	♗e6[6]	
2	♘f3	♗f4	♕c2[8]	e3	♗d3	♕xd3	h3	0-0	♗h6	∞/=
	♗e7[7]	c6	g6[9]	♗f5	♗xd3	♘bd7	0-0	♘h5[10]	♖e8[11]	
3	♗g5	e3	♗d3	♕f3[13]	♘ge2	h4	♗xf6	0-0-0	e4	±
	♗e7	0-0[12]	♘bd7	c6	♖e8	♘f8	♗xf6	♕d7	de[14]	
4	...	♘f3	♕b3	♕xb7[17]	♕xc6	g4[18]	♕a4	♗d2	♖c1	∞/=
	c6	♗f5[15]	♘bd7[16]	♖b8	♖xb2	♖b6	♗b4	♕c8[19]		
5	...	e3	♗d3	♕c2[20]	0-0-0[21]	f4	♗xf6	♘f3	♖dg1!	±
	...	♘bd7	♗d6	♘f8	♘g6[22]	h6	♕xf6	♗g4	♗xf3[23]	
6	...	...	♗d3[24]	♗xe7	♕c2[25]	♘ge2!	0-0	♖ae1	♘c1	∞/±
	...	♗e7	♘e4	♕xe7	♗f5	♘d7	♘df6	0-0	♘xc3[26]	
7	...	♕c2	e3	♗d3	♘f3[29]	♗h4	0-0	♖ab1	♗xe7	±
	...	♗e7[27]	♘bd7	♘f8[28]	♘e6	g6	0-0[30]	♘g4	♕xe7[31]	
8	...	...	...	...	♘ge2	0-0[32]	♖ab1[33]	b4	♘a4	±
	...	...	...	0-0	♖e8	♘f8	♗e6[34]	a6	♘6d7[35]	
9	...	...	...	...	♘f3	0-0-0[36]	h3	g4	♘xa4	=
	...	...	...	...	♖e8	♘f8	a5[37]	a4	♕a5[38]	
10	...	...	...	...	...	0-0	♖ab1[39]	a3	♗xe7	±
	...	...	...	...	...	♘f8	a5[40]	♘e4	♕xe7[41]	

[1] 5 ... c6 6 e3 ♗f5 7 ♘ge2 ♕b6 8 ♕d2 ♗e7 9 ♘g3 ♗g6 10 ♗d3 ♗xd3 11 ♕xd3 ♕a6 12 ♕xa6 ♘xa6 13 ♘f5 ± Barbero-Rasmussen, Plovdiv 1986

[2] 6 ♕c2 0-0 7 e3 c5 8 dc ♗xc5 9 ♘f3 ♘c6 10 ♗e2 d4! 11 ed ♘xd4 12 ♘xd4 ♕xd4 = Karpov-Kasparov, match (20) 1985

[3] 6 ... ♗f5 7 ♕b3 ♘c6 8 ♕xb7 ♘b4 9 ♗b5+ ♔f8 10 ♔d2! a6 11 ♗a4 ±/± Salov-Timoshchenko, Irkutsk 1986

[4] 7 ♘f3 ♗f5 8 h3 c6 9 g4 ♗g6 10 ♘e5 ♘fd7 11 ♘xg6 fg 12 ♗g2 ♘b6 13 0-0 ♔h8 = Karpov-Kasparov, match (22) 1985

[5] 9 ... ♗g4 10 dc ♗xc5 11 h3 ♗xf3 12 ♕xf3 d4 13 ♘e4! ♗e7 14 ♖ad1 ♕a5 15 ♘g3! ± Kasparov-Karpov, match (8) 1986

[6] 14 ♕c2 ♖e8 = Salov-Kruppa, USSR 1986

[7] 5 ... ♘bd7 6 ♗f4 c6 7 ♕c2 (7 e3 ♘h5 8 ♗g3 g6 9 ♗d3 ♘xg3 10 hg ♗g7 11 b4! a6 12 0-0-0 13 a4 ± Korchnoi-Csom, Titograd 1984) 7 ... ♘h5 8 ♗g5 ♗e7 9 ♗xe7 ♕xe7 10 g3 ♘b6 11 ♗g2 g6 12 0-0 ♗f5 13 ♕c1 0-0 14 ♖e1 ± Miles-R.Byrne, Reykjavik 1986

[8] 7 e3 ♗f5 8 ♗d3 ♗xd3 9 ♕xd3 ♘bd7 10 0-0 ♘h5 11 ♗e5 0-0 12 ♖ab1 ♘xe5 13 ♘xe5 ♗d6

[9] 7 ... ♘bd7 8 e3 0-0 (8 ... ♘h5 9 ♗e5 ♘xe5 10 de g6 11 0-0-0 ♘a5 12 ♘d4 ± Miles-Hartston, British Ch 1985) 9 ♗d3 ♖e8 10 0-0 (10 h3!? ♘f8 11 0-0-0 ♗e6 12 g4 ♖c8 13 ♔b1 b5 14 ♘g5 ♕b6 15 ♗e5 ± Miles-Jakobsen, Esbjerg 1984) 10 ... ♘f8 11 ♖ab1 a5 12 a3 ♘h5 13 ♗g3 ♗xg3 14 hg ± Browne-Hulak, Wijk aan Zee 1983

[10] 12 ... ♖e8 13 ♖ab1 a5 14 ♕c2 ♗f8 15 a3 ♘b6 = Smyslov-Geller, USSR 1955

[11] 14 ♖ab1 a5 15 e4 de 16 ♘xe4 ♘df6 ∞/= Meduna-Modr, Czechoslovakia 1983

[12] 6 ... ♘bd7 7 ♗d3 ♘f8 8 ♘f3 ♘e6 9 ♗h4 g6 10 0-0 0-0-0 11 b4 ±

6 ... h6 7 ♗h4 0-0 8 ♗d3 c5 9 dc ♘bd7 10 ♘ge2 ♘xc5 11 ♗c2 ♗e6 12 0-0 ♘ce4 13 ♕d3 ± Gulko-Lputian, Tashkent 1984

[13] 8 ♘ge2 b6 9 ♘g3 g6 10 h4 ± Gulko-Chiburdanidze, Frunze 1985

[14] 14 ♗xe4 ± Lerner-A.Petrosian, USSR 1983

[15] 6 ... h6 7 ♗h4 ♗c7 8 ♕c2 0-0 9 e3 ♘e4 10 ♗xe7 ♕xe7 11 ♗d3 f5 11 ♘e5 ±/±

[16] 7 ... ♕b6!? 8 ♗xf6 gf 9 e3 ♘d7 ∞/=

[17] 8 e4 ♗xe4 9 ♘xe4 de 10 ♘e5 ♕e7 11 0-0-0 ♘xe5 12 de ♕xe5 = Bejm-Khuzman, USSR

90

1986

[18] 10 ♗xf6!? Arkhipov

[19] Raičević-Arkhipov, Moscow 1986

[20] 8 ♘f3 ♘f8 9 ♕c2 (9 ♘e5 ♕b6 10 0-0 ♗xe5 11 de ♘6d7 12 ♗f4 ♘c5 13 ♘a4 ∞ Gulko-Smagin, Moscow Ch 1984) 9 ... ♘g6 10 ♘h4 0-0 11 0-0-0 h6 12 ♘xg6 fg 13 ♗h4 ∞/± Bagirov-Taimanov, USSR 1977

[21] 9 ♘ge2 ♘g6 10 ♘g3 h6 11 ♗xf6 ♕xf6 12 ♘h5 ± Bagirov

[22] 9 ... ♗g4 10 ♖e1 ♘g6 11 h3 ♗d7 12 e4 ± Knaak-Möhring, Leipzig 1981

[23] 14 gf ♘e7 15 ♔b1 0-0-0 16 ♘e2 ± Plachetka-Cvetković, Belgrade 1984

[24] 7 ♘f3 ♗f5 8 ♗d3 ♗xd3 9 ♕xd3 ♘bd7 10 0-0 0-0 11 ♖ab1 a5 12 a3 ♘e4 13 ♗xe7 ♕xe7 14 b4 b5 15 ♖fc1 ab 16 ab ♘d6 = Guseinov-Azmaiparashvili, Baku 1983

[25] 9 ♘f3 ♘d7 10 ♕c2 f5 11 0-0 0-0 12 ♖ae1 ± Korchnoi-Minev, Leipzig Ol 1960

[26] 14 bc ♗xd3 15 ♘xd3 ♘e4 = Hjartarson-Campora, Lone Pine 1981

14 ♗xf5 ∞/±

[27] 6 ... g6 7 e3 ♗f5 8 ♕b3 ±

6 ... ♘a6 7 a3 ♘c7 8 e3 ♘e6 9 ♗h4 ♗e7 10 ♘f3 g6 11 ♗d3 ± Vaganian-Westerinen, Moscow 1982

[28] 8 ... ♘h5 9 ♗xe7 ♕xe7 10 ♘ge2 g6 11 0-0-0 ♘b6 12 ♘g3! ♘f6 13 ♖he1 ♗e6 14 f3 ±/± Barlov-Campora, Bor 1985

[29] 9 ♘ge2! ♘e6 10 ♗h4 g6 11 0-0-0 ♘g7 12 f3! ♗f5 (12 ... ♘f5 13 ♗f2) 13 e4 Timman

[30] 11 ... ♘g7 12 b4 a6 13 ♖ab1 ♗f5 14 a4 0-0 15 b5 ab 16 ab ± Larsen-Smyslov, Copenhagen 1985

[31] 14 h3 ♘h6 15 ♖be1 ± Timman-Ljubojević, Amsterdam 1986

[32] 10 0-0-0 ♕a5 11 ♔b1 b5 12 ♘g3 h6 13 h4 ♘b6 14 ♗xf6 ♗xf6 15 ♘f5 ♗xf5 16 ♗xf5 ♘c4 ∞ Miles-Morovic, Tunis IZ 1985

10 h3 ♘f8 11 0-0-0 a5 12 ♔b1 b5 13 g4 a4 14 ♘g3 a3 15 b3 ♕a5 ∞/∓ Hulak-Spassky, Toluca IZ 1982

[33] 11 a3 a5 12 ♗xf6 ♗xf6 13 b4 ♗g4 14 h3 ♗xe2 15 ♘xe2 ± Cherepkov-Speelman, Leningrad 1984

[34] 11 ... a6 12 b4 ♗g4 13 ♘a4 ♗xe2 14 ♗xe2 ♘e4 15 ♗xe7 ♖xe7 16 ♘c5 ± Veingold-Nei, Tallinn 1983

[35] 14 ♗xe7 ♕xe7 15 ♘c5 ± Portisch-Yusupov, Bugojno 1986

[36] 10 h3 ♘f8 11 ♗f4 ♗e6 12 ♗e5 ♘6d7 13 ♗g3 a6 14 ♖d1 ♖c8 15 0-0 ♕b6 ∞/= Hort-Georgadze, Porz 1981-82

[37] 11 ... b5 12 ♗e5 ♗b7 13 ♔b1 ♕b6 14 g4 a6 ∞ Botterill-Csom, Hastings 1978-79

[38] 14 ♗xf6 ♗xf6 15 b3 b5 = Gheorghiu-Spassky, USSR 1981

[39] 11 h3 ♗e6 12 ♗f4 ♗d6 13 ♗xd6 ♕xd6 14 a3 ∞ Karpov-Belyavsky, Tilburg 1986

11 ♗xf6 ♗xf6 12 b4 ♗g4 13 ♘d2 ♗e7 14 ♖ab1 ♗d6 15 ♗f5 ♗h5 16 ♖fc1 g6 17 ♗d3 ♕g5 = Timman-Kasparov, World v USSR 1984

11 ♖ae1 ♘e4! 12 ♗xe7 ♕xe7 13 ♗xe4 de 14 ♘d2 f5 (14 ... b6 15 ♕a4 b5 16 ♕a5! ±/± Smejkal-Flear, Szirak 1986) 15 f3 ef 16 ♘xf3 ♗e6 17 e4 fe = Hjartarson-Short, Dubai Ol 1986, and Timman-Yusupov, Tilburg 1986

[40] 11 ... ♗d6 12 ♖fe1 ♗g4 13 ♘d2 ♘g6 14 e4 ♗f4 15 ♗xf6 ♕xf6 16 e5 ♕g5 17 ♘f1 ± Sveshnikov-Yusupov, Erevan 1982

11 ... ♘g6 12 ♗xf6 ♗xf6 13 b4 ♗g4 14 ♘d2 ♗e7 15 b5 ± Petrosian-Balashov, USSR Ch 1985

[41] 14 ♗xe4 de 15 ♘d2 f5 16 b4 ab 17 ab ♘g6 18 b5 ♗e6 19 ♖a1 ♖ad8 = Hansen-Inkiov, Plovdiv 1983

14 b4 ♗f5 15 ♗xe4 de 16 ♘e5 ab 17 ab ♕g5 18 ♘e2 ± Gligorić-Larsen, Copenhagen 1965

91

	4	5	6	7	8	9	10	11	12	
1	... ♗e7[1]	♗f4[2] 0-0[3]	e3 b6[4]	♖c1[5] c5	cd ed[6]	♗e2 ♗b7	0-0 ♘bd7	♘e5 ♘xe5[7]	♗xe5 ♘e4[8]	±
2	... ...	... ...	... c5	dc ♘c6[9]	cd ed	♗e2 ♗xc5	0-0 ♗e6	♖c1[10] ♖c8[11]	♕a4[12] a6[13]	±
3	... ...	... ...	... ...	... ♗xc5	cd[14] ♘xd5	♘xd5 ed	a3[15] ♘c6	♗d3 ♗b6	0-0 ♗g4[16]	=
4	... ...	... ...	... ...	... ...	a3 ♘c6[17]	♗e2[18] dc	♗xc4[19] ♘h5[20]	♗g5 ♗e7	♗xe7 ♕xe7[21]	=
5	... ...	... ...	... ...	... ...	♕c2 ♘c6	a3[22] ♕a5[23]	♘d2[24] ♗b4	♖c1[25] ♗xc3	♕xc3 ♕xc3[26]	=
6	... ...	... ...	... ...	... ...	... ...	♖d1 ♕a5	a3[27] ♗e7[28]	♖d2 ♘e4[29]	♘xe4 de[30]	∞/∓
7	... ...	... ...	... ...	... ...	... ...	... ...	... ...	♘d2 e5[31]	♗g5[32] d4[33]	=

[1] 4 ... ♘bd7 5 ♗f4 ♗b4 (5 ... dc!? 6 e3 ♘xd5 7 ♗xc4 ♘xf4 8 ef ♗e7 9 ♕c2 ± Byrne/Mednis) 6 cd ed 7 e3 c5 8 ♗d3 0-0 9 0-0 c4 10 ♗c2 ♗xc3 11 bc ♖e8 12 ♘d2 ♕a5 13 ♕c1 ± Adorjan-Kelečević, Sarajevo 1983

[2] 5 e3 0-0 6 ♗d3 dc 7 ♗xc4 a6 8 a4 c5 9 0-0 ♘c6 10 ♕d3 b6 11 ♖d1 ♗b7 12 ♕e2 ♕c7 = Hernandez-I.Zaitsev, Havana 1983

[3] 5 ... c5 6 dc ♘a6 7 ♗d6 0-0 8 cd ed 9 e3 ♗xd6 10 cd ♕xd6 11 ♗e2 ♕b6 12 ♕b3 ♕xb3 13 ab ♗b4 0-0 ± Tukmakov-Savon, Lvov 1978; 7 e3 ♘xc5 8 cd ed 9 ♗e2 ±

[4] 6 ... a6 7 ♕c2 (7 c5 b6 8 cb cb 9 ♗d3 ♗b7 10 0-0 ∞/±) 7 ... ♘bd7 8 cd ed 9 ♗d3 c5 10 g4 ± McCambridge-Hort, Dortmund 1982

6 ... c6 7 h3 ♘bd7 8 ♕c2 a6 9 ♖d1 ± Bagirov-A.Petrosian, Riga 1981

[5] 7 cd ♘xd5!? (7 ... ed 8 ♗d3 c5 9 0-0 ♗b7 10 ♘e5 ♘a6! = Bagirov-Lputian, Erevan 1982) 8 ♘xd5 ♕xd5 9 ♗d3 ♘a6 10 0-0 c5 11 ♗xa6 ♘xa6 12 ♕e2 ♕b7 = Zilberstein-Pigusov, USSR 1983

7 ♗e2 ♗b7 8 0-0 ♘bd7 9 h3 c5 10 ♗h2 a6 11 a4 ∞/± Karpov-Georgadze, USSR 1979

[6] 8 ... ♘xd5 9 ♘xd5 ed 10 ♗d3 ♘d7 11 0-0 ♗b7 12 ♕c2 ± Agdestein-Spassky, Gjovik 1983

[7] 11 ... ♖c8 12 dc! ♘xc5 13 ♘f3! ±

[8] 13 ♘xe4 de 14 ♕a4 ± Ree-Donner, Leeuwarden 1981

[9] 7 ... dc 8 ♕c2 ♗xc5 9 ♗xc4 a6 10 ♖d1 ♘bd7 11 ♗d3 b5 12 ♘e5 ±/± Miles-Barua, British Ch 1985

7 ... ♕a5 8 a3 dc 9 ♗xc4 ♕xc5 10 ♕e2 a6 11 e4 (11 b4 ♕h5 12 0-0 b5 13 ♗d3 ±) 11 ... b5 12 ♗d3 ♗b7 13 ♖c1 ± Portisch

[10] 11 ♘e5 ♗d6 12 ♘xc6 bc 13 ♕a4 ♗xf4 14 ♕xf4 ♕b8 15 ♕xb8 ♖axb8 16 b3 c5 17 ♖fd1 ♖fc8 18 ♖ac1 ± Cebalo-Rukavina, Yugoslav Ch 1982

[11] 11 ... ♗b6 12 ♕a4 ♕e7 13 ♖fd1 ♖fd8 14 ♗g5 h6 15 ♗h4 ♖ac8 16 ♘b5 ± Seirawan-R.Byrne, US Ch 1981

[12] 12 ♘b5 ♘e4 13 ♘d2 ♘xd2 14 ♕xd2 ♗b4 15 ♕d1 ♕b6 16 a3 ♗e7 = Korchnoi-Kasparov, Brussels 1986

[13] 13 ♖fd1 ♕b6 14 ♕c2 ♗e7 15 ♘e5 ♖fd8 16 ♗f3 ± Ribli-Unzicker, Baden-Baden 1981

[14] 8 ♗e2 dc 9 ♗xc4 ♕xd1 (9 ... a6 10 ♕e2 b5 11 ♗d3 ♗b7 12 0-0 ± Smyslov-Kasparov, match 1984) 10 ♖xd1 a6 11 ♗d3 ♘bd7 12 ♖c1 b6 13 ♘e4 ♗b7 =

[15] 10 ♗d3 ♗b4+ 11 ♔e2 ♘c6 12 ♕c2 h6 13 ♖hd1 ♗e6 14 ♖ac1 ♕f6 15 ♔f1 ♖fd8 16 ♗b5 ♗d6 = Mikhalchishin-Balashov, USSR Ch 1985

[16] 13 h3 ♗h5 14 b4 a6 (14 ... ♖e8 15 ♖a2! d4 16 g4 ♗g6 17 ♗xg6 hg 18 b5 ± Seirawan-Speelman, London 1984) 15 ♖a2 d4 16 e4 ♗c7 = Seirawan-Kir.Georgiev, Dubai Ol 1986

[17] 8 ... ♘e4!? 9 ♕c2 ♕a5 10 cd ♘xc3 11 bc

ed 12 ♗d3 h6 13 0-0 ♘c6 = Adorjan-Sibarević, Banja Luka 1983

[18] 9 b4 ♗e7 10 ♕c2 ♘d7! 11 ♗e2 ♖c8 12 0-0 dc 13 ♖ad1 ♕e8 14 ♖d2 a5 ∞ Christiansen-H.Olafsson, USA v Scandinavia 1986

[19] 10 ♕c2 b5 11 0-0 a6 12 ♖ad1 ♕b6 13 ♘g5 h6 14 ♘ge4 ♘xe4 15 ♘xe4 e5 = Adorjan-Karlsson, Gjovik 1983

[20] 10 ... a6 11 ♕c2 ♗e7 12 ♖d1 ♕a5 13 0-0 h6 14 e4 e5 15 ♗d2 ♕c7 ∞ Stohl-Bönsch, Potsdam 1985

[21] 13 0-0 ♖d8 14 ♕e2 ♗d7 = P.Nikolić-Kir.Georgiev, Dubai Ol 1986

[22] 9 ♗e2 ♘b4 10 ♕b3 dc 11 ♕xc4 b6 12 ♖d1 ♕e7 13 a3 ♗a6 14 ♘b5 ♖fc8 = Miles-Vaganian, Baden 1980

[23] 9 ... ♖e8 10 0-0-0 e5 11 ♗g5 d4 12 ♗e2 ♕a5 13 ed ♘xd4 14 ♘xd4 ♗xd4 15 ♘b5! ± Langeweg-van der Wiel, Dutch Ch 1983

9 ... ♕e7 10 cd (10 ♖d1 ±) 10 ... ed 11 ♗e2 ♗e6 12 0-0 ♖ac8 13 ♖fd1 ♖fd8 14 ♘a4 ± Suba-Lobron, Dortmund 1983

[24] 10 0-0-0 ♗e7 11 g4 ♖d8 (11 ... dc?! ± Gurevich-Sokolov, USSR Ch 1988) 12 h3 a6 13 ♘d2 e5? (13 ... ♗d7 = Gurevich-Kharitonov, USSR Ch 1988) 14 g5! ± Speelman-Short, match 1988

[25] 11 cd ed 12 ♘b3 ♗xc3+ 13 bc ♕a4 15 ♗d3 b6 = Agdestein-Hjartarson, Gjovik 1985

[26] 13 ♖xc3 e5 14 ♗g3 (14 ♗g5 ♗e6 =) 14 ... d4 15 ♖c1 ♗f5 = Gavrikov-Peshina, USSR 1981

[27] 10 ♘d2 ♗b4 11 ♘b3 ♕b6 12 ♗d3 e5 13 ♗g5 d4 14 ♗xf6 gf ∞ Littlewood-Speelman, Hastings 1981-82

[28] 10 ... ♖e8 11 ♘d2 e5 12 ♗g5 ♘d4 13 ♕b1! ± Korchnoi-Karpov, match (21) 1978

[29] 11 ... dc 12 ♗xc4 ♘h5 13 ♗d6 ♗xd6 14 ♖xd6 ♘f6 15 ♕d2 ♘e7 = Adorjan-Tisdall, Lugano 1983

11 ... ♖d8 12 cd ♘xd5 (12 ... ed 13 ♗e2 ♗g4 =) 13 ♘xd5 ed 14 ♗d3 h6 15 0-0 ♗f6 16 ♕b3 ♗g4 17 ♖fd1 ♖d7 18 h3 ♗xf3 19 gf d4 = Browne-Karpov, Tilburg 1982

[30] 13 ♕xe4 ♖d8 14 ♗e2 ♖xd2 (14 ... e5 15 b4! ♕xa3 16 ♖xd8+ ♗xd8 17 0-0 ± Meduna-Velikov, Trnava 1984) 15 ♘xd2 e5 16 ♗g3 ♗e6 $\overline{\overline{\infty}}$/∓

[31] 11 ... ♗d7 12 ♗e2 ♖fc8 13 0-0 ♕d8 14 cd ed 15 ♘f3 h6 16 ♘e5 ± Karpov-Spassky, Montreal 1979

[32] 12 ♘b3 ♕b6 13 ♗g5 ♗g4 (13 ... d4 14 ♗xf6 ♗xf6 15 ♘d5 ♕d8 16 ♗d3 g6 =) 14 f3 ♗e6 15 ♘a4 ♕c7 =

12 ♗g3 d4 13 ♘b3 ♕b6 14 ♘b5 (14 ed ♗f5 15 ♗d3 =) 14 ... a6 15 c5 ♕d8 16 ed ab 17 de ♕e8 = Kaidanov-Klovans, Pinsk 1986

[33] 13 ♘b3 ♕d8 14 ♗e2 (14 ed ed 15 ♗e2 ∞/=) 14 ... a5 15 ♘a4 g6 (15 ... h6!? 16 ♗h4 ♗d7 = Portisch-Tal, Montpellier C 1985) 16 ed ♗f5 17 ♕c1 ♘xd4 18 ♘xd4 ed 19 0-0 ♖c8 =

93

	4	5	6	7	8	9	10	11	12	
8	...	♕a4+[33]	e3[34]	♗d2	♕c2	c5	a3	♗b5	♕a4	=
	♗b4	♘c6	0-0	♗d7	♗d6[35]	♗e7	a5	b6	♘a7[36]	
9	...	...	cd	♗g5	♗xf6[39]	e3	♗e2	0-0	♖ac1[40]	=
	...	...	ed[37]	h6[38]	♕xf6	0-0	♗e6	a6	♗d6[41]	
10	...	cd	♗g5	♖c1[43]	dc	♕d4	♖xc3[44]	♗xf6	e3	±
	...	ed	c5[42]	♘bd7	♘xc5	♗xc3+	♘ce4	♘xf6	0-0[45]	
11	...	...	...	♗xf6[46]	♕b3[47]	dc[49]	bc	♖d1	♘d4	±
	...	...	h6	♕xf6	c5[48]	♗xc3+	♕c6	♗e6	♕xc5[50]	
12	...	...	...	e3	♗d3[51]	♗f5!	♕c2	0-0	♘d2[52]	±
	...	...	♘bd7	c5	c4	♕a5	0-0	♖e8	g6[53]	
13	...	♗g5	e3	♗d3[55]	0-0	bc	♗xc4	♗e2	dc	∞
	...	♘bd7[54]	c5	♕a5[56]	♗xc3	dc!	b5	♘e4	f6[57]	
14	...	...	e4	♗xc4	♘xd4	♗xf6	bc	♔f1	♔g1	±/±
	...	dc	c5[58]	cd	♕a5[59]	♗xc3+	♕xc3+	♕xc4+	♘d7[60]	
15	...	...	...	e5	♕a4+[61]	0-0-0	ef	fg	♘xd4	±
	...	...	...	cd	♘c6	h6[62]	hg	♖g8	♗xc3[63]	

³³ 5 a3 ♗xc3+ 6 bc dc 7 ♕a4+ ♗d7 8 ♕xc4 ♗c6 9 e3 0-0 10 ♗e2 ♘bd7 = Chandler-Hess, Dortmund 1980

³⁴ **6 ♘e5** ♗d7 7 ♘xd7 ♕xd7 8 a3 ♗xc3+ 9 bc 0-0 10 e3 a6 =
6 a3 ♗xc3+ 7 bc 0-0 8 ♗g5 ♘e7 9 e3 ♘e4 10 ♗xe7 ♕xe7 =

³⁵ 8 ... dc 9 ♗xc4 ♗d6 10 ♘g5 e5 ∞

³⁶ 13 ♗xd7 ♘xd7 14 cb ♘xb6 = Kristinsson-Bronstein, Reykjavik 1974

³⁷ 6 ... ♘xd5 7 ♗d2 0-0 8 e3 a6 9 ♕c2 ♗d6 10 a3 ♘f6 11 ♗e2 ±

³⁸ 7 ... 0-0 8 e3 ♗d6 9 ♗xf6 ♕xf6 10 ♗e2 ♗e6 11 0-0 a6 = Keres-Bronstein, Tallinn 1973

³⁹ 8 ♗h4 g5 9 ♗g3 ♘e4 10 ♖c1 h5 11 ♘e5 ♗d7 12 ♘xd7 ♕xd7 13 f3 ♘xg3 14 hg 0-0-0 ∓ Ubilava-Bagirov, USSR 1980

⁴⁰ 12 ♖fc1 ♗d6 13 ♕d1 ♖ae8 ∞ Portisch-Sosonko, Wijk aan Zee 1975

⁴¹ 13 ♕c2 ♖fe8 14 ♘a4 ♗g4 15 ♘c5 ♗xf3 16 ♗xf3 ♘xd4! 17 ed ♕f4 18 g3 = Hansen-Andersson, Denmark v Sweden 1986

⁴² **6 ... c6** 7 ♕c2 (7 e3 ±) 7 ... h6 8 ♗h4 ♘bd7 (8 ... ♗e6 9 e3 ♘bd7 10 ♗e2 0-0 11 0-0 ♗e7 12 ♖ab1 a5 = O.Rodriguez-Sosonko, Indonesia 1982; 9 ♕b3 ±) 9 e3 0-0 10 ♗d3 ♖e8 11 0-0 ♗d6 12 ♖ab1 ♘f8 13 b4 a6 14 a4 ± Polugayevsky-Zurachov, USSR Ch 1956
6 ... ♕d6 7 ♗xf6 ♕xf6 8 ♕b3 ♕d6 9 a3 ♗xc3+ 10 ♕xc3 0-0 11 e3 ♗f5 12 ♖c1 c6 13 ♕b3 ± Hort-Larsen, Hastings 1972-73

⁴³ 7 e3 0-0 8 dc ♘bd7 9 ♖c1 ♕a5 10 ♗xf6 ♘xf6 = Pytel-Diždar, London 1983

⁴⁴ 10 ♕xc3 ♘ce4 11 ♗xf6 ♕xf6 12 ♕xf6 ♘xf6 13 e3 ± Skembris-Kovačević, Sofia 1986

⁴⁵ 13 ♗d3 ± Miles-Pytel, London 1983

⁴⁶ 7 ♗h4 c5 (7 ... g5 8 ♗g3 ♘e4 9 ♘d2 ♘xg3 10 hg c5 11 dc ♘c6 12 e4 ♗xc3+ 13 bc ♕e7 14 ♕e2 ♗e6 = Polugayevsky-Sosonko, Tilburg 1983) 8 e3 g5 (8 ... ♘c6 9 dc g5 10 ♗g3 ♘e4 11 ♗b5 ♘xc3 12 ♗xc6+ bc = Korchnoi-Sosonko, Hastings 1975-76) 9 ♗g3 ♘e4 10 ♗b5+ ♔f8 11 dc ♘xc3 12 bc ♗xc3+ 13 ♔e2 ♗xa1 14 ♕xa1 f6 ∞ Kasparov-Sosonko, Tilburg 1981

⁴⁷ **8 e3** c5 9 ♗b5+ ♗d7 10 ♗xd7+ ♘xd7 11 0-0 ♗xc3 12 bc ♕c6 = Ree-Sosonko, Wijk aan Zee 1986; 8 ... 0-0 9 ♗e2 c5 =
8 ♖c1 ♗d6 9 e3 0-0 10 ♗e2 c6 11 0-0 ♘d7 12 a3 ♗a5 13 ♕c2 ♗d8 = Rashkovsky-Kupreichik, Erevan 1984

⁴⁸ 8 ... ♕d6 9 a3 ♗a5 10 ♕b5+ ♘c6 11 e3 a6 12 ♕b3 0-0 13 ♗d3 ± Smyslov-Antoshin, Sochi 1983

⁴⁹ 9 e3 0-0 10 ♕xd5 ♘c6 11 ♗d3 ♖d8 12 ♕e4 cd = Peyev-Korzubov, Pernik 1984

⁵⁰ 13 e4! ± Makarichev

⁵¹ **8 ♗b5** ♕b6 9 ♗xd7+ ♗xd7 10 0-0 ♗xc3 11 bc h6 12 ♗h4 0-0 = Lerner-Pytel, Jurmala 1983
8 ♗e2 ♕a5 9 0-0 0-0 10 dc ♗xc3 11 bc ♕xc5 = Tarjan-Kovačević, Indonesia 1983

⁵² 12 a3 ♗xc3 13 ♕xc3 ♕xc3 14 bc h6 15 ♗h4 ± Plachetka-Kovačević, Vinkovci 1982

⁵³ **13 ♗xd7** ♘xd7 14 a3 ♗xc3 15 bc ♘b6 16 f3 ♗d7 17 ♖fe1 ♗a4! ∞ Kasparov-Tatai, Dubai Ol 1986
13 ♗h3 ♔g7 14 a3 ♗xc3 15 ♕xc3 ♕xc3 16 bc b5 17 ♖fb1 a6 18 a4 ± Tukmakov-Kovačević, Hastings 1982-83

⁵⁴ **5 ... c5** 6 cd ♕xd5 7 ♗xf6 gf 8 ♕d2 ♘c6 9 ♘xd5 ed 10 dc ± Pekarek-Dejkalo, Polanica Zdroj 1986
5 ... h6 6 ♗xf6 ♕xf6 7 e3 0-0 8 ♖c1 (8 ♗e2 dc 9 0-0 b6 10 ♖c1 ♗b7 11 ♘b5 ± Karpov-Wockenfuss, Bad Lauterberg 1977) 8 ... c6 9 a3 (9 ♗d3 dc 10 ♗xc4 ♘d7 11 ♕b3 ♗xc3+ 12 ♕xc3 b6 13 0-0 ± Farago-Inkiov, Polanica Zdroj 1981) 9 ... ♗a5 10 b4 ♗c7 11 cd ed 12 ♘xd5 ± Stohl-Barlov, Biel 1985

⁵⁵ 7 cd! ± – 5 cd

⁵⁶ 7 ... 0-0 8 0-0 cd 9 ed dc 10 ♗xc4 ♗xc3 11 bc ♕c7 12 ♕d3 ± Ree-Stehouwer, Hilversum 1984

⁵⁷ **12 ... h6** 13 ♕d4! ♘xg5 14 ♘xg5 hg 15 ♕xg7 ♖f8 16 ♗f3 ±± Korchnoi-H.Olafsson, Wijk aan Zee 1983
12 ... f6 13 ♕d4 ♘dxc5 14 ♗h4 ∞

⁵⁸ 6 ... h6 7 ♗xf6 ♕xf6 8 ♗xc4 0-0 9 0-0 ♘d7 10 e5 ♕d8 11 ♕e2 ±/± Averkin-Nikolić, Sochi 1982

⁵⁹ **8 ... ♘bd7** 9 0-0 ♗xc3 10 bc ♕a5 11 ♗e3! 0-0 12 ♕c2 ± Barlov-Dejkalo, Dubai Ol 1986
8 ... ♗xc3+ 9 bc h6 10 ♗h4 ♘bd7 11 0-0 ±/±

⁶⁰ 13 ♖c1 ±/± Ermolinsky-Speelman, Leningrad 1984

⁶¹ **8 ef** gf 9 ♗h4 ♘c6 10 ♗xd4 ♘xd4 11 ♗xc4 ♗e7 ∞/=
8 ♘xd4 ♕a5 9 ef ±/∞ Ribli-Chernin, Subotica IZ 1987

⁶² 9 ... ♗d7 10 ♘e4 ♗e7 11 ef gf 12 ♗h4 ♖c8 13 ♔b1 ♘a5 14 ♕c2 ±

⁶³ 13 bc ♕a5 14 ♕xa5 (14 ♘xc6 ♕xc3+ 15 ♔b1 bc 16 ♕xc6+ ♔e7 17 ♕d6+ ♔f6 = Yusupov-Tukmakov, USSR Ch 1987) 14 ... ♘xa5 15 h4 g4 16 h5 ± Timman-Karpov, Amsterdam 1987

	QGD V		1 d4 d5 2 c4 e6 3 ♘c3 ♘f6 4 ♗g5						
	4	5	6	7	8	9	10	11	12
1	...	cd	♕xd4	e4	♕d2[2]	ed	f4	g3	gh	±
	c5	cd[1]	♗e7	♘c6	♘xd5[3]	♗xg5	♗h4+	ed	♕xh4+[4]	
2	...	e3	♘f3[6]	cd[8]	♕d2	♗d3[11]	bc	0-0[14]	♕e2	∞/±
	♘bd7	c6[5]	♕a5[7]	♘xd5[9]	♘7b6[10]	♘xc3[12]	♘a4[13]	♕xc3	♕b2[15]	
3	...	...	...	♘d2	♕c2	♗e2[18]	0-0[19]	♘b3	♘xd4	±
	...	...	...	♗b4[16]	0-0[17]	e5	ed	♕c7	dc[20]	

[1] 5 ... ♕b6 6 ♗xf6 ♕xb2 7 ♖c1 (7 ♕c1 ♕xc1+ 8 ♖xc1 gf 9 ♘f3 ± Furman-Kavalek, Harrachov 1966) 7 ... gf 8 e3 cd 9 ed ♗b4 10 ♗b5+ ♗d7 11 ♗xd7+ ♘xd7 12 ♘e2 ± Spassky-Uitumen

[2] 8 ♗b5 0-0 9 ♗xc6 bc = Tukmakov-Ubilava, USSR 1980

[3] 8 ... ♘e4 9 ♘xe4 ed 10 ♗xe7 ♕xe7 11 ♕xd5 0-0 12 f3 ± Saidy-Bisguier, Tallinn 1971

[4] 13 ♕f2 ♕e7+ 14 ♕e2 ♗e6 15 ♘f3 d4 16 ♘b5 0-0 17 f5! ± Furman-Dzindzihashvili, USSR 1969

[5] 5 ... ♗b4 6 cd ed 7 ♗d3 c5 8 ♘e2 c4 9 ♗c2 0-0 10 0-0 ♕a5 11 a3 ♗xc3 12 ♘xc3 ± Portisch-Tringov, Plovdiv 1983

[6] 6 ♗d3 ♕a5 7 ♗h4 dc 8 ♗xc4 b5 9 ♗b3 b4 10 ♘ce2 ♗a6 11 ♘f3 ♗e7 12 0-0 0-0 ∞ Korchnoi-Ljubojević, Tilburg 1986

6 cd!? cd 7 ♗d3 a6 8 ♘f3 ♗e7 9 0-0 0-0 10 ♖c1 ± Gavrikov-Panchenko, Leningrad 1984

[7] Cambridge Springs

[8] 7 ♗xf6 ♘xf6 8 ♗d3 ♗b4 9 ♕b3 c5 (9 ... dc 10 ♗xc4 c5 = Capablanca-Lasker, New York 1924) 10 cd ed 11 dc 0-0 12 ♖c1 ♗g4 13 ♘d4 ♖ac8 14 a3 ♗xc5 = Groszpeter-Inkiov, Plovdiv 1982

[9] **7 ... ed** 8 ♗d3 ♘e4 9 0-0 ♘xg5 10 ♘xg5 ♘f6 11 h3 ± Salov-Raičević, Moscow 1986

7 ... ♘e4 8 de fe 9 ♕a4 ♕xa4 10 ♘xa4 ♗b4+ 11 ♔e2 b5 12 ♘c5 ±

[10] 8 ... ♗b4 9 ♖c1 e5 (9 ... ♘7b6 10 ♗d3 f6 11 ♗h4 ♘xc3 12 bc ♗a3 13 ♖b1 c5 14 ♕c2 ± Vaganian-Smyslov, Montpellier C 1985) 10 a3 ♗xc3+ (10 ... ♗d6 11 de ♘xe5 12 ♘xe5 ♗xe5 13 b4! ± Kasparov-Smyslov, match 1984) 11 bc ♕a3 12 e4 ♘c7 13 ♗d3 ∞/±; 9 ... 0-0 10 ♗d3! e5 11 0-0 ed 12 ed f6 13 ♗h4 ♖d8 14 a3! ± Kasparov-Smyslov, match 1984

[11] 9 ♘xd5 ♕xd2 10 ♘xd2 ed 11 ♗d3 a5 =

[12] 9 ... ♗b4!? 10 ♖c1 ♘a4 11 0-0 ♘axc3 12 bc ♘xc3 13 ♕b2 ∞ Loginov-Panchenko, USSR 1986

[13] 10 ... ♘d5 11 0-0 ♕xc3 12 ♕e2 ♗d6 (12 ... ♗e7 13 ♗xe7 ♕xe7 14 ♘e5 ±/± Polugaevsky-Seirawan, Biel IZ 1985) 13 ♘d2 ♕a5 14 ♘c4 ♕c7 15 e4 (15 ♕h5 ♗e7 16 f4 ♘f6! ± Vaganian-Torre, Biel IZ 1985) 15 ... ♗xh2+ 16 ♔h1 ♗f4 17 ♗h4 ♘b6 18 ♕g4 ±/± Novikov-Smagin, USSR 1985

[14] 11 ♖c1!? ♘xc3 12 0-0 ♗b4 ∞ – 9 ... ♗b4

[15] 13 ♕d1 ♘c3 14 ♕e1 f6 15 ♗h4 ♗b4 16 a3 ∞/± E.Vladimirov-Nogueiras, Havana 1986; 16 e4 =

[16] 7 ... dc 8 ♗xf6 ♘xf6 9 ♘xc4 ♕c7 10 ♗e2 (10 ♖c1 ♗e7 11 g3 0-0 12 ♗g2 ♘d5 13 0-0 ♖d8 14 ♕e2 ♗d7 15 ♘e4 ± Polugaevsky-Sveshnikov, Kislovodsk 1982) 10 ... ♗e7 11 0-0 (11 a3 ♗d7 12 ♖c1 0-0 13 0-0 c5 14 dc ♕xc5 15 b4 ♕c7 16 ♘a5! ± Rashkovsky-Smagin, USSR Ch 1986) 11 ... 0-0 12 ♖c1 ♖d8 13 ♕c2 ♗d7 14 ♘e4 ± Kasparov-R.Rodriguez, Moscow IZ 1982

[17] 8 ... dc 9 ♗xf6 ♘xf6 10 ♘xc4 ♕c7 11 a3 (11 g3!? ±) 11 ... ♗e7 12 ♗e2 0-0 13 b4 b6 14 0-0 ± Ribli-Smyslov, Las Palmas IZ 1982

[18] 9 a3 dc!? (9 ... ♘e4 10 ♘cxe4 de 11 ♗h4 ♖e8 12 0-0-0 ± Timman-Yusupov, Linares 1983) 10 ♗xf6 ♘xf6 11 ♘xc4 ♗xc3+ 12 ♕xc3 ♕xc3+ 13 bc c5 14 ♗e2 ½-½ Kasparov-Smyslov, match 1984; 12 bc!? Smagin-Rezenberg, USSR 1984

[19] 10 ♗xf6 ♘xf6 11 de ♘e4 12 cd ♘xc3 13 bc ♗xc3 14 ♖c1 ♗xe5 15 dc bc ½-½ Kasparov-Smyslov, match 1984

[20] 13 ♗xc4 ♗xc3 (13 ... ♕e5 14 ♘f3 ♕e7 15 a3 ♗a5 16 ♖ad1 ± Belyavsky-Smagin, USSR Ch 1986) 14 bc ♘e5 15 ♗e2 ± Veingold-Kupreichik, USSR 1984

	5	6	7	8	9	10	11	12	13	
QGD VI			**1 d4 d5 2 c4 e6 3 ♘c3 ♘f6 4 ♗g5 ♗e7**							
1	♘f3	♕c2	a3[2]	dc	♖d1	cd	♗xe7	♘xd5	e3	=
	0-0	♘a6[1]	c5	♘xc5	b6	♘xd5![3]	♕xe7	ed	♕f6[4]	
2	...	♗xf6	♕d2[5]	e4	d5	e5	♕xd5	♗xc4	0-0	=
	h6	♗xf6	dc[6]	c5	ed	♗g5[7]	♘c6	0-0	♕xd5[8]	
3	...	♗h4	♕c2[9]	dc	e3	♗xc4	♗d3	a3	b4	=
	...	0-0	c5[10]	dc[11]	♕a5	♕xc5	♘c6	♗d7	♕h5[12]	
4	...	...	♖c1	e4[14]	e5	♗xe7	♗xc4	bc	♕e2	=
	...	...	dc[13]	♘c6[15]	♘d5	♘cxe7	♘xc3	b6	♗b7[16]	

[1] **6 ... dc** 7 e4 ♘c6 8 ♖d1 ♘b4 9 ♕b1 ♘d3+ 10 ♗xd3 cd 11 ♕xd3 ± Torre-Kurajica, Novi Sad 1984

6 ... h6 7 ♗xf6 ♗xf6 8 ♖d1 (8 0-0-0 c5 9 dc d4 10 ♘e4 e5 11 e3 ♘c6 12 ed ed 13 a3 ♗g4 ∞ Chekhov-Bönsch, Leipzig 1986; 8 e4 ±) 8 ... c6 9 e4 b6 10 ♗d3 de 11 ♗xe4 ♗b7 12 0-0 ♘d7 13 b4 ♕c7 14 ♖fe1 ± Romanishin-Tarjan, Hastings 1976-77

6 ... ♘bd7 7 0-0-0 c5 8 cd ♘xd5 9 ♗xe7 ♕xe7 10 e4 ♘xc3 11 ♕xc3 cd 12 ♖xd4 ♘b6 = Miles-Hansen, Reykjavik 1986

[2] 7 ♖d1 ♘b4 8 ♕b1 dc 9 a3 ♘bd5 10 e4 ♘xc3 11 bc b5 ∞ Dolmatov

[3] **10 ... ed?!** 11 e3 ♗b7 12 ♗e2 ♖c8 13 ♕b1 ♘e6 14 ♗h4! ± Dolmatov-Podgayets, USSR 1985

[4] Dolmatov

[5] **7 ♕c2** dc 8 0-0-0 a6 9 e4 b5 10 e5 ♗g5+ 11 ♔b1 ♗b7 12 h4 ∞ Bradbury-Wells, London 1985

7 e4 de 8 ♘xe4 ♘c6 9 ♘xf6+ ♕xf6 10 ♕d3 b6 11 ♕e4 ♗b7 = Tatai-Geller, Las Palmas 1979

7 ♕b3 c5 (7 ... c6 8 0-0-0 dc 9 ♕xc4 b5 10 ♕b3 a5 11 e4 a4 12 ♕c2 ± Timman-Yusupov, match 1986, and Thipsay-Barua, Dhaka 1986) 8 dc dc 9 ♕xc4 0-0 10 ♖c1 ♗d7 11 g3 ♕a5 12 ♗g2 ♗b5 = Lerner-Belyavsky, USSR Ch 1986

[6] **7 ... 0-0** 8 e4 c5 9 cd cd 10 ♘xd4 ed 11 ed ♘c6 = Tukmakov-Speelman, Moscow 1985

[7] 10 ... d4 11 ef dc 12 ♕e3+ ♗e6 13 fg ♖g8 14 ♕xc3 ±

[8] 14 ♗xd5 ♘b4 15 ♘xg5 (15 ♗e4 f5 16 ♗d5+ ♔xd5 17 ♘xd5 ♗d8 18 ♖fd1 ♖e8 = Ubilava-Dorfman, Tashkent 1984) 15 ... ♘xd5 16 ♘xd5 hg 17 f4 gf = Karpov-Kasparov, match (21) 1984-85

[9] 7 ♕b3 c5 8 dc ♘bd7 9 e3 ♘xc5 10 ♕c2 b6 = Kurajica-Kir.Georgiev, Sarajevo 1985

[10] **7 ... ♘a6** 8 ♖d1 b6 9 ♗xf6 ♗xf6 10 e4 c6 11 a3 ♗b7 12 ♗d3 dc 13 ♗xc4 b5 14 ♗e2 b4 = Torre-Karpov, Brussels 1986

7 ... b6 8 ♗xf6 ♗xf6 9 e4 ♘c6 10 0-0-0 de 11 ♕xe4 ♗b7 12 ♗d3 g6 13 h4 ♖b8 ∞ Ree-Hjartarson, Reykjavik 1984

[11] 8 ... ♘c6 9 e3 ♕a5 10 a3 ♗d7 11 ♖d1 ♕xc5 12 ♗e2 ♖fc8 13 ♕b1 ± Lerner-Geller, Moscow 1986

[12] Filip

[13] **7 ... b6** 8 cd ♘xd5 9 ♗xe7 ♕xe7 10 ♘xd5 ed and now:
11 ♕d2 ♗e6 12 g3 c5 13 ♘e5 ♘d7 = Savon-Balashov, Moscow 1982
11 ♕c2 ♘a6 12 e3 ♗xf1 13 ♔xf1 c5 ∞/= Ermolinsky-Podgayets, USSR 1981
11 g3 ♖e8 (11 ... ♗b7 12 ♗g2 c5 13 0-0 ♘d7 14 dc bc 15 ♘e1 ♖fd8 = Christiansen-Spassky, London 1982) 12 ♗g2 ♗a6 13 ♘e5 ♘d7 = Tukmakov-Vaganian, Hastings 1982-83

[14] 8 e3 c5 9 ♗xc4 cd 10 ed (10 ♘xd4 ♗d7 11 ♗e2 ♘c6 12 ♘b3 ♘d5 = Korchnoi-Karpov, match (17) 1981) 10 ... ♘c6 11 0-0 ♘h5 12 ♗xe7 ♘xe7 = Christiansen-Karpov, London 1982

[15] 8 ... c5 9 ♗xc4 ♘xe4 10 ♘xe4 ♗xh4 11 dc ♕xd1+ 12 ♖xd1 ♗e7 13 ♘e5 b6 ∞/= Vasyukov-Lputian, USSR 1983

[16] Tukmakov-Belyavsky, Tilburg 1984

	6	7	8	9	10	11	12	13	14	
1	Rc1	Bh4	cd[1]	Nxd5	Bxe7	Be2[2]	dc	Qxd5	Qxc5	=
	h6	b6	Nxd5	ed	Qxe7	c5[3]	bc	Bb7	Qxc5[4]	
2	Nf3	cd[5]	Rc1[6]	Bd3	0-0	Bf5[7]	Qc2	Bh3	Bxe7	±
	b6	ed	Bb7	Nbd7	c5	Re8[8]	g6	Ne4	Qxe7[9]	
3	...	Bxe7	cd[10]	bc	Qb3	c4[12]	Be2	Bxc4	Qxc4	±
	Ne4	Qxe7	Nxc3	ed	c6[11]	Be6	dc	Bxc4	Nd7[13]	
4	...	Bxf6	Qb3[14]	Rd1	Bd3	cd[16]	e4	Bxe4	0-0	=
	h6	Bxf6	c6	Nd7	b6[15]	cd	de	Rb8	b5[17]	
5	...	...	Qd2	Bxc4	dc	Ne4	Rd1[19]	b4	a3	=
	...	...	dc[18]	c5	Nd7	Be7	Qc7	a5	ab[20]	
6	...	...	Qc2	dc[21]	cd[23]	Bb5	0-0	ed	Nxd4	=
	...	...	c5	Nc6[22]	ed	Qa5[24]	d4!	Nxd4	Bxd4[25]	
7	...	...	Rc1	Bd3	cd	b4	0-0[28]	Qb3	a4	=
	...	...	c6[26]	Nd7	ed[27]	a6	Be7	Bd6	Nf6[29]	
8	...	...	...	...	0-0	Bxc4	h3[32]	ed	Bb3	±/=
	...	...	...	...	dc[30]	e5[31]	ed	Nb6[33]	Bf5[34]	
9	...	Bh4	Bxe7	cd[35]	bc	Qb3[36]	c4[38]	Bxc4	Be2!	±
	...	Ne4	Qxe7	Nxc3	ed	Rd8[37]	dc[39]	Nc6	Rd6[40]	

---

[1] 8 Bxf6 Bxf6 9 cd ed 10 g3 Be7 11 Bg2 c6 12 Nge2 Nd7 13 Qa4 Bb7 14 0-0 a5 = Adorjan-van der Sterren, Wijk aan Zee 1984

[2] 11 Ne2 Bb7 12 Nf4 c5 (12 ... Nd7 13 Be2 Nf6 14 Qa4 c5 15 0-0 Rfc8 = Petrosian-Fischer, Curaçao C 1962) 13 Be2 cd 14 Qxd4 Nc6 ∞ Portisch-Spassky, match 1980

[3] 11 ... a5 12 Bf3 Qb4+ 13 Qd2 c6 14 Rc3 Qd6 15 Ne2 ± Portisch-Ivkov, Wijk aan Zee 1972

11 ... Bb7 12 Bf3 c5 13 Ne2 Nd7 14 dc ± Portisch-Medina, Palma de Mallorca 1966

[4] 15 Rxc5 Bxg2 16 Bf3 Bxh1 17 Bxh1 = Neishtadt

[5] 7 Be2 dc 8 Bxc4 Bb7 9 0-0 Nbd7 (9 ... Nd5 10 Bxe7 Qxe7 11 Rc1 Nxc3 12 Rxc3 Rc8 13 Bd3 ±/± Inkiov-Radulov, Herculana 1982) 10 Qe2 Nd5 11 Bf4 Bd6 =

[6] 8 Bd3 Bb7 9 Qc2 Nbd7 10 h4 c5 11 0-0-0 cd (11 ... a6 12 g4 c4 13 Bf5 g6 14 Bxf6 Bxf6 15 g5 ± Spassky-Bobotsov, Havana Ol 1966) 12 Nxd4 Re8 13 Kb1 a6 14 g4 ±/± Alekhine-Yates, Hamburg 1910

[7] 11 Bb5!? Ne4 12 Bxe7 Qxe7 13 dc Nxc3 14 Rxc3 Nxc5 15 Qd4 ± Najdorf-Jimenez, Argentina 1971

[8] 11 ... c4 12 Ne5 g6 13 Bb1 Re8 14 f4 ± Kuligowski-Radulov, Smederevska Palanka 1979

[9] 15 Bxd7 Qxd7 16 dc bc 17 Nxe4 de

[18] Rfd1 ± Gligorić-Radulov, Venice 1971

[10] 8 Qc2 Nxc3 9 Qxc3 c6 (9 ... b6 10 cd ed 11 b4 c6 12 Rc1 Bb7 13 Bd3 ± Kasparov-Hübner, match 1985) 10 Bd3 Nd7 11 0-0 dc 12 Bxc4 b6 ±/=

8 Rc1 c6 9 Bd3 Nxc3 10 Rxc3 dc 11 Rxc4 Nd7 12 0-0 e5 13 Qc2 g6 14 Re1 Nb6 15 Rc5 Nd7 ∞ Portisch-Diždar, Sarajevo 1986

[11] 10 ... Rd8 11 c4 dc 12 Bxc4 Nc6 13 Be2 ±

[12] 11 Rb1 b6 12 Bd3 Be6 13 0-0 ∞/± Tukmakov-Lein, Hastings 1982-83

[13] 15 0-0 c5 16 Rac1 ± Tal-Kholmov, USSR 1959

[14] 8 cd ed 9 Qc2 Nc6 10 Be2 Ne7 11 0-0 Bf5 12 Bd3 Bxd3 13 Qxd3 Nc8 14 b4 Nb6 = Plachetka-Bönsch, Warsaw 1983

[15] 10 ... Qb6 11 Qc2 dc 12 Bxc4 c5 13 0-0 cd 14 ed Na5 15 Be4 Be7 16 d5 ± Hébert-Abramović, Hastings 1984-85

[16] 11 0-0 Bb7 12 Rfe1 a6 13 Bb1 g6 14 cd cd = Cserna-Pigusov, Copenhagen 1986

[17] 15 Rfe1 Qb6 16 Bb1 Bb7 = Kasparov-Karpov, match (3) 1985

[18] 8 ... c5 9 cd cd 10 Nxd4 ed 11 Bb5 Bd7 12 0-0 Bxb5 13 Ndxb5 a6 14 Nd4 ± Seirawan-Speelman, Wijk aan Zee 1983

8 ... c6 9 0-0-0 Nd7 10 h4 g6 11 g4 Bg7 12 g5 h5 13 e4! ± van der Sterren-Donner, Marbella 1982

8 ... b6 9 cd ed 10 Be2 (10 Rd1 Be6 11 g3

98

♕d6 12 ♗g2 ♘d7 Geller) 10 ... ♗e6 11 0-0
c5 12 dc bc 13 ♖fd1 ♗xc3 14 ♕xc3 ♘d7 =
Petrosian-Karpov, USSR Ch 1983

8 ... ♘c6 9 ♖c1 (9 cd ed 10 ♗e2 ♗f5 11 0-0
♘e7 12 b4 c6 13 ♖fc1 a6 = Kasparov-Karpov,
Moscow 1981) 9 ... a6 10 ♗e2 dc 11 ♗xc4 e5
12 d5 ♘a7 13 ♕c2 (13 0-0 ♗g4 14 ♗e2 ♘b5 ∞
D.Gurevich-A.Grünfeld, Beer-Sheva 1986)
13 ... ♘b5 14 ♘xb5 ab 15 ♗b3 ± Karpov-
Kasparov, match (19) 1984-85

[19] 12 c6 bc 13 0-0 ♘f6 14 ♕c2 ♘xe4 15 ♕xe4
♗f6 = Tukmakov-Petrosian, USSR Ch 1985

[20] 15 ab b6 = Pfleger-Kurajica 1971-72

[21] 9 0-0-0 cd 10 ed ♘c6 11 h4 ♕c7 12 ♔b1
♖d8 =

[22] **9 ... dc** 10 ♗xc4 ♕a5 11 0-0 ♗xc3 12 ♕xc3
♕xc3 13 bc ♘d7 14 c6 bc 15 ♖ab1 ♘b6
16 ♗e2 ± Karpov-Kasparov, match (27) 1984-85

9 ... ♕a5 10 cd ed 11 0-0-0 ♗e6 12 ♘xd5
♖c8 13 ♔b1 ♗xd5 14 ♖xd5 ♘c6 15 ♗c4 ±
Kasparov-Timman, USSR v World 1984

[23] 10 ♗e2 ♕a5 11 0-0 ♕xc5 12 ♖fd1 ♖d8
13 ♖ac1 dc 14 ♘e4 ♕e7 = Malanyuk-Klovans,
USSR 1985

[24] 11 ... ♗g4 12 ♗xc6 bc 13 ♘d4 ♗xd4 14 ed
♖e8+ 15 ♔f1 ♕f6 ∞ Douven-Geller, Eindhoven
v CSKA 1986

[25] 15 ♕a4 ♗xc3 16 bc ♕xa4 17 ♖xa4 ♗e6 =
Chernin-Geller, USSR Ch 1985

[26] 8 ... a6!? 9 a3 c6 10 ♗d3 ♘d7 11 0-0 b5
12 cb cb 13 ♗b1 ♗b7 = Portisch-Short, Brussels
1986

[27] 10 ... cd 11 0-0 b6 12 e4 de 13 ♗xe4 ♖b8
14 ♕e2 ± Gligorić-Spassky, Palma de Mallorca
1968

[28] 12 a4 ♗e7 13 b5 ab 14 ab ♗d6 15 0-0 ♘f6 =
Ivkov-Klovans, Riga 1981

[29] 15 ♖fe1 ♗e6 = Rajković-Abramović,
Yugoslav Ch 1984

[30] 10 ... ♗e7 11 ♘e5 ♗xe5 12 de dc 13 ♗xc4
♕a5 14 f4 ± Douven-van der Sterren, Dutch
Ch 1986

[31] **11 ... b6** 12 e4 ♗b7 13 e5 ♗e7 14 ♕e2 ∞/±
Karpov-Spassky, Lucerne 1985, and Portisch-
Spassky, London 1986

11 ... c5 12 ♕e2 a6 13 ♖fd1 cd 14 ♘xd4 ♕e7
15 ♘e4 ± Kasparov-Karpov, match (12) 1986,
and Kasparov-H.Olafsson, Dubai Ol 1986

[32] **12** ♘e4 ed 13 ♘xf6+ ♗xf6 14 ♕xd4 ♗g4
15 ♕f4 ♗xf3 16 ♕xf3 = Dorfman-Lputian,

USSR 1984

12 ♗b3 ed 13 ed ♖e8 14 ♕d2 (14 h3 ♘f8
15 d5 ♗d7 16 ♕d2 ♖c8 17 dc ♗xc6 = Smejkal-
Andersson, Reggio Emilia 1986) 14 ... ♘f8
15 d5 ♗f5 16 ♕f4 ♗g6 = Portisch-Spassky,
Bugojno 1986

[33] 13 ... c5 14 ♗b3 cd 15 ♘d5 b6 16 ♘xd4
♗xd4 17 ♕xd4 ± Kasparov-Karpov, match (10)
1986

[34] 15 ♖e1 and now:

15 ... ♗g5 16 ♖a1! ♘d7 17 d5! ± Kasparov-
Short, Brussels 1986

15 ... ♕d6 16 ♘e5 ♗xe5 17 de ♕xd1
18 ♖cxd1 ♖fd8 19 f4 h5 20 ♘e4 ± Oll-Gelfand,
USSR 1986

15 ... ♖e8 16 ♖xe8+ ♕xe8 17 ♕d2 ♕d7
18 ♖e1 ± Kasparov-Karpov, match (23) 1985

15 ... a5 16 a3 ♖e8 (16 ... ♕d7 17 ♘e5 ♗xe5
18 de ♕xd1 19 ♖cxd1 a4 20 ♗a2 ± Dohoyan-
Kruppa,Irkutsk 1986) 17 ♖xe8+ ♕xe8 18 ♕d2
♕d7 (18 ... ♘d7 19 ♕f4 ♗g6 20 h4! ♕d8
21 ♘a4 ± Kasparov-Karpov, match (22) 1986)
19 ♖e1 ♖e8 20 ♖xe8+ ♕xe8 21 ♕f4 ♗e6! ±/=
M.Gurevich-van der Sterren, Baku 1986, and
Benjamin-Hjartarson, Moscow 1987

[35] 9 ♕c2 ♘xc3 10 ♕xc3 dc 11 ♗xc4 b6 12 ♖c1
♗b7 13 ♗e2 ♘d7 14 0-0 ♖fc8 (14 ... c5 15 dc
♘xc5 16 b4 ♘a6 17 a3 ♖ac8 = Byrne) 15 ♖fd1
c5 16 ♕a3 ♖c7 17 ♖c3 ♖ac8 18 ♖dc1 ♘f6 =
Tal-Averkin, Sochi 1982

9 ♖c1 c6 10 ♗d3 (10 ♕c2 ♘xc3 11 ♕xc3
♘d7 12 a3 dc 13 ♗xc4 b6 14 0-0 ♗b7 =
Petrosian-Spassky, match (6) 1969) 10 ...
♘xc3 11 ♖xc3 dc 12 ♗xc4 (12 ♖xc4 ♘d7
13 ♗b1 e5 14 ♕c2 f5 =) 12 ... ♘d7 13 0-0 b6
(13 ... e5 =) 14 ♗d3 c5 15 ♗b5 ♖d8 16 ♗c6
♖b8 17 ♕c2 cd 18 ♘xd4 e5! = Smyslov-
Kasparov, match 1984

[36] 11 ♗e2 ♗e6 12 ♘e5 ♘d7 13 ♘d3 c5 14 0-0
c4 ∞ Spassky-Flesch, Tel Aviv Ol 1964

[37] 11 ... ♕d6 12 c4 dc 13 ♗xc4 ♘c6 (13 ...
♘d7 14 0-0 ♘b6 15 ♖fc1 ±) 14 ♕c3 b6 15 0-0
♗b7 16 ♖ac1 ±

[38] 12 ♗d3 c5 13 ♕a3 b6 14 0-0 ♘d7 15 ♖fe1
♗b7 ∞ Ftacnik-Inkiov, Banja Luka 1983

[39] 12 ... ♘c6 13 cd ♕b4+ 14 ♘d2 ♕xb3
15 ♘xb3 ♘b4 16 ♖c1 ♘d5 17 e4 ♖e8 18 f3 ±/±

[40] 15 0-0 ♖b8 (15 ... ♗e6 16 ♘c3 ♗d5 17 ♖fc1
♖e8 18 ♘e1 ± Korelov-Kholmov, USSR Ch
1963) 16 ♕c3 ± Belyavsky

	8	9	10	11	12	13	14	15	16	
1	cd[1]	♗xe7[3]	♘xd5[4]	♖c1[5]	♕a4	♕a3	♗e2[7]	0-0	b3	=
	♘xd5[2]	♕xe7	ed	♗e6[6]	c5	♖c8	a5[8]	♕a7	♘d7[9]	
2	...	...	...	...	♗d3	dc[10]	0-0	e4	♗xe4	=
	...	...	...	...	c5	bc	♘d7	de[11]	♖ab8[12]	
3	♕c2	♖d1[13]	cd	♗d3	0-0	♗f5	a4	♗xe7	♗xd7	=
	♗b7	♘bd7[14]	ed[15]	c5	a6	c4	♘e8	♕xe7	♕xd7[16]	
4	♕b3	♗xf6	cd	♖d1	a3[19]	♗d3[21]	dc	0-0	♕c2	=
	♗b7	♗xf6	ed[17]	♖e8[18]	♖e7[20]	c5	bc	♕b6	♘d7[22]	
5	♖c1	♗xf6	cd	b4[23]	bc	♗b5[25]	0-0	♕a4	♘xd4	=
	♗b7	♗xf6	ed	c5[24]	bc	♘a6	♘c7	cd	♗xd4[26]	
6	...	♗e2	♗xc4	0-0	♕e2[28]	a4	♘xd4[30]	♖fd1	♗g3	=
	...	dc[27]	♘bd7	c5	a6[29]	cd	♘c5	♕e8	♘fe4[31]	
7	...	♗d3	0-0	♕e2[32]	♖fd1[34]	♘xd4	♗xf6	cd	♕xd3	=
	...	♘bd7	c5	♖c8[33]	cd	♘e5	♗xf6	♘xd3	♗xd5[35]	
8	♗e2	♗xf6	cd	b4[36]	bc	♖b1	0-0	♗b5	♕c2[39]	=
	♗b7	♗xf6	ed	c5[37]	bc	♗c6[38]	♘d7	♕c7	♖fc8[40]	
9	♗d3	♗xc4	0-0	♕e2	♗g3	hg	♖fd1	gf	ed	=
	dc	♗b7	♘bd7	♘e4	♘xg3[41]	c5[42]	♗xf3!	cd	♗d6[43]	
10	...	0-0	♕e2	♖fd1	♗g3	ed[46]	hg	♘e5	♖ac1	=
	♗b7	♘bd7[44]	c5	♘e4[45]	cd	♘xg3	♘f6	♖c8!	dc[47]	

Header: QGD VIII   1 d4 d5 2 c4 e6 3 ♘c3 ♘f6 4 ♗g5 ♗e7 5 e3 0-0 6 ♘f3 h6 7 ♗h4 b6

[1]   8 ♗xf6 ♕xf6 9 cd ed 10 ♕d2 (10 ♗e2 ♗e6 11 0-0 c5 12 ♖c1 ♘d7 13 ♗a6 ♕c7 14 b4 c4 ∞ Alburt-Dlugy, New York 1983) 10 ... ♗e6 11 ♖d1 ♕e7 12 g3 c5 ∞/= Bischoff-Lobron, West German Ch 1984

[2]   8 ... ed 9 ♗d3 ♗b7 10 0-0 ♘e4 (10 ... c5 11 ♘e5! ± Kasparov-Belyavsky, match 1983) 11 ♗xe7 ♕xe7 12 ♕b3 (12 ♘e5 ♘d7 13 f4 ♘xe5 14 fe c5 15 ♕e1 ♖ad8 16 ♖d1 ♕g5 17 ♖f3 f6! = Kasparov-Belyavsky, match 1983) 12 ... ♖d8 13 ♖c1 c5 14 ♗b1 ♘c6 15 ♖fd1 ± Gligorić-Kurajica, Rovinj/Zagreb 1970

[3]   9 ♗g3 c5 10 ♗d3 ♗b7 11 0-0 ♘d7 12 ♕e2 cd 13 ed ♘xc3 14 bc ♖c8 = Razuvayev-Timman, Vilnius 1969

[4]   10 ♖c1 ♘f6 (10 ... ♗b7 11 ♘xd5 ♗xd5 12 ♗e2 ♖c8 13 0-0 c5 14 dc ♖xc5 15 ♖xc5 ♕xc5 16 ♕a4 ♗c6 17 ♕f4 ♘d7 18 b4 ♕f8 = Kasparov-Timman, USSR v World 1984; 12 ♕d4! ±/= Portisch-Karpov, Bugojno 1986) 11 ♗e2 ♗b7 12 0-0 ♘bd7 13 ♕a4 c5 14 ♕a3 ♖fc8 15 ♖fd1 ♕f8 = Filip-Fischer, Curaçao C 1962

[5]   11 ♗e2 ♗e6 12 0-0 ♘d7 13 ♕a4 c5 14 ♖fd1 ♖fc8 15 ♘e1 c4 16 b3 ♘f6 17 ♗f3 ♘e4 ∞ Larsen-Petursson, Reykjavik 1985

[6]   11 ... ♗b7 12 ♗d3 c5 13 0-0 ♘d7 14 b3 ♖fc8 15 ♖c2 ± Loginov-Gusev, USSR 1983

[7]   14 ♗b5 ♕b7! 15 dc bc 16 ♖xc5 ♖xc5 17 ♕xc5 ♘a6 18 ♗xa6 ♕xa6 = Timman-Geller, Hilversum 1973

[8]   14 ... ♕f8 15 dc bc 16 0-0 ♘d7 17 ♖fd1 a5 18 ♕c3 ♖cb8 19 ♘e5 ± Tarjan-Christiansen, USA 1983

14 ... ♕b7!? 15 b3 c4 16 bc dc 17 ♘d2 b5 18 ♗f3 ♗d5 ∞ Hernandez-Diaz, Cienfuegos 1983

[9]   Karpov-Kavalek, Linares 1981

[10]   13 b3 ♘d7 14 0-0 ♘f6 15 ♕e2 a5 16 ♗b5 ♖fc8 = Velikov-Short, Plovdiv 1984

[11]   15 ... d4 16 ♘d2! ±/±

[12]   17 b3 ♘b6 18 ♖e1 ♖fd8 19 ♕e2 ♘d5 = Danner-Lechtynsky, Dubai Ol 1986

[13]   9 ♗xf6 ♗xf6 10 cd ed 11 0-0-0 ♘c6! 12 h4 ♗c8 13 a3 ♘e7 ∞/= Cvitan-Cvetković, Opatija 1984

9 0-0-0!? ♘bd7 10 ♖g1 ∞ Spassky-Drimer, Reykjavik 1957

[14]   9 ... ♘e4 10 ♗g3 ♘d7 11 ♗d3 ♘xg3 12 hg ♘f6 13 e4 ♗b4 14 cd ed 15 e5 ♘e4 16 0-0 ± Romanishin-Chandler, Sochi 1982

[15]   10 ... ♘xd5 11 ♗g3 c5 12 ♗b5 cd 13 ♖xd4 ♗c5 14 ♖d1 ♘7f6 15 e4 ± Kir.Georgiev-Georgadze, Lvov 1984

[16] 17 b3 ♘d6 = Ubilava-Vasyukov, USSR 1982

[17] 10 ... ♗xd5 11 ♘xd5 ed 12 ♖c1 ♕d6 13 ♕c2 ♖c8 ∞ van der Sterren-van der Wiel, Dutch Ch 1983

[18] 11 ... ♕d6 12 ♗d3 c5 13 ♗b1 ♘d7 14 0-0 ♖fd8! = Basin-Gelfand, USSR 1984

[19] 12 ♗d3 c6 (12 ... c5 13 dc ♘d7 14 c6 ♗xc6 15 0-0 ♘c5 16 ♕a3 ± Kasparov-Belyavsky, USSR Ch 1978) 13 0-0 ♘d7 14 e4 ♘f8 15 ♖fe1 ∞/= Barbero-Lobron, Mendoza 1985

[20] 12 ... c6 13 ♗d3 ♘d7 14 0-0 ♘f8 15 ♗b1 g6 16 ♖fe1 ♘e6 17 ♗a2 ♗g7 (17 ... ♕c7 18 ♕a4 ♖ad8 19 b4 ♕b8 20 ♕c2! ± Korchnoi-Kasparov, match 1983) 18 ♕a4 b5! = Agzamov-Petrosian, USSR Ch 1985

[21] 13 ♗e2 c6 14 0-0 ♘a6 15 ♕a2 ♘c7 16 ♖d2 ♘e8 ∓ Witt-Geller, Baden-Baden 1985

[22] W.Schmidt-Bönsch, Dresden 1985

[23] 11 ♗e2 ♘d7 (11 ... ♗e7 12 0-0 ♘d7 13 ♕a4 a6 =) 12 0-0 ♗e7 13 ♕b3 ♘f6 14 ♖fd1 a6 15 ♘e5 ♕d6 = Dzindzihashvili-Hübner, Chicago 1982

[24] 11 ... c6 12 ♗d3 ♖e8 (12 ... ♕d6 13 ♕b3 ♘d7 14 0-0 ♗e7 15 ♖b1 a5 = Ivkov-Gligorić, Bled/Portorož 1979) 13 0-0 ♘d7 14 ♕b3 ♘f8 = Korchnoi-Spassky, match 1977-78

[25] 13 dc ♘d7 14 ♘b5 ♖c8 15 ♘d6 ♖xc5 16 ♘xb7 ♖xc1+ 17 ♕xc1 ♕b6 = Timman-Hübner, Tilburg 1979

[26] 17 ♕xd4 ♘e6 18 ♕e5 a6 19 ♗a4 d4! = Raičević-Geller, Moscow 1986

[27] 9 ... ♘bd7 and now:
10 0-0 c5 11 ♗g3 a6 12 cd ♘xd5 13 ♘xd5 ♗xd5 14 dc ♘xc5 15 b4 ♘e4 = Karpov-Kasparov, match (17) 1984-85
10 cd ed 11 0-0 c5 12 ♕a4! (12 dc bc 13 ♗b5 ♘b6 14 ♕e2 a6 15 ♗d3 ♘h5! = Ftacnik-Speelman, Hastings 1983-84; 13 ♖c2 ♖c8 14 ♖d2 ♕b6 15 ♕b3 ♖fd8 = Karpov-Kasparov, match (25) 1984-85) 12 ... a6 13 dc bc 14 ♖fd1 ♕b6 15 ♕b3 ♕a7 16 ♗g3 ± Karpov-Kasparov, match (31) 1984-85, and Chekhov-Bönsch, Potsdam 1985

[28] 12 dc ♘xc5 13 ♕e2 a6 14 ♖fd1 ♕e8 ∞/= Kasparov-Karpov, match (36) 1984-85

[29] 12 ... cd 13 ed ♘h5 14 ♗g3 ♘df6 15 ♖fd1 ♗d6 16 ♘e5 ♖c8 = Ftacnik-Belyavsky, Wijk aan Zee 1985

[30] 14 ed ♘h5 15 ♗xe7 ♕xe7 16 d5 ♘f4 17 ♕e3 ♕f6 = Kasparov-Karpov, match (34) 1984-85

[31] Yusupov-Karpov, Bugojno 1986

[32] 11 ♗g3 cd 12 ed dc 13 ♗xc4 a6 14 a4 ♘h5 = Romanishin-van der Wiel, Sarajevo 1984

[33] 11 ... ♘e4 12 ♗g3 ♘xg3 13 hg cd 14 ed dc 15 ♗xc4 ♘f6 16 ♖fd1 ♗b4 ∞/= Lobron-Grünfeld, Biel 1986

[34] 12 ♗g3 cd 13 ed dc 14 ♗xc4 ♘h5 15 ♗a6 ♘xg3 16 hg ♗xa6 17 ♕xa6 ♖c7 = Najdorf-Hort, Lugano Ol 1968

[35] Ftacnik-Cvetković, Stary Smokovec 1983

[36] 11 0-0 ♘d7 (11 ... ♕e7 12 ♕b3 ♖d8 13 ♖ad1 c5 14 dc ♗xc3 15 ♕xc3 bc = Veingold-Tal, Tallinn 1983) 12 ♕b3 c6 13 ♖ad1 ♗e7 14 ♖fe1 ♘f6 15 ♘e5 ♕d6 16 f4 c5 17 dc ♕xc5 = Timman-Karpov, Tilburg 1982

[37] 11 ... c6 12 0-0 ♕d6 13 ♕b3 ♖e8 14 ♖fd1 ♘d7 15 ♖ab1 a5 16 ba ♖xa5 17 a4 ♗a6 = Christiansen-Gudmundsson, Grindavik 1984

[38] 13 ... ♕a5 14 ♕d2 cd 15 ♘xd4 ♗xd4 16 ed ♗c6 ±/= Kasparov-Karpov, match (40) 1984-85

[39] 16 ♕d3 ♖fd8 17 ♖fd1 ♖ab8 18 ♗xc6 ♕xc6 19 ♖xb8 ♖xb8 20 dc ♗xc3 21 ♕xc3 ♕xc5 = Karpov-Kasparov, match (8) 1985

[40] **16 ...** ♖fd8 17 ♖fc1 ♖ab8 18 a4 ♕d6 19 dc ♘xc5 20 ♗xc6 ♕xc6 21 ♘b5 ♗e7 22 ♘xa7 (22 ♕f5 ♕e8 23 ♘e5 ♖b7 = Kasparov-Karpov, match (38) 1984-85) 22 ... ♕a6 23 ♘b5 ♕xa4 24 ♕xa4 ♘xa4 25 ♘fd4 ± Karpov-Kasparov, match (39) 1984-85
16 ... ♖fc8 17 ♖fc1 ♗xb5 18 ♘xb5 ♕c6 19 dc ♘xc5 20 ♕f5 ♕e6 21 ♘fd4 ♕xf5 22 ♘xf5 ♘e6 = Kasparov-Karpov, match (42) 1984-85

[41] 12 ... ♗d6 13 ♘xe4 ♗xe4 14 ♖fd1 ♕e7 15 ♖ac1 ♗xg3 16 hg c5 = Bukić-Sibarević, Banja Luka 1983

[42] 13 ... a6?! 14 ♖fd1 b5 15 ♗b3 ♕e8 16 e4 ± Smejkal-Sturua, Trnava 1980

[43] Gavrikov-Dolmatov, Tallinn 1985

[44] 9 ... c5 10 dc dc (10 ... bc ±) 11 ♗xc4 ♕xd1 12 ♖fxd1 ♗xc5 13 ♘e5! ±/± Belyavsky-Karpov, Tilburg 1986

[45] 11 ... cd 12 ed (12 ♘xd4 ♘e5 13 ♗xf6 ♗xf6 14 cd ♘xd3 15 ♕xd3 ♗xd5 16 ♕e2 ± Gheorghiu-A.Petrosian, Bagneux 1982) 12 ... a6 13 a4 ♘h5 14 ♗g3 ♘xg3 15 hg ♘f6 = Gheorghiu-Belyavsky, Baden 1980

[46] 13 ♘xd4 ♘xg3 14 hg ♘f6 15 ♖ac1 ♗b4 = Draško-Lputian, Sarajevo 1985

[47] 17 ♗xc4 ♘d5 = Gavrikov-Yusupov, Tunis IZ 1985

101

	7	8	9	10	11	12	13	14	15	
QGD IX			**1 d4 d5 2 c4 e6 3 ♘c3 ♘f6 4 ♗g5 ♗e7 5 e3 0-0 6 ♘f3 ♘bd7**							
1	♗d3[1]	♗xc4	0-0	a4	ed	♗b3	♕e2[4]	♖fd1	♘e5	=
	dc[2]	c5	a6[3]	cd	♘b6	♗d7	♗c6	♘bd5	h6[5]	
2	♕c2	cd[7]	♗xe7	♘xd5	♗d3	dc[9]	0-0	♘d4	♖ac1	±
	c5[6]	♘xd5[8]	♕xe7	ed	g6	♘xc5	♗g4	♖ac8	♕g5[10]	
3	...	h4[11]	0-0-0	♘xd4	f3	g4	♗xf6	g5	♖xd4	∞
	h6	c5	cd[12]	♘b6	♗d7	♖c8	♗xf6	♗xd4	h5[13]	
4	♖c1	cd	♕a4	♗b5[15]	0-0	♗xd7	dc	c6	♕g4	±
	b6[14]	ed	c5	♗b7	a6[16]	♘xd7	♗xg5	♘c5	♗f6[17]	
5	...	c5	♗d3[18]	de	♗f4	♗b1	♕c2[20]	♘d4	♗h6	=
	a6	c6	e5[19]	♘e8	♘xc5	♗g4	g6	♘e6	♘8g7[21]	
6	...	cd	♗d3	0-0	♗b1	♘e5	♗f4	♗xe5	♗xd6	±
	...	ed	c6[22]	♖e8	♘f8	♘6d7	♘xe5	♗d6	♕xd6[23]	
7	...	♕c2[24]	♗f4!?[26]	h3	♗d3	0-0	♘e5	f3	♗xe5	±
	c6	♘e4[25]	f5	♘df6	♗d7	♗e8	♘d7	♘xe5	♘xc3[27]	
8	...	...	a3[28]	c5	♗xe7	♗d3	♘e2!	de	♘xe5	±
	...	...	b5[29]	♘h5	♕xe7	g6	e5	♘xe5	♕xe5[30]	
9	...	♗d3	♗xc4	♗xe7[33]	0-0[34]	♖xc3	♕c2[36]	ed	♗b3[37]	=
	...	dc[31]	♘d5[32]	♕xe7	♘xc3[35]	e5	ed	♘b6	♗e6[38]	
10	...	...	...	...	...	...	de	♘xe5	f4[39]	±
	...	...	...	...	...	...	♘xe5	♕xe5	♕e4[40]	

---

[1] 7 ♕b3 c6 8 ♗d3 (8 ♗e2 ♘e4 9 ♗xe7 ♕xe7 10 ♘xe4 de 11 ♘d2 e5 =) 8 ... dc 9 ♕xc4 c5 ∞

[2] 7 ... c6 8 0-0 dc 9 ♗xc4 ♘d5 10 ♗xe7 ♕xe7 11 e4 ♘xc3 12 bc ± Korchnoi-Segal, Sao Paulo 1979

[3] 9 ... cd 10 ed ♘b6 (10 ... h6 11 ♗h4 ♘b6 12 ♗b3 ♗d7 13 ♕d3 ± Novikov-Tal, USSR 1985) 11 ♗b3 ♘fd5 12 ♗xe7 ♕xe7 13 ♖e1 ♖d8 14 ♖c1 ± Timman-Ree, Amsterdam 1984

[4] 13 a5 ♘bd5 14 ♗xd5 ♘xd5 15 ♘xd5 ed 16 ♗xe7 ♕xe7 17 ♖e1 ♕d6 = Seirawan-Timman, London 1984

[5] Spraggett-Prandstetter, Taxco IZ 1985

[6] 7 ... a6 8 cd ed 9 ♗d3 c5 10 dc ♘xc5 11 0-0 ♘xd3 12 ♕xd3 ♗e6 13 ♘d4 ± Rashkovsky-Lukov, Erevan 1984

  7 ... c6 8 ♖d1 b6 (8 ... dc 9 ♗xc4 ♘d5 10 ♗xe7 ♕xe7 11 0-0 ±) 9 ♗d3 ♗b7 10 0-0 h6 11 ♗f4 ± Polugayevsky-Partos, Biel IZ 1985

[7] 8 0-0-0 ♕a5 9 h4 cd 10 ♘xd4 ♗b4 11 ♘b3 ♕b6 12 ♔b1 dc 13 ♗xc4 ♕c6 = Cebalo-Campora, Sarajevo 1986

  8 ♖d1!? ♕a5 9 cd ed 10 ♗d3 h6 11 ♗h4 ♖e8 12 0-0 ± Velikov-Nenkov, Pernik 1984

[8] 8 ... cd 9 ♘xd4 ♘xd5 10 ♗xe7 ♘xe7 11 ♗e2 ♘f6 12 0-0 ♗d7 13 ♖fd1 a6 14 ♗f3 ±/± Adamski-Modr, Prague 1983

[9] 12 b3 b6 13 0-0 ♗b7 14 ♖ac1 ♖ac8 15 ♕e2 ♖fd8 = Veingold-Djurić, Tallinn 1981

[10] 16 ♗e2 ± Hort-Balashov, USSR 1981

[11] 8 cd!? ed (8 ... hg 9 de fe 10 ♘g5 ♘b6 11 h4! ∞) 9 ♗f4! c5 10 ♗e2 b6 11 0-0 ♗b7 12 ♖fd1 ♖c8 13 dc bc 14 a4! ± Kasparov-Portisch, Brussels 1986

[12] 9 ... ♕a5 10 ♔b1 dc 11 ♗xc4 cd (11 ... ♘b6 12 ♗xf6 gf 13 ♗e2 cd 14 ed ♗d7 15 ♖h3 ± Kasparov-Marović, Banja Luka 1979) 12 ed ♘b6 13 ♗b3 ♗d7 14 ♘e5 ±/± Bagirov-Kruppa, USSR 1984

[13] Ftacnik-Csom, Hastings 1983-84

[14] 7 ... dc 8 ♗xc4 c5 9 0-0 h6 10 ♗h4 cd 11 ed ♘h5 12 ♗xe7 ♕xe7 13 d5 ± Tal-Lechtynsky, Albena 1984

[15] 10 ♗a6 cd 11 ed ♗xa6 12 ♕xa6 ± Makarichev-Sturua, Frunze 1985

[16] 11 ... h6 12 ♗xd7 ♘xd7 13 ♗xe7 ♕xe7 13 ♕a3 ± Hertneck-Chiburdanidze, Bad Wörishofen 1986

[17] 16 cb ♖b8 17 ♖fd1 ± Podgayets-Chiburdanidze, USSR 1985

[18] 9 b4 a5 10 a3 ab 11 ab b6 12 ♗f4 bc 13 bc ♖a3 =

[19] 9 ... b6 10 cb c5 11 0-0 ♗b7 12 ♕e2 ♖e8 13 ♗b1 cd 14 ed ♕b6 15 ♖fd1 ± Christiansen-

Csom, Lucerne Ol 1982
[20] 13 h3 ♗h5 14 g4 ♗g6 15 ♗f5 ♘c7 16 h4 h5 ∞ Vaganian-Speelman, London 1984
[21] 16 0-0 ♖e8 17 ♕d2 ♘xd4 18 ed ♗f5 = Reshevsky-Lombardy, US Ch 1975
[22] 9 ... ♘b6 10 ♘e5 ♘e8 11 ♗f4 ♘d6 12 ♕c2 g6 13 h4 ± Hort-Plachetka, Czechoslovakia 1970
[23] 16 a3 ± Gligorić-Ivkov, Bugojno 1979
[24] 8 a3 h6 (8 ... ♘e4 9 ♗f4 ♗d6 10 ♗g3 ♕e7 11 ♗d3 ♘xc3 12 ♖xc3 h6 13 ♗h4 ± Korchnoi-Andersson, Wijk aan Zee 1984) 9 ♗h4 ♘e4 10 ♗g3 ♘df6 11 ♗d3 ♘xg3 12 hg dc 13 ♗xc4 c5 = Miles-Yusupov, World v USSR 1984
[25] 8 ... ♖e8 9 a3 dc 10 ♗xc4 ♘d5 11 ♗xe7 ♕xe7 12 0-0 ♘xc3 13 ♕xc3 b6 14 ♘e5 ± Groszpeter-Lechtynsky, Trnava 1983
[26] 9 ♗xe7 ♕xe7 10 ♗d3! (10 ♘xe4 de 11 ♕xe4 ♕b4+ =) 10 ... ♘xc3 11 bc h6 12 cd ed 13 0-0 ♘f6 14 c4 ± Timman-Prandstetter, Taxco IZ 1985
[27] 16 bc ± Pinter-Prandstetter, Taxco IZ 1985
[28] 9 c5 e5 10 de ♘e8 11 ♗xe7 ♕xe7 12 ♗d3 h6 13 0-0 ♘xe5 = Rivas Pastor-Toth, Rome 1984
[29] 9 ... ♖e8 10 h3 h6 11 ♗h4 dc 12 ♗xc4 b5 13 ♗a2 ± Hort-Toth, Biel 1982
[30] 16 ♕c3! ± Andersson-Arlandi, Rome 1985
[31] 8 ... h6 9 ♗h4 dc 10 ♗xc4 b5 11 ♗d3 a6 (11 ... ♗b7 12 0-0 ♖c8 13 ♕e2 ± Tal-Nei, USSR 1981) 12 a4 ba 13 ♘xa4 ♕a5 14 ♘d2 ♗b4

15 ♘c3 ♗b7 16 0-0 ± Hort-Rossetto, Skopje Ol 1972
[32] 9 ... b5 10 ♗d3 a6 11 e4 ±
[33] 10 h4 f6 (10 ... ♘xc3 11 bc ∞) 11 ♗f4 ♘xf4 12 ef ♘b6 13 ♗b3 ♘d5 ∞ Eingorn-Morovic, Bor 1985
[34] 11 ♘e4 ♘5f6 12 ♘xf6+ ♕xf6 13 0-0 c5 (13 ... e5 14 d5 e4 15 ♘d2 ♕g6 16 dc bc 17 ♗e2 ± Farago-Campora, Lucerne 1985) 14 dc ♘xc5 15 b4 ± W.Schmidt-Prandstetter, Prague 1985
[35] 11 ... ♖d8 12 ♕c2 ♘xc3 13 ♕xc3 b6 14 b4 ♗b7 15 ♗e2 ♖dc8 16 ♕b2 ± Karpov-Andersson, USSR v World 1984
[36] 13 ♗b3 ed 14 ed ♘f6 15 ♖ce1 ♕d6 16 h3 ♗d7 17 ♖ce3 ♘d5 = Ubilava-Kharitonov, USSR 1986
[37] 15 ♖e3 ♕d8 16 ♗b3 ♘d5 17 ♖e5 f6 18 ♗xd5 cd 19 ♖e3 ♗g4 = Farago-Prandstetter, Prague 1985
[38] 16 ♖e1 ♗xb3 17 ♖xb3 ♕d6 = Haik-Toth, Biel II 1986
[39] 15 a3 ♗f5! =
15 ♕b3 ♕e7 16 ♖d1 ♗f5 17 e4 ♗g6 18 f3 ♖fd8 =
[40] 15 ... ♕f6 16 f5! b5 17 ♗b3 b4 18 ♖c5 ♗a6 19 ♖f4 ± Bronstein-Gereben, 1949
15 ... ♕e4 16 ♕e2 ♗f5 17 ♗d3 ♕d5 (17 ... ♕e6 18 e4 ♖fe8 19 ♖e1 ♕d6 20 ♕f2 ± Garcia Gonzalez-Toth, Thessaloniki Ol 1984) 18 e4 ♕d4+ 19 ♕f2 ♕xf2+ 20 ♔xf2 Hertneck-Sonntag, West Germany 1986

103

Tarrasch and Semi-Tarrasch

 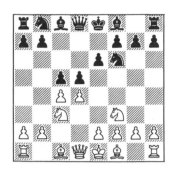

Tarrasch

This was once the focus for turbulent arguments between its inventor Siegbert Tarrasch and the rest of the chess world. Modern chess 'technology' is better placed to understand the dynamics of this defence. Voluntarily accepting an isolated d-pawn as well as granting White the ideal blockading square d4, Black receives excellent piece activity and open files as compensation. Revived by Keres and Spassky, its most dedicated adherent is Marjanović, though Chandler and Kasparov are notable part-time exponents. Despite setbacks during his first title match, Kasparov considers the Tarrasch fully viable. Those wishing to study the task of subduing Black's energetic counterplay and pressuring the isolated d-pawn should examine the virtuoso performances of Ulf Andersson and ex-champion Karpov.

It should be noted here that the main-line positions of the Tarrasch and Semi-Tarrasch often arise from the English, Réti and Catalan Openings.

The **von Hennig-Schara Gambit** is a lively bit of speculation. Black offers a pawn in return for quick development and the opportunity to castle long, guaranteeing an aggressive game and open combat. White should be able to keep his pawn and, correspondingly, the advantage, though he must be careful.

In the **Swedish Variation**, characterized by an early ... c4, Black avoids the tribulations of an isolated d-pawn and hopes to generate a healthy queenside initiative. Its drawback is the unwieldy pawn structure and Black must tread very carefully to ensure that a well-timed e4 break for White does not shatter his position. White is for choice but once again matters are far from simple.

The **Rubinstein Variation** is the Main Line and the crux of the Tarrasch argument. White's deployment is absolutely logical, the fianchettoed bishop bringing pressure to bear on Black's weak d-pawn. Black may fall just short of equality but his position is both active and extremely playable.

Semi-Tarrasch

In the Semi-Tarrasch Black captures on d5 with his king's knight, so avoiding the isolated queen's pawn. White gets an enduring initiative but Black has ample opportunity to pull level. His position is quite solid and he need not fear a kingside onslaught by White provided that the centre does not fall into enemy hands.

Reference: *The Closed Openings in Action* (Karpov)

	4	5	6	7	8	9	10	11	12	
1	cd	Qxd4[2]	Qd1	Qxd5[3]	Nf3[5]	Qd1	e3	a3[6]	Qc2	±
	cd[1]	Nc6	ed	Bd7[4]	Nf6	Bc5	Qe7	0-0-0	Kb8[7]	
2	...	Nf3[8]	Bg5	Bxe7	dc[10]	Ne4	Ned2[12]	Qc1	cb	=
	ed	Nc6[9]	Be7	Ngxe7	d4[11]	0-0	Qa5	b6	ab[13]	
3	...	...	e3	Be2	Nxd4[14]	0-0	b3[16]	Nxc6	Bb2	±
	...	...	Nf6	cd	Bd6[15]	0-0	Be5[17]	bc	Qd6[18]	
4	...	...	...	...	0-0	dc	a3[20]	b4	Bb2	=
	...	...	...	a6[19]	Bd6	Bxc5	0-0	Ba7	Re8[21]	
5	...	...	...	Bb5	dc[22]	0-0	b3[23]	Bb2	Be2	=
	...	...	...	Bd6	Bxc5	0-0	Bg4[24]	Rc8	Bd6[25]	

1 von Hennig-Schara Gambit

2 5 Qa4+ Bd7 6 Qxd4 ed 7 Nf3 Nc6 8 Qxd5 – 5 Qxd4

3 7 Nxd5 Nf6! 8 Nxf6+ Qxf6 ∓

4 7... Be6 8 Qxd8+ Rxd8 9 e3 Nb4 10 Bb5+ Ke7 11 Kf1! g6 12 Nf3 Bg7 13 Bd2 ±/± Mitev-Estrin, Albena 1970

5 8 Bg5 Nf6 9 Qd2 Qa5!? (9 ... Bb4 10 Nf3 h6 11 Bxf6 Qxf6 ∞∞) 10 Bxf6 gf 11 Nf3 0-0-0 12 Qc1 Bc5 13 e3 Kb8 ∞∞ Forintos-Hector, Budapest 1985

6 11 Be2 0-0-0 12 0-0 g5 13 b4 Bxb4 14 Qb3 g4 ∞/= Portisch-Velimirović, Rio de Janeiro IZ 1979

7 13 Be2 g5 14 b4 g4 15 Nd2 Bd6 16 Nc4 Bc7 17 Bb2 ± Cebalo-Marjanović, Novi Sad 1985

8 5 e4 de 6 d5 f5! 7 Bf4 Bd6 8 Bb5+ Kf7 9 Nh3 Nf6 10 Bc4 a6 11 a4 h6! ∓ Bronstein-Marjanović, Kirovakan 1978
5 dc Nf6 (5 ... d4!? 6 Na4 b5 7 cb ab ∞∞) 6 Be3 Nc6 7 Nf3 Qa5 8 a3 Ne4 = Karolyi-Wells, Malta 1984

9 5 ... Nf6 6 Bg5 Be6 7 e4 de 8 Nxe4 cd 9 Bb5+ Bd7 10 0-0! Be7 11 Bxf6 Bxb5 12 Bxe7 Qxe7 13 Re1 ± D.Gurevich-I.Ivanov, New York 1983

10 8 e3 c4 (8 ... cd 9 Nxd4 Qb6 =) 9 Be2 Rb8 10 b3 Qa5 11 Rc1 b5 12 bc bc 13 0-0 Bf5 = Tal-Vera, Malaga 1981

11 8 ... Qa5 9 e3 Bxc5 10 Be2 0-0 11 0-0 Be6 (11 ... Rd8!?) 12 Qa4 Qb6 13 Qa3 Nf5 14 Na4 Qa5 15 Rfd1 ± Korchnoi-Chandler, London 1984

12 10 g3 Qd5 11 Ned2 Qc5 12 Bg2 Qb6 13 Qb3 Qa5 = Condie-Motwani, Scotland 1984

13 13 g3 Ba6 14 Bg2 = Lputian-Arkhipov, Moscow 1985

14 8 ed Be7 (8 ... Bd6 9 Bg5 Be6 10 0-0 h6 11 Bh4 g5 12 Bg3 Ne4 13 Bxd6 Qxd6 ∞ Smyslov-Ribli, match 1983) 9 0-0 0-0 10 Ne5 Ne4 11 Be3 Nxc3 12 bc Bf5 13 Bg4 Bxg4 14 Qxg4 Qc8 = Murshed-Chandler, Hong Kong 1984

15 8 ... g6 9 Nxc6 bc 10 Bd2 Bg7 11 Rc1 0-0 12 0-0 Qd6 13 Bf3 Ba6 = Gavrikov-Lerner, USSR 1983

16 10 Ncb5 Bb8 11 b3 a6 12 Nxc6 bc 13 Nc3 Qd6 14 g3 Bh3 15 Re1 Re8 = Keene-Ftacnik, Aarhus 1983
10 Bf3 Be5 11 Qd3 Nb4 12 Qd2 Bxd4 13 ed Bf5 14 Qd1 Re8 = Karpov-Polugayevsky, Tilburg 1983
10 Nf3 a6 11 b3 Bb8 12 Bb2 Qd6 13 Rc1 Re8 14 Re1 d4 =/∞∞ Kantsler-Foisor, Tbilisi 1986

17 10 ... Re8 11 Bb2 Bb8 12 Rc1 Qd6 13 g3 Bh3 14 Re1 ± Gavrikov-Suba, Tunis IZ 1985

18 13 h3 Bf5 14 Rc1 Rfe8 15 Bd3 ± Portisch-Gligorić, Sarajevo 1986

19 7 ... Be7!? 8 0-0 0-0 9 b3 Ne4 10 Bb2 Bf6 11 Na4 Bg4 12 h3 Bxf3 13 Bxf3 cd 14 ed Ng5 =/∞ Miles-Petursson, Lone Pine 1978

20 10 b3 0-0 11 Bb2 Ba7 12 Na4 Ne4 13 Ba3 Re8 14 Rc1 Bg4 = Littlewood-D.Gurevich, Hastings 1982-83

21 13 Rc1 Bg4 14 Na4 Ne4 15 Nc5 Nxc5 16 bc = Yrjölä-Rogers, Tallinn 1985

22 8 Ne5 Qc7 9 Bxc6 bc 10 dc Bxc5 11 Be2 Bd6 12 h3 0-0 13 b3 Qe7 = Adorjan

23 10 Be2 a6 11 b3 Qd6 12 Bb2 Rd8 13 Rc1 Ba7 = Agzamov-Simić, Belgrade 1982

24 10 ... Qd6 11 Na4 Bb4 12 Bb2 Ne4 13 a3 Ba5 14 b4 Bc7 15 Bxc6 bc 16 Be5 ± Timman-Ljubojević, Tilburg 1981

25 13 Nb5 Bb8 14 Rc1 Ne4 15 Nbd4 Re8! ∞/= Sunye-Kasparov, Graz 1981

	Tarrasch II		1 d4 d5 2 c4 e6 3 ♘c3 c5 4 cd ed 5 ♘f3 ♘c6						

	6	7	8	9	10	11	12	13	14	
1	g3[1]	♗g2[3]	0-0	a3[4]	e4	ed	♘xd5	♘e5	a4	±
	c4[2]	♗b4	♘ge7	♗a5[5]	0-0!	♘xd5	♕xd5	♕b5	♕a6[6]	
2	...	♗g2	0-0[8]	♗f4[9]	♖c1	dc	♘e5	♘xc6	♗e5	±
	♘f6	♗e6[7]	h6	♖c8	a6	♗xc5	0-0	♖xc6	♘g4[10]	

[1] Schlechter-Rubinstein Variation

[2] Swedish Variation

[3] 7 e4 de 8 ♘g5 ♕xd4 9 ♗e3 ♕xd1+ 10 ♖xd1 h6 11 ♘d5 ♗b4+ 12 ♘xb4 ♘xb4 = A.Zaitsev-Mikenas, USSR Ch 1962

[4] 9 ♘e5 0-0 10 ♘xc6 bc 11 ♘a4 ♗f5 12 ♗d2 ♗e7 13 ♗c3 ♘d6 14 b3 cb 15 ab ♘b5 ∞ Kallinger-A.Mikenas, corr. 1983

9 e4 0-0 (9 ... de 10 ♘xe4 ♗g4 11 a3 ♗a5 12 ♗f4 ±/ ± Semkov-Nogueiras, Varna 1982) 10 ed ♘xd5 11 ♗g5 ♕a5 12 ♘xd5 ♕xd5 ∞/=

[5] 9 ... ♗xc3 10 bc 0-0 11 a4 ♖e8 12 ♗a3 ♗f5 13 ♘d2 ♘g6 14 ♖e1 ♕a5 15 ♕c1 ± Korchnoi-Ekström, Liechtenstein 1984

[6] 15 ♘xc6 bc 16 ♕h5!? ♗e6 17 ♖a3 ♗b4 18 ♖e3 ♖fe8 = Boleslavsky; 16 ♕f3 ±

[7] 7 ... ♗g4 8 ♗e3! cd 9 ♘xd4 ♗b4 10 0-0 0-0

[11] ♘b3 ♗xc3 12 bc ♖e8 13 ♖e1 ♕e7 14 ♖c1 ♖ad8 15 ♕c2 ± Panno-Garcia Palermo, Mar del Plata 1982

7 ... cd 8 ♘xd4 ♗c5 (8 ... ♕b6 9 ♘xc6 bc 10 0-0 ♗e7 11 b3 0-0 12 ♗b2 ♖e8 13 ♕c2 ♗a6 14 ♖fd1 ♘g4 15 e3 ± Furman-Mikenas, Tallinn 1966) 9 ♘b3 ♗b4 10 0-0 ♗xc3 11 bc 0-0 12 ♗g5 ♗g4 13 h3 ♗e6 14 ♘c5 ± Berry-Allan, Canadian Ch 1977

[8] 8 ♗g5 h6 9 ♗xf6 ♕xf6 10 0-0 cd 11 ♘b5 ♖c8 12 ♘fxd4 ♘xd4 13 ♘xd4 ♗c5 = Marshall-Capablanca, match 1909

[9] 9 b3 ♕a5 10 ♗b2 ± Boersma-Murey, Amsterdam 1983

[10] 15 ♗d4 ♗xd4 16 ♕xd4 ♖c4 17 ♕a7 ± Andersson-Murey, Moscow IZ 1982

| Tarrasch III | 1 d4 d5 2 c4 e6 3 ♘c3 c5 4 cd ed 5 ♘f3 ♘c6 6 g3 ♘f6 7 ♗g2 ♗e7 8 0-0 0-0[1] | | | | | | | |

	9	10	11	12	13	14	15	16	17	
1	b3[2]	♗b2	♘a4[4]	♖c1	dc	♘xb2	♘a4[6]	♖e1	♘d2[7]	∞
	♘e4[3]	♗f6	♖e8	b6[5]	♗xb2	bc!	♗a6	c4!	♕a5[8]	
2	♗e3	♘e5	♕a4[11]	♘xc6	b3	bc	♕d1	♘a4	♘b2	∞
	c4[9]	h6[10]	a6	bc	♖b8!	♖b4	♖xc4	♗f5	♖c3[12]	
3	dc	♘a4[14]	♗e3	♖c1	h3[16]	♘d4	♘xc6	♖e1[17]	♗d2	=
	♗xc5[13]	♗e7	♖e8[15]	♗g4	♗h5	♕d7	bc	♗b4	♗f8[18]	

[1] 8 ... h6 9 b3 0-0 10 ♗b2 ♗e6 11 ♖c1 ♖c8 12 dc ♗xc5 13 ♘a4 ♗e7 14 e3 ± Andersson-Handoko, Indonesia 1983
8 ... cd 9 ♘xd4 0-0 10 ♘b3! ♗e6 11 ♗e3 ♖c8 12 ♘b5 a6 13 ♘5d4 ±/±

[2] 9 ♗f4 ♗e6 10 dc ♗xc5 11 ♖c1 ♗b6 12 ♘a4 d4 13 a3 ♘d5 ∞/=

[3] 9 ... ♗f5 10 dc ♗xc5 11 ♗b2 a6 12 ♘a4 ♗a7 13 ♘d4 ± Georgadze-Bastian, Hanover 1983
9 ... ♖e8 10 ♗b2 ♗g4 11 ♖c1 ♖c8 12 dc (12 ♘e5 ♗h5 13 ♘xc6 bc 14 dc ♗xc5 15 ♕c2 ♗b6 16 e3 ♗g6 = Larsen-Spassky, Bugojno 1984) 12 ... ♗xc5 – 9 ... ♗g4
9 ... ♗g4 10 dc ♗xc5 11 ♗b2 ♖e8 12 ♖c1 a6 (12 ... ♗f8 13 ♖e1 ♕a5 14 a3 ± Farago-Raaste, Helsinki 1981; 13 ♘a4 ±

[4] 11 ♘xe4 de 12 ♘d2 ♗xd4 13 ♗xd4 cd 14 ♘xe4 ♗f5 15 ♕d2 ♖e8 = Mestel-Nunn, London 1984

[5] 12 ... cd 13 ♘xd4 ♗d7 14 ♘c5 ♘xd4 15 ♗xd4 ♗b5 16 ♖e1 ± Larsen-Amado, Buenos Aires 1983

[6] 15 ♘d2 ♕f6 16 ♘xe4 de 17 ♘a4 ♗g4 = Shvedchikov-Khenkin, USSR 1985

[7] 17 ♘h4 ♕a5 18 ♘f5 g6 19 ♘d4 ♖ac8 = Larsen-Kasparov, Nikšić 1983

[8] 18 ♗xe4 de 19 ♘xc4 ♗xc4 20 ♖xc4 ♖ad8 21 ♕c1 ♘d4 22 ♖c5 ♕a6 ∞ Bany-Kindermann, Naleczow 1984

[9] 9 ... ♗g4 10 h3 ♗xf3 11 ♗xf3 ♕d7 12 dc ♖ad8 13 ♗d4 ♕h3 14 ♗g2 ± Miles-Fernandez Garcia, Las Palmas 1980; 10 ♕a4 ±
9 ... ♘g4 10 ♗f4 ♗e6 11 dc ♗xc5 12 ♘a4

♗e7 13 ♘d4 ♘xd4 14 ♕xd4 ♕a5 15 ♖ac1 ♖ac8 16 ♘c3 ♗c5 17 ♕d2 ♕b6 = Agdestein-Petursson, Gausdal 1985

[9] 9 ... b6!? 10 dc bc 11 ♘a4 ♖b8 12 ♘xc5 ♖xb2 13 ♘d3 ♖b5 14 a4 ♖a5 ∞ I.Ivanov-McCambridge, New York 1984

[10] 10 ... ♗f5 11 ♕a4 ♘b4 12 ♖fc1 a6 13 ♕d1 ♖c8 14 ♗f4 ± Larsen-Ljubojević, Manila 1975
10 ... ♗e6 11 ♘xc4 dc 12 d5 ♘xd5 13 ♘xd5 ♗f6 14 ♘xf6+ ♕xf6 15 ♗xc6 bc 16 ♕d4 ± Miles-Petursson, Reykjavik 1980

[11] 11 b3 cb 12 ♘xc6 bc 13 ab a5 14 ♕c2 (14 ♖c1 ♗b4 15 ♘a4 ♖e8 16 ♗d2 ♗a6 17 ♖e1 ♗f8 18 ♕c2 ♘e4 ∓ Timoshchenko-Kasparov, USSR 1983) 14 ... ♗a6 15 ♘a4 ♗b5 =

[12] Larsen-Kasparov, Brussels 1987

[13] 9 ... d4 10 ♘a4 ♗f5 11 ♗f4! (11 ♘e1 ♕d7 12 ♘d3 ♖ad8 13 ♗d2 ♗h3 14 b4 ♖fe8 ∞ Vaisman-Urzica, Romanian Ch 1974) 11 ... ♗e4 12 ♖c1 ♕d5 13 ♕b3 ♕xb3 14 ab ♖ad8 15 ♘e1 (15 ♖fd1 ♘d5 16 ♘e1 ♘xf4 17 gf f5! ∞ Marjanović-Rogulj, Smederevska Palanka 1980) 15 ... ♗xg2 16 ♔xg2 ♘d7 17 ♘d3 ♖c8 18 ♖fd1 ±

[14] 10 b3 a6 11 ♗b2 ♖e8 12 e3 ♗f5 13 ♘e2 ♗e4 14 ♘ed4 ♘b4 15 ♗c3 ♖c8 = Osnos-Lputian, USSR 1983

[15] 11 ... ♗g4 12 ♘c5 ♗xc5 13 ♘xc5 ♕b6 14 ♘a4 ♕b5 15 ♖e1 ♖fe8 =

[16] 13 ♕b3 ♕d7 14 ♗c5 ♘e4 15 ♗xe7 ♖xe7 16 ♖fd1 d4 ∞ Hulak-Marjanović, Yugoslav Ch 1984

[17] 16 ♕c2 ♖ac8 17 ♗c5 ♗d8 18 e3 ♗g6 = Palatnik-Malevinsky, USSR 1979

[18] Ree-Petursson, Reykjavik 1984

1 d4 d5 2 c4 e6 3 ♘c3 c5 4 cd ed 5 ♘f3 ♘c6 6 g3 ♘f6 7 ♗g2 ♗e7 8 0-0 0-0 *continued*

	9	10	11	12	13	14	15	16	17	
4	dc	♗g5	♗xf6[19]	♘d5[20]	♘d2[21]	♖e1	♖c1	♕b3	♕a3[24]	=
	♗xc5	d4!	♕xf6	♕d8	♖e8[22]	a6[23]	♗a7	♖b8	♖e5![25]	
5	...	...	...	...	...	♖c1	♘b3[27]	♘f4	a3[28]	=
	...	...	...	...	...	♗b6[26]	♗e6	♕d6	♖ad8[29]	
6	♗g5	♘e5	♘xc6[31]	b3	♘a4[32]	e3	♗xf6[33]	dc	♘xc5[34]	±
	c4[30]	♗e6	bc	♕a5	♖fd8	c5	gf	♗xc5	♕xc5[35]	
7	...	♘xd4	♕a4[36]	e3[37]	♗xe7	♕a3	♕xc3	♖fd1	♕a3	±
	cd	♖e8	♗d7	♘e4	♘xe7	♘xc3	♕b6	♖ac8	♗g4[38]	
8	...	...	♗f4[39]	h3	♘b3	♘xd5	♗xd5	♘c1	♖b1	∞
	...	h6	♗g4[40]	♗h5[41]	a5	♘xd5	a4	♗f6	♘d4	
9	...	...	♗e3	♖c1[43]	♘xc6[45]	♘a4[46]	♗c5	♘xc5	♖e1	=
	...	...	♖e8[42]	♗f8[44]	bc	♗d7[47]	♗xc5	♗f5	♖b8[48]	
10	...	...	...	♕a4	♖ad1[49]	♕b3	a4[51]	♘c2[52]	♘xb4	=
	...	...	...	♗d7	♘b4[50]	a5	♖c8	b5	ba[53]	
11	...	...	...	♕b3	♕c2	♘f5[55]	♗d4	♗xc3	♖fe1	∞
	...	...	...	♘a5	♗g4[54]	♗b4[56]	♗xc3[57]	♘c4[58]	♖c8[59]	
12	...	...	...	a3	♕b3	♕a2	♘xd5	fe	♖ad1[61]	∞
	...	...	...	♗g4[60]	♘a5	♘c4	♘xe3	♕d7	♘xd5[62]	

---

[19] **11 ♘a4** ♗e7 12 ♖c1 h6 13 ♗xf6 ♗xf6·
14 ♘e1 ♖e8 15 ♘d3 ♕e7 16 ♖e1 ♗g5! =
Smyslov-Espig, Sochi 1974
    11 ♘e4 ♗e7 12 ♗xf6 ♗xf6 13 ♖c1 ♖e8
14 ♘e1 ♗e7 15 ♘d3 ♕b6 (15 ... ♗f8 16 ♕d2
a5 17 ♖fd1 ♗g4 18 ♘dc5 ± Nikolić-Kasparov,
Nikšić 1983) 16 a3 ♗g4 17 ♖e1 ♖ac8 18 ♘d2
♗g5 = Schüssler-Petursson, Neskaupstadur
1984

[20] 12 ♘e4 ♕e7 13 ♘xc5 ♕xc5 14 ♕d2 ♗g4
15 h3 ♗h5 16 b4 ♕b6 17 ♖ab1 a6 18 a4 ♗xf3
19 ♗xf3 ♘e5 = Speelman-Hodgson, England
1979

[21] 13 ♘f4 ♖e8 14 a3 a6 15 ♖c1 ♗a7 16 ♘d2
♗g4 17 ♗f3 ♗xf3 18 ♘xf3 ♕d7 19 ♖c2 ♖ad8 =
Lerner-Vera, Bratislava 1983

[22] **13 ...** ♗h3 14 ♗xh3 ♕xd5 15 ♗g2 ♕e6
16 ♖c1 ♗b6 17 ♘c4 ♖fe8 18 ♗f3 ± Cebalo-
Marjanović, Novi Sad 1984
    13 ... a6 14 ♖c1 ♗a7 15 ♘b3 (15 ♘c4
♗g4!?) 15 ... ♕d6 16 ♕d2 ♖e8 17 ♘f4 ♗f5
18 ♘a5! ± Plachetka-Nunn, Skara 1980

[23] **14 ... ♗c6** 15 ♘f4 ♗d7 16 ♖c1 ♗b6 17 ♕a4
(17 ♘xe6 ♕xe6 18 ♘c4 ♖ad8 19 a3 ♘e5!
20 ♘xe5 ♕xe5 21 ♕d3 ♖e7 ∞ Andersson-
Chandler, London 1984) 17 ... ♖ac8 18 ♘c4
♗d8 19 b4 a6 20 ♘b2 ♗g5 21 ♘bd3 ♕d6
22 ♖c5 ♗xf4 23 ♘xf4 ± Miles-Chandler,
London 1984
    14 ... ♗g4 15 ♘b3 ♗b6 16 ♖c1 ♗a5 17 ♘xa5

♕xa5 18 a3 ♖ad8 19 b4 ♕xa3 20 ♖a1 ♕b2 =
Rashkovsky-Lputian, USSR 1985; 18 b4 ♘xb4
19 ♕d2 ♘c6 20 ♕xa5 ♘xa5 ∞ Yusupov-
Petursson, Reykjavik 1985

[24] 17 ♘f4 ♖e5! 18 ♘c4 ♖b5 19 ♕a3 ♘b4! =
Miles-Hjorth, London 1984

[25] 18 ♘f4 ♖a5 19 ♕b3 ♖b5 20 ♕c2 ♗f5 =
Miles-Chandler, West Germany 1984

[26] 14 ... ♗f8!? 15 ♘b3 ♗f5 16 ♘f4 ♗e4
17 ♗xe4 ♖xe4 18 ♕d3 ♕e7 19 ♖fd1 ♖d8 =
Grooten-E.Vladimirov, Antwerp 1986

[27] 15 ♖e1 ♗e6 16 ♘f4 ♗xa2 17 b3 ♗a5 18 ♖c2
♗xb3 19 ♘xb3 d3 20 ♖xc6 ♗xe1 21 ♖c1 d2
22 ♖b1 a5 23 ♘d3 ± Karpov-Chandler, London
1984; 15 ... ♗g4! 16 ♘c4 = – 14 ♖e1

[28] 17 ♘xe6 ♕xe6 (17 ... ♖xe6 18 ♖c2 ♖ad8
19 a3 h5 ∞ Butnorius-Lputian, USSR 1981)
18 ♖c2 ♖ad8 19 ♖d2 h5 20 h4 ♕f6 21 a3 ♘e5 ∞
Spiridonov-Groszpeter, Polanica Zdroj 1985

[29] 18 ♖e1 ♗g4 19 ♘d3 ♗e7 20 ♘bc5 ♗xc5
21 ♘xc5 b6 = Jansa-Chandler, Plovdiv 1983

[30] **9 ... h6** 10 ♗xf6 ♗xf6 11 dc d4 12 ♘e4 ♗e7
13 ♕d3 ± Vilela-Braga, Havana 1984
    9 ... ♗e6 10 ♖c1 c4 (10 ... h6 11 ♗xf6 ♗xf6
12 dc d4 13 ♘e4 ♗e7 ± Pfleger-Andersson,
Tallinn 1973) 11 ♘e5 ♕a5 12 ♘xc6 bc 13 ♗xf6
♗xf6 14 b3 cb 15 ab ♖fe8 16 ♘a4 ♕b5 17 e3 ±
Zaltsman-Aronin, USSR 1972

[31] **11 ♕d2** ♘e8 12 ♘xc6 bc 13 ♗xe7 ♕xe7
14 f3 ♘c7 15 e4 a5 16 f4 f6 = Razuvayev-

Lputian, USSR 1985

11 f4 ♘g4 (11 ... ♘xe5 12 fe ♘e4 13 ♗xe7 ♘xc3 14 bc ♕xe7 15 e4 ♕d7 16 a4 ± Kasparov-Hjorth, Dortmund 1980) 12 ♘xg4 ♗xg4 13 ♗xd5 ♗xg5 14 fg ♕xg5 15 ♖f4 ♗e6 16 ♗g2 ♖ad8 = Salov-Lputian, USSR 1986-87

[32] 13 ♕c2 ♗b4 14 ♗d2 c5 15 a3 cb 16 ♕b2 ♗xc3 17 ♗xc3 ♕a4 = Bareyev-Lputian, Kharkov 1985

[33] 13 ♘xc5 ♗xc5 16 dc ♕xc5 17 bc dc 18 ♗xa8 ♖xd1 19 ♖fxd1 ♘d7 20 ♗f4 g5 ∞ Yusupov-Marjanović, Sarajevo 1984

[34] 17 ♕h5 ♖ac8 18 ♖fd1 c3 19 ♖ac1 ♗b4 20 ♖d4! ± Bagirov-Lputian, USSR 1980

[35] 18 ♕h5 ♖ac8 19 ♖fd1 ♕a3 20 bc dc 21 ♗e4 ♔f8 22 ♗f5 ± Kirov-Wedberg, Eksjö 1980

[36] 11 e3 h6 (11 ... ♗e6 12 ♘xe6 fe 13 ♗h3 ♗b4 14 ♘b5 ♕b6 15 ♘d4 ± Ribli-Handoko, Zagreb 1985) 12 ♗xf6 ♗xf6 13 ♘xd5 ♗xd4 14 ed ♗e6 15 ♖e1 ♗xd5 16 ♖xe8+ ♕xe8 17 ♗xd5 ♖d8 ∞∞ Yusupov-Petursson, Chicago 1983

[37] 12 ♖ad1 h6 13 ♗xf6 ♗xf6 14 ♘db5 d4 15 ♘e4 ♗e5 ∞ Polugayevsky-Chandler, London 1984

[38] 18 ♖d3 ± Suba-Zysk, Dortmund 1984

[39] 11 ♗xf6 ♗xf6 12 ♘b3 d4 13 ♘e4 ♗e7 14 ♖c1 ♕b6 15 ♘ec5 ♖d8 16 ♖c4 ♗xc5 17 ♘xc5 ♕xb2 18 ♕c2 = Seirawan-Kasparov, Nikšić 1983

[40] 11 ... ♖e8 12 ♖c1 ♗g4 13 h3 ♗e6 (13 ... ♗h5 14 g4 ♗g6 15 ♘cb5 ♖c8 16 ♘xc6 ♖xc6 17 ♘c7! ± Dlugy) 14 ♘cb5 ♘h5 15 ♗e3 ♕d7 16 ♘xe6 fe 17 g4 ♘f6 18 f4 ± Polugayevsky-Petursson, Biel IZ 1985

[41] 12 ... ♗d7 13 ♖c1 ♖c8 14 ♔h2 ± A.Rodriguez-E.Vladimirov, Havana 1986

[42] 11 ... ♗g4 12 ♕a4 ♘a5 (12 ... ♕d7 13 ♗xd5! ♘xd5 14 ♘xd5 ± Farago-Marjanović, Belgrade 1982) 13 ♖ad1 ♘c4 14 ♗c1 ♕c8 15 ♕b5 ♘b6 16 ♗f4 ± Kasparov-Palatnik, USSR 1981

[43] 12 ♘xc6 bc 13 ♗d4 ♘h7!? 14 ♘a4 ♘g5 15 ♖c1 ♘e6 ∞ Razuvayev-Nunn, London 1983

[44] 12 ... ♗g4 13 h3 ♗e6 14 ♘xe6 fe 15 f4 ± Spassky-Xu Jun, Dubai Ol 1986; 13 ♘b3 ♗e6 14 ♖e1 ♕d7 15 ♗c5 ♖ac8 16 ♗xe7 ♕xe7 17 e3 ± Petrosian-Spassky, match (4) 1969

[45] 13 ♕c2 ♗e6 14 ♖fd1 ♕d7 15 ♘xe6 fe

16 ♗d2 ♕f7 17 ♗e1 ♖ad8 ∞

[46] 14 ♗d4 ♘h7 (14 ... ♗g4?! 15 ♕a4! ♗d7 16 ♗xf6 ♕xf6 17 ♘xd5 ± Dorfman-Rantanen, Helsinki 1986) 15 ♘a4 ♗g4 16 ♖e1 ♕d7 17 ♗c5 ♘g5 ∞ Adorjan-Lobron, Indonesia 1983

[47] 14 ... ♕a5 15 ♖xc6! ♗d7 16 ♗d2 ♗b4 17 ♖c5 ± Ribli-Barle, Portorož/Ljubljana 1985

[48] 18 b3 ♕a5 19 ♘a4 ♕b4 = Sosonko-van der Sterren, Amsterdam 1982

[49] 13 ♖fd1 ♕c8 14 ♕b3 ♘a5 15 ♕c2 ♘c4 16 ♗f4 ♗h3 ∞ Fedorowicz-McCambridge, USA 1986

[50] 13 ... ♗f8 14 ♕b3 ♘a5 15 ♕c2 ♖c8 16 ♕b1!? ± Keene

[51] 15 ♖d2 a4 16 ♕d1 a3 ∞ Belyavsky-Kasparov, match 1983

[52] 16 ♖d2 ♗c5 17 h3 ♕b6 18 ♔h2 ♘e4 = Schüssler-H.Olafsson, Gausdal 1985

[53] 18 ♘xa4 ♗xb4 19 ♘c3 ♗xc3 20 bc a4 21 ♕a2 ♕e7 = Mayorov-Ehlvest, USSR 1983

[54] 13 ... ♗f8 14 ♖ad1 ♖e5 15 ♗f4 ♖h5 16 e4! ±/± Kuporosov-Ehlvest, USSR 1986

[55] 14 h3 ♗d7 15 ♖ad1 ♗e6!? Tal

[56] 14 ... ♖c8 15 ♗d4 ♗c5 16 ♗xc5 ♖xc5 17 ♘e3 ♗e6 18 ♖fd1 (18 ♖ad1 ∞/± Karpov-Kasparov, match (9) 1984-85) 18 ... ♕c7 19 ♕a4 ♖d8 20 ♖d3 ±

[57] 15 ... ♖c8 16 ♘e3! ♗e6 17 ♖ad1 ♘c4 18 ♘xc4 ♖xc4 19 ♕d3 ± Azmaiparashvili-Sturua, USSR 1986

[58] 16 ... ♖xe2 17 ♕d1 (17 ♕d3 ♖e8 18 ♘e3 ♗e6 19 ♕b5 b6 = Portisch-Chandler, Amsterdam 1984) 17 ... ♗h5 18 ♕d4 ♘c6 19 ♕f4 ±

[59] 18 ♖ad1 ♕d7 19 ♘xg7 ♔xg7 20 ♖xd5 ♕e7 21 h3 ♗e6 ∞

[60] 12 ... ♗e6 13 ♘xe6 fe 14 ♕a4 ♖c8 15 ♖ad1 ♔h8 16 ♔h1 a6 17 f4 ♘a5 18 ♗d4 (18 f5 b5 19 ♕h4 ♘g8 20 ♕h3 ♘c4 ∞ Smyslov-Kasparov, match 1984) 18 ... ♘c4 19 ♕b3 ±

12 ... ♗f8 13 ♕b3 ♖e5 14 ♖ad1 ♖h5 15 ♗f3 ♘a5 16 ♕a2 ♗g4 ∞ Kir.Georgiev-Kindermann, Plovdiv 1984

[61] 17 ♖ac1 ♖ac8 18 ♖xc8 ♖xc8 19 ♕b3 ♘xd5 20 ♗xd5 ♗f6 ∞∞

[62] 18 ♗xd5 ♗f6 19 e4 ♗e6 20 ♘f3 ♖ad8 21 ♖d2 ♕c7 ∞∞

Semi-Tarrasch I   1 d4 d5 2 c4 e6 3 ♘c3 ♘f6 4 ♘f3 c5

	5	6	7	8	9	10	11	12	13	
1	e3	cd[2]	♗e2	b3[3]	bc	0-0	♕c2	a4	ab	±
	a6[1]	ed	c4	b5	dc	♗b4	0-0	♗b7	♗xc3[4]	
2	...	♗d3[5]	♗xc4	ed	0-0	a3	♗a2	♗e3	♖c1	∞
	♘c6	dc	cd[6]	♗e7	0-0	a6[7]	♕d6	♖d8	b5[8]	
3	...	a3	ed	c5[10]	♗b5[11]	♕c2	♕xc3	0-0	♗f4[13]	±
	...	cd[9]	♗e7	♘e4	♗f6[12]	♘xc3	0-0	a5		
4	...	...	cd[14]	♗e2	♘xd4[15]	0-0	♘f3	b4	♗b2	=
	...	a6	ed	cd	♗d6	0-0	♗g4[16]	♖c8	♗b8![17]	
5	...	...	dc	b4	♗b2[20]	♕c2	♗xc4	♗d3	♖d1	=
	...	...	♗xc5[18]	♗d6[19]	0-0	dc[21]	b5	♗b7	♖c8[22]	

[1] 5 ... ♗e7 6 b3 0-0 7 ♗d3 cd 8 ed ♘c6 9 0-0 b6 10 ♗b2 ♘b4 11 ♗e2 ♗a6 ∞ Hort-Bastian, Baden-Baden 1981
5 ... cd 6 ♘xd4 (6 ed – Caro-Kann) 6 ... ♗e7 7 cd ♘xd5 8 ♗b5+ ♗d7 9 ♘xd5 ed 10 ♗e2 ♘c6 11 0-0 ♕b6 = Sunye-Chandler, Hastings 1981-82

[2] 6 dc ♗xc5 7 a3 0-0 8 b4 ♗a7 9 ♗b2 dc 10 ♗xc4 b5 11 ♗d3 ♗b7 12 0-0 ♘bd7 = H.Olafsson-Hjartarson, Reykjavik 1984
6 a3 dc 7 dc ♕c7 8 ♗xc4 ♗xc5 9 ♕e2 b5 10 ♗d3 ♗b7 11 ♗d2 ♘bd7 = Lputian-Tal, Erevan 1980

[3] 8 ♘e5 b5 9 0-0 ♗e7 10 a4 b4 11 ♘xd5!? ♘xd5 12 ♗xc4 ∞∞/∞ Portisch-Sosonko, Reggio Emilia 1985-86

[4] 14 ♕xc3 ab 15 ♗a3 ♖e8 16 ♖fb1 ± Sunye-Nogueiras, Thessaloniki Ol 1984

[5] 6 dc ♗xc5 7 a3 a5 8 ♕c2 ♕e7 9 ♗e2 0-0 10 0-0 ♖d8 11 ♖d1 h6 12 ♗d2 dc 13 ♗xc4 e5 ∞ Mestel-D.Gurevich, Hastings 1982-83

[6] 7 ... a6 8 0-0 b5 9 ♗b3 (9 ♗d3 ♗b7 10 a4 b4 11 ♘e4 =) 9 ... ♗b7 10 ♕e2 ♕c7 11 d5 ♘a5 12 de ♘xb3 13 ef+ ♕xf7 14 ab ♗d6 ∞∞ Lein-Marjanović, Vršac 1979

[7] 10 ... b6 11 ♕d3 ♗b7 12 ♗a2 ♖c8 13 ♗g5 ♘d5 ∞/= Lein-Christiansen, US Ch 1981

[8] Fries Nielsen-Short, Esbjerg 1984

[9] 6 ... ♗e7 7 dc ♗xc5 8 b4 ♗d6 9 cd ed 10 ♗b2 a5 11 b5 ♘e5 12 ♗e2 ♗e6 13 ♕d4 ± Podgayets-Vaganian, USSR 1971
6 ... dc 7 ♗xc4 a6 8 ♗d3 (8 0-0 b5 9 ♗a2 ♗b7 10 ♕e2 ♗e7 11 ♖d1 ±) 8 ... cd 9 ed ♗e7 10 0-0 0-0 11 ♗c2 b6 12 ♖e1 ± Vaganian-Bronstein, USSR 1973
6 ... ♘e4 7 ♕c2 (7 ♗d3 ∞/±) 7 ... ♘xc3 8 bc ♗e7 9 ♗d3 (9 ♗b2 0-0 10 ♗d3 h6 11 0-0 ♘a5 12 ♘d2 dc 13 ♘xc4 ♘xc4 14 ♗xc4 b6 = Petrosian-Fischer, match 1971) 9 ... dc 10 ♗xc4 0-0 11 ♗d3 h6 12 0-0 ± Inkiov-Hjorth, Thessaloniki Ol 1984

[10] 8 ♗g5 0-0 9 ♗d3 dc 10 ♗xc4 ♘d5 (Shamkovich-Kasparov, Malta Ol 1980) 11 h4!? ∞
8 ♗d3 dc 9 ♗xc4 0-0 10 0-0 a6 11 ♖e1 (11 ♗g5 b5 12 ♗d3 ♗b7 13 ♖c1 ♖c8 14 ♗b1 ♘a5 = Hecht-Vilela, Lucerne Ol 1982) 11 ... b5 12 ♗a2 ♗b7 13 d5 ♘xd5 14 ♗xd5 ed 15 ♗xd5 ♗f6 = Forintos-Tiller, Esbjerg 1983

[11] 9 ♕c2 ♘xc3 (9 ... 0-0 10 ♘xe4 de 11 ♕xe4 f5 ∞) 10 ♕xc3 a5 11 ♗b5 (11 ♗f4 a4 12 ♗b5 ♕a5 13 ♗xc6+ bc 14 ♘e5 ♗b7 ∞/∓ M.Gurevich, Gavrikov, USSR Ch 1986) 11 ... 0-0 12 b3 ♗d7 13 0-0 b6 =

[12] 9 ... ♘xc3 10 bc 0-0 11 ♗xc6 bc 12 0-0 ♕c7 13 g3 ♕a5 ∞ Williams-Hort, Nice Ol 1974; 12 ♘e5 ♗d7 13 0-0 f6 14 ♘xd7 ♕xd7 15 ♗f4 ± Alburt-Dlugy, USA 1982

[13] Hübner-de Firmian, Wijk aan Zee 1986

[14] 7 b3 ♗e7 8 ♗e2 0-0 9 dc ♗xc5 10 cd ed 11 ♗b2 ♗a7 = Vaganian-Littlewood, Hastings 1982-83; 7 ... cd 8 ed ♗e7 9 ♗e2 0-0 10 0-0 b6 =

[15] 9 ed ♘e4 10 ♕c2 ♘xc3 11 ♕xc3 ♗e7 = Reshevsky-Panno, Los Angeles 1963

[16] 11 ... ♖e8 12 b4 ♗c7 13 ♗b2 ♕d6 14 g3 ♗h3 15 ♖e1 ∞/± Najdorf-Kavalek, Buenos Aires 1980

[17] 14 ♖c1 ♕d6 15 g3 ♖fd8 = Spassov-Sosonko-Indonesia 1982

[18] 7 ... dc 8 ♕xd8+ ♘xd8 9 ♘a4 ±

[19] 8 ... ♗a7 9 ♗b2 0-0 10 ♕c2 (10 ♖c1 ♕e7 11 cd ♖d8 12 ♗e2 ed 13 ♘a4 ♘e4 ∞ Frey-Vilela, Bayamo 1983) 10 ... ♕e7 11 ♖d1 ♖d8 12 cd ed 13 b5 ab 14 ♘xb5 ♗b6 15 ♗e2 ± Ivkov-Fernandez Garcia, Torremolinos 1984

[20] 9 cd ed 10 ♗b2 0-0 11 ♗e2 ♗c7 12 0-0 ♕d6 13 g3 ♗h3 14 ♖e1 ♖ad8 ∞ Lerner-Tukmakov, USSR Ch 1983

[21] 10 ... ♗d7 11 ♖d1 ♖c8 12 ♗e2 ♘e5 ∞ Ivkov-Timman, Bugojno 1982

[22] 14 ♕b1 h6 = Ivkov-Bellon, Torremolinos 1983

1 d4 d5 2 c4 e6 3 Nc3 Nf6 4 Nf3 c5 5 cd Nxd5 6 g3 Nc6 7 Bg2 Be7 8 0-0 0-0

	9	10	11	12	13	14	15	16	17	
1	Nxd5[1]	dc[2]	Bg5[3]	Qxd5	Qd2	Be3	Qxe3	Rfb1	Nd2	=
	ed	Bxc5	Qb6[4]	Be6	h6	Bxe3	Qxb2	Qf6	Bf5[5]	
2	e4	d5	ed	Ne1[6]	Be3[7]	bc	Bxc5	Qd4[8]	Nd3	±
	Nb6	ed	Nb4	Bf6	Bxc3	N4xd5	Re8	Be6	Rc8[9]	
3	...	dc[10]	e5	a3	Qe2	Raxc1	Rfd1	Nd4	Rxd4	±
	Ndb4	Bxc5	Be7	Nd3	Nxc1	Qa5	a6[11]	Nxd4	Rd8[12]	
4	...	bc	d5	ed	Qc2[14]	Bf4	Ng5	Qe4	Bxd6	∞
	Nxc3	b6[13]	ed	Na5	Nc4	Bd6	g6	b5	Nxd6[15]	

[1]   9 Rb1 Bf6 (9 ... Qa5 10 dc Nxc3 11 bc Qxa2 12 Be3 e5 13 Ng5 ± Cebalo-Pinter, Taxco IZ 1985) 10 e3 cd 11 ed Qb6 12 Be3 Rd8 13 Ne4 Be7 14 Qe2 Bd7 15 Rfd1 Rac8 ∞ Cebalo-Marjanović, Kavala 1985

[2]   10 Be3 c4 11 Ne5 (11 b3 cb 12 ab Be6 13 Ne5 Qb6 ∞ D.Gurevich-Grünfeld, Las Vegas 1985) 11 ... f6 12 Nxc6 bc 13 Qc2 a5 14 Bf4 Bd6 = Bukić-Parma, Yugoslav Ch 1975

[3]   11 Ne1 d4 12 Nd3 Bb6 13 a4 Re8 14 Bd2 a6 = Panno-Karpov, Mar del Plata 1982

11 a3 Bf5 12 b4 Bb6 13 Ra2 Be4 14 Rd2 Qe7 15 Bb2 Rfe8 16 Qa1 f6 17 Rfd1 Qe6 = Portisch-Spassky, Bugojno 1978

11 b3 Qf6 12 Bg5 Qf5 13 Rc1 Bb6 14 Bf4 Rd8 15 e3 h6 = Uhlmann-Agzamov, Potsdam 1985

11 Qc2 Bb6 12 Ng5 g6 13 Qd1 Be6 14 Nh3 Bxh3 15 Bxh3 Re8 16 Bg2 Be7 ½-½ Adorjan-Dlugy, New York 1985

[4]   11 ... f6 12 Bd2 Be6 (12 ... Re8 13 Rc1 Bb6 14 e3 Bf5 15 Bc3 Be4 14 Qb3 ± Larsen-Agdestein, Gausdal 1985) 13 e3 Qb6 14 Rc1 d4 15 ed Nxd4 16 b4! ± Chernin-Dlugy Tunis IZ 1985

[5]   Barbero-Dlugy, Mendoza 1985

[6]   12 Ne5 Bf6 13 f4 Bf5 14 a3 Nc2 15 Ra2 Rc8 16 b3 = Tal-Petursson, Tallinn 1981

[7]   13 a3 Bxc3 14 ab Bxb4 15 Nc2 ∞ Boersma-Franco, Arnhem 1983

[8]   16 Bd4 Be6 17 Nd3 ± Ftacnik-A.Rodriguez, Thessaloniki Ol 1984

[9]   18 a4 ± Ehlvest-Lputian, USSR 1985

[10]   **10 d5** ed 11 ed Nd4 12 Ne1 Bf5 13 Bf4 Bd6 14 Bxd6 Qxd6 ∞ Garcia Palermo-Vilela, Cienfuegos 1984

10 a3 cd 11 ab dc 12 bc b6 13 Bf4 Bb7 14 Qb3 Qc8 = Polugayevsky-Radulov, Skara 1980

[11]   15 ... Rd8 16 Nb5 Qa6 17 Bf1 Bd7 18 Qe3 ± Korchnoi-Hübner, Johannesburg 1981

[12]   Povah-Diaconescu, corr. 1985

[13]   10 ... cd 11 cd b6 12 d5 ed 13 ed Nb4 14 Ne5 Bf6 15 Re1 Bb7 16 Ba3 ± Yusupov-Tukmakov, USSR 1979

[14]   13 Bf4 Bd6 (13 ... Bf6 14 Qd3 ± Hort-Zwaig, Halle 1967) 14 Ne5!? ∞

[15]   18 Qh4 h5 19 Qf4 ∞ Ftacnik-Lerner, Bratislava 1983

Semi-Tarrasch III				1 d4 d5 2 c4 e6 3 ♘c3 ♘f6 4 ♘f3 c5 5 cd ♘xd5 6 e4 ♘xc3 7 bc cd 8 cd					
	8	9	10	11	12	13	14	15	16
1	...	♗c4	♗e2[2]	♗d2	d5[4]	ed	0-0	♘xd2	♗f3[5]	±
	♘c6	b5[1]	♗b4+	♕a5[3]	ed	♘e7	♗xd2	0-0	♘f5[6]	
2	...	♗d2	♕xd2	♗c4[7]	0-0	♖fe1[9]	a4	♗d3	a5	±
	♗b4+	♗xd2+	0-0	♘d7[8]	♘f6	b6	♗b7	♖c8	♕c7[10]	
3	...	...	...	...	0-0	♖ad1![12]	♖fe1	d5	♗xd5	±
	...	...	...	♘c6	b6[11]	♗b7	♖c8[13]	ed[14]	♕c7[15]	

---

[1] 9 ... ♗b4+ 10 ♗d2 ♕a5 11 d5 ♗xd2+ 12 ♕xd2 ♕xd2+ 13 ♔xd2 ♘a5 14 ♖ac1 ♔e7 15 ♔e3 ♖d8 16 ♖hd1 ±/± Platonov-Krogius, USSR 1971

[2] 10 ♗d3 ♗b4+ 11 ♗d2 a6! 12 ♖c1 ♗xd2+ 13 ♕xd2 ♗b7 14 0-0 0-0 = Browne-Pinter, Las Palmas IZ 1982

[3] 11 ... ♗xd2+ 12 ♕xd2 a6 13 a4! ± Ftacnik-Paulsen, Dortmund 1981

[4] 12 ♗xb4!? ♕xb4+ 13 ♕d2 ♗b7 14 a3 ♕xd2+ 15 ♔xd2 a6 16 a4 ± Portisch-Pinter, Hungarian Ch 1984

[5] 16 ♘b3 ♖d8 17 ♗f3 ♘f5 18 ♖c1 ♘d6 19 ♕d4 ± Yusupov-Ribli, Montpellier C 1985

[6] 17 d6 ♖b8 18 ♘e4 ± Browne-D.Gurevich, US Ch 1983

[7] 11 ♗e2 ♘c6 12 ♖c1 ♕d6 13 0-0 ♗d7 (13 ... e5 14 d5 ♗g4 15 ♘h4 ♗d7 16 h3 ± Ljubojević-Kelečević, Yugoslav Ch 1982) 14 d5 ed 15 ♕xd5 ♕e7 16 ♗c4 ♗e6 = Larsen-Petrosian, Tilburg 1982

[8] 11 ... b6 12 0-0 ♗a6 13 ♖ac1 ♗xc4 14 ♖xc4 ± Anikayev-Bronstein, Minsk 1983

[9] 13 ♗d3 h6 14 ♕f4 ♗d7 15 ♖ad1 ♖c8 16 h4 ∞ Bagirov-Tal, USSR 1970

[10] 17 ab ab 18 ♖ac1 ♕b8 19 ♖b1 ± Yusupov-Eslon, Ca'n Picafort 1981

[11] 12 ... ♕d6 13 ♖ad1 ♖d8 14 ♖fe1 ♗d7 15 d5 ±/± Browne-H.Olafsson, Reykjavik 1980

[12] 13 ♖fd1 ♘a5! 14 ♗d3 ♗b7 15 ♕e3 ♖c8 16 ♖ac1 ♕e7 = A.Zaitsev-Polugayevsky, USSR Ch 1968-69

[13] 14 ... ♘e7 15 h4 (15 d5 ed 16 ed ♘f5 17 ♘e5 ± Petrosian-Korchnoi, match 1977) 15 ... ♖c8 16 ♗b3 ♕d6 17 h5 h6 18 ♘e5 ± Huss-Schauwecker, West Germany 1986

[14] 15 ... ♘a5 16 ♗d3 ed 17 e5! ± Polugayevsky-Tal, USSR Ch 1969

[15] 16 ... ♘a5 17 ♕f4 ± Spassky-Petrosian, match (5) 1969

16 ... ♕c7 17 ♕g5 h6 18 ♕g4 ♖fd8 19 h3 ± Swoboda-Plank, Vienna 1985

Semi-Tarrasch IV			1 d4 d5 2 c4 e6 3 ♘c3 ♘f6 4 ♘f3 c5 5 cd ♘xd5 6 e3 ♘c6[1]					

	7	8	9	10	11	12	13	14	15	
1	♗c4	ed	0-0	♖e1	bc	♗d3	h4[5]	♘g5	♗xg5	∞
	cd[2]	♗e7	0-0[3]	♘xc3[4]	b6	♗b7	♘a5!	♗xg5	♕d5[6]	
2	♗d3	ed	0-0	♖e1[8]	♗e4[10]	♘e5[12]	♗h6	♗xg7	♕f3	±
	cd[7]	♗e7	0-0	♗f6[9]	♘ce7[11]	g6	♗g7	♔xg7	♕b6[13]	
3	...	...	...		a3[14]	♕c2	♘xd5	♗e3[16]	♗h7+	=
	...	...	...	♕d6	♖d8[15]	h6	♕xd5	♗d7	♔h8[17]	

[1] 6 ... ♗e7 7 ♗d3 cd 8 ed 0-0 9 h4 (9 0-0 ♘c6! – 6 ... ♘c6 7 ♗d3) 9 ... ♘c6 10 ♕c2 f5 11 a3 b6 12 0-0 ♔h8 13 ♖e1 ♘f6 ∞ Sveshnikov-Kasparov, USSR Ch 1978

[2] 7 ... ♘xc3 8 bc ♗e7 9 0-0 0-0 10 ♕e2 b6 11 ♖d1 ♕c7 12 e4 ± R.Byrne-Fischer, US Ch 1959-60

7 ... ♗e7 8 ♗xd5 ed 9 dc ♗e6 10 0-0 ♗xc5 11 b3 0-0 12 ♗b2 ± Larsen-Tal, match 1969

[3] 9 ... ♘xc3 10 bc 0-0 11 ♗d3 b6 12 ♕e2 ♗b7 13 ♗b2 ± Spassky-Langeweg, Sochi 1967

[4] 10 ... a6 11 ♗b3! (11 ♗d3 ♘cb4 12 ♗b1 b5 ∞) 11 ... ♘xc3 (11 ... ♘f6 12 a3 b5 13 d5 ed 14 ♘xd5 ± Farago-Pachman, Baden-Baden 1985) 12 bc b5 13 ♕d3 ♖a7 14 ♗c2 g6 15 ♗h6 ♖e8 16 ♕e3 ± Sokolov-Karpov, match 1987

10 ... ♗f6 11 ♘e4 b6 12 a3 ♗b7 13 ♕d3 ♖c8 14 ♘fg5 ♗xg5 15 ♗xg5 f6 16 ♗d2 ♕d7 17 ♖ad1 ∞ Nikolić-Ribli, Portorož/Ljubljana 1985

[5] 13 ♕c2 g6 14 ♗h6 ♖e8 15 ♕d2 ♖c8 16 ♖ad1 ♗f6 ∞ Christiansen-Fedorowicz, US Ch 1984

[6] 16 ♕g4 f5 17 ♕g3 ♖ac8 ∞ Hernandez-Minguell, Valca 1984

[7] 7 ... ♗e7 8 0-0 0-0 9 ♖e1 (9 a3 ♘xc3 10 bc b6 11 ♗b2 ♗b7 12 ♕e2 ♕c7 13 ♖ad1 ♗f6 ∞ Psakhis-Sveshnikov, Sochi 1985; 9 ♗xd5 ♕xd5 10 e4 ♕h5 11 dc ♗xc5 12 ♗f4 b6 = Tukmakov-Eingorn, USSR 1980) 9 ... b6 10 ♗e4 ♘xc3

[8] 10 a3 ♗f6! 11 ♗e4 (11 ♕c2 h6 12 ♖d1 ♕b6 13 ♗c4 ♖d8 = Smyslov-Ribli, match 1983) 11 ... ♕d6 12 ♕d3 h6 13 ♖d1 ♗d7 14 ♕e2 ♖ac8 15 ♗c2 ♘ce7 16 ♘e4 ♕c7 = Alburt-Sax, Hastings 1983-84

[9] 10 ... ♘f6 11 a3 b6 (11 ... ♕d6 12 ♗e3 ♖d8 13 ♕c2 ♗d7 13 ♖ad1 ± Karpov-Hort, Malta Ol 1980) 12 ♗g5 (12 ♗c2 ♗b7 13 ♕d3 g6 14 ♗h6 ♖e8 15 ♖ad1 ± Velimirović-Böhm, Amsterdam 1976) 12 ... ♗b7 13 ♗c2 ♖c8 14 ♕d3 g6 15 ♖ad1 ♘d5 16 ♗h6 ♖e8 17 ♗a4 ± Belyavsky-Karpov, Trud v CSKA 1986

[10] 11 a3 ♘xc3 12 bc b6 13 h4 ♗b7 14 ♘g5 g6 15 ♕g4 h5 16 ♕g3 ♘e7 = Hansen-Ribli, Plovdiv 1983

[11] 11 ... ♕d6 12 ♗g5 ♗xg5 13 ♘xg5 h6 14 ♘f3 ♗d7 15 ♗xd5! ed 16 ♘e5 ±/± Gheorghiu-Petursson, USA 1979

[12] 12 a3 ♗d7 13 ♕d3 h6 14 ♘e5 ♘xc3 15 ♕xc3 ♗c6 = Rivas Pastor-Littlewood, Hastings 1981-82

[13] 16 ♗xd5 ♘xd5 17 ♘xd5 ed 18 ♕xd5 ♗e6 19 ♕c5 ± Ribli-Deze, Novi Sad 1982

[14] 11 ♕c2 h6! 12 a3 ♖d8 – 11 ... ♖d8

[15] 11 ... ♗d7 12 ♕c2 h6 13 ♖e4! ♖fd8 14 ♗d2 ± Jokšić-Commons, Plovdiv 1975

[16] 14 ♗e4 ♘xd4 15 ♘xd4 ♕xd4 16 ♗e3 ∞∞ Tal

[17] 16 ♗e4 ♕h5 17 ♘e5 ♕xe5 18 de ♖ac8 19 ♕e2 = Spassky-Korchnoi, match 1968

Slav and Semi-Slav

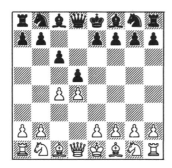 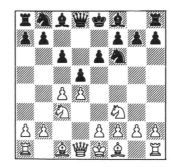

The Slav is a sensibly motivated defence to the Queen's Gambit. It is based on the same solid philosophy as the Orthodox defences, but here Black opts to bolster the centre without hemming in his queen's bishop, a source of congestion in the more classical lines of the QGD. The pawn on c6 paves the way for later expansion on the queenside, though this plan is best illustrated in the Meran Variation of the Semi-Slav (see below).

Both the Slav and Semi-Slav have received a great deal of attention, and the Czech Variation of the Slav in particular is extremely popular. The defence combines solidity with reasonable long-term chances to play for an edge. The Semi-Slav may lead to more chaotic play as there are a variety of ultra-sharp and well-examined lines at White's disposal. After some turbulent days weathering recent White assaults, these durable systems again seem secure for Black.

Slav

The **Exchange Variation** (3 cd cd) is the system that takes the fun out of playing the Slav. White's extra tempo in a symmetrical position gives him a chance to establish a slim but lasting pull at no risk. Black should hold the balance but this possibility robs the defence of much of its dynamic potential.

Czech Variation (3 ♘f3 ♘f6 4 ♘c3 dc 5 a4 ♗f5). A favourite of Smyslov, this safe and simple line provides Black with excellent prospects for full equality.

Semi-Slav

Marshall Gambit (3 ♘c3 e6 4 e4!?). Black does best to accept the challenge, though White's compensation is always evident. A difficult and obscure variant.

Abrahams Variation (3 ♘c3 e6 4 ♘f3 dc). A provocative and double-edged try for Black. White may be able to prove a small edge but it is a harrowing task.

Botvinnik System (3 ♘f3 ♘f6 4 ♘c3 e6 5 ♗g5). A violent system that leads to baffling tactical complications. Serious investigation is a must for the prospective defender.

Meran Variation (3 ♘f3 ♘f6 4 ♘c3 e6 5 e3 ♘bd7 6 ♗d3 dc 7 ♗xc4 b5). An enormous complex which embraces a large body of theory. Black's chances are sufficient for equality.

References: *The Slav for the Tournament Player* (Flear)
The Closed Openings in Action (Karpov)

	Slav I		1 d4 d5 2 c4 c6					
	3	4	5	6	7	8	9	10	11
1	♘c3[1]	e4[3]	♘f3	♛xd4	♘xd4	f3[5]	a4	♘d1	♗f4[7]	±
	dc[2]	e5[4]	ed	♛xd4	♘f6	b5[6]	b4	♗a6	♗c5[8]	
2	...	e3[9]	ed	♛b3	f4[13]	♘f3	♗b5	♘e5	♗d2	±
	♘f6	♗f5[10]	cd[11]	♗c8[12]	♘c6	g6	♗g7	♗d7	0-0[14]	
3	♘f3	e3	a4	ab	b3	♗d2	♘bxd2	bc	c5[17]	±
	dc[15]	b5[16]	e6	cb	♗b4+	♗xd2+	a5	b4	♘e7[18]	
4	...	♛c2[19]	♗f4	♘bd2	a3	♛xc4	♛c1	dc	e3[24]	=
	♘f6	g6[20]	♛a5+[21]	♘a6[22]	dc	♗e6	c5[23]	♛xc5	♖c8[25]	

[1] 3 e3 ♗f5 (3 ... ♘f6 =) 4 ♛b3 ♛b6 5 cd ♗xb1 =
  3 ♗f4 ♘f6 4 e3 ♗f5 5 ♘c3 e6 (5 ... ♛b6 6 ♛d2 ♘e4!? 7 ♘xe4 de ∞ Gulko-Chernin, USSR Ch 1985) 6 ♛b3 ♛c8 7 ♖c1 ♗e7 8 cd ♘xd5 9 ♗g3 0-0 10 ♘f3 ♘xc3 11 bc c5 = Miles-Portisch, Tilburg 1986
  3 cd cd 4 ♘c3 ♘f6 5 ♗f4 ♘c6 (5 ... ♛b6 6 e3! ♛xb2 7 ♖c1 ♘c6 8 ♗d3 ♗g4 9 ♘ge2 ± Rashkovsky-Arnason, Sochi 1980) 6 e3 ♗f5!? (6 ... a6 7 ♗d3 ♗g4 ∞/= Tukmakov-Chernin, USSR Ch 1985) 7 ♛b3 ♘a5 8 ♛a4+ ♗d7 9 ♗b5 ♘c6 = Plachetka-Mokry, Trnava 1985

[2] 3 ... e5 4 cd cd 5 ♘f3 e4 6 ♘e5 ♘c6 7 ♗f4 ± (7 ♛a4 ±) Suetin

[3] 4 ♘f3 b5 5 a4 b4 6 ♘a2 c5 =

[4] 4 ... b5 5 a4 ♛a5 6 ♗d2 b4 7 ♘a2 e6 8 ♗xc4 ♘f6 9 ♛c2 ± Lengyel-Rukavina, Sombor 1974

[5] 8 ♗c4 b5 (8 ... ♗b4 9 0-0 0-0 10 e5 ± Tukmakov-Skembris, Titograd 1982) 9 ♗d3 b4 =

[6] 8 ... ♗c5 9 ♗e3 ♘bd7 10 ♗c4 0-0 11 ♔f2 ± Portisch-Saidy, San Antonio 1972

[7] 11 ♗e3 ♘bd7 12 ♖c1 c5 =

[8] 12 ♘f5 0-0 13 ♖c1 ± Nei-Roizman, USSR 1964

[9] 4 ♗g5 dc 5 a4 ♘a6 6 e4 ♘b4 7 ♘f3 ♗g4 8 e5 ∞

[10] 4 ... ♗g4 5 f3 ♗c8 6 cd (6 ♗d3 e6 7 ♘ge2 c5 8 cd ed 9 0-0 ♘c6 10 ♔h1 ± Chernin-Meduna, Sochi 1986) 6 ... cd 7 ♗d3 (7 e4!? de 8 fe e6 9 ♘f3 ♗e7 10 ♗d3 ± Lukacs-Mokry, Polanica Zdroj 1986) 7 ... ♘c6 8 ♘ge2 e6 9 0-0 ♗e7 10 ♔h1 0-0 11 e4 ± Nogueiras-Flear, Szirak 1986

[11] 5 ... ♘xd5 6 ♗c4 e6 7 ♘ge2 ♘d7 8 e4 ±

[12] 6 ... ♛b6 7 ♘xd5 ♘xd5 8 ♛xd5 ♛b4+ 9 ♗d2 ♛xb2 10 ♖c1 ± Tal

[13] 7 ♘f3 e6 8 ♘e5 ♗e7 9 ♗d3 ±

[14] 12 0-0! ± Farago-Tiller, Helsinki 1983

[15] 3 ... ♗f5 4 ♘c3 e6 5 ♛b3 ♛b6 (5 ... b6?!

6 cd ed 7 e4! ±/± Ribli-Kurajica, Novi Sad 1982) 6 c5 ♛xb3 7 ab ♘a6 8 ♗f4 ±

[16] 4 ... ♗g4 5 ♗xc4 e6 6 h3 ♗h5 7 ♘c3 ♘d7 8 0-0 ♘gf6 9 e4 ± Ribli-Ljubojević, Amsterdam 1986

[17] 11 ♗d3 ♘f6 12 g4 ♗b7 13 g5 ♘fd7 14 h4 ♛c7 15 c5 h6 ∞ Lputian-Gurgenidze, USSR Ch 1985

[18] 12 ♗b5+ ♗d7 13 ♛a4! ± Neverov-Gurgenidze, Tbilisi 1985

[19] 4 ♘bd2 ♗f5 5 g3 e6 6 ♗g2 ♘bd7 7 0-0 ♗e7 8 b3 0-0 9 ♗b2 ♘e4 10 ♘xe4 ♗xe4 = Muco-Timman, Lucerne Ol 1982
  4 g3 ♗g4 (4 ... ♗f5 5 ♗g2 e6 6 0-0 ♘bd7 7 ♘c3 h6 8 ♗d2 ♗e7 9 b3 0-0 = Sveshnikov-Smagin, USSR 1984) 5 ♗g2 e6 6 0-0 ♘bd7 7 b3 ♗d6 8 ♗b2 0-0 9 ♘bd2 ♛b8 (9 ... ♛e7 10 a3 e5 11 cd cd ∞ Kurtenkov-Lukacs, Trnava 1986) 10 ♖e1 b5 11 c5 ♗c7 12 b4 a5 13 a3 h6 = Csom-Chernin, Järvenpää 1985

[20] 4 ... ♗g4 5 ♘e5 e6 6 ♛xg4 ♘xg4 7 e3 ♘d7 8 ♗e2 (8 ♘c3 f5 9 f3 ♘gf6 10 ♗d2 ± Miles-Torre, Bugojno 1984) 8 ... ♘gf6 9 0-0 ♗e7 10 ♘c3 0-0 11 b3 ♖e8 12 ♗b2 ♗f8 13 ♖ad1 ± Cserna-Chernin, Copenhagen 1986
  4 ... ♘a6!? ∞/=

[21] 5 ... ♗g7 6 e3 0-0 7 ♘bd2 ♗f5 8 ♛b3 ♛b6 = Dolmatov
  5 ... ♗f5 6 ♛b3 ♛b6 7 c5 ♛xb3 8 ab ♘bd7 (8 ... ♗xb1 9 ♖xb1 ♗g7 10 ♖a1 ♘bd7 11 h3 0-0 12 e3 ± Miles-Rivas Pastor, Linares 1985) 9 b4 ♗g7 10 h3 ♗xb1 11 ♖xb1 0-0 = Lein-Smyslov, Hastings 1981-82

[22] 6 ... c5 7 cd ♘xd5 8 ♗e5 f6 9 ♗xb8 ♖xb8 = Goldin-Khuzman, USSR 1986

[23] 9 ... ♗g7 10 b4 ♛d8 11 e3 ♘c7 12 ♗c4 ± Chernin-Knežević, Stary Smokovec 1984

[24] 11 b4!? ♛c8 12 ♛b2

[25] 12 ♛xc5 ♘xc5 13 ♗e5 ♗g7 = Sosonko-Chernin, Tunis IZ 1985

115

	3	4	5	6	7	8	9	10	11	
5	Nf3	e3	h3[27]	Nc3	g4	Ne5	h4	Nxg6	Bxc4	±
	Nf6	Bg4[26]	Bh5[28]	e6	Bg6	Nbd7[29]	dc	hg	Bb4[30]	
6	...	...	Bd3[31]	Nc3	0-0	b3[34]	Bb2	Ne2[35]	g3	=
	...	Bf5	e6[32]	Bg6[33]	Nbd7	Bd6	Ne4	Qb8	Nef6[36]	
7	...	cd	Nc3	Bf4	e3	Bg3[39]	Bd3	Rc1	Bh4[42]	=
	...	cd	Nc6[37]	e6	Bd6[38]	0-0![40]	b6[41]	Bb7	Be7[43]	
8	...	...	...	...	...	Bd3	0-0	Be5	a3[46]	=
	...	...	...	...	Be7	0-0	Nh5	f5[45]	Bd7[47]	
9	...	...	...	...	e3	Ne5[48]	Bxe5	Qb3[51]	de	∞
	...	...	...	Bf5	e6	Nxe5[49]	Nd7[50]	Nxe5	Be7[52]	
10	...	...	...	...	...	Bb5	Qa4[54]	0-0	Bxc6	=
	...	...	...	...	...	Nd7[53]	Rc8[55]	a6	Rxc6[56]	
11	...	Nc3	Ne5[58]	g3	Bf4	Bxe5	Bg2	de	a4	∞
	...	dc[57]	b5[59]	Nfd7	Nxe5	Nd7	Nxe5	Qb6[60]	Bb7[61]	
12	...	...	e4	e5	a4[62]	Ng5[64]	Nge4	Nb1	Nbd2	∞
	...	...	b5	Nd5	e6[63]	h6[65]	b4	Ba6[66]	c3[67]	
13	...	...	a4	e4[68]	Bxc4	Be3	0-0	a5[71]	Qb3	±
	...	...	Na6	Bg4	e6	Be7[69]	Nb4[70]	0-0	Bxf3[72]	
14	...	...	...	Ne5[73]	g3	Bg2	Nxc4[75]	Qd3[76]	0-0	=
	...	...	...	Bg4	Bh5	Bb4[74]	Nd5	Be7	0-0[77]	

[26] 4 ... g6 – Grünfeld

[27] **5 cd** Bxf3 6 Qxf3 cd 7 Nc3 e6 8 Qd1 Be7 9 Be2 0-0 10 0-0 Nc6 = Ribli-Dolmatov, Amsterdam 1980

5 Qb3 Qb6 6 Ne5 Bf5 7 cd Qxb3 8 ab Nd5 9 Nd2 f6 10 Nd3 Bg6 11 e4 ± Neverov-Ehlvest USSR 1986

[28] 5 ... Bxf3 6 Qxf3 e6 (6 ... g6 7 Nc3 Bg7 8 cd cd 9 Qd1 ± Taimanov) 7 Nc3 Nbd7 8 Bd3 Bd6 9 Bd2 Qe7 10 cd ±

[29] 8 ... Nfd7 9 Nxg6 hg 10 Qb3 Qc7 11 Bd2 ± Diesen-Hort, Stip 1977

[30] 12 Qb3 ± Chernin-Smagin, Kiev 1983

[31] **5 Qb3** Qb6 6 c5 Qc7 7 Bd3 e6 8 0-0 Nbd7 9 Nbd2 Be7 = Rivas Pastor-Ree, Hastings 1981-82

5 cd cd 6 Qb3 Qc7 (6 ... Qc8) 7 Nc3 e6 8 Bd2 Nc6 9 Rc1 Be7 10 Bb5 0-0 11 0-0 Rfc8 12 Ne2 Ne4 = K.Grigorian-Belyavsky, Baku 1980

5 Nc3 e6 6 Nh4 (6 Be2 Bd6 7 Nh4 Bg6 8 Nxg6 hg 9 g3 Nbd7 10 0-0 0-0 11 b3 Qe7 = Solozenkin-Khalifman, USSR 1986; 6 ... h6 =) 6 ... Be4 7 Qb3 Qb6 (7 ... Qc7 8 f3 Bg6 9 Bd2 Nbd7 10 Rc1 Rc8 11 g3! ± Smyslov-Chernin, Montpellier C 1985) 8 Qxb6 ab 9 Bd2 h6 10 cd

ed 11 f3 Bh7 12 g4 b5 = P.Nikolić-Belyavsky, Sarajevo 1982

[32] 5 ... Bxd3 6 Qxd3 e6 7 0-0 Nbd7 8 b3 Ne4 ∞/= Chernin-Portisch, Montpellier C 1985

[33] 6 ... Bxd3 7 Qxd3 Nbd7 8 0-0 Be7 9 b3 0-0 10 Bb2 (10 e4 de 11 Nxe4 Nxe4 12 Qxe4 Nf6 = Balashov-Kupreichik, Minsk 1982) 10 ... Qc7 11 e4 de 12 Nxe4 Nxe4 13 Qxe4 Nf6 14 Qc2 Rfd8 = Rivas Pastor-Taimanov, Plovdiv 1984

[34] 8 Qe2 Bb4 9 Bd2 a5 10 Nxg6 hg 11 cd ed = Seirawan-Larsen, Las Palmas 1981

[35] 10 Qc2 f5 11 Be2 Qf6 (11 ... Qb8 ∞) 12 Nf4 Bf7 = Hansen-P.Nikolić, Esbjerg 1982

[36] 12 Nf4 Bxd3 13 Nxd3 = Rivas Pastor-Mednis, Rome 1984

[37] 5 ... e6 6 Bg5 Nc6 7 e3 Be7 8 Bd3 0-0 9 0-0 ± Torre-Zsu.Polgar, New York 1985

[38] 7 ... Nh5 8 Bg5 Qb6 9 Bb5 h6 10 Bh4 g5 11 Ne5 Ng7 12 Bg3 Nf5 13 Qa4 ±/= Smejkal-P.Nikolić, Novi Sad 1982

[39] 8 Bxd6 Qxd6 9 Bd3 0-0 10 Rc1 e5 11 de Nxe5 12 Nxe5 Qxe5 13 Be2 Rd8 = Sosonko-Hübner, Tilburg 1981; 8 Bd3!?

[40] 8 ... Bxg3 9 hg Qd6 10 Bd3 Bd7 11 Rc1 Rc8 12 Bb1 ±

8 ... a6 9 Bd3 Bxg3 10 hg Qd6 11 Rc1

♗d7 12 a3 ♖c8 13 ♗b1 ± Keene-Pachman, Barcelona 1975

⁴¹ 9 ... a6 10 ♖c1 ♗xg3 11 hg g6 12 e4 ± Portisch-Ljubojević, Indonesia 1983

9 ... ♖e8!? 10 ♘e5 ♗xe5 11 de ♘d7 12 f4 ♘c5 ∞/=

⁴² 11 0-0 ♗xg3 12 hg ♕e7 13 ♖e1 ♖fc8 = Geller-Soos, Skopje 1967

⁴³ 12 0-0 ♘b4 13 ♗e2 ♘e4 = Hort-Ljubojević, Wijk aan Zee 1986

⁴⁴ 9 ♘e5 ♕b6 10 a3 ♘xe5 11 ♗xe5 ♗d7 12 ♕c2 h6 =

9 h3 b6 10 0-0 ♗b7 11 ♖c1 ♖c8 12 a3 a6 ∞ Tarjan-Henley, US Ch 1984

⁴⁵ 10 ... f6 11 ♗g3 ♘xg3 12 hg f5 13 ♗b5! ± Ubilava

⁴⁶ 11 ♖c1 ♘f6 12 ♗xf6 gf 13 ♘h4 ∞

⁴⁷ 12 ♘a4 ♘f6 13 ♗xf6 ♗xf6 14 ♘c5 ♕e7 15 ♖c1 ♗e8 = Andersson-Portisch, Tilburg 1980

⁴⁸ 8 ♗d3 ♘xd3 9 ♕xd3 ♗e7 10 0-0-0 0-0 11 ♗g5 ♘d7 = Timoshchenko-Yusupov, USSR Ch 1981

8 ♕b3 ♗b4 9 ♗b5 0-0 10 0-0 ♗xc3 11 ♕xc3 ♖c8 12 ♖fc1 ♕b6 = Seirawan-Yusupov, Indonesia 1983

⁴⁹ 8 ... ♗d6 9 ♗b5 ♖c8 10 ♗xc6! bc 11 0-0 0-0 12 ♖c1 ♕e7 13 ♘a4 ± Kasparov-Dolmatov, USSR Ch 1979

8 ... ♘d7 9 ♘xc6 bc 10 ♗e2 (10 ♗a6 ♕b6 11 ♕e2 ♘b8 12 ♗d3 ♗xd3 13 ♕xd3 ♕a6 = Keene-Torre, Bochum 1981) 10 ... ♕b6 11 ♕d2 (11 0-0 ♕xb2 12 ♘a4 ♕b4 ∞ I.Ivanov-Torre, Toluca IZ 1982) 11 ... ♗e7 12 0-0 a5 13 ♖fc1 0-0 14 ♘a4 ∞ Velikov-Mokry, Thessaloniki Ol 1984

⁵⁰ 9 ... a6 10 ♕b3 ♗d6 11 ♗xd6 ♕xd6 12 ♗e2 b5 13 0-0 ± Mikh.Tseitlin-Kirov, Prague 1983

⁵¹ 10 ♗g3 a6 11 ♗d3 ♗xd3 12 ♕xd3 ♗e7 13 0-0-0 ∞/∓ Spraggett-Yusupov, Montpellier C 1985

⁵² 12 ♗b5+ ♔f8 13 0-0 ♕b6 14 ♘a4 ♕c7 ∞ Yusupov

⁵³ 8 ... ♗b4 9 ♘e5 ♕a5 10 ♗xc6+ bc 11 0-0 ±

⁵⁴ 9 0-0 ♗e7 10 ♖c1 0-0 11 ♗xc6 bc 12 ♘a4 ♖c8 13 ♘e5 ♘xe5 14 ♗xe5 ♕a5 = Farago-Belyavsky, Novi Sad 1979

⁵⁵ 9 ... ♕b6 10 ♘h4 ♗e4 (10 ... ♗g4 11 h3 ♗h5 12 0-0 ±/±) 11 0-0-0 ♖c8 12 f3 ♗g6 13 ♘xg6 hg 14 ♔b1 ±/± Yusupov-Belyavsky, USSR Ch 1979

⁵⁶ 12 ♖fc1 ♗e7 13 ♘e2 ♕b6 = Kir.Georgiev-Khalifman, Plovdiv 1986

⁵⁷ 4 ... ♕b6 5 ♕b3 ♗f5 6 c5 ♕c7 7 ♗f4 ±; 6 ... ♕xb3 7 ab ♘fd7 8 ♗f4 f6 9 e3 e5 10 ♗g3 ± Miles-Bellon, Las Palmas 1980

4 ... a6 5 e3 (5 ♕b3 e6 6 ♗g5 b5 7 cd cd 8 ♖c1 ♗e7 9 e3 0-0 = Polugayevsky-Rivas Pastor, Linares 1985) 5 ... b5 6 b3 ♗g4 7 ♗e2 ♗xf3 8 ♗xf3 e6 9 0-0 ± Razuvayev-Pirttimäki,

Helsinki 1984

⁵⁸ 5 e3 b5 6 a4 b4 and now:
7 ♘a2 e6 8 ♗c4 ♗e7 (8 ... a5) 9 a5 ♕xa5 10 ♗d2 ♕b6 11 ♕a4 0-0 ∞ Miles-Portisch, Bugojno 1986

7 ♘b1 ♗a6 8 ♕c2 b3!? (8 ... e6 =) 9 ♕d1 e6 ∞ Adorjan-Torre, Toluca IZ 1982

⁵⁹ 5 ... e6 6 g3 ♗b4 7 ♗g2 ♘d5 8 ♗d2 ♘b6 9 ♘e4 a5 10 a3 0-0 = Benjamin-Murei, Jerusalem 1986

5 ... ♗e6 6 e4 b5 7 f4 g6 8 g4 ♗g7 9 f5 ♗c8 10 ♗g2 ♗b7 11 0-0-0-0 ∞ Stohl-Ehlvest, Tallinn 1986

⁶⁰ 10 ... ♗d7 11 a4 b4 12 ♘e4 ♕c7 13 ♕d4 ±/± Miles-Smyslov, Dortmund 1986

⁶¹ Torre

⁶² 7 ♘g5 f6 (7 ... h6) 8 ♘ge4 f5 9 ♘g5 e6 ∞ Wockenfuss-Wiemer, West Germany 1983

⁶³ 7 ... h6 8 ab ♘xc3 9 bc cb 10 ♗a3 ♗e6 11 ♗e2 ∞ Ermolinsky-Kupreichik, USSR 1986

⁶⁴ 8 ab ♘xc3 9 bc cb 10 ♘g5 ♗b7 11 ♕h5 ♕d7 ∞ Watson; 11 ... g6 12 ♕g4 ♗e7 13 h4 h5 14 ♕g3 ♘a6 15 ♖b1 ♕d7 ∞ Watson

⁶⁵ 8 ... ♕d7!? 9 ♗e2 ♗b7 10 0-0 ♘a6 ∞ Rajković-Velikov, Athens 1981

⁶⁶ 10 ... ♕h4 11 ♕f3 f5 12 ef ♘xf6 13 ♘bd2 ± Rajkovic-Vučičević, Bela Crkva 1986

⁶⁷ 11 ... ♘f4?! 12 ♕g4 ±/± Sosonko-Flear, Wijk aan Zee 1987

11 ... c3 12 ♘c4 cb 13 ♗xb2 ♗xc4 14 ♗xc4 ∞∞ Rajković-Meduna, Bad Wörishofen 1987

⁶⁸ 6 ♘e5 ♘g4 7 ♘xc4 e5 8 ♘xe5 ♘xe5 9 de ♕xd1+ 10 ♔xd1 ♗e6 11 ♗g5 h6 ∞ Whiteley-Speelman, London 1982

6 e3 ♗g4 7 ♗xc4 e6 8 h3 ♗h5 9 0-0 ♘b4 10 ♕e2 ± Belyavsky-Vasyukov, Frunze 1979

⁶⁹ 8 ... ♗b4 9 ♕d3 ♗xf3 10 gf ♕a5 11 ♔e2 ♗e7 12 ♖hg1 g6 13 ♖g5 ± Cebalo-Ivkov, Yugoslav Ch 1981

⁷⁰ 9 ... 0-0 10 ♗e2 c5 11 dc ♘xc5 12 e5 ♘d5 13 ♘xd5 ♕xd5 14 ♖c1 ± Cebalo-Kovačević, Novi Sad 1984

⁷¹ 10 h3 ♗h5 11 g4 ♗g6 12 ♘d2 0-0 13 f4 ∞/± Saeed-Speelman, Taxco IZ 1985

10 ♗e2 0-0 11 h3 ♗h5 12 a5 ± Smejkal-Plachetka, Czechoslovak Ch 1984

⁷² 12 gf ± Rogers-Hort, Biel 1985

⁷³ 6 e4 e6 7 ♗xc4 ♗b4 8 ♕b3 a5 9 0-0 ♗f3 10 gf ♕d4 ∞ Lputian-Haik, Sochi 1985

⁷⁴ 8 ... a5 9 0-0 ♗e7 10 ♘xc4 ♘a6 11 ♕d2 0-0 12 e4 ♘b4 13 f4 ± Rajković-Rukavina, Yugoslav Ch 1974

⁷⁵ 9 0-0 ♘d5 10 ♕c2 a5 11 ♘xc4 ♘b6 12 ♘xb6 ♕xb6 13 ♗e3 ♗g6 = Hjartarson-Yrjölä, Gjovik 1985

⁷⁶ 10 ♕b3 0-0 11 ♗d2 c5 12 dc ♘c6 13 ♘d6 ♘d4 14 ♕d1 ∞ Ftacnik-Ree, Wijk aan Zee 1985

⁷⁷ 12 a5 ♘a6 13 ♘e5 ♘ab4 ∞/= Vaiser-Khuzman, USSR 1986

117

Slav I   1 d4 d5 2 c4 c6 *continued*

	3	4	5	6	7	8	9	10	11	
15	Nf3	Nc3	a4	Ne5	f3[78]	Nxc4	Ne4[79]	Bd2	Bxb4[82]	±
	Nf6	dc	Bg4	Bh5	Nfd7	e5	Bb4+[80]	Qe7[81]	Qxb4+[83]	

[78] **7 h3** Nbd7 8 Nxc4 e6 9 g4 Bg6 10 Bg2 Bb4 11 0-0 Nb6 12 Ne5 ∞/± Khenkin-Khuzman, Sevastopol 1986
7 Nxc4 e6 8 Bg5 Bb4 9 f3 h6 10 Bh4 ± Schneider-Vainerman, USSR 1986

[79] 9 Nxe5 Nxe5 10 de Nd7 11 f4 Bb4 12 Qc2 Qe7 13 e4 g5! 14 Be2 ± Timman-Petrosian, Las Palmas IZ 1982

[80] 9 ... Nb6?! 10 Ne5 f6 11 Nd3! ±

[81] **10 ...** Qh4+ 11 g3 Qe7 12 de 0-0 13 Rc1 ±

Gavrikov-Rogers, Tallinn 1985
10 ... Bxd2+ 11 Qxd2 0-0 12 de b5 13 ab ±/± Lputian-Pergericht, Geneva 1986

[82] 11 de 0-0 12 f4 Ba6 13 Qb3 Bg6 ∞ Knaak-Tischbierek, Potsdam 1985; 12 Rc1 Na6 13 Bxb4 Nxb4! ∞ Zaid-Khuzman, USSR 1986

[83] 12 Qd2 Qxd2+ 13 Kxd2 ± Polugayevsky-Hübner, Tilburg 1985, and Adorjan-Flear, Szirak 1986

Slav II   1 d4 d5 2 c4 c6 3 Nf3 Nf6 4 Nc3 dc 5 a4 Bf5

	6	7	8	9	10	11	12	13	14	
1	Ne5[1]	e3[2]	Bxc4	0-0	Qe2	e4	Rd1	Bf4	Bb3	±
	Na6	Nb4	e6	Be7	h6[3]	Bh7	0-0	Qa5	Rad8[4]	
2	...	Nxc4	g3	de	Bf4	Qc1	Nxd6+	Bg2[7]	0-0	±
	Nbd7	Qc7[5]	e5	Nxe5	Rd8[6]	Bd6	Qxd6	a5[8]	0-0[9]	
3	...	f3	Bg5[11]	Bh4	dc	Kxd1	Nxd7	e4	Kc2	=
	e6	Bb4[10]	h6[12]	c5	Qxd1+	Nbd7	0-0-0	Rxd7+	Bh7[13]	
4	...	...	Nxc4	Bg5	Bh4	dc	Kxd1[17]	Kc1	e4	∞
	...	...	0-0[14]	h6[15]	c5[16]	Qxd1+	Rd8+	Na6	Nxc5[18]	
5	e3	Bxc4[19]	0-0	Qb3[20]	Na2[22]	Nh4	Nc3	Be2	Nxe4	=
	e6	Bb4	Nbd7	a5[21]	Be7	Be4[23]	Nb6	0-0	Nxe4[24]	
6	...	...	...	Nh4	Qb3[26]	g3	Nxg6	Rd1	Bf1[28]	±
	...	...	...	Bg6[25]	Qb6[27]	a5	hg	0-0-0	g5[29]	
7	...	...	...	Nh4[30]	f3	g4	e4[33]	g5	Nxg6	±
	...	...	0-0	Bg4[31]	Bh5[32]	Bg6	Qe7[34]	Nfd7	hg[35]	
8	...	...	...	...	f3[36]	Nxg6	Qc2	Na2	b4	±
	...	...	...	Nbd7	Bg6	hg	Qa5[37]	Be7	Qc7[38]	
9	...	...	...	Qe2	Bd3	bc	Qc2	Qxd3	Ba3[40]	±
	...	...	...	Ne4[39]	Bxc3	Nxc3	Bxd3	Nd5	Re8[41]	
10	...	...	...	...	e4	Rd1	h3[43]	Qxf3	d5	±
	...	...	...	Nbd7	Bg4	Qe7[42]	Bxf3	e5	Nb6[44]	
11	...	...	...	...	...	Bd3	Bf4[46]	e5	Nxd5	±
	...	...	...	...	Bg6	Bh5[45]	Re8	Nd5	ed[47]	

[1] 6 Nh4 Bc8 (6 ... e6 7 Nxf5 cf 8 e3 Bd6 9 Bxc4 0-0 10 Qf3 ± Inkiov-Meduna, Varna 1983) 7 e3 e5 8 de Qxd1+ 9 Nxd1 Bb4+ 10 Bd2 = Alekhine-Euwe, match (15) 1935; 8 Bc4 ed 9 ed ± Alekhine

[2] 7 f3 Nd7 8 Nxc4 e5 9 e4 ed 10 Ne2 (10 ef dc 11 bc Qf6 12 Qc2 Bc5 ∓ Timman-Hort, Volmac v Porz 1984) ∞ Kuzmin-Bagirov, Tashkent 1984

[3] 10 ... 0-0 11 e4 Bg6 12 Rd1 c5 12 Nxg6 hg 13 d5 ed 14 e5 ±/± Li Zunian-Vaganian, Biel IZ 1985

[4] Smejkal-Torre, Thessaloniki Ol 1984

[5] 7 ... Nb6 8 Ne5 e6 9 f3 (9 e3 Bb4 10 Bd2 Nfd7 11 Nd3 Be7 12 e4 Bg6 ∞/= Razuvayev-Chernin, USSR Ch 1985) 9 ... Nfd7 10 a5 Nxe5 11 ab Nd7 12 e4 ± Sosonko-Hort, West Germany 1982-83

[6] 10 ... ♘fd7 11 ♗g2 f6 12 0-0 ♗e6 13 ♘xe5 fe 14 ♗e3 ±

[7] 13 ♕e3 ♘fg4 14 ♕xa7 0-0 ∞ A.Rodriguez-Torre, Biel IZ 1985

[8] **13 ... 0-0** 14 a5 ♕e6 15 0-0 ± Adorjan-Osmanović, Sarajevo 1983, and Hübner-Rogers, Biel 1984

13 ... ♕e7 14 0-0 a5 15 h3 0-0 16 g4 ♗c8 17 ♕e3 ± E.Vladimirov-Barbulescu, Havana 1986

[9] 15 ♕e3 ± Spraggett-Rogers, Hong Kong 1984, and Browne-Miles, Indonesia 1982

[10] 7 ... c5 8 e4 cd 9 ef ♘c6 10 ♗xc6 bc 11 fe fe ±/= Hübner-Smyslov, match 1983, and Razuvayev-Hübner, London 1984

[11] 8 e4 ♗xe4 9 fe ♘xe4 10 ♕f3 ♘xd4 11 ♕xf7+ ♔d8 ∞ Moskalenko-Sergeyev, USSR 1984

[12] 8 ... c5 9 dc ♕a5 10 ♕d4 ± Sosonko-Hübner, Tilburg 1984

[13] 15 c6 bc 16 ♗c4 ♗d6 17 ♗d3 ♘h5 = Gulko-Anikayev, USSR 1981

[14] **8 ...** ♘bd7 9 ♗g5 (9 e4!?) 9 ... h6 10 ♗h4 b5 11 ab! cb 12 ♘d2 a6 13 e4 ± Bagirov-Mnatsakanian, Erevan 1982

8 ... c5 9 dc ♕xd1+ 10 ♔xd1 0-0 11 e4 ♗g6 12 ♘d6 ♖d8 13 ♔c2 ± Henley-Pavlović, Lugano 1983

[15] 9 ... c5 10 dc ♕xd1+ 11 ♖xd1 ♗c2 12 ♖d2 ♗b3 = Spassky-Petrosian, Moscow 1975

[16] 10 ... ♘a6 11 e4 ♗h7 12 ♘e3! c5 13 d5 ±/± Lin Ta-Chernin, Lucerne 1985

[17] 12 ♖xd1 ♗c2 13 ♖c1 ♗a4! ∞/∓ Belyavsky-Bareyev, USSR Ch 1986, and Bareyev-Ehlvest, USSR 1986

[18] 15 ♔c2 ♗h7 16 ♗e2 ∞

[19] 7 a5 ♘bd7 8 ♗xc4 b5 9 ab ab 10 ♖xa8 ♕xa8 11 0-0 ♗e7 12 ♖e1 0-0 = Sosonko-Kirov, Rome 1986

[20] **9 h3** h6 10 ♕e2 ♗h7 11 e4 ♗xc3 12 bc ♘xe4 13 ♗a3 ∞ Tukmakov-Kuzmin, USSR 1979

9 ♕e2 ♗g6 10 e4 (10 ♗d3 ♗xd3 11 ♕xd3 0-0 12 ♖d1 c5 13 d5 ed 14 ♘xd5 ♘xd5 15 ♕xd5 ♘f6 = Andersson-Ljubojević, Indonesia 1983) 10 ... ♗xc3 11 bc ♘xe4 12 ♗a3 ♕c7 13 ♖fc1 0-0-0 14 a5 ♖he8 15 ♕a2 ♘d6 ∞∞ Karpov-Hübner, Tilburg 1986

[21] 9 ... ♕b6 10 e4 ♗g6 11 ♗xe6 fe 12 a5 ♗xa5 13 ♕xe6+ ♔d8 14 e5 ∞ Novikov-Ehlvest, USSR 1986

[22] 10 ♘h4 ♗g4 11 f3 ♗h5 12 g3 0-0 (12 ... ♕b6 13 ♖f2 ♗e7 14 ♘g2 ♗g6 15 e4 ± Gavrikov-Chernin, match 1985) 13 e4 ♘b6 14 ♗e3 ♘xc4 15 ♕xc4 ♘d7 = Cebalo-Portisch, Reggio Emilia 1985-86

[23] 11 ... ♗g4 12 f3 ♗h5 13 g4 ♗g6 14 ♘c3 ±

[24] 15 ♘f3 ♘d5 16 ♘e5 ♘b4 = Kasparov-Kupreichik, USSR Ch 1981

[25] 9 ... ♗g4 10 f3 ♗h5 11 g4 (11 e4 ♘b6 12 ♗e2 ♘fd7 13 g3 a5 = Portisch-Smyslov, Amsterdam 1981) 11 ... ♘d5 (11 ... ♗g6 12 e4

♕a5 13 ♕e2 e5 14 ♘a2 ± Lputian-Smagin, USSR Ch 1986) 12 ♘g2 ♗g6 13 ♘a2 ♗e7 14 e4 ♘b6 15 ♗e2 ± Ivanchuk-Ehlvest, Minsk 1986

[26] **10 g3** 0-0 11 ♕b3 ♕b6 12 ♘xg6 hg 13 ♖d1 a5 14 ♕c2 c5 = Kasparov-Belyavsky, Tilburg 1981

10 f4!? ♘d5 11 ♕e1 ♗e7 12 ♘xg6 hg 13 a5 a6 14 e4 ± Lputian-Dokhoyan, Irkutsk 1986

[27] 10 ... a5 11 ♘a2 (11 g3 ♕b6 - 10 ... ♕b6) 11 ... ♗e7 12 g3 ♕c7 (12 ... ♗c8 13 ♘c3 0-0 14 ♘xg6 hg 15 ♖d1 e5 16 ♗f1 ± Kasparov-Belyavsky, USSR Ch 1981) 13 ♘c3 0-0 14 ♘xg6 hg 15 ♖d1 ± Tukmakov-Belyavsky, USSR Ch 1981

[28] 14 ♘a2 ♘g4!? 15 ♘xb4 ab ∞

[29] 15 ♘a2 ♗d6 16 ♕xb6 ♘xb6 17 b3 ♘bd5 18 ♗d2 ±

[30] 9 ♕b3 ♕e7 10 a5 c5 11 ♘e5 cd 12 ed ♘c6 =

[31] 9 ... ♗g6 10 ♘xg6 (10 ♕b3 ♕b6 11 ♘xg6 hg 12 ♖d1 ♘bd7 13 g3 ♖fd8 14 ♗f1 a5 ∞ Tukmakov-Smyslov, Tilburg 1984) 10 ... hg 11 ♕c2 ♘bd7 12 ♖d1 ♕e7 13 g3 ± Tukmakov-Kuijpers, CSKA v Eindhoven 1986

[32] 10 ... ♘d5 11 fg ♕xh4 12 ♕f3 ♘d7 13 ♗d2 a5 14 ♖ad1 ± Tukmakov-Kupreichik, USSR Ch 1981

[32] 12 ♘xg6 hg 13 e4 c5 14 ♘a2 ♕a5 15 ♘xb4 ♕xb4 16 b3 ♖d8 = Tukmakov-Ljubojević, Tilburg 1984

[34] 12 ... ♘bd7 13 ♘xg6 hg 14 g5 ♘h5 15 f4 ± Knaak-Meduna, Trnava 1981

[35] 15 f4 ± Uhlmann-Velikov, East Germany v Bulgaria 1982

[36] 10 ♕e2 - 9 ♕e2

[37] 12 ... ♖c8 13 ♖d1 (13 ♗a2 ♕e7 14 ♖d1 c5 15 d5 c4 Razuvayev-Dokhoyan, USSR 1986) ±

[38] 15 ♗d2 ♖fd8 16 ♖ab1 ± Yusupov-Smyslov, Montpellier C 1985

[39] 9 ... c5 10 ♘a2 ♘c6 11 ♘xb4 ♘xb4 12 ♗d2 ♘c2 13 ♖ad1 ± Balashov-Palatnik, USSR 1980

[40] 14 ♖b1 a5 15 ♗a3 ♘b4 16 ♗xb4 ab = Ivkov-Hébert, Rio de Janeiro IZ 1979

[41] 15 ♖ab1 b6 16 ♖fc1 ± Polugayevsky-Romanishin, USSR Ch 1978

[42] 11 ... ♕a5 12 h3 ♗xf3 13 ♕xf3 e5 14 d5 ♗xc3 15 bc ± Yusupov-Velikov, Bulgaria 1981

[43] 12 ♘a2 ♗a5 13 ♗g5 h6 14 ♗h4 e5 15 d5 ♖fd8 ∞ Rivas Pastor-Velikov, Plovdiv 1984

[44] 14 ... h6 15 dc bc 16 ♘e2 ♔h7 17 ♘g3 ± Polugayevsky-Agzamov, USSR Ch 1983

[45] 11 ... ♖e8 12 ♗f4 ♕a5 13 h3 ♖ac8 14 ♘a2 ♗f8 15 b4 ± Polugayevsky-Ribli, London 1986

[46] 12 e5 ♘d5 13 ♘xd5 cd 14 ♕e3 ∞ Smejkal-Mednis, Amsterdam II 1986, and Vaganian-Chernin, Sochi 1986

[47] **14 ... cd** 15 h3 a6 16 g4 ♗g6 17 h4 ± Magerramov-Bagirov, Baku 1986

14 ... ed 15 h3 ±

119

Semi-Slav I   1 d4 d5 2 c4 e6 3 ♘c3 c6[1]

	4	5	6	7	8	9	10	11	12	
1	e4[2]	♘xe4	♗d2[4]	♗xb4	♗e2[5]	♗c3[6]	♘f3[7]	0-0	♖e1	∞∞
	de	♗b4+[3]	♕xd4	♕xe4+	♘a6	♘e7	0-0	♘g6	f6[8]	
2	...	...	...	...	...	♗d6	♘f3	♘xe5[10]	♕xe2	=
	...	...	...	...	...	e5[9]	♗g4	♗xe2	♕xe2+[11]	
3	...	...	...	...	...	♗xc5	♕d4[12]	♗f3	♗b4!	∞/∞∞
	...	...	...	...	c5	♕xg2	♘d7[13]	♗g5	♕e5+[14]	

1 **3 ... ♗b4** 4 ♘f3 (4 a3 ♗xc3+ 5 bc ♘e7 6 e3 0-0 7 ♗d3 c5 8 ♘e2 ♘bc6 9 0-0 ∞ Kir.Georgiev-Velikov, Plovdiv 1984) 4 ... ♘e7 5 cd ed 6 ♗f4 0-0 7 e3 c5 8 ♗e2 ± Cebalo-Nogueiras, Taxco IZ 1985

3 ... a6 4 cd ed 5 ♗f4 ♘f6 6 e3 ♗d6 7 ♗xd6 ♕xd6 8 ♗d3 ♘c6 9 ♘ge2 0-0 10 a3 ±

2 **4 cd** ed 5 ♗f4 ♗d6! (5 ... ♘f6 6 e3 ±) 6 ♗g3 ♘e7 7 e3 ♘f5 8 ♗xd6 ♘xd6 9 ♘ge2 0-0 = Miles-Ljubojević, Tilburg 1981

4 ♗f4!? dc 5 e3 b5 6 a4 ♘f6 7 ab cb 8 ♘xb5 ♗b4+ 9 ♘c3 ♘d5 10 ♕c2 ∞ Christiansen-Nogueiras, Dubai Ol 1986

3 **5 ... ♘f6?!** 6 ♘xf6+ ♕xf6 7 ♘f3 ♗b4+ 8 ♗d2 ♗xd2+ 9 ♕xd2 ±

4 **6 ♘c3** c5 7 a3 ♗a5 (7 ... ♗xc3+ 8 bc ♘f6 =) 8 ♗e3 ♘f6 9 ♘f3 ♘c6 10 dc ♕xd1+ 11 ♖xd1 ♘e4 12 ♖c1 ♘xc3 13 bc e5 = Lerner-Lukacs, Polanica Zdroj 1986

5 **8 ♘e2** ♘e7 9 ♕d2 c5 10 ♗xc5 ♘bc6

Sveshnikov

6 9 ♗a5 ♘d7 10 ♘f3 ♘f6 11 ♕d6 ♕f6 ∞/∓

7 10 ♗xg7 ♖g8 11 ♗c3 ♘d5 12 cd ♕xg2 13 de ♗xe6 ∞/=

8 13 b4 ♘f4 14 ♗f1 ♕g6 15 g3 ∞∞ Estevez-Diaz, Bayamo 1984

9 9 ... b6!? 10 ♕d2 ♗b7 11 ♘f3 = Toshkov-Vera, Varna 1986

10 11 0-0 0-0-0 12 ♗d3 ♕f4 13 ♗xe5 ♕xe5 14 ♘xe5 ♗xd1 = Tal-Dorfman, USSR Ch 1978

11 13 ♔xe2 ♘h6 = Vaiser-Novikov, Volgodonsk 1983

12 10 ♘f3 ♕g5 11 ♗d6 ♘e7 12 ♘h3 ♕f6 13 ♖g1 ♘f5 14 ♗a3 ∞∞ Vladimirov-Monin, USSR 1980

13 10 ... ♘c6 11 ♕d6 ♘ge7 12 0-0-0 ♕e4 13 ♕c7! ∞∞/± Taimanov

14 13 ♘e2 ♕xd4 14 ♘xd4 ♘e5 15 0-0-0 ∞/∞∞ Larsen

Semi-Slav II   1 d4 d5 2 c4 e6 3 ♘c3 c6 4 ♘f3 dc

	5	6	7	8	9	10	11	12	13	
1	e4[1]	♗e2[2]	0-0	a4	♗g5	e5	♗h4	♗g3	♘e4	∞∞
	b5	♘f6	♗b7	a6	♘bd7	h6	g5	♘d5	♕b6[3]	
2	a4	e3[4]	♗d2[5]	ab	♗xc3	b3[7]	bc[8]	♗b2	♗d3	±
	♗b4	b5	a5[6]	♗xc3	cb	♗b7	b4	♘f6	♘bd7[9]	

1 **5 e3** b5 6 a4 b4 7 ♘c4 ♗a6 8 ♕c2 ♕d5 =

5 ♗g5 ♕c7 6 e4 b5 7 a4 ♗b4 8 ♘d2 a6 9 ab cb ∞ Bagirov-Chekhov, USSR 1982

2 **6 e5** ♗b7 7 ♗e2 a6 8 0-0 ♗b4 9 ♘e4 h6 10 ♗d2 ♗e7 ∞

3 Petrosian-Averbakh, USSR Ch 1950

4 **6 g3** a5 7 ♗e5 ♘f6 8 ♗g2 ♘d5 9 ♗d2 ♘b6 10 e3 ♘8d7 11 f4 ∞ Seirawan-Korchnoi, Bad Kissingen 1981

6 e4 b5 7 ab cb 8 ♗d2 ♗xc3 9 bc a6 10 g3 ♘f6 11 e5 ♘e4 ∞ D.Gurevich-Kaufman, USSR 1974

5 **7 ♘d2** ♕b6 8 ♗g4 ♔f8 9 g3 ♘f6 10 ♕f3 ♗b7 ∓ Speelman-Flear, London 1986

6 7 ... ♗b7 8 b3 a5 9 bc bc 10 ♗xc4 ♘f6 11 0-0 ± Spraggett-Klinger, Vienna 1986

7 ... ♘f6 8 ab ♗xc3 9 ♗xc3 cb 10 b3 0-0 11 bc bc 12 ♗xc4 ♕c7 13 ♕d3 ± Bagirov-Kupreichik, Lvov 1984

7 ... ♕e7 8 ♗e2 (8 ab ♗xc3 9 ♗xc3 cb 10 d5 ±) 8 ... ♘f6 9 0-0 ♘bd7 10 ♕c2 ±/±

7 10 d5?! ♘f6 11 de ♕xd1+ 12 ♔xd1 ♘e4 ∓ Donner-Pliester, Amsterdam 1982

8 11 d5 ♘f6 12 bc b4 13 ♗xf6 ♕xf6 ∞ Gavrikov-Karasev, USSR 1982

9 14 ♕c2 0-0 15 0-0 ± Saeed-Pliester, Amsterdam 1982

	5	6	7	8	9	10	11	12	13	
1	♕b3	♕xc4	♕d3[2]	e4[4]	♘a4	♗e2[5]	b3	e5	0-0	∞
	dc[1]	b5	♗b7[3]	b4	♘bd7	♕a5	c5	♘d5	cd[6]	
2	♗g5	♗h4	e4[7]	♗g3	♗e2	e5	h4	♖c1	♘d2	∞
	h6	dc	g5	b5[8]	♗b7[9]	♘d5	♕a5	g4	♘xc3[10]	
3	...	♗xf6	♕b3[11]	a3[13]	♘xa4	♕c2	♘c3	♖d1	g3	=
	...	♕xf6	a5[12]	a4	dc	♕d8	b5	♘d7	♗e7[14]	
4	...	...	g3	♗g2	0-0	♕d3	e4	♕xc4	♕e2	=
	...	...	♕d8[15]	♘d7	♗e7[16]	0-0	dc	♘b6	c5![17]	
5	...	...	e3	♗d3[18]	0-0[19]	♖c1[20]	e4	♗xc4	♗b3[21]	±
	...	...	♘d7	♕d8	♗e7	0-0	dc	b5	b4[22]	

---

[1] 5 ... ♘bd7 6 cd ed 7 ♗f4 ♘h5 8 ♗g3 ♗e7 9 e3 0-0 10 ♗d3 g6 11 0-0 ♘xg3 12 hg ♕b6 = Karpov-Ljubojević, Plovdiv 1983
5 ... ♗e7 6 g3 dc 7 ♕xc4 b5 8 ♕d3 ♗a6 9 ♕c2 0-0 10 ♗g2 ♘bd7 = Cebalo-Jovčić, Yugoslavia 1986
5 ... ♘e4 6 e3 f5 7 ♗d3 ♘d7 8 0-0 ♗d6 9 ♗d2 ♕f6 10 ♖ad1 ♕h6 11 g3 ♘df6 12 ♔g2 0-0 = F.Portisch-Vera, Bratislava 1983

[2] 7 ♕b3 a6!? 8 ♗g5 c5 9 dc ♗xc5 10 e3 ♘bd7 11 ♗d3 h6 12 ♗h4 ♗b7 = Romanishin-Sveshnikov, Erevan Z 1982

[3] 7 ... b4 8 ♘e4 ♗a6 9 ♘xf6+ gf 10 ♕c2 ±
7 ... a6 8 e4 c5 9 dc ♕xd3 10 ♗xd3 ♗xc5 11 e5 ♘fd7 12 ♗e4 ± Browne-Saeed, Taxco IZ 1985
7 ... ♘bd7 8 g3 ♗b7 9 ♗g2 ♗e7 10 0-0 0-0 11 ♗g5 b4 12 ♗xf6 ♘xf6 = Kavalek-Kogan, New York 1984

[4] 8 ♗g5 ♗e7 9 ♕c2 h6 10 ♗xf6 ♗xf6 11 e3 ♘d7 12 ♗e2 ∞ Miles-Mann, Copenhagen 1982

[5] 10 ♗e3 ♕a5 11 b3 ♗e7 12 ♖c1 0-0 13 ♗e2 ♖fd8 ∓ Romanishin-Sveshnikov, Sochi 1983

[6] 14 ♕xd4 ♗e7 ∞ Horvath-Sveshnikov, Sochi 1985

[7] 7 e3 b5 8 a4 ♗b4 9 ♘d2 ♗b7 10 ab ♗xc3 11 bc cb 12 ♕b1 ∞ Dlugy-Romero Holmes, Dubai Ol 1986

[8] 8 ... ♗b4 9 ♗xc4 ♘xe4 10 0-0 ♘xg3 11 fg ♘d7 ∞/∞ Lputian-Sveshnikov, USSR Ch 1985

[9] 9 ... b4 10 ♘a4 ♘xe4 11 ♗e5 ♘f6 12 0-0 ♘bd7 13 ♗xc4 ∞ Lputian-Smagin, USSR Ch 1985

[10] 14 bc h5 15 ♘e4 ♘d7 ∞
13 ... c5?! 14 ♘ce4! cd 15 0-0 h5 16 a4! ± Kasparov-Tal, Moscow IZ 1982

[11] 7 a3 dc 8 ♘e5 (8 g3 g6! 9 ♗g2 ♗g7 10 e3 0-0 ∞) 8 ... c5 9 ♗xc4 cd 10 ♘b5 ♕d8 11 ♕xd4 ♕xd4 12 ♘xd4 ♗d7 13 g3 ♗c5 = Kasparov-Sveshnikov, USSR Ch 1981

[12] 7 ... ♘d7 8 e4 dc 9 ♗xc4 b5 10 ♗d3 e5 11 de ♘xe5 12 ♘xe5 ♕xe5 13 0-0 ♗d6 =

[13] 8 e4 de 9 ♘xe4 ♗b4+ 10 ♕xb4 ab 11 ♘xf6+ gf = Polugayevsky-Sveshnikov, Manila 1982

[14] Smyslov-Pomar, Wijk aan Zee 1972

[15] 7 ... ♘d7 8 ♗g2 dc (8 ... ♗d6 9 0-0 ♕e7 10 e4 dc 11 ♘d2 ♘b6 12 e5 ♗e7 13 ♕e2 0-0 ∞ Bagirov-Fernandez, Cascais 1986) 9 0-0 ♗e7 10 e3 0-0 11 ♕e2 e5 12 ♕xc4 ed 13 ♘xd4 ♘e5 = Tukmakov-Sveshnikov, USSR 1986

[16] 9 ... dc 10 e3 c5 11 ♕a4 ♗e7 12 d5 ed 13 ♘xd5 0-0 14 ♕c4 ♘b6 = Oll-Novikov, Tallinn 1986

[17] 14 ♖fd1 ♗d7 15 dc ♗xc5 16 ♘e5 ♕e7 17 ♘xd7 ♘xd7 = Oll-Sveshnikov, Pinsk 1986

[18] 8 ♕c2 a6 9 0-0-0 ♗b4 10 ♔b1 0-0 11 ♗d3 b5 = Ree-Kuijf, Dutch Ch 1986
8 ♗e2 ♗d8 9 0-0 ♗e7 10 e4 de 11 ♘xe4 0-0 12 ♕c2 ♕c7 13 ♖ad1 ♘f6 14 c5 b6 = Peev-Velikov, Plovdiv 1984
8 a3 ♕d8 9 e4 de 10 ♘xe4 ♗e7 11 c5 b6 12 b4 0-0 13 ♗c4 a5 = Vladimirov-Chernin, USSR 1981

[19] 9 a3 ♗e7 10 ♕c2 0-0 11 h4 a6 12 cd ed 13 g4 ♘f6 14 g5 ♘g4 15 0-0-0 ∞ Polugayevsky-Sveshnikov, Moscow 1985

[20] 10 a3 0-0 11 e4 dc 12 ♗xc4 c5 13 dc ♗xc5 14 ♕e2 a6 15 e5 b5 ∞ Dolmatov-Sveshnikov, Moscow 1985
10 ♕e2 0-0 11 ♖fd1 a6 12 ♖ac1 f5 13 ♕c2 ♗d6 14 ♘e2 ♘f6 = Belyavsky-Sveshnikov, Kislovodsk 1982
10 e4 dc 11 ♗xc4 b5! 12 ♗b3 b4 13 ♘a4 0-0 14 ♕c2 ♗b7 15 ♖fd1 ♕a5 = Lukacs-Sveshnikov, Sochi 1984
10 cd!? ed 11 a3 a5 12 ♕e2 0-0 13 ♖ad1 ♗d6 14 e4 de 15 ♘xe4 ♘f6 16 ♘e5 ± Bönsch-Sveshnikov, Sochi 1984

[21] 13 ♗d3 ♗b7 14 e5 ♕b6 15 ♗e4 ± Rastjanis-Chernin, USSR 1985

[22] 14 ♘a4 ♗a6 15 ♖e1 ♖c8 16 d5 ed 17 ed ± Grivas-Votruba, Athens 1984

Semi-Slav III   1 d4 d5 2 c4 e6 3 ♘c3 ♘f6 4 ♘f3 c6   *continued*

	5	6	7	8	9	10	11	12	13	
6	♗g5	♗xf6	e3	♗d3	0-0	c5[24]	e4	♗xe4[25]	b4	±
	h6	♕xf6	♗d6	♕e7[23]	♘d7	♗c7	de	0-0	♖d8[26]	
7	...	...	♕c2	e3	a4[29]	ab	♘xb5	♘c3	♗e2	±
	...	...	dc[27]	b5[28]	♗b7[30]	cb	♗b4+	0-0	♘d7[31]	
8	...	e4[32]	a4[33]	♗xf6[35]	♗e2	0-0	d5	de	♘h4	∞
	dc	b5	♕b6[34]	gf	a6	♗b7	♗c5[36]	fe	♘d7[37]	
9	...	...	e5	♗h4	ef[38]	♘e5	a4[39]	♗e2	♗f3	∞
	...	...	h6	g5	gh	♕xf6	♗b4[40]	c5	cd[41]	
10	...	...	...	...	♘xg5	♘xf7[42]	♘xh8	♖c1[43]	♗e2	±/±
	...	...	...	...	♘d5	♕xh4	♗b4	♕e4+	♘f4[44]	
11	...	...	...	...	...	♗xg5	ef	♗e3[45]	g3	±/±
	...	...	...	...	hg	♗e7	♗xf6	♗g5[46]	♗b7[47]	

[23] 8... dc 9 ♗xc4 ♘d7 10 0-0 ♕e7 11 ♘e4 ♗c7 12 ♖c1 0-0 13 ♗b3 (13 ♕e2 e5 14 d5 ♘b6 15 dc bc 16 ♗a6 f5 17 ♘g3 ± Razuvayev-Dolmatov, USSR Ch 1981) 13... ♖d8 14 ♕c2 ♘f8 15 ♖fd1 ± Petrosian-Dorfman, USSR Ch 1976

[24] 10 ♖c1 0-0 11 ♕e2 dc 12 ♗xc4 e5 13 ♘e4 ed 14 ♘xd6 ♕xd6 15 ♖fd1 ♕e7 = Chekhov-Khuzman, USSR 1984

[25] 12 ♘xe4 0-0 13 ♖e1 ♖d8 14 b4 ♕f8 15 ♘c3 ♘f6 16 a3 ♗d7 = Ubilava-Sveshnikov, USSR 1986

[26] 14 ♖b1 ♘f6 15 ♗c2 ♘d5 16 ♕d3 g6 17 ♘xd5 ±/± Bukić-Barle, Ljubljana 1981

[27] 7... ♘d7 8 e4 ♗b4 9 ♗d3 ±; 8... de 9 ♕xe4 ♗d6 10 ♗d3 c5 11 d5 Agzamov-Gorelov, USSR 1982

[28] 8... ♗d6 9 ♗xc4 ♕e7 10 0-0 ♘d7 11 ♖fd1 0-0 12 ♗b3 b6 13 e4 ± Ftacnik-Hansen, Esbjerg 1982

[29] 9 ♘xb5 cb 11 ♕e4 ♗b4+ 12 ♔d1 ♕d8 13 ♕xa8 ♕c7 ∞ Sideif Zade-Gorelov, USSR 1983

[30] 9... a6?! 10 ab cb 11 ♘xb5 ♗b4+ 12 ♘c3 0-0 ±/± Farago-Djurić, Hastings 1984-85

[31] 14 0-0 e5 15 de ♘xc5 16 ♕xe5 ♕xe5 17 ♗xc4 ± Guseinov-Sveshnikov, USSR 1983

[32] 6 a4 ♗b4 7 e4 c5 (7... ♗xc3+ 8 bc ♕a5 9 e5 ♘e4 10 ♖c1 =) 8 ♗xc4 cd 9 ♘xd4 h6 10 ♗e3 ♘e4 11 0-0 ♗xc3 12 bc 0-0 13 ♕c2 ∞ Zaid-Ivanchuk, USSR 1985

[33] 7 ♕c2 ♘bd7 8 ♗e2 h6 9 ♗h4 ♗e7 10 0-0 0-0 11 ♖fd1 ♗b7 ∞/∓ Spraggett-Nogueiras, Taxco IZ 1985

[34] 7... ♗b7 8 ab cb 9 ♘xb5 ♗xe4 10 ♗xc4 ♗b4+ 11 ♘c3 ♘bd7 12 0-0 ♗xc3 13 bc 0-0 14 ♗d3 ± Ribli-Inkiov, Dubai Ol 1986

7... ♗b4 8 e5 h6 9 ef hg 10 fg ♖g8 11 h4 gh 12 ♖xh4 ♕f6 13 g3 (13 ♖h5!?) 13... ♘d7 14 ♗g2 ♗b7 15 ♔f1 ♗xc3 16 bc ± Wirthensohn-Flear, Graz 1984

7... b4 8 ♘b1 ♗a6 9 ♕c1 c3 10 bc ♗xf1 11 ♔xf1 h6 12 ♗xf6 ♕xf6 13 ♘bd2 ± Lerner-Chernin, USSR Ch 1984

[35] 9 e5 ♘d5 10 ♘e4 h6 10 ♗d2 ♘d7 11 b3 cb 12 ♕xb3 ♗a6 13 a5 ♕b7 ∓ Benjamin-Flear, Hastings 1984-85

[36] 11... cd 12 ed ♘d7 13 ab ab 14 ♖xa8+ ♗xa8 ∞/= Gorelov-Kishnev, USSR 1984

[37] 14 ♗g4 0-0-0 15 ♗xe6 ♔b8 ∞ Farago-Flear, Hastings 1984-85

[38] 9 ♗g3 ♘d5 10 h4 g4 11 ♘d2 h5 12 ♗e2 ♘d7 13 a4 ∞ Rajna-Lukacs, Hungarian Ch 1982

[39] 11 g3?! ♘d7 12 f4 ♗b7 13 ♗g2 ♘xe5 14 fe ♕e7 15 0-0 0-0-0 ∓ F.Portisch-Ribli, Warsaw 1979

11 ♗e2 ♘d7 12 0-0 ♘xe5 13 de ♕xe5 14 ♗f3 ♗b7 ∓ Ree-Hamann, Netanya 1968

[40] 11... ♗b7 12 ♗e2 c5 13 ♘xb5 cd 14 ♘c7+ ♔d8 15 ♕xd4 ♔xc7 16 ♕xc4+ ♘c6 ∞/± Piket-van der Wiel, match 1986

[41] 14 ♕xd4 ♘d7 15 ♘c6 ♕xd4 16 ♖xd4 ♖b8 17 ♘c6 ∞ Arencibia-Vera, San Juan 1985

[42] 10 ♘f3 ♕a5 11 ♖c1 ♗b4 12 ♕d2 ♘d7 13 ♗e2 ♗b7 ∞ Uhlmann-Inkiov, Plovdiv 1986

[43] 12 ♕d2 c5 13 0-0-0 ♘c6 14 dc ♘xe5 15 f4 ± Ribli-Nogueiras, Montpellier C 1985

[44] 14 a3! ♘xg2+ 15 ♔f1 ♘e3+ 16 fe ♕xh1+ 17 ♔f2 ♕xh2+ 18 ♔e1 ♗e7 19 ♔d2! ±/± Timman-Ljubojević, Buenos Aires 1980

[45] 12 ♗xf6 ♕xf6 13 a4 ♖h4 14 g4! b4 15 ♘e4 ♕f4 16 ♗g2 ± Novikov-Dreyev, USSR 1986; 13 g3 ♗b7 14 ♗g2 ♘a6 15 ♘e4 (15 a4 0-0-0 16 ab cb 17 ♗xb7+ ♔xb7 18 ♘xb5 e5 ∞ Ehlvest-Ivanchuk, USSR 1986

[46] 12... ♗b7 13 a4 b4 14 ♘e4 c5 15 ♘xc5 ♗d5 16 ♖c1 ♖g8 17 ♗c4 ± Nogueiras-Rogers, Dubai Ol 1986

[47] 14 ♗g2 ♗xe3 15 fe ♕c7 16 ♕f3 a6 17 0-0 ±/± Georgadze-Landero, Seville 1985

Semi-Slav IV **1 d4 d5 2 c4 e6 3 ♘c3 ♘f6 4 ♘f3 c6 5 ♗g5 dc 6 e4 b5 7 e5 h6**
8 ♗h4 g5 9 ♘xg5 hg 10 ♗xg5 ♘bd7

	11	12	13	14	15	16	17	18	19	
1	g3	ef	♘e4	♕f3[3]	♘c5[5]	♕xc6+	♕xc7+	dc	♖g1	∞
	♕a5[1]	b4	♗a6[2]	0-0-0[4]	♘xc5[6]	♔c7	♔xc7	♗b7	♖xh2[7]	
2	ef	g3[8]	d5	♗xh6	♗g2	♘e4	♘xc5	♗xd5[11]	♕xd5	=
	♗b7[7]	c5[9]	♗h6[10]	♖xh6	b4	♘xf6	♗xd5	♕xd5	♘xd5[12]	
3	...	...	♗g2	d5	0-0	♘a4[14]	a3[16]	ab	♕g4[18]	∞
	...	♕b6	c5[13]	0-0-0	b4	♕b5[15]	ed[17]	cb	d4[19]	

---

[1] **11 ... b4** 12 ♘e4 ♘xe4 13 ♗xd8 ♔xd8
14 ♗g2 f5 15 ef ♘exf6 16 ♕e2 ± Lipiridi-
Lutovinov, corr. 1984
  11 ... ♖g8 12 h4 ♖xg5 13 hg ♘d5 14 g6 fg
15 ♕g4+ Yusupov-Chekhov, USSR Ch 1980-81
  11 ... ♗b7 12 ♗g2 ♕c7 (12 ... ♖g8 13 ♗xf6
♘xf6 14 ef ♕xf6 15 a4 b4 16 ♘e4 ♕f5 17 ♖c1 ±;
12 ... ♕b6!? Timman-Tal, match 1988) 13 ef
c5 14 d5 ♕e5 15 ♕e2 0-0-0 16 de ♕xe2+
17 ♔xe2 ± Knaak-Vera, Tunja 1984

[2] 13 ... c3 14 bc bc 15 ♕d3 ♗b7 16 ♗e2 0-0-0
17 0-0 ♕f5 18 h4 ± Timman-Dolmatov, Amsterdam 1980

[3] **14 b3** 0-0-0 15 ♕c2 ♘b6 16 ♗e3 ♔b7
17 ♖c1 ♗a8 18 ♗e2 ♗b7 19 0-0 ♕f5 ∞
Novikov-Kaidanov, USSR 1986
  14 ♗e2 0-0-0 15 0-0 ♘c5 16 ♕c2 ♘xe4
17 ♕xe4 ♕d5 ∞ Schroer-Mercuri, USA 1986

[4] 14 ... ♕d5 15 ♖d1 0-0-0 16 b3 ♘b6 17 ♗e2
♗b7 ∞ Chernin-Torre, Bangalore 1981

[5] **15 b3** ♘b6 (15 ... cb 16 ♗xa6 ♕xa6 17 ♕xb3
♕b5 18 ♖c1! ± Kasparov-Miles, match 1986)
16 ♘c5 ♗b5 17 ♗e3 ♖d5 18 a4 ba! ∓ Oll-
Kaidanov, USSR 1986
  15 ♗g2 c3! 16 ♘xc3 ♘b8 ∓ Timman-
Pinter, Taxco IZ 1985
  15 ♗e2 ♗b7 16 0-0 ♕d5 17 ♗e3 ♖g8 = Flohr

[6] 15 ... ♘e5 16 de ♗xc5 17 ♗e2 b3+ 18 ♔f1
♖d5 19 ♔g2 ± Garcia Gonzalez-Braga, Cuba
1984

[7] Vladimirov

[8] 12 ♗e2 ♕b6 13 0-0 0-0-0 14 ♗f3 b4 15 ♘e4
♕c7 16 g3 ∞ Arbakov-Andrianov, Moscow Ch
1981

[9] 12 ... ♖g8 13 h4 c5 14 d5 ♕b6 15 ♗g2

0-0 16 0-0 b4 17 ♘a4 ± Chandler-Westerinen,
Wiesbaden 1981

[10] **13 ... ♘b6?** 14 de ♕xd1+ 15 ♖xd1 ♗xh1
16 e7 a6 17 h4!! ± Polugayevsky-Torre, Moscow
1981
  13 ... ♘e5 14 ♗g2 ♘d3+ 15 ♔f1 ♕d7
16 de fe 17 ♕e2 0-0-0 Hansen-Bagirov, Moscow
1975

[11] 18 0-0 ♗xg2 19 ♔xg2 ♕b6 ∞ Schneider-
Dvoretsky, Frunze 1983

[12] 20 ♖c1 ♖c8 21 ♖xc4 ♘b6 22 ♖c1 =
Azmaiparashvili-Dolmatov, USSR Ch 1986

[13] 13 ... 0-0-0 14 0-0 ♘e5 (14 ... ♗h6 15 ♗xh6
♖xh6 16 ♕d2 ♖dh8 17 ♘e4 ±) 15 de ♖xd1
16 ♖fxd1 ♗c5 17 ♘e4 ♗d4 18 ♘d6+ ♔c7
19 ♘f7 ♖f8 20 ♘d6 ♗e5 ∞ Vilela-Frey,
Havana 1985

[14] **16 de** ♗xg2 17 e7 ♗xf1 18 ♘d5 ♕b7 =
Suba-Tatai, Dortmund 1981
  16 ♖b1 ♕a6 17 de ♗xg2 18 e7 ♗a8
19 ed♕+ ♔xd8 20 ♘e2 ♔c8 Ermolinsky-
Makarov, USSR 1986

[15] 16 ... ♕d6 17 de ♕xe6 18 ♖e1 ♕f5 19 ♗xb7+
♔xb7 20 ♗f4 ± Agzamov-Timoshchenko, USSR
1982

[16] 17 de ♗xg2 18 ♔xg2 ♕c6+ 19 f3 ♕xe6
20 ♕c2 ♘e5 ∞ Nikolić-Tal, Nikšić 1983

[17] 17 ... ♘b8 18 ab cb 19 ♗e3 ♗xd5 20 ♗xd5
♖xd5 21 ♕e2 ♘c6 22 ♖fc1 ± Kasparov-
Timoshchenko, USSR Ch 1982, and Kasparov-
Dorfman, USSR Ch 1982

[18] 19 ♗e3 ♘c5 20 ♘xc5 ♗xc5 21 ♕g4 ♔b8 ∞
Kharitonov-Dorfman, USSR 1982

[19] 20 ♗xb7+ ♔xb7 21 ♕e4+ ♕c6 22 ♕xd4
♗d6 ∞ Zarubin-Andrianov, USSR 1982

Semi-Slav V — 1 d4 d5 2 c4 e6 3 Nc3 Nf6 4 Nf3 c6 5 e3 Nbd7[1]

	6	7	8	9	10	11	12	13	14	
1	Qc2[2]	b3[4]	Be2	bc	0-0	Bb2	Nd2	Rfe1[7]	f3	∞
	Bd6[3]	0-0	dc[5]	e5	Re8	e4[6]	Qe7	Nf8	ef[8]	
2	...	e4	Nxe4	Qxe4	de	ed	Qxe8+	Be3	0-0-0	∞
	...	de	Nxe4	e5[9]	0-0[10]	Re8	Qxe8+	Nf6!	Bf5[11]	
3	Bd3	a3[12]	0-0	Qc2	Bxc4	Ba2[15]	h3	e4	Be3	±
	Bb4	Ba5[13]	0-0	dc[14]	Bc7	e5	h6	Re8[16]	Qe7[17]	
4	...	e4[18]	Nxe4	Bxe4	0-0	Bc2	b3[21]	Re1	Rxe8+	±
	Bd6	de	Nxe4	0-0[19]	h6[20]	e5	Re8	ed	Qxe8[22]	
5	...	Bxc4	Be2	0-0[24]	Na4	a3[26]	b3	Bxa3	Rxa3	±
	dc	b5	Bb7[23]	b4[25]	Be7	ba	0-0	Bxa3	Qe7[27]	
6	...	...	Bb3	Na4[29]	Bd2	0-0	Qe2	dc	Bxb4	∞/±
	...	...	b4[28]	Bb7[30]	Be7	0-0	c5	Nxc5	Nxb3[31]	
7	...	...	Bd3	Ne4[32]	Bxe4	Qa4!	Nd2	a3	b4[34]	±/±
	...	...	b4	Nxe4[33]	Bb7	Qb6	Rc8	ba	Bxb4[35]	
8	...	...	...	e4[36]	Na4	e5[37]	Nxc5[38]	dc	Bb5+	±
	...	...	Bb7	b4	c5	Nd5	Bxc5[39]	Nxc5	Kf8[40]	

1   5 ... a6 6 c5 b6 7 cb Nbd7 8 Na4 Nxb6 9 Bd2 ± Euwe-Alekhine, match (8) 1935

2   6 a3 g6 7 Bd3 Bg7 8 0-0 0-0 9 b4 c5 10 cd ed 11 ed Nxd5 12 Nxd5 cd = Littlewood-Smyslov, Hastings 1981-82

3   6 ... a6 7 e4 de 8 Nxe4 Nxe4 9 Qxe4 Bb4+ 10 Bd2 Bxd2+ 11 Nxd2 ± Danner-Velikov, Albena 1983

4   7 Bd2 0-0 8 h3 (8 0-0-0 c5 9 cd cd 10 Be1 c4 11 g4 Nb6 12 h3 Re8 13 Bg2 Bd7 = Bischoff-Pinter, Plovdiv 1983) 8 ... a6 9 0-0-0 b5 10 c5 Bc7 11 g4 b4 ∞ Djurić-Petursson, Ljubljana 1981

5   **8 ... a6** 9 0-0 e5 10 cd cd 11 de Nxe5 12 Bb2 Be6 (12 ... Bg4!?) 13 Rac1 Rc8 14 Qb1 ± Portisch-Kasparov, Dubai Ol 1986
8 ... e5 9 cd Nxd5 10 Nxd5 cd 11 de Nxe5 12 Bb2 Bb4+ 13 Kf1 Bxf3 14 Bxf3 Be6 15 Qd3 Be7 16 Ke2 Qa5 17 Rhc1 ± Portisch-Hübner, Brussels 1986

6   11 ... ed 12 ed Nf8 13 Bd3 Bg4 14 Ne5 Bxe5 15 de N6d7 ∞ Draško-Sveshnikov, Sarajevo 1983

7   13 Rad1 Nf8 14 c5 Bc7 15 Nc4 Ng6 ∞ Kuzmin-Tatai, Dortmund 1981

8   15 Bxf3 Ng4 16 Nf1 Qh4 (16 ... Qg5 17 c5 Bc7 18 e4 ± Agdestein-Tal, Taxco IZ 1985) 17 g3 Qg5 18 Ne4 Qg6 ∞ Taimanov-Barbero, Montpellier 1986

9   **9 ... c5!?** 10 Bd2 Nf6 11 Qd3 0-0 12 Bc3 b6 13 0-0-0 cd 14 Qxd4 ± Ionescu-Hölzl, Dubai Ol 1986
9 ... Bb4+ 10 Bd2 Bxd2+ 11 Nxd2 0-0 12 0-0-0 ± Chandler-Torre, Hastings 1980-81

10   10 ... Qe7 11 Bf4 Bb4+ 12 Bd2 Bxd2+ 13 Nxd2 ± M.Gurevich-Novikov, USSR 1982

11   15 Bd3 Bxd3 16 Rxd3 Qe6 17 b3 a5 18 Rhd1 a4! 19 d7 Rd8 20 Bg5 ∞ Schneider-Chekhov, USSR 1982

12   **7 Bd2** Qe7 8 0-0 dc 9 Bxc4 0-0 10 Ne2 Bxd2 11 Qxd2 b6 12 Rfd1 Bb7 13 Nc3 c5 = Sahović-Tal, Lvov 1984
7 0-0 0-0 8 b3 (8 ... Bd6 9 Qc2 dc 10 Bxc4 e5 11 Rae1 Qe7 12 Ng5 h6 13 Nge4 Bc7 14 d5 ±/± Larsen-Flear, London 1985) 9 a3 Bd6 10 c5 Bc7 11 e4 de 12 Bxe4 Nxe4 13 Nxe4 Rd8 14 Qc1 ± Portisch-Hübner, Tilburg 1986

13   7 ... Bd6 8 e4 de 9 Nxe4 Nxe4 10 Bxe4 e5 11 0-0 0-0 12 Bc2 Re8 13 Re1 ± Kasparov-Hübner, Brussels 1986

14   9 ... Qe7 10 cd ed 11 Bd2 Bxc3 (11 ... Qd8

12 ♘e2 ♗b6 13 ♘g3 ♖e8 14 b4 a6 15 ♗c3 ±
Korchnoi-Hübner, Brussels 1986) 12 ♗xc3 ♖e8
13 ♘e5 ±

[15] 11 ♗d2 e5 12 de ♘xe5 13 ♘xe5 ♗xe5 14 h3 ±

[16] 13 ... ♘h5!?

[17] **14 ... ♘h5?** 15 ♖ad1 ± Kasparov-van der
Wiel, Brussels 1987

14 ... ♛e7 15 ♖fe1 ±

[18] 7 0-0 0-0 8 e4 dc 9 ♗xc4 e5 10 ♗g5 ♛e7
11 ♖e1 ♘b6 12 ♗e2 ♖d8 13 de ♗xe5 14 ♛c2
♖e8 15 ♖ad1 ♗d7 16 ♘xe5 ♛xe5 17 ♗h4 ±
Grünfeld-Pachman, Netanya 1983

[19] **9 ... c5** 10 0-0 ♛c7 11 ♖e1 ♘f6 12 ♗c2 ♗d7
13 ♘e5 ±/± Sosonko-Smyslov, Tilburg 1982

9 ... e5 10 0-0 ed 11 ♛xd4 ♛f6 12 ♛d1 ♘e5
13 ♖e1 ♗g4 14 ♗g5 ♛e6 15 ♛c2 ±/± O'Kelly-
Yanofsky, Barcelona 1964

[20] 10 ... ♘f6 11 ♗c2 c5 12 ♗g5 h6 13 ♗h4 cd
14 ♛xd4 ±/± Csom-Bellon, Malaga 1981

[21] 12 b4 ♗xb4 (12 ... ♖e8 13 c5 ♗c7 14 ♖e1 ±)
13 de ♘c5 14 ♛e2 ∞/±

[22] 15 ♛xd4 ± Gelfand-Raisky, USSR 1986

[23] 8 ... a6 9 e4 b4 10 e5 bc 11 ef cb 12 fg
♗xg7! 13 ♗xb2 ♛a5+ 14 ♘d2 ♖b8 15 ♛c1! ±
Schneider-Kishnev, USSR 1983

[24] **9 e4** b4 10 e5 bc 11 ef cb 12 fg ba♛
13 gh♛ ∞ Blackstock-Crouch, London 1980

9 a3 a6 10 b4 a5 11 ♖b1 ab 12 ab ♘d5
13 ♘xd5 ed = Bönsch-Pinter, Budapest 1986;
9 ... b4!? 10 ♘a4 ba 11 ba ♗e7 12 0-0 0-0 =
Karpov-Kasparov, match (29) 1984-85

[25] **9 ... a6** 10 e4 c5 11 e5 ♘d5 12 a4 ♘xc3 13 bc
c4 14 ♗g5 (14 ♘g5 ♗e7?! 15 ♗f3 ♗xf3
16 ♛xf3 0-0 17 ♛g4 ± Christiansen-Flear,
Szirak IZ 1987; 14 ... ♗d5 15 ♗h5 g6 16 ♗f3
♘b6 17 ♘e4 ∞ Christiansen) 14 ... ♗e7 =
Nogueiras-Tatai, Thessaloniki Ol 1984, and
Portisch-Flear, Szirak IZ 1987

9 ... ♗e7 10 e4 b4 11 e5 bc 12 ef ♘xf6
13 bc 0-0 14 ♖b1 ±/= Portisch-Chernin, Reggio
Emilia 1986-87

[26] 11 b3 0-0 12 ♗b2 c5 13 dc ♘xc5 14 ♘xc5
♗xc5 15 ♘e5 ♛e7 = Frias-Vera, Havana 1983

[27] 15 ♛c1 ± Donaldson

[28] 8 ... ♗b7 9 0-0 ♗e7 10 ♖e1 0-0 (10 ... b4
11 ♘e2 0-0 12 ♘f4 c5 13 ♘g5 ♛c8 14 e4 ±
Flear-Domont, Geneva 1986) 11 e4 b4 12 ♘a4
c5 13 e5 ♘d5 14 ♛d3 ± Korchnoi-Ribli, Montpellier C 1985

[29] 9 ♘e2 ♗e7 (9 ... ♗b7 10 0-0 ♗d6 11 ♘f4
0-0 12 ♖e1 ∞ Ligterink-Kuijpers, Hilversum
1984) 10 0-0 0-0 11 ♘f4 ♗b7 12 ♖e1 c5 =
Korchnoi-Tal, Havana 1963

[30] 9 ... ♗a6 10 ♗d2 ♗e7 11 ♖c1 0-0 12 ♗c4 ±
Speelman-Yusupov, Lucerne 1985

[31] 15 ♗xe7 ♛xe7 16 ab ♗d5 17 ♖a3 (17 ♘d2
♛b4 = Gelfand-Dreyev, Sochi 1986) 17 ...
♖ac8 18 ♘d4 ± Kapengut/Gelfand

[32] 9 ♘a4 c5 10 ♘xc5 ♘xc5 11 dc ♗xc5 12 0-0
0-0 13 e4 ♗b7 14 ♛e2 ±

[33] 9 ... ♗e7 10 ♘xf6+ ♘xf6 11 e4 ♗b7 12 ♛e2
♛b6 13 0-0 ♖c8 14 ♗g5 ±/± Tal-Ljubojević,
Milan 1975

[34] 14 b3 ♗a6 15 ♘c4 ♛b5 16 ♖a3 ±

[35] 15 ♗xa3 c5 16 ♗xb4 cb 17 0-0 ±/± Ogaard-
Sveshnikov, Bucharest 1976

[36] 9 0-0 b4 10 ♘e4 ♗e7 11 ♘xf6+ ♘xf6 12 e4
0-0 13 e5 ♘d7 14 ♗e4 f5 15 ef ♘f6 ±/= Tal-
Sveshnikov, Sochi 1986

[37] 11 dc ♗xc5 12 ♘xc5 ♘xc5 13 ♗b5+ ♔e7 =
Reshevsky-Stean, Beer-Sheva 1982

[38] 12 0-0 cd 13 ♖e1 g6 (13 ... ♗e7 14 ♘xd4
0-0 15 ♛h5 g6 16 ♛h6 ± Boleslavsky) 14 ♗g5
♛a5 (14 ... ♗e7 15 ♗xe7 ♛xe7 16 ♗b5 0-0
17 ♗xd7 ♛xd7 18 ♘c5 ±/± Gligorić-Ribli,
Nikšić 1978) 15 ♘d2 ♗a6 = Reshevsky-Dorfman,
Vilnius 1978

[39] 12 ... ♘xc5 13 dc ♗xc5 14 0-0 h6 15 ♘d2
♘c3 16 ♛c2 ± Polugayevsky-Mecking, Manila
1975

[40] 15 ♛d4 ♛b6 16 ♗e2 ± Lengyel-Hort,
Hungary 1966

	10	11	12	13	14	15	16	17	18	
1	d5	de[3]	ed+	0-0[4]	♖e1[5]	e5	♘e4[7]	♕xd3	♘g3	±
	c4[2]	cd	♕xd7	♗b7	♗e7[6]	♘d5	0-0	♕g4	♘b4[8]	
2	...	...	♗c2	0-0[9]	♕e2	♘g5	f4	a4[11]	♘d5	∞
	...	fe	♕c7	♗b7[10]	♗d6	♘c5	e5	b4	♘xd5[12]	
3	e5	♘xb5[14]	♘xe5	0-0[16]	♕e2	♗g5[18]	f4	♖f3	♖g3	±
	cd[13]	♘xe5[15]	ab	♕d5	♗a6[17]	♗e7	0-0	♗b7	g6[19]	
4	...	...	ef	0-0[21]	♗e4	♗xb7	♘xd4	f3	♕e2	±
	...	ab	♕b6[20]	gf	♗b7	♕xb7	♖g8	♖d8	♗c5[22]	

[1] 9 a4!? b4 10 ♘e4 c5 11 ♘ed2 ♗b7 12 ♘c4 ♗e7 13 a5! 0-0 14 0-0 ♕c7 15 h3! ± Korchnoi-Nogueiras, Wijk aan Zee 1987; 12 ... a5!?

[2] **10 ... e5** 11 b3 ♗d6 12 0-0 0-0 13 a4 c4 14 bc b4 15 ♘e2 ♘c5 16 ♘g3 ♕c7 17 ♗e3 a5 18 ♗xc5 ♗xc5 19 ♘d2 g6 20 ♘b3 ± van der Sterren-Bagirov, Baku 1986
10 ... ♗b7 11 0-0 ♗e7 12 ♗f4 ± Ribli-Smyslov, match 1983

[3] 11 ♗c2 ♘c5 12 ♗g5 b4 13 ♘e2 ed 14 e5 h6 15 ♗h4 g5 16 ♘xg5 hg 17 ♗xg5 ♕a5 ∞/± van der Sterren-Donaldson, Reykjavik 1986

[4] 13 ♘e5 ♕e7 14 ♗f4 ♘xe4 15 ♘xe4 ♕b4+

[5] 14 ♗g5 ♗e7 15 ♖e1 ♖d8! (15 ... 0-0 16 e5 ♘g4 17 ♗xe7 ♕xe7 18 ♕xd3 ♗xf3 19 ♕xf3 ♘e5 20 ♕g3 ♖ae8 21 ♖ad1 ± Korchnoi-Flear, Wijk aan Zee 1987) 16 e5 ♘g4 17 ♘e4 0-0 18 ♕d2 ♗xg5! 19 ♕xg5 ♗xe4 20 ♖xe4 f6! ∓/∓ Nenashev-Kaidanov, Pinsk 1986; 15 e5!? ♘d5 16 ♕xd3 ♘xc3 17 ♕xc3 ♗xg5 18 ♘xg5 ♕f5 19 f4 ± Farago-Boudre, Virton 1986

[6] 14 ... ♗b4 15 ♘e5 ♕c7 16 ♗f4 ♗xc3 17 bc ♕e7 18 ♘xd3 ±/± Suba-Xu, Dubai Ol 1986

[7] 16 ♕xd3 ♘xc3 17 ♕xc3 0-0 18 ♗g5 ♖ac8 ∞ Portisch-Yusupov, Montpellier C 1985

[8] 19 ♕f5 ± Groszpeter-Lukacs, Hungarian Ch 1986

[9] 13 ♘g5 ♘c5 14 f4 ♗b7 15 e5 ♖d8! ∞ Farago-Chandler, Belgrade 1982

[10] **13 ... ♗d6** 14 ♘d4 ♘b6 (Farago-Radulov, Herculana 1982) 15 a4! b4 16 a5 bc 17 ab cb 18 ♗xb2 ♕xb6 19 ♖b1 ± Farago
13 ... ♗c5 14 e5!? ♘xe5 15 ♗f4 ♗d6 16 ♘e4 ±

[11] 17 fe ♗xe5 18 ♘f3 ♗xc3 19 bc 0-0 20 e5 ♖ae8 = Dorfman-Sveshnikov, USSR Ch 1978

[12] 19 ed 0-0-0 20 ♕xc4 ef!? (20 ... h6 21 ♘h3 ♖hf8! 22 ♗e3 ef 23 ♗xf4 ♗xd5! = Farago-Schon, Budapest 1986) 21 ♗xf4 ♗xf4 22 ♖xf4

♗xd5 23 ♕xb4 a5 ∞ Farago

[13] 10 ... ♘g4 11 ♗f4 (11 ♗e4 ♖a7 12 0-0 ±) 11 ... cd 12 ♘e4 ♗b4+ 13 ♔f1 ♗b7 14 h3 ♘h6 15 ♗xh6 gh 16 a4 ± Kluger-Florian, Hungarian Ch 1951

[14] 11 ♘e4 ♘d5 12 0-0 h6 13 a4 b4 14 a5 ♗b7 15 ♖e1 ♗e7 = Bronstein-Dorfman, USSR Ch 1975

[15] 11 ... ♘g4 12 ♕a4! (12 ♘bxd4 ♗b4+ 13 ♗d2 ♗xd2+ 14 ♕xd2 ♗b7 15 ♖d1 0-0 16 0-0 ♘gxe5 17 ♗e2 ∞ Miles-Kasparov, match 1986) 12 ... ♘gxe5 13 ♘xe5 ♘xe5 14 ♘d6+ ♔e7 15 ♘xc8+ ♖xc8! (15 ... ♔f6?! 16 ♗e4 ♖xc8 ∞ Miles-Kasparov, match 1986; 16 ♗xa6! ♕xc8 17 ♕xd4 ±/±±) 16 ♗xa6 ♖a8 17 ♕b5 ♕d5! 18 ♕xd5 ed ±/= Ftacnik-Nogueiras, Szirak 1986; 14 ♘c7+ ♔e7 15 ♘xa8 ± Christiansen

[16] 13 ♗xb5+ ♗d7 14 ♘xd7 ♕a5+ 15 ♗d2 ♕xb5 16 ♘xf8 ♔xf8 17 a4 ♕xb2 18 0-0! (18 ♖b1 ♕a2 19 0-0 h6 ∞ Smyslov-Torre, Bugojno 1984) 18 ... ♘d5 19 ♖b1 ♕a3 20 ♖b7 ♕d3? 21 ♕h5 ± Vaganian-Kuczynski, Dubai Ol 1986; 20 ... h5! ∞/= Ftacnik

[17] 14 ... ♘d7 15 f4 ♗c5 16 b4 ♗a7 17 ♔h1 ± Miles-Hermann, West Berlin 1985

[18] 15 f4 ♗d6 16 ♗d2 0-0 17 ♖f3 ♗b7 18 ♖h3 g6 (18 ... ♖xa2? 19 ♖xa2 ♕xa2 20 ♘d7! ±± Cifuentes-Ribli, Dubai Ol 1986) =

[19] 19 h4 ♖fe8 (19 ... ♗d8 20 ♖e1 ♖xa2 21 h5 ± Kouatly-Iclicki, Brussels II 1986) 20 ♖e1 (20 h5 ♘e4! ∞ Ftacnik) 20 ... ♖xa2 (20 ... ♘d7 21 h5! ±) 21 h5 ♘xh5 22 ♕xh5 ♕xg2+ 23 ♖xg2 hg 24 ♖g3 ±

[20] 12 ... ♗b7 13 0-0 gf 14 ♘xd4 ♖g8 15 f3 ♗c5 16 ♗e3 ♕b6 17 ♗xb5 ♖d8 18 ♕d3 ±

[21] 13 fg ♗xg7 14 0-0 (14 ♕e2 0-0 15 0-0 ♘c5 =) 14 ... ♗b7 15 ♗f4 0-0 16 ♖e1 ♗d5 17 ♘e5 ∞/= Golombek-Szily, Trencianske Teplice 1949

[22] 19 ♗e3 ± Korchnoi

Benko Gambit and Benoni

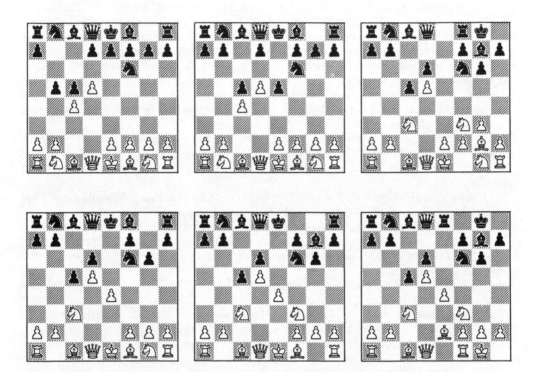

Benko Gambit

It is sad that the only river ever to have given its name to a chess opening should have been forced to cede this honour to a mere mortal. But the fact that an article written in 1946 by one Argunov who happened to live in Kuibishev on the River Volga considered the moves 1 d4 ♘f6 2 c4 c5 3 d5 b5 is generally considered less significant than the fact that grandmaster Pal Benko has by his games and writings transformed this little esteemed opening into one of Black's most successful defences to 1 d4.

If White accepts the pawn by 4 cb a6 5 ba ♗xa6 Black obtains a slight lead in development and (more important) lasting pressure on the queenside, where White's b-pawn is particularly vulnerable. White's king's bishop is also a problem piece. If he plays e4 he is forced to waste time castling artificially after ... ♗xf1 ♔xf1 followed by g3 and ♔g2. If he fianchettoes the bishop it is relegated to a passive position.

It is frustrating for White that even if he manages to reach an ending a pawn up such endings are rarely theoretically won – indeed they often favour Black. White's most promising strategy may be to forget the fact that he is a pawn up, consolidate his position and play for a break in the centre by e5.

Advances of theory and technique have robbed the Benko of some of its former lustre. While White still has difficulties utilizing his extra pawn, Black finds it ever harder to generate winning chances. The sharpest lines are those where White refuses or returns the gambit pawn. These variations offer a lively alternative to the ponderous duel between gambit pawn and counterplay of the Benko accepted.

Benoni

The Benoni, a relatively recent addition to Black's defensive arsenal against 1 d4, owes much of its popularity to the successes of ex-World Champion Mikhail Tal. The Modern Benoni (1 d4 ♘f6 2 c4 c5 3 d5 e6 4 ♘c3 ed 5 cd d6) offers the inventive and enterprising player a wealth of tactical opportunities. Black's counterplay springs from his queenside pawn majority (activated by the break ... b5), pressure along the half-open e-file and the strength of his fianchettoed king's bishop. White, on the other hand, enjoys more freedom and has an opportunity for pawn storms in the centre and on the kingside, as well as having an appealing target in the shape of Black's all-important pawn on d6. If White can undermine this pawn, the cornerstone of Black's position, the defender will often find himself beset with insurmountable problems.

As predicted in the first edition, the systems with 7 ♗f4 achieved tremendous popularity, eclipsing even the Main (Classical) Line. After some rough handling Black advocates have begun turning the tide and chances now appear roughly balanced in this complex variation.

The **Main Line** (6 e4 g6 7 ♘f3 ♗g7 8 ♗e2 0-0 9 0-0) and **Fianchetto Variation** (6 ♘f3 g6 7 g3) remain popular with White players of a temperate nature.

The swashbuckling **Mikenas Variation** (with 7 f4 and 8 ♗b5+) has scored so many violent successes that many defenders now only venture the Benoni from the move order 2 ... e6 3 ♘f3 c5. Die-hard Benoni players must have something ready to combat this ambitious attacking plan.

For a short time **Systems with ♗g5** scored great successes, but now Black can once again face them with confidence.

The **Nimzowitsch System** (6 ♘f3 g6 7 ♘d2) is a very direct attempt to stifle the Benoni positionally. Black's lead in development should suffice to provide him with equality.

The **Czech Benoni** (3 d5 e5) is out of fashion. Black's position is congested and a bit ponderous, but it remains solid.

The so-called "Schmid Benoni" (1 d4 c5), rarely seen, is a quiet and fairly passive continuation. We deal with it under '1 d4: Early Divergences' on page 65.

References: *Benko Gambit* (Gufeld)
            Benoni for the Tournament Player (Nunn)

	4	5	6	7	8	9	10	11	12	
1	a4[1]	♘d2[3]	e4	♘gf3[5]	g3	♗g2[6]	0-0	cd	♖e1	∞
	b4![2]	g6[4]	d6	♗g7	e6!	ed	0-0	♗a6	♘bd7[7]	
2	♘f3	a4[9]	ab	♖xa8	♘c3	♗f4![12]	♘d2	♘b5	cd	±
	♗b7[8]	a6[10]	ab	♗xa8	♕a5[11]	d6	b4	♘xd5[13]	♕xb5[14]	
3	...	cb[15]	♘c3[16]	e4[17]	♘b5[18]	e5	♘xe5	♗c4	0-0	∞/±
	g6	a6	ab	b4	d6[19]	de	♗g7	0-0	♗b7[20]	

[1]   4 ♗g5 ♘e4 5 ♗f4 e6 6 ♕c2 ♘xf2! (6 ... ♘d6 7 ♘c3 ♕a5 8 cb ♘xb5 9 ♗d2 ± Kaidanov-Arkhipov, Moscow 1985) 7 ♔xf2 ♕f6 8 ♘h3 e5 9 ♕c3 d6 10 ♔e1 ♗xh3! ∞ Kormanyos-Arkhipov, Harkany 1983
   4 ♕c2 ♘a6! 5 cb ♘b4 6 ♕xc5 ♘fxd5 7 ♗d2 ∞ Quinteros-Ermenkov, Baden-Baden 1985
   4 ♘d2 d6 5 e4 bc 6 ♗xc4 g6 7 b3 ♗g7 8 ♗b2 0-0 9 ♘gf3 ♘bd7 10 0-0 ♘b6 11 ♕c2 ♖b8 = Ornstein-Bielczyk, Gausdal 1983

[2]   4 ... bc 5 ♘c3 d6 6 e4 g6 (6 ... ♗a6 7 f4 ♘bd7 8 ♘f3 g6 9 a5! ± Fridh-Ernst, Sweden 1986) 7 ♗xc4 ♗g7 8 ♘f3 0-0 9 0-0 ♗a6 10 ♗b5!? ♗xb5 11 ab ♘bd7 12 ♕e2 ± Legky-Lputian, USSR 1983

[3]   5 g3 e5! 6 ♗g2 d6 7 e4 g6 8 b3 ♗g7 9 ♗b2 0-0 10 ♘d2 a5 11 ♘e2 ♖a7 ∓ Witt-Ermenkov, Baden-Baden 1985

[4]   5 ... e5 6 e4 d6 7 b3 ♗e7 8 ♗b2 ♘bd7 9 g3 ±

[5]   7 b3 ♗g7 8 ♗b2 0-0 ∞ Tukmakov

[6]   9 ♗h3?! ed 10 ♗xc8 ♕xc8 ∓ W.Schmidt-Kasparov, Dubai Ol 1986

[7]   Kasparov

[8]   4 ... b4?! 5 a3! (5 ♗g5 d6 6 ♘bd2 g6 7 e4 ♗g7 8 ♗d3 0-0 = Gulko-D.Gurevich, Somerset (USA) 1986) 5 ... a5 6 ♘bd2 g6 7 e4 d6 8 ab ± Seirawan-D.Gurevich, US Ch 1986
   4 ... bc 5 ♘c3 d6 6 e4 g6 7 e5! (7 ♗xc4 ♗g7 8 0-0 0-0 9 ♕e2 a5!? 10 h3 ♘fd7 ∞ Markzon-Parsons, New York 1985) 7 ... de 8 ♘xe5 ♗g7 9 ♗xc4 0-0 10 0-0 ± Browne-Wolff, US Ch 1985

[9]   5 ♘c3 b4 6 ♘a4 e6 7 ♗g5 d6 8 e4 ♗e7 ∞ Anikayev-Vaganian, USSR Ch 1982
   5 ♕b3 ♕b6 6 ♘c3 b4 7 ♘a4 ♕c7 8 ♕c2 d6 9 a3 g6 ∞ Ubilava-Grigorian, Minsk 1983

[10]   5 ... b4 6 ♘bd2 d6 7 e4 e5 8 g3 g6 9 ♗g2 ♗g7 10 0-0 ♘bd7 11 ♘h4 ± Tukmakov

[11]   8 ... b4 9 ♘b5 ♕b6 10 ♕a4! ±

[12]   9 ♘d2 b4 10 ♘b3 ♕b6 ∞ Kan-Keres, USSR Ch 1955

[13]   11 ... g6 12 e4 ♘bd7 13 ♘b3 ♕b6 14 ♕a1 ♗b7 15 ♕a5! ± Dorfman-Mochalov, USSR 1981

[14]   13 e4 ♕a5 14 ♘c4 ♕a2 15 ♗d3 ♘d7 16 0-0 ± Gorelov-Yanovsky, Moscow 1984

[15]   5 ♕c2 ♗g7 (5 ... bc 6 e4 ♗g7 7 ♗xc4 d6 8 0-0 0-0 9 h3 ♗a6 10 ♘a3! ±) 6 e4 d6 7 cb (7 ♘c3 bc 8 ♗xc4 0-0 9 0-0 ♗a6! 10 ♘d2 ♘fd7! ∞ Pachman-Despotović, 1984) 7 ... 0-0 8 ♘c3 a6 9 ♗e2! (9 a4 e6! 10 ♗xe6 11 ♗e2 d5 Gorelov-Kishnev, Moscow 1984) 9 ... ab 10 ♘xb5 ∞/±
   5 a4 bc 6 ♘c3 ♗g7 7 e4 0-0 8 ♗xc4 ♗a6 9 ♗xa6 ♘xa6 10 e5 ♘g4 11 ♕e2 ♘b4! Romanishin-Deže, Novi Sad 1982

[16]   6 e3 d6 7 ♘c3 ♗g7 8 a4 0-0 9 ♗e2 ab 10 ♗xb5 ♗a6 ∞ Frias-Alburt, Santiago 1981
   6 ♕c2 ♗g7 7 e4 (7 ♕xc5 0-0 8 ♘c3 d6 9 ♕b4 ab 10 ♗xb5 ♘a6 ∞) 7 ... 0-0 8 ♘c3 ♗b7 9 a4 e6 10 d6 ab ∞ Balashov-Glek, USSR 1984

[17]   7 d6 b4 (7 ... ♕a5 8 e3 ± Gulko-Renet, Marseilles 1986; 7 ... ed 8 e4 ±) 8 ♘b5 ♘a6 ∞ Gulko

[18]   8 e5!? bc 9 ef ef! (9 ... ♕a5 10 bc ♕xc3+ 11 ♗d2 ♕xf6 12 ♖c1 ♗g7 13 ♗c4 ± Christiansen-Andersson, New York 1985) 10 bc ♗g7 11 ♕e2+ ♕e7 ∞

[19]   8 ... ♘xe4 9 ♕e2 f5 10 d6! (10 ♘g5 d6 11 ♘xe4 fe 12 ♕xe4 ♗g7 13 ♗c4 0-0 ∞ van der Wiel-Hodgson, Brussels 1985) ±

[20]   13 d6 ♘c6 14 ♗f4 ♘xe5 15 ♗xe5 ∞/± Ftacnik-Plachetka, Czechoslovakia 1985

129

	5	6	7	8	9	10	11	12	13	
4	e3²¹	♘c3	♘f3²³	a4	♖b1²⁵	de	♗e2	ab	0-0	±
	g6²²	♗g7	0-0	♗b7²⁴	e6	fe	ab	♗d5	♘bd7²⁶	
5	...	♗xb5	♘c3	♘e2²⁸	0-0	♗c4	♗xa6	e4	♗f4	±
	ab²⁷	♕a5+	♗b7	♘xd5²⁹	♘c7	♗a6	♕xa6	e6	d6³⁰	

1 d4 ♘f6 2 c4 c5 3 d5 b5 4 cb a6 5 ba ♗xa6 6 ♘c3 d6

	7	8	9	10	11	12	13	14	15	
6	e4³¹	♔xf1	g3³³	♔g2	♘f3³⁴	♖e1	♕e2	♗d2	♖ab1	∞
	♗xf1³²	g6	♗g7	0-0	♘bd7	♖a7!?³⁵	♕a8	♖b8	♘e8³⁶	
7	...	...	...	...	...	h3	♕e2³⁷	♘d1	♖b1	±
	...	...	...	...	...	♘b6	♘a4	♕d7	e6³⁸	
8	♘f3	g3³⁹	♗g2⁴⁰	0-0	♕c2⁴¹	♗d2	h3	♖fe1	b3	±
	g6	♗g7	♘bd7	0-0	♕a5⁴²	♖fb8	♘e8	♘c7	c4⁴³	
9	...	...	...	...	♖e1⁴⁴	♘d2⁴⁶	♖b1⁴⁸	b3	♘xd5	∞
	...	...	...	♘b6	0-0⁴⁵	♕c7⁴⁷	♕b7!	♘fd5	♘xd5⁴⁹	

²¹ **5 b6** e6 (5 ... d6 6 ♘c3 ♘bd7 7 ♘f3 g6 =) 6 ♘c3 ♕xb6 7 e4 ♗b7 8 ♘f3 g6 = Fedorowicz-Alburt, New York 1984

5 f3 g6 6 e4 d6 7 ♘c3 (7 ♘a3 ♗g7 8 ♘e2 ♘bd7 9 ♘c3 0-0 10 ♗e2 ♘e8 ∞ Corral-T.Georgadze, Pontevedra 1986) 7 ... ♗g7 8 a4 0-0 9 ♗c4 (9 ♗d2 ♘bd7 ∞ Cebalo) 9 ... ♘bd7 10 ♘ge2 ♘e5 11 b3 ♘fd7 ∞ Chandler-Alburt, Hastings 1980-81

²² 5 ... e6 6 ♘c3 ed 7 ♘ge2 ♗b7 8 ♘f4 ab 9 ♗xb5 ♗d6 10 ♘xfd5 ♘xd5 11 ♘xd5 ± Novikov-Bareyev, USSR 1986

²³ **7 e4** d6 8 ♗d2 0-0 9 a4 e6 10 de fe 11 e5 ♘d5! ∞ Farago-Sznapik, Belgrade 1984

7 d6 ♗b7 8 ♘f3 0-0 9 ba ♘xa6 10 ♗c4 ♘b4 11 0-0 e6 = Ree-Miles, Amsterdam 1981

7 a4!? 0-0 8 ♗c4 e6! (8 ... ♗b7 9 ♘ge2 ab 10 ♗xb5 ♘a6 11 0-0 ♘b4 12 e4 e6 13 ♗g5! ± Pinter-Hjartarson, Malta Ol 1980) 9 ♗d2 ab 10 ♗xb5 (10 ♘xb5 ed 11 ♗xd5 ♘c6! 12 0-0 ♗a6 13 ♖a3 ♘xd5 14 ♕xd5 ♕e7 = Farago-Vaganian, Hastings 1982-83) 10 ... cd 11 ♘xd5 ♗b7 12 ♗c4 ± Spassov-Hebden, Silkeborg 1983

²⁴ 8 ... d6 9 e4 (9 ♖a3 ♘e8 10 ♗d2 ♘d7 11 ♗e2 ♘c7 12 0-0 f5 = Franco-Bellon, 1985) 9 ... ab 10 ♗xb5 ♗a6 11 ♗d2 ♘bd7 12 0-0 ♕g4 13 ♕e2 ♕a5 14 ♖a3! ± Belyavsky-Hodgson, London 1985

8 ... e6 9 de fe 10 ♕d6 ♗b7 11 ♕xc5 ♘e4 12 ♘xe4 ♗xe4 13 ♕b4! ± Tomaszewski-Kaidanov, Moscow II 1986

²⁵ **9 ba** ♘xa6 10 ♗c4 ♘e8!? 11 0-0 ♘d6 12 ♗e2 ♘c7 = I.Ivanov-Hartman, Canadian Ch 1985

9 c4 e6! 10 ♖b1 ed 11 ed ab ∞ Agzamov-Vaganian, Erevan Z 1982

9 ♖a3 e6 10 de fe 11 ♕d6 ab (11 ... ♖e8 12 ♕xc5! ♗f8 13 ♕d4 ♗xa3 14 ba ± Plaskett-Popović, Gausdal 1985) 12 ♗xb5 ♕c8 13 0-0 ♘e8 ∞ Ravikumar-Miles, London 1985

²⁶ 14 b4 c4 15 ♘d4 ♕e7 16 e4! ± Gligorić-Rajković, Yugoslavia 1984

²⁷ 5 ... ♗b7 6 ♘c3 ♕a5 7 ba ♘xa6 8 ♗d2 ♕b6 9 e4 e6 10 ♘f3! ± Benjamin-Alburt, US Ch 1986

²⁸ 8 ♗d2 ♕b6 9 ♕b3 e6 10 e4 ♘xe4 11 ♘xe4

♗xd5 12 ♕d3 ♕b7! (12 ... f5 13 ♘g3 ♗xg2
14 a3 ♗e7 15 ♘f3! ± Novikov-Palatnik, Lvov
1986) 13 f3 c4 14 ♗xc4 ♖xc4 15 ♕xc4 d5
16 ♕c2 de 17 ♕xe4 (17 ♖c1 ♘d7 ∞ Litvinchuk-
Wolff, USA 1985) 17 ... ♕xe4+ (17 ... ♕xb2!?)
18 fe ♘d7 = Karpov-Miles, Tilburg 1986;
10 ♗c4 ♕xb3 11 ♗xb3 ♘a6! (11 ... ed 12 ♘ge2
♘a6 13 0-0 ♗e7 14 ♖fd1 0-0 ∞ Hjartarson-
Fedorowicz, Hastings 1985-86) 12 ♘ge2
(12 ♘f3? ed ∓ D.Gurevich-Benjamin, Chicago
1986) 12 ... ♘b4 13 de ♘d3+ ∞ Benjamin
[29] **8 ... e6** 9 0-0! ed 10 ♕b3 ♗c6 11 ♗xc6 dc
12 e4 ± Farago-Zsu.Polgar, Amsterdam II
1985
   8 ... ♗xd5 9 0-0! ♗c6 10 ♕d3 ♗xb5
11 ♘xb5 ♘c6 12 ♗d2 ♕b6 13 a4! ± Farago-
Stangl, Altensteig 1987
[30] 14 a4! ± Farago-Ermenkov, Albena 1985
[31] 7 f4 g6 8 ♘f3 ♗g7 9 e4 ♗xf1 (9 ... 0-0
10 e5 de 11 fe ♘g4 12 ♗f4 ± Murei-D.Gurevich,
Hastings 1982-83) 10 ♖xf1 ♕b6 11 e5!? de
12 fe ♘g4 13 ♕e2 ♘d7 (13 ... ♕a6!? 14 ♗f4
♘d7 D.Gurevich-Bukal, Lugano 1983) 14 e6
fe 15 de ♘de5 16 ♘xe5 ♘xe5 = Christiansen-
D.Gurevich, US Ch 1986
[32] 7 ... g6 8 ♗xa6 ♘xa6 9 ♘f3 ♗g7 10 0-0
0-0 11 ♗f4 ±
[33] 9 ♘f3 ♗g7 10 h3 0-0 11 ♖g1 ♘bd7 12 ♔h2
♕a5 13 ♖e1 ♖fb8 ∞ Tukmakov
[34] 11 ♘ge2 ♕b6 12 ♖b1 ♘a6 13 b3 ♘c7 14 f3
e6 ∞
[35] **12 ...** ♘b6 13 ♖e2 ♕d7 14 ♕d3 ♘a4
15 ♖b1 ∞/± Salov-Tseshkovsky, USSR Ch
1987
   12 ... ♕b8 13 ♕c2 ♕b7! 14 a4 ♖fb8 ∞
Monin-Kaidanov, USSR 1986
   12 ... ♕b6 13 ♖e2 ♖fb8 14 h3 ♕a6 ∞
Hjartarson-Alburt, Scandinavia v USA 1986
   12 ... ♕a5 13 ♗d2 ♖fb8 14 ♕c2 ♘g4
15 b3!? Tukmakov
[36] 16 ♗f4 ♘b6 ∞ Dlugy-Fedorowicz, US Ch

1985
[37] 13 ♖e1 ♕d7 14 ♕c2 ♕b7 15 ♖b1 e6 =
Fokin-Lanka, USSR 1986; 14 a4 ♕b7 15 ♖a2
♘fd7 16 ♕c2 ± Khuzman-Lanka, USSR 1986
[38] 16 de fe 17 b3 ♘b6 18 ♘c3 ♘h5 19 ♗b2
d5 20 a4 ± Belyavsky-Tseshkovsky, USSR Ch
1987
[39] 8 ♘d2 ♗g7 (8 ... ♕a5!?) 9 e4 0-0 10 ♗xa6
♘xa6 11 0-0 ♘d7 12 ♘c4 ♘b6 13 ♘e3 (13 ♕e2
♘xc4 14 ♕xc4 ♕b6 ∞ Ivkov-Browne, 1970)
13 ... ♕c7 14 ♗d2 ♖fb8 15 ♕e2 c4 ∞ Tukmakov
[40] 9 ♗h3 ♘bd7 10 0-0-0 0-0 11 ♕c2 (11 ♖e1 ♕c7
12 ♗f4 ♖fb8 13 ♕d2 ♖b4 14 ♖ac1 h5! =
Belyavsky-Vaganian, USSR 1977) 11 ... ♗c4
12 ♖d1 ♖a7 13 e4 ♕a8 ∞ Furman-Geller,
USSR 1975
[41] 11 ♖e1 ♕a5 12 h3 ♖fb8 13 e4 ♘e8 14 h4
♘c7 15 h5 ♘b5 ∞
[42] **11 ...** ♕c7 12 ♖d1 ♖fb8 13 ♖b1 ♖b4
14 ♗d2 ± Bukić-Bellon, Pula 1975
   11 ... ♕b6 12 ♖b1 ♖fb8 13 b3 ♘e8 14 ♘d2
♕a5 15 ♗b2 ± Korchnoi-Quinteros, Leningrad
IZ 1973
[43] 16 ♖ac1 cb 17 ab ♘b5 18 ♘xb5 ♕xb5
19 ♕e4 ± Donner-Browne, Wijk aan Zee 1975
[44] **11 ♘d2** ♖a7!? 12 ♕c2 ♕a8 13 ♖d1 0-0
14 ♘f1 ♖fb8 15 b3 ♘bd7 16 ♖b1 ♘e8 ∞ van
der Sterren-Miles, London 1981
   11 ♗f4 h6 12 h4 ♕d7 13 ♖e1 ♘g4 14 ♕c2
♕f5 ∞ Ehlvest-Vasyukov, USSR 1982
[45] **11 ...** ♕c7 12 ♖b1! ± Sosonko-Miles,
Hastings 1975-76
[46] 12 ♗f4 ♘h5!? (12 ... ♘c4 13 ♕c1 ♕a5
14 ♘d2 ♖fb8 15 ♘xc4 ♗xc4 16 ♗d2! ± Nikolić-
Grünfeld, Thessaloniki Ol 1984) ∞ Schwarz
[47] 12 ... ♖a7 13 h3 ♕a8 14 e4 ♘fd7 15 f4 ♖b8
16 ♕c2 ♘c4 17 ♘f3! ± Kakageldiev-Peshina,
USSR 1979
[48] 13 ♘b3!? ♘c4 14 h3 ♖fb8 15 ♕c2 ♕b6!? ∞
[49] 16 ♘e4 ♖ad8 17 ♗b2 ♗xb2 18 ♖xb2
♕b4! ∞

131

	6	7	8	9	10	11	12	13	14	
	Czech Benoni			**1 d4 ♘f6 2 c4 c5 3 d5 e5 4 ♘c3 d6 5 e4 ♗e7**						
1	g3[1]	♗g2[2]	♘ge2[4]	f4	gf	♘g3	0-0	♘cxe4	♗d2	±
	0-0	♘e8[3]	♗g5[5]	ef	♗h4+[6]	f5	fe	h6	♘d7[7]	
2	♘f3	h3[9]	g4	♗d3	a4	♖g1	♗h6	♕e2[13]		±
	0-0[8]	♘bd7	♘e8	a6[10]	♖b8[11]	g6[12]	♘g7			

[1] **6 ♗d3** 0-0 7 ♘ge2 (7 h3 a6 8 a4 a5 9 g4 ♘e8 10 ♗e3 ♘a6 ∞ Li-Partos, Biel 1985) 7 ... ♘h5 (7 ... ♘e8 8 a3 ♗g5) 8 ♗e3 ♗g5 9 ♕d2 ♗xe3 10 ♕xe3 ♕f6 11 g3 a6 12 0-0-0 b5 ∞ Dlugy-Ivanov, New York 1983

6 ♘ge2 a6 7 ♘g3 h5!? 8 ♘f5 ♗xf5 9 ef ∞ Benjamin-Dozorets, Hollywood 1985

6 ♗e2 0-0 7 ♘f3 ♘bd7 (7 ... a6 8 0-0 ♘bd7 9 a3 ♘e8 10 ♖b1 ♔h8 11 b4 b6 ∞ Blees-Piket, Wijk aan Zee II 1986) 8 0-0 ♘e8 9 a3 g6 10 ♗h6 ♘g7 11 ♕d2 ♘f6 (11 ... ♔h8 12 ♘e1 a6 13 b4 b6 14 ♘d3 ± Ligterink-Hoi, Reykjavik 1986) 12 ♘e1 ♔h8 13 ♘d3 ∞/± Schmidt-Podzielny, Trnava 1984

[2] 7 ♗h3!? ♘a6 8 ♗xc8 ♕xc8 9 ♘f3 ♘c7 10 a4 a6 ∞ Ftacnik-Mokry, Trencianske Teplice 1985

[3] 7 ... ♘bd7 8 ♘ge2 ♔h8 9 0-0 ♘h5 10 f4 ±

[4] 8 ♘h3 ♘d7 9 0-0 g6 10 ♕d3 ♘g7 11 ♗d2 f5 ∞ Miles-Seirawan, Brussels 1986

[5] 8 ... ♘d7 9 0-0 g6 10 ♗h6 ±

[6] 10 ... ♗h6 11 0-0 ♗g4 12 ♕d3 ±

[7] Ostermeyer-Gscheidlen, West Germany 1983-84

[8] 6 ... ♘bd7 and now:

7 ♗e2 ♘f8 8 0-0 ♘g6 9 ♘e1 0-0 10 ♗d3 h6 11 g3 ∞ Agzamov-Lerner, USSR Ch 1985

7 g3 a6 8 a4 b6 9 ♗g2 0-0 10 0-0 ♘e8 11 ♘e1 ♖b8 12 ♘d3 ± Hort-Nunn, West Germany 1985-86

7 ♗d3 a6 8 a4 b6 9 h3 0-0 10 ♗e3 ♘e8 11 ♕d2 ± Miralles-Dussol, Montpellier 1984

[9] 7 ♗d3 ♘e8 8 0-0 g6 9 a3 ♘d7 10 b4 ♗xf3 11 ♕xf3 ♗g5 ∞

[10] 9 ... g6 10 ♗h6 ♘g7 11 ♕d2 ♘f6 12 ♔e2! (12 0-0-0 ♔h8 13 ♖dg1 ♘g8 14 ♗e3 a6 ∞) 12 ... ♔h8 13 ♖ag1 ♘g8 14 h4! ± Fedorowicz-Illescas, Dubai Ol 1986

[11] 10 ... g6 11 ♗h6 ♘g7 12 ♕d2 ♘f6 13 ♘g1! ± Gurevich-Guseinov, Baku 1986

[12] 11 ... ♘c7?! 12 b3 ♖e8 13 h4! b5 14 g5 ♘f8 15 h5 ± Kasparov-Miles, match 1986

[13] Kasparov

Benoni I   1 d4 Nf6 2 c4 c5 3 d5 e6 4 Nc3 ed 5 cd d6 6 Nf3 g6

	7	8	9	10	11	12	13	14	15	
1	Nd2	e4[1]	Nc4	Ne3	Bd3[3]	0-0	a4	a5	Be2	±
	Nbd7	Bg7	Nb6[2]	0-0	Re8	a6[4]	Nbd7	Ne5	g5[5]	
2	...	Nc4	Bg5[6]	Bh4[8]	e3	a4	Be2[10]	Bg3	Bxc4	∞/=
	Bg7	0-0	h6[7]	b6[9]	Ba6	Qe7	g5	Bxc4	Ne4[11]	
3	Bg5	Bh4[12]	Bg3	e3	hg	Bd3[14]	Qc2	a4[16]	Rb1[17]	±
	h6	g5	Nh5	Nxg3[13]	Bg7	Nd7[15]	Qe7	a6	0-0[18]	
4	...	Nd2[19]	Bh4	Bg3	Qa4+	e3	hg	Qc2[21]	Be2	∞
	Bg7	h6	g5[20]	Nh5	Kf8	Nxg3	Nd7	Ne5	Qe7[22]	
5	Bf4	e4	Qa4+	Qb3	Bxd6	e5[26]	ef	Qxb2	Be5	∞
	a6	Bg7[23]	Bd7[24]	b5[25]	b4	bc	cb	Bxf6	Qe7[27]	

---

[1]   8 Nc4 Nb6 9 e4 Nxc4 10 Bxc4 Bg7 11 0-0 0-0 12 Bg5 h6 13 Bh4 g5 14 Bg3 a6 = Inkiov-Antonov, Varna 1977

[2]   9 ... Qe7 10 Be2 0-0 11 f3 Ne5 12 Ne3 a6 13 a4 Rb8 14 0-0 ± Gorelov-Khasin, Moscow 1977

[3]   11 g3 a6 (11 ... Nbd7 12 a4 ±) 12 Bg2 Rb8 13 a4 Na8 14 Nc4 Ne8 15 a5 ±

[4]   12 ... c4 13 Bc2 Nd7 14 a4 Rc8 15 f4 Na8 16 Qe2 ±

[5]   16 h3 ± Kapengut

[6]   9 Bf4 Na6 (9 ... Ne8 10 Qd2 Bxc3 11 bc b5 12 Nb2 f5 13 e3 g5 14 Bg3 Qe7 ∞ Seirawan-D.Gurevich, USA 1985; 13 a4! Qa5 14 Qc1 ba 15 e3 ±) 10 Bxd6 Re8 11 e3 Ne4 (11 ... Nh5!?) 12 Nxe4 Rxe4 13 Bg3 b5 14 Nd6 Rb4 15 Be2 Bxb2 16 0-0 c4 ∞.

[7]   9 ... Qe7 10 e3 Nbd7 11 Nb5 (11 a4?! Ne5 12 Na3 h6! 13 Bh4 g5 14 Bg3 Nfd7! ∓ Dlugy-Klinger, Sharjan 1985) 11 ... a6 12 Nbxd6 b5 13 Nxc8 Raxc8 = Dlugy

[8]   10 Bf4 Ne8 11 Qc1 g5 12 Bd2 Nd7 (12 ... Nc7 13 a4 Nba6 14 h4 f6 ∞ Portisch-Spassky, Turin 1982) 13 h4 f6 14 e4 Qe7 ∞ Andruet-Seret, French Ch 1985

[9]   10 ... Na6!? 11 e3 Nc7 12 a4 b6 13 Be2 Ba6 14 0-0 Qd7 ∞ Popov-Nunn, Birmingham 1974

[10]   13 Qc2 Nbd7 14 Rd1 Bxc4 15 Bxc4 g5 16 Bg3 Nh5 17 Qf5 ∞

[11]   16 Nxe4 Qxe4 17 Qb3 Qe7! (17 ... Nd7 18 Bxd6 Qxg2 19 0-0-0 Yusupov-Christiansen, Mexico 1980) ∞/= Yusupov

[12]   8 Bf4 Nh5 9 Bg3 Bg7 10 Nd2 Nxg3 11 hg Nd7 12 e3 0-0 =

[13]   10 ... Bg7 11 Bb5+ Kf8 12 Bd3 Nxg3 13 hg (13 fg Qe7 14 0-0 Nd7 15 Bf5 Nf6 ∞ Yusupov-Gavrikov, USSR 1981) 13 ... Nd7 14 Qc2 Qe7 15 Bf5 Rb8 16 a4 ∞ Antoshin-Psakhis, Moscow 1981

[14]   12 Nd2 Nd7 13 Nc4 Nb6 (13 ... Ne5 14 Nxe5 Bxe5 15 Qc2 a6 ∞ M.Tseitlin-Karasev, Leningrad 1982) 14 Nxb6 Qxb6 ∞ Bagirov-Savon, Baku 1972

[15]   12 ... 0-0 13 Qc2 f5 14 Nd2 Na6 = Lerner-Dolmatov, Kislovodsk 1982

[16]   14 Nd2 Ne5 15 Bf5 Bxf5 16 Qxf5 c4 17 Ke2 ± Psakhis-Gavrikov, Erevan Z 1982

[17]   15 Bf5 Ne5 16 a5! Bxf5 17 Qxf5 ± Tukmakov-Agzamov, Erevan Z 1982

[18]   16 0-0 Ne5!? (16 ... Rb8 17 b4 ± Hartston-Nunn, London 1976) 17 Nxe5 Qxe5 18 a5 ± Hartston-Nunn, London 1981

[19]   8 e3 0-0 9 Nd2 h6 (9 ... Nbd7 10 a4 a6 11 Be2 Re8 12 0-0 Rb8 13 h3! Qc7 14 Kh1 ± Tukmakov-Larsen, Las Palmas 1978) 10 Bh4 Na6 11 Nc4 Re8 12 Be2 Nc7 13 a4 b6 14 0-0 Ba6 ∞

[20]   9 ... a6 10 a4 g5 11 Bg3 Nh5 12 Nc4 Nxg3 13 hg ±

[21]   14 Nc4 Ne5 15 Nxe5 Bxe5 16 Qc2 g4!? ∞ Kapengut

[22]   16 0-0-0 a6 17 e4 b5 18 Rdf1 c4 ∞

[23]   8 ... b5 9 Be2 (9 e5 de 10 Nxe5 Bd6 11 Be2 0-0 12 0-0 b4 13 Nc6 Qc7 ∞ Schüssler-Petrosian, Tallinn 1983) 9 ... Nh5 10 Bg5 Be7 11 Bh6 Bf8 12 Qe3 Bxh6 (12 ... b4 13 Nd1 Nf6 14 Bxf8 Kxf8 15 Qh6+ Kg8 16 Bd3 ± Tarjan-Fedorowicz, USA 1984) 13 Qxh6 Nd7 14 a4 b4 15 Nd1 ± Agdestein-Arnason, Oslo 1984

[24]   9 ... Nfd7 10 Qc2 Qc7 11 a4 0-0 12 Be2 Re8 13 0-0 ±

[25]   10 ... Bc8 11 a4 0-0 12 Be2 Nh5 13 Bg5 f6 14 Be3 f5 15 gf gf 16 Ng5! ± Tarjan-Agzamov, Vršac 1983

[26]   12 Na4 Nxe4 13 Bxc5 Nxc5 14 Nxc5 Qe7+ 15 Qe3 ∞

[27]   16 0-0-0 Nxe5 17 Qxe5 Qxe5 18 Nxe5 Ba4 ∞ Sosonko-Lobron, Bad Kissingen 1981

Benoni I		1 d4 ♘f6 2 c4 c5 3 d5 e6 4 ♘c3 ed 5 cd d6 6 ♘f3 g6						*continued*	
	7	8	9	10	11	12	13	14	15
6	♗f4	a4	e4	♗e2	0-0[29]	♗xf3	♖e1[32]	a5	♘a4	±
	a6	♗g7	0-0	♗g4[28]	♗xf3[30]	♕e7[31]	♘bd7	♖ab8[33]	♖fe8[34]	
7	...	e4	♘d2[35]	♗e2	♗g3	ef[38]	0-0	a4	♘de4	∞
	♗g7	0-0	♗g4[36]	♘e5	f5[37]	♗xf5	a6	♘bd7![39]	♘b6[40]	
8	...	♕a4+	♕b3[42]	e4	♗e2[43]	♗e3	♘d2	0-0[46]	♖ac1	∞
	...	♗d7[41]	♕c7	0-0	♘h5!?[44]	a6[45]	b5	♖a7	♖b7[47]	

[28] 10 ... ♕e7 11 ♘d2 ♘bd7 12 0-0 ♘e5 13 h3 ♘fd7 14 ♕c2 ± Burger-Spraggett, New York 1983

[29] 11 ♘d2 ♗xe2 12 ♕xe2 ♘h5 13 ♗e3 ♘d7 14 0-0 f5 15 ef ♖xf5 ∞ Tarjan-Kudrin, USA 1984

[30] 11 ... ♖e8 12 ♘d2 ♗xe2 13 ♕xe2 ♘h5 14 ♗e3 ♘d7 15 a5 ± Browne-Yap, Thessaloniki Ol 1984, and Browne-de Firmian, US Ch 1985

[31] 12 ... ♘e8 13 ♕d2 ♕e7 14 ♗g5 ♕e5 15 ♖fe1! ± Gligorić-Barlov, Yugoslav Ch 1982

[32] 13 e5!? de 14 d6 ♕e6 15 ♖e1 ♘bd7 16 ♗xb7 ∞/± Browne-D.Gurevich, New York 1984

[33] 14 ... ♘e5 15 ♗e2 ♖fb8 16 ♕c2 b5 17 ab ♖xb6 18 ♖a2 ± W.Schmidt-Abramović, Niš 1983

[34] 16 ♕d2 ♕f8 (16 ... ♘e5 17 ♗xe5 ♕xe5 18 ♘b6 ♕e7 19 e5! ± Browne-Kudrin, US Ch 1984) 17 h3 h5 18 ♖ac1 ± van der Sterren-Hulak, San Bernardino 1985

[35] 9 ♗e2 b5!? 10 ♕c2 a6 11 0-0 ♖e8 12 a3 ∞ Klinger

[36] 9 ... ♘e8 10 ♗e2 f5 11 ef ♗xf5 12 0-0 ♘d7 13 ♘c4 ± Sahović-de Firmian, Bor 1984

9 ... ♘h5 10 ♗e3 ♘d7 11 ♗e2 ♘e5 12 0-0 ♕h4 13 ♘f3 ♘xf3+ 14 ♗xf3 ± Tukmakov-Lau, Plovdiv 1983

[37] 11 ... g5 12 0-0 a6 13 a4 ♘bd7 14 ♕c2 ±

[38] 12 f4 ♘f7 (12 ... ♘g4 Kapengut) 13 0-0 a6 14 a4 fe 15 ♘dxe4 ♗f5 ∞ Eingorn-Pigusov, Kharkov 1985

[39] 14 ... ♕c7 15 ♘de4 ♘f7 16 ♖c1 ♘d7 17 b4!? ∞/± Polugayevsky-Agzamov, USSR 1985

[40] 16 ♗xe5 ♗xe5 17 a5 ♘c8 ∞ Agzamov

[41] 8 ... ♔f8 9 e4 ♘h5 10 ♗e3 ♘d7 11 ♕c2 a6 12 a4 ♖b8 13 ♗e2 ±

[42] 9 ♕c2 0-0 10 e4 ♕e7 11 ♗e2 ♖e8 12 ♘d2 b5 ∞ Herzog-Klinger, Zug 1985

[43] 11 ♘d2 ♘h5 12 ♗e3 f5 (12 ... ♗d4!?) 13 ef gf 14 ♗e2 ♗e8 15 ♘f3 h6 16 ♘b5 ♕e7! ∞ Lebredo-Arencibia, Camaguey 1985

[44] 11 ... a6 12 e5! de 13 ♗xe5 ♕c8 14 ♗xf6! ♗xf6 15 ♘e4 ± Kapengut

11 ... b5 12 e5 (12 ♗xb5 ♘xe4 13 ♘xe4 ♕a5+ 14 ♗d2 ♕xb5 15 ♕xb5 ♗xb5 16 ♘xd6 ♗d3! ∞ Haag) 12 ... ♘h5 13 ed ♕a5 14 ♗d2 ♖e8 15 ♘d1 Starck-Stratil, East Germany 1985

[45] 12 ... ♗g4 13 h3 ♗xf3 14 ♗xf3 ♘d7 (14 ... ♘f6?! 15 e5! Hjartarson-Sigurjonsson, Reykjavik 1984) 15 0-0 ♘hf6 16 ♗b5 ♕b8 17 ♗f4 ± G.Garcia-Velimirović, Moscow IZ 1982

[46] 14 a4 ba 15 ♘xa4 ♗b5!? 16 ♗xb5 ab 17 ♕xb5 f5 ∞∞ Nogueiras-Garcia, Havana 1983

[47] 16 ♖fe1 ♘f6 17 h3 ♖e8 18 ♕c2 b4 ½-½ Ribli-Ljubojević, Tilburg 1984

Benoni II		1 d4 ♘f6 2 c4 c5 3 d5 e6 4 ♘c3 ed 5 cd d6 6 ♘f3 g6 7 g3 ♗g7 8 ♗g2 0-0							
	9	10	11	12	13	14	15	16	17
1	0-0	♘d2[2]	♘c4[3]	♘xe5	a4	a5	♗f4	♕b3	♖fe1	±
	♕e7[1]	♘bd7	♘e5	♕xe5	a6	♖e8[4]	♕e7	♘d7	♘e5[5]	
2	...	♘d2[6]	♘c4[7]	♗f4[9]	♘a5	♘e4	♘c6	♖b1	♘xc5	∞
	♘a6	♘c7	♘fe8[8]	b5	b4	♗xb2	♕d7	♗g7	dc[10]	
3	...	♘d2[11]	a4	h3[14]	♘c4[16]	♘a3[18]	e4[19]	♕d3	♗e3[21]	±
	♖e8	♘bd7[12]	a6[13]	♖b8[15]	♘b6[17]	♗d7	♘c8	♕c7[20]	♘a7[22]	

134

	9	10	11	12	13	14	15	16	17	
4	...	♗f4	a4	♖e1[25]	e4	♘d2![26]	♗f1	♗e3	h3	±
	...	a6[23]	♕c7[24]	♘bd7	♘g4	♘ge5	♖b8	♘f8	f5[27]	
5	...	a4	♗f4[28]	h3[30]	e4	ab[32]	♖e1	♕e2[33]		∞/±
	a6	♘bd7	♕e7[29]	♖b8[31]	b5	ab	♘e8			

[1] **9 ... b6** 10 ♗f4 ♖e8 (10 ... ♘e8 11 ♕d2 ♘d7 12 ♗h6 ± Pfleger-Lengyel, Tel Aviv Ol 1964) 11 ♖e1 a6 12 a4 ♖a7 13 e4 ±
9 ... ♗g4 10 ♘d2 ♕d7 11 f3! ♗h3 12 e4 ♗xg2 13 ♔xg2 ±

[2] 10 ♖e1 ♘bd7 11 e4 ♘g4 12 ♘h4 ♘b6!? =

[3] 11 a4 ♘h5 12 e4 ♘e5 13 ♕e2 f5 14 f4 ♘g4 ∞ Hort-Nunn, Hastings 1975-76

[4] 14 ... ♖b8 15 ♕b3 ♕e7 16 ♗f4 ♘d7 17 ♘a4 ± Kapengut

[5] 18 ♘a4 ♗d7 19 ♘b6 ± Gligorić-Petrosian, Zürich C 1953

[6] 10 h3 ♗d7 11 a4 c4 12 ♗f4 ♖e8 13 ♘d2 ♘h5 14 ♗xd6 ♗xh3 15 ♗xh3 ♕xd6 16 ♘de4 ±

[7] 11 a4 b6 12 ♘c4 ♗a6 13 ♕b3 (13 ♘a3 ♖e8 14 ♖e1 ♘g4! ∓) 13 ... ♗xc4 14 ♕xc4 a6 15 ♖b1 ♘d7 16 b4 b5! = Quinteros-G.Garcia, Las Palmas 1974

[8] 11 ... ♘h5!? 12 a4 f5 (12 ... b6 13 ♕c2 ♗a6 14 b3 ±) 13 e3 b6 14 ♕c2 ♗a6 15 b3 ♕d7 16 ♗b2 ♖ae8 17 ♖ad1 ± Marović-Honfi, Maribor 1977

[9] 12 a4 b6 13 ♕c2 ♘a6 14 ♘a2 ♘ac7 = Alburt-Shamkovich, New York 1986

[10] 18 d6 ♘e6 ∞ Alburt-D.Gurevich, New York 1986

[11] 10 h3 ♘bd7 11 ♗f4 ♘e4! 12 ♘xe4 ♖xe4 13 ♘d2 ♖b4 ∞ Draško-Kovačević, Pula 1986

[12] 10 ... ♘g4 11 ♘c4 (11 ♘de4?! a6! 12 ♗g5 f6 13 ♗f4 ♘e5 14 a4 ♘f7! ∓ Kharitonov-Agzamov, USSR 1986) 11 ... ♘e5 12 ♘xe5 ♗xe5 13 ♕c2 ±

[13] 11 ... ♘e5 12 f4 ♘eg4 13 ♘c4 ♘h5 14 ♘b5 ±

[14] **12 ♖a2** ♖b8 13 a5 b5 14 ab ♘xb6 15 b3 h5 ∓ Shapiro-Fedorowicz, Somerset (USA) 1986
12 e4 ♘e5 13 ♕c2 ♘h5 14 h3 g5! ∞ Razuvayev
12 ♘c4 ♘b6 13 ♘a3 ♗f5!? (13 ... ♗d7 14 ♗d2 ♖b8 15 ♖e1 ± Neverov-Magerramov, Baku 1986) 14 f3 ♗d7 15 ♕b3 ♖b8 ∞

[15] 12 ... ♘h5 13 ♔h2 f5 14 e4 (14 ♘c4 ♘e5 15 ♘xe5 ♗xe5 16 e3 ♖b8 ∓ Timoshchenko-Kindermann, Baden-Baden 1985) 14 ... ♘e5 15 ef ♗xf5 16 g4!? ±

[16] 13 a5 b5 14 ab ♘xb6 15 e4 ♘fd7 16 f4 f5 17 ♖e1 ∞

[17] 13 ... ♘e5 14 ♘a3 ♘h5 15 e4 ♖f8 (15 ... ♗d7!? 16 a5 ♕xa5 17 g4 Hulak-Nunn, Toluca IZ 1982) 16 ♔h2 ♗d7 17 ♕e2 ♕e8 18 g4! ± Kapetanović-Martić, corr. 1986

[18] 14 ♘e3 ♘bd7 15 ♖b1 b5 16 ab ab 17 b4 ♘h5 ∞ Kapengut

[19] **15 a5** ♘c8 16 ♘c4 ♗b5 (16 ... ♕c7 17 ♗d2! ± Tal-Andersson, Biel IZ 1976) 17 ♕b3 ♗xc4 18 ♕xc4 ♘d7 19 ♖a3 ∞ Rubinetti-Gheorghiu, Buenos Aires 1979
15 ♕c2 ♘c8 (15 ... ♕c7 16 ♗d2 ♘xa4 17 ♘xa4 b5 ∞ Timoshchenko-Quinteros, Baden-Baden 1985) 16 ♖b1 ♕c7 17 ♗d2 c4! ∓ Petran-Sindik, West Berlin 1986

[20] 16 ... b5?! 17 ab ab 18 ♘axb5 ♗xb5 19 ♘xb5 ♘d7 20 ♘c3 ± Ljubojević-Barlov, Vrbas 1980

[21] 17 ♖b1 c4! 18 ♕c2 b5 19 ab ab 20 b4 cb! ∓ Ljubojević-Hulak, Yugoslavia 1981

[22] Kapengut

[23] **10 ... ♘e4** 11 ♘xe4 ♖xe4 12 ♘d2 ♖b4 13 a3! ♖xb2 14 ♘c4 ±
10 ... ♘h5 11 ♗g5 ♕b6 12 ♕c1! ± Alburt-D.Gurevich, US Ch 1985

[24] 11 ... ♘e4 12 ♘xe4 ♖xe4 13 ♘d2 (13 ♖a2 ♗g4! = Csom-Savon, Esbjerg 1980) 13 ... ♖b4 14 ♘e4 ± Tal-Savon, USSR 1970

[25] 12 ♖c1 ♗g4!? 13 ♘g5 ♘h5 14 ♗d2 h6 15 h3 ♗d7 ∞

[26] 14 h3 ♘ge5 15 ♘xe5 ♘xe5 16 ♗f1 ♕b6! ∓ Kapengut

[27] 18 f4 ♘f7 19 ♗f2 ± Smyslov-Vuković, Bor 1980

[28] 11 h3 ♖b8 12 ♖e1 ♖e8 13 ♗f4 ♕c7 14 ♘d2 ♘h5 15 ♗e3 b5 ∞ Razuvayev-Panchenko, Minsk 1985
11 ♖e1 ♕c7 (11 ... ♖b8 12 ♗f4 ♘e8 13 e4 b5 = Csom-Pinter, Hungary 1981) 12 ♘d2 ♖b8 13 a5 b5 14 ab ♘xb6 15 ♖a2 ♘fd7 = Alburt-Hjartarson, Philadelphia 1986
11 ♘d2 ♖b8 (11 ... ♘h5 12 ♘ce4 ♘df6 13 ♘xf6+ ♗xf6 14 ♘c4 ♗d4 15 e3 ♗g7 16 e4 ± Nikolić-de Firmian, Wijk aan Zee 1986) 12 ♘c4 ♘e8 13 ♗f4 ♘b6 ∞ Reefschläger-Sax, Lugano 1986

[29] 11 ... ♕c7 12 e4 ♖e8 13 ♕c2 ♖b8 14 a5 ♘h5 15 ♗e3 ± Polugayevsky-Vaiser, Sochi 1981

[30] 12 ♖e1 ♖b8 13 e4 ♘g4 14 ♘d2 ♘ge5 = Smyslov-Portisch, Budapest 1978

[31] 12 ... ♖e8 13 e4 ♘h5 14 ♗g5 ♗f8 15 ♖e1 ± Draško-Cebalo, Yugoslav Ch 1986

[32] 14 ♖e1 b4 15 e5 bc 16 ef ♕xf6 17 ♗g5 c2 ∞ Zaitsev-Abramović, Moscow 1982

[33] Razuvayev-Psakhis, Irkutsk 1986

	7	8	9	10	11	12	13	14	15	
1	f3[1]	♗g5	♕d2	a4	♗e3	♘ge2	♘d1[5]	♘ec3	♗e2	=
	♗g7	0-0[2]	a6[3]	h6[4]	♖e8	♘bd7	♘e5	♔h7[6]	♕a5[7]	
2	...	♗e3	♘ge2[8]	♘c1[10]	♗e2	0-0	♘d3	♘f2	♕d2	∞
	...	0-0	♘bd7[9]	h5!	♘h7[11]	♕e7	♘e5	f5	a6[12]	
3	♗d3	♘ge2	0-0[13]	h3[15]	♘g3	f4	♗xc4	♗d3	♗xb5	∞
	♗g7	0-0	♘a6[14]	♖e8[16]	♖b8[17]	c4[18]	b5	♘c5	♖xb5[19]	
4	...	...	...	a4	h3[22]	f4[23]	♗e3[24]	♘g3	♗c2	∞
	...	...	a6[20]	♕c7[21]	♘bd7	♖b8	♖e8	c4[25]	♘c5[26]	
5	f4	♗b5+[28]	♗d3[30]	♘f3	0-0	♔h1	a4	a5[34]	ab	=
	♗g7[27]	♘fd7[29]	0-0[31]	♘a6[32]	♖b8[33]	♘c7	a6	b5	♘xb6[35]	
6	...	...	a4	♘f3	0-0	♖e1[39]	♗f1[40]	h3	♗e3	±
	...	...	0-0[36]	♘a6[37]	♘b4[38]	a6	♖e8	♖b8[41]	b6[42]	

[1] 7 ♗b5+ ♘bd7 8 a4 a6 9 ♗e2 ♗g7 10 ♘f3 0-0 11 0-0 ♖e8 = Forintos-Vaganian, Kirovakan 1978

  7 ♘ge2 ♗g7 8 ♘g3 0-0 9 ♗e2 ♘a6 10 0-0 ♘c7 11 a4 ♖b8 12 ♖b1 b6 = Szabo-Borik, Dortmund 1974

[2] 8 ... a6 9 a4 ♘bd7 10 ♘h3! h6 11 ♗e3 ♘e5 12 ♘f2 g5 13 ♗e2 ± Gulko-Kasparov, USSR 1981

[3] 9 ... ♖e8 10 a4 ♘a6 11 ♗b5!? ♗d7 12 ♘ge2 ♗xb5 13 ab ♘c7 14 0-0 a6 = Ionescu-Panno, Dubai Ol 1986

  9 ... h6 10 ♗e3 ♖e8 11 ♘ge2 ♘bd7 12 ♘c1 a6 13 a4 a5 ∞ Rodriguez-Quinteros, Biel IZ 1985

[4] 10 ... ♖e8 11 ♘ge2 ♘bd7 12 ♘g3 ♖b8 13 ♗e2 ♕c7 14 0-0 c4 15 ♗e3 b5 16 ab ab 17 b4 ± Seirawan-Hardarson, Reykjavik 1986

  10 ... ♕a5 11 ♖a3 ♖e8 12 ♘ge2 ♘bd7 13 ♘g3 ♖b8 14 ♗e2 ♘b4 15 0-0 ± Lputian-Palatnik, Lvov 1986

[5] 13 ♘c1 ♘h7 14 ♗e2 g5 15 ♖a3 ♕e7 = Vasyukov-A.Kuzmin, Moscow II 1986

[6] 14 ... ♘h7 15 ♗e2 f5 16 0-0 ♘f7 17 ♘f2 ♗d7 18 ♔h1 ± Foisor-Cvitan, Tbilisi 1986

[7] 16 ♖a3 ♕b4!? = Foisor

[8] 9 ♕d2 a6 10 a4 ♘bd7 11 ♘h3 ♖b8 (11 ... ♘e5 12 ♘f2 ♗d7 13 ♗e2 b5 14 ab ab 15 ♖xa8 ♕xa8 16 ♘xb5 ± Seirawan-Sax, Biel IZ 1985) 12 ♘f2 ♖e8 13 ♗e2 ♘c7 ∞ Raičević-Hulak, Niš 1985

[9] 9 ... ♖e8 10 ♘g3 h5 11 ♗e2 h4 12 ♘f1 ♘h7 13 ♘d2 a6 14 a4 ♘d7 15 0-0 f5 16 a5 f4! ∞ Cebalo-Ilić, Yugoslavia 1986

[10] 10 ♘g3 a6 11 a4 ♘e5 12 ♗e2 ♗d7 13 0-0 b5! ∞ Spraggett-Hazai, Szirak 1986

[11] 11 ... ♘e5 12 0-0 ♘h7 13 ♕d2 f5 ∞ Ionov-Kuzmin, USSR 1986

[12] 16 a4 g5 17 ef ♗xf5 ∞ Dolmatov-Khalifman, USSR Ch 1986

[13] 9 ♗g5 a6 10 a4 ♘bd7 11 0-0 ♖b8 12 ♔h1 ♕c7 13 ♖c1 ♘e5 14 f4 ♘xd3 15 ♕xd3 b5! ∞ Hartston-Nunn, London 1981

[14] 9 ... b6 10 ♗g5! h6 11 ♗h4 ♘a6 12 f4 ♗xd3 13 ♕xd3 ♘bd7 14 a4 a6 15 ♔h1 ±

[15] 10 f3 ♗d7 (10 ... ♘c7 11 ♗g5 a6 12 a4 ♗d7 13 a5 ♖b8 = Miles-Arnason, Manchester 1981) 11 ♗g5 ♖c8 12 ♗c4 ♘c7 13 a4 a6 14 a5 h6! 15 ♗e3 ♗b5 ∞ Rivas Pastor-Suba, 1980

[16] 10 ... ♗d7 11 ♗f4! ♘e8 12 ♕d2 ♖b8 13 ♗g5 ±

  10 ... ♘c7 11 a4 b6 12 ♗g5! h6 13 ♗h4 ♗a6 14 f4 ± Ivkov-Toran, Palma de Mallorca 1966

[17] 11 ... ♘c7 12 a4 b6 13 f4 (13 ♗f4 ♗a6 14 ♗xa6 ♖xa6 15 ♕d2 c4 16 ♖ae1 ♘c5 ∞ Hartston-Ribli, Moscow 1977) 13 ... ♗a6 14 ♔h1 ♘d7 15 e5! ±

[18] 12 ... ♘b4 13 ♗c4! ♘g4 14 e5! ±

  12 ... ♘c7 13 a4 ±

[19] 16 ♘xb5 ♕b6 ∞ Kapengut

[20] 9 ... ♖e8 10 h3 ♗d7 11 ♗g5 ♕c7 12 ♕d2 c4 13 ♗c2 b5 14 a3 ♘a6 15 ♘g3 b4 = Spassky-Ljubojević, Manila IZ 1976

[21] 10 ... b6 11 h3 ♘bd7 12 ♘g3 ♕c7 13 ♗e3 c4 14 ♗c2 ♖b8 15 f4 ±

[22] 11 b3 ♘bd7 12 ♔h1 ♖e8 13 f3 ♖b8 14 a5 b5 ∞ Miles-Grünfeld, Riga IZ 1979

[23] 12 ♘g3 ♖b8 13 ♕e2 ♖fe8 14 ♗e3 h5 ∞ Kapengut

[24] 13 ♘g3 c4 14 ♗c2 b5! 15 ab ab 16 ♗e3 b4! ∞ Hess-Danner, Reggio Emilia 1980

[25] 14 ... ♘xe4 15 ♗xe4 f5 16 ♗xf5! ± Knaak-Rajković, Novi Sad 1979

[26] 16 ♗d4 b5 17 ab ab 18 e5 de 19 fe ♖xe5 20 ♕f3! ♖g5 ∞ Knaak-Enders, East Germany 1982

27 **7 ...** ♕e7 8 ♘f3 ♗g4 9 h3 ♗xf3 10 ♕xf3
♗g7 11 ♗d3 ±

7 ... a6 8 e5! ♘fd7 9 ♘f3 ♗g7 10 ♘e4 de
11 ♘d6+ ♔f8 12 ♗e2 ± Kapengut
28 8 e5 ♘fd7 9 ♘b5 de 10 ♘d6+ ♔e7 11 ♘xc8+
♕xc8 12 ♘f3 ♖e8 13 fe ♘xe5 14 ♗b5 ♘bd7
15 ♘xe5 ♔f8! Shakarov-Shmulenson, corr. 1976
29 **8 ...** ♘bd7 9 e5! de 10 fe ♘h5 11 e6 fe
12 de 0-0 13 ♘f3! ♖xf3 14 ♕xf3 ±
30 9 ♘f3 a6 10 ♗d3 b5 11 0-0 0-0 12 ♔h1 b4!
(12 ... c4 13 ♗c2 ♘c5 14 ♗e3 ♘bd7 15 ♗d4 ±
Gulko-Basin, Minsk 1985) 13 ♘a4 ♘b6 =
31 **9 ...** ♕h4+!? 10 g3 ♕e7 11 ♘f3 0-0 12 0-0
♘b6 13 ♔g2 (13 f5!? Psakhis) 13 ... ♗g4 14 h3
♗xf3 15 ♕xf3 c4 16 ♗c2 ♘a6 = Lau-Dolmatov,
Graz 1981
32 10 ... a6 11 a4 ♘f6 12 0-0 (12 h3 ♖e8
13 0-0 ±) 12 ... ♗g4 13 h3 ♗xf3 14 ♕xf3 ♘bd7
15 ♗d2 ± Pinter-Djurić, Bajmok 1980
33 11 ... ♘c7 12 a4 a6 (12 ... ♘f6 13 ♗c4! ♗g4
14 h3 ♗xf3 15 ♕xf3 ± Timman) 13 ♕e1 ♖b8
14 e5 ♘b6 15 f5! ± Gulko-Savon, Lvov 1978
34 14 ♕e2 ♘f6 15 ♘d2 ♖e8 ∞
35 16 f5 gf! 17 ef ♘bxd5 18 ♗g5 ± Dorfman-
Psakhis, USSR 1980
36 **9 ...** ♕h4+ 10 g3 ♕e7 11 ♘f3 0-0 12 0-0
♘a6 13 e5! de 14 d6 ♕d8 15 ♘d5 ± Kouatly-

Hulak, Toluca IZ 1982
9 ... ♘a6!? 10 ♘f3 ♘c7 (10 ... ♘b4? 11 0-0
a6 12 ♗xd7+ ♗xd7 13 f5! ± Kasparov-Nunn,
Lucerne Ol 1982) 11 0-0 ♘xb5 (11 ... a6
12 ♗xd7+ ♗xd7 13 f5! 0-0 14 ♗g5 ± Baumbach-
Danner, corr. 1985) 12 ab 0-0 13 ♗d2 ♘b6 =
Kapengut
9 ... a6 10 ♗e2 ♕h4+ 11 g3 ♕d8 12 ♘f3
0-0 13 0-0 ♖e8 14 ♕c2 ± Cebalo-Lobron,
Reggio Emilia 1985-86
37 10 ... a6 11 ♗e2 ♕c7 (11 ... ♘f6 12 0-0
♕c7? 13 e5! ♘e8 14 e6! ± Kasparov-Kuijpers,
Dortmund 1980) 12 0-0 c4 13 ♘d2 b5 14 ab
♘b6 15 ♔h1 ± Li Zunian-Sax, Biel IZ 1985
38 11 ... ♘c7!? (Kapengut) 12 ♗c4 ♖e8 13 ♖e1
♘b6 14 ♗b3 ±
39 12 ♗d2 a6 13 ♗e2 ♖b8 14 ♗e1 ♖e8
15 ♔h1 ♘f6 16 ♘d2 b6 ∞ Doroshkevich-
Anikayev, USSR 1976
40 13 ♗c4 ♘b6 14 ♗e2 ♗g4 15 h3 ♗xf3
16 ♗xf3 ♕h4 17 ♔h2 ♖fe8 + Watson-Nunn,
England 1980
41 14 ... ♘f6 15 ♗c4 ♘d7 16 ♗e3 ♘b6 17 ♗f1
♗d7 18 ♗f2 ♖c8 19 g4 ± Horvath-Bönsch,
Kestelyi 1981
42 16 ♕d2 ♗b7 17 ♗f2 ♕e7 18 ♗c4 ±
Enevoldsen-Filipowicz, Siegen Ol 1970

Benoni IV		**1 d4 ♘f6 2 c4 c5 3 d5 e6 4 ♘c3 ed 5 cd d6 6 ♘f3 g6 7 e4 ♗g7**						
	8	9	10	11	12	13	14	15	16
1	♗g5	♗h4[1]	♗g3	♗b5+![2]	e5[4]	♗e2[6]	fg	♘h4	0-0	±
	h6	g5	♘h5	♔f8[3]	a6[5]	♘xg3	g4[7]	♗xe5	♕g5[8]
2	...	♘d2	♗h4	♗e2[10]	♕c2[11]	a4	♘d1	0-0[14]	♗g3	∞
	a6	h6[9]	b5	0-0	♘bd7[12]	b4[13]	♖e8	g5[15]	♘xd5[16]

[1] 9 ♗f4 g5 10 ♗b5+ ♔f8 11 ♗e3 ♘g4
12 ♗d2 a6 13 ♗e2 ♘d7 14 h4!? ∞
[2] 11 ♘d2 ♘xg3 12 hg a6 13 a4 ♘d7 14 ♗e2
♕e7 15 a5 ∞
[3] 11 ... ♗d7?! 12 ♗xd7+ ♕xd7 13 ♘e5! de
14 ♕xh5 ±
[4] O'Kelly
12 ♗e2 ♘xg3 13 hg ♘d7 14 ♘d2 a6 15 a4
♕e7 ∞ Mecking-Keene, Hastings 1966-67
[5] **12 ... g4** 13 ♗h4! ♕b6 14 0-0 gf 15 e6! ±
12 ... ♘xg3 13 fg de (13 ... g4?! 14 0-0! a6
15 ♗d3 gf 16 ♕xf3 ±) 14 0-0 a6 15 ♗d3 b5
16 ♕e2! ±
12 ... ♗g4!? (Timman) 13 ed ♘xg3 14 hg
♕xd6 15 ♕a4 ±
[6] 13 ♗d3 de 14 ♗xe5 g4! ∞ Keene-Timman,
Weissingen 1975
[7] 14 ... de 15 0-0 ♖a7 16 a4 b6 17 ♕b3 ±

Stean-Nunn, Birmingham 1976
[8] 17 ♔h1 ± Kapengut
[9] 9 ... b5 10 ♗e2 (10 a4 b4 11 ♘cb1 ∞) 10 ...
0-0 11 0-0 ♘bd7 12 ♕c2 ♖e8 13 a4 b4 14 ♘d1 ±
[10] 11 a4 b4 12 ♘cb1 0-0 13 ♗e2 ♖e8 14 f3
g5 15 ♗f2 ♘h5 16 ♘c4 a5! + Lambert-Nunn,
London 1977
[11] 12 0-0 ♘bd7 (12 ... g5 13 ♗g3 ♕e7 14 ♕c2
♘bd7 15 ♖ae1 ±) 13 ♕c2 c4! 14 f4 ♕c7 15 ♔h1
♘c5 ∞ Zaid-Magerramov, USSR 1978
[12] 12 ... ♖e8 13 0-0 ♘bd7 14 a4 – 12 ... ♘bd7
[13] 13 ... ba 14 0-0 ♘b6 15 f4 ♕c7 16 ♗f3 ±
[14] 15 f3 g5 16 ♗f2 ♘e5 17 ♘e3 ♗g6 18 g3
♖b8 19 0-0 b3! + Tatai-Hulak, Amsterdam 1977
[15] 15 ... ♕e7 16 ♘e3 ♘f8 17 ♘ec4 ± Timman-
G.Garcia, Buenos Aires 1978
[16] 17 ♘c4 ♘f4 18 ♗xf4 gf 19 ♘xd6 ♖e6 ∞
Shashin-Agapov, Leningrad 1980

	8	9	10	11	12	13	14	15	16	
3	♗g5	♘d2	♗e2	♗h4	0-0	♗g3	a4	♕c2	a5	∞
	0-0[17]	♘bd7[18]	h6[19]	♕e7[20]	g5	a6	♘e5	♗d7[21]	♖ae8[22]	
4	♗e2	♗g5	♗h4	♗g3	♘d2	hg	♘c4[25]	♕c2[27]	♘e3	∞
	0-0	h6	g5[23]	♘h5[24]	♘xg3	♘d7	♕e7[26]	♘e5	♖e8![28]	
5	...	...	...	...	...	...	♘c4[29]	ef	0-0	∞
	...	...	...	...	...	f5	♘a6[30]	♗xf5	♕f6[31]	
6	...	♘d2	0-0	a4	♘c4	♗f4![33]	♗xc4	♕c2[34]	♖fe1	=
	...	♘a6	♘c7	b6[32]	♗a6	♗xc4	♖e8	a6	♖b8[35]	
7	...	...	0-0	a4	♖e1[38]	♕c2	h3	♘c4	♗f4	=
	...	♘bd7	♕e7[36]	a6[37]	b6[39]	♖e8	♖b8	♘e5	♘xc4[40]	

[17] 8 ... ♗g4 9 ♕a4+! ♗d7 10 ♕b3 ♕c7 11 ♗e2 ±

[18] 9...b6 10 ♗e2 h6 11 ♗h4 ♗a6 12 0-0 ♗xe2 13 ♕xe2 ± Miles-Robatsch, Biel 1977

   9...♘a6 10 ♗e2 h6 11 ♗h4 ♖e8 12 0-0 ♘c7 13 f4 b6 14 a4 ♖b8 15 ♔h1! ±

[19] 10...a6 11 a4 ♖e8 12 0-0 ♕c7 13 ♗h4 ♖b8 14 h3 ± Kavalek-Ljubojević, Manila IZ 1976

[20] 11...a6 12 a4 ♖e8 13 0-0 ♕c7 14 ♕c2 ♖b8 15 h3 g5 16 ♗g3 ♘e5 17 f4! ±

[21] 15...♘fd7 16 ♘d1 ♘g6 17 ♗g4 ± Polugayevsky-Kapengut, Riga 1975

[22] 17 ♘d1 ♘g6 18 ♘e3 ♘f4 19 ♗f3 h5 ∞ A.Rodriguez-Ortega, Bayamo 1982

[23] 10...b5!? 11 ♗xb5 (11 ♗xf6 ♗xf6 12 ♗xb5 ♕a5 13 ♕d3 ♘d7 ∞̄) 11...g5 12 ♗g3 ∞

[24] 11...b5 12 ♘d2 a6 13 0-0 ♖e8 14 ♕c2 ± Najdorf-Fischer, Santa Monica 1966

[25] 14 0-0 ♕e7 15 ♗g4 ♗d4 16 ♗f5 a6 17 a4 ♘f6 18 ♕f3 ♔g7 =

[26] 14...♘b6 15 ♘e3 f5 16 ef ♗xf5 17 g4 ♗g6 18 ♗d3 ±

[27] 15 ♘e3 ♘f6 16 ♕c2 ♖e8 17 f3 ♘h7 18 g4 ♘f8 ∞ Larsen-Fischer, Santa Monica 1966

[28] Uhlmann-Gligorić, Skopje 1968

[29] 14 ef ♗xf5 15 0-0 ♘d7 16 ♘c4 ♘e5 17 ♘e3 ♗g6 =

[30] 14...a6 15 a4 f4 16 gf ♖xf4 17 g3! ± Portisch

[31] 17 g4 ♗g6 18 ♗d3 ♘b4 19 ♗xg6 ♕xg6 20 ♘e3 ∞

[32] 11...♕e7 12 ♖e1 b6 13 ♘c4 (13 h3 ♖e8 14 ♘c4 ♗a6 15 ♗g5 h6 16 ♗h4 ♘d7 = A.Petrosian-Tal, Lvov 1981) 13...♗a6 14 e5! ±

   11...♘d7 12 ♘c4 ♘e5 13 ♗f4 (13 ♘e3 f5 14 f4 ♘f7 15 ef gf 16 ♗d3 ∞ Stohl-Dejkalo, Tallinn 1986) 13...♘xc4 14 ♗xc4 ♖e8 15 ♕d3 h5 16 ♖ae1 a6 17 a5 ± Wilder-de Firmian, US Ch 1986

[33] 13 ♗g5 ♕d7! Dlugy-Hulak, Montpellier 1985

[34] 15 ♖e1 ♘h5 16 ♗d2 a6 17 ♖b1 ♗d4! ∞

[35] 17 e5 de 18 ♗xe5 ♘fxd5 19 ♗xg7 ♘b4 20 ♕b3 ♔xg7 21 ♗xf7 = Kapengut

[36] 10...♘e8 11 ♔h1 (11 a4 f5 12 ef gf 13 f4 ♘df6 14 h3 ± Pinter-Bischoff, Dubai Ol 1986; 11...♘c7 12 ♔h1 b6 13 ♘c4 ♘e5 14 f4! ±) 11...♘c7 12 f4 f5 13 ♘c4 ♘b6 14 e5 ± Farago-Renet, Lucerne 1985

   10...a6 11 a4 ♘e8 12 ♘c4 ♘e5 13 ♘e3 f5 14 f4 ♘f7 15 ef gf 16 ♗d3 ∞/±

[37] 11...♘e5 12 ♖a3 g5 13 ♖e1 ± Bagirov

[38] 12 f4 ♖b8 13 ♔h1 ♖e8!? 14 ♕c2 ♘b6 ∞ Kapengut

[39] 12...♖b8 13 f4 b6 14 ♗f3 b5 15 ab ab 16 ♖a5 ± A.Petrosian-Kapengut, Moscow 1972

[40] Tisdall-Nunn, London 1976

1 d4 ♘f6 2 c4 c5 3 d5 e6 4 ♘c3 ed 5 cd d6 6 e4 g6 7 ♘f3 ♗g7 8 ♗e2 0-0

	9	10	11	12	13	14	15	16	17	
1	0-0	h3[1]	♗xf3	♗f4[2]	a4	♗e2	♕d2[4]	♖fe1	♗f1	±
	♗g4	♗xf3	♘bd7	♘e8	a6	♕e7[3]	♘c7	♖fb8	♕f8[5]	
2	...	a4	♗g5	♗xf3	♗e2[7]	♕c2	b3[8]	♗d2	♔h1[9]	=
	a6	♗g4	♗xf3[6]	♘bd7	♖e8	♕a5	♖e7	♖ae8	♕c7[10]	
3	...	...	♗f4	♗xf3	♕d2	♗g5[13]	h4	♗e2	♕f4	±
	...	...	♗xf3[11]	♘e8[12]	♘d7	♗f6	♘c7	♖e8	♕e7[14]	
4	...	...	h3	♗xf3	♕c2[16]	♗d2	b3[17]	b4	♖fe1	∞
	...	...	♗xf3	♘bd7[15]	♖e8	♕c7	c4	♖e7[18]	♖ae8[19]	
5	...	...	...	...	♗f4	♕c2[20]	a5![21]	♖a4[23]	♗xe5[25]	∞/±
	...	...	...	...	♕c7	♖fe8	c4[22]	♘e5[24]	♖xe5[26]	

[1] 10 ♘d2 ♗xe2 11 ♕xe2 ♖e8 12 ♘c4 b5 13 ♘xb5 ♘xe4 14 ♕c2 a6 ∞ Bagirov-Karasev, USSR 1974
10 ♗g5 h6 11 ♗h4 ♕b6! 12 ♖b1 ♘bd7 ∞ Zilberman-Kapengut, USSR 1980
10 ♗f4 ♕b6 11 ♖b1 ♘bd7 12 h3 ♗xf3 13 ♗xf3 ♖fe8 = Ivkov-Greef, Lone Pine 1981

[2] 12 ♕c2 ♖e8 13 ♗d2 c4 14 ♗e3 a6 15 a4 ♖c8 16 a5 ♘c5 ∞ Nikolac-Rajković, Yugoslavia 1978

[3] 14 ... ♕c7 15 ♖c1 ♖b8 (15 ... c4 16 b3 cb 17 ♕xb3 ♘c5 18 ♕a3 ± Boleslavsky) 16 b3 ♘ef6 17 ♕c2 ♖fe8 18 ♗h2 ± Smyslov

[4] 15 ♕c2 ♘c7 16 ♖fe1 ♖ab8 17 ♗f1 ♖fe8 ∞ Kapengut

[5] 18 ♔h1 b6 19 ♗h2 ± Kapengut

[6] 11 ... ♘bd7 12 ♘d2 ♗xe2 13 ♕xe2 ♖e8 14 f4 ♕c7 15 ♕f3 c4 16 ♔h1 ♖ab8 17 ♖ae1 ± Timman-Nunn, London 1975
11 ... h6 12 ♗h4 ♗xf3 (12 ... ♘bd7 13 ♘d2 ± Schmidt-de Firmian, Smederevo 1981) 13 ♗xf3 ♘bd7 14 ♗e2 ♖e8 15 ♕c2 ± Antunac-Kuligowski, New York 1981

[7] 13 ♕d2 ♖e8 14 a5 c4 15 ♖a4 ∞ Hansen-Agdestein, Gjovik 1985

[8] 15 ♖fe1 ♖ac8 16 f4?! c4 17 ♗h4 ♘c5 ∓

[9] 17 ♘b5 ♕d8 18 ♘xd6 ♘xe4 19 ♘xe8 ♗xa1 20 ♖xa1 ♘xd2 21 ♕xd2 ♕xe8 ∓

[10] 18 f3 ♘b6 19 a5 ♘c8 20 ♗g5 ♘a7 = Timman-Kavalek, Wijk aan Zee 1975

[11] 11 ... ♖e8 12 ♘d2 ♗xe2 13 ♕xe2 ♘h5 14 ♗e3 ♘bd7 15 g4 ♘hf6 16 f3 h6 17 ♔h1 ♘e5 ∞ Portisch-Kasparov, Moscow 1981
11 ... ♕e7!? 12 ♕c2 ♖e8 13 ♖ae1 (13 ♖fe1 = Petrosian) 13 ... ♘bd7 14 ♘d2 ♗xe2 15 ♖xe2 ♘h5

16 ♗e3 ♘e5 ∞ Torre-Lobron, Hamburg 1982

[12] 12 ... ♕e7 13 ♖e1 ♘bd7 14 a5 h5 (14 ... ♖ab8 15 ♘a4 ♘e5 16 ♗xe5 ♕xe5 17 ♖b1 ♘d7 18 b4 ♕d4 19 ♕e2 ∞ Browne-D.Gurevich, US Ch 1985) 15 g3 ♘e8 (15 ... ♖ab8 16 ♘a4 ♘e8 17 ♖c1! ± Gligorić-Psakhis, Sarajevo 1986) ∞

[13] 14 ♗e2!? ∞/± Portisch-Lobron, Reggio Emilia 1985-86

[14] 18 ♖fe1 ± Zaid-E.Vladimirov, USSR 1977

[15] 12 ... ♖e8 13 ♕c2 ♕e7 14 ♖e1 ♘bd7 15 a5 ± Rubinetti-Castro, Kyto 1976

[16] 13 g3 ♖e8 14 ♕c2 ♖c8 15 a5 c4 16 ♖a4 ♘e5 17 ♗g2 ♘fd7 = ECO

[17] 15 a5 ♖ac8 16 ♖a4 ♕d8 17 g3 c4! 18 ♖e1 ♘e5 ∓ Kapengut

[18] 16 ... ♖ac8 17 ♖ae1 ♘e5 18 ♗e2 ♘fd7 ∞ Portisch-Gligorić, Vrnjačka Banja 1966

[19] 18 ♖ac1 h6 19 a5 ∞ Petrosian-Ivkov, Santa Monica 1966

[20] 14 ♕d2 ♖fe8 15 a5 ♖ac8 16 g4 ♖e7 17 ♖fe1 ♘e8 18 ♗g2 ♖b8 ∞ Vaganian-Tal, Leningrad 1971

[21] 15 ♖fe1 c4 16 ♗e2 ♖ac8 17 a5 ♘c5! =
15 ♗e2 ♖e7 16 ♖fe1 ♖ae8 17 ♗f1 ♘e5 18 ♖ad1 c4 19 b4 ½-½ Podgayets-Zaid, Kharkov 1980

[22] 15 ... ♘e5 16 ♗e2 ♘fd7 17 ♗d2 c4 18 ♘a4 ♘c5 19 ♘b6 ± Ree-Keene, Havana Ol 1966

[23] 16 ♘b1 ♘c5 17 ♕xc4 ♘fxe4 18 ♖a2 f5 = Portisch-Timman, Hastings 1969-70

[24] 16 ... b5 17 ab ♘xb6 18 ♖a5 ♘fd7 19 ♗e3 ♘e5 20 ♗e2 ± Najdorf-Torre, Manila 1973

[25] 17 ♗e2?! ♘fd7 18 ♗xe5 ♖xe5 19 f4 ♘d3! ∓

[26] 18 ♖d1! ♘d7 19 ♖d4 b5 20 ab ♘xb6 ∞/±

Benoni VI   1 d4 ♘f6 2 c4 c5 3 d5 e6 4 ♘c3 ed 5 cd d6 6 e4 g6 7 ♘f3 ♗g7 8 ♗e2 0-0 9 0-0 ♖e8

	10	11	12	13	14	15	16	17	18	
1	♕c2	♗f4[2]	♕b1	♗g5	♗e3[5]	a3	ab[7]	♗xf3	♘e4[8]	=
	♘a6[1]	♘b4[3]	♘h5[4]	f6	f5	fe[6]	ef	cb		
2	♘d2	♖e1[9]	♗xa6	♘c4	♗f4	a4	♗d2	h3![12]	g4[13]	±
	b6	♗a6[10]	♘xa6	♘c7[11]	♗f8	♘h5	♕d7	♖ad8		
3	...	a4	♖a3	a5[15]	♕c2	f4	♘c4	♔h1[17]	♗xg4	∞
	♘bd7	a6[14]	♖b8	♕c7	♘e5[16]	♘eg4	♘h5	♕d8	♗xg4[18]	
4	...	♕c2	a4[19]	♖a3[21]	♘d1[23]	g3[24]	♘e3	♗xf3	♘f5	±
	...	♘e5	g5[20]	g4[22]	♘h5	♕f6	♘f3+	gf	♗xf5[25]	
5	...	♖e1[26]	a4	h3![28]	♗b5[29]	♗c6	♘f3!	dc	♗f4	±
	♘a6	♘c7[27]	b6	♖b8	♖e7[30]	♗d7	♗xc6	♕e8	♕xc6[31]	
6	...	f3	a4	♔h1[32]	♘c4	♘e3	ef	f4	♗d3	±
	...	♘c7	♘d7	b6[33]	♘e5	f5[34]	gf	♘g6	♖f8[35]	
7	...	...	...	♘c4	♗g5[36]	♕d2[38]	♗xc4	♕d3	♗d2	±
	...	...	b6	♗a6	♕d7[37]	♗xc4	a6	h6	♕e7[39]	
8	...	...	...	...	...	♗e3[40]	♗xc4	♕d2	♖ab1	±
	...	...	...	...	h6	♗xc4[41]	a6	♔h7	♖b8[42]	

¹ 10 ... b6 11 ♖e1 ♘a6 12 ♗b5 ♖e7 13 ♗f4 ±

² 11 ♗g5 h6 12 ♗h4 ♘b4 13 ♕b1 g5 14 ♗g3 ♘h5 ∞

11 a3 ♘c7 (11 ... ♗g4!? 12 ♗f4 c4 ∞/=) 12 ♖e1 ♖b8 13 ♗f4 b5 14 b4 ♘xe4!? ∞

11 ♖e1 ♗g4 12 ♗f4 c4! 13 ♗xc4 ♗xf3 14 gf ♘h5 15 ♗g3 ♗e5 ∞ Nemet-Rogulj, Karlovac 1979

³ 11 ... ♗g4 12 h3 ♗xf3 13 ♗xf3 ♕b6 14 b3 ♘d7 15 a3 ± Balashov-Savon, Leningrad 1971

⁴ 12 ... ♗g4!? 13 a3 ♘a6 14 ♖e1 c4 ∞ Gliksman-Matulović, Sarajevo 1976

⁵ 14 ♗d2 f5 15 ♘g5 ♗f6 16 ♘e6 ♗xe6 17 de ♘g7 18 ♘d5 ♘c6 ∞ Filip-Bilek, Budapest 1961

⁶ 15 ... f4 16 ♗xc5 ♘xd5 17 ♘xd5 dc 18 ♖d1 ± Marić

⁷ 16 ♘g5 ♘d3 17 ♗xh5 gh 18 ♘gxe4 c4 ∞ Portisch-Adamski, Raach 1969

⁸ Tal

⁹ 11 a4 a6 12 ♕c2 ♘bd7 13 ♖a3 ♖b8 14 ♘c4 ♘e5 15 ♘xe5 ♖xe5 16 h3 ♖e7 17 ♗d3 ♕c7! = Burger-Tisdall, Brighton 1981

¹⁰ 11 ... ♘bd7 12 ♗b5! ♗f8 13 ♘c4⁻a6 14 ♗c6 ± Farago-Dorfman, Cienfuegos 1977

¹¹ **13 ... b5** 14 ♘xb5 ♖xe4 15 ♗f4 ♘xf2 16 ♕f3! ±

13 ... ♕d7 14 a4 ♘g4 15 ♘b5 ♗f8 16 ♗f4! ± Polugayevsky

¹² 17 e5?! de 18 ♘xe5 ♕d6 ∓ Douven-van Baarle, Holland 1980

¹³ Kapengut

¹⁴ **11 ... g5** 12 ♖e1 ♘f8 13 ♗b5 ♖e7 14 ♘f3 g4 15 ♘h4 ± Tukmakov-Suba, Las Palmas 1982

11 ... ♘e5 12 ♖a3 (12 ♘db1 h6 13 f4 ♘ed7 14 ♗f3 c4 ∞ Lukacs-Kovačević, Balatonbereny 1985) 12 ... g5 (12 ... ♗d7 13 f4! ±) 13 ♖e1 a6 14 ♘f1 g4 15 ♗g5 h6 16 ♗h4 ♗d7 17 ♘g3 ± Browne-Nunn, London 1980

¹⁵ 13 ♔h1 ♕c7 14 f4 h5 15 h3 ♘h7 ∞/∓

¹⁶ 14 ... b5 15 ab ♖xb6 16 ♘c4 ♖b4 17 ♗f4 ♗f8 18 ♗g3 ±

¹⁷ 17 e5 de 18 d6 ♕d8 ∓ Toth-Nunn, Geneva 1979

¹⁸ 19 e5 ♕h4 20 ♘e4 ∞ Nunn

¹⁹ 12 f4?! ♘eg4 13 ♘f3 ♘xe4! 14 ♘xe4 ♗f5 15 ♗d3 c4 16 ♕xc4 ♖c8 ∓

²⁰ 13 ♘h5 13 ♗xh5 gh 14 ♘d1 b6 15 ♖a3 ♗a6 16 ♖e1 ± Podgayets-Zaichik, USSR 1986

²¹ **13 ♘c4** ♘xc4 14 ♗xc4 ♘g4 15 ♘e2 ♕f6!? 16 f3 ♘e5 17 ♗b5 ♖f8 ∞ G.Gonzalez-Andres,

Havana 1985

13 ♘d1!? g4 (13 ... ♘g6 14 ♘e3 ♕e7 15 ♗b5! ±) 14 ♖a3! – 13 ♖a3

²² 13 ... ♘fg4 14 ♘d1 ♖f8 15 f3 ± W.Schmidt-Barbero, Vinkovci 1986

²³ **14 b3** a6 15 a5 ♘h5 16 ♘c4 ♕f6 ∓
14 ♘c4 ♘h5 15 ♘e3 ♘f4 16 ♗b5 ♖f8 ∓

²⁴ **15 ♘e3** ♘f4 16 ♗d1 b6 17 ♘dc4 ♘xc4 18 ♘xc4 ♘g6 ∞ Antunac-Grünfeld, New York 1981

15 f4!? gf 16 ♖xf3 ∞/± Kapengut

²⁵ 19 ef ± Nunn

²⁶ 11 ♗xa6?! ba 12 f3 ♗d7 13 a4 ♘h5 14 ♘c4 ♖b8 ∓

²⁷ 11 ... ♖b8 12 ♗f1 ♘g4 13 h3! ♖xf2 14 ♔xf2 ♗d4+ 15 ♔e2! (15 ♔e3? ♕h4+ 16 ♔e2 ♗xe3 17 ♔xe3 f5 ∓ West-Levy, Australian Ch 1985-86) 15 ... ♕h4 16 ♘f3! ♕f2+ 17 ♔d3 ♘b4+ 18 ♔c4 ± Rogers

²⁸ 13 ♕c2 ♖b8 14 ♘c4 ♗a6 15 ♗f4 ♗xc4 16 ♗xc4 ♘h5 ∓

²⁹ 14 ♗f1 a6 15 ♘f3!? b5 16 e5! ∞/±

³⁰ 14 ... ♗d7 15 ♘c4! a6 16 ♗xd7 ♕xd7 17 ♗f4 ♗f8 18 e5 ±

³¹ 19 ♕xd6 ♕xd6 20 ♖xd6 ♖d7 21 ♖ad1 ± Pelts-Sorokin, USSR 1975

³² 13 ♘c4 ♘e5 14 ♘e3 b6 15 ♖e1 ♖b8 16 f4 ♘d7 17 ♘c4 ♗d4+ 18 ♔h1 ♘f6 ∞

³³ 13 ... h5 14 f4 ♘f6 15 f5! gf 16 ♗xh5 ± Gligorić

13 ... f5 14 ef gf 15 ♘c4 ♘e5 16 ♘xe5 ♗xe5 17 f4 ♗g7 18 ♗h5 ± Gligorić-Portisch, Manila 1974

13 ... ♕e7 14 ♘c4 f5 15 ♗f4 ♘e5 16 ♘xe5 ♗xe5 17 ♗xe5 ♕xe5 18 f4 ♕d4 19 e5! ± Peev-Spassov, Bulgaria 1976

³⁴ 15 ... ♖b8 16 ♗d2 a6 17 f4 ♘d7 18 ♘c4 ± Gligorić

³⁵ 19 ♗d2 ♘a6 20 ♕b1! ♕f6 21 ♘b5 ± Bagirov-Sorokin, USSR 1973

³⁶ 14 ♗d2 ♗xc4 15 ♗xc4 a6 16 ♖b1 ♘d7 ∞/∓ Adamski-Matulović, Lugano Ol 1968

³⁷ 14 ... ♖b8 15 b3 h6 16 ♗d2 ±/±

³⁸ 15 ♖b1 h6! 16 ♗d2 b5 17 ab ♘xb5 18 ♘xb5 ♗xb5 19 ♘e3 a5 = Kapengut

³⁹ 19 ♖ae1 ±

⁴⁰ 15 ♗h4 ♕d7 16 ♗d2 ♗xc4 17 ♗xc4 a6 ∞/∓ Boleslavsky

⁴¹ 15 ... ♖b8 16 ♕d2 ♔h7 17 ♖b1 ±

⁴² 19 b4 b5 20 ab ab 21 ♗e2 c4 22 ♖a1 ♖a8 23 ♗d4 ± Reshevsky-Matulović, Palma de Mallorca IZ 1970

King's Indian Defence

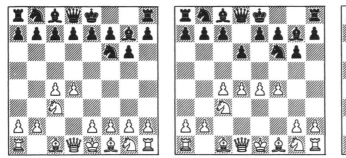

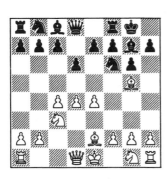

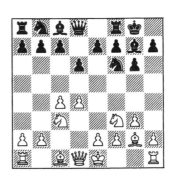

A perennial favourite of aggressive, ambitious players such as Fischer, Bronstein, Gligorić and co-author Kasparov, the King's Indian is an old defence re-armed with modern ideas. Black allows White to establish a broad pawn centre with e4, hoping to use it as a target or work around it. White must take care not to release the Indian Bishop, whose latent power down the long diagonal gives the defence added bite. The locking of the centre leaves the players to their own devices in their separate sectors, which leads in general to White storming the queenside and Black pulling out all the stops on the kingside. Obviously, this hostile indifference to the plans of the opponent causes unbalanced play, and Black does not need to equalize completely in order to gain dynamic chances.

The **Classical Line** (4 e4 d6 5 ♘f3 0-0 6 ♗e2 e5 7 0-0) is the most analysed and the most often encountered. White claims an edge in space, and settles down to the task of breaking into the queenside, usually via the c-file, before Black's kingside counterattack reaches frightening proportions.

The **Sämisch** (5 f3) is now considered White's most reliable choice, combining aggression with solidity. Maintaining options of attack on either side of the board, White has a plethora of viable plans from which to choose and Black must play with great care against all of them.

White's other major alternative is the **Fianchetto Variation** (g3). A quiet positional continuation, its scheme is to focus the king's bishop on the centre in order to nurture White's spatial plus. Black's position is quite solid and he can confidently adopt the system which best suits his style, with the Panno Variation (6 ... ♘c6) being the sharpest and least explored.

The **Four Pawns Attack** (5 f4) swings in and out of fashion depending on the outcome of constant theoretical arguments about its soundness. Too violent and chaotic to gain widespread acceptance, it is nevertheless enjoying a renaissance as latest results have favoured White. How long it will be before the Attack fades from the scene once again remains to be seen. A volatile weapon, it can often backfire, and should only be chosen by those who relish living dangerously.

Systems with ♗g5 for White include the **Smyslov** (4 ♘f3, 5 ♗g5) and the **Averbakh** (4 e4, 5 ♗e2, 6 ♗g5). The Smyslov is an indirect and positionally esoteric line. Very rarely encountered, and slightly underestimated, it carries a subtle sting that can catch the unwary defender by surprise, though Black can equalize by accurate play. The Averbakh, with links to the Benoni and the Maroczy Bind, tries to provoke Black into weakening his pawn structure by tempting him to kick the annoying bishop off the d8-h4 diagonal. The play is much more complex than in the Smyslov, and White can develop a formidable initiative if not carefully watched. Its greatest adherent is undoubtedly East German grandmaster Wolfgang Uhlmann.

References: *The Semi-Closed Openings in Action* (Karpov)
              Understanding the King's Indian (Bellin and Ponzetto)

	King's Indian I		1 d4 ♘f6 2 c4 g6 3 ♘c3 ♗g7						
	4	5	6	7	8	9	10	11	12
1	♘f3	♗g5!?[1]	e3	♗e2	♕c2[4]	♖d1	0-0	♗h4	♗g3	∞
	d6	0-0[2]	♘bd7[3]	c6	e5	♕e7	h6	g5	♘h5[5]	
2	e4	♘ge2	♘g3	d5[8]	♗e2	ed	a4	♗f4	♕d2	=
	d6	0-0[6]	c5[7]	e6	ed	a6	♖e8	♕c7	♘bd7[9]	

[1] **5 ♗f4** ♘h5 6 ♗g5 h6 7 ♗e3 0-0 8 ♕d2 ♔h7 9 h3 f5 10 g4 fg 11 hg ♗xg4 ∞ Vaganian-Kupreichik, USSR Ch 1979

5 e3 0-0 6 ♗e2 ♘bd7 7 0-0 e5 8 b3 ♖e8 9 ♗a3 ed 10 ♘xd4 ♘c5 =

[2] **5 ... h6** 6 ♗h4 g5 7 ♗g3 ♘h5 8 e3 ♘d7 9 ♕e2 e6 (9 ... e5 10 ♖d1 ♕a5 11 ♗e2 ♘df6 12 a3 0-0 13 dc ♕xc5 14 ♘d5 ± Kovačević-Damljanović, Novi Sad 1985) 10 ♗e2 ♘df6 11 ♘d2 ♘xg3 12 hg ♕e7 13 ♖d1 ♗d7 14 b4 ± Kovačević-Barlov, Novi Sad 1985

[3] **6 ...c5** 7 ♗e2 ♕a5 8 ♕d2 ♗g4 9 0-0 ♘bd7 10 h3 ♗xf3 11 ♗xf3 ♖ac8 12 ♗xb7 cd 13 ed ♖xc4 = Smyslov-Geller, USSR 1966

[4] **8** 0-0 h6 9 ♗h4 g5 10 ♗g3 ♘h5 11 ♘d2 ♘xg3 12 hg ♘f6 13 b4 e5! = Smyslov-Gligorić, Zagreb 1970

[5] 13 de de 14 ♘d2 ½-½ Bagirov-Ciocaltea, Baja 1971; 14 ... ♘f4!? 15 ef ef 16 ♗xf4 gf ∞ Hartston

[6] **5 ...e6** 6 ♘g3 ♘bd7 7 ♗e2 h5 8 ♗g5 a6 9 ♕d2 b5 10 f3 0-0 11 ♖d1 e5 = Miles-Romanishin, Tilburg 1985

5 ... c5!? 6 d5 b5 7 cb a6 8 ♘g3 0-0 9 ba h5 10 ♗e2 ♕a5 ∞ Martin-Fedorowicz, Hastings 1984-85

[7] **6 ...e5** 7 d5 c6 8 ♗e2 cd 9 cd a5 10 ♗e3 ♘a6 11 0-0 h5 = Forintos-R.Byrne, Monte Carlo 1968

6 ... a6 7 ♗e2 c6 8 0-0 b5 9 e5 ♘e8 10 f4 ♘d7 11 ♗e3 ♗b7 ∞ Miles-Nunn, OHRA 1985

[8] **7** dc dc 8 ♗e3 ♕a5 =

[9] 13 0-0 b6 14 ♗h6 ♗h8 = Szabo-Petrosian, Sarajevo 1972

	4	5	6	7	8	9	10	11	12	
3	e4	h3	Nf3	d5	Bd3	ed	Be3	0-0	fe	±
	d6	0-0[10]	c5[11]	e6	ed	Re8+[12]	Nh6[13]	Bxe3	Nbd7[14]	
4	...	...	...	d5[15]	Be3	Nh2	Be2	Bf3	h4[17]	∞
	...	...	e5	Na6[16]	Nh5	Qe8	Nf4	f5	Qe7[18]	
5	...	...	Bg5[19]	d5	cb	a4	Bd2	f3	Qc2	∞/=
	...	...	c5[20]	b5!?[21]	a6	Qa5	Qb4[22]	Nfd7	c4[23]	

[10] 5 ... e5 6 d5 Nbd7 7 Bg5 h6 8 Be3 Nc5 9 Qc2 a5 10 g4 ± Katalimov-Uusi, USSR 1980

[11] 6 ... c6 7 Be3 a6 8 Bd3 (8 a4 d5! 9 e5 Ne4 10 Bd3 Bf5 = Yap-Sax, Rome 1985) 8 ... b5 9 e5 Nfd7 10 e6 fe 11 Ng5 Nf6 12 h4 ±/± Portisch-Minić, Zagreb 1965

[12] 9 ... Qe7+ 10 Qe2 Re8 11 Qxe7 Rxe7 12 Kd1 Nbd7 13 Bg5 ± Bagirov-Borisenko, USSR 1974

[13] 10 ... b5 11 Nxb5! Ne4 12 0-0 a6 13 Nc3 Nxc3 14 bc Bxc3 15 Rb1 ± Timman-Velimirović, Skopje 1976

[14] **13 Qd2** Ne5 14 Nxe5 Rxe5 15 Rf2 Nh5 16 e4 ± Polugayevsky-Rodriguez, Manila 1982
13 e4 Qe7 14 Qd2 Rf8 15 Rf2 Ne8 16 Raf1 ±

[15] 7 de de 8 Qxd8 Rxd8 9 Bg5 Nbd7 10 0-0-0 Rf8 11 Be3 c6 = Hébert-Watson, Hastings 1984-85

[16] **7 ... Nh5** 8 Nh2! Qe8 9 Be2 Nf4 10 Bf3 f5 11 g3! Nxh3 12 Bg2 f4 13 Nf3 g5 14 Rxh3 ±

Vizhmanavin-Chiburdanidze, Moscow 1981

7 ... a5 8 Bg5 Nbd7 9 Be2 Nc5 10 Nd2 Bd7 11 b3 ± Larsen-Gligorić, Monte Carlo 1967

[17] 12 0-0 b6 13 h4 Nc5 14 Bxc5 bc 15 g3 Nh3+ 16 Kg2 h5 ∞ Korchnoi-Romanishin, Tilburg 1985

[18] 13 g3 Nb4! 14 Qb3 Nfd3+ 15 Ke2 f4 16 Bd2 (Kavalek-Kasparov, Bugojno 1982) 16 ... Nxf2!! ∓; 14 0-0! g5 ∞

[19] 6 Be3 Nbd7 (6 ... e5 7 d5 Nbd7 8 Nf3 Nc5 9 Nd2 a5 10 g4 Qe7!?) 7 Nf3 =

[20] 6 ... a6 7 Nf3 Nbd7 8 Be2 h6 9 Be3 c5 10 0-0 cd 11 Bxd4 b6 12 e5 ± Suba-Georgiev, Prague Z 1985

[21] 7 ... e6 8 Bd3 ed 9 ed Nbd7 10 f4 Qa5 11 Qd2 a6 12 Nge2 b5 13 cb ab 14 Bxb5 Rb8 15 a4 ± Suba-Sznapik, Dortmund 1981

[22] 10 ... ab 11 Bxb5 Ba6 12 Ra3 Nbd7 13 Nf3 ±

[23] 13 Nd1 Qc5 ∞/= Suba-Ermenkov, Prague Z 1985

	6	7	8	9	10	11	12	13	14	
1	Nf3	Be2[3]	Be3	Bxf3	e5[5]	Qa4	Qxa5	Qd5	Qe4	±
	Bg4[2]	Nfd7	Bxf3[4]	Nc6	Na5	Nb6	Nxc4	Nxe3	Nc4[6]	
2	...	d5[7]	Be2	e5	fe	cd	bc	0-0	Rxf3	=
	c5	e6[8]	cd	de[9]	Ne4![10]	Nxc3	Bg4	Bxf3	Nd7![11]	
3	...	...	...	ed	0-0	Bd3	h3	a3	g4	=
	...	...	...	Re8[12]	Bf5	Qd7[13]	Na6	Nc7	Bxg4![14]	
4	...	...	de	Bd3	0-0	Ng5	Qe1	f5	Nh3	∞
	...	...	fe[15]	Nc6	Nd4[16]	Qe7[17]	e5	h6	gf[18]	

	9	10	11	12	13	14	15	16	17	
5	...	e5[19]	fe	Bg5[20]	ef	Qd2!	Nxb5	0-0	Bc4[22]	±
	b5	de	Ng4	f6[21]	Bxf6	Bf5	Nd7	Qb6		

144

	9	10	11	12	13	14	15	16	17	
6	...	0-0	h3[24]	♗xf3	♖e1	a4	♗e3	♕e2	♕f2	=
	♗g4	♘bd7[23]	♗xf3	♖e8[25]	a6	♕c7	c4	♖ac8	♘c5[26]	
7	...	e5	fe	♗g5[27]	0-0	d6	♘d5	♘e7+	de	=
	♖e8	de	♘g4	♕b6[28]	♗f5[29]	♕xb2	♘xe5	♖xe7	♘bc6[30]	
8	...	♘d2	a4	♗xg4[33]	g3	♕xg4	♔f2	h3	♔g2	∞
	...	a6[31]	♘g4[32]	♕h4+	♕xg4	♗xg4	♘d7	♗d4+	♗xc3[34]	

[1] 5 ... c5 6 d5 0-0 7 ♗d3 a6!? 8 ♘ge2 b5 9 cb ab 10 ♘xb5 ♗a6 ∞ Hernandez-Kasparov, Banja Luka 1979

[2] 6 ... e5 7 de de 8 ♕xd8 ♖xd8 9 ♘xe5 ♖e8 (9 ... ♘xe4 10 ♘xe4 f6 11 c5! ±) 10 ♗d3 ♘xe4 11 ♗xe4 f6 12 ♗d5+ ♔f8 13 ♗f7 ±
6 ... ♘c6 7 ♗e2 ♘d7 8 ♗e3 e5 9 fe dc 10 d5 ± Alekhine

[3] 7 h3 ♗xf3 8 ♕xf3 ♘c6 9 ♗e3 e5 10 fe de 11 d5 ♘d4 12 ♕f2 c5 ∞ Marjanović-Kozul, Sarajevo 1985

[4] 8 ... ♘c6 9 d5 ♗xf3 10 gf ±

[5] 10 0-0 e5 11 fe de 12 d5 ♘d4! ∓
10 d5 ♘a5 11 ♕d3 c6 12 b4 ♘xc4 13 ♕xc4 cd 14 ♕d3 de 15 ♗xe4 d5 16 ♗xd5! ±

[6] 15 ♕e2 ♘a5 16 ♖d1 e6 17 h4 ± Nogueiras-Kozul, Sarajevo 1985

[7] 7 dc (♕c5 8 ♗d3 ♕xc5 (8 ... ♘fd7 9 cd!? ♗xc3+ 10 bc ♕xc3+ 11 ♕d2 ♕xa1 12 de ♖e8 13 e5 ∞ Ljubojević-van der Wiel, Wijk aan Zee 1985) 9 ♕e2 ♘c6 10 ♗e3 h5 11 h3 ♘g4 12 ♗d2 ∞
7 ♗e2 cd 8 ♕xd4 ♘a6! (8 ... ♘c6 9 ♗e3 ♗g4 10 ♘xc6 ♗xe2 11 ♘xd8 ♗xd1 12 ♖xd1 ♖fxd8 13 ♔e2 ♖dc8 14 c5± Uhlmann-Gligorić, Sarajevo 1963) 9 ♗e3 ♘c5 10 ♗f3 ♕b6 (10 ... ♗h6!?) 11 ♘b3 ♕b4 12 0-0 ♗e6 ∞ Pribyl-Martz, Decin 1979

[8] 7 ... a6 8 ♗d3 b5 9 e5 de 10 fe ♘g4 11 ♕e2 ♘bd7 12 ♗f4 ♕c7 13 0-0± Korchnoi-Gheorghiu, Vienna 1986; 8 a4 e6 9 de ♗xe6 10 ♗d3 ♗g4 11 0-0 Danner-Uhlmann, Budapest 1985
7 ... b5 8 cb a6 9 a4! e6!? (9 ... ab 10 ♗xb5 ♗a6 11 ♖b1 ♗xb5 12 ab ♘bd7 13 0-0 ♘b6 14 ♕e2 ± Vaiser-S.Garcia, Bayamo 1985) 10 de ♗xe6 11 ♗e2 ab 12 ♗xb5 ♘a6 13 0-0 ♗b4 ∞ Gorelov-Gufeld, USSR 1981

[9] 9 ... ♘g4 10 cd ed 11 h3 e4 12 hg ef 13 gf ♖e8 14 f5 ± Nielsen-Mortensen, Esbjerg 1985
9 ... ♘e4!? 10 cd ♘xc3 11 bc ♘d7! ∞ Li-Gheorghiu, Dubai Ol 1986

[10] 10 ... ♘g4 11 ♗g5 ♕a5 12 0-0 (12 cd ♘xe5 13 0-0 ♘bd7 ∞ Novak-Georgiev, Plovdiv 1985) 12 ... ♘c6 13 ♘d5 ∞of/± Kouatly-Zsu.Polgar, Brussels 1985

[11] 15 e6 ♘e5 16 ef+ ♔h8 17 ♖f1 ♖xf7 = Chekhov-Vasyukov, Moscow II 1986

[12] 9 ... ♘h5 10 0-0 ♗xc3 11 bc f5 12 ♘g5 ♘g7 13 ♗f3 ♘d7 = Forintos-Gligorić, Ljubljana 1969

[13] 11 ... ♘e4 12 ♘xe4 ♗xe4 13 ♗xe4 ♖xe4

14 ♘g5 ± ECO

[14] 14 ... ♗xd3 15 ♕xd3 b5 16 cb ♖eb8 ∞ Geller
14 ... ♗xg4 15 hg ♕xg4+ 16 ♔h2 ♕h5+ = Conquest-Mestel, Hastings 1986-87

[15] 8 ... ♗xe6 9 ♗d3 ♗g4 10 h3 ♗xf3 11 ♕xf3 ♘c6 12 ♗e3 ♕b6 13 0-0 ♖fe8 14 ♖ad1 ± Nikolić-Popović, Sarajevo 1982

[16] 10 ... ♕e7 11 ♕e1 ♘d7 12 ♗d2 a6 13 ♔h1 b5 14 e5! ± Marjanović-Popović, Sombor 1978
10 ... a6!?

[17] 11 ... e5 12 f5?! (12 fe) 12 ... h6 13 ♘h3 gf 14 ef b5! ∓ Christiansen-Kasparov, Moscow IZ 1982

[18] 15 ef e4! ∞

[19] 10 ♗xb5 ♘xe4 11 ♘xe4 ♕a5+ 12 ♔f2 ♕xb5 13 ♘xd6 ♕b6 ∞ A.Zaitsev-Bogdanovich, Sochi 1967

[20] 12 ♗f4 b4 13 ♘e4 ♘d7 ∓
12 ♗xb5 ♘xe5 13 0-0 ♗g4 14 ♗e2 ♗xf3 15 ♗xf3 ♘bd7 =/±

[21] 12 ... ♕b6 13 0-0 ♘xe5 14 ♘xe5 ± Nunn

[22] Sosonko-Reshevsky, Amsterdam 1973

[23] 10 ... ♗xf3 11 ♗xf3 ♘bd7 12 ♔h1 a6 13 a4 ♖c8 14 a5 ± Peev-Pavlov, 1971

[24] 11 a4 ♖e8 12 h3 ♗xf3 13 ♗xf3 c4! 14 ♗e3 ♕a5 ∞
11 ♘d2 ♗xe2 12 ♕xe2 ♖e8 13 ♕f3 ♕e7 14 a4 c4 15 ♔h1 ♘c5 ∞ Peev-Tseshkovsky, Albena 19??

[25] 12 ... c4!? 13 ♗e3 ♕a5 14 ♕e2 ♖ac8 ∞ Kaplan-Sigurjonsson, Hastings 1975-76

[26] Lputian-Mikhalchishin, USSR Ch 1985

[27] 12 ♗f4 ♘xe5 13 0-0 ♘bd7 14 d6! ♖b8 15 ♘b5! ∞

[28] 12 ... f6 13 ef ♗xf6 14 ♕d2 ♗f5 15 0-0 ♘d7 16 h3 ♗xg5 17 ♕xg5 ♗e3 ∞/= Szabo-Timman, Amsterdam 1975

[29] 13 ... ♘xe5 14 d6 c4+ 15 ♔h1 ♘d3 16 ♗xd3 cd 17 ♕xd3 ♗e6 18 ♖ac1 ± ECO

[30] 18 ♔h1 ♘xf3 19 ♗xf3 ♕xa1 20 ♕xa1 ♗xa1 21 ♖xa1 f6 = Filip

[31] 10 ... ♘a6 11 0-0 ♘c7 12 a4 a6 (12 ... b6 13 ♔h1 ♗a6 14 ♖e1 ♗xe2 15 ♖xe2 ♘g4 16 h3 ± Savon-Belyavsky, USSR Ch 1973) 13 ♗f3 ♖b8 14 ♘c4 b5 15 ab ab 16 ♘xd6 ♕xd6 17 e5 ECO

[32] 11 ... ♘bd7 12 0-0 c4! 13 ♗f3 ♕e7 14 ♔h1 ♖b8 15 a5 b5 16 ab ± Grigorian-Lutikov, USSR 1971

[33] 12 ♘c4 h5 ∞

[34] 18 bc ♗e2 19 ♖e1 ♗d3 20 ♖e3 c4 21 ♗a3 ∞

King's Indian III 1 d4 ♘f6 2 c4 g6 3 ♘c3 ♗g7 4 e4 d6 5 f3

	5	6	7	8	9	10	11	12	13	
1	...	♘ge2[2]	♗g5	♕d2[3]	d5	cd	♘g3	♗e2	♗e3	±
	e5[1]	c6	♘bd7	0-0	cd	♘c5	♕b6	♗d7	a5[4]	
2		♗e3	♗d3[5]	♘ge2[6]	0-0	♕d2[8]	♖ad1	a3	♘c1	±
	c6	a6	b5	♘bd7[7]	0-0	♖e8[9]	e6	♕e7	bc[10]	
3	...	♗e3	♕d2[12]	0-0-0	dc	e5	ed	♘d5	♗g5	±
	0-0	a6[11]	b6[13]	c5	bc	♘e8[14]	♘xd6	♘d7	f6[15]	
4	...	...	♗d3[16]	♘ge2	♗c2	d5	♗b3	♕d2	f4	±
	...	b6	♘fd7[17]	c5	♘c6	♘b4	♖e8[18]	♘e5	♘g4[19]	
5	...	...	♘ge2	♕d2	d5[21]	cd[22]	g4	h3	0-0-0	∞
	...	e5	c6[20]	♘bd7	cd	a6	h5	♘h7	h4[23]	
6	...	...	d5	♕d2[24]	g3[26]	♕f2	♕xh4	♔e2!	♖e1![27]	±
	...	...	♘h5	♕h4+[25]	♘xg3	♘xf1	♘xe3	♘xc4	♘a6[28]	
7	...	...	...	♕d2[29]	cd	♘ge2	g4[31]	h3[32]	0-0-0	∞
	...	...	c6	cd	♘bd7[30]	a6	h5	♘h7	h4[33]	
8	...	♗g5	d5	♕d2[36]	cd[37]	a4	♗e3	♘ge2	♘f4[39]	∞/±
	...	c5[34]	e6[35]	ed	a6	h6	♘h7[38]	♘d7	♘e5[40]	
9	...	...	♘ge2	♕d2	h4[43]	0-0-0	♗h6	♗xg7	de	∞/=
	...	♘c6	a6[41]	♖b8[42]	h5	b5	e5!	♔xg7	de[44]	

[1] 5 ... c5 6 dc dc 7 ♕d8+ ♔xd8 8 ♗g5 ♘fd7 9 f4 ♘c6 10 ♘f3 ♘d4 11 0-0-0 ± Petrosian-Kärner, Tallinn 1983

5 ... ♘c6 6 ♗e3 a6 7 ♕d2 ♗d7 8 0-0-0 b5 9 c5 dc 10 d5 ♘d4 11 e5 ± Miles-Spassky, Linares 1985

[2] 6 d5 ♘h5 7 ♗e3 f5 8 ♕d2 ♕h4+ 9 ♗f2 ♕e7 10 ♘ge2 0-0 11 0-0-0 a6 12 ♔b1 ± Seirawan-Zuckerman, New York 1985

[3] 8 d5 h6 9 ♗e3 ed 10 ed a6 11 ♘g3 0-0 12 ♗e2 b5 13 ♕d2 ♔h7 14 0-0 ♘b6 ∞ Spassov-Lanc, Trnava 1985

[4] 14 0-0 a4 15 ♖ac1 ± Portisch-Zapata, Tunis IZ 1985

[5] 7 c5 0-0 8 ♘ge2 ♘bd7 9 ♘f4 e5!? ∞/±

[6] 8 e5 ♘fd7 9 f4 ♘b6 10 b3 ∞ Portisch-Kavalek, Wijk aan Zee 1975

[7] 8 ... 0-0 9 0-0 bc 10 ♗xc4 d5!? Fedorowicz-Djurić, Hastings 1984-85

[8] 10 b3 ♗b7 11 ♕d2 e6 12 ♖ad1 ♖e8 = Gligorić-Kavalek, Manila 1975

[9] 10 ... e5 11 cb ab 12 b4 ♗b7 13 ♖fd1 ed 14 ♘xd4 ± Ree-Zakharov, Sochi 1976

[10] 14 ♗xc4 ± Portisch-Hort, Montreal 1979

[11] 6 ... c5 7 dc (7 ♘ge2 ♘c6 8 d5 ♘e5 9 ♘g3 a6 10 f4 ♘eg4 11 ♗d2 e5 12 de fe 13 h3 ♘h6 14 ♗e3 ± Dlugy-Zsu.Polgar, New York 1985) 7 ... dc 8 ♕xd8 ♖xd8 9 ♗xc5 ♘c6 10 ♗a3!

♘d7 11 0-0-0 ♗xc3 12 bc b6 13 ♘e2 e5 14 ♔c2 ±/± Knaak-Vogt, East German Ch 1986

[6] 6 ... ♘bd7 7 ♘h3! e5 8 d5 ♘h5 9 g4 ♘f4 10 ♘xf4 ef 11 ♗xf4 ♘e5 12 ♗e2 f5 13 gf gf 14 ♕d2 fe (14 ... ♕h4+ 15 ♗g3 ♕h5 16 f4 ♘f3+ 17 ♗xf3 ♕xf3 18 ♖f1 ♗xc3 19 ♖xf3 ♗xd2+ 20 ♔xd2 fe 21 ♖b3! ±/±) 15 ♘xe4 ♕h4+ 16 ♗g3 ♕h5 17 ♘g5 ♗xf3+ 18 ♘xf3 ♖xf3 19 ♗xf3 ♕xf3 20 ♖f1 ∞/± Seirawan-Nunn, Lugano 1987; 11 ... f5!? 12 gf gf 13 ♕d2 ♘e5 14 ♗e2 fe! 15 ♘xe4 ♕h4+ 16 ♗g3 ♕h5 17 0-0 ∞ Beaton-Watson, Cap d'Agde 1986

[12] 7 ♗d3 c5 8 dc dc 9 e5 ♘fd7 10 f4 ♘c6 11 ♘f3 f6 ∞ Piasetski-Eslon, Alicante 1977

[13] 7 ... ♘bd7 8 ♗d3! c5 9 ♘ge2 cd 10 ♘xd4 ± Knaak-Ničevski, Trnava 1980

7 ... ♘c6 – 6 ... ♘c6

[14] 10 ... ♘fd7 11 ed ed 12 ♗h6 ±

[15] 14 ♗e3 ± Knaak-Fernandez, Halle 1978

[16] 7 ♕d2 e5 8 ♘ge2 ♘c6 9 d5 ♘c5 10 ♘g3 e6 11 ♗e2 ed 12 ed a6 13 a4 ♗d7 14 0-0 b5! ∞ Ghitescu-Schaufelberger, Bath 1973

[17] 7 ... c5? 8 e5!

7 ... a6 8 ♘ge2 c5 9 e5 ♘e8 10 ♗e4 ♖a7 11 dc bc 12 ♗xc5 ♖d7 13 ♗e3 ♗b7 14 ♗xb7 ♖xb7 15 b3 ± Gligorić-Torre, Manila 1975

7 ... ♗b7 8 ♘ge2 c5 9 d5 e6 10 ♗g5 ♘bd7

11 f4 a6 12 a4 ♕c7 13 0-0 ± Gligorić-Pazz, Lone Pine 1975

[18] 11 ... ♘e5 12 0-0 ♗a6 13 a3 ♘xc4 14 ♗xc4 ♗xc4 15 ab cb 16 b3 bc 17 bc ± Zsu.Polgar-Root, Vienna 1986

[19] 14 ♗g1 ♘a6 15 h3 ♘f6 16 ♗c2 ± Timman-Cvitan, Zagreb 1985

[20] 7 ... ♘bd7 8 ♕d2 ♘b6 9 b3 ed 10 ♘xd4 ± Khasin-Spassky, Leningrad 1954

7 ... ♘c6 8 d5 ♘e7 9 g4 ♗e8 10 ♕d2 f5 11 h3 ♘f6 12 0-0-0 ± Quinteros-Afifi, Switzerland 1985

7 ... ed 8 ♘xd4 c6 9 ♕d2 d5 10 cd cd 11 e5 ♘e8 12 f4 f6 13 ♗b5! fe 14 fe ♕h4+ 15 g3 ♕e7 ±

[21] 9 0-0-0 a6 10 ♔b1 b5! 11 ♘c1 ed 12 ♗xd4 ♖e8 ∞ Mishkov-Petrushin, USSR 1980

[22] 10 ed!?

[23] 14 ♔b1 ♗f6 15 ♖c1 ♗g5 ∞Visier-Gheorghiu, Las Palmas 1974

[24] 8 ♘ge2!? f5 9 ♕d2 ♘d7 10 0-0-0 ♘hf6 11 h3 ∞/± Seirawan-Ardiansyah, Dubai Ol 1986

[25] 8 ... f5 9 0-0-0 ♗d7 10 ef gf 11 ♘h3 ♘df6 12 ♗g5 ± Möhring-Uhlmann, Leipzig 1975

[26] 9 ♗f2 ♕e7 10 0-0-0 f5 11 ♔b1 ♘d7 12 ef gf 13 ♘h3 e4!? ∞ Miles-van der Wiel, Wijk aan Zee 1987

[27] 13 ♘b5 ♘a6 14 ♖c1 ♗d7 15 ♘xc7 ♘xc7 16 b3 f5 ∞ Hölzl-Duriga, Vienna 1986

[28] 14 ♘d1 ♘b6 15 ♘e3 (15 ♘h3 f6 16 ♖g1 ♗d7 17 ♘e3 ♖ae8! 18 ♖g2 ♖e7 ∞∞ Spycher-Piket, Groningen 1986-87) ± Karpov-Velimirović, 1976

[29] 8 ♗d3 b5! 9 ♘ge2 b4 (9 ... bc 10 ♗xc4 c5 11 0-0 ♘bd7 12 a3 ♖b8 13 b4 ∞ Ligterink-Spraggett, Wijk aan Zee 1985) 10 ♘b1 a5 11 a3 ♘a6 12 ab ♘xb4 13 dc ♕c7 14 ♘ec3 ♘xd3+ 15 ♕xd3 ♕xc6 = Speelman-Balashov, Taxco IZ 1985

[30] 9 ... a6 10 ♗d3 intending ♘ge2, 0-0 ±

9 ... ♘a6 10 0-0-0 ♗d7 11 ♔b1 ♘c5 12 ♘ge2 b5 13 b4 ♘a4 14 ♘xa4 ba 15 ♘c3 ♘e8 16 ♗d3 ±/± Gheorghiu-Timman, Moscow 1981

9 ... ♘e8 10 g4! f5 11 gf gf 12 0-0-0 f4 13 ♗f2 ♘d7 14 ♔b1 ±/± Larsen-Donner, The Hague 1958

[31] 11 ♘c1 ♘h5 12 ♘d3 b5 13 0-0-0 ♘b6 14 ♘b4 ♗d7 ∓ Szabo-Petrosian, Amsterdam C 1956

[32] 12 ♗g5 hg 13 fg ♘c5 14 ♘g3 ♗xg4 15 b4 ∞ Botvinnik-Tal, match (10) 1960

[33] 14 ♔b1 ∞

[34] 6 ... a6 7 ♕d2 c6 8 0-0-0 b5 9 h4 ♕a5 10 ♔b1 ♖e8 11 ♗h6 ♗xh6 12 ♕xh6 ♘bd7 13 h5! ± Dorfman-Georgiev, Moscow 1985

6 ... ♘a6 7 ♕d2 c5 8 d5 ♘c7 9 a4 a6 10 a5 ♖b8 11 ♗d3 b5 12 ab ♖xb6 13 f4 h6 14 ♗h4 ± Tomoshchenko-Bastian, Baden-Baden 1985

[35] 7 ... ♘a6 8 ♕d2 ♘c7 9 a4 a6 10 ♗d3 ♖b8 11 a5 b5 12 ab ♖xb6 13 f4 ♗d7 14 ♘f3 ± Psakhis-Minić, Banja Luka 1985

7 ... h6 8 ♗e3 e6 9 ♕d2 ed 10 cd ♖e8 (10 ... ♔h7 11 ♘ge2 ♘bd7 12 ♘g3 a6 13 a4 ♘e5 14 ♗e2 ± Dorfman-Keene, Manila 1979) 11 ♘ge2 ♘bd7 12 ♘c1 a6 13 a4 h5 14 ♗e2 ♕a5 15 0-0 ♘e8 16 ♖a3 ± Rodriguez-Quinteros, Biel 1985

7 ... a6 8 a4 e6 9 ♕d2 ed 10 cd ♖e8 11 ♘ge2 ♘bd7 12 ♘g3 ♕a5 13 ♖a3! h5 14 ♗e2 ♘h7 15 ♗f4 ± Timoshchenko-Loginov, USSR 1984

[36] 9 ♘ge2 ed 9 cd a6 (9 ... ♘a6 10 ♘g3 ♗d7 11 ♕d2 ♘c7 12 ♗e2 b5 13 ♘d1 ♕e7 14 0-0 ± Adorjan-Hazai, Hungary 1984) 10 a4 ♘bd7 11 ♘g3 ♖b8 (11 ... h6!? 12 ♗e3 h5 13 ♗e2 h4 14 ♘f1 ♘h7 15 h3 ± Spassov-Belov, Moscow II 1985) 12 ♗e2 ♕d7 13 0-0 c4 14 ♗e3 b5 15 ab ab 16 ♖a7 ± Chernin-Chekhov, USSR 1984

[37] 9 ♘xd5 ♗e6 10 ♘xf6+ ♗xf6 11 h4 b5 12 cb a6 13 ba ♖xa6 ∞∞ Djurić-Cebalo, Novi Sad 1985

[38] 11 ... ♖e8 12 ♘ge2 ♘bd7 13 ♘c1 ♘h7 14 ♗e2 ♘e5 15 0-0 g5 16 f4 ± Yusupov-Ermenkov, Tuniz Z 1985

[39] 13 ♘c1 ♘e5 14 ♗e2 f5 15 0-0 g5 ∞ Olafsson-Mortensen, Esbjerg 1985

[40] 14 ♗e2 ♖b8 15 0-0 ♘f6 16 b3 g5 17 ♘d3 ∞/± Adorjan-Mestel, Switzerland 1985

[41] 7 ... e5 8 d5 ♘a5 9 ♘c1 c5 10 ♕d2 a6 11 ♗e2 ♗d7 12 0-0 ♖b8 13 a4 ± Kallai-Uhlmann, Budapest 1985

[42] 8 ... ♗d7 9 h4 h5 10 ♕e3 b5 11 0-0-0 ♘a5 12 ♘f4 ♘h7 ∞ Kotronias-Gufeld, Athens 1985

[43] 9 0-0-0 b5 10 h4 e5 11 h5 ♕e8! ∞ Agdestein-Nunn, Norway 1983

9 d5!? ♘e5 10 ♘g3 c6 11 ♗e2 cd (11 ... b5 12 cb cd 13 ♗xf6 ♗xf6 14 ♘xd5 ♗g7 15 a4 ± Polugayevsky-Nunn, Plovdiv 1983) 12 cd b5 ∞/=

[44] Mestel-Gufeld, Hastings 1986-87

King's Indian IV 1 d4 ♘f6 2 c4 g6 3 ♘c3 ♗g7 4 e4 d6 5 f3 0-0 6 ♗e3 ♘c6

	7	8	9	10	11	12	13	14	15	
1	♘ge2[1]	♕d2[3]	h4[4]	0-0-0	♗h6	♕e3	d5	♘g3	♗d3	∞
	♖b8[2]	♖e8	h5[5]	a6	♗h8[6]	e5	♘a5	c5	b5![7]	
2	...	...	♖b1	h4	cb	d5	♘d4	♘cxb5	de	±
	...	...	a6[8]	b5[9]	ab	♘e5	♗d7	e6	fe[10]	
3	...	♕d2[11]	0-0-0[13]	g4[15]	d5	♘g3	c5	c6	♕xc3	=
	a6	♖b8[12]	b5[14]	e5	♘a5	♗d7	b4	bc	♘xc6[16]	
4	...	...	h4	h5[18]	d5[20]	♘g3	♘d1	♘f2	b3![22]	±
	...	...	b5[17]	e5[19]	♘a5	b4[21]	c6	♗d7		
5	...	...	...	0-0-0[23]	♘d5[24]	♘xf6+[25]	g4!	♘c3	gh	∞
	...	...	h5	b5	bc	♗xf6	♘b4!	♗e6![26]	c5[27]	
6	...	...	♘c1	♘b3[28]	♘xd4	♗e2[30]	♘c2	b3	0-0	=
	...	...	e5	ed	♘e5[29]	c5![31]	♗e6	♕a5	b5[32]	
7	...	...	...	d5	♘1e2[34]	♗xe2	0-0-0![36]	c5	♗f2	±
	...	...	...	♘d4[33]	♘xe2[35]	♘h5	f5	f4[37]	♗f6[38]	

[1] 7 ♕d2 a6 8 0-0-0 ♖b8 9 ♗h6 (9 h4 e5! 10 d5 ♘d4 11 ♘ge2 c5 12 dc bc 13 ♘xd4 ed 14 ♗xd4 ♗e6 ∞/∞ Afifi-Messa, Lucerne Ol 1982) 9 ... e5 10 ♘ge2 b5 11 h4 bc 12 ♗xg7 ♔xg7 13 h5 ♘g8 ∞ Razuvayev-Kupreichik, USSR 1974

[2] 7 ... e5 8 d5 ♘e7 9 g4 c6 10 ♘g3 ±

[3] 8 d5 ♘e5 9 ♘g3 c5! (9 ... a6 10 ♗e2 e6 11 f4 ♘eg4 12 ♗a7! ♖a8 13 ♗d4 ♗h6 14 e5 ± Knaak-Westerinen, Moscow 1982) =
   8 ♘c1 c5 9 ♘b3 ed 10 ♘xd4 ♖e8! 11 ♕d2 d5 12 cd ♘xd5 13 ♘xd5 ♘xd4 14 0-0-0 ♘e6 = Gligorić-Kavalek, Manila 1974

[4] 9 g3 a6 10 ♗g2 b5 11 cb ab 12 b3 b4 13 ♘a4 ♗a6 14 ♖c1 ♕d7 = Muller-Nogues, Hastings 1979-80
   9 0-0-0 a6 10 ♕e1 ♗d7 (10 ... b5 11 h4 h5 12 e5 ±/± Spassky-Keene, Dortmund 1973) 11 h4 h5 12 g4 hg 13 fg ♗xg4 14 e5 ♘h5 15 e6 fe 16 ♖g1 ♗f5 17 ♘g3 ∞ Ghitescu-Whiteley, Nice Ol 1974

[5] 9 ... a6 10 h5 b5 11 hg fg 12 ♗h6 ♗h8 13 cb ab 14 ♘f4 ± Raičević-Mestel, Hastings 1979-80

[6] 11 ... e5 12 ♗xg7 ♔xg7 13 d5 ♘e7 14 ♔b1 ♗d7 15 ♘c1 ± Ornstein-Dueball, Glucksberg 1977
   11 ... b5 12 g4 e5 13 d5 b4 14 dc bc 15 ♘xc3 hg 17 ♗g5 ± Begovac-Portisch, Sombor 1980

[7] 16 ♘f1 ♘d7 17 g4 ♘b6 18 gh ♘bxc4 19 ♕g1 ♘h7 20 hg+ fg ∞ Barden

[8] 9 ... a5 10 g3 e5 11 d5 ♘e7 12 ♗g2 c6 Petrosian

[9] 10 ... ♗d7 11 g3! ± Gresch-Veroci, Budapest 1977

[10] 10 ♗e2 ± Polugayevsky-Gufeld, USSR Ch 1975

[11] 8 ♖b1 b5 9 cb ab 10 d5 ♘e5 11 ♘d4 e6! 12 de fe 13 ♘dxb5 ♘h5 ∞ Boleslavsky
   8 ♘c1 e5 9 d5 ♘d4 10 ♘b3 ♘xb3?! (10 ... c5!? 11 dc bc 12 ♘xd4 ed 13 ♗xd4 ♖b8 14 ♕d2 ♕a5 15 ♖c1 ♖d8! = A.Rodriguez-Kuzmin, Minsk 1982) 11 ♕xb3 c5 12 dc bc 13 0-0-0 ♕e7! 14 ♕h6 ♗b7 ∞ Timman-Kasparov, Moscow 1981
   8 a3 e5 (8 ... ♗d7 9 b4 ♕b8 10 g3! b5 11 c5 ± Karolyi-Coleman, London 1986) 9 d5 ♘e7 10 c5 ♘e8 11 ♕d2 f5 12 0-0-0 dc 13 ♗xc5 ♘d6 ∞ Agdestein-Nunn, Naestved 1985

[12] 8 ... ♖e8 9 ♘c1 e5 10 d5 ♘d4 11 ♘1e2 c5 12 dc ♘xc6 13 ♘d5 b5! ∞ Belyavsky-Kasparov, Moscow 1981

[18] 9 ♖b1 b5 (9 ... ♗d7 10 b4 ♕e8 11 b5 ♘a5 12 ♘f4 c6 13 b6 ± Gulko-Kupreichik, USSR Ch 1985) 10 cb ab 11 b4 e5 12 d5 ♘e7 13 g4 c6 ∞/=
   9 d5 ♘a5 10 ♘g3 c5 11 ♖c1 ♗d7 12 ♗d3 b5 = Lutikov-Gufeld, USSR 1980
   9 a3 ♗d7 10 b4 b5 11 cb ab 12 d5 ♘e5 13 ♘d4 c6 ∞/=
   9 ♗h6 b5 (9 ... ♗xh6! 10 ♕xh6 e5 11 0-0-0 b5 12 h4 ed 13 ♘xd4 ♘xd4 14 ♕xd4 ♕e7 = Razuvayev-Rashkovsky, USSR 1979) 10 h4 e5 11 ♗xg7 ♔xg7 12 h5 ♔h8 13 ♘d5 bc 14 hg fg 15 ♕h6 ♘h5 16 g4 ♖xb2! ∞ Bagirov-Gufeld, USSR 1973

[14] 9 ... ♗d7 10 ♗h6 b5 11 h4 e5 12 ♗xg7

♔xg7 13 gh ± Benko-Harris, USA 1968

[15] 10 h4 e5 11 d5 ♞a5 12 ♞g3 b4 ∞ Knaak-Gufeld, Jurmala 1978

[16] Kraidman-Portisch, Manila 1974

[17] 9 ... e5!? 10 d5 ♞a5 11 ♞g3 c5 12 h5 ♝d7 13 ♝h6 ♝xh6 14 ♛xh6 b5 15 ♝e2 ♛e7 ∞/= Gheorghiu-Andersson, Las Palmas 1972

[18] 10 cb ab 11 ♝h6 e5 12 ♝xg7 ♔xg7 13 h5 ♛e7 ∞ Sherbakov-Zhelnin, USSR 1976

[19] 10 ... bc 11 hg fg 12 ♞f4 ± Romanishin-Tseshkovsky, Vilnius 1975

[20] 11 0-0-0!? ed 12 ♞xd4 ♞xd4 13 ♝xd4 ♝e6 14 ♞d5 ∞/± Ree-Mortensen, Malta Ol 1980

[21] 12 ... bc?! 13 0-0-0 ± Timman-Kasparov, Bugojno 1982

[22] Petursson-Sznapik, Ljubljana 1981

[23] 10 ♞d5 b5 (10 ... ♞h7 11 g4 hg 12 h5 e6 13 ♞dc3 gf 14 hg fg 15 ♞f4 ♞d4 16 0-0-0 ±/± Petursson-Westerinen, Gausdal 1985) 11 cb ab (11 ... ♜xb5?! 12 ♞ef4 ♜b8 13 ♜c1 ♝d7 14 ♞xf6+ ♝xf6 15 ♞d5 ♝g7 16 ♝g5 ±/± Murei-Nunn, London 1983) 12 ♜c1 ♝d7 13 ♞xf6+ ef! =

10 ♝h6 ♝xh6 (10 ... b5 11 ♝xg7 ♔xg7 12 0-0-0 e5 13 cb ab 14 de ♞xe5 15 ♞f4 ± Rivas Pastor-Mestel, Marbella Z 1982) 11 ♛xh6 e5 12 0-0-0 ed 13 ♞xd4 ♞xd4 14 ♜xd4 ♛e7 15 g4 ♛e5 16 ♜d2 ♝e6 ∞ Gligorić-Cigan, Portorož 1985

[24] 11 ♝h6 e5 12 ♝xg7 ♔xg7 13 de ♞xe5 = Gligorić-Quinteros, Lone Pine 1980

11 ♞f4 bc (11 ... ♝d7 12 g4 ♞xd4! 13 ♝xd4 e5 14 ♝xe5 de 15 g5 b4 ∞ Ree-Nunn, Wijk aan Zee 1983) 12 ♝xc4 (12 g4) 12 ... e5! Ree-Mestel, Plovdiv 1983) 13 de ♞xe5 14 ♝b3 ♛e8! ∞ Didishko-Gelfand, Minsk 1986

[25] 12 g4 ♞xd5 13 cd ♞b4 14 ♞c3 c6 15 ♝xc4 cd 16 ♝b3 ♛b6! ∞/= Kuligowski-Nunn, Wijk aan Zee 1983

[26] 14 ... c5 15 ♝xc4 cd 16 ♝xd4 ♛c7 17 ♝b3 ♝xd4 18 ♛xd4 ♝e6 ± Schmidt-Sznapik, Prague Z 1985

[27] 16 hg ♛a5 17 a3 ∞

[28] 10 de ♞xe5 =

[29] 11 ... ♞xd4 12 ♝xd4 c5!? 13 ♝e3 b5 14 cb ab 15 ♝xb5 d5 16 ♞xc5 de 17 ♜d1! ± Andrianov-Chiburdanidze, USSR 1981; 12 ... ♝e6 13 ♝e2 c5 14 ♝e3 b5! ∞ Ledić-Chiburdanidze, Vinkovci 1982

11 ... ♝d7 12 ♝e2 ♞h5 13 ♞xc6 bc 14 ef gf 15 0-0 ♛e8 = Didishkov-Yuferov, Minsk 1979

[30] 12 ♜d1 c5 13 ♞c2 ♝e6 14 ♛xd6 ♛xd6 15 ♜xd6 ♞xc4 =

[31] 12 ... c6 13 ♜d1! b5 14 cb ab 15 b4 ♝d7 16 0-0 ± Pachman-Ciocaltea, Havana Ol 1966

[32] 16 cb ab 17 ♜fd1 ♜fe8! = Belyavsky-Gufeld, USSR 1979

[33] 10 ... ♞e7 11 b4 ♞e8 12 ♝e2 f5 13 0-0 f4 14 ♝f2 g5 15 e5 ± Huerta-Pecorelli, Bayamo 1985

[34] 11 ♞b3 ♞xb3 12 ab c5 13 g4 (13 ♝d3 ♞d7 14 g4 ♛h4+ =) 13 ... h5 14 h3 ♞h7 15 gh ♛h4+ 16 ♛f2 ♛xf2+ 17 ♔xf2 gh = Boleslavsky

[35] 11 ... c5 12 dc ♞xc6 13 ♜d1 ♝e6 14 ♞d5 ♞d7 15 g3 f5 16 ♝h3 ±/± Savon-Gufeld, USSR 1967

[36] 13 0-0 f5 14 c5 ♞f6 15 ♛c2 f4 16 ♝f2 g5! ∓ Boleslavsky

[37] 14 ... b6?! 15 cb! ♔h8 16 g3 f4 17 ♝f2 ♝f6 18 g4 ♞g7 19 h4 ±

[38] Kaufman-Morris, USA 1979

149

	6	7	8	9	10	11	12	13	14	
1	... ♘bd7[1]	♕d2 e5	d5 ♘c5	f3 a5	h4[2] c6[3]	g4[4] a4	h5 ♕a5	♘h3 cd	cd ♗d7[5]	±
2	... h6	♗e3 e5[6]	d5 c6[7]	dc[8] bc	♕d2 h5	♖d1 ♕a5	♗f3 ♗e6	b3 ♖d8	♘ge2 ♘a6[9]	∞
3	... c5	dc ♕a5	♗d2 ♕xc5	♘f3 ♗g4[10]	0-0 ♘bd7[11]	b3 a6	h3 ♗xf3	♗xf3 ♖ab8	♖c1 ♖fc8[12]	=
4	... ...	d5 b5!?[13]	cb a6	a4[14] ♕a5[15]	♗d2 ♕b4[16]	♕c2[17] ab	♗xb5 ♗a6	f3 ♗xb5	♘xb5 ♕xb5[18]	∞∞
5	... ...	... e6	♕d2[19] ed	ed ♖e8[20]	♘f3 ♗g4	0-0 ♘bd7	h3 ♗xf3	♗xf3 a6	a4 ♕b6[21]	±

	8	9	10	11	12	13	14	15	16	
6	♗e3[22] e6	♕d2[23] ed	ed[24] ♔h7	h3 ♖e8[25]	♗d3[26] ♘a6[27]	♘f3 ♘b4	♗b1 ♗f5	a3 ♗xb1	♖xb1 ♘a6[28]	=
7	♗f4 e6	de ♗xe6	♗xd6[29] ♖e8	♘f3 ♘c6[30]	0-0 ♘d4	e5[31] ♘d7	♘xd4 cd	♕xd4[32] ♘xe5	♗xe5 ♕xd4[33]	±

1 6 ... c6 7 ♕d2 a6 8 ♘f3 b5 9 a3 bc 11 ♗xc4 ♘xe4 12 ♘xe5 d5 13 ♗d3 de 14 ♗xe4 ± Tukmakov-Utasi, Szirak 1985; 8 a4 ±

2 10 0-0-0 ♗d7 11 ♔b1 ♕e8 12 g4 ♘a4 13 ♘xa4 ♗xa4 14 ♖c1 c5 15 h4 ± Alburt-Cebalo, Taxco IZ 1985

3 10 ... ♕e8 11 g4 h5 12 0-0-0 hg 13 ♗xf6 ♗xf6 14 fg ♕e7 15 g5 ♗g4 16 ♘f3 ± Lerner-Georgadze, Moscow 1985

4 11 h5 cd 12 cd ♗d7 13 g4 a4 14 ♘h3 ∞/± Alburt-Spraggett, Taxco IZ 1985

5 15 ♗f2 b5 16 ♘cd1 ± Fedorowicz-Kr. Georgiev, Dubai Ol 1986

6 7 ... c5 and now:
   8 dc ♕a5 9 ♗d2 ♕xc5 (9 ... dc 10 e5 ♘h7 11 f4 ♘c6 12 ♘f3 ♕d8 13 ♗e3 b6 14 0-0 ♕xd1 15 ♖axd1 ♗b7 16 ♗d3 ± Yakovich-Rashkovsky, USSR 1986) 10 ♘f3 ♗g4 11 ♖c1 ♘c6 12 ♗e3 ♕b4 13 ♕d2 ♗xf3 14 gf ♔h7 = Sanguinetti-Liberzon, Biel IZ 1976
   8 e5 de 9 de ♕xd1+ 10 ♖xd1 ♘g4 11 ♗xc5 ♘xc5 12 ♘d5 ♘a6 (12 ... ♘bc6 13 f4 ♘g4 14 h3 ♘f6 15 ♗f3! ±/± Shereshevsky-Dementiev, USSR 1976) 13 ♗xe7 ♖e8 14 b3 ♗f5 15 ♘h3 (15 ♔f1 ♘c6 16 ♗f6 ♘cb4 17 ♗xg7 ♔xg7 18 ♘f3 ∞ Agzamov-Yurtayev, Frunze 1985) 15 ... ♘c6 16 ♘f6+ ♗xf6 17 ∞/= Lputian-Chekhov, USSR 1986

7 8 ... ♔h7 9 g4 ♘e8 10 h4 c6 11 h5 g5 12 ♘h3 a6 13 f3 ± Hernandez-Pecorelli, Havana 1985
   8 ... ♘bd7 9 ♕d2 (9 g4 ♘c5 10 f3 a5! 11 h4 h5 12 g5 ♘h7 13 ♘h3 f6 ∓ Gunnarsson-Keene, Reykjavik 1976) 9 ... h5 10 f3 ♘h7 11 ♘h3 ♘c5 12 ♘f2 a5 13 0-0-0 b6 14 g4 hg 15 fg f5 16 gf gf 17 ef ♕h4 ∞ Polugayevsky

8 9 h4 h5 10 f3 a6 11 ♕d2 cd 12 cd b5 13 ♘h3 ♘bd7 14 ♘f2 ♘b6 ∞ Agzamov-Pähtz, Potsdam 1985

9 Portisch-Cigan, Portorož 1985

10 9 ... b6!? 10 0-0 ♗b7 11 ♗e3 ♕c7 12 ♘d2 ♘bd7 13 ♖c1 e6 14 f3 ♖ad8 ∞ Nieves-Ree, Madrid 1982

11 10 ... ♗xf3 11 ♗xf3 ♘c6 12 ♗e2 ♘d7 13 ♖c1 a6 14 b3 ♖ac8 15 ♗e3 ♗d4! = Fuller-Evans, Haifa Ol 1976

12 15 ♗e3 ♕a5 = Adamski-Hazai, Vrnjačka Banja 1985

13 7 ... a6 8 a4 ♕a5 9 ♗d2 e6 10 ♘f3 ed 11 ed ♗g4 (11 ... ♕c7!?) 12 0-0 ♘bd7 13 h3 ♗xf3 14 ♗xf3 ♕c7 15 ♖e1 ♘e8 16 ♕c2 ± Agzamov-Szekely, Frunze 1985; 11 cd ♖e8 12 0-0 ♕c7 13 ♕c2 ♗g4 14 h3 ♗xf3 15 ♗xf3 ♘db7 16 a5 c4! = Gligorić

14 9 ♕d2!? ♕a5 10 f3 ∞/± Forintos-Reshevsky,

Dubna 1979

15 9 ... h6 10 ♗d2 e6 11 de ♗xe6 12 ♘f3 ab 13 ♗xb5 ♘a6 14 0-0 ♘c7! 15 ♖e1 ∞ Tukmakov-Kasparov, USSR Ch 1981

16 10 ... ♘bd4?! 11 ♖a3! ± Kasparov-Spassky, Tilburg 1981

17 11 ♕e1!?; 11 f3!?

18 15 ab ♖xa1+ 16 ♘c1 ♘bd7 ∞

19 8 ♘f3 ed 9 ed h6 11 ♗e3! – 7 ... h6

20 9 ... ♕b6 10 0-0-0 (10 ♘f3 ♗f5 11 0-0 ♘e4 12 ♘xe4 ♗xe4 = Meduna-Zaichik, Brussels 1979) ±

21 14 ... ♕e7 15 ♖ae1 ♕f8 16 ♗d1 ± Uhlmann-Gligorić, Hastings 1970-71
   14 ... ♕b6 15 ♕c2 h5 16 ♖ae1 ♘h7 17 ♗d2 ± Lukacs-Damljanović, Vrnjačka Banja 1985

22 8 ♗d2 c6 9 ♘f3 ed 10 ed ♘a6 11 0-0 ♗f5 12 ♕c1 ♔h7 13 ♘h4 ♗d7 = Lputian-Sax, Sarajevo 1985

23 9 h3 ed 10 ed ♖e8 11 ♘f3 ♗f5 12 g4 ♗e4 13 0-0 ♗xf3 14 ♗xf3 ♘bd7 15 ♗f4 ♘b6 = Averbakh-Geller, USSR 1974
   9 de ♗xe6 10 ♕d2 ♔h7 11 h3 ♘c6 12 ♘f3 ♕e7 13 0-0 ♖ad8 14 ♖ad1 ♖fe8 15 ♖fe1 ♕f8 = Donner-Gligorić, Amsterdam 1971

24 10 cd ♕e7 (10 ... ♖e8 11 f3 h5 12 ♗g5 a6 13 a4 ♕c7 14 ♖a3 ♘bd7 15 ♘h3 ♘e5 16 ♘f2 ♗d7 ∞ Fedorowicz-Grünfeld, USA 1985) 11 f3 h5 12 ♗g5 a6 13 a4 ♖e8 14 ♗d3 ♕f8 15 ♘ge2 ½-½ Browne-Nunn, Naestved 1985

25 11 ... ♘a6 12 ♘f3 ♗f5 13 ♗d3 ♕d7 14 0-0 ♖fe8 15 ♖fe1 ♘b4 16 ♗xf5 ♕xf5 17 a3 ♘c2! = Uhlmann-Fischer, Siegen Ol 1970

26 12 ♘f3 ♗f5 13 0-0 ♘e4 14 ♘xe4 ♗xe4 15 ♘e1 ♘d7 16 ♖c1 b5! ∞ Karlsson-Sznapik, Helsinki 1981

27 12 ... ♘bd7 13 ♘f3 ♘e5 14 ♘xe5 ♖xe5 15 0-0 a6 16 a4 ♘h5 17 ♖ae1 ± Belyavsky-Vogt, Sukhumi 1970

28 12 ♕d3 ♕e7 = Spassov-Ermenkov, Bulgarian Ch 1973

29 10 ♕d2!? ♕b6 11 ♗xh6 ♗xh6 12 ♕xh6 ♕xb2 13 ♖c1 ♘c6 14 h4 ∞ Gaprindashvili-Hartoch, Wijk aan Zee II 1987

30 11 ... ♕b6 12 e5!? (12 ♗xb8 ♖axb8 13 ♕e2 ♘h5 14 g3 ♗h3 15 ♘d2 ♘f6 ±) 12 ... ♘fd7 13 ♘b5 ♘e5 14 c5 d3! ∞ Uhlmann-Schmidt, Brno 1975

33 17 ♗xd4 ♗xd4 18 ♖ac1 ♖ad8 19 b3 ♗xc3 20 ♖xc3 ♖d2 21 ♗f3 ♖xa2 22 ♗xb7 ♖b8 23 ♗f3 (23 ♗c6 ♖a3 = Uhlmann-Schmidt, Polanica Zdroj 1975) 23 ... ♖a3 24 ♗d1 a5 25 ♖e3! (25 ♖c1 ♖c8 26 ♖e1 a4 27 ba ♖xc4 = Polugayevsky-Kasparov, Bugojno 1982) ± Barlov-Ramayrat, New York 1986

	6	7	8	9	10	11	12	13	14	
King's Indian VI				**1 d4 ♘f6 2 c4 g6 3 ♘c3 ♗g7 4 e4 d6 5 ♘f3 0-0 6 ♗e2[1]**						
1	...	0-0	♕c2[3]	♖d1	e5	♗f4	♗xc4	♗b3	♕e2	±/±
	c6[2]	a6	b5	♘bd7	♘e8	bc	♘b6	♗g4	♘c7[4]	
2	...	0-0[5]	d5	♗f4[7]	h3	de	♗xd6	♗xc5	♗d4	±/±
	c5	♘c6[6]	♘a5	a6	e5[8]	♗xe6	♖e8	♕c8	♗xc4[9]	
3	...	de[10]	♕xd8	♗g5	♘d5[12]	cd	♗c4	♗xd5	♘d2[15]	±/=
	e5	de	♖xd8	♖e8[11]	♘xd5	c6	cd[13]	♘d7[14]	♘b6[16]	
4	...	♗e3	♗g5	♗c1[18]	h3	0-0	♗e3	c5	cd	±
	...	♘g4[17]	f6	♘c6[19]	♘h6[20]	♘f7[21]	♔h8	f5	♘xd6[22]	
5	...	...	d5[23]	♗g5	♗h4	♘d2[26]	a3	b3	h3	=
	...	♕e7	♘g4[24]	f6	h5[25]	a5	♗d7[27]	♘a6	♘h6[28]	

[1] 6 ♗e3 e5 7 de de 8 ♕xd8 ♖xd8 9 ♘d5 ♖d7 10 ♘xf6+ ♗xf6 11 c5 ♖d8 12 ♗c4 ± Rivas Pastor-Kristiansen, Linares 1985; 6 ... ♘bd7 intending ... c5

[2] 6 ... ♘c6 7 d5 ♘b8 (7 ... ♘b4 8 0-0 ♗g4 9 ♗e3 c5 10 h3 ♗xf3 11 ♗xf3 ♘a6 12 ♕d2 ± Dorfman-Karasev, USSR 1975) 8 0-0 e6 9 ♗g5 h6 10 ♗h4 ed 11 cd ♖e8 12 ♘d2 c6 13 ♖c1 a6 14 ♗g3 ± Toran-Westerinen, Malaga 1967

6 ... ♘bd7 7 e5 de 8 de ♘g4 9 e6 fe 10 0-0 ♘de5 11 ♗g5 ♘xf3+ 12 ♗xf3 ♘e5 13 ♗e2 ♗d7 14 ♕d2 ♗f6 15 ♖ad1 ½-½ Maroczy-Kindermann, Budapest 1985; 7 0-0 ±

[3] 8 h3!? b5 9 e5 ♘e8 10 ♗f4 ♘d7 11 ♕d2 ♗b7 12 ed ed 13 ♖ad1 ± Hort-Westerinen, Nice Ol 1974

8 a4 a5 9 h3 ♘a6 10 ♗e3 ♘d7 11 ♕d2 ♖e8 12 ♖ad1 ♕c7 13 ♘h2! ± Ungureanu-Taimanov, Bucharest 1973; 11 ... e5!?

8 e5 ♘e8 9 ♗f4 b5 10 ♖e1 f6 11 ed ed 12 h3 ♔h8 13 ♖c1 g5 14 ♗e3 h6 15 b4 a5 16 a3 ab 17 ab bc 18 d5! ±/±

[4] 15 h3 ♗f5 16 ♗g5 ♘bd5 17 ♗g3 ±/± Lein-London, USA 1985

[5] 7 d5 e6 8 0-0 ♖e8 9 ♗f4! ed 10 ed ♘e4 11 ♘xe4 ♖xe4 12 ♕d2 ± Sosonko-Keene, Hastings 1975-76

[6] 7 ... ♘a6 8 d5 ♘c7 9 ♗f4 (9 ♗g5 h6 10 ♗f4 g5 11 ♗d2 e6 12 h4 gh 13 ♕c1 ∞ Belov-Tseshkovsky, Moscow 1985) 9 ... a6 10 a4 b6 11 h3 ♗d7 12 e5 ♘fe8 13 ♕d2 ± Sofrevski-Velimirović, Skopje 1976

[7] 9 h3 e6! (9 ... e5 10 ♗g5 h6 11 ♗d2 ♘e8 12 ♘e1 f5 13 ef gf 14 ♘c2 b6 15 ♕e1 ♗d7 16 ♔h2 ± Groszpeter-Maroczy, Budapest 1985) 10 ♗g5 h6 11 ♗e3 ed 12 ed a6 13 a3 ♘e8 14 ♖c1 b5 ∞ Dorfman-Tseshkovsky, Tashkent 1980

[8] 10 ... ♖b8 11 e5 ♘e8 12 ♕d2 ±/±

[9] 15 ♗xc4 ♕xc4 16 ♗xf6 ♗xf6 17 ♘d5 ±/± Adamski-Perenyi, Budapest 1978

[10] 7 ♗g5 h6 8 ♗xf6 ♕xf6 9 ♘d5 ♕d8 10 de de 11 0-0 ♘c6 12 c5 ∞ Orlov-Sahović, Yugoslavia 1985

[11] 9 ... ♘bd7 10 0-0-0 ♖f8 11 ♘e1 ♘c5 (11 ... c6 12 ♘c2 ♘c5 13 f3 ± ECO) 12 f3 c6 13 ♘c2 a5 14 ♗e3 ♘fd7 15 b3 ♖e8 16 ♖d2 ♗f8 17 ♖hd1 f6 18 ♔b2 ♘b6 19 ♗f1 ± H.Olafsson-Kristiansen, Denmark 1985; 11 ♘d2!? c6 12 b4 a5 13 a3 ± Andersson-Balashov, Moscow 1981

9 ... ♘a6 10 ♘d5 (10 0-0 ♖e8 11 ♖ad1 h6 12 ♗c1 c6 = Pilarte-A.Rodriguez, Havana 1983) 10 ... ♖d6 11 ♗xf6 ♗xf6 12 ♗xf6+ ♖xf6 13 ♘xe5 ♗e6 14 f4 ♖e8 15 0-0-0 ± D.Gurevich-Murei, Brighton 1982

[12] 10 ♖d1 h6 11 ♗xf6 ♗xf6 12 ♘d5 ♗d8 13 ♘xe5 ♖xe5 14 ♘b6 ab 15 ♖d8+ ♔g7 16 ♖xc8 ♖xa2! =

10 0-0-0 h6 11 ♗e3 c6 12 ♘e1 ♗e6 13 f3 ♗f8 14 b3 ♘a6 15 ♘c2 ♔g7 16 ♖d2 ♘d7 17 ♖hd1 ♘b6 18 ♔b2 ♘c5 19 g3 a5 = Nei-Tal, Tallinn 1973

[13] 12 ... b5 13 ♗b3 ♗b7 14 ♖c1 a5 (14 ... ♖c8 15 ♗e3 a5 16 a3 a4 17 ♗a2 ∞/±) 15 a3 ♖a6 16 0-0 a4 17 ♗a2 ♗d7 18 dc ♖xc6 19 ♖xc6 ♗xc6 20 ♖c1 ± Miles-Marjanović, Bled 1979

[14] 13 ... h6 14 ♗e3 ♘d7 15 ♘d2 ♘f6 16 ♗b3 ♗e6 17 f3 b6 18 ♗xe6 ♖xe6 19 ♖c1 ♖d8 20 ♔e2 ± Grünberg-Vogt, East Germany 1980

13 ... ♘a6 14 ♔e2 ♘b4!? (14 ... ♘c7 15 ♗b3 ♗e6 16 ♖hd1 ♗xb3 17 ab ♘e6 18 ♗e3 ± Andersson-Biyiasas, Hastings 1980-81) 15 ♗c4 ♗g4 16 ♖hc1 ♖ac8 17 ♗b5 ♖xc1 18 ♖xc1 ♖c8 19 ♖xc8 ♗xc8 20 a3 a6 ∞/= Lengyel-Uhlmann, Budapest 1985

[15] 14 0-0-0!? h6 15 ♗h4 ♘b6 16 ♗b3 ♗g4

17 ☒d3 ☒ac8 18 ♔b1 a5 19 a3 a4 20 ♗a2 ±/=
Georgiev-Uhlmann, Szirak 1985
[16] 14 ... ♗f8 15 ☒c1 h6 16 ♗e3 ♘f6 17 ♗b3
♘g4 18 ♗c5 ♗e6 19 ♗xe6 ☒xe6 19 ♔e2 ±
Andersson-Sigurjonsson, Munich 1979
14 ... ♘b6 15 ♗b3 ♗e6 16 ♔e2 ♗f8
17 ☒hc1 ±/= Andersson-Byrne, Sao Paulo 1979
[17] 7 ... e6 8 ♘xd4 ☒e8 9 f3 c6 10 ♕d2 (10 ♗f2
d5 11 ed cd 12 0-0 ♘c6 13 c5 ♘h5 14 ♕d2 ♗e5
15 g3 ♘g7!? 16 ☒fe1 ♘e6! = Hort-Gligorić,
Tilburg 1977) 10 ... d5 11 ed cd 12 0-0 dc
13 ♗xc4 a6 14 ☒ad1 ± Gheorghiu-Browne,
USA 1971
7 ... h6 8 h3 (8 de ♘g4 9 ♗f4 ♘xe5 10 ♕d2
♔h7 11 ♘d4 ♘bc6 12 ♗e3 ♘xd4 13 ♗xd4 e5
14 ♗e3 ♗e6 ∞ Speelman-Kindermann, Switzerland 1985) 8 ... ed 9 ♘xd4 ☒e8 10 ♕c2 ♕e7
11 ♗d3 ♘a6 12 ♕d2 ♘c5 13 f3 ♘xd3+
14 ♕xd3 ± Portisch-Nunn, London 198?
7 ... ♗g4 8 d5 ♘fd7 9 0-0 f5 10 ♘g5 f4
11 ♗xg4 ♕xg5 12 ♗d2 h5 13 ♗e6+ ♔h8
14 b4 ± Damljanović-Kobas, Novi Sad 1985;
8 ... ♘g4 9 ♗c1 f5 10 0-0 ♘d7 11 g3! ± Lukacs
7 ... ♘c6 8 d5 ♘e7 9 ♘d2 c5 (9 ... ♘d7
10 b4 f5 11 f3 a5 12 ba ☒xa5 13 ♘b3 ☒a8
14 c5 ± Magerramov-Lechtynsky, Baku 1980)
10 g4 ♘e8 11 g5 ♗h3 12 ☒g1 a6 13 a4 ☒b8
14 ♗g4 ♗xf4 15 ♕xg4 b6 16 ☒b1 ± Portisch-
Andersson, Siegen Ol 1970
[18] 9 ♗h4 ♘c6 10 d5 ♘e7 11 ♘d2 ♘h6 12 f3

c5 13 ♗f2 (13 a3 g5 14 ♗f2 f5 15 b4 b6 16 bc
bc 17 ☒b1 ♘g6 = Damjanović-Hazai, Vrnjačka
Banja 1985) 13 ... f5 14 ♘f1 f4 15 g4 g5 16 h4
gh 17 ♗xh4 ♔h8 ∞/= Sahović-Hazai, Niš 1985
[19] 9 ... f5 10 ♗g5! ♕e8 11 de ♘xe5 12 ♘xe5
♕xe5 13 ef ♕xf5 14 ♗e3 ♘c6 15 ♕d2 ±
Reshevsky-Byrne, Chicago 1973
[20] 10 ... ed 11 ♘xd4 ♘xd4 12 ♕xd4 ♘e5
13 ♕d5+ ♔h8 14 0-0 ± Hort-Sigurjonsson,
Reykjavik 1978
[21] 11 ... ♔h8 12 ♗e3 ed 13 ♘xd4 f5 14 ♘xc6
bc 15 ♕d2 ±
[22] 15 ♘xe5 ♘xe5 16 de ♘xe4 (Miles-Hort,
Tilburg 1977) 17 ♘xe4 fe 18 ♕c2 ±
[23] 8 de de 9 0-0 c6 10 ♕c2 ♘g4 11 ☒fd1 ♘a6
12 ☒d2 ♗xf3 13 ♗xf3 ♘c5 14 ☒ad1 ♘e6 =
Karpov-Quinteros, Malta Ol 1980
[24] 8 ... a5 9 ♘d2 h5 10 f3 ♘h7 11 a3 f5 12 b4
♘d7 13 0-0 f4 14 ♗f2 g5 ∞ Donner-Kavalek,
Amsterdam 1969
[25] 10 ... ♕e8 11 h3 ♘h6 12 g4 a5 13 g5 fg
14 ♗xg5 ♘a6 15 ♕d2 ♘f7 16 ♗e3 ♘c5 17 0-0-0
c6 ∞ Tal-Sax, Malta Ol 1980
[26] 11 h3 ♘h6 12 ♘d2 a5! = Kasparov-
Chiburdandidze, Baku 1980
[27] 12 ... ♘h6 13 f3 ♘f7 14 ♗d3 ♗h6 15 ♕e2
♘d7 16 ♗c2 ± Smejkal-Moles, Skopje Ol 1972
12 ... ♘a6!?
[28] 15 f3 ♘f7 16 ♕b1 ♘h6 17 ♗f2 f5 = Ivkov-
Torre, Manila 1973

| King's Indian VII | 1 d4 ♘f6 2 c4 g6 3 ♘c3 ♗g7 4 e4 d6 5 ♘f3 0-0 6 ♗e2 ♗g4 | | | | | | | |

	7	8	9	10	11	12	13	14	15	
1	0-0	♗e3[2]	d5	♘e1	♕xe2	f3	♗f2	♘b5	♘d3	±
	e5[1]	♘fd7[3]	a5[4]	♗xe2	f5	f4	♗f6	♘a6	☒f7[6]	

---

[1] 7 ... c6 8 ♗e3 ♘bd7 9 ♘d2! (9 h3 ♗xf3
10 ♗xf3 e5 11 d5 cd 12 cd a6 ∞ Gufeld) 9 ...
♗xe2 10 ♕xe2 e5 11 d5 c5 12 ☒ab1 ♘e8 13 f3
f5 14 b4 ± Petrosian-Simagin, Moscow 1956
7 ... c5 8 ♗e3 (8 d5 ♘a6 9 ♗g5 ♘c7
10 ♘d2 ± Petrosian) 8 ... ♗f3 (8 ... cd!? Tisdall)
9 ♗xf3 cd 10 ♗xd4 ♘c6 11 ♗e3 ♕a5 12 a3
♘e5 13 ♗e2 ☒fc8 14 b4 ± Kapengut-Peev,
Lublin 1973
7 ... ♘c6 8 ♗e3 (8 d5 ♗xf3 9 ♗xf3 ♘e5
10 ♗e2 c6 11 ♗e3 ♕a5 ∞ Kouatly-Spassky,

Toluca IZ 1982) ±
[2] 8 d5 a5 (8 ... ♘fd7 9 ☒b1 a5 10 a3 ♘a6
11 b4 ±) 9 ♗g5 h6 10 ♗e3 ♘a6 11 ☒b1 ±
Gavrikov-Sugulski, Naleczow 1984
[3] 8 ... ♘bd7 9 ☒b1 c6 10 d5 cd 11 cd ♘c5
12 ♘d2 ±
[4] 9 ... f5 10 ef gf 11 ♘g5 f4 12 ♗xg4 ♕xg5
13 ♗d2 ±
[5] 12 ... ♘a6 13 ♘d3 b6 14 a3 ±
[6] 16 a3 ± Antunac-Andersson, Wijk aan Zee
1970

153

1 d4 Nf6 2 c4 g6 3 Nc3 Bg7 4 e4 d6 5 Nf3 0-0 6 Be2 Bg4

	7	8	9	10	11	12	13	14	15	
2	0-0	Be3[7]	Ne1[8]	Nxe2	d5	Nd3	f3	Nc3	Bf2	±
	Nfd7	Nc6	Bxe2	e5[9]	Ne7	f5	Nf6	f4	g5[10]	
3	...	...	d5	a3	Rb1	Bxf3	b4[12]	ab	Be2	±
	...	e5	a5	Na6[11]	Bxf3	f5	ab[13]	Rf7	f4[14]	
4	h3	Bxf3	Be3[15]	Ne2[17]	d5	h4!	h5	Bd2	hg	±
	Bxf3	Nfd7	Nc6[16]	e5	Ne7	f5	f4	Nf6	hg[18]	
5	Be3	d5[20]	Bxf3	Be2	0-0	Rc1	dc[22]	Qb3	Rfd1	±
	Nc6[19]	Bxf3	Ne5	c6	Re8[21]	e6	Nxc6	Qe7	Red8[23]	
6	...	Ng1[24]	Ngxe2	0-0[26]	Qd2	f3	Nxd4	Rad1	Ndb5!	±
	Nfd7	Bxe2	e5[25]	a5[27]	Nc6	ed	Nc5	Ne6[28]	Re8[29]	
7	...	Rc1	d5	a3[31]	Rb1	Bxf3	b4	Bd2	ab	±
	...	e5	a5[30]	Na6[32]	Bxf3[33]	f5	f4	ab	Kh8[34]	

[7] 8 d5 Na6! 9 Be3 Nac5 10 Bd4 Bxf3 11 Bxf3 Bxd4 12 Qxd4 e5! ∓

[8] 9 d5 Bxf3 10 Bxf3 (10 gf!? Ncb8 11 Qd2 e5 12 f4 ef 13 Bxf4 Nc5 14 f3 a5 = Belyavsky-Tseitlin, USSR 1976) 10 ... Na5 11 Be2 Bxc3 12 bc e5 13 de fe 14 f4 Qe7 ∞ Cuellar-Tal, Leningrad IZ 1973

[9] 10 ... e6 11 Rc1 Qe7 12 d5 Nd8 13 Nd3 c5 14 a3 ±

[10] 16 c5 Ng6 17 Rc1 ± Rizen-Popović, Novi Sad 1977

[11] 10 ... f5 11 Ng5 Bxe2 12 Qxe2 Nc5 13 ef gf 14 f4 ±

[12] 13 ef gf 14 Be2 Qh4 15 f3 Rf6 ∓

[13] 13 ... b6 14 Bd2 Qe7 15 Qe2 Rf7 16 Nb5! ±/±

[14] 16 Bc1 h5 17 Qc2 Bf8 18 Nd1 ± Spiridonov-Peev, Bulgaria 1981

[15] 9 d5 Na6 10 Bd2 Nac5 11 0-0 a5 12 Re1 e5 = Sher-Kochiev, USSR 1976

[16] 9 ... e5 10 d5 f5 11 h4! Nf6 12 Qe2 f4 13 Bd2 c5 14 g4! ± Keene-Avner, Orebro 1968

[17] 10 d5 Na5 11 Be2 Nb6 12 Bd4 ± Panno-Hug, Biel 1977

[18] 16 g3 ± Keene-Fuller, Sydney 1979

[19] 7 ... Bxf3 8 Bxf3 e5 9 d5 Nbd7 10 g4! a6 11 h4 Rb8 12 h5 ± Panno

7 ... e5 8 d5 Nh5 9 g3 a5 10 h3 Bd7 11 Nd2 Nf6 12 g4! ± Henley-Taulbut, Mexico 1978

[20] 8 0-0 Nd7 (8 ... Re8 9 d5 Bxf3 10 Bxf3 Ne5 11 Be2 c6 12 Rc1 Na5 13 f3 Rab8 14 b3 ± Polugayevsky-Spassky, Toluca IZ 1982) 9 d5 Bxf3 10 Bxf3 Nce5 11 Be2 Nb6 12 Qb3 c6 13 Rac1 Nec7 14 Rfd1 e5 15 Qc2 ± Sahović-

Barlov, Valjevo 1984

[21] 11 ... Qc7 12 Rc1 (12 f4 Ned7 13 Rb1 e6 14 Kh1 ± Petursson-Angantysson, Reykjavik 1980) 12 ... Rfe8 13 h3 Ned7 14 Re1 ± Larsen-Spassky, Linares 1985

11 ... cd 12 ed Qe8 13 b3 Ng4 14 Bd2 ± Yrjölä-Barlov, Sochi 1984

[22] 13 f4 Nxc4! 14 Bxc4 ed ∞

[23] 16 Rd2 Rd7 17 Rcd1 Rad8 18 Qa3 ± Dorfman-Balashov, USSR Ch 1984

[24] 8 d5 Na6 9 Nd4 Bxe2 10 Qxe2 Nac5 11 h4 Nf6 12 f3 Qd7 ∞ Hort-Hug, Malta Ol 1980

8 Qd2 e5 9 d5 Bxf3 10 Bxf3 f5 11 ef gf 12 Bg5 Nf6 ∞ Gufeld

[25] 9 ... c5 10 0-0 cd 11 Nxd4 Nc6 12 Rc1 Rc8 13 b3 ± Nogueiras-Braga, Mexico 1980

[26] 10 d5 f5 11 f3 Bh6!

[27] 10 ... Nc6 11 f3 f5 12 ef gf 13 de de 14 c5! ±

[28] 14 ... Nxd4 15 Bxd4 Bxd4 16 Qxd4 ±

[29] 16 Qc1 ± Kasparov-Bukić, Banja Luka 1979

[30] 9 ... f5 10 Ng5 f4 11 Bxg4 Qxg5 12 h4 Qe7 13 Bd2 ± Ftacnik-Züger, Biel 1984

[31] 10 0-0 Na6 11 a3 Ndc5 12 Nd2 Bd7 13 Nd2 Bd7 14 b3 f5 15 f3 Bf6 16 Rb1 Bg5 ∞ Pribyl-Tseitlin, 1981

[32] 10 ... Bf6 11 b4 ab 12 ab Bxf3 13 Bxf3 Bg5 14 Bxg5 Qxg5 15 0-0 ± Gavrikov-Kaksov, USSR 1978

[33] 11 ... f5 12 b4! Bf6 13 0-0 ± Cvetković-Zügler, Lugano 1983

[34] 16 0-0 g5 17 Bg4 ± Pinter-Maroczy, Hungary 1980

King's Indian VIII		1 d4 ♘f6 2 c4 g6 3 ♘c3 ♗g7 4 e4 d6 5 ♘f3 0-0 6 ♗e2 e5						
	7	8	9	10	11	12	13	14	15
1	d5	♗g5[1]	♗h4	♗g3	h4[5]	♘d2[7]	ef	♗xg4	fg	∞
	♘bd7	h6[2]	g5[3]	♘h5[4]	g4[6]	f5	♘df6	♘xg3	♘xg4[8]	
2	...	♗g5[9]	♗h4[10]	♗g3	♘d2	♔f1!?[11]	♗g4	♗xc8	h4	±/∞
	c5	h6	g5	♘h5	♘f4	♘d7	♘f6	♖xc8	g4[12]	
3	...	♗g5[13]	♗h4	0-0	♘d2	f3	♖b1	b3	a3	=
	a5	h6	♕e8[14]	♘h5[15]	♘f4	♘a6	♗d7	f5	♘c5[16]	

[1] 8 ♗e3 ♘g4 9 ♗g5 f6 10 ♗h4 ♘h6 (10 ... h5 11 h3 ♘h6 12 g4 hg 13 hg g5 14 ♗g3 ♘xg4 15 ♘h2 ♘xh2 16 ♖xh2 ∞ Naranja-Planinc, Nice Ol 1974) 11 ♘d2 g5 12 ♗g3 f5 13 ef ♘f6 14 ♘de4 ♘xe4 15 ♘xe4 ♗xf5 16 ♗d3 g4 17 ♕d2 ♗xe4 18 ♗xe4 ♘f5 19 ♕d3 ♕g5 = Mecking-Gligorić, Palma de Mallorca IZ 1970

[2] 8 ... a5 9 ♘d2 h6 10 ♗e3 ♘e8 11 g4 (11 ♕c2 f5 12 f3 ♘c5 13 ♘b3 b6 14 ♘xc5 bc 15 0-0-0 ♕e7 16 ♗d3 f4 17 ♗d2± Visier-Olsson, Lugano Ol 1968) 11 ... b6 12 h4 ♘c5 13 h5 g5 14 f3 ♗d7 15 ♕c2 c6 16 0-0 cd 17 cd ♖c8 18 ♖fc1 ± Zinser-van Kleef, Strasbourg 1973

[3] 9 ... a5 10 ♘d2 ♘c5 11 g4 a4 12 f3 c6 13 ♗f2 ♕a5 14 ♖b1 ♗d7 15 0-0 cd 16 cd b5 17 a3 Mecking-Panno, Buenos Aires 1967

[4] 9 ... a6 10 ♘d2 ♕e8 11 0-0 (11 b4 ♘h7 12 f3 f5 13 ♗f2 ♕e7 14 ♕c1 h5 15 ♘b3 ♘df6 16 ♗d3 fe 17 ♘xe4 ♘xe4 18 ♗xe4 ∞/± Rogers-Kochiev, Tallinn 1985) 11 ... ♘h7 12 b4 ♘g5 (12 ... ♗f6 13 ♗xf6 ♘hxf6 14 ♘b3 ♕e7 15 ♕d2 ♔h7 16 ♕e3! ♘g8 17 c5 ± Tal-Fischer, Bled/Zagreb C 1959) 13 f3 f5 14 ♖e1 ♕e7 15 ♔h1 ♘f6 16 c5 ♘h5 17 c6! b6 18 ef gf 19 g3 ± Petrosian-Gligorić, Bled/Zagreb C 1959

[5] 10 ... ♘xe4 11 ♘xe4 f5 12 ♘fd2 fe 13 ♘xe4± Mikhalchishin-Kovacs, Debrecen 1967
10 ... ♘c5 11 ♘d2 a5 12 h4 ♘h7 13 ♘b3± Gligorić-Aloni, Netanya 1965

[6] 11 0-0 ♘f4 12 ♘e1 ♘xe2+ 13 ♕xe2 f5 14 ef ♘f6 15 ♘d3 ♗xf5 16 f3 ♕e8 = Boleslavsky

[7] 11 ... ♘xg3 12 fg hg 13 ♘xh4 ♕g5 14 ♗g4±/± Ivkov-Timman, Wijk aan Zee 1972
11 ... ♘f4 12 hg hg 13 ♕c2 f5 14 ef ♘c5 15 ♗xf4 ±/±

[8] 12 ♘h2 ♘xg3 13 fg h5 14 0-0 ♗h6 15 ♗d3 ♘c5 16 ♗c2 a5 17 ♕e2 f6 18 ♖f2 (Hort-Janošević, Wijk aan Zee 1970) 18 ... ♗d7 ∞ Hort

[8] 16 ♕xg4 ♗xf5 17 ♕e2 e4! 18 0-0 ♕d7 19 ♕e3 c5 ∞ Hort-Vogt, Leipzig 1973

[9] 8 0-0 ♘e8 9 ♘e1 ♗d7 10 ♘d3 f5 11 ef gf 12 f4 ♕e7 13 ♔h1 e4 14 ♘e1 ♘df6 15 ♘c2 ♕f7 16 ♘e3 ♕g6 = Gligorić-Quinteros, Leningrad IZ 1973

[10] 9 ♗d2 ♘h5 10 ♕c1 (10 g3!? ♘d7 11 ♕c2 ♘df6 12 h3 ♗d7 13 a4 ± Larsen-Quinteros, Mar del Plata 1981) 10 ... ♔h7 11 h4 ♘f4 12 ♗xf4 gf 13 ♕xf4 f5 14 ♕d2 ± Euwe

[11] 12 0-0 ♘xe2+ 13 ♕xe2 ♘d7 14 a3 ♖e8 15 f3 ♘f8 16 ♗f2 ♘g6 17 g3 ♘e7 18 b4 b6 19 ♖fb1 f5 = Ivkov-Korchnoi, Havana 1963

[12] 16 ♔g1 ±/∞ Kapengut-Abramasov, USSR 1966

[13] 8 27e3 ♘g4 9 ♗g5 f6 10 ♗h4 ♘a6 (10 ... ♕e8!? 11 ♘d2 f5 12 h3 ♘f6 13 g4 ♘xe4 14 ♘dxe4 fe 15 ♘xe4 ♘a6 16 f3 ∞ Djurić-Tringov, Vrnjačka Banja 1975; 10 ... ♘h6 11 ♘d2 ♘f7! = Hort) 11 ♘d2 ♘h6 12 f3 ♗d7 13 0-0 ♘f7 14 ♘b3 b6 15 ♘c1 ♘c5 16 ♘d3 ♕e8 17 b3 f5 = Gligorić-Geller, Belgrade 1970

[14] 9 ... g5 10 ♗g3 ♘h5 11 h4 g4 12 ♘d2 ♘xg3 13 fg h5 14 0-0 ♘h6 15 ♗d3± Mecking-Cuellar, Sousse IZ 1967
9 ... ♘a6 10 ♘d2 ♕e8 11 0-0 ♘h7 (11 ... ♗d7 12 b3 ♘h7 13 f3 h5 14 a3 ♗h6 15 ♔h1 ♗e3 16 ♖b1 ♘e5 17 ♕c2 f5 18 b4 ab 19 ab ♘a4 20 ef ± Zlotnik-Yuferov, USSR 1980) 12 a3 ♗d7 13 b3 ♗f6 14 ♗xf6 ♘xf6 15 ♕c2 b6 16 ♖ab1 ± Ivanchuk-Piket, Groningen 1986-87

[15] 10 ... ♘h7 11 ♘d2 ♗f6 12 ♗xf6 ♘xf6 13 b3 c5 14 dc ♘xc6 15 ♘f3 ♕e8 16 ♕d2 ♔g7 17 ♖fd1 ♖d8 18 ♖ac1 ± Lukacs-Uhlmann, Budapest 1985

[16] 16 ♔h1 ♗f6 17 ♗f2 h5 18 ♕c2 h4 19 ♗e3 ♗g5 = Stempin-Georgiev, Prague Z 1985

155

King's Indian VIII *continued*
1 d4 ♘f6 2 c4 g6 3 ♘c3 ♗g7 4 e4 d6 5 ♘f3 0-0 6 ♗e2 e5

	7	8	9	10	11	12	13	14	15	
4	0-0	♘xd4	f3	♔h1[18]	cd	♗g5	fe[20]	♘db5!	♗f4	±
	ed	♖e8	c6[17]	d5	cd	de[19]	♘bd7	♖e5	♘xe4[21]	
5	...	d5[22]	cd	♗g5	♗h4	♗g3	♘d2	♘c4!	f3	±
	c6	cd[23]	♘bd7[24]	h6	g5	♘h5	♘f4	♘f6	♕e7[25]	
6	...	♗e3[26]	♗g5	♗d2[28]	b4[30]	de[31]	♕b3	♖fd1	♗e3	±
	♘bd7	♘g4[27]	f6	♘h6[29]	♘f7	fe	h6	♔h7	c6[32]	
7	...	...	♕c2[33]	♗g5	♗d2[35]	ef	de	♘g5	♖ad1	∞/±
	...	c6	♘g4[34]	f6	f5[36]	gf	de	♘df6	♕e7[37]	
8	...	...	♕c2[38]	♗g5	♗h4[39]	♖ad1	♗g3	ef	♘xd4[41]	±
	...	a5	♘g4	f6	♘h6[40]	g5	f5	ed		
9	...	♖e1	♗f1[43]	♖b1[45]	d5	b3	dc	♕c2[48]	♗a3	±
	...	c6[42]	a5[44]	♖e8	♘c5	♗d7[46]	♗xc6[47]	♖c8	♕b6[49]	
10	...	...	...	...	♘xd4	f3[50]	♗f4!	cd	ed	±
	...	...	...	ed	♖e8	♘c5[51]	d5	♘xd5	♖xe1[52]	
11	...	...	...	♘xd4	♗f4[54]	♕c2	♘b3[55]	♗g3	♖ad1	∞/±
	...	...	ed	♖e8[53]	♘c5	♘g4	♘e6	♗e5	♕g5[56]	
12	...	♗e3	de[58]	♕xd8[59]	♗g5	♗d1	♗a4	♗e3		∞/±
	♘c6	♖e8!?[57]	de	♖xd8	♖d7!?	♘e8	f6	♖d6[60]		

[17] 9 ... ♘c6 10 ♗e3 ♘e5 11 ♕d2 c6 12 ♖ad1 a6 13 a4 ±/± Taimanov-Kupreichik, Jurmala 1978

[18] 10 ♘c2!? d5 11 cd cd 12 ed ♘a6 (12 ... ♗f5 13 ♘e3 ♗d7 14 ♔h1 ♘a6 15 ♗d2 ♕b6 16 ♘c4 ± Ribli-Gheorghiu, Baden 1981) 13 ♔h1 ♕b6 14 ♗c4 ±

[19] 12 ... ♘c6 13 ♗b5! ♕b6 14 ♘xc6 bc 15 ♗xf6 ♗xf6 16 ♘xd5 cd 17 ♗xe8 ± Tal

[20] 13 ♗c4!? h6 14 ♗h4 ♘c6 15 ♘xc6 bc 16 ♕a4 ±/± Didishko-Litvinov, Minsk 1973

[21] 16 ♗xe5 ♗xe5 17 ♘xe4 ♕h4 18 h3 ♕xe4 19 ♕b3 ± Tal-Spassky, Montreal 1979

[22] 8 ♗e3 ed 9 ♘xd4 (9 ♘xd4 ♖e8 10 f3 d5 =) 9 ... ♘bd7 10 ♕c2 ♕e7 (10 ... ♘bd7 11 ♖ad1 ♕e7 12 ♖fe1 c5 13 ♗e3 ♘xe4 14 ♘b5 ♘df6 15 ♗f4 ♗f5 ∞/± Vlam-Scheeren, Wijk aan Zee II 1983) 11 ♖fe1 c5!? 12 ♗e3 ♘xe4 13 ♘xe4 ♕xe4 14 ♕d2 ∞ Tal

8 ♖e1 ed 9 ♘xd4 ♖e8 10 ♗f1 ♘g4 11 h3 ♕f6 12 hg ♕xd4 13 g5 ♘d7 14 ♗e3 ± Rashkovsky-Szabo, Sochi 1973

[23] 8 ... c5 9 ♘e1! ♘bd7 (9 ... a6 10 ♗g5 h6 11 ♗e3! ♘bd7 12 a3 ♖e8 13 ♕d2 ♔h7 14 ♘d3 ± Trifunović-Toran, Palma de Mallorca 1966) 10 ♗g5 h6 11 ♗h4 a6 12 a3 ♕c7 13 b4 ± Donner-Kurajica, Wijk aan Zee 1970

[24] 9 ... ♘a6 10 ♘d2 ♘e8 11 ♘c4 f5 12 f3 f4 13 a4 g5 14 ♘b5 ♖f6 15 g4! ± Hübner-Kaplan, Houston 1974

[25] 16 ♗f2 ♗d7 17 a4 ± Geller-Puig, Oberhausen 1961

[26] 8 d5 ♘c5 9 ♕c2 a5 10 ♗g5 h6 11 ♗e3 b6 (11 ... ♘h5 12 g3 b6 13 ♘d2 ♗h3 14 ♖fe1 ♗d7 ∞ Hess-Lobron, Beer-Sheva Z 1985) 12 ♘d2 ♗g4 (12 ... h5 ∞) 13 f3 ♗d7 14 b3 ♘h5 15 g3 ½-½ Banas-Lanc, Trnava 1985

8 ♕c2 ed 9 ♘xd4 ♖e8 10 ♖d1 ♘c5 11 f3 ♘h5 12 g4 ♘f6 13 ♗g5 a5 14 ♘db5 h6 15 ♗h4 ♗d7 Bönsch-Vogt, Leipzig 1986; 10 ♗e3 ♘b6 11 ♖ad1 ± Lukacs-Vogt, Leipzig 1986

[27] 8 ... ♖e8 9 d5 ♘g4 10 ♗g5 f6 11 ♗h4 ♘f8 12 ♘d2 h5 13 ♗xg4 hg 14 f3 gf 15 ♕xf3 ± Najdorf-Geller, Moscow 1967

8 ... h6 9 de (9 h3 ed 10 ♘xd4 ♘c5 11 ♕c2 ♖c8 12 ♗f3 c6 13 ♖ad1 ♕e7 14 ♖fe1 ± Veingold-Yrjölä, Tallinn 1985) 9 ... de 10 ♘e1 ♘h7 11 ♕d2 ♘g5 12 ♖ad1 ♔h7 13 ♗g4 f5 14 ef ♗xf5 15 ♕c2 ± Cvitan-Lobron, Zagreb 1985

8 ... ♕e7 9 ♕c2 c6 10 ♖ad1 ♖d8 11 de de 12 ♘a4 ♘g4 13 ♗g5 f6 14 ♗d2 ♘f8 15 c5 ± Thorsteins-Bjarnason, Iceland 1985

[28] 10 ♗h4 c6 11 ♕c2 ♕e7 12 ♖ad1 h5 13 h3 ♘h6 14 b4 ♔h8 15 de de 16 c5 ∞/± Schmid-

Hausner, Trnava 1985

10 ♗c1 ♘h6 11 ♖b1 ♘f7 12 b4 c6 13 d5 c5 14 a3 b6 15 ♘e1 f5 16 ♘d3 ♘f6 17 ef ♗xf5 18 ♗e3 g5 ∞ Hansen-Bjarnason, Iceland 1985

[29] 10 ... c6 11 b4 f5 12 d5 f4 13 ♗c1 c5 14 ♘b5 ♘df6 15 ♘g5! ±/± Uhlmann-Knaak, Leipzig 1977

[30] 11 ♕c2 c6! (11 ... ed?! 12 ♘xd4 ♘e5 13 ♖ad1 f5 14 ♕c1! ± Spassov-Sahović, Vrnjačka Banja 1976) ∞ Gufeld

[31] 12 ♕b3 c6 13 ♖ad1 ♕e7 14 ♗e3 ± Miles-Ciocaltea, Montilla 1978

[32] 16 ♖d2 a5 17 b5 ± Alburt-Shirazi, US Ch 1985

[33] 9 d5 ♘g4 10 ♗g5 f6 11 ♗d2 f5 12 ♗g5 ♘df6 13 h3 ♘h6 14 dc bc ∞ Chekhov-Knaak, Potsdam 1985

[34] 9 ... ♕e7 10 ♖fe1 ed 11 ♗xd4 ♘e5 (11 ... ♘c5 12 ♘d2 ♖e8 13 ♖ad1 h5 ∞ Pinter-Tal, Moscow IZ 1982) 12 ♖ad1 ♘fd7 13 ♕d2 ♘c5 14 h3 ♘e6 =/± Olafsson-Hjartarson, Copenhagen 1985

[35] 11 ♗h4 h5! 12 h3 ♘h6 13 ♖ad1 g5 14 ♗g3 g4 ∞

[36] 11 ... ♕e7 12 ♖ad1 (12 d5 f5 13 ♘c1 ♘df6 14 f3 ♘h6 15 ♘d3 c5 16 ♘f2 f4 17 ♖ab1 g5 ∞ Bukić-Hausner, Banja Luka 1981) 12 ... ♘h6 13 ♗c1 f5 14 ef gf 15 ♖fe1 ±; 13 b4!?

[37] 16 a3 ♔h8 17 b4 ♗d7 18 ♕c1 ♖ad8 19 b5 ♕e8 20 bc bc 21 ♘a4 f4 ∞ Uhlmann-Knaak, Potsdam 1985

16 ♕c1 ♗d7 17 b4 ♔h8 18 f3 ♘h6 19 c5 ♘d5 20 a3 f4 21 ♘ge4 ∞/± Uhlmann-Knaak, Szirak 1985

[38] 9 de de 10 ♕c2 ♘g4 11 ♗d2! c6 12 ♘a4 h6 13 h3 ♘gf6 14 ♗e3 ± Uhlmann-Knaak, Leipzig 1980

[39] 11 ♗d2 ed 12 ♘xd4 ♘c5 13 ♘b3 (13 h3 f5! 14 hg ♗xd4 15 ef gf 16 ♗h6 fg! ∓ Miles-Cramling, Gausdal 1980) 13 ... ♘xb3 14 ab f5 15 ♗xg4 fg 16 ♘d5 c6 17 ♘e3 ♗e6 18 ♗c3 ♗e5 = R.Byrne-Vukčević, USA 1969

[40] 11 ... c6 12 ♖ad1 ♕e7 13 a3 ♘h6 14 ♗g3 ♘f7 15 ♖fe1 ± Hort

[41] Bukić-Ničevski, Yugoslavia 1980

[42] 8 ... ed 9 ♘xd4 ♘c5 10 f3 a5 11 ♘db5 ♘e8 (11 ... ♗d7 12 ♗e3 ♗xb5 13 ♘xb5 ♕e7 14 ♕d2 a4 15 ♖ad1 ♖fd8 16 ♗f1 ± Taimanov-Kestler, Hamburg 1965) 12 ♗e3 b6 13 ♕d2 ♗b7 14 ♖ad1 f5 15 ef ♖xf5 16 ♘d4 ± Nesis-Thiele, corr. 1985

8 ... ♖e8 9 d5 a5 10 ♗g5 h6 11 ♗h4 g5 12 ♗g3 ♘h5 13 ♘d2 ♘f4 14 ♗g4 ♘c5 15 ♗xc8 ♕xc8 16 ♘f1 ± Najdorf-Andersson, Wijk aan Zee 1971

8 ... h6 9 ♕c2! ♘h7 10 de de 11 ♗e3 ♖e8

[12] ♖ad1 ± Andersson-Kasparov, Moscow IZ 1982

[43] 9 ♖b1 ♖e8 (9 ... a5 10 b3 ed 11 ♘xd4 ♖e8 12 ♗f1 ♘g4 ∞) 10 ♗f1 ed 11 ♘xd4 ♘g4 12 h3 ♕b6 13 hg ♕xd4 ∞ Shabalov-Oll, USSR 1986

[44] 9 ... a6 10 ♖b1 b5 11 b4 ed 12 ♘xd4 ♗b7 13 ♗g5 ♕e7 14 ♖c1 ± Petursson-Angantysson, Iceland 1985; 10 ... ed 11 ♘xd4 ♖e8 12 ♗g5 h6 13 ♗h4 ♘e5 14 f4 ± Bjarnason-Soltis, New York 1985

9 ... ♘g4 10 h3 ed 11 ♘xd4 ♕b6 12 ♕xg4 (12 hg ♕xd4 13 ♗f4 ♕xd1 14 ♖axd1 ♘e5 15 g5 ♗e6 16 ♖d6 ♗c4 17 ♗c1 ♖fd8! = Dokhoyan-Romanishin, Irkutsk 1986) 12 ... ♗xd4 13 ♕e2 ♘e5 14 ♗h6 ♖e8 15 ♖ad1 ± Moskalenko-Monin, Pinsk 1986

9 ... ♕b6!?

[45] 10 de de 11 ♘a4 ♖e8 12 ♕c2 ♕e7 13 c5 ♗f8 14 ♗g5 h6 15 ♗e3 ♘g4 16 ♖ac1 ∞ Mochalov-Podgayets, USSR 1980

[46] 12 ... ♕c7 13 ♘d2 ♗g4 14 ♗e2! ♘d3 15 ♗xg4 ♘xg4 16 ♖f1 ± Timman-Sigurjonsson, Reykjavik 1978

[47] 13 ... bc 14 h3 ♕c7 15 ♗a3 ♘h5 16 ♘a4! ± Popov-Knaak, Polanica Zdroj 1976; 14 ... ♗f8!?

[48] 14 ♗d3!? Csom

[49] 16 ♖bd1 ♖cd8 17 ♕b1 ♗h6 18 h3 ♖f8 19 ♘d2 ♖c8 20 ♖c1 ± Knaak-Möhring, Leipzig 1975

[50] 12 ♗f4 ♘c5 13 ♕c2 ♘g4 14 ♖bd1 ♗e5 15 ♗xe5 de 16 ♘b3 ± Smejkal-Kochiev, Dortmund 1977

[51] 12 ... d5 13 cd cd 14 ♘db5! ±/±

[52] 16 ♕xe1 ♗xd4+ 17 ♗e3 ♗xe3+ 18 ♕xe3 ± Tal-Grigorian, USSR Ch 1977

[53] 10 ... ♘g4 – 9 ... ♘g4 (note 44)

[54] 11 ♖b1 a5 12 b3 ♘c5 13 f3 ♘h5 14 g4 ♘e6 15 ♗e3 ♘hf4 ∞ Kovačević-Rukavina, Novi Sad 1985

[55] 13 ♖ad1 ♗xd4! 14 ♖xd4 ♕f6 15 ♘e2 ♘xf2!? Gufeld

[56] 16 ♕d2 ∞ Cvitan-Morović, Bor 1985

[57] 8 ... ♘g4 9 ♗g5 f6 10 ♗c1 (10 ♗h4 ♔h8 11 de de 12 ♘d5 ♘e7 13 ♘d2 ♘h6 14 ♕c2 c6 15 ♘xe7+ ♕xe7 16 f3 ♘f7 ∞ Najdorf-Uhlmann, Moscow 1967) 10 ... ♔h8 11 d5 ♘e7 12 h3 ♘h6 13 b4 f5 14 ♗d2 ♘f7 15 a4 ♗h6 16 c5 ♗xd2 17 ♕xd2 f4 ∞ Chekhov-Uhlmann, Potsdam 1985

[58] 9 d5 ♘d4! 10 ♖e1 ♘xe2+ 11 ♕xe2 ♘g4 12 ♗g5 ∞

[59] 10 h3 ♗e6 11 c5 a6 12 ♕a4 ♕e7 13 ♖fd1 ♖ad8 14 ♗c4 ♘d4 = Garcia-Kasparov, Banja Luka 1979

[60] Chekhov-Ehlvest, Tallinn 1980

157

King's Indian IX   1 d4 ♘f6 2 c4 g6 3 ♘c3 ♗g7 4 e4 d6 5 ♘f3 0-0 6 ♗e2 e5 7 0-0 ♘c6 8 d5 ♘e7

	9	10	11	12	13	14	15	16	17	
1	b4	c5[2]	♗xf4	♖c1	♘d2[4]	♘c4	a4	cd	a5	∞
	♘h5[1]	♘f4	ef	h6[3]	g5	a6	♘g6	cd	♖e8[5]	
2	♗d2	♖c1	♕b3[8]	ef	♘g5	f4	fe	c5	♘xd5	∞
	♘e8[6]	f5[7]	b6	gf	♘f6[9]	h6	de	♘fxd5	♘xd5[10]	
3	♘d2	♖b1[12]	a3	b4	ab	f3	♕b3	♗a3	c5[16]	∞/=
	a5[11]	♘d7[13]	f5	ab[14]	♔h8[15]	f4	g5	♘f6		
4	...	♖b1[17]	b4	bc[19]	♗b2[21]	♗d3	♘e2	f4	♕e1	=
	c5	♘e8[18]	b6	dc[20]	♗d7	♘d6	f6	♕c7	♘f7[22]	
5	♘e1	f3	g4	♘d3[25]	♔g2[26]	♗e3	♕d2	♗xh6[27]		=
	♘d7[23]	f5	♔h8[24]	♘g8	a6	♗h6	♕h4	♘xh6		
6	...	♘d3	♗d2[28]	f3	c5	cd[30]	♘f2	h3	♕c2	±
	...	f5	♘f6[29]	f4	g5	cd	h5[31]	♘g6	♘e8[32]	

[1] 9 ... a5 10 ba ♖xa5 (10 ... c5!? 11 ♘d2 ♕xa5 12 ♘b5 ♕d8 13 ♗b2 ♘e8 14 a4 ♗h6 15 ♖a3 f5 ∞ Sosonko-Ligterink, Amsterdam 1979; 11 ♗d2 ±) 11 ♘d2 b6 12 ♘b3 ♖a8 13 a4 ± Schmidt-Atanasov, Leipzig 1973
     9 ... ♘e8 10 ♘d2 f5 11 c5 ♘f6 12 f3 f4 13 ♘c4 g5 14 a4 ♘g6 15 ♗a3 ♖f7 16 b5 ±
     9 ... ♘d7 10 c5 dc 11 bc ♘xc5 12 ♗a3 b6 13 ♗xc5 bc 14 ♘a4 ± Sahović-Ligterink, Jurmala 1978
[2] 10 ♘d2 ♘f4 11 ♗f3 f5 12 a4 g5! 13 ef ♘xf5 ∓ Keene-Kavalek, Teesside 1975
     10 g3 f5 11 ♘g5 ♘f6 12 f3 f4 13 c5 fg 14 hg h6 15 ♘e6 ♗xe6 16 de ±/=; 12 ... ♔h8 ∞
[3] 12 ... a5 13 cd (13 ♘b5 a6 14 cd cd 15 ♕b3 ♗g4 ∞ Bönsch-Uhlmann, Potsdam 1985) 13 ... cd 14 ♕d2 ab 15 ♘b5 ♗g4 16 ♖c7 ±
[4] 13 h3 g5 14 a4 ♘g6 15 ♘b5 a6 16 ♘bd4 ♖e8 17 ♖c4 ♕f6 18 ♕c2 h5 ∞/∓ Suba-Schmidt, Prague Z 1985
[5] 18 h3 ♖b8 ∞ Keene-Gligorić, Bad Lauterberg 1977
[6] 9 ... ♘d7 10 ♖c1 (10 g3 f5 11 ef ♘xf5 12 ♘e4 ♘f6 13 ♗g5 h6 14 ♗xf6 ♗xf6 15 ♗d3 ♗g7 16 h4 c6 ∞ Vogt-Gufeld, Baku 1980) 10 ...f5 11 ♘g5 (11 ef ♘xf5 12 ♘e4 ♘f4 13 ♖e1 ♘xe2+ 14 ♕xe2 b6 ∞ Taimanov-Spassky,

Moscow 1973) 11 ... ♘f4 12 ♗xf4 ef 13 ♗f3 fe 14 ♗xe4 ♘f5 15 ♘e6 ♗xe6 16 de c6 ∞ Korchnoi-Spraggett, Montreal 1983
[7] 10 ... h6 11 ♘e1 f5 12 ♘d3 f4 13 c5 g5 14 ♗g4! ±/± Vogt-Hesse, East Germany 1980
[8] 11 ♘g5 h6 12 ♘e6 ♗xe6 13 de ♕c8 14 ♕b3 c6 15 f4 ∞ Ftacnik-Georgiev, Groningen 1976-77
[9] 13 ... h6 14 ♘e6 ♗xe6 15 de ♕c8 16 ♘d5 ♕xe6 17 ♘xe7+ ♕xe7 18 c5+ ♔h8 ∞
[10] 18 cb ab 19 ♖c6 ♔h8 ∞ Taimanov-Fischer, match 1971
[11] 9 ... ♗d7 10 b4 c6 11 ♗a3 a6 12 dc ♗xc6 13 ♖e1 b5 14 ♗f1 ♕b6 15 ♘b3 ± Korchnoi-I.Zaitsev, USSR Ch 1970
[12] 10 b3 ♘d7 11 ♗a3 ♘c5 (11 ... f5 12 b4 ab 13 ♗xb4 ♔h8 14 a4 ♘g8 15 ♘b3 b6 16 a5 ± Lputian-Dorfman, Moscow 1986) 12 b4 ab 13 ♗xb4 ♗a6 14 ♗a3 b6 15 ♘b3 f5 ∞
[13] 10 ... c5 11 a3 ♘e8 12 b4 ab 13 ab b6 14 bc (14 ♕b3 f5 15 bc bc 16 ♕b6 ♕d7 17 ♘f3 h6 ∞ Ftacnik-Sznapik, Prague Z 1985) 14 ... bc 15 ♘b3 f5 16 f3 (16 ♗g5!? ♗f6 17 ♗d2 ♖f7 18 ♖a1 ♖b8 19 f3 f4 20 ♘b5 ∞/± Eingorn-Marjanović, Bor 1985) 16 ... ♘f6 17 ♗d2 ♘h5 (17 ... ♗d7 18 ♕c2 ± Farago) 18 ♖a1! ♖xa1 19 ♕xa1 ♘f4 20 ♕a5 ♕xa5 21 ♘xa5 ±

Farago-Sznapik, Warsaw Z 1987

[14] **12 ... b6** 13 f3 f4 14 ♘a4 ab 15 ab g5 16 c5 ♘f6 17 cd cd 18 b5 ±/± Kasparov-Smirin, USSR Ch 1988

12 ... ♔h8 13 ♕c2 b6 14 ♘b3 ab 15 ab fe ∞ Gavrikov-Kasparov, USSR Ch 1988

[15] **13 ... ♗h6** 14 ♔h1 ♔g7 15 ♗b2 ♘f6 16 ♗d3 ♘eg8 17 c5 ♘h5 ∞ Farago-Kristiansen, Esbjerg 1985

[16] Krasenkov-Glek, Pinsk 1986

[17] 10 dc bc 11 b4 d5 12 b5 (12 ♗a3 a6 13 ♖e1 h5 14 ♖b1 ♖e8 15 ♗f1 ♗g4 16 ♕b3 de 17 ♘dxe4 ♘f5 ∓ Sinkovics-Uhlmann, Stary Smokovec 1985; 12 ♖e1 ♖e8! 13 b5 ♗e6 = Plachetka-Kr.Georgiev, Dubai Ol 1986) 12 ... d4 13 ♘a4 d3 14 ♗f3 cb 15 cb ♗d7 16 ♘c5 ♗xb5 17 a4 ♗c6 18 ♗a3 ♖e8 19 ♖c1 ♘d7! (19 ... ♖c8 20 ♖c3 ♘f5 21 ef e4 22 fg hg 23 ♘dxe4 ± Farago-Gavrić, Banja Luka 1985) = Farago-Piket, Amsterdam II 1985

[18] 10 ... ♘d7!? 11 ♘b5 (11 b4 cb 12 ♖xb4 ♘c5 13 ♘a4 b6 14 ♘xc5 bc 15 ♖b2 f5 = Grünberg-Vogt, Potsdam 1985) 11 ... ♕b6 12 a3 a6 13 ♘c3 ♕c7 14 b4 b6 15 ♘b3 f5 = Farago-Piket, Wijk aan Zee 1987

[19] 12 a4 a5 13 bc bc 14 ♕b3 ♘c7 15 ♕b6 ♖a6 16 ♕b8 ♖a8 = Fedorowicz-Watson, Hastings 1984-85

[20] 12 ... bc 13 ♘b3 f5 14 ♗g5 ± Pekarek-Sznapik, Warsaw Z 1987

[21] 13 a4 a5 14 ♖b3 ♗d7 15 ♗b2 ♘d6 16 ♕a1 ♗h6 17 ♘db1 f6 ∞ Bönsch-Vogt, Potsdam 1985

[22] 18 ♕g3 f5 = Pekarek-Kr.Georgiev, Warsaw Z 1987

[23] 9 ... ♘e8 10 f3 f5 11 g4 c5 12 ♖b1 h5 13 g5 h4 14 ♘d3 f4 15 ♔h1 ♔f7 16 ♖g1 ± Dorfman-Fernandez, Mexico 1977

[24] 11 ... ♘f6 12 ♘d3 c6 13 ♗e3 (13 ♘f2 ♔h8 14 ♗d2 a5 15 a3 ♗d7! 16 ♖b1 ♕b8 17 b3 ♖f7 18 ♕c1 ♕c7 19 b4 ab 20 ♖xb4 ♖af8 = Taimanov-Kavalek, Montilla 1977) 13 ... ♔h8 14 h3 b5 15 ♘b4 cd (15 ... bc 16 ♘xc6 ♘xc6 17 dc ♗e6 18 ♕a4 ± Pinter-Mortensen, Copenhagen 1985) 16 ♘bxd5 ♘exd5 17 ♘xd5 ♗b7 18 ♘xf6+ ♕xf6 19 cb d5 20 ed ♖ad8 21 ♗c4 ± Pinter-Sznapik, Prague Z 1985

[25] 12 ♗e3 ♘g8 13 ♕d2 a6 14 ♘g2 f4 15 ♗f2 h5 ∞/= Pinter-Nunn, Dubai Ol 1986

[26] 13 ♗e3 ♗h6 14 ♗f2 ♖f7 15 ♔g2 ½-½ Garcia-Uhlmann, Potsdam 1985

[27] ½-½ Pinter-Uhlmann, Szirak 1985

[28] 11 ef ♘xf5 12 f3 ♘d4 13 ♘f2 ♘f6 14 ♗d3 c5 15 ♗e3 ♘h5 16 ♗e4 ♖f7 17 ♖b1 b6 18 ♕d2 ♘f5 19 ♗g5 ♗f6 = Hort-van der Wiel, Reykjavik 1985

[29] **11 ... fe** 12 ♘xe4 ♘f6 (12 ... ♘f5 13 ♗c3 ♘f6 14 ♗f3 ♘h4 15 ♘xf6+ ♕xf6 16 ♗e4 ♗f5 17 ♕e2 ♗xe4 18 ♕xe4 ±/± Ftacnik-Mortensen, Esbjerg 1985) 13 ♘xf6+ ♗xf6 14 ♗c3 ♘f5 15 ♗f3 ♗g7 16 ♖e1 (16 ♗e4 ♕h4 17 ♖e1 b6 18 g3 ♕g5 = Polugayevsky-Tal, USSR 1980) 16 ... ♔h8 17 ♖c1 ♖f7 18 ♗g4 ± Didishko-Ehlvest, Tallinn 1980

11 ... ♔h8 12 ♖c1 f4 13 f3 ♘g8 14 b4 ♘df6 15 c5 g5 16 cd cd 17 ♘b5 ♘e8 18 a4 h5 19 ♘f2 ♘h6 20 h3 ♖g8 21 ♖c3! ± Cebalo-Cvitan, Yugoslav Ch 1986

[30] 14 ♖c1 ♘g6 15 cd cd 16 ♘b5 ♖f7 17 ♕c2 ♘e8 18 a4 h5 19 ♘f2 ♗f8 20 h3 ♖g7 21 ♕b3 ♘h4 22 ♖c2 a6 23 ♘a3 ♘f6 24 ♗e1 g4 25 hg hg! = Ftacnik-Zsu.Polgar, Trencianske Teplice 1985; 19 ... ♗d7 20 ♕b3 ♗f6 21 ♖c2 ♕b8 = Davidović-Sahović, Niš 1985

[31] 15 ... ♘g6 16 ♕c2 ♖f7 17 ♖fc1 h5 18 h3 g4 19 hg hg 20 fg ♘e8 21 a4 ± Sosonko-Hellers, Wijk aan Zee 1985

[32] 18 a4 ♗f6 19 ♖a3 ♕c7 20 ♖c1 ♗d8!? 21 ♘b5 ♕b8 22 a5 a6 23 ♘c3 ± Karpov-van der Wiel, Brussels 1987

King's Indian X	1 d4 ♘f6 2 c4 g6 3 ♘f3 ♗g7 4 g3 0-0 5 ♗g2 d6 6 0-0 c6 7 ♘c3								
	7	8	9	10	11	12	13	14	15
1	...	♘h4[2]	f4	♔h1	b3	f5	cb	♗g5	♗xf6	±
	♗f5[1]	♗d7[3]	♕b6	♕a6	d5	b5	cb	b4	bc[4]	
2	...	e4[5]	d5	cd	♖e1[7]	a3	♘a4	b3	=
	♕a5	e5[6]	cd	b5	♘a6	b4[8]	♗d7	♖fb8[9]	
3	...	h3	e4	♘xd4	♘b3	♗e3	e5	♘c5[13]	♗xf8	±
	...	e5[10]	ed[11]	♕c5	♕b4[12]	a5	de[14]	♕xc4	♗xf8[15]	
4	...	...	d5[16]	♘d4	cd[18]	♘b3[19]	e4	♗e3	♗d4	±
	...	♗e6	cd[17]	♗d7	♖c8	♕d8	♗e8	♘bd7	♘b6[20]	

[1] 7 ... a6 8 e4 ♘fd7 (8 ... b5 9 e5 ♘e8 10 c5 ♗g4 11 cd ed 12 ♗f4 ± Khalifman-Georgiev, Moscow 1985) 9 ♖e1 b5 10 e5 bc 11 e6 fe 12 ♘g5 ♘b6 13 ♗h3 ♔h8 14 ♗xe6 ♕e8 15 ♗xc8 ♘xc8 16 ♘e6 ±/± Andersson-Kozul, Sarajevo 1985

[2] 8 b3 ♘e4 9 ♗b2 a5!? 10 ♘h4 ♘xc3 11 ♗xc3 ♗c8 12 ♘f3 ♘d7 13 ♕c2 e5 14 ♖d1 ♕e7 ∞ Velikov-Romanishin, Frunze 1985

[3] 8 ... ♗e6 9 b3 d5 10 cd ♘xd5 11 ♗b2 ♘xc3 12 ♗xc3 ♘a6 13 ♕c2 ♘c7 14 ♖fd1 ± Kirov-Pähtz, Potsdam 1985

[4] 16 ♗xg7 ♔xg7 17 ♕c1 ♕d6 18 ♕xc3 ± Tukmakov-Romanishin, Moscow 1985

[5] 8 ♕d2 e5 9 b3 ed 10 ♘xd4 ♘h5 11 ♕g5 ♕xg5 12 ♗xg5 h6 13 ♗f4 ♖d8 14 ♖ad1 ♘a6 ∞ Rukavina-Barlov, Novi Sad 1985
8 d5 ♕b4!? 9 ♘d2 ♗d7 10 e4 a5 11 ♖e1 ♘a6 12 a3 ♕b6 ∞ Ivkov-Larsen, Zagreb 1977

[6] 8 ... ♕h5 9 ♖e1 e5 10 b3 ♗g4 11 d5 ±
8 ... ♗g4 9 h3 ♗xf3 10 ♕xf3 e5 11 d5 cd 12 cd ♘bd7 13 ♗g5 ♖fc8 14 ♖fe1 ♕b4 15 ♖ab1 ♘e8 16 h4 ± Djurić-Sibarević, Banja Luka 1985

[7] 11 ♘d2 b4 12 ♘b3 ♕a6 13 ♘e2 ♗d7 14 ♗d2 ♗b5 ∞ Savon-Kavalek, Sarajevo 1967

[8] 12 ... ♗d7 13 b4 ♕c7 14 ♗d2 ♖fc8 15 ♗f1 ♕b7 16 ♕e2 ±

[9] Makarov-Dementiev, Erevan 1981

[10] 8 ... ♕a6 9 ♕b3 (9 b3 b5 10 cb cb 11 b4 ♗b7 12 a4 ba 13 ♖xa4 ∞ Nikolić-Gavrikov, Tunis IZ 1985) 9 ... ♘bd7 10 e4 e5 11 ♖d1 ♖e8 12 ♗e3 h6 13 ♖ac1 g5 14 de de 15 ♘d2 ♗f8 16 ♘a4 ± Smejkal-Ermenkov, Baden-Baden 1985

[11] 9 ... ♗e6 10 d5 cd 11 cd ♗d7 12 ♗e3 ♖c8 13 ♘d2 ±
9 ... ♘bd7 10 ♖e1 ♖e8 (10 ... ed 11 ♘xd4 ♕c5 12 b3 ♘e8 13 ♗e3 ♕a5 14 ♕c2 ±) 11 d5 cd 12 cd a6 13 a3 ♕d8 14 a4 ♖f8 15 ♘d2 ± Pigusov-Pecorelli, Bayamo 1985

[12] 11 ... ♕xc4 12 ♕xd6 a5 13 ♗f4 ♘h5 14 ♗e3 ♘d7 15 ♖ac1 ±

[13] 12 ♗f4 ♘e8 13 ♖e1 ♗e6 (13 ... ♕xc4 14 ♗xd6 ♘xd6 15 ♕xd6 ♕e6 16 ♘c5 ♘d7 ± Vladimirov-Chekhov, Baku 1979) 14 e5 ∞

[14] 13 ... ♘fd7 14 a3 ± Quinteros-Torre, Olot 1973

[15] 16 ♘xa5! ± Podgayets-Klimenko, USSR 1981

[16] 9 ♘d2!? ♘a6 10 a3 ♘c7 (10 ... ♕b6 11 e3 c5 12 d5 ♗d7 13 ♖e1 ♕d8 14 ♖b1 ± Marović-Bertok, Zagreb 1965) 11 e4 ♕a6 12 d5 ♗d7 13 ♖e1 ♖fe8 14 ♗f1 ± Csom-Nielsen, Esbjerg 1985

[17] 9 ... ♗d7 10 e4! ♘e8 11 a3 cd 12 cd ♕b6 13 ♕e2 ± Smejkal-Jakobsen, Raach 1969

[18] 11 ♘b3 ♕b4! (11 ... ♕d8 12 cd a5 13 ♗e3 ♘a6 14 ♘d4 ♖c8 = Morović-Vukić, Bor 1985) 12 cd ♖c8 13 ♗e3 ♗a4 14 ♘xa4 ♕xa4 15 ♗d4 ♘a6 = Pavlović-Hulak, Niš 1984

[19] 12 ♗e3 ♘a6 13 ♕d2 ♘c5 14 ♖fb1! ♘a4 15 b4 ♕d8 16 ♘xa4 ♗xa4 17 b5 ± Browne-Vukić, Banja Luka 1979
12 e4 ♗e8 13 ♗e3 ♘bd7 14 ♕e2 ♘b6 15 ♖fd1 ± Agdestein-Plachetka, Malmö 1986-87

[20] 16 ♘c1 ♘c4 17 ♘d3 ± Kir.Georgiev-Plachetka, Malmö 1986-87

160

King's Indian XI			1 d4 ♘f6 2 c4 g6 3 ♘c3 ♗g7 4 ♘f3 d6 5 g3 0-0 6 ♗g2 ♘bd7 7 0-0 e5						

	8	9	10	11	12	13	14	15	16	
1	b3[1]	♗b2[3]	e4	♘xd4	♕c2	♖ad1	a3	h3	♖xd4	∞
	♖e8[2]	c6	ed	♘c5	a5	♕b6	♘g4	♗xd4	♕xb3[4]	
2	♕c2	♘xd4	♖d1[6]	♘cb5	♕xc4	♘xb5	a4	♕b3	♘d4	=
	ed[5]	♘b6	♘xc4	a6	ab	♗d7[7]	d5	c6	♕c8[8]	
3	e4	♗e3[10]	♗g5	♗c1	h3	♗e3	♕c2	♖ad1	b4	±
	♖e8[9]	♘g4	f6[11]	♘h6[12]	♘f7	♘f8	c6	♕c7	♗d7[13]	
4	...	♕c2[14]	♖d1	b3[16]	♘xd4	f3	♖e1	♘ce2	♗f4	=
	c6	♖e8	♕e7[15]	ed	♘c5	a5	♘fd7	♘e5	♕c7[17]	
5	...	♘xd4	h3	♖e1	♗g5[19]	♗f4	♗e3	♖b1	♕c2	∞
	ed	♖e8	♘c5	a5[18]	h6	♘fd7	a4	c6	♕a5[20]	

[1] 8 de de 9 ♕c2 c6 10 ♖d1 ♕e7 11 e4 ♘e8 12 ♗g5 f6 13 ♗e3 f5 14 ♕d2 ♘b6 15 ♗g5 ♕f7 16 b3 f4 ∓ Yabra-Polugayevsky, Siegen Ol 1970

[2] 8 ... c6?! 9 ♗a3 ed 10 ♘xd4 ♘c5 11 b4! ♘e6 12 ♘xe6 ♗xe6 13 b5 ±

[3] 9 ♕c2 c6 10 ♗b2 e4 11 ♘g5 e3 12 fe ♗g4 13 ♘xf7 ♘e3 14 ♕d2 ♕e7 15 ♘e4 ♘xg2 ∓ Spraggett-Brendel, Vienna 1986; 14 ♕d3!? Klinger

[4] 17 ♕e2 ♘e5 18 f4 ♗e6 19 fe de ∞ Karlsson-Rantanen, Helsinki 1981

[5] 8 ... c6 9 ♖d1 ♖e8 10 ♗g5 ♕b6 11 h3 ♕a6 12 de de 13 ♘d2! =

[6] 10 ♗g5 h6 11 ♗xf6 ♕xf6 12 ♖fd1 c6 13 ♘e4 ♕e7 ∞ Boleslavsky

[7] 13 ... ♘e8 14 ♘c3 c6 15 e4 ♗g4 16 ♖e1 ♗e6 =

[8] Geller

[9] 8 ... a6 9 ♕c2 ed 10 ♘xd4 ♘g4 (10 ... ♘e5 11 b3 c5 12 ♘de2 ♖b8 13 ♗b2 b5 14 cb ab 15 f4 ± Tukmakov-Knaak, Szirak 1985) 11 ♘de2 ♘c5 12 b4 ♘e6 13 ♗b2 ♘e5 14 ♘d5 c6 15 ♘e3 ♕b6 16 ♗c3 ± Saeed-Balashov, Taxco IZ 1985; 9 d5 b5 10 ♘d2 ♘c5 11 ♘b3 ♘xb3 12 ab ♗d7 13 ♕e2 ± Velikov-Vogt, Sofia 1986

[10] 9 d5 ♘c5 10 ♘e1 a5 11 h3 ♘h5! =

[11] 10 ... ♗f6 11 ♗c1! ♗g7 12 h3 ♘f6 13 ♗e3 ± Geller

[12] 11 ... ed 12 ♘xd4 ♘c5 13 b4 ♘e6 14 ♘f5! ±/± Botvinnik-Boleslavsky, USSR 1952

[13] 17 d5 ± Geller

[14] 9 ♖b1 ed (9 ... ♕e7 10 ♖e1 a6 11 b3 b5 12 ♖e2 ♖d8 13 a3 ± Flear-Watson, Hastings 1984-85) 10 ♘xd4 ♕b6 11 b3 ♘c5 12 ♘de2 a5 = Olafsson-Timman, Amsterdam 1976
9 b3!? ed 10 ♘xd4 ♘c5 11 h3 ♖e8 12 ♖e1 a5 13 ♖b1 ♗d7 14 ♗f4 ± Smejkal-Uhlmann, Sarajevo 1982

[15] 10 ... a6 11 h3 ♕a5 12 ♗e3 b5 13 c5 b4 14 ♘a4 ± Najdorf-Szabo, Mar del Plata 1955

[16] 11 d5 c5 12 ♘e1 ♘g4 13 h3 ∞

[17] Boleslavsky

[18] 11 ... ♘fd7 12 ♗e3 ♘e5 13 b3 c6 14 ♖b1 a5 15 ♖e2 a5 16 ef gf 17 ♕c2 ∞/± Andersson-Ljubojević, Lanzerote 1973

[19] 12 ♕c2 a4 13 ♗e3 c6 14 ♖ad1 ♘fd7 15 ♖e2 ♕a5 16 ♖ed2 ♕e4 ∞ Hjartarson-Kristiansen, Denmark 1985
12 ♖b1 ♘fd7 13 ♗e3 c6 14 ♕c2 ♕e7 15 b3 ♘e5 16 ♖bd1 a4 17 f4 ab 18 ab ♘ed7 ∞/= Zsu.Polgar-Hausner, Vienna 1986
12 ♘db5 ♘fd7 13 ♗e3 ♘e5 14 b3 (14 ♗xc5 dc 15 ♕xd8 ♖xd8 16 ♘xc7 ♖b8 17 ♖ed1 ♗e6 18 ♘xe6 fe 19 ♗f1 ♘c6 ∞ Boleslavsky) 14 ... ♘ed3 15 ♖e2 c6 16 ♘d4 a4 17 ♖d2 ∞/∞ Geller

[20] Gutman-Martin, Hastings 1984-85

161

1 d4 ♘f6 2 c4 g6 3 ♘c3 ♗g7 4 ♘f3 d6 5 g3 0-0 6 ♗g2 ♘bd7 7 0-0 e5 8 e4 c6 9 h3

	9	10	11	12	13	14	15	16	17	
1	... ♕b6[1]	♖e1[2] ed[3]	♘xd4 ♘e8[4]	♘b3[5] ♕b4	♗f1 ♘c5	♗g5[6] f5	♗d2! ♘xb3	ab ♕b6	♗e3 ♕c7[7]	±
2	... ♕a5	♖e1[8] ed[9]	♘xd4 ♘e5[10]	♗f1 ♖e8	♗e3 ♗e6	♘xe6[11] ♖xe6	♔g2! ♖ae8	f3 a6[12]		±
3	... ♖e8	♖e1[13] a5	♖b1[14] ed[15]	♘xd4 ♘c5	♗f4 ♘e6[16]	♘xe6 ♗xe6	♗xd6 ♗xc4	b3 ♗e6	♘a4 ♘d7[17]	±

[1]   9 ... ♕e7 10 ♗e3 ed 11 ♘xd4 ♘c5 12 ♕c2 ♖e8 13 ♖fe1 a5 14 ♖ad1 ±/± Morović-Milanović, Yugoslavia 1985

  9 ... a6 10 ♖b1 b5 11 c5 b4 12 ♘a4 d5 13 de ♘xe4 14 ♘d4 ± Pachman-Tatai, Netanya 1973

  9 ... a5 10 ♗e3 a4 11 ♕c2 ♕a5 12 ♖ab1 b5 13 cb cb 14 de de 15 b4 ± Boleslavsky

[2]   10 ♖b1 ♕b4! 11 ♕b3 (11 de ♘xe5 12 ♘xe5 de 13 ♕d3 ♘d7 = Berger-Gligorić, Amsterdam IZ 1964) 11 ... a5 12 ♗e3 ed 13 ♗xd4 ♖a6 14 ♖fd1 ♖e8 15 ♕c2 h6 16 ♗d2 a4 = Diesen-Watson, Lone Pine 1976

  10 b3 ed (10 ... ♖e8 11 ♗e3 ed 12 ♘xd4 ♘c5 13 ♕c2 ♕c7 14 ♖ad1 h6 15 ♖fe1 ♗d7 16 ♖e2 ± Velikov-Thipsay, Frunze 1985) 11 ♘a4 ♕a5 12 ♘d4 d5 ∞

  10 d5 ♘c5 (10 ... c5 11 ♘e1 ♘e8 12 ♘d3 a6 13 ♗e3 ♕c7 14 ♕d2 ♖b8 15 a4 f5 16 ef gf 17 f4 ± Barcza-Tringov, Ljubljana 1969) 11 ♘e1 cd 12 cd ♗d7 13 ♘d3 ♘xd3 14 ♕xd3 ♖fc8 15 ♖b1 ♘h5 16 ♗e3 ♕b4 17 ♕e2 ♖c4 18 ♖fc1 ♖ac8 19 ♔h2 f5 = Botvinnik-Tal, match (6) 1960

[3]   10 ... a5!? 10 ♖b1 ed 11 ♘xd4 ♘g4! 12 ♘ce2 ♘ge5 13 b3 ♘xc4 14 ♘c2! ∞ Ilić-Klauser, Switzerland 1979

  10 ... ♖e8 11 d5 ♘c5 (11 ... c5 12 ♗e3 a6 13 ♕d2 ♖f8 14 ♘h2 ♕c7 15 a4 ♘h5 16 ♕e2 b6 17 ♗f3 ± Ribli-Biyiasas, Manila IZ 1976) 12 ♖b1 a5 13 ♗e3 (13 ♗f1 ♗d7 14 ♗e3 ♕c7 15 ♕d2 cd 16 cd ♖ec8 17 a4 ∞/± Garcia Palermo-Roth, Vienna 1986) 13 ... ♕c7 14 ♕d2 ♗d7 15 ♗f1 ♖ab8 16 a3 cd 17 cd ±

[4]   11 ... ♖e8 12 ♘a4 (12 ♘b3 a5 13 ♘a4 ♕b4 14 ♘d2 ♘c5 15 ♘xc5 ♕xc5 16 ♕e2 a4 = Geller-Didishko, USSR 1981) 12 ... ♕a5 13 ♗f4 ♘e5 14 b3 ♘fd7 15 ♗d2 ♕d8 16 ♗c3 ♘c5 17 ♘b2 a5 18 a3 ♘e6 19 ♘xe6 ♗xe6 20 ♕c2 ± Karpov-Balashov, Moscow 1981

[5]   12 ♘ce2 ♘c7 13 ♘b3 ♕b4 14 ♘c3 a5

[6]   15 ♘d2 a4 16 a3 ♕a5 ∓ Bukal-Smyslov, Linz 1980

  12 ♘c2 ♘c5 13 ♕d2 a5 14 b3 f5 15 ♖b1 ♗e5 16 ef ♗xf5 ∞/∓ Bukal-Hulak, Zagreb 1982

  12 ♘f3!? ♘e5 13 ♘xe5 de 14 ♗e3 ♕a5 15 a3 ♗f6 16 b4 ± Nikolić-Hausner, Banja Luka 1981

[6]   14 ♗e3 ♘a4 15 ♘xa4 ♕xa4 16 ♕d2 a5 17 ♗d4 ♕b4 18 ♕e3 a4 19 ♘d2 ± Portisch-Westerinen, Malta Ol 1980

[7]   18 ♕d2 ± Portisch-Ermenkov, Malta Ol 1980

[8]   10 ♕c2 ed 11 ♘xd4 ♕c5 12 ♘ce2 d5 13 cd cd 14 ed ♖e8 15 ♕xc5 ♘xc5 16 ♖d1 ♗d7 17 ♗e3 ♘ce4 18 ♗xe4 ♖xe4 19 ♘c3 ♖e5 20 ♘f3 ♖h5 ∞ Michalov-Bobovich, USSR 1978

  10 ♗e3 ♘b6 11 ♘d2 ed 12 ♗xd4 ♗e6 ∞ Zaltsman-Soltis, Lone Pine 1981

[9]   10 ... b5?! 11 cb cb 12 d5 ♗b7 13 ♗d2 a6 14 a4 ba 15 ♘xa4 ♕c7 16 ♖c1 ♕b8 17 b4 ± Kavalek-Saidy, Netanya 1969

  10 ... ♖e8 11 d5 cd 12 cd b5 13 ♗f1 a6 14 ♗d2 ♕c7 15 b4 ♗b7 16 a4 ± Ribli-Szilagyi, Hungarian Ch 1974

[10]   11 ... ♘b6!? 12 ♗f1 ♖e8 13 ♘b3! ♕h5 14 ♕xh5 ♘xh5 15 g4! ♘f6 16 ♗f4 ± Marović-Bilek, Yugoslavia 1974

  11 ... ♖e8 12 ♗e3 ♕b4 13 a3 ♕a5 14 b4 ♕c7 15 ♖c1 ± Vladimirov-Savon, USSR 1961

[11]   14 ♘b3 ♕c7 15 ♘d2 ± Lengyel-Minić, Hungary v Yugoslavia 1968

[12]   Boleslavsky/Geller

[13]   10 b3!? ed 11 ♘xd4 ♘c5 12 ♖e1 a5 13 ♗f4 h6 14 ♕c2 ♘fd7 15 ♖ad1 ± Quinteros-Li Zunian, Biel IZ 1985

[14]   11 ♕c2 ed 12 ♘xd4 ♘c5 13 ♗e3 a4 14 ♖ad1 (14 ♖ab1 ♗d7 15 b4 ab 16 ab ♕e7 17 f3 ♘h5 ∞ Minić) 14 ... ♘fd7 15 ♖e2 ♕a5 16 ♖ed2 ♘e5! (16 ... ♕b4 17 ♘b1 ♘b6 18 ♘a3

♗d7 19 ♘e2 ± Averbakh-Dittmann, Dresden 1956) 17 ♗f1 a3 18 b3 ♘f3+! = Diesen-Browne, Lone Pine 1976

[15] 11 ... ♕e7 12 b3 ed 13 ♘xd4 ♘c5 14 ♗f4 ♘fd7 15 ♗e3 ♘f8 16 ♕d2 ♘fe6 ± Jansa-Honfi, Zalaegerszeg 1969

[16] 13 ... ♕b6 14 ♘b3 ♘e6 15 ♗xd6! a4 16 c5 ± Portisch-Planinc, Vrčac 1971

13 ... ♘h5 14 ♗e3 ♕c7 15 ♕d2 ♘f6 16 ♕c2 ♗d7 17 ♖bd1 ± Donner-Kavalek, Lugano 1970

13 ... a4 ♕d2! (14 b4 ab 15 ab ♘h5 16 ♗e3 ♖a3 17 g4 ♘f6 18 ♕c1 ♖a8 = Pachman-Browne, Mannheim 1975) 14 ... ♘h5 15 ♗e3 ♕c7 16 b4 ab 17 ab ± Filip

[17] 18 ♖c1 ± Pigusov-Tseitlin, Sochi 1985

King's Indian XIII				1 d4 ♘f6 2 c4 g6 3 ♘c3 ♗g7 4 ♘f3 d6 5 g3 0-0 6 ♗g2 c5 7 0-0[1] ♘c6 8 dc dc				
9	10	11	12	13	14	15	16	17
♗e3	♕a4[3]	♖ad1	♘d5	♖d2	♕b5	♗xd4	♘xd4	♘xb6
♗e6[2]	♘d7[4]	♕c8[5]	♖e8	♘b6	♘d4	cd	♕xc4	ab[6]
♗f4	♘e5	♘d3	♘xc5	gf	♖c1	♘xb7	e3[10]	♘xa5
♗e6[7]	♘a5![8]	♘h5	♘xf4	♗xc4	♕c7	♕xf4[9]	♕e5	♕xa5[11] =

[1] 7 d5 e6 8 de ♗xe6 9 ♘g5 ♗xc4 10 ♗xb7 ♘bd7 ∞; but note 1 d4 ♘f6 2 c4 g6 3 ♘f3 ♗g7 4 g3 d6 5 ♗g2 0-0 6 0-0 c5 7 d5 e6? 8 de ♗xe6 9 ♘g5 ♗xc4 10 ♗xb7 ♘bd7 11 ♘a3! ±

[2] 9 ... ♕a5 10 ♕a4 (10 ♗d2 ♗f5 11 ♘d5 ♕d8 12 ♘h4 ♗g4 13 h3 ♗d7 14 ♗c3 e5! 15 e3 ♖e8 = Smejkal-Gligorić, Hastings 1968-69) 10 ... ♕xa4 11 ♘xa4 b6 12 ♘g5 ♗b7 13 ♗xc5 h6 14 ♘e4 ♘xe4 15 ♗xe4 bc 16 ♘xc5 ♖ab8 17 ♘xb7 ♖xb7 18 ♗xc6 ♖xb2 19 ♗f3 ♖c8 =

[3] 10 ♗xc5 ♕a5 (10 ... ♗xc4 11 ♕c2 ♕c7 12 ♖fd1 ♖fd8 13 ♖xd8+ ♖xd8 14 ♖d1 ♗e6 = Lukov-Kr.Georgiev, Sofia 1984) 11 ♗a3 ♗xc4 12 ♘d4 ♗xd4 13 ♕xd4 ♖ac8 14 ♕f4 ♘h5 15 ♕e3 ♗xc3 16 ♕xc3 ♕xc3 17 bc ♗e2 18 ♖fe1 ♗a6 19 ♗xe7 ♖fe8 =; 17 ... ♖c7 = Tal

[4] 10 ... ♘d4 11 ♖ad1 ♗g4 (11 ... ♗d7 12 ♕a3 ♘c2 13 ♕xc5 b6 14 ♕g5 h6 15 ♕f4 g5 15 ♕e5 ♖c8! ∞ Grigorian-Kasparov, USSR Team Ch 1981) 12 ♗xd4 cd 13 ♘d5 ♗d7 (13 ... ♗xd5?! 14 cd ♕xd5 15 h3 ♘e5

16 ♘xd4 ♕c4 17 ♕a3! ± Vaganian-Mestel, London 1986) 14 ♕a3 e6 15 ♘f4 e5 16 ♘d5 ♖e8 = Caifas-Hertneck, Lucerne 1985

[5] 11 ... ♕b6 12 ♘g5!? ±

[6] 18 ♕xb6 ♖ad8! 19 e3 ♕xa2 = Mikhalchishin-Velimirović, Sarajevo 1985

[7] 9 ... ♘h5 10 ♗e3 ♘d4 11 ♖c1!? (11 ♘d2 ♖b8! 12 ♘b3 b6 13 ♗xd4 cd 14 ♘b5 ♗b7! 15 ♘5xd4 ♗xg2 16 ♔xg2 ♖c8 = Adorjan-Gufeld, Hastings 1986-87; 11 ... e5 12 ♘d2 f5 13 ♘b3 f4 14 ♗xd4 cd 15 ♘e4 ♘h6 16 ♘bd2! ♗f5 17 c5 ± Agdestein-Sigurjonsson, Gausdal Z 1987

[8] 10 ... ♘xe5 11 ♗xe5 ♘d7 12 ♗xg7 ♔xg7 13 ♗xb7 ♖b8 14 ♗d5 ♘h3 15 ♖e1 e6 16 ♗c6 ♘e5 17 ♕xd8 ♖fxd8 18 ♗b5 ± Lisenko-Muratov, Moscow 1986

[9] 15 ... ♘xb7 16 ♘d5! Tal

[10] 16 ♘xa5?! ♗e5 17 ♖e1 ♖ad8! 18 ♕a4 ♕xh2+ 19 ♔f1 ♗e6 ∓

[11] 18 ♗xa8 ♗xf1 = Tal-Kasparov, Moscow (speed chess) 1987

	8	9	10	11	12	13	14	15	16	
1	b3[2]	♗b2[3]	cb	♖c1	♘b1	♘e1[5]	♘d3	♕c2	♖fd1	±/=
	♖b8	b5	ab	b4[4]	♘a7	c6	♗a6	♘d7[6]	♕b6[7]	
2	h3	♗e3	♘d2	cb[9]	♘xb5	♕a4	♔xg2	♘c3	♘xa4	=
	♖b8	b5	♗b7!?[8]	ab	♘a5	♗xg2	♕d7!	♕xa4	♘d5[10]	
3	...	e4	e5[12]	e6[13]	d5	cd	♗e3	♘g5	dc	±
	...	b5[11]	♘d7	fe	ed	♘a7[14]	♘b6	c5	e6[15]	
4	...	...	...	de	♖xd1	e6	cb	♗e3[16]	♘a4[17]	±
	...	...	de	♕xd1	♘d7	fe	ab	b4	♘de5[18]	

1 d4 ♘f6 2 c4 g6 3 ♘c3 ♗g7 4 ♘f3 d6 5 g3 0-0 6 ♗g2 ♘c6 7 0-0 a6[1]

[1] 7 ... ♖b8 8 d5 ♘a5 9 ♘d2 c5 10 ♕c2 e5 11 b3! intending ♗b2, e4 ± Ribli

7 ... ♗f5 8 ♘e1 (8 d5 ♘a5 9 ♘d2 ♘e8! 10 e4 ♗d7 11 ♕c2 c6 12 b3 b5 ∞ Hjartarson-Murei, London 1986) 8 ... ♕c8 9 e4 ♗h3 10 ♘c2 ♗xg2 11 ♔xg2 e5 12 d5 ♘e7 13 ♘e1 ♘d7 14 ♘d3 a5 15 ♗g5 f6 16 ♗e3 ± Portisch-Korchnoi, Brussels 1986

7 ... ♗g4 8 h3 ♗xf3 9 ♗xf3 ♘d7 10 e3 e5 11 de de 12 ♕b3 ♕c8 13 ♖d1 ♘h8 14 ♘a4 ± Lau-Kindermann, Beer-Sheva Z 1985

[2] 8 e3?! ♖b8 9 ♕e2 b5 10 ♘d2 ♘a7 11 b3 ♗g4 ∓ Euwe

8 ♗g5 ♗d7 9 ♖c1 b5 10 d5 ♘a5 11 b3! ± Kasparov-Nunn, London (exhibition game) 1987

8 ♗d2 ♖e8 9 ♖c1 b5 10 cb ab 11 d5 ♘a7 12 b4 c5 13 dc ♘xc6 = Tukmakov-Sax, Szirak 1985

8 ♕d3 ♖b8 (8 ... ♗g4 9 d5 ♘b4 10 ♕d2 a5 11 h3 ♗xf3 12 ♗xf3 ♕c8 13 ♗g2 c6 14 a3 ♘a6 15 ♖b1 ± Csom-Sznapik, Prague Z 1985) 9 d5 ♘a7 10 a4 c5 11 ♖e1 ♕c7 12 a5 b5 13 ab ♖xb6 14 ♘a4 ♖b8 15 c4 ∞/± Suba-Zapata, Tunis IZ 1985

[3] 9 a4 ♘a5 (9 ... a5 10 h3 ♗f5 11 ♘h4 ♗d7 12 e4 ♕c8 13 g4 h5 ∞ Pomar-Keene, Palma de Mallorca 1971) 10 ♘d2 ♘d7 11 ♗b2 c5 12 d5 ♘f6 13 ♕c2 e5 14 e4 ♘h5 15 ♖a2 ♗h6 Quinteros-Zsu.Polgar, Baden-Baden 1985

9 ♘d5 ♗f5 (9 ... ♘xd5 10 cd ♘b4 11 e4 f5 12 ♘g5 ± Romanishin-Kantsler, Frunze 1985) 10 ♗b2 e6 11 ♘e3 ♗e4 12 ♖c1 ♘d7 13 ♘h3 ♗xf3 14 ef e5 15 de ♘cxe5 ∞ Adorjan-Perez, Dubai Ol 1986; 9 ... e6!? 10 ♘xf6+ ♗xf6 11 ♗b2 e5 12 de de ∞

[4] 11 ... ♗d7 12 ♘e1 e5 13 ♘xb5 ♖xb5 14 ♗xc6 ♗xc6 15 ♖xc6 ♕a8 16 ♖c2 ♕xa2 17 de ±/= Nikolić-Hellers, Wijk aan Zee 1985

[5] 13 ♘bd2 ♘b5 14 e4 ♘d7 15 ♘c4 c5

16 ♕d2 ♗b7 = Ta-Mestel, Switzerland 1985

[6] 15 ... ♘d5!?

[7] Romanishin-Keene, Dortmund 1982

[8] 10 ... ♘a5 11 cb ab 12 b4 ♘c4 13 ♘xc4 bc 14 b5 d5 15 a4 ± Hjartarson-Ernst, Gausdal Z 1987

10 ... ♗d7 11 ♖c1 ♘a5 12 cb ab 13 b4 ♘c4 14 ♘xc4 bc 15 b5! ± Beil-W.Schmidt, Sofia 1985

[9] 11 ♖c1 ♘a5 12 cb ab 13 b4 ♘c4 14 ♘xc4 bc 15 d5 e6 ∞ Poutiainen-Pinter, Budapest 1975

[10] 17 ♖ab1 ♗xd4! 18 ♗xd4 ♘b4 = Grünfeld-Nunn, Biel 1986

[11] 9 ... ♘d7 10 ♗g5 h6 11 ♗e3 ♘a5 12 b3 c5 13 ♕d2 ♔h7 14 ♖ac1 ♘c6 15 ♖fd1 e5 16 dc dc 17 ♘d5 ± Donchev-Ghinda, Prague Z 1985

[12] 10 cb ab 11 ♗e3 b4 12 ♘d5 ♘xe4 13 ♕c2 e6 14 ♕xc6 ♗b7 ∞ Adianto-Zapata, Jakarta 1986

[13] 11 ♘g5 ♘xd4 12 ♕xd4 ♘xe5 13 ♕d1! Keene

11 cb ab 12 ♘g5 de (12 ... ♘xd4 13 ♕xd4 ♘xe5 14 ♕h4 h6 15 ♘f3 ♘xf3+ 16 ♗xf3 ± Thorsteins-van der Wiel, Reykjavik 1985) 13 ♗xc6 ed 14 ♘xb5 ♘e5!? (14 ... ♖b6 15 ♘a7 h6 16 ♘f3 ♗a6 17 ♖e1 ♘b8 18 ♗e4 ± Nikolić-Nunn, Wijk aan Zee 1982) intending 15 ♘xd4 ♖b6 ∞

[14] 13 ... ♘a5 14 ♘d4 ♘e5 15 ♘ce2! ± Portisch-Vigh, Hungary 1986

[15] 17 ♖c1 ± Kanko-Tiemann, corr. 1985

[16] 15 ♗f4 ♘de5 16 ♘e1 ♘b4 17 a3 ♘a6 18 ♖ac1 ∞∞ Vaganian-Sax, Switzerland 1985

15 ♘g5 ♘d4 16 ♗e3 c5 17 ♘ce4 e5 18 ♗xd4 cd 19 ♖ac1 ∞∞

[17] 16 ♘e4 ♗xb2 17 ♖ab1 ♘de5 18 ♖xb2 ♘xf3+ 19 ♔h1 e5 ∞ Korchnoi-Grünfeld, Jerusalem 1986

[18] 17 ♘e1 b3 18 ab ♖xb3 19 ♖ac1 ♘b4 20 ♖xc7 ± Geller-Piket, Amsterdam 1986

King's Indian XV
1 d4 ♘f6 2 c4 g6 3 ♘c3 ♗g7 4 ♘f3 d6 5 g3 0-0 6 ♗g2 ♘c6 7 0-0 a6 8 d5 ♘a5 9 ♘d2 c5

	10	11	12	13	14	15	16	17	18	
1	♖b1	b3	♗b2	de	cb	♘de4	♘xf6+	♘e4	♖xb2	∞/=
	♖b8[1]	b5	e5[2]	fe	ab	b4	♗xf6	♗xb2	♘b7[3]	
2	♕c2	b3	♗b2[4]	♖ae1[6]	♘d1	e3	♘e4	bc	♗a3	±
	♖b8	b5	e5[5]	♘h5	♗h6	♗f5	bc	♕b6	♗g7[7]	
3	...	...	...	de[8]	cb	♘ce4	♖ad1	♘xf6+	♗xf6	=
	...	...	e6	fe[9]	ab	♗b7[10]	♕e7	♗xf6	♕xf6[11]	
4	...	...	...	bc	♘cb1!	♗c3	♘a3	♗xb4	♘ab1	±
	...	...	...	bc	♗h6	♗d7	♖b4	cb	♕c7[13]	
5	...	...	...	f4[14]	bc	de[16]	♘d5	♕xb2	♕c1[17]	±
	...	...	...	♗h6	bc	♗xe6	♖xb2!?	♗g7	♘g4[18]	

[1]   10 ... e5 11 b3 a6 12 ♗b2 ♖b8 13 f4 ef 14 ♖xf4 ♗c8 15 ♘ce4 ♘h5 16 ♗xg7 ♔xg7 17 ♖f1 ± Gutman-Eng, Beer-Sheva Z 1985

[2]   12 ... bc 13 bc e6 (13 ... ♗f5 14 e4 ♘xe4 15 ♗xe4 ♖xb2 16 ♖xb2 ♗xc3 17 ♖c2 ± van der Sterren-Hellers, Wijk aan Zee 1985; 14 ♗a1 ♖b4 15 a3 ♖xb1 16 ♕xb1 ed 17 ♘xd5 ♗f5 18 ♕b2 ± Vaganian-van der Wiel, Biel IZ 1985

[3]   19 ♖c2 ♕c7 20 ♕c1 ♗d7 21 h4 ♗c6 ∞/= Kirov-Hazai, Niš 1985

[4]   12 ♖e1 e6 13 ♗b2 ♖e8 14 ♖fe1 h5 15 de ♗xe6 16 cb ab 17 ♘ce4 ♗f5 = Ornstein-Kindermann, Vienna 1986

[5]   12 ... ♗d7 13 ♖ab1 e5 14 de fe 15 ♘ce4! ±/± Korchnoi-Ciocaltea, Hamburg 1965

[6]   13 ♖ac1 ♘g4 (13 ... ♘h5 14 ♘d1 ♗h6 15 e3 ±) 14 h3 ♘h6 15 e4 f5 16 ef gf 17 ♘d1 f4 ∞ Vukić-Velimirović, Yugoslavia 1983

[7]   19 f4 ef 20 gf ♖fe8 21 ♘df2 ♘f6 22 ♗xf6+ ♗xf6 23 e4 ± Langeweg-Westerinen, Wijk aan Zee 1970

[8]   13 e4!? bc 14 bc ♘d7 15 ♖ab1 ♗d4 16 ♘e2 ♗xb2 17 ♖xb2 ♖xb2 18 ♕xb2 e5 ±/= Ornstein-Djurić, Järvenpää 1985
     13 ♖ab1 ♖e8 14 e4!? Spassky

[9]   13 ... ♗xe6?! 14 cb ab 15 ♘xe4 ♘xe4 16 ♘xe4 ♗xb2 17 ♕xb2 f5 18 ♘c3 b4 (18 ... ♕f6 19 ♕d2 b4 20 ♘d5 ♗xd5 21 ♗xd5+ ± Keene-Sharpe, England 1967) 19 ♘d5 h6 20 ♖ad1 = Panchenko-Peev, Lublin 1975

[10]   15 ... ♘xe4 16 ♘xe4 ♗xb2 17 ♕xb2 ♗b7 18 ♖ad1 ♗xe4 19 ♗xe4 d5 20 ♗g2 ± Ftacnik-Schmidt, Prague Z 1985

[11]   19 ♘e4 ♗xe4 20 ♗xe4 d5 21 ♗g2 ♖bc8 22 e3 ♖fd8 = Donner-Penrose, Holland v England 1966

[12]   14 ... ♗d7 15 ♘c3 ♕c7 16 ♘b3! ♘xb3 (16 ... ♗a7 17 e3! ± Ribli-Bouaziz, Las Palmas IZ 1982) 17 ab ♗c8 18 e4 ♗g7 19 ♘d2 ± Goldin-Oll, USSR 1983

[13]   18 ... ♕b6 19 ♘b3 ♘b7 20 ♘1d2 ♖c8 21 a3 ± Petrosian-Toran, Bamberg 1968
     18 ... ♕c7 19 c5! (19 e3 ♗f5 20 ♘e4 ♗xe4 21 ♗xe4, Timman-Kasparov, Tilburg 1981, 21 ... ♘xe4 22 ♗xe4 f5 ∞) 19 ... ♘xc5 20 ♕b2 ♘g4 21 ♘e4 ♕b6 22 ♗f3 ± Kurajica-Filipović, Banja Luka 1983

[14]   13 cb ab 14 ♘de4 ♗g7 15 h4 b4 ∞ Magerramov-Loginov, USSR 1983
     13 ♘cb1 e5 14 cb ab 15 a3 ♗d7 16 b4 cb 17 ab ♖c8 ∞ Djurić-Watson, Hastings 1984-85

[15]   14 ... ♗g7 15 ♖ab1 e6 16 ♘d1 ± Stohl-Pähtz, Potsdam 1985

[16]   15 ♖ae1 ef 16 gf ♘h5 17 e3 ♗g7 18 ♘d1 ♗f5 19 ♗e4 ♗xb2 20 ♘xb2 ♖xb2!! ∞/∓ Kasparov

[17]   18 ♕a3 ♘xc4 19 ♗xc4 ♘xd5 ∞ Hübner-Nunn, Wijk aan Zee 1982

[18]   19 ♖b1 ♗xd5 20 ♗xd5 ♘e3 21 ♖e1 ♖e8 22 ♘f3 ♘f6 (22 ... h6 23 h3 g5 24 fg hg 25 ♕d2 g4 26 hg ♘axc4 27 ♗xc4 ♘xc4 28 ♕f4 ± Danailov-Ornstein, Pamporovo 1981) 23 ♔h1 ♔f8 24 ♕a3! ♘c2 25 ♕d3 ♘xe1 26 ♘xe1 ♕c7 27 ♘c2 ± Hansen-Ernst, Lugano 1987

165

Grünfeld

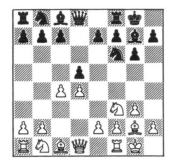 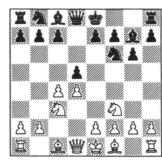 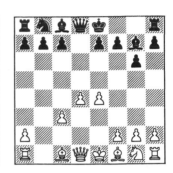

Austrian theoretician Ernst Grünfeld's creation is based on one of the fundamental strategies of the hypermodern school: that a large pawn centre can be a target as well as a strategical asset. Although Grünfeld himself grew fearful of White's central preponderance, subtle developments by exponents like Smyslov, Korchnoi, Fischer, Timman and co-author Kasparov have shaped the defence into a reliable weapon.

The seemingly eternal argument between Kasparov and Karpov will be central to the Grünfeld's status. Karpov's assaults have centred around the two systems which historically posed Black the greatest problems.

The **Exchange Variation** (4 cd ♘xd5 5 e4) has been the main theoretical battleground for the defence. In the "Classical" Exchange (white knight on e2) White establishes the vaunted pawn centre, often as a basis for a direct attack, while Black tries to negotiate its collapse. Karpov's latest attempt, the "Seville" Variation (see p. vi), poses the defender new and subtle problems.

Fashion now smiles upon the Classical rather than the Modern Exchange (white knight on f3). The teeth of the white advantage in the Modern have, for the time being, been drawn, though this could suddenly change.

The **Smyslov System** (4 ♘f3 ♝g7 5 ♕b3) has the most sting of White's less direct options. After a shaky period in the 1986 world title match, Kasparov succeeded in bolstering Black's defences in the Smyslov. Extremely complex, the variation is attractive for those with a taste for exploration.

White also has a number of quiet tries (lines with ♝f4 or ♝g5) but the consensus is that Black can achieve equality in all lines.

The **Neo-Grünfeld** is a closely related system. White delays the development of his queen's knight in order to chase the black knight on d5, which can no longer exchange itself on c3. This line offers White prospects of a slight edge, but the player who is content to fight back quietly against the white centre will probably also find these positions to his liking.

References: *Winning with the Grünfeld* (Adorjan and Dory)
The Semi-Closed Openings in Action (Karpov)

	Grünfeld I	1 d4 ♘f6 2 c4 g6 3 g3[1] d5 4 ♝g2 ♝g7 5 cd ♘xd5								
	6	7	8	9	10	11	12	13	14	
1	♘c3	bc	e3	♘e2	0-0	cd	♝b2	♘f4	♔xg2	=
	♘xc3[2]	c5	0-0	♘c6	cd	♝e6[3]	♝d5	♝xg2	♖c8[4]	

166

	6	7	8	9	10	11	12	13	14	
2	e4	d5	a3[5]	♘c3	♗f4[6]	ed	♘f3	0-0	♖e1	±
	♘b4	c6	♕a5	cd	♘4c6	♘d4	♗g4	0-0	♖e8[7]	
3	...	♘e2	♘bc3[9]	0-0	de[11]	♕c2	♗h6	♗xg7	♖fd1	=
	♘b6	0-0[8]	c6[10]	e5	♗xe5	♘a6	♗g7	♔xg7	♕e7[12]	
4	♘f3	0-0	e4	e5	dc	♕e2	♖d1	b4	b5	=
	0-0	c5[13]	♘f6	♘d5	♘a6[14]	♘xc5[15]	b6	♗a6	♗b7[16]	
5	...	...	♘c3	bc	cd[18]	♗e3	♕d2	♖fd1	♗h6	=
	...	...	♘xc3	cd[17]	♘c6	♗e6	♗d5	♖c8	♕a5[19]	
6	...	...	dc	♘g5[20]	♘c3	♘f3	♖xd1	♗e3	♖ac1	±
	...	...	♘a6	♘db4	h6[21]	♕xd1[22]	♘xc5	♘e6	♘c6[23]	
7	...	...	♘c3	d5[24]	e4	♗g5[26]	♕c1	dc	♖d1[28]	=
	...	♘b6	♘c6	♘a5[25]	c6	♘ac4[27]	♗g4	bc	♕c8[29]	

---

[1] 3 f3 d5 4 cd ♘xd5 5 e4 ♘b6 6 ♘c3 ♗g7 7 ♗e3 0-0 8 f4 ♘c6 (8 ... f5!? 9 ♕b3+ e6 10 e5 ♘c6 11 ♘f3 a5 12 a3 ♘e7 = Speelman-Gavrikov, London 1985) 9 d5 ♘a5 10 ♗d4 e5 (10 ... ♗g4 11 ♕d3 e5 12 fe ♘ac4 13 ♕g3 h5 14 ♘f3 ♕e7 15 ♗xc4 ♘xc4 16 0-0 ± Banas-Ftacnik, Czechoslovak Ch 1986) 11 ♗xe5 ♗xe5 12 fe ♕h4+ 13 g3 ♕e7 14 ♕d4 ♖d8 15 b4 ♘ac4 16 ♘f3 ♗g4 = Gheorghiu-Granda Zuniga, New York 1987

[2] 6 ... ♘b6 7 e3 ♘c6 8 ♘ge2 e5 9 d5 ♘e7 10 e4 c6 11 0-0 cd 12 ed 0-0 = Szabo-Tukmakov, Buenos Aires 1970

[3] 11 ... ♗f5 12 ♗a3 ♕d7 13 ♕b3 ♖fd8 14 ♖ac1 ♖ac8 = Gligorić-R.Byrne, Hastings 1967-68

[4] 15 ♖c1 ♕b6 = Vaganian-Szekely, Tallinn 1983

[5] 8 ♘e2 cd 9 ed ♗f5 10 0-0 0-0 11 ♘bc3 ♘8a6 =

[6] 10 ♗e3 d4 11 ab ♕d8 12 ♗xd4 ♗xd4 13 ♘ge2 ♗b6 14 0-0 0-0 15 ♕xd8 ♗xd8 = Evans-Pachman, Helsinki Ol 1952

[7] 15 ♗e5 ± Djurić-Smejkal, New York 1986

[8] 7 ... ♘c6 8 d5 ♘a5 9 0-0 0-0 10 ♕d2 ♘ac4 11 ♕c2 ♗d7 12 ♘bc3 ± Osnos-Karasev, USSR 1971

 7 ... c5 8 d5 e6 9 0-0 0-0 10 ♘ec3 ♘a6 11 a4 ed 12 ed ∞/± Vaganian-Ftacnik, Naestved 1985

[9] 8 0-0 e5 9 d5 c6 10 ♘bc3 – 8 ♘bc3

[10] 8 ... ♘c6 9 d5 ♘a5 10 a4 c5 11 0-0 c4 12 ♗e3 ±/± Korchnoi-Stepak, Beer-Sheva 1984

[11] 10 d5 cd 11 ed ♘a6 12 b3 ♗f5 13 ♗a3 ♖e8 14 d6 ♕d7 ∞ Timoshchenko-Mikhalchishin, USSR Ch 1981

[12] Priehoda-Banas, Trnava 1986

[13] 7 ... ♘c6 8 e4 ♘b6 9 d5 ♘a5 10 ♕e1 ♘ac4 11 ♘c3 e6 12 b3 ± Korchnoi-Kouatly, Cannes 1986

[14] 10 ... ♘c6 11 ♕e2 ♕a5 12 ♘bd2 ♕xc5 13 ♘b3 ♕b6 14 ♖d1 e6 15 h4 ± Botvinnik-Ragozin, USSR 1951

[15] 11 ... ♕c7 12 ♖d1 ♕xc5 13 ♘bd2 ♘db4 14 a3 ♘c6 15 ♘e4 ± Olafsson-Cuellar, Moscow Ol 1956

[16] 15 ♗b2 ♕c7 = Henriksen-Altshuler, corr. 1964

[17] 9 ... ♘c6 10 dc ♕a5 11 ♗e3 (11 ♘d4!? Palatnik-Stohl, Tallinn 1986) 11 ... ♗xc3 12 ♖c1 ♗g7 13 ♕b3 ± Vakhidov-Ermolinsky, USSR 1982

[18] 10 ♘xd4 ♕a5 11 ♗e3 ♘c6 12 ♕b3 (12 ♘xc6 bc 13 ♗xc6 ♖b8 =) 12 ... ♕a6 13 ♖ab1 ♘xd4 14 cd ♕xe2 15 ♕a3 ♗f6 16 ♖fe1 ⫶∞ Portisch-Korchnoi, Tilburg 1986

[19] 15 ♗xg7 ♔xg7 16 ♕f4 ♕c7 = Saltzberg-I.Ivanov, New York 1985

[20] 9 ♘a3 ♘db4 10 ♘c4 ♕xd1 11 ♖xd1 ♗e6 = Bradford-Gutman, Lone Pine 1981

 9 c6 bc 10 ♘a3!? Romanishin-Lanka, Jurmala 1983

[21] 10 ... ♘xc5 11 ♗e3 ♘ca6 12 ♕b3 h6 13 a3 ♘c6 14 ♖fd1 ♕e8 15 ♘ge4 ± Keene-Barreras, Camaguey 1974

[22] 11 ... ♗f5 12 ♘h4 ♗g4 13 ♗e3 ♕xd1 14 ♖axd1 g5 15 ♘f3 ±/± Helmers-Gutman, Randers 1982

[23] 15 b3 ± Helmers-Lobron, Lucerne 1979

[24] 9 ♗f4 ♗e6! 10 ♕c1 ♘xd4 11 ♘xd4 ♕xd4 12 ♖d1 (12 ♗xb7 ♖ab8 13 ♖d1 ♕b4 14 ♗f3 ♘a4 = Lechtynsky-Stohl, Trencianske Teplice 1985) 12 ... ♕c4 13 ♗xb7 ♖ad8 14 ♗f3 = Donchev-Ftacnik, Prague Z 1985

[25] 9 ... ♗xc3 10 dc ♗g7 11 cb ♗xb7 12 ♕c2 a5 ∞ Ilić-Rogers, Niš 1983

[26] 11 ♘d4 cd 12 ed e6 13 ♘b3 ♘xb3 14 ab ed 15 ♘xd5 ♗e6 = Priehoda-Plachetka, Trnava 1986

[27] 11 ... h6 12 ♗f4 ♘ac4 13 b3 ♗xc3 14 ♖c1 ∞ A.Petrosian-Grigorian, Erevan 1980

[28] 14 h3?! ♗xf3 15 ♗xf3 ♕d6! ∓ Smejkal-Hulak, Zagreb/Rieka 1985

[29] Smejkal

167

	6	7	8	9	10	11	12	13	14	
8	♘f3	0-0	♘c3	e3	♘e1[31]	d5	e4	♘c2	ed	±
	0-0	♘b6	♘c6	♖e8[30]	e5	♘a5	c6[32]	cd	♘ac4[33]	
9	...	...	...	...	d5	e4	♗g5[35]	♗e3	♗xb6[36]	∞
	...	...	...	e5	♘a5[34]	c6	f6	cd	♕xb6[37]	
10	...	...	...	...	...	e4	a4[38]	a5	a6[39]	=
	...	...	...	...	♘e7	♗g4	c6	♘c4	ba[40]	

30 9 ... ♗e6 10 b3 h6 11 ♗a3 ± Botvinnik-Tukmakov-Gavrikov, USSR Ch 1985
  9 ... a5 10 d5 ♘b4 11 e4 c6 12 a3 ♘a6 13 dc bc 14 ♕c2 ±

31 10 d5 ♘a5 11 ♘d4 ♗d7 12 e4 c5?! 13 ♘b3 ♘xb3 14 ♕xb3 c4 15 ♕c2 ± Kharitonov-Podgayets, USSR 1985

32 12 ... ♘ac4 13 a4! a5 14 b3 ♘d6 15 ♘d3 f5 16 ♘c5 ± Vaganian-Chandler, Thessaloniki Ol 1984

33 15 b3 ± Nikolić-Ftacnik, Naestved 1985

34 10 ... e4 11 dc ♕xd1 12 ♖xd1 ef 13 ♗xf3 bc 14 ♗xc6 ♖b8 ∞ Akhmilovskaya-Chiburdanidze, match 1986

35 12 ♖e1 ♖e8 13 ♗f1 cd 14 ed ∞ Timman-Ree, Wijk aan Zee 1981

36 14 ed ♘ac4 15 ♗c5 ♖f7 16 b3 ♘d6 ∞

37 15 ♘xd5 ♕d8 16 ♖c1 ♘c6 ∞ Dorfman-Yrjöla, Helsinki 1986

38 12 h3 ♗xf3 13 ♕xf3 c6 14 ♖d1 cd 15 ♘xd5 ♘exd5 16 ed ♕d6 = Tukmakov-Mikhalchishin, USSR 1981
  12 ♕b3 c6 13 ♘h4 cd 14 ed ♘ec8 15 a4 ♘d6 16 a5 ♘bc4 17 ♕b3 ♖c8 18 h3 ♗h5 19 ♖a2 ∞ Vukić-Ftacnik, Banja Luka 1983

39 14 ♕b3 ♘a5 15 ♕a2 b5 16 b4 ♘b7 ∞/= Spraggett-Ftacnik, New York 1983

40 15 ♕b3 cd 16 ed ♘d6 (16 ... ♘b6 17 ♘h4 ♖b8 18 ♕a2 h6 19 h3 ± Portisch-Smejkal, Reggio Emilia 1985-86) 17 ♖xa6 ♗c8 18 ♖a2 ♘ef5 = Smejkal-Doncevic, West Germany 1985-86

	6	7	8	9	10	11	12	13	14	
1	...	♘a3[2]	♘xc4	b3	♗b2	a4[5]	♖c1	♖a1	e3	±
	dc[1]	♘c6	♗e6	♗d5[3]	a5[4]	♘b4	♘a2	♘b4	♗e4[6]	
2	...	...	♘xc4	dc	♕xd8[8]	♘a5	♗e3	♖ad1	♘d4	=
	...	♘a6	c5	♗e6[7]	♖fxd8	♗d5	♘e4	♘exc5	♗xg2[9]	
3	...	...	bc	♘e5[10]	♘ac4[11]	♘xc6	♘e5	♗b2	♘d3[12]	∞
	...	c3	c5	♘c6	♗e6	bc	♘d5	♕c7	♖ab8[13]	
4	...	♘bd2[14]	b3	♗b2	♘h4	♕xd2	e4	♗xe4	♖fd1[17]	=
	c6	♗f5[15]	♘e4	♘d7[16]	♘xd2	♗e6	de	♗h3	♕c7[18]	
5	...	cd	♘e5[19]	♘xg4[20]	♘c3	h3[21]	e3	b3	♗d2	=
	...	cd	♘g4	♗xg4	♘c6	♗d7!	e6	♕a5	♕c7[22]	
6	...	...	...	♘c3	♘f3[23]	♗f4	♘e5	♕d2	♗xe5	=
	...	...	e6	♘fd7	♘c6	♘f6[24]	♗d7	♘xe5	♗c6[25]	
7	...	...	♘c3	♘e5	♘xc6[27]	♘a4	♗f4	♗d6[29]	b4	=
	...	...	♘c6	e6[26]	bc	♘d7	♕a5[28]	♖e8	♕d8[30]	
8	...	...	...	♘e5[31]	bc	♘xd7	♕b3	a4	a5	=
	...	...	♘e4	♘xc3[32]	♘d7[33]	♕xd7	♖d8	b6	♗a6[34]	

1 6 ... ♘c6 7 cd ♘xd5 8 e4 – 5 cd
   6 ... c5 7 dc dc 8 ♘c3 ±

2 7 ♘e5 c5 8 dc ♕c7 9 ♘xc4 ♕xc5 ∓ Partos-Gheorghiu, Romanian Ch 1973
   7 ♕a4 ♘c6 8 ♖d1 ♘d7 9 ♕xc4 ♘b6 = Alburt-Ribli, Lucerne Ol 1982

3 9 ... a5 10 ♗b2 a4 11 ♘g5 ♗d5 12 e4 ♗xc4 13 bc h6 14 ♘h3 ± Portisch-Ilijevski, Skopje 1968

4 10 ... ♕c8 11 ♘e3 ♗e4 12 ♘e5 ♗xg2 13 ♔xg2 ♘xe5 14 de ♖d8 15 ♕c2 ± Nikolić-Dvoiris, Sochi 1982

5 11 ♖c1 ♕c8 12 ♘e3 (12 a3 ♖d8 13 e3 ♕e6 14 ♕c2 h6 = Bilek-Rogulj, Zagreb 1986) 12 ... ♗e4 13 ♘e5 ♗xg2 14 ♔xg2 ♘xe5 (14 ... ♘b4 15 a3 ± Miles-Schmid, London 1980-81) 15 de ♖d8 = Miles

6 15 ♘e1 ♗xg2 16 ♔xg2 ± Kurajica-Rogers, Reggio Emilia 1984-85

7 9 ... ♘xc5 10 ♗e3 ♘ce4 11 ♕a4 ♗d7 12 ♕b3 ± Boleslavsky

8 10 ♘ce5 ♘xc5 11 ♗e3 ♘fe4 (11 ... ♕a5 12 ♗d4 ♗d5 13 e3 ± Timman-Henley, Arnhem/Amsterdam 1983) 12 ♖c1 ♖c8 = Vaganian

9 15 ♔xg2 ♘a4 = Nikolić-Smejkal, Sarajevo 1983

10 9 ♕b3 ♘c6 10 ♖d1 ♘a5! 11 ♕c2 ♗f5 12 ♕d2 ♗e4 ∓ Voiska-Chiburdanidze, Dubai Ol 1986
   9 ♘c4 ♘c6 10 ♗b2 ♕c7 11 ♘ce5 ♖d8 12 ♘xc6 bc 13 ♘d2 ♖b8 = Semkov-Ftacnik, Sochi 1982; 10 ♘ce5 ♘d5 11 ♗d2 ♘xe5 12 ♘xe5 ♘b6 13 ♗f4 ♘d5 ½-½ Smyslov-Kasparov, Moscow 1981

11 10 ♘xc6 bc 11 ♕a4 (11 ♕d3 ♘d5 12 ♖d1 ♕a5 13 ♗b2 ♖b8 ∓/∓ Granda Zuniga-Kasparov, Dubai Ol 1986) 11 ... ♘d5 12 ♗d2 cd 13 cd ♘b6 = Smyslov-Gufeld, USSR 1979

12 14 e4? ♘xc3 15 ♗xc3 cd 16 ♗xd4 ♗xe5 17 ♗xe5 ♕xe5 ∓ Pomar-Chiburdanidze, Barcelona 1979

13 15 ♕c1 cd 16 cd c5! (16 ... ♘b4?! 17 ♗c5 ±) ∞

14 7 b3 a5 8 ♘c3 ♘e4 9 ♗b2 ♘xc3 10 ♗xc3 ♘d7 =

15 7 ... a5 8 b3 ♘e4 9 ♗b2 a4 10 ba ♘c5 11 a5 ♕xa5 12 ♘b3 ♕b4 = Kavalek-Cooper, Thessaloniki Ol 1984

16 9 ... ♕a5 10 a3 ♘d7 11 b4 ♕d8 12 ♕b3 ♘df6 13 a4 ± Ribli-Andersson, Wijk aan Zee 1973
   9 ... a5 10 e3 a4 11 ♘xe4 ♗xe4 12 cd cd 13 ba ♘c6 = Pelts-Westerinen, Thessaloniki Ol 1984

17 14 ♖fe1 ♖e8 =

18 15 ♗g2 ♗xg2 16 ♘xg2 ♖ad8 17 ♕e2 ♖fe8 = Razuvayev-Vogt, Leipzig 1983

19 8 ♗f4 ♘e4 9 ♗e5 f6 10 ♗xb8 ♖xb8 11 ♘c3 e6 12 ♕d3 ♔h8 13 e3 b6 14 ♖fc1 ♘d6 = Romanishin-Henley, Indonesia 1983

20 9 f4 ♘xe5 10 de e6 11 ♘c3 ♘c6 = Nikolić-Watson, Bor 1986

21 11 ♗xd5 ♘xd4 12 ♗xb7 ♘xe2+ 13 ♘xe2 ♕xd1 14 ♖xd1 ♗xe2 15 ♗xa8 ♗xd1 = Veličković-Henley, Tbilisi 1983

22 15 ♖c1 ♖ac8 = Polugayevsky-Kasparov, Moscow 1981

23 10 ♘xd7 ♗xd7 11 ♗f4 ♘c6 12 e3 ♘a5 = Jansa-Ftacnik, Prague Z 1985
   10 f4 f6! (10 ... ♘xe5 11 de?! ♕b6+ 12 ♔h1 ♘c6 13 b3 ♗d7 14 ♘a4 ♕b5 15 ♗a3 ♖fd8 = Portisch-Nunn, Brussels 1986; 11 fe ♘c6 12 e4! de 13 ♗e3 f5 14 ef ♖xf6 15 ♘xe4 ♖xf1+ 16 ♕xf1 ± Kasparov-Nunn, Brussels 1986) 11 ♘f3 ♘c6 12 ♗e3 ♘b6 13 ♗f2, Karpov-Kasparov, match (13) 1986, 13 ... ♗d7 = Dorfman

24 11 ... ♕b6 12 ♘a4 ♕a5 13 ♖c1 b5 14 ♘c5 ♘xc5 15 ♖xc5 ♗d7 = Akhmilovskaya-Chiburdanidze, match 1986

25 15 ♖fd1 ♘d7 16 ♗xg7 ♔xg7 17 ♖ac1 ♘f6 = Karpov-Kasparov, match (3) 1986

26 9 ... ♗f5 10 ♘xc6 bc 11 ♘a4 ♘d7 12 b3 e5 13 de ♗xe5 14 ♗h6 ±
   9 ... ♗d7!? 10 ♗g5 ♗e8 11 ♗xf6 ♗xf6 12 ♘xd5 ♗g7 13 e3 ♘xe5 14 de ♗xe5 15 ♕b3 e6 = Korchnoi-Ljubojević, Brussels 1986

27 10 ♗f4 ♘xe5 11 ♗xe5 ♗d7 12 ♕d3 ♕b6 13 ♖fc1 ♖fc8 14 ♖c2 ♘e8 15 ♗xg7 ♔xg7 = Azmaiparashvili-Malanyuk, Tbilisi 1986

28 12 ... ♗a6 13 ♕d2 ♕e7 14 ♖ac1 ♖fc8 15 ♖fe1 ± Boleslavsky

29 13 a3 ♗a6 14 b4 ♕d8 = Akhmilovskaya-Chiburdanidze, match 1986

30 15 e4 ♗a6 = Chiburdanidze

31 9 ♗f4 ♘xc3 10 bc ♘c6 11 ♖c1 ♘a5 12 ♖e1 ♗f5 = Browne-Kavalek, Buenos Aires 1980
   9 ♘xe4 de 10 ♘e5 ♕b6 11 ♘c4 ♕a6 12 b3 ♖d8 13 ♗b2 ♘c6 14 e3 f5 = Marović-Mariotti, Rome 1982

32 9 ... ♗f5 10 ♗f4 f6 (10 ... ♘xc3 11 bc ♘c6 12 ♕b3 ♘xe5 13 ♗xe5 ♗xe5 14 de ±/= Kirov-Andersson, Rome 1986) 11 ♘d3 ♘c6 12 ♘c5 ♘xc3 13 bc b6 = Browne-Hübner, Chicago 1982

33 10 ... ♘c6 11 ♘xc6 bc 12 ♗a3 ♖e8 13 e4 ♗a6 14 ♖e1 e6 = Kärner-Sturua, Tbilisi 1983

34 15 ab ab 16 ♗f4 ♕c6 = Gutman-Andersson, Biel IZ 1985

Grünfeld III   1 d4 ♘f6 2 c4 g6 3 ♘c3 d5

	4	5	6	7	8	9	10	11	12	
1	♗g5[1]	♗h4[2]	bc	cd	e3	♕xd4	cd	♗d3[6]	♗g3	=
	♘e4	♘xc3[3]	c5[4]	♕xd5	cd[5]	♕xd4	e6!	♗e7	♘c6[7]	
2	...	...	...	e3	cd	♕f3[8]	♗c4	♘e2	ed[10]	=
	...	...	♗g7	c5	♕xd5	♕d7!?[9]	0-0	cd	♘c6[11]	
3	♗f4	e3[12]	dc	♖c1[13]	cd	♕d2	bc	♗c4	♘f3[17]	=
	♗g7	c5	♕a5	♘e4	♘xc3	♕xa2[14]	♕a5[15]	♘d7[16]	0-0[18]	
4	...	...	♕b3[19]	♗xc4	♗e2	♘f3	e4[22]	0-0	♕d1	∞
	...	0-0	dc[20]	♘c6[21]	a5!	♘b4	c6	♗e6	b5[23]	
5	...	...	cd	♘xd5	♗xc7	♗xa6[25]	♘f3	0-0	♗e5	∞/=
	...	...	♘xd5	♕xd5	♘a6[24]	ba[26]	♗b7[27]	♖ac8	♗xe5[28]	

[1] 4 e3 ♗g7 5 ♕b3 e6 6 ♕a3 ♘c6 7 ♘f3 ♘e7 8 ♕a4+ c6 9 ♗e2 0-0 10 0-0 ♕c7 = Knežević-Ftacnik, Trnava 1983
    4 ♕b3 dc 5 ♕xc4 ♗e6 6 ♕b5+ ♗d7 7 ♕b3 ♘c6 8 ♘f3 ♗g7 9 e4 0-0 ∞ Ree-Sax, Teesside 1972

[2] 5 cd?! ♘xg5 6 h4 ♘e4 7 ♘xe4 ♕xd5 8 ♕d3!? ♘c6 9 ♘f3 ∞ Gipslis
    5 ♗f4 ♘xc3 6 bc dc 7 e3 ♗e6 8 ♖b1 b6 9 h4 h6 10 ♘f3 ♗g7 11 e4 ♘d7 ∞ Grigorian-Tukmakov, USSR Ch 1971

[3] 5 ... c5 6 e3 ♕a5 7 ♕b3 cd 8 ed ♗h6 ∞

[4] 6 ... dc!? 7 e3 ♕d5 8 ♕a4+ b5 9 ♕a5 c6 ∞ Alburt-Faibisovich, USSR 1971

[5] 8 ... ♘c6 9 ♕f3! ± Taimanov-Uhlmann, Belgrade 1970

[6] 11 ♗b5+ ♗d7 12 ♖b1 ♗e7 13 ♗xe7 ♔xe7 = Jones-Ghinda, Lucerne Ol 1982

[7] 13 ♘f3 = Hoi-W.Schmidt, Malmö 1979

[8] 9 ♗e2 cd 10 ed ♕a5! 11 ♕d2 e5 12 ♘f3 ♘c6 = Ogaard-Timman, Helsinki 1972

[9] 9 ... ♕d8 10 ♗b5+ ♗d7 11 ♘e2 cd 12 ed 0-0 13 0-0 a6 (13 ... ♘f6 14 ♖fe1 ♗g4 =) 14 ♗d3 ♕c7 = Levin-Tukmakov, USSR 1970

[10] 12 cd ♕a4! =

[11] 13 0-0 e6 14 ♗f6 ♗xf6 15 ♕xf6 ♕e7 = Vilela-Popović, Polanica Zdroj 1982

[12] 5 ♖c1 dc 6 e4 c5 7 dc ♕a5 8 ♗xc4 0-0 = Lin Ta-Kouatly, Dubai Ol 1986

[13] 7 ♘f3 ♘e4 8 ♗e5 ♗xe5 9 ♘xe5 ♘xc3 10 ♕d2 ♗e6 11 cd ♗xd5 12 bc ♕xc5 = Pinter-Ghinda, Prague Z 1985
    7 ♕b3 ♘e4 8 ♕b5+ ♕xb5 9 ♘xb5 ♘a6 = Ruban-Semenyuk, USSR 1986; 7 ... ♘c6 =

[14] 9 ... ♘d7 10 ♘e2 ♘xc5 11 ♘xc3 ♗d7 12 ♗c4 ± van der Sterren-Timman, Holland 1986

[15] 10 ... ♕xd2+ 11 ♔xd2 ♘d7 12 ♗b5 0-0 13 ♗xd7 ♗xd7 14 e4 f5 ∞ Karpov-Kasparov, match (5) 1986

[16] 11 ... ♕xc5 12 ♗a2 0-0 13 ♘e2 b6 14 e4 ♗a6 15 c4 ± van der Sterren-van Mil, Copenhagen 1984

[17] 12 ♘e2 ♘xc5 13 0-0 0-0 14 ♘d4 (14 f3 e5! 15 ♗g3 b5 16 ♗a2 ♕b6! ∓ Rashkovsky-Mikhalchishin, USSR 1984) 14 ... ♗d7 15 ♕b2 ♖fc8 16 ♗e2 b6 17 c4 e5 = Polugayevsky-Timman, match 1980

[18] 13 0-0 ♘xc5 14 ♗e5 ♗xe5 15 ♘xe5 f6 16 ♘f3 (16 ♖a1 ♘e4! = Razuvayev-Mikhalchishin, Minsk 1985) 16 ... b5 17 ♖a1 ♕d8 18 d6+ bc 19 ♕d5+ ♗e6 20 ♕xc5 ed = van der Sterren-de Boer, Holland 1986

[19] 6 ♖c1 c5 7 dc ♗e6 8 ♘ge2 ♘c6 9 cd ♘xd5 10 ♘xd5 ♕xd5 11 ♕xd5 ♗xd5 = Paunović-Ghinda, Nikea 1986

[20] 6 ... c5 7 dc (7 cd cd 8 ed – Caro-Kann) 7 ... ♘e4 8 cd ♕a5 9 ♘e2 ∞ Boleslavsky

[21] 7 ... ♘bd7 8 ♘f3 ♘b6 9 ♗e2 ♗e6 10 ♕c2 ♘fd5 11 ♘xd5 ♘xd5 12 ♗g3 ± Garcia Gonzalez-Sigurjonsson, Nice Ol 1974

[22] 10 0-0 ♗e6 11 ♗c4 ♗xc4 12 ♕xc4 ♘bd5 13 ♘xd5 ♘xd5 = Mecking-Hort, Palma de Mallorca IZ 1970

[23] 13 a3 ♘a6 ∞ Pomar-Toran, Malaga 1967

[24] 8 ... ♘c6 9 ♘e2 ♗g4 10 f3 ♖ac8 11 ♘c3 ♕e6 12 ♗f4 ♘xd4 (12 ... ♗xd4 13 fg g5 14 ♗xg5 ♖fd8 15 ♕c1 ± Wiersma-Zapletal, corr. 1980, and Smit-Sapundzhiev, corr. 1980) 13 fg ♖fd8 14 ♗d3 ♘c6 15 ♕b1! ± Timman-W.Schmidt, Indonesia 1983
    8 ... ♗f5 9 ♘e2 ♖c8! 10 ♘c3 ♕c6 11 ♗g3 ♘a6 12 a3 e5! 13 d5 ♕b6 ∞ Tamme-Gulko, USSR 1977

[25] 9 ♗g3 ♗f5 10 a3 ♖ac8 11 ♘f3 ♖c2 12 b4 ♕b3 ∞ Evans-Saidy, USA 1983

[26] 9 ... ♕xg2 10 ♕f3 ♕xf3 11 ♘xf3 ba 12 ♖g1 ♗b7 (12 ... ♗e6 13 ♔d2 ±/= Littlewood-Pein, London 1985) 13 ♔e2 f6 14 ♖gd1 ♖ac8 15 ♖ac1 ♗d5 16 b3 ±/= Stahlberg-Donner, Munich Ol 1958

[27] 10 ... ♗f5 11 ♕b3 ♕c6 12 ♕c3 ♕b5 13 ♕b3 ♕c6 14 ♗g3 ♗e4 15 0-0! ± Lputian-Gavrikov, Irkutsk 1986

[28] 13 de ♕e6 14 b3 ♖fd8 15 ♕e2 ♗xf3 16 ♕xf3 ♕xe5 ∞/=

	5	6	7	8	9	10	11	12	13	
1	♕a4+ ♗d7![2]	♕b3 dc	♕xc4 0-0	e4 b5![3]	♘xb5[4] ♘xe4	♘xc7 ♘c6	♘xa8 ♕a5+	♗d2 ♘xd2	♘xd2 ♘xd4[5]	$\overline{\infty}/\mp$
2	cd ♘xd5	♕b3[6] ♘xc3[7]	bc c5	e3 0-0	♗e2[8] ♕c7	0-0 b6	♗a3 ♘d7	e4 e5	d5 ♘f6[9]	=
3	... ...	♗d2 0-0[10]	♖c1 ♗g4[11]	e3 e5[12]	♕b3 ♗xf3	gf ♘b6	de ♗xe5	f4 ♗g7	♗g2 ♘a6![13]	=
4	♗g5 ♘e4[14]	♗h4[15] c5[16]	cd ♘xc3	bc ♕xd5	e3 ♘c6	♗e2 cd[17]	cd ♕a5+[18]	♕d2 ♗e6	♕xa5 ♘xa5[19]	=
5	... ...	cd ♘xg5[20]	♘xg5 e6[21]	♕d2 ed[22]	♕e3+ ♔f8	♕f4 ♗f6	h4 h6[23]	♘f3 c6[24]	e4[25] de[26]	=

[1]   4 ... c6 5 cd cd 6 ♗f4 ♗g7 7 e3 0-0 (7 ... ♘c6 8 ♘e5 0-0 9 ♗e2 ± Yusupov-Pfleger, Lucerne 1985) 8 h3 ♘c6 9 ♗e3 ♘e4 10 ♖c1 ♗f5 11 ♕b3 ± Spraggett-Lein, Montreal 1986

[2]   5 ... c6 6 cd ♘xd5 7 e4 ♘xc3 8 bc 0-0 9 ♗a3 ♕c7 10 ♗e2 c5 = Razuvayev

[3]   8 ... ♘a6 9 e5 ♘e8 10 ♗e2 c6 11 0-0 ♗e6 12 ♕a4 ♘ac7 = Sideif Zade-Dorfman, USSR 1980

[4]   9 ♕b3 c5 10 e5 (10 dc ♘a6 11 e5 ♘g4 ∓ Ubilava-Kengis, USSR 1984) 10 ... ♘g4 11 ♗xb5 cd 12 ♘xd4 ♗xb5 13 ♘dxb5 a6 14 ♘a3 ♕d4! ∓ Hübner-Kasparov, Brussels 1986

[5]   14 ♕c7 ♕xc7 15 ♘xc7 ♘c2+ 16 ♔d1 ♘xa1 17 ♗d3 ♗xb2 $\overline{\infty}/\mp$ Bönsch-Jasnikowski, Harkany 1985

[6]   6 ♕a4+ ♘c6! =

[7]   6 ... ♘b6 7 ♗g5 h6 8 ♗h4 ♗e6 9 ♕c2 ♘c6 10 ♖d1 ♘b4 11 ♕b1 0-0 ∞ Tisdall-Jansa, Aarhus 1983

[8]   9 ♗a3 b6 10 ♖d1 ♕c7 11 ♗e2 ♘d7 = Pribyl-Smejkal, Bratislava 1983

[9]   14 ♕c2 ♘e8! intending ... ♘d6 = Rogers-de Wit, Wijk aan Zee II 1985

[10]   6 ... c5 7 ♖c1 ♘xc3 8 ♗xc3 cd 9 ♘xd4 0-0 10 e3 ♘d7 (10 ... ♕d5 11 ♘b4! ♕xd1+ 12 ♖xd1 ♘c6 13 ♗xg7 ♔xg7 14 ♗e2 ± Petrosian-Fischer, Belgrade 1970) 11 ♗e2 ♘b6 = Ivkov-Simić, Yugoslav Ch 1984

[11]   7 ... ♘b6 8 ♗g5 h6 9 ♗f4 ♘c6 10 e3 g5 11 ♗g3 g4 ∞/= Martinović-Timman, Amsterdam 1985

    7 ... ♘c6 8 e4 (8 e3 e5 9 ♘xd5 ♕xd5 10 ♗c4 ♕d6 11 d5 ♘e7 12 e4 c6 = Kholmov-Platonov, USSR Ch 1970) 8 ... ♘b6 9 d5 ♘b8 10 ♗b5 c6 11 dc ♘xc6 12 h3 ♗e6 = Henley-Gavrikov, Tbilisi 1983

[12]   8 ... ♘xc3 9 ♗xc3 ♕d5 = Pomar-Korchnoi, Palma de Mallorca 1972

[13]   Hort-Hübner, match 1979

[14]   5 ... c6 6 e3 0-0 7 ♗d3 ♗e6 8 cd (8 ♕e2 ♘bd7 9 0-0 h6 10 ♗h4 ♗g4 11 cd cd 12 h3 ± Kasparov-Smyslov, match 1984) 8 ... ♘xd5 9 0-0 ♘d7 10 h3 ±

    5 ... dc 6 e4 c5 7 ♗xc4 (7 d5 b5 8 e5 b4 9 ef ef 10 ♕e2+ ♔f8 11 ♗e3 ∞ Flear-Kouatly, Brussels 1986) 7 ... ♕a5 8 e5 ♘g4 9 0-0 ± Browne-Strauss, Lone Pine 1973

[15]   6 ♕c1 h6 7 ♗f4 ♘xc3 8 bc c5 = Zaitsev-Tukmakov, Erevan 1982

[16]   6 ... ♘xc3 7 bc dc and now:
    8 e3 ♗e6 9 ♗e2 (9 ♕b1!?) 9 ... ♘d7 10 ♘g5 ♗d5 11 e4 h6 12 ed hg 13 ♘xg5 ♘b6 14 ♗xc4 = Ristić-Kapetanović, Yugoslavia 1985
    8 ♕a4+ ♕d7 9 ♕xc4 b6 10 e3 ♗a6 11 ♕b3 ♗xf1 12 ♔xf1 = Meduna-Plachetka, Trnava 1981

[17]   10 ... 0-0 11 0-0 b6 12 ♕d2! cd 13 ♗f3 ♕d7 14 cd ±

[18]   11 ... 0-0 12 0-0 e5 13 de ♕a5 ∞ Petran-Okhotnik, Eger 1984

[19]   14 0-0 ♗c4 = Bagirov-Neverov, Baku 1986

[20]   6 ... ♘xc3 7 bc ♕xd5 8 e3 (9 ♕b3!? ♗e6 10 ♕xd5 ♗xd5 11 ♘d2 f5 ∞ Rogers-Hort, Biel 1984) 8 ... c5 9 ♗e2 ♘c6 10 0-0 cd 11 ed (11 cd 0-0 12 ♕b3 ♗e6 13 ♕a3 ♖fe8 ∞ Lobron-Wittmann, Beer-Sheva 1985) 11 ... 0-0 12 c4 ♕d6 13 d5 ± Rogoff-Zaltsman, Lone Pine 1978

[21]   7 ... c6 8 dc ♘xc6 9 e3 e5 10 d5 ♕xg5 11 dc 0-0 12 h4 ♕e7 13 ♘d5 ♕d6 14 c7 ±/± Hübner-Ftacnik, Biel 1984

[22]   8 ... h6 9 ♘h3 ed 10 ♕e3+ ♔f8 11 ♘f4 c5 12 dc d4 13 ♕d2 ∞/±

[23]   11 ... ♗g7 12 e4! de 13 0-0-0 ♕d6 14 ♕xd6 cd 15 ♘gxe4 ± Hort-Miles, Montilla 1978

[24]   12 ... ♗g7 13 0-0-0 ♗e6 14 e3 c6 = − 12 ... c6

[25]   13 e3 ♗e6 14 ♗d3 ♔g7 15 ♕g3 ♘d7 16 ♗e2 ∞/= Legky-Bagirov, USSR 1984

[26]   14 ♘xe4 ♔g7 15 ♗c4 ♕a5+ (15 ... ♘d7?! 16 ♘d6 ♖f8 17 h5 ± Lechtynsky-Torre, Baku 1980) 16 ♔f1 ♕f5 17 ♕xf5 ♗xf5 18 ♘d6 c5! = Marović-W.Schmidt, Rome 1979

	5	6	7	8	9	10	11	12	13	
6	♗g5	cd	♘xg5	♘f3	e3²⁷	♗e2	0-0	♘e1³⁰	♗d3	=
	♘e4	♘xg5	e6	ed	a5²⁸	0-0	c6²⁹	♗f5	♗xd3³¹	
7	♗f4	♖c1	e4	♗xc4	gf	♗e3	♘e2	♘g3	♕d2	=
	0-0³²	dc	♗g4³³	♗xf3	♘h5	e6³⁴	♕f6!	♘f4	♘g2+³⁵	
8	...	...	dc	e3³⁷	♗e2	♘d4³⁹	ed	bc	0-0	=
	...	c5	♗e6³⁶	♘c6	♘e4³⁸	♘xd4	♘xc3	dc	♗d5⁴⁰	
9	...	e3	dc⁴¹	♖c1	♗xc4	♗b3	0-0	h3	♘d4⁴⁵	=
	...	c5	♕a5⁴²	dc⁴³	♕xc5⁴⁴	♘c6	♕a5	♗f5	♗d7⁴⁶	
10	...	...	♖c1⁴⁷	♕b3	c5⁴⁹	ab	♗xb8	♗e2	b4	=
	...	c6	♗e6⁴⁸	♕b6	♕xb3	♘h5⁵⁰	♖axb8	♘f6	a6⁵¹	
11	e3	b4⁵²	♗b2⁵⁴	bc⁵⁵	♖c1	♘xd4	♗e2⁵⁶	♘xc6	0-0	=
	0-0	b6⁵³	c5!	bc	cd	♗b7	♘c6	♗xc6	dc⁵⁷	
12	...	cd	♗c4	bc	0-0	♗e2⁵⁹	a4	♘d2	♘c4	=
	...	♘xd5	♘xc3⁵⁸	c5	♕c7	b6	♘c6	♖d8	♗a6⁶⁰	
13	...	♗e2	0-0	ed	h3⁶³	♘e5	♗f3	♖e1	cd	=
	...	c5⁶¹	cd⁶²	♘c6	b6⁶⁴	♗b7	♘a5	♖e8	♘xd5⁶⁵	
14	...	♗d3	0-0	h3	♕xf3	♖d1	b3⁶⁹	♗f1	cd	±/=
	...	c6⁶⁶	♗g4⁶⁷	♗xf3	e6⁶⁸	♘bd7	♖e8	e5⁷⁰	e4⁷¹	

²⁷ 9 b4 ♕d6 (9 ... ♗f8!? ∞ W.Schmidt-Ghinda, Prague Z 1985) 10 a3 0-0 11 e3 c6 12 ♗e2 ♗f5 13 0-0 ♘d7 = Seirawan-Kasparov, Dubai Ol 1986

²⁸ 9 ... 0-0 and now:
10 ♗e2 c6 11 0-0 ♕d6 12 ♘e1 (12 a3 ♗e6 13 ♘a4 ♘d7 14 b4 ♖fc8 ∞ Donner-Botterill, Cambridge 1971) 12 ... ♗e6 13 ♘d3 ♘d7 = Didishko-Mikhalchishin, Minsk 1986
10 b4 ♗e6 (10 ... c6 11 ♗e2 a5 12 b5 a4 13 0-0 ♕a5 = Ostermeyer-Korchnoi, Biel 1984) 11 ♗e2 ♘d7 12 0-0 f5 13 ♖e1 g5 14 ♖c1 ♔h8 15 ♗d3 a6 (15 ... c6 16 b5 g4 17 ♘d2 ± Karpov-Korchnoi, London 1984) 16 ♘a4 c6 17 ♕c2 = Ivkov-Jansa, Bor 1984

²⁹ 11 ... ♘c6 12 ♖c1 ♘e7 13 a3 ♘f5 14 ♗d3 ± Amos-Korchnoi, Toronto 1985

³⁰ 12 ♖c1 ♘d7 13 ♘a4 ♖e8 14 ♘e1 ♗f8 15 ♘d3 ♗d6 ∞/= Schüssler-Yrjölä, Gausdal 1985

³¹ 14 ♗xd3 ♘d7 15 ♖c1 ♘b6 = Schneider-Veingold, USSR 1985

³² 5 ... c5 6 dc ♕a5 7 cd ♘xd5 8 ♕xd5 ♗xc3+ 9 ♗d2 ♗e6 ∞ Dreyev-Epishin, USSR 1986

³³ 7 ... c5 8 dc ♘a6 (8 ... ♕xd1+ 9 ♖xd1 ♘a6 =) 9 ♗xc4 ♘xc5 10 ♕e2 ♗e6 ∞ Martz-Larsen, USA 1970

³⁴ 10 ... e5 11 de ♗xe5 12 ♕b3!? Gipslis

³⁵ 14 ♔e2 ♘xe3 15 fe c5 = Nogueiras-Timman, Montpellier C 1985

³⁶ 7 ... dc 8 ♕xd8 ♖xd8 9 e3 ♘a6 10 c6 bc 11 ♗xc4 ∞/± Dlugy-London, New York 1985

³⁷ 8 ♘d4 ♘c6 9 e3 (9 ♘xe6 fe 10 e3 ♕a5 11 ♗e2 e5 12 cd ef 13 dc bc = Kavalek-Ribli, Las Palmas 1973) 9 ... ♘xd4 10 ed dc 11 ♗e2 ♖c8 12 0-0 b6 = D.Gurevich-Henley, Hastings 1982-83

³⁸ 9 ... ♕a5 10 ♘g5 ♖ad8 11 ♘xe6 fe 12 ♕a4 ∞/± Jacobs-Rogers, British Ch 1983

³⁹ 10 0-0 ♘xc3 11 bc dc 12 ♘g5 ♗d7 13 ♗xc4 ♘a5 = Farago-W.Schmidt, Polanica Zdroj 1981

⁴⁰ 14 ♗f3 ♕d7 15 ♖e1 ♖fe8 16 ♗xd5 ♕xd5 = Farago-Tukmakov, Helsinki 1983

⁴¹ 7 ♕b3 cd 8 ♘xd4 dc 9 ♗xc4 ♕a5 10 ♘f3 ♘e4 = Pedersen-Stohl, Trnava 1985

⁴² 7 ... ♘e4!? 8 ♖c1 (8 ♕b3?! ♘a6! 9 cd ♘axc5 10 ♕c4 b5! ∓ Behrhorst-Kasparov, Hamburg 1985) 8 ... ♘xc3 9 bc dc 10 ♕xd8 ♖xd8 11 ♗xc4 ♘d7 12 ♗c7 ♖e8 (12 ... ♖f8 13 c6 bc 14 ♘d4 ♘b6 15 ♗xb6 ab ∞ Georgiev-Mikhalchishin, Lvov 1984) 13 ♗b5 a6 14 ♗a4 ♖f8 15 ♗b6 ♘xb6 16 cb ♗e6 = A.Rodriguez-Milos, Havana II 1986

⁴³ 8 ... ♘a6!? 9 cd ♘xc5 10 ♕d2 ♗g4 11 ♘e5 ♖ac8 12 f3 ♗d7 13 ♗e2 b5 ∞ Farago-Gutman, Luxembourg 1986

⁴⁴ 9 ... ♘c6 10 0-0 ♕xc5 11 ♕a4 ♗d7 12 ♕b5

♕xb5 13 ♗xb5 ♖ac8 = Karpov-Kasparov, match (1) 1986

[45] 13 ♕e2 ♘e4 14 ♘d5 (14 ♘xe4 ♗xe4 = Hansen-Wiedenkeller, Helsinki 1986) 14 ... e5 15 ♗h2 (15 ♖xc6?! ef 16 ♘c7 ± Karpov-Kasparov, match (11) 1986; 15 ... bc! 16 ♘e7+ ♔h8 17 ♘xc6 ♕b6 18 ♘cxe5 ♗e6! ∞ Kasparov) 15 ... ♗e6 16 ♖fd1 ♖ad8 = Moran-Wittmann, Dubai Ol 1986

[46] 14 ♕e2 ♘xd4 15 ed e6! 16 ♗d2 ♕b6 = Karpov-Kasparov match (9) 1986

[47] 7 ♗e2 dc 8 ♗xc4 ♗g4 9 h3 ♗xf3 10 ♕xf3 ♘fd7 =

7 ♕c2 ♗f5 8 ♕b3 ♕b6 9 c5 ♕xb3 10 ab ♘bd7 11 h3 ♘e4 = Miles-Agdestein, Oslo 1984

7 ♕b3 ♕a5 8 ♘d2 ♘bd7 9 ♗e2 ♘h5 10 ♗xh5 dc 11 ♘xc4 ♕xh5 12 0-0 e5! = Inkiov-Ghinda, Athens 1981

[48] 7 ... ♗g4 8 h3 ♗xf3 9 ♕xf3 e6 (9 ... ♕a5 10 ♗d3 ♘bd7 11 0-0 dc 12 ♗xc4 e5 =) 10 ♗d3 ♘bd7 11 0-0 ♖e8 12 cd ♘xd5 13 ♘xd5 ed 14 b4 a6 = Hausner-Lechtynsky, Hradec Kralove 1981

[49] 9 ♕xb6 ab 10 ♘g5 ♗d7 11 cd ♘xd5 12 ♘xd5 cd = Skembris-Z.Nikolić, Vrnjačka Banja 1983

[50] 10 ... b6 11 b4 a5 12 ♘a4 ∞ Rogers-Jansa, Niš 1983

[51] Rogers-Korchnoi, Biel 1984

[52] 6 ♗d2 c5 (6 ... c6 7 ♗d3 ♗g4 8 ♕b3 ♗xf3 7 gf dc 10 ♗xc4 ♕b6 11 0-0 ± Nogueiras-Meduna, Plovdiv 1982) 7 dc ♘a6 8 cd ♘xc5 9 ♗c4 ♗f5 10 0-0 ♖c8 = Lombardy-Tarjan, US Ch 1975

[53] 6 ... ♗e6!? 7 c5 ♘e4 8 ♗b2 ♘d7 9 ♕c2 ♘xc3 10 ♕xc3 c6 = Plaskett-Tukmakov, Hastings 1982-83

6 ... ♘e4 7 ♗b2 c6 8 ♗d3 ♘xc3 9 ♗xc3 dc 10 ♗xc4 ♘d7 =

[54] 7 b5 c5 8 bc ♘xc6 9 ♗a3 ♗b7 10 ♖c1 a6 = Bagirov-Mikhalchishin, USSR 1981

7 ♕b3 dc (7 ... c5 8 cd cd 9 ♘xd4 ♗b7 = Draško-Jansa, Sarajevo 1981) 8 ♗xc4 c5 9 ♘e5 e6 10 bcbc 11 ♗a3 ♘bd7 ∞ Mikhalchishin-Tseshkovsky, USSR 1985

[55] 8 ♕b3 dc 9 ♗xc4 cb 10 ♕xb4 ♘c6 = Bellon-F.Garcia, Torremolinos 1985

[56] 11 ♕b3 ♘c6! =

[57] 14 ♕xd8 ♖fxd8 15 ♗xc4 ♘d5 = Andrianov-Gorelov, Moscow 1981

[58] 7 ... ♘b6 8 ♗b3 c5 9 0-0 cd 10 ed (10 ♘xd4 ♘c6! 11 ♘xc6 bc 12 ♕f3 a5 13 ♘a4 ♕c7 = Panno-Gheorghiu, Las Palmas 1973) 10 ...

♗g4 (10 ... ♘c6 11 d5 ♘a5 12 ♖e1 ♗g4 13 h3 ♗xf3 14 ♕xf3 ♕d7 15 ♗g5 ± Belyavsky-Peresipkin, USSR 1976) 11 d5 a5 12 a3 ♘a6 13 h3 ♗xf3 14 ♕xf3 ± Nei-Belyavsky, USSR 1975

[59] 10 ♕e2 b6 (10 ... ♗g4 =) 11 ♗b2 ♘c6 12 ♖ac1 ♗b7 13 ♖fd1 e6 = Kuzmin-Kochiev, USSR 1976

[60] Plachetka-Tukmakov, Decin 1977

[61] 6 ... dc 7 ♗xc4 c5 8 h3 cd 9 ed ♘bd7 10 0-0 ♘b6 11 ♗b3 ♘bd5 12 ♖e1 ± Ghitescu-Smejkal, Lugano Ol 1968

6 ... c6 7 0-0 and now:

7 ... ♗g4 8 cd cd 9 ♕b3 b6 10 h3 ♗xf3 11 ♗xf3 e6 12 ♗e2 a6 13 ♗d2 ± Timman-Smyslov, Las Palmas IZ 1982

7 ... dc 8 ♗xc4 ♗g4 9 h3 ♗xf3 10 ♕xf3 ♘bd7 11 ♖d1 ♘b6 (11 ... e5 12 d5 e4 13 ♕f4 ♕e7 14 dc bc 15 ♗d2 ± Portisch-Draško, Sarajevo 1986) 12 ♗b3 ♘fd5 13 e4 ♘xc3 14 bc ♕c7 15 h4 ± Korchnoi-Hübner, Tilburg 1986

7 ... ♗e6 8 cd ♘xd5 9 ♕c2 ♗xf3 10 ♗xf3 ♘bd7 11 ♖d1 ♕c7 12 e4 e5 13 d5 ± Larsen-Smyslov, Bugojno 1984

[62] 7 ... dc 8 ♗xc4 a6 9 ♕e2 ♕c7 10 ♖d1 cd 11 ed ♗g4 12 ♗b3 ♘c6 13 h3 ± Inkiov-Hebden, Moscow 1986

[63] 9 ♗e3 ♗g4 10 c5 ♘e4 11 ♕a4 e5! = Sunye-Mokry, Zenica 1986

9 ♗f4 ♗g4 10 c5 ♘e4 11 ♖c1 e6 12 ♘e1 ♘xc3 13 bc = Nei-Jansa, Tallinn 1983

[64] 9 c5 ♘e4 11 ♗f4 ♘xc3 12 bc b6 = Sturua-Gavrikov, Tbilisi 1983

[65] 14 ♗xd5 ♗xd5 15 ♗f4 e6 = Marjanović-Smejkal, Marseilles 1986

[66] 6 ... c5!? ∞/= Bagirov

[67] 7 ... ♗e6 8 b3 ♘bd7 9 ♗a3 ♕a5 10 ♕c1 ± Portisch-Hort, Lucerne Ol 1982

7 ... ♗f5 8 ♗xf5 gf 9 cd cd 10 ♕b3 b6 11 ♗d2 ♘c6 12 ♖fc1 ♖c8 13 ♖c2 ± Tarjan-Shamkovich, Lone Pine 1981

[68] 9 ... ♖e8 10 ♖d1 ♕b6 11 e4 de 12 ♗xe4 ± Ribli-Smyslov, match (8) 1983

9 ... ♕d6 10 ♖d1 ♘bd7!? Chernin/M.Gurevich

[69] 11 ♕e2 ♖e8 12 b3 e5 13 de ♘xe5 14 ♗b2 d4! = Ftacnik-Lechtynsky, Trnava 1983

[70] 12 ... ♗f8 13 ♗b2 ♗d6 14 e4 de 15 ♘xe4 ♘xe4 16 ♕xe4 ± Portisch-Hort, Reggio Emilia 1984-85

[71] 14 ♕e2 cd!? (14 ... ♘xd5 15 ♘xd5 cd 16 ♕b5 ± Ribli-Smyslov, match (6) 1983) ±/= Bagirov

1 d4 ♘f6 2 c4 g6 3 ♘c3 d5 4 ♘f3 ♗g7 5 ♕b3 dc¹ 6 ♕xc4 0-0 7 e4

	7	8	9	10	11	12	13	14	15	
1	...	♕b3²	♗c4	0-0	♗xb3	♗f4	♗e5	♖ad1	♖fe1⁴	±
	c6	♕b6³	♘a6	♕xb3	♘c7	♘e6	♗d7	♖ad8		
2	...	♗e2⁵	d5!	♘xe5	♕b3	0-0	ed	♗e3	♖ad1	±
	♘c6	♘d7⁶	♘de5	♘xe5	e6	ed	♕h4	c6	a5⁷	
3	...	♕b3⁸	dc	c6¹⁰	♗e2	0-0	♕c2	♗g5	♖fd1	±
	a6	c5⁹	♘bd7	bc	♕c7	♖b8	c5	♗b7¹¹	♖fe8¹²	
4	...	♗e2¹³	d5	0-0¹⁴	ed	♗f4¹⁵	♖ad1	♗d3¹⁸	♗xd6	∞/=
	♘a6	c5	e6	ed	♗f5	♖e8¹⁶	♘e4¹⁷	♘d6	♗xd3¹⁹	
5	...	♗e3²⁰	♖d1²¹	♗e2²²	♕c5²⁴	e5²⁵	dc	h3²⁶	♗xf3	=
	♗g4	♘fd7	♘c6	♘b6²³	♕d6	♕xc5	♘c8	♗xf3	♗xe5²⁷	
6	...	...	♕b3	♖d1	♗e2	♘g1³⁰	♘gxe2	0-0	a3	=
	...	...	♘b6²⁸	e6²⁹	♘c6	♗xe2	♕e7	♖fd8	h6³¹	
7	...	...	...	...	d5	♗e2	gf	♖g1³³	♖g3	=
	...	...	...	♘c6	♘e5	♘xf3+	♗h5³²	♕d7³⁴	c6³⁵	

[1] 5 ... c6 6 cd cd (6 ... ♘xd5 7 e4 ♘b6 8 ♕c2! ±/±) 7 ♗g5 e6 8 e3 0-0 9 ♗d3 ♘c6 10 h3 b6 11 ♘e5 ∞/± Bagirov-Gurgenidze, USSR 1959

[2] 8 ♗f4!? ♗g4 9 ♗e2 ♘fd7 10 ♖d1 ± Didishko-Dorfman, Minsk 1986

[3] 8 ... e5 9 de ♘g4 10 ♗e2 ♕b6 11 0-0 ± Sosonko-Ree, Wijk aan Zee 1975

[4] Belyavsky-Korchnoi, Tilburg 1986

[5] 8 e5 ♘d7 9 ♗e3 ♘b6 10 ♕c5 a5 11 ♗e2 ♘b4 12 0-0 ♘d7 = Gulko-Gavrikov, USSR 1983

8 h3 e5 (8 ... ♘d7 =) 9 de ♘d7 10 e6 fe 11 ♕xe6+ ♔h8 ∞ Portisch-Korchnoi, match 1983

[6] 8 ... e5 9 d5 ♘d4 10 ♘xd4 ed 11 ♕xd4 c6 12 ♕d1 ♖e8 13 0-0 ± Eingorn-Kuzmin, USSR 1985

[7] 16 dc bc 17 ♗c5 ± Eingorn-Gavrikov, USSR Ch 1986

[8] 8 a4?! b5! 9 ♕b3 c5 10 dc ♗e6! ∓ Adorjan

8 ♗f4 b5 9 ♕xc7 ♘xc7 10 ♗xc7 ♗b7 11 ♗d3 b4 12 ♘a4 ♗xe4 = Adorjan

8 ♗e2 b5 9 ♕b3 c5 10 dc ♘bd7 11 e5 ♘xc5 12 ♕b4 ♘fd7 = Ree-Mecking, Wijk aan Zee 1978

[9] 8 ... b5 9 e5 ♘g4 (9 ... ♘fd7 10 h4! ±) 10 h3 ♘h6 11 ♗f4 c5 12 ♖d1 cd 13 ♘xd4 ∞/± Ivkov-Sax, Osijek 1978

[10] 10 ♕b4 ♕c7 11 ♗e3 ♘g4 12 ♗g5 a5! = Miles-F.Garcia, Dubai Ol 1986

[11] 14 ... ♖e8!? F.Garcia

[12] 16 h3 ± Portisch-F.Garcia, Dubai Ol 1986

[13] 8 ♗f4 c5 9 dc ♕a5 10 ♕b5 ♕xb5 11 ♗xb5 ♘xc5 12 e5 ♘fe4 13 ♘xe4 ♘xe4 = Sosonko-Smejkal, Lucerne Ol 1982

8 ♕a4 c5 9 d5 ♕b6 10 ♗xa6 ba 11 0-0 e6 12 ♖e1 ♗b7 13 de ♕xe6 = Nesis-G.Andersson, corr. 1980

8 ♕b3 c5 9 d5 e6 =

[14] 10 ♗g5 ed 11 ♘xd5 ♗e6 12 0-0-0 ♗xd5 13 ♖xd5 ♕b6 ∞ Belyavsky-Kasparov, Belfort 1988

[15] 12 ♖d1 ♖e8 13 d6 h6 14 ♗f4 ♘d7! ∞ Karpov-Kasparov, match (21) 1987

[16] 12 ... ♕b6 13 ♘h4 ♗g4! = Bareyev-Gavrikov, Irkutsk 1986

[17] 13 ... ♘d7!? 14 ♗g5 ♕c8 15 ♖d2 h6 16 ♗e3 ♘b6 ∞ Gavrikov-Schneider, Jurmala 1983

[18] 14 ♘b5 ♗d7 ∞ Smyslov; 14 ... ♕f6 15 ♗d3 ♖ad8! ∞ Dzhandzhava-Kasparov, Baku 1987

[19] 16 ♖xd3 ♕xd6 ∞/= Renet-Kouatly, Marseilles 1986

[20] 8 ♗e2 ♘c6 9 d5 ♗xf3 10 gf ♘e5 11 ♕b3 c6 12 f4 ♘ed7 13 dc bc 14 e5 ±; 8 ... ♘fd7 9 ♗e3 - 8 ♗e3

[21] 9 0-0-0 ♘b6 10 ♕c5 e5 (10 ... e6 11 h3 ♗xf3 12 gf ♘8d7 ∞ Sosonko-Smejkal, Amsterdam 1979) 11 d5 ♘8d7 12 ♕a5 ♗xf3 13 gf ♕h4 = Hartston

9 ♗e2 ♘b6 10 ♕d3 ♘c6 11 0-0-0 e5 12 d5 ♗xf3 13 gf ♘d4 =

[22] 10 ♕b3 e5! 11 de ♘cxe5 12 ♗e2 ♗e6 = Hartston

10 ♕b5 ♘b6 11 d5 ♘e5 12 ♗e2 ♘xf3+ 13 gf ♗h5 = Belyavsky-Ornstein, Vienna 1986

[23] 10 ... ♗xf3 11 gf ♘b6 (11 ... e5 12 de ♘cxe5 13 ♕a4 ±) 12 ♕c5 e6 13 h4 ± Chernin-Ornstein, Järvenpää 1985

[24] 11 ♕d3 ♕c8 12 ♕c2 e5 = Andersson-Korchnoi, London 1984

[25] 12 h3 ♗xf3 13 gf ♘d7 (13 ... ♖fd8 14 e5 ♕xc5 15 dc ♖xd1+ 16 ♔xd1 ♘d7 17 f4 g5 = Fischer) 14 ♕c4 ♘b6 = W.Schmidt-Ftacnik, Herculana Z 1982

[26] 14 ♘b5 ♖b8 15 ♘xc7 e6! ∞ Karpov-Kasparov, match (15) 1986

[27] 16 ♗xc6 bc 17 ♗d4 ♗f4 18 0-0 e5! (18 ... a5? 19 ♖fe1 ± Karpov-Kasparov, match (17) 1986) 19 ♗e3 ♗xe3 20 fe ♘e7 21 ♖d7 ♘f5 22 ♖xc7 ♖fc8! = Karpov-Timman, Tilburg 1986

[28] 9 ... c5 10 d5 ♘a6 11 ♗e2 ♕a5 12 0-0 ♖ab8 13 ♗f4 ± Sturua-Henley, Tbilisi 1983

[29] 10 ... ♗xf3 11 gf e6 12 d5 (12 ♗e2 ♘c6 13 d5 ed 14 ♘xd5 ♘xd5 15 ♖xd5 ♕h4 ∞ Eingorn-Lputian, USSR Ch 1986) 12 ... ♕e7 13 de fe 14 ♗h3 ♖e8 15 f4 ± Eingorn-Belyavsky, USSR Ch 1986

[30] 12 e5 ♘e7 13 0-0 ♗xf3 14 ♗xf3 ♘f5 = Ree-Ftacnik, Kiev 1978

[31] 15 ... ♘a5 16 ♕b5 ♘ac4 16 ♗g5 f6 17 ♗c1 a5 = Gligorić-Smejkal, Novi Sad 1982

15 ... h6 16 ♘a4 ♘a5 17 ♕c2 ♘ac4 18 ♗c1 ♘xa4 19 ♕xa4 ♘b6 = Meduna-Jansa, Trnava 1982

[32] 13 ... ♗h3?! 14 ♖g1 ♕c8 15 f4 ♘d7 16 f5 ±

[33] 14 f4 ♗xe2 15 ♘xe2 ♕d7 (15 ... c6!?) 16 ♗d4 ♗xd4 17 ♖xd4 c6 = Averbakh-Petrosian, Moscow 1966

[34] 14 ... ♕c8 15 ♖g3 c6 16 a4 ± Sosonko-Timman, Wijk aan Zee 1981

[35] 16 dc ♕xc6 17 ♘b5 ♖fc8 18 ♘xa7 ♖xa7 19 ♗xb6 ♖aa8 (19 ... ♖xa2 20 ♕xa2 ♕xb6 21 b3 ± Sosonko-Timman, Bergen 1984) = Keene-Tarjan, Torremolinos 1975

Grünfeld VI			1 d4 ♘f6 2 c4 g6 3 ♘c3 d5 4 cd ♘xd5 5 e4 ♘xc3[1] 6 bc ♗g7						

	7	8	9	10	11	12	13	14	15	
1	♗a3	♖c1[3]	d5	♕b3	♘f3	♗e2	d6	0-0	♕b2	=
	♘d7[2]	c5	♕a5	0-0	♘b6	e6!	♗d7	♗a4	♗c6[4]	
2	♗e3	♕d2[5]	d5[7]	♗xc5	♗d4	cd	e5	♗e2	ef	∞
	c5	0-0[6]	e6[8]	♕c7	♗xd4	ed	♘c6	f6	♖xf6[9]	
3	♘f3	♗b5+	0-0	cd	♗xc6[12]	♗a3	♗c5	♖c1	♕xf3	=
	c5[10]	♘c6[11]	cd	0-0	bc	♗g4	♖e8	♗xf3	♗xd4[13]	
4	...	♗e2	d5[15]	♗d2	♕xa1	♘xd4	♕xd4	0-0	♗c4	=
	...	♘c6[14]	♗xc3+	♗xa1	♘d4	cd	0-0[16]	♖e8	e5[17]	
5	...	♗e3	♖c1[19]	♕d2	cd	♘xd2[21]	♘b3	♗g5	♗e3	=
	...	0-0[18]	♕a5[20]	cd	♕xd2+	e6[22]	♖d8[23]	f6	♗f8[24]	
6	...	...	♖c1[25]	♕d2	gf	dc[28]	♗e2	♕b2	h4	∞
	...	♗g4	♕a5[26]	♗xf3[27]	e6	♘xc6	0-0	♕c7	h5[29]	
7	...	...	♕d2[30]	♖b1[31]	♖c1	cd	♔xd2	d5[34]	ed	=
	...	♕a5	♘c6	a6[32]	cd	♕xd2+	e6[33]	ed	♘e5[35]	
8	...	♖b1	♗e2	0-0[37]	♗xf3	cd	♖xb7[39]	♕a4[40]	♗a3	=
	...	0-0[36]	♗g4	♗xf3	♗xf3	cd	♗xd4[38]	♘c6	♗c5[41]	
9	...	...	...	0-0	♕d3	cd	♕e3	♗xa6	♕a3	∞
	...	...	b6	♗b7	cd	♗a6[42]	♕d7	♘xa6	♕b7[43]	
10	...	...	...	0-0[44]	♗d2	♕c2	♖xb7[46]	♖b3	♖xa3	=
	...	...	♕a5	♕xc3[45]	♕a3	♗d7	♗c6	♗a4	♗xc2[47]	
11	...	...	...	d5	♘xe5	♕d2[49]	f4	c4	cd	∞∞
	...	...	♘c6	♘e5[48]	♗xe5	e6[50]	♗g7	ed[51]	♗d4[52]	
12	...	...	....	cd	♕d2[53]	♗xd2	♖c1[54]	♗d3	♔e2	=
	...	...	cd	♕a5+	♕xd2+	b6	♗b7	♘a6	♖fc8[55]	

[1] 5 ... ♘b6 6 h3 ♗g7 7 ♘f3 0-0 8 ♗e3 (8 ♗e2 ♘c6 9 ♗e3 ±) 8 ... a5 9 ♗e2 a4 10 ♖c1 (10 0-0 c6 11 ♕d2 ♗e6 12 ♗h6 ± Alburt-Gutman, Thessaloniki Ol 1984) 10 ... a3 11 b3 f5 12 ef ♗xf5 13 0-0 ♘c6 14 ♕d2 ± I.Sokolov-Djurić, Novi Sad 1986

[2] 7 ... 0-0 8 ♘f3 b6 9 ♗c4 ♗b7 10 ♕d3 c5 11 0-0 ♘c6 12 ♖ad1 ♕c7 = Hernandez-Mikhalchishin, Havana 1982

[3] 8 ♘f3 c5 9 ♕b3 0-0 10 ♗d3 b6 11 ♖e1 e6 12 0-0 ♕c7 ∞ Dolmatov-Bagirov, Frunze 1983

[4] Garcia Gonzalez-Lechtynsky, Cienfuegos 1985

[5] 8 ♖c1 ♕a5 9 ♕d2 cd 10 cd ♕xd2+ 11 ♗xd2 0-0 12 d5 e6 = W.Schmidt-Jansa, Vrnjačka Banja 1983

[6] 8 ... cd 9 cd ♘c6 10 ♘f3 ♗g4 11 ♖d1 0-0 12 ♗e2 ♖c8 13 0-0 b6 = Haik-Granda Zúñiga, Dubai Ol 1986

[7] 9 ♖c1 ♘d7 10 d5 ♘f6 11 f3 e6 12 c4 ♖e8 ∞ Spassov-Tseshkovsky, Moscow II 1985

[8] 9 ... ♕a5 10 ♖c1 f5 11 ef ♗xf5 12 ♘f3 ♘d7 13 ♗e2 ± Zaltsman-Hansson, Reykjavik 1982

[9] Birnboim-Ribli, Lucerne Ol 1982

[10] 7 ... b6 8 ♗b5+ c6 9 ♗c4 0-0 10 0-0 ± Kasparov-Pribyl, Skara 1980
7 ... 0-0 8 ♗e2 b6 9 ♗g5! c5 10 0-0 ± – 7 ... c5

[11] 8 ... ♗d7 9 ♗xd7+ ♕xd7 (9 ... ♘xd7 10 0-0 0-0 11 ♖b1 b6 12 ♗g5 ± F.Portisch-Pribyl, Trnava 1981) 10 0-0 0-0 11 ♖b1 ♘c6 12 ♗e3 ± Speelman-Sisniega, Taxco IZ 1985

[12] 11 ♗e3 ♕a5 12 ♕a4 ♕xa4 13 ♗xa4 ♗d7 14 ♖ab1 b6 = Guseinov-Razuvayev, USSR 1983

[13] 16 ♖fd1 e5 = Alburt-Kudrin, New York 1986

[14] 8 ... 0-0 9 0-0 b6 10 ♗g5 cd 11 cd ♗b7 12 ♕d3 ± Veingold-Lanka, USSR 1980

[15] 9 ♗e3 ♗g4 10 e5 cd 11 cd 0-0 12 0-0 ♕d7

13 ♕d2 ♖fd8 ∞ Langeweg-Timman, Wijk aan Zee 1981

[16] 13 ... f6 14 0-0 0-0 15 e5 fe 16 ♕xe5 ♕d6 17 ♕b2 b6 = Lputian-Tukmakov, USSR Ch 1984

[17] 16 ♕d3 ♗d7 17 f4 ♖c8 = Ruderfer-Gorelov, USSR 1980

[18] 8 ... ♘c6 9 ♖c1 cd 10 cd 0-0 11 d5 ♘e5 12 ♘xe5 ♗xe5 13 ♗c4 b5 14 ♗b3 a5 15 0-0 a4 16 ♗c2 ± Miles-Gligorić, Bled/Portorož 1979

[19] 9 ♗e2 ♕a5 10 0-0 ♕xc3 11 ♖c1 ♕a3 12 ♖xc5 ♕xa2 13 ♘g5 ∞

[20] 9 ... e6 10 ♗c4 ♕a5 11 0-0 b5 12 ♗c3 c4 13 ♗b1 ♘d7 14 ♕d2 ♖e8 15 ♗h6 ± Gligorić-Popović, Yugoslavia 1981

[21] 12 ♔xd2 ♖d8 13 ♗b5 ♗g4 14 ♖c7 ♘c6 15 d5 ♖ab8! = Tseitlin-W.Schmidt, Lodz 1980

[22] 12 ... ♘c6 13 ♘b3 ♖d8 14 d5 ♘b4 ∞ Portisch-Adorjan, Hungarian Ch 1981

[23] 13 ... b6 14 ♗b5 ♗b7 15 f3 ♖c8 ∞/= Krnić

[24] 16 ♗c4 ♘c6 17 ♔e2 ♗d7 18 ♖hd1 ♔g7 = Johansen-Hort, Martigny 1986

[25] 9 ♕a4+ ♘c6 10 ♘e5 and now:
10 ... cd 11 ♘xc6 bc 12 cd 0-0 13 ♖c1 ♗d7 14 ♖c5! ± Kasparov-Romanishin, USSR Ch 1979
10 ... ♗xe5 11 de ♕c7 12 f4 0-0 ∞

[26] 9 ... 0-0 10 ♗e2 ♕a5 11 ♕d2 ♘d7 (11 ... e6 12 d5 ed 13 ed ♗xf3 14 ♗xf3 c4 15 0-0 ♘d7 16 d6! ± Kasparov-Kouatly, Graz 1981) 12 d5 c4 13 ♗d4 ♗xf3 14 gf ∞ Itkis-Tseshkovsky, USSR 1980

[27] 10 ... ♘d7 11 d5 b5 12 ♗e2 0-0 13 c4 b4 14 0-0 ♖ac8 ∞ Portisch-Korchnoi, match 1983

[28] 12 ♖b1 cd 13 cd ♕xd2+ 14 ♔xd2 0-0 15 e5 ♘c6 = Sande-Nesis, corr. 1985

[29] Renman-Ornstein, Uppsala 1985

[30] 9 ♗d2 ♗g4 10 ♗e2 0-0 11 0-0 ♖d8 = Belyavsky

[31] 10 ♖c1 cd 11 cd ♕xd2+ 12 ♔xd2 0-0 13 d5 (13 ♗b5 f5! 14 ef ♗xf5 = Browne-Vaganian, Thessaloniki Ol 1984) 13 ... ♖d8 14 ♔e1 ♘a5 = Tatai-Ftacnik, Dortmund 1981

[32] 10 ... b6 11 ♖c1 e6 12 d5 ed 13 ed ♘e7 14 ♗g5 ∞/± Yusupov-Timman, Indonesia 1983

[33] 13 ... f5 14 ♗d3 0-0 15 d5 ♘b4 16 ♗c4 fe ∞ Agdestein-Ftacnik, Gjovik 1983

[34] 14 ♗d3 0-0 15 ♖c4 f5 16 ♔e2 ♗d7 = Ftacnik-Sax, Herculana Z 1982

[35] 16 ♘xe5 ♗xe5 17 g3 ♗f5 = Ftacnik-Jansa, Bratislava 1985

[36] 8 ... cd 9 cd ♕a5+ 10 ♕d2 ♕xd2+ 11 ♗xd2 0-0 12 ♗c4 e6 13 d5 ± van der Sterren-Sokolowski, Dortmund 1986

[8] ... a6 9 ♗e2 ♕a5 10 0-0 ♕xa2 11 ♗g5 ♕a5 12 d5 h6 13 ♗e3 ♘d7 14 c4 ± Petursson-Gutman, Biel IZ 1985

[37] 10 ♖xb7 ♘c6 11 0-0 (11 ♕a4 ♕c8 = Fedorov-V.Ivanov, USSR 1982) 11 ... cd! 12 cd ♗xf3 13 ♗xf3 ♕c8 = Polovodin, Fedorov

[38] 12 ... ♕xd4 13 ♖xb7 ♘c6 14 ♗e3 ♕xd1 15 ♖xd1 ♖fc8 16 ♗e2 ± Lerner-Vakhidov, USSR 1983

[39] **13 ♗h6!?** ♗g7 14 ♗xg7 ♔xg7 15 ♖xb7 ♘c6 16 ♕d5! (16 ♕a4 ♕d6! 17 ♖d1 ♕f6 18 ♖c7 ♖ac8 = Schmidt-Kouatly, Lucerne Ol 1982) 16 ... ♕xd5! (16 ... ♖c8 17 ♗d7 ♖d8 18 ♗g4! ♕a6 19 e5 ±/±; 16 ... ♖c8 17 ♗d7 ♕b6 18 e5 ±/± Henley) 17 ed ♘d4 18 ♗e4 Ubilava-Henley, Tbilisi 1983

13 e5!? ♘c6 14 ♗h6 ♖e8 15 e6! fe 16 ♕b3 Henley

[40] 14 ♗h6 ♖e8 15 ♕a4 ♖c8 16 ♗e2 ♕a5 = Commons-Tarjan, US Ch 1978

[41] Rubinetti-Sax, Lucerne Ol 1982

[42] 12 ... e6 13 ♗g5 ♕d6 14 ♕e3 ♖c8 15 ♖fd1 ± Lputian-Lalić, Sarajevo 1985

[43] 16 ♗e3 e6 17 h4 ∞ Cvitan-Gavrikov, Vršac 1985

[44] 10 ♖b5 ♕xc3+ 11 ♗d2 ♕a3 12 ♖a5 ♕b2 13 ♖xc5 ♕xa2 ∞

[45] 10 ... ♕xa2 11 ♗g5 cd 12 cd ♖e8 13 ♗b5 ♗d7 14 ♗xd7 ♘xd7 15 ♖xb7 ± Foisor-Gulko, Sochi 1985; 11 ... ♕e6!? 12 e5 ♖d8 ∞/= Grünberg-Ghinda, Potsdam 1985

[46] 13 dc ♗c6 14 ♗b5 ♘a6 15 ♖fc1 ♘c7 ∞ Belyavsky-Tukmakov, USSR Ch 1983

[47] Miniböck-Konopka, Eger 1985

[48] 10 ... ♗xc3+ 11 ♗d2 ♗xd2+ 12 ♕xd2 ♘a5 13 h4 ♗g4 ∞ Westermeier-Stohl, Lugano 1986

[49] 12 c4 ♕c7 13 h3 f5 14 ef ♗xf5 = Danner-Nesis, corr. 1985

[50] 12 ... b6!? 13 f4 ♗g7 14 0-0 e6 ∞ Pergericht-Jansa, Metz 1985

[51] 14 ... ♖e8 15 e5! f6 16 d6 fe 17 ♗b2 ef 18 ♗xg7 ♔xg7 19 0-0 ±/± Novikov-Tukmakov, USSR Ch 1984

[52] 16 ♗b2 ♕b6! 17 ♗d3 c4! 18 ♖xc4 ♖e8 ∞∞ H.Olafsson-Helmers, Gjovik 1985

[53] 11 ♗d2 ♕xa2 12 0-0 b6 (12 ... ♕e6 13 ♕c2 ♕d7 14 d5 ± Conquest-Korchnoi, Lugano 1986) 13 ♖c1 ♕e6 14 ♗c4 ♕xe4 15 ♖e1 ♕b7 16 ♗b4 ∞∞ Gelfand-Dorfman, Minsk 1986

[54] 13 0-0 ♗b7 14 d5 ♗a6 15 ♖fe1 ♗xe2 16 ♖xe2 ♘a6 = Khalifman-Tseshkovsky, Minsk 1985

[55] 16 a4 ♘c7 17 ♗e3 e6 = de Boer-Mikhalchishin, Cascais 1986

Grünfeld VII   1 d4 ♘f6 2 c4 g6 3 ♘c3 d5 4 cd ♘xd5 5 e4 ♘xc3 6 bc ♗g7 7 ♗c4 0-0[1]

	8	9	10	11	12	13	14	15	16	
1	♘e2[2]	0-0	♕d3[3]	e5	♘f4	♕h3	♗e2	♗e3	cd	±
	♕d7	b6	♗b7	♘c6	e6	♘a5	c5	cd	♖fd8[4]	
2	...	h4[5]	♗d5[7]	h5	♗b3	hg	♗h6	♖xh6	♕d2	±
	b6	♘c6[6]	♕d7	e6	e5	hg	♗xh6	♔g7	♗a6[8]	
3	...	0-0[9]	♗e3	♖c1[11]	f4	f5	♗d3	ef	♖f2	∞
	♘c6	b6[10]	♗b7	♕d6	e6	♘a5	ef	♕c6	♘c4[12]	
4	...	0-0	♗e3	♖c1	♗f4[15]	d5[17]	♗d3[18]	c4	♗d2	±
	c5	♘c6	♕c7[13]	♖d8[14]	♕d7[16]	♘a5	b6[19]	e5	♘b7[20]	
5	...	...	...	...	♕d2	♖fd1	♕b2[23]	♕xb5	♗xb5	±
	...	...	...	...	♕a5[21]	♗d7[22]	b5	♕xb5	♘xd4[24]	
6	...	...	...	f3	♗d5[25]	♖b1[26]	♗f4[27]	♕d2[28]	♗b3	=
	...	...	♗g4	♘a5	♗d7	♕c7	♕c8	e6	♘xb3[29]	

1 d4 ♘f6 2 c4 g6 3 ♘c3 d5 4 cd ♘xd5 5 e4 ♘xc3 6 bc ♗g7 7 ♗c4 0-0 8 ♘e2 c5 9 0-0 ♘c6 10 ♗e3 cd 11 cd

	11	12	13	14	15	16	17	18	19	
7	...	♗d3[31]	♗b5	f3	♖b1	♘f4	♗e2	d5	de	∞
	♘a5[30]	♘c6[32]	♗g4	♗d7	e6	a6	b5	♘e5	fe[33]	
8	...	f3	♗d5[35]	♖b1	♗xb7	♗d5	a4	♕xe2	♗c4	=
	♗g4	♘a5[34]	♗d7	a6	♖a7[36]	♗b5[37]	♗xe2	e6	♗xd4[38]	
9	...	...	♗d3	♖c1[39]	♕a4[40]	d5	♕b4	♘c3	♗a6	∞
	...	...	♗e6	♗xa2	♗e6	♗d7	e6[41]	b6	♕f6[42]	
10	...	...	...	d5	♕xa1	♖b1[43]	e5[45]	♕xe5	♕xe7[47]	∞
	...	...	...	♗xa1	f6	♗d7[44]	fe[46]	♕b8	♖e8[48]	

---

[1] **7 ... b6** 8 ♕f3 0-0 9 e5 ♗a6 10 ♗d5 c6 11 ♗b3 ♕d7 (11 ...♕c7 12 h4 c5 13 h5 ± Yusupov-Timman, match 1986) 12 ♘e2 e6 13 0-0 c5 14 ♖d1 ♘c6 15 ♗g5 ± Yusupov-Timman, Bugojno 1986

7 ... c5 8 ♘e2 ♘c6 (8 ... 0-0 – 7 ... 0-0) 9 ♗e3 cd 10 cd b5 (10 ... ♕a5+ 11 ♗d2 ♕a3 12 ♖b1 0-0 13 0-0 a5 14 e5 e6 15 ♗g5 ±/± Lukacs-Pavlov, Herculana Z 1982) 11 ♗d5 ♗d7 12 ♖c1 ♖c8 13 0-0 0-0 14 ♗xc6 ♖xc6 15 ♖xc6 ♗xc6 16 d5 ♗d7 17 ♕d2 ± Polugayevsky-Bagirov, USSR Ch 1978

[2] 8 ♗e3 b6 9 h4 ♗b7 10 ♕f3 ♕d7 11 ♘e2 h5 12 ♗g5 ♘c6 13 ♘f4 ± Kasparov-Sax, Moscow IZ 1982; 8 ... c5! =

[3] 10 e5 ♗b7 11 ♘f4 e6 12 ♕g4 c5 13 ♗e3 ♘c6 14 ♖ad1 ± Balashov-Gulko, USSR Ch 1976

10 ♗e3 ♗a6 (10 ... ♗b7 11 f3 ♘c6 12 ♗b5 ±) 11 ♗xa6 ♘xa6 12 ♗g5 ±

[4] 17 ♖ad1 ♕e7 18 ♕g3 ± Gligorić-Vaganian, Yugoslavia v USSR 1975

[5] 9 ♗d5!? c6 10 ♗b3 ♗b7 11 ♗g5 ♕d7 12 0-0 c5 13 d5 ± Pinter-Groszpeter, Hungarian Ch 1978

[6] 9 ... ♗a6 10 ♗xa6 ♘xa6 11 h5 c5 12 hg hg 13 ♕d3 ♕c8 14 ♕g3 ± Womack-Menzel, USA 1970

[7] 10 e5 ♘a5 11 ♗d3 c5 12 h5 cd 13 cd ♗g4 14 ♗e4 ♖c8 15 f3 ♗e6 16 ♘f4 ± Vaiser-Chekhov, Sochi 1983

[8] Boersma-Timman, Holland 1977

[9] 9 ♗g5 ♘a5 10 ♗b3 b6 11 ♕d3 ♕d7 12 0-0 ♗b7 13 ♖ad1 ♖ac8 = Portisch-Filip, Leipzig Ol 1960

[10] 9 ... e5 10 d5 ♘a5 11 ♗d3 c6 12 c4 ± Rashkovsky-Ermolinsky, USSR 1985

[11] 11 f4 ♘a5 12 ♗d3 f5! ∞ Haldarsson-Stean, Graz 1972

[12] 17 ♗g5 ♘b2 18 ♕c2 ♘xd3 19 ♕xd3 ∞ Najdorf-Sanguinetti, Argentina 1973

[13] **10 ... ♗d7** 11 ♖b1 ♘a5 (11 ... ♖c8 12 ♗d3 ♘a5 13 d5 e6 14 ♕d2 ± Farago-Filipović, Banja Luka 1985) 12 ♗d3 ♕c7 13 ♕d2 ♖fd8

178

14 d5 c4 15 ♗c2 ± Polugayevsky-Romanishin, Tilburg 1985

10 ... b6 11 dc ♕c7 12 ♘d4 ♘e5 13 ♗e2 ± Portisch-Ftacnik, Wijk aan Zee 1985

10 ... ♘a5 11 ♗d3 b6 12 ♖c1 ♗b7 13 d5 c4 14 ♗c2 ± Portisch-Uhlmann, Zagreb 1965

[14] 11 ... ♘a5 12 ♗d3 b6 13 ♘f4 ♗b7 14 e5 ♖ad8 15 ♕g4 ♘c6 16 ♖fd1 ± Kavalek-Tseshkovsky, Manila IZ 1976

[15] **12 h3 b6** 13 f4 e6 14 ♕e1 (14 g4 ♘a5 15 ♗d3 f5 16 ♘g3 oo) 14 ... ♘a5 15 ♗d3 f5 16 g4 oo Spassky-Fischer, Siegen Ol 1970

12 ♕a4 ♗d7 13 ♕a3 ♗f8 14 ♕b2 b5 =

12 ♕e1 ♕a5! 13 ♖d1 cd 14 cd ♕xe1 15 ♖fxe1 b6 =

12 f4 ♗g4 (12 ... e6 13 f5 ef 14 ♗g5 ⁼⁼) 13 f5 gf 14 h3 (14 ef ♕d6! oo/=) 14 ... ♗h5 (14 ... ♗xe2 15 ♕xe2 cd 16 cd ♕d6 =) oo Bellon-Conquest, Hastings 1985-86

[16] 12 ... **e5** 13 ♗g5 ♖d6 14 ♗d5 ± Peev-Georgiev, Plovdiv 1984

[17] 13 dc ♕e8 14 ♗d5 ♗d7 15 ♗g5 ♘a5 = Botvinnik/Estrin

[18] 14 ♗b3 b5 15 ♗e3 ♕c7 16 c4 bc! 17 ♗xc4 ♘xc4 18 ♖xc4 ♗a6 19 ♖xc5 ♕e5 = Dolmatov-Lputian, USSR Ch 1986

[19] 14 ... e5 15 ♗e3 b6 16 f4 ef 17 ♗xf4 ± Polugayevsky-Tukmakov, Moscow 1985

[20] 17 a4 ± Polugayevsky-Gutman, Biel IZ 1985

[21] 12 ... ♘e5 13 ♗b3 ♘g4 14 ♗f4 e5 15 ♗g3 ♕e7 16 ♗d5 ♗e6 17 de ± Toth-Castro, Rome 1980

[22] **13 ... cd** 14 cd ♕xd2 15 ♖xd2 ♗d7 16 d5 ♘a5 17 ♗d3 b6 18 ♘d4 ± Tarjan-Algeo, USA 1980

13 ... b6 14 ♗h6 ♗a6 15 ♗xa6 ♕xa6 16 ♗xg7 ♔xg7 17 d5 ± Gligorić

13 ... ♗g4 14 f3 ♘e5 15 ♗d5 ♖xd5 16 ed ♘c4 17 ♕d3 ♘b2 18 ♕b1 ± Ftacnik-Stohl, Trnava 1984

[23] 14 ♗h6 ♗h8 (14 ... cd 15 ♗xg7 ♔xg7 16 ♕f4 ±/± Gligorić) 15 ♕e3 ♗e8 16 e5 ± Vaiser-Lputian, Sochi 1985

[24] 17 ♘xd4 cd 18 ♗xd7 ± Pinter-Jansa, Prague Z 1985

[25] **12 ♗d3** cd 13 cd – 10 ... cd

12 ♗xf7+ – see Introduction

[26] 13 ♗g5 ♗b5 14 ♖b1 ♗a6 15 f4 oo Spassky-Timman, Montreal 1979

[27] 14 a3 a6 15 dc e6 16 c6 ♗xc6 17 ♗b6 ♕e7! ⁼ Ehlvest-Gavrikov, USSR 1984

[28] 15 a3 a6 16 ♖f2 ♗b5 17 ♗a2 ♗c4 = Polugayevsky-Timman, Tilburg 1985

[29] 17 ab cd 18 cd ½-½ Plachetka-Smejkal, Czechoslovak Ch 1986

[30] 11 ... ♗d7 12 ♖b1 ♘a5 13 ♗d3 b6 14 ♕d2 ♖c8 15 ♖fc1 ± Kaidanov-Zilberstein, USSR 1983

[31] 12 ♗b5 ♗d7 13 ♕a4 ♗xb5 14 ♕xb5 a6 15 ♕b4 b5 = Didishko-Ehlvest, USSR 1982

[32] **12 ... b6** 13 ♖c1 e6 14 ♗d2 ♕d6 15 ♗f4 oo/±

Belyavsky-Tukmakov, USSR 1975

12 ... ♗g4!? 13 ♖b1 a6 14 d5 b5 15 ♕d2 f5 oo Vaiser-Simić, Vrnjačka Banja 1986

[33] Murei-Ftacnik, New York 1986

[34] 12 ... ♗d7 13 ♖b1 a6 14 ♕d2 ♖c8 15 ♗d3 b5 16 ♖fc1 e6 17 ♖c2 ♗e8 18 ♖bc1 ± Knaak-Tseshkovsky, Rostock 1984; 13 ... e6!?

[35] 13 ♗xf7+ ♖xf7 14 fg ♖xf1+ 15 ♔xf1 ♕d7 16 h3 ♕e6 ∞ Spassky-Korchnoi, USSR Ch 1953

13 ♗b3 ♗d7 14 ♖b1 e6 15 ♕d2 ♗b5 = Razuvayev-Ftacnik, Moscow 1985

13 ♗b5 ♗d7 14 ♖b1 ♖c8 15 ♕d3 a6 16 ♗xd7 ♕xd7 = Tunik-Veingold, USSR 1984

[36] 15 ... ♘xb7 16 ♖xb7 ♗b5 17 ♖e1 ♕a5 18 a4 ± Dolmatov-Maliskauskas, USSR 1985

[37] 16 ... e6 17 ♗b3 ♘xb3 18 ab ♗b5 oo/= Dolmatov-Kuzmin, USSR 1985

[38] 20 ♖fd1 ♗xe3+ 21 ♕xe3 ♖d7 22 ♗e2 ♖xd1+ 23 ♖xd1 ♕c8 (23 ... ♕c7 24 ♗xa6 ♕c2 25 ♕d4 e5 26 ♕a1 ± Yusupov-Korchnoi, Lucerne 1985) 24 ♕c1 (24 e5 ♕c2 25 ♖d4 ♖b8 = Farago-W.Schmidt, Prague Z 1985) 24 ... ♕b7 25 ♕c5 ♘b3 26 ♕e3 ♘a5 27 ♖d6 ♕b4 = Spassky-Timman, Bugojno 1978

[39] 14 ♕a4 a6 15 d5 b5 16 ♕b4 ♗xa1 17 ♖xa1 ♗d7 18 ♕d4 f6 =

[40] 15 d5 e6! = Knaak-Szymczak, East Germany v Poland 1977

[41] 17 ... b5 18 f4 a6 19 e5 ± Glek-Kozlov, Pinsk 1986

17 ... b6 18 f4 e6 19 d6 ♘c6 20 ♕b3 ⁼⁼ Dolmatov-Gavrikov, USSR Ch 1986

[42] 20 f4 ed 21 ♘xd5 ♕b2 22 ♘e7+ ♔h8 23 ♕xb2 ♗xb2 24 ♖c7 ⁼⁼ Spassky-Dueball, Dortmund 1973

[43] **16 ♕b1 ♗d7** 17 ♗h6 ♖e8 intending ... ♕b6 ∓ Hartston

16 ♗h6 ♖e8 and now:

17 ♘d4 ♗d7 18 e5 e6! ∓/∓

17 ♖b1 a6 18 ♕d4 ♗f7 19 f4 ♖c8 20 f5 b5 21 fg hg ∓

16 ♕d4 ♗d7 17 ♘f4 b6 18 ♗d2 ♕c7 19 ♕b4 ♕d6 20 ♗a6 ∞ Toften-Martin, London 1984

[44] **16 ... b6** 17 ♗h6 ♕d6 18 ♗xf8 ♖xf8 = Vaiser-Zakharov, USSR 1984

16 ... ♗f7 17 ♗h6 ♖e8 18 ♗b5 ♕d6! 19 ♗xe8 ♗xe8 20 ♕c3 b6 = Pinter-Pribyl, Sochi 1981

[45] 17 ♗h6 ♖f7 18 e5 e6 (18 ... fe 19 ♕xe5 ♕b8 20 ♕xb8 ♖xb8 21 ♗d2 ± Haik-Chiburdanidze, Montpellier 1986) 19 ♘f4 fe 20 ♘xe6 ♗xe6 21 de ♖e7 = Polugayevsky-Chandler, Amsterdam 1984

[46] 17 ... ♗f5 18 ♗xf5 gf 19 ef ♖xf6 20 ♘f4 ⁼⁼ Knaak-Gauglitz, Dresden 1985

[47] 19 ♕d4 ♕d6 20 ♗d2 b6 21 ♘c3 ♕f6 = Lukacs-W.Schmidt, Trnava 1986

[48] 20 ♕c5 b6 21 ♕c1 ± Miles-Bor, Utrecht 1986

179

Bogo-Indian

Queen's Indian

"It is safe to assume that this defence [the Queen's Indian] is not likely to decrease in popularity until White decides to bypass it and face up to the Nimzo-Indian." This statement from the first edition holds more than a grain of truth. While the defence has declined somewhat in frequency, this has had little to do with its own merits.

The defence still enjoys an irreproachable reputation; solid, resilient and with potential for active counterplay. Many White players have preferred to reopen investigation into the Nimzo-Indian, which leads to more unbalanced play.

Nimzowitsch also popularized the Queen's Indian, and the rediscovery of his 4 ... ♗a6! in the 4 g3 Classical Variation led to a wholehearted revival of the defence. Black's scheme of development exerts pressure on the key square e4, and the combined influence of the ♘f6 and the fianchettoed queen's bishop makes the acquisition of this square, an integral part of successful White strategy, extremely difficult to achieve.

The latest attempt by White to prove advantage, 4 a3, popularized by Petrosian, Gheorghiu and, lately, Kasparov, can lead to positions directly related to the Benoni. Another complex occurs if Black responds with ... d5, accepting a slightly disadvantageous pawn structure but gaining dynamic equality through excellent piece activity.

The attacking system 4 ♘c3 and 5 ♗g5 (examined under the Nimzo) is an aggressive modern line that leads to extremely complex play. Quiet lines such as 4 ♗f4 and 4 e3 avoid such heated debates, but promise White less chance of an advantage.

The other reason for fewer Queen's Indians is the recent examination of the Bogo-Indian. Fresh ideas like 4 ♗d2 c5!? have opened up fresh fields for investigation. Though less dynamic than the Queen's Indian, it offers a solid and less explored alternative.

Those who prefer confusion and risk can try the Blumenfeld Gambit (3 ♘f3 c5 4 d5 b5). White is preferred by theory, but there is plenty of room for argument.

References: *Winning with the Queen's Indian* (Ribli and Kallai)
The Semi-Closed Openings in Action (Karpov)

					1 d4 ♘f6 2 c4 e6 3 ♘f3				
	3	4	5	6	7	8	9	10	11
1	...	d5[2]	de[4]	cb	e3[5]	♘c3	e4!	♘g5	♕c2	±
	c5[1]	b5[3]	fe	d5	♗d6	♗b7	de[6]	♗d5	♘bd7	
2	...	...	♗g5	♗xf6	♘c3	♘b5	e4	e5	♗d3!	±
	...	...	h6[7]	♕xf6	b4	♘a6	g5	♕f4	g4[8]	

[1] 3 ... d5 – 1 d4 d5 2 c4 e6 3 ♘f3 ♘f6.
3 ... ♘e4 4 ♘fd2 ♗b4 5 ♕c2 d5 6 ♘c3 f5 7 ♘dxe4 fe 8 ♗f4 0-0 9 e3 ± Alekhine-Marshall, New York 1927.
[2] 4 ♘c3 cd 5 ♘xd4 – 1 c4 c5 2 ♘f3 ♘f6 3 d4 cd 4 ♘xd4 e6 5 ♘c3.
[3] Blumenfeld Gambit
4 ... ed 5 cd b5 (5 ... d6 – Benoni) 6 ♗g5 ♕b6!? (6 ... ♕a5 7 ♘c3 ♘e4 8 ♗d2 ♘xd2 9 ♘xd2 ± Browne-Ljubojević, Buenos Aires 1979) 7 ♘c3 b4 8 ♗xf6 ♕xf6 9 ♘e4 ∞ Browne.
[4] 5 e4!? ♘xe4 6 de fe 7 ♗d3 ♘f6 8 ♘g5 (intending 9 ♗xh7!) 8 ... ♕e7 9 cb d5 ∞ Gipslis.
5 a4 bc (5 ... ed!? 6 cd b4 ∞) 6 ♘c3 ♗b7 7 e4! ♘xe4 8 ♘xe4 ed 9 ♘c3 d4 10 ♗xc4 dc

11 ♗xf7+ ♔xf7 12 ♕b3+ ∞ Rubinstein-Spielmann, Vienna 1922.
[5] 7 ♗g5 ♗e7 8 e3 ♘bd7 9 ♘c3 ♗b7 10 ♗e2 0-0 11 0-0 ♕c7! ∞ Kan-Goldenov, USSR 1946.
[6] 9 ... d4? 10 e5 ±.
9 ... ♘bd7!?
[7] 5 ... ed 6 cd d6 7 e4! a6 8 a4 ♗e7 (8 ... b4 9 ♘bd2 ±) 9 ♗xf6 ♗xf6 10 ab ♗xb2 11 ♖a2 ♗f6 12 ♘bd2 ± Vaganian-K.Grigorian, USSR Ch 1971.
5 ... ♕a5+ 6 ♗d2 (6 ♘c3 ♘e4 7 ♗d2! ±) 6 ... ♕xd2+ 7 ♘bxd2 bc 8 ♗xf6 gf 9 e4 ±.
[8] 12 ♕d2 ♕xd2+ 13 ♘xd2 ± Polugayevsky-Ljubojević, Manila 1975.

181

| | Bogo-Indian | | 1 d4 ♘f6 2 c4 e6 3 ♘f3 ♗b4+ | | | | | |

	4	5	6	7	8	9	10	11	12	
1	♘bd2	a3	♗xd2²	♘xd4	♗e3	g3	♗g2	0-0	♗xb7	∞
	c5¹	♗xd2+	cd³	♘e4⁴	0-0	b6	♗b7	♘d6	♘xb7⁵	
2	...	a3⁶	♕xd2⁷	e3	♗e2⁹	♕d3	0-0	♕xc4	♕c2	=
	b6	♗xd2+	♗b7	0-0⁸	♘e4	d5¹⁰	dc	♗a6	♗xe2¹¹	
3	♗d2	♕xd2¹³	♘c3	e3	♖c1	♕c2	♗xc4	0-0	dc	±
	♗xd2+¹²	0-0¹⁴	d5¹⁵	♕e7¹⁶	♖d8¹⁷	dc	c5	♘c6	♕xc5¹⁸	
4	...	g3¹⁹	♕c2	♗g2	♕xc4	♕d3²²	♕xe4	a3	♗e3!²⁵	±
	a5	d5²⁰	♘c6²¹	dc	♕d5	♕e4²³	♘xe4	♗d6²⁴	♘f6²⁶	
5	...	g3	♗g2	♕xd2²⁸	♕c2	0-0	♘c3³⁰	♕xc3	c5³²	±
	♕e7	0-0²⁷	♗xd2+	♘e4²⁹	f5	d6	♘xc3	♘d7³¹	dc³³	
6	...		♗g2	♘bxd2	0-0	e4	d5	c5³⁵	cd	∞/=
	...	♘c6	♗xd2+	d6	a5³⁴	e5	♘b8	0-0³⁶	cd³⁷	
7	...	...	♘c3	♗xc3	♖c1	♕a4	♗g2	0-0⁴⁰	♖xc3	±
	...	...	♗xc3³⁸	♘e4	♘b4³⁹	a5	0-0	♘xc3	d6⁴¹	

¹ 4 ... d6 5 g3 (5 e3 0-0 6 ♗e2 ♕e7 7 0-0 ♗xd2 8 ♘xd2 e5 =) 5 ... ♘c6 6 ♗g2 0-0 7 0-0 e5 (7 ... ♗xd2 8 ♕xd2 ♘e4 9 ♕e3 f5 10 b3 ± Polugayevsky-Razuvayev, Moscow 1967) 8 d5 ♗xd2 9 ♗xd2 ♘e7 10 ♘e1 ♘d7 11 f4 ± Quinteros-Hecht, Wijk aan Zee 1974

4 ... 0-0 5 a3 ♗xd2+ 6 ♗xd2 ♘e4 and now:
7 g3 d6 8 ♗g2 ♘d7 9 0-0 ♕e7 10 ♖c1 f5 11 c5 ♘df6 12 ♘g5 ♘xd2 13 ♕xd2 e5 ∞ Lputian-Psakhis, USSR Ch 1987
7 ♗e3 d5 8 ♖c1 dc 9 ♖xc4 ♕d5 10 ♕c2 ♗d7 11 g3 ♗b5 12 ♖b4 ♗c6 13 ♗g2 ± Cebalo-Korchnoi, Biel 1986

4 ... d5 5 ♕a4+ ♘c6 6 a3 ♗xd2+ (6 ... ♗e7 7 e3 a5!? 8 ♗d3 0-0 9 0-0 ♗d7 10 ♕c2 a4 ∞ Gurevich-Salov, USSR Ch 1987) 7 ♗xd2 ♘e4 8 ♖d1 (8 ♗f4 g5!? 9 ♗e3 f5 10 ♘e5 ♗d7 ∞ Malanyuk-Salov, USSR Ch 1987) 8 ... 0-0 9 e3 ♘e7 10 ♕c2 b6 11 ♗d3 ♗b7 12 0-0 ♘g6 13 b4 f5 = A.Petrosian-Spassky, Sarajevo 1986

² 6 ♕xd2 cd 7 ♘xd4 ♘c6 8 e3 d5 9 cd ed 10 ♘xc6 bc 11 b4 0-0 12 ♗b2 a5 = Browne-Djurić, New York 1986

³ 6 ... d6 7 ♕c2 ♘c6 8 e3 ± Gipslis

⁴ 7 ... d5?! 8 cd ♕xd5 9 e3 0-0 10 ♗b4 ± Lobron-Korchnoi, Biel 1986

⁵ 13 ♕c2 ∞ Cebalo-Djurić, Yugoslav Ch 1986

⁶ 5 e3 ♗b7 6 a3 ♗xd2+ 7 ♕xd2 0-0 8 ♗e2 d6 9 b3 ♘bd7 = Baumbach-Lein, Moscow 1970

⁷ 6 ♗xd2 ♗b7 7 ♗g5 d6 8 e3 ♘bd7 9 ♗d3 (9 ♕c2!? h6 10 ♗h4 Yusupov-Hort, Reykjavik 1985) 9 ... h6 10 ♗h4 g5 11 ♗g3 ♕e7 12 ♕c2

h5 13 h3! h4 14 ♗h2 g4 ∞ Nikolić-Seirawan, Wijk aan Zee 1986

⁸ 7 ... ♘e4 8 ♕c2 0-0 9 ♗d3 f5 10 0-0 ♖f6 11 ♖d1 (11 ♘d2 ♖h6 12 f3 ♗d6 13 ♖f2 ♘c6 ∞ Miles-Karlsson, Portorož/Ljubljana 1985) 11 ... d6 12 ♘d2 ♘xd2 13 ♗xd2 ♖g6 = Polugayevsky-Cebalo, Biel 1986

⁹ 8 b4 a5 9 ♗b2 d6 10 ♗e2 ♘e4 11 ♕d3 f5 12 0-0 c5 13 dc bc 14 b5 ♘d7 = Browne-Arnason, USA v Scandinavia 1986

¹⁰ 9 ... d6 10 0-0 ♘d7 11 b4 f5 12 ♗b2 ± Miles-Mascarinas, Lugano 1986

¹¹ 13 ♕xe2 ♕d5! 14 ♖d1 ♘d7 15 ♘e1 f5! Miles-Nikolić, Reykjavik 1986

¹² 4 ... c5 5 ♗xb4 (5 g3?! ♕b6! = Kasparov-Korchnoi, Brussels 1986) 5 ... cb 6 a3 ba 7 ♖xa3 b6 8 ♘c3 ♗b7 9 e3 0-0 10 ♗d3 d5 11 cd ♘xd5 12 0-0 ♘c6 13 ♕b1 ± Christiansen-Timman, Linares 1985

4 ... ♗e7 – Catalan

¹³ 5 ♘bxd2 d6 6 e4 0-0 7 ♗d3 e5 =

¹⁴ 5 ... d5 6 g3 ♘bd7 7 ♗g2 c6 8 b3 0-0 9 0-0 ± Sosonko-Andersson, Reggio Emilia 1985-86

¹⁵ 6 ... d6 7 g3 ♘c6 8 ♗g2 e5 9 d5 ♘e7 10 e4 a6 11 0-0 b5 12 cb ab 13 b4 ± Razuvayev-Makarichev, USSR 1972

¹⁶ 7 ... ♘bd7 8 ♖c1 c6 9 ♗d3 ♕e7 10 0-0 dc 11 ♗xc4 e5 12 e4 ±

¹⁷ 8 ... ♘bd7 9 cd (9 ♗d3 dc 10 ♗xc4 e5 = Tatai-Andersson, Rome 1986) 9 ... ed 10 ♗d3 c6 11 ♕c2 ♖e8 12 0-0 ± Quinteros-Andersson, Rio de Janeiro 1985

[18] 13 ♘e4 ♕e7 14 a3 ♗d7 15 ♖fd1 ± Psakhis-Rashkovsky, USSR Ch 1987

[19] 5 ♕c2!? d6 6 ♘c3 0-0 7 ♗g5 ♘bd7 8 e3 b6 9 ♗h4 ♗b7 10 ♗d3 ♗xc3+ 11 bc ♕e8 12 0-0 e5 13 ♘d2 ∞/± Eingorn-Rashkovsky, Kiev 1986

[20] 5 ... d6 6 ♗g2 ♘bd7 7 0-0 e5 8 ♕c2 0-0 9 ♘c3 ♖e8 10 e4 ±

[21] 6 ... ♖a6!? 7 a3 ♗xd2+ 8 ♘bxd2 ♘c6 9 ♗g2 0-0 10 0-0 dc 11 ♕xc4 ♗d7 12 ♖ac1 ±

[22] 9 ♕xd5 ed 10 0-0 ♗g4 11 ♗e3 ♘e4 12 ♖c1 ♗xf3 13 ♗xf3 0-0-0 14 ♘c3 f5 15 ♘b5 ± Kogan-Vaisman, USA 1986

[23] 9 ... 0-0 10 ♘c3 ♕h5 11 e3 ♖d8 12 ♕e2 ± Hertneck-Smyslov, Dortmund 1986

[24] 11 ... ♗xd2+ 12 ♘bxd2 ♘xd2 13 ♔xd2 ±

[25] 12 ♗f4 a4 13 ♘e5 ♘xd4! 14 ♗xe4 ♘b3 ∞ Groszpeter-Barlov, Sochi 1984

[26] 13 ♘c3 a4 14 0-0 ♘d5 15 ♗d2 ♘a5 16 e4 ± Gligorić-Barlov, Budva 1986

[27] 5 ... ♗xd2+ 6 ♕xd2 d5 7 ♗g2 0-0 8 0-0 b6 (8 ... dc 9 ♘a3 c5 10 dc ♕xc5 11 ♖ac1 ♘c6 12 ♘xc4 ± Kasparov-Petrosian, Bugojno 1982) 9 cd ed 10 ♘c3 ♗b7 11 ♕f4 ± Razuvayev-Inkiov, Calcutta 1986

[28] 7 ♘bxd2 d6 8 e4 e5 9 d5 a5 10 ♘h4 ♘a6 = Tatai-Hernandez, Rome 1986

[29] 7 ... d6 8 ♘c3 e5 9 h3! ♖e8 10 e4 a5 11 0-0 ♘a6 12 ♖ad1 ± Bouwmeester-Markland, corr. 1986

7 ... d5 8 0-0 ♖d8 9 ♕c2 ♘c6 10 cd ed 11 ♘c3 ± Timman-Korchnoi, Tilburg 1986, and Pinter-Petran, Szirak 1985

[30] 10 ♘fd2 ♘xd2 11 ♕xd2 ♘d7 12 ♘c3 c6 13 ♖ad1 ♘f6 14 ♖fe1 ±

[31] 11 ... ♘c6 12 d5 ♘d8 13 de ♘xe6 14 b4 ± Vizhmanavin-Balashov, USSR Ch 1984

[32] 12 ♖ac1 ♘f6 13 c5 ♘d5 14 ♕a3 Rivas Pastor-Ivanović, 1986

[33] 13 ♖ac1 cd 14 ♕xc7 ± Barlov-Rivas Pastor, 1986

[34] 8 ... 0-0 9 e4 e5 10 d5 ♘b8 11 de (11 b4 ±) 11 ... ♗xe6 12 ♘d4 ♘c6 13 ♘b5 ♘e5 14 ♕e2 ± Hort-Rogers, Biel 1986

[35] 11 ♘e1 h5! 12 ♘ef3 ♘bd7 13 ♕c2 h4 ∞ Popov-Rogers, Berlin 1986

11 ♕e2 ♘a6 12 ♘b1 ♗g4 13 ♘c3 0-0 14 h3 ♗xf3 15 ♕xf3 = Ehlvest-Eingorn, USSR Ch 1987

[36] 11 ... dc?! 12 ♘c4 ♘bd7 13 d6! ♕e6 14 ♖c1! ± Belyavsky-Dückstein, Vienna 1986

[37] 13 ♘h4 g6 14 ♖c1 ♘bd7 15 ♖e1 ♘c5 = Barlov-Cebalo, Bela Crkva 1986

13 a3 ♘a6!? 14 b4 ♗d7 15 ♕b3 ab 16 ab ♗b5 17 ♖fc1 ♖fc8 = Kir.Georgiev-Cebalo, Sofia 1986

[38] 6 ... d5 7 cd ed 8 ♗g2 0-0 9 0-0 ♖e8 10 ♕b3 a5 11 ♗g5 ± Sideif Zade-Salov, USSR 1983

[39] 8 ... 0-0 9 ♗g2 d6 10 d5 ♘b8 11 de fe 12 0-0 ♘xc3 13 ♖xc3 a5 14 h4 ± Farago-Ekström, Budapest 1986

[40] 11 ♘d2 ♘xc3 12 bc ♘c6 13 c5 d5 14 cd cd 15 ♖b1 ∞/± Tukmakov-Rashkovsky, USSR Ch 1987

[41] 13 a3 ♗d7 14 ♕d1 ♘a6 15 ♘e1 ♖ab8 16 c5! ± Gligorić-Rajković, Budva 1986

183

Queen's Indian I   1 d4 ♘f6 2 c4 e6 3 ♘f3 b6

	4	5	6	7	8	9	10	11	12	
1	e3	♗d3	0-0	♘c3	ed	cd	♗b5+[1]	♗c4[2]	♕e2[3]	=
	♗b7	c5	♗e7	cd	d5	♘xd5	♗c6	0-0	♘xc3[4]	
2	...	...	...	b3	♗b2	ed	♘bd2	♕e2	♖ac1	=
	...	...	...	0-0	cd	d5	♘c6[5]	♖c8[6]	♖e8[7]	
3	...	...	0-0	cd[8]	♘c3	♕c2	e4	e5	♕xd3	±
	...	d5	♘bd7	ed	♗d6	c5[9]	c4	cd	♗e7[10]	
4	...	...	...	b3[11]	♗b2	♘c3[13]	♖c1[14]	♘a4	♘e5	=
	...	...	♗d6	♘bd7	0-0	a6	♕e7[15]	♘e4[16]	dc[17]	
5	♗f4	e3[18]	♘fd2[20]	a3	♘c3	cd	♘xd5	♕c2[22]	dc	=
	♗b7	♗b4+[19]	0-0	♗e7	d5[21]	♘xd5	♗xd5	c5	♗xc5[23]	
6	...	...	h3[24]	♘c3	cd	♘xd5	♗d3[27]	♔e2	dc	=
	...	♗e7	0-0	d5	♘xd5[25]	♕xd5[26]	♕a5+	c5	♖d8[28]	
7	...	...	...	dc[29]	♘c3	♗e2	0-0	♕c2	♖ad1	=
	...	...	c5	bc	0-0	♘c6	d6[30]	♕b6	♖fd8[31]	
8	♘c3	♗g5[32]	♗h4	♗g3	e3[34]	fg[35]	♗d3	0-0	♖c1	∞
	♗b7	h6[33]	g5	♘h5	♘xg3	♗g7	♘c6[36]	♕e7	0-0-0[37]	
9	...	...	e3	♗h4	♗g3[39]	♕c2	♗d3	bc	hg	=
	...	♗e7	h6	♘e4[38]	♗b4	d6	♗xc3+	♘xg3	♘d7[40]	
10	...	...	♕c2	♗h4	dc[43]	e3	♖d1[44]	♗e2	0-0	∞
	...	...	h6[41]	c5[42]	bc	0-0	d6	♕b6	♖d8[45]	

[1]   10 ♘xd5 ♗xd5 11 ♘e5 0-0 12 ♕h5 f5 13 ♕e2 ♗f6 (13 ... ♘d7 14 ♘c6! ± Speelman-Short, Hastings 1983-84) 14 ♗f4 ♗xe5 15 ♗xe5 ♘c6 = Speelman

[2]   11 ♕a4 ♕d7 11 ♘xd5 (11 ♘e5? ♗xc3) 11 ... ♕xd5 12 ♗xc6+ ♘xc6 ∓

[3]   12 ♘e5 ♘xc3 13 bc ♗d5 14 ♗b3 ± Diždar-Lobron, Sarajevo 1984; 12 ... ♗b7 =

[4]   13 bc ♗d5 14 ♗d3 ♘c6 = M.Gurevich-Yudasin, USSR Ch 1986

[5]   10 ... ♘e4 11 ♖e1 ♘xd2 12 ♘xd2 ♘d7 = Karpov-Portisch, Malta Ol 1980

[6]   11 ... ♕d6 12 ♖ad1 ♖ac8 13 ♖fe1 ♕f4 14 g3 ♕h6 ∞ Winants-Karpov, Brussels 1986

[7]   13 ♖fd1 ♗f8 14 h3 g6 15 ♕e3 ♗g7 16 ♘e5 dc 18 bc ♘e7 = Portisch-Sosonko, Tilburg 1983, and Smyslov-Ribli, match 1983

[8]   7 b3 ♗d6 - 6 ... ♗d6
  7 ♘c3 ♗d6 8 ♕e2 ♘e4! = Nogueiras-Dzindzihashvili, Thessaloniki Ol 1984

[9]   9 ... 0-0 10 ♘b5 ±
  9 ... a6 10 e4 ±

[10]   13 ef ♘xf6 14 ♕b5+ ♕d7 15 ♖e1 ± Portisch-Timman, match 1984

[11]   7 ♘c3 0-0 8 ♕e2 c5 9 cd ed 10 b3 ♘c6

11 ♘b5 ♗e7 12 dc bc 13 ♖d1 ♖e8 ∓ Averkin-Polugayevsky, USSR 1979

  7 b4 dc 8 ♗xc4 ♘bd7 9 b5 0-0 10 ♗b2 ♘e4 = Gulko-Khalifman, USSR 1985

[12]   8 ... ♘e4 9 ♕c2 a6 10 ♘e5 ♗xe5 11 de ♘ec5 = Portisch-Ljubojević, Bugojno 1986

[13]   9 ♘bd2 ♘e4 10 ♘e5 (10 ♕c2 f5 11 ♖ad1? ♘xd2 12 ♘xd2 dc 13 ♘xc4 ♗xh2+! ∓∓ Diždarević-Miles, Biel 1985) 10 ... ♗xe5 11 de ♘dc5 12 ♗e2 ♘xd2 13 ♕xd2 dc 14 ♕xd8 ♖fxd8 15 ♗xc4 ♗a6 ∓ Hradeczky-Farago, Balatonbereny 1984

[14]   10 ♕e2 ♘e4 11 ♖ac1 f5 12 ♗b1 ♖f6 ∓ Spassky-Miles, Bugojno 1984

[15]   10 ... ♘e4 11 ♗e2 ♕e7 12 ♘e5 ♖fd8 13 cd ed 14 ♘c6 ± Gligorić-P.Nikolić, Portorož/Ljubljana 1985

[16]   11 ... dc 12 bc ♘e4 13 ♕e2 f5 14 ♖fd1 ♖fc8 ∞ Portisch-P.Nikolić, Tunis IZ 1985

[17]   13 ♘xc4 ♗xh2+! (13 ... ♖fc8 14 ♕e2 ± Portisch-Miles, Tunis IZ 1985) 14 ♔xh2 ♕h4+ 15 ♔g1 ♘g5 16 f3 ♘h3+ = Salov

[18]   5 ♘c3 ♗b4 6 ♕b3 ♗a5 7 e3 ♘e4 ∞ Seirawan-Dzindzihashvili, US Ch 1984

[19]   5 ... c5 6 d5! ed 7 ♘c3 ± Lputian-Vaganian,

Erevan 1980

[20] 6 ♘bd2 ♗e7 7 ♗d3 c5 8 0-0 0-0 9 e4 cd 10 ♘xd4 d6 11 ♗g3 ♘bd7 = Hübner-Andersson, Buenos Aires Ol 1978

[21] 7 ... c5 8 d5! ± Miles-Timman, Wijk aan Zee 1979

[22] 11 ♖c1 c5 12 dc ♗xc5 13 ♗c4 ♗b7! 14 0-0 ♗d6 = Miles-Hübner, England v West Germany 1979

[23] 13 ♘e4 ♘d7 14 ♖d1 ♕c8 = Miles-Unzicker, South Africa 1979

[24] 6 ♘c3 ♘h5! = Miles-Andersson, Amsterdam 1978, and Spassky-Karpov, Montreal 1979

[25] 8 ... ed 9 ♗d3 c5 10 0-0 ♘c6 11 ♘e5 ± Miles-Spassky, Montilla 1978 and Buenos Aires Ol 1978

[26] 9 ... ♗xd5 10 ♗d3! ♗b4+ 11 ♔e2 ±/∞ Miles-Browne, Amsterdam 1978, Miles-Rivas, Buenos Aires Ol 1978, and Miles-Reshevsky, Lone Pine 1979

[27] 10 a3 c5 (10 ... ♘d7!? 11 dc ♕xc5 12 ♖c1 ♕a5+ 13 ♕d2 ♕xd2+ 14 ♘xd2 ♘a6 = Yusupov-Zaitsev, USSR 1980

[28] 13 ♕d2 ♗a6 14 ♘e1 ♕xd2+ 15 ♔xd2 ♘c6 16 ♗d6 ♗xd6 17 ♗xa6 ♗xc5+ 18 ♔e2 = Lputian-Andrianov, USSR 1983

[29] 7 ♘c3 cd 8 ♗xd4 (8 ed 0-0 9 ♗d3 d5 10 0-0 dc 11 ♗xc4 ♘c6 =/∓ Rivas-Hübner, Linares 1985) 8 ... 0-0 9 ♘db5 ♘e8 ∞/∓ Miles-Kupreichik, Reykjavik 1980, and Djurić-Ornstein, Pamporovo 1981

[30] 10 ... d5 11 cd ed 12 ♖c1 d4 13 ♘a4 ♕d5 14 ♕b3 ♘b4 ∞ Lputian-A.Ivanov, USSR 1979

[31] Lputian-A.Mikhalchishin, USSR 1979

[32] 5 ♕c2 c5 6 e4 cd 7 ♘xd4 ♗c5 8 ♘b3 ♗b4 9 ♗d3 ♘c6 10 ♗f4 ♗e7 11 ♗e2 ♘b4 12 ♕b1 d6 = Speelman-Razuvayev, Moscow 1985

5 a3! – 4 a3

[33] 5 ... ♗b4 – Nimzo-Indian

[34] 8 ♗e5 ♖g8!? (8 ... f6 9 ♕d3 fe 10 ♕g6+ ♔e7 11 ♕xh5 ed 12 ♘xd4 ♗g7 ∓ Shamkovich-Polugayevsky, USSR 1963) 9 e3 d6 10 ♗g3 ♘d7 11 ♘d2 ♘df6 ∓ Qi-Speelman, China 1981

[35] 9 hg ♗g7 10 g4 ♘c6 11 ♗d3 ♕e7 12 ♕a4 a6 13 ♖c1 ♘b4 14 ♗b1 c5 ∞ Taimanov-Polugayevsky, USSR 1979

[36] 10 ... d6 11 0-0 ♘d7 12 ♗c2 ♕e7 13 ♕d3 a6 14 ♘d2 c5 15 ♘de4! ± Romanishin-Ribli, Riga IZ 1979

[37] 12 ... a6 13 ♕e2 h5 ∞ Plachetka-Kristiansen, Esbjerg 1980

12 ... 0-0-0 13 ♕a4 ♔b8 14 c5 g4 15 ♘h4 ♗f6 ∞ Speelman-Stean, London 1980

[38] 7 ... 0-0 8 ♗e2 (8 ♗d3 c5 9 0-0-0 cd 10 ed ♗xf3 11 ♕xf3 ♘c6 ∞ Spassky-Portisch, match 1977) 8 ... ♘e4 (8 ... c5 9 0-0 d6 10 dc bc 11 ♕c2 ± Karpov-Polugayevsky, Bugojno 1980) 9 ♗xe7 ♕xe7 10 ♘xe4 ♗xe4 = Martinović-M.Gurevich, Vršac 1985

[39] 8 ♗xe7 ♕xe7 9 ♘xe4 ♗xe4 10 ♖c1 c5 11 ♗e2 0-0 12 0-0 d6 = Karpov-Balashov, USSR 1980

[40] 13 e4 ♕e7 14 0-0 0-0 = Korchnoi-Ligterink, Wijk aan Zee 1984

[41] 6 ... c5 7 dc bc 8 ♖d1 ♘c6 9 e3 0-0 10 ♗e2 d6 11 0-0 ♕b6 12 ♖d2 ±/∞ Lputian-Prandstetter, Erevan 1984

6 ... d5 7 cd ♘xd5 8 ♗xe7 ♕xe7 9 e4 ♘xc3 10 bc 0-0 11 ♗c4 c5 12 0-0 ±/∞ Plaskett-Chandler, London 1986

[42] 7 ... d5 8 cd ♘xd5 9 ♘xd5 ed 10 ♗xe7 ♕xe7 11 g3 0-0 12 ♗g2 c5 = Polugayevsky-Korchnoi, USSR v World 1984

[43] 8 ♖d1 ♗xf3 9 gf cd 10 ♖xd4 ♘c6 11 ♖d1 ♖c8 ∞ Ree-Korchnoi, Wijk aan Zee 1985

[44] 10 ♗e2 d5 11 cd ed 12 0-0 ♘bd7 – Queen's Gambit

[45] 13 ♖d2 ♘bd7 14 ♖fd1 a6 15 ♗g3 ♘f8 ∞ Lerner-Makarichev, USSR 1984

	Queen's Indian II		1 d4 Nf6 2 c4 e6 3 Nf3 b6 4 g3						
	4	5	6	7	8	9	10	11	12

	4	5	6	7	8	9	10	11	12	
1	...	Bd2	Qxd2	Na3[2]	Bg2	0-0	Rfd1	Rac1	Nb5	∞
	Bb4+	Bxd2+	Na6[1]	0-0	Bb7[3]	d6	Nbd7	Qe7	a6[4]	
2	...	Bg2	d5	Nh4[6]	cd	0-0	a4	b3[7]	Bb2	∞
	Bb7	c5[5]	ed	b5	d6	g6	b4	Bg7	0-0[8]	
3	...	...	Bd2[9]	Nc3	0-0	Ne5[12]	Kxg2	e4[14]	Qf3	±
	...	Bb4+	Be7[10]	0-0	Na6[11]	Bxg2[13]	Qb8	Qb7	c6[15]	
4	...	...	...	Qxd2	0-0[16]	Nc3[18]	Nxe4	Qf4	e4	±
	...	...	Bxd2+	0-0	d6[17]	Ne4[19]	Bxe4	Bb7	Nd7[20]	
5	...	...	Nc3	Bd2	d5	Qc2	b3	Rd1	0-0	±
	...	Be7	Ne4[21]	f5[22]	0-0[23]	Nd6[24]	Bf6	Na6	Qe7[25]	
6	...	...	0-0	d5	Nh4[26]	cd	Nf5	Nc3	e4	∞
	...	...	0-0	ed	c6	Nxd5[27]	Nc7[28]	d5[29]	Bf6[30]	
7	...	...	...	Nc3	cd[31]	Qc2[33]	Rd1	Bf4	Rac1	±
	...	...	...	d5	ed[32]	Na6	Qc8[34]	Rd8	c5[35]	
8	...	...	...	...	Qc2[36]	Qxc3	Rd1[38]	b3[39]	Bb2	=
	...	...	...	Ne4	Nxc3	c5[37]	d6	Bf6	Nd7[40]	
9	...	...	...	...	Bd2	d5	Rc1	a3[41]	cd	=
	...	...	...	...	f5	Bf6	Na6	ed[42]	c5[43]	
10	...	...	...	...	...	Rc1	d5	Nxd2[46]	Nde4	±
	...	...	...	...	Bf6	d6[44]	Nxd2[45]	Kh8	Bxc3[47]	
11	...	...	...	...	...	...	cd	Bf4[48]	Qc2	=
	...	...	...	...	...	d5	ed	Na6[49]	c5[50]	

1. 6 ... Bb7 7 Bg2 – 4 ... Bb7
2. 7 b3! – 4 ... Ba6 5 b3
3. 8 ... c6 9 0-0 d5 10 Rac1 ± Belyavsky-P.Nikolić, Tunis IZ 1985
4. 13 Nc3 Ne4 14 Qd3 f5 ∞ Belyavsky-Miles, Tilburg 1986
5. 5 ... g6 6 0-0 Bg7 7 Nc3 Ne4 8 Nxe4 Bxe4 9 Bg5 ± Portisch-Spassky, match 1980
6. 7 Ng5 Qc7 (7 ... Ne4!?) 8 cd h6 9 Nh3 d6 10 Nc3 a6 11 a4 g6 12 0-0 Bg7 13 e4 0-0 14 f4 Nbd7 15 Nf2 b5 ∞ Nei-Tal, Tallinn 1983
7. 11 Nd2 Bg7 12 Nc4 0-0 13 Bf4 Ba6 14 Qc2 Bxc4 15 Qxc4 Nh5 16 Bc1 Nd7 = Andrianov-Mateu, Moscow v Catalonia 1981
8. 13 e4 Re8 14 Re1 Nbd7 ∞ Shnaider-Andrianov, USSR 1983
9. 6 Nbd2 c5 (6 ... 0-0 7 0-0 d5 8 a3 Be7 9 b4 c5 =) 7 a3 Bxd2+ 8 Bxd2 (8 Qxd2 cd 9 Qxd4 Nc6 =) 8 ... cd 9 Bb4 Na6 10 Bd6 Ne4 11 Qxd4 Nxd6 = Korchnoi
10. 6 ... a5 7 0-0 0-0 8 Bg5 Be7 9 Qc2 h6 10 Bxf6 Bxf6 11 Nc3 ± Kasparov-Karpov, match (24) 1986, and Karpov-Korchnoi, Tilburg 1986

6 ... c5 7 0-0 (7 Bxb4 cb ∞ Ljubojević-Kir.Georgiev, Thessaloniki Ol 1984, and Gligorić-Kir.Georgiev, Sarajevo 1986) 7 ... 0-0 8 Nc3 Na6 9 d5! ed 10 Nh4 Nc7 11 a3 Bxc3 12 Nxc3 ± Djurić-Tukmakov, Szirak 1985, and Gheorghiu-Carlier, Ostend 1986

11. 8 ... d5 9 cd Nxd5 10 Qc2 ±
   8 ... Ne4 – 5 ... Be7 6 0-0 0-0 7 Nc3 Ne4 8 Bd2 but with an extra tempo for White
12. 9 Rc1 Re8 10 Qa4 c5 11 d5 ed 12 cd Nc7 13 e4 ± Plaskett-Polugayevsky, London 1986
13. 9 ... Qb8 10 d5! ± Polugayevsky-Larsen, London 1986
14. 11 e3 c5 12 Qf3 cd 13 ed Nb4 14 Bg5 ± Lerner-Romanishin, USSR Ch 1979
15. 14 Rfe1 Nb4 = Timman-Polugayevsky, Wijk aan Zee 1979
   14 Nd3 ± Polugayevsky
16. 8 Nc3 Ne4 9 Nxe4 (9 Qc2 Nxc3 10 Ng5 Qxg5 11 Bxb7 Nxe2! ∞ Portisch-Andersson, Tilburg 1983) 9 ... Bxe4 10 0-0 d5 (10 ... d6 – 8 0-0 d6) 11 Rac1 ± Timman-Hübner, Tilburg 1980
17. 8 ... Qe7 9 Nc3 d5 10 cd Nxd5 11 Rac1 ±

Sosonko-Hecht, Malta Ol 1980

8 ... ♘c6 9 ♘c3 ♘a5 10 b3 d5 11 cd ed 12 ♘e5 ± Kurajica-Ivanović, Yugoslav Ch 1984

8 ... c5 9 ♘c3 cd 10 ♘xd4 ♗xg2 11 ♔xg2 d5 12 cd ♘xd5 13 ♖fd1 ± Burger-Arnason, Reykjavik 1986

[18] 9 ♕c2 c5 10 ♘c3 cd 11 ♘xd4 ♗xg2 12 ♔xg2 a6 13 ♖fd1 ♕c7 = Ligterink-Andersson, Wijk aan Zee 1984

[19] 9 ... ♕e7 10 ♖ac1 c5 11 d5 ± Browne-Kogan, USA 1981

[20] 13 ♖fe1 ♕e7 14 ♖ad1 e5 15 ♕d2 ± Eingorn-Kharitonov, USSR Ch 1984

[21] 6 ... 0-0 7 ♕c2 d5 (7 ... c5 8 d5 ed 9 ♘g5 ± Korchnoi-Karpov, match 1974) 8 cd ♘xd5 9 0-0 ♘d7 10 ♘xd5 ed 11 ♖d1 ♘f6 12 ♘e5 ± Karpov-Spassky, USSR 1975

[22] 7 ... d5 8 cd ed 9 ♕a4+ ♕d7 10 ♕c2 ± Kasparov-Gligorić, Nikšić 1983

7 ... ♗f6! 8 0-0 (8 ♖c1 ♗xd4!) 8 ... 0-0 - 6 0-0

[23] 8 ... ♗f6 9 ♕c2 ♘xd2 10 ♘xd2 0-0 11 0-0 a5 12 ♖ad1 ± Tukmakov-Timman, Las Palmas IZ 1982

[24] **9** ... ♘xd2 10 ♘xd2 e5 11 0-0 d6 12 f4 e4 13 g4! ± Nesis-Koskinen, corr. 1984

9 ... ed 10 ♘xd5 ♘c6 11 0-0 ± Tukmakov-Razuvayev, USSR Ch 1985

[25] **12** ... ♘b4 13 ♕b1 ed 14 ♘b5! ± Dlugy-Korchnoi, Toronto 1985

12 ... ♕e7 13 e3 g6 14 e4! ± Ribli-P.Nikolić, Dubai Ol 1986

[26] 8 ♘d4 ♗c6! 9 cd ♗xd5 10 ♗xd5 ♘xd5 11 e4 ♘b4 ∞ Polugayevsky-Korchnoi, match 1980

[27] 9 ... cd 10 ♘c3 ♘a6 11 ♘f5 ♘c7 12 ♗f4 ± Timman-Gligorić, Bugojno 1982, and Panchenko-Inkiov, Plovdiv 1982

[28] **10** ... ♗c5 11 e4 ♘e7 12 ♘xg7! ♔xg7 13 b4 ± Polugayevsky-Korchnoi, match 1980

10 ... ♘f6 11 e4 d5 12 ♘c3 de 13 ♗g5 h6 14 ♗f4! ± Sturua-Kengis, USSR 1981

10 ... ♗f6 11 ♖e1 ♗a6 12 e4 ♘e7 13 ♘e3! ± Timman-Portisch, London 1982

[29] **11** ... d6 12 ♗f4 ♘e8 13 ♕d2 ±

11 ... ♘e6 12 e4 ♘a6 13 f4 ±

[30] 13 ♗f4 ♗c8 14 g4! ∞∞ Kasparov-Karpov, match (2) 1984-85, and Sosonko-Tukmakov, Tilburg 1984

[31] 8 ♘e5 ♘a6 9 b3 c5 10 ♗b2 ♖e8 (10 ... ♘c7 11 dc bc 12 ♘a4 ♖c8 13 ♖c1 ± Smyslov-Psakhis, Las Palmas IZ 1982, and Quinteros-Portisch, Lucerne Ol 1982) 11 ♖c1 ♕b8 12 cd ed 13 e3 ♕d6 14 ♘b5 ♕d8 ±/∞ Ribli-Tukmakov, Tilburg 1984

[32] 8 ♘xd5 9 ♘xd5 ed (9 ... ♗xd5 10 ♕c2 ±) 10 ♕c2 ♘d7 11 ♖d1 ♗d6 12 ♗g5 ± Ribli-Sosonko, Tilburg 1984

[33] 9 ♘e5 ♘a6 10 ♕a4! ♕e8 11 ♕b3 ♖d8 12 ♘b5 ± Rajković-Abramović, Belgrade 1986

[34] **10** ... c5 11 dc bc (11 ... ♘xc5 12 ♘g5!) 12 ♘g5! ♘b4 13 ♕b1 h6 14 ♘ge4 ± Chernin-Afifi, Tunis IZ 1985

10 ... h6 11 ♗f4 ♖e8 12 a3 c5 13 ♗e5 ♘c7 14 ♘h4! ± Yusupov-Kuzmin, USSR Ch 1981

[35] 13 ♗e5 ♘e4 14 dc ♘xc3 15 ♗xc3 bc 16 ♘e5! ± Gavrikov-Yudasin, USSR Ch 1981

[36] 8 ♘xe4 ♗xe4 9 ♘h4 ♗xg2 10 ♘xg2 d5 11 ♕a4 dc 12 ♕xc4 c5 13 ♗e3 cd 14 ♗xd4 ♕c8 = Portisch-Karpov, Tilburg 1986

[37] 9 ... f5 10 b3 (10 d5 ♗f6 11 ♕c2 ♘a6 ∞) 10 ... ♗f6 11 ♗b2 d6 12 ♖ad1 a5 13 ♘e1 ♗xg2 14 ♘xg2 ♘c6 = Polugayevsky-Korchnoi, match 1980

[38] 10 b3 cd 11 ♘xd4 ♗xg2 12 ♔xg2 ♗f6 = Spassky-Portisch, Nikšić 1983

[39] 11 ♗f4 ♘c6 12 ♕d2 (12 ♕d3 ♕c8 13 d5 ♘b4 14 ♕b3 e5 15 ♗d2 b5! ∓ Sosonko-Portisch, Tilburg 1980) 12 ... ♘xd4 13 ♘xd4 ♗xg2 14 ♘xe6 fe 15 ♔xg2 ♕d7 16 f3 ♖ad8 = Ftacnik-S.Marjanović, Novi Sad 1984

[40] Andersson-Karpov, Tilburg 1983, London 1984 and World v USSR 1984

[41] **11** ♘e1 ♘ac5 12 b4 ♘xc3 13 ♗xc3 ♘e4 14 ♗xf6 ♕xf6 = Plachetka-Prandstetter, Czechoslovak Ch 1986

11 ♗e1 ♗xc3 12 ♗xc3 ♘xc3 13 ♖xc3 ♘c5 = Tukmakov-Anand, Delhi 1986, and Khuzman-Tukmakov, USSR 1986

[42] 11 ... ♘ac5 12 b4 ♘xc3 13 ♗xc3 ♘e4 14 ♗xf6 ♕xf6 15 ♕d4 ± Chiburdanidze-Akhmilovskaya, match 1986

[43] 13 dc dc 14 ♕c2 c5 15 ♖fd1 ♕e7 = Panno-Hjartarson, Dubai Ol 1986

[44] 9 ... c5 10 d5 ed 11 cd ♘xd2 12 ♘xd2 d6 13 ♘de4 ± Kasparov-Ligterink, Malta Ol 1980, Pinter-Belyavsky, Lucerne 1985, and van der Sterren-de Firmian, Wijk aan Zee 1986

[45] **10** ... ♗xc3 11 ♗xc3 ♘xc3 12 ♖xc3 e5 13 ♘d2 ♘d7 14 f4 ± Tukmakov-Petrosian, Las Palmas IZ 1982

[46] 11 ♕xd2 ♘d7 12 ♘d4 ♗xd4 (12 ... e5 13 ♘c6) 13 ♕xd4 e5 14 ♕d2 ± Pinter-Ribli, Hungarian Ch 1981

[47] **12** ... ♗e7 13 f4 c6 14 ♕d2 f5 15 ♘f2 ± Rashkovsky-Anikayev, USSR 1979

12 ... ♗xc3 13 ♖xc3 ♘d7 14 f4 ± Ftacnik-Karpov, Dubai Ol 1986

[48] 11 e3 ♘a6 12 ♕a4 c5 13 ♖fd1 ♖e8 14 dc ♘exc5 15 ♕g4 ♘d3 ∓ Pytel-Kuzmin, Polanica Zdroj 1984

[49] 11 ... ♘xc3 12 ♖xc3 c5 13 ♗e5 ♗e7 14 dc bc 15 ♕b3 ♕c8 ∞ Novikov-Rozentalis, USSR 1985

[50] 13 ♖fd1 ♕e7 14 dc ♘xc3 15 bc ♘xc5 = Velikov-Sturua, Frunze 1985

	5	6	7	8	9	10	11	12	13	
1	♕c2	♗g2¹	dc²	a3	♕a4³	0-0	♘c3	♗g5	♘d2	=
	c5	♘c6	♗xc5	♖c8	♗b7	0-0	♗e7	♘a5	♗xg2⁴	
2	♕b3	♘bd2	♕a4⁷	♗g2	0-0	♕c2	♘xd4	♔xg2	e4	=
	♘c6⁵	♘a5⁶	♗b7	c5	♗c6	cd	♗xg2	♖c8	♗c5⁸	
3	♕a4	♘c3	cd	♗g2	♗g5	♘e5	♕c2	♘a4		∞
	c6⁹	d5¹⁰	ed	♗d6	0-0	b5	b4	♖e8¹¹		
4	...	♗g2	0-0	♘xd4	♔xg2	♘c3	♖d1	f3¹²	♗f4	=
	c5	♗b7	cd	♗xg2	♕c7	♗e7	0-0	a6	♕b7¹³	
5	...	...	dc	0-0	♘c3	♗f4	♖ad1¹⁶	♕c2	♘b5	∞
	...	...	♗xc5¹⁴	0-0	♗e7	♘a6¹⁵	♘c5	♕c8	♘ce4¹⁷	
6	♘bd2	♕c2¹⁸	♗g2	♕b3	♗xd2	0-0	♕a3	♖ac1	♖fd1	±
	♗b4	♗b7¹⁹	♗e4	♗xd2+²⁰	0-0	d6	♘bd7	♕e7	♖fe8²¹	
7	...	e4²²	e5	h3	♗g2	0-0	♕a4²⁴	♘e4	♗d2	∞
	c5	cd	♘g4²³	♘h6	♘c6	♘f5	♕c8	h5	♗b7²⁵	
8	...	♗g2	e4	e5	0-0²⁸	♕xd2²⁹	♗xf3	♕f4	♗xc6	=
	♗b7	c5²⁶	cd	♘e4²⁷	♘xd2	♗xf3	♘c6	♕c7	dc³⁰	

1 6 d5 ed 7 cd ♗b7 8 e4 ♕e7 9 ♗g2 ♕xe4+ 10 ♕xe4 ♘xe4 11 0-0 ♘d6 (11 ... ♗e7 12 ♖e1 f5 13 ♘c3 0-0 14 ♘d2 ∞ Vaganian-Razuvayev, USSR 1981) 12 ♖e1+ ♔d8 ∓ Eingorn-Kengis, USSR 1982

2 7 0-0 cd 8 ♖d1 ♖c8 9 ♕a4 ♘a5 ∞

3 9 b4 ♗e7 10 0-0 (10 b5? ♗xb5 11 cb ♘b4 ∓) 10 ... ♗b7 11 ♗b2 0-0 12 ♘bd2 (11 ♘c3 a5! 12 b5 ♘b8 ∓ Bachtiar-Ribli, Indonesia 1982) 12 ... d5! =

4 14 ♔xg2 ♕c7 = Skembris-P.Nikolić, Dubai Ol 1986

5 5 ... d5 6 cd ♕xd5 (6 ... ed 7 ♘c3 ♗e7 8 ♗g2 0-0 9 ♘e5 ± Vaganian-Spassky, Montpellier C 1985) 7 ♕c2 ♗b4+ 8 ♘c3 ♗xc3+ 9 bc ♕e4 10 ♕b2 ± Torre-van der Wiel, Brussels 1986

5 ... ♗b7 6 ♗g2 ♕c8 7 ♘c3 ♘c6 8 0-0 (8 ♕d1 ♗b4 =) 8 ... ♘a5 9 ♕c2 ♘xc4 10 e4 ∞ Barlov-Eingorn, Bor 1986

5 ... c6 6 ♘c3 d5 =

6 6 ... ♗b4 7 d5 ♗xd2+ 8 ♕xd2 ♘a5 9 ♕a4! ± Vaganian-Nogueiras, Montpellier C 1985

7 7 ♕c2 c5 8 e4 cd 9 e5 ♘g8 10 ♗d3 ♗e7 11 ♗xh7 ♖c8 ∓ Timman-Polugayevsky, Bugojno 1982

8 Chandler-Hort, Bochum 1981

9 5 ... ♗e7 6 ♘c3 0-0 7 e4 ♗b7 8 ♗d3 d5 9 cd ed 10 e5 ♘e4 ∞ Antoshin-Speelman, Frunze 1979

10 6 ... b5 7 cb cb 8 ♘xb5 ♕b6 9 ♘c3 (9 e3 ♗b7 ∞ Timman-Gulko, Nikšić 1978) 9 ... ♗b4 10 ♗g2 0-0 (10 ... ♘c6!? Seirawan) 11 0-0! ♗xc3 12 bc ♗xe2 13 ♖e1 ± Bagirov-Zaichik, Kirovakan 1978

11 13 ♘d3?! h6 14 ♗d2 ♗b5 ∓ Dlugy-Chandler, London 1986

13 ♗xf6 ♕xf6 14 f4 ∞

12 12 ♗g5 a6 13 ♘e4 ♘xe4 14 ♗xe7 ♖c8 15 f3 (15 ♗a3!?) 15 ... ♘c5 16 ♕c2 d5 = P.Nikolić-A.Sokolov, Novi Sad 1984

13 14 e4 d6 15 ♘de2 ♖d8 16 ♖d2 ♘c6 17 ♕d1 b5 = Gavrikov-Sosonko, Tunis IZ 1985

14 ♖d2 ♖c8 15 ♖ad1 ♘c6 16 ♘xc6 ♕xc6 17 e4 b5! = P.Nikolić-Browne, Reykjavik 1986

14 7 ... bc 8 0-0 ♗e7 9 ♘c3 0-0 10 ♖d1 d6 11 ♗f4 ♕b6 (11 ... a6 12 ♖d2 ♕c7 13 ♖ad1 ♖d8 14 b4! ± Inkiov-de Boer, Lugano 1985) 12 ♖d2 ♖d8 13 ♖ad1 a6 14 ♘g5! ± Dlugy-Sigurjonsson, Dubai Ol 1986

15 10 ... a6 11 ♖fd1 d6 12 ♖d2 ♕c7 13 ♖ad1 ♖d8 14 ♗g5 ♗xg2 15 ♔xg2 ♘c6 16 ♘ge4 ♘e8 = Zaltsman-Arnason, New York 1986

16 11 ♖ac1 ♘c5 12 ♕c2 ♕c8 13 ♖fd1 ♘ce4 = Dlugy-Adorjan, New York 1984

17 14 ♘fd4 a6 15 ♘c7 ♖a7 16 f3 g5! ∓ Dlugy-Browne, USA 1984

14 ♘c7 g5 15 ♗e5 d6 16 ♗xf6 ♕xc7 ∞

18 6 ♕b3 c5 7 a3 ♗xd2+ 8 ♗xd2 ♘c6 9 d5 (9 ♗g2 cd 10 ♕a4 ♕c8 11 0-0 ♗b7 ∓) 9 ... ♘a5 ♗xa5 ba ∓ Fedorowicz-Seirawan, USA 1981

6 ♕a4 c5 7 a3 ♗xd2+ 8 ♗xd2 cd 9 ♗g2 ♗b7 = Hawksworth-Korchnoi, London 1982, and Kulgowski-Andersson, Wijk aan Zee

19 6 ... c5 7 ♗g2 ♘c6 8 dc ♗xc5 – 5 ♕c2, but with an extra tempo for White

20 8 ... ♘c6 9 0-0 ♗xd2 10 ♗xd2 0-0 11 ♖fd1 ♖e8 12 ♕c3 a5 13 b3 ± Romanishin-Lein, Lone Pine 1981

21 14 b4 e5 15 c5! ± Romanishin-Timman, Taxco IZ 1985

22 6 ♗g2 ♘c6 7 ♘e5 ♘xd4 8 ♗xa8 ♕xa8 9 0-0 ♗e7 ∞ Taborov-Aseyev, USSR 1983

23 7 ... ♘g8 8 ♗g2 ♗b7 (8 ... ♘c6 9 0-0 ♘ge7 10 ♕a4 ♗b7 11 ♘xd4 ±) 9 0-0 ♘e7 (9 ... d6 10 ♘xd4! ± Sosonko-Gheorghiu, Wijk aan Zee 1981) 10 ♘xd4 ♗xg2 11 ♔xg2 ♘ec6 12 ♘2f3 ♘xd4 13 ♕xd4 ± Razuvayev-Rashkovsky, USSR 1980

24 11 b3 d5 ∓ Romanishin-Aseyev, Irkutsk 1986

25 14 ♖fe1 ∞ Geller-Georgadze, USSR Ch 1980-81

26 6 ... ♗e7 and now:

7 0-0 0-0 8 ♕c2 d5 9 cd ed 10 ♘e5 c5 11 dc ♗xc5! (11 ... bc?! ± Yusupov-A.Sokolov, Tilburg 1987) = Timman-A.Sokolov, Tilburg 1987

7 e4!? ♘xe4 8 ♘e5 ∞ Khuzman-Eingorn, USSR 1983, and Timman-A.Sokolov, Montpellier C 1985

27 8 ... ♘g4 9 0-0 ♕c7 10 ♖e1 h5 (10 ... ♘c6 11 h3 ♘h6 12 ♘e4 ± Dorfman-Platonov, USSR 1980; 10 ... f6, Timman-S.Agdestein, Reykjavik 1987, 11 ♘e4! ♘xe5 12 ♘xe5 fe 13 ♗g5 ± Timman; 10 ... ♗c5? 11 ♘e4! ±/±± Adorjan-Kudrin, New York 1987) 11 h3 ♘h6 12 ♘xd4 ♗xg2 13 ♔xg2 ♘c6 ∞ Timman-Ljubojević, Amsterdam 1981

28 9 ♘xd4? ♘c3 ∓ Chow-Ljubojević, New York 1984

9 ♘xe4 ♗xe4 10 ♕xd4 ♗b4+ 11 ♗d2 ♗xf3 12 ♗xf3 ♘c6 =

29 10 ♗xd2 ♗xf3 (10 ... ♘c5!? 11 b4 ♗e7 =) 11 ♕xf3! ♘c6 12 ♕xc6! dc 13 ♗xc6+ ♕d7 14 ♗xd7+ ♔xd7 15 ♖fd1 ♔c6 ∞ Adorjan

30 14 ♕xd4 ♗c5 = Tunik-M.Gurevich, USSR 1984

189

Queen's Indian IV   1 d4 ♘f6 2 c4 e6 3 ♘f3 b6 4 g3 ♗a6 5 b3

	5	6	7	8	9	10	11	12	13	
1	...	♗g2	♘e5	♔f1[3]	♘xc4[5]	♗b2	♘cd2[6]	a3	♘c3	∞
	d5[1]	dc[2]	♗b4+	♘fd7[4]	c6	b5	0-0	♗e7	♕b6[7]	
2	...	cd	♗g2	♗d2	♕xd2[10]	0-0	♕b2	b4	b5	∞
	...	ed[8]	♗b4+[9]	♗xd2+	0-0	♘e4	♘d7	c5	♗b7[11]	
3	...	♗g2	♗d2	0-0	♕c2[12]	♗g5	♗xf6	e4	ba	∞
	♗b7	♗b4+	a5	0-0	♕e7[13]	h6	♕xf6	a4	♘c6[14]	
4	...	♗d2	♕xd2[15]	♘c3[17]	e4	♘xe4	♗g5	♘xe4	♗g2[19]	±
	♗b4+	♗xd2+	c6[16]	d5	♘xe4[18]	de	♘d7	♘f6		
5	...	...	♗g2	cd	0-0	♘c3	♘e5	♖c1[22]	♗e3	±
	...	♗e7	d5[20]	ed	0-0	♗b7	♘a6[21]	♖e8	h6[23]	
6	...	...	...	0-0	0-0	♘c3	♘xd5	♖c1[24]	♖c2[26]	±
	...	...	...	♘xd5	0-0	♘d7	ed	♖e8[25]	c5[27]	
7	...	...	...	♗c3[28]	♘e5	0-0	♘xd7	♘d2	e4[31]	=
	...	...	c6	d5	0-0[29]	♘fd7[30]	♘xd7	♖c8	dc[32]	
8	...	...	...	...	♘bd2	0-0	♖e1[33]	e4	♘xe4	=
	...	...	...	...	♘bd7	0-0	c5	de[34]	♗b7[35]	
9	...	...	♘c3	e4	cd	♔xf1	e5	♕e2[38]	♗xc3	±
	...	...	0-0[36]	d5[37]	♗xf1	ed	♘e4	♘xc3[39]	♕d7[40]	
10	...	...	...	e4	e5[41]	♗d3	♗xc3	dc[42]	♕e2[44]	=
	...	...	c6	d5	♘e4	♘xc3	c5	bc[43]	♗b7[45]	

---

[1] 5 ... b5 6 cb ♗xb5 7 ♗g2 c5 8 0-0 ♗c6 9 ♗a3 ♘a6 10 ♘bd2 ± Tarjan-Browne, US Ch 1984, and Smyslov-Belyavsky, Tilburg 1984

[2] **6 ... ♗d6** 7 0-0 ♘bd7 8 ♗b2 ♖c8 9 cd ed 10 ♘e5 ± Polugayevsky-G.Garcia, Wijk aan Zee 1979

  6 ... c5 7 0-0 ♘c6 8 cd ed 9 ♗b2 ♖c8 10 ♘c3 ♗e7 11 ♖c1 0-0 12 dc bc 13 ♘a4 ±/∞ Smyslov-Sosonko, Tilburg 1984

[3] 8 ♗d2 cb! 9 ab ♗xd2+ 10 ♕xd2 ♘d5 11 0-0 0-0 12 ♖c1 ∞

[4] 8 ... ♗d6 9 ♘xc4 ♘d5 10 e4 ♘e7 11 ♗b2 (11 ♔g1? ♗xc4 12 bc ♗e5! ∓) 11 ... ♘bc6 12 ♘d2 0-0 13 ♔g1 ± Burger-Petursson, Reykjavik 1986

[5] 9 ♗xa8 ♘xe5 10 bc 0-0 ∞

[6] 11 ♘e3 0-0 12 ♘d2 ♘f6 ∞ Langeweg-van der Wiel, Montpellier 1985

[7] Magerramov-Yudasin, Baku 1986

[8] **6 ... ♕xd5** 7 ♗g2 ♘c6 8 0-0 0-0-0 9 ♗b2 ± Psakhis-Plaskett, Sochi 1984

  6 ... ♘xd5 7 e4 ♗xf1 8 ♔xf1 ♘f6 ±/∞

[9] 7 ... ♗d6 8 0-0 0-0 9 ♘c3 ♘bd7 10 ♘e1 c6 11 ♘d3 ± Eingorn-Khalifman, USSR Ch 1986

[10] 9 ♘bxd2 0-0 10 0-0 c5 = van der Sterren-Ljubojević, Wijk aan Zee 1986

[11] Torre-Ljubojević, Brussels 1986

[12] **9 ♗g5** ♗e7 10 ♘c3 ♘e4 = Kasparov-Hübner, match 1985, and Hansen-Short, Naestved 1985

  9 ♘c3 d5 10 ♕c2 ♘a6 11 cd ed 11 ♗g5 ♗xc3 = Chernin-Spassky, Montpellier C 1985

  9 ♗f4 d5 10 ♘bd2 c5 11 ♖c1 ♘c6 = Polugayevsky-Hübner, Biel 1986

  9 ♗c3!? d5 10 ♘e5 ♕c8 11 ♗b2, Pinter-Korchnoi, Zagreb IZ 1987, 11 ... ♗e7 ± Pinter

[13] 9 ... c5 10 ♖d1 (10 dc ♗xc5 11 ♘c3, Nikolić-Korchnoi, Tilburg 1987, 11 ... ♘a6!? 12 ♖ad1 d5 13 cd ♘b4 = Korchnoi) 10 ... ♗xd2 11 ♘bxd2 ♘c6 12 ♘e4 a4 = Torre-Short, Biel IZ 1985

[14] Polugayevsky-Hort, Biel 1986

[15] 7 ♘bxd2 ♗b7 8 ♗g2 c5 = Andersson-Short, Naestved 1985

[16] **7 ... d5** 8 cd ed 9 ♕e3+ ♕e7 10 ♕xe7+ ♔xe7 11 ♘c3 ± Timman-Short, Montpellier C 1985

  7 ... 0-0 8 ♘c3 d5 9 cd ed 10 ♗g2 ♖e8 11 ♘e5 c5 12 0-0 ± Magerramov-King, Baku 1986

[17] 8 ♕f4 d5 9 ♘bd2 0-0 10 e4 de (10 ... c5!?) 11 ♘xe4 ± Korchnoi-Kudrin, Titograd 1984

[18] 9 ... de 10 ♘g5 0-0 11 ♗g2 ♘bd7 12 ♘gxe4 ♖c8 13 0-0 ± Didishko-Balashov, USSR 1979

[19] Dzindzihashvili-Miles, Tilburg 1985

[20] 7 ... ♗b7 8 ♘c3 0-0 9 0-0 d5 (9 ... c5 10 d5 ed 11 ♘e1 ♘a6 12 cd d6 13 ♘c2 ± Dorfman-Eingorn, USSR 1984) 10 ♘e5 ♘bd7 11 cd ♘xd5 12 ♘xd5 ed 13 ♘d3 ± Yusupov-Sokolov, match 1986

[21] 11 ... ♘bd7 12 ♗f4 ♖e8 13 ♖c1 ♘f8 14 ♗g5 ♘e6 15 ♗xf6 ♗xf6 16 e3 ± Petrosian-Korchnoi, match 1977, and Portisch-Sosonko, Tilburg 1984

[22] 12 ♗f4 ♕c8 13 ♗g5 ♖d8 14 e4 ± Xu Jun-Lau, Lucerne 1985

[23] 14 ♕c2 c6 15 f4 ± Pinter-Sax, Szirak 1985

[24] 12 b4 c5 13 bc bc 14 ♖e1 ♖e8 15 ♖c1 ♗c4 16 ♗c3 cd 17 ♘xd4 ♖c8 18 ♘f5 ± van der Sterren-Douven, Holland 1985, and van der Heijden-Bewersdorff, Guernsey 1986

[25] 12 ... c5 13 ♗e3 ♖e8 14 ♖c2 ♘f6 15 ♖e1 ♘e4?! 16 dc bc 17 ♘d2! ± Gavrikov-Sokolov, USSR Ch 1985

[26] 13 ♖e1 c5 14 ♗e3 ♗b7 15 ♗h3 cd 16 ♗xd4 ♘f6 17 ♖c2 ♗b4 18 ♖f1 ♗a6 ±/= Karpov-Sokolov, match 1987

[27] 14 ♗e3 ♘f6 15 ♖e1 ♖c8 16 ♕c1 ♕d7 17 dc bc 18 ♗xc5 ±/= Petursson-Sokolov, Biel IZ 1985

14 ♗f4 ♗b7 15 ♕c1 a5 16 ♖d1 a4 17 dc ab 18 ab ♘xc5 19 ♕b2 ± Belyavsky-Dolmatov, USSR Ch 1985

[28] 8 ♗g5 d5 9 ♘bd2 ♘bd7 10 0-0 0-0 11 ♕e2 c5 = Ribli-Timman, Bugojno 1984

8 0-0 d5 9 ♕c2 (9 ♘e5 ♘fd7 =) 9 ... ♘bd7 10 ♖d1 0-0 11 ♘e1 ♖c8 12 ♘bd2 c5 = Sahovic-Spassov, Vrnjačka Banja 1984

[29] 9 ... ♘e4 10 0-0 ♘xc3 11 ♘xc3 0-0 12 ♖e1 ♗b7 13 cd cd 14 e4 ♗b4 = Yusupov-Sokolov, match 1986

[30] 10 ... ♗b7 11 ♘d2 ♘a6 12 e4 c5 13 ed ed 14 ♖e1 cd 15 ♗xd4 ♘c5 16 ♘g4 dc =/∞ Torre-Adorjan, Wijk aan Zee 1984

[31] 13 ♖e1 c5 14 cd ed = Portisch-Timman and Petrosian-Timman, Tilburg 1982

[32] 13 ... de 14 ♘xe4 (14 ♘xe4 b5! ∓ Yrjölä-H.Olafsson, Gjovik 1985) 14 ... c5 15 d5 ed 16 ♗xd5 ♗f6 =

13 ... dc 14 bc b5 15 ♖e1 bc 16 ♕c2 ♕c7

[17] ♘f1 e5 = Karpov-Kasparov, match (21) 1986

[33] 11 ♕c2 c5! = Gligorić-Ljubojević, Nikšić 1983

[34] 12 ... dc 13 bc (13 ♘xc4!?) 13 ... cd 14 ♘xd4 ♘e5 15 ♘xe6 fe 16 ♗xe5 ♗c5 17 ♖f1 ♕d3 ∞ Farago-Lerner, Polanica Zdroj 1986

[35] 13 ... ♘xe4 14 ♖xe4 ♗b7 15 ♖e3 ± Pinter-Tukmakov, Las Palmas IZ 1982, and Portisch-Hübner, Tilburg 1982

13 ... ♗b7 14 ♘fg5 cd 15 ♗xd4 ♕c7 = Kasparov-Karpov, match (18) 1984-85, and Eingorn-Lerner, USSR Ch 1986

[36] 7 ... d5 8 cd ♘xd5 9 e4 (9 ♘xd5! ed 10 ♗g2 – 7 ♗g2) 9 ... ♘xc3 10 ♗xc3 ♕c8 11 ♗d3 0-0 12 0-0 ♖d8 = Shnaider-Sokolov, USSR 1984

[37] 8 ... ♗b7 9 ♗d3 d5 10 cd ed 11 e5 ♘e4 12 0-0 c5 13 ♖c1 ± Pinter-Adorjan, Prague Z 1985, Szirak 1985, and Szirak 1986

[38] 12 ♖c1 c5 13 ♔g2 ♘c6 14 ♖e1 ♘xc3 15 ♗xc3 ♕d7 = Karpov-Sokolov, match 1987

12 ♔g2 f5 13 ef (13 ♖c1 ♕d7 14 ♘e2 c5 ∞) 13 ... ♗xf6 14 ♖e1 ♘c6! = van der Sterren-Magerramov, Baku 1986

[39] 12 ... f5 13 ef ♘xd2+ 14 ♕xd2 ♗xf6 15 ♔g2 ♘c6 16 ♖he1 ± van der Sterren-Ree, Wijk aan Zee 1984

[40] 14 ♔g2 c5 (14 ... ♘c6 15 ♖he1 ♘d8 16 ♘g1! c5 17 f4 ± Karpov-Sokolov, match 1987) 15 ♖ad1 ♘c6 16 ♖d2 ± Pinter-Stoica and Polugayevsky-Sosonko, Thessaloniki Ol 1984

[41] 9 ♕c2 de 10 ♘xe4 ♗b7 11 ♗g2 c5 = Seirawan-Browne, US Ch 1981

[42] 12 cd ♕xd5 13 ♗xa6 ♘xa6 14 dc ♕e4+ 15 ♕e2 ♘xc5 ∓ Tarjan-Polugayevsky, Riga IZ 1979

12 0-0 ♗b7 13 ♕e2 ♘d7 14 cd ♗xd5 15 ♗e4 ♗xe4 16 ♕xe4 cd 17 ♗xd4 0-0 = Portisch-Timman, Tilburg 1984

[43] 12 ... ♗xc5 13 ♕e2 ♗b7 14 0-0 dc (14 ... 0-0 15 ♖ad1 ♕e7? 16 b4! ±± Christiansen-Ligterink, Lucerne Ol 1982) 15 bc ♘c6 16 ♖ad1 ♕c7 17 ♗e4 h6 18 h4 ♖d8 ∞ Levin-Lerner, USSR 1983

[44] 13 cd ed 14 ♗xa6 ♘xa6 15 ♕d3 ♘c7 16 ♗a5 d4 = Timman-Portisch, Indonesia 1983

[45] 14 0-0-0 d4 15 ♗e4 ♘c6 16 ♗d2 ♕b6 17 ♕d3 ♖b8 ∞ Korchnoi-Timman, match 1982

14 0-0 0-0 15 ♖ad1 d4 16 ♗d2 ♘d7 17 ♗e4 ♗xe4 18 ♕xe4 ♕c7 19 ♖fe1 ♖fe8 20 h4 a5 = Ribli-Chandler, Sarajevo 1985

Queen's Indian V 1 d4 ♘f6 2 c4 e6 3 ♘f3 b6 4 a3

	4	5	6	7	8	9	10	11	12	
1	...	d5[2]	♕c2	cd	♘c3	g3[6]	♗g2	0-0	♖e1	±
	c5[1]	♗a6[3]	ed[4]	g6[5]	♗g7	0-0	d6	♖e8	♘bd7[7]	
2	...	♕c2[8]	♘c3	e3	ed	♗d3	gf	♗e3	0-0	∞
	♗a6	♗b7[9]	c5	cd[10]	♗e7	♗xf3[11]	♘c6	♖c8	♘a5[12]	
3	...	...	...	dc	♗g5[13]	e3	♗e2	♗xe7	b4	=
	...	...	...	bc	♗e7	d6	♘h5[14]	♕xe7	♘c6[15]	
4	...	...	...	e4	♘xd4	♘xc6	♗f4[17]	♗e3[19]	♗xc5	±
	...	...	...	cd	♘c6[16]	♘xc6	♘h5[18]	♗c5	bc[20]	
5	...	...	...	...	...	♘b3	♗g5[21]	♗h4	0-0-0	±
	...	...	...	...	♗c5	♘c6	h6[22]	d6	♕e7[23]	
6	...	♘c3	d5[25]	e4	♗e2	0-0	♘d4	f3	♗e3	±
	♗b7	g6[24]	♗g7[26]	0-0	d6	♘bd7	♘c5	a5	a4[27]	
7	...	...	♘xe4	♘d2[28]	e4	e5[31]	♘f3	♗e2	0-0	±
	...	♘e4	♗xe4	♗b7[29]	♕f6[30]	♕g6[32]	♗e7	0-0	f6[33]	
8	...	...	cd[34]	♗g5[35]	♕a4+[36]	e3	♗d3	♗xe4	♘xg5	=
	...	d5	ed	♗e7	c6[37]	0-0	♘e4	♗xg5	♕xg5[38]	
9	...	...	...	♕a4+	g3	♗g2	♘h4	♘f5	0-0	=
	...	...	...	c6[39]	♘bd7[40]	♗d6	0-0	♗c7	♖e8[41]	
10	...	...	...	♗f4	e3	♗d3[42]	0-0	♘e5	♘xc6	±
	...	...	...	♗e7	0-0	c5	♘c6[43]	cd	♗xc6[44]	
11	...	...	...	...	♗g3[45]	e3	♗e2[47]	♕c2	0-0[48]	=
	...	...	...	♗d6	0-0	c5[46]	♕e7	♘bd7	♗xg3[49]	
12	...	...	...	g3	♗g2	0-0	♕c2[52]	♖d1	♕f5	=
	...	...	...	♗e7[50]	0-0	c5[51]	♘bd7[53]	♖c8	g6[54]	

1 4 ... ♘e4 5 ♘fd2 d5 6 e3 ♗b7 7 cd ed 8 ♘xe4 de 9 ♘c3 ♗d6 10 ♗b5+! ± Glek-Rozentalis, USSR 1985

2 5 e3 g6 6 ♘c3 ♗g7 7 e4 cd 8 ♘xd4 0-0 9 ♗g5 h6 10 ♗h4 d5 = Miles-Timman, Amsterdam 1981

3 5 ... ed 6 cd g6 7 e4! ♘xe4 8 ♗d3 ♘f6 9 0-0 ± Benjamin-de Firmian, US Ch 1986; 7 ... d6 8 ♗b5+ ±

4 6 ... ♕e7 7 ♗g5 ed 8 ♘c3! ♗xc4 9 e4 h6 10 ♗xf6 ♕xf6 11 ed ♗xf1 12 ♔xf1 d6 13 ♖e1+ ♗e7 14 ♕a4+! ♔f8 15 ♕g4 ± Miles-Kudrin, London 1982

5 7 ... ♗b7 8 e4 ♕e7 9 ♗d3 ♘xd5 10 0-0 ∞

6 9 ♗f4 d6 10 ♕a4+ ♕d7 11 ♗xd6 ♕xa4 12 ♘xa4 ♘xd5 13 0-0-0 ♘e7 = Browne-Timman, Las Palmas IZ 1982

7 **12 ... ♕c7** 13 e4 ♘bd7 15 ♗f4 ♘h5 16 ♗e3 ♖ac8 17 g4! ♘hf6 18 h3 b5 18 ♗f4 ± A.Petrosian-Foisor, Baile Herculana 1984

 12 ... ♘bd7 13 h3 ♘e5 14 ♘xe5 ♖xe5 15 e4 ± Yusupov-Timman, match 1986

8 5 e3 d5 6 ♘c3 (6 ♘bd2 ♗e7 7 b4 0-0 8 ♗b2 c5 =) 6 ... ♗e7 7 ♘e5 0-0 8 ♗e2 c6 9 0-0 ♘fd7 = Browne-Benjamin, US Ch 1984

9 5 ... d5 6 cd ed 7 g3 ♗d6 8 ♗g5 0-0 9 ♘c3 c6 10 0-0-0! h6 11 ♗xf6 ♕xf6 12 ♗g2 ♖c8 13 e4 ± Epishin-Burkovsky, USSR 1985

10 7 ... g6 8 ♗e2 ♗g7 9 0-0 0-0 10 ♖d1 cd 11 ♘xd4 a6 12 e4 ± Portisch-Timman, Tilburg 1986

11 9 ... ♕c8 10 0-0 ♗xf3 11 gf ♘c6 12 ♗e3 0-0 13 ♔h1 g6 14 ♖g1 ± Portisch-Korchnoi, match 1983

12 **12 ... 0-0** 13 ♖ad1 ♘a5 14 d5 ♖e8 15 ♕e2 ± Plaskett-Polugayevsky, Lucerne 1985

 12 ... ♘a5 13 ♕e2 0-0 14 d5 ♘h5! ∞ Polugayevsky

13 8 ♗f4 ♘h5 9 ♗g5 ♗e7 10 ♗xe7 ♕xe7 = Yusupov-Miles, USSR v World 1984

14 10 ... ♘c6 11 0-0 h6 12 ♗h4 ♘h5 13 ♗xe7 ♕xe7 14 b4 ♘f6 15 b5 ♘a5 = Timman-Miles, Thessaloniki Ol 1984

15 13 bc dc 14 ♖b1 ♘f6 15 0-0 0-0 16 ♖b5 ♖ac8 = Yusupov-Timman, match 1986

16 8 ... d6 9 ♗e2 (9 ♗g5 ♘bd7 10 0-0-0 a6 11 f4 ± Szabolcsi-Schneider, Budapest 1986) 9 ... ♘bd7 10 ♗e3 ♗e7 11 f4 a6 12 0-0-0 ± Vizhmanavin-Razuvayev, Irkutsk 1986

17 10 ♗e2 ♕b8! 11 ♗e3 ♗c5 12 ♗xc5 bc

13 0-0 ♕e5 $\overline{\mp}$ Christiansen-Miles, Linares 1985

[18] **10 ... d6** 11 ♗e2 ♗e7 12 ♖d1 ♕b8 13 0-0 $\pm$

10 ... ♗c5 11 ♗e2 0-0 12 ♖d1 a5 13 0-0 $\pm$ M.Gurevich-Yudasin, Tbilisi 1985

[19] **11 ♗d2 ♕b8** 12 g3 f5 13 ♗d3 ♗d6 14 0-0-0 f4 ∞ Polugayevsky-Arnason, Reykjavik 1987

[20] **13 g3 0-0** 14 ♗d3 ♘f6 15 0-0-0 d6 16 f4 $\pm$ Bareyev-Eingorn, USSR Ch 1986

[21] **10 ♗f4 e5** 11 ♗g5 h6 12 ♗h4 0-0 13 ♘xc5 bc 14 ♗d3 ♘d4 15 ♕d1 a5 ∞ Christiansen-Seirawan, US Ch 1984

10 ♘xc5 bc 11 ♗d3 d6 12 0-0 0-0 13 ♗g5 h6 14 ♗h4 g5 15 ♗g3 e5 ∞ Vizhmanavin-Salov, Irkutsk 1986

[22] **10 ... a6** 11 0-0-0 ♕c7 12 ♔b1 $\pm$ Kasparov-van der Wiel, Amsterdam 1988

[23] **13 ♗e2 g5** (13 ... 0-0-0!? M.Gurevich) 14 ♗g3 e5 (14 ... 0-0-0 M.Gurevich) 15 ♘d5 ♘xd5 16 cd ♘d4 17 ♘xd4 ♗xd4 18 ♖xd4! $\pm$ M.Gurevich-Lerner, Moscow 1987

[24] **5 ... ♗xf3** 6 gf ♗e7 7 f4 d5 8 f5! ef 9 ♗g2 $\pm$ Petrosian-Spassky, match (18) 1966

5 ... ♗e7 6 d5 0-0 7 e4 d6 8 ♗d3 c6 9 0-0 $\pm$ Reshevsky-Blocker, New York 1984

[25] **6 ♕c2 c5** (6 ... d5 7 cd ed 8 ♗f4 $\pm$) 7 e4 cd 8 ♘xd4 ♗g7 9 ♗g5 h6 10 ♗f4 0-0 11 ♘db5 $\pm$ Kuligowski-Speelman, Wijk aan Zee 1983

[26] **6 ... ed** 7 cd ♗g7 8 ♗g5 h6 9 ♗h4 0-0 10 e3 c6 11 ♗c4 $\pm$ Ermolinsky-Danailov, Tbilisi 1986

[27] **13 ♘db5** $\pm$ Zichichi-Spassky, Reggio Emilia 1983-84

[28] **7 e3 ♗e7** 8 ♗d3 d5! 9 ♕c2 ♗xd3 10 ♕xd3 0-0 = Romanishin-Portisch, Indonesia 1983

7 ♗f4!? ♗xf3!? (7 ... ♗e7 8 e3 c5 9 d5 $\pm$ Ftacnik-Csom, Szirak 1986) 8 gf ♗d6 9 ♗xd6 cd 10 f4 ♘c6 ∞ A.Petrosian-Gurgenidze, USSR 1985

[29] **7 ... ♗g6** 8 g3 ♘c6 9 e3 $\pm$ Kasparov-Andersson, Tilburg 1981, and Psakhis-Gurgenidze, USSR Ch 1985

[30] **8 ... g6** 9 ♗d3 ♗g7 10 ♘f3 d6 11 0-0 0-0 12 ♗g5 ♕d7 13 ♕d2 $\pm$ Polugàyevsky-Christiansen, Thessaloniki Ol 1984

8 ... d5 9 cd ed 10 e5 c5 11 ♗d3 ♕d7 12 0-0 ♗a6 13 ♗xa6 ♘xa6 14 ♘f3 $\pm$ Christiansen-Portisch, Linares 1985

[31] **9 d5 ♗c5** 10 ♘f3 ed 11 cd ♕g6 12 ♗d3! ♕xg2 13 ♖f1 c6 14 b4 cd 15 ed ♗e7 16 ♗b2 ♗xd5 17 ♗e2 ♗b7 18 ♖g1 ♕h3 19 ♖xg7 ∞ Glek-Krasenkov, USSR 1985

[32] **9 ... ♕d8** 10 ♘f3 d5 11 ♗e3 ♘d7 12 cd ♗xd5 13 ♗d3 c5 14 0-0 $\pm$ Polugayevsky-Unzicker, Lucerne Ol 1982

[33] **13 ♗f4** $\pm$ Polugayevsky-Speelman, London 1986

[34] **6 ♗g5 ♗e7** 7 e3 0-0 8 ♖c1 h6 9 ♗h4 ♘bd7 10 ♗d3 c5 = Andersson-Karpov, World v USSR 1984

6 ♕a4+ ♕d7 7 ♕xd7+ ♘bxd7 8 ♘b5 ♗d6 = Christiansen-Korchnoi, Linares 1985

[35] **7 e3 ♘bd7** 8 ♗e2 ♗d6 9 b4 0-0 10 0-0 a6 11 ♕e3 ♕e7 12 ♖b1 ♘e4! $\overline{\mp}$ Spassky-Petrosian, match (11) 1969

7 b4 a5 8 b5 ♗d6 9 e3 ♘bd7 10 ♕b3 0-0 11 ♗d3 ♘e4! 12 0-0 (12 ♘xd5 ♘dc5) 12 ... ♖e8 = Gheorghiu-Bobotsov, Siegen Ol 1970

[36] **8 ♗xf6** ♗xf6 9 g3 0-0 10 ♗g2 ♖e8 11 0-0 ♘a6 12 b4 c5 = Kasparov-Bukić, Banja Luka 1979

8 e3 0-0 9 ♗d3 ♘bd7 10 ♖c1 c5 11 0-0 ♘e4 12 ♗f4 ♘xc3 13 ♖xc3 c4 14 ♗b1 b5 = Plaskett-Psakhis, Troon 1984

[37] **8 ... ♘bd7** 9 ♗xf6 ♗xf6 10 g3 c5 11 ♗h3 $\pm$ Browne-Chandler, Naestved 1985

[38] **13 ♗f3 ♘a6** = Ftacnik-Short, Naestved 1985

[39] **7 ... ♕d7** 8 ♕xd7+ ♘bxd7 9 ♘b5 $\pm$

7 ... ♘bd7 8 ♗f4 a6 9 g3 c5 10 ♗g2 b5 11 ♕c2 ♕b6 12 ♘e5 $\pm$ Razuvayev-A.Ivanov, Minsk 1985

[40] **8 ... ♗e7** - 7 g3

8 ... g6 9 ♗g2 ♗g7 10 0-0 0-0 11 ♗g5 $\pm$ Christiansen-Kurajica, Thessaloniki Ol 1984

[41] Christiansen-Hübner, Linares 1985

[42] **9 ♗e2 ♘bd7** 10 ♘e5 ♘xe5 11 de ♘e4 12 ♘xe4 de 13 ♕c2 ♗g5 = Portisch-Ljubojević, Tilburg 1986

[43] **10 ... ♘a6** 11 ♘e5 ♘c7 12 ♕a4 $\pm$ Inkiov-Augustin, Lodz 1979

[44] **13 ed ♗d6** 14 ♗g5 $\pm$ Portisch-P.Nikolić, Portorož/Ljubljana 1985

[45] **8 ♗xd6 ♕xd6** 9 ♖c1 ♕e7 10 g3 0-0 11 ♗g2 c5 = Browne-I.Ivanov, Los Angeles 1982, and A.Petrosian-Yudasin, USSR 1983

[46] **9 ... ♘e4** 10 ♕b3 ♘xc3 11 ♕xc3 c5 12 ♗e2 ♗xg3 13 hg $\pm$ Portisch-Chernin, Tunis IZ 1985, and Chernin-Chandler, Lucerne 1985

[47] **10 ♗d3 ♖e8** 11 0-0 ♗xg3 12 hg ♘bd7 13 dc bc 14 b4 d4! = Portisch-Tal, Montreal 1979

[48] **12 ♗xd6 ♕xd6** 13 0-0 ♖fd8 14 dc bc 15 b4 ♖a8 = Ivkov-Gligorić, Vrbas 1980

[49] **13 hg ♖fc8** 14 dc bc 15 ♖fd1 ♖ab8 = Malanyuk-A.Ivanov, Minsk 1985

[50] **7 ... ♗d6** 8 ♗g2 0-0 9 0-0 ♖e8 10 ♗g5 ♘bd7 11 ♘b5 h6 12 ♘xd6 cd 13 ♗xf6 ♘xf6 14 ♘e1 $\pm$ Kasparov-A.Ivanov, USSR 1981

7 ... c5 8 ♘e5 ♘bd7 9 ♗g2 cd 10 ♕xd4 $\pm$ Portisch-Tukmakov, Tilburg 1984

[51] **9 ... ♖e8** 10 ♗f4 a6 13 ♖c1 ♗d6 14 e3 ♗xf4 15 gf $\pm$ Vaganian-Speelman, London 1986

9 ... ♘bd7 10 ♗f4 c6 11 ♕b3 $\pm$ Tal-Vaiser, Sochi 1984

[52] **10 ♘h4 ♕d7** 11 dc ½-½ Karpov-Portisch, Bugojno 1986

10 ♘e5 ♘c6 11 ♘xc6 ♗xc6 =

10 ♗g5 ♘a6 11 e3 ♘e4 =

[53] **10 ... ♘a6** 11 ♗g5 h6 12 ♗xf6 ♗xf6 13 ♖fd1 ♖e8 = Yusupov-Hjartarson, Thessaloniki Ol 1984

[54] **13 ♕h3 ♖e8** 14 dc bc 15 ♘g5 ♘f8 = Kharitonov-Vladimirov, Irkutsk 1983

Queen's Indian V   1 d4 ♘f6 2 c4 e6 3 ♘f3 b6 4 a3 *continued*

	4	5	6	7	8	9	10	11	12	
13	...	♘c3	cd	g3	♗g2	0-0	♗f4	♘e5[56]	dc	=
	♗b7	d5	ed	♗e7	0-0	c5	♘a6[55]	♘c7	bc[57]	
14	...	...	...	...	♕a4+	♗h3[59]	0-0	♖d1	♘h4	±
	...	...	...	...	♘bd7[58]	0-0	a6	♗d6[60]	b5[61]	
15	...	...	...	...	...	♗g2[62]	0-0	♗f4	♖ad1	±
	...	...	...	...	c6	0-0	♘bd7[63]	♘h5[64]	♘xf4[65]	

[55] **10 ... ♘bd7** 11 ♘e5 ♖e8 12 ♖c1 ♘f8 13 dc bc 14 ♘c4 ± P.Nikolić-Chandler, Naestved 1985

10 ... ♘c6 11 dc bc 12 ♘e5 ♘d4 13 ♘c4 intending ♘e3 ± Gulko-Panchenko, Moscow Ch 1981, and A.Petrosian-Kengis, USSR 1984

[56] 11 ♕c2 ♕c8 12 ♖ad1 ♖d8 13 ♗e5 ♘e4 14 dc ♘xc3 15 ♗xc3 bc 16 e3 ♕e6 = Kengis-Yudasin, USSR 1984

[57] **13 ♘c4 ♖b8!** 14 ♗xc7 ♕xc7 15 ♘xd5 ♗xd5 16 ♗xd5 ♖bd8 17 e4 ♘xe4 = Timoshchenko-Psakhis, USSR Ch 1981

13 ♕a4 ♗d6! 14 ♘c6 (14 ♖fd1? g5) 14 ... ♗xc6 15 ♕xc6 ♗xf4 16 gf ♖b8 ∞ Grooten-Kurajica, Ramsgate 1982

[58] 8 ... ♕d7 9 ♕xd7+ ♘bxd7 10 ♘b5 ± Ivkov-Polugayevsky, Bugojno 1982

[59] 9 ♘e5 c5 10 ♗e3 0-0 11 ♘xd7 ♘xd7

[60] 12 ♗g2 ♘f6 13 0-0 c4 ∞ Browne-Short, Naestved 1985

[61] 13 ♕c2 ♘e4 14 ♘f5 ± Belyavsky-Chernin, Tunis IZ 1985

[62] 9 ♗h3 0-0 10 0-0 c5 11 ♖d1 c4 (11 ... ♘c6!? 12 ♗g5 ♖e8 Yusupov-Ljubojević, Bugojno 1986) 12 ♘e5 a6 ∞ Tukmakov-Yudasin, Kuibishev 1986

[63] 10 ... c5 11 ♖d1 ♘a6 (11 ... c4 12 ♘e5 a6 13 ♕c2 b5 14 b3 ±) 12 ♗f4 ± Lputian-P.Popović, Sarajevo 1985

[64] **11 ... a5** 12 ♘e5 b5 13 ♕c2 ♘b6 (13 ... a4 14 e4 ±) 14 a4 ± Browne-Peters, US Ch 1984

11 ... ♖e8 12 ♖ad1 ♘h5 13 ♗c1 ♕c7 14 e4 ± Belyavsky-Short, Montpellier C 1985

[65] 13 gf ♘f6 14 ♘e5 ± Yusupov-Short, Dubai Ol 1986

Queen's Indian VI   1 d4 ♘f6 2 c4 e6 3 ♘f3 b6 4 a3 ♗b7 5 ♘c3 d5 6 cd ♘xd5

	7	8	9	10	11	12	13	14	15	
1	♗d2[1]	♕c2	e4	♗xc3	♘xd4	♗e2	0-0	h3	♖fe1	=
	♘d7[2]	c5[3]	♘xc3[4]	cd	a6	♕c7	♗e7	0-0	♖fd8[5]	
2	♕a4+	♘xd5	♗f4	g3	♗h3	♖c1	0-0[7]	♖fe1	♗e5	±
	♘d7[6]	ed	c6	♗e7	0-0	♗f6	♖e8	♘f8	♗xe5[8]	
3	...	...	♕c2[9]	e4	♗e3	♖d1	d5	ed	♕e4+	∞
	...	♗xd5	c5[10]	♗b7	a6	♕c7	ed	♗d6	♔f8[11]	
4	♕c2	e4	bc	♗d3	0-0	cd	♕e2	♗b2	♕xd3	±
	♗e7[12]	♘xc3	0-0	c5	cd	♕c8	♗a6	♗xd3	♕a6[13]	
5	...	♕xc3[14]	♗g5	e3[17]	♕b3	♕a4+	♕a6	♗b5+	♕a4	±
	♘xc3	♘d7[15]	♘f6[16]	♖c8	♕d5	♗c6	♗b7	♘d7	c6[18]	
6	...	...	e3[19]	♗b5+	♗a4[20]	0-0	♖d1	b4	♗b2	±
	...	h6	♗c7	c6	0-0	♘d7	♖c8	♕c7	♖fd8[21]	
7	...	dc	♗g5	♖c1	♘xd5[23]	b4	♘e5	♕b2[24]	♕xe5	∞
	c5	♗xc5	♕c8[22]	h6	hg	g4	♖h5	♖xe5	♗xb4+[25]	
8	...	e4	bc	♗b2	d5	♖d1	ed	♘xe5	♗b5+	±
	...	♘xc3	♘c6[26]	♗e7[27]	ed	♗f6	♘e5	♗xe5	♔f8[28]	
9	...	...	...	♗f4[29]	cd	♕b3	♗d3	♕b5+[32]	♘e5	∞
	...	...	♘d7	cd	♖c8	♗e7[30]	♘f6[31]	♕d7	♕xb5[33]	

¹ 7 e4 Nxc3 8 bc Bxe4 9 Ne5 Qh4! ∓ Nogueiras-Belyavsky, Thessaloniki Ol 1984, and Lewis-Miles, England 1984

² 7 ... c5 8 e4! Nxc3 9 Bxc3 Bxe4 10 Ne5 a6 11 Qh5 ± Romanishin-Panchenko, Sochi 1983

7 ... Be7 8 Qa4+ Qd7 9 Qc2 0-0 10 e4 Nxc3 11 Bxc3 ± Romanishin-Vaganian, Lvov 1984

³ 8 ... Nxc3 9 Bxc3 Nf6 10 e3 a6 11 Bd3 Qd5 12 Ne5 Qxg2 13 0-0-0 ∞ Tal-Belyavsky, Bugojno 1984

⁴ 9 ... N5f6 10 Rd1 cd 11 Nxd4 a6 12 Be2 (12 Bg5!?) 12 ... Qc7 13 Qb1 Bd6 = Tukmakov-Polugayevsky, USSR 1984

⁵ Lputian-Rodriguez, Erevan 1984

⁶ 7 ... c6 8 e4 Nxc3 9 bc Be7 10 Bd3 0-0 11 0-0 c5 12 Rd1 ± Rashkovsky-Makarichev, USSR 1982

7 ... Qd7 8 Qc2 Nxc3 9 Bxc3 Bd6 10 g3 Be4 11 Bg2 Qc6 12 Be3 ± Rashkovsky-Ehlvest, Sverdlovsk 1984

⁷ 13 Rxc6 Nc5! 14 Rxc5 bc 15 dc Qe8! 16 Bd7 Qe4 ∞ Kasparov

⁸ 15 ... Be7 16 Rxc6 Bxc6 17 Qxc6 ± Christiansen-Ornstein, Reykjavik 1984

15 ... Bxe5 16 Nxe5 c5 17 e3 Qd6 18 Bg2 Red8 19 f4 ± Novikov-Orlov, USSR 1986

⁹ 9 Ne5 a6 10 Bf4 (10 Nc6 Nc5! 11 dc Qd7 =) 10 ... Bd6 ∞ Ilić-Stean, London 1983

9 Bg5 Be7 10 Bxe7 Qxe7 11 Ne5 (11 Rc1 0-0!) 11 ... a6 12 Nc6 Qd6 13 Rc1 b5 =

¹⁰ 9 ... Be7 10 e4 Bb7 11 Bb5 0-0 12 Bc6 Bxc6 13 Qxc6 Nf6 14 Bg5 ± Malanyuk-Novikov, Lvov 1986

¹¹ 16 Bc4 Re8 ½-½ Malanyuk-Novikov, USSR 1986

¹² 7 ... Nd7 8 Nxd5 ed 9 Bg5 ± Kasparov-Karpov, match (32) 1984-85

¹³ 16 Qd2 Nd7 17 Rfe1 Rfd8 18 d5 ed 19 ed Bf6 20 d6 ± Kengis-Danailov, Albena 1986

16 Qe3 Nd7 17 Rad1 Rfe8 18 Qf4 ± Podgayets-Georgadze, USSR 1986

¹⁴ 8 bc Qd5 (8 ... c5! 9 e4 – 7 ... c5; 8 ... Be7!? 9 e3 Qc8! 10 Bb2 c5 11 Bb5+ Bc6! intending ... c4 =/∓ Timman-Karpov, Tilburg 1988) 9 e3 Nd7 10 Bd3 c5 11 e4 Qc6 12 d5! ± Miles-Karklins, Reykjavik 1986

¹⁵ 8 ... Be7 9 Bf4 ±
8 ... Bd6 9 Bg5 ±

¹⁶ 9 ... f6 10 Bf4 Bd6 11 Bg3 0-0 12 e3 ± Kir.Georgiev-Korchnoi, Wijk aan Zee 1985

9 ... Qc8 10 e3 Bd6 11 Bb5 ± Ermolinsky-Tukmakov, Kuibishev 1986

¹⁷ 10 e4 and now:
10 ... Rc8 11 Bxf6! gf (11 ... Qxf6 12 Ba6! Bxa6 13 Qc6+ Kd8 14 Ne5 Qe7 15 d5 Qe8

16 Nxf7+! ± Spraggett-Karklins, Toronto 1985) 12 d5 ed 13 0-0-0 ∞

10 ... c6 11 Bxf6 gf 12 d5 ed 13 0-0-0 Qd6 14 ed 0-0-0 ∞ Benjamin-Razuvayev, Dortmund 1985

¹⁸ 16 Bc4 Qa5+ 17 Qxa5 ba 13 Ke2 ± Kharitonov-Bandza, USSR 1985

¹⁹ 9 Bf4 Bd6 10 Bxd6 cd 11 d5 e5 = Burger-Reshevsky, Reykjavik 1986

9 b4 Be7 10 Bb2 0-0 11 e3 Nd7 12 Rd1 Rc8 13 Bb5 c6 14 Be2 (14 Ba4? a6 ∓ Hardicsay-Adorjan, Hungary 1986) 14 ... c5 15 dc Bf6 =

²⁰ 11 Be2 0-0 12 0-0 Nd7 13 Rd1 Rc8 14 b4 c5 = Vaganian-Adorjan, Dubai Ol 1986

²¹ 16 Rac1 Nf6 17 Ne5 (17 Qe1 c5 = Lputian-Lerner, Kharkov 1985) 17 ... c5 18 dc Rxd1+ 19 Bxd1 bc 20 Bf3 ± Lputian

²² 9 ... Qc7 10 Rc1 f6 11 Nxd5 Bxd5 12 e4 ± Vizhmanavin-Novikov, Tashkent 1984

9 ... Be7 10 Nxd5 ed 11 Bxe7 Qxe7 12 e3 ±

9 ... f6 10 Bd2 0-0 11 e3 Nc6 12 Nxd5 Qxd5 13 Bc4 ±

²³ 11 Ne4 Nd7 12 Nxc5 Nxc5 = Ligterink-Belyavsky, Wijk aan Zee 1985

11 Bh4 a5 = Spraggett-Portisch, Montpellier C 1985

11 Bd2 Nf6 = Chekhov-Timoshchenko, Berlin 1986

²⁴ 14 Qa4+ Nc6 15 bc Rxe5 ∓ Petersson-C.Hansen, Borgarnes 1985

²⁵ 16 Kd1 Nc6 17 Rxc6 Qxc6 18 Nxb4 0-0-0+ 19 Nd3 f6 ∞ Dreyev-Gelfand, USSR 1986

²⁶ 9 ... Be7 10 Bb5+ Bc6 11 Bd3 Nd7 12 0-0 h6 13 Rd1 Qc7 14 d5 ± Kasparov-Gheorghiu, Moscow IZ 1982

²⁷ 10 ... g6 11 Rd1 Bg7 12 d5 ± Petrosian-Sosonko, Tilburg 1982

10 ... Rc8 11 Rd1 cd 12 cd b5, Lputian-Belyavsky, USSR Ch 1987, 13 Qd2! ±

²⁸ 16 0-0 ± Tukmakov-Oll, Kuibishev 1986

²⁹ 10 Bd3 Qc7! 11 Qb1 (11 Bb2 cd =; 11 Qd2 g6 =) 11 ... g6 ∞ Hort-Miles, Lucerne Ol 1982

³⁰ 12 ... Bxe4 13 Bb5 Bc6 14 Ba6 Ra8 15 Rc1 ±

12 ... Qf6 13 Qe3 Qg6 14 Bd3 Be7 15 0-0 ± Gelfand-Mikhalchishin, Minsk 1986

³¹ 13 ... 0-0 14 0-0 Nf6 (14 ... Nb8 15 Rad1 Bd6 16 Bd2 ± Portisch-Korchnoi, Montpellier C 1985) 15 Rfe1 Nh5 16 Bd2 ± Khalifman-Blatny, Groningen 1985-86

³² 14 d5 ed 15 Rd1 0-0 16 0-0 de! 17 Bxe4 Nxe4 18 Rxd8 Rfxd8 ∞ Miles-Polugayevsky, Sarajevo 1987

³³ 16 Bxb5+ Kf8 17 f3 Ne8 ∞ Browne-Miles, New York 1987

	7	8	9	10	11	12	13	14	15	
10	e3	♗b5+[35]	♗c4[36]	e4	bc	♗g5	♕d3	♖d1	0-0	∞
	g6[34]	c6	♗g7	♘xc3	c5	♕d6	♘c6	0-0	♘a5[37]	
11	...	♘xd5	b4	♕b3	♗e2[40]	♗b2	0-0	a4	a5	±
	...	ed[38]	♗g7[39]	0-0	♘bd7	c6	♕e7	♖ac8	♖c7[41]	
12	...	♗b5+	♗d3[42]	bc	0-0[44]	e4	♗e3[46]	cd	♗b1	=
	♗e7	c6	♘xc3[43]	c5	♘c6[45]	0-0	cd	cd	♗f6[47]	
13	...	...	...	...	...	♗b2	♕e2	♖ad1	cd	±
	...	...	...	...	...	♖c8	0-0	cd[48]	♗f6[49]	
14	...	♗d3	e4	♗f4[52]	d5	♘xd5	ed	♕c2[54]	0-0	±/∞
	♘d7	c5[50]	♘5f6[51]	a6[53]	ed	♘xd5	♗xd5	♘f6	♗d6[55]	

[34] **7 ... ♘xc3** 8 bc g6 9 a4 ♗g7 10 ♗a3 ± Portisch-Adorjan and Portisch-Miles, Linares 1985

   7 ... c5 8 ♗b5+ ♗c6 9 ♗d3 cd 10 ed ♘d7 11 0-0 ♗e7 12 ♖e1 0-0 (12 ... ♖c8 13 ♘xd5 ♗xd5 14 ♗a6 ± Timman-van der Wiel, Wijk aan Zee 1980) 13 ♗c2 ♕c7 14 ♕d3 g6 15 ♗h6 ♖fc8 16 ♗b3 ± Grigorian-Oll, Pinsk 1986

[35] **8 h4 ♗g7** 9 h5 0-0 10 hg hg ∓ Miles-Adorjan, Reggio Emilia 1984-85, and Cebalo-Timman, Zagreb 1985

[36] **9 ♗d3 ♗g7** 10 e4 ♘xc3 11 bc c5 12 ♗g5 ♕d6 13 e5 ♕d7 14 0-0 (14 dc?! 0-0 ∓ Kasparov-Korchnoi, match 1983) 14 ... 0-0 15 ♕d2 ∞

[37] **16 ♗a2** c4 17 ♕e3 ♕xa3 18 ♗b1 ♖fe8 19 h4 ∞ Browne-Olafsson, New York 1984

[38] **8 ... ♕xd5** 9 ♕c2 ±

[39] **9 ... ♗d6!?**

[40] **11 a4** ♘d7 12 ♗a3 ♖e8 13 ♖c1 ± Kir. Georgiev-Ornstein, Stockholm 1983-84

[41] **16 ♖fc1** ± Miles-Miralles, Metz 1985

[42] **9 ♘xd5** ed (9 ... ♕xd5 10 ♗d3 0-0 11 ♕c2 ±) 10 ♗d3 ♘d7 =

[43] **9 ... c5** 10 ♕a4+ ♕d7 11 ♕c2 ± Timman-Petrosian, Moscow 1981

   9 ... 0-0 10 ♕c2 h6 11 e4 ± Portisch-Mokry, Reggio Emilia 1984-85

[44] **11 ♕c2** ♕c7! = McKay-Miles, match 1983

[45] **11 ... 0-0** 12 ♕c2 g6 13 e4 ♘c6 (13 ... ♕c7 14 ♕e2 ♖d8 15 h4 ± Polugayevsky-Petrosian, Moscow 1981) 14 ♗h6 ♖e8 15 ♖fd1 ± Kasparov-Petrosian, Moscow 1981

[46] **13 ♗b2** cd 14 cd ♗f6! 15 e5 ♗e7 = Ftacnik-Farago, Baile Herculana Z 1982

[47] **16 ♖a2** ♖c8 17 ♕d3 ♕d7 = Kasparov-Karolyi, Dortmund 1980

[48] **14 ... ♕c7** 15 c4! ± Kasparov-Portisch, Nikšić 1983

[49] **16 h4** ♗xh4 ∞ Yusupov-Sokolov, match 1986

   16 e4 ♘a5 (16 ... ♘xd4 17 ♗xd4 ♗xd4 18 ♗b5 ±; 16 ... g6 17 h4! ±) 17 ♖fe1 ♖c7 (17 ... ♗c6 18 d5 ed 19 e5! ♗e7 20 e6 ± Browne-Gheorghiu, Wijk aan Zee 1981) 18 h4 ♗xh4 19 d5 ed 20 ♘xh4 ♕xh4 21 ed ± Epishin-Aseyev, Leningrad Ch 1987; 17 ... ♖e8! ±

[50] **8 ... ♘xc3** 9 bc ♗d6 10 e4 e5 11 ♗g5 ± Browne-Sunye, Wijk aan Zee 1980

[51] **9 ... ♘xc3** 10 bc ♗e7 11 0-0 0-0 12 ♕e2 a6 13 a4 cd 14 cd ♘b8 15 ♗b2 ♘c6 16 ♖fd1 ♘b4 17 ♗b1 a5 18 ♘e5 ± de Boer-Pokojowczyk-Copenhagen 1983

[52] **10 0-0** cd 11 ♘xd4 ♗e7 =

   10 d5 ed 11 ed ♗d6! = Kasparov-Karpov, match (10) 1984-85

[53] **10 ... ♗e7** 11 d5 ed 12 ♘xd5 ♗xd5 13 ed ♘xd5 14 ♗g3 0-0 15 ♗a6 ± Portisch-H.Olafsson, Gjovik 1985

[54] **14 ♗xh7** ♕e7+ 15 ♔f1 ♘f6! 16 ♗d3 ♕b7 ∞

   14 0-0 ♗e7 15 ♖e1 ♘f6 (15 ... ♘f8 16 ♗e4 ± Kozul-Kir.Georgiev, Sarajevo 1985) 16 ♕e2 0-0 ∞

[55] **16 ♕e2+** ♔f8 17 ♘e5 ±/∞ Portisch-Miles, Thessaloniki Ol 1984

Nimzo-Indian

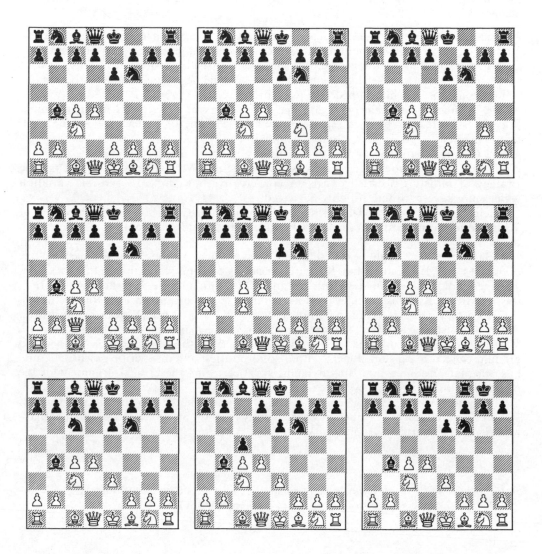

Aron Nimzowitsch's greatest contribution to opening theory, this defence offers Black excellent chances to play for a win without exposing himself to unnecessary risk. His third move exerts indirect influence on the e4 square, a pressure necessary to avoid the construction of a formidable White pawn centre. Acquiring the bishop pair is easily accomplished by White but the resulting configurations make it a difficult and laborious project to attain the open lines that would allow them to cause damage. In return for ceding the two bishops, Black achieves a substantial lead in development and often saddles White with a pair of weak c-pawns which may come under attack for the duration of the game. A successful White strategy hinges on a number of thematic possibilities: the liberation of the bishop pair, the successful advance of his central pawn wedge or gradual aggressive inroads afforded by his space advantage.

An opening system of vast strategical subtlety and complexity, the Nimzo-Indian has been adopted, at one time or another, by nearly every modern GM. With its durability and dynamism, it is the QP equivalent of the Ruy Lopez, offering a stern test of skill to both players.

The **Sämisch Variation** (4 a3) is an arrogant reaction, investing a tempo to force Black to implement his strategy of doubling the white c-pawns. White tries to start an immediate attack by expanding in the centre and smoking out the opposing king. This show of aggression is not to be taken lightly and Black needs to be well acquainted with the dangers which lie in store for him in order to react properly.

The **Leningrad Variation** (4 ♗g5), analysed by Zak and bestowed upon his pupil, Boris Spassky, had an ephemeral spell of popularity. The line allows several ways for Black to equalize but a few players, notably Timman, continue to employ it for White.

The **Classical Variation** (4 ♕c2) is rising in popularity despite having an established reputation for innocuousness. At the cost of a little time, White neutralizes Black's prime strategy of inflicting doubled pawns. A conservative but eminently sensible variation which may have been unjustifiably neglected.

Spielmann's Variation (4 ♕b3) is similar in plan to the Classical but the placement of White's queen is more awkward and so it, too, promises little for the ambitious player with the white pieces.

4 g3/4 ♘f3 and g3 might be called the **Kasparov System**. Although it was once a pet line of Soviet GM Oleg Romanishin, Kasparov arguably owes his world title to this variation. The theory of the line is still in its infancy and, as a result, obscure. For those with faith in the initiative and the bishop pair, it offers dynamic new ground against the Nimzo-Indian. While Kasparov does not claim a definite plus for White, his results have been impressive.

The **Rubinstein Variation** (4 e3) continues to be the main line of the Nimzo-Indian. White develops patiently but efficiently, planning a methodical opening of lines and gradual central expansion. Black, with a solid position and a superior pawn structure, has adequate resources and this dynamic balance forms the critical argument of the Nimzo-Indian.

The system with ♘f3, ♗g5 forms a bridge between the Nimzo-Indian and Queen's Indian. In practice it arises much more frequently from the 3 ♘f3 sequence, and it perhaps represents the sharpest system available in that move order.

References: *How to Play the Nimzo-Indian Defence* (Keene and Taulbut)
           The Semi-Closed Openings in Action (Karpov)

	4	5	6	7	8	9	10	11	12	
1	♕b3[1]	dc	a3[2]	♘f3	♕c2[3]	e4	♗d3[4]	0-0	b4	∞
	c5	♘a6	♗xc5	b6	♗b7	0-0	♘g4	f5	♕b8[5]	
2	...	...	♘f3[6]	♗d2	♘xd2	e3[9]	♗e2	0-0[10]	♘de4	=
	...	♘c6	♘e4	♘xd2[7]	♗xc5[8]	0-0	b6	♗b7	♖b8[11]	
3	f3	a3	cd[13]	e4	bc	♗d3	♘e2	♗e3	cd	∞
	d5	♗e7[12]	♘xd5	♘xc3	c5	♘c6	0-0	cd	♕a5+[14]	
4	...	d5[15]	g3[16]	bc	e4	de[19]	♘e2	♗g2[20]	♖xh2	∞
	c5	♘h5	♗xc3+[17]	f5	f4[18]	♕f6!	fg	gh[21]	g6[22]	
5	♗g5[23]	d5[24]	e3[26]	cd	♗d3[27]	♘e2	0-0	bc	♗c2[28]	∞∞
	c5	d6[25]	ed	♘bd7	♕a5	♘xd5	♗xc3	c4!	0-0[29]	

[1] 4 ♗d2 0-0 (4 ... d5 5 a3 ♗e7 =) 5 a3 ♗xc3 6 ♗xc3 ♘e4 7 ♕c2 f5 8 g3 b6 9 ♗g2 ♗b7 10 ♘f3 ♘xc3 11 ♕xc3 d6 12 0-0 ♘d7 13 ♖fd1 ♕e7 14 b4 ♘f6 15 ♖ac1 ♘e4 16 ♕b2 ♖ab8 = Idema-Dünhaupt, corr. 1985

[2] 6 ♗g5 ♕a5 7 ♗xf6 gf 8 e3 ♘xc5 9 ♕c2 ♗xc3+ 10 bc b6 ∓ Taimanov
6 ♗d2 0-0 7 ♘f3 ♕e7 8 e3 ♘xc5 9 ♕c2 b6 = Filip-Fischer, Curaçao C 1962

[3] 8 ♗g5 ♗b7 9 e3 (9 e4 h6) 9 ... ♗e7 10 ♗e2 0-0 11 0-0 ♘c5 12 ♕c2 ♘fe4 =

[4] 10 b4!? ♗e7 11 ♗d3

[5] Szymczak-Nogueiras, Varna 1978

[6] 6 ♗g5 h6 7 ♗xf6 (7 ♗h4 g5! 8 ♗g3 ♘e4 ∓) 7 ... ♕xf6 8 e3 0-0 9 ♘f3 a5! 10 a4 ♕e7 11 ♗e2 ♗xc5 12 0-0 b6 = Zimmerman-Grünfeld, corr. 1937-38

[7] 7 ... ♘xc5 8 ♕c2 f5 9 a3 ♗xc3 10 ♗xc3 0-0 11 b4 (11 ♘d2 a5) 11 ... ♘e4 12 ♗b2 d6 13 e3 e5 =

[8] 8 ... f5 9 e3 (9 g3 ♕a5 10 ♖c1 b6! 11 cb ♘d4 12 ♕d1 ♗b7 ∞∞) 9 ... 0-0 10 ♗e2 ♗xc5 intending ... b6, ... ♗b7 =

[9] 9 ♘de4 d6 10 e3 (10 ♖d1 ♘d4) 10 ... f5 11 ♘xc5 dc =

[10] 11 0-0-0 ♕e7 12 ♘f3 ♗b7 13 ♖d2 ♖ac8 =

[11] 13 ♖ad1 f5 14 ♘xc5 bc = Barczay-Tal, Miskolc 1963

[12] 5 ... ♗xc3+ - 4 a3

[13] 6 e4 de 7 fe e5 8 d5 0-0 9 ♘f3 ♗g4 10 ♗d3 ♗c5 11 ♗g5 (11 h3! Malanyuk/Moskalenko) 11 ... h6 12 ♗h4 g5 13 ♗f2 ♗xf2+ 14 ♔xf2 c6 ∞ Malanyuk-Rashkovsky, USSR Ch 1987
6 e3 0-0 7 c5 a5 8 ♖b1 b6 9 b4 ab 10 ab bc 11 bc e5! 12 de ♘fd7 ∞∞ Raičević-Lerner, Moscow 1986

[14] 13 ♔f2 b5 ∞ Nogueiras-Sax, Sarajevo 1985

[15] 5 a3 cd (5 ... ♗xc3+ - 4 a3) 6 ab dc 7 bc d5 = Taimanov.

[16] 6 ♘h3! V.Raičevic

[17] 6 ... 0-0 7 e4 f5 8 f4 ♘f6 9 e5 ♘e4 10 ♗d2 ♗xc3 11 ♗xc3 d6! ∞ Armas-Barbalescu, Havana 1986

[18] 8 ... ♕f6 9 f4! ♘xg3 10 hg ♕xc3+ 11 ♗d2 ♕xg3+ 12 ♔e2 fe 13 ♕b3! ± Nogueiras-Kindermann, Dubai Ol 1986

[19] 9 ♘e2 e5 10 d6 ♘c6 11 ♗h3 b6 12 ♗g4 ♘f6 13 gf ♘xg4 14 fg ef 15 ♗xf4 0-0 ∞ Vulfson-Veselovsky, USSR 1986

[20] 11 ♘xg3 ♘xg3 12 hg ♕xc3+ 13 ♗d2 ♕d4 14 ed+ ♗xd7 ∞

[21] 11 ... ♕xe6 12 hg ± Nogueiras-Rodriguez, San Juan 1985

[22] Arkhipov-Foisor, Tbilisi 1986

[23] Leningrad

[24] 5 ♘f3 cd 6 ♘xd4 0-0 7 ♖c1 ♘c6 8 e3 d5 9 a3 ♗e7 10 cd ♘xd4 11 ♕xd4 ♘xd5 = Gulko-Tal, Biel IZ 1976
5 ♖c1 cd 6 ♘xd4 ♘c6 7 ♗xf6 ♕xf6 8 ♕xf6 gf 9 ♘f3 b6 10 a3 ♗xc3+ 11 ♖xc3 ♗b7 12 e3 ♖g8 = Ionescu-Benjamin, Moscow 1987

[25] 5 ... ♘xd5 6 ♗xd8 ♘xc3 7 ♕b3 ♘e4+ 8 ♔d1 ♘xf2+ 9 ♔c1 ♘xd8 10 ♕f3 ♘xh1 11 ♕xf7 ±

[26] 6 f3 ed 7 cd 0-0 8 e4 ♘bd7 9 ♕c2 (9 ♗d3 ♘e5 10 ♘e2 c4 11 ♗c2 ♗c5 ∓) 9 ... a6 10 0-0-0 b5 ∞

[27] 8 ♗b5 ♗xc3+ 9 bc a6 10 ♗xd7+ ♗xd7 11 ♘e2 ♗b5 = Moiseyev

[28] 12 ♗f5 ♘7b6! ∓ Ionescu-Eingorn, Sochi 1986

[29] 13 ♗h4 ♘xc3 14 ♘xc3 ♕xc3 15 ♖c1 ∞∞ Rajković-Stoica, Sofia 1986

Nimzo Indian I — 1 d4 Nf6 2 c4 e6 3 Nc3 Bb4 *continued*

	4	5	6	7	8	9	10	11	12	
6	Bg5	d5	Bh4[30]	e3[32]	de	cb	Nf3	Bxf6	Qc1[34]	∞/±
	c5	h6	b5[31]	Bb7[33]	fe	0-0	Qa5	Rxf6		
7	...	...	...	e3	bc	f3	Bd3	Ne2[37]	Bg3	∞
	...	...	d6	Bxc3+[35]	e5	Nbd7[36]	Qe7	g5	e4[38]	
8	...	...	...	...	...	Bd3	f4	Ne2	fg	∞
	...	...	...	...	...	Nbd7[39]	Qe7[40]	g5	Ng4[41]	

[30] 6 Bd2 0-0 7 e3 Bxc3 8 Bxc3 ed 9 cd d6 10 Ne2 Nbd7 11 Nf4?! (11 g3) 11 ... Ne4 12 Be2 b5! ∓ Hort-Adorjan, Oslo 1984

[31] 6 ... ed 7 cd d6 8 e3 g5 (8 ... Nbd7 9 Bd3 Qa5 10 Ne2 Nxd5 11 0-0 Bxc3 12 bc Nxc3 13 Nxc3 Bxc3 14 Be2 ±) 9 Bg3 Ne4 10 Qc2 Qe7 11 Bd3 Bxc3+ 12 bc Nxg3 13 hg ± Timman-Lobron, Amsterdam 1983

[32] 7 de fe 8 cb d5 9 e3 0-0 ∞∞ Spassky-Tal, Tallinn 1973, and Cooper-Adamski, Nice Ol 1974

[33] 7 ... 0-0 8 Qf3 Bb7 9 Bxf6 Qxf6 10 Qxf6 gf 11 0-0-0 ± Timman-Yusupov, match 1986

[34] 12 Qd2?! a6 13 ba Bxf3 14 gf Nc6 15 Be2 d5 16 a3 d4 ∞ Timman-Ligterink, Wijk aan Zee 1977

12 Qc1! ∞/±

[35] 7 ... Qe7 8 Bd3 Bxc3+ 9 bc Nbd7 10 Nf3 (10 Ne2 Ne5 ∓ Miles-Karpov, Tilburg 1986) 10 ... e5 11 Nd2 ±/∞ Timman-Romanishin, Tilburg 1985

7 ... g5 8 Bg3 Ne4 9 Qc2 Qf6 10 Rc1 ed 11 cd Bf5 ∞ Hort-de Firmian, Wijk aan Zee 1986, and Kouatly-Winants, Brussels 1986

[36] 9 ... Qa5 10 Qc2 Nbd7 11 Rb1 e4 12 Bg3! ± Malanyuk-Rashkovsky, USSR Ch 1986

[37] 11 Qc2 g5 (11 ... Kd8 12 Ne2 Qc7 13 Ng3 Qe8 14 Bxf6 Nxf6 ∞ Bagirov-Nagy, Budapest 1983) 12 Bg3 b5 13 cb Nxd5 14 Bf2 a6 ∞ Bagirov-Speelman, Baku 1983

[38] 12 ... Rg8 13 Qc2 h5 14 h4 g4 ∞ Timman-Polugayevsky, Linares 1985

12 ... e4 13 Bxe4 Nxe4 14 fe Nf6 ∞ Timman-Hulak, Zagreb 1985, and Yrjölä-Schüssler, Gjovik 1985

[39] 9 ... e4 10 Bc2 Nbd7 11 f4 ef 12 Nxf3 Qe7 13 0-0 ±/∞ Hort-Suba, Tunis IZ 1985

[40] 10 ... Rg8 11 Nh3 ± Cooper-Petrosian, Buenos Aires Ol 1978

[41] 13 Ng3 Nxe3 14 Qf3 hg 15 Qxe3 gh 16 Nf5 Qf6 17 0-0 Nf8 ∞ Miles-Polugayevsky, Tilburg 1985

Nimzo-Indian II — 1 d4 Nf6 2 c4 e6 3 Nc3 Bb4 4 Nf3

	4	5	6	7	8	9	10	11	12	
1	...	Qc2	g3	Bg2	0-0	bc	c5	c4![5]		±
	Ne4[1]	f5	Nc6[2]	0-0	Bxc3	Na5[3]	d6[4]			
2	...	Bg5	Bh4	e3	ed	Rc1	Bxc4	0-0	Re1	±
	0-0	h6	c5	cd[6]	d5[7]	dc[8]	Nc6	Be7	b6[9]	
3	...	Qb3[10]	g3[12]	Bg2	Qc2	ba	0-0	Raxc1	Nb5	±
	b6	a5[11]	Nc6[13]	a4	a3[14]	Bxa3	Bxc1	Ba6	0-0[15]	
4	...	...	a3[16]	Bf4[17]	Rd1[19]	e3	Nxd4	Qc2	bc[20]	∞
	...	c5	Ba5	Bb7[18]	0-0	cd	Ne4	Bxc3+		
5	...	Bg5	e3[21]	Bh4	Bg3	Nd2	bc	Rc1	h4	∞∞
	...	Bb7	h6	g5[22]	Ne4	Nxc3[23]	Bxc3	Bb4	gh[24]	
6	...	...	...	...	...	Qc2	bc	Bd3	d5	±
	...	...	...	...	...	Bxc3+	d6[25]	f5[26]	Nc5[27]	
7	...	...	...	...	bc	Bd3	0-0	Nd2	Bg3	∞
	...	...	...	Bxc3+	d6	Nbd7[28]	Qe7[29]	g5	h5[30]	
8	...	...	...	...	...	Nd2	Bg3	h4[33]	Rb1	∞
	...	...	...	...	...	g5[31]	Nbd7[32]	Be7[34]	Ne4[35]	

[1] 4 ... c5 5 d5 (5 e3 – 4 e3; 5 g3 – 4 g3) 5 ... Ne4 6 Qc2 Qf6 7 Bd2 Bxc3 8 bc Nxd2 =

[2] 6 ... b6 7 Bg2 Bb7 8 Nd2 Bxc3 9 bc Nd6 10 e4 ±

[3] 9 ... d6 10 d5 Na5 11 Nd4 Nc5 12 de Qf6 13 Ba3 Bxe6 14 Qa4 ± Richardi-Hecht, Dubai Ol 1986

[4] 10 ... b6 11 c4! Ba6 12 Nd2 Nxd2 13 Bxd2 Nxc4 14 Bb4! ± Kasparov

[5] 11 ... b6 12 Bd2! Nxd2 13 Qxd2 ± Kasparov-Karpov, match (19) 1985

11 ... dc 12 Rd1 ±; 12 Ba3 ±

[6] 7 ... Qa5 8 Bxf6 (8 Bd3!?) 8 ... Bxc3+ 9 bc Qxc3+ 10 Nd2 gf 11 Rc1 Qa3 12 h4 ∞ van der Sterren-Dehmelt, Reykjavik 1986

[7] 8 ... Qa5 9 Bd3 Bxc3+ 10 bc Qxc3+ 11 Kf1 Nc6 12 Bxf6 gf 13 Rb1 d6 14 h4 ∞/± Rashkovsky-Razuvayev, Minsk 1985

[8] 9 ... Be7 10 c5 b6 11 b4 ±

9 ... Nc6 10 c5 g5!? 11 Bg3 Ne4 Kasparov

[9] 13 a3 Bb7 14 Bg3 Rc8 15 Ba2 Bd6 (Kasparov-Karpov, match (11) 1985) 16 Be5 ±

[10] 5 e3 – 4 e3

5 Qc2 Bb7 6 a3 Bxc3+ 7 Qxc3 0-0 – 4 Qc2

[11] 5 ... Qe7 6 g3 Bb7 7 Bg2 Nc6 (7 ... Ne4 8 0-0 Bxc3 9 bc 0-0 10 c5 ±) 8 0-0 Na5 9 Qc2 Bxc4 10 Nb5 d5 11 Nxc7+! Qxc7 12 Qa4+ ± Tadadian-Sturua, USSR 1985

[12] 6 a3 a4? 7 Qxb4? Nc6

[13] 6 ... Bb7 7 Bg2 0-0 8 0-0 Bxc3 9 bc d6 10 c5 ± Efimov-Podgayets, USSR 1984

[14] 8 ... Ba6 9 0-0 Bxc4 10 Ne5 Bxe5 11 de Nd5 12 Nxa4 b5 13 Nc3 ± Georgadze-Gomez, Seville 1985

[15] 13 a4 ± Georgadze-A.Sokolov, Nikolayev 1983

[16] 6 e3 Ba6 7 a3 Ba5 8 Bd2 0-0 9 0-0-0 Qe7 ∞ Browne-Korchnoi, Chicago 1982

6 dc Bxc5 7 Bg5 Bb7 8 e3 Be7 9 Be2 Na6 10 0-0 h6 11 Bh4 Nc5 12 Qc2 Nce4 = Basin-A.Ivanov, Minsk 1985

6 Bf4 Nc6 7 e3 cd 8 Nxd4 Nxd4 9 ed Qe7 10 Be2 Bb7 11 0-0 0-0 = Khalifman-Lerner, USSR Ch 1986

[17] 7 Bg5 Bb7 8 e3 Bxf3 9 gf cd 10 ed Nc6 11 0-0-0 Bxc3 12 Qxc3 Rc8 ∞ Korchnoi-Polugayevsky, Reykjavik 1987

[18] 7 ... 0-0 8 Rd1 Ba6 9 e3 cd 10 Nxd4 d5 = Garcia Palermo-Eingorn, Havana 1986

[19] 8 dc Na6! 9 c6 Bxc6 10 Qc2 Bxc3+ 11 Qxc3 Nc5 12 Nd4 Rc8 = Chekhov-Lerner, Kharkov 1985

[20] ½-½ Portisch-Polugayevsky, Linares 1985

[21] 6 Nd2 h6 7 Bh4 c5 8 a3 Bxc3 9 bc d6 10 f3 Nbd7 11 e4 Qc7 12 Be2 Nh5 = Farago-Bauer, Budapest 1986

6 Qc2 h6 7 Bh4 c5 8 a3 Be4 9 Qb3 Ba5 ∞

[22] 7 ... c5 8 Bd3 cd 9 ed Bxf3 10 Qxf3 Nc6

11 Qe3 Be7 12 Bg3 Nb4 13 Bb1 Nh5 14 0-0 0-0 15 a3 Nc6 16 Rd1 ± Tukmakov-Salov, USSR Ch 1987

[23] 9 ... Nxg3 10 hg Bf8 11 f4 Bg7 12 Qa4 Qe7 13 0-0-0 ± Kasparov-Miles, Dubai Ol 1986

[24] 12 ... Rg8 13 hg hg 14 Qc2 ∞∞

12 ... gh 13 Rxh4 Bd6 14 Qg4 ∞∞ Kasparov-Timman, match 1985, and Agdestein-Hellers, Gausdal Z 1987

[25] 10 ... Nxg3 11 hg Nc6 12 Rh5! ± Ionescu-Kengis, Timisoara 1987

[26] 11 ... Nxg3 12 hg Nd7 13 Be4 (13 g4!? Be7 14 e4 Nf6 15 0-0-0 Nxg4 16 Qe2 ∞∞ Goldin-Levin, USSR 1984) 13 ... Bxe4 14 Qxe4 Nf6 15 Qd3 g4 16 Nd2 Qe7 17 a4 a5 18 Rb1 ± Christiansen-de Firmian, USA 1985

[27] 12 ... ed 13 cd Bxd5 14 Nd4 ± Ribli-Seirawan, Malta Ol 1980

12 ... Nd7 13 Bxe4 fe 14 Qxe4 Qf6 15 0-0 0-0-0 (15 ... Nc5 16 Qd4 ± Kharitonov-Vaiser, USSR 1984) 16 Qxe6 Qxe6 17 de Nc5 18 Nd2 Nxe6 19 f3 ± Kharitonov

12 ... Nc5 13 h4 g4 14 Nd4 Qf6 15 0-0 Nba6 (15 ... Nxd3 16 Qxd3 e5 17 Nxf5 Bc8 18 f4! ± Miles-Belyavsky, Tilburg 1986) 16 Nxe6 Nxe6 17 Bxf5! Ng7 18 Bg6+ Kd7 19 f3 ± Kasparov-Timman, match 1985, and Miles-Timman, Tilburg 1986

[28] 9 ... 0-0 10 0-0 Nbd7 (10 ... g5 11 Nxg5!) 11 Nd2 Re8 12 f4 ± Tukmakov-Petran, Szirak 1985

[29] 10 ... g5 11 Bg3 Ne4 12 Nd2 Nxd2 13 Qxd2 f5 14 f3 ± Kir.Georgiev-Ionescu, Sofia 1986

[30] 12 ... 0-0-0 13 c5! dc 14 Qa4 ± Spassky-Seirawan, Linares 1983, and Greenfeld-Ambroz, Biel 1985

12 ... h5 13 h4 (13 f3 h4 ∞ Karpeshov-Yudasin, USSR 1985, and Johansen-Hjartarson, Dubai Ol 1986) 13 ... Rg8 (13 ... Ng4!?) 14 f3 ∞ Petursson-Greenfeld, Hastings 1985-86, and Farago-Rechlis, Beer-Sheva 1987

[31] 9 ... Nbd7 10 f3 Qe7 11 e4 e5 (11 ... g5!? 12 Bf2 Nh5 13 Qa4 c5 ∞ Tukmakov-Chernin, USSR Ch 1987) 12 Bd3 (12 Qa4 g5 13 Bf2 Kf8 14 Be2 Nh5 ∞ Salov-Dokhoyan, Irkutsk 1986) 12 ... g5 13 Bf2 Nh5 14 Nf1 Nf4 15 Ne3 g4!? ∞ Razuvayev-Stoica, Nikea 1986

[32] 10 ... Qe7 11 a4 a5 12 h4 ± Kasparov-Karpov, match (18) 1986, and Kozlov-Tukmakov, USSR 1986

[33] 11 f3 Qe7 12 e4 Nh5 13 Bf2 f5 14 g3 0-0-0 ∞ Rashkovsky-Salov, USSR Ch 1987

[34] 11 ... Rg8 12 hg hg 13 Qa4 Ke7 (13 ... Qe7 14 f3 a5 15 0-0-0 ±) 14 f3 Rh8 15 Rg1 ± Bareyev-Gavrikov, USSR Ch 1987

[35] 13 Nxe4 Bxe4 14 Rb2 Qg8 ∞ Ftacnik-Short, Dubai Ol 1986

	Nimzo-Indian III		1 d4 ♘f6 2 c4 e6 3 ♘c3 ♗b4 4 g3						
	4	5	6	7	8	9	10	11	12
1	... ♗xc3+	bc 0-0	♗g2 d6[1]	♘f3 ♘c6	0-0 ♖b8[2]	♕d3[3] b6	♘d2 ♗b7[4]	♘b3 ♖e8	e4 e5[5]	∞
2	... d5	♗g2 0-0	♘f3 dc[6]	0-0 ♘c6[7]	♖e1[8] ♖b8[9]	a3 ♗e7[10]	e4[11] b5	d5 ♘a5	♘d4 a6[12]	∓
3	... ...	... ...	... ...	... ...	a3 ♗e7[13]	e4 ♘a5	♗f4[14] c6	♕e2 b5	♖ad1 ♗b7[15]	∞
4	... c5	♘f3 ♘c6[16]	♗g2 ♘e4[17]	♕d3 ♕a5[18]	d5 ♘e7	♕xe4 ♗xc3+	♘d2 f5	♕c2 ♗f6	0-0 ♕c7[19]	∞
5	... ...	... ...	... ...	♗d2 ♘xd2[20]	♕xd2 cd	♘xd4 0-0[21]	♘c2 ♗e7	0-0 a6	♖fd1 ♕c7[22]	∞
6	... ...	... ♘e4	♕d3[23] ♕a5	♕xe4 ♗xc3+	♗d2 ♗xd2+	♘xd2 ♘c6[24]	d5 ♘d4	♗g2 ♘b3	♖d1 ♘xd2[25]	∞
7	... ...	... ...	... cd	♘xd4 ♕a5[26]	♘b3 ♕f5[27]	♕e3 0-0	♗g2 ♘xc3	bc ♗e7	0-0 ♘c6[28]	∞
8	... ...	... cd	♘xd4 0-0[29]	♗g2 d5	♕b3[30] ♗xc3+	bc[31] ♘c6[32]	cd ♘a5[33]	♕c2 ♘xd5	♕d3[34] ♕c7![35]	∞

202

1 6 ... ♘c6 7 ♘f3 ♖b8 8 ♕d3 b6 (8 ... d6 – 6 ... d6) 9 ♗g5 h6 10 h4! ♖e8 11 ♘e5 ± Makarichev-A.Sokolov, Moscow Ch 1982

2 8 ... e5!? 9 ♖e1 ♖e8 10 e4 ed 11 ♘xd4 ♘a5 12 ♕a4 b6 13 e5 ♗d7 14 ♕d1 de 15 ♗xa8 ♕xa8 ∞ I.Sokolov-Kurajica, Sarajevo 1987

3 9 ♕c2!? b6 10 e4 e5 11 c5 Romanishin
   9 c5!? d5 (9 ... dc 10 ♗a3) 10 ♘e5 Gulko

4 10 ... ♘a5 11 ♘b3 ♗a6 12 ♘xa5 ba 13 ♗c6! ±/∞ Tielmann-Petrosian, Oberwart 1981

5 Gulko-A.Sokolov, USSR Ch 1985

6 6 ... c5 7 cd ♘xd5 8 ♗d2 cd 9 ♘xd5 ♗xd2+ 10 ♕xd2 ♕xd5 11 ♕xd4 ± Azmaiparashvili-Kholmov, Minsk 1985
   6 ... c6 7 0-0 ♘bd7 8 ♕b3 ♗e7 9 ♗f4 ± Romanishin-Korchnoi, Wijk aan Zee 1985

7 7 ... ♘bd7 8 ♕c2 c5 9 ♖d1 cd 10 ♖xd4 ♗c5 11 ♖xc4 b5! 12 ♘xb5 ♕b6 ∞ Gulko-Barlov, Sochi 1985

8 8 ♗g5 ♗e7 9 e3 ♘d5 10 ♗xe7 ♕xe7 11 ♘d2 ♘b6 12 ♕e2 ♘a5 ∓ Ubilava-Agzamov, Sevastopol 1986

9 8 ... ♘d5 9 ♕c2 ♗e7 10 ♘e4 ∞ Bradford-Peters, US Ch 1980, and Gulko-Lputian, Sochi 1985

10 9 ... ♗xc3 10 bc ♘a5 11 ♖b1 b6 12 e4 ∞ Romanishin-Savon, Erevan 1976

11 10 ♕a4 b5! 11 ♘xb5 ♗d7 12 ♖xa7 ♘xd4 13 ♕xc4 ♘b3 14 ♖b1 c5 ∓ Diždar-Cebalo, Yugoslavia 1980

12 Catalan-Tatai, Dubai 1984

13 8 ... ♗xc3 9 bc ♘a5 10 ♖b1 b6 11 ♘e5 ∞

14 10 ♗e3 b6 11 ♕c2 ♗b7 12 ♖ad1 c6 13 ♘e5 ♕e8 14 ♖fe1 ♘d7 ∓ Ricardi-Sunye, Rio de Janeiro 1985

15 13 ♖fe1 a6 14 ♘e5 ∞ Gulko-Popović, Clichy 1986-87

16 5 ... ♗xc3+ 6 bc ♕a5 7 ♕d3 ♘e4 8 ♗d2 (8 ♗g2!?) 8 ... f5 9 ♗g2 ♘c6 (Polugayevsky-Korchnoi, Linares 1985) 10 0-0 ±
   5 ... b6 6 ♗g2 ♗xc3+ 7 bc ♗b7 8 dc bc 9 0-0 ♘c6 10 ♗e3 d6 11 ♗f4 ♔e7 12 ♖b1 ± de Firmian-Short, Wijk aan Zee 1986

17 6 ... d5 7 0-0 (7 cd ♘xd5 8 ♗d2 cd 9 ♘xd4 ♗xd4 10 ♘xd5 ♗xd2+ 11 ♕xd2 ♘c6 ±/= Kasparov-Karpov, match (2) 1986) 7 ... dc 8 dc ♕xd1 9 ♖xd1 ♗xc5 10 ♘d2 ± Romanishin-Tal, Sochi 1984
   6 ... ♕a5 7 0-0 ♗xc3 8 bc ♕xc3 9 ♗f4 ♕xc4 10 ♖c1 ♕xa2 11 dc 0-0 12 ♗d6 ♖d8 13 ♘d4 ± Rashkovsky-Novikov, Kuibishev 1986

18 7 ... cd 8 ♘xd4 ♗xc3 9 bc ♘e5 10 ♕c2 ♗c5 (10 ... ♗e7 11 ♕b3 0-0 12 ♗f4 ± Gulko-Balashov, USSR 1983) 11 ♕a4 0-0 12 ♘b3 ± Rashkovsky-Khalifman, USSR Ch 1986

19 13 e4 0-0 14 ef (Frias-Arnason, New York 1986) 14 ... ♘xf5 15 de de ∞ Arnason

20 7 ... ♗xc3 8 bc 0-0 9 0-0 ♘a5 (9 ... f5 10 ♗e3 ♘xc3 11 ♕d3 ± Kasparov-Karpov, match (13) 1985) 10 dc (10 ♗f4!?) 10 ... ♕c7 (Kasparov-Karpov, match (17) 1985) 11 ♗e3 ♘xc4 12 ♗d4 ±/∞

21 9 ... ♘e5 10 ♕c2 ♗e7 (10 ... ♘xc4 11 ♕d4 ±) 11 ♘e3 f5 (11 ... a6 12 ♘e4 ± Spraggett-Kir. Georgiev, Montreal 1986) 12 0-0 a6 13 f4 ♘f7 14 ♘c2 ± Farago-Hawelko, Polanica Zdroj 1986

22 13 ♘e4 ♘e5 14 b3 b5 15 ♘d6 ♖b8 16 cb ab 17 ♖ac1 ♖b6 ∞ H.Olafsson-Christiansen, Scandinavia v USA 1986

23 6 ♗d2 ♘xd2 7 ♕xd2 cd 8 ♘xd4 ♘c6 9 ♗g2 – 5 ... ♘c6

24 9 ... ♕b6 10 dc ♕xb2 11 ♖b1 ♕c3 (11 ... ♕a3 12 ♕d4 0-0 13 ♗g2 ± Itkis-A.Ivanov, Borzomi 1984, and Ubilava-Rozentalis, Kharkov 1985) 12 ♕d3! ♕xd3 13 ed ± Kasparov-Karpov, match (1) 1985

25 13 ♖xd2 ♕xa2 14 0-0 0-0 15 de fe 16 ♖fd1 ∞ Rogers-Lau, Dortmund 1985

26 7 ... ♗xc3+ 8 bc ♘c5 9 ♕d2 b6 10 ♘b5 0-0 11 ♘d6 ±
   7 ... ♗xc3 8 bc ♗e7 9 ♘b5 ± Stean-Timman, London 1980

27 8 ... ♘xc3 9 ♗d2 ♗e4 10 ♕xe4 ♗xd2+ 11 ♘xd2 0-0 12 ♗g2 ♘c6 13 ♕e3 d5 14 0-0 d4 15 ♕d3 e5 ±/∞ Cvitan-Nikolić, Sarajevo 1987

28 12 ... ♘a6 13 c5! ♗xc5 (13 ... ♘xc5? 14 g4) 14 ♘xc5 ♗xc5 15 ♕xc5 ♘xc5 16 ♗a3 d6 17 ♖fd1 ± Donchenko-Shakarov, USSR 1976
   12 ... ♘c6 13 ♖d1 (13 c5 b6! = Khuzman-Tukmakov, USSR 1983) 13 ... b6 14 ♗e4 ♕h3 15 c5 bc 16 ♗a3 d5 17 ♗g2 ♕h5 18 ♗xc5 ♗a6 ∞ Dorfman-Wiedenkeller, Helsinki 1986

29 6 ... ♘e4 7 ♕d3 – 5 ... ♘e4
   6 ... ♕c7 7 ♕d3 a6 (7 ... ♘c6 8 ♘db5! ♕b8 9 ♗f4 ♘e5 10 ♕d4 d6 11 ♘xd6+! ♗xd6 12 0-0-0 ± Polugayevsky-Seirawan, London 1984) 8 ♗g2 ♘c6 9 ♘xc6 dc 10 0-0 ±

30 8 cd ♘xd5 9 ♗d2 ♘xc3 10 bc ♗c5 =
   8 0-0!? dc ♕a4 ∞ Romanishin-Ribli, Reggio Emilia 1985-86, and Karpov-Portisch, Tilburg 1986

31 9 ♕xc3 e5 intending ... d4 =

32 9 ... dc 10 ♕a3! (10 ♕xc4 e5 11 ♘b5 a6 12 ♘c7 ♖a7 =) 10 ... ♘bd7 (10 ... e5 11 ♘b5 ∞) 11 0-0 ♘b6 12 ♘b5 (12 f4!?) 12 ... ♗d7 13 ♖d1 ♘fd5 14 ♘d6 ∞ Karpov-Portisch, Lucerne 1985

33 10 ... ed 11 0-0 ♖e8 12 ♗g5! ♘xd4 13 cd ♖xe2 14 ♖fe1 ±

34 12 0-0 ♗d7 13 ♗a3 ♖e8 14 c4 ♖c8 15 c5 b6 ∞

35 12 ... ♗d7 13 c4 ± Kasparov-Karpov, match (4) 1986
   12 ... ♕c7! ∞ Kasparov-Suba, Dubai Ol 1986, and Izeta-Smagin, Novi Sad 1986

	4	5	6	7	8	9	10	11	12	
1	...	♘f3	a3	♕xc3	♕c2	de	e3[4]	♗d3	♕xd3	∞
	♘c6[1]	d5[2]	♗xc3+	♘e4	e5[3]	♗f5	♘g3	♗xd3	♘xh1[5]	
2	...	a3	♕xc3	♕c2	dc	cd[6]	♘f3	b4	♗b2	∞
	d5	♗xc3+	♘e4	c5	♘c6	ed	♗f5	0-0	b6[7]	
3	...	cd	♗g5	♗xf6[9]	a3	♕xc3	e3	♘e2[11]	♘g3[12]	±/=
	...	ed[8]	h6	♕xf6	♗xc3+	0-0[10]	♗f5	♖c8		
4	...	dc	♘f3[14]	♗d2[15]	a3	♗xc3	♗xf6	e4	♗d3	=
	c5	0-0[13]	♘a6	♘xc5	♗xc3	♘ce4[16]	♘xf6	d6	e5[17]	
5	...	...	a3	♘f3	♗g5[18]	♘xd4[19]	e3	ed	♕d2[20]	±
	...	...	♗xc5	♘c6	♘d4	♗xd4	♕a5	♕xg5	♕xd2+[21]	
6	...	...	...	...	♗f4[22]	♖d1	e3[24]	♗e2	0-0	∞
	...	...	...	b6	♗b7	♘c6[23]	♗e7[25]	♖c8	♘a5[26]	
7	...	a3[27]	♕xc3	♗g5	e3	f3[28]	♗d3	♘e2	0-0	=
	0-0	♗xc3+	b6	♗b7	d6	♘bd7	c5	♖c8	♗a6[29]	
8	...	...	...	♘f3	e3[30]	b4[32]	b5[34]	♗b2	♕c2	∞
	...	...	...	♗b7	d6[31]	a5[33]	♘bd7	♘e4	f5[35]	

[1]   4 ... d6 5 a3 ♗xc3+ 6 ♕xc3 0-0 7 g3 a5 8 b3 ♗d7 9 ♗g2 ♘c6 10 ♘f3 ± Belyavsky-Quinteros, Moscow IZ 1982

[2]   5 ... d6 6 ♗d2 0-0 7 a3 ♗xc3 8 ♗xc3 ±

[3]   8 ... 0-0 9 e3 ♖e8 10 b4 e5 11 cd ♘xd4 12 ed ed 13 ♗e2 ♗f5 ∞ Naumkin-Gurgenidze, Borzomi 1984

[4]   **10 ♕a4** 0-0 11 ♗e3? d4 12 ♖d1 de! ∓ Gerusel-Lombardy, Toronto 1957

    10 ♕b3!? ♘a5 11 ♕a4+ c6 12 cd ♕xd5 13 ♗e3 Taimanov

[5]   13 cd ♘e7 14 e4 c6 15 d6 ♘g6 16 ♗e3 0-0 17 0-0-0 ∞ Kakageldiev-Antoshin, USSR 1974, and Kakageldiev-Naumkin, Borzomi 1984

[6]   **9 e3** ♕a5+ 10 ♗d2 ♘xd2 11 ♕xd2 dc =

    9 ♘f3 ♕a5+ 10 ♘d2 ♘d4 ∞/= *ECO*

[7]   13 b5 bc 14 bc ♕a5+ 15 ♘d2 ♖ab8 ∞ Grigorian-Gulko, USSR 1975, and Chekhov-Vaiser, USSR 1982

[8]   5 ... ♕xd5 6 ♘f3 c5 7 ♗d2 ♗xc3 8 ♗xc3 cd 9 ♘xd4 (9 ♖d1 ♘c6 10 ♘xd4 0-0 11 f3 ♕xa2! ∞ Glek-Gulko, Tashkent 1984) 9 ... e5 (9 ... ♘c6 10 ♘xc6 ♕xc6 11 ♖c1 ±) 10 ♘f3 ♘c6 11 ♖d1 ♕c5 12 e3 ±

[9]   7 ♗h4 c5 8 ♘f3 (8 0-0-0 ♗xc3 9 ♕xc3 g5! 10 ♗g3 cd 11 ♕xd4 ♘c6 12 ♕a4 ♗f5 ∓

Keres-Botvinnik, USSR Ch 1941) 8 ... ♘c6 9 e3 cd =

[10]   9 ... c6 10 e3 0-0 11 ♘f3 ♗f5 12 ♗e2 ♘d7 13 0-0 a5 14 b4 ± Larsen-Seirawan, Mar del Plata 1981

[11]   11 ♘f3 ♘d7 12 ♖c1 ♖fc8 13 b4 a5 14 ba c5 ∞ Nogueiras-A.Sokolov, Leningrad 1987

[12]   **12 ... ♗e6** 13 b4 a5 (13 ... b6!?) 14 ♗e2 ab 15 ab ± Seirawan-Tal, Nikšić 1983

    12 ... c5!? 13 ♘xf5 ♕xf5 14 dc b6 Parma

[13]   **5 ... ♘a6** 6 a3 ♗xc3+ 7 ♕xc3 ♘xc5 8 f3 a5 9 e4 ± Vaiser-Lechtynsky, Berlin 1982

    5 ... ♕c7 6 a3 ♗xc5 7 b4 ♗e7 8 ♘b5 ♕c6 9 ♘f3 d6 10 ♘fd4 ♕d7 11 e4 ± Kaidanov-Shestoperov, USSR 1986

    5 ... ♗xc5 6 ♘f3 ♕b6!? 7 e3 ♕c7 8 ♗e2 a6 9 0-0 b6 10 b3 ♗b7 11 ♗b2 ♗e7 12 ♖ac1 d6 = Seirawan-Romanishin, Brussels 1986

[14]   **6 ♗e3** ♘a6 7 a3 ♗xc3+ 8 ♕xc3 ♘e4 9 ♕d4 (9 ♕e5 ♕a5+ 10 b4 ♘xb4 =) 9 ... ♘axc5 = Bronstein-Andrianov, Moscow Ch 1981

    6 ♗f4 ♘a6 7 ♗d6 ♖e8 8 a3 ♕a5 9 ♖c1 ♗xc3+ 10 ♕xc3 ♕xc3+ 11 ♖xc3 ♘e4 = Tal-Andersson, match 1983

    6 ♗g5 ♘a6 7 a3 ♗xc3+ 8 ♕xc3 ♘xc5

9 ♗xf6 (9 f3 ♘fe4! ∓) 9 ... ♕xf6 10 ♕xf6 gf =

15 7 a3 ♗xc3+ 8 ♕xc3 ♘xc5 9 e3 (9 b4 ♘ce4 10 ♕c2 a5 ∓) 9 ... a5 10 b3 b6 11 ♗e2 ♗a6 = Kogan-Seirawan, US Ch 1981

16 9 ... b6 10 ♘g5 ♖e8! (10 ... g6 11 b4 ♘a6 12 h4 ± Toth-Sax, Rome 1984) 11 b4 (11 ♗xf6 ♕xf6 12 ♕xh7+ ♔f8 ∓) 11 ... h6 12 h4 hg 13 bc gh 14 ♖xh4 bc 15 g4 ∞ A.Geller-Kondratiev, USSR 1963

17 Haik-Langeweg, Montpellier Z 1985

18 8 ♗f4 d5 9 ♖d1 (9 e3 – QGD) 9 ... e5! 10 ♗g5 (10 ♗g3 ♘d4! ∓ Oll-Yailian, USSR 1984) 10 ... d4 11 ♘d5 ♗e7 = Seirawan-van der Wiel, Tilburg 1983

19 9 ♕d3 ♘xf3+ 10 ♕xf3 ♗e7 11 0-0-0 d5 = Lputian-Gligorić, Sarajevo 1983

20 12 g3 d6 13 ♕d2 (13 f4 ♕a5 14 b4 ♕c7 15 ♗e2 b6 =) 13 ... ♕a5 14 ♗g2 ♕c7 15 b3 ♗d7 = Donner-Polugayevsky, Amsterdam 1981

21 13 ♔xd2 ± Karpov-Portisch, Amsterdam 1981, and Suba-Nogueiras, Lugano 1987

22 8 ♗g5 ♗b7 9 e4 h6 10 ♗h4 ♗e7 11 ♖d1 ♘h5 12 ♗xe7 ♕xe7 =/∞ Toth-Gheorghiu, Rome 1983

23 9 ... d5 10 cd ed 11 e3 ± Smyslov-Hübner, match 1983

9 ... ♕c8 10 e3 d5 11 cd ♘xd5 12 ♘xd5 ♗xd5 13 ♗d3 h6 14 0-0 ± Lputian-Shnaider, USSR 1983

24 10 e4 ♘e7 11 ♗e2 ♘g6 12 ♗g3 ♘h5 13 ♕d2 ♘xg3 14 hg ♗c6 ∞/= Suba-Grünberg, Sochi 1983

25 10 ... ♘h5 11 ♗g3 f5 12 b4 ♗e7 13 ♗e2 ± Reshevsky-Christiansen, match 1984

26 13 ♘b5 ♗xf3 14 gf a6 15 ♘d6 ♖c6 ∓ Soos-Hübner, Lucerne 1979

13 ♘e5 ♗a6 14 b3 d5 15 e4 ♗d6 16 ed ♕c7 17 ♗g3 ♘xb3 ∞ Kaidanov-Kengis, Moscow 1986

27 5 e4 d5 6 e5 ♘e4 7 ♗d3 (7 a3 ♗xc3+ 8 bc c5 9 ♗d3 ♕a5 ∓ Kelečević-Abramović, Yugoslavia 1984) 7 ... c5 8 dc ♘d7! 9 ♘f3 ♘dxc5 ∓/∞

Bareyev-Podgayets, Toliatti 1985

5 ♗g5 h6 6 ♗h4 c5 7 e3 (7 d5 ed 8 cd ♖e8 9 e3 d6 ∞ Watson-Browne, USA 1984) 7 ... cd 8 ed ♘c6 9 ♘f3 ♗e7 10 a3 d5 11 ♖d1 b6 12 ♗d3 dc 13 ♗xc4 ♘d5 = Ree-van der Wiel, Dutch Ch 1986

5 ♘f3 c5 6 a3 ♗xc3+ 7 ♕xc3 cd 8 ♕xd4 ♘c6 9 ♕h4 d5 10 e3 ♘a5 = Forintos-Schneider, Eksjö 1981

28 9 ♘f3 ♘bd7 10 ♗d3 c5 11 0-0 cd 12 ed h6 13 ♗h4 ♖c8 14 ♘d2 d5 = Salov-A.Sokolov, Burevestnik v Trud 1984

29 13 b4 cd 14 ♕xd4 h6 15 ♗xf6 ♕xf6 16 ♕xf6 ♘xf6 17 ♖ac1 ♘d7 = Gheorghiu-Timman, Malta Ol 1980

13 b3 h6 14 ♗h4 cd 15 ♕xd4 (15 ed b5) 15 ... d5 =

30 8 g3 ♕e7 9 ♗g2 c5 10 0-0 ♖c8 11 b3 a5 12 dc bc = Kakageldiev-Aseyev, Borzomi 1984

31 8 ... c5 9 dc bc 10 b4 ♘e4 11 ♕c2 cb 12 ab a5 13 ♗d3 f5 14 b5 d6 ∞ Miles-Tukmakov, Wijk aan Zee 1981

32 9 b3 ♘bd7 10 ♗b2 ♕e7 11 ♖d1 ♘e4 12 ♕c2 f5 13 ♗e2 a5 14 0-0 ♘df6 = Browne-McCambridge, Fort Worth 1984

33 9 ... ♘bd7 10 ♗b2 ♘e4 11 ♕c2 f5 12 ♗d3 ♕e7 (12 ... ♕e8 13 0-0 ♕h5 14 d5! ± Oll-Makarichev, USSR 1983) 13 0-0 ♖ae8 14 d5! ed 15 cd ♗xd5 16 ♗c4 ± Dreyev-Rozentalis, USSR 1986

34 10 ♗b2 ♘bd7 11 ♗e2 ♘e4 12 ♕b3 (12 ♕d3 ab 13 ab ♖xa1+ 14 ♗xa1 ♕a8 15 ♕b1 ♕a3 = Hort-Seirawan, Linares 1983) 12 ... ab 13 ab ♖xa1+ 14 ♗xa1 b5!? 15 cb ♗g5 ∞ Nogueiras-Kir.Georgiev, Leningrad 1987

35 13 ♗d3 ♖f6 (13 ... ♕e8 14 0-0 ♕h5 15 d5 ♘dc5 =) 14 d5 ♖g6 15 ♘d4 ♘dc5 = Oll-Novikov, Kuibishev 1986

13 ♗e2 ♖f6 14 c5 ♗d5 15 ♗c4 (15 c6 ♘f8 16 ♗c4 ♕e7 17 0-0 ♖h6 = Browne-Andersson, Brasilia 1981) 15 ... ♗xc4 16 ♕xc4 bc 17 dc ♖g6 ∞ Knežević-Gerusel, Porz 1981-82

	5	6	7	8	9	10	11	12	13	
1	...	e3[2]	♝d3[4]	♘e2[5]	0-0	a4	c5	♕xd3	f3	±
	♘e4[1]	0-0[3]	f5	b6	♘c6	♝a6	♝xd3	bc	♘f6[6]	
2	...	f3	e4	♝g5[9]	♝e3	♝d3	♝f2	♘e2	♘g3	∞
	d6	e5[7]	♘c6[8]	h6	♘d7	♕h4+	♕g5[10]	♕xg2	♕h3[11]	
3	...	f3	e4	e5[13]	♘h3	♕a4	♘f2[15]	♘e4	♝f4	±
	b6	♝a6	♘c6[12]	♘g8	♘a5	h6[14]	♘e7	0-0[16]		
4	...	f3[17]	cd	e3	♘e2	g4[20]	♘f4	h4	♘xg6	∞
	0-0	d5[18]	ed	♝f5[19]	c5	♝g6!	♘bd7	h6	fg[21]	
5	...	f3[22]	e4	♘e2[23]	♝g5[24]	♝e3	d5	♘g3	♝d3	∞
	c5	d6	♘c6	b6	h6	e5[25]	♘a5	g6	♝a6[26]	
6	...	...	cd	dc[27]	e4[28]	♕c2	♝d3	c4[30]	♝xe3	=
	...	d5	♘xd5	f5	fe	e3[29]	♘d7	♘f4	♕a5+[31]	
7	...	...	...	...	e4	♕d4[33]	f4[34]	♕c4	♝e3	=
	...	...	...	♕a5	♘c7[32]	f6	♘c6[35]	0-0	♔h8[36]	
8	...	e3	♝d3[38]	♘e2	0-0[40]	e4	d5	f3	♝e3	±/=
	...	♘c6[37]	e5	d6[39]	0-0	h6[41]	♘e7	♘g6	♝d7[42]	
9	...	...	...	♘e2[43]	e4	e5[44]	ef	♝e3	♕c2	=
	...	...	0-0	b6	♘e8	f5[45]	♕xf6	♝a6	g6[46]	
10	...	...	...	...	...	0-0	f4	♘g3[48]	ef	∞
	...	...	...	...	...	♝a6	f5[47]	♘e7[49]	♘xf5[50]	

[1] 5 ... d5 6 cd ed 7 e3 ± – 4 e3

[2] 6 ♕c2 f5 7 ♘h3 (7 f3?! ♕h4+ 8 g3 ♘xg3 9 hg ♕xh1 10 ♘h3 d6 11 ♔f2 e5 12 ♝g2 ♕h2 13 ♝f4 ef 14 gf ♘c6 15 ♖h1 ♕xh1 16 ♝xh1 ♝d7 ∓) 7 ... 0-0 8 f3 ♘f6 9 c5 (9 e4 fe 10 fe e5 =) 9 ... b6 10 cb cb 11 e3 ♕c7 = Botvinnik-Tal, match (18) 1960

[3] 6 ... f5 7 ♕h5+! g6 8 ♕h6 ± Botvinnik-Tal, match (20) 1960, and Gutman-Knežević, Baden-Baden 1984

[4] 7 ♘e2 b6 8 f3 ♘d6 9 ♘g3 ♝a6 10 e4 ♝xc4 11 ♝xc4 ♘xc4 12 ♕d3 d5 13 0-0 ∞ Vaganian-Rashkovsky, USSR Ch 1977

[5] 8 ♕c2 b6! 9 ♝xe4 (9 ♘e2 ♝b7 10 0-0 ♕h4 ∞) 9 ... fe 10 ♕xe4 ♘c6 11 ♘f3 ♝a6 =

[6] 14 ♝a3 d6 15 dc ± Dolmatov-Rashkovsky, USSR Ch 1986

[7] 6 ... ♘h5!? 7 ♘h3 e5 8 ♘f2 0-0 9 e4 ♘c6 10 g4 ♘f6 ∞ Diez-del Corral-Korchnoi, Buenos Aires Ol 1978

[8] 7 ... 0-0 8 ♝g5 ♘c6 9 ♘e2 b6 10 g4 ♝a6 11 ♘g3 ±
     7 ... c5 8 ♝d3 ♘c6 9 ♘e2 b6 10 ♝e3 ♘a5 11 ♘g3 ♕c7 12 0-0 ♝a6 13 ♕e2 0-0-0 14 f4 ±

[9] 8 ♝e3 0-0 9 ♝d3 ♘a5 10 ♘e2 ♕e8 11 0-0 ♘d7! 12 ♘g3 ♘b6 ∞ Gutman

[10] 11 ... ♕e7 12 ♘e2 h5 13 ♘g3 g6 14 ♘f1! ± Gutman-Kurajica, Thessaloniki Ol 1984

[11] 14 ♘f5 ∞ Gutman

[12] 7 ... d5 8 ♝g5 h6 9 ♝h4 ♝xc4 10 ♝xc4 dc 11 ♕a4+ ♕d7 12 ♕xc4 ± Alekhine-Eliskases, Hastings 1933-34, and Lilienthal-Capablanca, Hastings 1934-35

[13] 8 ♝d3 ♘a5 9 ♕e2 d6 10 ♝g5 h6 11 ♝h4 ♕d7 ∞ Zsu.Polgar-Browne, New York 1986
      8 ♘h3 ♘a5 9 ♕a4 0-0 10 ♝g5 d6 11 e5 ♕d7 ∞ Timman-Seirawan, Tilburg 1983
      8 ♝g5 ♕c8 9 ♝d3 ♘a5 10 ♕e2 ♝b7!? ∞ Williams-Dzindzihashvili, Thessaloniki Ol 1984

[14] 10 ... ♘e7 11 ♝d3 (11 ♝g5!) 11 ... 0-0 (11 ... h6!) 12 ♝g5 h6 13 ♝h4 d5 (13 ... ♕e8!) 14 ♝b1! g5 15 ♕c2 ♘g6 16 ♘f4!! ±± Kotov-Keres, Budapest 1950

[15] 11 ♝d3 ♘e7 12 ♘f4 0-0 13 h4 d6 ∞ Niklasson-Adamski, Poland 1978

[16] 12 ... ♕c8 13 ♖b1 ♘f5 14 h4 ♕d8 15 h5 ± Gutman-Abramović, Hastings 1984-85

[17] 6 e3 c5 – 5 ... c5

[18] 6 ... ♘e8 7 e4 ♘c6 8 ♝d3 b6 9 a4 ♝a6 10 ♝a3 d6 11 f4 ♘a5 12 ♕e2 ♕d7 13 ♝b4 ♘b7 14 ♘f3 c5 15 ♝a3 ♘a5 16 0-0 ♖c8 17 e5! ± Gutman-Taimanov, USSR 1974, and Gutman-

Unzicker, West Germany 1985-86

[19] 8 ... ♘h5 9 g3 b6 10 ♗d3 f5 11 ♘e2 ♗a6 12 ♗xa6 ♘xa6 13 ♕d3 ♕c8 14 c4 ±

[20] 10 ♘g3 ♗g6 11 ♗d3 ♘c6 12 0-0 ♕d7 13 ♖a2 ♖fe8 14 ♖e2 ♖ad8 =

[21] 14 ♗d3 ♕c7 15 ♔e2 ♕d6! ∞ Bareyev-Rozentalis, USSR 1986

[22] 6 e4 ♕a5! 7 e5 ♘e4 8 ♗d2 ♘c6 9 ♘e2 b6 10 f4 cd 11 cd ♘xd2 12 ♕xd2 ♕xd2+ 13 ♔xd2 ♗a6 ∓

[23] 8 ♗e3 ♕a5 9 ♕d2 (9 d5 ♘e5 10 ♗d2 0-0 ∓ Murei-Stean, Beer-Sheva 1980) 9 ... b6 10 ♗d3 cd 11 cd ♕xd2+ 12 ♔xd2 ♗a6 =/∓ Gutman-Savon, USSR 1977

[24] 9 ♘g3 ♕a5 10 ♗d3 (10 f4 0-0 11 e5 ♘e8 ∓ Spassky-Hübner, Turin 1982) 10 ... ♗a6 11 ♗e3 0-0 12 ♕e2 ♖c8 13 ♖c1 ∞

[25] 10 ... ♕d7 11 ♘g3 ♗a6 12 ♗d3 0-0-0 13 a4 ∞/± Gutman-Spassky, West Germany 1985-86

[26] 14 ♘f1 ♕d7 15 ♘d2 ♘h5 16 g3 g5 ∞ Gutman-Ivkov, Manchester 1983

[27] 8 ♕d2 ♕a5 9 ♗b2 ♘b6 10 e3 ♘a4 =
8 ♕d3 cd 9 cd ♘c6 10 e4 ♘b6 11 ♗e3 0-0 12 ♖d1 ♗d7 13 ♗e2 f5 (13 ... ♘a5!?) 14 ♘h3 fe 15 ♕xe4 ♘d5 ∞

[28] 9 c4 ♕f6 10 ♗d2 ♘c3 =
9 ♘h3 ♕a5 10 e4 fe 11 ♘g5 e3 ∞
9 ♕c2 f4 10 ♗xf4?! (10 e4 fe – 9 e4) 10 ... ♗xf4 11 ♕a4+ ♘c6 12 ♕xf4 e5 13 ♕a4 ♕e7 14 ♕b5 a6 15 ♕b6 e4 ∞ Ernst-C.Hansen, Gausdal Z 1985

[29] 10 ... 0-0 11 fe ♕h4+ 12 g3 ♕f6 13 ♗d3 ♕xc3+ 14 ♗xc3 ♘xc3 15 ♗f4! ± Hollis
10 ... ♕a5 11 fe ♕xc3+ 12 ♕xc3 ♘xc3 13 ♗d3 ♗d7 14 ♗d2 ♘a4 15 ♖c1 ♗c6 16 ♘f3 ♘d7 = Ruderfer-Gulko, USSR 1966

[30] 12 ♘e2 ♘xc5 13 0-0 ♗d7 ∓ Diez del Corral-Polugayevsky, Kapfenberg 1970

[31] 14 ♔f2 ♘xd3+ 15 ♕xd3 0-0 = Furman-Polugayevsky, USSR Ch 1963

[32] 9 ... ♘e7 10 ♗e3 ♘xc3+ 11 ♔f2 0-0 12 ♘e2 ♕a5 13 ♕d2! ♕xd2 14 ♗xd2 ± Vladimirov-Tavadian, USSR 1983
9 ... ♘f6 10 ♗e3 0-0 11 ♕b3 ♘a6 12 ♗xa6 ♕xa6 13 ♘e2 ± Moskalenko-Shnaider, USSR 1985

[33] 10 ♗e3 0-0 11 ♕b3 ♘ba6 12 ♗c4 e5 13 ♘e2 ♗e6 = Arkhipov-Eingorn, Sochi 1985

[34] 11 ♕b4 ♘c6 12 ♕xa5 ♘xa5 13 ♖b1 ♗d7 14 ♗d2 0-0-0 15 c4 ♘c6 = Yudasin-Farago, Albena 1985

[35] 11 ... e5 12 ♕b4 ♘c6 13 ♕xa5 ♘xa5 14 fe ♘b3 15 ♖b1 ♘xc5 16 ef gf ∞ Kouatly

[36] 14 ♘f3 e5 15 f5 ♗d7 16 ♘d2 ♘a6 17 ♘b3 ♕c7 18 ♖d1 ♗e8 19 ♗e2 ♖c8 = Kouatly-Farago, Brussels 1986

[37] 6 ... b6 7 ♗d3 (7 ♘e2!? ♗a6 8 ♘g3 ♕c7 9 e4 cd 10 cd ♗xc4 11 ♕c2 d5 12 ♗d3 ∞∞ Vaganian-Gulko, USSR 1977) 7 ... ♗b7 8 f3 ♘c6 9 ♘e2 0-0 10 e4 ♘e8 11 0-0 ♗a6 (11 ... ♖c8!?) 12 f4 – 6 ... ♘c6

[38] 7 ♘e2 d6 8 ♘g3 e5 9 d5 ♘e7 10 ♗d3 h5! 11 h4 g6 12 e4 ♔f8 ∓ Szabo-Lein, Vršac 1979

[39] 8 ... e4 9 ♗b1 b6 10 ♘g3 ♗a6 11 f3 ±/∞ Spassky-Tal, USSR Ch 1958, and Psakhis-Plaskett, Bor 1985

[40] 9 e4 ♘h5 (9 ... ed 10 cd cd 11 0-0 ♕a5?! 12 ♗f4 ± Kasparov-Belyavsky, USSR 1983) 10 0-0 g5 ∞ Bronstein-Smyslov, Budapest 1950

[41] 10 ... b6 11 d5 ♘a5 12 ♘g3 ♖b8 13 a4 ♖e8 14 h3 ♘d7 15 ♘f5 ± Vizhmanavin-Belyavsky, USSR Ch 1984

[42] 14 ♕d2 ♖b8 15 a4 b6 16 ♘g3 ±/= Balashov-Lerner, USSR Ch 1985

[43] 8 e4 cd 9 cd d5 10 cd ed 11 e5 ♘e4 12 ♘e2 f6! ∓

[44] 10 ♗e3 ♗a6 11 ♘g3 (11 dc ♘e5 12 0-0 ♗xc4 13 ♗xc4 ♘xc4 14 ♕d4 ♘xe3 15 ♕xe3 ♘f6 = Korzubov-Chernin, USSR 1984) 11 ... ♖c8 12 e5 f5 13 ef ♖xf6 14 ♕e2 cd 15 cd ♘a5 16 ♖c1 d5 = Korzubov-Neverov, USSR 1985

[45] 10 ... ♗a6 11 ♘g3 cd?! 12 cd ♕xd4 13 ♗b2 ♘c6 14 ♕h5 g6 15 ♕h6 ± Pliester-Ligterink, Amsterdam 1982

[46] 14 h4! d6 15 h5 ♘xc4 16 hg hg 17 ♗xc4 ♗xc4 18 ♖h6 ♘e7! (18 ... ♕f5 19 ♖xg6+ ♔f7 20 ♕xf5+ ef 21 ♖d6 ± Heuer-Shakarov, corr. 1970) 19 ♘f4 ♕f5 =

[47] 11 ... ♘a5 12 f5 f6 13 ♘f4 ∞ Timman-Polugayevsky, Tilburg 1983

[48] 12 d5 ♘a5 13 e5 ♗xc4 14 ♗xc4 ♘xc4 15 d6 b5 ∞ Ziatdinov-Georgadze, USSR 1985
12 ef ef 13 dc bc 14 ♘g3 ♘e7 15 ♗e3 ♕c7 ∞/∓ Korzubov-Kharitonov, USSR 1985

[49] 12 ... g6 13 ♗e3 ♘a5 14 dc ♘xc4 15 ♗xc4 ♗xc4 16 ♖f2 ± Christiansen-Rodriguez, Moscow IZ 1982
12 ... ♘d6 13 ef ♘xf5 14 dc bc 15 ♗xf5 ef 16 ♕d5+ ♔h8 17 ♘xf5 ♕f6 18 ♘d6 ♕xc3 19 ♖b1 ♕d4+ 20 ♕xd4 ±/= Bagirov-Neverov, USSR 1985

[50] 14 ♘xf5 ef 15 dc bc 16 ♖b1 ♖b8 17 ♗e3 d6 ∞/= Martin-Short, London 1985

Nimzo-Indian VI   1 d4 ♘f6 2 c4 e6 3 ♘c3 ♗b4 4 e3 b6

	5	6	7	8	9	10	11	12	13	
1	♗d3	♘f3	♕c2	0-0	bc	♘e1[2]	f3	♗a3[4]	e4	∞
	♗b7	♘e4	f5[1]	♗xc3	0-0	c5[3]	♘d6	♘a6	fe[5]	
2	...	...	0-0	bc	♘e1	f3	♘c2	♗d2	♕e2	±
	...	...	♗xc3[6]	0-0[7]	f5	♘f6[8]	c5	♕e7	d6[9]	
3	...	...	0-0	cd	♘e5	f4	♕f3[10]	♗d2[11]	♘xc6	=
	...	0-0	d5	ed	♗d6	c5	♘c6	cd	♗xc6[12]	
4	...	...	...	a3	cd[13]	b4	♕b3	a4	♘xd5	∞
	...	...	...	♗d6	ed	a6[14]	♘bd7[15]	♘e4[16]	♘g5[17]	
5	...	...	...	♘a4	ed	a3	b4	♖e1	♗b2	±/∞
	...	...	c5	cd	♗e7[18]	d6	♘bd7	a5[19]	ab[20]	
6	...	...	...	bc	♘d2[22]	e4[23]	cd	e5	♘e4[24]	∞
	...	...	♗xc3	c5[21]	♘c6	cd	♘xd4	♘e8		
7	♘e2	a3	d5	♘g3[26]	♗e2	e4	ed	cd	0-0	±
	♗b7	♗e7[25]	0-0	d6	c6	cd	ed	♖e8[27]	♘bd7[28]	
8	...	a3	♘f4	cd	♔xf1	♕f3[32]	g3	♔g2	♖d1	±
	♗a6	♗e7[29]	d5[30]	♗xf1	♘xd5[31]	c6	0-0	♘d7	♕c7[33]	
9	...	♘g3	bc	♗a3	♗xc4	0-0	e4[36]	♖b1	♗b4	±
	...	♗xc3+[34]	d5	♗xc4[35]	dc	♕d7	♕b5	♕a6	♘c6[37]	
10	...	♕c2	a3	♘xc3	♕xc3	b4[39]	♗b2	d5	♖d1	±/=
	♘e4	♗b7	♗xc3+	♘xc3[38]	0-0	d6	♘d7	♘f6	♕e7[40]	

[1] 7 ... ♘g5 8 ♘xg5 ♕xg5 9 f3 ♕h4+ 10 g3 ♕h5 11 0-0 ± Gulko-Romanishin, USSR Ch 1981

[2] 10 ♘d2 ♘xd2 11 ♗xd2 ♘c6 12 e4 (12 f3 ♘a5) 12 ... fe 13 ♗xe4 ♕h4 = Portisch-P.Nikolić, Nikšić 1983

[3] 10 ... ♘c6 11 f3 ♘g5 12 ♕e2 ♕e7 (12 ... e5!?) 13 ♘c2 e5 14 ♗a3 d6 15 c5 ± Portisch-van der Wiel, Wijk aan Zee 1985

[4] 12 ♕e2 ♘c6 13 ♗a3 ♕c7 14 ♘c2 (14 dc bc 15 ♗xc5 ♘e5 16 ♗a3 ♗a6 ∞) 14 ... ♘a5 ∞/= Zysk-Razuvayev, Athens 1986

[5] 13 ... ♕e7 14 e5 ♘f7 15 f4 g5 ∞ Yusupov-Timman, match 1986

   13 ... fe!? 14 fe ♖xf1+ 15 ♔xf1 e5! Timman

[6] 7 ... ♘xc3 8 bc ♗e7 (8 ... ♗xc3 9 ♖b1 ♘c6 10 ♖b3 ♗a5 11 e4 ± Balashov-Romanishin, Lvov 1978) 9 e4 d6 10 ♗e3 ♘d7 11 ♘d2 0-0 12 ♕g4 ± Farago-Romanishin, Kiev 1978

   7 ... f5 8 ♘e2 ♗d6 9 b3 ♕e7 10 ♕c2 ♘a6 11 a3 c5 12 ♗b2 0-0 13 ♘e5 ± Tisdall-Keene, New York 1981

[7] 8 ... ♘xc3 9 ♕c2 ♗xf3 10 gf ♕g5+ 11 ♔h1 ♕h5 12 ♖g1! ♗xf3+ 13 ♖g2 f5 14 ♗a3 ∞/± Keres-Spassky, match 1965

   8 ... f5 9 ♘e1 ♘xc3 10 ♕h5+ g6 11 ♕h6 ♕f6 12 f3 ± Bronstein

[8] 10 ... ♘d6 11 ♗a3 ±

[9] 14 e4 ± Gligorić-Kuzmin, Bled/Portorož 1979

[10] 11 ♖f3 g6 12 ♗d2 ♘c6 13 ♖h3 cd 14 ♘xc6 ♗xc6 15 ed ♘e4 16 f5 ♕f6 = Knaak-Petrosian, Tallinn 1979

[11] 12 ♕h3 g6 13 ♗d2 cd 14 ♘xc6 ♗xc6 15 ed ♘e4 = Farago-Lerner, Kiev 1978

[12] 14 ed ♖e8! = Knaak-Lukacs, Leipzig 1986

[13] 9 b4 dc 10 ♗xc4 ♘bd7 11 ♗b2 a5 12 b5 e5 13 ♖e1 e4 14 ♘d2 ♕e7 = Portisch-Petrosian, Lone Pine 1978, and Portisch-Hübner, match 1980

[14] 10 ... ♘bd7 11 ♕b3 c6 (11 ... ♖e8 12 a4 c6 13 ♗a3 ± Ree-Ligterink, Dutch Ch 1983) 12 ♖e1 ♖e8 13 ♗b2 ♖b8 14 ♕c2 ♖c8 15 ♖ad1 Timman-van der Vliet, Dutch 1983

[15] 11 ... ♕e7 12 b5 ♖d8 13 a4 ± Polugayevsky-Christiansen, Linares 1985

[16] 12 ... ♖e8 13 ♗a3 g6 14 b5 ± Gligorić-Petrosian, Bugojno 1982

[17] 14 ♘xg5 ♕xg5 15 e4 ♗xd5 = Ftacnik-Ligterink, Wijk aan Zee 1985

   14 ♗e2 ♘c5 15 bc ♗xd5 16 ♕d1 ♘xf3+ 17 ♗xf3 ♗xf3 18 ♕xf3 bc =

   14 ♘e1!? Ftacnik

[18] 9 ... ♖e8 10 a3 (10 c5 ♗xf3! 11 ♕xf3 ♘c6 12 ♗e3 e5 = Ogaard-Adorjan, Gjovik 1983)

10 ... &f8 11 &g5 d6 12 &c3 &e7 (12 ... &bd7 13 d5 ±) 13 &e1 ± Kharitonov-Chernin, USSR Ch 1984

[19] 12 ... &e8 13 &b2 &c8 14 &c3 g6 15 &f1 a6 16 &d2 &h5 17 d5 ± Polugayevsky-Seirawan, Toluca IZ 1982

[20] 14 ab &e8 (14 ... b5!? 15 cb &b6 Lein-de Firmian, US Ch 1986) 15 &d2 e5 16 &b3 ed 17 &xd4 &f8 ±/oo Lerner-Polugayevsky, USSR Ch 1983

[21] 8 ... &e4 9 &e2 c5 10 &d2 &b7 11 f3 ±

[22] 9 &e1 &e4 10 &c2 f5 11 &b2 &e8 ∓ Tal-Short, Montpellier C 1985

[23] 10 &b3 d6 11 e4 a5 oo Ree-Korchnoi, Wijk aan Zee 1984

[24] 13 ... &c6? 14 &h5 ± Ree-Kudrin, Wijk aan Zee 1985
13 ... d6 14 &a3 de oo; 14 &g5!? Parma
13 ... f5 oo Ree

[25] 6 ... &xc3+ 7 &xc3 0-0 8 &d3 d5 (8 ... c5 9 d5 ±) 9 cd ed 10 b4 ±

[26] 8 e4 &e8! 9 g3 (9 e5? &g4) 9 ... b5! oo Marin-Suba, Romanian Ch 1985

[27] 12 ... &a6 13 0-0 &c7 14 &f3 ± Lerner-Gavrikov, USSR 1981

[28] 14 &f4 g6 15 &c1 a6 = Ehlvest-Khalifman, Kuibishev 1986
14 &f5 &f8 15 &f4 ± M.Gurevich-Khalifman, USSR Ch 1987

[29] 6 ... &xc3+ 7 &xc3 d5 8 b3 0-0 9 &e2 &c6 10 0-0 &a5 11 &b1! c6 (11 ... &e7 12 e4! ± Henley-Dzindzihashvili, US Ch 1984; 11 ...

c5!?) 12 a4 &e7 13 &d2 ± Hort-Lombardy, Reykjavik 1978

[30] 7 ... d6 8 b4 c6 9 &b2 0-0 10 &e2 e5 11 &h3 &bd7 12 0-0 ± Henley-Benjamin, US Ch 1984

[31] 9 ... ed 10 &f3 c6 11 g4 g5 12 &h5 &xh5 13 gh ±

[32] 10 &cxd5 ed 11 &h5 &g5 12 e4 (12 &e6 g6 13 &xg5 fe 14 &e5 &d7 oo) 12 ... &xf4 13 &xf4 &c6! oo/= Saeed-Timman, Taxco IZ 1985

[33] 14 e4 &xc3 15 &xc3 &ac8 16 &e3 ± D.Gurevich-H.Olafsson, Reykjavik 1982, and D.Gurevich-Bonin, USA 1985

[34] 6 ... 0-0 7 e4 &c6 8 &d3 (8 &g5!? h6 9 h4 Plachetka-Schneider, Lucerne Ol 1982) 8 ... e5 (8 ... &a5 9 &g5 h6 10 h4 ± Knaak-Adorjan, Szirak 1985) 9 d5 &xc3+ 10 bc &a5 11 &e2 c6 12 &f5 ± Spassky-Hübner, Munich 1979

[35] 8 ... dc 9 &e2 &d7 10 e4 &c6 11 0-0 0-0-0 12 &c2 h5 13 &fd1 h4 14 &f1 ± Portisch-Fischer, Siegen Ol 1970, Gligorić-Cosulich, Venice 1971, and Najdorf-Donner, Wijk aan Zee 1971

[36] 11 &b1 h5 12 h4 &c6 13 e4! ± Cebalo-P.Nikolić, Kavala 1985

[37] 14 a4 0-0-0 15 &e2 ± Plachetka-Skrobek, Warsaw 1983

[38] 8 ... f5 9 d5 &xc3 10 &xc3 ±

[39] 10 &c2 &h4 11 b4 a5 12 b5 d6 13 &b2 &d7 ∓ Ravisekhar-Kuzmin, Bangalore 1981

[40] 14 &e2 c6 ±/= Ivkov-Korchnoi, Amsterdam 1976

	Nimzo-Indian VII			1 d4 &f6 2 c4 e6 3 &c3 &b4 4 e3 &c6				
	5	6	7	8	9	10	11	12	13
1	&e2[1]	a3	cd	&f4	&b3!?[4]	&a2	b4	&xc4	&xc4	⹀
	d5	&e7[2]	ed	0-0[3]	&a5	c6[5]	&c4	dc	a5[6]	
2	&d3	&e2[8]	ed	c5!?[10]	0-0	bc	&g3	&a3	&f3	±
	e5?![7]	ed[9]	d5	0-0	&xc3	h6	b6	&e8	&g4[11]	

---

[1] 5 a3 &xc3+ - 4 a3
5 &d2!?

[2] 6 ... &f8!? 7 cd (7 &g1!? g6 8 &f3 &g7 Taimanov) 7 ... ed 8 &f4 &e7 9 b4 a6 10 g3 c6 11 &g2 &f5 12 0-0 &d6! = Osnos-Taimanov, Tbilisi 1967

[3] 8 ... &f5 9 &b3!

[4] 9 &e2 &f5 10 g4! &e6 11 g5 &d7 12 h4 &b6 13 &d3 ±; 9 ... &b8!? intending ... c6 Botvinnik

[5] 10 ... &e6 11 &xe6 fe = Pritchett

[6] Taimanov

[7] 5 ... d5 6 a3 dc 7 &xc4 &d6 8 f4! ± Keene-Fedorowicz, New York 1981

[8] 6 d5!? e4?! 7 &c2 &e5 oo Darga-Pachman, European Team Ch 1957

[9] 6 ... d5!? 7 0-0 dc 8 &xc4 ed 9 ed 0-0 10 &g5 &e7 = Pritchett; 7 cd &xd5 8 e4 &b6 9 d5 &e7 10 a3 &d6 11 &g5 h6 12 &h4 c6! = Lipnitsky-Borisenko, USSR Ch 1950

[10] 8 cd &xd5 9 0-0 0-0-0 10 a3 &e7 11 &b3 &f6 12 &d1 a6 13 h3 &d6 14 &g5 h6 = Matanović-Taimanov, Stockholm 1951

[11] 14 &f4 &e7 15 &ae1 &e6 16 &c1 bc 17 &xc5 ± Gligorić-Pachman, Havana Ol 1966

	5	6	7	8	9	10	11	12	13	
3	♘f3	♗d3	0-0[12]	h3!	♗xc4	e4	♗e3	♘xd4	♖e1[13]	=
	0-0	d5	a6	dc	♗d6	e5	ed	♗d7	♘e5[14]	
4	...	...	...	♗xc4	♗b5[16]	♗xc6	ed[18]	♗g5	♖e1	=
	...	...	dc	♗d6[15]	e5![17]	ed	bc	♖e8	♖xe1+[19]	

[12] 7 a3 dc 8 ♗xc4 ♗d6 9 b4 e5 10 ♗b2 ♗g4 11 d5 ♘e7 12 h3 ♗d7 13 ♘g5 (Botvinnik-Tal, match (3) 1961) 13 ... h6! 14 ♘ge4 ♘xe4 15 ♘xe4 f5! Pritchett; 11 de ♘xe5 12 ♗e2 ♕e7 13 ♘b5 ♖fd8 14 ♕c2 a6 = Botvinnik-Tal, match (5) 1961

[13] Taimanov-Fischer, Buenos Aires 1960

[14] 14 ♗b3 ♘g6 = Taimanov

[15] 8 ... ♕e8!? 9 a3 (9 e4!? ♗xc3 10 bc ♘xe4 11 ♗d3 f5 ∞ Taimanov) 9 ... ♗d6 10 e4 e5 11 d5 ♘e7 12 h3 ± Pritchett

[16] 9 ♘b5 ♗e7 10 ♕c2 a6 11 ♘c3 ♗d6 =

Medina-Zuckerman, Malaga 1968
9 e4 e5 10 d5 ♘e7 11 ♗g5 ♘g6 12 ♖c1 a6 = **9 h3!?** e5 10 ♕c2 ♕e7 11 ♗d2 ♗d7 12 ♖ae1 ♖ae8 = Bolbochan-Pachman, Helsinki 1952

[17] 9 ... ♕e7 10 e4 e5 11 ♗xc6 bc 12 de (12 ♗g5!?) 12 ... ♗xe5 13 ♘xe5 ♕xe5 ∞ Lipnitsky

[18] **11 ♗xb7** ♗xb7 12 ♘xd4 ♕d7 13 ♘db5 ♕c6 14 f3 ♗e5! ∞ Furman-Lipnitsky, USSR 1951

11 ♘xd4 bc 12 ♘xc6 ♕e8 13 ♘d4 ♗b7 14 ♘f5 ♗e5 15 ♕c2 ♕e6 16 f3 g6 17 ♘d4 ♕d6 ∓

[19] 14 ♕xe1 ♗f5 15 ♘e5 c5! = Pritchett

	5	6	7	8	9	10	11	12	13	
1	♗d3[1]	♘f3	bc	e4	d5[2]	♘h4[3]	g3[4]	♘g2	♘e3	=
	♘c6	♗xc3+	d6	e5	♘e7	h6	g5[5]	♗h3	♕d7[6]	
2	...	...	...	0-0	♘g5	f4[8]	cd	♘f3	ed	=
	...	...	...	e5	0-0[7]	ed	h6[9]	cd	d5[10]	
3	...	...	...	...	♘d2	d5[12]	♕c2	a4[13]	f4	=
	...	...	...	...	0-0[11]	♘e7	g6	♘h5	ef[14]	
4	...	♘e2	ed	cd[16]	0-0	♕c2[18]	♖d1	a3	♘xd5	=
	...	cd[15]	d5	♘xd5[17]	0-0	h6	♗d6[19]	♗d7	ed[20]	
5	...	...	...	...	...	♗c2	a3	♗g5	♕d3	±/∞
	...	...	...	...	...	♗e7[21]	♘f6[22]	b6	g6[23]	
6	♘e2	a3	♘xc3	ed	♗xc4	♗e3	0-0	♖e1	♗a2	±
	d5	♗xc3+[24]	cd	dc[25]	♘c6	0-0	b6[26]	♗b7	h6[27]	
7	...	ed	c5[28]	♗d2	♕xd2	a3	♘xc3	♗d3[30]	cb!	±/∞
	cd	d5	♘e4	♘xd2	a5	♗xc3	a4[29]	b6	♕xb6[31]	
8	...	...	a3	d5[32]	cd	♗e3![33]	♗d4	♕d3	♘g3[36]	±
	...	0-0	♗e7	ed	♖e8	♘g4[34]	♘h6[35]	d6	♗f6+[37]	
9	...	...	...	...	...	♘d4[38]	♗e3	♗e2	0-0	±/∞
	...	...	...	...	♗c5	♖e8+[39]	d6	♘bd7	a6[40]	

[1] 5 ♘f3 ♘c6 6 d5?! (6 ♗d3 – 5 ♗d3) 6 ... ♘e7 7 d6?! (7 de =) 7 ... ♘f5 ∓ Christiansen-Browne, US Ch 1981

[2] 9 h3 h6 10 ♗e3 b6 11 0-0 ♕c7 12 d5 ♘e7 13 ♘h4 g5 14 ♕f3 ♘fg8 15 ♘f5 ♘xf5 16 ef ♘f6 = Portisch-Timman, Mar del Plata 1982

[3] **10 ♘d2** ♗d7 11 ♘f1 ♕c7 12 ♘g3 0-0-0 =

Gligorić-Andersson, Tilburg 1977
10 ♖b1 h6 11 h4 0-0 **12** ♘h2 ♘h7 13 g4 ♘g6 14 g5 ♘xh4 15 gh g6 ∓ Gligorić-Adorjan, Sarajevo 1983

[4] 11 f4 ♘g6! 12 ♘xg6 fg 13 0-0 (13 fe de ∓ Spassky-Fischer, match (5) 1972) 13 ... 0-0 14 f5 ♗d7 ∞ Vaidya-Miles, British Ch 1984

5   11 ... 0-0 12 0-0 ♗h3 13 ♘g2 ♕a5 14 ♖b1
♕xa2 15 ♖xb7 ∞/± Tukmakov-M.Gurevich,
Leningrad 1987

6   14 f3 0-0-0 ∞/= Hübner-Timman, Tilburg
1981

7   9 ... ♕e7 10 ♕c2 h6 11 ♘e4 0-0 (11 ...
♘xe4 12 ♗xe4 0-0 13 dc dc 14 ♗d5±) 12 ♘xf6+
♕xf6 13 ♗e4 cd 14 cd ± Danner-Lalev, Albena
1983

8   10 ♘e4 ed 11 cd ♗f5 12 ♘xc5 dc 13 ♗xf5
cd = Knaak-Garcia Gonzalez, Cienfuegos 1984

9   11 ... cd 12 ed ♘xd4 13 ♗b2 ♘f5 14 ♕c2
♘e3 15 ♗xh7+ ♔h8 16 ♕d3 ♘xf1 17 ♖xf1 ±
Kuuskmaa-Uogele, corr. 1983, and Pliester-
Bergström, Andorra 1986

10   14 ♗a3 ♖e8 15 ♘e5 dc 16 ♗xc4 ♗e6
17 ♗xe6 ♖xe6 ∓ Pliester-Mednis, Amsterdam
1986

14 ♘e5 dc 15 ♗xc4 ♗e6 16 ♗xe6 fe =
Mednis

11   9 ... cd 10 cd ed 11 ed ♘xd4 12 ♖e1+ ♘e6
13 ♗a3 0-0 14 ♘b3 ± Portisch-Timman, Wijk
aan Zee 1978

9 ... ♕e7 10 d5 ♘b8 11 e4 0-0 12 ♖b1 ±
Taimanov-Agzamov, USSR 1983

12   10 ♘b3 e4! 11 ♗e2 b6 12 ♗d2 ♘e7 ∓
Portisch-Miles, Nikšić 1983

13   12 e4 ♘h5 ∓ Gligorić-Seirawan, Baden 1980
12 f4 ♘g4 13 ♘f3 ef 14 ef ♘f5 ∓ Donner-
Stean, Marbella 1982

14   14 ef ♘f6 15 ♘f3 ♘f5 = Spassky-Timman,
match 1983

15   6 ... d5 7 cd ed 8 a3 cd 9 ab dc 10 b5 ♘e5
11 ♘xc3 ♘xd3+ 12 ♕xd3 0-0 13 b3 ±/∞ Miles-
Romanishin, World v USSR 1984

16   8 0-0 dc 9 ♗xc4 0-0 – 4 ... 0-0

17   8 ... ♕xd5 9 0-0 ♕h5 10 ♘e4 ♘xe4
11 ♗xe4 0-0 12 ♕d3 ♗d6 13 ♘f4 ♗xf4
14 ♗xf4 ♖d8 15 ♕e3! ± M.Gurevich-Benjamin,
Moscow 1987

18   10 ♘xd5 ed 11 ♘f4 ♗d6 12 ♖e1 g6 =
Lerner-Razuvayev, Moscow 1986

19   11 ... ♘ce7 12 ♘f4 (12 ♘g3!? ♗d6 13 ♕e2
Polugayevsky) 12 ... ♗d6 13 ♘fxd5 ♘xd5 =
Speelman-Polugayevsky, Moscow 1985

20   Chernin-Geller, Sochi 1986

21   10 ... ♖e8 11 ♕d3 g6 12 ♖d1 ♗f8 13 ♕f3 ±
Timoshchenko-Arnason, Helsinki 1986, and
M.Gurevich-Razuvayev, Moscow 1987

10 ... ♗d6!? Tal

22   11 ... ♘xc3 12 bc b6 (12 ... e5 13 d5 ♘a5
14 f4! ± Timoshchenko-Vizhmanavin, USSR
1986) 13 ♕d3 g6 14 ♖e1 ♗b7 15 ♘f4 ±/∞
Knaak-Stohl, Potsdam 1985

23   14 ♖ad1 ♗b7 15 ♖fe1 ♖e8 16 h4 ±/∞
Bagirov-Aseyev, Sevastopol 1986

24   6 ... ♗a5 7 dc dc 8 ♕xd8+ ♔xd8 9 ♗d2 ±
6 ... cd 7 ab dc3 8 ♘xc3 ± Garcia Palermo-
Matanović, Vienna 1986

25   8 ... ♘c6 9 c5 0-0 10 ♗e2 ♘e4 11 ♘xe4

de 12 ♗e3 f5 13 ♕d2 ♕f6 14 g3 e5 15 de
♘xe5 16 0-0-0 ± M.Gurevich-Zaid, USSR 1984

26   11 ... h6 12 ♖e1 ♘e7 (12 ... b6 13 ♕f3
♗b7 14 ♕g3 ± D.Gurevich-Browne, US Ch
1986) 13 ♗f4 ♗d7 14 ♗e5 ± Miles-Hulak,
Bad Worishofen 1985

27   13 ... ♘e7 14 ♗g5 ♘g6 15 d5 ± Cebalo-
Hulak, match 1982

13 ... h6 14 ♕f3 ♖b8 15 ♕h3 ♘e7 16 ♖ad1 ±
M.Gurevich-Andersson, Leningrad 1987

28   7 a3 ♗e7 8 c5 b6 9 b4 0-0 10 g3 bc 11 dc
a5 12 ♖b1 ♘c6 13 ♗g2 ♖b8! 14 ♗f4 (14 b5
♗xc5! 15 bc ♖xb1 16 ♘xb1 ♕b6 ∞̄) 14 ... ab!
15 ♗xb8 bc ∞̄ Salov-M.Gurevich, Leningrad
1987

29   11 ... ♗d7 12 ♗d3 a4 13 0-0 0-0 14 f4 ±
Korchnoi-Karpov, match (3) 1978

30   12 ♗b5+ ♗d7 13 0-0 0-0 14 f4 g6 15 ♖ac1
(15 ♖ae1!? ♗xb5 16 ♘xb5 b6 Miles-Short,
Esbjerg 1984) 15 ... ♗xb5 16 ♘xb5 ♘c6
17 ♖c3 ±/∞ W.Schmidt-Stempin, Prague Z
1985

31   14 ♗c2 ♗d7 15 0-0 0-0 16 ♖fe1 ♗c6
17 ♕d3 g6 18 h4 ♘d7 ±/∞

32   8 ♘f4 d5 (8 ... d6!? 9 ♗e2 e5 Hort-van der
Wiel, Amsterdam 1983) 9 cd ♘xd5 10 ♘cxd5
ed 11 ♗d3 ♘c6 12 0-0 ♗g5 13 ♖e1 ♕d6 =
Chernin-Eingorn, USSR Ch 1984

33   10 g3 ♗c5 11 ♗g2 d6 12 h3 a6 13 0-0
♘bd7 14 ♘d4 ♘e5 = Chandler-Andersson,
Malta Ol 1980

10 d6 ♗f8 11 g3 ♖e6 12 ♗f4 ♘h5 13 ♗e3
♖xd6 14 ♕c2 ∞̄ Korchnoi-Kindermann, Beer-
Sheva 1984

34   10 ... d6 11 h3 ♘bd7 12 ♘g3 ± Kasparov-
Andersson, Moscow 1981

35   11 ... d6 12 ♘g3 ♗f6+ (12 ... ♘h6
13 ♗b5! ± Gligorić-Sosonko, Plovdiv 1983)
13 ♗e2 ± Kir.Georgiev-Littlewood, Plovdiv
1983

11 ... ♗f6 12 h3 ♗xd4 (12 ... ♘e5 13 ♘e4 ±)
13 ♕xd4 ♘e5 14 f4 ♘g6 15 g3 ± Seirawan-
Karlsson, Lucerne Ol 1982

36   13 f4? ♗f5 14 ♕d2 ♘d7 ∓ Lukov-Horvath,
Plovdiv 1983

37   14 ♗e2 ♗xd4 (14 ... ♘f5 15 ♗xf6 ♕xf6
16 0-0 ± Paunović-Maksimović, Yugoslavia
1983) 15 ♕xd4 ♘f5 16 ♕f4 ± Kir.Georgiev-
Qi, Thessaloniki Ol 1984

38   10 b4 ♗b6 11 ♘a4 ♖e8 12 ♘xb6 ab 13 d6
♘e4 14 ♗b2 b5! ∓ Davidović-Maksimović,
Niš 1985

39   10 ... d6 11 ♗e2 a6 12 0-0 ♘bd7 13 ♗g5?!
(13 ♗e3 ♖e8 – 10 ... ♖e8) 13 ... h6 14 ♗h4?!
♖e8 15 ♖c1 ♘f8 ∓ Gligorić-Short, London
1980-81

40   14 h3?! ♘e4 = Bagirov-Robatsch, Erevan
1982

14 ♕c2 ±/∞

14 ♖c1 ±/∞

211

	5	6	7	8	9	10	11	12	13	
1	♘e2	cd	g3	♗g2	0-0	f3	e4	fe	♗g5	=
	d5[1]	ed[2]	c6	♖e8[3]	♘bd7[4]	♘b6	de	♗g4	♗e7[5]	
2	...	a3	cd[7]	b4[8]	♘g3	♗d3	0-0	b5	a4	∞
	...	♗e7[6]	ed	♘bd7[9]	♘b6	c6	♘e8	♘c7	a5[10]	
3	...	...	...	♕c2[11]	♗d2[12]	g3	♗g2	♘xd4	0-0	=
	...	...	♘xd5	♘d7	♘5f6[13]	e5	ed	♘e5	c5[14]	
4	♗d3	a3[16]	♗xc4[17]	♘f3[18]	e4[19]	d5	h3	0-0	♖e1	±
	d5[15]	dc	♗d6	♘c6	e5	♘e7	a6	h6	♘g6[20]	
5	...	...	bc	♗xc4	♘e2[22]	0-0	♗b2[24]	f3	♕b3[25]	=
	...	♗xc3+	dc[21]	c5	♘c6[23]	e5	♗f5	♕b6	♘a5[26]	
6	...	♘e2	0-0[27]	ed	♗xc4	a3[28]	♕d3	d5	♘xe4	∞
	...	c5	cd	dc	♘c6	♗d6[29]	e5[30]	e4	♘e5[31]	
7	...	...	cd	a3[33]	ab	♘xc3	b5	0-0	♗e2	±/∞
	...	...	ed[32]	cd	dc	♘c6[34]	♘e5	♕c7[35]	♖d8[36]	
8	...	...	♗xc4	0-0[37]	a3[39]	♘b5	♘xd6	h3	b3	∞
	...	dc	e5	♘c6[38]	♗d6	e4	♕xd6	♗e6	♖fe8[40]	

[1] 5 ... ♖e8 6 a3 ♗f8 7 d5 a5 (7 ... ed 8 cd c5 9 ♘g3 d6 10 ♗e2 a6 11 a4 g6 12 0-0 ♘bd7 13 e4 h5! ∞ Bagirov-Didishko, USSR 1984) 8 g3 ♘a6 9 b3 ♘c5 10 ♗b2 c6 ∞ D.Gurevich-Kavalek, US Ch 1985

[2] 6 ... ♘xd5 7 ♗d2 ♘d7 (7 ... ♘f6 8 ♘g3 c5 9 a3 ♗xc3 10 bc ♘c6 11 f4 b6 ∞ Lerner-Osnos, USSR 1981) 8 g3 ♘xc3 9 bc ♗a5 10 ♗g2 e5 11 0-0 ♖e8 ∞ Taimanov-Speelman, Baku 1983

[3] 8 ... a5 9 0-0 ♘a6 10 f3 c5 (10 ... ♖e8 11 e4 ± Oll-A.Sokolov, USSR 1985) 11 a3 ♗xc3 12 bc ± Utasi-Sax, Szirak 1985

[4] 9 ... ♘f8 10 h3 (10 f3 c5 11 dc ♗xc5 12 ♘f4 ♖xe3! = M.Gurevich-Tukmakov, Jurmala 1985) 10 ... ♘a6 11 g4 h5 12 f3 hg 13 fg ♘c7 14 ♘g3 ♘h7 15 ♗d2 g6 ∞ Arkhipov-Geller, USSR 1983

[5] 14 e5 ♗xe2 15 ♘xe2 ♘fd5 16 ♗xe7 ♕xe7 = Garcia Palermo-Spassky, Vienna 1986

[6] 6 ... ♗d6 7 c5 ♗e7 8 b4 b6 (8 ... ♘bd7!? 9 g3 e5 D.Gurevich-Dzindzihashvili, USA 1984) 9 ♘g3 c6 10 f4 ♘e8 11 ♗d3 f5 = Kasparov-Kurajica, Banja Luka 1979

[7] 7 ♘g3 c5 =
7 ♘f4 c6 8 b3 ♘bd7 9 ♗d3 ♗d6! = Hort-

Scheeren, Wijk aan Zee 1983

[8] 8 h3 c6 9 g4 a5 10 ♘g3 g6 11 g5 ♘e8 12 h4 ♗e6 13 f4 ♘d6 ∞ Züger-Kindermann, Biel 1986
8 g3 c6 9 ♗g2 ♖e8 10 0-0 a5 11 h3 ♘bd7 12 ♕c2 ♘f8 13 ♗d2 ♘e6 14 ♖ad1 ♘g5 15 g4 h6 16 ♗c1 b5 ∞ M.Gurevich-Geller, USSR Ch 1985

[9] 8 ... c6 9 ♘g3 ♖e8 10 ♗d3 a5 11 b5 c5 12 0-0 ♘bd7 ∞ Henley-Peters, US Ch 1984

[10] Salov-Gavrikov, USSR Ch 1987

[11] 8 e4 ♘xc3 9 ♘xc3 (9 bc c5 10 g3 cd 11 cd e5! 12 d5 f5! ∓ Kagan-Shakarov, USSR 1981) 9 ... c5 10 d5 ed 11 ♘xd5 ♘c6 12 ♗c4 ♘f6! = Torre-Korchnoi, Lucerne Ol 1982

[12] 9 g3 ♘xc3 10 ♘xc3 c5 11 dc ♘xc5 12 b4 ♘d7 13 ♗g2 a5 = D.Gurevich-Korchnoi, Beer-Sheva 1987

[13] 9 ... c5 10 ♘xd5 ed 11 ♘f4 cd 12 ♘xd5 de 13 ♘xe3 ♘f6 = Petrosian-Korchnoi, match 1980

[14] 13 ... c6 14 h3 ♖e8 15 ♖ad1 ± Garcia Palermo-Suba, Dortmund 1985
13 ... c5 =

[15] 5 ... c5 6 d5 (6 ♘e2 d5 = 5 ... d5) 6 ... b5! 7 de bc 8 ef+ ♔h8 9 ♗xc4 d5 10 ♗d3 ♘c6 ∞∞

Bagirov-Averbakh, USSR 1980

[16] 6 cd ed 7 ♘e2 ♗d6 8 a3 a5 9 ♕c2 (9 ♘g3 ♖e8 10 0-0 c6 11 ♕c2 ♘a6 12 ♗d2 c5! = Martin-Farago, Hastings 1984-85) 9 ... ♘a6 10 ♗d2 c6 11 ♘g3 ♖e8 12 ♘ce2 ♘c7 13 f3 ♘e6 = Chernin-Kavalek, Subotica IZ 1987

[17] 7 ♗xh7+ ♘xh7 8 ab ♘c6 9 b5 (9 ♘f3!? ♘xb4 10 0-0) 9 ... ♘b4 10 ♘f3 ♘d3+ 11 ♔f1 ♘f6 12 ♘d2 e5 13 ♘xc4 ed 14 ♕xd3 dc $\overline{\infty}$

[18] 8 ♕c2 ♘bd7 9 ♘f3 c5 10 dc ♗xc5 11 0-0 b6 = Vaganian-A.Sokolov, match 1986

[19] **9 ♗b5** e5 10 ♗xc6 ed 11 ed bc 12 0-0 ♘d5 = Christiansen-Tal, Moscow IZ 1982

9 b4 e5 10 d5 ♘e7 11 ♗b2 ♗g4 12 ♕c2 ± Christiansen-Garcia Gonzalez, Moscow IZ 1982

[20] 14 ♗f1 ♗d7 15 ♗e3 ♕e7 16 ♘d2 ± Lerner-A.Sokolov, USSR Ch 1984

[21] 7 ... c5 8 cd ed 9 ♘e2 b6 (9 ... ♘c6 10 0-0 b6 11 f3 ♖e8 12 ♖a2 ♘a5 13 ♘g3 ♗b7 14 ♖e2 ± M.Gurevich-Agzamov, USSR Ch 1985) 10 0-0 ♗a6 11 f3 ♗xd3 12 ♕d3 ♖e8 13 ♘g3 ♘c6 14 ♖a2 ♖c8 15 ♖e2 ± -

[22] 9 ♗b2 ♕a5 10 ♕d2 ♘e4 11 ♕c2 ♘d6 12 ♗d3 cd 13 ed e5 14 ♘e2 ed (14 ... e4?! 15 ♗xe4 ♘xe4 16 ♕xe4 ♕b5 17 ♕c2 ♗f5 18 c4 ♖c8 19 ♖c1! ±) 15 ♗xh7+ (15 0-0 ♗f5) 15 ... ♔h8 16 0-0 g6 17 ♗xg6 fg 18 ♕xg6 ♘c4 19 ♕h6+ = Shakarov

[23] 9 ... ♕c7 10 ♗d3 (10 ♗a2 b6 11 0-0 ♗a6 12 ♖e1 ♘c6 13 ♘g3 ♖ad8 14 ♗b2 e5 15 ♖c1 ♘a5 16 e4 ♗c4 = Glazstein-Shakarov, USSR 1980) 10 ... b6 11 0-0 ♗a6 12 e4 ± Timman-Kavalek, Bugojno 1980

[24] 11 ♗a2 cd 12 cd ed 13 ed ♗e6 14 ♗xe6 fe =

[25] 13 ♕d2 ♘a5 14 ♗a2 ♗e6 15 de ♗xa2 ∓ McCambridge-King, Reykjavik 1984, and Raičević-Plaskett, Troon 1984

[26] Razvalayev-Shakarov, corr. 1985

[27] 7 a3 ♗xc3 8 bc – 6 a3

[28] 10 ♕d3 ♘a5 11 ♗b5 ♗d7 12 ♗g5 ♗e7 = 10 ♗g5 ♗e7 11 a3 a6 12 ♖c1 b5 13 ♗a2 ♗b7 14 ♕d3 ♘e5 15 ♕h3 ♘c4 = Hoi-Chernin, Copenhagen 1984

[29] 10 ... ♗xc3 11 bc e5 12 ♗g5 ♕d6 13 ♗a2! ± Chekhov-Makarichev, Moscow 1986

[30] 11 ... b6 12 ♖d1 ♗b7 13 ♕h3 ♘a5 14 ♗a2 ♖c8 ∞ D.Gurevich-Fedorowicz, New York 1982, and Kir.Georgiev-Langeweg, Amsterdam 1985

[31] 14 ♕d4 ♘xe4 15 ♕xe4 ♗g4 ∞ Zakharov-Vaiser, USSR 1982, and Meulders-Kasparov, Brussels 1987

[32] **7 ... cd** 8 ed ♘xd5 9 0-0 ♘c6 – 4 ... c5
7 ... ♘xd5 8 a3 cd 9 ab dc 10 bc ♘c6 11 e4 ♘b6 (Meulders-Karpov, Brussels 1987) 12 f4 ±

[33] 8 0-0 ♘c6 9 a3 cd 10 ed ♗d6 (10 ... ♗xc3 11 bc ± Kasparov-Tal, Brussels 1987) 11 f3 h6 12 ♔h1 (12 g4!? Tal) 12 ... ♘h5! ∞ Tal-Sax, Subotica IZ 1987

[34] 10 ... ♗g4 11 f3 ♗h5 12 ♗e2 ♗g6 13 b5 ♕d6 14 ♖a4 ± Bareyev-Agdestein, Gausdal 1986

[35] 12 ... ♗g4 13 f3 d4 14 ♗xh7+! ♔xh7 (14 ... ♔xh7 15 ed!) 15 ♕xd4 ± Kir.Georgiev-Spassov, Bulgarian Ch 1984

[36] 14 ♕d4 b6 15 b3 ♘eg4 (15 ... ♗f5 16 ♗b2 ♘g6 17 g4! ± Keene-Langeweg, Holland 1980) 16 ♗xg4 ♘xg4 17 f4 ±/∞ Cebalo-Gligorić, Yugoslav Ch 1986

[37] 8 a3 ♗d6 9 de ♗xe5 10 ♕xd8 ♖xd8 = D.Gurevich-Speelman, Hastings 1983-84, and Tatai-Sax, Rome 1985

[38] 8 ... ed!? 9 ♘xd4 ♘bd7

[39] 9 d5 ♘e7 10 e4 ♘g6 11 a3 ♗d6 12 f3 ♘h5 ∞ Suba-Szekely, Tallinn 1983

[40] **13 ...** ♘a5 14 ♗d2! ± Cebalo-Suba, Vršac 1983
13 ... ♖fe8 14 a4 a5 15 ♗a3 ♘b4 ∞ Cebalo

213

Nimzo-Indian X | 1 d4 ♘f6 2 c4 e6 3 ♘c3 ♗b4 4 e3 0-0 5 ♗d3 d5 6 ♘f3 c5 7 0-0[1]

	7	8	9	10	11	12	13	14	15	
1	...	cd	♘e5	♗d2	a3	♗xc3	♘xc6	dc	b4	±
	b6[2]	ed	♗b7[3]	♘c6	♗xc3	♖e8	♗xc6	bc	d4[4]	
2	...	♗xc4	♕e2[6]	a4	♘a2	♗d3	b4![8]	ab	♗a3	±
	dc	♘bd7[5]	a6[7]	♕c7	b5	♗a5	cb	b3	ba[9]	
3	...	...	ed	♕e2	♖d1	♗d3	♗d2	♗a6[14]	♖ac1	=
	...	cd	b6[10]	♗b7	♘bd7[11]	♖c8[12]	♗d6[13]	♕c7	♕b8[15]	
4	...	...	...	♗g5	♖c1	♖e1[16]	♗d3[17]	♕e2	♗b5	=
	...	...	...	♗b7	♘bd7	♖c8	♖e8[18]	♗e7[19]	♘d5[20]	
5	...	...	...	...	♘e5	♕e2[22]	bc	♘xd7	♖ac1	=
	...	...	...	...	♘bd7[21]	♗xc3	♕c7	♘xd7	e5[23]	
6	...	a3	bc	cd[26]	♘h4[27]	g3[28]	♖e1	♗g2	f3	∞
	♘c6	♗xc3[24]	♕c7[25]	ed	♘e7	♗h3	♘g6	♕d7	♗f5[29]	

1 d4 ♘f6 2 c4 e6 3 ♘c3 ♗b4 4 e3 0-0 5 ♗d3 d5 6 ♘f3 c5 7 0-0 ♘c6 8 a3 ♗xc3 9 bc dc 10 ♗xc4 ♕c7[30]

	11	12	13	14	15	16	17	18	19	
7	♗d3[31]	♕c2	e4[32]	cd	♕xc5[34]	gf	♗e3[36]	♗xe4	fe	=
	e5	♖e8	ed[33]	♗g4	♗xf3![35]	♕d7	♘xe4	♖xe4	♕g4+	
8	♗e2	d5[38]	♘e1[39]	f4	gf	♖f2[40]	e4	♗f4[41]	♗xe5	=
	e5[37]	e4	♘e5	ef	♗h3	♖ad8	h6	♘h5	♕xe5[42]	

---

1 7 a3 cd 8 ed (8 ab dc3 9 c5 b6! ∓) 8 ... ♗xc3+ 9 bc dc 10 ♗xc4 ♕c7 11 ♕d3 ♘bd7 12 0-0 e5 =

2 7 ... ♘bd7 8 a3 ♗a5 9 cd ed 10 b4! cb 11 ♘b5 a6 12 ♕b3! ba 13 ♘d6 ♗c7 14 ♗xa3 ♗xd6 15 ♗xd6 ♖e8 16 ♖fc1 ±/± Gligorić-Andersson, Berlin 1971, and Pinter-Gheorghiu, Baile Herculana Z 1982

3 **9 ... ♗xc3** 10 bc ♗a6 11 f3 ± Portisch-Panno, Wijk aan Zee 1978

9 ... ♖e8 10 ♗d2 ♗a6 11 ♗xa6 ♘xa6 12 ♕a4 ± Portisch-Spassky, match 1977

4 16 ed cd 17 ♗b2 ♕d5 18 f3 ± Gligorić-Ljubojević, match 1979, and Gligorić-Bukić, Yugoslavia 1979

5 **8 ... ♗d7** 9 ♕e2 ♗c6 10 ♖d1 ♕e7 11 a3 ♗a5 (11 ... ♗xc3 12 bc ♘bd7 13 a4 ± Gligorić-Taimanov, Montilla 1977) 12 ♗d2 ♗xf3 13 ♕xf3 ♘c6 14 dc ♕xc5 15 ♗f1 ± Korchnoi-Matanović, Palma de Mallorca 1968, and Boudy-Vilela, Cuban Ch 1982

8 ... ♕e7 9 a3 ♗a5 10 ♕d3 ♘bd7 (10 ... ♖d8 11 ♘e4 ±) 11 ♘e4 ♗c7 12 ♘xf6+ ♘xf6 (12 ... ♕xf6 13 ♗d2 ±) 13 e4 ±

8 ... ♘c6 9 a3 ♗a5 (9 ... ♗xc3 - 7 ... ♘c6) 10 ♗a2 ♗b6 (10 ... a6 11 ♗b1 ♗b6 12 ♕c2! g6 13 dc ♗xc5 14 b4 ± Polugayevsky-Karpov, match 1974) 11 dc ♗xc5 12 b4 ±

6 9 a3 cd 10 ♕xd4 (10 ab dc 11 bc ♕c7

12 ♕b3 ♘b6 13 ♗e2 e5 = Timman-Keene, Reykjavik 1976) 10 ... ♗xc3 11 ♕xc3 ♕c7 12 ♕b3 (Miles-Ribli, Tilburg 1984) 12 ... ♘b6 intending ... ♗d7 = Miles

7 9 ... b6 10 d5 (10 ♖d1 cd 11 ed ♗b7 - 8 ... cd) 10 ... ♗xc3 11 de ♘e5 12 ef+ ♔h8 13 bc ♗g4 14 e4 ♕e7 15 ♖e1 (15 ♖d1 ♘xc4 16 ♕xc4 ♕xe4 = Portisch-Ljubojević, Montreal 1979) 15 ... b5 16 ♗xb5 ♘h5 17 ♗c4 ♕f6 18 ♗g5! ♗xf3 19 ♗xf6 ♗xe2 20 ♗d5! ± Knaak-Lukacs, Berlin 1982

8 13 ab ab 14 ♗xb5 ♗b7 15 ♖d1 ♖fb8 = Karpov-Portisch, Moscow 1981

9 16 ♗xf8 ♕xf8 (16 ... ♘xf8 17 ba ± Azmaiparashvili-Rashkovsky, Baku 1983) 17 ba ♘d5 18 ♕xa2 ♗c3 19 ♖ac1 ♕a5 ± Azmaiparashvili-A.Sokolov, USSR 1984

10 9 ... a6 10 a4 ♘c6 (10 ... ♕a5 11 ♗g5 ♘d5 12 ♘e4 ± Spassky-Petrosian, USSR 1975) 11 ♗g5 h6 12 ♗h4 ♗e7 13 ♖e1 ♗d7 14 ♗g3 ♘b4 15 ♘e5 ± Pinter-Psakhis, Las Palmas IZ 1982

11 11 ... ♗xc3 12 bc ♘bd7 (12 ... ♕c7 13 ♗d3! ♕xc3 14 ♗b2 ♕c7 15 d5 ± Belyavsky-Kasparov, match 1983) 13 ♗d3 ♖c8 14 c4 ± Plachetka-Groszpeter, Trnava 1983

12 12 ... ♖e8 13 ♗g5 ♗xc3 14 bc ♕c7 15 ♖ac1 (15 c4 e5!) 15 ... h6 16 ♗h4 ♘h5 = Knaak-Suba, East Germany v Romania 1983

[13] 13 ... ♗xc3 14 bc ♕c7 15 ♖ac1 ♖fe8 16 ♖e1 ♕d6 = Scheeren-Ribli, Wijk aan Zee 1983

[14] 14 ♗g5 h6 15 ♗h4 ♕c7 16 ♘b5 ♕b8 17 ♘e5 ♗xe5 18 de ♕xe5 19 ♘d6 ∞/= Knaak-Pinter, East Germany v Hungary 1980

[15] Petran-Sax, Hungary 1983

[16] 12 ♗d3 ♗e7 13 ♗b1 ♖e8 14 ♕d3 ♘f8 15 ♘e5 ♘g6! = Dolmatov-A.Rodriguez, Moscow 1985

12 ♕e2 ♗xc3 13 ♖xc3 (13 bc ♕c7 14 ♗d3 ♘g4 15 ♗e4 =) 13 ... ♕b8 14 ♗h4 ♘e4 15 ♖e3 ♕f4 16 ♖e1 ♖ac8 = Knaak-Inkiov, East Germany v Bulgaria 1982

[17] 13 ♕b3 ♗xc3 (13 ... ♕e7? 14 ♗d5! ± Browne-Ljubojević, Tilburg 1978) 14 ♖xc3 h6 15 ♗h4 ♗d5! = Podgayets-Ubilava, USSR 1979

[18] 13 ... ♗e7 14 ♕e2 ♘d5 15 ♕e4 (15 ♘xd5 ♗xg5 16 ♖xc8 ♗xc8 17 ♘b4 ♗b7 18 ♗e4 ♗e7 = Timman-Polugayevsky, Moscow 1981) 15 ... g6 16 ♗h4 ♗xg5 17 ♘xg5 ♘7f6 18 ♕h6 ∞ ½-½ Gligorić-Polugayevsky, Plovdiv 1983

... ♗xc3 14 bc ♕c7 15 ♗h4 ♕f4 ∞ Flear-Tatai, Graz 1984

[19] 14 ... ♗xc3 15 bc ♕c7 16 ♗h4 ♘h5 17 ♕e3 (17 ♗xh7+? ♔xh7 18 ♘g5+ ♔g6 19 g4 ♕f4! 20 gh+ ♔h6 ∓ Knaak-Sturua, Trnava 1980) 17 ... ♘df6 18 ♘e5 ♘d5 ∞ Gligorić-Browne, Novi Sad 1979, and Littlewood-Chandler, England 1981

[20] Balashov-Sosonko, Hanover 1983

[21] 11 ... ♘c6 12 ♗xf6 ♕xf6 13 ♘d7 ♕h4 14 ♘xf8 ♖xf8 ∞/± Farago-Rigo, Hungarian Ch 1976

11 ... h6 12 ♗h4 ♗e7 13 ♖e1 ♘c6 (13 ... ♘d5!? 14 ♗xe7 ♘xe7 15 ♘xf7!? Stoica) 14 ♗a6! ± F.Portisch-Stoica, Athens 1985

[22] 12 ♘xd7 ♕xd7 13 ♗xf6 gf 14 ♕g4+ ♔h8 15 ♕h4 ♖g8! 16 d5 ♗xc3 17 bc ♖g6 18 ♖fd1 ♗xd5 19 ♗xd5 ed 20 c4 ♕g4 21 ♕xg4 ♖xg4 22 c4 ♖c4 = Nekrasov-Vdovin, corr. 1979

[23] 15 ... ♖ac8 16 ♗d3 ♕c6 17 f3 ± Knaak-Vaiser, Szirak 1985

15 ... e5 16 ♗b5 ♗c6 = Vaiser

[24] 8 ... ♗a5 9 cd ed 10 dc ♗xc3 11 bc ♗g4 (11 ... ♕a5 12 ♕c2 ♕xc5 13 a4 ±) 12 c4 ♘e5 13 cd ♗xf3 (13 ... ♘xf3+ 14 gf ♗h3 15 e4 ±) 14 gf ♕xd5 15 ♗e2 ♕xc5 16 ♗b2 ±

8 ... cd 9 ed ♗xc3 10 bc dc 11 ♗xc4 ♕a5 12 ♕e1 (12 ♕c2 e5 =) 12 ... b6 13 ♗g5 ♘d5 14 ♗d3! ♗a6 15 c4 ± Eingorn

[25] 9 ... b6 10 cd ed 11 ♘e5 ♕c7 12 ♘xc6 ♕xc6 13 f3 ±

[26] 10 ♕e2 dc, 10 ♖e1 dc, 10 ♗b2 dc – 9 ... dc

[27] 11 a4 ♖e8 12 ♗a3 c4 13 ♗c2 ♘e4 =

11 h3 c4 12 ♗c2 ♘e7 13 ♘d2 ♗f5 14 a4 ♖fe8 = Azmaiparashvili-Shnaider, USSR 1983

[28] 12 a4 ♖e8 13 ♗a3 c4 14 ♗c2 ♘g6 15 ♘f5 ♘e4 16 ♗xe4 ♖xe4 17 ♘g3 ♖e8 18 ♕h5 ♕d7 19 a5 f5 ∞ Portisch-Byrne, Bugojno 1978

12 ♖a2 ♘g6 13 ♘xg6 hg 14 f3 ♗f5 15 ♗e2 ♖ac8 16 g4 ♗d7 ∞ Yusupov-A.Sokolov, match 1986

[29] 16 ♗xf5 ♕xf5 17 g4 ♕c8 18 g5 ♘e8 19 a4 ♘d6 ∞ Knaak-Averbakh, Polanica Zdroj 1976

16 ♗f1 h5! (16 ... cd 17 g4! ♗e6 18 cd ± Shashin-Osnos, USSR 1980) 17 ♖a2 ♖ac8 ∞

[30] 10 ... ♕e7 11 a4 ± Portisch-Miles, Tilburg 1981

[31] 11 a4 e5 12 ♗a3 e4 13 ♘d2 b6 =

11 ♖e1 e5 12 d5 ♘a5 13 d6 ♕d8 14 ♘xe5 ♘xc4 15 ♘xc4 ♗e6 16 ♘b2 (16 ♕d3? ♘g4! ∓ O.Rodriguez-F.Olafsson, Las Palmas 1978) 16 ... ♘e4 =

11 ♕e2 e5 12 d5 e4 13 dc ♗g4 (13 ... ♘g4 14 g3 ef 15 ♕xf3 ♘e5 =) 14 cb ♕xb7 (14 ... ♖ae8!?) 15 ♕b2 ♕xb2 16 ♗xb2 ef = Hübner-Chandler, Biel 1987

11 ♕c2 e5 12 ♗b5 e4 13 ♘g5 a6 14 ♗c4 ♘a5 15 ♗a2 ♗f5 16 f3 ♖ae8 17 fe ♘g6! = H.Olafsson-Zaltsman, Reykjavik 1982

[32] 13 ♘xe5 ♘xe5 14 de ♕xe5 15 f3 ♗d7 16 a4 ♖ad8 17 e4 (17 ♖a3 ♗c6 18 c4 ♖d6 ∞ Hort-Miles, Amsterdam 1981) 17 ... ♗c6 18 ♗c4 ♖d7 = Portisch-Spassky, match 1977

[33] 13 ... c4 14 ♗xc4 ed 15 cd ♘a5 16 ♗d3 ♕xc2 17 ♗xc2 ♘xe4 18 ♖e1 ♗f5 19 ♗f4 ♘d6 20 ♗a4 b5 21 ♗xd6 ± Kiprov-Yudovich, corr. 1976

[34] 15 e5 ♗xf3 16 ef ♘xd4 17 ♗xh7+ ♔h8 18 fg+ ♔xg7 19 ♗b2 ♖ad8 20 ♖fc1! (20 gf? ♖h8 21 ♔h1 ♔f8 22 ♕e4 f5! 23 ♕h4 ♖xh7 24 ♕f6+ ♘e8 25 ♖fe1+ ♔d7 26 ♖e5 ♔c8 27 ♗xd4 cd 28 ♕xf5+ ♔b8 ∓) 20 ... ♖h8 21 ♕xc5 ♕xc5 22 ♖xc5 ♔xh7 23 ♗xd4 ♖hg8 24 ♗e5 = Euwe

[35] 15 ... ♘xe4 16 ♗xe4 ♖xe4 17 ♘g5 ± Bronstein-Euwe, Zürich C 1953

[36] 17 d5? ♘e5 18 ♗e2 ♕h3 19 ♕e3 ♘xd5 20 ed ♘g6 ∓ Rovner

[37] 11 ... ♖d8 12 c4 e5 13 d5 e4 14 ♘d2 ♘e5 15 f4 ef 16 gf ± Gligorić-Ljubojević, Bugojno 1982

11 ... b6!? 12 a4 ♗b7 13 ♗a3 ♖fd8 14 ♕c2 ♘a5 =

[38] 12 ♕c2 e4 (12 ... ♗g4 13 d5! ♘a5 14 e4 ± Knaak-Prandstetter, Bratislava 1983) 13 ♘d2 ♗f5 =

[39] 13 dc ♘g4 14 g3 ef 15 ♗xf3 ♘e5 16 ♗g2 ♘xc6 =

[40] 16 ♘g2 ♖ad8 17 e4 ♘g6 18 ♗g5 ♕e5 19 ♕d2 ♗xg2 20 ♔xg2 h6 21 ♗xf6 ♘f4+ 22 ♔h1 ♕xf6 ∓ Knaak-Tomoshchenko, Polanica Zdroj 1976

[41] 18 ♗g2?! ♘g6 19 ♕d2 ♘h5 20 f4 ♗xg2 21 ♔xg2 ♘f6 22 ♗d3 ♖fe8 23 ♖e2 c4 ∓ Kats-Shakarov, corr. 1977

18 ♘d3!?

[42] 20 ♘d3 ♕g5+ 21 ♔h1 ♘f4 =

1 d4 ♘f6 2 c4 e6 3 ♘c3 ♗b4 4 e3 0-0 5 ♗d3 d5 6 ♘f3 c5 7 0-0 ♘c6 8 a3 ♗xc3 9 bc dc 10 ♗xc4 ♕c7[30]

	11	12	13	14	15	16	17	18	19	
9	♗a2	h3[43]	♘h2	♘g4	hg	a4	♕e2[45]	♗a3	♗c4[46]	∞
	e5	e4	♗f5[44]	♘xg4	♗g6	♖ad8	♖fe8	b6	♘a5[47]	
10	♗b2	♗e2	♕c2	de	c4	gf	♖ad1	♕b3		=
	e5	♖d8[48]	♗g4	♘xe5	♘xf3+	♗h5[49]	♗g6	♘d7[50]		

[43] **12 d5** e4 13 dc ef 14 ♕xf3 ♗g4 15 ♕g3 ♕xc6 =
12 ♕c2 e4 13 ♘d2 (13 ♘g5 ♗f5 14 f3 ♖ae8 15 g4?! ♗g6 ∓ Belyavsky-Kupreichik, USSR 1983) 13 ... ♗f5 14 f3 ♖ae8 ∞

[44] 13 ... ♘a5!? 14 f3 b6! ∞ Keene-Zaltsman, New York 1980

[45] 17 f4 ef 18 ♕xf3 ♖fe8 19 ♗a3 cd 20 cd ♖xd4! 21 ed ♘xd4 = Shakarov

[46] **19 ♖ad1** ♔h8 20 ♖d2 f5 = Kagan-Shakarov, corr. 1977
19 f4!?

[47] 20 ♗a6 f6 ∞ Knaak-Kir.Georgiev, East Germany v Bulgaria 1986

[48] 12 ... e4 13 ♘d2 ♗f5 14 c4 ♖fe8 15 d5 ♘e5 16 ♖e1 ♖ad8 (16 ... ♗g6 17 a4 ♖ab8 18 ♖a3 ♘fd7 19 f4 ± Flear-Spassky, London 1986) 17 a4 ♕e7 ∞

[49] 16 ... ♗h3 17 ♖fe1! (17 ♖fd1 ♖xd1 18 ♖xd1 ♖d8 =) 17 ... ♕c6 18 ♖ad1! (18 ♕c3 ♖d2! 19 ♗f1! ♕xf3 20 ♕xd2 ♗g4+ =) 18 ... ♖xd1 19 ♖xd1 ♖e8 20 ♕c3 ♘h5 21 ♔h1 ± Shakarov

[50] Korchnoi-Draško, Sarajevo 1984

Modern and Pirc

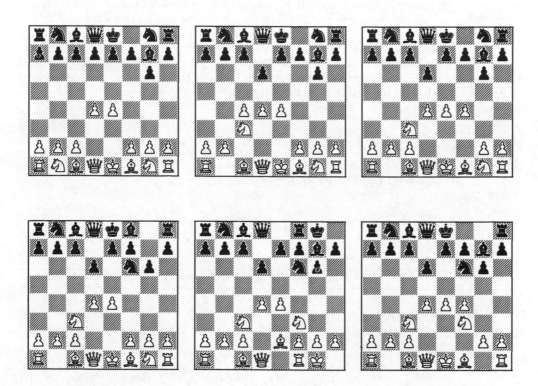

Modern (1 e4 g6 2 d4 d6 or 2 ... ♗g7)

Blood-brother of the Pirc in strategical aim, the Modern embraces subtle differences in move order. Co-author Keene has, for example, used this possibility to forge a new system against the Austrian Attack. The major difference between the Pirc and the Modern is that the lack of pressure on e4 (usually exerted by Black's recalcitrant king's knight) allows White to play 3 c4 and steer the game into channels that approximate to, or transpose into, the King's Indian Defence. Very interesting play can result from Black attempts to pressure White's d-pawn with an early ... ♘c6 or ... c5. This defence gives ample scope for innovation and improvisation, often of a highly tactical nature. It is a truly 'modern' system and has allowed players with a creative temperament (particularly Suttles and Timman) to pose problems at an early stage of the game. White must beware of reflex response in order to emerge with an edge.

217

Pirc (1 e4 d6 2 d4 ♘f6)

The paternity claims to this defence have been numerous but in common parlance Pirc has won out over Robatsch, Ufimtsev and other more peripheral characters. It was not until relatively recently that the merits of Black's system became clearly understood. Disparaged for many years as passive and eccentric, the mechanics of Pirc counterplay are now well defined. Ideally, the strategy is to undermine and explode the White centre and to establish the latent power of the fianchettoed king's bishop. As is the case with defences of a hypermodern turn, White is allowed a superiority in space which it is his task to maintain.

The first player has a wide choice of weapons, but the toughest questions are posed by the Austrian Attack (3 ♘c3 g6 4 f4). White tries to enforce a central clamp, followed by direct kingside hostilities. Black requires thorough preparation, though Seirawan appears to have defused White's attacking chances in the line 5 ... c5 (note 8, page 225). More subtle but no less threatening is the Classical Variation (3 ♘c3 g6 4 ♘f3 ♗g7 5 ♗e2). White restricts his ambitions to ensuring that his space advantage will endure – a humble goal which, however, he can almost certainly achieve. Still, his edge is not intimidating and the Pirc devotee can attain a solid position, though full equality is a more difficult matter.

Other tries for White (4 ♗c4, 4 ♗g5, 4 ♗e3) carry their own brand of trouble but are less likely to procure a pull against accurate play. Nonetheless, there is always danger involved in provocative defence and Black must be well prepared to cope with an opponent bent on his outright destruction.

References: *The Complete Pirc* (Nunn)
The Semi-Open Game in Action (Karpov)

	Modern I	1 e4 g6 2 d4 ♗g7							
	3	4	5	6	7	8	9	10	11
1	c3[1]	♘f3	♗d3[4]	0-0	♗g5[7]	♗h4	de	♘a3	♖e1	∞
	d6[2]	♘f6[3]	0-0[5]	♘c6[6]	h6[8]	e5[9]	de[10]	♗e6	♕e8[11]	
2	...	f4[12]	e5	fe	♘f3	♗c4	dc[16]	♕d4	♕e4	∞
	...	♘f6[13]	de[14]	♘d5	0-0	c5![15]	♗e6	♘c6	♘a5![17]	
3	♘c3	dc[18]	♗d2[19]	♘d5	♘f3	♗c3	♘xc3	♕d2	0-0-0	±
	c5	♕a5	♕xc5	♘a6	e6	♗xc3	♘f6	0-0	♘g4[20]	
4	...	♗e3[21]	♕d2	f3	♘h3	♘f2[25]	♗xd4	♗e2	g4	∞/±
	d6	a6[22]	♘d7[23]	b5	c5[24]	cd	♘gf6	♗b7	h6[26]	
5	...	♗c4!	♕f3	♘ge2	♗d3	ed[29]	♗f4	0-0-0	h3[30]	±
	c6	d6[27]	e6	d5[28]	♘d7	ed	♘e7	0-0		
6	♘f3	♘c3	♗e3	♗e2	d5[33]	♘d2	g4!	♖g1	g5	±
	d6	♗g4[31]	♘c6	e5[32]	♘ce7	♗d7	c5	♘c8	h6[34]	
7	...	♗c4	♕e2	♗b3	0-0	♖d1	♘bd2	e5	♘f1	±
	...	♘f6[35]	c6[36]	0-0	♘a6[37]	♘c7	d5	♘fe8	♗g4[38]	

[1] 3 f4 c5 (3 ... d6 4 ♘f3 ♘f6 5 e5 de 6 fe ♘d5 7 ♗c4 ♘b6 8 ♗b3 c5 9 c3 ± Belyavsky-Azmaiparashvili, USSR Ch 1986) 4 c3 d5 (4 ... cd =) 5 e5 ♘c6 (5 ... f6!? 6 ef ♘xf6 7 dc 0-0 ∞ Ivkov) 6 dc f6 7 ♘f3 fe 8 fe ♘xe5 9 ♘xe5 ♗xe5 ∞ Plachetka-Rakić, 1978

[2] 3 ... c5?! 4 dc ♘a6 5 ♗e3 ♕c7 6 ♗xa6 ba 7 ♘d2! ±
3 ... d5 4 ed! ♕xd5 5 ♗e2 c5 6 ♗f3 ♕e6+ 7 ♘e2 ±

[3] 4 ... e6 5 ♗d3 ♘e7 6 a4! ♘d7 7 0-0 a5 8 ♘a3 ± Benko-Planinc, Novi Sad 1972

[4] 5 ♕c2 0-0 6 ♗g5 c6 7 ♘bd2 h6 8 ♗h4 g5 9 ♗g3 ♘h5 =

[5] 5 ... ♘bd7 6 e5 ±

[6] 6 ... ♘bd7 7 ♖e1 e5 8 h3 ♖e8 9 ♗g5 ± Panno-Larsen, Buenos Aires 1983
6 ... ♘h5!? 7 ♖e1 e5 ∞ O.Rodriguez-Keene, Barcelona 1980

[7] 7 d5 ♘b8 8 c4 ♗g4! 9 h3 ♗xf3 10 ♕xf3 ♘a6 = Korchnoi-Sznapik, Lucerne Ol 1982
7 ♖e1 e5 8 h3 h6 9 ♗e3 ♘h5 10 ♘bd2 ♘f4 ∞/= Dolmatov-Kuzmin, USSR 1982

[8] 7 ... ♘d7 8 a4 ♕e8 (8 ... f6 9 ♗h4 e5 ± Vaganian) 9 ♘a3 a6 10 ♕d2 f6 11 ♗h6 e5 12 ♗xg7 ♔xg7 13 b4 ♘d8 14 a5! ± Vaganian-Ermenkov, Thessaloniki Ol 1984

[9] 8 ... ♘h5 9 ♘a3 ♘f4 10 ♗c2 ♗g4 11 ♕d2 ± Tal-Hoi, Jurmala 1985

[10] 9 ... ♘xe5 10 ♘xe5 de 11 ♘a3 ♘e8 12 f3 ± Bischoff-Bilek, Budapest 1985

[11] 12 ♗b5 ♘d7 13 ♘c4 f6 ∞ Yusupov-Seirawan, Montpellier C 1985

[12] 4 ♗g5 ♘f6 5 ♘d2 0-0 (5 ... h6 6 ♗h4 e5 7 de de 8 ♘gf3 ± E.Vladimirov-Ivkov, Havana 1986) 6 f4 c5! 7 dc dc 8 ♗c4 ♘c6 9 ♘gf3 ♘a5!? 10 ♗e2 ♗g4 11 ♗b5 ♕b6! ∞ Klarić-Kasparov, Graz 1981

[13] 4 ... e5 5 de ♕h4+ 6 g3 ♕e7 7 ed ♕xe4+ 8 ♕e2 ± Portisch-Suttles, Siegen Ol 1970

[14] 5 ... ♘d5 6 ♘f3 0-0 7 ♗d3 c5 8 ♗e4 ♘c7 9 dc de 10 ♕xd8 ♖xd8 11 ♘xe5! ± Hort

[15] 8 ... ♗g4 9 0-0 e6 10 ♕b3 ♗xf3 11 ♖xf3 ♘b6 12 ♗e2 ± Petrosian

[16] 9 0-0 cd 10 ♕xd4 e6 11 ♗g5 ♘c6! ∓

[17] 12 ♗e2 ♕c7 13 ♘g5 ♕xe5 14 ♕xe5 ♗xe5 15 ♘xe6 fe ∞ Hort

[18] 4 ♘f3 ♘f6 (4 ... cd – Accelerated Fianchetto) 5 d5 0-0! 6 ♘d2 d6 7 ♗e2 ♘a6 8 0-0 ♘c7 9 a4 b6 10 ♘c4 ♗a6! = Browne-Gheorghiu, London 1980

[19] 5 ♘e2 ♘f6 6 e5 ♘g4 7 f4 ♕xc5 8 ♘e4 ♕b6 ∞

[20] 12 ♗xa6 ba 13 ♖hf1 ± Barle-Forintos, Maribor 1977

[21] 4 ♗c4 ♘c6! 5 ♗e3 ♘f6 6 f3 0-0 7 ♘ge2 e6 8 ♗b3 b6 9 ♕d2 ♗a6 ∞ Kristiansen-Keene, Reykjavik 1972
4 ♗g5!? c6 (4 ... a6 5 ♕d2 b5 6 f4 ♘d7 7 ♘f3 ♗b7 8 a4 b4 = Puhm-Keene, Haifa Ol 1976) 5 ♕d2 b5 6 f4 ♘d7 7 ♘f3 b4!? 8 ♘d1 ♕b6 9 ♘e3 h6! = Nunn

[22] 4 ... c6 5 ♕d2 b5 6 0-0-0 (6 f3!? ♘d7 7 h4 ± Hort) 6 ... ♘d7 7 ♔b1 ♕a5 ±

[23] 5 ... b5 6 0-0-0!? ♗b7 7 f3 ♘d7 8 h4 h6 9 ♘h3 ± Gufeld-Kindermann, Dortmund 1983

[24] 7 ... ♘b7 8 ♗e2 c5 9 a4! b4 10 ♘d1 ♘gf6 11 a5! ± Cardoso-Larsen, Orense 1975

[25] 8 dc?! ♘xc5 9 ♘f2 ♘d7 10 ♗e2 ♕c7 11 a3 ♖c8 ∓ Rantanen-Keene, Gausdal 1979

[26] 12 a3 ♘e5 13 ♘d5 ∞/± Ciocaltea-Botterill, Hastings 1971-72

[27] 4 ... d5 5 ed b5 6 ♗b3 b4 7 ♘ce2 cd 8 ♗d2! (8 ♘f3 ♘f6 9 0-0-0 10 a3 ba 11 ♖xa3 ± Nunn-Dresen, West Germany 1985-86) 8 ... a5 9 a3! ba 10 ♖xa3 ♘c6 11 ♘f3 ♘f6 12 ♘e5! ± Ghinda-Schneider, Dortmund 1986

[28] 6 ... ♘d7 7 a4 a5 8 h4 ±

[29] 8 e5 ∞/± Wolff-Lief, USA 1986

[30] Wilder-Zlotnikov, USA 1986

[31] 4 ... a6 5 ♗e2 (5 ♗e3 ♘d7 6 ♕d2 b5 7 a4 b4 8 ♘e2 ♘gf6 9 ♘g3 h5! ∞ Hort-Keene, Dortmund 1982) 5 ... b5 6 0-0 ♘d7 7 ♖e1 ♗b7 8 ♗g5 ± Grünfeld-Soltis, Lone Pine 1979
4 ... c6 5 ♗c4 b5 6 ♗b3 b4 7 ♘d5 a5 8 ♘e3 ± Pribyl-Kosanski, Osijek 1980

[32] 6 ... e6 7 0-0 ♘ge7 8 ♕d2 0-0 9 ♖ad1 ± Kuijpers-Keene, Wijk aan Zee 1974

[33] 7 de de 8 ♕xd8+ ♖xd8 9 ♘d5 ♖c8 10 ♗g5 ± Browne-Timman, Amsterdam 1972

[34] 12 h4 hg 13 hg a6 14 a4 ± Psakhis-Belov, USSR 1977

[35] 4 ... c6 5 ♗b3 ♘f6 6 ♕e2 – 4 ... ♘f6
4 ... e6 5 ♗b3 ♘e7 6 0-0 0-0 7 c3 b6 8 ♖e1 c5 9 a4 ♗a6 10 ♘a3 ♕d7 11 ♘c4 cd 12 ♖xd4 ± Kovačević-Plaskett, Hastings 1982-83

[36] 5 ... ♘c6 6 c3 0-0 7 0-0 ♗g4 8 h3 ♗xf3 9 ♕xf3 e5 10 ♗b5 ±

[37] 7 ... ♗g4 8 ♘bd2 ±
7 ... a5 8 e5 ♘d5 9 a4 de 10 ♘xe5 ±

[38] 12 h3 ♗xf3 13 ♕xf3 ± Shamkovich

Modern II   1 e4 g6 2 d4 ♗g7 3 c4 d6 4 ♘c3

	4	5	6	7	8	9	10	11	12	
1	...	♘f3[1]	♗e3	♗e2	♗xf3	0-0	g3	h3	♗g2	±
	c6	♗g4	♘d7	♗xf3	♘gf6	a6	h5	e5	0-0[2]	
2	...	ef	♘f3[4]	♗e2	0-0	d5	♘g5	♗d3	♘e2	±
	f5	♗xf5[3]	♘h6	0-0	♘a6	c5	♘c7	♗d7	♘f7[5]	
3	...	♘f3	d5	♗e2	0-0	a3	♖b1	♔h1	♘e1	±
	e5	♗g4	a5[6]	♘a6	♘e7	0-0	c5	♗d7	f5[7]	
4	...	♗e3	♗xd4	f3![8]	♗e3	♘ge2	♘f4	♕b3	♖d1	=/∞
	...	ed!	♘f6	♘c6	0-0	♘e5	c6	♘fd7	♕h4+![9]	
5	...	de	♕xd8+	♗g5+[10]	0-0-0+	♗e3	♗xh6	h4	h5	=
	...	de	♔xd8	f6	♘d7	♗h6!	♘xh6	c6	♔e7[11]	
6	...	d5	♗e3	♗xh6	♕d2	h3	♗d3	♘ge2	a3	=
	...	♘d7!?[12]	♗h6	♘xh6	♘g4	♘gf6	a6	♕e7	c6[13]	
7	...	♘f3[14]	♗e2[15]	0-0	♖e1[17]	♗f1	de	b3	♘b5	±
	♘d7	e5	♘e7[16]	0-0	h6	♔h7	de	c5	♘c6[18]	
8	...	♘ge2[19]	d5	♘g3[20]	♗d3	h4	a3	♗g5	♕d2	±
	♘c6	e5	♘ce7	c5	h5	a6	♘f6	0-0	♘h7[21]	
9	...	♗e3	d5![23]	g4	gf!	♕h5+	ef	♕f3	♘b5	∞
	...	e5[22]	♘ce7![24]	f5	gf	♘g6[25]	♕h4	♘6e7	♔d8	
10	...	...	...	...	h3	g5	♕d2	♘f3	0-0-0	∞
	...	...	...	♘f6![26]	h5	♘h7	0-0	♗d7	♕b8![27]	
11	...	...	...	...	g5!	h4	gh	♗xh6	♕d2	∞
	...	...	...	...	♘d7[28]	h5	♗xh6	♖xh6		

[1] 5 f4 ♕b6! 6 ♘f3 ♗g4 7 d5 ♘f6 = Uhlmann-Olafsson, Reykjavik 1968

[2] Schmid-Bronstein, Monaco 1969

[3] 5 ... gf?! 6 ♕h5+ ♔f8 intending ... ♘f6 ±

[4] 6 ♗d3 ♗xd4 7 ♗xf5 ♗xc3+ 8 bc gf 9 ♕h5+ ♔d7 = Portisch-Bilek, Sousse IZ 1967

[5] Polugayevsky-Bilek, Lipeck 1968

[6] 6 ... ♘e7 7 ♗e2 0-0 8 ♘d2 ♗c8! = Cobo-Ivkov, Havana Ol 1966

[7] Korchnoi-Hübner, Wijk aan Zee 1971

[8] 7 ♗e2 0-0 8 ♘f3 ♘c6 =

[9] Donner-Ivkov, Wijk aan Zee 1971

[10] 7 f4!? ♗e6 (7 ... ♘c6 8 fe ♗e6 9 ♗g5+ ♔c8 10 ♘f3 h6 ± Uhlmann-Larsen, Aarhus 1971; 7 ... ♘d7 8 ♘f3 c6 9 ♗e2 f6 10 0-0 ♔e8 11 g3 ± Hübner-Benko, Hungary 1978) 8 ♘f3 (8 fe ♘c6) 8 ... ♘d7 9 ♗e2 h6 10 0-0 ♘e7 11 ♘d5 ± Tarjan-Mestel, Hastings 1977/78; 9 ... c6!?

[11] 13 hg hg 14 ♘f3 ♘f8 15 ♘h4 ♗e6 = Janošević-Benko, Majdanpek 1976

[12] 5 ... ♘f6 – King's Indian

[13] Ivkov-Panno, Caracas 1970

[14] 5 f4 e5 6 d5 – King's Indian
5 ♘ge2!? e5 6 ♗e3 – cf. KI Sämisch

[15] 6 g3 ♘e7 7 ♗g2 0-0 8 0-0 ♘c6 = Velimirović

[16] 6 ... c6 7 0-0 ♘h6 ∞

[17] 8 ♗e3 f5! 9 ef gf 10 de de 11 ♗g5 h6 12 ♗h4 ± Kozma-Plachetka, Luhacovice 1969

[18] 13 ♘d6 ± Filip-Suttles, Palma IZ 1970

[19] 5 d5 ♘d4 (5 ... ♘b8!? Hartoch) 6 ♗e3 c5 7 ♘ge2 ♕b6 8 ♘a4 (8 ♕d2 ♘f6! ∞; 8 ♗xd4 cd 9 ♘a4 ♕a5+ 10 ♗d2 ±; 9 ... de!? 10 ♘xb6 ef+ 11 ♔xf2 ab ōō !?) 8 ... ♕a5+ 9 ♗d2 ♕a6 10 ♘xd4 ±

[20] 7 h4 h5 8 g3 intending ♗h3 ± *Archives*

[21] 13 ♗h6! ±/= Forintos-Uhlmann, Monaco 1968

[22] 5 ... ♘h6?! 6 h3 f5 7 ♕d2 ♘f7 8 d5 ±/± Lehmann-Shamkovich, Palma 1966

5 ... ♘f6!? (Keene) 6 f3 – King's Indian Sämisch; 6 ♗e2 e5 7 d5 ♘d4 8 ♗xd4 ed 9 ♕xd4 0-0 ōō Ligterink-Keene, Rotterdam 1981. 6 d5 ♘e5 7 f4 ♘ed7 ∞ Tal-Christiansen, Wijk aan Zee 1982; 7 ... ♘eg4!? 8 ♗d2 ♘h5! ∞

[23] 6 ♘ge2 ♘h6 7 f3 f5 8 ♕d2 ♘f7 9 0-0-0 0-0 10 ♔b1 a6 11 d5 ±

[24] 6 ... ♘d4 7 ♘ge2 ♘xe2 8 ♗xe2 ±

[25] 9 ... ♔f8 10 ♗h3 ±/±

[26] 7 ... f6 8 h4 ♘h6 9 g5 ♘f7 10 gf ♗xf6 11 ♕f3 ♗g7 12 0-0-0 ♖f8 ±/± Polugayevsky-Zaitsev, Moscow 1969

7 ... a6 8 f3 f5 9 c5 ♘f6 10 h3 0-0 11 ♕d2 ±
7 ... c5!?

[27] 13 ♔b1 ♖d8 14 c5 ♘c8! ∞

[28] 8 ... ♘h5!? intending ... ♘f4

Modern III   1 e4 g6 2 d4 Bg7 3 Nc3 d6 4 f4

	4	5	6	7	8	9	10	11	12	
1	...	Nf3	Bd3	Qe2	e5	d5	Bxb5+	dc	Bc4	±
	a6[1]	b5	Bb7	Nc6[2]	Nh6	Nb4	c6	Nxc6	0-0[3]	
2	...	Nf3	Be3	Qd2[4]	gf	0-0-0	Kb1	a3[6]	Rg1	±
	c6	Bg4	Qb6	Bxf3	Nd7[5]	Qa5	b5	Rb8	Nb6[7]	
3	...	Be3[8]	h3	g4	de	f5	ef[11]	Bg2	Qd2	±/∞
	Nc6	Nf6[9]	0-0	e5	de	gf[10]	Nd4	Qe7	Rd8[12]	

[1] 4 ... c5 5 dc Bxc3+ (5 ... Qa5 6 cd) 6 bc dc 7 Qxd8+ Kxd8 8 Bc4 e6 9 f5 ±/± Brinck Claussen-Larsen, Danish Ch 1963

[2] 7 ... **Nf6** 8 e5 ± Ljubojević-Panno, Palma de Mallorca 1972

7 ... **c5** 8 dc dc 9 e5 ± Tal-Szabo, Sochi 1973

7 ... **Nd7** 8 e5 e6 9 a4 b4 10 Ne4 ± Jansa-Vogt, Leipzig 1973

[3] 13 e6 ± Peters-Christiansen, US Ch 1984

[4] 7 Qd3 Nf6 8 Ne5 (8 0-0-0 d5 9 e5 Ne4! =) 8 ... d5! = Arnason-Soltis, New York 1986

[5] 8 ... Qxb2 9 Rb1 Qa3 10 Rxb7 ± de Firmian-Soltis, US Ch 1983

[6] 11 f5 Ngf6 12 Bd3 b4 13 Ne2 ±

[7] 13 f5 Nc4 14 Bxc4 bc 15 Ka2 ±

Mnatsakanian-Tseshkovsky, USSR 1983

[8] **5 d5** Nd4 6 Be3 c5 = Handoko-Keene, Indonesia 1982

5 Nf3 Bg4 6 Be3 Bxf3 7 gf d5 8 Qd2 e6 9 0-0-0 Nge7 10 h4 h5 ∞ de Firmian-Kristiansen, Copenhagen 1985

[9] 5 ... Nh6 6 Nf3 Bg4 7 Qd2 d5 8 Nxd5! e6 9 Nc3 Bxf3 10 gf Bxd4 (10 ... Nxd4 11 0-0-0 Nc6 12 Qf2 Qc8 13 f5 ±) 11 0-0-0 Bxe3 12 Qxe3 Qh4 13 Bb5 ± Boleslavsky

[10] 9 ... h6 11 Nf3 Qe7 12 g5 hg 13 Bxg5 ± Arnason-Goodman, Reykjavik 1982

[11] 10 gf Qxd1+ 11 Rxd1 Nd4 =

[12] 13 Qf2 h6 14 0-0-0 c5 15 Nge2 ±/∞ Arnason-Keene, London 1981

Pirc I   1 e4 d6 2 d4 Nf6 3 Nc3[1] g6[2]

	4	5	6	7	8	9	10	11	12	
1	Be3[3]	Qd2[5]	Bd3[7]	Nf3[8]	Bh6	Nd1	Qxh6	c3		∞
	c6[4]	b5[6]	Nbd7	Qc7	b4	Bxh6	c5	Bb7		

[1] 3 Bd3 g6 4 c3 Bg7 5 f4 e5! (5 ... 0-0 6 Nf3 c5 7 dc dc 8 e5 Nd5 9 Be4 Nb6 10 Qe2! ± Qi Jingxuan-Balashov, Taxco IZ 1985) 6 Nf3 Nh5!? 7 fe de 8 Bg5 f6 ∞ Nunn

3 Nd2 g6 4 Ngf3 Bg7 5 Be2 (5 Bc4 0-0 6 Qe2 Nc6 7 c3 e5 8 de Nh5! = Jansa-Adorjan, Sombor 1972) 5 ... 0-0 6 c3 Nc6 (6 ... c5!?) 7 0-0 Nd7 8 b4 a6 9 Nc4 b5 10 Ne3 Nb6 ∞ Lengyel-Hort, Moscow 1975

[2] 3 ... c6 4 Qd3 Bg4 5 h3 Bh5 6 Be2 e6 7 Bf4 Be7 8 Nd2! Bxe2 9 Qxe2 d5 10 e5 ± Zaichik-Tseitlin, Prague Z 1985; 9 ... 0-0!? intending 10 0-0-0 d5 Jansa/Pribyl

[3] 4 Bf4 Bg7 5 Qd2 0-0 6 0-0-0 Nc6 7 Bh6 ∞

Kholmov-Chikovani, USSR 1976

[4] 4 ... Bg7 5 Qd2 Ng4 6 Bg5 h6 7 Bh4 g5 8 Bg3 e5 9 de ± Parma

[5] 5 a4 Bg7 6 h3 0-0 7 Nf3 Nbd7 8 e5 de 9 de Nd5 = Peters-Christiansen, US Ch 1981

[6] 5 ... Qa5 6 Nf3 b5 7 Bd3 b4 8 Ne2 Ba6 9 0-0 Bxd3 10 cd ± Zapata-van der Wiel, Brussels 1986

[7] 6 e5 Ng4 (6 ... de 7 de Qxd2+ 8 Bxd2 Ng4 9 Nf4 ±) 7 ed Qxe3 8 Qxe3 Nxd6 9 a4 Bg7 10 Nf3 ∞ van der Wiel-Piket, Leiden 1986

[8] 7 Bh6 Bxh6 8 Qxh6 Bb7 9 Nf3 e5 10 0-0 a6 11 Rad1 Qe7 = Corden-Botterill, England 1970-71

	4	5	6	7	8	9	10	11	12	
2	♗c4	♕e2	e5	♗d2	♗b3[11]	a4	de	♘f3	♗xd5	∞
	♗g7	c6[9]	♘d5[10]	0-0	a5	de	♘a6	♘c5	cd[12]	
3	g3	♗g2	♘ge2[13]	h3[15]	a4[17]	0-0	♗e3[19]	♗xd4	f4	=
	♗g7	0-0	e5[14]	c6[16]	a5[18]	♘a6	ed	♘b4	♖e8[20]	
4	♗e2	h4	dc	♔f1[22]	♗e3	h5	♗xh5	bc	♗d4[24]	∞
	♗g7	c5[21]	♕a5	♕xc5	♕a5	♘xh5[23]	♗xc3!	gh		
5	f3	♗e3	♕d2	♘h3[26]	0-0-0[28]	♔b1	g4	g5	♘f2	∞
	c6	♘bd7[25]	b5	♗b7[27]	a6	♕c7	e5	♘h5	♖d8[29]	
6	...	♗e3	♕d2	♘h3	♘f2[33]	♗e2	0-0	♗h6	♗xg7	=
	♗g7	c6[30]	♘bd7[31]	b5[32]	a6	♕c7	0-0	e5[34]	♔xg7[35]	
7	...	...	...	♗d3[36]	♘ge2	a4	0-0	♔h1	♘g3	=
	...	...	b5	♘bd7	a6[37]	♗b7	0-0	♕c7	e5[38]	
8	♘f3	♗c4[39]	♗b3[41]	h3	0-0	ab	♗e3	♕d2	♖ad1	=
	♗g7	0-0[40]	♘c6[42]	♘a5	♘xb3	♘d7	a6	♖e8	e6[43]	
9	...	h3	♗e3[45]	a4[47]	a5[49]	♗e2[51]	de	0-0	♕b1	=
	...	0-0[44]	c6[46]	♘bd7[48]	♕c7[50]	e5	de[52]	♖d8	♘f8[53]	

[9]   5 ... ♘c6 6 e5 ♘g4 and now:

7 ♗b5 0-0 8 ♗xc6 bc 9 h3 ♘h6 10 ♘f3 c5 ∞ Sigurjonsson-Timman, Wijk aan Zee 1980

7 e6!? d5 (7 ... ♘xd4 8 ♕xg4 ♘xc2+ 9 ♔f1 ♘xa1 10 ef+ ♔f8 11 ♕h4 ∞ van der Plassche-Piket, Hilversum 1985) 8 ♗xd5 ♘xd4 9 ♕xg4 ♘xc2+ 10 ♔e2 ♘xa1 11 ef+ ♔f8 12 ♕h4 ∞ Bezemer-Piket, Amsterdam II 1986

[10]   6 ... de 7 de ♘d5 8 ♗d2! ♗e6 9 0-0-0 ♘d7 10 f4 ♘7b6 11 ♗b3 ± Galloway-D.Gurevich, USA 1985

[11]   8 h4!? b5! (8 ... ♗e6 9 h5 ♘xc3 10 ♗xc3 ♗xc4 11 ♕xc4 de 12 hg ± Schubert-Ditt, West Germany 1984) 9 ♗b3 ♘xc3 10 ♗xc3 a5 ∞ Smejkal

8 0-0-0!? Parma

[12]   Tan-Smyslov, Petropolis IZ 1973

[13]   6 ♘gf3 ♗g4 7 ♗e3 ♘c6 8 h3 ♗xf3 9 ♕xf3 e5 10 de de 11 0-0 ♘d4 = Spassky-Timman, Tilburg 1978

[14]   6 ... c6 7 a4 d5 8 e5 ♘e8 9 0-0 a5 10 ♘f4 ♘c7 11 ♘ce2 ± Rukavina-Kosanović, Budva 1986

6 ... ♘fd7!? 7 0-0 c5 8 h3 cd 9 ♘xd4 ♘c6 10 ♘de2 ♖b8 11 a4 b6 12 ♖e1 ♗b7 = Rukavina-Lević, Vrnjačka Banja 1986

[15]   7 0-0 ♘c6 8 de de 9 ♗g5 ♗e6 10 ♕e1 ♘d4 11 ♘xd4 ♕xd4 12 ♖d1 ♕c5 13 h3 c6 = Speelman-Sznapik, Dortmund 1981

[16]   7 ... a6 8 a4 b6 9 0-0 ♗b7 10 d5 c6 11 dc ♘xc6 12 ♗g5 h6 13 ♗e3 ♔h7 = Wessendorf-van der Wiel, San Bernardino 1986

7 ... b6 8 0-0 ♗b7 9 g4?! ed 10 ♘xd4 ♖e8 11 ♗g5 h6 12 ♗h4 = Klinger-Quinteros, Zürich 1985

7 ... ♘c6 8 ♗e3 ♗d7 (8 ... ♖e8!? 9 0-0 a6 10 a4 ed 11 ♘xd4 ♗d7 12 ♖e1 ♘a5!? ∞ Wockenfuss-Plaskett, Lugano 1986) 9 0-0 ed 10 ♘xd4 ♖e8 11 ♖e1 a6 12 f4 ♕c8 13 ♔h2 h5 ∞ Abramović-Terzić, Zenica 1986

[17]   8 0-0 b5 9 a3 ♘bd7 10 d5 cd 11 ♘xd5 ♗b7 12 ♘xf6+ ♘xf6 13 ♘c3 a6 = Klinger-Cuijpers, Vienna 1984

[18]   8 ... d5 9 ed ed 10 ♘xd4 ♘xd5 11 ♘xd5 cd 12 0-0 ± Klinger-Carr, Oakham 1986

8 ... ed 9 ♘xd4 a5 10 0-0 ♘bd7 11 ♗f4! Popović-Rukavina, Budva 1986

[19]   10 ♗g5 ♘c7 11 ♕d2 ♗e6 12 ♗e3 c5 ∞ Belyavsky-Zilberman, USSR 1979

[20]   13 g4 d5! 14 e5 ♘d7 = Martinović-Gligorić, Yugoslav Ch 1986

[21]   5 ... h6 6 ♗e3 c6 7 ♕d2 b5 8 a3 ♘bd7 9 ♖d1 ±

5 ... **h5** 6 ♗g5 ♘c6 7 ♕d2 a6 8 0-0-0 b5 9 e5 ±

5 ... ♘c6 6 h5 gh (6 ... e5 7 h6 ♗f8 8 ♘f3 ± Malanyuk-Guseinov, Kiev 1984) 7 ♗g5 (7 ♗b5!? ♗d7 8 ♘ge2 a6 9 ♗xc6 ♗xc6 10 ♘g3 ∞/± Smejkal-Ftacnik, Novi Sad 1984) 7 ... ♗g4 8 f3 ♗d7 9 ♕d2 e5 10 de de 11 0-0-0 ± Kuijf-Piket, Wijk aan Zee 1986

5 ... ♘bd7 6 ♗e3 c5!? 7 dc ♕a5 8 ♕d2 ♘xc5 9 e5 ♘g4 ∞

[22] 7 ♗d2 ♕xc5 8 h5 gh 9 ♘h3 ♘c6 10 ♘f4 ♘g4 11 ♘d3 ♕d4 ∞ Malanyuk-Azmaiparashvili, USSR Ch 1986

[23] 9 ... gh 10 f3!? ♘c6 11 ♕d2 (11 ♘h3 ♗xh3 12 ♖xh3 0-0-0 13 ♖g3 ± Mesing-Rukavina, Sarajevo 1971) 11 ... ♘e5 12 ♘h3 ± Delavilla-Lopez Colon, Spain 1985

[24] 12 ♖xh5 ♕xc3 13 ♘e2 ♕c4 14 f3 ♘c6 15 ♔f2 ♗e6 ∓

12 ♗d4 ∞

[25] 5 ... ♕b6 6 ♖c1 (6 ♕d2 ♕xb2 7 ♖b1 ♕a3 8 ♗c4 ♘bd7 9 ♘ge2 ∞̄) 6 ... ♗g7 7 ♘ge2 0-0 8 g4!? ♘bd7 9 h4 ♕a5 10 h5 e5 11 ♕d2 b5 12 a3 ∞

[26] 7 ♘ge2 ♘b6 8 b3 ♕c7 9 g4 e5 10 ♗g2 b4 11 ♘d1 a5 = Hennings-Smyslov, Havana 1967

[27] 7 ... a6 8 ♘f2 e5 9 ♗e2 ♕c7 10 0-0 ♗g7 11 de de 12 a4 ± Geller-Andersson, Hilversum 1973

7 ... ♘b6 8 ♘f2 ♕c7 9 ♗e2 a6 10 0-0 ♗b7 11 a4 ♗g7 12 ♗h6 ±

[28] 8 ♗e2 e5 9 0-0 a6 10 ♖ad1 ♗g7 11 ♘f2 0-0 = Jimenez-Botvinnik, Palma de Mallorca 1967

[29] 13 ♘e2 c5 14 d5 ♗g7 15 ♘g3 ∞ Torre-Jansson, Siegen Ol 1970

[30] 5 ... ♘c6 6 ♕d2 a6 7 0-0-0 e6 8 g4 b5 9 h4 h5 10 gh ♘xh5 11 ♘ge2 ♗d7 12 ♗h3 ± Short-Kavalek, Dubai Ol 1986

5 ... **0-0** 6 ♕d2 e5 (6 ... ♘c6 7 0-0-0 e5 8 d5 ♘e7 9 g4 ♘e8 10 ♘ge2 ∞/± Sveshnikov-Quinteros, Rio de Janeiro 1985) 7 d5 c̄6 8 0-0-0 cd 9 ♘xd5 ♘xd5 10 ♕xd5 ♘c6 ∞ Yudasin-Zaichik, USSR 1985

[31] 6 ... ♕a5 7 ♘ge2 ♘bd7 8 ♗h6 (8 ♘c1 b5 9 ♘b3 ±) 8 ... ♗xh6 9 ♕xh6 b5 10 ♘c1 ♕b6 11 ♘b3 ± Hartston-Littlewood, British Ch 1968

[32] 7 ... ♕a5 8 ♘f2 b5 9 ♗e2 a6 10 0-0 ♗b7 11 ♗h6 ± Geller-Liebert, Kapfenberg 1970

[33] 8 ♗h6 0-0 9 ♘f2 e5 10 ♗xg7 ♔xg7 11 0-0-0 ♕a5 12 ♔b1 ♖e8 ∞/= Karpov-Gipslis, USSR 1972

[34] 11 ... c5 12 ♗xg7 ♔xg7 13 d5 ♗b7 14 a4 b4 15 ♘d1 e6 = Hartston-Rukavina, Vrnjačka Banja 1972

[35] 13 f4 b4 14 ♘d1 ed 15 ♕xd4 c5 ∞ Hennings-Timman, Sochi 1973

[36] 7 ♘ge2 ♘bd7 8 ♘c1 ♘b6 9 ♗h6 0-0 =

Hartston-Torre, Nice Ol 1974

7 ♗h6 ♗xh6 8 ♕xh6 ♕a5 9 ♗d3 ♘bd7 10 ♘h3 b4 = Belyavsky-Hort, Moscow 1975

7 h4 h5 8 ♘h3 ♘bd7 9 ♘g5 a6 10 0-0-0 ♕c7 11 ♘e2 c5 = Hecht-Torre, Amsterdam 1973

[37] 8 ... ♘b6 9 ♗h6 0-0 10 ♗xg7 ♔xg7 11 0-0 = Parma

[38] 13 de de 14 ♕f2 ♖fe8 15 ♖fd1 ♘f8 = Geller-Hort, Amsterdam 1970

[39] 5 ♗g5 0-0 6 ♕d2 d5 7 ♗xf6 ef 8 ed ♖e8+ 9 ♗e2 ♘d7 =

5 ♗f4 ♘c6 6 h3 (6 ♕d2 0-0 7 d5 e5! =) 6 ... 0-0 7 ♕d2 e5 8 de de 9 ♕xd8 ♖xd8 10 ♗e3 ♗e6 = Kuzmin-Popović, Kladovo 1980

[40] 5 ... c6 6 e5 ♘d5!? 7 ♗xd5 cd 8 ♘xd5 ♕a5+ 9 ♘c3 de =

[41] 6 0-0 ♗xe4 7 ♗xf7+ ♖xf7 8 ♘xe4 h6 9 h3 ♕f8 = Honfi-Adorjan, Hungarian Ch 1971

6 ♕e2 ♗g4 7 ∞ Hort

[42] 6 ... c6 7 0-0 ♗g4 8 h3 ♗xf3 9 ♕xf3 ♘bd7 10 ♗e3 ♕a5 11 ♖ad1 ± Jansa-Ebalard, Metz 1985

6 ... ♗g4 7 h3 ♗xf3 8 ♕xf3 ♘c6 9 ♘e2 e5

[43] 13 e5 b6 = Gufeld

[44] 5 ... a6 6 ♗d3 ♘fd7 7 ♘e2 c5 8 c3 ± Spassky-van der Wiel, Baden 1980

[45] 6 ♗g5 c5 (6 ... c6 7 ♕d2 e5 8 de de 9 ♕xd8 ♖xd8 10 ♘xe5 ± Kaidanov-Azmaiparashvili, Moscow II 1986) 7 d5 b5 8 ♗xb5 ♘xe4 9 ♘xe4 ♕a5+ = Armas-Garcia Martinez, Granma 1986

[46] 6 ... a6 7 a4 b6 8 ♗c4 ♗b7 9 e5 ♘e4 10 ♘xe4 ♗xe4 11 ♘g5! ± Spassky-Seirawan, Zürich 1984

6 ... ♘a6 7 ♗e2 c5 (7 ... c6 8 a4 ♘b4 9 0-0 a5 10 ♖c1 ♕c7 11 ♕d2 ± Braga-Piket, Wijk aan Zee II 1986) 8 dc ♘xc5 9 e5! ♘fe4 10 ♘xe4 ♘xe4 11 ♕d5 ± Nunn-Davies, London 1985

6 ... ♘c6!? 7 ♕d2 e5 8 0-0-0 ed 9 ♘xd4 ♘xd4 10 ♗xd4 ♗e6 = Knoppert-Nijboer, Dieren 1986

6 ... b6 7 ♗d3 ♗b7 8 0-0 ♘bd7 9 a4 a6 10 ♖e1 e5 11 d5 c6 = Eingorn-Guseinov, Kiev 1984

[47] 7 ♕d2 b5 8 ♗d3 ♘bd7 9 e5 b4! Arnason-Fries Nielsen, Vejle 1984; 9 ♗h6 e5! = Short-Torre, Biel 1985

[48] 7 ... a5 8 ♗e2 ♘a6 9 0-0 ♘b4 10 ♕c1! ♖e8 11 e5 ± Gutman-Rukavina, Oberwart 1986

[49] 8 e5 de 9 de ♘d5 10 ♘xd5 cd 11 ♗f4 ∞ Brynell-Pribyl, Malmö 1985-86

[50] 8 ... e5 9 de de 10 ♕d6 ♘e8 11 ♕b4 ♗f6 12 ♗e2 ± Kindermann-Haik, Biel II 1986

[51] 9 ♕d2 e5 10 de ♘xe5 11 ♗e2 ♖e8 = Sharif-Bernard, Clermont Ferrand 1985

[52] 10 ... ♘xe5 11 0-0 ♖e8 12 ♘d2! ♘ed7 13 ♘c4 ♘xe4 14 ♘xe4 ♖xe4 15 ♕xd6 ± Short-van der Wiel, Biel 1985

[53] Spassky-van der Wiel, Reykjavik 1985

223

	4	5	6	7	8	9	10	11	12	
10	♗g5	♕d2	♗h6⁵⁶	♕xh6	♗d3⁵⁷	♘f3	♘g5	h3	0-0	±/∞
	♗g7⁵⁴	c6⁵⁵	♗xh6	♕a5	♘a6⁵⁸	♗g4	♘c7⁵⁹	♗e6	♘g8⁶⁰	

⁵⁴ 4 ... c6 5 ♕d2 b5 6 f3 ♘bd7 7 ♘h3 h6 8 ♗e3 ♗g7 9 ♘f2 ♗b7 10 ♗e2 ♕c7 11 0-0 a6 12 a4 ± Hübner-van der Sterren, Wijk aan Zee 1984

⁵⁵ 5 ... h6 6 ♗f4 ♘c6 (6 ... g5 7 ♗g3 ♘h5 8 0-0-0 ± Fischer-Mednis, US Ch 1958) 7 ♗b5 ♗d7 8 ♘ge2 a6 9 ♗xc6 bc (Korzubov-Hoi, Copenhagen 1984) 10 0-0-0! intending ♖he1 ± Korzubov

⁵⁶ 6 f4 0-0 7 ♘f3 b5 8 ♗d3 ♘bd7 (8 ... ♗g4 9 e5 b4 ∞ Peters-van der Sterren, London 1978) 9 0-0 ♘b6 10 ♖ael b4 11 ♘e2 c5 ∞

⁵⁷ 8 0-0-0 b5 9 e5 b4 10 ef bc ∓ Ornstein-Pribyl, Helsinki 1984

⁵⁸ 8 ... b5 9 ♘f3 b4 10 ♘e2 ♘bd7 (10 ... b3+ 11 ♘c3 bc 12 ♗xc2 ♘a6 13 0-0-0 ±) 11 0-0 e5 12 a3 ± Kupreichik-Sznapik, Zenica 1985

⁵⁹ 10 ... ♕b4 11 e5 de 12 de ♕xb2 13 0-0 ♕xc3 14 ef ♕xf6 15 ♗xa6 ba 16 ♖ab1 ∞ van der Wiel

⁶⁰ 13 ♕h4 h6 14 d5 ±/∞ van der Wiel-van Wijgerden, Dutch Ch 1984

	6	7	8	9	10	11	12	13	14	
1	...	e5	♗g5	ef	♗e3	d5	♕d2	♖ae1	h3⁴	±
	♘bd7²	♘e8³	f6	ef	c6	c5	♖f7	♘f8		
2	...	d5⁵	a4⁷	h3⁹	♗e3	♖e1	♗f1	♘c4	♖e2!¹⁰	±
	♘c6	♘b8⁶	a5⁸	c6	♘a6	♘b4	e5	♗d7		
3	...	a4¹¹	h3¹³	♗e3¹⁴	♕d2¹⁵	♖ad1	♖fe1	e5	♘xd5	=
	c6	a5¹²	♘a6	♘b4	♕c7	♖e8	♗d7	♘fd5	cd¹⁶	
4	...	h3	e5¹⁸	♗c4²⁰	♗b3	♗g5	♗h4	♘e2	ef	±
	...	♘bd7¹⁷	♘e8¹⁹	♘b6	♘c7	♘e6	d5	f6	ef²¹	
5	...	♗e3²²	d5²⁴	♗xf3	♗e2	a4²⁵	♖a3	♖b3	♕d4	∞
	♗g4	♘c6²³	♗xf3	♘e5	c6	♕a5²⁶	♖fc8²⁷	♖ab8	c5²⁸	
6	...	...	♕d2	de	♖ad1	♕c1	♖xd8+	♖d1	h3	±/=
	...	...	e5²⁹	de	♕c8³⁰	♖d8	♕xd8³¹	♕f8	♗xf3³²	
7	...	...	...	d5	♖ad1³⁴	♘e1³⁶	♗xg4	f3	f4	∞∞
	...	...	...	♘e7³³	♗d7³⁵	♘g4³⁷	♗xg4	♗d7	♗g4³⁸	

¹ 6 h3 c6 7 a4 ♘bd7 8 ♗e3 e5 9 de de 10 ♘d2 ♕e7 11 ♘b3 ♘e8 12 ♕d2 ♘c7 = Chiburdanidze-Piket, Amsterdam 1986

² 6 ... c5 7 dc dc 8 ♗e3 b6 9 ♕xd8 ♖xd8 10 ♖fd1 ± Andersson-Torre, Leningrad 1987

   6 ... e5 7 de de 8 ♕xd8 ♖xd8 9 ♗g5 ♖e8 10 ♖fd1 ±

   6 ... b6 7 ♖e1 ♗b7 8 e5 ♘d5 9 ♘xd5 ♗xd5 10 c4 ± Marić-Quinteros, Bor 1977

   6 ... a6 7 a4 b6 8 e5! de 9 ♘xe5 ± Gheorghiu-Espig, Romania v East Germany 1984

   6 ... ♘a6 7 ♖e1 c5 8 e5 ♘g4 9 ed ♕xd6 10 ♘e4 ± Geller-Sax, Budapest 1973

³ 7 ... de 8 de ♘g4 9 e6! ± Kasparov-Sendur, Wattignies 1976

⁴ Spassky-Khodos, USSR 1962

⁵ 7 ♗e3 ♘g4 8 ♗g5 h6 9 ♗h4 ♘f6 10 d5 ± Andersson-Kavalek, Buenos Aires 1980

⁶ 7 ... ♘b4 8 ♖e1 e6 9 a3 ♘a6 10 de ♗xe6 11 ♘d4 ± Stohl-Jansa, Prague 1986

⁷ 8 ♖e1 c6 (8 ... ♗g4!? – 6 ... ♗g4) 9 ♗f1 ♘bd7 10 ♗g5 h6 11 ♗f4 ± Karpov-Pfleger, London 1977

⁸ 8 ... e5 9 de ♗xe6 10 ♘d4 ♗d7 11 ♖e1 ♘c6 12 ♘xc6 ♗xc6 13 ♗b5 ± Georgadze-Razuvayev, USSR Ch 1978

⁹ 9 ♗c4 ♗g4 10 h3 ♗xf3 11 ♕xf3 ♘fd7 12 ♕e2 ♘a6 ∞ Gurgenidze-Gulko, USSR 1979

¹⁰ Miles-Quinteros, Dortmund 1986

¹¹ 7 e5 ♘d5 8 ♘xd5 cd 9 ♗f4 de 10 ♗xe5 ♘c6 = Hulak-Rukavina, Yugoslav Ch 1981

   7 ♖e1 and now:

7 ... ♘a6 8 e5! de 9 de ♘d5 10 ♘xd5 cd 11 ♗xa6 ba 12 ♘d4 ± Speelman-Ghinda, Thessaloniki Ol 1984

7 ... ♕c7 8 ♗f4 ♘bd7 9 e5 ♘h5 10 ed ed 11 ♗e3 f5 12 d5! ± Andersson-van der Wiel 1984

7 ... ♘bd7 8 ♗f4 ♕a5! 9 ♕d2 (9 ♘d2 ♕c7 10 a4 e5 11 de de 12 ♗e3 ♖d8 13 ♕c1 ♗f8!? ∞ Pigusov-Azmaiparashvili, USSR 1986) 9 ... e5 10 ♗g5 ed 11 ♘xd4 ♘xe4 12 ♘xe4 ♕xd2 13 ♗xd2 d5! = A.Sokolov-van der Wiel, Biel IZ 1985

[12] 7 ... ♕c7 8 h3 e5 9 de de 10 ♗e3 (10 ♗c4!? ±) 10 ... ♘h5 11 ♖e1!? ♘f4 12 ♗f1 ♘a6 13 ♘d2 ♖d8 14 ♕c1 ♘e6 15 a5 ± Szmetan-Schweber, Buenos Aires 1985

7 ... ♘bd7 8 h3 e5 9 de de 10 ♗e3 ♕e7 11 ♕d3 ♘h5 12 ♖fd1 ± Nun-Ftacnik, Czechoslovak Ch 1986

[13] 8 ♗e3 ♘g4 9 ♗g5 h6 10 ♗h4 ♘a6 11 ♖e1 ♘b4 = Browne-Hort, Wijk aan Zee 1975

8 ♖e1 ♘a6 9 ♗f1 ♗g4 10 h3 ♗xf3 11 ♕xf3 ♘d7 = Poutiainen-Planinc, Nice Ol 1974

[14] 9 ♖e1 ♘b4 10 ♗f1 e5 11 ♗g5 h6 12 ♗e3 ♕e7 13 ♕d2 ♔h7 ∓ Lobron-Seirawan, Bad Kissingen 1981

9 ♗f4 ♘b4 10 ♕d2 ♕b6 11 ♖ac1 ♖d8 12 ♗h6 e5 ∞ Salov-Gurevich, USSR 1978

[15] 10 ♘d2 e5 11 de de 12 ♘c4 ♗e6 = Sznapik-Nunn, Helsinki 1981

[16] 15 c3 ♘c6 16 ed ed = Spassky-Hort, match 1977

[17] 7 ... ♕c7 8 ♗f4! ♘bd7 (8 ... ♘h5 9 ♗e3 e5 10 ♕d2 ♘d7 11 a4 ±) 9 e5 de 10 ♘xe5 ♕d8 11 ♖e1 ♘d5 12 ♘xd5 cd 13 ♗f3 ± Gligorić-Nikolić, Budva 1986

[18] 8 ♗f4 ♘h5 9 ♗g5 ♖e8 10 ♕d2 ♕c7 11 ♖fd1 ± Vasyukov-Andersson, Camaguey 1974

[19] 8 ... de 9 de ♘d5 10 ♘xd5 cd 11 ♗f4 ♕c7 (11 ... ♘c5 12 ♕d2 ± Gligorić-Tringov, Skara 1980) 12 ♕xd5 ♕xc2 13 ♗b5 ± Ermolinsky-Azmaiparashvili, USSR 1986

[20] 9 ♗f4 de 10 de ♘c7 11 ♖e1 ♘e6 12 ♗g3 ♕a5 = Liberzon-Torre, Geneva 1977

[21] Shamkovich-Torre, Rio de Janeiro IZ 1979

[22] 7 h3 ♗xf3 8 ♗xf3 ♘c6 9 d5 ♘e5 10 ♗e2 c6 11 f3 ♘ed7 ∞ Georgadze-Tseitlin, USSR 1975

7 ♗g5 ♘c6 8 h3 ♗xf3 9 ♗xf3 ♘d7 10 ♘e2 h6 11 ♗e3 e5 12 c3 ♘b6 = Smyslov-Timman, Amsterdam 1971

[23] 7 ... ♘bd7?! 8 h3 ♗xf3 9 ♗xf3 e5 10 g3 c6 11 ♗g2 ♕a5 12 ♕d2 ♖fe8 13 ♖ad1 ± Karpov-Nunn, Tilburg 1982

[24] 8 h3 ♗xf3 9 ♗xf3 e5 (9 ... ♘d7 10 d5 ± Short-Botterill, Brighton Z 1984) 10 de de 11 ♘e2 ♕e7 12 c3 ♖fd8 = Speelman-McNab, Brighton Z 1984

8 ♘e1 ♗xe2 9 ♕xe2 e5 10 de ♘xe5 11 ♖d1 ♖e8 = Geller-Balashov, Moscow 1981

8 ♘d2 ♗xe2 9 ♕xe2 e5 10 d5 ♘e7 11 ♖fd1 ♕c8 12 f3 ♘h5 ∞ Keene

8 ♕d3 ♘d7 9 ♘e1 (9 ♖ad1 ♘b6 10 a3 d5 11 h3 ♗xf3 12 ♗xf3 e5 = Belyavsky-Nunn, Baden 1980) 9 ... ♗xe2 10 ♘xe2 e5 11 c3 ♘e7 12 ♘f3 ed 13 ♗xd4 ♘e5 = Karpov-Timman, Amsterdam 1980

[25] 11 f4 ♘ed7 12 dc bc 13 ♕d2 a5 14 ♗f3 ♘b6 15 b3 ∞

[26] 11 ... ♕c7 12 a5 a6 13 f4 ♘ed7 14 ♗f3 ± Kuzmin-Benko, Hastings 1973-74

11 ... cd 12 ed ♕a5 13 ♖a3! ♖fc8 14 ♖b3 ♕c7 15 ♖e1 ± Kengis-Hoi, Jurmala 1985

[27] 12 ... ♘ed7 13 ♕d2 ♖fc8 14 ♖b1! ± Gavrikov-Mäki, Leningrad 1984

[28] 15 ♕d1 a6 16 f4 ♘ed7 17 g4 ♘e8 ∞ Panchenko-Ehlvest, Leningrad 1984

[29] 8 ... ♖e8 9 ♗fe1! a6 (9 ... e5 10 d5 ♗xf3 11 ♗xf3 ♘d4 12 ♗xd4 ed 13 ♘b5 ±) 10 ♖ad1 e5 (10 ... ♗xf3 11 ♗xf3 e5 12 de de 13 ♘a4 ♕e7 14 c3 ± Karpov-Spassky, Hamburg 1982) 11 de de 12 ♕c1 ♕e7 13 ♘d5 ± Geller-Pribyl, Sochi 1984

[30] 10 ... ♕xd2 11 ♖xd2 ♖fd8 12 ♖fd1 ♖xd2 13 ♖xd2 ♘e8 14 ♗b5!? ± Parma

[31] 12 ... ♘xd8!? ∞ Keene-Pritchett, China 1981

[32] 15 ♗xf3 ♖d8 (15 ... a6 16 ♘b1! ± Petrosian-Sax, Tallinn 1979) 16 ♘b5 (16 ♖xd8!?) 16 ... ♖xd1+ 17 ♕xd1 ♕b8 18 c3 ♗f8!? (18 ... h5 19 ♘a3 ♕c8 20 ♕b3 ± Hansen-Hoi, Naestved 1985) ±/= Ivanchuk-Azmaiparashvili, Tallinn 1986

[33] 9 ... ♘b8 10 ♖ad1 ♘bd7 11 h3 ♗xf3 12 ♗xf3 ± Tal-Hort, Montreal 1979

[34] 10 ♖e1 ♗xe2 11 ♕xe2 c6 12 dc bc = Vokacs-Jansa, Czechoslovak Ch 1986

[35] 10 ... ♘d7 11 ♘g5 ♗xe2 12 ♘xe2 h6 13 ♘h3 ♔h7 14 b3 f5 15 ef ♘xf5 16 f3 ± Timman-Seirawan, Las Palmas 1981

10 ... ♗xf3 11 ♗xf3 ♘d7 12 ♗e2 f5 13 f4 a6 14 g4 ±

10 ... b5 11 ♗xb5 (11 a3 ♕b8 12 ♘e1 ♗d7 13 f3 a5 ∞ Barlov-Jansa, Bor 1985) 11 ... ♘xe4 12 ♘xe4 (12 h3!?) 12 ... f5 13 ♘eg5 f4 14 ♘e6 (14 ♗c5 dc 15 ♗c4 ± Negrini) 14 ... ♗xe6 15 de fe 16 ♕xe3 c6 17 ♗c4 ± Venni-Segatini, Caorle II 1986

10 ... ♘c8 11 h3 ♗d7!? Parma

[36] 11 ♗h6 ♘c8 12 ♗xg7 ♔xg7 13 ♘e1 c5 ∞ Groszpeter-Mednis, Budapest 1978

11 h3 ♔h8 12 ♘e1 ♘fg8 13 ♘d3 f5 ∞ Vogt-Plachetka, Berlin 1979

[37] 11 ... b5!? 12 ♘d3 a5 13 b4 c6 ∞ Psakhis-Gufeld, USSR 1979

[38] 15 ♘f3 f5 16 ♖de1 ♗xf3 17 ♖xf3 ♕d7 18 fe de = Geller-Timman, Wijk aan Zee 1977

15 ♖b1 c6 16 h3 ♗d7 17 fe (17 dc ♗xc6 18 ♖d1 ef 19 ♖xf4 f5 ∓ Karpov-Adorjan, Las Palmas 1977) 17 ... de 18 ♗c5 cd ∞∞ Torre-Chandler, Penang 1978

225

	5	6	7	8	9	10	11	12	13	
1	...	dc[1]	♗d3[2]	♕e2	♗e3	0-0	h3[5]	♕xf3	a3	=
	c5	♕a5	♕xc5	0-0	♕a5[3]	♗g4[4]	♗xf3	♘c6	♘d7[6]	
2	...	♗b5+	e5[7]	e6	ef+	♘xb5[9]	♘c3	♘xd4	h3	∞
	...	♗d7	♘g4	♗xb5[8]	♔d7	♕a5+	cd	h5[10]	♘c6[11]	
3	...	...	...	h3	♕xd4	♘xb5	♕e4	♕e2[14]	♗e3	=
	...	...	...	cd	♗xb5[12]	♘c6	♕b6[13]	♘h6	♕a5+[15]	
4	...	...	...	♗xd7+	d5	h3	♘xe4[16]	♘xf6+[17]	0-0	±/=
	...	...	...	♕xd7	de	e4	♘f6	♗xf6	0-0[18]	
5	...	e5[19]	h4	h5	♕xd4[21]	♕f2[22]	♘g5	hg	♘cxe4[23]	=
	0-0	♘fd7[20]	c5	cd	de	e4	♘f6	hg	♘xe4[24]	
6	...	♗e3	dc	♗d3[26]	♗d2	♕e2	0-0-0	♘a4	♕e3	±
	...	c5[25]	♕a5	♘g4	♕xc5	♘f6	♘c6[27]	♘d4	♘g4[28]	
7	...	...	e5	♗g1	♗c4[30]	♕xd4	h3	0-0-0	♕f2	∞
	...	b6	♘g4[29]	c5	cd	♗b7	♘h6	♘c6	♖c8[31]	
8	...	...	♕d2	0-0-0[32]	♗g1[33]	♘xd4	♘de2	♘xf4	♗d4	=
	...	♘bd7	c5	♘g4	cd	e5	ef	♕a5	♘ge5[34]	
9	...	...	♗e2[35]	♗g1	fe[36]	d5	h3	♗e3	0-0	∞
	...	♘c6	♘g4	e5	de	♘b8	♘f6	c6	cd[37]	
10	...	♗d3	0-0	fe	d5	♘xe5	♘xf7	bc	♖xf7	∞
	...	♘c6[38]	e5[39]	de	♘e7[40]	♘fxd5[41]	♘xc3	♖xf7	♔xf7[42]	
11	...	...	e5	fe[43]	♗e2	♗e3	ef	♕d2	0-0-0	±
	...	...	de	♘h5[44]	♗g4[45]	f6	ef[46]	♕e7	♖fe8[47]	
12	...	...	0-0[48]	d5	♕e1[50]	♕h4	f5!	a3	cd	∞
	...	♘a6	c5	♖b8[49]	♘b4	b5	c4	♘xd3	cd[51]	

---

[1]   6 e5 ♘fd7 7 e6 (7 ed 0-0! ∞ Sax-Sigurjonsson, London 1975) 7 ... fe 8 ♘g5 ♘f6 9 dc ♘c6 10 ♗c4 d5 11 ♗b5 d4 ∞ Vasyukov-Tseshkovsky, USSR Ch 1974

[2]   7 ♕d3 ♕xc5 8 ♗e3 ♕a5 9 ♕b5+ ♕xb5 10 ♘xb5 ♘a6 11 ♗d3 0-0 12 ♗xa7 h5! ∞ A.Sokolov-M.Gurevich, USSR Ch 1985

[3]   9 ... ♕b4 10 0-0 ♕xb2 11 ♘b5 ♘e8 12 a3 ± Fridstein

    9 ... ♕c7 10 0-0 ♗g4 11 ♕e1 ♗xf3 12 ♖xf3 a6 13 ♕h4 ± van der Wiel-Wilder, Lone Pine 1979

[4]   10 ... ♘c6 11 h3 ♗d7 (11 ... e5 12 fe de 13 ♕f2 ♗e6 14 ♕h4 ±) 12 a3 ♖ac8 13 ♕f2 intending ♕h4 ±

[5]   11 ♕e1 ♗xf3 12 ♖xf3 ♘c6 13 ♔h1 ♘b4 ∞

[6]   14 ♗d2 ♕d8 (14 ... ♕b6+ 15 ♔h1 ♘c5 16 ♖ab1 ♘xd3 17 cd f5! ∞/=) 15 ♔h1 e6 = Arnason-Kristiansen, Gausdal Z 1987

[7]   7 ♗xd7+ ♘bxd7! 8 e5 ♘h5 9 ♗e3 (9 g4 cd) 9 ... 0-0 10 ♕d2 cd 11 ♗xd4 ♗h6 12 ♗e3 ♘b6 13 b3 ♖c8 ∞ Hort-Suttles, Indonesia 1982

[8]   8 ... fe 9 ♘g5 ♗xb5 10 ♘xe6 (10 ♕xg4 ♗c4 11 b3 ♗xd4 12 ♗d2 ♗d5 13 ♘xd5 ed 14 0-0-0 ♕d7 15 ♘e6 ♘c6 16 f5 ♗f6 17 ♖he1 ♘d8! ± Nunn-Benjamin, Thessaloniki Ol 1988) 10 ... ♗xd4 11 ♘xd8 ♗f2+ ½-½ Sax-Seirawan, Brussels 1988

[9]   10 ♘g5!? h5 11 h3 (11 ♕f3 ♗c6 12 d5 ♗xc3+ 13 bc ♗b5 14 ♕e4 ∞ Stader-Vinke, corr. 1983) 11 ... ♘h6 12 ♕f3 ♘c6 13 ♕e4 ∞ Lehmann-Stempka, corr. 1986

[10]   12 ... ♗xd4 13 ♕xd4 ♘c6 14 ♕c4 ♕b6 15 ♕e2 h5 16 ♗d2 ♘d4 17 ♕d3 ♘f5 18 ♘e4 ♖ac8 19 0-0-0 ± Timman-van Wijgerden, Dutch Ch 1983, and Hellers-Ivanchuk, Champigny 1984

[11]   14 ♘de2 ♘h6 15 ♗e3 ♖af8! 16 ♕d3 ♘f5 17 ♗f2 ♖xf7 ∞ Oll-M.Gurevich, Tallinn 1987

[12]   9 ... de 10 ♕d5 ± Sigurjonsson-Vogt, Cienfuegos 1976

[13]   11 ... ♕a5+ 12 ♘c3 ♘h6 13 g4 ± Timman-Sigurjonsson 1977

[14] 12 hg ♕xb5 13 ed 0-0-0 14 ♘g5 ed 15 ♘xf7 ♖d7 ∓ Guljas-Bockinas, corr. 1983

[15] 14 ♗d2 ♕b6 = Grodzensky-Kudinov, corr. 1975

[16] 11 hg ef 12 ♕xf3 ♘a6 13 ♗d2 ♘c7 14 0-0-0 0-0-0 ∞ Barber-Agnos, British Ch 1986

[17] **12 ♘xc5** ♕xd5 13 ♕xd5 ♗xd5 14 ♘xb7 ♘c6 ∞∞

12 ♘e5 ♕d8 13 ♘xf6+ ef 14 ♘f3 0-0 15 0-0 f5 =

[18] **14 c4** e6 = Adorjan-Pfleger, Lanzarote 1975

14 ♗e3 e6 15 ♗xc5 ♖d8 16 ♗d4 ♗xd4 17 ♕xd4 ♕xd5 18 ♕xd5 ♖xd5 19 ♖ad1 ♘c6 20 ♖xd5 ed 21 ♖d1 ♖d8 22 g4 ±/= Dolmatov-Chernin, Sverdlovsk 1984

[19] 6 ♗e2 c5 7 dc ♕a5 8 0-0 ♕xc5+ 9 ♔h1 ♘bd7 10 ♗d3 a6 11 ♕e1 b5 12 ♗e3 ♕c7 13 a3 ♗b7 14 ♕h4 ♖ae8?! 15 f5 e6 16 ♗g5! ± Kuijf-Piket, Wijk aan Zee 1987; 14 ... e6, 14 ... ♖fe8 ∞∞

[20] 6 ... de 7 fe (7 de ♕xd1+ 8 ♔xd1 ♘h5 = Ljubojević-Timman, Bugojno 1980) 7 ... ♘d5 8 ♗c4 ♘b6 9 ♗b3 ♗g4 10 0-0 ♘c6 11 ♗e3 ♘a5 ∞ Inkiov-Sznapik, Warsaw 1979

[21] 9 hg?! dc 10 gf+ ♖xf7 ∓ *ECO*

[22] 10 ♕g1 e4 11 ♘xe4 ♘f6 12 ♘xf6+ ef 13 hg ♖e8+ 14 ♔f2 hg 15 ♕h2 ♘d7 16 ♕h7+ ♔f8 17 b3 ♘c5 ∓ Gasić-Keene, Bognor Regis 1967

[23] 13 ♕h4 ♕d4!

[24] 14 ♘xe4 ♕d4 =

[25] 6 ... c6 7 ♗d3 ♘bd7 8 e5 ♗g4 9 ♗g1 c5 10 ♕e2 cd 11 ♗xd4 de 12 fe ♕a5 13 e6 ± Lanka-Hoi, Trnava 1987

[26] 8 ♕d2 dc 9 ♘b5 ♕a4! = Belyavsky-Timman, Tilburg 1986

[27] 11 ... ♘a6 12 e5 ± Tal-Mednis, Riga IZ 1979

[28] 14 ♘xc5 ♘xe3 15 ♗xe3 dc 16 ♗xd4 cd 17 e5 ± Timman-Hartoch, Dutch Ch 1981

[29] 7 ... ♘fd7 8 ♗g5 h6 9 ♗xf7 ± A.Sokolov-Partos, Biel IZ 1985

[30] 9 h3 ♘h6 10 d5 ♘a6 11 ♕d2 ♘c7 ∞ Schneider-Short, Hamburg 1981

[31] 14 ♗d5 b5 ∞ Mikhalchishin-Sznapik, Dortmund 1984

[32] 8 dc ♘xc5 9 e5 ♘fe4 10 ♘xe4 ♘xe4 11 ♕b4 d5 ∞ Khalifman-Azmaiparashvili, USSR Ch 1986

[33] 9 dc ♘xe3 10 ♕xe3 ♘xc5 11 e5 ♕a5 ∞ Sideifzade-Gipslis, USSR 1983

[34] 13 ... ♘de5 14 ♔b1 ♘f6 = Mikhalchishin-Azmaiparashvili, Baku 1983

13 ... ♘ge5 14 ♔b1 ♘c5 = Belyavsky-Azmaiparashvili, USSR Ch 1983, and Sax-Ftacnik, Hastings 1983-84

[35] **7 d5** ♘b8 8 ♗e2 c6 9 0-0 ♘g4 10 ♗d4

♗xd4+ 11 ♕xd4 ♕b6 = Shakarov-Chikovani, USSR 1975

7 ♕d2 ♘g4 8 ♗g1 e5 9 fe de 10 d5 ♘b8 11 h3 ♘f6 12 0-0-0 ♘bd7 13 d6 c6 ∞ Dvoiris-Azmaiparashvili, USSR Ch 1986

[36] 9 de de 10 ♕xd8 ♖xd8 11 h3 ♘h6 12 g4 f5 ∞ Fridstein

[37] 14 ed ♘h5 (14 ... e4 15 ♘e5 ± Balashov-Tseshkovsky, USSR Ch 1976) 15 ♘e4 ♗f5 16 ♘c5 ♘g3 ∞ Fridstein

[38] 6 ... ♘bd7 7 0-0 e5 8 fe de 9 d5 ± *ECO*

6 ... ♗g4 7 h3 ♗xf3 8 ♕xf3 ♘c6 9 ♗e3 e5 10 de de 11 f5 ± Fischer-Benko, US Ch 1964, and Parma-Planinc, Portorož 1977

[39] 7 ... ♗g4 8 e5 de 9 de ♘d5 10 h3 ± Balashov-Pfleger, Hanover 1983, and Thipsay-Bell, London 1986

[40] 9 ... ♘b4 10 ♗c4 ± Balashov-Timman, Moscow 1981

9 ... ♘d4 10 ♘xe5 ♘xd5 11 ♘xd5 ♗xe5 12 ♗f4 ± Dolmatov-Kuzmin, USSR 1981, and Marjanović-P.Nikolić, Sarajevo 1982

[41] 10 ... c6 11 ♗g5 ± Dolmatov-Kuzmin, USSR Ch 1980-81, and Moiseyev-Labunsky, USSR 1986

[42] 14 ♗c4+ e6 15 ♕f1+ ♗f6 16 ♗xe6+ ♔xe6 17 ♕c4+ ♔d7 18 ♗a3 ♕g8 ∞ Berecz-Den Broeder, corr. 1986

[43] 8 de ♘d5 9 ♗d2 ♗g4 10 ♗e4 e6 =

[44] 8 ... ♘d5 9 ♘xd5 ♕xd5 10 c3 ♗e6 11 0-0 f6 12 c4 ♕d7 13 d5 ♘b4 14 ♗e2 ♗g4 15 e6 ♕d6 16 ♗e3 ± van der Sterren-Marangunić, Brussels 1984

[45] 9 ... f6 10 e6! f5 11 d5 ±

[46] 11 ... ♗xf6!? 12 ♘e4 ♕d5 13 ♘xf6+ ef Katalimov-Kuzmin, USSR 1980

[47] 14 ♖he1 ♔h8 15 ♗h6 ± Timman-Nijboer, Holland 1985-86

[48] 7 e5 ♘d7 and now:

8 h4 c5 9 h5 cd 10 hg hg 11 ♘g5 ♘xe5! 12 fe dc ∞∞/∓ de Firmian-van der Wiel, Wijk aan Zee 1986

8 ♗e3 ♘b4 9 ♗e2 ♘b6 = Timman-Nunn, London 1982

[49] 8 ... ♘c7 9 ♕e1 ♗g4 10 f5 ♗xf3 11 ♖xf3 ± van der Sterren-Hartoch, Dutch Ch 1981

8 ... ♗g4 9 h3 ♗xf3 10 ♖xf3 ♘c7 11 a4 ± Ehlvest-Azmaiparashvili, USSR 1986

[50] **9 ♕e2** ♘c7 10 a4 a6 11 a5 b5 12 ab ♖xb6 13 ♘a4 ♖b8 14 c4 e6! ∞ Dolmatov-Gipslis, USSR 1985

9 ♔h1 ♗g4 10 ♕e1 ♘b4 ∞ Velimirović-van der Wiel, Sarajevo 1984, and Stehouwer-van der Wiel, Dutch Ch 1984

[51] 14 ♗h6 ∞∞ Sznapik-van der Wiel, Amsterdam 1984

1 e4; Centre Counter; Nimzowitsch

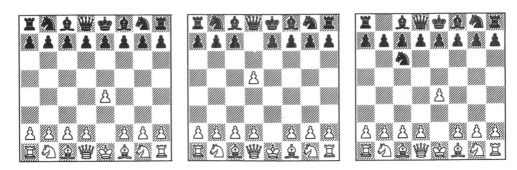

1 ... g5 and **1 ... a6**. These highly unusual first moves have been championed by the irrepressible English IM Michael Basman. They are of great psychological value but are positionally suspect, though it must be noted that Basman's compatriot Miles adopted 1 ... a6 to defeat Karpov. The moves remain, despite this success, rather distrusted by the public in general and should be recommended only to the adventurous.

1 ... b6. This move enjoyed a brief revival at the hands of American IM Regan and Yugoslav GM Sahović. Unfortunately, the attention it received unearthed more accurate lines for White and it is currently considered insufficient.

1 ... d5. The Centre Counter, or Scandinavian, has been adopted by Australian GM Ian Rogers, who employed some witty ideas in the solid 2 ... ♕xd5 line. However, White seems in the process of consolidating an advantage against this opening. The 2 ... ♘f6 3 c4 c6 variation transposes to the Panov-Botvinnik Attack in the Caro-Kann, but Black can try the virtually unexplored gambit 3 ... e6!? 4 de ♗xe6.

1 ... ♘c6. The Nimzowitsch Defence, envisaged by its namesake as a system akin to the French, has never been fully accepted as a dependable opening. Nevertheless it is sound and offers the maverick spirit a great deal of foreign territory to explore.

References: *Unorthodox Openings* (Benjamin and Schiller)
The English Defence: ... e6, ... b6, ... ♗b7 (Keene, Plaskett and Tisdall)

	1	2	3	4	5	6	7	8	9	
					1 e4					
1	...	d4[2]	♘f3[3]	♗d3[4]	♕e2[5]	0-0[6]	c3	e5	dc	±
	a6[1]	b5	♗b7	♘f6	e6	c5	d5[7]	♘fd7[8]	♘xc5[9]	
2	...	d4	♘c3	a3[10]	♗d3	e5	♘ce2	c3	♘f3	±
	b6	♗b7	e6	♘f6[11]	d5[12]	♘fd7[13]	c5	♘c6	cd[14]	
3	...	...	♗d3	♘c3[16]	♘ge2[18]	d5	a4	ed	♘xd5	±
	...	...	e6[15]	♘f6[17]	c5[19]	a6	ed	♘xd5	♗xd5[20]	⩲

[1] St George's Defence

1 ... g5 2 d4 h6 3 ♗d3 (3 h4!? gh 4 ♖xh4 d5 5 ed e6 6 ♖h5 ♘f6 7 de ∞ Speelman-Basman, British Ch 1980) 3 ... d6 4 ♘e2 c5 5 c3 ♘c6 6 0-0 ♘f6 7 ♘d2 ± Nunn-Basman, British Ch 1980 (Basmaniac Defence)

[2] 2 c4!? (Miles) 2 ... c5 3 ♘f3 ± – O'Kelly Sicilian

[3] 3 a4 ♗b7 4 ab?! ♗xe4! 5 ba ♗b7 ∓ Miles

3 ♗d3 e6 (3 ... ♗b7 4 f3 e6 5 ♗e3 ±) 4 ♘f3 ♗b7 5 0-0 c5 6 c3 ♘f6 7 ♖e1 ± Miles-Thomas, London 1984

3 ♗g5!? Larsen

[4] 4 e5!? (Chandler) 4 ... e6 5 c4 bc 6 ♗xc4 ♗b4+ 7 ♘c3 ♘e7 Miles

[5] 5 ♘bd2 e6 6 0-0 c5 7 c3 ♘c6 8 ♖e1 cd 9 cd ♖c8 10 a3 ± Torre-Winants, Brussels 1986

[6] 6 a4 c5 (6 ... b4!? Miles) 7 dc ♗xc5 8 ♘bd2

b4 9 e5 Nd5 10 Ne4 Be7 = Karpov-Miles, Skara 1980

[7] 7 ... Nc6 8 e5 (8 d5 Ne7 9 de de 10 e5 Nfd5 11 Ng5 Ng6 12 f4 c4! = De Rosende-Hodgson, Hastings II 1980-81) 8 ... c4 9 Bc2 Nd5 10 b3 ±

[8] 8 ... Ng8 9 dc Bxc5 10 Bxb5+! ± Hulak

[9] 10 Bc2 Nc6 11 Nd4 Be7 12 Nd2 0-0 13 N2f3 ± Larsen

[10] 4 Nf3 Nf6 5 Bd3 – 3 Bd3
   4 Nge2!? Larsen

[11] 4 ... g6?! 5 Nf3 Bg7 6 d5 Ne7 7 Bc4 0-0 8 0-0 ± Shamkovich-Basman, London 1978

[12] 5 ... c5 6 Nf3 cd 7 Nxd4 d6!? (7 ... Nc6 8 Nxc6 Bxc6 9 e5 Nd5 10 Ne4 Qc7 11 Qh5 ± Meyer-Werner, West Germany 1980) ± Larsen

[13] 6 ... Ne4 7 Nce2!

[14] 10 cd a6 11 0-0 ± Kovačević

[15] 3 ... f5?! 4 ef Bxg2 5 Qh5+ g6 6 fg Bg7 7 gh+ (7 Qf5!? Nf6 8 Bh6! ± Bruder-Vegener, corr. 1982) 7 ... Kf8 8 Be2! Bxh1 9 Nf4 Nf6 10 Ng6+ Ke8 11 Nxh8+ ± Lalev-Trifonov, Bulgaria 1985

[16] 4 Nf3 c5 5 c3 Nf6 6 Qe2 Be7 7 0-0 Nc6 (7 ... d5 8 e5 Nfd7 9 a3 ± Matulović-Sahović, Bled 1984) 8 e5 Nd5 9 dc bc 10 Na3 ± Larsen

[17] 4 ... g6 5 Nge2 Bg7 6 h4!? Nc6 7 Bg5 Nge7 8 h5! ± Rogers-Spassky, Reggio Emilia 1983-84

[18] 5 Nf3 Bb4 6 Qe2 d5 7 ed Nxd5 8 Bd2 Nxc3 9 bc Be7 ∞ Kagan-Sahović, Biel 1976
   5 Qf3 d6 6 Nge2 Nbd7 7 Qh3 g6 8 Bg5 Bg7 9 0-0-0 h6 10 Be3 Qe7 ∞ Murei-Keene, Netanya 1977

[19] 5 ... d5 6 e5 Nfd7 7 Nf4 ±

[20] 10 Nf4 Be6 11 Be4 Ra7 12 0-0 ± Speelman-Basman, British Ch 1984

	Centre Counter (Scandinavian)				1 e4 d5 2 ed				
2	3	4	5	6	7	8	9	10	
1 ...	Nc3	d4	Bc4![3]	Nge2	Bg5	Qd2	f3	g4	±/±
Qxd5	Qd8[1]	Nf6[2]	Bg4[4]	e6	Be7	Nbd7	Bf5	Bg6[5]	
2 ...	...	d4[6]	Nf3[8]	Bc4[10]	Bd2![12]	Qe2	Ne5[14]	Nxd7[15]	±
...	Qa5	Nf6[7]	Bf5[9]	c6[11]	e6[13]	Bb4	Nbd7	Nxd7[16]	

[1] 3 ... Qd6 4 d4 Nf6 5 Nf3 (5 Bc4 a6 6 Nge2 Qc6 7 Bb3 Qxg2 8 Rg1 Qxh2 9 Bf4 ∞ Vera-Utasi, Havana 1986) 5 ... Bg4 (5 ... a6?! 6 Be3 Nc6 7 Qd2 Bg4 8 Ng5! ± Karpov-Lutikov, USSR 1979) 6 Be2 ±

[2] 4 ... g6 5 Bf4 Bg7 (5 ... Nh6 6 Be5! f6 7 Bf4 ± Fischer) 6 Qd2! Nf6 (6 ... Qxd4 7 Qxd4 Bxd4 8 Nb5 ± Fischer) 7 0-0-0 Nd5 8 Be5 0-0 9 h4 h5 10 Nge2 ± Fischer

[3] 5 Nf3 Bg4 6 Be2 e6 ∞/±

[4] 5 ... Bf5 6 Qf3! Qc8 7 Bg5 Bxc2 8 Rc1 Bg6 9 Nge2 ± Fischer-Addison, Palma de Mallorca IZ 1970

[5] 11 h4 h6 12 Bf4 ± ECO

[6] 4 Nf3 and now:
   4 ... Bg4 5 h3 Bh5 6 g4 Bg6 7 Bg2 ± Chiburdanidze-Klarić, Banja Luka 1985
   4 ... Nc6 5 Bb5! a6 6 Bxc6+ bc 7 Qe2! Nf6 8 Ne5 ± Karpov-Hort, Oslo 1984
   4 ... Nf6 5 d4 – 4 d4

[7] 4 ... e5 5 Nf3 (5 de Bb4 6 Bd2 Nc6 7 a3 ±) 5 ... Bg4 6 h3 ed 7 Qxd4! ± Keene

[8] 5 Bd2 Bg4 6 Be2 Bxe2 7 Ncxe2 Qb6 8 Nf3 Nbd7 9 0-0 e6 = Karpov-Larsen, Montreal 1979

[9] 5 ... Nc6 6 Bb5 Bd7 7 d5 ± Shamkovich-Leverett, USA 1977
   5 ... c6 6 Bc4 (6 Bd2 Qc7 7 Bc4 ± Tal) 6 ... Bg4 7 h3 Bh5 8 g4 (8 Bd2 e6 9 g4 Bg6 10 Qe2 ± Nunn) 8 ... Bg6 9 Ne5 e6 10 Nxg6 hg 11 Bd2 ± Radulov-K.Berg, Silkeborg 1986

[10] 6 Ne5 c6 7 g4 Be6 8 Bd2 Nbd7 9 Nxd7 Nxd7 10 Bg2 Qc7 ∞ Pinal-Bellon, Havana 1986
   6 Bd3 e6 7 Bxf5 Qxf5 8 Ne5 h5 9 0-0 Nbd7 = Barle-Larsen, Bled/Portorož 1979

[11] 6 ... Nbd7 7 Bd2! c6 – 6 ... c6

[12] 7 Ne5 e6 8 0-0 Nbd7 9 Nxd7 (9 Qe2 Bb4 10 Nxd7 Nxd7 = Fedorowicz-Cirić, Manchester 1981) 9 ... Nxd7 10 Re1 Nf6 11 a3 Bd6 = Lerner-Sokolov, USSR Ch 1984

[13] 7 ... Nbd7 8 Qe2 e6 9 d5! ± Spassky-Larsen, Montreal 1979

[14] 9 0-0-0 Nd5 10 Nxd5 Bxd2+ 11 Nxd2 cd 12 Nb3 ∞/± Ljubojević-Kurajica, Bugojno 1980

[15] 10 0-0-0 Nxe5 11 de Nd5! (11 ... Nd7 12 a3 b5 13 Ba2 ± Jansa-Taulbut, Copenhagen 1981) 12 Bxd5 ed 13 g4 Be6 14 f4 0-0-0 ∞ Nijboer-Stehouwer, Holland 1985-86

[16] 11 a3 Bb6 12 0-0 ± Chandler-Rogers, Bath 1983

	2	3	4	5	6	7	8	9	10	
3	...	Nc3	d4	Nf3	h3[17]	g4[19]	Ne5	Bg2[21]	Bxe4	±
	Qxd5	Qa5	Nf6	Bg4	Bh5[18]	Bg6	e6[20]	Be4[22]	Nxe4[23]	
4	...	Bb5+	Bc4[25]	f3	Nc3[28]	Qe2	Bb3	d6	Nb5	∞
	Nf6	Bd7[24]	Bg4[26]	Bf5[27]	Nbd7	Nb6	Qd7!	Qxd6[29]	Qd7[30]	
5	...	d4	c4	Nf3	h3[33]	Nc3	Be3[34]	Qd2	d5	∞
	...	Nxd5	Nb6[31]	g6[32]	Bg7	0-0	Nc6	e5	Ne7[35]	
6	...	...	Nf3	h3[37]	g4	Ne5	Nxg6[39]	Bg2	Nc3	±
	...	...	Bg4[36]	Bh5	Bg6	Nc6[38]	hg	Qd6	Nf4[40]	
7	...	...	...	Bc4!?[41]	0-0	c3	Re1	Bb3	Bf4[43]	∞/±
	...	...	g6	Bg7	0-0	Nc6	Nb6	Bg4[42]	e5!?[44]	

[17] 6 Bb5+ c6 7 Be2 e6 8 0-0 Bd6 = Radulov-Bitman, Albena 1981

[18] 6 ... Bxf3 7 Qxf3 c6 8 Bd2 Nbd7 9 0-0-0 e6 10 Bc4 ± Gufeld

[19] 7 Bd2!? e6 8 Bc4 c6 9 Nd5 (9 Qe2 Bb4 10 g4 Bg6 11 0-0-0 Nbd7 12 Kb1 0-0-0 13 a3 ± Dolmatov-Rogers, Tallinn 1985) 9 ... Qd8 10 Nxf6+ gf (10 ... Qxf6?! 11 g4 Bg6 12 Qe2 ± Chandler-Rogers, Hong Kong 1984) 11 c3 Nd7 12 Qe2 Qc7 13 0-0-0 ± Abramović-Rogers, Bor 1984

[20] 8 ... Ne4 9 Bg2 Nxc3 10 Qd2 c6 11 bc e6 12 Rb1 ± Belyavsky-Böhm, Le Havre 1977
8 ... c6 9 h4 Nbd7 10 Nc4 Qc7 11 h5 ± Matulović-Govedarica, Vrnjačka Banja 1986

[21] 9 Nc4 Qa6 10 Rh3 Bxc3+ (10 ... c6 11 Bd2 Qb6 12 h5 Be4 13 Re3! ± Karpov-Rogers, Bath 1983) 11 bc Nbd7 12 Nxd7 (12 Nxg6 hg 13 Rb1 0-0 14 Rb5 Qa4 ∞ Lobron-Rogers, Biel 1984) 12 ... Nxd7 13 h5 Be4 14 Bd2 0-0 15 Re3 Be6 16 c4 Qg5 = Timman-Rogers, Reggio Emilia 1984-85

[22] 9 ... c6 10 h4 Be4 (10 ... Nbd7 11 Nc4 Qa6 12 Bf1 b5 13 h5 ± Karpov-Larsen, Mar del Plata 1982) 11 Bxe4 Nxe4 12 Qf3 Nd6 13 Bf4 ± Karpov

[23] 11 Qf3 Nd6 12 0-0! ± Jansa-Rogers, Niš 1985

[24] 3 ... Nbd7 4 c4 a6 5 Bxd7+ Qxd7 6 d3 b5 7 Nf3 ±

[25] 4 Be2 Nxd5 5 d4 Bf5 6 Nf3 e6 7 0-0 Be7 =

[26] 4 ... b5 5 Be2 (5 Bb3 a5 6 a4 ba 7 Bc4 Bg4 8 f3 Bc8 9 Nc3 Bb7 10 Nge2 Bxd5 ∞ Kupreichik-Smagin, USSR Ch 1985) 5 ... Bxd5 6 d4 e6 7 Nf3 Bd6 8 0-0 Nc6 9 a4! ± Matulović-Bronstein, Hamburg 1965

[27] 5 ... Bc8 6 Nc3 Nbd7 7 d4 Nb6 8 Bb3 Nbxd5 9 Nxd5 Nxd5 10 c4 ±

[28] 6 g4 Bc8 7 Nc3 c6 (7 ... a6!? Gipslis) 8 dc Nxc6 9 d3 e5 (9 ... g6!? Larsen) ∞

[29] 9 ... cd 10 a4 a5 11 d3 ±

[30] 11 Qe5 0-0-0 12 Nxa7+ Kb8 13 Nb5 Nfd5 14 a4 e6! ∞ Peters

[31] 4 ... Nb4 5 Qa4+ N8c6 6 a3 Na6 7 Nf3 (7 Be3 ±) ±
4 ... Nf6 5 Nf3 g6 6 Nc3 Bg7 7 h3 0-0 8 Be3 Nbd7 9 Qd2 c6 10 Be2 Re8 11 Rd1 ± Tal-Bronstein, Moscow 1967

[32] 5 ... Bg4 6 c5 N6d7 7 Bc4 e6 8 h3! Bh5 9 Be3 ± Byrne-Rogoff, US Ch 1978

[33] 6 Be2 Bg7 7 0-0 (7 Be3 0-0 8 0-0 Nc6 9 h3 e5 10 d5 e4! 11 Nd4 Ne5 12 Qb3 a5! Moen-Ostenstad, Gausdal 1985) 7 ... 0-0 8 Nc3 Bg4 9 h3 Bxf3 10 Bxf3 Nc6 = Granat-Martin, London 1985; 8 ... Nc6 9 d5! Ne5 (9 ... Na5 10 c5!) 10 Nxe5 Bxe5 11 Bh6 ± J.Polgar-Stefansson, Iceland 1988

[34] 8 Be2 Nc6 9 Be3 e5 10 de Nxe5 11 Nxe5 Bxe5 12 Qxd8 Rxd8 13 Rc1 Be6 = Westerinen-Ostenstad, Gausdal 1985

[35] 11 g4 e4! 12 Nxe4 f5 13 Nc5 fg ∞ Tseshkovsky-Smagin, USSR Ch 1986

[36] 4 ... Bf5 5 Bd3 Bxd3 6 Qxd3 c6 7 0-0 e6 8 c4 Nf6 9 Nc3 ± Zuckerman-Shamkovich, New York 1980

[37] 5 Be2 Nc6 6 0-0 e6 7 Re1 Be7 8 c3 0-0 9 Nbd2 a6 = Damjanović-Gipslis, 1979-80

[38] 7 ... Nd7 8 Nxg6 hg 9 Bg2 c6 10 c4 ± Razuvayev-Gipslis, USSR 1973

[39] 8 Nxc6 bc 9 Bg2 Qd6 10 Na3 h5 ∞

[40] 10 ... Nxc3 11 bc 0-0-0 12 Rb1 Kb8 13 0-0! ±
10 ... Nf4 11 Bxf4 Qxf4 12 Qd3 ±

[41] 5 Be2 Bg7 6 0-0 0-0 7 Na3 (7 h3 Nc6! 8 c4 Nb6 9 d5 Ne5! ∞ Yakovich) 7 ... a5 (7 ... Nc6 8 Nc4 Bg4 9 c3 Nb6 10 Ne3 ∞) 8 Nc4 a4 9 Bd2 c5 10 dc Qc7 11 Qc1 ∞ Yakovich-Smagin, USSR Ch 1986

[42] 9 ... Bf5 10 Nbd2 (10 a4 Na5 11 Ba2 c5! ∞ Glek-Smagin, USSR 1984) ±

[43] 10 h3 Bxf3 11 Qxf3 a5 12 a4 e5!? Chekhov

[44] 11 de Qxd1 12 Bxd1 Nc4 13 Nbd2! ∞/± Klovan-Dautov, USSR 1986

	Nimzowitsch		1 e4 ♘c6						

	2	3	4	5	6	7	8	9	10	
1	♘f3[1]	d4	♘c3[3]	♗b5[5]	♗xc6+	♗g5![6]	♗h4	h3	♕e2	±
	d6	♘f6[2]	♗g4[4]	a6	bc	h6	g6	♗d7	♗g7[7]	
2	d4	de[8]	♘f3[9]	♗e2[11]	♘bd2[13]	♗xf3	0-0	♘c4[14]	c3	±
	e5	♘xe5	♕f6[10]	♗b4+[12]	♘xf3+	♘e7	0-0	d6		
3	...	e5[15]	♘e2[17]	♘g3	h4[19]	♘e2	♘f4	c3	♘d2	∞
	d5	♗f5[16]	e6	♗g6[18]	h5[20]	♗f5	g6	♕d7	f6[21]	
4	...	♘c3	d5	♗f4[23]	♗g3	♘h3![25]	de	♘b5	♗xd6[26]	±
	...	de	♘e5[22]	♘g6	f5[24]	e5	♗xe6	♗d6	cd[27]	

[1]   2 f4 d5 3 e5 d4 4 ♘f3 ♗f5 5 ♗b5 e6 ∞ Coates-Smith, British Ch 1978

[2]   3 ... ♗g4 4 ♗b5 (4 d5 ♘b8 5 c4 ±) 4 ... a6 5 ♗a4 b5 (5 ... ♘f6 6 c4! ±) 6 ♗b3 ♘f6 7 c3 e6 8 ♕e2 ♗e7 9 0-0 0-0 10 ♘bd2 ±

[3]   4 c3!? ♗g4 5 ♗e3 e5 6 ♘bd2 ed 7 cd d5 8 e5 ♘e4 9 ♗b5 ± Sarapu-Corry, New Zealand 1985

[4]   4 ... a6 5 ♗g5 ♗g4 6 ♗e2 e6 7 h3 ♗h5 8 d5 ± Salov-Kuijf, Mexico 1981
4 ... e5 5 d5 (5 de ♘xe5 6 ♘xe5 de 7 ♕xd8+ ♔xd8 8 ♗c4 ±) 5 ... ♘e7 6 ♗e2 ♘g6 7 0-0 ♗g4 8 ♘d2! ♗d7 9 ♘c4 ± Marić-Metstrović, Tjentiste 1986

[5]   5 d5 ♘b8 (5 ... ♘e5 6 ♗b5+ c6 7 dc ♘xc6 8 e5 ± Timman-Miles, Tilburg 1981) 6 ♗e2 g6 7 ♗g5 (7 ♘d4 ♗xe2 8 ♕xe2 c6 9 ♗g5 ♗g7 10 0-0-0 0-0 11 f4 ± A.Sokolov-Torre, USSR v World 1984) 7 ... ♗g7 8 ♕d2 0-0 9 h3 ± London-Benjamin, New York 1985
5 ♗e3 e6 6 ♗e2 ♗e7 7 ♕d2 0-0 8 0-0 ♖e8 9 ♖ad1 d5 10 e5! ± Wedberg-Miles, Oslo 1984

[6]   7 h3 ♗h5 8 ♕e2 e6 9 ♗g5 (9 g4 ♗g6 10 ♘h4 d5! 10 e5! ± Hulak-Miles, Indonesia 1982) 9 ... ♗e7 10 ♗xf6 ♗xf6 11 g4 ♗g6 12 ♕c4! ± Sax-Kindermann, Lucerne 1985

[7]   11 0-0-0 ± Timman-Kuijf, Holland 1984-85

[8]   3 d5 ♘ce7 4 c4 ±
3 ♘f3 – Scotch

[9]   4 f4 ♘g6 (4 ... ♘c6 5 ♗c4 ♗b4+ 6 ♗d2 ♕h4+ 7 g3 ♕e7 8 ♕e2 ± Hübner-Hort, West Germany 1984-85) 5 ♗e3 ♗b4+ 6 c3 ♗e7!? Larsen

[10]   4 ... ♘xf3+ 5 ♕xf3 ♕f6 6 ♕g3 ♕g6 7 ♕xc7 ♕xe4+ 8 ♗e3 ± Lombardy-Calvo, Siegen Ol 1970

[11]   5 ♘xe5 ♕xe5 6 ♗d3 ± Tarve-Ritov, USSR 1976

[12]   5 ... ♘xf3+ 6 ♗xf3 ♗c5 7 ♘c3 (Paulsen-Alapin, Breslau 1889) 7 ... ♘e7 ± Larsen

[13]   6 c3 ♗c5 7 0-0 ♘e7 8 ♘bd2 d6 9 ♘b3 ♗b6 = Tarve-Keres, Tallinn 1969

[14]   9 ♘b3 ♘c6 10 g3 ± Keres-Kevitz, USSR v USA 1954

[15]   3 de!? ♕xd5 4 ♘c3!? ♕xd4 5 ♕e2!? Marshall

[16]   3 ... f6 4 f4 ♗f5 5 ♘e2 e6 6 c3 fe 7 fe ♘ce7 (7 ... ♗e7 8 ♘f4! ♕d7 9 ♗d3 ± Sax-Kastro, Budapest 1977) 8 ♘g3 ♗g6 9 ♘d2 ± Larsen

[17]   4 h4 ♕d7 (4 ... f6?! 5 g4 ♗e6 6 f4 fe 7 de g6 8 ♗d3 ± Plaskett-Crawley, British Ch 1986) =

[18]   5 ... ♘ge7 6 ♘xf5 ♘xf5 7 c3 f6 8 ef ♕xf6 9 ♘d2 ±

[19]   6 f4 ♘b4 7 ♘a3 c5 8 c3 ♘c6 ∞

[20]   6 ... f6 7 h5 ♗f7 8 f4 ♕d7 9 ♗b5!? a6 10 ♗a4 ♘h6 ∞ Randall-Harding, England 1978

[21]   Romanishin-Mariotti, Leningrad 1977

[22]   4 ... ♘b8 5 ♗c4 (5 f3 e6! =) 5 ... ♘f6 6 ♗f4 a6 7 ♕e2 b5 8 ♗b3 c5 9 dc ♘xc6 10 ♖d1 ± Keres-Larsen, Stockholm 1966-67

[23]   5 ♕d4 ♘g6 6 ♗b5+!? (6 ♕xe4 a6 7 ♗e3 ♘f6 8 ♕d4 e5 9 de ♗xe6 10 0-0-0 ♗d6 ∞ West-Miles, London 1981) 6 ... ♗d7 7 ♘ge2 (7 ♗c4 f5 8 f3 e5! 9 de ∞) 7 ... ♘f6 8 ♗g5 ± Campora-Wockenfuss, Amsterdam II 1985

[24]   6 ... a6 7 ♗c4! ♘f6 8 ♕e2 ± Rogers

[25]   7 ♗b5+ ♗d7 8 ♘h3!? (8 ♘ge2 a6 9 ♗c4 b5 10 ♗b3 c5 ∞) 8 ... c6 9 ♗c4 ± Schwarz

[26]   10 ♘xd6 cd 11 ♗xd6 ± Rogers

[27]   11 ♕d4! ± Rogers-Dunne, Philadelphia 1986

Alekhine

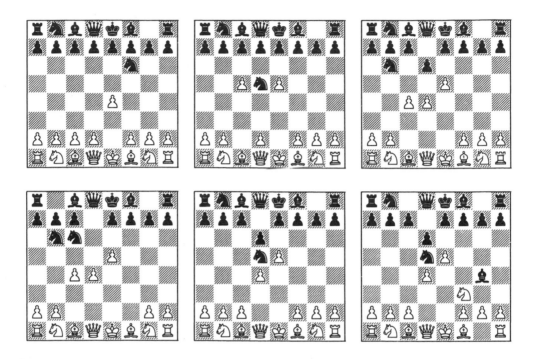

Alekhine's Defence, in the best hypermodern tradition, attempts to lure White's centre forward in order to fix and, later, to sabotage it. In practice, the defence leads to positions of an obscure order, but there are several ways for White to maintain an edge and the choice is a matter of temperament. Of modern GMs only Alburt, Kovačević, Palatnik and Bagirov seem comfortable with the difficult and unique problems native to the defence.

Reference: *The Alekhine for the Tournament Player* (Alburt and Schiller)

	2	3	4	5	6	7	8	9	10	
1	♘c3[1]	e5	ef	fg	♕xd2[2]	♗xd2	0-0-0	♗b5	♘f3	=
	d5	d4	dc	cd+	♕xd2+	♗xg7	♘c6[3]	♗d7	0-0-0[4]	
2	...	...	♘ce2	c3[6]	♘xd4[8]	♕a4+	♕xd4	cd	♗c4	∞∞
	...	♘e4	d4[5]	♘c6[7]	♘xd4	c6	♕xd4	♘g5	♘e6[9]	
3	...	...	e6[10]	d4	♘f3	dc	h4	♗b5	♗f4	∞
	...	♘fd7	fe	c5[11]	♘c6	g6[12]	♘f6[13]	♗g7	0-0[14]	
4	...	ed	♗c4[15]	♘f3[17]	0-0	d4	♘e4	♕e2	♖d1	=
	...	♘xd5	e6[16]	♗e7	0-0	b6	♗b7	♘d7	c5	

Alekhine I   1 e4 ♘f6

	2	3	4	5	6	7	8	9	10	
5	e5	♘c3[19]	d4[21]	♘f3	♘xe5	bc	♗f4	♘c4		±
	♘d5[18]	e6[20]	d6	de[22]	♘xc3	♘d7	c5	♘b6[23]		
6	...	...	bc	f4	♘f3	d4	♗e2[25]	0-0	fe	∞/∓
	...	♘xc3!	c5[24]	d6	g6	♗g7	0-0	de	♘c6[26]	
7	...	...	dc	♘f3[28]	♕xd8+	♘xe5	♗c4[29]	♗e3[30]	♘d3	∞
	...	...	d6[27]	de	♔xd8	♔e8	e6	♗d6	♗d7[31]	

---

[1] **2 ♗c4 ♘xe4!** 3 ♗xf7+ ♔xf7 4 ♕h5+ ♔g8 5 ♕d5+ e6 6 ♕xe4 d5 7 ♕e2 c5 ∞/∓

2 d3 e5 (2 ... c5 =) 3 ♘f3 ♘c6 4 ♗e2 d5 5 ♘bd2 ♗e7 6 0-0 0-0 7 c3 a5 = Tompa-Orev, Budapest 1969

[2] 6 ♗xd2 ♗xg7 7 ♕f3 ♗xb2 8 ♖d1 ♕d4 9 ♘e2 ♕g4 10 ♕b3 ♗f6 ∞

[3] 8 ... ♗f5!? 9 ♘e2 ♘c6 10 ♗c3 ♖g8 11 ♗xg7 ♖xg7 12 ♘g3 ♗d7 =

[4] 11 ♖he1 e6 12 ♘g5 ♖df8 13 ♗e3 a6 = Chekhov-Barlov, Tjentiste 1975

[5] **4 ... ♘c5** 5 d4 ♘e6 6 f4 g6 7 ♗e3 ♗g7 8 ♕d2 b6 9 h3 e6 10 ♘f3 ± Gaprindashvili-Alexandria, match 1975

4 ... f6 5 d3 ♘g5 6 ♗xg5 fg 7 h4 gh?! 8 ♘f4 g6 9 ♖xh4 ♗g7 10 d4 c5 11 ♗d3 ± Vorotnikov-Kengis, Tallinn 1983; 7 ... g4! ∞ Alburt, Schiller

[6] 5 d3 ♘c5 6 b4 ♘e6 7 ♘f3 c5! 8 bc ♘c6 ∞

[7] 5 ... dc 6 ♕a4+ ♘d7 7 ♕xe4? ♘c5! ∓

[8] 6 cd ♘g5 7 ♕a4 a6 8 f4 ♘e6 9 ♘f3 b5 ∞

[9] 11 ♘e2 ♘c7 12 d3 a5 ∞ Yakovich-Kengis, USSR 1984

[10] **4 ♘xd5** ♘xe5 5 ♘e3 c5 6 b3 ♘ec6! 7 ♗b2 e5 8 g3 ♗d6 9 ♗g2 0-0 10 ♘e2 f5 = Groszpeter-Suba, Kecskemet 1979

4 f4 e6 5 ♘f3 c5 6 g3 ♘c6 7 ♗g2 ♗e7 8 0-0 a6 (8 ... 0-0 9 ♔h1 b5 10 ♘xb5 ♖a6 11 a4 ♕a5 12 ♕e2 ∞/± Kupreichik-Balashov, Kiev 1984) 9 a4 ♕a5 ∞

[11] 5 ... g6 6 h4 ♗g7 7 h5 ♘f8 8 ♘f3 ∞ Bagirov; 8 ... c5!?, 8 ... ♘c6 intending ... e5

[12] 7 ... a6 8 ♗e3 ♘f6 9 ♗g5 ♕c7 10 g3 ±

[13] 8 ... ♗g7 9 h5 gh 10 ♗e2 ♕a5 11 ♘g5 ±

[14] 11 ♗xc6 bc 12 ♗e5 ♕a5 = Bagirov

[15] **4 ♘ge2** e6 5 g3 ♘xc3 6 ♘xc3 ♗d7 7 ♗c4 c5 8 0-0 ♘c6 = Keres-Marović, Erevan 1971

4 g3 b6 5 ♗g2 ♗b7 6 ♘f3 e6 7 0-0 ♗e7 8 ♖e1 0-0 9 ♘e4 ♘d7 Westerinen-Timman, Tallinn 1973

[16] 4 ... ♘b6 5 ♗b3 ♘c6 (5 ... c5 6 ♕h5! e6 7 d3 ♘c6 8 ♗g5! ±) 6 ♘f3 g6 7 ♘g5 e6 8 d3 ♘d4 9 0-0 ♗g7 10 ♘ce4 h6 = Rozentalis-Bagirov, USSR 1985

[17] 5 ♕f3 ♘b4 6 ♗b3 ♘8c6 7 ♘ge2 ♘a5 8 ♗a4+ ♗d7 9 a3 ♘d5 =

[18] 2 ... ♘g8!? Berwick v Edinburgh, corr. 1860-61) 3 d4 d6 and now:

4 ♘f3! ♗g4 (4 ... c6!?, 4 ... c5!? Alburt, Schiller) 5 h3! ± Smejkal-Vesely, Czechoslovakia 1968

4 ed ed (4 ... ♕xd6 – Scandinavian) 5 ♗d3 ♘c6 6 c3 ♘f6 7 ♘e2 ♗g4 8 0-0 ♕d7 9 ♖e1 0-0-0 ∞ Forster-Schiller, England 1982

[19] **3 ♗c4** ♘b6 4 ♗b3 d5 5 ed ed 6 d4 ♗e7 7 ♘f3 0-0 8 0-0 ♗g4 =

3 ♘f3 d6 4 ♗c4 ♘b6 5 ♗b3 ♗f5! = Alburt, Schiller

3 b3?! g6! ∓

3 ♕f3 e6 4 ♗c4 ♘b6 = Wedberg-Niklasson, Lund 1974

[20] 3 ... c6 4 d4 d6 5 f4 ♗f5 6 ♘xd5 cd 7 ♘f3 ♘c6 8 ♗d3 ♗xd3 9 ♕xd3 ± Zaitsev-Westerinen, Moscow 1982

[21] 4 ♘xd5 ed 5 d4 d6 (5 ... ♗e7 6 ♗d3 0-0 7 ♕h5 g6 8 ♕h6 ♘c6 9 ♘f3 ±/± Andreescu-Orev, Romania 1982) 6 ♘f3 ♘c6 7 ♗e2 ♗e7 8 ♗f4 0-0 9 0-0 f6! =

[22] 5 ... ♘c6 6 ♗b5 ♘xc3 7 bc de 8 ♘xe5 ♗d7 9 ♘xd7 ♕xd7 10 0-0 ±

[23] Bagirov

[24] **4 ... d6** 5 f4 ♗f5 (5 ... c5 6 ♘f3 ♘c6) 6 ♘f3 e6 7 d4 ♗e7 8 ♗d3 ♗xd3 9 ♕xd3 =/±

4 ... d5 5 d4 c5 6 ♘f3 ♘c6 7 ♗e2 ♗g4 8 0-0 e6 9 ♖b1 ∞ Nikolić-Schmidt, Smederevska Palanka 1978

[25] 8 ♗b5+ ♗d7 9 ♗xd7+ ♕xd7 10 0-0 =

[26] 11 ♗f4 ♗g4 ∞/∓ Hennings-Gipslis, Havana 1971

[27] 4 ... d5 5 c4 c6 6 ♘f3 ♗g4 7 h3 ♗xf3 8 ♕xf3 e6 9 cd ♕xd5 10 ♕xd5 cd ∓ Kuzmin-Alburt, USSR 1974

[28] **5 ♗f4** ♘c6 6 ♘f3 de! 7 ♕xd8 ♘xd8 8 ♗xe5 c6 9 0-0-0 f6 10 ♗g3 e5 = Boleslavsky

5 ♗c4 ♘c6 6 ♘f3 de 7 ♕xd8+ ♘xd8 8 ♘xe5 f6 9 ♘d3 e5 =

[29] 8 ♗e3 ♘d7 9 ♘f3 e5 10 0-0-0 f6 11 ♘d2 ♗c5 =

[30] 9 ♗f4 ♗d6 10 0-0-0 ♘d7 11 ♖he1 = Pfleger-Schmidt, Polanica Zdroj 1971

[31] 11 0-0-0 ♗c6 12 f3 ♘d7 13 ♘b4 ♘b6 = Radulov-Jansa, Erebro 1966

	5	6	7	8	9	10	11	12	13	
1	♘c3	dc	cd[1]	♗c4[2]	♗f4	♗xe5	♕xd8	♘f3	0-0-0	±
	♘xc3	d6	ed	♗e7	de	0-0	♗xd8	♗g4	♘d7[3]	
2	...	♘xd5[4]	d4	cd	♘f3	♗e2	0-0	♗f4	♕d2	=
	e6	ed	d6[5]	cd	♘c6	♗e7[6]	0-0	♗g4	♖e8[7]	
3	...	d4	cd	♘f3	ed[8]	♗d3	♗xf4	♕e2[9]	♗b5+	=
	...	d6	cd	♘c6	♗xd6	♘f4	♗xf4	♘b4[10]	♗d7[11]	
4	...	♗c4	♕b3[13]	♘xd5	♗xd5	♗xb7	♕xb7	♕c8+	♕c7+	∞
	c6	d6[12]	de[14]	cd	e6	♗xb7	♕d5[15]	♔e7	♔f6[16]	
5	♗c4	♘c3	♘xd5	♗xd5	♗xf7+	cd	♕f3+	♕e3	♘ge2	∞
	e6[17]	d6[18]	ed	c6	♔xf7	♕e8[19]	♔g8	♗e6	♘d7[20]	
6	...	...	dc	♗f4	cb[23]	♘f3	0-0	♕e2	ef	±
	...	♘xc3	♘c6[21]	b6[22]	ab	♗e7	0-0	f5	♗xf6[24]	
7	...	...	...	...	♕g4	♗xg5[25]	♘h3[26]	f4	fe	∞
	...	...	...	♗xc5!	g5	♖g8	♗e7	♘xe5	♗xg5[27]	
8	...	d4	cd	♕e2[29]	♘f3	0-0	♕e4	♗d3	♗h6	∞/=
	...	d6[28]	cd	♘c6	♗e7[30]	0-0	b6[31]	g6	♖e8[32]	

[1] 7 ♗c4 d5! 8 ♕xd5 ♕xd5 9 ♗xd5 e6 10 ♗e4 ♗xc5 =
7 ♗g5 de (7 ... f6!?) 8 ♕b3 ♕d7 9 ♖d1 ♕f5 10 ♗c4 ♘c6 11 ♗d5 h6 12 ♕b5 ♕g6 ∞; 10 ... ♘d7! ∓

[2] 8 ♘f3 ♗e7 9 ♗c4 de 10 ♕xd8+ ♗xd8 11 ♘xe5 0-0 = Estrin-Bagirov, USSR 1960

[3] 14 ♗f4 ♘b6 15 ♗b3 ± Krogius-A.Zaitsev, Rostov 1971

[4] 6 ♗c4 – 5 ♗c4

[5] 7 ... b6 8 ♗e3 bc 9 dc c6 10 ♗d3 ♘a6 (10 ... ♗a6 11 b4! ±) 11 ♖c1 ♕a5+ 12 ♗d2! ♕xa2 13 ♖a1 ♕xb2 14 ♗xa6 ♗xa6 15 ♖xa6 ♕xe5+ 16 ♘e2 ♗xc5 17 0-0 ±/± Hennings-Smejkal, Kapfenberg 1970

[6] 10 ... de 11 ♘xe5 ♗b4+ 12 ♗d2 ♕b6 13 ♘xc6 bc = Vaskanian-Shmit, Riga 1975

[7] 14 ♖fd1 ♖ac8 15 ♖ac1 a6 = Ničevski-Vasyukov, Skopje 1969

[8] 9 ♕b3 ♗e7 10 ed ♕xd6 =

[9] 12 0-0 0-0 13 ♖e1 g6 14 ♗f1 ♗h6 = Csom

[10] 12 ... ♘xd4?! 13 ♘xd4 ♕xd4 14 g3 ♗c7 15 ♗b5+ ♔e7 16 0-0 ± Damjanović-Buljovčić, Belgrade 1966

[11] 14 d5 0-0 15 ♗xd7 ♕xd7 = Bagirov

[12] 6 ... ♘xc3 7 dc d5 8 cd ed 9 ♘f3 d5 10 ♗d3 ♗g4 11 h3 ♗h5 12 ♗f4 ±

[13] 7 cd cd 8 ♘f3 ♗e7 9 0-0 (Mechkarov-Suba, Bankya 1977) 9 ... ♘xc3! 10 dc 0-0 = Alburt

[14] 7 ... ♘d7!? 8 ♗xd5 ♘xc5! 9 ♘c7+ ♕xc7!? 10 ♗xf7+ ♔d8 11 ♕c2 g6! =; 8 cd ♘xe5 9 ♘xd5 cd 10 ♗xd5 e6 ∞

[15] 11 ... ♘d7 12 b4 ♖b8 13 ♕e4 f5 14 ♕c4 ±

[16] 14 d4 ♘c6 ∞ Sveshnikov-Palatnik, USSR 1974

[17] 5 ... c6 6 ♕e2 e6!? 7 d4 b6 8 cb ab 9 ♘f3 ♗e7 10 ♘bd2 ∞/± Shabalov-Shmit, Riga 1983

[18] 6 ... c6 7 ♘e4 b6 8 ♗d6+ ♗xd6 9 cd ∞/± Szabolcsi-Knežević, Budapest 1982
6 ... ♗xc5 7 d4 (7 ♕g4 0-0!) 7 ... ♗b4 8 ♗xd5 ed 9 ♕g4 ♔f8 10 ♘f3 d6 11 ♕g3 ∞∞/±

[19] 10 ... ♗e6 11 ♘f3 (11 ♘h3!?) 11 ... ♘d7 12 0-0 g6 13 d3 h6 14 ♘d4 ±

[20] 14 0-0 ♘xe5! 15 ♕xe5 ♗c4 16 ♕xe8 ♖xe8 ∞ Vasyukov-Spassky, Tbilisi 1959

[21] 7 ... b6!? 8 cb ab 9 ♘f3 d5 10 ed cd 11 0-0 ♗e7 ∞/= Sveshnikov-Bagirov, USSR 1967
7 ... ♗xc5 8 ♕g4 ♔f8 9 ♘f3 ♘c6 10 ♗g5 ♗e7 11 h4 ± Ozsvath-Garcia, Moscow 1968; 8 ... ♕e7 9 ♕xg7 ♕f8 ∞

[22] 8 ... ♕h4!? (Suba) 9 ♕d2 ♘xe5 10 ♗e2 ♘g6 11 ♗xc7 ♗xc5 12 ♗g3 ∞∞ Angelov-Suba, Varna 1975

[23] 9 ♕g4 ♗b7 10 ♘f3 ♘e7 11 ♖d1 ∞ Hort

[24] 14 ♖fd1 d5 15 ♗g3 ± Marklund-Ghizdavu, Reggio Emilia 1973

[25] 10 ♕xg5 ♕xg5 11 ♗xg5 ♘xe5 12 ♗f6 ♘xc4 13 ♗xh8 ♘xb2 ∓ Kirov-Orev, Bulgaria 1962

[26] 11 ♗xd8 ♖xg4 12 ♗e2 ♖xg2 13 ♗xc7 b6! ∞

[27] 14 ♕h5 ♖g7 15 0-0 ♕e7 = Angelov-Orev, Sofia 1971

[28] 6 ... b6 7 cb ab 8 ♘e2 ♗a6 9 ♗xd5 ed 10 ♘bc3 c6 ∞ Semenyuk-Mikhalchishin, USSR 1975

[29] 8 ♘f3 ♘b6 9 d3 ♘c6 10 0-0 ♘b4 = Hort

[30] 9 ... de 10 de ♘a5 11 ♗xd5 ♕xd5 12 0-0 ♕c4! = Gurgenidze-Mikenas, Kharkov 1967

[31] 11 ... ♔h8!? 12 ♗d3 f5 13 ef ♘xf6 14 ♕e2 ♕b6 = Chekhov-Dorfman, USSR 1975

[32] 14 ♘bd2 ♘cb4 15 ♗b1 ♗a6 ∞/= Dvoretsky-Taimanov, USSR 1975

	5	6	7	8	9	10	11	12	13	
1	ed	♞c3[1]	♝e3[2]	♝d3	♞ge2	0-0[3]	f3	b3	♕xd3	=
	cd	g6	♝g7	0-0	♞c6	♝g4[4]	♝f5	♝xd3	e5[5]	
2	...	♞f3	♝e2	0-0	h3[6]	♞c3	♝e3[7]	c5	♝xc4[8]	∞
	...	g6	♝g7	0-0	♞c6	♝f5	d5	♞c4	dc[9]	
3	...	...	...	...	♝e3	♞bd2	c5	♕b3[11]	de	=
	...	...	...	...	♞c6	d5[10]	♞d7	e5	♞dxe5[12]	
4	...	...	...	...	...	♞c3	b3	c5	b4[14]	=
	...	...	...	...	...	♝g4	d5[13]	♞c8	a6[15]	
5	...	♞c3	h3[17]	♞f3	♝e2	0-0	♝f4	b3	♝h2	=
	ed	♝e7[16]	0-0	♖e8[18]	♝f5	♞8d7	♞f8	♞g6	c6[19]	
6	f4	♞c3	♝e3	c5![22]	dc	h4	h5	♕a4[23]	♞xa4[24]	±
	g6[20]	♝g7[21]	0-0	dc	♞6d7	c6	♕a5	♕xa4		
7	...	♞c3	♝e3	♞f3	♝d3![26]	♕xd3	b3	bc	0-0	±/±
	♝f5	e6	♝e7[25]	0-0	♝xd3[27]	d5	dc	♞c6	♞a5[28]	

[1]   6 ♝d3 e5! 7 ♞e2 ♞c6 8 d5 ♞b4 9 ♞bc3 f5 10 ♝b1 a5 11 0-0 ♝e7 = Sigurjonsson-Hort, Hastings 1974-75

[2]   7 a4!? a5 8 c5 dc 9 ♝b5+ ♞6d7 10 ♝f4 ♝g7 11 ♞d5 e5! 12 de 0-0 13 ♞f3 ♞c6 ∞ Perović-Begovac, Yugoslavia 1985
    7 h4 h5 8 ♝e3 ♝g7 9 ♝e2 ♞c6 10 d5 ♝xc3+ 11 bc ♞a5 12 ♕d4 ♖g8 ∞ Kurajica-Bagirov, Erevan 1971

[3]   10 b3 d5 11 c5 ♞d7 12 ♝b5 e5 13 0-0 ♞xc5! ∓ Minić-Fischer, Palma de Mallorca IZ 1970

[4]   10 ... e5?! 11 d5 ♞e7 12 b3 ♞d7 13 ♞e4 ♞f5 14 ♝g5 f6 15 ♝d2 ± Fischer-Berliner, New York 1961

[5]   14 ♖c1 d5 15 c5 ♞c8 = Minić-Gipslis, Erevan 1971

[6]   9 b3 ♞c6 10 ♝b2 ♝g4 11 ♕d2 e6 12 ♞a3 d5! = Karpov-Vaganian, Leningrad 1969.

[7]   11 ♝f4 h6 12 ♝e3 d5 13 b3 dc 14 bc ♖c8 15 ♖c1 ♞a5 16 c5 ♝bc4 ∞ Karpov-A.Petrosian, Rostov 1971

[8]   13 ♝c1 b6 14 cb ab 15 a3 ♖a5 = Dementiev-Gipslis, Riga 1970

[9]   14 ♕a4 ♝d3 15 ♖fd1 ♕a5 (15 ... f5 16 d5 ♞e5 17 ♞e1 f4 18 ♝d4 ♕c8 19 ♞xd3 cd 20 ♖xe5 ♝xe5 21 ♕c4 ±) 16 ♕xa5 ♞xa5 ∞ Espig-Pribyl, Leipzig 1983

[10]   10 ... ♝g4 11 d5! ♞e5 12 ♞xe5 ♝xe2 13 ♕xe2 ♝xe5 14 ♞f3 ♝g7 15 ♖ad1 ± Bronstein-Bagirov, Leningrad 1963
    10 ... e5!? 11 de de 12 ♝c5 ♖e8 13 ♞e4 ∞/±

[11]   12 b3 e5 13 de ♞dxe5 =

[12]   14 ♞xe5 ♞xe5 15 ♖fd1 ♞g4 =

[13]   11 ... e6 12 ♕d2 d5 13 c5 ♞d7 14 ♖ac1 ± Bagirov

[14]   13 h3 ♝xf3 14 ♝xf3 e6 15 ♕d2 ♞8e7 = Browne-Fischer, Zagreb 1970

[15]   14 ♖b1 e6 15 a4 ♞8e7 16 b5 ab 17 ab ♝xf3 18 ♝xf3 ♞a5 19 ♝e2 ♞f5 = Klovan-Bagirov, USSR 1969

[16]   6 ... g6 7 ♝d3 ♝g7 8 ♞ge2 0-0 9 0-0 ♞c6 10 ♝e3 ♞e7! (10 ... d5 11 c5 ♞d7 12 ♝b5 ±) 11 b3 ♝f5 12 ♞g3 ♝xd3 14 ♕xd3 = Bagirov

[17]   7 ♞f3 0-0 8 ♝e2 ♝g4 9 b3 ♞c6 10 h3 ♝xf3 11 ♝xf3 ♝f6 12 ♝e3 ∞/= Minić-Vukić, Yugoslavia 1976

[18]   8 ... ♝f6 9 ♝e2 ♖e8 10 0-0 ♞c6 11 ♝e3 ♝f5 12 b3 h6 13 ♖c1 ♖e7 = Suetin-Vukić, Odessa 1975

[19]   14 ♕d2 ♝f6 15 ♖fe1 a5 = Serper-Dreyev, USSR 1986

[20]   5 ... g5?! 6 ♕h5! de 7 c5 ♞d5 8 fe ♞f4 9 ♝xf4 gf 10 ♝c4 ±/± Durao-Pomar, Madrid 1983

[21]   6 ... de 7 fe ♝g7 8 ♝e3 0-0 9 h4! ± Estrin-Pytel, Polanica Zdroj 1971; 7 de ±

[22]   8 ♞f3 ♝e6!? ∞ Ivanchuk-Sergeyev, USSR 1984

[23]   12 a3 ♖d8 13 ♕a4 ♕xa4 14 ♞xa4 ♞f8 15 h6 ♝h8 16 ♞f3 ± Rogers-Depasquale, Australian Ch 1985-86

[24]   Rogers

[25]   7 ... ♞a6 (Trifunović) 8 ed cd 9 ♞f3 ♝e7 10 ♝e2 0-0 11 ♖c1 ±

[26]   9 ed cd 10 b3 d5 11 c5 ♞6d7 12 ♝d3 ♝xd3 13 ♕xd3 b6 = Uitumen-Fischer, Palma de Mallorca IZ 1970

[27]   9 ... d5 10 ♝xf5 ef 11 c5 ♞c4 12 ♝f2 ♞xb2 13 ♕b1 ♞c4 14 ♕xb7 ± Stein-Mikenas, Erevan 1962

[28]   Bagirov

Alekhine III 1 e4 ♘f6 2 e5 ♘d5 3 d4 d6 4 c4 ♘b6 *continued*

	5	6	7	8	9	10	11	12	13	
8	f4	fe	d5	♘c3	cd	♘f3	♕d4[31]	gf	♗xc4	±
	de	c5	e6	ed[29]	c4[30]	♗g4	♗xf3	♗b4	0-0[32]	
9	...	...	♘c3	♘f3[33]	♗e2[34]	0-0	♗e3	♘xe5	♘f3	=
	...	♗f5	e6	♗e7	0-0	f6[35]	fe	♘8d7	h6[36]	
10	...	...	...	...	♗d3[37]	0-0	c5	bc	♕e1	±
	...	...	...	♗b4	♗g4[38]	♘c6	♗xc3	♘d5	♘de7[39]	

29 8... ♕h4+ 9 g3 ♕d4 10 ♗d2 ♕xe5+ 11 ♗e2 ∓

30 9... ♕h4+ 10 g3 ♕d4 11 ♗b5+ ♗d7 12 ♕e2 (12 ♗xd7+ ♘8xd7 13 ♘f3 ♕xd1+ ∞ Chiburdanidze-Palatnik, Moscow 1982) 12... ♘xd5 13 e6 fe 14 ♕xe6+ ♘e7 15 ♘f3 ± Balashov-K.Grigorian, Riga 1967

31 11 ♗xc4!? ♘xc4 12 ♕a4+ ♘d7 13 ♕xc4 ♗xf3 14 gf ♘xe5 15 ♕e2 ♘e7 16 0-0! ± Browne-Ničevski, Skopje 1970

32 **14 ♖g1** g6 15 ♗g5 ♕c7 16 ♗b3 ♗c5 17 ♕f4 ♗xg1 Grünfeld-Ljubojević, Riga IZ 1979; 18 d6 ♕c5 19 ♘e4 ♕d4 20 ♖d1 ♕xb2 21 ♘f6+ ♔h8 22 ♖d2! ± Mourg-Rinaldi, corr. 1983

14 ♗h6 ♘8d7 15 ♖g1 g6 16 e6 ♘e5 17 ♗e2 ± Martin-Gonzalez, Lucerne Ol 1982

33 8 ♗e3 ♗b4! (Keene) 9 ♗d3 ♗xd3 10 ♕xd3 c5 11 0-0-0 cd 12 ♗xd4 ♘c6 ∓

34 9 ♗d3 ♗g4 10 ♗e4 ♘c6 11 ♗xc6+ bc 12 0-0 0-0 ∞ Bagirov

35 10... ♘c6 11 ♗e3 f6 – 6... ♘c6

36 14 c5 ♘d5 15 ♘xd5 ed = Suetin-Mikenas, USSR 1961

37 9 ♗e3 c5 10 ♗e2 ♘c6 11 0-0 cd 12 ♘xd4 ♘xd4 13 ♗xd4 ♗c2 14 ♕d2 ♖c8 ∞ Pritchard-Williams, England 1972

38 **9... ♗xd3** 10 ♕xd3 c5 11 0-0 cd 12 ♘e4! ±/± Ivkov-Timman, Amsterdam 1974

9... c5 10 d5! ♗xd3 11 ♕xd3 ed 12 ♘g5! ± Jokšić-Hazai, Budapest 1975

39 14 ♖b1 ♖b8 15 ♘g5 ± Velimirović-Martz, Vrnjačka Banja 1973

Alekhine IV 1 e4 ♘f6 2 e5 ♘d5 3 d4 d6 4 c4 ♘b6 5 f4 de 6 fe ♘c6

	7	8	9	10	11	12	13	14	15	
1	♘f3	e6	c5	♗b5	0-0[2]	♘bd2[3]	♕a4	♘xf3		∞
	♗g4	fe	♘d5![1]	♕d7!	g6	♗g7	♗xf3![4]	0-0		
2	♗e3	♘c3	♘f3	♖c1[6]	a3	♖xc3	♗e2	0-0	♔h1	$\overline{\overline{\infty}}$
	♗f5[5]	e6	♗b4	0-0[7]	♗xc3+	♕d7	♖ad8	♗g4	♗xf3[8]	
3	...	...	♘f3	♕d2[9]	0-0-0	h3	gf	f4	♕c2	∞/±
	...	...	♗g4	♗e7[10]	♕d7[11]	♗xf3	0-0-0	♗b4	♔b8[12]	
4	...	...	...	♖c1	♗e2	0-0[14]	dc[15]	a3	b4	±
	...	...	♘b4	c5	♗e7[13]	0-0	♘d7	♘c6	♘dxe5[16]	
5	...	...	...	♗e2[17]	0-0	c5	♘xd5	♘g5[19]	♕xe2	±
	...	...	♕d7	0-0-0[18]	♗g4	♘d5	♕xd5	♗xe2	♘xd4[20]	
6	...	...	...	...	...	d5[21]	♘xe5	a4[22]	♘b5	±
	...	...	...	...	f6	♘xe5	fe	a5	♗b4[23]	

---

1 e4 ♘f6 2 e5 ♘d5 3 d4 d6 4 c4 ♘b6 5 f4 de 6 fe ♘c6 7 ♗e3 ♗f5 8 ♘c3 e6 9 ♘f3 ♗e7

	10	11	12	13	14	15	16	17	18	
7	♗e2	0-0	ef[24]	♕d2[25]	♖ad1	♕c1	♔h1	h3	♗g1	=
	0-0	f6	♗xf6	♕e7[26]	♖ad8	h6[27]	♔h8	♗h7	♖fe8[28]	

	10	11	12	13	14	15	16	17	18	
8	d5	Rc1[29]	a3	ab	Bxd4	Nxd4[32]	Nxf5	Be2	c5	±
	Nb4	ed[30]	c5[31]	d4	cd	Qb8	Qxe5+	Qxf5	Nd7[33]	
9	...	cd[34]	Nd4	e6[36]	de	Qg4	g3	Bb5+[38]	0-0-0	∞
	ed	Nb4	Bd7[35]	fe	Bc6	Bh4+	Bxh1[37]	c6	0-0[39]	

---

[1] **9 ... Nc8?!** 10 Bb5 Bxf3 11 Qxf3 Qd5 12 Nd2 g6 13 0-0 Qxf3 14 Nxf3 Bg7 15 Be3 ±/± Bagirov
9 ... Nd7 10 Be2 e5 11 0-0 ed 12 Ng5 Bxe2 13 Qxe2 ∞

[2] 11 Nbd2 g6 12 Qa4 Bg7 13 Ne5 Bxe5 14 de Ne3! ∓ Ilyin Zhenevsky-Levenfish, Leningrad 1936

[3] 12 Qa4 Bxf3 13 Rxf3 Bg7 14 Kh1 Rf8 15 Rxf8+ Kxf8 ∓ Kalantar-Bagirov, USSR 1961

[4] 13 ... 0-0?! 14 Ne5 Bxe5 15 de Bf5 16 Nf3 ± Winiwalter-Hort, Krems 1967

[5] 7 ... h5!? intending 8 ... Bg4 Rohde

[6] 10 Be2 0-0 11 0-0 Bxc3 12 bc Na5 13 Nd2 Qd7 14 g4!? Bg6 15 h4 h6 ∞; 14 Rf4 Bg6 15 Qf1 c5 (Zuidema-Hort, Amsterdam 1971) 16 h4 ± Alburt

[7] 10 ... Na5 11 c5! Bd5 12 Bd2 c6 13 Nxd5 Bxd2+ 14 Qxd2 ed 15 b3 ± Bagirov

[8] 16 Bxf3 Nxd4 17 Bg5 ∞∞

[9] 10 Be2 Bxf3 11 gf Qh4+ 12 Bf2 Qf4 13 c5 Nd7 14 Ne4 ±

[10] 10 ... Bb4!? 11 a3 Be7 Kremenetsky-Vaganian, Moscow 1981

[11] 11 ... a5 12 h3 Bh5 13 g4 Bg6 14 h4 Nb4 ∞/±

[12] Bagirov

[13] **11 ... Bg4** 12 0-0 Bxf3 13 Bxf3 Nxc4 14 Bf2! ± Kadrev-Bogdanov, Sofia 1963
11 ... cd 12 Nxd4 Bg6 13 c5! Nd5 14 Qa4+ ± Alburt, Schiller; 13 Ndb5 Qxd1+ 14 Rxd1 ±/± Boleslavsky

[14] 12 a3!? cd 13 Nxd4 Nc6 14 Nxf5 ef 15 0-0 0-0 16 Rxf5 ± Lutovinov-Kopilov, corr. 1983

[15] 13 a3 cd 14 Nxd4 Nc6 15 Nxf5 ef 16 Rxf5 g6 17 Rf1 ± Estrin-Kopilov, corr. 1971

[16] 16 Nb5! ± Mikhalchishin-Karsa, Lvov 1983

[17] 10 Rc1 0-0-0 11 h3 f6! 12 ef gf ∓ Yuferov-Nekrasov, Minsk 1984

[18] 10 ... Rd8 11 Qd2 Be7 12 0-0 0-0 13 Rad1 ∞/±

[19] 14 b4 Qe4 15 Qb3 Nxd4 16 Nxd4 Bxe2 17 Rf4 ∞ Platonov-Kupreichik, Moscow 1969

[20] 16 Bxd4 Qxd4+ 17 Kh1 Qd2 18 Qxd2 Rxd2 19 Rxf7 Bxc5 20 Nxe6 Bd4! 21 Nxd4 Rxd4 ±/= Gipslis-Kengis, Jurmala 1983

[21] 12 ef gf 13 d5 Qg7!? ∞ Hecht-Cafferty, Teesside 1972

[22] 14 Rc1!? Yudovich

[23] 16 d6 c5 17 Qc1 (17 Bd2 Qxd6!? 18 Nxd6+ Rxd6 Sozin) ± Bagirov

[24] 12 Nh4 fe 13 Nxf5 ef 14 d5 Nd4! 15 Bxd4 ed 16 Qxd4 Nd7 ∓

[25] 13 h3 Qe8! 14 g4 Qg6 15 Kh1 Be4 16 Nxe4 Qxe4 ∓

[26] **13 ... Rf7** 14 Rad1 Rd7 15 c5 Nd5 16 Nxd5 ed 17 Ne5! ± Hernandez-Pomar, Barcelona 1984
13 ... Qe8 14 Bg5! Rd8 15 Bxf6 Rxf6 16 Rad1 Bg4 17 Ne4 ± Ignatiev-Larsen, Moscow 1962

[27] **15 ... e5** 16 d5 Nd4 17 Nxd4 ed 18 Bxd4 Bg5 19 Qa1 ±
15 ... Rfe8 16 Rf2 Bg6 17 b3 ± Stein-Podgayets, USSR 1971

[28] Hecht-Timman, Wijk aan Zee 1971

[29] 11 Nd4 Bg6 12 a3 c5 13 Nxe6 fe 14 ab cb 15 Na4! 0-0 16 Nxb6 ab 17 Rxa8 Qxa8 18 d6 Bd8 19 Be2 b3! ∞/= Bagirov

[30] 11 ... f6 12 a3 Na6 13 g4! ± Tringov-Rodriguez, Havana 1971

[31] 12 ... Na6 13 cd 0-0 14 b4! Nb8 15 Be2 ± Korelov-Ignatiev, USSR 1974

[32] 15 Qxd4!? Bxb4 16 c5 Nd5 17 Bb5+ Bd7 18 Bxd7+ Qxd7 ∞ Maryasin-Kengis, Tallinn 1981

[33] Velimirović-Marović, Yugoslavia 1977

[34] 11 Bxb6 ab 12 cd Nb4 13 Nd4 Bg6! 14 d6 0-0! (14 ... Bh4+ 15 g3 0-0 16 a3 c5 17 Nf3 Nc2+ 18 Kf2 ± Murei-Kovačević, Hastings 1982-83) 15 a3 cd ∞ Chandler-Kengis, Jurmala 1983

[35] 12 ... Bc8 13 Bb5+ c6 14 dc 0-0 15 0-0 ±/± Yudovich-Ignatiev, Moscow 1974

[36] **13 Qf3** c5! 14 dc bc 15 a3 Nd5 16 Nxd5 Nxd5 17 Bc4 Qa5+! = Ljubojević-Hartston, Las Palmas 1974
13 Qb3 c5 14 dc bc 15 Rd1 Nd5 16 Nxd5 Nxd5 17 Bc4 Rb8 ∞ Timman-Kovačević, Wijk aan Zee 1980
13 Nf3!? Bg4 14 Bxb6 ab 15 Be2 Bc5 ∞/= Geller-Vaganian, Sochi 1986

[37] 16 ... Bf6?! 17 0-0-0! ± Gligorić

[38] 17 0-0-0 Qf6 18 gh 0-0 19 Bb5! Qe5 20 Bg5 ∞; 20 Bh6!? ∞/± Kveinis-Panchenko, USSR 1979; 19 ... c5! ∞/= Murei-Alburt, Beer-Sheva 1980

[39] 19 gh and now:
19 ... Qf6 20 Bg5 Qe5 21 e7 cb 22 Nf5! ∞/± Roth-Etmans, corr. 1986
19 ... h5! 20 Qg3 cb 21 Bg5 Qb8 22 e7 Re8 ∞ Velimirović-Kovačević, Yugoslav Ch 1984

	4	5	6	7	8	9	10	11	12	
1	♗c4[1]	♗b3	♕h5[4]	de	c3	♘f3	♕g4	♕e4	♗f4	=
	♘b6[2]	de[3]	e6	c5!?[5]	♘c6	g6	♕e7	♗g7	♗d7[6]	
2	♘f3	c4	♗e2[8]	ed	♘c3	♗e3	♕d2	0-0	♖ad1	±
	c6[7]	♘c7	g6[9]	♕xd6	♗g7	♘a6	♗g4	0-0	♖ad8[10]	
3	...	c4[11]	e6!?[12]	h4[13]	d5	♘xd4	♕xd4[14]	♗e2	de	∞
	♘c6	♘b6	fe	e5	♘d4	ed	♕d7[15]	e5	♕xe6[16]	
4	...	...	...	♘g5	d5![18]	♗d3![19]	♗xf5	♗e3!	g4	±
	...	...	...	e5[17]	♘d4	♗f5	♘xf5	g6[20]	♘g7[21]	
5	...	♘xe5	♘xf7!	♕h5+	c4[23]	d5+	♕f7![24]	♘c3	♗f4+	±
	de	♘d7[22]	♔xf7	♔e6	♘5f6	♔d6	♘b6[25]	♕e8	♔d7[26]	
6	...	...	♗c4[27]	♘c3![29]	♘e4	de	♘c5	♗xe3	b3	±
	...	g6	♗e6[28]	♗g7	♗xe5	♘c6	♘e3![30]	♗xc4	b6[31]	
7	...	♘g5	♗c4[33]	♕e2	0-0	de	♘f3	♘bd2	h3	=
	g6	c6[32]	♗g7	0-0	de[34]	h6	♗g4	♕c7	♗xf3[35]	
8	...	♗c4!	0-0	ed	♖e1[36]	♗g5	♘bd2	♗b3	♗h4	±/±
	...	c6	♗g7	♕xd6	0-0[37]	♗g4	♖e8	h6	♘d7[38]	
9	...	...	♗b3	a4[40]	0-0	h3	♕e2	♘c3	♗f4	±
	...	♘b6	♗g7[39]	a5	0-0	♘c6	d5[41]	♗e6	♕d7[42]	

[1]   4 ♗g5 de 5 de ♘c6 6 ♘f3 ♗g4 = Lutikov-Kopulov, corr. 1968; 6 ♗b5 ♗f5 7 ♘f3 ♗b4! = A.Steiner-Alekhine, Budapest 1921
  4 ed ♕xd6!? 5 ♘f3 ♗g4 6 ♗e2 ♘c6 7 0-0 0-0-0 8 c3 ♘f4 = Yates-Kmoch, Budapest 1926
  4 f4 ♗f5 (4 ... de 5 fe ♘c6 6 ♘f3 ♗g4 7 ♗e2 e6 8 0-0 ♗e7 9 c3 0-0 10 ♖e1 ± Zapata-Kovačević, Zenica 1986) 5 ♘f3 e6 6 ♗d3 ♗xd3 7 ♕xd3 c5 8 dc ♕a5+ 9 ♗d2 ♕xc5 = Bokhosian-Orev, Pernik 1975
  4 ♗e2 ♗f5 (4 ... de 5 de ♘c6 6 ♘f3 ♗g4 7 c3! e6 8 ♕a4 ♗xf3 9 ♗xf3 ♕d7 10 ♕e4 ± Kupreichik-Palatnik, Kislovodsk 1982) 5 ♘f3 e6 6 0-0 ♗e7 7 c4 ♘b6 8 ed cd 9 ♘c3 0-0 10 ♗f4 ♘8d7 ∞ Kupreichik-Kengis, Lvov 1984

[2]   4 ... c6 5 ♕e2 (5 f4 ±) 5 ... de 6 de ♗f5 7 ♘f3 e6 8 0-0 ♗g4 9 ♘bd2 ♘d7 10 ♗b3 ♘c5 ∞/± Mestel-Popov, Malta Ol 1980

[3]   5 ... ♗f5!? 6 ♕f3 ♕c8 7 ♘h3 c5!? 8 dc dc 9 ♗xf7+ ♔xf7 10 g4 g6 11 ♘g5+ ♔e8 ∞ Arnason-Hansen, Dortmund 1980; 7 ... ♘c6! = Arnason-Alburt, Lone Pine 1980

[4]   6 ♕f3 e6 7 de a5! 8 c3 a4 9 ♗c2 ♗d7 10 ♕g3 ♗b5 11 ♗g5 ♕d5 ∓ Gufeld-Vasyukov, Kislovodsk 1968

[5]   7 ... a5 8 a4 ♘a6 9 ♘c3 ♘c5 10 ♗g5 ♗e7 11 ♖d1 ♗d7 12 ♗e3 0-0 13 ♘f3 ± Hecht-Hartmann, West Germany 1985-86

[6]   13 ♘bd2 ♘a5 14 ♗c2 ♗c6 = Fedorov-Gipslis, Tbilisi 1973

[7]   4 ... ♗f5 5 ♗d3 ♕d7 6 0-0 ♘c6 7 c4 (7 ♗xf5 ♕xf5 8 c4 ♘b6 9 ed ed 10 ♖e1+ ♗e7+ Timman-Ljubojević, Hilversum 1973) 7 ... ♗xd3 8 ♕xd3 ♘b6 9 ed ed 10 ♖e1+ ♗e7 11 d5 ♘d8 12 ♕e2 ±
  4 ... ♘b6 5 a4 a5 (5 ... c6 6 a5 ♘d5 7 ♗e2 g6 8 0-0 ♗g7 9 c4 ♘c7 10 ed ♕xd6 11 ♘c3 ± Sigurjonsson-Larsen, Ljubljana/Portorož 1977) 6 ♗b5+! c6 7 ♗e2 g6 8 h3 ♗g7 9 0-0 0-0 10 ♗f4 ± Ciocaltea-Hecht, Dortmund 1973

[8]   6 ed ed 7 ♗d3 ♗g4 8 0-0 ♗e7 9 ♘bd2 ♘d7 = Rodriguez-Petrosian, Buenos Aires Ol 1978

[9]   6 ... ♗g4 7 ♘g5 ♗xe2 8 ♕xe2 de 9 de h6 10 ♘f3 ♘e6 11 0-0 ± Parma-Suba, Buenos Aires Ol 1978

[10]   13 ♕c1 ± Dolmatov-Petrosian, Moscow 1981

[11]   5 ♗b5 a6 6 ♗xc6+ bc 7 0-0 e6 8 ♘bd2 ♗e7 9 ♘c4 a5 10 ♖e1 a4 = Egin-Grigorian, Erevan 1984

[12]   6 ed ed 7 d5 ♘e5 8 ♘xe5 de 9 ♗d3 ♗b4+ 10 ♘c3 0-0 11 0-0 f5 = Przewoznik-Böhm, Polanica Zdroj 1980

[13]   7 ♘c3 g6 8 h4 ♗g7 9 ♗e3 d5! 10 c5 ∞ Nunn-Vaganian, London 1986
  7 ♗d3 e5! 8 d5 ♘b4 9 ♘g5 ♘xd3+ 10 ♕xd3 e6! ∞

[14]   10 ♗d3 ♕d7! 11 ♗g5 h6 12 ♗d2 ♕g4

13 &e2 ♕e4 ∞ Tal-Larsen, match 1969

[15] 10 ... &f5 11 ♘c3 ♕d7 12 &e2 e5 13 ♕d1 ♕f7 14 g4 ± Cramling-Berchorst, Lugano 1983

[16] 13 ♖h3! c5 14 ♕c3 &e7! 15 ♖e3 ♕f7 ∞ Nei-Honfi, Zalaegerszeg 1969

[17] 7 ... ♕d7?! 8 &e3 e5 9 d5 ♘d8 10 &e2 c6 11 ♕c2 ±

[18] 8 ♕f3 ♘xd4! 9 ♕f7+ ♔d7 10 &e3 h6! =∓

8 &d3!? ♘xd4 9 &xh7 ♖xh7! 10 ♘xh7 &f5 11 ♘a3 ♖xc4 12 ♘xc4 ♘c2+ 13 ♔f1 ♘xa1 14 ♘xf8 ♔xf8 15 ♘e3 ♕d7 ∞ Wolfe-Podgorny, corr. 1979

[19] 9 &e3 ♘f5 (9 ... e6? 10 &d3 g6 11 ♘c3 ♘f5 12 h4! ±) ∞/= Bagirov

[20] 11 ... ♕d7 12 g4 ♘xe3 13 fe 0-0-0 14 ♘d2 ± Blatny-Horn, Groningen 1985-86

[21] 13 ♕f3 ♕d7 14 ♘d2 ± Haba-Freisler, Czechoslovak Ch 1986

[22] 5 ... e6 6 ♕f3 ♕f6 7 ♕g3 h6 8 ♘c3 ♘b4 9 &b5+ c6 10 &a4 ♘d7 11 ♘e4 ♕f5 12 f3 ±/± Tal

[23] 8 g3 b5! 9 a4 c6 10 ab g6 11 ♕e2+ ♔f7 12 bc ∞∞

[24] 10 ♕h3 ♘c5 11 ♕a3 e5 12 &e3 b6 13 ♘c3 ♔e7 ∞

[25] 10 ... ♘e5 11 &f4 c5 12 ♘c3 a6 13 b4! ± Bagirov

10 ... ♘b8 11 c5+! ♔xc5 12 &e3+ ♔d6 13 ♘a3! ±

[26] 13 ♕e6+ ♔d8 14 ♕e5 ♕d7 15 0-0-0 ±/± Bagirov

[27] 6 c4 ♘f6 7 ♘c3 &g7 8 &e3 0-0 9 &e2 ♘bd7 10 ♘d3 ♘b6 11 b3 &f5 ∞/= Ljubojević-Williams, Nice Ol 1974

[28] 6 ... c6 7 0-0 &g7 8 ♖e1 0-0 9 c3 &e6 10 ♘d2 ♘d7 11 ♘ef3 ± A.Ivanov-Schmidt, Riga 1982

[29] 7 0-0!? &g7 8 ♘d2 0-0 9 ♖e1 ♘d7 10 ♘ef3 ♘7f6 11 &f1! ± Unzicker-Williams, Buenos

Aires Ol 1978

[30] 10 ... ♘xe5 11 ♘xb7 ♕d7 12 ♘c5 ♕c6 13 ♘xe6 fe 14 ♕d4! ± Bagirov

[31] 13 bc bc 14 &xc5 ♘xe5 16 &d4 ± Larsen

[32] 5 ... f6 6 c4! ♘b6 7 e6! fg 8 d5 &g7 9 a4 a5 10 h4 gh 11 ♖xh4 ±/± O'Kelly-Golombek, Amsterdam 1951

5 ... de 6 de &g7 7 &c4 c6 8 e6 &xe6 9 ♘xe6 fe 10 ♘d2 ∞∞ Panchenko-A.Petrosian, Riga 1973

[33] 6 ed ed 7 &c4 ♕e7+ 8 ♕e2 ♕xe2+ 9 ♔xe2 h6 10 ♘f3 ♘b4! ∞/=∓ Qi-Timman, Taxco IZ 1985

[34] 8 ... e6?! 9 ♘c3 ♘xc3 10 bc d5 11 &d3 c5 12 ♕g4 ±/± Vasyukov-Larsen, Moscow 1959

[35] 13 ♘xf3 e6 = Bagirov

[36] 8 ♘bd2 0-0 9 h3 &f5 10 ♘b3 ♘d7 11 ♖e1 h6 12 ♘h4 ± Kavalek-Böhm, Wijk aan Zee 1977

[37] 8 ... &g4 9 h3! (9 ♘bd2 0-0 10 h3 &xf3 11 ♘xf3 e6 12 &f1 b5! = Nunn-Vaganian, London 1984) 9 ... &xf3 10 ♕xf3 e6 11 ♘c3 0-0 12 &g5 ± Chandler-Vaganian, London 1984

[38] 13 c4 ♘f4 14 c5! ±/± Tal-Ljubojević, Wijk aan Zee 1973

[39] 6 ... a5 7 a4 &g7 8 ♘g5 e6 9 f4 de 10 fe c5 11 0-0-0 12 c3 ± Kasparov-Palatnik, USSR 1978

[40] 7 ♘g5 d5 (7 ... e6 8 ♕f3! ±) 8 f4 f6 9 ♘f3 ♘c6 (9 ... 0-0 10 0-0 ♘c6 11 c3 fe 12 fe &f5 13 ♘h4 ± Panchenko-Uusi, Jurmala 1980) 10 &e3 &g4 11 ♘bd2 ♕d7 12 0-0 0-0-0 13 c3 ± Matulović-Ljubojević, Yugoslavia 1972

[41] 10 ... de 11 de ♘d4 12 ♘xd4 ♕xd4 13 ♖e1 e6 14 ♘d2 ± Bagirov

[42] 13 ♖ad1 ♖a6 14 ♕d2 ± Keres-Kupka, Kapfenberg 1970

	Alekhine VI	1 e4 ♘f6 2 e5 ♘d5 3 d4 d6 4 ♘f3 &g4						
	5	6	7	8	9	10	11	12	13
1	h3[1]	♕xf3	de	♕e4[3]	&c4	♕e2	0-0[4]	♕xc4	=
	&xf3	de[2]	e6	♘d7	♘c5	♘b6	♘xc4	♕d5[5]	

[1] 5 &c4 e6 6 h3 &h5 7 ♕e2 ♘b6 8 &b3 ♘c6 = Adorjan-Alburt, USSR 1970

[2] 6 ... c6 7 c4 ♘c7 8 ed ♕xd6 9 &f4 ±

[3] 8 a3 ♘d7 9 ♕g3 h5! 10 &e2!? (10 ♘bd2 h4 11 ♕b3 ♖h5! ∓ Panov-Mikenas, Moscow 1943) 10 ... h4 11 ♕b3 ♖b8 12 0-0 ∞/=∓

8 &c4 ♘c6 9 ♕e4 ♘de7 10 &e3 ♘f5 11 0-0 ♕h4! ∞∓

[4] 11 &b3 a5 12 a3 ♘xb3 12 cb &e7 =∓ Kupreichik-Bagirov, USSR 1970

[5] Bagirov

239

	5	6	7	8	9	10	11	12	13	
2	c4	d5!?[6]	ed	♞c3	cd	h3	g4	♝g2	♞xd5	=
	♞b6	e6[7]	♕xd6	ed	c6	♝h5![8]	♝g6	♞xd5	cd[9]	
3	♝e2	♞g5[10]	♕xe2	de	0-0[12]	c4[13]	♞c3	♞f3	♖e1	±
	c6	♝xe2[11]	de	e6	♞d7	♞e7[14]	♞f5	♕c7	♝b4[15]	
4	...	c4[16]	ed	0-0	♞c3[18]	b3	♝e3	c5	h3	∞/±
	♞c6	♞b6	ed[17]	♝e7	0-0	♝f6	d5	♞c8	♝e6[19]	
5	...	0-0	c4	ed	d5	cd	gf[22]	♝b5+	♕d4	±
	e6	♞c6	♞b6[20]	cd	ed[21]	♝xf3	♞e5	♞ed7	♕f6[23]	

---

1 e4 ♞f6 2 e5 ♞d5 3 d4 d6 4 ♞f3 ♝g4 5 ♝e2 e6 6 0-0 ♝e7 7 c4 ♞b6

	8	9	10	11	12	13	14	15	16	
6	ed	b3	♝b2[24]	♞bd2	c5	a3	b4	♖e1	♞f1	∞/∓
	cd	♞c6	0-0	d5[25]	♞d7[26]	a6	♕c7	b6	♝f6[27]	
7	...	♞c3	♝e3	c5	♝xf3	♝f4	b3	♖c1	cb[29]	=
	...	0-0	d5[28]	♝xf3	♞c4	♞c6	♞4a5	b6	♕xb6[30]	
8	h3	ed	♞bd2	b3	♝b2	a3	♞c3	♖e1[32]	♞f1[33]	=
	♝h5	cd	♞c6	0-0	♝g6[31]	a5	♝f6	e5	e4[34]	
9	...	♞c3	♝e3[35]	cd[37]	♞d2[39]	♞xe2	f4	♕xd2		∞
	...	0-0	d5[36]	ed[38]	♝xe2	♝b4	♝xd2	f5[40]		
10	...	...	...	c5	♝xf3	♝f4[41]	b3	♖c1[43]	dc	∞/=
	...	...	...	♝xf3	♞c4	b6[42]	♞a5	bc	♞ac6[44]	
11	...	...	...	...	gf!	b4[46]	♝d3	♕c2	b5	∞
	...	...	...	...	♞c8[45]	♝h4[47]	♞e7	g6	f6[48]	
12	...	...	...	...	...	f4!	b4[50]	a3[52]	♝d3	±
	...	...	...	...	...	♞c6[49]	a6[51]	♝h4	g6[53]	

[6] A.Vitolins
6 ♝e2 de 7 c5 (7 ♞xe5 ♝e2 8 ♕xe2 ♕xd4 9 ♞a3!? Alekhine) 7 ... e4 8 ♞g5 ♝xe2 9 ♕xe2 ♞d5 10 0-0 ♞c6 11 ♖d1 ∞ Alekhine

[7] 6 ... de 7 h3 ♝xf3 8 ♕xf3 ±/±

6 ... ♞8d7 7 e6 fe 8 h3 (8 ♝e2 ed 9 cd ♞f6 10 ♞c3 c6 11 0-0 ∞ Vitolins-Palatnik, Jurmala 1981) 8 ... ♝xf3 9 ♕xf3 ♞e5 10 ♕b3 ed 11 cd g6 ∞ Vitolins-Bagirov, Riga 1981

[8] 10 ... ♝xf3?! 11 ♕xf3 ♕e5+ 12 ♕e3 ♝d6 13 f4! ± Vitolins-Kengis, Riga 1984

[9] 14 0-0 ♝e7 = Vitolins-Kengis, USSR 1984

[10] 6 0-0 ♝xf3 7 ♝xf3 de 8 de e6 9 ♕e2 ♞d7 (9 ... ♕c7!? 10 b3 ♞d7 11 ♝b2 ♞f4 12 ♕e4 ♞g6 13 ♖e1 0-0-0 ∞ Sax-Kovačević, Sarajevo 1982) 10 ♖e1 ♕c7 11 ♝d2 ♞c5 12 c4 ♞e7 13 ♝c3 a5 14 ♞d2 ∞

6 c4 ♞b6 7 ♞bd2!? (Levenfish) 7 ... de 8 ♞xe5 ♝f5 (8 ... ♝e6 9 ♞e4! f6 10 ♞c5! ♝g8 11 ♞f3 ± Vogt-Bagirov, Riga 1981) 9 ♞f1 ♞8d7 10 ♞f3 ♝e4 11 ♞e3 e6 12 0-0 ♝e7 13 b3 0-0 14 ♝b2 a5 ∞ Ghinda-Agzamov, Potsdam 1985

[11] 6 ... ♝f5 and now:
7 ♝d3 ♝xd3 8 ♕xd3 h6 (8 ... de 9 ♕f5!) 9 ♞f3 de 10 de e6 11 0-0 ♞d7 12 ♕e2 ♕c7 13 ♝d2 a5 14 ♖e1 ♞c5 = Smagin-Agzamov, Riga 1985

7 ♝h5!? g6 8 ♝g4 ♝xg4 9 ♕xg4 de 10 de h6 11 ♞e4 ♕d7 ∞ Marjanović-Kovačević, Pula 1984

7 e6 fe (7 ... ♞xe6 8 ♞xe6 fe 9 ♕d3 ♞f6 10 0-0 ♞bd7 11 f4 g6 12 ♞d2 ± Ivanović-Kovačević, Novi Sad 1984) 8 g4 ♝g6 9 ♝d3 ♝xd3 10 ♕xd3 g6 11 ♕f3 ♞f6 12 ♞xe6 ♕d7 13 ♕e2 ± Oll-Kulinsky, USSR 1983

7 ♝g4 ♕d7!? 8 ♝xf5 ♕xf5 ∞ Svenn-Krüger, Dortmund 1981

[12] 9 ♕h5!? g6 10 ♕e2 Sax

[13] 10 ♖e1 h6 11 ♞f3 ♕c7 12 ♞bd2 ∞/± Balashov-Yusupov, Moscow 1982

[14] 10 ... ♞5b6 11 ♖e1 ♝e7 12 ♞f3 0-0 13 ♞c3 ♕c7 14 ♝g5 ± Short-Kovačević, Hastings 1982-83

[15] 14 ♗d2 ± Bagirov
[16] 6 0-0 ♘b6 (6 ... de 7 ♘xe5 ♗xe2 8 ♕xe2 ♘xd4 9 ♕c4 c5 10 ♗e3! a6 11 ♘c3 e6 12 ♗xd4 ± Thorsteins-Hansen, Reykjavik 1985) 7 h3 ♗xf3 8 ♗xf3 de 9 de ♕xd1 10 ♖xd1 e6 11 b3 ± Novopashin-Mikenas, Erevan 1962
[17] 7 ... cd 8 d5 ♗xf3 9 ♗xf3 ♘e5 10 ♗e2 g6 11 ♗e3 ♗g7 12 ♗d4 0-0 13 ♘c3 ± A.Sokolov-Vaganian, match 1986
[18] 9 ♗e3 0-0 10 b3 f5 11 ♘c3 f4 12 ♗d2 ♗f6 = Kavalek-Larsen, Solingen 1970
[19] 14 b4 a6 15 ♖b1 ♘8e7 16 a4 ∞/±
[20] 7 ... ♘de7 8 ed! ♕xd6 9 ♘c3 ♗xf3 10 ♗xf3 0-0-0 11 ♘b5! ♕d7 12 ♕b3 ± Matulović-Knežević, Bajmok 1975
[21] 9 ... ♗xf3?! 10 gf ♘e5 11 f4 ♘ed7 12 de fe 13 ♖e1 ± Atanasov-Stavrev, Bulgaria 1982
[22] 11 ♗xf3 ♘e5 12 ♗e4 ♗e7 13 a4 0-0 14 a5 ♘bd7 15 ♘c3 ± Lepeshkin-Nisman, Moscow 1983
[23] 14 ♖e1+ ♗e7 15 ♕xf6 gf 16 ♘c3 ± Vogt-Uddenfeld, Skopje Ol 1972
[24] 10 ♘c3 0-0 11 ♗e3 d5! 12 c5 ♘c8 13 b4 a6 14 ♖b1 ♗f6 15 a4 ♘8e7 ∞/∓ Mikhalchishin-Hort, Banja Luka 1974
[25] 11 ... ♗f5 12 a3 a5 13 ♖e1 d5 14 c5 ♘d7 15 ♘f1 e5! =
11 ... ♕b8!? Bagirov
[26] 12 ... ♘c8?! 13 ♗c3 a5 14 a3 ♘8a7 15 b4 b5 16 ♕c2 ±/± Shakarov-Bagirov, USSR 1970
[27] Makarichev-Palatnik, USSR 1974
[28] 10 ... ♘8d7?! 11 b3 ♘f6 12 ♖c1 a6 13 h3 ♗h5 14 g4 ♗g6 15 ♘h4 ± Chandler-Christiansen, Hastings 1981-82
10 ... ♘c6 11 d5! ♗xf3 (11 ... ed 12 ♘xd5 ±) 12 ♗xf3 ♘e5 13 de fe 14 ♗g4 ♘exc4 15 ♗xe6+ ♔h8 16 ♗xb6! ♕xb6 17 ♕b3 ± Timman-Bagirov, Tbilisi 1971
[29] 16 ♕d2 bc 17 dc ♖c8 18 ♘b5 a6 19 ♘d6 ♖b8 ∞ Taberov-Palatnik, Kiev 1984
[30] 17 ♗e3 ♖ac8 (17 ... ♗f6 18 ♘a4 ♕b4 19 ♕d3 ±) 18 ♘a4 ♕b8 19 ♘c5 ♗xc5 20 ♖xc5 ♘b7 21 ♖c3 ♘e7 = Short-Bagirov, Baku 1983
[31] 12 ... d5 13 c5 ♘d7 14 ♗c3!? (14 a3 f6 15 b4 a6 16 ♖e1 ♗f7 17 ♘f1 b6 = Vogt-Schmidt, Brno 1975) 14 ... b6 15 b4 bc 16 bc ♕c7 17 ♕a4 ∞/± Kapengut-A.Ivanov, USSR 1976
[32] 15 b4?! ♘a4! 16 ♕xa4 ab 17 ♕xa8 ♕xa8 18 ab ♕b8 19 b5 ♘e7 ∓/∓ Janošević-Kovačević, Yugoslavia 1978
[33] 16 de de = Hulak-Vukić, Belgrade 1978
16 d5 ♘d4 17 ♖c1 = Bagirov
[34] Tal-Bagirov, Leningrad 1977
[35] 10 ♗f4!? ♘c6 11 ed cd 12 d5 ed 13 ♘xd5 ♗xf3 14 ♗xf3 ♘xc4 15 ♕b3 ♘4e5 Böhm-Jansa, Amsterdam 1975
[36] 10 ... a5!? 11 b3 (11 g4 ♗g6 12 d5 ♘8d7 13 ed cd 14 de fe 15 ♘d4 ♘c5 ∞/∓

Damljanović-Bagirov, Baku 1986) 11 ... d5 12 c5 ♘6d7 13 ♕d2 b6 14 cb ♘xb6 15 ♘e1 ± Sax-Kovačević, Belgrade 1976; 11 ... ♘a6!? Bagirov
[37] 11 b3 ♘c6 12 c5 ♘c8 (12 ... ♘d7 13 b4! ±) 13 b4 a6 14 ♕b3 ♗xf3 15 ♗xf3 ♗g5 =
[38] 11 ... ♘xd5 12 ♕b3 ♘b6 13 a4 a5 14 ♖ad1 (14 ♖fd1 c6 15 ♘d2 ♗xe2 16 ♖xe2 ♘a6 17 ♘f4 ♘b4 ∞/= Balashov-Palatnik, Kislovodsk 1982) ∞/± Gligorić-Vukić, Novi Sad 1976
[39] 12 ♗d3 ♘c6 13 g4 ♗g6 14 ♗f5 ♕e8! = Gulko-Bagirov, Baku 1977
[40] Djukić-Bagirov, Prague 1984
[41] 13 b3 ♘xe3 14 fe ♘c6! (14 ... b6?! 15 e4 c6 16 b4 bc 17 bc ♕a5 18 ♘xd5! ±/± Spassky-Fischer, match (19) 1972, and van der Gracht-Prins, corr. 1986) 15 ♖b1 f6 16 ef ♗xf6 17 b4 ♘e7 18 ♗g4 ♕d7 = Olafsson-Andersson, Nice Ol 1974
13 b4 b6 14 ♖c1 c6 15 ♗e2 a5 16 ♗xc4 dc ∞Belyavsky-Palatnik, USSR 1974; 13 ... ♘c6! 14 b5 ♘xe3 15 fe ♘xe5 16 de ♗xc5 intending 17 ... ♕g5 Alburt
[42] 13 ... ♘c6 14 b3 ♘4a5 15 ♖c1 b6 16 ♘a4 ± Geller-Timman, Teesside 1975; 15 ... ♗g5 16 ♘e2 ♗xf4 17 ♘xf4 ♘e7! 18 ♗g4 ♘ac6 19 ♕d2 ♔h8 20 ♖c3 ∞/± Hübner-Hort, Biel 1984; 15 ... ♕d7! 16 ♗e3 f6 = Geller-Bagirov, USSR Ch 1979
[43] 15 ♘a4 ♘d7 16 ♕d2 ♘c6 17 b4 bc 18 bc ♖b8 = Gufeld-Palatnik, Kirovabad 1973
15 b4 ♘c4 16 ♖c1 c6 17 ♗e2 a5 18 ♗xc4 dc = Lukin-Bagirov, USSR 1975
[44] 17 ♖e1 ♗g5 Kavalek-Schmidt, Nice Ol 1974
[45] 12 ... ♘6d7 13 ♔h1 f6 14 f4 f5 15 b4 ♖f7 16 ♖g1 ± Ciocaltea-Böhm, Wijk aan Zee 1975
[46] 13 ♔h1 ♗h4 14 ♗d3 ♘e7 15 f4 g6 16 ♕g4 ♘f5 ∞ Ciocaltea-Bagirov, Tbilisi 1974
[47] 13 ... f6 14 f4 fe 15 fe ♕e8 16 ♗d3 ♗d8 17 ♕g4 ± Matanović-Vukić, Novi Sad 1975
13 ... ♘c6 14 b5 ♘a5 15 ♕a4 b6 16 c6 ♗h4 ∞ Minev-Palatnik, Albena 1975
[48] 17 f4 fe 18 fe ♘f5 ∞ Bellon-Schmidt, Lodz 1980
[49] 13 ... ♗h4 14 ♗d3 g6 15 ♕g4 ♔h8 16 b4 ♘c6 17 a3 f5 18 ♕d1 ± Psakhis-Agzamov, Moscow 1983
[50] 14 ♗d3 g6 15 f5!? ef 16 ♕f3 ♗xc5 17 dc d4 18 ♗h6 ∞/± Sokolov-Veingold, Tallinn 1981
[51] 14 ...♗h4 15 ♖b1 ♔h8 16 ♗d3 g6 17 ♕g4 ♖g8 18 ♔h2 ± Wolff-Alburt, US Ch 1985
[52] 15 ♔h2 ♗h4 16 ♗d3 g6 17 a3 ♘8e7 18 ♖g1 ± Spassky-Bagirov, Moscow 1979
15 f5 ef 16 f4 ♘b8 17 ♗d3 ∞/±
[53] 17 ♕g4 f5 18 ♕d1 ♔h8 19 ♔h2 ± Solozhenkin-Bagirov, USSR 1986

241

French

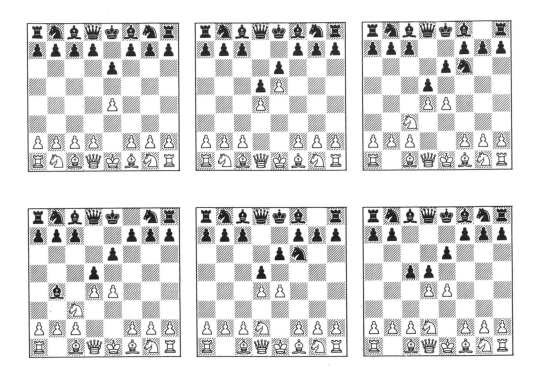

The French is a defence in the truest sense of the word, appealing to players who are content to endure cramped or passive positions in the hope of emerging with a superior pawn structure or an eventual counterattack. It was honed into a formidable weapon by ex-World Champion Botvinnik and the defence's most dedicated and successful practitioners are now undoubtedly Uhlmann and Korchnoi. As the times and the players setting opening trends change, so do the popularity and assessments of White's main choices against this opening.

The solid **Tarrasch Variation** (3 ♘d2) enjoyed nearly universal appeal during the reign of Karpov. The former world champion's mastery versus the isolated QP and the fact that the Tarrasch avoids any positional concession made it a safe and effective weapon. Black's counterplay has always been sufficient, and the Tarrasch owed much of its success to the success of Karpov.

The **Winawer Variation** (3 ♘c3 ♗b4) is the most difficult and dynamic French, and was the usual topic of discussion in the heyday of Tal, Spassky and Fischer. White accepts a gashed formation for the bishop pair and a spatial plus. When Karpov dropped the quieter Tarrasch, the revival of the brawling 3 ♘c3 was complete. The richness of the position is indicated by the fact that Nigel Short remains successful from both sides of this system.

The **Classical Variation** (3 ♘c3 ♘f6) is showing signs of resurgence as the Winawer becomes more analysed. It is a solid alternative to the Winawer; less ambitious, but also less explored.

The **Advance Variation** (3 e5), advocated by Nimzowitsch, has waned in popularity. It is not without its dangers for the second player, and it must be studied carefully by anyone who wishes to employ the defence in tournament play.

The **MacCutcheon Variation** (4 ♗g5 ♗b4) currently suffers from neglect, since it may involve Black in the disadvantages of the Winawer without its compensatory chances for counterattack. However, this line still holds unclear possibilities for those who wish to study it.

	2	3	4	5	6	7	8	9	10	
French I					**1 e4 e6**					
1	♘f3[1]	♘c3[2]	e5	a3[4]	dc	♗f4	♕d2	♗e2	♗g3	=
	d5	♗b4[3]	♘e7	♗xc3	c5	♘bc6	♗d7	♘g6	♘ce7[5]	
2	♕e2	g3	♘f3	♗g2	0-0	c3[8]	d4	cd	♗f4	∞
	c5[6]	♘c6	g6[7]	♗g7	♘ge7	e5	cd	ed	d6[9]	
3	d3	♘d2	♘gf3	g3[12]	de	♗b5+[13]	♗e2	e5	♘e4	=
	d5	♘f6[10]	b6[11]	de	♗b7	c6	♗e7	♘fd7	0-0[14]	
4	d4	ed	c4[15]	♘c3	♘f3	♗e2	♗xc4	♗e3	0-0[17]	∞
	d5	ed	♘f6	♗b4[16]	0-0	dc	♗g4	♘d5		
5	...	...	♗d3	♕f3[19]	c3	h3	♘e2	♗g5	♗e3	∞
	...	...	♗d6[18]	♘c6	♘f6	0-0	♖e8	♗e7	♘e4[20]	

[1]   **2 b3** d5 3 ♗b2 de 4 ♘c3 ♘f6 5 ♕e2 ♗e7 6 0-0-0 ♘c6 7 d3 (7 ♘xe4 ♘d4 ∓) 7 ... ♘d4 8 ♕e1 ed 9 ♗xd3 ♗d7 ∞ Kärner-Ritov, Tallinn 1973

    2 c4 d5 3 ed ed 4 cd ♘f6 5 ♘c3 (5 ♗b5+ ♘bd7 6 ♘c3 ♗e7 =) 5 ... ♘xd5 6 ♗c4 ♘b4 7 ♘f3 ♘d3+ 8 ♔f1 ♗e7 ∞ Velimirović-P.Nikolić, Novi Sad 1984

[2]   **3 e5** c5 4 b4!? (4 d4 – 2 d4) 4 ... cb 5 a3 ba 6 d4 ♘c6 7 c3 f5 8 ♗d3 ♗d7 9 g4 ∞ Mortensen-Karlsson, Copenhagen 1985

[3]   **3 ... d4** 4 ♘e2 c5 5 c3 dc (5 ... ♘f6!?) 6 bc ♘f6 7 ♘g3 ♗e7 8 d4 =/± Ljubojević-S.Garcia, Palma de Mallorca 1971

[4]   5 d4 – 2 d4

[5]   11 ♗d3 ♕b6 12 0-0 ♗b5 = Kuzmin-Lputian, USSR Ch 1980-81

[6]   2 ... e5 3 ♘f3 ♘c6 4 c3 d5 5 ♕b5 de 6 ♘xe5 ♕d6 7 d4 ed 8 ♘xc6 bc 9 ♕xd3 ♘f6 = Sax-P.Nikolić, Banja Luka 1981

[7]   4 ... ♗e7 5 ♗g2 d5 6 d3 ♘f6 7 0-0 h6 (7 ... b6 8 e5 ♘d7 9 c4± Balashov-Lputian, USSR Ch 1980-81) 8 ♖e1 b6 9 e5 ♘h7 10 c4± Vasyukov-Lputian, USSR Ch 1980-81

[8]   7 d3 0-0 8 c3 b6 9 h4 h6 10 ♘bd2 ♗b7 11 ♖e1 d6 = Smyslov-Kurajica, Bar 1980

[9]   Hjorth-Speelman, Brighton 1984

[10]   3 ... c5 4 ♘gf3 ♘c6 5 g3 – 1 ♘f3 d5 2 g3 c5

[11]   4 ... ♘c6 5 c3 a5 6 ♕c2 (6 e5 ♘d7 7 d4 f6 ∞) 6 ... g6 7 d4 ♗g7 8 ♗b5 0-0 9 ♗xc6 bc 10 0-0 c5 ∞ Kupreichik-Lputian, USSR Ch 1985

[12]   5 e5 ♘fd7 6 d4 c5 7 c3 – 2 d4 d5 3 ♘d2 ♘f6, but with an extra tempo for White

[13]   7 ♗g2 ♘xe4 8 ♘e5 ♘xc3! (8 ... ♘c5? 9 ♘xf7!) 9 ♕h5 g6 ∓ Kobas-Diždar, Zenica 1985

    7 ♕e2 ♘c6 8 ♗g2 a5! ∓

[14]   11 0-0 c5 12 ♘d6 ♗d5 13 c4 ♗c6 14 ♘b5 = Szmetan-Huss, Haifa Ol 1976

[15]   4 ♘c3 ♗b4 – 3 ♘c3 ♗b4

[16]   5 ... ♗e7 6 ♘f3 0-0 7 cd ♘bd7 8 ♗c4 ♘b6 9 ♗b3 ♘bxd5 = Nunn-Short, Brighton 1983

[17]   Gulko-Psakhis, USSR Ch 1985

[18]   4 ... c5 5 ♘f3 ♘c6 6 ♕e2+? ♗e7 7 dc ♘f6 8 h3 0-0 9 0-0 ♗xc5 10 c3 ♖e8 11 ♕c2 ♕d6 12 ♘bd2? ♕g3! ∓∓ Tatai-Korchnoi, Beer-Sheva 1978; 6 0-0 ∞

[19]   5 ♘f3 ♗e7 6 0-0 ♗g4 7 c3 ♘bc6 8 ♖e1 ♕d7 9 ♘bd2 0-0-0 ∞ Z.Nikolić-Barlov, Yugoslav Ch 1986

[20]   11 ♗xe4 de 12 ♕xe4 ♗b4! 13 ♔d1 ♘d5 ∞ Malanyuk-Psakhis, USSR Ch 1983

	3	4	5	6	7	8	9	10	11	
1	...	Nf3	c3[2]	a4[3]	Na3	Bxa6	0-0	Qd3	Nc2	±
	b6[1]	Ne7	Qd7	a5	Ba6	Nxa6	c6	Nc7	c5[4]	
2	...	Nf3[5]	Bd3[6]	0-0	Qe2	Nxe5	Qxe5	Bb5+	Qxd4	∞
	c5	Nc6	cd	f6[7]	fe	Nxe5	Nf6	Kf7	Bd6	
3	...	c3	Nf3	Be2[8]	c4[9]	Bxc4	Nbd2	a3	Qe2	±
	...	Qb6	Bd7	Bb5	Bxc4	Qb4+	dc	Qb5	cd[10]	
4	...	...	Nf3	Na3[12]	cd	Nc2	Bd2	Bc3	Bd3	∞
	...	Nc6	Nge7[11]	cd	Nf5	Qa5+[13]	Qb6	Bd7	Be7[14]	
5	...	...	...	a3	h4[16]	h5	g3	Nbd2	Nh4	∞
	...	...	Bd7	c4[15]	Nge7	h6	Na5	Nc8	Nb6[17]	
6	...	...	...	Be2	Na3	cd	0-0[20]	ba	Be3	∞
	...	...	...	Nge7[18]	cd[19]	Nf5	Bxa3[21]	Qb6	0-0[22]	
7	...	...	...	Bd3	cd	0-0[23]	Nxd4	Nc3	Qe2	∞
	...	...	Qb6	cd	Bd7	Nxd4	Qxd4	a6[24]	Ne7[25]	
8	...	...	...	Be2	cd	Nc3	Na4	Bd2	Bc3	=
	...	...	...	cd[26]	Nh6	Nf5	Qa5+	Bb4	Bxc3+[27]	
9	...	...	...	a3	Nbd2	Rb1[30]	Be2	Nf1	Bf4	±
	...	...	...	c4[28]	Bd7[29]	Na5	Ne7	Qb3	Ba4[31]	
10	...	...	...	...	b4[32]	cd	Bb2	Nbd2[34]	Bxc4	∞
	...	...	...	Bd7	cd	Rc8	Na5[33]	Nc4	dc[35]	

[1]   3 Bd7!? 4 Nf3 a6 5 c4 dc 6 Bxc4 Nc6 7 0-0 Ne7 ∞ Lau-Benjamin, New York 1985

[2]   5 c4 Bb7 6 Nc3 Qd7 7 cd Nxd5 8 Bd3 c5 9 0-0 ±/∞ Kupreichik-Vaganian, USSR 1980

[3]   6 Nbd2 a5 7 h4 h5 8 Ng5 Ba6 9 Bxa6 Nxa6 10 Nf1 Nf5 11 Ng3 ± Kupreichik-Vaganian, USSR 1984

[4]   12 h4 ± Sveshnikov-Vaganian, Moscow 1985

[5]   4 Qg4 cd 5 Nf3 Nc6 6 Bd3 Qc7 7 0-0 (7 Bf4 Nge7 8 0-0 Ng6 ∓) 7 ... Nxe5 (7 ... Nge7!?) 8 Nxe5 Qxe5 9 Bf4 Qf6 10 Bg5 Qe5 =

[6]   5 dc Bxc5 6 Bd3 f6 7 Qe2 (7 Bf4? fe 8 Nxe5 Nf6 ∓; 7 ef Bxf6 ∓) 7 ... fe 8 Nxe5 Nxe5 9 Qxe5 Qf6 =

[7]   6 ... Bc5 7 Bf4 Nge7 8 Nbd2 Ng6 9 Bg3 Bd7 10 Nb3 Bb6 11 Re1 Rc8 12 h4 ± Spraggett-M.Gurevich, Havana 1986

[8]   6 a3 Bb5 (6 ... Nc6 - 4 ... Nc6) 7 c4 Bxc4 8 Bxc4 dc 9 Nbd2 (9 d5 Ne7 10 de ±) 9 ... Qa6 10 Qe2 ± Sveshnikov-Ehlvest, Leningrad 1984

[9]   **7 dc** Bxc5 8 b4 Bxf2+! 9 Kf1 Bc6! 10 Qd2 d4 11 Kxf2 d3+ 12 Qe3 Qxe3+ 13 Bxe3 de ∓ Matousek

    7 0-0 Bxe2 8 Qxe2 Qa6 9 Qd1 c4 = Hecht-Karpov, Bath 1973

[10]   12 Nxd4 Qd5 13 N4f3 (13 N2f3 Bc5

14 Be3 Bxd4 15 Bxd4 Nc6 16 0-0-0 ∞ Ivell-Belyavsky, London 1985) 13 ... Nd7 14 Nxc4 ± Pinter-Ornstein, Budapest 1977

[11]   5 ... Nh6!? 6 Bxh6 gh 7 dc Bxc5 8 Bd3 f6! 9 b4 Bf8 10 b5 Nxe5 ∓ Khalifman-Kaidanov, Moscow 1987; 8 b4!? Kaidanov

[12]   6 Bd3!? cd 7 cd Nf5 8 Bxf5 ef 9 Nc3 Be6 10 Ne2 Be7 11 h4 ± Kupreichik

[13]   8 ... Be7 9 Nd3 0-0? (9 ... Qb6) 10 g4! Nh4 11 Nxh4 Bxh4 12 g5 ± Sveshnikov-Farago, Hastings 1984-85

    8 ... Nb4 9 Nxb4 Bxb4+ 10 Bd2 Bxd2+ 11 Qxd2 Qb6 12 Bd3 Bd7 13 Bxf5 ef 14 0-0 ± Psakhis-Chernin, USSR Ch 1985

    8 ... Qb6 9 Bd3 Bb4+ 10 Kf1 Be7 11 h4! (11 g3 Bd7 12 Kg2 Rc8 13 Bxf5 ef ∓ Short-Vaganian, Montpellier C 1985) 11 ... h5 (11 ... Bd7 12 g4 ±) 12 g3 ± Malanyuk-Lputian, USSR Ch 1986

[14]   Marjanović-P.Popović, Yugoslavia 1986

[15]   6 ... Rc8 7 Bd3 cd 8 cd Qb6 9 Bc2 g5!? 10 h3 Nxd4 ∞ Sveshnikov-Chernin, USSR Ch 1985

    6 ... Nge7 7 Bd3 (7 b4 cd 8 cd Nf5 9 Bb2 Be7 10 Bd3 Qb6 ∞ Gorelov-Yudasin, Minsk 1985) 7 ... cd 8 cd Nf5 9 Bxf5 ef 10 Nc3 Be6 11 b4 Be7 ∞ Marjanović-Abramović, Yugoslavia 1985

    6 ... f6!? 7 ef (7 b4 fe 8 dc e4 ∓ Popčev-

Dolmatov, Polanica Zdroj 1987) 7 ... gf 8 ♘h4 ♕e7 ∞

[16] 7 ♗f4 ♘ge7 8 h4 ♘c8 9 ♘bd2 h6 10 g3 ♘b6 11 ♗h3 ♗e7 12 h5 ♘a5 ⩲ Khalifman-Yusupov, USSR Ch 1987

7 b4 cb 8 ♕xb3 ♘a5 9 ♕c2 b5 10 ♗d3 h6 11 0-0 ♘e7 12 ♖e1 ♖c8 ⩲ Khalifman-Bareyev, USSR Ch 1987

[17] 12 ♘g2 ♕c7 13 ♘e3 0-0-0 14 f4 ∞ Malanyuk-Bareyev, USSR Ch 1987

[18] 6 ... f6 7 0-0 fe 8 ♘xe5 ♘xe5 10 de ♕c7 10 c4 0-0-0 (10 ... ♕xe5 11 ♗h5+! g6 12 ♗f3 0-0-0 13 ♖e1 ± Romanishin-Ivanchuk, Irkutsk 1986) 11 cd ♕xe5 12 ♗f3 ± Sveshnikov-Psakhis, Sochi 1984

[19] 7 ... ♘g6 8 h4 cd 9 cd ♗b4+ 10 ♔f1 h6 11 ♘c2 ♗e7 12 h5 ± Sveshnikov-Gulko, Tashkent 1984

[20] 9 ♘c2 ♘b4 10 ♘e3 ♘xe3 11 fe ♗e7 12 a3 ♘c6 13 b4 a6 ∞ Spassky-Korchnoi, match 1977-78

[21] 9 ... ♕b6 10 ♘c2 a5 11 g4 ♘fe7 12 ♘h4 ♘g6 13 ♘g2 ♗e7 14 f4 ± Sveshnikov-Gulko, USSR Ch 1985

[22] Sveshnikov

[23] Milner Barry Gambit

8 ♗c2 ♘b4 ⩲ Steinitz-Burn, Vienna 1898

[24] 10 ... ♕xe5 11 ♖e1 ♕b8 13 ♘xd5 ♗d6 14 ♕g4 ♔f8 15 ♗d2 h5 16 ♕h3 ♗c6 (16 ... ed 16 ♕xd7 ♗xh2+ 17 ♔h1 ♘f6 18 ♕f5 ± Borg-P.Nikolić, Kavala 1985) 16 ♘e3 ♘f6 17 ♗c3 ∞ Borg

[25] 12 ♔h1 ♘c6 13 f4 ♘b4 14 ♖d1 ♘xd3 15 ♖xd3 ♕b6 16 ♗e3 ♗c5 17 ♗xc5 ♕xc5 18 f5 d4 ∞ Messere-Dijkstra, corr. 1977

[26] 6 ... ♘h6 7 ♗xh6 ♕xb2? 8 ♗e3 ♕xa1 9 ♕c2 cd 10 ♘xd4 ±; 7 ... gh ±

[27] 11 ... b5 12 a3 ♗xc3+ 13 ♘xc3 b4 =

11 ... ♗xc3+ 12 ♘xc3 ♕b6 13 ♗b5 ♗d7 14 ♗xc6 ♗xc6 = Hennings-Knaak, Leipzig 1981

[28] 6 ... a5 7 ♗d3 (7 ♗e2 ±) 7 ... ♘ge7 8 0-0 cd 9 cd ♘f5 10 ♗xf5 ef 11 ♘c3 ♗e6 12 ♘a4 ± Georgadze-Draško, Tbilisi 1985

[29] 7 ... f6 8 ♗e2 fe 9 ♘xe5 ♘f6 (9 ... ♘xe5 10 de ♘h6? 11 ♗xc4! dc 12 ♗xh6 ± Pähtz-Uhlmann, Erfurt 1985) 10 f4 ♗d6 11 ♗h5+ g6 12 ♗f3 ± Pähtz-Uhlmann, East German Ch 1986

[30] 8 g3 ♘a5 9 h4 0-0-0 10 ♗h3 f5 11 0-0 ♘h6 12 ♘e1 ♘f7 ∞ Klinger-Portisch, Dubai Ol 1986

[31] 12 ♕xb3 ♗xb3 13 ♘e3 ± Sveshnikov-Eingorn, Sochi 1985

[32] 7 ♗e2 ♘ge7 8 dc ♕c7 9 0-0 ♘xe5 10 ♘xe5 ♕xe5 11 ♘d2 ♕c7 12 b4 g6 ∞ Romanishin-Foisor, Tbilisi 1986

[33] 9 ... ♘xb4? 10 ab ♕xb4+ 11 ♕d2 ♖c2 12 ♗a3! ± Parma

[34] 10 ♗c3 ♘c4 11 ♗d3 ♗e7 12 0-0 ♘h6 ⩲ Klinger-Arencibia, Gausdal 1986

[35] 12 ♖c1 ♕a6 (12 ... c3!? 13 ♖xc3 ♖xc3 14 ♗xc3 ♕a6 ∞ Arencibia) 13 ♘e4 ♗c6 15 ♘fd2 b5 ∞ Nikolenko-Naumkin, Moscow 1986

French III   1 e4 e6 2 d4 d5 3 ♘c3

	3	4	5	6	7	8	9	10	11	
1	...	♘xe4	♘f3	♘xf6+	♗d3[3]	♕e2	♗g5	0-0-0	♔b1	±
	de[1]	♘d7[2]	♘gf6	♘xf6	♗e7	0-0	c5	♕a5	cd[4]	
2	...	e5	♘xe4	♗c4[5]	a4	♘h3	♘f4	♗e3	0-0	±
	♘f6	♘e4	de	a6[6]	b6	♗b7	♘c6	♘e7[7]	g6[8]	

---

[1] 3 ... ♘c6 4 ♘f3 ♘f6 5 ed ed 6 ♗b5 ♗b4 (6 ... ♗g4 7 h3 ♗xf3 8 ♕xf3 ± Fischer-Petrosian, match 1971) 7 0-0 0-0 8 ♗xc6 bc 9 ♘e5 ± Korchnoi-Short, Reykjavik 1987

[2] 4 ... b6 5 ♕f3! c6 6 ♗g5 ♗e7 7 ♗xe7 ♘xe7 8 0-0-0 ±

4 ... ♗d7 5 ♘f3 ♗c6 6 ♗d3 ♘d7 7 0-0 ♘gf6 8 ♘g3 ♗e7 9 c4 ♗xf3 10 ♕xf3 c6 11 ♗f4 ±

4 ... ♕d5 5 ♘c3 ♗b4 6 ♘f3 ♘f6 7 ♗d3 ♘e4 8 0-0 ♗xc3 9 bc ♗xc3 10 ♖b1 ♘c6 11 ♗e3 ♗d7 12 ♖b5! ♕d6 13 ♖xb7 ±

4 ... ♘f6 5 ♘xf6+ ♕xf6 6 ♘f3 h6 7 ♗d3 ±
4 ... ♗e7 5 ♘f3 ♘f6 6 ♘xf6+ ♗xf6 7 c3

0-0 8 ♗d3 c5 9 dc ♕c7 10 ♕c2 ± Ghinda-Ree, Thessaloniki Ol 1984

[3] 7 ♗g5 c5 8 ♗b5+ ♗d7 9 ♗xd7+ ♕xd7 10 ♕e2 cd 11 0-0-0 ± Mihalchishin-Chernin, Cienfuegos 1981

[4] 12 h4 ♗d7 13 ♘xd4 ± Nunn-Skembris, Paris 1983

[5] 6 ♗e3 c5 7 dc ♘d7 8 ♕g4 ♘xc5 9 ♗b5+! ♘d7 10 ♘e2 ♕a5+ 11 ♘c3 a6 12 ♗xd7+ ♗xd7 13 ♗d4 ± A.Ivanov-Malanyuk, USSR 1981

[6] 6 ... c5 7 d5 ♘d7 8 de fe 9 f4 ±

[7] 10 ... ♗e7 11 ♕g4 g6 12 c3 ±

[8] 12 ♕e2 ♘f5 13 ♖fd1 ♗h6 14 a5 ± Aseyev-Lputian, USSR Ch 1984

	3	4	5	6	7	8	9	10	11	
3	...	e5	f4[9]	♘f3	♗e3	♕d2	dc	♗d3[12]	♕f2	±
	♘f6	♘fd7	c5	♘c6	a6[10]	b5	♘xc5[11]	♗b7	♘xd3+[13]	
4	...	...	...	...	...	♘a4	c3	b4	cb	±
	...	...	...	...	♕b6	♕a5+	cd	♘xb4[14]	♗xb4+[15]	
5	...	...	...	...	...	♘xd4	♕d2	♗xd4	♕xd4	±
	...	...	...	...	cd	♗c5[16]	♘xd4	♗xd4	♕b6[17]	
6	...	♗g5	♘xe4	♗xf6	♘f3	♕d2	0-0-0	♗d3	♘xf6+	±
	...	de	♗e7	♗xf6[18]	♕d7[19]	♗e7[20]	♘f6	0-0	♗xf6[21]	
7	...	...	e5	h4[23]	hg	♘h3	♘f4	♕g4	0-0-0	∞∞
	...	♗e7	♘fd7[22]	♗xg5[24]	♕xg5	♕e7	♘c6[25]	♘xd4	♘f5[26]	
8	...	...	...	...	♕g4[27]	ef	♕g3	dc	0-0-0	∞
	...	...	...	0-0	f5	♘xf6	c5	♘bd7	♘xc5[28]	

1 e4 e6 2 d4 d5 3 ♘c3 ♘f6 4 ♗g5 ♗e7 5 e5 ♘fd7 6 ♗xe7 ♕xe7

	7	8	9	10	11	12	13	14	15	
9	f4[29]	♘f3	dc	♕d2	♗d3	a3	♕f2	ab	0-0[32]	±
	a6	c5	♘c6	♕xc5[30]	b5	h6[31]	b4	♕xb4		
10	...	♘f3	♕d2[33]	dc	♗d3	ef	0-0-0	♖he1		∞
	0-0	c5	♘c6	♕xc5[34]	f6	♘xf6	♖b8[35]	b5[36]		
11	...	...	dc	♕d4[38]	♕xc5	a3	ef	g3[40]		±
	...	...	♕xc5[37]	♘c6[39]	♘xc5	f6	♖xf6			

9 **5 ♘ce2** c5 6 c3 ♕a5 7 f4 b5 8 dc b4! 9 a3 ♗xc5 10 cb ♗xb4+ = Kristiansen-Chernin, Copenhagen 1984

5 ♘f3 c5 6 dc ♘c6 7 ♗f4 ♗xc5 8 ♗d3 f6 9 ef ♕xf6 (9 ... ♘xf6 10 0-0 0-0 11 ♘e5 ♗d7 = Spassky-Petrosian, match (19) 1966) 10 ♗g3 0-0 11 0-0 ♘d4 = Rogers-Draško, Tallinn 1985

10 7 ... b6 8 ♗b5 ♗b7 9 0-0 ♗e7 10 f5! ± Gipslis-Shereshevsky, USSR 1981

11 9 ... ♕a5 10 ♗d3 b4 11 ♘e2 ♗xc5 12 0-0 ± Short-Agdestein, Naestved 1985

12 10 ♕f2 ♘e4 ∞ Nunn-Andersson, Naestved 1985

13 12 cd ± Gheorghiu-Belkadi, Skopje Ol 1972

14 10 ... ♕c7 11 ♘xd4 ♘xd4 12 ♗xd4 ♘b8 13 a3 ±

15 12 ♗d2 ♗xd2+ 13 ♘xd2 ⊥ Timman-Yusupov, Bugojno 1986, Timman-Korchnoi, Brussels 1987, and Chandler-M.Gurevich, Leningrad 1987

16 **8 ...** ♘xd4 9 ♗xd4 ♘b8 10 ♗d3 ♘c6 11 ♗f2 ♗e7 (11 ... ♕a5 12 0-0 ♗c5 13 ♘b5 ±) 12 ♕h5 ± Nunn-Sutton, England 1984

8 ... ♕b6 9 a3 ♗c5 10 ♘a4 ♕a5+ 11 c3 ± Sax-Klinger, Szirak 1985

17 **12 ♘b5** ± Short-Chernin, Montpellier C 1985

12 ♕xb6 ♘xb6 13 ♘b5 ± Timman-Korchnoi, Brussels 1986

18 6 ... gf 7 ♘f3 f5 8 ♘c3 ♗f6 9 ♕d2 (9 ♗c4 ♘c6 ∞ Rohde-Speelman, London 1984) 9 ... ♘c6 10 ♗b5 ±

19 7 ... ♗d7 8 ♕d2 ♗c6 9 ♘xf6+ ♕xf6 10 ♘e5 0-0 11 0-0-0 ± Spassky-Petrosian, match (23) 1966

20 **8 ...** b6 9 ♗b5 ♗b7 10 ♘xf6+ gf 11 ♕c3 ±
8 ... 0-0 9 0-0-0 b6 10 ♕f4 ♗b7 11 ♗d3 ± Ljubojević-Quinteros, Orense 1975

21 12 ♕f4 ± Fischer-Benko, Curaçao C 1962

22 5 ... ♘e4 6 ♗xe7 ♘xc3 (6 ... ♕xe7 7 ♘xe4 de 8 ♕e2 b6 9 0-0-0 ♗b7 10 g3 ±) 7 ♗xd8 (7 ♕g4!?) 7 ... ♘xd1 8 ♗xc7 ♘xb2 9 ♖b1 ♘c4 10 ♗xc4 dc 11 ♘f3 ± Spassky-R.Byrne, Moscow 1975

23 Alekhine-Châtard Attack

24 **6 ... f6** 7 ♕h5+ ♔f8 (7 ... g6 8 ef!) 8 ef ♘xf6 9 ♕f3 ±
6 ... c5 7 ♗xe7 ♕xe7 8 ♘b5 ±
6 ... h6 7 ♗e3 c5 8 ♕g4 g6 9 ♘f3 ± Hellers-Bareyev, Gausdal 1986
6 ... a6 7 ♕g4 ♗xg5 8 hg c5 9 g6 f5 10 ♕g3

h6 11 ♘f3 0-0 12 0-0-0 ♘c6 13 ♘e2 ±/∞

25 **9 ... f5** 10 ♕h5+ ♕f7 11 ♘xe6! g6 12 ♘xc7+ ♔d8 13 ♕f3 ±

9 ... ♘f8 10 ♕g4 f5 11 ef gf 12 0-0-0 ± Alekhine-Fahrni, Mannheim 1914

9 ... a6 10 ♕g4 ♔f8 11 ♕f3 ♔g8 12 ♗d3 c5? (12 ... h6) 13 ♗xh7+! ±± Keres-Wade, USSR v England 1954

26 12 ♘fxd5 ∞∞

27 7 ♗d3 f5 8 g4 c5 9 gf cd 10 f6 ♗xf6! 11 ef ♘xf6 12 ♘ce2 e5 13 f3 ♕b6 14 c3 ♕xb2 15 cd ♘c6 ∞ Shabalov-Supatashvili, USSR 1985

28 12 ♗d3 b5 ∞ Kupreichik-Moskalenko, USSR 1986

29 7 ♕g4 0-0 8 ♘f3 c5 9 ♗d3 f5 10 ef ♖xf6 ∓

7 ♕d2 0-0 8 ♘ce2 c5 9 c3 f6 10 f4 cd 11 cd fe 12 fe ♘c6 =

7 ♘b5 ♘b6 8 c3 a6 9 ♘a3 c5 10 f4 ♘c6 11 ♘c2 ♘a4 12 ♖b1 b5 =

30 10 ... ♘xc5 11 0-0-0 b5 12 ♗d3 b4 13 ♘e2 a5 14 ♘ed4 ±

31 12 ... ♗b7 13 ♕f2 ♖c8 14 ♘e2 ♕xf2+ 15 ♔xf2 f6 16 ♘ed4 ± Bednarski-Raičević, Trencianske Teplice 1974

32 15 ... ♕xb2 16 ♘b5 0-0 17 ♖fb1 ab 18 ♖xb2

♖xa1+ 19 ♘e1 ± Hebden-Raičević, Moscow 1986

33 **9 ♘b5?** a6! (9 ... cd!? 10 ♘c7 ♘xe5 Bronstein) 10 ♘d6 cd 11 ♗d3 f6 12 0-0 ♘c6 ∓ Stecko

9 ♗d3 cd (9 ... f5 10 ef ♕xf6 11 ♗g5 ♕xf4! 12 ♗xh7+ ♔h8 13 ♕h5? ♘f6; 13 ♕d2 ∞) 10 ♗xh7+ ♔xh7 11 ♘g5+ ♕xg5 12 fg dc 13 ♕d3+ ♔g8 14 ♕xc3 ♘c6 ∓ Lanka-Gauens, corr. 1984

34 10 ... ♘xc5 11 0-0-0 f6 12 ef ♕xf6 13 g3 ±

35 13 ... ♗d7 14 ♔b1 a6 15 ♖he1 b5 16 ♘e2 ♔h8 17 ♘g3 a5 ∞ Utasi-Garcia Gonzalez, Havana 1985

36 Kupreichik-Bareyev, USSR Ch 1987

37 9 ... ♘c6 10 ♗d3 (10 ♕d2 – 9 ♕d2) 10 ... f6 11 ef ♕xf6 (11 ... ♘xf6 12 0-0 ♕xc5+ 13 ♔h1 ±; 11 ... ♖xf6 12 ♕d2 ±) 12 g3 ♘xc5 13 0-0 ±

38 10 ♕d2 ♘b6 (10 ... ♘c6 – 9 ♕d2) 11 ♘b5 ♘c6 12 c3 f6 13 ef ♖xf6 = van der Sterren-Korchnoi, Wijk aan Zee 1984

39 10 ... b6!?

40 14 ... ♗d7? 15 b4 ± Vera-Klüger, Havana 1986

French IV	1 e4 e6 2 d4 d5 3 ♘c3 ♘f6 4 ♗g5 ♗b4

	5	6	7	8	9	10	11	12	13	
1	ed[1]	♗xf6[3]	bc	♕d2	c4	♘e2	f3			=
	♕xd5[2]	♗xc3+[4]	gf	♘d7	♕e4+	b6[5]	♕c6[6]			
2	e5	♗e3[7]	♕g4[8]	a3	bc	♗d3	h4	h5	f4	±
	h6	♘e4	g6[9]	♗xc3+	♘xc3[10]	♘c6	♕e7[11]	g5	gf[12]	

[1] 5 ♗d3 de 6 ♗xe4 h6 =

5 ♘e2 de 6 a3 ♗e7 7 ♗xf6 ♗xf6 8 ♘xe4 e5 =

[2] 5 ... ed 6 ♗d3 ♘c6 7 ♘e2 ♗e7 8 a3 ±

[3] 6 ♘f3 ♘e4 (6 ... c5 7 ♗d2 ♗xc3 8 ♗xc3 ♘e4 9 ♕d3 ♘d7 10 ♗e2 ♘xc3 11 ♕xc3 cd 12 ♕xd4 ± Malanyuk-M.Gurevich, USSR Ch 1987) 7 ♗d2 ♗xc3 8 bc ♘xd2 9 ♕xd2 ∞

[4] 6 ... gf 7 ♘e2 intending 8 a3 ±

[5] 10 ... ♘b6 11 f3 ♕c6 12 c5 ♘d5 13 c4 ♘e7 14 ♘c3 ± Capablanca-Alekhine, New York 1924

[6] 11 ... ♕g6 12 ♘g3 ♗b7 13 ♗d3 ± Alekhine

11 ... ♕c6 =

[7] 6 ♗xf6 gf 7 ♘f3 f5 8 ♗d3 c5 ∓ Steinitz-MacCutcheon, New York 1885

6 ef hg 7 fg ♖g8 8 h4 gh 9 ♕g4 (9 ♘f3 ♖xg7 10 ♖xh4 ♖g8 =) 9 ... ♕f6 10 ♖xh4 ♕xg7 11 ♕xg7 ♖xg7 12 ♖h8+ ♗f8 = Heuer-Dvoretsky, USSR 1976

6 ♗h4 g5 7 ♗g3 ♘e4 8 ♘e2 f5 9 ef ♕xf6 10 ♕d3 ♘c6 11 0-0-0 ♘xg3 12 ♘xg3 ♗d7 ∞

Purdy-Miller, Australia 1955

6 ♗c1 ♘e4 7 ♕g4 ♔f8 8 a3 (8 ♘e2 c5 9 a3 ♗a5 ∓) 8 ... ♗xc3+ 9 bc ♘xc3 10 ♗d3 c5 11 dc ♘c6 12 ♗d2 f5 = Malich-Fuchs, East Germany 1963

[8] 7 ♘e2 c5 8 a3 ♗xc3 9 ♘xc3 ♗xc3+ 10 bc ♘c6 11 ♕g4 ♔f8 intending ... ♕a5 =

[9] 7 ... g5 8 a3 ♗xc3+ 9 bc c5 10 ♗d3 h5 11 ♕f3 ♘xc3 12 dc ♘c6 13 ♕g3 ♕a5 14 ♔f1 ± Veselovsky-Glek, USSR 1984

[10] 9 ... c5 10 ♗d3 ♕a5 11 ♘e2 cd 12 ♗xd4 ♘c6 13 0-0 ♘c5 14 ♗xg6 ♖g8 15 ♗xf7+ ♔xf7 16 ♕h5+ ♔e7 17 ♕xh6 ± Shamkovich-Chistyakov, USSR 1961

[11] 11 ... ♗d7 12 ♗xg6 ♖g8 13 ♗xf7+ ♔xf7 14 ♕h5+ ♖g6 15 ♘h3 ∞∞

11 ... ♘e7 12 f3 ♗d7 13 ♕f4 ♘f5 14 ♗f2 c5 15 dc d4 16 ♗xf5 gf 17 ♗xd4 ♘d5 18 ♕d2 ± Kurajica-Dvoretsky, Wijk aan Zee 1976

[12] 14 ♕xf4 ♗d7 15 ♘h3! 0-0-0 16 0-0 ♖df8 17 ♕f6 ±

	5	6	7	8	9	10	11	12	13	
3	e5	Be3	Qg4	a3	bc	Bd3	dc	Bd2	Nf3	∞
	h6	Ne4	Kf8	Bxc3+[13]	c5[14]	Nxc3[15]	Qa5[16]	Nc6[17]	Qxc5	
4	...	Bd2	bc[18]	Qg4	h4[19]	Rh3	Bd3	Kxd2	Be2	±
	...	Bxc3	Ne4	Kf8	c5	Nc6[20]	Nxd2	c4[21]	b5[22]	
5	...	...	...	...	...	ef	Nf3	Qf4	Qxd2	±
	...	...	...	...	f5	Qxf6	Nc6	Nxd2	e5[23]	
6	...	...	...	...	Be3[24]	Bd3	dc	Nf3	Kf1	∞
	...	...	...	g6	Nxc3	c5	Qa5	Ne4+	Bd7[25]	
7	...	...	...	...	Bd3	Kxd2	Nf3[27]	Rab1[28]	cd	±/∞
	...	...	...	...	Nxd2	c5[26]	Nc6	cd[29]	Qa5+[30]	

[13] 8 ... Ba5 9 Ne2 c5 10 dc Nc6 11 b4 Nxc3 12 Nxc3 Nxe5 13 Qd1 Bc7 14 Nb5 ± Klovans-Harding, corr. 1982

[14] 9 ... Nxc3 10 Bd3 b6 11 h4 Ba6 12 Rh3 ±

[15] 10 ... Qa5 11 Ne2 cd 12 Bxd4 Nc6 13 0-0 Nc5 14 c4 ±

10 ... cd 11 cd Qa5+ 12 Kf1 Bd7 13 h4 ±

[16] 11 ... Nc6 12 Nf3 f5 13 ef Qxf6 14 Qh5 e5 15 Bg6 Bd7 16 0-0 ±/∞ Klovans-Shereshevsky, USSR 1977

[17] 12 ... Qxc5 13 Ne2 ±

12 ... Qa4 13 Qb4 ±

[18] 7 Bxc3 Ne4 8 Bb4 (8 Ba5 0-0! 9 Bd3 Nc6 10 Bc3 Nxc3 11 bc f6 ∓ Fischer-Petrosian, Curaçao C 1962; 8 Ne2) 8 ... c5 9 Bxc5 (9 dc? Nxf2) 9 ... Nxc5 10 dc Nd7 11 Qd4 Qc7 12 Nf3 Nxc5 =

[19] 9 Bd3 Nxd2 10 Kxd2 Qg5+ (10 ... c5 11 h4 Qa5 ∞) 11 Qxg5 hg =

[20] 10 ... Qa5 11 Bd3 Nxd2 12 Rg3! g6 13 Kxd2 cd 14 Qxd4 Nc6 15 Qf4 d4 16 Nf3 Qxc3+ 17 Ke2 Qxa1 18 Qf6 Rg8 19 h5 ±± Maroczy

10 ... cd 11 cd Qb6 12 Nf3 Nc6 13 Bd3 Nxe5 14 Nxe5! Qxd4 15 Qf4 Qxa1+ 16 Ke2 ±± Keres

[21] 12 ... Qa5 13 Rg3 g6 14 Bxg6 ±±

12 ... cd 13 cd Qb6 14 Rg3 g6 15 Ne2 ± Keres

[22] 14 Qf4 Bd7 15 Rh5 Qe7 16 Ne2 Rb8

17 a3 Rb6 (17 ... a5!?) 18 g4 Ra6 19 g5 ± Shakarov-Monin, corr. 1983

[23] 14 0-0-0 Bg4 (14 ... e4 15 Ne5 ±) 15 Nxe5 Nxe5 16 de Qxe5 17 Re1! Qd6 18 h5 Re8 19 Bd3 ± Shakarov-Monin, corr. 1986

[24] 9 h4 c5 10 Bd3 Nxd2 – 9 Bd3

9 Bc1 Nxc3 10 Bd3 c5 11 dc Qa5 12 Bd2 Qa4 =

[25] 13 ... Nxc5 14 Bxg6 ± Maroczy

13 ... Bd7 14 Bxe4 de 15 Qxe4 Bc6 16 Qd4 Na6 ∞ Fjelstad-Sauermann, corr. 1976

[26] 10 ... Qg5+ 11 Qxg5 hg 12 g4 ±

[27] 11 h4 Qa5 12 Rh3 Nc6 (12 ... cd 13 Bxg6 Qc7 ∞ Euwe-Maroczy, The Hague 1921) 13 Bxg6 Nxd4! ∓ Harding

11 dc Bd7 12 Bb5 Qc7 13 Qd4 0-0 14 Bxd7 Nxd7 15 Nf3 Rfc8 = Martinović-Padevsky, Kragujevac 1984

[28] 12 Qf4 Qa5 (12 ... Qc7 13 Qf6 Rg8 14 h4 ±) 13 Rhb1 b6 14 a4 Ba6 15 Bb5 Rc8 16 dc bc 17 Bxc6+ Rxc6 18 Rb8+ Rc8 = Fischer

[29] 12 ... c4 13 Be2 b6 14 Qf4 Bd7 15 h4 Qe7 16 h5 g5 17 Qf6 0-0-0 18 Qxe7 Nxe7 19 Nh2 ± Spraggett-Ree, Wijk aan Zee 1985

[30] 14 Ke2 b6 15 Qf4 Ba6 16 Rhc1 Rc8 17 Kf1 Qa3 ∞ Matulović-Tsvetkov, Varna 1965

14 Ke3 b6 15 Qf4 Ba6 16 Rhc1 ±/∞

French V   1 e4 e6 2 d4 d5 3 ♘c3 ♗b4

	4	5	6	7	8	9	10	11	12	
1	ed[1]	♗d3[2]	a3	bc	♕f3[4]	♖b1	♘h3	♘g5	♘xe6	∞
	ed	♘c6[3]	♗xc3+	♘ge7	♗e6	b6	♕d7	h6	♕xe6+[5]	
2	♗d3	♗xe4	♗f3[6]	a3	bc	♘e2	a4	0-0	g3	∞
	de	♘f6	c5	♗xc3+	♘c6	c4[7]	0-0	♘d5	b6[8]	
3	♕d3	♕xe4	♕h4	dc	bc	♕b4	♘f3	♗b5	♗g5	=
	de[9]	♘f6	c5	♗xc3+[10]	♕a5	♕c7	♘c6	e5	0-0[11]	
4	♗d2	♕g4	♘f3[13]	♕xe6+[14]	♘xd4	♘xe4	♘xd2			=
	de[12]	♕xd4	♘h6	♗xe6	♗d7	♗xd2+	♘c6			
5	♘e2	a3	♘xe4	♗f4	♕d3	0-0-0	♘2c3[16]	♘xd5	♗g3[17]	=
	de[15]	♗e7	♘c6	♘f6	0-0	b6	♘d5	ed	♗e6[18]	
6	...	...	♘xc3	♗b5[19]	♗g5[20]	♗e3	♕d2	0-0-0	♗xc6	∞
	...	♗xc3+	♘c6	♘e7	f6	0-0	f5[21]	a6[22]	♘xc6[23]	

---

[1] 4 ♕g4 ♘f6 5 ♕xg7 ♖g8 6 ♕h6 ♖g6 7 ♕e3 c5 8 a3 ∞

[2] 5 ♕f3 ♕e7+! 6 ♘e2 (6 ♕e3 ♘c6 ∓) 6 ... ♘c6 7 ♗e3 ♘f6 ∓

[3] **5 ... c5** 6 dc ♘c6 7 ♘f3 d4 8 a3 ± van der Wiel-Vaganian, Amsterdam 1986

5 ... ♘e7 6 ♕h5 c5 7 a3 ♗xc3+ 8 bc c4 9 ♗e2 ♗f5 10 ♗d1 ♘bc6 ∞ Smyslov-Portisch, Reggio Emilia 1986-87

[4] 8 ♕h5 ♗e6 9 ♘e2 ♕d7 10 ♘g3 (10 0-0 ♗f5 =) 10 ... 0-0-0 11 0-0 ♖de8 12 a4 g6 13 ♕f3 h5 ∞ Casper-Uhlmann, Leipzig 1982

[5] 13 ♔d1 0-0 14 ♖e1 ♕d7 15 ♕g3 ♔h8 ∞ Kavalek-Yusupov, Dubai Ol 1986

[6] 6 ♗d3 c5 7 dc (7 a3 ♗xc3+ 8 bc 0-0 9 ♘f3 ♕c7 10 0-0 c4 11 ♗e2 ♘d5 ∓ Barlov-Sahović, Vrnjačka Banja 1984) 7 ... ♘bd7 8 ♗d2 ♘xc5 9 ♗b5+ ♘cd7 =

[7] 9 ... e5 10 ♗g5 cd 11 cd ed 12 ♗xc6+ bc 13 ♕xd4 ♕a5+ 14 ♗d2 ♕d5 = Hort-Pietzsch, Kecskemet 1964

[8] Sariego-Vaiser, Bayamo 1985

[9] 4 ... c5 5 ed ed 6 a3 ♗xc3+ 7 ♕xc3 c4 8 ♕g3 ±

[10] 7 ... ♘c6 8 ♗d2 ♗xc5 9 ♘f3 0-0 10 0-0-0 ± Kuzmin-Draško, Tallinn 1985

[11] **12 ... ♗d7** 13 ♗xc6 ♗xc6 14 ♗xf6 gf 15 0-0-0! ± Chiburdanidze-Bareev, USSR 1985

12 ... 0-0 13 ♗xc6 ♕xc6 =

[12] 4 ... ♘e7 5 ♗d3 de (5 ... b6 6 ed ed 7 ♕h5± Timman-Hübner, Tilburg 1986) 6 ♘xe4 ♕xd4 7 ♘f3 ♗xd2+ 8 ♕xd2 ♕d5 9 0-0-0 ♘bc6 10 ♕c3 f6 ∞ Timman-Vaganian, Amsterdam 1986

[13] 6 0-0-0 f5 (6 ... h5 7 ♕e2! ♗d7! 8 ♘xe4 ♗xd2+ 9 ♖xd2 ♕a4 10 a3 ♘a6! ∓ Uhlmann) 7 ♕g3 ♗d6 8 ♗f4 ♗xf4+ 9 ♕xf4 ♕c5 10 f3 ♘f6! 11 fe e5 12 ♕g5 0-0 13 ef ♘c6 14 ♘f3 h6 ∓ Vaganian

[14] 7 ♕f4 e5! 8 ♕xe5+ ♕xe5 9 ♘xe5 ♗xc3 (9 ... ♘g4 =) 10 ♗xc3 ∞

[15] 4 ... ♘f6!? 5 e5 ♘fd7 6 ♕d3 0-0 ∞ Mokry-Timman, Reggio Emilia 1984-85

[16] 10 ♘xf6+ ♗xf6 11 ♕g3 ♗h4 12 ♕e3 ♗b7 ∞ Stoica-Farago, Albena 1983

[17] 12 ♘c3 ♗f6 13 ♕f3 ♗e6 14 ♗e3 ♘e7 15 g4 c5 = Stoica-Uhlmann, Bucharest 1978

[18] 13 ♕c3 ♗d6 14 ♘h5 ♘e7 15 ♗xd6 ♕xd6 16 ♕g3 ♘f5 = Mokry-Short, Thessaloniki Ol 1984

[19] 7 ♗e3 ♘f6 8 ♕d2 ♘e7 (8 ... h6 9 0-0-0 ♘e7 10 f3 ef 11 gf ♘ed5 12 ♖g1 ∞ Ermenkov-Belyavsky, Tunis IZ 1985) 9 ♗g5 ♘ed5 10 0-0-0 ♗d7 ∞ Kotronias-Foisor, Moscow 1987

[20] 8 ♗e3 0-0 9 ♕d2 e5 (9 ... f5 – 8 ♗g5) 10 de (10 d5 ♘d4 ∓ Garcia Martinez-Uhlmann, Leipzig 1983) 10 ... ♘xe5 11 ♘xe4 ♗f5 = Mokry-Knaak, Bratislava 1983

[21] **10 ... e5** 11 d5 ♘d4 12 ♗xd4 ed 13 ♕xd4 ♘f5 ½-½ Sax-Barczay, Hungary 1982; 11 de! ♕xd2+ 12 ♗xd2 ± Gipslis-Toshkov, Jurmala 1987

10 ... a6!? 11 ♗xc6 ♘xc6 = Gipslis-Casper, Jurmala 1987

[22] 11 ... ♘d5 12 ♘xd5 ed 13 ♗xc6 bc 14 ♗f4± Miles

[23] **13 ♗g5** ♕e8 14 f3 ef 15 gf ∞ Miles-Reefschläger, Porz 1981-82

13 f3 e5 (13 ... ef 14 gf e5 15 d5 ♘a5 16 ♕e2 b5 17 ♖hg1 ∞ Ciocaltea-Ornstein, Smederevska Palanka 1981) 14 d5 ♘a5 15 ♕e2 b5 16 fe f4 17 ♗c5 ♖f7 ∞ Stoica

French V   1 e4 e6 2 d4 d5 3 ♘c3 ♗b4   *continued*

	4	5	6	7	8	9	10	11	12	
7	a3	bc	♕g4	♕xg7	♕h6	♘e2[25]	g3[27]	♗g2	0-0	∞
	♗xc3+	de	♘f6	♖g8	♘bd7[24]	c5[26]	b6	♗b7	♕e7[28]	
8	...	...	...	...	...	♘h3	♗e2	♗d2	♘g5[31]	±/∞
	...	...	...	...	...	c5[29]	♕a5	♖xg2[30]		

[24] **8 ... b6** 9 ♗g5 ♖g6 10 ♕h4 ♗b7 11 ♘e2 ± Watson-Whiteley, Bristol 1968
8 ... ♖g6 9 ♕e3 (9 ♕d2 b6 =) 9 ... ♘c6 10 ♘e2 ♘e7 11 ♘g3 ♗d7 12 ♘xe4 ♘xe4 13 ♕xe4 ♗c6 ∞ Vorotnikov-Epishin, USSR 1983

[25] 9 h3 b6 10 g4 ♗b7 11 ♗g2 ♕e7 12 g5 ♕f8! 13 ♕xf8+ ♘xf8 ∓ Vorotnikov-Uhlmann, Leningrad 1984

[26] 9 ... b6 10 ♘g3 (10 ♗g5 ♕e7 11 ♕h4 ♗b7 12 ♘g3 h6! ∓ Fischer-Kovačević, Zagreb 1970) 10 ... ♗b7 11 ♗e2 ♕e7 12 a4 ♖g6 13 ♕h4 0-0-0 14 0-0 ♕f8 15 a5 ♕g7 ∞

[27] 10 ♘g3 ♕c7 11 ♕e3 (11 ♗b5!?) 11 ... ♕c6 12 a4 a6 13 dc ♕xc5 ∞ Fischer-R.Byrne, US Ch 1966-67

[28] 13 a4 ♘g4 14 ♕f4 f5 ∞ Kir.Georgiev-Psakhis, Sarajevo 1986

[29] 9 ... b6! 10 ♗g5 ♗b7 11 ♗b5 ♖g6! = Byrne-Raičević, Philadelphia 1987

[30] 11 ... ♕a4 12 0-0 cd (12 ... ♕xc2 13 ♖fc1 ♕a4 14 ♖cb1 intending ♗b5) 13 cd ♕xd4 14 ♖fd1 ∞∞ Ftacnik

[31] Ljubojević-Korchnoi, Tilburg 1986

French VI   1 e4 e6 2 d4 d5 3 ♘c3 ♗b4 4 e5

	4	5	6	7	8	9	10	11	12	
1	...	♕g4[2]	♕g3	♘h3[3]	♗xa6	♘f4	a3	♕xc3[5]		±
	♕d7[1]	f5	b6	♗a6[4]	♘xa6	0-0-0	♗xc3+			
2	...	♕g4	♗g5[6]	f4[7]	♘f3[8]	♗xe7	♗b5	♗d3	♕h3	∞
	b6	♗f8	♕d7	♘c6	♘ge7	♘xe7	c6	h5	♖h6[9]	
3	...	♗d2	♕g4[11]	♘f3	♗xa6	♖d1[12]	bc[13]	h4	♖c1	∞
	...	♘e7[10]	0-0	♗a6	♘xa6	♗xc3	♕d7	♕a4	♘f5[14]	
4	...	a3!	♘f3[15]	♗b5	♗a4	♘e2	♗b3	c3	0-0	∞
	...	♗f8	♕d7[16]	c6[17]	♗a6	♗b5!	c5	♘c6	♘ge7[18]	
5	...	...	bc	♕g4[19]	♕g3	♗xa6	♘e2	a4	h4	±
	...	♗xc3+	♕d7	f5	♗a6	♘xa6	♔f7[20]	♘e7	c5[21]	
6	...	...	...	♕g4	h4	♕f3[23]	♗g5	♗xa6	a4[25]	±
	...	...	♘e7	♘g6[22]	h5	♗a6[24]	♕d7	♘xa6		

[1] 4 ... ♘e7 5 a3 (5 ♕g4 c5! and 5 ♗d2 c5! – 4 ... c5) 5 ... ♗xc3+ 6 bc c5 – 4 ... c5; 6 ... b6 – 4 ... b6

[2] 5 a3! ♗f8 (5 ... ♗xc3+ 6 bc b6 – 4 ... b6) 6 ♘ce2 b6 7 ♕f4 c5 8 dc bc 9 c4 ♘c7 10 ♘f3 ♗b7 11 ♗e2 d4 12 ♘d3 ♕c7 13 ♗f4 ♘d7 14 h4 ± Fedorowicz-Seirawan, US Ch 1986

[3] 7 ♗d2 ♗a6 8 ♗xa6 ♘xa6 9 0-0-0 0-0-0 10 h4 ±

[4] 7 ... a5 8 ♘f4 (intending ♘xe6) 8 ... ♕f7 9 a3 ♗xc3+ 10 ♕xc3 ± Ljubojević-Seirawan, Tilburg 1983

[5] Ljubojević

[6] 6 a4 ♘e7 7 ♘f3 ♗a6 8 ♘b5 ♘g6 9 ♘g5 ♕d7 10 h4 c6 ∞ Murei-Vaganian, Hastings 1982-83
6 ♘f3 ♕d7 7 ♗e2 ♘e7 8 0-0 ♘f5 9 a4 ♗a6 ∞∞ van der Wiel-Vaganian, Tilburg 1983
6 ♘h3 ♘e7 7 ♗g5 ♘8c6 8 ♗b5 ♗d7 9 0-0 h6 10 ♗e3 ♘b4 11 a3 ♗xb5 12 ♘xb5 ♘bc6 ∞ Sax-Vaganian, Biel IZ 1985

[7] 7 0-0-0 ♘c6 8 ♔b1 ♗b7 9 ♘ge7 h6 10 ♕h3 ♘ge7 11 g4 ♗a5 12 ♗c1 c5 ∞ Aseyev-Khuzman, USSR 1986

[8] 8 0-0-0 ♘ge7 9 ♘ge2 ♗b7 10 ♘g3 h6 11 ♗xe7 ♘xe7 12 h4 ∞ Lputian-Psakhis,

Sochi 1985

[9] Timman-Portisch, Bugojno 1986

[10] 5 ... ♕d7 6 ♗b5! c6 7 ♗a4 a5 8 a3 ♗xc3 (8 ... ♗f8 9 ♘ce2! ♗a6 10 c3 ± Nunn-Hübner, Brussels 1986) 9 ♗xc3 ♗a6 10 ♗d2! ♘e7 11 c3 ♘f5 12 ♘e2 ± Nunn-Lutz, Krefeld 1986

[11] 6 f4 ♗a6 7 ♗xa6 ♘xa6 8 ♕e2 ♘b8 9 ♘f3 ♘bc6 10 0-0-0 h5 ∞ Mikhalchishin-Eingorn, Moscow 1984

6 ♘ce2 ♗xd2+ 7 ♕xd2 0-0 8 f4 c5 9 c3 ♗a6 10 ♘f3 ♘bc6 = Marjanović-Psakhis, Bor 1985

6 ♘f3 ♗a6 7 ♘e2 ♗xd2+ 8 ♕xd2 ♕d7 9 g3 c5 10 c3 ♘bc6 = Sax-Vaiser, Szirak 1985

[12] 9 h4 c5 10 h5 ♘f5 11 ♘h4 f6 ∞

9 a3 ♗xc3 10 bc ♕d7 11 a4 c5 12 h4 ♖fc8 ∞ Hübner

[13] 10 ♗xc3 c5 11 ♗d2 ♘b4 ∞

[14] 13 ♕h3 c5 14 g4 ♘e7 15 h5 ♘c6 16 h6 g6 17 ♕h4 f5 18 ef cd ∓ Hübner

13 h5 ♗c5 14 ♘h4 ♘e4 15 ♘xf5 ef 16 ♕xf5 ♕c6 ∞∞ Timman-Hübner, Linares 1985

[15] 6 f4 ♘e7 7 ♗e3 h5 8 ♘f3 ♘f5 9 ♗f2 ± Diaz-Psakhis, Cienfuegos 1983

6 ♗b5+ c6 7 ♗a4 ♘e7 8 ♘ce2 ♘f5 9 c3 ± Rogers-Diždar, West Berlin 1986; 7 ... ♗d7!? 8 ♗b3 ♘e7 9 ♘ce2 c5 = Cabrilo-Bronstein, Panchevo 1987

[16] 6 ... c5 7 ♗g5 ♗e7 8 h4 a6 9 ♕d2 ± Kurajica-Korchnoi, Amsterdam 1976

6 ... ♘e7 7 h4 ♕d7 (7 ... c5 8 h5 h6 9 ♘e2 ♗a6 10 c3 ♘ec6 11 b4! ± Dolmatov-Gulko,

USSR 1985) 8 ♗b5 c6 9 ♗a4 a5 10 h5 h6 11 ♘e2 ♗a6 12 c3 ± Short-Psakhis, Banja Luka 1985

[17] 7 ... ♘c6 8 ♕e2 ♗b7 9 0-0 0-0-0 10 b4 ±

[18] 13 ♖e1 0-0-0 Chandler-Timman, Amsterdam 1987

[19] 7 h4 c5 (7 ... ♗a6 8 ♗xa6 ♘xa6 9 ♕d3 ♘b8 10 h5 ± Short-Huss, Lugano 1985) 8 h5 f5 9 h6 g6 10 a4 ♗a6 11 a5 ± Nunn-Levitt, London 1985

[20] 10 ... 0-0-0 11 a4 ♔b7 12 0-0 ♕f7 13 c4! ± Fischer-Bisguier, US Ch 1957-58

10 ... ♘b8 11 ♘f4 ♘c6 12 ♘xe6 ♕xe6 13 ♕xg7 ♕g6 14 ♕xh8 0-0-0 15 ♗e3! ♖d7 16 0-0-0! h5 17 g4! ± Schiller

[21] 13 ♕d3 ♕b7 14 ♗g5 cd 15 ♗xe7 ♔xe7 16 cd ± Sveshnikov-Gulko, USSR Ch 1976

[22] 7 ... 0-0 8 ♗g5 ♘d7 9 ♗d3 f5 10 ♕g3 ♕e8 11 h4 ♔h8 12 ♘h3 ± Benjamin-Kogan, Hollywood 1985

7 ... ♘f5 8 ♗d3 h5 9 ♕h3 c5 10 ♘f3 ♕c7 (10 ... c4 11 ♗xf5 ef 12 ♕g3 ± Unzicker-Herzog, Graz 1984) 11 0-0 ♘c6 12 a4 ± Tseshkovsky-Smyslov, USSR Ch 1976

7 ... ♔f8!? Spassky-Rodgaard, Thessaloniki Ol 1984

[23] 9 ♕d1 ♗a6 10 ♗g5 ♕d7 11 ♗xa6 ♘xa6 12 ♘e2 ♕a4 13 ♖h3 ± Ivkov-R.Byrne, Varna Ol 1962

[24] 9 ... ♘xh4 10 ♕h3 ♘g6 (10 ... ♘f5 11 g4 ±) 11 ♗d3 ♕d7 12 ♕g3 ± Parma-Ivkov, Bled 1961

[25] Ivkov-R.Byrne, Havana Ol 1966

	French VII	1 e4 e6 2 d4 d5 3 ♘c3 ♗b4 4 e5 c5							
	5	6	7	8	9	10	11	12	13
1	♕g4	♘f3[1]	♘xd4	♗d2[4]	f4	♘xc6	a3	♗d3	ef	=
	♘e7	cd[2]	♘g6[3]	0-0	♘c6	bc	♗a5	f5	♕xf6[5]	
2	♘f3	dc	♕d4	♗d2	♕g4	♗d3	♘xe5	♗xh7+	♕h5+	=
	♘e7[6]	♘d7[7]	♕a5[8]	♘c6	0-0	♘cxe5	♘xe5	♔xh7	♔g8[9]	

[1] 6 dc ♘bc6 7 ♗d2 0-0 8 ♘f3 f5 9 ♕h4 ♘g6 10 ♕xd8 ♖xd8 11 ♘a4 ♗d7 = Mednis

[2] 6 ... ♘bc6 7 a3 (7 ♗d2 0-0 8 ♗d3 f5 = Sax-Mednis, Budapest 1976) 7 ... ♗a5 (7 ... ♕a5!? Murei-Ambroz, Biel 1985) 8 ♕xg7 ♖g8 9 ♕xh7 cd 10 b4 ♘xb4 (10 ... dc 11 ba – 5 a3 ♗a5) 11 ab ♗xb4 12 ♗d2 ♗xc3 13 ♗xc3 dc 14 h4 ∞ Agapov-Malanyuk, USSR 1985

[3] 7 ... ♕c7 8 ♗b5+ ♘bc6 9 0-0 ♗xc3 10 bc ♗d7 11 ♗xc6 bc 12 ♗a3 ± Spassky-Uhlmann, Manila IZ 1976

[4] 8 ♘f3 ♘c6 9 ♗d2 d4 10 ♘e4 ♗xd2+ 11 ♘exd2 ♕a5 12 0-0 ♕xa2 13 h4 ∞ Kuzmin-Dolmatov, Minsk 1982

[5] 14 ♗xg6 ♕xg6 15 ♕xg6 hg 16 0-0-0 ♗c7 ½-½ Short-Farago, Banja Luka 1985

[6] 5 ... ♘c6 6 ♗b5 (6 dc ♘ge7 – 5 ... ♘e7) 6 ... ♘e7 7 0-0 ♗d7 8 dc ♗xc3 9 ♗xc6 ♘xc6 10 bc ♕a5 11 ♗e3 ♕xc3 12 ♖b1 ♖b8 13 ♖b3 ♕a5 ∞ Winants-Suba, Dubai Ol 1986

[7] 6 ... ♘bc6 7 ♗d3 d4 8 a3 ♗a5 9 b4 ♘xb4 10 ab ♗xb4 11 0-0 ♗xc3 12 ♖b1 ∞ Honfi-Farago, Hungarian Ch 1974

[8] 7 ... ♗xc5 8 ♕g4 ♘g6 9 ♗d3 ♗e7 10 ♗xg6 hg 11 h4 ± Watson-Farago, Wijk aan Zee 1987

[9] 14 ♕xe5 ♕xc5 15 0-0-0 ♗d7 16 a3 ♕d6 17 ♕xd6 ♗xd6 18 ♘e4! = Jadoul-Korchnoi, Brussels 1986

251

	5	6	7	8	9	10	11	12	13	
3	Bd2	Nb5	Qxd2	Nxd4	Qxd4	Nf3[11]	Bd3	Qe3	0-0	±
	Nc6[10]	Bxd2+	Nxd4	cd	Ne7	0-0	Nc6	f5	Bd7[12]	
4	...	Nb5[13]	Qxd2	c3	f4	Nd6	cd	0-0-0[17]		∞
	Ne7	Bxd2+	0-0	Nbc6[14]	a6[15]	cd	f6[16]			
5	a3	Bd2	Nb5	Nf3	Nbxd4	Nxd4	Qxd2	Bb5+	Nf3	∞̄
	Ba5[18]	cd	Nc6[19]	f6[20]	Nxd4	Bxd2+	fe	Kf8	Qd6[21]	
6	...	...	Nb5	Nxd4	Bb5+	Bxd7+	Nf3	Qxd2	0-0	±/=
	...	Nc6	Nxd4	cd[22]	Bd7	Kxd7	Bxd2+	Qb6	Ne7[23]	
7	...	b4	Nb5	f4[25]	Nf3	Nbxd4	c3[28]	cd	Bd3	∞
	...	cd[24]	Bc7	Ne7[26]	Bd7[27]	Nbc6	Nxd4	Nf5[29]	Bb6[30]	
8	...	...	Qg4	ba	Qxg7	Qxh7	Nf3[32]	Bb5	0-0[35]	∞
	...	...	Ne7	dc	Rg8	Nbc6[31]	Qc7[33]	Bd7[34]	Nxe5[36]	
9	...	...	...	Nb5	Qxg7	Qxh7	Nxc7+	Ne2	Bb2	±
	...	...	...	Bc7	Rg8	a6[37]	Qxc7	Qxe5	Qf6[38]	
10	...	bc	Qg4	Qxg7	Qxh7	cd[40]	Qd3	Bd2	Rc1	±
	Bxc3+	Nc6	Nge7[39]	Rg8	cd	Nxd4[41]	Qa5+	Qa4	Bd7[42]	
11	...	...	Bd2	Qg4[43]	Qd1!	h4	h5	Rh4	Bxa6	±
	...	Qa5	Qa4	Kf8[44]	b6	Ne7	h6	Ba6	Nxa6[45]	
12	...	...	Nf3	dc	Bd3!	Bd2	Bb4	Bd6	Nd2[49]	∞̄
	...	Qc7	Bd7[46]	Qxc5[47]	Qxc3+[48]	Qc7	Nc6	Qa5+		
13	...	...	Qg4	Nf3[50]	cd	Qh5+!	Bd2	Qxe5	Nxe5[52]	±
	...	...	f6	cd[51]	fe	Kf8	Nf6	Qxe5		
14	...	...	...	Qh5+	Qd1	Nf3	Rb1	Be2	0-0	±/∞
	...	...	f5	g6[53]	Bd7[54]	Ba4	Nd7[55]	h6	c4[56]	
15	...	...	...	Qg3	cd	Bd2[59]	Bd3	Ne2	Nf4	±
	...	...	...	cd[57]	Ne7[58]	0-0	b6	Ba6	Qd7[60]	

---

[10] 5 ... cd 6 Nb5 Bxd2+ 7 Qxd2 Nc6 8 f4 Nge7 9 Nd6+ Kf8 10 Nf3 Qa5 11 Qxa5 Nxa5 12 Nxd4 ±

[11] 10 0-0-0 Nc6 11 Qg4 0-0 12 Nf3 Bd7 13 Bd3 h6 14 h4 Qb6 = Santo Roman-Korchnoi, Cannes 1986

[12] 14 Rfd1 Qc7 15 a3 Bc8 16 Nd4 Nxd4 17 Qxd4 b5 18 f4 ± Zagorovsky-Abramov, corr. 1977

[13] 6 a3 Bxc3 7 Bxc3 Nbc6 8 Nf3 cd 9 Nxd4 (9 Bxd4 Nf5 10 c3 Bd7 =) 9 ... Nxe5 10 Nxe6 Bxe6 11 Bxe5 0-0 = Ljubojević-Nogueiras, Wijk aan Zee 1987

[14] 8 ... f6 9 ef (9 f4 fe 10 fe Nf5 ∓; 9 Nf3 fe 10 Nxe5 Nbc6 =) 9 ... Bxf6 10 dc Nd7 11 b4 b6 12 cb Qxb6 ∞̄ Przewoznik-Malanyuk, Lvov 1986

[15] 9 ... cd 10 cd f6 11 ef Rxf6 12 Nf3 Bd7 13 Ne5 Nf5 14 Bd3 ±/∞ Marjanović-Nogueiras, Reggio Emilia 1985-86

[16] 11 ... Nf5 12 Nxf5 ef 13 Nf3 ± Timman-Vaganian, Linares 1985

[17] **12 Nf3 Bg6!** ∓ Timman-Agdestein, Taxco IZ 1985

12 0-0-0 ∞ Timman

[18] 5 ... cd 6 ab dc 7 Nf3 cb 8 Bxb2 ∞̄/±

[19] **7 ... Bxd2+** 8 Qxd2 Nc6 9 f4 Nh6 10 Nd6+ Kf8 11 Nf3 f6 12 Bb5! ± Sax-Korchnoi, Lugano 1986

7 ... Bc7 8 f4 Ne7 9 Nf3 Nbc6 10 Bd3 a6 11 Nbxd4 Bb6 12 c3 ± Ghinda-Ionescu, Romanian Ch 1985

[20] 8 ... Nge7 9 Bd3 Ng6 10 Bxg6 hg 11 0-0 Bc7 12 Bg5 Qd7 13 Nxc7+ Qxc7 14 Re1 ± Kurajica-Enklaar, Amsterdam 1971

[21] 14 Qg5 e4 15 Ne5 ∞̄ A.Sokolov-Vaganian, match 1986

[22] 8 ... Bxd2+ 9 Qxd2 cd 10 Qxd4 (10 Nf3 Ne7 11 Nxd4 0-0 12 f4 Nc6 13 0-0-0 ± Nunn-Hug, Biel 1986) 10 ... Ne7 11 Nf3 0-0 12 Bd3

♘c6 13 ♕e3 ± A.Sokolov-Vaganian, match 1986

23 14 ♘xd4 ♖hc8 15 c3 h6 ±/= Rogers-Korchnoi, Biel 1986

24 6 ... cb 7 ♘b5 ♘c6 8 ab ♗xb4+ 9 c3 ♗e7 10 ♗d3 ∞/±

25 8 ♘f3 ♘c6 9 ♗f4 ♘ge7 10 ♘xc7+ ♕xc7 11 ♗d3 ♘g6 12 ♗g3 a5 13 h4 (13 b5 ♘cxe5 ∓ Kindermann-Lputian, Moscow 1985) 13 ... ab 14 ab ♖xa1 15 ♕xa1 0-0 ∞ Horvath-Lputian, Sochi 1985

26 8 ... ♗d7 9 ♘f3 ♗xb5 10 ♗xb5+ ♘c6 11 0-0 ♘e7 12 ♗d3 a6 13 ♔h1 h6 14 ♕e2 ♕d7 15 ♗b2 ♗b6 16 ♖ae1 ± Chandler-Vaganian, London 1986

27 9 ... ♘bc6 10 ♗d3 a6 (10 ... ♗b8 11 ♘bxd4 ±) 11 ♘xc7+ ♕xc7 12 0-0 ♗d7 13 ♗b2 ♕b6 14 ♔h1 0-0-0 15 a4! ± Nunn-Hug, Zürich 1984

28 11 ♗d3 ♘xd4 12 ♘xd4 ♗b6 13 ♗e3 ♕c7 14 ♕d2 ♖c8 (14 ... 0-0!? intending ... f6) 15 a4 a5 ∞ Ljubojević-Vaganian, Biel IZ 1985

29 12 ... 0-0 13 ♗e2 ♘c8 14 0-0 ♘b6 15 a4 a6 16 ♗d3 ±/∞ Dolmatov-Lputian, USSR 1983

30 14 ♗b2 ♘e3 15 ♕e2 ♘c4 16 ♗xc4 dc 17 ♕xc4 ♖c8 ∞ Klovans-Legky, USSR 1983

31 10 ... ♘d7 11 ♘f3 ♕c7 12 ♗b5 a6 13 ♗xd7+ ♗xd7 14 0-0 d4 15 ♘xd4 ♕xe5 16 ♕d3 ±

10 ... ♕c7 11 ♘f3 ♗d7 12 ♗f4 ♘bc6 13 a6 b6 14 ♗g3 0-0-0 ∞ Psakhis-Eingorn, USSR Ch 1987

32 11 f4 ♕xa5 12 ♖b1 ♗d7! 13 ♖xb7 ♘d4 14 ♕d3 ♘ef5 ∞ Timman-Vaganian, Montpellier C 1985, and Dolmatov-Lputian, Irkutsk 1986

33 11 ... ♕xa5 12 ♘g5 ♖f8 13 f4 ♗d7 14 h4 (14 ♖b1 0-0-0 15 ♘xf7 ♖xf7 16 ♕xf7 ♗e8! 17 ♕xe6+ ♗d7 18 ♕f6 ♗f5 19 ♗e2 ♕c5 ∓ Fichtl-Blatny, 1964) 14 ... ♘d4! ∞ van der Heijden-Timmer, Holland 1986

34 12 ... ♖xg2 13 ♔f1 ♖g8 14 ♖g1 ♖xg1+ 15 ♔xg1 ± Fischer

35 13 ♗xc6 ♗xc6 14 0-0 d4 15 ♘g5 ♕xe5 16 ♕xf7+ ♔d7 ∓ Fischer

36 13 ... 0-0-0 14 ♗xc6 (14 ♗g5 ♘xe5 = Fischer-Tal, Leipzig Ol 1960) 14 ... ♗xc6 15 ♕xf7 ± Fischer

13 ... ♘xe5 14 ♘xe5 ♕xe5 15 ♗xd7+ ♔xd7 16 ♕d3 d4 ∞ Chandler-Vaganian, Naestved 1985

37 10 ... ♗xe5 11 ♘f3 ♖h8 12 ♕d3 ♗f6 13 ♗f4 ±

10 ... ♘bc6 11 f4 a6 12 ♘xc7+ ♕xc7 13 ♕d3 ± Timman-Hug, Nice Ol 1974

38 13 ... ♘bc6 14 0-0-0 ♕d6 15 f4 ± Klovans-Lputian, USSR 1985

13 ... ♕f6 14 f4 ♘bc6 15 ♕d3! ♘f5 16 0-0-0 ♕h6 17 ♖e1 ♗d7 18 ♕d2! ± Klovans-Legky, USSR 1986

39 7 ... g6 8 ♘f3 intending h4 ±

40 10 f4!? ♕a5 11 ♖b1! ♕xc3+ 12 ♗d2 ♕xa3 13 ♘f3 ∞

41 10 ... ♕c7 11 ♗b2 (11 ♘f3 ♘xd4; 11 ♕d3 ♘xe5) 11 ... ♕a5+ 12 ♔d1 ♕b6 13 ♔c1 ♘xd4 14 ♕d3 ♘dc6 15 f4 ± Zhuravlev-Panchenko, USSR 1974

42 14 ♘e2 ♘xe5 15 ♗xe2 ♖xg2 16 h4 ± 0-0-0 17 ♗g5 ± Shakarov-V.Ivanov, corr. 1986

43 8 ♕b1 a6 (8 ... c4 9 ♘f3 ♘c6 10 g3 ±) 9 ♘f3 ♘e7 10 ♕b3 ♕xb3 11 cb ± Ljubojević-Kavalek, Montreal 1979

44 8 ... g6 9 ♕d1 cd 10 cd ♕xd4 11 ♘f3 ∞

45 14 ♖f4 ± Fischer-Hook, Siegen Ol 1970

46 7 ... ♘e7 – 6 ... ♘e7

7 ... b6 8 a4 ♗a6 9 ♗xa6 ♘xa6 10 ♕d3 ♘b8 11 0-0 ♘e7 12 a5 ± Fischer-Mednis, USA 1971

47 8 ... ♘e7 9 ♗d3 ♘a6 10 ♗xa6 ba 11 0-0 ♕xc5 12 a4 ♕xc3 13 ♗a3 ± Tsaturian-Bodisko, corr. 1985

48 9 ... ♗a4 10 0-0 ♘c6 11 ♖b1 0-0-0 12 ♕d2! ♖d7 13 ♕f4 ± Nunn-Morović, London 1985

49 Nunn

50 8 ♗b5+? ♔f8! ∓

51 8 ... c4 9 ♕g3 ± (intending 10 ef ♕xg3 11 f7+)

8 ... ♘c6 9 ♕g3 ♕f7 10 dc ♘ge7 11 ♗d3 ± Smyslov-Botvinnik, match (20) 1957

52 Agapov-Epishin, USSR 1985

53 8 ... ♕f7 9 ♕xf7+ ♔xf7 10 c4! ♘c6 11 dc ♘xe5 12 cd ed 13 ♗b2 ♘c6 14 0-0-0 ± Shakarov-Gorin, corr. 1980

54 9 ... ♘c6 10 ♘f3 ♗d7 11 a4 intending ♗a3 ±

55 11 ...- cd 12 ♕xd4 ♗xc2? 13 ♖b2 ♗e4 14 ♘g5 ±±

56 14 ♘h4 ♘e7 15 f4 0-0-0 ±/∞ Velimirović-Morović, Vršac 1985

57 8 ... ♘e7 9 ♕xg7 ♖g8 10 ♕xh7 cd 11 ♔d1 ♗d7 (11 ... ♕xc3 12 ♖b1 d3 13 ♗xd3 ♕xe5 14 ♕h5+ ±; 11 ... ♘bc6 12 ♘f3 ♘xe5 13 ♗g5! ♘5g6 15 ♗f6 intending h4 ± Euwe) 12 ♕h5+ ♘g6 (12 ... ♔d8 13 ♘e2 ± Ivkov-Portisch, Bled 1961) 13 ♘e2 ± Tal-Botvinnik, match (1) 1960

58 9 ... ♕xc2 10 ♗d2 ♕c7 11 ♖c1 ∞

59 10 ♔d1!? 0-0 11 ♘f3 b6 12 ♗h6 ♘g6 13 ♗d2 ♗a6 14 ♗d3 ♗xd3 15 cd ♘c6 16 h4 ± Mnatsakanian-Prandstetter, Erevan 1984

60 14 ♗b4 ♖f7 15 h4 ± Hort-Petrosian, Kapfenberg 1970

French VIII   1 e4 e6 2 d4 d5 3 Nc3 Bb4 4 e5 c5 5 a3 Bxc3+ 6 bc Ne7

	7	8	9	10	11	12	13	14	15	
1	Nf3[1]	Bb5+[2]	Bd3	h4	h5	g3[3]	Be3	0-0	Nh4	∞
	b6	Bd7	Ba4	Nbc6	h6	Rc8[4]	Na5	Qd7	Bb5[5]	
2	...	a4	Bb5+[6]	ab	0-0	Qe2[9]	Bg5	Ra2	Bd2	±
	...	Ba6	Bxb5	Qc7[7]	Nd7[8]	0-0	Rfe8	h6	Rab8[10]	
3	...	Be2[11]	a4[13]	0-0	ef	c4[14]	dc	Nd2	Nxc4	∞
	Qc7	Bd7[12]	Nbc6	f6	gf	dc[15]	0-0-0	Ne5	Nxc4[16]	
4	...	Bd3	0-0	a4	Be2	Re1	Ba3	de	Nxe5	±
	...	Nbc6[17]	Bd7	c4	f6	Ng6[18]	fe	Ncxe5	Nxe5[19]	
5	...	Bd3	0-0	Be2	Bd2	Rb1	Ra1			=
	Nbc6	Qa5	c4[20]	Qxc3[21]	Qb2	Qxa3				
6	...	Be2	0-0	Qd2	Rb1	Re1	Bd1	ef	Qg5[23]	±
	...	Qa5[22]	c4	Qa4	0-0	b6	f6	Rxf6		
7	...	dc[24]	Bd3	Rb1[26]	Nxe5	Rxb7	Rb4	0-0	Qxd3	=
	Bd7	Nbc6[25]	Ng6	Ncxe5[27]	Nxe5	Qc8[28]	Qxc5	Nxd3	Qxd3	
8	...	h4	h5	Rb1	Bf4	Bd3	Be2	Kf1[29]	Qc1	±/=
	...	Nbc6	h6	Qc7	0-0-0	c4	f5	Kb8	Ka8[30]	
9	...	Bd2	Be2[31]	cd	Be3[33]	Qd3	Nd2	0-0	Rfc1	∞/∓
	Qa5	Nbc6	cd[32]	Qa4	b6	Na5[34]	Bd7	Rc8	0-0[35]	
10	...	...	a4	Be2	ef[37]	c4[38]	cd	c4[39]	dc	∞
	...	...	Bd7	f6[36]	gf	Qc7	Nxd5	Nde7	0-0-0[40]	
11	...	...	...	Bb5	0-0	Re1	Bd3	Qc1	Bf1	∞
	...	...	...	Qc7[41]	0-0[42]	b6[43]	h6	c4	f6[44]	
12	...	Qd2	a4	Be2	Ba3	cd	Kxd2	h4	Rhb1	±/=
	...	Nbc6[45]	Bd7[46]	f6[47]	cd	Qxd2+	Na5[48]	h5[49]	Rc8[50]	

---

1 **7 a4** Nbc6 8 Nf3 Qa5 – 7 Nf3

   7 h4 Nbc6 8 h5 Qa5 9 Bd2 cd (9 ... h6 10 Qg4 ±; 9 ... Bd7!? intending ... 0-0-0 Uhlmann) 10 cd Qa4 11 Bc3 b6 ∞ Short-Korchnoi, Wijk aan Zee 1987

2 8 Ng5 h6 9 Qh5 g6 10 Qh3 Qc7 ∞ A.Sokolov-Yusupov, match 1986

3 **12 Rh4** c4 13 Be2 Kd7! 14 Be3 Qg8 15 Qd2 Qh7 ∞ A.Sokolov-Yusupov, match 1986

   12 0-0 Qc7 (12 ... c4!?) 13 Re1 c4 14 Bf1 0-0-0 ∞ Spassky-Short, London 1982

4 12 ... c4 13 Bf1 Kd7! 14 Bh3 Qg8 15 0-0 Qh7 ∞ Dolmatov-Hertneck, Lugano 1986

5 16 Qg4 Bxd3 17 cd cd 18 cd g5 ∞ Dolmatov-Dokhoyan, USSR 1986

6 9 Bxa6 Nxa6 10 0-0 Nb8 11 Ng5 (11 dc bc 12 c4 0-0 13 cd Nxd5 = A.Sokolov-Yusupov, match 1986) 10 ... h6 11 Qh5 g6 12 Qh3 ±/∞ Karpov-Short, London 1982

7 **10 ... a5** 11 dc bc 12 c4 0-0 13 Bg5 ± Tseshkovsky-Grünberg, Halle 1984

   10 ... Qd7 11 Qe2 c4 12 Ba3 Qxb5 13 Ng5 Qd7 14 Qh5 Ng6 15 0-0 ∞ Gulko-Eingorn, USSR 1983

8 11 ... 0-0 12 Qd3 h6 13 dc bc 14 c4 Nd7 15 cd ed 16 Re1 ± Tseshkovsky-Vladimirov, USSR 1984

9 12 Qd3 h6 13 Ra4 0-0 14 Bd2 Rfc8 15 Rc1 ±/= Karpov-Mednis, Vienna 1986

10 16 Rfa1 Rb7 17 Ne1 ± Mokry-Prandstetter, Prague 1986

11 **8 a4** Nbc6 (8 ... b6 9 Bb5+ Bd7 10 0-0 Bxb5 11 ab – 7 ... b6 8 a4 Ba6 9 Bb5+) 9 Be2 Bd7 – 8 Be2

   8 h4 b6 9 h5 h6 10 Bd3 Ba6 11 0-0 Bxd3 12 cd c4! = Tseshkovsky-Vaiser, Sochi 1983

12 8 ... Nbc6 9 0-0 Bd7 10 Re1 f6 11 Bf4 Ng6 12 Bg3 fe (12 ... f5 13 h4 ±) 13 Bd3 0-0-0 14 Bxg6 hg 15 Nxe5 ± Nunn-Huss, Lugano 1986

13 9 0-0 Ba4 10 c4 dc 11 dc Nd7 =

14 12 dc e5 13 c4 Be6 14 cd Nxd5 15 Nd2 0-0-0 16 Ne4 Nc3 17 Nd6+ Qxd6 18 cd Nxd1 19 Rxd1 Nd4 = Panchenko-Bagirov, USSR 1972

15 12 ... 0-0-0 13 Ba3 ±

16 16 Bxc4 Rhg8 17 Qe2 Nf5 18 Bxe6

♕c6 19 ♗xg8 ♖xg8 20 f3 ♘h4 ∞ Dolmatov-Vaiser, USSR 1983

[17] 8 ... b6 9 0-0 ♗a6 10 ♗xa6 (10 ♘g5 ♗xd3 11 cd ±) 10 ... ♘xa6 11 ♘g5 h6 12 ♘h3 ♖c8 13 ♕g4 ±

[18] 12 ... fe 13 de 0-0 14 ♗a3 ± Ciocaltea-Padevsky, Vrnjačka Banja 1975

[19] 16 ♕d4 ♘g6 17 ♗h5! ± Fischer-Larsen, match 1971

[20] 9 ... ♕xc3? 10 ♗d2 ♕b2 11 ♖b1 ♕xa3 12 ♖b3 ♕a2 13 ♕c1 ±

[21] 10 ... ♗d7 11 a4 ♘c8 12 ♕d2 ♘b6 13 ♕g5! 0-0 14 ♕g3 ± Korchnoi

[22] 8 ... ♗d7 9 0-0 ♕c7 - 7 ... ♕c7

[23] Chandler-Draško, Sarajevo 1985

[24] **8 ♗d3 c4 9 ♗e2 ♗a4 =**
8 ♗e2 ♗a4 9 0-0 ♕c7 =
8 a4 ♕a5 - 7 ... ♕a5

[25] 8 ... ♕a5 9 ♗d3 ♘a6 10 0-0 ♘xc5 11 ♖b1 h6 12 ♖b4 0-0-0 13 ♘d4 ± Petrushin-Dolmatov, USSR 1983

8 ... ♗a4 9 ♖b1 ♘d7 10 ♗e3 (10 ♖xb7 ♘xc5 11 ♖b4 ♕a5 12 ♗d2 ± Chandler-Agdestein, Naestved 1985) 10 ... ♕a5 11 ♖xb7 ♕xc3+ 12 ♗d2 ♕xc5 13 ♗d3 ± Gavrikov-van der Wiel, London 1985

[26] **10 ♗xg6 hg 11 0-0 ♘a5 12 ♕d4 ♕c7 13 ♗e3 ♘c4 ∞ Tischbierek-Knaak, East German Ch 1986**

10 0-0 ♘cxe5 11 ♘xe5 ♘xe5 12 ♗f4 ♕f6 13 ♕d2 ♘xd3 13 cd d4 ∞ Chandler-Belyavsky, London 1985

[27] 10 ... ♕c7 11 0-0 ± ♘cxe5 12 ♘xe5 ♘xe5 13 ♗f4 0-0-0 14 ♕e2 f6 15 ♗a6! ±± Balashov-Chen De, Hanover 1983

[28] 12 ... 0-0 13 ♗xh7+ ± Belyavsky-Uhlmann, Sarajevo 1982

[29] 14 ef ♕xf4 15 fe ♖de8 ∓ Klovans-Dolmatov, USSR 1983

[30] 16 ♘h4 ♖c8 17 ♕b2 ♖hf8 18 ♖h3 ±/= Klovans-Dolmatov, USSR 1985

[31] 9 ♗d3 c4 10 ♗f1 f6 11 ef gf 12 ♘h4 0-0 13 g3 ♖f7 = R.Byrne-Korchnoi, London 1979

9 h4 ♗d7 10 h5 h6 11 ♖h4 (11 ♖b1 ♕c7 12 ♗f4 - 7 ... ♗d7 8 h4) 11 ... c4 12 ♖g4 ♖g8 13 ♘h4 0-0-0 ∞ Rantanen-Vaganian, Tallinn 1979

[32] 9 ... ♗d7 10 0-0 and now:

10 ... f6 11 c4 ♕c7 12 cd ♘xd5 13 c4 ♘de7 14 ef gf 15 ♗c3 0-0-0 16 d5 ± Hazai-Raičević, Niš 1985

10 ... c4 11 ♘g5 h6 12 ♘h3 ♘g6 13 ♗h5 ♘ce7 14 a4 ± Planinc-Timman, Amsterdam 1974

10 ... ♕c7 11 ♖e1 f6 12 c4 cd 13 ef gf 14 ♘h6! dc 15 ♘xd4 ± Gurgenidze-Psakhis, USSR 1985

[33] **11 c3 ♕xd1+ 12 ♔xd1 ♘a5 13 ♔c2**

♗d7 =/∓ Pritchett-Garcia Martinez, Dubai Ol 1986

11 ♗c3 b6 12 ♕d3 a5 13 ♕d2 ♗a6 =/∓ de Firmian-Garcia Martinez, Dubai Ol 1986

[34] 12 ... ♘b4 13 ♕b5+ = Short-Korchnoi, Brussels 1986

[35] A.Sokolov-Yusupov, match 1986

[36] **10 ... c4 11 ♘g5 ±**

10 ... ♕c7 11 0-0 0-0 12 ♖e1 h6 13 ♗c1 ± Vasyukov-Vaganian, Erevan 1976; 13 ♕c1 ± Kurajica-Timman, Skopje 1976

[37] 11 ♖b1 ♕c7 (11 ... fe!? 12 ♖xb7 e4 13 ♘g5 c4! ∞ Knaak) 12 ♗f4 ♘g6 13 ♗g3 fe 14 0-0 cd 15 cd 0-0 16 ♗b5 ♘f4 ∞ Wedberg

[38] 12 0-0 0-0-0 13 ♖e1 c4 14 ♕c1 ♖hg8 ∞ Tringov-Timman, Plovdiv 1983

[39] 14 c3 0-0-0 15 0-0 ♖hg8 16 ♖e1 e5 17 c4 ♗h3 18 ♗f1 ♘b6 19 d5 ♘xc4 20 dc ♕xc6 ∞/= Spassky-Korchnoi, match 1977-78, and Dünhaupt-Stern, corr. 1984

[40] 16 ♗c3 e5 17 ♕d6 ♘f5 18 ♕xc7+ ♔xc7 ∓ Timman-Korchnoi, match 1976

16 0-0 e5 17 ♗e3 ♖hg8 18 ♕c2 ♗h3 19 ♘h4 ♘d4 20 ♗xd4 ♖xd4 21 f4 ∞ Oll-Psakhis, USSR 1983

[41] 10 ... c4 11 0-0 0-0-0 (11 ... ♘b8 12 ♕b1! ± Rogers-P.Nikolić, Bor 1986) 12 ♖e1 a6 13 ♗xc6 ♘xc6 14 ♕c1 h6 15 ♕a3 ± Hazai-Grünberg, Leipzig 1983

10 ... f6 11 0-0 (11 ef gf 12 dc a6 13 c4 ♕c7 14 cd ♘xd5 15 ♗c4 ♘ce7 ∞ Hjorth-Garcia Gonzalez, Dubai Ol 1986) 11 ... fe 12 c4 ♕c7 13 cd ed5 14 ♘xe5 ♘xe5 15 ♗f4 ♘7g6 16 ♗xe5 ♘xe5 17 ♖e1 0-0 18 ♖xe5 ♗c6 = Nunn-Agdestein, Dortmund 1987

[42] 11 ... ♘a5 12 ♗d3 c4 13 ♗e2 0-0-0 14 ♗c1 ♔b8 15 ♕d2 h6 16 ♕f4 ± Nunn-Farago, Dortmund 1987

[43] 12 ... h6 13 ♗f4 (13 ♗c1!?) 13 ... ♘g6 14 ♗g3 ♘ce7 = R.Byrne-Vaganian, Moscow 1975

[44] Rogers-Nogueiras, Szirak 1986

[45] **8 ... ♕a4 9 ♖b1 c4 10 g3 ♘bc6 11 ♗h3 ±**

8 ... ♗d7 9 ♖b1 ♘c6 10 ♗d3 ♘d7 11 0-0 c4 12 ♗e2 h6 13 h4 ± Short-Timman, Reykjavik 1987

[46] **9 ... cd 10 cd ♗xd2+ 11 ♗xd2 ♘f5 12 ♗c3 ±**

9 ... b6 10 ♗b5 ♗a6 11 ♖b1 0-0 12 0-0 cd 13 ♕d3 ±

[47] 10 ... ♖c8 11 ♗a3 cd 12 cd ♕xd2+ 13 ♔xd2 ♘f5 14 c3 ♘a5 15 ♖hb1! h5 (15 ... ♗xa4 16 g4! ♘h6 17 ♗d6 ♘b3+ 18 ♖xb3 ♗xb3 19 ♖xa7 ±) 16 ♗b4 ± Rodriguez-Eingorn, Havana 1986

[48] 13 ... ♘f5 14 ♖hb1 b6 15 c3 ♘a5 16 ♗b4 ± Abramović-Farago, Belgrade 1984

[49] 14 ... ♖c8 15 h5 h6 16 ♘h4 ± Tisdall-Renman, Oslo 1985

[50] 16 ♗b4 ♘ec6 17 ♗c3 ♔f7 ±/=

French IX   1 e4 e6 2 d4 d5 3 ♘c3 ♝b4 5 e5 c5 5 a3 ♝xc3+ 6 bc ♘e7 7 ♕g4

	7	8	9	10	11	12	13	14	15	
1	...	♘f3	ef	♗g5	♗xf6	♔e2[2]	♖c1	h4	h5	±
	0-0[1]	f5	♖xf6	♕a5	♕xc3+	♘g6	gf	♘c6	e5[3]	
2	...	...	♗d2	♗d3	♗xh7+	♕h4+	♕xe7	♕h4[6]	0-0	±
	...	♕a5	♕a4[4]	c4[5]	♔xh7	♔g8	♘c6	♕xc2	f6[7]	
3	...	...	♗d3	ef	♗g5	♗xe7[9]	♕h4	0-0	♗g6	±
	...	♘bc6	f5	♖xf6	♖f7[8]	♖xe7	h6	c4[10]	♗d7[11]	
4	...	...	...	...	...	...	...	0-0	♗e2	±
	...	...	...	...	...	...	g6	c4	♗d7[12]	
5	...	♕xg7	♕xh7	♔d1	♘f3	♘g5[14]	f4[15]	fe	♕h5+	∞
	♕c7	♖g8	cd	♘bc6	dc[13]	♘xe5	f6[16]	fg	♔d8[17]	

1 e4 e6 2 d4 d5 3 ♘c3 ♝b4 4 e5 c5 5 a3 ♝xc3+ 6 bc ♘e7
7 ♕g4 ♕c7 8 ♕xg7 ♖g8 9 ♕xh7 cd 10 ♘e2 ♘bc6 11 f4 ♗d7 12 ♕d3 dc

	13	14	15	16	17	18	19	20	21	
6	♖b1[18]	♘xc3	g3	♘e2	♗g2	ef	0-0	♖f2	♗b2	∞
	0-0-0[19]	♘a5[20]	♘c4	♖gf8	f6	♘f5	♕c5+	♖xf6	♖g6[21]	
7	...	♘xd4	♕xd4	♕f2[22]	♖b4[23]	♖g1	♗d3[24]	♖c4	h3	∞
	d4	♘xd4	♘f5	♕c6	♕d5	♗c6	♖d8[25]	♖h8	♘h4[26]	
8	♘xc3	♖b1	h4	♖h3	h5	♖b4	h6	h7	♘e2	±
	a6	♘a5[27]	♘f5	0-0-0	♘c4[28]	♗c6[29]	♖g6	♖h8	♖g7[30]	
9	...	...	h4[31]	♖h3	h5	♗d2	♖xb7	♘xb5	♔f2	±
	...	♖c8	♘f5[32]	♘cd4[33]	♕a5[34]	♕xa3	♗b5	♕a1+	ab[35]	
10	♕xc3	♖b1[36]	♕d3	♖g1	g4	ef	♖xg4	f7[38]		±
	♘f5	d4	0-0-0	f6[37]	♘h6	♖xg4	♘xg4			
11	...	...	♗d2	♕d3	♘xd4	♕xd4	♕xa7	♕xb7	♕b8+	±
	...	♖c8	d4[39]	♘ce7	♘xd4	♘f5[40]	♕xc2	♖c7	♖c8[41]	
12	...	♖b1[42]	♕d3[44]	g3	ef	♗g2	fe	♕b3	♕e6+	±
	0-0-0	d4[43]	♘d5	f6	♘xf6	e5	♘xe5	♗c6	♘fd7[45]	

---

[1]   7 ... ♕a5 8 ♗d2 ♘g6 9 h4 ±

7 ... ♘f5 8 ♗d3 h5 9 ♕f4 cd 10 cd ♕h4 11 ♕xh4! ♘xh4 12 ♗g5 ± Yanofsky-Uhlmann, Stockholm IZ 1962

7 ... cd 8 ♕xg7 (8 cd ♕c7 9 ♔d1 0-0 ∞ Spassky-Korchnoi, match 1977-78) 8 ... ♖g8 9 ♕xh7 ♕a5 (9 ... ♕c7 - 7 ... ♕c7) 10 ♘e2 dc 11 ♘g3 ♘d7 12 ♘h5 d4 13 f4 ± Timman-Korchnoi, match 1976

[2]   12 ♔d1 ♕xa1+ 13 ♔d2 ♘g6 14 ♗d3 ♕xh1 15 ♗xg6 (15 ♗xg7 = Chandler-Nogueiras, Leningrad 1987) 15 ... gf 16 ♕h4!? (16 ♗c8+ = Kupreichik-Kosten, Minsk 1986) 16 ... hg 17 ♕xf6 ± Blatny-Szymczak, Trnava 1987

[3]   16 ♕g3 e4 17 hg ef+ 18 ♔d1 ♗f5 (18 ... ♕xd4+? 19 ♗d3 ♗f5 20 ♖h4! ±± Hellers-

Arencibia, Gausdal 1986) 19 ♖xh7 ♕xd4+ 20 ♗d3 ♘e5 (20 ... ♗xd3? 21 ♖h8+!) 21 ♖h4 ♗g4 22 gf! ± Lau-Hertneck, West Germany 1987

[4]   9 ... c4 10 h4 ♘bc6 11 h5 f6 12 h6 g6 13 ef ♖xf6 14 ♕h4 ± Ehlvest-Bareyev, USSR Ch 1987

[5]   10 ... ♘f5 11 ♕h3 c4 12 g4 cd 13 gf ±

[6]   14 ♕g5 ♕xc2 15 h4 f6 (15 ... ♕e4+ 16 ♔f1 ♕f5 17 ♕xf5 ef 18 h5 ♘a5? 19 h6 ♘b3 20 ♗g5! ±± Balashov-Farago, Dortmund 1987) 16 ef ♖xf6 17 h5 ± Lputian-Psakhis, USSR 1985

[7]   16 ef gf 17 ♖ae1 ♘e7 18 g4 ± Spassky-Kanani, Dubai Ol 1986

[8]   11 ... e5 12 ♗xh7+! (12 ♕g3? ♖xf3! 13 gf

c4 14 ♗e2 ♕a5 ∓) 12 ... ♔xh7 13 ♕h5+ ♔g8 14 ♗xf6 gf 15 de ±

[9] 12 ♕h4 h6 13 0-0 c4 14 ♗xe7 (14 ♗g6? ♖xf3! ∓) 14 ... ♖xe7 – 12 ♗xe7

12 ♕h5 g6 13 ♕h4 c4 14 ♗e2 ♕a5 15 ♗d2 ♘f5 16 ♕g5 ♗d7 17 g4 ♘d6 18 h4 ∞ Ljubojević-Korchnoi, Linares 1985

[10] 14 ... cd 15 cd ♗d7 16 ♖fe1 ± Murei-Short, Brighton, 1982

[11] 16 ♖fe1 ♗e8 17 ♗xe8 ♖xe8 18 ♕h3 ± Sax-Farago, Hungarian Ch 1981

[12] 16 ♖fe1 ♕f8 (16 ... ♕a5 17 ♘e5 ±; 16 ... ♔g7 17 ♗f1 ± Mestel-Korchnoi, London 1984) 17 ♗f1 ♖ae8 18 ♖e2 ♖g7 19 ♘g5 ± Sax-Schmidt, Warsaw Z 1987

[13] 11 ... ♘xe5 12 ♗f4 ♕xc3 13 ♘xe5 ♕xa1+ 14 ♗c1 ♖f8 15 ♗d3 ♗d7 16 ♔e2 ∞

[14] 12 ♗g5 ♗d7 13 ♗f6 0-0-0 14 h4 ♘g6! 15 ♗xd8 ♖xd8 16 ♕g7 ♘gxe5 17 ♘xe5 ♘xe5 18 h5 d4 19 h6 d3 ∓ Lukin-Cherepkov, USSR 1983

12 ♗f4 ♕b6! 13 ♗e3 ♕b2 14 ♖c1 ♗d7 15 h4 0-0-0 ∓ Steil-Farago, Budapest 1986; 13 ♗g3 ♕b2 14 ♖c1 ♕xa3 15 ♗d3 ∞ Schiller

[15] 13 ♗f4 ♕b6! 14 ♗xe5 ♖xg5 15 h4 ♖g8 16 ♔e1 ♗d7 ∓ Matulović-Uhlmann, match 1967

[16] 13 ... ♖xg5 14 fg ♘5g6 15 h4 e5 16 h5 ♘f8 17 ♕g7 ♗g4+ 18 ♔e1 0-0-0 ∞ Stein-Farago, Lugano 1985

[17] 16 ♗xg5 ♕c5 17 ♕h4 (17 ♗d3 ♔c7 ∓ Sisniega-Agdestein, Taxco IZ 1985) 17 ... ♗d7 18 ♗d3 ♗c6 19 ♖f1 ♔d7 ∞/∓ Stein-Bukal, Balatonbereny 1985

[18] 13 ♗e3 d4 (13 ... ♘f5!?) 14 ♗f2 0-0-0 15 ♗xd4 ♘xd4 16 ♕xd4 b6 ∞ Spassky-Korchnoi, match 1977-78

13 h4 ♘f5 14 h5 0-0-0 15 h6 ♖g6 16 h7 ♖h8 17 ♖b1 f6 18 ef ♗e8 ∞ Vasyukov-Doroshkevich, USSR 1967

13 ♘g3 0-0-0 14 ♗e2 ♘f5 15 ♘xf5 ef 16 0-0 d4 17 ♗f3 ♗e6 = Sveshnikov-Webb, Hastings 1977-78

[19] 13 ... ♖c8 14 h4! ± Tseshkovsky-Priehoda, Trnava 1986

13 ... ♘f5 14 h3! d4 (14 ... 0-0-0 15 g4 ♘h4 16 ♘xc3 ±) 15 g4 ♘h4 16 ♕h7 ♘f3+ 17 ♔f2 0-0-0 18 ♔xf3 ± Horvath-Uhlmann, Szirak 1985

[20] 14 ... ♘f5 15 g3 ♔b8 16 ♘b5 ♕a5+ 17 ♕d2 ♖h8 18 ♗g2 ♕a6 19 ♕d3 ♘a5 20 ♘d6 ± Anand-MacDonald, London 1986

[21] Blatny-Agdestein, Gausdal 1986

[22] 16 ♕b4 0-0-0 17 ♖b3 ♗c6 18 ♖xc3 ♖d4 ∞

[23] 17 ♖g1 ♕e4+ 18 ♕e2 ♕d4 20 ♕f2 =

[24] 19 ♗e2 ♕a2 20 ♗d3 ♖d8 21 g4? ♘h4!

22 ♕xh4 ♖xd3 ∓∓ Strand-F.Larsen, corr. 1985; 21 ♕xa7 ∞ F.Larsen

[25] 19 ... 0-0-0 20 ♖c4 ♔b8 21 ♖xc3 ♘h4 22 ♔f1 ♖xg2 23 ♖xg2 ♕xg2+ 24 ♕xg2 ♗xg2+ 25 ♔f2 ± Liberzon-Pietzsch, Leipzig 1965

[26] 22 ♖c5 ♕a2 23 ♖xc3 ♕a1 24 ♔d2 ♘f5 ∞ Matanović-Rolland, Le Havre 1966

[27] 14 ... 0-0-0? 15 ♕xa6!

[28] 17 ... ♗g4 18 ♕f3! ♖dg8 (18 ... ♘h6? 19 f5!) 19 h6 ♘4g6 (19 ... ♘xh6? 20 ♖xh6 ♖g3 24 ♖h8) 20 h7 ♖h8 21 g4 ± Khasin-Carbonell, corr. 1977

17 ... d4 18 ♘e4 ♗b5 19 ♖xb5! ab 20 ♘f6 ♖h8 21 g4 ± Yurtayev-Lputian, USSR 1975

[29] 18 ... b5!?

[30] 22 g4! ♖xg4 23 ♘d4 ± Yurtayev

[31] 15 ♗d2 ♘a5 16 h4 ♘c4 ∞ Hort-Agdestein, Oslo 1984

15 ♘e2!? ♘f5 16 h3 d4 17 g4 ± Spassky-Miralles, Cannes 1987

[32] 15 ... ♘xe5 16 fe ♕xc3+ 17 ♕xc3 ♖xc3 18 h5 ±

[33] 16 ... ♘a7 17 h5 ♘b5 18 ♘e2! ± Yurtayev-Bukhman, USSR 1984

[34] 17 ... ♘xc2+ 18 ♕xc2 d4 19 g4! ♘e7 20 h6 ±

[35] 22 h6 ♖h8 23 h7 ♕a8 24 ♖xb5 ± Filipenko-Bikhovsky, USSR 1986

[36] 14 ♗d2 ♕b6! 15 ♖c1 ♖c8 16 ♕b3 ♕c7 ∞ Hartmann-Uhlmann, Budapest 1986

[37] 16 ... ♕a5+!? 17 ♗d2 ♕d5 18 g4 ♘h4 19 ♖g3 Balashov

[38] Balashov-Kosten, Minsk 1986

[39] 15 ... b6 16 ♕d3 ♘ce7 17 ♖b2 ♗a4 18 ♘c3 ♗c6 19 ♖g1 ± Borg-Walker, England 1985

15 ... ♕d8 16 ♕d3 ♘a5 17 g3 ± Borg-Skalkotas, Kavala 1985

15 ... ♘ce7 16 ♖xc7 ♖xc7 17 c3 ± Mestel-Depasquale, Southampton 1986

[40] 18 ... ♗c6!? 19 ♕xa7 ♗xg2 20 ♖g1 ♗xf1 21 ♖xg8+ ♘xg8 22 ♔xf1 ♕xc2 23 ♕xb7 ♘e7 ∞ Makarichev

[41] 22 ♕b4 ♗d4 23 ♔f2 ± Karpov-Agdestein, Oslo 1984

[42] 14 ♘g3 ♖h8 15 ♗d2 ♖dg8 16 0-0-0 ∞ Spassky-Nogueiras, Montpellier C 1985

[43] 14 ...♘f5 15 ♖g1 (15 ♗d2 d4 16 ♕d3 f6! 17 ef e5 ∞ Kir.Georgiev-Rasidović, Sarajevo 1986) 15 ... f6 16 g4 ♘h6 17 ef ♖xg4 18 ♗e3 ± Mecking-Uhlmann, Manila IZ 1976

[44] 15 ♕c5 b6 16 ♕c4 ♔b8 17 ♗d2 ♗c8 18 g3 (18 ♘g3 ♗b7 19 ♗d3 ♘d5! 20 0-0 ♕e7 ∞ Spraggett-Belyavsky, Wijk aan Zee 1985) 18 ... ♗b7 19 ♗g2 d3 20 cd ♘xe5 21 ♕xc7+ ♔xc7 22 fe ♖xg2 23 ♖g1 ± Shakarov

[45] 22 ♗xc6 ♖xc6 23 ♗f4 ♕a5+ 24 ♔f2 ♖ge8 25 ♕c4 ± Balashov-Agdestein, Dortmund 1987

	3	4	5	6	7	8	9	10	11	
1	...	c3	ed²	Ngf3	Bc4	Nxd4	cd	Qa4+	Qb3	±
	Nc6¹	e5	Qxd5	ed	Qf5³	Nxd4	Be6	Bd7	0-0-0⁴	
2	...	Ngf3	e5	Bd3⁵	ef⁷	0-0	c4	Nb3	Re1	=
	...	Nf6	Nfd7	f6⁶	Qxf6	Bd6⁸	0-0	h6	b6⁹	
3	...	...	...	Be2	ef	Nf1	Ne3	0-0	c4	∞
	...	...	...	f6¹⁰	Qxf6¹¹	Bd6	0-0	Qg6	Nf6¹²	
4	...	...	...	Nb3	a4	Bf4	c3	h4	Bb5	±
	...	...	...	a5¹³	b6¹⁴	Be7	Bb7¹⁵	Qc8	Nd8¹⁶	
5	...	Ngf3	ed¹⁷	dc	Nb3	Bd3¹⁸	Qe2+	Qxe7+	0-0	±
	a6	c5	ed	Bxc5	Ba7	Nf6¹⁹	Qe7	Kxe7	Nc6²⁰	
6	...	...	...	...	...	c3²¹	Bg5	Qc2	Bh4	±
	...	...	...	...	Be7	Nf6	0-0	h6	Nh5²²	
7	...	...	...	Be2	0-0	Re1²⁴	Nb3	Bg5	Bh4	±
	...	...	...	cd²³	Bd6	Ne7	Nbc6	0-0	Qb6²⁵	
8	...	...	...	...	0-0	b3²⁷	c3²⁹	a4	Ba3	±
	...	...	...	c4	Bd6²⁶	b5²⁸	Ne7	Bb7	0-0³⁰	

258

¹ 3 ... g6 4 ♘gf3 ♗g7 5 ♗d3 ♘e7 6 c3 ♘d7 7 e5 c5 8 h4 ± Nemet-Planinc, Yugoslav Ch 1972

3 ... f5 4 ef ef 5 ♘df3 ♘f6 6 ♗g5 ♗e7 7 ♗d3 ♘e4 8 ♗xe7 ♕xe7 9 ♘e2 ± Karpov-Enevoldsen, Skopje Ol 1972

3 ... b6 4 ♘gf3 ♘f6 (4 ... ♗a6 5 ♗xa6 ♘xa6 6 c3 ±) 5 e5 ♘fd7 6 c4 ± A.Sokolov-Gulko, Moscow Ch 1983

3 ...♗e7 4 ♘gf3 ♘f6 5 e5 ♘fd7 6 c4 ± Kholmov-Suetin, Moscow Ch 1983

² 5 de de 6 ♕a4 e3 7 fe ♗c5 8 ♗b3 ♗b6 9 ♘f3 ♘e7 ∞ Lau-Hug, Beer-Sheva Z 1985

³ 7 ... ♕h5 8 cd ♘f6 9 0-0 ♗e7 10 ♖e1 (10 ♘e5 ± Marjanović-Kovačević, Yugoslav Ch 1984) 10 ... 0-0 11 h3 ♗d6 12 ♘f1 ± A.Sokolov-Kovačević, Novi Sad 1984

⁴ 12 0-0 ♗d6 (12 ... ♗e6 13 ♖e1 ♗xc4 14 ♘xc4 ± Korchnoi-Hug, Palma de Mallorca 1972) 13 ♘f3 ♘h6 14 ♖e1 ± A.Sokolov-Vaganian, Biel IZ 1985

⁵ 6 ♗b5 a6 7 ♗xc6 bc 8 ♘b3 a5 (8 ... c5 9 ♗g5 ♗e7 10 ♗xe7 ♕xe7 11 0-0 ± Popović-Kovačević, Novi Sad 1984) 9 ♗g5 ♗e7 10 ♗xe7 ♕xe7 11 ♕d2 ♕b4! 12 0-0 (12 c3 ♕b5 =) 12 ... ♕xd2 13 ♘bxd2 c5 = Khalifman-Monin, Leningrad Ch 1985

⁶ 6 ... ♘b4 7 ♗e2 c5 8 c3 ♘c6 9 0-0 cd 10 cd f6 11 ♗d3! fe 12 ♘xe5 ♘dxe5 13 de g6 14 ♘f3 ± Faibisovich-Monin, USSR 1979

⁷ 7 ♗g5 ♘dxe5! 8 de fg 9 ♕h5+ g6! 10 ♗xg6+ ♔d7 11 f4 gf 12 ♗d3 ♘b4 ∞ Faibisovich-Monin, USSR 1979

⁸ 8 ... ♘xd4 9 ♘xd4 ♕xd4 10 ♖e1 ♘f6 11 ♘e4! ± Ghinda-Urzica, Romania 1984

⁹ Dorfman-Vaganian, USSR 1978

¹⁰ 6 ... ♗e7 7 ♘f1 f6 8 ef ♗xf6 9 ♗g5 ♘e4 10 ♗xe7 ♕xe7 11 c3 ♗d7 12 ♘e3 0-0 13 0-0 ♗e8 ±/= Hodgson-Short, Wijk aan Zee 1986

¹¹ 7 ... ♘xf6 8 0-0 ♗d6 9 c4 0-0 10 c5 ♗f4 11 ♗b5 ♗d7 12 ♗xc6 ♗xc6 13 ♘b3 ± Mikh.Tseitlin-Gusev, USSR 1986

¹² 12 c5 ♗f4 13 ♖e1 ♗d7 14 ♘f1 ♗xc1 15 ♖xc1 ♘e4 ∞ Kindermann-Hug, Beer-Sheva Z 1985

¹³ 6 ... f6 7 ♗b5 fe (7 ... a6 8 ♗xc6 bc 9 0-0 c5 10 ♖e1 ± Evans-Kaner, USA 1976) 8 de ♗e7 9 ♘bd4 ♘db8 10 ♘g5 ± Estrin-Bagirov, Baku 1958

6 ... a6 7 ♘g5 ♕e7 8 c3 ± Hübner-Hug, Biel 1986

¹⁴ 7 ... ♗e7 8 ♗b5 ♘a7 9 ♗d3 b6 (9 ... c5 10 ♘xc5 ± Matulović-Kovačević, Yugoslavia 1984) 10 0-0 0-0 11 c3 c5 12 ♗c2 ± Rogers-Hug, Biel 1986

¹⁵ 9 ... ♗a6 10 ♗xa6 ♖xa6 11 ♘c1 ♘cb8 12 h4 c5 13 ♖h3 ± Kupreichik-Böhm, Polanica Zdroj 1981

¹⁶ 12 ♗g5 ♗f8 13 h5 ± Spassky-Draško, Sarajevo 1986

¹⁷ 5 dc ♗xc5 6 ♗d3 ♘e7 7 0-0 ♘bc6 8 c3 0-0 9 ♕e2 ♘g6 10 ♘b3 ♗d6 = Kholmov-Dolmatov, Volgodonsk 1983

¹⁸ 8 ♗g5 ♘f6 (8 ... ♘e7 9 ♕d2 ♘bc6 10 ♗e3 ± van der Wiel-Seirawan, Biel IZ 1985) 9 ♕e2+ ♗e6 10 ♘bd4 ♕e7 11 0-0-0 0-0 ∞ Jansa-Andersson, Biel IZ 1985

8 ♕e2+ ♘e7 9 ♗e3 0-0 10 0-0-0 ♘bc6 11 ♗xa7 ♖xa7 12 ♕d2 ♗g4 ∞ Renet-Raičević, Panchevo 1985

8 ♗e2 ♘f6 9 0-0 0-0 10 ♘fd4 ♖e8 11 c3 ♘c6 12 ♗e3 ± Garcia Martinez-Spraggett, Havana 1986

¹⁹ 8 ... ♕e7+ 9 ♕e2 ♘c6 10 ♗g5 ♕xe2+ 11 ♔xe2 ± Gufeld-Lebredo, Cienfuegos 1984

²⁰ 12 ♖e1+ ♗e6 13 ♗e3 ♗xe3 14 ♖xe3 ♔d6 15 ♖ae1 ♖he8 16 c3 ± Mestel-Karlsson, Esbjerg 1984

²¹ 8 ♗d3 ♘f6 9 ♗g5 ♗g4 10 h3 ♗h5 11 ♕e2 0-0 12 0-0-0 ♖e8 (12 ... ♘c6 13 ♖he1 ± Yudasin-M.Gurevich, Baku 1986) 13 ♖he1 ♘bd7 ∞

8 ♗e2 ♘f6 9 0-0 0-0 10 ♘fd4 ♘c6 11 ♗f4 ♘e4 12 c3 ± Yakovich-Chernin, Sochi 1986

²² 12 ♗g3 ♘c6 13 ♗e2 ♗g4 14 ♖d1 ♘xg3 15 hg ♕c7 16 ♘fd4 ± van der Wiel-P.Nikolić, Wijk aan Zee 1986

²³ 6 ... ♘f6 7 0-0 ♗e7 (7 ... c4 – 6 ... c4) 8 dc ♗xc5 9 ♘b3 – 6 dc, but with an extra tempo for White

²⁴ 8 ♘b3 ♘c6 9 ♘bxd4 ♘ge7 10 ♘xc6 bc 11 c4 ± Chiburdanidze-Levitina, match 1984

²⁵ 12 ♘fxd4 ♗g6 13 ♗g3 ♗e7 14 a4 ♘xd4 15 ♕xd4 ± Yudasin-Dolmatov, USSR Ch 1986

²⁶ 7 ... ♘f6 8 ♖e1 ♗e7 9 b3 b5 10 a4 c3 11 ab cd 12 ♗xd2 0-0 13 c4 dc 14 bc ♗b7 15 ♗a5 ∞ Hulak-P.Nikolić, Yugoslav Ch 1984

²⁷ 8 ♖e1 ♘e7 9 b3 cb 10 ab ♘bc6 11 ♘f1 ♗g4 12 ♘g3 0-0 13 c3 ± A.Sokolov-Miralles, Dubai Ol 1986

²⁸ 8 ... cb 9 ab ♘e7 10 c4 dc (10 ... 0-0 11 c5 ♗c7 12 b4 ±) 11 bc ±

²⁹ 9 a4 c3 10 ab cd 11 ♗xd2 ♗b7 12 ba ♘xa6 13 ♗xa6 ♖xa6 (13 ... ♗xa6? 14 ♖xa6) 14 ♕e2+ ♕e7 15 ♕xa6!? (15 ♕b5+ ♕d7 16 ♕e2+ =) 15 ... ♗xa6 16 ♖xa6 ∞ Geller-Kekki, Mätynkylä 1986

³⁰ 12 ♕c2 ♗g6 13 ♖fe1 ♖e8 14 ♕b2 ♗xa3 15 ♕xa3 ± Chandler-Dolmatov, Minsk 1982

French XI   1 e4 e6 2 d4 d5 3 ♘d2 ♘f6

	4	5	6	7	8	9	10	11	12	
1	e5	♗d3[1]	♗xd2	dc[2]	♘f3	0-0	♗c3	♗d4		±
	♘e4	♘xd2	c5	♘d7[3]	♘xc5	♕b6	♗d7			
2	...	♗d3	c3	♘e2[5]	♗xa6[6]	0-0	♖e1[8]	♘f4	b3[9]	±
	♘fd7	c5[4]	b6	♗a6	♘xa6	b5[7]	♗e7	c4		
3	...	...	...	♘gf3	0-0	cd	♘xd4	♘f3	♕c2[12]	∞
	...	...	♘c6	♕b6[10]	cd	♘xd4[11]	♕xd4	♕b6	♕c5[13]	
4	...	...	...	...	...	♖e1	♘f1[15]	dc	♘d4	∞
	...	...	...	...	♗e7	g5[14]	g4	♗xc5	♘dxe5[16]	

1 e4 e6 2 d4 d5 3 ♘d2 ♘f6 4 e5 ♘fd7 5 ♗d3 c5 6 c3 ♘c6 7 ♘e2

	7	8	9	10	11	12	13	14	15	
5	...	cd	0-0	f4	♘f3	a3	♘c3	h3[20]		±
	cd[17]	♘b6[18]	♗d7	h5[19]	♖c8	a5	♘a7			
6	...	...	♘f4	♕h5+	ef+[21]	♘g6+	♕xh8	♘f3	gf	∞
	...	f6	♘xd4	♔e7	♘xf6	hg	e5[22]	♘xf3+	♗f5[23]	
7	...	...	ef	0-0	♘f3	♖e1	♘f4	♗e3[27]	g3	±
	...	...	♘xf6[24]	♗d6	♕b6[25]	0-0	♗d7[26]	♕c7[28]	♖ae8[29]	
8	...	...	...	...	...	...	♘c3	♗g5[30]	♗h4	±
	...	...	...	...	...	...	♗d7	♘g4	♘h6[31]	
9	...	...	...	...	...	♗g5	♖c1	♘g3[32]	♗b5[34]	∞
	...	...	...	...	♕c7	0-0	♘g4	g6[33]	♗d7[35]	
10	...	...	...	...	...	g3	♗f4	♖c1	♘xf4	±
	...	...	...	...	...	0-0	♗d7[36]	♗xf4[37]	♕b6[38]	
11	...	...	...	...	...	♘c3	♗g5	♗h4	♖c1[39]	±
	...	...	...	...	...	a6	0-0	♘h5	g6[40]	

1 5 ♘xe4 – 3 ♘c3

2 7 ♘f3 ♕b6?! (7 ... cd) 8 dc ♕xb2 9 0-0 ± Geller-Vaganian, USSR Ch 1983

   7 c3 ♘c6?! (7 ... ♕b6) 8 ♘f3 ♕b6 9 dc ± Pytel, Jurmala 1983

3 7 ... ♘c6 8 ♘f3 ♗xc5 9 0-0 a6 10 a3 h6 11 ♕e2 ♕c7 12 ♖fe1 b6 13 b4 ♗e7 14 c4 ± Geller-Vaganian, Erevan Z 1982

4 5 ... b6 6 ♘e2 ♗a6 7 ♗xa6 ♘xa6 8 0-0 c5 9 c4! ♘c7 10 ♘f4! ± Tal-Granda Zúñiga, Termas de Rio Hondo 1987

5 7 ♘h3 ♗a6 8 ♗xa6 ♘xa6 9 0-0 b5 (9 ... ♘c7 10 ♘f4 – 7 ♘e2) 10 ♘f3 c4 11 ♘f4 g6 (11 ... ♘c7 12 ♘h5 ±) 12 h4 ± Zapata-Nogueiras, Thessaloniki Ol 1984

6 8 ♗b1 cd (8 ... b5!? 9 0-0 ♘c6 10 ♖e1 ♕b6 11 ♘f3 b4 ∞) 9 cd ♘c6 10 ♘f3 ♗b4+ 11 ♗d2 ♗xd2+ 12 ♕xd2 ♕e7 = de Firmian-Despotović, Smederevska Palanka 1981

8 ♘f3 ♗xd3 9 ♕xd3 ♘c6 10 0-0 ♗e7 11 b3 0-0 12 ♗d2 a6 13 g3 b5 = Ljubojević-Short, Biel IZ 1985

7 9 ... ♘c7 10 ♘f4 ♗e7 11 ♕g4 ± Razuvayev-Bagirov, USSR Ch 1973

8 10 f4 g6 11 ♘f3 h5 12 ♗e3 c4 (Cirić-Short, Manchester 1983) 13 g3 ♗e7 14 h3 intending g4 ± Cirić

   10 ♘f4 ♘c7 11 ♖e1 c4 12 b3 ♘b6 13 a4 ± Stoica-Miralles, Lucerne 1985

9 Jansa-Prandstetter, Czechoslovak Ch 1984

10 7 ... cd 8 cd f6 9 ♘g5 fg 10 ♕h5+ g6 11 ♗xg6+ hg 12 ♕xg6+ ♔e7 13 ♘f3 ♘f6 14 ♗xg5 ♘d7 15 ♗xf6 ♕a5+ 16 ♔f1 ♕b5+ 17 ♔g1 ♖h6 18 ♕f7+ ♗e7 19 ♘g5 ♕xb2 20 ♖f1 ♕xd4 21 ♘xe6 ♖xf6 ∞ Bryson

   7 ... ♗e7 8 0-0 g5!? Paavilainen-Vaiser, Tallinn 1986

11 9 ... ♗e7 10 ♖e1 ♘xd4 11 ♘xd4 ♕xd4

12 ♘b3! ♕a4 (12 ... ♕b6 13 ♕g4) 13 ♗c2 ± Hartman-Benjamin, USA 1986

[12] 12 ♕a4 ♕b4 (12 ... ♗e7 13 ♕g4) 13 ♕c2 ♘c5! (13 ... h6 14 ♗d2 ♕b6 15 ♖ac1 ♗e7 16 ♕a4 ± Sax-Vih, Hungary 1986; 13 ... ♕c5 – 12 ♕c2) 14 ♗d2 ♕a4 15 b3 ♕d7 16 ♗e2 ♗e7 ∞

[13] 12 ... h6 13 ♖b1 ♗e7 14 ♗e3 ♗c5 15 ♗d2 ♗b4 16 ♗f4 ∞̄ de Wit-Weyns, Belgium 1985-86

12 ... ♕c5 13 ♕e2 ♕b6 14 ♗e3 ♕d8 15 ♖ac1 ♗e7 16 ♖c3 ∞̄ Hellers-de Wit, Amsterdam 1985

[14] 9 ... cd 10 cd – 8 ... cd
9 ... 0-0 10 c4 cd 11 cd ed 12 ♘b3 ±

[15] 10 dc ♗xc5 11 ♕e2 g4 12 ♘d4 ♘dxe5 ∓ Plaskett-Chernin, Järvenpää 1985

[16] 13 ♗f4 ♘xd3 14 ♕xd3 ∞̄ Riskin-Korzubov, USSR 1985

[17] 7 ... f6 8 ♘f4 ♕e7 9 ef ♕xf6 10 ♘f3 cd 11 0-0 ∞̄ Grünfeld-Schmittdiel, Dortmund 1984

[18] 8 ... a5 9 0-0 ♘b6 (9 ... a4 10 f4!) 10 ♘f3 (10 f4!) 10 ... ♗e7 11 ♘f4 g6 12 ♘h3 h6 13 ♘f4 ± Marjanović-Lalić, Yugoslav Ch 1983

8 ... ♕b6 9 ♘f3 f6 10 ♘c3?! (10 ef ♘xf6 – 8 ... f6) 10 ... fe 11 de g6 12 ♗e3 ♕a5 (12 ... ♕xb2 13 ♘b5 ∞̄) 13 ♗d2 (Shamkovich-Watson, USA 1976) 13 ... ♗g7! ∞

[19] 10 ... g6 11 ♘f3 h5 12 a3 a5 13 g3 intending h3, g4 ±

[20] 14 ... ♘c4 15 f5 ± Lputian-Agzamov, USSR Ch 1985
14 ... g6 15 g4 ±
14 ... h4 15 ♘g5 intending ♕g4 ±

[21] 11 ♘g6+ hg 12 ef+ ♔xf6!? 13 ♖xh8 ♔f7 14 f4 (14 0-0 ♘c5 15 ♗b1 e5 ∓ Barle-Portisch, Portorož 1973) 14 ... ♘c5 15 ♗b1 ∞ Sigurjonsson-Hjartarson, Westmannaeyjar 1985

[22] 13 ... ♔f7 14 0-0 (14 ♕h4 e5 15 ♘f3 ♘xf3+ 16 gf ♗f5 ∞ van der Wiel-Timman, Brussels 1986) 14 ... e5 15 ♘f3 ♘xf3+ 16 gf ♘h5? (16 ... ♗f5; 16 ... e4) 17 ♗xg6+! ♔xg6 18 ♔h1 ± Ernst-Rodgaard, Copenhagen 1986

[23] 16 ♗xf5 gf 17 ♗g5 ♕a5+ 18 ♔f1 ∞ Yandemirov-Dreyev, USSR 1985, and Prandstetter-Yurek, Karvina 1986

[24] 9 ... ♕xf6 10 0-0! ♘xd4 (10 ... ♗d6 11 ♘f3 0-0 12 ♘g3 ±) 11 ♘xd4 ♕xd4 12 ♘f3 ♕f6 13 ♗g5 ♕f7 13 ♕c2 g6 14 ♖ac1 ±

[25] 11 ... 0-0 12 ♗f4 ♗xf4 13 ♘xf4 ♘e4 14 ♕c1 ± Dvoiris-Gleizerov, USSR 1987

[26] 13 ... ♗xf4 14 ♗xf4 ♕xb2 15 ♗d6 ♖e8 16 ♗e5 ±
13 ... ♘e4 14 g3 ♗xf4 15 ♗xf4 ♕xb2 16 ♖e2 ♕a3 17 ♗xe4 ±

[27] 14 ♘xe6 ♖fe8 15 ♗f5 ♗b4! 16 ♗d2 ♗xd2 17 ♕xd2 ♘e7 18 ♗xg7 ∞

[28] 14 ... ♕xb2 15 ♖b1 ♕xa2 16 ♖xb7 ∞̄
14 ... ♖ae8!?

[29] 16 ♖c1 ♕b8 17 ♘g5! h6 18 ♘f3 ♘g4 (18 ... ♘e4 19 ♘g6 ± Georgiev-Farago, Dubna 1979) 19 ♘g6 ♖f6 20 ♗b1 ±

[30] 14 ♗e3 ♗h8 15 a3 ♗e8! 16 ♘g5 ♗h5 ∞ van der Wiel-Ree, Dutch Ch 1985

[31] 16 ♗g3 ♗e7 (16 ... ♗xg3 17 hg ± van der Wiel-Short, Biel 1985) 17 ♘a4 ♕a5 18 a3 ♖xf3 (18 ... ♘xd4 19 ♘xd4 ♗xa4 20 ♕b1 ±) 19 gf ♘xd4 20 ♘c3 ±

[32] 14 h3 ♖xf3! 15 hg ♖f7 16 ♗b1 g6 ∞ Hellers-Chernin, Wijk aan Zee 1986

[33] 14 ... h6 15 ♗d2 ♕e7 16 ♗b1 ♗d7 17 ♕c2 ± Tseshkovsky-Chernin, USSR Ch 1987

[34] 15 ♘h4 e5 16 ♗e2 ♘f6 17 de ♗xe5 18 b4 ♗f4 = Smagin-Dolmatov, USSR 1986; 15 ... ♘f6 16 ♕d2! ± Geller-Vaiser, Delhi 1987

[35] 16 ♘h4 ♘f6 17 ♕d3 ♖f7! ∞ A.Sokolov-Yusupov, match 1986

[36] 13 ... ♘e4 14 ♗xe4 de 15 ♘g5 ±
13 ... ♘g4 14 ♖c1 ♗xf4 15 ♗xf4 ♖xf4 16 gf ♕xf4 17 ♗e2 ± Rozentalis-Lputian, USSR 1985
13 ... ♗xf4 14 ♘xf4 ♕b6 15 ♕d2 ♔h8 16 ♕e3 ♕xb2 17 ♖ab1 ♕a3 18 ♘g5 ± Rozentalis-Ivanchuk, USSR 1986

[37] 14 ... ♘h5 15 ♗xd6 ♕xd6 16 ♘c3 g6 17 ♖e1 a6 18 ♘e5 ± Dvoiris-Dolmatov, USSR Ch 1986

[38] 16 b3 ♖ae8 17 ♖e1 ± Yakovich-Belyavsky, USSR Ch 1986

[39] 15 ♗g3 ♘xg3 16 hg g6 17 ♖c1 ♕g7 18 ♗b1 g5 ∓ Smagin-Vaiser, Barnaul 1984
15 ♖e1 g6 16 ♗f1 (16 ♖c1 ♕g7 17 ♗f1 ♗d7 ∞ Karpov-Mestel, London 1984) 16 ... ♕g7 17 ♘a4 ♗d7 18 ♘b6 ♖ae8 ∞ Belyavsky-M.Gurevich, USSR Ch 1986

[40] 16 ♗b1 ♕g7 17 ♘a4 ♖xf3! 18 gf ♗d7 ±
16 ♗e2! ♕g7 17 ♘a4 ± Sznapik-Pokojowczyk, Poland 1986

French XII   1 e4 e6 2 d4 d5 3 Nd2 Nf6 4 e5 Nfd7 5 f4

	5	6	7	8	9	10	11	12	13	
1	...	Ndf3	Ne2	g3	Nexd4	Nxd4	c3	Nb3	a4	∞
	c5[1]	Nc6	Qb6[2]	cd	Nxd4![3]	Nb8	Nc6	Bd7	a5[4]	

1 e4 e6 2 d4 d5 3 Nd2 Nf6 4 e5 Nfd7 5 f4 c5

	6	7	8	9	10	11	12	13	14	
2	c3	Ndf3[6]	g3	a4[9]	cd	Kf2	h3[10]	Be3	Rc1	±
	Nc6[5]	Qb6[7]	a5[8]	cd	Bb4+	g5	f6	0-0	Rf7[11]	
3	...	...	cd	g4![13]	Ne2	Kf2	Bh3	f5	Kg3!?	±
	...	cd	Nb6[12]	a5[14]	a4	Bd7	Nc4[15]	Qb6	Nxb2[16]	
4	...	...	...	g3	Kf2	Kg2	Bd3	ef	Nxg5[19]	±
	...	...	Qb6	Be7[17]	0-0	f6	g5[18]	Bxf6		
5	...	...	...	...	Kf2	Kg2	Bd3	Be3![21]	fe	±
	...	...	...	Bb4+	f6[20]	0-0	Nxd4	fe	Bc5[22]	
6	...	...	...	...	...	fg![23]	Nxe5	Kg2[24]	Nf3	±
	...	...	...	...	g5!?	Ndxe5	Nxe5	Nc4[25]	Bd7[26]	

1 5 ... b6 6 Ndf3 Ba6 7 Ne2 Nc6 8 g4! ± Gipslis-Taimanov, USSR 1972

2 7 ... Qa5+ 8 c3 (8 Bd2?! Qb6 9 Bc3 Be7 ∞ Kavalek-Ree, Wijk aan Zee 1982) 8 ... cd 9 Nexd4
7 ... b5 8 Be3 Qa5+ 9 Kf2 Be7 10 g3 h5 11 dc! ± Ghinda

3 9 ... Bc5 10 c3 0-0 11 Bd3 Nxd4 12 cd Be7 13 0-0 f5 14 Rf2 Nb8 15 Rg2! ± Ghinda-Czerveny, Romania 1986

4 14 Bb5 ∞ Ghinda-Foisor, Romanian Ch 1985

5 6 ... b6 7 Ndf3 Ba6 8 Bxa6 Nxa6 9 f5! ± Matanović-Panno, Yugoslavia 1962
6 ... f5 7 Ndf3 Be7 8 h4 h5 9 Ng5 Nf8 10 Be3 ± Westerinen-Keene, Alicante 1975
6 ... cd 7 cd Nc6 8 Ndf3 (8 Ngf3 a5!? 9 a4?! Bb4 10 Kf2 f6 11 g3 Qb6 ∞/∓ Smagin-Gurevich, USSR Ch 1986) – 6 ... Nc6

6 7 Ngf3 f6 8 b3 cd 9 cd fe 10 de Qb6 11 Be2 Be7 12 g3 0-0 13 a3 a5 ∓ Westerinen-Ivanović, Metz 1987

7 7 ... Rb8!? 8 Bd3 b5 9 Ne2 Qb6 10 0-0 b4 11 Kh1 Ba6 12 f5! ± Glek-Ivanchuk, USSR 1986
7 ... Qa5 8 dc!? (8 Kf2 Be7 9 Bd3 cd 10 cd f6 11 Ne2 Qb6 = Hübner-Ree, Wijk aan Zee 1982; 8 Be3 ±) 8 ... Qxc5 9 Bd3 Be7 10 Ne2 Qb6 11 Ned4 ± Minić-Yudovich, Zagreb 1970
7 ... f5 8 Bd3 Be7 9 Ne2 0-0 10 h3 a5 11 g4 ± Inkiov-Ambroz, Herculana Z 1982

8 8 ... Be7 9 Ne2 (9 Bh3 Qa6?! 10 Ne2 cd 11 cd Nb6 12 0-0 0-0 13 Rf2! ± Sznapik-Farago, Herculana Z 1982; 9 ... cd 10 cd 0-0 11 Ne2 f6!? ∞ Sznapik) 9 ... 0-0 10 Bh3 cd 11 cd a5 12 0-0 a4 13 a3 Qa7 14 Qc2 ± Ljubojević-Hübner, Wijk aan Zee 1986

9 9 a3 f5 (9 ... Ndb8 10 Ne2 Bd7 11 Bg2 a4 12 0-0 Ba5 13 f5 ± Kindermann-Rodriguez, West Germany 1985-86) 10 Ne2 Be7 11 h3 Nf8 ∞ Kindermann-Zsu.Polgar, Baden-Baden 1985

10 12 fg Ndxe5 13 Kg2 Nxf3 14 Kxf3 ±

11 15 Rh2 Nf8 16 Qd2 ± Karpov-Ljubojević, Brussels 1986

12 8 ... h5 9 Bd3 Nb6 10 Ne2 Bd7 11 0-0 a5 12 a3 Be7 13 b3 g6 14 Kh1 Nf8 15 Rg1 ± Balinas-Lim Kok Ann, Manila 1968

13 9 Bd3 Bd7 10 Ne2 Nb4 11 Bb1 Ba4 12 b3 Bd7 13 0-0 h5 14 f5 ef 15 Nf4 ∞ Adorjan-Kovačević, Sarajevo 1982

14 9 ... h5 10 gh Rxh5 11 Ne2 g6 12 Ng3 Rh8 13 h4! ±

15 12 ... h5 13 gh Rxh5 14 Bg4 ±

16 15 Nxb2 Qxb2 16 Nf4 ± Georgadze-Mnatsakanian, USSR 1982

17 9 ... f6 10 Bd3! (10 Bh3 fe 11 fe Bb4+ 12 Kf1 0-0!? 13 Kg2 Ndxe5 14 de Nxe5 ∞∞) 10 ... fe 11 fe Bb4+ 12 Kf1 0-0 13 Kg2! ± Medina-Keene, Torremolinos 1976

18 12 ... fe!? intending ... Kh8

19 Degerman-Reefschläger, Stockholm 1984-85

20 10 ... f5 11 Kg2 Qd8 12 Bd3 Nb6 13 Ne2 Bd7 14 h3 Be7 15 g4 ±

21 13 Nxd4 fe 14 fe Nxe5 15 Ngf3 Nxf3 16 Nxf3 e5 ∞∞

262

22 15 ♗xd4 ♗xd4 16 ♘xd4 ♕xb2+ 17 ♗c2! ± Yakovich-Bareyev, USSR 1985

23 11 ♗e3 f6 (11 ... g4!? 12 ♘d2 f6! 13 ♘b3 fe 14 de ♗c5 15 ♘xc5 ♗xc5 ∞ Yakovich-Machulsky, USSR 1985) 12 ♗h3 0-0 13 ♗g4 fe 14 fe ♗c5!! 15 ♗xe6+ ♔h8 16 dc ♕xb2+ 17 ♗d2 g4! ∓ Emms-Kosten, British Ch 1985
   11 h3 f6 ∞

24 13 ♗e3 ♘c4! (13 ... ♘c6 14 ♘f3 ♗d7 15 ♖c1 ± Anand-Ravikumar, India 1985) 14 ♗xc4 dc = Ghinda-Foisor, Romania 1986

25 13 ... ♘c6 14 ♘f3 ♗f8 15 b3 ♗g7 16 ♗b2 ♗d7 17 ♖c1 h6 18 ♕d2! ±/± Gruzman-Glek, corr. 1986

26 15 b3 ♘d6 16 ♗f4 ♘e4 17 ♖c1 ♗d6 18 ♗d3 ± Glek-Vaiser, Tallinn 1986

French XIII   1 e4 e6 2 d4 d5 3 ♘d2 c5

	4	5	6	7	8	9	10	11	12	
1	♘gf3	♗b5	♘xe4	♗g5	♘c3	♗xc6	d5	0-0	♘e5	∞
	♘c6[1]	de[2]	♗d7	♕a5+	a6[3]	♗xc6	♗xd5	♗c6	♕c7[4]	
2	ed	♘gf3	♗c4	0-0	♘b3	♗bxd4[6]	♕xd4	♘xd4	♗e2[7]	±
	♕xd5	cd	♕d6[5]	♘f6	♘c6	♘xd4	♕xd4	a6	♗d7[8]	
3	...	...	...	...	...	...	♘xd4	a4[10]	b3	±
	...	...	...	...	...	...	♗d7[9]	♕c7[11]	0-0-0[12]	
4	...	♗b5+	♕e2+[14]	dc	♘b3	♗e3[15]	♘f3[16]	♗d3	♘fd4	∞
	ed	♗d7[13]	♗e7	♘f6	0-0	♖e8	a6[17]	♗a4	♘bd7[18]	

---

[1] 4 ... de 5 ♘xe4 cd 6 ♕xd4 ±
4 ... cd 5 ed ♕xd5 – 4 ed ♕xd5
4 ... ♘f6 5 ed ♘xd5 6 ♘b3 cd 7 ♘bxd4 ♗e7 8 ♗c4 (8 g3 0-0 9 ♗g2 ♗d7 10 0-0 ♘c6 11 ♘xc6 ♗xc6 12 ♘e5 ∓ Jansa-Korchnoi, Nice Ol 1974) 8 ... 0-0 9 0-0 ♘c6 10 c3 ♗f6 11 ♖e1 ± Eingorn-Nogueiras, Havana 1986

[2] 5 ... cd 6 ♘xd4 ♗d7 7 ♗xc6 ♗xc6 8 ♗xc6+ bc 9 c4 ♘f6 10 ♕a4 ♕d7 11 e5 ♘g4 12 ♘f3 ♖b8 13 a3 c5 14 ♕c2 ± Kuzmin-Kholmov, Moscow Ch 1987

[3] 8 ... cd 9 ♘xd4 ± Tal-Uhlmann, Moscow 1971
8 ... h6 9 ♗d2 ± Tischbierek-Casper, East German Ch 1985

[4] 13 ♖e1 ♘f6 ∞ Ničevski-Uhlmann, Skopje 1976

[5] 6 ... ♕c5 7 0-0 ♘c6 8 ♕e2 ♘f6 9 ♘b3 ♕b6 10 ♖d1 ±

[6] 9 ♖e1 ♗e7 10 ♘bxd4 ♘xd4 11 ♘xd4 0-0 12 b3 e5 = Ljubojević-Hübner, Tilburg 1986

[7] 12 ♗f4 b5 13 ♗e2 ♗b7 14 ♘b3 ♗e7 15 c4 bc 16 ♘a5 ± Hübner-Klinger, Biel 1986

[8] 12 ... e5 13 ♘b3 ♗f5 14 c3 0-0-0 15 ♗g5 ♗e7 16 ♖fe1 ± Chernin
12 ... ♗d7 13 ♗f4 ♘d5 14 ♗g3 ♗c5 15 ♖fd1 ± van der Wiel-Chernin, Wijk aan Zee 1986

[9] 10 ... ♗e7 11 b3 0-0 12 ♗b2 e5 13 ♘b5 ± Tal-Uhlmann, Moscow 1967

[10] 10 ... a6 11 b3 (11 ♖e1 ♕c7 12 ♗d3 ♗d6 13 ♘f5! ± Shamkovich-Seirawan, US Ch 1980) 11 ... ♕c7 12 ♗b2 ♗d6 13 ♖e1 0-0 14 ♘f3 ± Psakhis-Chernin, USSR Ch 1987

[10] 11 b3 0-0-0 12 ♗b2 ♕c7 13 ♕e2 h5! ∞ Grünfeld-Lobron, New York 1985, and Matulović-Marjanović, Yugoslavia 1986

[11] 11 ... 0-0-0 12 ♘b5 ±

[12] 12 ... ♗c5 13 ♗b2 ♕f4 14 g3 ♕h6 15 ♕f3 0-0-0 16 ♗a6! ± Tseshkovsky-M.Gurevich, USSR Ch 1987
12 ... 0-0-0 13 ♕e2 ♗c5 14 ♘b5 ± Ljubojević-Lobron, Reggio Emilia 1985-86

[13] 5 ... ♘c6 6 ♘gf3! – 5 ♘gf3

[14] 6 ♗xd7+ ♘xd7 7 ♘gf3 ♘gf6 8 0-0 ♗e7 9 dc ♘xc5 10 ♘b3 ♘ce4 11 ♘fd4 ♕d7 12 ♕f3 0-0 13 ♘f5 ♗d8 14 ♗e3 g6 15 ♘g3 ♕c6 = Rozentalis-Bareyev, USSR 1985

[15] 9 ♗g5 ♖e8 10 0-0-0 a5! ∓ Radulov-Uhlmann, Albena 1983

[16] 10 0-0-0 a5! ∓ Gurgenidze-Psakhis, USSR 1985

[17] 10 ... ♗xc5 11 ♘xc5 ♕a5+ 12 ♕d2 ♕xb5 13 0-0-0 ♗g4 (13 ... b6 14 ♘xd7 ± Karpov-Korchnoi, match (22) 1978) 14 h3! ± Tseshkovsky-Vaganian, Lvov 1978

[18] 13 0-0-0 ♗xb3 (13 ... ♘xc5 14 ♘f5 ± Tal-Portisch, Montreal 1979) 14 ♘xb3 a5! 15 ♘d4 ♗xc5 16 ♕f3 a4 ∞ Yakovich-Shereshevsky, USSR 1985

	4	5	6	7	8	9	10	11	12	
5	ed	♘gf3	♗b5	dc	0-0	♘b3	♖e1[21]	♗g5[22]	c4	±
	ed	♘c6[19]	♗d6[20]	♗xc5	♘e7	♘b6	0-0	♕d6[23]	h6[24]	

1 e4 e6 2 d4 d5 3 ♘d2 c5 4 ed ed 5 ♘gf3 ♘c6 6 ♗b5 ♗d6 7 dc ♗xc5 8 0-0 ♘e7 9 ♘b3 ♗d6

	10	11	12	13	14	15	16	17	18	
6	♖e1[25]	♗g5[26]	♗e2	c3	♗h4	♘fd4	♖xe2	♘xd4	♘f5	=
	0-0	♗g4[27]	♖e8[28]	a6	♕b6	♗xe2	♘xd4	♘c6	♗e5[29]	
7	...	...	♗h4	♗g3	hg	♗d3	♗xh7+[32]	♗d3	♘bd2	∞
	...	...	♖e8[30]	♗xg3	♕b6	a5[31]	♔f8	a4	♘f5[33]	
8	♘bd4	c3[34]	♕a4	♖e1[35]	♗f1	g3	♘h4	♘df5[36]	♘xf5	=
	0-0	♗g4	♗h5	♕c7	a6	♘a5	♘c4	♘xf5	♗c5	
9	...	♗e3	h3[37]	♕d2	♖fe1	♗e2	c3	♖ad1	♗f4[40]	±
	...	♗g4	♗h5	♖c8[38]	a6	♘g6	♗e4	♗b8[39]		

---

19 **5 ...** c4 6 ♗e2 a6 – 3 ... a6
5 ... ♘f6 6 ♗b5+ ♗d7 – 5 ♗b5+

20 **6 ... cd** 7 ♕e2+ ♕e7 8 ♘xd4 ± Hübner-Korchnoi, match (5, 7, 9) 1980-81
6 ... ♕e7+ 7 ♗e2 cd 8 0-0 ±

21 **10** ♗e3 ♗xe3 11 ♗xc6+ bc 12 fe 0-0 13 ♕d2 ♕b6 14 ♕c3 ♖b8 15 ♘fd4 (15 ♖ab1!?) 15 ... ♗a6 16 ♘f5 ♘xf5 17 ♖xf5 ♗c4 ∞ van der Wiel-Korchnoi, Brussels 1987

22 **11** ♗e3 ♗f5 (11 ... ♗g4 12 ♗xb6 ♕xb6 13 ♗xc6 ±) 12 c3 ±

23 **11 ...** h6 12 ♗h4 g5 (12 ... f6!?) 13 ♗g3 ♘f5 14 ♕d2 ± Karpov-Vaganian, Budapest 1973

24 **13** ♗e3 ♗xe3 14 ♖xe3 ♗g4 15 ♗xc6 bc 16 c5 ♕c7 17 ♘bd4 ± Geller-Wilder, Reykjavik 1986

25 **10** ♗xc6+ bc 11 ♕d4 0-0 12 ♗f4 ♘f5 13 ♕a4 (13 ♕d2 ♕b6 14 ♘fd4 ♖d8 ∞) 13 ... a5 14 ♖fe1 ♗e6 15 ♘g5 c5 ∞ Smagin-Balashov, USSR Ch 1986
10 ♗g5 0-0 11 ♗h4 ♕b6! 12 ♗d3 a5 13 a4 ♘f5 14 ♗g5 (14 ♗xf5 ♗xf5 ∓ Balashov-Gulko, Moscow Ch 1974) 14 ... h6 15 ♗d2 ♗e6 = Rozentalis-Psakhis, Sevastopol 1986

26 **11** h3 ♘f5! 12 c3 ♗c7 13 ♗d3 ♕d6 = Belyavsky-Vaganian, Sochi 1986

27 **11 ...** a6 12 ♗e2 ♗f5 13 c3 ♕c7 14 ♗xe7 ♘xe7 15 ♗d3 ± Rodriguez-Uhlmann, Berlin 1979
11 ... ♕c7 12 c3 h6 13 ♗xe7 ♘xe7 14 ♘bd4 a6 15 ♗d3 ± Hübner-Korchnoi, Johannesburg 1981

28 **12 ...** h6 13 ♗xe7 ♗xe7 14 h3 ♗f5 (14 ... ♗h5 15 c3 ♗f6 16 ♘h2 ♗g6 17 ♗f3! ± Sisniega-Prandstetter, Taxco IZ 1985) 15 ♗d3 ♕d7 16 c3 ± van der Wiel-Short, Wijk aan Zee 1986

29 Khalifman-Uhlmann, Plovdiv 1986

30 **12 ...** h6 13 ♗g3 ♗xg3 14 hg ♘f5 15 ♕d3 ± Balashov-Lputian, USSR 1985

31 **15 ...** h6 16 ♕d2 ♗xf3 17 gf ± A.Sokolov-Spraggett, Montpellier C 1985

32 **16** a4 ♘f5 = Przewoznik-Lputian, Lvov 1986

33 **18 ...** ♕xb2 19 ♖b1 ♕xa2 20 ♕c1 a3 21 ♘g5 ± Oll-Temirbayev, USSR 1986
18 ... ♘f5 19 ♖xe8+ ♖xe8 20 ♘f1 ♕xb2 ∞ A.Sokolov-Vaganian, match 1986

34 **11** h3 ♘xd4 12 ♕xd4 ♗f5 = Tukmakov-Uhlmann, Hastings 1972-73
11 b3 ♘xd4 12 ♘xd4 (12 ♕xd4 ♘c6 =) 12 ... ♗e5 =

35 **13** ♗xc6 bc 14 ♘xc6 ♘xc6 15 ♕xc6 ♗xf3 17 gf ♖c8 ∓
13 ♗d3 h6 14 ♗e3 a6 15 ♖fe1 ♕c7 16 h3 ♘a5 = Karpov-Korchnoi, match 1974

36 **17** ♕c2 ♖fe8 18 ♗g5 ♘c6 19 ♘df5 ♗f8 20 ♘e3 ♕a5! ∓ A.Sokolov-Vaganian, Montpellier C 1985

37 **12** ♕d2 ♕c7 13 h3 ♗xf3 (13 ... ♗h5 12 h3) 14 ♘xf3 ♖ad8 15 c3 ♘g6 16 ♖fe1 A.Sokolov-Lputian, USSR Ch 1985

38 **13 ...** ♕c7 14 ♘h4 ♘xd4 15 ♗xd4 ±

39 **17 ...** ♖e8 18 ♘xc6 bc (18 ... ♘xc6 19 ♘g5 ±) 19 b4 a5 20 ♘d4 ± Gulko

40 Marjanović-Gulko, Marseilles 1986

Caro-Kann

Christened in honour of the analytical efforts of H.Caro of Berlin and M.Kann of Vienna who adopted the opening towards the end of the 19th century, the Caro-Kann is another opening that owes a great deal of its present status to the work of Botvinnik. Although it has a reputation for being unnecessarily dull, as the theory of this defence has developed so it has expanded to include variations ranging from the quiet to the chaotic. Every year this once maligned defence adds new converts to its ranks and its adherents include GMs of a wide variety of tastes – Andersson, Larsen, Speelman and Seirawan, to name just a few.

The Classical System (**2 d4 d5 3 ♘c3 de 4 ♘xe4 ♗f5**) continues to attract players who prefer to postpone the fight until they have secured a solid position and who enjoy chipping away at the ambitiously advanced boundaries of White's position. White must tread a narrow line between aggression and over-extension. Black must always be wary of the retribution that such a provocative stance can entail.

The aggressive system championed by Bent Larsen (**2 d4 d5 3 ♘c3 de 4 ♘xe4 ♘f6 5 ♘xf6+ gf**) has enjoyed a healthy measure of success. Black's unorthodox pawn structure provides tactical counterplay on the half-open g-file and the kingside in general. As White came to grips with the system its popularity declined, though it remains a vigorous option for the second player.

For the more peacefully inclined, **5 ... ef** offers chances of a solid equality and is a favourite of GM Ulf Andersson. Korchnoi has used this variation with success as well, finding the kingside pawn mass useful both for defence and attack. **2 d4 d5 3 ♘c3 de 4 ♘xe4 ♘d7** is also in tune with the basically solid mood of the Caro-Kann. Unambitious, it nevertheless poses problems as far as White's intentions to demonstrate an opening advantage are concerned.

2 d4 d5 3 ♘c3 de 4 ♘xe4 ♘d7 enjoys tremendous popularity, despite its basically unassuming nature. A number of original ideas by Speelman, combined with the essential resilience of the defence, created a system that consistently frustrated White attempts to secure an advantage. When Karpov selected it as his main defence for his 1987 matches against Sokolov and Kasparov, its stock soared. Future Kasparov-Karpov encounters will doubtless influence this variation's final value. See, for example, Kasparov's win against Karpov in the introduction to this volume.

Alternative attempts to handle the Caro-Kann are the Two Knights, **2 ♘c3 d5 3 ♘f3**, the Exchange Variation, **2 d4 d5 3 ed cd** (both of which were tried by Fischer), the Advance, **2 d4 d5 3 e5** and the Panov-Botvinnik Attack, **2 d4 d5 3 ed cd 4 c4**. The last two are White's sharpest options. Black must be theoretically prepared and, in the case of the Panov-Botvinnik, conversant with the various transpositional possibilities in order to equalize.

	Caro-Kann I			1 e4 c6						
	2	3	4	5	6	7	8	9	10	
1	d3	♘f3[1]	g3	♗g2	0-0	d4	de	b3	♕e2	=
	e5	d6	g6[2]	♗g7	♘e7	0-0	de	c5	♘bc6[3]	
2	...	♘d2	♘gf3	g3[5]	♗g2	0-0	h3	b3[8]	♗b2	=
	d5	e5[4]	♗d6	♘f6[6]	0-0	♗g4[7]	♗h5	♘bd7	♖e8[9]	
3	c4	d4	de[11]	♕d4	♘d2	♗xd2	♕d5	♕xd2	0-0-0	∞
	e5	♘f6[10]	♘xe4	♗b4+	♘xd2	c5	♗xd2+	0-0	♘c6[12]	
4	...	♘f3	♘c3[13]	♘xe5	♗e2	♘d3	dc	0-0[14]	cd	±
	...	♘f6	♗b4	0-0	♖e8	♗xc3	♘xe4	d5	♕xd5[15]	
5	...	cd	ed	♕a4+[17]	♘c3	d4[19]	♕b3	♗g5	♗xf6	∞
	d5	cd	♘f6[16]	♘bd7[18]	g6	♗g7	0-0	♘b6	♗xf6[20]	
6	...	...	...	♗b5+	♘c3	♕a4[23]	♘f3	0-0	♗xd7	∞
	...	...	...	♘bd7[21]	a6[22]	g6[24]	♗g7	0-0	♗xd7[25]	
7	♘c3	♘f3	h3	♕xf3	d3[28]	♗d2	g4	h4	a3	±
	d5	♗g4[26]	♗xf3	♘f6[27]	e6	♘bd7	g6[29]	♗b4	♗a5[30]	
8	...	...	...	ed[31]	♗b5+[32]	g4	♘e5	d4	h4	∞
	...	...	...	cd	♘c6	♗g6	♖c8[33]	e6	f6[34]	

---

1 e4 c6 2 ♘c3 d5 3 ♘f3 ♗g4 4 h3 ♗h5 5 ed cd 6 ♗b5+ ♘c6 7 g4 ♗g6 8 ♘e5 ♖c8 9 d4 e6

	10	11	12	13	14	15	16	17	18	
9	♕e2	h4	h5	f3[35]	♘xc6[36]	♗xc6[37]	0-0[38]	bc	♗d2[39]	=
	♗b4	♘e7	♗e4	0-0	♘xc6	♖xc6	♗xc3	♖xc3	♖xc2[40]	

---

[1] **3 f4 ef 4 ♗xf4 d5** =
   3 g3 g6 4 d4 ♘f6! 5 ♘c3 ♕a5 6 ♗g2 d6 = Dolmatov-Kasparov, USSR 1978

[2] **4 ... ♘f6 5 ♗g2 ♗e7 6 0-0 0-0 7 h3 ♘bd7 8 ♘bd2 ♖e8 9 a4 ♗f8 10 a5 d5** = Ljubojević-Bilek, Bath 1973

[3] 11 c3 b6 12 ♖d1 ♗a6! =/∓ Zakharov-Kasparov, USSR 1978

[4] 3 ... g6 4 ♘gf3 ♗g7 5 ♗e2 e5 6 0-0 ♘e7 7 b4 ∞/± Ljubojević-Speelman, London 1980, and Ljubojević-Hübner, Lucerne Ol 1982

[5] 5 ♗e2 ♘e7 6 0-0 0-0 7 ♖e1 f5 = Ljubojević-Lobron, Indonesia 1983

[6] 5 ... f5 6 ♗g2 ♘f6 7 0-0 0-0 8 c3 ♔h8 ∞ Hübner-Miles, Tilburg 1986

[7] 7 ... ♖e8 8 ♖e1 ♘bd7 = Ljubojević-Portisch, Bugojno 1978, and Ljubojević-Karpov, Buenos Aires 1980

[8] 9 c3 ♘bd7 10 ♕c2 a5 11 a4 ♖e8 12 ♖e1 ♗f8 13 ♘f1 de 14 de ♘c5 = Romanishin-Psakhis, USSR 1983

[9] 11 ♕e2 a5 12 a3 ♕e7 13 ♖fe1 ♗c7 14 ♕f1 de 15 de ♕c5 = Belyavsky-Bagirov, USSR 1978

[10] 3 ... ♗b4+ 4 ♗d2 ♗xd2+ 5 ♕xd2 d6 6 ♘c3 ♘f6 7 f4 ± Tal-Nei, Pärnu 1971

[11] 4 ♘c3 ♗b4 5 de ♘xe4 ∞ Tal-Garcia Gonzalez, Sochi 1986

[12] 11 f4 d6 12 ed ♘d4 13 ♘f3 ♗g4 14 ♘xd4 ♗xd1 15 ♘f5 ⯑ Ivanchuk-Epishin, USSR 1982

[13] 4 ♘xe5 d6 5 ♘f3 ♘xe4 =

[14] 9 ♘f4 d6 10 0-0 ♘d7 11 ♗e3 ♘df6 12 ♖e1 ♗f5 ∞ Belyavsky-Garcia Gonzalez, Sochi 1986

[15] 11 ♗e3 ♘d7 12 ♘f4 ± Gheorghiu-Mednis, Riga IZ 1979

[16] 4 ... ♕xd5 5 ♘c3 ♕d6 6 d4 ♘f6 7 ♘ge2 (7 ♘f3 e6 8 ♗d3 ♗e7 9 0-0 0-0 10 a3 ♘c6 11 ♗c2 ♖d8 = Dolmatov-Douven, Amsterdam 1986) 7 ... e6 8 g3 ♗e7 (8 ... ♗d7 9 ♘f4 ♕b6 10 ♗g2 ♗c6 = Mestel-Dlugy, London 1986) 9 ♗g2 0-0 10 0-0 ♖d8 11 ♕c2 ♕a6 12 ♗e3 ♘c6 = Nunn-Miles, Biel 1986

[17] 5 ♘c3 ♘xd5 6 ♘f3 (6 ♗c4 ♘b6 7 ♗b3 ♗f5 =) 6 ... ♘c6 (6 ... ♘xc3 7 bc g6 8 h4?! ♗g7 9 h5 ♘c6 ∞ A.Sokolov-Karpov, match 1987; 8 d4 ♗g7 9 ♗d3 ♘c6 10 0-0 0-0 11 ♖e1 ♗g4 12 ♗e4 ♖c8 13 ♗g5 ± Nunn-Petrosian, Tilburg 1982) 7 ♗b5 (7 d4 ♗g4 – Panov-Botvinnik) 7 ... e6 8 0-0 ♗e7 9 ♘e5 ♗d7 =

[18] 5 ... ♗d7 6 ♕b3 ♘a6! ∞ Vizhmanavin-Smagin, Moscow Ch 1984

[19] 7 g3 ♗g7 8 ♗g2 0-0 9 ♘ge2 ♘b6 10 ♕b3 a5 ⯑

7 ♘f3 ♗g7 8 ♕b3 a6 9 a4 ♘b6 10 ♗c4 ♘xc4 11 ♕xc4 0-0 intending ... b5 ⯑

[20] 11 ♘f3 ♗g7 12 ♗e2 e6 ⯑ Larsen-Karpov, Montreal 1979

[21] 5 ... ♗d7 6 ♗c4 ♕c7 7 d3 (7 ♕b3? b5 ∓∓; 7 ♗b3 ♘xd5 =) 7 ... b5 8 ♗b3 a5 9 a3 ♘a6 10 ♘c3 ±

[22] 6 ... g6 7 d4 ♗g7 8 d6 ed 9 ♕e2+ ♕e7 10 ♗f4 ♕xe2+ 11 ♗xe2 ♘e7 12 ♗f3 ∞/± Smagin-Vizhmanavin, USSR 1984

[23] 7 ♗a4 b5 =

7 ♗xd7+ ♕xd7 8 ♕b3 ♕g4 ∞

[24] 7 ... ♖b8 8 ♗xd7+ ♗xd7 9 ♕f4 ±

[25] 10 ... ♕xd7 11 ♕xd7 ♗xd7 12 ♖e1 ♖fe8 13 d4 ♖ad8 14 ♗g5 ∞/±

10 ... ♗xd7 11 ♕b3 (11 ♕h4 h6! 12 ♖e1 ♗c8 13 h3 g5 ⯑ Glek-Meduna, Prague Z 1985) 11 ... b5 12 d4 ♗c8! 13 ♗g5 ♗b7 14 ♗xf6 ♗xf6 15 a4 ♕d6 16 ab ab 17 ♖xa8 ♖xa8 18 ♕xb5 ♗a6 19 ♕a4 ♕b8 ⯑ Markovich-Shakarov, corr. 1986

[26] 3 ... de 4 ♘xe4 ♗g4 (4 ... ♘f6 5 ♘xf6+ gf 6 d4 – 2 d4) 5 h3 ♗h5 6 ♘g3 ♗xf3 (6 ... ♗g6 7 h4 h6 8 ♘e5 ±) 7 ♕xf3 ±

[27] 5 ... de 6 ♘xe4 ♘d7 7 d4 ±

5 ... e6 6 d4 de 7 ♘xe4 ♘xd4 8 ♗d3 ♘f6 9 ♗e3 (9 c3 ♕d8 10 0-0 ♗e7 11 ♖d1 ⯑ Korchnoi-Spassky, USSR Ch 1959) 9 ... ♕d8 (9 ... ♗b4+ 10 ♔e2 ♕d8 11 ♖hd1 ⯑) 10 0-0-0 ♘bd7 11 ♗c4 ⯑ Boleslavsky-Flohr, USSR Ch 1950

[28] 6 d4 de 7 ♕e3 ♕a5 (7 ... ♘d5 8 ♕xe4 ♘xc3 9 bc ±; 7 ... ♘bd7 8 ♘xe4 ♘xe4 9 ♕xe4 ♘f6 10 ♕d3 ± Fischer-Keres, Bled 1961) 8 ♗d2 ♕f5 9 g4 ♕f3 10 ♖g1 e6 11 g5 ♕xe3+ 12 fe ±

[29] 8 ... h6 9 h4 ♘e5 10 ♕g3 ♘exg4 11 e5 ♗c5 12 ♘d1 ♕c7 13 f4 ± Timman-Miles, Amsterdam 1985

8 ... ♗b4 9 a3 ♗a5 10 g5 ♘g8 11 h4 d4 12 ♘b1 ±

[30] 11 ♗h3 d4 12 ♘b1 ♗xd2+ 13 ♘xd2 ♕c7 14 0-0-0 ± Tseshkovsky-Razuvayev, USSR Ch 1980-81

[31] 5 ♗e2 de 6 ♘xe4 ♘d7 =

[32] 6 d4 ♘c6 7 g4 ♗g6 8 ♘e5 e6 9 h4 ♘xe5 10 de ♗b4 11 h5 ♗e4 ∞ Ghinda-Lobron, Lucerne Ol 1982

[33] 8 ... ♕d6 9 d4 f6 10 ♘xg6 hg 11 ♕d3 0-0-0 (11 ... ♔f7? 12 ♗xd5) 12 ♗xc6 ♕xc6 13 ♕xg6 ±

[34] 11 ♘xg6 hg 12 ♕d3 (12 ♗d3 f5 ⯑ Kupreichik-Christiansen, Hastings 1981-82) 12 ... ♔f7 13 h5 (13 ♗xc6!? ♖xc6 14 ♗d2) 13 ... gh 14 gh ♘ge7 15 ♗e3 ♘f5 ⯑ Fischer-Smyslov, Yugoslavia 1959

[35] 13 0-0 0-0 14 ♗xc6 ♗xc3 15 bc (15 ♗xb7? ♗xb2! 16 ♗xb2 ♖xc2 17 ♕b5 ♘f5 ⯑) 15 ... ♘xc6 16 ♘xc6 ♖xc6 17 f3 – 13 f3

[36] 14 fe? ♘xd4 15 ♕d3 ♗xc3+ 16 bc ♘xb5 17 ♕xb5 ♕c7 ∓∓

[37] 15 ♗e3 ♕f6 16 fe ♘xd4 17 ♗xd4 ♕xd4 18 ♖d1 (18 ♕d3 ♕e5 ⯑) 18 ... ♗xc3+ 19 bc ♕xc3+ 20 ♔f1 (20 ♖d2 de 21 0-0 ♖c5 ⯑ Grefe-Commons, US Ch 1975) 20 ... de 21 ♕xe4 f5! ⯑ van der Wiel-Timman, Amsterdam 1986

[38] 16 ♔f1 f5 17 fe fe+ 18 ♔g2 ♗xc3 19 bc ♖xc3 ⯑

16 ♖d1 ♕b6 17 ♗e3 (17 fe? ♖xc3) 17 ... ♗xc3 18 bc ♖xc3 19 fe de ∞/⯑ Shakarov

[39] 18 fe ♖g3+ 19 ♔f2 ♕h4 ⯑

[40] 19 fe de 20 ♖fc1 ♕xd4+ 21 ♗e3 ♖xe2 22 ♗xd4 (intending g5) 22 ... h6 23 ♗xa7 ♖a8 ½-½ Bobkov-Shakarov, corr. 1982

	3	4	5	6	7	8	9	10	11	
1	f3[1]	fe	♘f3	c3[3]	♗d3	♕e2	♘bd2	0-0		≐
	de	e5	♗e6[2]	♘f6	♘bd7	♗d6	♕e7	0-0-0[4]		
2	...	♘c3	♗e3	♖b1[5]	fe	♘f3	♘xd4	♗c4	0-0	=
	g6	♗g7	♕b6	de[6]	e5	ed[7]	♕c7	♘f6	0-0[8]	
3	...	♘c3[9]	♘e2[11]	fe	♘g3	♕f3	♗e3	♗d3	♗g1	∞/∓
	e6	♗b4[10]	de	♕h4+	♘f6	e5	0-0	♘g4	ed[12]	
4	e5	c3[14]	♗e3	♘d2	f4	♘gf3	♘xe5	fe	♕h5[16]	=
	♗f5[13]	e6	♘d2[15]	♘e7	f6	fe	♘xe5	♘g6	♕b6[17]	
5	...	♘e2	♘g3[18]	h4	♗e2	c3[20]	♗e3[21]	dc	0-0	=
	...	e6	♗g6	h5[19]	c5	♘c6	♕b6	♕xb2	0-0-0[22]	
6	...	h4	c4[24]	♘c3	♗xc4	♘ge2	♘g3	♘ce4		∞
	...	h5[23]	e6[25]	dc[26]	♘d7	♗e7[27]	♗g6	♘h6[28]		
7	...	♘c3	g4	♘ge2	h4[31]	h5	de	f4	♘d4	±/∞
	...	e6[29]	♗g6	f6[30]	fe	♗f7	♘d7	♕b6	0-0-0[32]	
8	...	...	...	...	♗e3	dc	♘d4	♗b5	♗a4	∓
	...	...	...	c5	♘c6[33]	♘xe5[34]	♘d7[35]	a6	♗xc5[36]	
9	...	...	...	...	h4	♘xd4	♗b5+[38]	f4[39]	f5	∞
	...	...	...	...	cd[37]	h5	♘d7	hg	♖xh4[40]	
10	...	...	...	...	...	♗e3[41]	♕d2[42]	h5[44]	0-0-0	∞
	...	...	...	...	h6	♕b6	♘c6[43]	♗h7	c4[45]	
11	ed	♗d3	c3	♗f4[47]	♘f3	0-0	♘bd2	♗e3	♘b3	±
	cd	♘c6	♘f6[46]	g6[48]	♗g7	0-0	♘h5[49]	f5[50]	f4[51]	

[1] Tartakower

[2] 5 ... ed 6 ♗c4 ♗b4+ 7 c3 dc 8 ♗xf7+ ♔e7 9 ♕b3 ±
    5 ... ♗g4 6 ♗c4 ♘d7 7 c3 b5 8 ♗b3 ♘gf6 9 0-0 ±

[3] 6 ♗g5 ♗e7 7 ♗xe7 ♕xe7 8 ♘c3 ♗g4 9 ♗c4 ♘d7 10 d5 ♘gf6 ∞ Murei-Seirawan, New York 1985

[4] Kasparian-Kholmov, USSR 1949

[5] 6 ♕d2 ♕xb2 7 ♖b1 ♕a3 8 ed ♘f6 9 dc bc 10 ♘c4 0-0 11 ♘ge2 ♘bd7 12 0-0 ♘b6 13 ♗b3 ♗a6 = Geenen-Watson, Brussels 1986

[6] 6 ... ♘f6 7 e5 ♘g8 8 f4 h5 9 ♗d3 ♘h6 10 ♘f3 ♗f5 ∞ Geenen-Miles, Geneva 1986

[7] 8 ... ♘d7 9 ♗c4 ♘gf6 10 ♕e2 ♕c7 11 ♗xf7+! ♔xf7 12 ♕c4+ ± Barczay-Spiridonov, Zrenyanin 1980
    8 ... ♗g4 9 ♕d2 ♗xf3 10 de ±

[8] Barczay

[9] 4 ♗e3 de 5 ♘d2 ef 6 ♘gxf3 ♘f6 7 ♘c4 (7 ♘e5 ♘bd7 8 ♕f3 ♗d6! 9 ♘dc4? ♘xe5

[10] de ♗xe5 ∓) 7 ... ♗e7 8 ♗d3 0-0 ∞/∓

[10] 4 ... ♘f6 5 e5! (5 ♗g5 h6 6 ♗h4 ♕b6 7 a3 c5! ∓ Smyslov-Botvinnik, match (15) 1958) 5 ... ♘fd7 6 f4 – French

[11] 5 ♗d3 de 6 ♗xe4 f5 ∓

[12] 12 ♗xd4 c5 13 ♗f2 ♘c6 ∞/∓ Fernandez-Hodgson, Seville 1986

[13] 3 ... c5 4 dc e6 (4 ... ♘c6 5 ♗b5) 5 ♗e3 ♘e7 6 c3 ♘f5 7 ♗d4 ♕c7 8 ♗d3 ±
    3 ... ♘a6 4 c3 ♘c7 5 ♗d3 ±

[14] 4 g4 ♗e4 5 f3 ♗g6 6 h4 h5 ∓
    4 ♗d3 ♗xd3 5 ♕xd3 e6 6 ♘c3 ♕a5 7 ♘e2 ♕a6 8 ♕h3 ♘e7 =
    4 c4 e6 5 ♘c3 dc 6 ♗xc4 ♘d7 =
    4 ♘f3 e6 5 ♗e2 c5 6 0-0 ♘c6 = Vogt-Kasparov, Baku 1980

[15] 5 ... ♕b6 6 ♕b3 ♘d7 7 ♘d2 h5 8 f4 ♘h6 9 ♘gf3 ♗e7 10 h3 f6 11 ♗e2 0-0 = Yudasin-Bagirov, USSR 1984

[16] 11 ♗e2 ♗e7 12 0-0 ♗g5 ∓ Tal

[17] 12 b4 ♗e7 = Zaichik-Tal, Tbilisi 1986

[18] 5 ♘f4 c5 = Ciocaltea-Golombek, Moscow

1956

[19] 6 ... h6 7 h5 ♗h7 8 ♗d3 ♗xd3 9 cd (9 ♕xd3
c5 =) 9 ... ♕b6 10 ♗e3 c5 (10 ... ♕xb2 11 ♘d2 ∞
Kuzmin-Bordonada, Nice Ol 1974) 11 dc ♗xc5
12 d4 ♗f8 13 0-0 ♘c6 14 ♘c3 f5 = Grünfeld-
Campora, Graz 1981

[20] 8 f4 ♘c6 9 dc ♗xc5 10 ♗d3 ♕b6 ∓ Bellin-
Seirawan, Hastings 1979-80

8 dc ♗xc5 9 ♘d2 ♘c6 10 ♘b3 ♗b6
11 ♗xh5 ♘xe5 = Bronstein-Botvinnik, USSR
1966

[21] 9 ♘xh5 ♗xh5 10 ♗xh5 g6 11 ♗f3 ♖xh4 ∓
Espig-Vadasz, Trnava 1979

[22] 12 ♕h3 ♕xb3 13 ab a6 ½-½ Spassky-
Dzindzihashvili, 1978

[23] 4 ... c5 5 dc ♘c6 6 ♗b5 ± Nunn-Lobron,
Wijk aan Zee 1985

[24] 5 ♘e2 e6 6 ♘g3 ♗g6 – 4 ♘e2
5 ♗d3 ♗xd3 6 ♕xd3 e6 = Spassky-Larsen,
Bugojno 1982

[25] 5 ... ♗xb1?! 6 ♖xb1 ± Spassky-Seirawan,
London 1982

[26] 6 ... ♗e7!? 7 ♘f3 ♗g4 Nunh-Miles, Amsterdam 1985

[27] 8 ... ♘b6 9 ♗b3 ♘e7 10 ♗g5 ♕d7 11 0-0
♘ed5 12 ♘g3 ♗g6 13 ♘ce4 ± Spassky-Lobron,
Hamburg 1982

[28] 11 ♘g5?! ♕a5+ 12 ♗d2 ♗b4 ∓ Chandler-
Speelman, British Ch 1985

11 ♗g5 ♗xe4 12 ♘xe4 ♘f5 ∞

[29] 4 ... h5 5 ♗d3 ♗xd3 6 ♕xd3 e6 7 ♘f3
♘h6 8 0-0 ♘f5 9 ♘e2 ± Nunn-Dlugy, London
1986

4 ... ♕d7 5 ♗e3 h6 6 h3 e6 7 g4 ♗h7 8 f4
♗b4 9 ♘e2 ♘e7 10 a3 ± van der Wiel-Hort,
Wijk aan Zee 1986

4 ... ♕b6 5 g4 ♗d7 6 ♘a4 ♕c7 7 ♘c5
e6 8 ♘xd7 (8 ♗d3 h5 ∓ Klinger-Hodgson,
Oakham 1984) 8 ... ♘xd7 9 f4 c5 ∞ Velimirović-
Kasparov, Moscow IZ 1982

[30] 6 ... ♗b4 7 h4 ±

6 ... ♗e7 7 ♗e3 ♘d7 8 ♕d2 ±

[31] 7 ♘f4 fe 8 ♘xe6 (8 ♘xg6 hg 9 de ♘d7
10 ♗f4 ♕b6 11 ♕d3 0-0-0 12 0-0-0 ♗b4 ∓;
8 de ♗f7 9 ♘e2 ♘d7 ∓) 8 ... ♕e7 9 ♗xf8 ed+
10 ♗e2 dc 11 ♘xg6 hg 12 ♕d3 ♘f6 13 ♕xc3
♘bd7 ∞ Nunn-Andersson, London 1982

[32] 11 ... ♗c5 12 ♘a4 ♕a5+ 13 c3 ± van der
Wiel-Messa, Graz 1981

11 ... 0-0-0 12 a3 c5 13 ♘f3 ♗e7 14 b4 ±/∞
Marjanović-Campora, Niš 1985

[33] 7 ... cd 8 ♘xd4 ♘c6 9 ♗b5 ♘e7 10 f4 a6
11 ♗a4 ♕c7 ∞ van der Wiel-Scheeren, Dutch
Ch 1982

7... ♕b6 8 dc ♗xc5 ∓ Nunn-Seirawan, Wijk
aan Zee 1983; 8 ♕d2!?; 8 f4!?

[34] 8 ... ♕h4 9 ♘b5 ♘xe5 (9 ... ♗e4 10 ♘c7+
♔d7 ∞ van der Wiel-Sosonko, Amsterdam
1982; 9 ... ♘h6 10 h3 ♖c8 11 ♘g3 ♘xe5 ∞

Nunn-Sosonko, Tilburg 1982) 10 ♘g3 ♖c8
11 ♘xa7 ♖xc5 12 c3 ♘f6 13 ♕a4+ ♘fd7
14 0-0 ♗d6 15 ♗e2 0-0 ∞ Klinger-S.Garcia,
Havana 1985

[35] 9 ... ♘c6 10 ♗b5 ♖c8 11 ♕e2 ♘f6 12 0-0-0
♗xc5 13 h4 h5 14 g5 ♘d7 15 ♘xe6! ± Kuijf-
van den Berg, Amsterdam 1982

9 ... ♘f6 10 f4 (10 ♗b5+!? ♘ed7 11 ♕e2)
10 ... ♘exg4 11 ♗b5+ ♔e7 12 ♕e2 ∞ Timman

[36] 12 ♘xe6 fe 13 ♗xd7+ ♕xd7 14 ♗xc5
♘f6 15 ♕e2 ♖c8 16 ♗d4 0-0 ∓ Biro-Berg,
Budapest 1986

[37] 7 ... h5 8 ♘f4 ♗h7 9 ♘xh5 cd 10 ♕xd4
♗xc2 ∞

[38] 9 f4 ♕d7 10 f5 ef 11 gf ♗xf5 12 ♘xf5
♕xf5 13 ♗xd5 ♘c6 ∞ Korolev-Kastarkov,
corr. 1984

[39] 10 ♗g5 ♗e7 11 f4 hg 12 ♕xg4 ♗xg5 13 fg
♗h5 ∞/∓ Hort-Seirawan, Bad Kissingen 1981

[40] 12 ♖g1 ♗h5 (12 ... ♖h5!?) 13 fe fe 14 ♘xe6
♕b6 ∞ van der Wiel-Speelman, Wijk aan Zee
1983

12 ♖f1 ef (12 ... ♖h2? 13 ♗xd7+ ♔xd7
14 ♕xg4 ± Moore-Mills, USA 1984) 13 e6
fe 14 ♘xe6 ♕e7 15 ♕e2 ♖h2! 16 ♕e5 ♘f6
17 ♗f4 ♖xc2 18 ♘c7+ ♔f7 ∞ Kotliar-Retter,
Israel 1986

[41] 8 ♘f4 ♗h7 9 ♗e3 ♘e7 10 dc ♘ec6 11 ♗b5
♘d7 12 ♕e2 ♕c7 13 0-0 ♕xe5 ∞ Korchnoi-
Bivshev, USSR 1951

8 h5 ♗h7 9 ♗e3 ♘c6 10 f4 cd 11 ♘xd4
♘xd4 12 ♕xd4 ♘e7 13 ♗b5+ ♘c6 14 ♕a4
♕c8 15 f5 a6 16 ♗xc6+ ♕xc6 = Kengis-
Korsunsky, USSR 1979

[42] 9 h5 ♗h7 10 dc ♗xc5 11 ♗xc5 ♕xc5
12 ♕d4 ♕a5 13 b4 ♕b6 14 ♕xb6 ab = Oll-
Tukmakov, USSR 1986

9 f4!?

[43] 9 ... ♕xb2 10 ♖b1 ♕xc2 11 ♕xc2 ♗xc2
12 ♖xb7 ±

[44] 10 0-0-0 h5! 11 dc ♗xc5 12 ♗xc5 ♕xc5
13 ♘f4 ♘ge7 ∓ A.Sokolov-Karpov, match
1987

[45] 12 f4 ♕a5 13 f5 b5 ∞ Nunn-Seirawan,
Lugano 1983

[46] 5 ... g6 6 ♘f3 ♗h6!? 7 h3 (7 0-0 ♗f5
8 ♗xh6?! ♗xd3 =) 7 ... ♗f5 8 ♗xh6 ♗xh6
9 ♗xf5 gf ∞ Nunn-Chandler, Wijk aan Zee
1982

[47] 6 ♗g5 ♗g4 7 f3 (7 ♕b3 ♕d7 =) 7 ... ♗h5
8 ♘e2 ♗g6 =

6 h4 e5 7 de ♘xe5 =

[48] 6 ... ♕b6 7 ♕b3 ♕xb3 (7 ... ♗g4 8 ♘a3 ±)
8 ab ±

[49] 9 ... ♗f5 10 ♗xf5 gf 11 ♘e5 ±

[50] 10 ... ♕d6 11 ♖e1 ♗d7 12 ♘b3 ♖ad8
13 ♕d2 ±

[51] 12 ♗d2 ♕d6 13 ♖e1 ♗g4 14 ♗e2 ♖ae8
(Fischer-Czerniak, Netanya 1968) 15 ♘e5 ±

Caro-Kann II   1 e4 c6 2 d4 d5 *continued*

	3	4	5	6	7	8	9	10	11	
12	ed	♗d3	c3	♗f4	♕b3	♘d2	♘gf3	0-0[53]	♘e5	=
	cd	♘c6	♘f6	♗g4	♕c8[52]	e6	♗e7	0-0[54]	♗h5[55]	

[52] 7... ♘a5 8 ♕a4+ ♗d7 9 ♕c2 e6 10 ♘f3 ♕b6 11 a4! (11 ♘bd2 ♗b5 =) 11... ♖c8 12 ♘bd2 ♘c6 13 ♕b1 ± Fischer-Petrosian, World v USSR 1970

7... ♕d7 8 ♘d2 e6 9 ♘gf3 ♗xf3 10 ♘xf3 ♗d6 11 ♗xd6 ♕xd6 12 0-0 (12 ♕xb7 ♖b8 13 ♕a6 0-0 $\overline{\infty}$) 12... 0-0 13 ♖ae1 ♖ab8 14 ♘e5 b5 ∞ Semenyuk-Shakarov, USSR 1981, and Benjamin-Christiansen, US Ch 1981

[53] 10 ♘e5 ♗h5! (10... ♘xe5 11 ♗xe5 0-0 12 ♕c2 ±) 11 ♕c2 ♘xe5 12 ♗xe5 a6 (12...

♗g6? 13 ♕a4+) 13 0-0 ♗g6 = Kasparov-Morgulev, USSR 1977

[54] 10... ♗h5!? 11 ♘e5 ♘xe5 12 ♗xe5 0-0 intending... ♗g6 =

[55] 12 ♖fe1 ♘xe5 13 ♗xe5 ♕c6 = Sznapik-Seirawan, Malta Ol 1980

12 ♕c2 ♗d6 (12... ♗g6 13 ♘xg6 hg 14 ♘f3 ± Browne-Larsen, San Antonio 1972) 13 ♘xc6 ♕xc6 14 ♗e5 ♗g6 = Timman-Hübner, Bugojno 1982

Caro-Kann III   1 e4 c6 2 d4 d5 3 ed cd 4 c4 ♘f6 5 ♘c3

	5	6	7	8	9	10	11	12	13	
1	...	cd[2]	♕b3[4]	♗b5+[6]	♘f3	♘e5	♘xd7	0-0	♖d1[7]	±
	g6[1]	♘xd5[3]	♘b6[5]	♗d7	♗g7	0-0	♘8xd7	♘f6		
2	...	♕b3	cd	♘ge2[8]	g3	♗g2	♘f4	a4[11]	h4	±
	...	♗g7	0-0	♘bd7[9]	♘b6	♗f5[10]	h6	a5[12]	♕d6[13]	
3	...	...	...	♗e2	♗f3	♘ge2[15]	♘f4	♘fe2	♘g3	±
	...	...	...	♘bd7[14]	♘b6	♗f5[16]	g5	g4	♗g6[17]	
4	...	♘f3	cd	♕b3[18]	gf	♕xb7	♗b5+	♕c6+	♕xb5[19]	∞
	♘c6	♗g4	♘xd5	♗xf3	e6	♘xd4	♘xb5	♔e7	♘xc3[20]	
5	...	...	...	...	...	♗e3[21]	♖g1[22]	0-0-0	d5	=
	...	...	...	...	♘b6	e6	g6[23]	♗e7[24]	ed[25]	
6	...	♗g5	♗d2[27]	♗xc4	♘f3[29]	♘d5	♘xe7	0-0	♗g5	±
	...	♕a5[26]	dc[28]	e6	♗e7[30]	♕d8	♘xe7	♗d7	♗c6[31]	
7	...	...	♕d2[32]	c5[34]	♘xe4	♕xa5	♗d2[35]	♗c3	♘e2	=
	...	♗e6	♕a5[33]	♘e4	de	♘xa5	♘c6	0-0-0	♗c4[36]	
8	...	...	c5[37]	♗b5+[38]	♗xc6[39]	♘f3	♗xe7	0-0	bc	=
	...	e6	♗e7	0-0	bc	♘e4	♕xe7	♘xc3	♕c7[40]	

[1] 5... ♗e6 (Basman) 6 ♘ge2 (6 c5 g6 ∞; 6 cd ♗xd5 7 ♘f3 ♘c6 8 ♘xd5 ♕xd5 9 ♗e2 g6 = Hmadi-Miles, Tuniz IZ 1985) 6... dc 7 ♘f4 ♗c8 8 ♗xc4 ± Hebden-And.Martin, British Ch 1985

[2] 6 ♘f3 ♗g7 7 ♗g5 0-0 (7... ♘e4 8 cd ♘xg5 9 ♘xg5 0-0 $\overline{\infty}$) 8 ♗xf6 ♗xf6 9 ♘xd5 ♗g7 10 ♘e3 (10 ♘c3 ♗g4 11 ♗e2 ♘c6 12 d5

♗xf3 13 ♗xf3 ♘a5 $\overline{\infty}$ Pachman-Andersson, Geneva, 1977) 10... ♕a5+ 11 ♕d2 ♕xd2+ 12 ♔xd2 ♖d8 $\overline{\infty}$ Lputian-Gufeld, USSR 1981

[3] 6... ♗g7 7 ♗c4 0-0 8 ♘ge2 ♘bd7 9 ♘f4 ±

[4] 7 ♗b5+ ♘c6 8 ♕a4 ♘xc3 9 bc ♗g7 ∞ Karpov-Miles, Amsterdam 1981

7 ♗c4 ♘b6 8 ♗b3 ♗g7 9 ♘f3 ♘c6 10 0-0 0-0 11 d5 ♘a5 12 ♗g5 ±/∞ Nunn-Seirawan,

London 1984

[5] 7 ... ♘xc3 8 ♗c4! e6 9 bc ±

[6] 8 d5 ♗g7 9 ♘e3 0-0 10 ♖d1 ♘a6 11 ♗e2 ♕d6 12 ♘f3 ♘c5 13 ♕b5 ♘ca4 ∞ Schulz-Miles, West Germany 1983

[7] Ang.Martin-Seirawan, Biel IZ 1985

[8] 8 ♗g5 ♕a5 9 ♗xf6 ef 10 0-0-0 ♘d7 ∞‾ Vasyukov-Bronstein, Kislovodsk 1968

8 g3 e6! 9 de ♘c6 10 ef+ ♔h8 11 ♘ge2 ♕e7 12 ♗e3 ♘g4 ∞‾ Gheorghiu-Johannessen, Havana Ol 1966

[9] 8 ... ♘a6 9 g3 ♕b6 10 ♕xb6 ab 11 ♗g2 ♘b4 12 0-0 ♖d8 13 d6! ± Spassky-Petrosian, match (5) 1966

8 ... ♖e8 (intending 9 g3 e6!) 9 ♘f4 ±

[10] 10 ... a5 11 a4 ♗f5 12 0-0 ♗d3 13 d6 ed 14 ♗xb7 ♖b8 15 ♗f3 ± Hübner-Smyslov, Tilburg 1984

[11] 11 0-0 g5 12 ♘fe2 ♕d7 ∞

[12] 12 ... ♕d7 13 a5 ♘c8 14 ♘a4 ± Suba-Dvoiris, Sochi 1983

[13] 13 ... ♖c8 14 0-0 ♖c4 15 ♕d1 ±

13 ... ♕d6 14 0-0 ♕b4 15 ♕d1 ±

[14] 8 ... a5 9 ♗f3 ♘a6 10 a3 ±

8 ... ♘a6 9 ♗f3 ♕b6 10 ♕xb6 ab 11 ♘ge2 ♘b4 12 0-0 ♖d8 13 d6 ♖xd6 14 ♗f4 ±

[15] 10 ♗f4 ♗f5 11 ♖d1 ♕d7 12 h3 h5 13 ♘ge2 ♖fd8 = Georgadze-Vaganian, USSR 1983

10 ♗g5 ♗g4 11 ♗xf6 ♗xf3 12 ♘xf3 ef 13 0-0 ♕d7 14 ♖fe1 (14 ♖ac1 ♗h6 15 ♖c2 ♗f4 = Botvinnik) 14 ... ♖ad8 ±/=

[16] 10 ... ♗g4 11 ♗xg4 ♘xg4 12 a4 a5 13 0-0 ♕d6 14 ♗f4 ♕b4 15 ♕d1 ±

[17] 14 ♗e2 ♘bxd5 15 ♕xb7 ♖b8 16 ♕xa7 ♘b4 ∞‾; 15 h3 ± Botvinnik

[18] 8 ♗b5 ♖c8 9 h3 ♗h5 10 0-0 e6 11 ♖e1 ♗e7 12 ♗e5 ♘xc3 13 bc ♗g6 = Khasin-Bagirov, USSR Ch 1961

[19] 13 ♘xb5 ♖b8 14 0-0 (14 ♘d4 ♕d7 ‾+) 14 ... ♕b6 15 ♕xb6 ab ‾+

[20] 13 ... ♕d7 14 ♘xd5+ (14 ♕a5 ♘xc3 15 ♕xc3 f6 16 ♗e3 ♔f7 = Tseitlin-Kasparov, USSR 1978) 14 ... ♕xd5 15 ♕xd5 ed 16 0-0 ♔e6 17 ♖e1+ ♔f5 18 ♖d1 ♖d8 19 ♗e3 ± Belyavsky-Wells, London 1985

13 ... ♘xc3 14 bc f6 (14 ... ♕d7 15 ♖b1 ±) 15 ♗a3+ ♔f7 16 ♖d1 ♕c8 17 ♖d7+ ♔g8 ∞ Christiansen-Shamkovich, US Ch 1981

[21] 10 d5 ♘d4 11 ♗b5+ (11 ♕d1 e5 12 de fe 13 ♗e3 ♗c5 14 b4 ♕f6 15 bc ♘xf3+ 16 ♔e2 0-0 17 cb ♖ad8! ∞ Hermlin-Pishkin, corr. 1976) 11 ... ♘d7 12 ♕a4 ♗xb5 13 ♕xb5 g6 ∞ Hübner-Hermann, West Germany 1983-84

[22] 11 0-0-0 ♗e7 12 d5 ed 13 ♗xb6 ♕xb6 (13 ... ab 14 ♘xd5 0-0! 15 ♖g1! ♗f6 16 ♖g4 ± Short-Miles, Brighton 1984) 14 ♕xb6 ab 15 ♘xd5 0-0 (15 ... ♖xa2 16 ♔b1 ♖a5 17 ♗b5 ♔f8 = Ribli-Miles, Indonesia 1982) 16 ♔b1 (16 ♘xe7+ ♘xe7 17 ♖d7 ♖ac8+ 19 ♔b1

♖fd8 =) 16 ... ♗c5 = Ehlvest-Kasparov, USSR 1977

[23] 11 ... ♖c8 12 ♖d1 (12 0-0-0 ♗b4 =) 12 ... g6 13 d5 ♘xd5 14 ♕xb7 ♗b4 15 ♗b5 ♕c7 = Velimirović-Nikolac, Yugoslav Ch 1978

[24] 12 ... ♗g7? 13 d5 ♘xd5 14 ♘xd5 ed 15 ♗c5 ± Sveshnikov-A.Ivanov, USSR 1976

[25] 14 ♘xd5 ♘xd5 15 ♖xd5 ♕c7 16 ♕c3 ♗f6 17 ♕c5 ♗e7 = Sveshnikov-Hodgson, Sochi 1986

[26] 6 ... dc 7 d5 ♘e5 8 ♕d4 ♘d3+ 9 ♗xd3 cd 10 ♘f3 ± Botvinnik-Flohr, match 1933

6 ... ♗g4 7 ♗e2 ♗xe2 8 ♘gxe2 dc 9 d5 ♘e5 10 0-0 ± Tal-Bronstein, USSR Ch 1971

6 ... ♕b6 7 cd ♘xd4 (7 ... ♕xb2 8 ♖c1 ±) 8 ♗e3 (8 ♘f3 ±; 8 ♘ge2) 8 ... e5 9 de ♗c5 10 ef+ ♔e7 11 ♗c4 ± ECO

[27] 7 ♕d2 ♗e6 - 6 ... ♗e6

7 ♘f3 ♗g4 8 ♕b3 (8 ♗e2 dc ‾+) 8 ... 0-0-0 ∞

7 ♗xf6 ef 8 cd ♗b4 9 ♕d2 ♗xc3 10 bc ♕xd5 = Belyavsky-Bagirov, USSR Ch 1978, and Ornstein-Shamkovich, Gausdal 1984

[28] 7 ... ♕d8 8 ♘f3 e6 9 c5 ± Kindermann-Goldenberg, Trouville 1982

[29] 9 d5 ed 10 ♘xd5 ♕d8 11 ♕e2+ ♗e6 12 ♘f4 ♘d4 13 ♘xe6 fe 14 ♕d3 ± Bronstein-Bagirov, Tallinn 1981

[30] 9 ... ♕d8 10 ♗e3 ♗e7 11 0-0 0-0 12 ♘e5 ±

[31] 14 ♖e1 ± Tal-Marović, Malaga 1981

[32] 7 ♘f3 ♘e4 8 ♗xe4 de 9 d5 ef 10 de ♕a5+ 11 ♗d2 ♕e5+ 12 ♗e3 ♗xe6 13 ♕xf3 0-0-0 = Estrin-Flohr, USSR 1960

7 g3 ♕a5 8 ♗g2 ♘e4 9 ♗xe4 de 10 d5 0-0-0 11 ♗d2 ♘b4 ∞ Tal-Hodgson, Sochi 1986

7 ♗xf6 gf 8 ♕d2 ♕a5 9 c5 0-0-0 ∞ Miles-Yusupov, Tunis IZ 1985

[33] 7 ... g6 8 g3 (8 ♗xf6 ef 9 ♗e2 h5 10 ♗f3 ♗h6 11 ♕d1 ♗e7 ∞) 8 ... ♗g7 (8 ... ♘a5 9 ♗xf6 ef 10 c5 ± Sveshnikov-Tseitlin, Sochi 1985; 8 ... ♕a5!? 9 ♗g2 0-0-0 10 ♗xf6 ef 11 cd ♗xd5) 9 ♗g2 ♘a5 10 ♗xf6 ♘xc4 11 ♗xg7 ♘xd2 12 ♗xh8 ♕b6 ∞

[34] 8 ♗xf6 - 7 ♗xf6

8 ♘f3 dc 9 ♗xf6 ef 10 d5 0-0-0 ‾+ Skrobek-Lechtynsky, Pamporovo 1981

[35] 11 ♗b5+ ♘c6 12 ♘e2 0-0-0 13 ♗xc6 bc ‾+ Suba-Hort, Dortmund 1985

[36] 14 ♘g3 ½-½ Ribli-Torre, match 1983

[37] 7 ♘f3 ♗e7 8 ♖c1 0-0 9 c5 - 7 c5

7 cd ed 8 ♗b5 (8 ♗xf6 ♕xf6 9 ♘xd5 ♕d8 =) 8 ... ♗e7 9 ♘ge2 0-0 10 0-0 h6 11 ♗h4 ♘h5 = Suba-Kuijf, Narbonne 1984

[38] 8 ♘f3 0-0 9 ♖c1 ♘e4 10 ♗xe7 ♕xe7 11 ♗e2 ♖d8 12 0-0 e5 13 ♘xe5 ♘xe5 14 de ♘xc3 15 ♖xc3 d4 = Liberzon-A.Zaitsev, USSR Ch 1969

[39] 9 ♘f3 ♘e4 10 ♗xe7 ♘xe7 11 0-0 ♘xc3 12 bc b6 = Suba-Rogers, Malta Ol 1980

[40] 14 ♖e1 f6 = Bade-Shakarov, corr. 1986

	5	6	7	8	9	10	11	12	13	
9	...	♘f3	c5	♗d3[42]	b4	♘a4	♗f4[45]	c6	dc	∞
	e6	♗e7[41]	0-0	b6	a5[43]	♘bd7[44]	ab[46]	♘c5	bc	
10	...	...	cd	♗b5+[48]	♕b3[50]	♕xb5+	♘e5	♘xb5	0-0	±
	...	...	ed[47]	♗d7[49]	♗xb5	♕d7	♕xb5	♘a6	0-0[51]	
11	...	...	cd[52]	♗b5+[53]	♕e2+	0-0	bc	♗d3[54]	♕b2	∞
	...	♗b4	ed	♗d7[49]	♘e4	♗xc3	0-0	♘xc3[55]	♕c8[56]	
12	...	...	...	♕c2	♗d3	0-0	a3[59]	♖d1	♕e2	=
	...	...	♘xd5	0-0[57]	h6	♘c6[58]	♗d6[60]	♘ce7	♗d7[61]	
13	...	...	...	♗d2	♗d3	0-0	a3	♕c2	♗e3[64]	∞
	...	...	...	0-0	♘c6[62]	♗e7[63]	♗f6	h6	♘ce7[65]	

[41] 6 ... ♘c6 7 c5 ♗e7 8 ♗b5 (8 a3 – 1 d4 d5 2 c4 e6 3 ♘c3 ♘f6 4 ♘f3 c5 5 e3 ♘c6 6 a3 cd 7 ed ♗e7 8 c5) 8 ... 0-0 9 0-0 ♗d7 10 ♖e1 ♕c7 11 ♗g5 ♖fd8 12 ♖h4 ♘e8 13 ♗g3 ♕c8 14 ♕e2 ♘h5 = Gobet-Hort, Biel 1984

[42] 8 b4 ♘e4 9 ♕c2 ♘c6 10 b5 (10 a3 e5) 10 ... ♘xd4! 11 ♘xd4 ♗xc5 12 ♘xe4 ♗xd4 13 ♘c3 ♗d7 ∞ Estrin-Borngasser, corr. 1980

[43] 9 ... bc!? 10 bc ♗a6 Skrobek-Spiridonov, Polanica Zdroj 1981

[44] 10 ... ♘fd7 11 h4 (11 b5 bc 12 dc e5! 13 c6 e4 =) 11 ... h6 (11 ... ab 12 ♗xb6 ♘xb6 13 ♗xh7+! ±; 11 ... f5 12 ♘g5 ♕e8 13 ♗b5 ♗a6 14 ♗xa6 ♘xa6 15 b5 ±) 12 ♖h3 e5 13 ♗xh6 ♗f6 (13 ... e4!?) 14 ♗e3 e4 15 ♘g5 g6 16 ♗b5 ±

[45] 11 a3 ab 12 ab bc 13 bc e5 14 ♘xe5 ♗xc5 =

[46] 11 ... ♘h5 12 ♗d2 ab 13 c6 ♘b8 14 ♘e5 f5 15 ♖c1 ± Simagin-A.Zaitsev, USSR 1966

[47] 7 ... ♘xd5! – Semi-Tarrasch

[48] 8 ♗d3 0-0 9 h3 (9 ♘e5 ♘c6 10 0-0 ♘xd4 11 ♗xh7+ ♘xh7 12 ♕xd4 ♗e6 = Speelman-Dolmatov, Moscow 1985) 9 ... ♘c6 10 0-0 ♗e6 12 ♖e1 ♖c8 13 ♗f4 ♕b6 14 ♘a4 ♕d8 14 ♘c5 (14 ♖c1 ♘e4) 14 ... ♘xd4 = Portisch-Larsen, Nikšić 1983

[49] 8 ... ♘c6 9 ♘e5 ♗d7 10 0-0 0-0 11 ♖e1 ±

[50] 9 ♗xd7+ ♘bxd7 10 0-0 0-0 11 ♗g5 (11 ♕b3 ♕a5) 11 ... ♕a5 12 ♘e5 ♖fe8 13 ♕b3 ♘xe5 14 de ♘e4 = Sveshnikov-Dzindzihashvili, Hastings 1978-79

[51] 14 ♗g5 ♖fe8 15 ♖ac1 ± Timman-Benko, Wijk aan Zee 1972

[52] 7 ♗d3 dc 8 ♗xc4 – Nimzo-Indian
   7 ♗g5 ♕a5 =
   7 ♕b3 ♘c6 8 ♗g5 0-0 ∞

[53] 8 ♕a4+ ♘c6 9 ♗b5 0-0 10 0-0 ♕a5 = Peresipkin-Bagirov, USSR 1977

[54] 12 ♗xd7+ ♘xd7 13 c4 ♖e8 14 ♗e3 (14 ♕b2 dc 15 ♕xb7 ♘b6 ∓ Tatai-Larsen, Las Palmas 1977) 14 ... ♗b6 ∓ Nun-Meduna, Trnava 1985

[55] 12 ... ♗f5 13 ♗a3 ♖e8 14 ♕b2 ♕c8 15 ♖fe1 ± Jansa-Hansen, Borgarnes 1985
   12 ... ♖e8 13 ♘e5 ♘c6 14 ♘xd7 ♕xd7 15 ♕b2 ± Meister-Vizhmanavin, USSR 1985

[56] 14 ♕b3 ♗a4 15 ♕a3 ∞ Sveshnikov-Meduna, Sochi 1986

[57] 8 ... ♘c6 9 ♗d3 ♗a5 (9 ... ♘xc3 10 bc ♘xd4 11 ♘xd4 ♕xd4 12 0-0 ♕xc3 13 ♗b5+ ± Nunn-Lobron, Biel 1982) 10 a3 (10 0-0 ♘db4 =) 10 ... ♘xc3 11 bc ♘xd4 ∞ Kindermann-Speelman, Plovdiv 1983

[58] 10 ... ♗e7 11 ♕e2 ♘d7 12 ♘xd5 ed 13 ♘e5 ± Sveshnikov-Dolmatov, Erevan Z 1982

[59] 11 ♖d1 ♗d6 12 ♕e2 ♖e8 13 a3 ♗d7 14 ♘e4 ♗f8 15 ♘e5 f5 16 ♘c3 ♘xe5 17 ♕xe5 ♘xc3 18 bc ♗a4 = Hebden-Burger, New York 1983

[60] 11 ... ♗e7 12 ♖d1 ♗f6 13 ♗h7+ ♔h8 14 ♗e4 ♕d6 15 ♕e2 ♖d8 16 ♗c2 ♕f8 = Speelman-Suba, Hastings 1983-84

[61] 14 ♘e5 ♗xe5 15 de ♘xc3 16 bc ♘g6 17 ♗xg6 fg = Mortensen-Lobron, Plovdiv 1983

[62] 9 ... b6 10 ♘xd5 ♗xd2+ 11 ♘xd2 ed 12 0-0 ±

[63] 10 .., ♘f6 11 ♗g5 ♗e7 12 ♖c1 (12 a3 h6 13 ♗h4 ♘h5 =) 12 ... h6 13 ♗e3 (13 ♗h4 ♘h5 14 ♗xe7 ♘xe7 15 ♗b1 ♘f6 16 ♕d3 ♕b6 = Greenfeld-Shvidler, Beer-Sheva 1985) 13 ... ♘b4 14 ♗b1 b6 15 ♘e5 ♗b7 = Podgayets-Vaiser, USSR 1984

[64] 13 ♖ad1 ♗d7 14 ♘xd5 ed 15 ♕b3 ± Suba-Petrosian, Tallinn 1983; 13 ... ♗xd4!

[65] 13 ... ♘xc3 14 bc e5 15 ♗h7+ ♔h8 16 ♗e4 ed 17 cd ♗g4 18 ♗xc6 ♖c8 = Sveshnikov-Speelman, Moscow 1985
   13 ... ♘ce7 14 ♘e4 ♘f5 15 ♕d2 b6 16 ♖ac1 ♗b7 ∞ Vaganian-Sveshnikov, Sochi 1986

Caro-Kann IV   1 e4 c6 2 d4 d5 3 Nd2 g6

	4	5	6	7	8	9	10	11	12	
1	Ngf3	c3[1]	Nxe4	Bc4[2]	Nxf6+	0-0	Re1	Ne5	Qe2[3]	±
	Bg7	de	Nd7	Ngf6	Nxf6	0-0	a5	Nd5		
2	...	...	Bd3	0-0	Re1[5]	h3[6]				±
	...	Nh6	0-0	Nd7[4]	Re8					

1 e4 c6 2 d4 d5 3 Nc3 g6

	4	5	6	7	8	9	10	11	12	
3	Nf3	h3[7]	Bf4[9]	Nxe4	c3	Bd3	0-0	Re1[11]		±
	Bg7	Nh6[8]	de[10]	Nf5	0-0	Nd7	Nb6			
4	...	...	Bd3[12]	Nxe4	Bxe4	0-0	c3[14]	Bc2	Nxd4	±/=
	...	Nf6	de	Nxe4	Nxe4	0-0[13]	Nd7	c5	cd	e5[15]
5	e5	f4	Be3[17]	Nf3	Be2	Qd2	g3	Bf2	h3	∞
	Bg7	h5[16]	Nh6	Bg4	e6	Nd7	Nf5	Bf8	Bxf3[18]	

[1] 5 Bd3!? de 6 Nxe4 Bxd4 7 Nxd4 Qxd4 8 Bd2 ∞

[2] 7 Bd3 Ngf6 8 Nxf6+ Nxf6 9 0-0 0-0 10 Qe2 ± Savon-Tseshkovsky, Vilnius 1975

[3] 12 Nd3 b6? 13 Bg5 ± Ljubojević-Skembris, Thessaloniki Ol 1984; 12 ... Bf5
12 Qe2 e6 13 Bg5± (13 ... Nc7? 14 Bxe6 Nxe6 15 Nxf7) Ljubojević

[4] 7 ... f6 8 Re1 Nf7 9 c4 ±

[5] 8 e5 Re8 9 h3 f6 10 ef ef = Prasad-Skembris, Dubai Ol 1986

[6] Balashov

[7] 5 Bd3 Bg4 6 e5 e6 7 h3 Bxf3 8 Qxf3 Nd7 9 0-0 Ne7 10 Ne2 c5 = de Firmian-Dzindzihashvili, US Ch 1984
5 Bf4 Bg4?! (5 ... de 6 Nxe4 ±) 6 ed cd 7 Nb5 Na6 8 Bd3 Nf6 9 h3 Bxf3 10 Qxf3 ± Soltis-Brasket, New York 1977

[8] 5 ... de 6 Nxe4 Nd7 7 Bc4 (7 Bd3 Ngf6 8 Nxf6+ Nxf6 9 0-0 0-0 10 Re1 Qd6 11 Bg5± Kottnauer-Hübner, Hastings 1968-69) 7 ... Ngf6 8 Nxf6+ Nxf6 9 0-0 0-0 10 Re1 Bf5 11 Bb3 Qd6 12 Qe2 ± Balashov-Petrosian, USSR Ch 1976

[9] 6 e5 f6 7 Bf4 0-0 8 Qd2 Nf7 9 0-0-0 fe 10 de e6 11 h4 c5 12 h5 Nc6 13 hg hg 14 Re1 c4 15 Rh3 ± Tseitlin-Varlamov, Leningrad Ch 1986

[10] 6 ... f6 7 ed cd 8 Nb5 Na6 9 c4 Nf7 10 cd Qxd5 11 Nc3 Qe6+ 12 Be2 0-0 13 0-0 ± Prandstetter-Nun, Czechoslovak Ch 1986

[11] Stefanov-Grigorev, Varna 1982

[12] 6 e5 Ne4 7 Bd3 (7 Nxe4 de 8 Ng5 c5 9 dc Qa5+ 10 Bd2 Qxc5 11 Bc3 Nc6!

[12 continued] 12 Nxe4 Qb6 = Dvoretsky-Zilberstein, USSR 1973) 7 ... Nxc3 8 bc c5 9 dc (9 0-0!?) 9 ... 0-0 10 Be3 Nd7 11 Bd4 Qc7 12 0-0 Nxe5 ∞ Chandler-Gufeld, Hastings 1986-87

[13] 8 ... Bf5 9 Bxf5 Qa5+ 10 c3 Qxf5 11 0-0 Nd7 (11 ... 0-0 12 Re1 Re8 13 Bg5 e6 14 Re5! ±) 12 Re1 e6 13 Qb3 ± Lobron-Grünfeld, Lucerne 1979

[14] 10 Bg5 h6 (10 ... Re8 11 c3 Qb6 12 Qd2 ± de Firmian-Seirawan, Wijk aan Zee 1986) 11 Be3 c5 12 dc Qc7 13 Qe2 Rb8 14 Qb5 Nf6 15 Bd3 e5 ∞ Chandler-Christiansen, Thessaloniki Ol 1984
10 Re1 c5 11 c3 cd 12 cd (12 Nxd4!?) 12 ... Nf6 13 Bc2 b6 (13 ... Be6 14 Rxe6! ± Mariotti-Tseshkovsky, Manila IZ 1976) 14 Bf4 Bb7 =

[15] 13 Nb5 a6 14 Nd6 ± Bronstein-Tseshkovsky, USSR Ch 1974

[16] 5 ... Nh6 6 Nf3 Bg4 7 h3 (7 Be2 f6 8 Be3 0-0 9 0-0 Nf5 10 Bf2 Bxf3 11 Bxf3 fe 12 de e6 ∞ Sveshnikov-Yurtayev, USSR Ch 1983) 7 ... Bxf3 8 Qxf3 Qb6 9 Ne2 f6 10 g4 fe 11 de Na6 12 Bg2 0-0-0 13 Be3 d4 14 Bf2 Rhf8 15 0-0 Qxe5 16 c3 ± Sveshnikov-Orlov, USSR 1986

[17] 6 Nf3 Bg4 7 h3 Bxf3 8 Qxf3 e6 9 g3 (9 Be3 Qb6! 10 0-0-0 h4 ∞) 9 ... Qb6 10 Qf2 Ne7 11 Bd3 Nd7 12 Ne2 0-0-0 13 c3 f6 = Fischer-Petrosian, World v USSR 1970

[18] 13 Bxf3 h4 (13 ... Bb4 14 a3 Qa5 ∞ Pasman-Ciocaltea, Beer-Sheva 1982) 14 g4 Ng3 15 Rg1 Qb6 16 0-0-0 Qa6 ∞ Arnason-Christiansen, Reykjavik 1986

	4	5	6	7	8	9	10	11	12	
6	e5	f4	♗e3	♘f3	h3	♕xf3	♗d3	0-0	♗f2	±
	♗g7	h5	♘h6	♗g4	♗xf3	h4[19]	e6	♘f5	♘d7[20]	

[19] 9 ... ♕b6 10 ♖b1 ♘f5 11 ♗f2 ♘xd4 12 ♕d3 ± A.Sokolov

[20] 13 ♘e2 ♗f8 14 b3 ♗a3 (14 ... ♕a5 15 a3 b5 16 c4 ± A.Sokolov-Seret, Thessaloniki Ol 1984) 15 ♖ab1 ♗e7 16 c4 ± Gagarin-Lyubimov, USSR 1985

Caro-Kann V   1 e4 c6 2 d4 d5 3 ♘c3 de 4 ♘xe4 ♘f6 5 ♘xf6+[1] ef

	6	7	8	9	10	11	12	13	14	
1	♗c4[2]	♘e2[3]	0-0	♗f4	♗d3[5]	c3	♗xd6	♕d2	♖fe1	±
	♗d6	0-0	♘d7[4]	♘b6	♗e6	♘d5	♕xd6	♖ad8	g6[6]	
2	...	♕e2[7]	♗b3[8]	c3	ab	♗f4	♗g3	♔d2	♘xe2	±/=
	♕e7+	♗e6	♘a6	♗xb3	♘c7	♘d5	a6	♕xe2+	0-0-0[9]	
3	c3	♗d3	♕c2	♘e2	h4	h5	♗h6[11]	0-0-0		±
	♗d6	0-0	♖e8+	g6	♘d7[10]	♘f8	♕c7[12]	b5[13]		
4	...	...	...	...	0-0[14]	♘g3[15]	♕d1	♕h5	♘e4	±
	...	...	...	h6	♕c7	♘d7[16]	♘f8	♗f4	♘h7[17]	

1 e4 c6 2 d4 d5 3 ♘c3 de 4 ♘xe4 ♘f6 5 ♘xf6+ gf

	6	7	8	9	10	11	12	13	14	
5	♗c4[18]	♗f4[20]	♘f3	0-0	♗g3	♖e1	♘h4	c3	♕f3	±/=
	♗f5[19]	e6[21]	♘a6	♘c7	♗d6	♕d7	♗g6	0-0-0	f5[22]	
6	♘e2	♕d3	h3	♘f4	♕b3	c3	♗c4	♕d1	♕f3	±/=
	♗g4[23]	♘a6[24]	♗h5	♗g6	♕b6	♘c7	e6	0-0-0	♗e7[25]	
7	c3	♘e2	♘g3	h4	♗e2	b4	♘xh5	♘f4	♘xg6	±/∞
	♗f5	♘d7[26]	♗g6	h5[27]	♕a5	♕c7	a5[28]	ab	fg[29]	
8	♘f3	♗e2[30]	h3	0-0	c4	d5	dc	♘d4		±
	♗g4	♕c7[31]	♗h5[32]	e6[33]	♘d7	0-0-0	bc			
9	...	c3[34]	g3[36]	♗g2	0-0	♗xh3	a4	a5	b3	±
	♗f5	♘d7[35]	♘b6	♕d7	♗h3	♕xh3	♕h5	♘c4	♘d6[37]	
10	...	...	g3	♗g2	0-0	♖e1	b4	♕a4	♗xf3	±
	...	♕c7	♘d7	0-0-0[38]	e6	♗g4[39]	h5	♗xf3	♔b8[40]	

[1] 5 ♘g3 and now:

   5 ... g6 6 ♘f3 ♗g7 7 ♗e2 0-0 8 0-0 ♕b6 9 b3 a5 = Sax-Larsen, Tilburg 1979

   5 ... c5 6 dc ♕xd1+ 7 ♔xd1 e6 8 b4 a5 ∞ Ivanović-Matulović, Yugoslavia 1980

   5 ... h5 6 h4 (6 ♗g5 h4 7 ♗xf6? hg 8 ♗e5 ♖xh2 9 ♖xh2 ♕a5+ intending ... ♕xe5 ∓) 6 ... ♕c7 7 ♗c4 ♗g4 8 ♘1e2 e6 9 f3 ♗d6 ∞ Kupreichik-Skembris, Zenica 1985

[2] 6 ♗e3 ♗f5 7 ♗d3 ♗d6! 8 ♘f3 0-0 9 ♗xf5 ♕a5+ 10 ♕d2 ♕xf5 11 0-0 c5 12 c4 ♖d8 = Ivanović-Matulović, match 1985

6 ♘f3 ♗d6 7 ♗e2 0-0 8 0-0 ♖e8 9 ♖e1 ♗f5 10 ♗e3 ♘d7 11 h3 ♗e4 = Karpov-Hort, Tilburg 1979

[3] 7 ♕e2+ ♕e7 8 ♕xe7+ ♔xe7 9 ♘e2 ♗e6 10 ♗d3 ♘d7 11 ♗f4 ± Matulović-Smyslov, Siegen Ol 1970

[4] 8 ... ♕c7 9 ♘g3 ♘d7 10 ♕h5 c5 (10 ... ♘b6 11 ♗d3 g6 12 ♕h4 ±) 11 ♘f5 g6 12 ♘h6+ ♔g7 13 ♕h4 ±

[5] 10 ♗b3 ♗g4 11 f3 ♗xf4 12 ♘xf4 ♗f5 13 c3 ± Liberzon-Korchnoi, Lone Pine 1979

[6] 15 ♖ad1 ± Karpov-Korchnoi, match (20)

1978

[7] 7 $\triangle$e2!? $\triangle$c7 8 $\triangle$f3 $\triangle$d6 9 0-0 0-0 10 c4

[8] 8 $\triangle$d3 c5 9 dc $\triangle$xc5 10 $\triangle$f3 $\triangle$c6 11 0-0 $\triangle$d6 ±/= Jovčić-Andersson, Titovo Uzice 1978

[9] Keres-Smyslov, Amsterdam 1971

[10] 10 ... c5 11 h5 f5 12 hg hg 13 g4 ± Vogt-Möhring, Halle 1981

10 ... f5 11 h5 $\triangle$f6 12 hg fg 13 $\triangle$b3+ $\triangle$h8 14 $\triangle$g5! $\triangle$g7 15 0-0-0 ± Sznapik-Plachetka, Bratislava 1983

[11] 12 hg fg 13 $\triangle$h6 (13 $\triangle$b3+ $\triangle$e6 14 $\triangle$xb7 $\triangle$d5 $\overline{\infty}$) 13 ... $\triangle$e6 14 0-0-0 $\triangle$e7 15 $\triangle$h4 $\triangle$f7 ∞ Bednarski-Möhring, Kecskemet 1982

[12] 12 ... f5 13 0-0-0 $\triangle$f6 14 hg hg 15 $\triangle$d2 $\triangle$e6 16 $\triangle$g5 $\triangle$g7 17 $\triangle$g3 $\triangle$xa2 18 $\triangle$h4 ± Tisdall-Chandler, Brighton 1981

[13] 13 ... $\triangle$e6?! 14 c4 c5 (14 ... $\triangle$ad8 15 hg fg 16 c5 $\triangle$e7 17 $\triangle$f4 $\triangle$f7 18 $\triangle$c4 ± Kavalek-Andersson, match 1978) 15 d5 $\triangle$c8 16 hg fg 17 $\triangle$h4 ± Sznapik-Kostro, Poland 1980

13 ... b5 ±

[14] 10 $\triangle$e3!? $\triangle$d7 11 0-0-0 $\triangle$a5 12 $\triangle$b1 b5 ± Jansa-Pedersen, Aarhus 1983

[15] 11 h3 $\triangle$d7 (11 ... $\triangle$e6 12 $\triangle$e3 $\triangle$d7 13 c4 ±) 12 $\triangle$e3 $\triangle$f8 13 $\triangle$ae1 $\triangle$d7 14 c4 c5 15 d5 b6 = Matulović-Cirić, Yugoslavia 1982

[16] 11 ... c5 12 dc $\triangle$xc5 13 $\triangle$h5 $\triangle$g4 14 $\triangle$f4 $\triangle$d6 15 $\triangle$a4 $\triangle$d7 16 $\triangle$d4 ± Hazai-Lechtynsky, Halle 1981

[17] 15 $\triangle$h4 $\triangle$xc1 16 $\triangle$axc1 ± van der Wiel-Pedersen, Aarhus 1983

[18] 6 $\triangle$f4 $\triangle$b6 (6 ... $\triangle$f5 7 $\triangle$c4 – 6 $\triangle$c4) 7 $\triangle$f3 $\triangle$xb2 8 $\triangle$d3 ∞

6 $\triangle$e2 $\triangle$g8 (6 ... $\triangle$f5 7 $\triangle$f3 – 6 $\triangle$f3) 7 $\triangle$f3 e5 8 $\triangle$e2 $\triangle$g4 ∞ Timman-Bellon, Amsterdam 1978

6 $\triangle$d3 $\triangle$a6 7 $\triangle$d2 (7 a3 $\triangle$g4 8 $\triangle$e2 $\triangle$d7 9 $\triangle$e3 $\triangle$c7 ∞ Matulović-Chandler, Vršac 1981) 7 ... $\triangle$e6 8 0-0-0 $\triangle$d6 9 c4 0-0-0 ∞ Lederman-Grünfeld, Israeli Ch 1984

[19] 6 ... $\triangle$c7 7 $\triangle$h5 e6 8 $\triangle$e2 $\triangle$a6 9 $\triangle$f4 ± Jamieson-Tal, Nice Ol 1974

6 ... h5 7 $\triangle$d3 $\triangle$d7 8 $\triangle$f3 $\triangle$b6 9 $\triangle$b3 $\triangle$g4 10 $\triangle$h4 ± Hort-Miles, match 1983

[20] 7 $\triangle$e2 h5 (7 ... e6 8 $\triangle$g3 $\triangle$g6 9 $\triangle$f4 h5 10 h4 $\triangle$d6 11 $\triangle$xd6 $\triangle$xd6 = Unzicker-Marović, Rome 1982) 8 $\triangle$f4 h4 9 c3 e6 10 $\triangle$e2 $\triangle$d6 11 d5 cd 12 $\triangle$xd5 $\triangle$d7 ∞ Rigo-Skembris, Rome 1984

[21] 7 ... $\triangle$b6 8 $\triangle$b3 a5 9 a4 $\triangle$d7 10 $\triangle$f3 $\triangle$a6 11 $\triangle$h4 ± Tal-Larsen, Las Palmas 1977

[22] 15 $\triangle$e5 $\triangle$xe5 16 $\triangle$xe5 $\triangle$he8 ±/= Tal-Larsen, Riga IZ 1979

[23] 6 ... $\triangle$f5 7 $\triangle$g3 $\triangle$g6 8 h4 h5 9 c3 $\triangle$d7 – 6 c3

6 ... h5 7 $\triangle$d3 $\triangle$a5+ 8 $\triangle$d2 $\triangle$f5 9 $\triangle$g3 (9 $\triangle$b3!? $\triangle$h4 10 0-0-0) 9 ... $\triangle$xd3 10 $\triangle$xd3 h4 11 $\triangle$e4 $\triangle$g7 12 c3 ± Maeder-Engel, corr. 1981

[24] 7 ... $\triangle$h5 8 $\triangle$b3 $\triangle$c8 9 $\triangle$f4 $\triangle$g6 10 $\triangle$c4 ± Bednarski-Ermenkov, Varna 1972

[—] 7 ... $\triangle$d7 8 h3 $\triangle$xe2 9 $\triangle$xe2 ± Browne-Kavalek, US Ch 1971

[25] Unzicker-Shvidler, Beer-Sheva 1984

[26] 7 ... e5 8 $\triangle$g3 $\triangle$e6 9 $\triangle$e3 ±

7 ... h5 8 $\triangle$g3 $\triangle$g4 9 f3 $\triangle$e6 (9 ... h4 10 fg hg 11 h4 ±) 10 $\triangle$f4 $\triangle$a5 11 $\triangle$d3 h4 12 $\triangle$e4 $\triangle$d7 13 0-0 ± Estrin-Stecko, USSR 1974

[27] 9 ... h6 10 h5 $\triangle$h7 11 $\triangle$d3 $\triangle$xd3 12 $\triangle$xd3 $\triangle$c7 13 $\triangle$f3 e6 14 $\triangle$f4 ± Adorjan-Hübner, match 1980

[28] 12 ... $\triangle$xh5 13 $\triangle$xh5 a5 14 $\triangle$e2 ab 15 cb e5 16 b5 ±

12 ... e5 13 $\triangle$g3 0-0-0 14 h5 $\triangle$h7 15 $\triangle$g4 (15 $\triangle$b3 $\triangle$b6 $\overline{\infty}$ Peters-Seirawan, US Ch 1984) 15 ... $\triangle$b8 16 $\triangle$e3 ±

[29] 15 cb c5 $\overline{\infty}$ Adorjan-Bellon, Buenos Aires Ol 1978

15 $\triangle$d3 0-0-0 (15 ... bc 16 $\triangle$xg6+ $\triangle$d8 17 g3 ± Liberzon-Pasman, Beer-Sheva 1984) 16 cb e5 17 $\triangle$b1 ±/∞

[30] 7 c3 $\triangle$d7 8 h3 $\triangle$h5 9 g4 $\triangle$g6 10 $\triangle$h4 e6 11 $\triangle$g2 f5 12 $\triangle$xg6 hg ∞ Popchev-Damljanović, Vrnjačka Banja 1985

[31] 7 ... $\triangle$a6 8 0-0 $\triangle$c7 9 c4 ±

7 ... e6 8 $\triangle$f4 $\triangle$d6 9 $\triangle$d2 $\triangle$xf4 10 $\triangle$xf4 $\triangle$xf3 11 $\triangle$xf3 ± Gurgenidze-Bagirov, Tbilisi 1972

7 ... $\triangle$d7 8 $\triangle$f4 $\triangle$a5+ 9 c3 $\triangle$g8 10 $\triangle$h4 $\triangle$h5 11 f3 $\triangle$h3 12 g3 e5 13 $\triangle$e3 ± Spassky-Khaled, Vienna 1986

[32] 8 ... $\triangle$xf3 9 $\triangle$xf3 $\triangle$d7 10 c4 0-0-0 11 0-0?! $\triangle$e5 12 $\triangle$e2 $\triangle$g6 ∞ Popović-Campora, Vršac 1981; 11 $\triangle$c2 ±

[33] 9 ... $\triangle$d7 10 d5 $\triangle$b8 11 c4 $\triangle$b6 12 $\triangle$e3 $\triangle$xf3 13 $\triangle$xb6 ab 14 $\triangle$xf3 ± Smyslov-Pachman, Amsterdam 1964

[34] 7 $\triangle$e2 e6 8 0-0 $\triangle$c7 9 c4 $\triangle$d7 10 d5 $\triangle$g8 11 $\triangle$e3 $\triangle$e4 ∞ Timman-Speelman, London 1980

7 $\triangle$d3 $\triangle$xd3 (7 ... $\triangle$g6 8 0-0 e6 9 c4 ±; 7 ... $\triangle$g8!?) 8 $\triangle$xd3 $\triangle$c7 9 $\triangle$e3 (9 $\triangle$e4!? intending $\triangle$f4) 9 ... e6 10 0-0-0 ±

[35] 7 ... e6 8 g3 $\triangle$e4 (8 ... $\triangle$d5 9 $\triangle$g2 $\triangle$c4 10 $\triangle$h4 $\triangle$d3 11 $\triangle$d2 $\triangle$g6 12 $\triangle$xg6 hg 13 b3 $\triangle$b5 14 $\triangle$b2 ± Kholmov-Bronstein, Moscow Ch 1983) 9 $\triangle$g2 f5 10 0-0 $\triangle$e7 11 $\triangle$e1 $\triangle$d7 (11 ... h5!?) 12 $\triangle$f4 $\triangle$f6 13 a4 ± Chandler-Bellon, Indonesia 1982

[36] 8 $\triangle$f4 $\triangle$b6 9 $\triangle$d3 $\triangle$xd3 10 $\triangle$xd3 $\triangle$xb2 11 0-0 $\triangle$a3 12 $\triangle$fb1 $\overline{\infty}$ Karpov-Miles, Oslo 1984

[37] 15 c4 ± Popović-Korchnoi, Titograd 1984

[38] 9 ... e6 10 0-0 $\triangle$g4 11 $\triangle$f4 $\triangle$d6 12 $\triangle$xd6 $\triangle$xd6 13 $\triangle$b3 0-0-0 14 $\triangle$d2 ± Hecht-Meitner, West Germany 1985-86

[39] 11 ... $\triangle$d6 12 b4 $\triangle$g4 13 $\triangle$a4 ± de Firmian-Miles, Oslo 1984

[40] 15 $\triangle$f4 $\triangle$d6 16 $\triangle$xd6 $\triangle$xd6 17 $\triangle$ad1 h4 12 c4 ed ± Firmian-Conquest, London 1986

	5	6	7	8	9	10	11	12	13	
1	Bd3[1]	Ng5[2]	N1f3	Nxe6[4]	0-0	Bg6+	Bf4	a3	Qe2[5]	∞
	Ngf6	e6[3]	h6	Qe7	fe	Kd8	Qb4	Qxb2		
2	Nf3	Ng3[7]	Bd3	c3[10]	Nxd4	Bc2	0-0	Re1	Be3	=
	Ngf6[6]	e6[8]	c5[9]	cd[11]	Bc5	0-0[12]	Qc7[13]	Rd8	b6[14]	
3	...	Nxf6+	Ne5[15]	Be2	0-0	c4[17]	Be3	f4[19]	Nf3	±
	...	Nxf6	Be6[16]	g6	Bg7	0-0	Ne4[18]	f6	Bf7[20]	
4	...	...	...	Bf4[21]	Bxe5	c4[23]	Qe2	Qxe4	f3	=
	...	...	Nd7	Nxe5	Qd5[22]	Qe4+	Bf5	Bxe4	Bf5[24]	
5	...	...	Bc4	Qe2[25]	Bg5	0-0-0	h3	Qxf3	Bxe7	±/=
	...	...	Bf5	e6	Be7	Ng4[26]	Bxf3	Nd5	Qxe7[27]	
6	Bc4	Nxf6+	c3	Nf3	Qd3	Ne5	Nxg4	g3	Qf3	±/=
	Ngf6[28]	Nxf6	Qc7[29]	Bg4	e6	Bd6	Nxg4	0-0-0	h5	
7	...	Ng5	Qe2	Bb3	N5f3	Bf4[33]	Be5	Nd2	Nf3	=
	...	e6[30]	Nb6	h6[31]	c5[32]	Nbd5[34]	Qa5+	cd[35]	Be7[36]	

	10	11	12	13	14	15	16	17	18	
8	dc[37]	Ne5[39]	Ngf3	0-0[40]	Bf4	Rfe1	Nxe5	Rad1	Bg3	±
	Bxc5[38]	Nbd7	Qc7	0-0	Bd6	Nxe5[41]	b6	Bb7	Rad8[42]	
9	...	...	...	Nxe5	0-0	Bf4[44]	Rad1	c3	Rd2	=
	...	...	Nxe5	0-0	b6[43]	Bb7	Qe7	Rfd8	a6[45]	

---

[1] 5 Qe2 Ndf6 =
   5 Ne2 Ndf6 6 N2f3 Nxe4 7 Nxe4 Bf5 = Panchenko-Speelman, Sochi 1982
   5 Ng5!? – see Kasparov-Karpov, Amsterdam 1988, in the Introduction

[2] 6 Qe2 Nxe4 7 Qxe4 Nf6 8 Qh4 Bf5! =

[3] 6 ... h6 7 Ne6! ± Tal-Oll, USSR 1986

[4] 8 Ne4 Nxe4 9 Bxe4 Nf6 10 Bd3 c5 ±/= Gufeld-Speelman, Hastings 1986-87

[5] Geller-Meduna, Sochi 1986

[6] 5 ... Ndf6 6 Neg5! Bg4 (6 ... h6? 7 Nxf7; 6 ... Bf5 7 Ne5 ±) 7 Be2 (intending Nxf7) 7 ... Bxf3 8 Nxf3 ± Gligorić-Rabar, Yugoslav Ch 1948

[7] 6 Nc3 e6 (6 ... Nb6 intending ... Bf5/ ... Bg4 =) 7 g3 b6 8 Bg2 Ba6 9 Ne2 Be7 = Spassky-Speelman, London 1982

[8] 6 ... g6 7 Bc4 Bg7 8 0-0 0-0 9 Re1 ± Vogt-Garcia Gonzalez, Havana 1985
   6 ... c5 7 Bd3 cd 8 Nxd4 g6 9 0-0 Bg7 10 Re1 ±/= Plachetka-Meduna, Trnava 1982

[9] 7 ... Be7 8 0-0 0-0-0 9 Qe2 b6 10 Bf4 ± Tal-Miles, Cologne 1982

[10] 8 0-0 cd 9 Nxd4 Bc5 10 Nb3 (10 c3 Bxd4 11 cd 0-0 =; 10 Nf3 0-0 11 Qe2 b6 12 Bf4 Bb7 13 Rad1 Nd5 = Ivanović-Speelman, Thessaloniki Ol 1984) 10 ... Bb6 11 Qe2 0-0 12 c4 a5 = Aseyev-Vizhmanavin, USSR Ch 1984

[11] 8 ... Be7 9 0-0 0-0-0 10 Qe2 Qc7 11 Re1 b6 12 Ne5 (12 Ng5 h6 13 Nd2 Bb7 = Zapata-Dlugy, Tuniz IZ 1985) 12 ... cd (12 ... Bb7!?) 13 cd ± Tischbierek-Spiridonov, Calimanesti 1984

[12] 10 ... Ne5 11 0-0 Bxd4 11 cd Bxd4 12 cd Nc6 13 Nh5! ± Bagirov
   10 ... b6 11 Ne4 ± Tseitlin-Bagirov, USSR 1982

[13] 11 ... Ne5 12 Bg5 h6 13 Bxf6 Qxf6 14 Re1 ± Tseshkovsky-Bagirov, USSR 1982
   11 ... Re8 12 Bg5 a6 13 Qf3 ±/= Taulbut-Speelman, Hastings 1981-82

[14] 14 Qe2 Bb7 = Thipsay-Speelman, Brighton 1984

[14] ♘e4!? Speelman

[15] 7 h3 ♗f5 (7 ... e6 8 ♗g5 ♗e7 9 ♗d3 0-0 10 ♕e2 b6 11 0-0-0 ± Spassky-Dlugy, London 1986) 8 ♗d3 ♗g6 = Spassky-Speelman, London 1986

[16] 7 ... ♗f5 8 c3 and now:
8 ... ♘d7 9 ♘xf7 ♔xf7 10 ♕f3 ± Spassky-Donner, San Juan 1969
8 ... e6 9 g4 ♗g6 10 h4 ± Karpov-Hort, Bugojno 1978
8 ... ♗g6 9 h4 ♘d7 10 ♘c4 h5 11 ♗g5 ± Karpov-Spassky, Bad Kissingen 1980

[17] 10 c3 0-0 11 ♖e1 ♘d7 12 ♘d3 ♗f5 13 ♗g5 h6 14 ♗h4 ♖e8 15 ♗f1± Kavalek-Christiansen, US Ch 1985

[18] 11 ... ♕c7 12 ♕c1 ♖ad8 13 ♖d1 ♘d7 14 ♘f3 ± Grünfeld-Christiansen, Philadelphia 1985
11 ... ♘d7 12 ♘f3 ♘f6 (12 ... ♗g4 13 h3 ±) 13 h3 ♘e4 14 ♕c1 ± Belyavsky-Korchnoi, Montpellier C 1985
11 ... ♘e8 12 f4 ♘d6 13 b3 ± Ivanović-Watson, Bor 1986

[19] 12 ♕c2 ♘d6 13 b3 c5! = A.Sokolov-Karpov, match 1987

[20] 14 ♕c2 ♘d6 15 ♗d3± Psakhis-Tukmakov, USSR Ch 1987

[21] 8 ♘d3 g6 9 ♗e3 (9 c3 ♗g7 10 ♗f4 ♕a5 11 ♕d2 0-0 12 ♗e2 e5 = Karpov-Sosonko, Amsterdam 1980) 9 ... ♗g7 10 ♕d2 ♘b6 11 ♘e5 ♗e6 ∞ Timman-Korchnoi, Montpellier C 1985

[22] 9 ... ♕b6 10 ♗d3! ± Larsen-Rogoff, Lone Pine 1978
9 ... ♗f5 10 ♗d3 ♗xd3 11 ♕xd3 ±

[23] 10 ♗e2 ♕xg2 11 ♗f3 ♕g5 ∞

[24] 14 d5 f6 (14 ... e6? 15 dc ± Hulak-Speelman, Wijk aan Zee 1983) 15 ♗c3 e5 16 dc bc =

[25] 8 ♘e5 e6 9 g4 ♗g6 (9 ... ♗e4 10 f3 ♗d5 11 ♗e2! ±) 10 h4 ♘d7 11 ♗f4 ♘xe5 12 ♗xe5 h5 =

[26] 10 ... h6 11 ♗h4 ♘e4 12 g4 ♗h7 13 ♗g3 ♘xg3 14 fg ± Tal-Füster, Portorož 1958
10 ... b5 11 ♗d3 ♗xd3 12 ♕xd3 ♕d5 13 ♔b1 0-0 ∞ Lerner-A.Ivanov, USSR 1977

[27] Fischer-Petrosian, Bled 1961, and Matanović-Petrosian, Yugoslavia v USSR 1969

[28] 5 ... ♘b6 6 ♗b3 ♗f5 7 ♘c5 ♕c8 8 ♘f3 ± Romanishin-Kholmov, USSR 1978

[29] 7 ... ♗f5? 8 ♕b3 ++
7 ... e6 8 ♘f3 ♗e7 9 0-0 0-0 10 ♕e2 ± Tseshkovsky-Meduna, Trnava 1986

[30] 6 ... ♘d5 7 ♘1f3 h6 8 ♘e4 ♘7b6 9 ♗b3 ♗f5 10 ♘g3 ♗h7 11 0-0 ±

[31] 8 ... ♕xd4? 9 ♘1f3 intending ♘e5 ++
8 ... c5 9 dc ♗xc5 10 ♘1f3 h6 11 ♘e4 ♘xe4 12 ♕xe4 intending ♗d2, 0-0-0 ±

[32] 9 ... a5 10 a3 a4 (10 ... g6 11 ♗d2 ♗g7 12 0-0-0 ± Kupreichik-Tukmakov, USSR Ch 1987) 11 ♗a2 c5 12 c3 ♗d7 13 ♘e5 ± Karpov-Petrosian, Tilburg 1982

[33] 10 dc ♗xc5 11 ♘e5 0-0 12 ♘gf3 ♘bd5 13 ♗d2 a5 ∞
10 ♗e3 ♕c7 11 ♘e5 a6 12 ♘gf3 ♘bd5 =
10 c3 ♕c7 11 ♗e3 ♘bd5 =

[34] 10 ... ♘fd5 11 ♗d2 ±
10 ... ♗d7 11 ♘e5 cd 12 0-0-0 ± Kupreichik-Kharitonov, USSR 1984

[35] 12 ... b5 13 c4 bc 14 ♗xc4 ♘b6 15 b4!? ∞ Short-Speelman, Hastings 1988-89

[36] 14 0-0 0-0 15 ♗xd4 ♗d7 16 a3 (16 c4 ♘b4 17 ♘4f3 ♗a4 =) 16 ... ♕c5 17 c4 ♘f4 = Suetin-Filip, Sochi 1973

[37] 10 ♗f4 cd 11 0-0-0 ♘bd5 12 ♗e5 ♕a5 13 ♗c4 ♘c3! ∞
10 ♗e3 a6 11 c3 (11 0-0-0 c4 12 ♗xc4 ♘xc4 13 ♕xc4 b5 ∞ Tseshkovsky-Razuvayev, USSR 1977) 11 ... ♘bd5 12 ♘e5 ♗d6 13 ♘gf3 cd 14 ♗xd4 ♘f4 = Adorjan; 11 c4!? intending 11 ... cd 12 ♗xd4 ♗b4+ 13 ♔f1 Shamkovich, Schiller

[38] 10 ... ♘bd7 11 c6 (11 b4 ♘d5 12 ♗d2 ♕f6 13 ♖b1 a5 14 a3 g5 ∞ Sax-Speelman, Hastings 1983-84) 11 ... bc 12 ♗d2 ♗e7 13 ♘d4 ♕b6 14 ♘gf3 ±

[39] 11 ♗d2 ♘bd7 12 0-0-0 ♕c7 (12 ... 0-0 13 ♘h3 ♕c7 14 g4 ±) 13 ♘h3 g5 14 ♘e1 b6 15 f4 g4 16 ♘f2 ♗xf2 17 ♕xf2 ♗b7 ∞

[40] 13 ♗d2? ♘xe5 14 ♘xe5 ♗xf2+! ++
13 ♗f4 ♘d6 (13 ... ♗b4+!?) 14 0-0-0 ♘d5! (14 ... ♘h5 15 g3 ±) 15 ♗g3 ♘c3! ∞ Chandler-Speelman, London 1986

[41] 15 ... ♘h5 16 ♗d2 ♘c5 17 ♗c4 ±
15 ... ♘c5 16 ♖ad1 b6 17 ♗b5 ± Klovans-Vizhmanavin, USSR 1983

[42] 18 ... ♖fd8 19 c3 ♗d5 20 ♗b1 ♖ac8 21 ♖d4 ♕b7 22 ♘g4 ± Horvath-Chandler, Keszthely 1981
18 ... ♖ad8 19 c3 ♗a8 20 ♗b1 ♕b7 21 f3 ± Gufeld-Dlugy, Athens 1984

[43] 14 ... ♕c7 15 ♘g4 ±
14 ... ♕e7 15 ♗f4 b6 16 ♗g3! ♗b7 17 ♗h4 ±

[44] 15 ♗xh6 gh 16 ♕f3 ♘d5 17 c4 ♕g5 ∞ Mecking-Flesch, Strasbourg 1976
15 ♕f3 ♕c7! = Hübner-Lobron, Biel 1986
15 b4 ♗d6 16 ♗b2 ♗b7 17 ♖fd1 ♕e7 18 b5 ♖ac8 19 a4 ♘d5 ∞ Klovans-Khalifman, USSR 1987

[45] Prandstetter-Speelman, Taxco IZ 1985

1 e4 c6 2 d4 d5 3 Nc3 de 4 Nxe4 Nd7 5 Bc4 Ngf6 5 Ng5 e6 6 Qe2 Nb6 7 Bd3 h6 8 N5f3 c5

	10	11	12	13	14	15	16	17	18	
10	dc	Ne5	Ngf3	Nxe5	Bd2	0-0-0[47]	c3	Bxh6	Bg5[49]	±/∞
	Bxc5	Nbd7	Nxe5	0-0	Qd5[46]	Qxa2	b5	Bb7[48]	b4[50]	

[46] 14 ... Qc7 15 0-0-0 b6 16 g4 ±

[47] 15 0-0 Bd4 (15 ... b5 16 Kh1 Bb7 17 f4 ± Chandler-Speelman, British Ch 1986) 16 Nf3 (16 Bf4 Bxb2 17 Rad1 Qc5! ∓ Khalifman-Tukmakov, USSR Ch 1987; 16 Nc4 Bd7 =) 16 ... Bxb2 17 Rab1 Ba3 18 Nc3 ∞ de Firmian-Dlugy, US Ch 1985

[48] **17 ... gh** 18 Qf3 ± Bielczyk-Szabolcsi, Kikinda 1983

17 ... b4 18 Ng4 Ne8 19 Bxg7 ±

[49] **18 Ng4?** Qa1+ 19 Bb1 Ne4 ∓

18 Nd7 Nxd7 19 Qg4 Qa1+ 20 Bb1 g6 21 Rxd7 Ba3 = Adorjan-Flesch, Hungarian Ch 1975

18 Bb1 Qa4 (18 ... Qa1? 19 Nd7 ± Bielczyk-Zelić, Bugojno 1985) 19 Bg5 ∞

[50] **18 ... Be7?** 19 Nd7 Rfd8 20 Bxf6 Bxf6 21 Nxf6+ gf 22 Qg4+ Kf8 23 Qb4+ Kg7 24 Bxb5 ± Shakarov-Grivainis, corr. 1987

18 ... b4 19 c4 Be7 ∞

Caro-Kann VII   1 e4 c6 2 d4 d5 3 Nc3 de 4 Nxe4 Bf5

	5	6	7	8	9	10	11	12	13	
1	Qf3[1]	Be3[3]	Bd3	Ng5!	Bxg6	0-0-0	Kb1	h4		∞
	e6[2]	Nd7[4]	Bg6	Ngf6	hg	Qa5	Be7			
2	Nc5	Bd3	Nxd3	Nf3[6]	0-0	c4	Re1	Bf4	Nfe5	=
	Qc7[5]	Bxd3	e6	Nd7	Ngf6	Be7	0-0	Bd6	Rfd8[7]	
3	...	Nf3[8]	Bb3	Bd3	Qxd3	c4	Ke2	Rd1	Bf4	=
	Qb6	e6	Nf6	Bxd3	Qa6[9]	Bb4+	Be7	0-0	Nbd7[10]	
4	Ng3	h4[11]	f4[13]	Nf3	h5	Bd3	Qxd3	Bd2	Qe2[16]	=
	Bg6	h6[12]	e6	Nd7[14]	Bh7	Bxd3	Qc7	0-0-0[15]	c5[17]	
5	...	N1e2[18]	h4	Nf4	Bc4	0-0	Bb3	Re1	Bxf7	±
	...	Nd7	h6	Bh7	Ngf6[19]	Nb6	Qc7[20]	0-0-0	e5[21]	
6	...	...	Nf4	Nxg6[23]	Ne4	g3	Bg2	Bxe4	0-0	±
	...	e6	Bd6[22]	hg	Be7[24]	Nf6	Nxe4	Nd7	Qa5[25]	
7	...	...	Nf4[26]	Nxg6[28]	de	Bd2	Qe2	Qxe5+	Nc3	=
	...	Nf6	e5[27]	hg	Qa5+	Qxe5+	Nbd7[29]	Nxe5	Ned7[30]	
8	...	Bc4	N1e2	h4	Nf4	0-0[32]	Nxe6[34]	Bxe6	Re1	∞∞
	...	e6	Nf6[31]	h6	Bh7	Bd6[33]	fe	Qc7[35]	Nbd7[36]	
9	...	...	...	Nf4	Bb3[37]	Qf3	h4[39]	Nxg6	Be3	=
	...	...	...	Bd6	Qc7[38]	Nbd7	e5	hg	0-0-0[40]	

1   5 ♗d3 ♘d7 (5 ... ♕xd4 6 ♘f3 ♕d8 7 ♕e2 ∞)
6 ♘f3 (6 ♕f3 ♗g6 – 5 ♕f3) 6 ... ♘gf6! =

2   5 ... ♕d5 6 ♗d3 ♗xe4 7 ♕xe4 ♕xe4
8 ♗xe4 ±
5 ...♗g6 6 ♗d3 (6 ♘e2!? ♘d7 7 ♗f4) 6 ...
♘d7 (6 ... ♕xd4 7 ♘e2 ∞) 7 ♘e2 ♘gf6 =

3   6 ♗d3 ♕xd4 (6 ... ♘d7 7 ♘e2 ♗g6 8 ♗f4
♘df6 9 ♘g5! ± Tal-Balashov, USSR Ch 1971)
7 ♘e2 ♕d8 8 ♘g5 ♘f6 9 ♗xf5 ♕a5+ ∞

4   6 ... ♘f6 7 ♗xf6+ ♕xf6 8 0-0-0 ±
6 ... ♕a5+ 7 ♗d2!? ♕d5 8 ♗d3 ♕xd4
9 ♘e2 ♕xb2 10 0-0 ∞

5   5 ... b6 6 ♗b3 e6 7 ♘f3 ♗d6 8 g3! ±
Bronstein-Petrosian, USSR 1966
5 ... e5 6 ♘xb7 ♕e7 (6 ... ♕xd4 7 ♕xd4
ed 8 ♘f3 ±; 6 ... ♕b6 7 ♘c5 ed 8 ♘b3 ♗b4+
9 ♗d2 ♘f6 10 ♗d3 ± Arnason-Bonin, New
York 1986) 7 ♘a5 ed+ 8 ♗e2 ♕b4+ 9 ♗d2
♕xb2 10 ♗d3 ± Klovans-Machulsky, USSR
1978

6   8 ♗f4 ♕a5+ 9 c3 ♘d7 10 ♘f3 ♘gf6
11 0-0 ♗e7 = Bronstein-Barcza, Tallinn 1971

7   14 ♕f3 ♘f8 15 ♖ad1 ♘g6 16 ♗g3 ♕a5
17 a3 ♗xe5 18 de ♘h5 = Sigurjonsson-Burger,
Brighton 1981

8   6 g4 ♗g6 7 f4 e6 8 ♗e2 ♗e7 9 h4 h5 10 f5
ef 11 g5 ♘d7! ∓ Bronstein-Belyavsky, USSR
Ch 1975

9   9 ... ♘bd7 10 0-0 ♕c7 11 c4 ♗d6 12 ♗d2
0-0 13 ♗c3 ♖fe8 14 ♖ae1 e5 = Klinger-
Rodriguez, Havana 1985

10   14 ♔f1 c5 = Arnason-Garcia Palermo,
Dubai Ol 1986

11   6 f4 e6 7 ♘f3 ♗d6 8 ♗d3 ♗e7 9 0-0 ♘d7
10 ♔h1 ♕c7 11 ♘e5 ♖d8 12 ♕e2 ♗xd3
13 ♘xd3 0-0 ∓ Marshall-Capablanca, New
York 1927

12   6 ... h5 7 ♘h3 ±

13   7 ♘h3 e5?! (7 ... ♘f6! 8 ♘f4 – 6 ♘1e2)
8 de ♕a5+ 9 ♗d2 ♕xe5+ 10 ♗e2 ♕xb2
11 0-0 ♕xc2 12 ♕e1 ♗e7 13 ♖c1 ♕a4 14 ♘f4
♘d7 15 ♗c4 ± Espig-Böhnisch, East German
Ch 1979

14   8 ... ♗d6 9 ♘e5 ♗xe5 10 fe ± Arnason-
Adianto, Dubai Ol 1986

15   12 ... ♘gf6 13 ♘e5 (13 ♕e2 c5 14 dc ♗xc5
15 0-0-0 ♖c8 ∓ Marjanović-Douven, Amsterdam 1986) 13 ... ♗d6 14 0-0-0 0-0 15 ♘e2 c5
(15 ... ♖fd8!?) 16 ♘xd7 ♘xd7 17 ♔b1 ♖fd8
18 g4 ± Dückstein-Hort, Czechoslovakia 1968

16   13 0-0-0 ♗d6 =

17   14 ♘e5 ♗b6 15 dc ♗xc5 16 0-0-0 ♘f6 =
Hort-Garcia Palermo, Reggiò Emilia 1984-85

18   6 ♘h3 e5?! (6 ... ♘f6! 7 ♘f4 – 6 ♘1e2)
7 de ♕a5+ 8 c3 ♕xe5+ 9 ♗e2 ♘f6 10 0-0
♘bd7 11 ♖e1 0-0-0 12 ♕a4 ±

19   9 ... e6 10 ♕e2 ♗d6 (10 ... ♘gf6 11 ♗xe6 ±)
11 ♘gh5! ±
9 ... e5 10 ♘d3! ed 11 0-0 ♘gf6 12 ♘h5 ±

20   11 ... ♘bd5 12 c4 ♘xf4 13 ♗xf4 e6 14 d5! ±

21   14 ♗e6+ ♔b8 15 ♘d3 ♖xd4 ∞ Ravinsky-
Petrosian, USSR 1950
14 ♘e6!? ±

22   7 ... ♘f6 8 h4 ±
7 ... ♕h4 8 c3 ♗d6 9 ♘gh5 ♗xh5 10 ♕xh5 ±
Popović-Lobron, Sarajevo 1984

23   8 h4 ♕c7 = (9 ♘gh5 ♗xh5 10 ♘xh5 g6 ∓)
8 ♘gh5 ♘f6! = (9 ♘xg7+ ♔e7 10 h4 ♗xf4
11 ♗xf4 h5 ∓)
8 c3 ♘f6 9 h4 ♕c7 10 h5 (10 ♕f3 ♘bd7
11 h5 ♗c2 ∞) 10 ... ♗xf4 11 ♗xf4 ♕xf4 12 hg
fg = Boleslavsky-Petrosian, Zürich C 1953

24   9 ... ♖h4 10 ♕f3 ♘f6 11 ♘xd6+ ♕xd6
12 c3 ± Serper-Khenkin, USSR 1987

25   14 c3 ♘f6 15 ♗g2 ± Byrne-Kavalek, US
Ch 1981

26   7 h4 h6 8 ♘f4 ♗h7 9 ♗c4 e5 (9 ... e6 –
6 ♗c4) 10 ♕e2 ♕xd4 11 0-0 ♘bd7 ∞

27   7 ... ♘bd7 8 ♗c4 e5 9 ♕e2 ± Ljubojević-
Portisch, Tilburg 1978

28   8 de ♕a5+ (8 ... ♕xd1+ 9 ♔xd1 ♘g4
10 ♘xg6 hg 11 ♘e4 ± Fischer-Foguelman,
Buenos Aires 1960) 9 ♗d2 (9 c3 ♕xe5+ 10 ♕e2
♘bd7 11 h4 0-0-0 ∞) 9 ... ♕xe5+ 10 ♗e2
♘bd7 ∞

29   11 ... ♕xe2+ 12 ♗xe2 ♘bd7 13 0-0-0
(13 0-0!?) 13 ... ♗c5 14 f4 0-0 = Tseshkovsky-
Bagirov, Lvov 1978

30   14 ♗c4 ♖h4 15 ♗b3 ♘c5 = Avshalumov-
Kasparov, USSR 1977

31   7 ... ♗d6 8 h4 h6 9 ♘f4 ♗xf4 (9 ... ♗h7
10 ♘gh5) 10 ♗xf4 ±

32   10 ♕e2 ♗d6 11 c3 (11 ♗xe6? 0-0; 11 ♗e3
♘bd7 12 ♘gh5 ♗xh5 13 ♘xh5 ♖g8 14 g4
♕c7 15 g5 ♗g6! ∓ Tal-Botvinnik, match (5)
1960) 11 ... 0-0 (11 ... ♘bd7 12 ♗xe6 ∞ Keres-
Olafsson, Bled 1961) 12 ♘d3 ♘bd7 ∓ Hébert-
Vranesić, Montreal 1981

33   10 ... ♘d5 11 ♕g4 ♘f6 (11 ... ♘d7 12 ♗xd5
cd 13 ♘xd5!) 12 ♕e2 ±

34   11 ♘gh5 0-0 ∓ Bellon-Seirawan, Las
Palmas 1981

35   12 ... ♗xg3 13 fg ♕e7 14 ♖e1 ♗e4 15 ♗f5
0-0 (15 ... ♗xf5!?) 16 g4 ♕f7! = Shakarov

36   14 ♗g8+ ♔f8 15 ♗xh7 ♖xh7 16 ♘f5 ∞
Tal-Botvinnik, match (9) 1960

37   9 h4?! ♕c7
9 0-0 ♘d5! (9 ... ♕c7 10 ♕f3 ♗xc2 11 ♘fh5
♘xh5 12 ♘xh5 0-0 13. ♗h6 ±) 10 ♘gh5 0-0 =
Tal-Botvinnik, match (2) 1961

38   9 ... ♘d5 10 ♘xg6 hg 11 ♘e4 ± Korchnoi-
Petrosian, Stockholm IZ 1962

39   11 0-0 0-0 (11 ... e5 12 ♘xg6 hg 13 c3 ±
Simagin-Dubinin, corr. 1969) 12 h4 e5 ∞
11 ♗e3 0-0-0 12 0-0-0 c5 = Kupreichik-
Chandler, Hastings 1981-82

40   14 ♗xf7? ed 15 ♗xd4 ♘e5 ∓
14 0-0-0 ed 15 ♗xd4 ♘c5 =

Caro-Kann VII   1 e4 c6 2 d4 d5 3 ♘c3 de 4 ♘xe4 ♗f5   continued

	5	6	7	8	9	10	11	12	13	
10	♘g3	♗c4	♘1e2	0-0	f4	♗d3[42]	♕xd3	b3	♗b2	=
	♗g6	e6	♘f6	♗d6	♕d7[41]	♗xd3	g6	♘a6	♗e7[43]	
11	...	♘f3	h4	h5[44]	♗d3	♕xd3	♗d2[45]	0-0-0	♘e4[46]	=
	...	♘f6	h6	♗h7	♗xd3	e6	♗e7	0-0	♘xe4[47]	
12	...	...	♗c4	0-0	♕e2	♖e1	c3[50]	♗g5	♗h4	=
	...	♘d7	e6	♘gf6[48]	♗e7[49]	0-0	♕c7	h6	♖ad8[51]	
13	...	...	♗d3	0-0	c4	b3[54]	♗xg6	♗b2	♕e2	=
	...	...	e6	♘gf6[52]	♗e7[53]	0-0	hg	♕c7[55]	a5[56]	
14	...	...	h4	♗d3	♕xd3	♗d2	0-0-0	♔b1[59]	c4	=
	...	...	h6[57]	♗xd3	♕c7[58]	e6	♘gf6	0-0-0	c5[60]	

[41] **9 ... ♕c7** 10 f5! ef 11 ♘xf5 ♗xf5 (11 ... ♗xh2+ 12 ♔h1 0-0 13 g3 ♗xf5 14 ♖xf5 ♗xg3 15 ♖xf6! ± Keres-Golombek, Moscow 1956; 12 ... ♗xf5 13 ♖xf5 ♗d6 14 ♗h6! ±) 12 ♖xf5 ♘bd7 ±

9 ... ♗f5 10 ♘xf5 ef 11 ♘g3 g6 12 ♖e1+ ♔f8 13 ♕f3 ♕c7 14 b3 ± Hartmann-Lobron, Hanover 1983

[42] **10 ♔h1** h5! ∓ Eolian-Kasparov, USSR 1977

[43] van der Wiel-Seirawan, Baden 1980

[44] 8 ♘e5 ♗h7 9 ♗c4 e6 10 ♕e2 ♘d5 11 0-0 (11 ♗b3!? ♘d7 12 ♗d2 intending 0-0-0) 11 ... ♘d7 12 h5 ♗d6 13 ♖e1 0-0 = Liao-Campora, Lucerne Ol 1982

[45] 11 ♗f4 ♗d6 12 ♗xd6 ♕xd6 13 0-0-0 ♘bd7 = Marjanović-Campora, Bor 1983

[46] **13 ♕e2** a5!? (13 ... ♘bd7 = 6 ... ♘bd7)
13 ♔b1 c5!? (13 ... ♘bd7 – 6 ... ♘bd7)

[47] 14 ♕xe4 ♕d5 = Milanović-Campora, Panchevo 1985

[48] 8 ... ♕c7 9 ♕e2 0-0-0 10 c3 ± Kholmov-Kasparov, USSR 1978

[49] 9 ... ♗d6 10 ♘e5 ♕c7 (10 ... 0-0? 11 ♗xe6) 12 ♖e1 0-0 =

[50] 11 ♗b3 ♘d5 12 c4 ♘b4 13 a3 (13 ♖d1 a5 14 a3 a4!) 13 ... ♘d3 14 ♖d1 ♘xc1 15 ♖axc1 ♖e8 =

[51] Hübner-Portisch, Montreal 1979

[52] 8 ... ♕c7 9 c4 0-0-0 (9 ... ♘gf6 10 ♗xg6 hg 11 ♕e2 ♗d6 12 ♗d2 ♗f4 13 ♗c3 0-0-0 ∞ Chistyakov-Furman, USSR 1960) 10 ♗xg6 hg 11 ♕a4 ♔b8 12 b4 ♘h6 13 ♕b3 ♘f5 14 a4 (14 ♖e1 ♗e7 15 a4 ♗f6 16 ♗b2 g5 ∞) 14 ... e5 ∞ Dückstein-Petrosian, Varna Ol 1962

[53] 9 ... ♗d6 10 b3 0-0 11 ♗xg6 hg 12 ♗b2 ♕c7 13 ♕e2 ♖fe8 14 ♘e4 ♘xe4 15 ♕xe4 ♗e7 = Spassky-Karpov, match 1974

[54] 10 ♖e1 0-0 11 ♗xg6 hg 12 ♗f4 (12 ♕e2 a5 13 ♗f4 a4 16 ♘e5 ♕a5 = Trepp-Garcia Palermo, Dubai Ol 1986) 12 ... ♖e8 13 ♕c2 c5 = Najdorf-Kotov, Zürich C 1953

[55] 12 ... ♕b6 13 ♖e1 ♖fe8 13 ♕c2 c5 = Spassky-Portisch, Montreal 1979

[56] 14 ♖fd1 ♖fe8 15 ♘e4 a4 = Fedoruk-Kasparov, USSR 1978

[57] 7 ... h5 8 ♗d3 ♗xd3 9 ♕xd3 e6 10 ♗d2 ♘gf6 11 0-0-0 ♕c7 12 ♘g5 ± Boleslavsky

[58] 9 ... e6 10 ♗f4 ♘gf6 11 0-0-0 ♘d5 (11 ... ♗e7!?) 12 ♗d2 b5 13 ♔b1 ♗d6 (13 ... ♗e7 14 ♘h5 ♗f6 15 g4 ±) 14 ♘e4 ♘7f6 15 ♖hg1 ± Matanović-Wade, Opatija 1953

[59] 12 c4 0-0-0 (12 ... b5!? 13 c5 ∞) 13 ♗c3 (13 ♔b1 – 12 ♔b1) 13 ... ♗d6 14 ♘e4 ♗f4+ 15 ♔b1 ♘e5! = Szabo-Barcza, Leningrad 1967

[60] **14 ♕e2** ♗d6 (14 ... cd 15 ♘xd4 a6 16 ♘b3! intending ♗a5 ±)15 ♘e4 ♘xe4 16 ♕xe4 ♘f6 17 ♕e2 cd 18 ♘xd4 a6 19 ♗c3 ♖d7! = Smyslov-Botvinnik, match (3) 1958 (by transposition)
14 ♗c3 cd 15 ♘xd4 a6 16 ♘f3 (16 ♘b3 ♘c5 =) 16 ... ♗c5 17 ♕e2 ♗d6 = Spassky-Petrosian, match (1) 1966

Caro-Kann VIII 1 e4 c6 2 d4 d5 3 Nc3 de 4 Nxe4 Bf5
5 Ng3 Bg6 6 Nf3 Nd7 7 h4 h6 8 h5 Bh7 9 Bd3 Bxd3 10 Qxd3

	10	11	12	13	14	15	16	17	18	
1	...	Bf4	0-0-0	Ne5[2]	Qe2[4]	Kb1	c4	de	Rd2	=
	e6	Ngf6[1]	Be7	0-0[3]	Qa5[5]	Rad8	Nxe5	Nd7	Bg5[6]	
2	...	Bd2	0-0-0	Qe2[8]	Ne5	Rhe1[10]	Ng6	Nxe7+	d5[11]	±
	...	Ngf6	Be7[7]	Rc8[9]	c5	0-0	Re8	Qxe7		
3	...	Rh4[12]	Bf4	Bd2	0-0-0	Rhh1[14]	c4[15]	Kb1	Ne2	=
	Qc7	e6	Qa5+[13]	Qb6	Be7	Ngf6	Qa6	Bd6	Ng4[16]	
4	...	Bd2	Qe2[17]	c4[19]	Nf5	Bxf4	Ne3	Nd5[22]	cd	=
	...	e6	Ngf6[18]	Bd6[20]	Bf4[21]	Qxf4	c5	Nxd5	0-0[23]	
5	...	...	0-0-0	Kb1[25]	c4	Qe2[27]	Ne4	Qxe4	Qe2	=
	...	...	Ngf6[24]	0-0-0[26]	c5	Bd6	Nxe4	Nf6	Qc6[28]	

[1] 11 ... Qa5+ 12 c3 (12 Bd2! Qc7 – 10 ... Qc7) 12 ... Ngf6 13 a4 Nd5 14 Bd2 Qc7 ∞ Panchenko-Bronstein, USSR 1981

[2] 13 Ne4 Nxe4 14 Qxe4 Nf6 15 Qd3 Qd5 16 c4 Qe4 =
13 Kb1 a5 14 Ne4 Nxe4 15 Qxe4 a4 = Karpov-Larsen, Linares 1983

[3] 13 ... a5 14 Rhe1 a4? (14 ... 0-0 15 Qe2 – 13 ... 0-0) 15 Ng6! ± Belyavsky-Larsen, Tilburg 1981

[4] 14 Nxd7 Qxd7 15 Be5 Rad8 16 Qe2 Qd5 ∞ Timman-Hübner, Tilburg 1982
14 c4 c5 (14 ... Qa5 15 Kb1 Rad8 16 Qe2 – 14 Qe2) 15 d5 ∞ Karpov-Hübner, Tilburg 1982

[5] 14 ... a5 15 c4 a4 ∞ Timman-Lobron, Plovdiv 1983

[6] Belyavsky-Tal, USSR 1981

[7] 12 ... c5? 13 Rhe1 Be7 14 d5! ± Kavalek-Hübner, Montreal 1979

[8] 13 Ne4 Nxe4 14 Qxe4 Nf6 15 Qe2 Qd5 16 c4 Qe4 = Ivanović-Kavalek, Bugojno 1982

[9] 13 ... a5 14 Rhe1 0-0 15 Nf5 ± Glatt-Burger, Budapest 1982
13 ... c5 14 Rhe1 0-0 15 Nf5 ± Vogt-Delezal, Budapest 1985

[10] 15 dc Nxe5 16 Bxh6 ∞ van der Wiel-Lobron, Sarajevo 1984

[11] Grünfeld-Lobron, New York 1986

[12] 11 0-0?! e6 12 c4 Ngf6! (12 ... 0-0-0 13 b4 ∞) 13 Re1 Bb4 ∓

[13] 12 ... Bd6 13 Bxd6 Qxd6 14 Ne4 Qe7 15 Qa3 Qxa3 16 ba Ke7 17 Rb1 b6 18 Ne5 Nxe5 19 de f6! (19 ... f5 20 Ng3 ± Belyavsky-Pomar, Las Palmas 1974) 20 Rd1 fe 21 Rg4 Rh7! intending ... Nf6 = Dorfman

[14] 15 Rg4!? Ngf6 16 Rxg7 Bf8 17 Rxf7

[15] 16 Rhe1!? 0-0-0 (16 ... a5 17 Ne5 a4 18 Nxf7! ± Watson-Miles, British Ch 1985) 17 Qe2 intending Ne5

[16] 19 Be1 0-0-0 = Gilezetdinov-Shakarov, corr. 1976

[17] 12 c4 Ngf6 13 c5 0-0-0 (13 ... b6 14 b4 a5 15 cb Qxb6 16 ba Qa6 =∞ Rom-Porath, Israel 1976) 14 Qe2 (14 Qa3 e5! ∓) 14 ... Rg8 15 b4 g6 ∞ Karpov-Hort, Portorož/Ljubljana 1975

[18] 12 ... 0-0-0 13 Ne5 Nb6 14 c3 Nf6 15 0-0! ± Nikitin-Lazarev, USSR 1966
12 ... Bd6 13 Nf5 Bf4 14 Bxf4 Qxf4 15 Ne3 ±

[19] 13 Ne5 Bd6 (13 ... c5 14 Nxd7 Qxd7 15 dc Bxc5 16 0-0-0 Qa4 17 Bc3 ± Tal-Kasparov, USSR 1980) 14 f4 0-0 15 0-0-0 ∞

[20] 13 ... 0-0-0 14 Ne5 (14 Bc3 c5 15 0-0-0 – 12 0-0-0) 14 ... Nxe5 (14 ... Nb8!?) 15 de Nd7 16 f4 Nc5 17 0-0-0 Nd3+ 18 Kb1 Nxb2! =∞ Klovans-Andreev, corr. 1976

[21] 14 ... 0-0 15 Nxd6 Qxd6 16 0-0-0 b5! 17 g4! bc 18 g5 hg 19 h6 g6 20 h7+ Nxh7 21 Nxg5 Qxg5 22 Bxg5 c3! (22 ... f6? 23 Qe4 ±) 23 Qe5! cb+ 24 Kb1 Qxe5 25 de f6 26 Rxd7 fg 27 Rhh7 = Kasparov

[22] 17 d5 Ne5! ∓
17 0-0-0 cd 18 Rxd4 Qc7 =

[23] 19 de Rfe8 = Tal-Portisch, Bugojno 1978

[24] 12 ... Bd6 13 Ne4 Bf4 14 Qa3 ± Timman-Ivanović, Nikšić 1978

[25] 13 c4 0-0-0 (13 ... b5!? 14 c5 Be7) 14 Bc3 Bd6 15 Ne4 Bf4+ 16 Kc2 Ne5 17 Nxe5 Bxe5 18 Nc5 Bd6 19 Nb3 Qe7 = Bronstein-Kotov, Amsterdam 1968

[26] 13 ... c5 14 Qe2 cd 15 Nxd4 Bc5 (15 ... a6? 16 Nxe6!) 16 Nb3 Be7 = Diaz-Garcia Palermo, Havana 1986

[27] 15 Bc3 cd 16 Nxd4 a6 17 Nb3 (17 Nf3 Bc5 18 Qe2 Bd6 19 Ne4 Nxe4 20 Qxe4 Nf6 21 Qe2 Qc5 22 Ne5 Bxe5 =) 17 ... Be7 18 Ba5 b6 19 Bc3 Nc5 20 Qf3 Qb7 = Spassky-Portisch, match 1980

[28] 18 ... Rhe8 19 Bc3 Re7 20 Ne5 ± Kavalek-Karpov, Montreal 1979
18 ... Qc6 19 Ne5 Nxe5 20 de Qe4+ 21 Qxe4 Nxe4 = Vasyukov-A.Zaitsev, USSR Ch 1969

	10	11	12	13	14	15	16	17	18	
6	...	♗d2	0-0-0	♕e2	♘e5	♗a5[31]	♗xb6[33]	f4[34]	♔b1	∞
	♕c7	e6	♘gf6	0-0-0[29]	♘b6[30]	♖d5[32]	ab	♗d6	♖d8[35]	
7	...	...	...	...	♖h4[36]	dc	♖c4[38]	♖c3	♘d4	=
	...	...	...	c5	♗e7[37]	♘xc5	b5	♕b7	♘fe4[39]	
8	...	...	...	♘e4	♘xd6+[41]	♕e2	♔b1	♖h4[43]	g3	∞
	...	...	...	♗d6[40]	♕xd6	♕d5	b5[42]	a5	b4[44]	
9	...	...	...	...	g3[45]	♕xe4	♕e2	c4	♗c3[49]	=
	...	...	...	0-0-0	♘xe4[46]	♘f6[47]	♗d6[48]	c5	cd[50]	

[29] 13 ... ♗d6 14 ♘f5 ♗f4 15 ♗xf4 ♕xf4+ 16 ♘e3 ±

[30] **14 ... ♘b8** 15 ♖h4 ♗d6 16 ♘c4! ± Ivanović-Nikolac, Vukovar 1976

14 ... ♘xe5 15 de ♘d7 16 f4 ±

[31] 15 ♖h4 ♗d6 16 ♗a5 ♗xe5 17 de ♖xd1+ 18 ♔xd1 ♘fd7 19 ♖e4 (19 ♖g4? ♘xe5) 19 ... ♕d8+! 20 ♕d2! =

[32] 15 ... c5 16 ♖h4! ♗d6 17 dc ♗xe5 (17 ... ♗xc5 18 ♖xd8+ ♖xd8 19 ♖c4 ±) 18 ♖xd8+ ♖xd8 19 cb ± Ubilava-Peresipkin, USSR 1974

[33] 16 b4 ♖xa5 17 ba ♗a3+ 18 ♔b1 ♘a4 ∞̄

[34] 17 c4 ♖d8 18 ♘e4 ♘xe4 19 ♕xe4 ♗d6 20 f4 (20 ♘f3 ♗e7 intending ... ♗f6 =) 20 ... f5 21 ♕e2 ♗xe5 22 ♕xe5 ♕xe5 23 de g5! 24 hg ♖dg8 =

[35] **19 c3 c5!** (19 ... ♔b8 20 ♘f1 ± Romanishin-Bagirov, USSR 1978) 20 ♘f1 cd 21 cd ♗c5 ∞ Kasparov

19 c4 ♖a5 20 ♖d2 b5 21 c5 ♗xe5 22 fe ♖a4! ∞ Marczell-Shakarov, corr. 1977

[36] **14 ♔b1** – 13 ♔b1

14 c4 cd 15 ♘xd4 ♖c8 = Marjanović-Seirawan, Niš 1979

14 ♘f5 0-0-0 15 ♘e3 ♘b8 16 ♖h4 ♘c6 = Faibisovich-Okhotnik, USSR 1979

14 ♖he1 cd 15 ♘xd4 ♖c8 16 ♗c3 ♕c4 = Vogt-Garcia Palermo, Havana 1985

[37] 14 ... ♖c8 15 ♗f4 ♕a5 16 d5 ♕xa2 17 c4 (17 de!?) 17 ... ♗e7! 18 ♗d6! ♗xd6 19 dc 0-0 20 ♘f5 ∞/± Kanani-Shakarov, corr. 1982

[38] 16 ♖d4 0-0 = Butnorius-Bagirov, USSR 1975

[39] 19 ♘xe4 ♘xe4 20 ♕f3! ♖b8! 21 ♖b3 ♘xd2 22 ♔xd2 ♕xf3 = Levin-Shakarov, corr. 1982

[40] **13 ... ♖d8** 14 ♘xf6+ ♘xf6 15 ♘e5 ± Wedberg-Stean, Lucerne Ol 1982

13 ... ♗e7 14 ♘xf6+ ♘xf6 15 ♕e4 ± Karpov-Seirawan, Linares 1983

[41] 14 g3 b5 15 ♔b1 a5 16 ♘xf6+ ♘xf6 17 ♘e5 ∞ Chandler-Seirawan, London 1984

[42] 16 ... ♘xh5 17 ♘e5 ♘hf6 18 f3 ∞̄ Karpov-Seirawan, Tilburg 1983

[43] 17 ♘e5 ♕e4 = Adianto-Seirawan, Indonesia 1983

[44] 19 ♘e5 ♕b5 ∞ Pchelkin-Akopov, corr. 1986

[45] 14 ♔b1 c5 = van der Wiel-Portisch, Budapest 1985

[46] 14 ... ♘c5 15 ♘xc5 ♗xc5 16 c4 ± Christiansen-Chandler, Wijk aan Zee 1982, and Tal-Miles, Bugojno 1984

[47] **15 ... c5** 16 dc! ♘f6 (16 ... ♗xc5 17 ♕c4 intending ♗f4 ±) 17 ♕e2 ♗xc5 18 ♖h4! ± Tal-Hübner, Montreal 1979

15 ... ♗e7 16 ♔b1 ♖he8 17 ♕e2! ± Geller-Kasparov, USSR Ch 1979

[48] 16 ... ♖d5 17 c4! ♖xh5 18 ♗f4 ♕a5 19 ♘e5 ± Horvath-Vadasz, Hungary 1980

[49] 18 ♔b1 cd 19 ♘xd4 ♗xg3 20 ♘b5 (20 ♘xe6? ♖he8! ∓) 20 ... ♕e5 ∞/∓

[50] **19 ♗xd4 ♕a5** 20 ♔b1 ♗c7 = Polovodin-Kharitonov, USSR 1980

19 ♘xd4 a6 20 ♖d2 (20 ♘b3 ♕c6 =) 20 ... ♕c5 21 ♔c2 ♗c7 22 g4 ♗a5 23 ♘b3 ♕c6 = Cabrilo-Vadasz, Trnava 1981

Sicilian

I

II

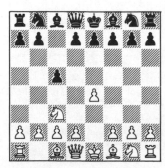

III

IV

V

VI

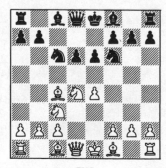

VII-VIII

IX

X-XI

XII

XIII

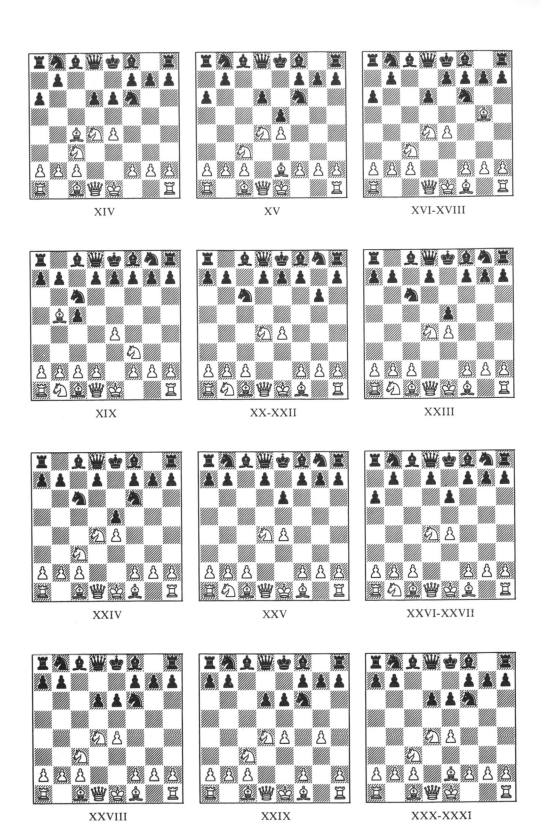

XIV

XV

XVI-XVIII

XIX

XX-XXII

XXIII

XXIV

XXV

XXVI-XXVII

XXVIII

XXIX

XXX-XXXI

284

The most popular reply to 1 e4, the Sicilian steers clear of symmetrical defence in favour of a more dynamic pawn structure. By trading his c-pawn for White's d-pawn Black guarantees pressure down the half open c-file and chances to fashion his central pawn majority into a strong centre. In return for these long-term possibilities White gets a lead in development which, combined with an edge in space and the half-open d-file, can lead to quick and violent attacks.

The balance is delicate in this opening and through continuous tournament practice many recurring tactical themes for attack and defence have been mapped. A classic example is Black's c-file pressure culminating in an exchange sacrifice on c3 to undermine White's pawn centre. This idea cuts across all variations of the Sicilian but is predominant in the Scheveningen and Dragon.

White's initiative can reach hurricane proportions if Black neglects his king safety or piece development while engaged in more esoteric pursuits. Black's most reliable stratagem in the face of White storming his bastions is to fall back on a truism that will serve the Sicilian player well, and that is the wisdom of meeting a flank attack with a reaction in the centre. Here Black's central preponderance makes this an extremely effective tack, and a well-timed blow in this sector of the board can completely turn the game around.

Another critical theme for the defence is the acquisition of the e5 square. Whether or not Black can seize this post for defence is often the difference between success and failure for the attack.

A common strategical formation is the stationing of white pawns on c4 and e4, the well-known 'Maroczy Bind'. White's strategy is ambitious, attempting to restrict Black's expansion on the queenside and in the centre. However, if White is up to the task Black suffers from his lack of space and may be slowly strangled.

In the **Closed Sicilian** (2 ♘c3 ♘c6 3 g3), White's refusal to trade a centre pawn for Black's c-pawn leads to a slow, strategical battle where the first player has a choice of a gradual kingside storm or erecting a formidable centre with c3 and d4. Generally, Black relies on a full-scale onslaught on the queenside to provide adequate counterplay. Although not without danger for Black, the closed systems have never caught on as a really serious threat to the Sicilian. Lines with ♘c3 and f4 (the "Grand Prix Attack") have proved very popular in British swiss events.

Open Systems

The **Dragon** (2 ♘f3 d6 3 d4 cd 4 ♘xd4 ♘f6 5 ♘c3 g6) is in many ways the most logically motivated of Sicilians, emphasizing quick development and with all of Black's pieces seeking aggressive posts. The acid test has always been the Yugoslav attack, a direct and unabashed attempt to give mate. Like so many popular variations, the Yugoslav Dragon has acquired a vast body of theory, and the play in this line is so complex that it is foolhardy to enter into it without doing one's 'homework'. World-renowned specialists in this line are Miles, Mestel and Gufeld.

Against the two knights' formation (2 ♘f3 d6 3 d4 cd 4 ♘xd4 ♘f6 5 ♘c3 ♘c6) White's main choices are the **Sozin/Velimirović Attack** (6 ♗c4) and the **Richter-Rauzer** (6 ♗g5). Both variations rest their hopes on producing dividends through the use of violence. The play is razor-sharp, characterized in most cases by castling on opposite sides and full-scale attacks. Theory is not as extensive here as in variations like the Najdorf or Dragon and Black success depends on a sophisticated combination of defence and counterattack.

The **Najdorf** (2 ♘f3 d6 3 d4 cd 4 ♘xd4 ♘f6 5 ♘c3 a6) is one of the most reliable Sicilians, though it is fraught with dangers for both sides and requires considerable expertise. It tends to attract sharp and ambitious players who intend to specialize in the intricacies of this defence. Fischer, Polugayevsky and Browne are good examples of players devoted to the Najdorf, and it has served each of them well.

The **Pilnik/Pelikan/Lasker/Sveshnikov** (2 ♘f3 ♘c6 3 d4 cd 4 ♘xd4 ♘f6 5 ♘c3 e5) owes its status to Soviet GM Sveshnikov, who forged this complex system from a lifetime of inventive analysis. His success catapulted the variation to huge popularity, which has begun to decline in recent years. Black accepts an odd pawn structure and a gaping hole on d5 in return for the bishop pair and a wealth of possibilities for active play. The system's current loss of support seems due to a dearth of fresh ideas rather than concrete problems for the defence. Sveshnikov has begun experimenting with 2 ♘f3 ♘c6 3 d4 cd 4 ♘xd4 e5 5 ♘b5 d6 with good results – the next variation to bear his name?

The **Taimanov** (2 ♘f3 e6 3 d4 cd 4 ♘xd4 ♘c6), like its close relative the Kan, may transpose into the Scheveningen at several junctures. In its own territory, however, it offers scope for sophisticated manoeuvring and it justifiably bears the name of Soviet GM Mark Taimanov, who has constantly discovered imaginative new strategical possibilities, infusing the line with his own brand of defensive versatility.

In the **Kan** (2 ♘f3 e6 3 d4 cd 4 ♘xd4 a6) Black essays slow development to construct a pawn shell that he hopes will deter aggressive demonstrations from White's more active pieces. Miles, Karpov and Gheorghiu are the masters of the options that this extremely flexible variation has to offer.

The **Scheveningen** (2 ♘f3 e6 3 d4 cd 4 ♘xd4 ♘f6 5 ♘c3 d6) is the classic Sicilian. Black is subjected to persistent pressure on the kingside in return for counterplay on the queenside and the c-file. The defender must exercise great care in order not to succumb to direct attack, but he has rich opportunities for counterattack as the reward for success.

References:　*Sicilian: ... e6 and ... d6 Systems* (Kasparov and Nikitin)
The Sicilian for the Tournament Player (Gufeld)
The Sicilian Pelikan (Sveshnikov)
Najdorf for the Tournament Player (Nunn)
The Sicilian Defence: Taimanov System (Taimanov)
The Sicilian Dragon: Yugoslav 9 ♗c4 (Sapi and Schneider)

	Sicilian I	1 e4 c5								
	2	3	4	5	6	7	8	9	10	
1	b4[1]	d4[2]	e5[3]	a3	♘e2!?[4]	ab	♘a3	♘f4	♕g4	∞
	cb	d5	♘c6	♕b6	♗f5	♘xb4	♖c8	♗xc2	e6[5]	
2	b3	♗b2[7]	♗b5+	♗xd7+	♗xf6	♕h5	♘c3	♕xf5	ef	=
	d6![6]	♘f6[8]	♗d7	♕xd7	gf	♘c6[9]	f5!	♕xf5	♘d4[10]	
3	g3	♗g2	f4[11]	♘f3	d3	c3[14]	0-0	♗xf4	♘a3	=
	g6	♗g7	♘c6	d6[12]	e5[13]	♘ge7	ef[15]	0-0	♘e5[16]	
4	...	ed	♘f3	♗g2	♔f1	h3[19]	♘c3[21]	d3	♗f4[22]	∞/=
	d5!	♕xd5	♗g4	♕e6+[17]	♘c6![18]	♗h5[20]	♕d7	e6	♘f6[23]	
5	f4	ed	♗b5+[26]	c4	♗xd7+	d4	♘f3	0-0	de	∞
	d5[24]	♘f6!?[25]	♘bd7[27]	a6	♗xd7	♗g4	cd	e6	♗xe6[28]	
6	d4	c3	♘xc3	♘f3	♗c4	0-0	♕c2	♖d1	h3	=
	cd	dc[29]	♘c6[30]	d6[31]	e6	♘f6[32]	♗e7[33]	e5!	0-0[34]	

[1]　2 ♗c4 e6 3 ♕e2 ♘c6 4 c3 ♗e7 5 d3 d5
6 ♗b3 ♘f6 =
　2 ♘e2 e6 3 d3 d5 4 ♘d2 ♘c6 5 g3 ♘f6

6 ♗g2 ♗e7 = Cardoso-Lombardy, Manila 1973
[2]　3 ♗b2 ♘f6 4 e5 ♘d5 5 ♘f3 e6 6 d4 b6 ∓
Taimanov

286

3 a3 d5! 5 ed ♕xd5 6 ♗b2 e5 6 ab ♗xb4
7 ♘a3 ♘c6 ∞/∓

[3] 4 ed ♘f6! 5 ♗b5+ ♗d7 6 ♗c4 ♗g4 7 f3
♗f5 8 a3 ♘xd5 ∓

[4] 6 ♗e3 ♗f5 7 ♗d3 ♗xd3 8 ♕xd3 e6
9 ♘ge2 ♘ge7 ∞

[5] 11 ♗b5+ ♘c6 12 ♘xd5 ∞ Mariotti-
Kuzmin, Leningrad 1977

[6] 2 ... ♘f6 3 e5 ♘d5 4 ♘c3 e6 5 ♘e4 f5
6 ef ♘xf6 7 ♗d3 ♘xe4 8 ♗xe4 ♕f6 ∞
Gurgenidze-Lukin, USSR 1979

[7] 3 ♗b5+ ♗d7 4 c4 ♗xb5 5 cb a6 6 ♘c3
♘f6 7 ♘f3 g6 = Lein-Polugayevsky, Buenos
Aires Ol 1978

[8] 3 ... a6?! 4 f4! ♘c6 5 ♘f3 e6 6 g3 ♘f6
7 e5 ± Spassky Hébert, Bucnos Aires Ol 1978

3 ... ♘c6 4 ♗b5 (4 g3 e5 5 ♗g2 g6 6 ♘c3
♗g7 7 ♘d5 ♘ge7 8 h4 h5 = Bellin-Spassov,
Skara 1980) 4 ... ♗d7 5 ♘e2 e6 6 0-0 ♘f6
7 d3 ♗e7 8 ♘d2 0-0 9 ♘g3 ± Gurgenidze-
Zaichik, USSR 1979

3 ... e5!? ∞/=

[9] 7 ... ♖g8!? 8 ♘e2 ♕g4 =

[10] Spassky-Hübner, Buenos Aires Ol 1978

[11] 4 ♘e2 ♘c6 5 c3 e5 6 0-0 ♘ge7 (6 ... d6
7 ♘a3 ♘ge7 8 ♘c2 d5 9 ed ♘xd5 10 d4! ±
Short-Ree, Hastings 1981-82) 7 d3 0-0 8 ♗e3
(8 a3 d5! 9 ed ♘xd5 10 c4 ♘c7 = Dorfman-
Magerramov, USSR 1979) 8 ... d6 9 ♘a3
(9 d4 ed 10 cd ♗g4 11 f3 cd =) 9 ... b6 10 ♕d2
♗a6 11 b4 ♗b7 12 ♖fd1 cb 13 cb d5! ∞

[12] 5 ... e6!? 6 c3 ♘ge7 7 ♘a3 d5 8 e5 d4!? ∞
Hebden-Ftacnik, Hastings 1982-83

[13] 6 ... e6 7 c3 ♘ge7 8 0-0 0-0 (8 ... d5 9 e5!
b6 10 ♘a3 a6 11 ♗e3 ± Chandler-Cebalo,
Vršac 1981) 9 ♗e3 b6 10 ♗f2 ♕c7 11 ♖e1
h6 12 d4 ± Makarichev-Dolmatov, USSR Ch
1979

6 ... ♘f6 7 0-0 0-0 8 h3 (8 c3 ♖b8 9 ♕e2
♘e8 10 ♗e3 ± Korchnoi-Karpov, match (11)
1978) 8 ... ♖b8 9 g4 b5 10 f5! ± Sveshnikov-
Sideif Zade, USSR 1980

[14] 7 0-0 ♘ge7 8 f5 gf 9 ♘h4 fe 10 de h5!? ∓
Varlamov-Karasev, Leningrad 1983·

[15] 8 ... 0-0?! 9 f5! gf 10 ♘h4! ±

[16] 11 ♕d2 ♗g4 12 ♘e1 ♖c8 13 ♘ac2 ♕d7 =
Chandler-Andersson, Hastings 1981-82

[17] 5 ... ♘c6 6 h3 ♗h5 7 0-0 ♕d7 8 d3 e6
9 ♘bd2 ± Taimanov-Korchnoi, USSR 1965

[18] 6 ... ♗h3 7 d4! (7 b4 cb 8 a3 g6! 9 ♗b2
♘f6 10 ab ♘c6 ∓) 7 ... cd 8 ♗xd4 ♕d7! (8 ...
♕d5?! 9 ♕f3 ♕xf3 10 ♘xf3 ♗xg2+ 11 ♔xg2
♘c6 12 c4! ± Gurgenidze-Azmaiparashvili,
Kiev 1984) 9 ♘c3 ♘c6 ∞ Volchok

[19] 7 ♘c3 ♗h3 8 d3 0-0-0 9 ♗e3 ♕f5! =

[20] 7 ... ♗f5 8 ♘c3! (8 d3 ♖d8! 9 ♘c3 ♕c8! ∓
Mestel-Simić, Belgrade 1982) ±

[21] 8 d3 ♕d7 9 ♗e3 e6 10 ♘bd2 ♘f6 11 ♘b3

♘d5!? ∞ Fuller-Keene, Brisbane 1979

[22] 10 g4 ♗g6 11 ♘h4 ♘f6 12 ♘xg6 hg
13 ♗e3 ♘d4! 14 ♘e4 ♘d5 =

[23] 11 g4 ♗g6 12 ♘e5 (12 g5 ♘h5! 13 ♘e5
♘xe5 14 ♗xe5 ♗d6! =) 12 ... ♘xe5 13 ♗xe5
♗d6! 14 ♕e2 ♗xe5 (14 ... 0-0-0!? Short-
Chandler, Dortmund 1983) 15 ♕xe5 ♖c8 ∞/=
Chandler-Hübner, Wijk aan Zee 1982

[24] 2 ... ♘f6 3 ♘c3 d5 4 e5 d4 5 ef dc 6 fg
cd+ 7 ♕xd2 ♕xd2+ 8 ♗xd2 ♗xg7 9 0-0-0 ±
Bisguier-Hartston, Hastings 1975-76

2 ... e6 3 ♘f3 d5 4 ♗b5+ ♗d7 5 ♗xd7+
♕xd7 6 d3 ♘e7 7 ♘c3 g6 8 ♕e2! ±

2 ... ♘c6 3 ♘c3 – 2 ♘c3

[25] 3 ... ♕xd5 4 ♘c3 ♕d8 5 ♘f3 ♘f6 (5 ...
g6 6 ♘e5 ♗g7 7 ♗b5+ ♘d7 8 d4 cd 9 ♕xd4 ±
Hebden-Kudrin, Hastings 1983-84) 6 ♘e5 e6
(6 ... ♘bd7 7 b3 e6 8 ♗f3 ♗d6 9 ♘c4 ♗e7
10 ♗b2 ±) 7 ♕f3 ♗e7 8 b3 0-0 (8 ... ♘fd7
9 ♗b5! ± Westerinen-Ornstein, Gausdal 1982)
9 ♗b2 ♗d5! 10 0-0-0 f6 11 ♘c4 ♘c6 ∞
Fadeyev-Lerner, USSR 1982

[26] 4 c4 e6 5 de ♗xe6 6 ♘f3 ♘c6 ∞ Hodgson-
Salov, Leningrad 1983

4 ♘c3 ♘xd5 5 ♘f3 e6 6 ♘e5 ♘d7 7 ♗b5
♗d6 8 0-0 0-0 = Plaskett-Yrjölä, Sochi 1984

[27] 4 ... ♗d7 5 ♗xd7+ ♕xd7 6 c4 e6 7 ♕e2
♗d6 8 f5 ♘a6! (8 ... 0-0 9 fe fe 10 de ♕e8
11 ♘f3 ♕h5 12 ♘c3 ± Hebden-Davis, Nottingham 1983) ∞

[28] 11 ♖e1 ♗e7 12 b3 0-0 ∞ Westerinen-
Burger, Brighton 1981

[29] 3 ... d5 – 2 c3

3 ... ♘f6 – 2 c3

3 ... d3 4 ♗xd3 ♘c6 5 c4 (5 ♘f3 g6 6 0-0
♗g7 7 ♕e2 d6 8 ♖d1 ♗g4 9 ♘bd2 ±) 5 ...
♘f6 6 ♘c3 d6 7 h3 g6 8 ♘f3 ♗g7 9 0-0 ♘d7
10 ♗e3 ± Chandler-Sunye, Wijk aan Zee 1982

[30] 4 ... e6 5 ♘f3 ♘c6 6 ♗c4 ♘f7 7 0-0 0-0
8 ♗g5 f6 9 ♗f4 g6 10 ♗g3 ∞ Chandler-
Timman, Wijk aan Zee 1982

[31] 5 ... g6 6 ♗c4 ♗g7 7 0-0 ♘f6 (7 ... d6
8 h3 ♘f6 9 ♗f4 0-0 10 ♕d2 ∞) 8 e5 ♘g4
9 ♗xf7+ ♔xf7 10 ♘g5+ ♔g8 11 ♕xg4 ♘xe5
12 ♕e4 e6 ∞ Tompa-Ribli, Hungarian Ch
1976

5 ... e6 6 ♗c4 a6 (6 ... ♗b4?! 7 0-0 ♘ge7
8 ♕e2 0-0 9 ♖d1 ♗xc3 10 bc d5 11 ♗d3 ±)
7 0-0 ♘ge7 8 ♗g5 f6 9 ♗e3 b5 10 ♗b3 ♘g6
11 ♖e1!? Gheorghiu

[32] 7 ... ♘ge7 8 ♗g5 a6 9 ♕e2 h6 10 ♗e3
♘g6 11 ♖ad1 ±

[33] 8 ... a6!? 9 ♖d1 ♕c7 10 ♗g5 ♗e7 11 ♖ac1
0-0 12 ♗b3 h6 13 ♗f4 e5 = Fischer-Korchnoi,
Buenos Aires 1960

[34] 11 ♗e3 ♗e6 12 ♗xe6 fe 13 ♖ac1 ♖c8
14 b4 a6 = Pokojowczyk-Gligorić, Yugoslavia
1971

	2	3	4	5	6	7	8	9	10	
1	...	d4	f3[2]	cd	d5[5]	♗e3	♗d3	♘e2	♗f2	∞
	d6[1]	♘f6	cd[3]	e5[4]	♗e7	0-0	♘fd7	♗g5	♘c5[6]	
2	...	d4	ed	♘f3	♗e3[9]	b3	ab	♗e2	♗g5	=
	e6	d5	ed[7]	♘c6[8]	c4[10]	cb	♘f6[11]	♗d6	h6[12]	

1 e4 c5 2 c3 d5 3 ed ♕xd5 4 d4

	4	5	6	7	8	9	10	11	12	
3	...	♘f3	♗e2	cd	h3[15]	♘c3	d5!	♘d4	♗xh5	±
	♘c6[13]	♗g4	cd[14]	e6	♗h5	♕a5	ed[16]	♘xd4	♘e6[17]	
4	...	♘f3	♗d3[18]	0-0	c4[20]	dc	♕e2	♗c2	♘c3	∞
	e6	♘f6	♗e7[19]	0-0	♕d8[21]	♘bd7[22]	♘xc5	b6	♗a6[23]	
5	...	...	♗e2	cd	0-0	♘c3	♗f4	♖c1	♘b5	∞/=
	...	...	cd[24]	♘c6	♗e7	♕d8[25]	0-0	b6	♘d5[26]	

1 e4 c5 2 c3 ♘f6 3 e5 ♘d5 4 d4 cd

	5	6	7	8	9	10	11	12	13	
6	♕xd4[27]	♘f3[28]	♕e4	ef[30]	♕h4[31]	♗d3	♗g6+	♗c2	♗g6	∞
	e6	♘c6	f5[29]	♘xf6	d5[32]	♗d6	♔e7	h6	♗d7[33]	
7	♘f3	cd	♘c3[35]	bc	♗d3[37]	0-0	♘xe5	de	♗e4	±
	e6	d6[34]	♘xc3[36]	♘c6	♕a5	de	♘xe5	♗d7	♕c7[38]	

---

[1] **2 ... ♕a5?!** 3 ♘f3 ♘c6 4 d4 cd 5 b4 ♕c7 6 b5 ♘e5 7 ♘xe5 ♕xe5 8 ♕d4 ± Makropoulos-Ljubojević, Athens 1981

2 ... b6 3 d4 e6 (3 ... ♗b7 4 ♗d3 ♘f6 5 ♕e2 ±) 4 ♘f3 ♗b7 5 ♗d3 ♗e7 6 h4 ♘bc6 7 a3 ± Sveshnikov-Tseshkovsky, USSR Ch 1980

[2] **4 ♗d3** cd 5 cd g6! 6 ♘e2 ♗g7 7 0-0 0-0 8 ♘bc3 ♘c6 9 a3 e5 10 d5 ♘d4 = Rozentalis-Gelfand, USSR 1987

4 dc ♘c6 5 ♘d2 (5 f3 d5 6 ed ♕xd5 7 ♕xd5 ♘xd5 8 ♗c4 ♗e6! 9 ♗xd5 ♗xd5 10 ♗e3 ♘e5 = Klinger-Cebalo, Biel 1986) 5 ... dc 6 ♘gf3 g6 7 g3 ♗g7 8 ♗g2 ♕d3 = Sveshnikov-Dorfman, USSR 1981

[3] 4 ... ♘bd7 5 ♗e3 e5 6 dc dc 7 a4 ± Sveshnikov-Gufeld, USSR 1983

[4] 5 ... g6 6 ♘c3 ♗g7 7 ♗e3 0-0 8 ♕d2 e5 9 ♘ge2 ±

[5] 6 de de 7 ♕xd8+ ♔xd8 8 ♗c4 ♗b4+ =

[6] Sveshnikov

[7] 4 ... ♕xd5 - 2 ... d5

[8] 5 ... ♗d6 6 dc! (6 ♗e3 c4! 7 b3 cb 8 ab ♘e7 9 c4 ♘bc6 10 c5 ♗c7 = Short-Kasparov, Dortmund 1980) 6 ... ♗xc5 7 ♗e2 - 5 ... ♘c6

[9] **6 ♗b5** ♗d6 7 ♗e3 cd 8 ♗xd4 ♘e7! 9 ♗xg7 ♖g8 10 ♗d4 ♖xg2 11 ♘bd2 ♕c7 = Sveshnikov-Polugayevsky, USSR Ch 1976

6 ♗e2 ♗d6 (6 ... ♘f6 7 0-0 ♗e7 8 ♗e3 cd 9 ♘xd4 0-0 10 ♘d2 ± Hort-Karpov, Tilburg 1977) 7 dc ♗xc5 8 0-0 ♘ge7 9 ♘bd2 a6 10 ♘b3 ♗a7 11 ♗f4 0-0 ∞ Kr.Georgiev-Ermenkov, match 1979

[10] 6 ... cd 7 ♗xd4 ♘xd4 8 ♕xd4 ♘f6 9 ♗b5+ ♗d7 10 ♗xd7+ ♕xd7 11 0-0 ♗e7 = Sveshnikov-Tal, USSR Ch 1976

[11] 8 ... ♗d6 9 ♗d3 ♘ge7 10 0-0 0-0 11 ♖e1 h6 12 ♕c1 ♗f5 oo Castro-Schmidt, Budapest 1977

[12] 11 ♗h4 0-0 12 0-0 ♖e8 = Makarichev-Gulko, Frunze 1985

[13] 4 ... e5 5 de ♕xe5+ 6 ♗e3 ♘f6 7 ♘f3 ♕c7 8 ♗a3! a6 9 g3! ±

4 ... cd 5 cd e5 6 ♘f3 ed 7 ♘xd4 ♗c5 8 ♗e3 ♘f6 9 ♘c3 ♕e5 10 ♗b5+ ♗d7 11 0-0 (11 ♕f3 ♗e7 12 0-0 ♗xe3 13 ♖e1 ♘g4! = Makropoulos-Armas, Herculana 1984) ±

4 ... ♘f6!? 5 ♘f3 ♗g4 6 ♗e2 e6 7 h3 ♗h5 8 0-0 ♘c6 9 ♗e3 ±

[14] 6 ... e6 7 h3 ♗h5 8 c4 ♕d7 9 g4 ♗g6 10 d5 ± Adamski-Schneider, Breslau, 1981

[15] 8 ♘c3 ♕a5 9 0-0 ♘f6 10 h3 ♗h5 11 ♗e3 ♗e7 12 ♕b3 ♕b4 13 ♕xb4 ♗xb4 14 g4 ± Sveshnikov-Hansen, Copenhagen 1984

[16] 10 ... 0-0-0 11 ♘d2! ±

[17] 13 0-0 ± Benjamin-Zsu.Polgar, New York 1985

[18] 6 ♘bd2 ♘c6 7 ♗c4 ♕h5!? 8 ♗e2 cd 9 ♘xd4 ♕d5 10 ♘xc6 ♕xc6 = van der Sterren

6 ♘a3 ♕d8 (6 ... ♗e7 7 ♘b5 ♘a6 8 ♗e2 0-0 9 0-0 ♕d8 10 ♗f4 ♗d7 = Malanyuk-Eingorn, USSR 1987) 7 ♘c2 (7 ♘c4 ♘c6 8 ♘ce5 cd 9 ♗b5 ♕d5! 10 ♕a4 a6 = Rozentalis-Yudasin, USSR 1984) 7 ... ♗e7 8 ♗d3 0-0 9 ♕e2 ♘bd7 10 ♗f4 a6 11 ♘e5 b5 = Vera-Horvath, Sochi 1985

[19] 6 ... cd 7 cd ♘c6 8 ♘c3 ♕d8 9 0-0 ♗e7 10 a3 0-0 11 ♗c2 ♕a5 12 ♕d3 ♖d8 13 ♗f4 ± Braga-Haag, Berlin 1984

6 ... ♘c6 7 0-0 ♗e7 8 ♗e3 cd 9 cd 0-0 10 ♘c3 ♕d8 11 a3 b6 12 ♖c1 ♗b7 13 ♖b1 ♖c8 14 ♕d3 g6 15 ♗a2! ± Borg-Hawes, Thessaloniki Ol 1984

[20] 8 ♗e3 ♘c6 9 dc (9 c4 ♕h5 = Ambroz-Adorjan, Riga 1981) 9 ... ♖d8 10 ♗e2 ♕f5 11 ♕a4 ♗xc5! = Sveshnikov-Gufeld, USSR 1982

8 ♕e2 cd (8 ... ♘c6 9 dc ♕xc5 10 ♘bd2 ♖d8 11 ♖d1 ± Short-Andersson, London 1980) 9 cd ♘c6 10 ♖d1 ♘b4 11 ♘c3 ♕d8 12 ♗c4 (12 ♗b1 b6 13 ♘e5 ♗b7 14 a3 ♘bd5 oo Braga-Karpov, Mar del Plata 1982) 12 ... b6 13 ♘e5 ♗b7 14 a3 ♘bd5 = Braga-Portisch,

Mar del Plata 1982

[21] 8 ... ♕h5 9 dc ♖d8 10 ♗f4 ♕xc5 11 ♕e2 ♘c6 12 ♘c3 ♘d4 oo/± Rozentalis-Novikov, USSR 1984

[22] 9 ... ♗xc5 10 ♘c3 ♘c6 11 ♗g5 h6 12 ♗h4 ♗e7 = Zyck-Lobron, Dortmund 1984

[23] 13 ♘e5 ♕c8 14 ♗g5 ♘ed7! oo Sax

[24] 6 ... ♗e7 7 0-0 0-0 (7 ... ♘c6 8 ♗e3 cd 9 cd 0-0 10 ♘c3 ♕d8 11 ♘e5 ± Sveshnikov-Sokolov, USSR 1983) 8 ♘e5 (8 ♗e3 ♘g4 9 ♗f4 ♖d8! 10 ♕c2 ♘c6 11 ♖d1 cd 12 cd ♘b4! Hulak-Adorjan, Banja Luka 1983) 8 ... cd 9 cd ♖d8 10 ♗e3 ♘c6 11 ♘c3 ♕a5 12 ♘c4! ±

[25] 9 ... ♕d6 10 ♗e3 (10 ♘b5 ♕d8 11 ♗f4 ♘d5 12 ♗g3 0-0 13 ♘c4 a6 14 ♗xd5 ed oo Sveshnikov-Foisor, Sochi 1985) 10 ... 0-0 11 ♖c1 ♖d8 12 ♕d2 ± Mikhalchishin-Tukmakov, USSR Ch 1985

[26] 13 ♗g3 ♗b7 oo Handoko-Timman, Indonesia 1983

[27] 5 ♗c4 ♕c7! 6 ♕e2 ♘b6 7 ♗d3 ♘c6 8 ♘f3 g6 9 0-0 dc 10 ♘xc3 ♗g7 11 ♖e1 0-0 oo Miles-Sax, Bath 1973

[28] 6 ♗c4?! ♘c6! 7 ♕e4 ♘de7! 8 ♘f3 ♘g6 9 ♗b5 ♕c7 ∓ Semenyuk-Yuferov, USSR 1977

[29] 7 ... ♕c7 8 ♘bd2 ♘de7 9 ♘c4 ♘g6 10 ♗f4 f6 11 0-0-0 b5! oo Vasyukov-Sideif Zade, USSR 1979

7 ... d6 8 c4!? f5 9 ♕e2 ♕a5+ 10 ♗d2 ♘db4 11 ed ♗xd6 12 ♗c3 ♗e7 13 ♘bd2 oo Short-Browne, London 1980

[30] 8 ♕e2 ♕c7 9 g3 b6 10 c4 ♗a6 11 b3 ♗b4+ 12 ♗d2 oo Vorotnikov-Georgadze, USSR 1979

[31] 9 ♕c2 ♕c7 10 ♗g5 ♘e5! = Hort-Hartston, Hastings 1975-76

[32] 9 ... ♕c7 10 ♘bd2 ♗e7 11 ♗d3 ♘e5 12 ♘xe5 ♕xe5 = Taimanov

[33] Novopashin-Sveshnikov, USSR 1981

[34] 6 ... b6 7 ♗d3 ♗b4+ 8 ♗d2 ♗xd2+ 9 ♕xd2 ♗a6 10 ♘c3 (10 ♗e4 ± Sveshnikov) 10 ... ♗xc3 11 bc 0-0 12 0-0 ♗xd3 13 ♕xd3 ♘c6 14 ♖ad1 ± Barlov-Rajković, Kragujevac 1977

[35] 7 a3 ♗d7 (7 ... ♗e7 8 ♗d3 ♘c6 9 0-0 b6 10 ♘bd2 oo/±) 8 ♗d3 ♘c6 9 0-0 ♘d7 10 ♖e1 de 11 de ♗e7 12 b4 ♘5b6 13 ♘bd2 a5! oo Kholmov-Polugayevsky, USSR 1980

[36] 7 ... ♘c6 8 ♗d3 de 9 de ♘db4 10 ♗e4 ♕xd1+ 11 ♔xd1 ± Byrne, Mednis

[37] 9 ed ♗xd6 10 ♗d3 ±

[38] Sveshnikov

	5	6	7	8	9	10	11	12	13	
8	♘f3	♗c4	♗b3	ed	0-0[41]	♘a3[43]	♕xb3[45]	♖d1	♘b5	∞
	♘c6	♘b6	d6[39]	♕xd6[40]	♗e6[42]	♗xb3[44]	e6[46]	♕d5[47]	0-0-0[48]	
9	...	cd	♗c4[49]	♗b5	♘xe5	♘c3[53]	de	♘xb5	♔xd1	=
	...	d6	♘b6[50]	de[51]	♗d7[52]	♘xe5[54]	♗xb5	♕xd1+	♘d5[55]	

[39] 7 ... d5 8 ed – 7 ... d6

[40] 8 ... ed 9 ♘xd4 ♗e7 10 0-0 0-0 11 h3 d5 12 ♗f4 ♗f6 13 ♘b5 ♗e6 = Malanyuk-Savon, USSR 1982

[41] 9 cd ♗e6 10 ♘c3 ♗xb3 11 ♕xb3 ♕b4 12 ♕c2 ♕c4! ∓ Genin-Varlamov, USSR 1981

[42] **9 ... d3** 10 ♘a3 ♗f5 11 ♘b5 ♕d7 12 ♗f4 ±
  9 ... ♗f5 10 ♘xd4 ♘xd4 11 cd e6 12 ♘c3 ♗e7 13 ♕f3 ± Kantsler-Salov, USSR 1980
  9 ... dc 10 ♘g5 e6 11 ♕h5 g6 12 ♕f3 ♕e7 13 bc ♗g7 14 ♕g3 ± Mascarinas-Palatnik, 1979

[43] 10 ♗xe6 ♕xe6 11 ♘xd4 ♘xd4 12 ♕xd4 ♖d8 (12 ... ♕d7 13 ♕e5 e6 14 ♘d2 ♕d5 15 ♕e2 ♗e7 16 c4 ± Vorotnikov-Georgadze, USSR 1985) 13 ♕h4 ♕e2 (13 ... ♕c6 14 ♖e1! e6 15 ♗g5 ♖d5 16 ♘d2 ± Sveshnikov) 14 ♘d2 h5!? (14 ... e6 15 ♕g3 h5!? ∞) 15 ♘e4 ♕g4 =; 14 ♗d2 h5 15 h3 ♖xd2!? ∞ Sveshnikov

[44] 10 ... dc 11 ♗xe6 (11 ♘b5 ♕xd1 12 ♖xd1 ♖c8 13 ♗xe6 fe 14 bc ♘c4 15 ♗g5 e5 16 ♘e6 ♔f7 ∞ Smagin-Gavrikov, USSR Ch 1986) 11 ... ♕xd1 12 ♖xd1 fe 13 bc ♘a4 14 ♗d2 e5 15 ♘g5 ∞/± Smagin-Dvoiris, USSR Ch 1986

[45] 11 ab e6 12 ♘b5 ♕d7 13 ♘fxd4 ♘xd4 14 ♘xd4 ♗c5 =

[46] **11 ... ♕d7** 12 ♖d1 e6 13 ♘xd4 ♘xd4 14 ♖xd4 ♕c6 15 ♘c4± Vorotnikov-Panchenko, USSR 1985
  11 ... ♕d5!? 12 ♘b5 ♖c8 13 ♘fxd4 ♘xd4 14 ♘xd4 e6 (14 ... ♕xb3 15 ab a6 16 ♖d1 e6 17 b4 ± Rashkovsky-Georgadze, USSR 1985) 15 ♖d1 ♗c5 16 ♕b5+ ♕d7 17 ♕e2 ♕e7 ∞/± Rozentalis-Pigusov, USSR 1986

[47] 12 ... ♗e7 13 ♘b5 ♕b8 14 ♘bxd4 0-0 15 ♘xc6 bc 16 c4 ± Glek-Pigusov, USSR 1985

[48] **14 ♘xa7+** ♘xa7 15 ♕xb6 ♗c5 16 ♕a5 ♘c6 17 ♕a8+!? (17 ♕a4 d3! ∓ Rozentalis-Sideif Zade, USSR 1985) 17 ... ♔c7 18 ♕a4 ∞ Glek
  14 ♗f4 ♕xb3 15 ab ♘d5 16 ♘xa7+ ♘xa7 17 ♖xa7 ♘xf4 = Panchenko-Baikov, USSR 1986

[49] **7 ed** ♕xd6 8 ♘c3 g6 9 ♗c4 ♘b6 10 ♗b3 ♗g7 11 0-0 0-0 =
  7 ♘c3 de 8 de ♗e6 (8 ... ♘db4!? Boleslavsky) 9 ♘d4 ♘xc3 10 bc ♗d5 11 e6 fe ∞

[50] **7 ... de!?** 8 de ♘db4 9 0-0 ♕xd1 10 ♖xd1 ♗g4 11 e6! fe 12 ♘c3 g6! ∞ Sveshnikov-Hartston, Sochi 1979
  7 ... e6 8 0-0 ♗e7 9 ♕e2 0-0 10 ♘c3 de 11 de ♘xc3 12 bc ♕c7! ∞ Semenyuk-Gufeld, USSR 1976

[51] 8 ... ♗d7 9 ed ed 10 ♘c3 ± Sveshnikov

[52] 9 ... ♕d5?! 10 ♗xc6+ bc 11 0-0 c5 12 ♘c3 ± Makropoulos-Ljubojević, 1978

[53] 10 ♗xc6 ♗xc6 11 ♘xc6 bc 12 0-0 g6 13 ♕c2 ♖c8 14 ♖d1 ♗g7 15 ♘c3 0-0 16 ♗g5 ♕d7 = Westerinen-Rantanen, Helsinki 1979

[54] 10 ... e6 11 ♗xc6 ♗xc6 12 ♘xc6 bc 13 ♕g4 ♘d5! 14 0-0 h5 15 ♕f3 ♕f6! = Lerner-Gutman, USSR 1979

[55] **14 ♔e2** a6 15 ♖d1 0-0-0 16 ♘a3 e6 17 ♘c4 ♗e7 18 ♗d2 b6! ∓ Sveshnikov-Kasparov, USSR Ch 1979
  14 ♗d2 a6 (14 ... e6 15 ♔e2 ♗e7 16 ♖ac1 ♔d7 17 ♖hd1 ♖hc8 = Sveshnikov-Andersson, Wijk aan Zee 1981) 15 ♘c3 ♖d8 16 ♔e2 e6 17 ♖hd1 ♗e7 = Sveshnikov-Tal, USSR Ch 1980

	2	3	4	5	6	7	8	9	10	
1	...	f4[2]	♘f3[3]	♗c4	f5!?[4]	d3	0-0	♘h4	ed	±
	d6[1]	g6	♗g7	e6	gf[5]	♘e7	h6	d5	♗xc3[6]	
2	...	g3[7]	♗g2[8]	d3	♘ge2	♘xe4	♗xe4	0-0	♗g2	=
	e6	d5	♘f6[9]	♗e7	de	♘xe4	0-0	♘d7	♘f6[10]	
3	...	f4[11]	♘f3	♗c4[13]	f5	fe	d3	♗g5!?	♗h4	∞
	♘c6	g6[12]	♗g7	e6	♘ge7	fe[14]	0-0[15]	h6	g5[16]	

[1] 2 ... g6 3 d4 cd 4 ♕xd4 ♘f6 5 ♗b5! a6 6 e5! ±

[2] 3 ♘ge2 ♘f6 (3 ... a6 4 g3 b5!? 5 ♗g2 e5 6 0-0 ♘c6 7 d3 h5 8 h4 g6 ∞ Suetin-Chekhov, USSR 1980) 4 g3 b5 5 ♗g2 ♗b7 6 0-0 e6! 7 d3 b4 8 ♘b1 ♘fd7! ∞/= Lau-Gutman, Wippertal 1986

[3] 4 d4 cd 5 ♕xd4 ♘f6 6 e5 ♘c6 7 ♗b5 ♘h5!? 8 ♗e3 ♗g7 9 ♕d1 de ∞ Romanishin-Portisch, Tilburg 1979

[4] 6 0-0 ♘e7 7 d4 cd 8 ♘xd4 a6 9 f5 ±

[5] 6 ... ef 7 d3 ♘c6 8 0-0 ♘ge7 – 2 ... ♘c6 3 f4

[6] 11 bc ♘xd5 12 ♕e1 ♘e7 13 ♕e5 ± Dobosz-Pokojowczyk, Prague 1978-79

[7] 3 ♘ge2 ♘c6 (3 ... d5 4 ed ed 5 d4 ♘c6 6 ♗e3 cd 7 ♘xd4 ♗b4 8 ♘xc6 ± Spassky-Polugayevsky, Bugojno 1982) 4 g3 ♘f6 (4 ... a6?! 5 ♗g2 b5 6 0-0 ♗b7 7 d3 b4 8 ♘a4 ± Franzoni-Polugayevsky, Lucerne 1985) 5 ♗g2 – 2 ... ♘c6 3 g3 e6

3 f4 d5 4 d3 ♘c6 5 ♘f3 ♘f6 6 ♗d2 ♗e7 7 g3 a6 8 e5 ♘d7 9 ♗g2 b5 10 0-0 g6 ∞ Hort-Wirthensohn, Biel 1981

[8] 4 d3 ♘c6 5 ed ed 6 ♗g2 d4 7 ♘e4 ♘f6 8 ♘e2 ♘xe4 9 ♗xe4 ♗d6 10 0-0 ♗g4 = Hug-Korchnoi, Biel 1986

4 ed ed 5 ♗g2 ♘f6 6 ♘ge2 d4 7 ♘e4 ♘xe4 8 ♗xe4 ♘d7 9 0-0 (9 d3 ♘f6 10 ♗g2 ♗d6 11 0-0 0-0 12 ♗f4 ♗g4 = Spassky-Korchnoi, match 1968) 9 ... ♘f6 10 ♗g2 ♗d6 11 c3 d3!? (11 ... 0-0 12 cd cd 13 d3 ♖e8 = Kasparov) 12 ♘f4 0-0 ∞ Spassky-Kasparov, Bugojno 1982

[9] 4 ... d4!? 5 ♘ce2 ♘c6 6 d3 b6! 7 f4 ♗b7 8 ♘f3 ♘f6 ∞ Sturua-Veličković, Tbilisi 1983

[10] 11 d4 ♕b6 12 c3 cd 13 ♘xd4 ♖d8 = Marjanović-Masić, Subotica 1978

[11] 3 ♘ge2 e5 4 ♘d5 g6 5 ♘ec3 a6 6 a4 ♗g7 7 ♗c4 ♘ge7 8 d3 ♘xd5 9 ♘xd5 d6 = Inkiov-Gheorghiu, Warsaw 1979

3 ♗b5 g6 4 ♗xc6!? dc 5 d3 ♗g7 6 ♗e3 b6 7 ♘ge2 ∞ Spassky-Hübner, match 1989

[12] 3 ... d6 4 ♘f3 g6 5 ♗c4 ♗g7 6 0-0 ♘f6 (6 ... e6 7 f5 ef 8 d3 ♘ge7 9 ♕e1 ± Ermenkov-Kuligowski, Warsaw 1979) 7 d3 0-0 8 f5 gf 9 ♕e1 fe 10 de ♗g4 11 ♕h4 ± Hodgson-Nunn, England 1979

3 ... e6 4 ♘f3 d5 (4 ... ♘ge7 5 d4 ♘xd4 6 ♘xd4 cd 7 ♕xd4 ♘c6 8 ♕f2 d5 = Hug-Smyslov, Petropolis IZ 1973) 5 ♗b5 ♘e7 6 0-0 (6 ♕e2!?) 6 ... de 7 ♘xe4 a6 8 ♗xc6+ ♘xc6 9 d3 ♗e7 10 ♗e3 b6 ∞ Romanishin-Ljubojević, Tilburg 1985

[13] 5 ♗e2 e6 6 d4 ♘xd4 7 ♘xd4 cd 8 ♘b5 d6 9 c3 ♘e7 10 ♘xd4 a6 = Romanishin-Polugayevsky, Tilburg 1985

5 ♗b5 ♘d4 6 d3 (6 ♘xd4 cd 7 ♘e2 ♕b6 =) 6 ... d6 (6 ... e6 7 ♘xd4 cd 8 ♘b5 d6 9 c3 ♘f6 10 ♘xd4 e5 = Benjamin-Geller, Lone Pine 1980) 7 ♘xd4 cd 8 ♘e2 ♘f6 (8 ... ♘h6?! 9 c3 dc 10 dc 0-0 11 0-0 d5 12 e5 ± Dzindzihashvili-Hübner, Tilburg 1985) 9 0-0 0-0 10 c3 e5 11 cd ed = Basman-Adorjan, London 1975

[14] 7 ... de 8 d3 0-0 9 0-0 ♘a5 10 ♗b3 ♘ec6 11 ♗e3 ± Bangiev-Kartman, USSR 1980

[15] 8 ... d5 9 ♗b3 b5! 10 ed (10 a3 c4! ∓ Chernov-Serper, USSR 1986) 10 ... ed 11 ♘xb5 ♕a5 ∞ Kosanović-Cebalo, Yugoslav Ch 1986

[16] 11 ♗f2 d5 12 ♗b3 g4 13 ♘d2 c4! ∞ Hebden-Speelman, British Ch 1983

	3	4	5	6	7	8	9	10	11	
4	g3	♗g2	d3	f4[19]	♘f3	0-0	♗d2	♖b1	♘e5	∞
	g6[17]	♗g7	e6[18]	♘ge7	d5	b6	♗b7	♘d4	0-0[20]	

1 e4 c5 2 ♘c3 ♘c6 3 g3 g6 4 ♗g2 ♗g7 5 d3 d6

	6	7	8	9	10	11	12	13	14	
5	♘ge2[21]	0-0	h3	f4	f5	g4	♘f4	♔h1	♘ce2	∞/=
	♘f6[22]	0-0	♘d4[23]	♘d7	b5	♗b7	♗e5	e6	♕h4[24]	
6	f4	♘h3[26]	0-0	f5!?	♕h5[28]	♖f2	♗e3	♖af1	♘d5	∞
	e5[25]	♘ge7[27]	♘d4	gf	h6	♗e6	♕d7	0-0-0	fe[29]	
7	...	♘f3	0-0	♗d2	♖b1	♘e2[32]	g4	gf	c4	=
	e6	♘ge7	0-0[30]	b6[31]	♗b7	♕d7[33]	f5	ef	♘d8[34]	
8	...	...	...	♗e3	♗f2[36]	♗xf3	♗g2	♖b1	♕d2	=
	...	...	...	♘d4[35]	♘xf3+[37]	♘c6	♖b8	b6	♗b7[38]	
9	♗e3	♕d2	♘ge2	0-0	♘d5[41]	ed	♕d1	♕xe2	c3	∞
	e5[39]	♗e6[40]	♘ge7	0-0	♗xd5	♘d4	♘xe2+	b5	a5[42]	
10	...	♕d2	♘ge2[44]	0-0	♖ae1	♘d1	♕xa5	♘xd4	♗d2	=
	e6	♘ge7[43]	♘d4	0-0	♘ec6	♕a5!	♘xa5	cd	♘c6[45]	

¹⁷ 3 ... ♖b8!? 4 f4 g6 5 ♘f3 ♗g7 6 ♗g2 b5
7 a3 ♕a5 8 0-0 b4 = Spassky-Ljubojević,
Bugojno 1978

3 ... e6 4 ♗g2 ♘f6 5 ♘ge2 d5 6 ed ed 7 d4
cd 8 ♘xd4 ♗b4 9 0-0 0-0 10 ♗g5 ♗xc3 11 bc
h6 = Spassky-Garcia Gonzalez, Linares 1981

¹⁸ 5 ... b6 6 ♘h3!? ♗b7 7 0-0 d6 8 f4 h6 9 f5 ±
Smyslov-Portisch, match 1971

5 ... ♖b8 6 ♘h3 b5 7 0-0 e6 8 ♗g5 ♘ge7
9 ♕d2 b4 10 ♘d1 d5 = Spassky-Ljubojević,
Bugojno 1981

¹⁹ 6 ♘h3 ♘ge7 7 0-0 0-0 8 ♗e3 b6 9 ♕d2
d5 10 ♗h6 d4 =

6 ♗e3 ♘d4 7 ♘ce2 b6 8 c3 ♘xe2 9 ♘xe2
♗b7 10 ♕d2 f5 11 0-0 ♘e7 = Medina-Mecking,
Palma de Mallorca 1969

²⁰ 11 ♖e1 ♕c7 ∞ Marjanović-Kuzmin, Bled/
Portorož 1979

²¹ 6 ♘f3 e5 7 0-0 ♘ge7 8 a3 0-0 9 ♖b1 h6
10 b4 b6 11 ♘d2 ♗e6 = Popović-Schmidt,
Sombor 1978

²² 6 ... e6 7 0-0 ♘ge7 8 ♗g5 b6 9 ♕d2 h6
10 ♗e3 ♗a6 11 ♖fe1 ♘d4 12 f4 ♖c8 = Spassky-
Panno, Lucerne 1985

6 ... e5 7 0-0 ♘ge7 8 a3 0-0 9 ♖b1 f5
10 ♗d2 a5 11 a4 ♗e6 12 ♘d5 h6 = Spassky-Hort,
West Germany 1985-86; 7 ♘d5 ♘ge7 8 ♘ec3
♖b8 9 h4 h6 ∞ Spassky-Suba, Reggio Emilia
1986-87

²³ 8 ... ♖b8 9 f4 ♗d7 10 a3 ♘d4 11 ♘xd4
cd 12 ♘e2 ♕b6 = Shamkovich-Browne, US
Ch 1977

²⁴ Lutikov-Romanishin, Tbilisi 1979

²⁵ 6 ... ♘f6 7 ♘f3 0-0 8 0-0 ♖b8 9 h3 b5
10 a3 (10 g4 b4 11 ♘e2 c4! = Lobron-Keene,
Bochum 1981) 10 ... a5 11 ♗e3 b4 12 ab ab
13 ♘e2 ± Spassky-Geller, match 1969

6 ... ♖b8 7 ♘f3 b5 8 0-0 b4 9 ♘d5 e6
10 ♘e3 ♘ge7 11 a3 a5 ∞ Roos-Miles, Amsterdam 1978

6 ... f5 7 ♘f3 ♘f6 8 0-0 0-0 9 ♔h1 ♗d7
10 ♗e3 ♖b8 11 ♕e2 ± Smyslov

²⁶ 7 ♘f3 ♘ge7 8 0-0 0-0 9 ♗e3 ef 10 gf ♘d4
11 ♕d2 ♘ec6 12 ♖ab1 ♗g4 = Bastian-Ribli,
Baden-Baden 1981

²⁷ 7 ... ef!? 8 ♗xf4 ♘ge7 9 0-0 h6 10 ♕d2
(10 ♖b1 0-0 11 a3 ♗e6 12 ♗e3 ♘e5 ∞ Spassky-
Portisch, match 1977) 10 ... g5 11 ♗e3 ♘ce5
12 ♘f2 0-0 ∞ Hodgson-Kudrin, Hastings 1986-
87

²⁸ 10 ♘g5!? h6 11 ef hg 12 f6 ♗f8 13 fe
♗xe7 ∞ Seret-Birnboim, Malta Ol 1980

²⁹ 15 ♘xe7+ ♕xe7 16 ♗xd4 cd 17 ♖xf7 ∞
Spassky-Hort, Bugojno 1978

³⁰ 8 ... ♗d7 9 ♗e3 ♘d4 10 ♖b1 ♖c8 11 ♗f2
♘ec6 12 ♘e2 ± Spassky-Hort, West Germany
1981

³¹ 9 ... ♖b8 10 ♖b1 b5 11 a3 a5 (11 ... f5
12 ♗e3 ♕c7 13 ♗f2 ♔h8 14 ♖e1 b4 15 ab
cb 16 ♘e2 ± Spassky-Larsen, match 1968)
12 a4 b4! 13 ♘b5 d5 14 c4 bc 15 bc ± Spassky-
Larsen, match 1968

³² 11 a3 ♕d7 12 ♘e2 ♘d4 13 ♘exd4 cd
14 ♕e2 ♖ac8 = Balashov-Adorjan, Munich 1979

³³ 11 ... f5!? 12 c4 ♕d7 13 a3 d5 ∞ Lobron-
Ree, Malta Ol 1980

³⁴ 15 ♘c3 ♘e6 = Spassky-Portisch, match
1980

³⁵ 9 ... b6?! 10 d4! ♗a6 11 ♖e1 ± Evans-
Lombardy, USA 1973

³⁶ 10 ♖b1 b6 (10 ... ♗d7 11 ♘e2 ♘xf3+
12 ♗xf3 ♕c7 13 ♕d2 ♖ad8 14 c4 b6 =
Christiansen-Andersson, Mar del Plata 1981)
11 ♘e2 ♘xf3+ 12 ♗xf3 ♖b8 ∞ Spassky-
Portisch, Toluca IZ 1982

³⁷ 10 ... ♘ec6 11 ♘xd4 ♘xd4 12 ♖b1 ♗d7
13 ♘e2 ♕a5 ∞ Spassky-Miles, Gjovik 1983

³⁸ Spassky-Karpov, Linares 1983

³⁹ 6 ... ♘f6 7 h3 0-0 8 ♕d2 ♘d4 9 ♘ce2 e5
10 c3 ♘c6 11 f4 ± Ljubojević-Sunye, Brasilia
1981

6 ... b5 7 e5 ♗b7 (7 ... ♕d7 8 ed ed 9 ♘ge2
♘ge7 10 d4 ± Romanishin-Torre, Indonesia
1983) 8 ed ed 9 ♘b5 ♘ge7 10 ♘e2 (10 ♘c3
♕b6 11 ♖b1 ♘e5 ∞∞ Ljubojević-Miles, London
1982) ± Miles

6 ... ♖b8!? 7 ♕d2 (7 f4 ♘d4 8 ♘f3 b5
9 ♖b1 b4 10 ♘e2 e5 = Norwood-Benjamin,
Toronto 1985) 7 ... b5 8 ♘ge2 b4 9 ♘d1 ♘d4
10 0-0 e6 = Ljubojević-Tringov, Lucerne Ol
1982

⁴⁰ 7 ... ♘ge7 8 ♗h6 ♗xh6 (8 ... 0-0 9 ♗xg7
♔xg7 10 f4 ♘d4 11 ♘f3 ♗g4 12 0-0 ± Ljubojević-
van der Wiel, Tilburg 1983) 9 ♕xh6 ♘d4
10 ♖c1 ♗e6 11 ♘f3 ♕b6 ∞ Rohde-Dlugy,
US Ch 1986

⁴¹ 10 f4 ♘d4 11 ♖ae1 ♕d7 12 ♘c1 ♖ad8
13 ♘d1 b6 =

⁴² Hort-Larsen, Sousse IZ 1967

⁴³ 7 ... ♕a5 8 ♘f3 ♘d4 9 0-0 ♗d7 10 ♗f4
♕b6 11 ♖ab1 ♖c8 12 ♖fe1 ♘e7 13 e5 ±
Ljubojević-A.Rodriguez, Biel IZ 1985

7 ... ♖b8 8 ♘ge2 ♘d4 9 0-0 b5 10 ♘d1
♘e7 11 ♘c1! b4 12 a3 a5 13 ab ab 14 c3 ±
Spassky-Portisch, match 1980

⁴⁴ 8 ♗h6 ♗xh6 9 ♕xh6 ♘d4 10 0-0-0 ♘ec6
11 ♘ge2 ♗d7 = Ljubojević-Quinteros, Mar del
Plata 1981

8 ♘h3 0-0 9 0-0 (9 ♗h6 ♗xh6 10 ♕xh6 f6
11 0-0 ♘d4 12 ♕d2 e5 = Balashov-Timman,
Rio de Janeiro IZ 1979) 9 ... b6!? 10 ♗h6 d5
11 ed ed 12 ♗xg7 ♔xg7 13 ♘f4 d4 ∞ Spassky-
Kavalek, Linares 1981

⁴⁵ 15 c4!? = Polugayevsky

293

Sicilian IV 1 e4 c5 2 ♘f3

	2	3	4	5	6	7	8	9	10	
1	...	d4	♘xd4	♘c3	♗g5	♗c4	♕e2	♗d5	0-0	±/±
	b6[1]	cd	♗b7	d6[2]	♘d7	a6	b5	♕c8	♘gf6[3]	
2	...	d4[4]	♘xd4[5]	♘c3	♘de2[6]	♘g3	♕d2	♘a4	♘xc5	=
	a6	cd	♘f6	e5	♗c5	♕b6[7]	0-0	♕c6	♕xc5[8]	
3	...	c3	ed	c4[11]	de	d4[12]	♘xd4	♗e3	♘c3[13]	∞∞
	...	d5[9]	♘f6![10]	e6	♗xe6	cd	♗c5	♘g4	♘xe3[14]	
4	...	d4[15]	♕xd4	♗b5![17]	♗xc6[19]	♕xd8+	♘c3	♗e3	♗f4	±
	g6	cd[16]	♘f6	♘c6[18]	dc[20]	♔xd8	♔e8	♘g4	♗g7[21]	
5	...	c3	d4	cd	e5[24]	h3	♘c3	♗g5	♗b5	±
	...	♗g7	cd[22]	d5[23]	♘c6[25]	♗f5[26]	e6	♕b6	♗e4[27]	
6	...	♘c3	d4[29]	ed	♘xd5[30]	♗e3	♘xd4	c3[32]	♕xd4	∞/±
	♘f6	♘c6[28]	d5	♘xd5	♕xd5	cd	♗d7[31]	♘xd4	♕xd4[33]	
7	...	e5	d4[35]	♕xd4	♗c4[36]	♕e4	ed[38]	♕e2	0-0	±
	...	♘d5[34]	cd	e6	♘c6	d6[37]	♘f6	♗xd6	0-0[39]	
8	...	...	♘c3	♘e4	c4	b3[43]	ed	♘xc5	d4	∞
	...	...	e6[40]	♘c6[41]	♘b6[42]	d5!	f5[44]	e5	♗xd6[45]	
9	...	...	...	♘xd5	d4	♗b5+[46]	0-0	c4	♗e3	±/±
	...	...	...	ed	d6	♘c6[47]	♗e7	♗e6	♕b6[48]	
10	...	...	...	...	...	dc[49]	♕xd5[50]	ed	♕e4+!?[52]	∞/±
	...	...	...	...	♘c6	♗xc5	d6[51]	♕b6	♗e6[53]	

---

[1] 2 ... ♕c7 3 c3!? (3 ♘c3; 3 d4 cd 4 ♘xd4 ♘c6 – 2 ... ♘c6) 3 ... ♘f6 4 e5 ♘d5 5 d4 cd 6 cd d6 7 ♗d3 de 8 ♘xe5 e6 9 0-0 ± Timman-Quinteros, Mar del Plata 1982

[2] 5 ... e6 6 ♘db5 a6 7 ♘d6+ ♗xd6 8 ♕xd6 ±
5 ... a6 6 ♗d3 d6 7 0-0 ♘f6 8 f4 e6 9 ♕e2 ± Panchenko-Sahović, Dubna 1979
5 ... ♘c6 6 ♗f4! ± Belyavsky-Quinteros, Vienna 1986

[3] 11 ♖ad1 ±/± Panchenko-Psakhis, USSR 1978

[4] 3 ♘c3 e6 (3 ... b5?! 4 d4 cd 5 ♘xd4 ♗b7 6 ♗g5 ±/± Shamkovich-Marcland, USA 1977) 4 d4 cd 5 ♘xd4 – 2 ... e6
3 c4 e6 4 d4 cd 5 ♘xd4 – 2 ... e6

[5] 4 c3!? dc 5 ♘xc3 e6 – 2 d4

[6] 6 ♘f3 ♗b4 7 ♗c4 ♕c7 8 ♕d3 (8 ♗b3 0-0 9 0-0 ♗xc3 10 bc d6 11 ♖e1 = Gligorić) 8 ... b5 9 ♗b3 ♗b7 ∞
6 ♘b3 ♗b4 7 ♗d2 0-0 8 ♗d3 ♗xc3 9 ♗xc3 d5 10 ed ♕xd5 = Suetin

[7] 7 ... d6 8 ♗e2 ♗e6 9 0-0 0-0 10 ♔h1 d5 =

[8] 11 c4 = Uitumen-Taimanov, Palma de Mallorca IZ 1970

[9] 3 ... d6 4 d4 ♘d7 5 ♗d3 e6 6 0-0 ♘gf6 7 ♕e2 ±
3 ... ♘f6 4 e5 ♘d5 5 d4 cd 6 cd d6 7 ♘c3 ♘xc3 8 bc e6 9 ♗d3 ±

[10] 4 ... ♕xd5 5 d4 ♘f6 6 ♗e2 e6 7 0-0 ♘c6

8 c4 ♕d8 9 ♗e3 cd 10 ♘xd4 ♘xd4 11 ♗xd4 ± Dolmatov-A.Ivanov, USSR 1980

[11] 5 ♕a4+ ♘bd7 6 c4 b5! 7 cb ♘xd5 8 ba ♘b4 9 d4 ♗xa6 ∞
5 d4 cd (5 ... ♘xd5 6 ♗d3 cd 7 cd g6 8 ♘c3 ± Nunn-Boey, Amsterdam II 1976) 6 ♕a4+! ♕d7 7 ♕xd7+ ♘bxd7 (7 ... ♗xd7 8 c4 ± Shalnev-Korsunsky, USSR 1982) 8 c4 b5 9 b3 bc 10 bc ♘c5 ∞

[12] 7 ♘c3 ♘c6 8 ♗e2 ♕c7! (8 ... ♘d4?! 9 d3 ♘xe2 10 ♕xe2 ♗e7 11 0-0 ± Olafsson-Bazan, Mar del Plata 1960) 9 0-0 0-0-0 ∞

[13] 10 ♗e2?! ♘xe3 11 fe ♕h4+ 12 g3 ♕h6! ∓

[14] 11 fe ♕h4+ 12 g3 ♕h6 13 ♕f3 0-0 14 ♕f4! (14 ♗e2? ♘c6 15 ♖ad1 ♖ae8 16 ♘xc6 bc ∓ Kuindzhi-Govashelishvili, USSR 1982) 14 ... ♕xf4 15 gf ♘c6 ∞∞

[15] 3 c4 ♘c6 – 2 ... ♘c6
3 c4!? ♗g7 4 0-0 ♘c6 5 c3 d6 6 d4 ♘f6 7 d5 (7 e5 ±) ±

[16] 3 ... ♗g7 4 d5 – 1 d4 c5; 4 ♘c3 (4 dc ♕a5+ 5 ♘c3 ♘f6 6 ♗d3 ♕xc5 7 ♗e3 ♕a5 8 ♕d2 ± Sveshnikov-Romanishin, USSR Ch 1977) 4 ... ♕a5 5 d5 ♗xc3+ 6 bc ♘f6 7 ♘d2! ♕xc3 8 ♖b1 ± Mortensen-Keene, Gausdal 1983

[17] 5 e5 ♘c6 6 ♕a4 ♘d5 7 a3 ♕b6 8 ♕e4 ♘c7 9 ♘c3 ♗g7 ∞ Hulak-Barlov, Yugoslavia 1975

[18] 5 ... ♕a5+?! 6 ♕c3! ♘c6 7 ♕xa5 ♘xa5

[8] ♘c3 a6 9 e5 ♘g4 10 ♘d5 ± Kavalek-Lehmann, West Germany 1985-86

[19] 6 ♕a4!? ♗g7 7 0-0 ♕c7 8 ♘c3 a6 9 ♗g5 ± Krnić-Kupreichik, Wijk aan Zee 1977

[20] 6 ... bc 7 e5 ♘d5 8 0-0 ♗g4 9 ♕h4 f6 10 c4 ♘c7 11 ♗h6 ± Sax-Tatai, Rome 1986

[21] 11 e5 g5 12 ♗g3 h5 13 h4 ± Pribyl-Sikora, Czechoslovak Ch 1980

[22] 4 ... ♕a5 5 ♗bd2 (5 ♗e2 cd 6 b4 ♕b6 7 cd ♘c6 8 ♘c3 ∞ Miles-Quinteros, Buenos Aires 1979) 5 ... cd 6 ♘b3 ♕b8 7 cd ♘f6 8 ♗d3 0-0 9 0-0 ♘c6 10 e5 ±

[23] 5 ... ♘f6 6 e5 ♘e4 7 ♗d3 d5 8 ♘c3 ± Adorjan-Sikora, Warsaw 1979

[24] 6 ed ♘f6 7 ♗b5+ ♘bd7 - 1 e4 c6 2 c4

[25] 6 ... ♗g4 7 ♘bd2!? ♘c6 8 ♗d3 ± Westerinen-Filipowicz, Esbjerg 1977

[26] 7 ... ♘h6!? 8 ♘c3 0-0 9 ♗b5 ♔h8 10 0-0 ± Andersson-Dueball, Berlin 1971

[27] 11 0-0 ♗xf3 12 ♕xf3 ± Sanz-Gurgenidze, Tbilisi 1980

[28] 3 ... e6 4 d4 d5 5 ed ♘xd5 6 ♘xd5 ♕xd5 7 ♗e3 ♘d7 8 ♗e2 ± Dolmatov-Murei, Amsterdam 1986

3 ... d5 4 ed ♘xd5 5 ♗b5+ ♘c6 (5 ... ♗d7 6 ♕e2 ♘xc3 7 dc a6 8 ♗xd7+ ♕xd7 9 ♘e5 ±) 6 ♘e4 e6 7 0-0 ♗e7 8 ♗xc6+ bc 9 b3 0-0 10 ♘e5 ± Kozlov-Osnos, USSR 1978

[29] 4 e5 ♘g4 5 ♕e2 ♕c7 6 ♘d5 ♕b8 7 d4 cd 8 ♗f4 e6 9 h3 ∞ Krnić-Mozetić, Yugoslavia 1982

[30] 6 ♗b5 ♘xc3 7 bc cd 8 ♘xd4 ♗d7 9 ♖b1 g6 ∞/=

6 dc!? ♘xc3 7 ♕xd8+ ♔xd8 8 bc ♗d7 (8 ... g6 9 ♗e3 ♗g7 10 ♗b5 ± Kuzmin-Pribyl, Tallinn 1985) 9 ♗e3 g6 (9 ... ♖c8?! 10 ♘e5! ♗a4 11 ♖b1! ± Romero-Casafus, Dubai Ol 1986) 10 0-0-0 ♗g7 11 ♗d4 ♗h6+ 12 ♔b2 0-0 13 ♘e5 ♗e6 ∞ Krnić-Wedberg, Eksjö 1978

[31] 8 ... ♘xd4 9 ♕xd4 ♕xd4 10 ♗xd4 ♗d7 11 0-0-0 ♗c6 12 f3 (12 f4!?) ±

8 ... ♕a5+ 9 c3 ♘xd4 10 b4 ♕e5 11 ♕xd4 ♕xd4 12 ♗xd4 ± Spassky-Pribyl, Tallinn 1973

8 ... a6 9 c3 e5 10 ♕b3 ♕xb3 11 ♘xb3 ♗e6 12 0-0-0 ±

[32] 9 ♘b5 ♕xd1+ 10 ♖xd1 ♖c8 11 ♘xa7 ♘xa7 12 ♗xa7 ♖xc2 13 ♗d4 e5!? ∞

[33] 11 ♘xd4 ♘c6 12 0-0-0 e6 13 h4 h5 14 ♖h3 ∞/± Speelman-Wedberg, Skara 1980

[34] 3 ... ♘g4 4 h3 ♘h6 5 c3 ♘c6 6 d4 ± Peters-Shirazi, Los Angeles 1982

[35] 4 g3 e6 (4 ... d6 5 ♗g2 ♘c6 6 ed ♕xd6 7 0-0 ♗g4 8 h3 ♗h5 9 d4 ± Veličković-Mnatsakanian, Tbilisi 1983) 5 ♗g2 d6 6 0-0 ♘c6 =

4 c4 ♘c7 5 b4!? cb 6 d4 d5 7 a3 ♘c6 8 ab ♘xb4 9 ♘c3 ∞ van der Wiel-Ostermeyer, Porz 1981-82

[36] 6 c4 ♘c6 7 ♕e4 ♘de7 ∞/∓
6 a3 ♘c6 7 ♕e4 b6!? ∞

[37] 7 ... f5 8 ♕e2 ♘de7 9 ♘c3 a6 10 h4! ± Tal-Zaitsev, Sochi 1977

[38] 8 0-0 de 9 ♘xe5 ♘f6 10 ♘xc6 ♕c7 (10 ... ♘xe4 11 ♘xd8 ±) 11 ♕f3 ♗d7 ∞ Timoshchenko-Garcia Palermo, Havana 1981

[39] 11 ♘c3 a6 12 ♗g5 ± Balashov-Pribyl, Moscow 1977

[40] 4 ... ♘c7 5 d4 cd 6 ♕xd4 ♘c6 7 ♕e4 ±

4 ... ♘xc3 5 dc ♘c6 (5 ... d5 6 ed ♕xd6 7 ♕xd6 ed 8 ♗f4 ±) 6 ♗f4 e6 (6 ... h6!? 7 ♕e2 ♕c7 8 0-0-0 b6 9 ♘e3 e6 ∞ van der Wiel-Murei, Moscow IZ 1982) 7 ♗c4 (7 ♕d2 ♕c7) 7 ... ♕c7 8 0-0 b6 9 ♖e1 ± Boleslavsky

[41] 5 ... f5 6 ef!? (6 ♘c3 ♘c6 7 ♗c4 ♘b6 8 ♗b5 ♕c7 9 ♗xc6+ ♕xc6 10 0-0 d5 ∞ Georgadze-Ostermeyer, Porz 1981-82) 6 ... ♘xf6 7 ♕xf6+ ♕xf6 8 d4 cd 9 ♘xd4! ♘c6 10 ♗e3 d5 11 c3 a6 12 ♗e2 ± Dolmatov-Pribyl, Tallinn 1985

[42] 6 ... ♘f4?! 7 b4! cb 8 d4 ♘g6 9 h4! ± Kindermann-Biro, Budapest 1986

6 ... ♘db4 7 a3 ♕a5 8 ♕b3 d5 9 ed e5 10 ♖b1 ♘a6 11 g4! ±/± Kopilov-Korolev, corr. 1983

[43] 7 b4!? Gurgenidze

[44] 8 ... ♗xd6 9 d4 f5 10 ♘xd6+ ♕xd6 11 ♗a3 ± Gipslis-Mnatsakanian, USSR 1977

[45] 11 ♗e3 ♕e7 12 d5 ∞ Kuporosov-Mnatsakanian, Sochi 1979

[46] 7 ed ♗xd6 8 ♗e3 c4 9 ♗e2 0-0 10 0-0 ♘c6 =

7 ♗g5 ♕a5+ 8 c3 cd 9 ♕xd4 (9 ♗d3!? dc 10 0-0 ♘c6 11 ♖e1 ♗e6 12 bc de 13 ♘xe5 ♘xe5 14 ♖xe5 ♗d6 ∞) 9 ... ♘c6 10 ♕e3 ♗e6 11 ♘d4 ∞ Kelečević-Kozomara, Sarajevo 1968

[47] 7 ... ♗d7 8 ♗xd7+ ♕xd7 9 0-0 ♘c6 10 ed ± Boleslavsky

[48] 11 a4! ±/± Unzicker-Pomar, Bad Aibling 1968

[49] 7 c3!? d6 8 ♗b5 ♗e7 9 ed ♕xd6 10 0-0 0-0 11 dc ♕xc5 12 ♕a4 ∞/± Geller-Kirov, Moscow 1977

[50] 8 ♗d3!? d6 9 ed 0-0 10 0-0 ♕xd6 11 c3 h6 12 ♗c2 ♗g4 13 ♕d3 ± Biyiasas-Peters, Hastings 1978-79

[51] 8 ... ♕b6 9 ♗c4 ♗xf2+ 10 ♔e2 0-0 11 ♖f1 ♗c5 12 ♘g5 (12 c3 d6 13 b4 ♗xb4! 14 cb ♗e6 ∞) 12 ... ♘d4+ (12 ... ♘xe5?! 13 ♕xe5 d5 14 ♕xd5 ± Spassky) 13 ♗d1 ♘c6 14 ♘e4! d6 15 ed ♖d8 16 ♕f5!? (16 ♗d3 ± A.Rodriguez-Diaz, Cuban Ch 1983) 16 ... ♗xd6 17 ♘xd6 ♕xd6 18 ♗d3 ± Short

[52] 10 ♗c4 ♗xf2+ 11 ♔e2 0-0 12 ♖d1 ♗e6 13 ♕e4 ♖ae8 14 ♔f1 ♗d7! = Keller-Schiffer, corr. 1976

[53] 11 d7+ ♕xd7 12 ♗e3 ♗xe3 13 ♖d1+ ♔c7 14 fe ♖ad8! =/∓ Kasparov, Keene

11 ♕h4 ♗xd6 12 ♗e2 (12 c3?! ♗e7 13 ♕g3 0-0-0 ∓) 12 ... ♗e7 13 ♕e4 0-0-0 13 0-0 ∞/± Chandler-Bartsch, West Germany 1985

	3	4	5	6	7	8	9	10	11	
1	♗b5+	d4	♘c3[2]	♕xd4	♕d3	♗e3[5]	0-0	♗c4	♗b3	±
	♘d7[1]	♘f6	cd[3]	e5[4]	h6	♗e7	0-0[6]	♘b6	♗e6[7]	
2	...	♗xd7+	0-0[9]	c3	d4[10]	cd	e5	♘e1	f3	∞
	♗d7	♕xd7[8]	♘c6	♘f6	cd[11]	d5	♘e4	f6[12]	♘g5[13]	
3	c3	♗e2[14]	0-0	d3	♗g5	♘bd2	♖e1	♗f1	d4	=
	♘f6	e6[15]	♗e7	0-0	b6	♗b7	♘bd7	♘e5	♘xf3+[16]	
4	...	h3	♗d3[18]	♗c2	0-0	d4	cd	e5	♘c3	±
	...	♘c6[17]	g6[19]	♗g7	0-0[20]	cd	d5[21]	♘e8[22]	♘c7[23]	
5	d4	♕xd4	e5[25]	♗b5	♘c3	♘xb5	♘fxd4	♘c7+	♘xa8	=
	cd	♘f6[24]	♘c6	♕a5+	♕xb5	♘xd4	de	♔d7[26]	ed[27]	
6	...	...	♗b5	♗xc6	♘c3[28]	♗g5	0-0-0	♖he1	♕d2[29]	∞
	...	♘c6	♗d7	♗xc6	♘f6	e6	♗e7	0-0	♕c7[30]	

[1] 3 ... ♘c6 – 2 ... ♘c6 3 ♗b5

[2] **5 dc** ♕a5+ 6 ♘c3 ♘xe4 7 c6 bc 8 ♗xc6 ♘xc3 9 ♗d2 ♕a6 10 ♗xd7+ ♕xd7 11 ♗xc3 e5 ∓ Konopka-Kengis, Moscow 1986
  5 e5 ♕a5+ 6 ♘c3 ♘e4 7 ♗d2 ♘xc3 8 ♗xd7+ ♕xd7 9 ♗xc3 ♕a6 ∞
  5 0-0 cd 6 ♕xd4 a6 7 ♗xd7+ ♕xd7 8 ♗g5 h6 9 ♗xf6 gf 10 ♘c3 e6 ∞/= Fernandez Garcia-Csom, Malaga 1981

[3] 5 ... a6 6 ♗xd7+ ♘xd7 7 ♗e3 (7 0-0 e6 8 ♗g5 ♕c7 9 dc ♘xc5 10 ♖e1 ± Ghinda-Ftacnik, Bratislava 1983) 7 ... e6 8 a4 b6 9 0-0 ♗e7 10 d5 ± Rozentalis-Dokhoyan, USSR 1986

[4] **6 ... e6** 7 ♗g5 ♗e7 8 e5 ± Vasyukov-Belyavsky, USSR 1975
  6 ... g6 7 ♗g5 ♗g7 8 0-0-0 0-0 9 e5 ± Stean-Dueball, England v West Germany 1974

[5] 8 ♘d2 ♗e7 9 ♘c4 0-0 10 ♗xd7 ♗xd7! 11 ♘e3 (11 ♘xd6?! ♕c7 12 ♘f5 ♗xf5 13 ef e4 ∞̄ Mednis-Csom, Cleveland 1975) 11 ... ♗e6 = Rogers-Suba, Dortmund 1985

[6] 9 ... a6!? 10 ♗c4 ♕c7 11 ♘h4 g6!? Stanciu-Suba, Romanian Ch 1985

[7] 12 ♘h4 ♖c8 (12 ... ♕d7 13 ♗xe6 fe 14 ♘b5 ± Kupreichik-Polugayevsky, USSR Ch 1976) 13 ♘g6 ♖e8 14 ♖fd1 ± Chandler-Mestel, Brighton 1984

[8] 4 ... ♘xd7 5 0-0 ♘gf6 6 ♕e2 ♖c8 (6 ... e6 7 d4 cd 8 ♘xd4 ♘c5 9 f3 ♕b6 10 ♕b5+ ± Korchnoi-Miles, Linares 1985) 7 c3 e6 8 d4 cd 9 cd d5 10 e5 ♘e4 ∞/= Ghinda-Chandler, Lucerne 1985

[9] 5 c4 ♘c6 6 d4 cd 7 ♘xd4 ♘f6 8 ♘c3 e6 9 0-0 ♗e7 10 ♘c2 (10 ♗e3 0-0 11 f3 ♖fd8 = Bouaziz-Tseshkovsky, Riga IZ 1979) 10 ... 0-0 11 ♗f4 ♖fd8 12 ♘e3 ♖ac8 = Ghinda-Kir.Georgiev, Sofia 1986

[10] 7 ♕e2 e6 8 d4 cd 9 cd d5 10 e5 ♘e4 = Fernandez Garcia-Ljubojević, Dubai Ol 1986

[11] 7 ... ♘xe4 8 d5 intending 9 ♖e1 ∞̄/±

[12] 10 ... h6 11 ♗e3 e6 12 ♘d3 ♗e7 13 ♕g4 g6 ∞ Sharif-Cebalo, Marseilles 1986

[13] 12 ♗xg5 fg 13 ♘c3 e6 14 ♘e2 ♗e7 15 ♘d3 0-0 ∞ Ristić-Gutman, St Wendel 1986

[14] 4 e5 de 5 ♘xe5 ♘bd7 =
  4 ♗d3 ♘c6 5 ♗c2 (5 h3 – 4 h3) 5 ... ♗g4 6 d3 e6 7 ♘bd2 ♗e7 8 h3 ♗h5 9 ♘f1 d5 10 ♘g3 ♗g6 = Martinović-Jansa, Vrnjačka Banja 1981, and Ostermeyer-Tal, Porz 1981-82

[15] **4 ... ♘c6** 5 d4 (5 d3!? g6 6 0-0 ♗g7 7 d4! Ljubojević-van der Wiel, Amsterdam 1986) 5 ... cd 6 cd ♘xe4 7 d5 ♕a5+ 8 ♘c3 ♘xc3 9 bc ♘e5 (9 ... ♘d8 10 0-0 e5 11 de ♘xe6 12 ♘d4 ± Martinović-Jansa, Bor 1985) 10 ♘xe5 de (10 ... ♕xc3+ 11 ♗d2 ♕xe5 12 0-0 ± Basman-Stean, Hastings 1973-74) 11 0-0 e6 12 ♖b1 ± Kr.Georgiev-Sindik, West Berlin 1986
  4 ... ♘bd7 5 d3 b6 6 0-0 ♗b7 7 ♘bd2 g6 8 ♖e1 ♗g7 9 ♗f1 0-0 10 d4 e6 = Kr.Georgiev-Ftacnik, Prague Z 1985

[16] 12 ♕xf3 cd 13 cd ♘d5 = Romanishin-Korchnoi, Tilburg 1985

[17] 4 ... e6 5 ♗d3 ♗e7 6 ♗c2 0-0 7 d4 b5 8 ♕e2 ♗b7 9 0-0 ♘bd7 10 ♖e1 ± Martinović-

de Firmian, Vrnjačka Banja 1983

[18] 5 d4?! cd 6 cd Nxe4 7 d5 Qa5+ 8 Nc3 Nxc3 9 bc Ne5 10 Nxe5 Qxc3+ 11 Bd2 Qxe5+ 12 Be3 Qc3+ 13 Bd2 Qe5+ 14 Be3 Bd7! ∓ Fucak-Ghinda, Nikea 1985

[19] 5 ... e5!? 6 0-0 Be7 7 Bc2 d5

[20] 7 ... e5 8 d4 ed 9 cd 0-0 (9 ... cd 10 Nxd4 0-0 11 Nxc6 bc 12 Nc3 Re8 13 Qf3 ± Marjanović-Kudrin, Titograd 1984) 10 d5 Nb4 11 Nc3 Nxc2 12 Qxc2 Re8 13 Re1 a6 14 a4 ± Barlov-Vera, Sochi 1985

[21] 9 ... Nb4 10 Bb3 d5 11 e5 Ne4 12 Nc3 Bf5 13 Ne2! ± A.Rodriguez-Garcia Martinez, Havana 1985

[22] 10 ... Ne4 11 Nc3 Nxc3 (11 ... Bf5 12 Ne2! f6 13 ef Rxf6 14 Nf4 ⊥ Marjanović-Browne, Thessaloniki Ol 1984) 12 bc f6 13 ef ef 14 Re1 Re8 16 Rb1 ± Marjanović-Ivanović, Novi Sad 1984

[23] 12 Be3 f6 13 ef ef = Qi-Sisniega, Taxco IZ 1985

12 Re1 b6 (12 ... f6 13 ef ef 14 Bb3 intending Bf4 ±) 13 Be3 Nb4 14 Bb1 ± Stoica-Szekely, Athens 1986

[24] 4 ... Bd7 5 c4 Nc6 6 Qd2 Nf6 7 Nc3 g6 8 b3 Bg7 9 Bb2 0-0 10 Be2 ±

4 ... a6 5 Bg5 Nc6 6 Qd2 ±

[25] 5 Nc3 a6 6 Be3 (6 Bg5 Nc6 7 Qe3 e6 ∞) 6 ... Nbd7 (6 ... Nc6 7 Qb6 ±) 7 0-0-0 e5 8 Qa4 Be7 ∞

[26] 10 ... Kd8 11 Nxa8 ed 12 Bf4 Qd5 13 0-0-0 Nxf4 14 Rxd4+ Bd7 15 Rxf4 g6 16 Rc4 Bh6+ 17 Kb1 Bc6 18 b4 ± Messa-Nunn, Lugano 1982

[27] 12 Bf4 Qd5 13 0-0-0 e6 14 Rxd4 Bc5 15 Rc4 (15 Rd2 Kc6) 15 ... b6 16 Bg3 Bb7 17 Nc7 Rxc7 18 Bxc7 Qd5 20 Rxc5 = Dmitriev-Zilberstein, USSR 1984

[28] 7 c4 f5 8 ef (8 Nc3 e5 9 Qd3 fe 10 Nxe4 Nf6 11 Nxf6+ gf 12 Qf5 Qd7! ∓ Silli-Pantaleoni, corr. 1985) 8 ... Qa5+ 9 Nc3 Qxf5 ∞ Damjanović-Groszpeter, Prague 1986

[29] 11 e5 de 12 Qh4 Qe8 (12 ... Qc7 13 Nxe5 Rfd8 = Adorjan-Tal, Sochi 1977) 13 Nxe5 h6 14 Bxh6 gh 15 Qxh6 Nh7 16 f4 Kh8 ∞ Svensk-Hellers, Sweden 1985

11 Kb1 Qc7 12 Qd2 Rfc8 13 Nd4 b5! 14 f3 (14 Ndxb5 Bxb5 15 Nxb5 Qc5 16 Nc3 Rab8 ∞∞) 14 ... b4 15 Nce2 Be8 16 h4 a5 ∞/∓ Malanyuk-Lukov, Erevan 1984

[30] 12 Nd4 Rfd8 (12 ... b5!? Grottke-Kalinichev-Potsdam 1986) 13 f4 Rac8 14 g4 b5 ∞ Mariotti-Tal, Leningrad 1977, and Johansen-Speelman, British Ch 1985

Sicilian VI (Dragon)			1 e4 c5 2 Nf3 d6 3 d4 cd 4 Nxd4 Nf6 5 Nc3 g6					

	6	7	8	9	10	11	12	13	14
1	Bc4[1]	h3	0-0	Bb3[2]	Bg5	Re1	Nd5	Nxf6+	Qd3	∞
	Bg7	0-0	a6	b6!?[3]	Bb7	Nbd7	e6	Nxf6	Qc7[4]

---

[1] 6 h4 Nc6 7 h5?! Nxh5 8 g4 Nxd4! 9 gh Nc6 10 hg fg ∓ Velimirović-Watson, Bor 1986

6 Bg5 Bg7 7 Qd2 (7 Nb3 0-0 8 Be2 a6 9 0-0 b5 10 Nf3 Ra7 11 Nc1 Nbd7 ∞ Tringov-Miles, Plovdiv 1983) 7 ... Nc6 8 Nb3 0-0 9 Be2 a5 10 a4 Be6 = Ivanović-Sax, Lucerne Ol 1982

[2] 9 Re1 b5 (9 ... Nc6 10 Be3 Na5 11 Bf1 Bd7 12 Nf3 ± Kaidanov-Ehlvest, USSR 1986) 10 Bb3 Bb7 11 a4 Nbd7 12 ab ab 13 Rxa8 Qxa8 14 Ndxb5 Nxe4 ∞ Stoica-Martin Gonzalez, Dubai Ol 1986

[3] 9 ... b5 and now:

10 a4 Bb7 11 Re1 Nc6 12 Nxc6 Bxc6 13 ab ab 14 Rxa8 Qxa8 Kir.Georgiev

10 Nd5 Bb7 11 Nxf6+ Bxf6 12 Bh6 Bg7 13 Qd2 e5 ∞ Kindermann-Kir.Georgiev, Lugano 1986

10 Re1 Bb7 11 Bg5 Nbd7 12 Nd5 ±

[4] Short-Watson, Lugano 1986

297

	6	7	8	9	10	11	12	13	14	
2	g3	♗g2[5]	♕xd4	0-0[6]	♕b4!?[7]	a4[8]	a5[10]	♗e3	bc	∞/±
	♘c6	♘xd4	♗g7	0-0	♕c7	♗e6[9]	♘d7	♗xc3!?[11]	♘e5[12]	
3	f4	♘f3	♗c4	♗b3	♗e3	♕d3	0-0-0	♗d4	g3	∞
	♘bd7[13]	♗g7	♘b6	0-0	♗d7[14]	♘c6	♘fd7[15]	♗h6		
4	...	♗b5[16]	♗xc6	e5	♘xd5[18]	♕f3	♗d2	fe	♕f2	=
	♘c6	♗d7	bc	♘d5[17]	cd	e6	de	♕h4+	♕e4+[19]	
5	...	♘xc6	e5	ed[21]	♗e3[22]	♕d2[24]	0-0-0	♗e2	h4	∞
	...	bc	♘d7[20]	ed	♗e7[23]	0-0[25]	♘b6	d5	h5[26]	
6	♗e2	0-0	♘b3	♔h1	f4	f5	e5[29]	♘xe2	ed	∞
	♗g7	0-0	♘c6	♗e6[27]	♘a5[28]	♗c4	♗xe2	♘g4![30]	♘c4[31]	
7	...	...	...	♗g5	♔h1	f4	a3	♗f3	♖e1	∞/=
	...	...	...	♗d7!?[32]	a6[33]	b5	♖b8	a5	♕c8[34]	
8	♗e3	h3[35]	♗c4	♗b3[36]	0-0	f4[38]	♕f3	a3	♖ad1	∞
	♗g7	0-0	♘c6	♗d7[37]	♖c8	a6	b5	♘a5	♘c4[39]	
9	...	♗e2	♘b3[40]	f4[42]	g4	g5	♗d4	h4[44]	♗xg7	∞
	...	♘c6	0-0[41]	♗e6	♘a5[43]	♘d7	f6	fg	♔xg7[45]	
10	...	...	...	...	a4	♗f3[46]	0-0	♘d4	♖f2	=
	...	...	...	a5	♗e6	♘b4	♘d7	♗c4	e5[47]	
11	...	...	0-0	♕d2[48]	♗xg4	♘d5[50]	c4	b3	♖ae1	∞
	...	...	0-0	♘g4[49]	♗xg4	♖c8[51]	♗e6	♕d7	♘xd4[52]	
12	...	...	...	...	ed[53]	♘xc6[54]	♖fd1[55]	♗d4	♗c5	=
	...	...	...	d5	♘xd5	bc	♕c7	e5	♖d8[56]	

5 7 ♘de2 and now:

7 ... ♗d7 8 ♗g2 ♕c8 9 h3 ♗g7 10 ♗e3 0-0 11 ♖c1 b5 12 b3 ♖b8 13 ♕d2 ± Abramović-Petursson, New York 1986

7 ... ♗g4 8 ♗g2 ♕d7 9 h3 ♗e6 10 ♘d5 ♗g7 11 ♘ef4 ± Arnason-Hansen, Helsinki 1986

7 ... ♗g7 8 ♗g2 0-0 (8 ... ♖b8 9 a4 a6 10 0-0 b5 11 ab ab 12 ♘d5 0-0 13 ♗g5 ± Nunn-Miles, Baden bei Wien 1980) 9 0-0 ♖b8 10 b3 b5 11 ♖b1 b4 12 ♘d5 ♗a6 = Condie-Kir. Georgiev, Dubai Ol 1986

6 9 ♕b4!? ♘d7 10 0-0 ♘e5 11 ♘d5 ♘c6 12 ♕b3 0-0 13 c3 ♖e8 14 ♗g5 ∞/± Ambroz-Robach, Prague 1986

7 10 ♕d1 ♗g4 11 f3 ♕b6+ 12 ♔h1 ♗e6 13 ♖e1 ♖ac8 = Cabrilo-Georgiev, Varna 1983

10 ♕d3 ♗e6 11 ♘d5 ♘xd5 12 ed ♗f5 13 ♕e2 b5!? ∞ Hartman-Sosonko, Hanover 1983

8 11 ♗g5 ♗e6 12 ♘d5 ♗xd5 13 ed b5!? 14 c3 ♖ab8 ∞ Yakovich-Lerner, USSR Ch 1986

9 11 ... a5 12 ♕b3 ♗e6 13 ♘d5 ♘xd5 14 ed ♗f5 15 c3 ♗d3 16 ♖e1 ± Popović-Velimirović, Titograd 1984

10 12 ♘d5 ♗xd5 13 ed ♕xc2! 14 ♕xb7 ♖fe8 15 a5 ♘g4 ∞ Popović-Timman, Zagreb/Rieka 1985

11 13 ... ♘e5 14 ♘d5! ♗xd5 15 ed ♖fc8 16 c3 ± Kudrin-Tal, Titograd 1984

12 15 f4 ♘c4 16 ♗d4 f6 17 ♖fe1! (17 ♖fb1 ♖fb8 18 ♗f2 ♔g7 = Popović-Kir.Georgiev, Sarajevo 1985) ∞/± Kotronias-Kir.Georgiev,

Sofia 1986

[13] 6 ... ♗g7 7 e5 ♘h5 (7 ... de 8 fe ♘fd7 9 e6 ♘e5 10 ♗b5+ ♘ec6 11 ef+ ♔f8 ∞) 8 ♗b5+ ♗d7 9 e6 fe 10 ♘xe6 ♗xc3+ 11 bc ♖c8 12 ♕d3 ♘c6 = Peters-Mestel, Hastings 1980-81

[14] 10 ... ♗e6!? Geller

[15] 12 ... ♗g4?! 13 h4! ♘xe3 14 ♕xe3 ♘d7 15 h5 ♕b6 16 ♕e1 ±/± Hecht-Whiteley, Nice Ol 1974

[16] 7 ♘b3 ♗g7 8 ♗e2 ♕b6! ∓ Cabrilo-Lerner, Lvov 1981

7 ♘f3 ♗g7 8 ♗d3 ♕b6 (8 ... ♗g4 =) 9 h3 e5 10 fe de 11 ♕e2 0-0 = Sax-Sosonko, London 1980

[17] 9 ... de 10 fe ♘g4 11 e6 ♗xe6 12 ♕f3 ♕d7 13 ♗f4 ♗g7 = Euwe

[18] 10 ed ♘xc3 11 bc c5! 12 ♘f3 ♗g7 =

[19] Tsaplinsky-Tolush, USSR 1952

[20] 8 ... ♘g8!? 9 ♗e3 ♗g7 10 ed ed 11 ♕d2 ♘e7 12 0-0-0 0-0! ∞ Peters-Ivanov, Lone Pine 1981; 9 ♗d3!? ± Geller

8 ... de 9 ♕xd8+ ♔xd8 10 fe ♘d5 11 ♗d2 ♔c7 12 0-0-0 ±

[21] 9 ♕f3 ♗g7 (9 ... d5 10 h4 h5 11 e6 ♘f6 ∞/= Ubilava) 10 ♗b5 de 11 ♗xc6 ♖b8 12 ♗e3 ♖xb2 13 0-0-0 e4 =

[22] 10 ♕d4 ♘f6 11 ♗e3 ♗e7 12 ♗e2 0-0 13 ♗f3 d5 14 ♕d2 ♕a5 = Kasparov-Balashov, Moscow 1981

[23] 10 ... ♕e7 11 ♕d4 ♘f6 12 0-0-0 d5 13 ♖e1 ♗e6 14 g4 ±/± Peters-Zaltsman, US Ch 1980

10 ... ♘f6 11 ♕d2 ♗g7 12 0-0-0 d5 13 ♗c5 ♗e6 = Nunn-Miles, London 1982

[24] 11 ♗e2 0-0 12 0-0 d5 13 ♘a4 ♖e8 14 ♕d2 ♘f6 = Nunn-Sax, Teesside 1974

[25] 11 ... ♘f6 12 0-0-0 ♗e6 ∞

[26] 15 g4 ♗xg4 16 ♗xg4 ♘c4 17 ♕d3 ♕b8 ∞ Larsen-Lein, Lone Pine 1979

[27] 9 ... a6 10 f4 b5 11 ♗f3 ♗d7 12 ♗e3 ♖c8 = Lobron-Keene, Dortmund 1982

9 ... a5 10 a4 ♗e6 11 f4 ♕b6 12 ♘d5 ♗xd5 13 ed ♘b4 14 ♗f3 ♕a6 = Larsen

[28] 10 ... ♕c8 11 ♗f3 ♗g4 12 ♘d5 ♗xf3 13 ♕xf3 b5 14 c3 b4 ±/= Kavalek-Sosonko, 1979

[29] 12 ♘xa5 ♗xe2 13 ♕xe2 ♕xa5 14 ♗d2 ♖ac8 15 ♖ae1 ♕b6 16 ♗c1 e6 ∞ Glek-Lerner, Tallinn 1986

[30] 13 ... ♘e8 14 fg hg 15 e6! ♘c6 16 ♘f4 ♘e5 17 ♘d4 ± Psakhis-Lerner, Moscow 1986

[31] 16 ♘ed4! ♘ce3 16 ♗xe3 ♗xe3 17 de ♕xe7 18 ♖e1 ∞ Abramović-Rajković, Yugoslavia 1986

[32] 9 ... a5 10 a4 ♗e6 11 ♔h1 ♖c8 (11 ... ♘d7 12 f4 ± Karpov-Sosonko, Bad Lauterberg 1977) 12 f4 ♘b4 13 ♗h4 ± Lederman-Sikora, Skara 1980

9 ... a6 10 f4 b5 11 ♗f3 b4 12 ♘a4 ♗d7

[13] ♖f2 ± Mencinger-Petursson, Ljubljana 1981

9 ... ♗e6 10 f4 ♘a5 11 f5 ♗c4 12 ♔h1 ♖c8 13 ♗d3 ± Larsen-Miles, Las Palmas 1978

[33] 10 ... ♖b8!? 11 f4 b5 12 ♗f3 a5 13 e5 de 14 ♗xc6 ♗xc6 15 ♕xd8 ♖fxd8 16 fe ♘g4 ∞ Szell-Liptay, Hungary 1986

[34] A.Sokolov-Ljubojević, Bugojno 1986

[35] 7 ♗c4 ♘g4 8 ♗b5+ ♔f8 9 ♗g5 h6 10 ♗h4 g5 11 ♗g3 ♕b6 = Ljubojević-Sosonko, Buenos Aires Ol 1978

[36] 9 0-0 ♗d7 (9 ... ♘xe4 10 ♗xf7+ ♖xf7 11 ♘xe4 ± Stoica-Makropoulos, Bucharest 1983) 10 f4 ∞

[37] 9 ... ♘a5 10 0-0 b6 11 ♕d3 ♗xb3 12 ab ♗b7 13 ♖fd1 a6 14 ♘de2 ± Ljubojević-Adorjan, Amsterdam 1978

[38] 11 ♖e1 a6!? ∞ Geller

[39] 15 ♗c1 ∞ Dueball

[40] 8 h4 h5 9 f3 0-0 10 ♕d2 d5 11 ♘xc6 bc 12 e5 ♘e8 13 f4 f6 = Smyslov-Botvinnik, match (9) 1958

8 ♕d2 0-0 9 ♖d1 ♘g4 10 ♗xg4 ♗xg4 11 f3 ♗d7 12 0-0 ♖c8 13 ♖f2 ♘e5 ∞ Larsen-Miles, Reykjavik 1986

[41] 8 ... ♗e6!? 9 f4 ♖c8 10 g4 a6 11 f5 ♗xb3 12 ab ♘d7!? Geller

[42] 9 g4 d5! 10 ed ♘b4 11 ♗f3 ♘xg4 =

[43] 10 ... d5 11 f5 ♗c8 12 ed ♘b4 13 ♗f3! gf 14 a3! ±/± Fischer

10 ... a5!? 11 f5 ♗c8 12 g5 ♘d7 13 ♘d4 ♘b6 ∞ Gulko-Lukin, USSR 1979

[44] 13 gf ♗xf6 14 ♖g1 ♗f7 15 ♕d2 ♖c8 16 f5 ♕c7! ∓ Osterman-Nesis, corr. 1980

[45] 15 ♘d4 ♗g8 16 f5 ♕b6! ∞ Geller

[46] 11 ♘d4 ♕b6! 12 ♘xe6 ♕xe3 13 ♘xf8 ♘g4! ∓ Gufeld

[47] 15 ♘db5 ef 16 ♗xf4 ♗xb5 17 ab ♗e5 = Gufeld

[48] 9 ♘b3 ♗d7 10 f4 b5! 11 a3 a5 12 ♗f3 b4 = Short-Miles, Dortmund 1986

[49] 9 ... ♗d7 10 ♖ad1 ♖c8 11 f4 a6 12 h3 ± Kovacs-Nikolić, Reggio Emilia 1978-79

[50] 11 f4 ♘xd4 12 ♗xd4 e5 13 ♗e3 ef 14 ♖xf4 ♗e6 = Radulov-Mestel, Belgrade 1982

[51] 11 ... ♗e6 12 c4 ♕d7 13 a4 ♗xd5 14 ed ♘xd4 15 ♗xd4 ♗xd4 16 ♕xd4 ± Timman-Ljubojević, Bugojno 1986

[52] 15 ♗xd4 ♗xd4 16 ♕xd4 ♖c5 17 f4 ♗xd5 18 ed b5 ∞ Timoshchenko-Makarichev, USSR Ch 1979

[53] 10 ♘xc6 bc 11 e5 ♘e8 12 f4 f6 13 ♗f3 ♖b8 = Minev-Gufeld, Sofia 1967

[54] 11 ♘xd5 ♗xd4 12 c4 e5 13 f4 ♗e6 = Panchenko-Gufeld, USSR 1978

[55] 12 ♖ad1 ♕c7 13 ♗d4 e5 14 ♗c5 ♖d8 15 ♘e4 f5 = Timoshchenko-Belyavsky, USSR 1977

[56] 15 ♗c4 ♗g4 16 ♖e1 ♘b6 = Mariotti-Parma, Rome 1981

Sicilian VII (Dragon)

1 e4 c5 2 ♘f3 d6 3 d4 cd 4 ♘xd4 ♘f6 5 ♘c3 g6 6 ♗e3 ♗g7 7 f3 0-0 8 ♛d2 ♘c6[1]

	9	10	11	12	13	14	15	16	17	
1	0-0-0	♗xd4	♔b1[3]	h4	h5	h6[4]	a3	♗xh8	♘d5	±
	♘xd4[2]	♗e6	♛c7	♖fc8	♛a5	♗h8	♘d7	♔xh8	♛xd2[5]	
2	...	ed[6]	♘xc6	♗d4[7]	♗c5	♘e4[8]	♗c4[10]	h4	♗b3[12]	±
	d5	♘xd5	bc	e5	♗e6	♖b8[9]	♖e8[11]	a5		
3	...	...	...	...	...	♘xd5[13]	♛xd5[14]	♖xd5	♖d6[15]	±/∞
	...	...	...	...	♖e8	cd	♛xd5	♗e6	♗xa2[16]	
4	g4	0-0-0[18]	♗xd4	a3	h4	♘d5[20]	♖xd2	♗xg7[22]	ed	±
	♗e6[17]	♘xd4[19]	♛a5	♖ab8	♖fc8	♛xd2+	♘xd5[21]	♔xg7[23]	♗d7[24]	
5	...	...	...	...	...	♘d5	♖xd2	ed	♔b1	∓/=
	...	...	...	...	b5	♛xd2+	♗xd5	a5	♘d7[25]	
6	♗c4	♗xd4	♗b3	0-0-0	♔b1	h4	cb	a3[28]	b4	±
	♘xd4[26]	♗e6	♛a5	♖fc8[27]	♖c6	♗xb3	b5	♖ac8	♛a6[29]	
7	...	h4	♗b3	♛d3	h5	hg	0-0-0	♗h6[32]	♗xg7	±
	♘d7	♘a5	♘b6[30]	♗d7[31]	♖c8	hg	♘bc4	e5[33]	♔xg7[34]	
8	...	0-0-0[35]	♗b3	h4	♗h6	h5	hg!	♗g5	♗xc4+	±
	♗d7	♛c7	♖fc8	♘e5	♗h8	♘c4	fg[36]	b5	♛xc4[37]	
9	...	...	h4	♘dxb5[39]	♗e2	a3	ab	♘xe2	b5	±
	...	♛b8	b5[38]	♖c8	♘b4	♗xb5	♗xe2	a5	♛xb5[40]	
10	...	...	h4	♗b3	♔b1[41]	♗xc4	♘b3	♗d4[44]	h5	±
	...	♛a5	♖fc8	♘e5	♘c4[42]	♖xc4	♛c7[43]	♗e6	a5[45]	

---

1   8 ... d5 9 e5 ♘fd7 (9 ... ♘e8 10 f4 f6 11 0-0-0! fe 12 fe ♗xe5 13 ♘f3 ±) 10 f4 ♘b6 11 ♗e2 ♘c6 (Popović-Sax, Vršac 1981) 12 0-0-0 ♗d7 13 ♘b3 ± Geller

2   9 ...♗e6 10 ♘xe6 fe 11 ♗h6 ♗xh6 12 ♛xh6 ♘e5 13 ♗b5! ± Akopian-Alterman, USSR 1986

   9 ... ♗d7 10 g4 ♖c8 11 h4 ♛a5 12 ♔b1 ♖fd8 13 ♘b3 ♛c7 14 h5 ± Hübner-Hort, match 1979

3   11 ♘d5 ♗xd5 12 ed ♛c7 13 g4 ♖ac8 14 c3 ♛a5 15 h5 ♘xh5 16 ♗xg7 ♔xg7 17 ♗h3 (17 ♔b1 e5! ∞ Timman-Sosonko, Wijk aan Zee 1978) 17 ... ♛xa2! 18 ♗xc8 ♖xc8 ∞ A.Sokolov-Velimirović, Novi Sad 1984

4   14 hg hg 15 a3 ♖ab8 (15 ... ♘c4 16 ♖h3! ± Short-Velimirović, Banja Luka 1985) 16 ♗d3 ♗c4 (16 ... b5 17 ♛g5 ♛c7 18 e5 ± van der Wiel-Sax, Plovdiv 1983) 17 ♗xc4 ♖xc4 18 ♗xf6 ♗xf6 19 ♘d5 ♛xd2 20 ♖xd2 (20 ♘xf6+ ♔g7!) 20 ... ♔g7 = Marjanović-Mesing, Bela Crkva

1984

5   18 ♖xd2 ♗xd5 19 ed ♔g8 20 f4 ♘f6 21 ♖h3 ± Psakhis-Taborov, USSR 1979

6   10 h4 de 11 h5 ♘xd4 12 ♗xd4 e5! (12 ... ♘xh5? 13 ♛e3 ±) 13 ♗xe5 ♛xd2+ 14 ♖xd2 ef 15 hg hg 16 gf ♗e6 =

   10 ♘xc6 bc 11 ♗h6 ♛c7 (11 ... ♛a5 12 ♗xg7 ♔xg7 13 ed cd 14 g4 e6 = Timman-Sax, Nikšić 1983; 13 e5 ∞) 12 ♗xg7 ♔xg7 13 ed cd 14 h4 h5 15 ♘xd5 ♘xd5 16 ♛xd5 ♗e6 17 ♛d4+ ♔g8 18 ♗d3 ♖fd8 ∞ A.Sokolov-Kudrin, Lugano 1985

7   12 ♘xd5 cd 13 ♛xd5 ♛c7 14 ♛c5 (14 ♛xa8?! ♗f5) 14 ... ♛b7 15 b3 ♗f5 16 ♗d3 ♖ac8 17 ♛a5 (17 ♛xa7 ♗xd3 18 ♛xb7 ♖xc2+ =) 17 ... ♖c3! 18 ♗xf5 ♖xe3 19 ♗e4 ♛b8 ∞ Smirin-Basin, USSR 1985

8   14 ♗xf8?! ♛xf8 15 ♘xd5 cd 16 ♛a5 ♖b8 17 ♖d3 d4! ∞/∓ Maryasin-I.Botvinnik, USSR 1984

9   14 ... ♖e8 15 h4 h6 (15 ... f5 16 ♘g5 ±;

300

15 ... Rb8 16 g4 ±) 16 g4 Nf4 (16 ... Qc7 17 g5! h5 18 Bc4 ±) 17 Qc3 Bd5 18 h5 f5 (18 ... g5 19 Qa3 Qc7 20 Ba6 ± Psakhis-Vasyukov, USSR Ch 1981) 19 gf gf 20 Rg1 ±

[10] **15 h4 Qc7!** 16 Bxf8 (16 h5? Rfd8 17 hg Nb4! ∓ Jasnikowski-Perenyi, Hungary 1984) 16 ... Bxf8 ∞∞

15 g4 f5 16 gf gf 17 Ng5 e4 ∞

15 c4 Qc7 16 Bxf8 (16 Ng5!?) 16 ... Bxf8 17 cd cd+ 18 Qc3 Qe7 ∞∞ Oll-Basin, USSR 1985

[11] **15 ... f5** 16 Ng5 e4 17 Bb3 ±

15 ... Qh8 16 h4 f5 17 Ng5 Bg8 18 h5 ± Sigurjonsson-Kudrin, Gausdal 1983

[12] Popović-Sax, Subotica IZ 1987

[13] **15 Ne4 f5** 15 Nd6 (15 Bc4 fe 16 fe Qh4! ∞ Sax-Mestel, Hastings 1983-84) 15 ... Bf8 16 c4 Bxd6 = Velimirović-Miles, Vrbas 1980

14 Bc4 Qa5 15 Ne4 Qxd2+ 16 Rxd2 Bh6 = Zapata-Ernst, Subotica IZ 1987

[14] **15 Bb5?!** d4 16 Bxe8 Qxe8 ∓ Dolmatov-Dorfman, Erevan 1982

[15] **17 Rd3 Bf5** 18 Ra3 Rec8 19 Ra5 Bh6+ 20 Kd1 Rd8+ 21 Bd3 = Ilić-Jovičić, Yugoslavia 1985

[16] **18 b3 Rec8** 19 Rd5 a5! 20 Kb2 a4 = A.Ivanov-Peshina, USSR 1980, and Gufeld-Kudrin, Hastings 1986-87

18 b4 a5 19 Bb5 Rec8 20 Bd7 (van der Wiel-Sosonko, Wijk aan Zee 1986) 20 ... Rc7 21 Rhd1 (21 Bb6 Rb7 22 ba Rxa5! 23 Bc8 Bf8! 24 Bxb7 Rb5 =) 21 ... ab 22 Bc6 Rf8 23 Bxb4 ±/∞

[17] **9 ... e5** 10 Nxc6! bc 11 g5 Ne8 12 0-0-0 ± Nunn

9 ... e6 10 0-0-0 d5 11 g5 Nh5 12 f4! ± Zapata-Armas, Havana 1986

9 ... Nxd4 10 Bxd4 Be6 11 Nd5 ± Karpov-Mestel, London 1982

[18] **10 h4?** d5! ∓ van der Wiel-Miles, Utrecht 1986

[19] **10 ... Ne5** 11 h4 Bc4 12 Bh3 Ba6 13 b3 Qa5 14 Kb1 Qa3 15 g5 Nh5 16 f4 Nc6 17 Bg4 ± Anand-Mestel, London 1985, and Anand-Jassem, Sharjah 1985

[20] **14 h5 b5** 15 h6 b4! (15 ... Bh8 16 Nd5 ± Tal-Sax, Moscow IZ 1982, and Short-Kir. Georgiev, Oakham 1984) 16 Nb5 (16 hg ba 17 Qh6 ab+ 18 Kd2 Bxg4! ∓/∞ Plaskett-Watson, Brighton 1983) 16 ... Rxb5 17 Bxb5 Qxb5 18 hg ba ∞ Shirov-Golubev, USSR 1985

[21] **15 ... Bxd5** 16 ed a6 17 Bh3 ± Miles-Keene, London 1982

[22] **16 ed Bxd5** 17 Bxg7 Bxf3 18 Rh3 Bxg4 19 Rg3 Kxg7 20 Rxg4 b6 ∞/= Marjanović-Velimirović, Yugoslav Ch 1983

[23] **15 ... Ne5** 17 Bd4 Nxf1 18 Rxf1 b6 19 g5! ± Short-Sax, Hastings 1983-84

[24] **18 h5 h6!** (18 ... b5 19 hg hg 20 Rdh2 ±

Campora-Velimirović, Bor 1985) 19 hg fg = Nunn-Karlsson, Helsinki 1983

18 Be2! intending f4 ± Nunn

[25] **18 Bxg7 Bxg7** 19 f4 h6 ±/= Timman-Nunn, Utrecht 1986

[26] **9 ... Na5** 10 Bb3 Nxb3 11 ab d5 12 e5 Nd7 13 f4 Nc5 14 Ndb5 ±

9 ... a5 10 Bb3 Bd7 11 a4 Nxd4 12 Bxd4 Be6 13 0-0-0 (13 Bxe6 fe 14 0-0 ± Larsen-Byrne, San Juan 1979) 13 ... Qd7 14 Kb1 Rfc8 15 Rhe1 ±/± Hardicsay-Honfi, Hungary 1977

[27] **12 ... b5** 13 Kb1 b4 14 Nd5 Bxd5 15 ed Qb5 16 Qd3! ±

12 ... Bxb3 13 cb Rfd8 14 Kb1 Bd7 15 h4 Rad8 16 Qf2 b5 17 h5 ±

[28] **16 h5 b4** 17 Bxf6 bc 18 Bxc3 Bxc3 19 bc Qxc3 20 hg hg 21 Qxc3 Rxc3 22 Rc1 Rxc1+ 23 Rxc1 f5! = Shakarov-Alterman, USSR 1974

[29] **18 e5** ± Gipslis-Nei, USSR 1961

[30] **11 ... Ne5** 12 Qe2 h5 13 0-0-0 Bd7 14 g4 hg (14 ... Bc8 15 gh ± Mikhalchishin-Barczay, Cienfuegos 1981) 15 f4 Nxb3 16 cb Nc6 17 h5 ±

[31] **12 ... Bxb3** 13 ab d5 14 Ndb5 ±

[32] **16 Ng5!?** Nxb3+ 17 cb Qa5 18 Bxe7 Ne5 19 Qc2! Kruppa-Savchenko, USSR 1984

[33] **16 ... e6** 17 f4 e5 18 Nf5! ± Fischer-Purevzhav, Varna Ol 1962

[34] **18 Nde2 Qg5+** 19 Kb1 b5 20 g3 ± Fleck-Kozul, Cesme 1983

[35] **10 h4 Nxd4?** (10 ... Rc8! ∞) 11 Bxd4 b5 12 Bb3 a5 13 Nd5 e6 14 Bb6 Qb8 15 Bc7 ±/±± Nunn-Mestel, London (quickplay) 1988

[36] **15 ... hg** 16 Bxc4 Qxc4 17 Bf8! Rxf8 18 Rxh8+ Kxh8 19 Qh6+ Kg8 20 Nd5 ±±

[37] **18 Bxf6 Bxf6** 19 Nd5! Bxd4 20 Nxe7+ Kf7 (20 ... Kf8 21 Nxc8 Rxc8 22 c3 ±) 21 Rxh7+ Kg7 22 c3 Rh8 23 Qf4+ Bf5 24 Bxf5 ± Milstein-Lagutkin, corr. 1978

[38] **11 ... Rc8** 12 Bb3 a5 13 a4 Nxd4 14 Bxd4 b5 15 Nd5 e5 16 Bxe5! ba 17 Bxf6 ± d'Alamo-Tepelke, corr. 1986

[39] **12 Nd5 bc!** (12 ... Nxd4? 13 Nxe7+ Kh8 14 Bxd4 bc 15 Qc3 ±) 13 Nxc6 Nxd5! 14 Nxb8 Bxb2+ 15 Kxb2 (15 Kb1 Raxb8 ∓) 15 ... c3+ ∓ Gomez

[40] **18 Bd4** ± Geller

[41] **13 h5 Nxh5** 14 Bh6 (14 g4 Nf6 15 Bh6 Rxc3 ∞∞) 14 ... Bxh6 15 Qxh6 Rxc3 ∞∞

13 g4 Nc4 14 Bxc4 Rxc4 15 h5 Rxc3 16 Qxc3 Rxa2 ∞

[42] **13 ... b5?!** 14 Ncxb5 ±

[43] **15 ... Qa6** 16 e5 Ne8 (16 ... de 17 Nc5 Qd6 18 Qe2 ±) 17 h5 ±

15 ... Qd8 16 Bh6 Rh8 17 h5 Rac8 18 hg fg 19 e5 ±

[44] **16 h5 Rxc3** 17 Qxc3 Qxc3 18 bc Nxh5 ∞∞

[45] **18 hg hg** 19 a4 ± Gheorghiu-Geller, Moscow 1967

Sicilian VIII (Dragon) 1 e4 c5 2 ♘f3 d6 3 d4 cd 4 ♘xd4 ♘f6
5 ♘c3 g6 6 ♗e3 ♗g7 7 f3 0-0 8 ♕d2 ♘c6 9 ♗c4 ♗d7 10 0-0-0 ♖c8 11 ♗b3 ♘e5 12 h4[1]

	12	13	14	15	16	17	18	19	20	
1	...	♗h6[3]	♕xh6	bc	♔b1!	f4	♕g5	fe	cb	±
	h5[2]	♗xh6	♖xc3	♕c7	a5[4]	♘fg4[5]	a4	ab	♘f2[6]	
2	...	...	...	...	♔b1	g4[7]	gh	♗xc4	♖d3	±
	...	...	...	♕a5	♖c8	♕xc3	♘c4[8]	♖xc4	♕b4+[9]	
3	...	...	♗xc4	♗xg7	g4[10]	h5	hg	f4	fe[12]	±
	...	♘c4	♖xc4	♔xg7	hg	♖h8	fg	e5[11]	de[13]	
4	...	♗xc4	h5![14]	g4	♘b3[16]	e5	fg	♖dg1	♕xd8	∞
	♘c4	♖xc4	♘xh5[15]	♘f6	♖e8[17]	♘xg4	♗xg4	de[18]	♖xd8[19]	
5	...	...	...	...	♘de2	♗d4[21]	g5	♗xg7	♘f4	±
	...	...	...	...	♖e8[20]	♕a5	♘h5	♔xg7[22]	♘xf4[23]	
6	...	...	...	...	e5	fg	♖dg1	♖xg4	♕e2[27]	±
	...	...	...	...	♘xg4[24]	♗xg4[25]	de	h5[26]	ed[28]	
7	...	...	...	hg	♔b1[29]	g4	♕h2[31]			±
	...	...	♕c7	fg	♖c8	b5[30]				

[1] 12 ♗g5 ♘c4 (12 ... ♕a5 13 ♖he1 ± Mikhalchishin-Watson, Hastings 1985-86) 13 ♗xc4 ♖xc4 14 e5 de 15 ♘b3 (15 ♘db5 a6 16 ♗xf6 ♗xf6 17 ♕xd7 ♕b6 ∞ Mikhalchishin-Basin, Minsk 1985; 15 ... ♕b6!?) 15 ... ♖c7 16 ♘b5 ♖c8 (16 ... ♗f5 17 ♘xc7 ♕xc7 18 ♔b1 ♖c8 19 ♔a1! ± Shirov-Petrenko, USSR 1984) 17 ♘xa7 ½-½ A.Kuzmin-Basin, Kostroma 1984

[2] 12 ... a5 13 a4 ♘c4 14 ♗xc4 ♖xc4 15 b3 ♖c8 16 h5 (16 ♘db5 ±) 16 ... ♘xh5 17 g4 ♘f6 18 ♗h6! ♗xh6 19 ♕xh6 ♖xc3 20 g5 ±± Oim-Stern, corr. 1980

[3] 13 ♗g5 ♖c5 14 ♔b1 b5 15 g4 a5 (15 ... hg 16 h5 ± Karpov-Sznapik, Dubai Ol 1986) 16 ♗xf6 ♗xf6 17 gh (17 a3 hg ∓ Karpov-Kir.Georgiev, Dubai Ol 1986) 17 ... a4 18 ♗d5 e6 19 hg ed 20 h5 ♗g5! 21 f4 ♘c4 22 ♕g2 ♘e3 ∞ Shulman-Basin, USSR 1987; 22 ♕h2 ♗h6 23 ♘xd5 Nunn

[4] 16 ... ♕xc3 17 ♘e2 ♕c5 18 ♘f4 e6 19 g4 ±
16 ... ♖c8 17 g4 a5 18 gh a4 19 hg (19 ♗d5 ♘xd5! 20 ed ♕xc3 21 hg ♕b4+ 22 ♔c1 fg 23 ♖hg1 ♗f5 24 ♘xf5 ♕a3+ 25 ♔b1 ♕b4+ = Gobet-Kudrin, Berne 1988) 19 ... ab 20 gf+ ♔xf7 21 cb ♕xc3 22 ♖hg1 ♗h3!, Bierenbroodspot-Riemersma, Wijk aan Zee 1987, 23 ♖g3! ♘d3 24 ♖g7 ♔e8 25 ♖xe7+ =

[5] 17 ... ♘c4 18 f5 ±

[6] 20 ... de 21 ♘f5! ±± Hübner-Miles, West Germany 1986
20 ... ♘f2 21 e6! ♖xe4 (21 ... ♘xh1 22 ed ♘f2 23 ♘e6!) 22 ♕h6 ♘xc3+ 23 ♔b2 ♘xd1+ 24 ♖xd1 ±/±± Short-H.Olafsson, Wijk aan Zee 1987, and van der Wiel-Kir.Georgiev, Lugano 1987

[7] 17 ♕d2 b5 ∞

[8] 18 ... ♘xh5 19 ♖hg1 ♘c4 20 ♗xc4 ♖xc4 21 ♕xh5 ♖xd4 22 ♖xg6+ ±± Grünfeld-Findlay, Toronto 1984

[9] 21 ♘b3 ♘xh5 ±

[10] 16 ♘d5 e5 17 ♘e2 ♘xd5 18 ♕xd5 ♗e6 19 ♕xd6 ♕a5 ∞
16 ♔b1 ♕a5 17 ♘b3 ♕c7 18 g4 hg 19 h5 gf! ∞ Short-Fleck, West Germany 1986

[11] 19 ... ♖c5 20 e5 de 21 ♘b3 ±±
19 ... ♕b8 20 ♖xh8 ♕xh8 21 e5 ±± Ady-Kudrin, London 1986

[12] 20 ♘de2! Nunn

[13] 21 ♘e6+ ♔xe6 22 ♕xd8 ♖xd8 23 ♖xd8 ♘xc4 ∞/∓
21 ♘de2! ♖c8! ±

[14] 14 g4 ♕a5 (14 ... ♕c7 15 h5 ♖c8 16 hg fg 17 ♔b1 b5 – 14 h5) 15 h5 ♖xc3 16 ♕xc3 ♕xa2 17 hg hg 18 ♕b3 ♕a6 ∞ Klovans-Yurtayev, USSR 1981

[15] 14 ... b5 15 hg fg 16 e5 de 17 ♘e6 ♕c8 18 ♘xf8 (18 ♘xg7 ♖f7!) 18 ... ♗xf8 19 ♔b1

b4 20 Nd5 ± Parma-Szilagyi, Reggio Emilia 1966

[16] 16 Qh2 Rxc3 17 bc Qa5 18 Nb3 Qa3+ 19 Kb1 Be6 ∞∞

16 Bh6 Nxe4 17 Qe3 Rxc3 18 bc Nf6 19 Bxg7 Kxg7 20 Rh2 Qc7 (20 ... Rg8 21 Ne2 Qa5 22 g5 Nh5 23 Qxe7 ± Short-Ernst, Subotica IZ 1987) 21 Qxe7 Qxc3 22 Qxd6 Rc8 ∞

16 Nd5 Nxd5 17 ed Qc7 18 Qh2 h5 19 gh (19 Kb1!?) 19 ... Rc8 20 hg fg 21 Kb1 Kf7 ∞ Pinkas-Tolnai, Katowice 1986

[17] 16 ... Rxc3 17 bc a5 18 e5 ±±

16 ... a5 17 Bh6 a4 (17 ... Bxh6!?) 18 Bxg7 Kxg7 19 Qh6+ Kg8 20 Nd5 Re8 21 g5! 1-0 Loktev-de Visser, corr. 1977

[18] 19 ... h5 20 e6 f5 (20 ... Bxe6 21 Rxh5) 21 Nd5 Qc8 22 Nd4! Bxd4 (22 ... Kh7? 23 Rxg4! fg 24 Qd3 ±± Ye Jiangchuan-Velimirović, Asia v Yugoslavia 1984) 23 Bxd4 Qxe6 24 Ne3 ± Velimirović

[19] 21 Nd2 Rxc3 22 bc h5 ∞

[20] 16 ... Qa5 17 Bh6 Bxh6 18 Qxh6 Rfc8 19 Rd3! Be6 (19 ... N4c5 20 g5! Rxg5 21 Rd5! ± Karpov-Korchnoi, match 1974) 20 g5 Nh5 21 Ng3 Qe5 22 Nxh5 gh 23 Qxh5 Kf8 (23 ... Qg7 24 f4 d5 25 Rhd1 Qg6 26 Qh6! ±) 24 Qxh7 Qxg5+ 25 Kb1 Ke8 26 Qh2 Qa5? 27 Rxd6! ed 28 Qxd6 1-0 Yoffe-Reshko, USSR 1980

[21] 17 Bh6 Bh8 18 e5 Nxg4 19 fg Bxe5 ∞ Klovans-Belyavsky, USSR 1977

[22] 19 ... Nxg7 20 Rh2 ±
[23] 21 Qxf4 Be6 22 Rxh7+! Kxh7 23 Qh4+ Kg8 24 Rh1 Qe5 25 Qh7+ Kf8 26 Qh8+ ± Lagland-Endzelins, corr. 1980
[24] 16 ... Ne8 17 Qh2 ±

16 ... de 17 Nb3 Rc6 18 Bc5! b6 19 g5 ±
[25] 17 ... Bxe5 18 Qg2 Re8 19 Rxh7! ±± Adorjan-Ostojić, Olot 1974
[26] 19 ... ed 20 Bh6 ±±

19 ... Rxd4!? 20 Bxd4 ed 21 Ne4 Qd5 Hellers-Ernst, Sweden 1987
[27] 20 Rxh5 Rxd4 (20 ... ed? 21 Rh1! Rc6 22 Qh2 f5 23 Rxd4 ±± Dvoiris-Asanov, USSR 1977) 21 Bxd4 ed 22 Ne4 gh 23 Rxg7+ =
[28] 20 ... hg? 21 Qh2 ±±

20 ... Qc8? 21 Nf5! ±±

20 ... Rxd4 21 Rgg1! ±

20 ... ed 21 Rxg6 fg 22 Qxc4+ Kh8 23 Rd1 e5 24 Ne4 ± Vitomskis-Koifman, corr. 1985
[29] 16 Bh6 Nxe4 17 Qe3 Nxc3 18 Bxg7 Rf7! 19 Rxh7 Ne2+ 20 Nxe2 Rxc2+ 21 Kb1 Rxe2 = Belunovich-Starodub, corr. 1972

16 Nde2 Rc8 ∞ Matulović-Velimirović, Novi Sad 1976
[30] 17 ... Rxc3 18 Qxc3 Qxc3 19 bc Rxc3 20 Rd3 ±

17 ... Qa5 18 Nb3 Qe5 19 Bd4 (19 f4 Qxc3! ∞∞) 19 ... Qe6 20 Qh2 Qf7 21 e5 ± Nesis-Oechsldin, corr. 1979
[31] 18 Nd5 Nxd5 19 ed a5 20 Qh2 h6! 21 Rd2 g5 ∞ Pirisi-Szalanczy, Hungary 1981

18 Qh2 ±

Sicilian IX	1 e4 c5 2 Nf3 d6 3 d4 cd 4 Nxd4 Nf6 5 Nc3 Nc6								
	6	7	8	9	10	11	12	13	14
1	f4[1]	Nb3[3]	Qe2	Be3	g4	g5[4]	a4	h4	Bg2	∞
	Qb6[2]	e6	Be7	Qc7	a6	Nd7	b6	Nb4[5]	Bb7[6]	

[1] 6 f3 e5 7 Nb3 Be6 8 Be3 d5 9 ed Nxd5 10 Nxd5 Qxd5 =

6 g3 Bg4 (see note 2) 7 f3 Bd7 8 Be3 (8 Bg2 a6 9 Nb3 e6 10 Be3 b5 =) 8 ... e6 9 Qd2 (9 g4 h6 10 h4 a6 11 Rg1 b5 12 g5 Nh5 ∞ Mestel-Timman, Lone Pine 1978) 9 ... a6 10 g4 Nxd4 (10 ... b5 11 g5 Nh5 12 0-0-0 ± Short-Tukmakov, Hastings 1982-83) 11 Bxd4 Bc6 12 g5 Nd7 ∞

[2] 6 ... g6 – Dragon

6 ... e6 – Scheveningen

6 ... e5 7 Nf3 Be7 8 Bd3 0-0 9 0-0 ef 10 Bxf4 Ne5 11 Kh1 Ng6 12 Bg5 Ng4 = Zapata-Speelman, Mexico 1980

[3] 7 Be3 Qxb2 8 Ndb5 Bg4 9 Qb1 ∞/∓ Ang.Martin-Tatai, Las Palmas 1977

[4] 11 0-0-0 b5 12 g5 Nd7 13 h4 Bb7 ∞/= Kirov-Pähtz, Bialistok 1979

[5] 13 ... Nc5?! 14 h5 Nb4 15 Bg2 Bb7 16 0-0 0-0 17 f5 ± Kochiev-Belyavsky, Lvov 1978

[6] Gulko

	6	7	8	9	10	11	12	13	14	
2	♗e3	♗g5!?[8]	♗b5	0-0	♗e3!	fe	♗xc6	♕f3	♕h5+	∞/±
	♘g4[7]	♕b6	♗d7	h6	♘xe3[9]	e6	bc	f6	♔e7[10]	
3	♗c4	0-0[12]	♘xc6	f4	♕d3	h3[16]	e5	ed	de	±
	♗d7[11]	g6[13]	bc[14]	♗g4[15]	♗g7	♗c8	♘d7	♘b6	♕xe7[17]	
4	...	♘db5[18]	♗e3	♘d4	0-0	♗b3	f4	♗xd4	f5	=
	♕b6	a6[19]	♕a5[20]	e6[21]	♗e7	0-0	♘xd4	♗d7[22]	♖ac8[23]	
5	...	♘b3	0-0[24]	♗g5[26]	♗xf6	♕h5	♔h1	f4!	a4	±
	...	e6	♗e7[25]	a6[27]	gf	♗d7[28]	0-0-0!?	♖df8	♕c7[29]	
6	♗e2	♘b3	0-0	f4[31]	a4[33]	♔h1	f5	♗g5	♗xf6	=
	e5	♗e7	0-0[30]	a5[32]	♘b4[34]	♗e6	♗d7	♗c6	♗xf6[35]	
7	...	...	...	♔h1	f4	♗xf4	e5	♗d3	ef	=
	...	...	...	♗e6[36]	ef	d5!	♘e4[37]	f5	♗xf6[38]	
8	...	♘f3	0-0[40]	♖e1[42]	h3	♗f1	b3	♗b2	♕d2	=
	...	h6[39]	♗e7[41]	0-0	♖e8[43]	♗f8	a6	b5	♗b7[44]	

---

[7] **6 ... e5** and now:
7 ♘f3 ♗e7 8 ♗c4 0-0 9 ♕e2 ♗e6 10 ♖d1 ♕c8 11 ♗b3 ♘a5 12 ♘d5 ± Kapengut-Yuferov, USSR 1976
7 **♘b3** ♗e6 (7 ... ♗e7 8 ♗e2 – 6 ♗e2) 8 ♕d2 d5 9 ed ♘xd5 10 ♘xd5 ♕xd5 11 ♕xd5 ♗xd5 12 0-0-0 0-0-0 13 f3 f5 14 ♗b5 ± Timman-van der Wiel, Amsterdam 1986
6 ... e6! – Scheveningen

[8] 7 ♗b5 ♘xe3 8 fe ♗d7 9 0-0 e6 10 ♗xc6 bc 11 e5 ♗e7 12 ♕h5 0-0 13 ed ♗xd6 14 ♘e4 ♗e7 = Gipslis-Tukmakov, USSR 1977

[9] 10 ... ♖c8 11 ♘d5 ♕d8 12 ♗c1! ± Yakovich-Oll, USSR 1986

[10] Rohde-D.Gurevich, USA 1986

[11] 6 ... e6 – 5 ... e6 6 ♗c4 ♘c6

[12] 7 ♗b3 g6 (7 ... ♖c8 8 0-0! g6 9 ♘xc6 ♗xc6 10 ♗g5 ♗g7 11 ♘d5 ± Nunn-Robatsch, Cleveland 1979) 8 f3 ♘xd4 10 ♕xd4 ♗g7 10 ♗g5 0-0 11 0-0-0 b5 =

[13] 7 ... e6 8 ♔h1 ♗e7 9 f4 0-0 10 f5! ±/± Euwe

[14] 8 ... ♗xc6 9 ♘d5 ♗d7 10 ♗g5 ♗xd5 11 ed 0-0 12 ♕e2 (12 ♗e2!?) ± Euwe

[15] 9 ... ♕c7 10 e5! de 11 fe ♕xe5 12 ♗xf7+! ±

[16] 11 e5 ♘d7 12 ed ♘b6 13 ♗a6 0-0 ∞ Nunn-Balashov, Toluca IZ 1982

[17] 15 ♗b3 0-0 16 ♗e3 ± Chandler-Kupreichik, Minsk 1982

[18] 7 ♘de2 e6 8 0-0 ♗e7 9 ♗b3 (9 ♗e3 ♕c7 10 ♘g3 a6 11 f4 b5 12 ♗b3 ♘a5 = Ivanović-Fedorowicz, Lone Pine 1981) 9 ... 0-0 10 ♗g5 ♘a5 11 ♘g3 h6 12 ♗e3 ♕c6 = Thipsay-Dorfman, New Delhi 1982
7 ♘xc6 bc 8 0-0 e6! 9 b3 ♗e7 10 ♗b2 0-0 11 ♕e2 ♘d7! = Peres-Radulov, Torremolinos 1975

[19] 7 ... ♗g4 8 f3 ♗d7 9 ♕e2 a6 10 ♗e3 ♕a5 11 ♘d4 b5 12 ♗b3 e6 13 a3 ± Sax-Csom, Hungarian Ch 1976

[20] 8 ... ♕d8 9 ♘d4 ♘g4!? (9 ... e6 10 ♕e2 – Velimirović Attack) 10 ♘xc6 bc 11 ♗g5 ♕b6 12 ♕d2 h6 13 ♗h4 g5 14 ♗g3! ∞

[21] 9 ... ♘g4 10 ♘xc6 bc 11 ♗d2 g6 12 ♕e2 ♗g7 13 0-0 ∞/± Sax-Radulov, Vrnjačka Banja 1974
9 ... ♘e5 10 ♘b3 ♕c7 11 ♗d3 e6 12 f4 ♘c4 13 ♗c1 b5 14 ♕e2 ± Kristiansen-Arnason, Reykjavik 1986

[22] 13 ... e5 14 ♗f2 ef 15 ♗d4 ♗e6 16 ♖xf4 ± Velimirović-Mihaljčišin, Banja Luka 1981

[23] 15 fe ♗xe6 = Bilek-Hort, Göteborg 1971

[24] 8 ♗g5!? ∞/±

[25] 8 ... a6 9 a4 ♗e7 (9 ... ♘a5 10 ♗e3 ♕c7 11 ♘xa5 ♕xa5 12 f4! ± Gulko) 10 a5 ♕c7 11 ♗e2 ♗d7 12 ♗e3 ♘b4 13 f4 0-0 14 ♗f3 ± Nunn-Csom, Moscow 1977

[26] 9 ♗e3 ♕c7 10 f4 0-0 11 ♗d3 ♖d8 12 ♕f3 a6 13 ♘a4 ♘d7 14 ♕f2 b5 = Hartston-Dorfman, New Delhi 1982
9 a4 0-0 10 a5 ♕c7 11 ♗e2 ♖d8 12 f4 ♘b4 13 ♗e3 e5! = Nunn-I.Ivanov, Lugano 1982

[27] 9 ... ♘e5 10 ♗e2 ♗d7 11 ♔h1 ♘g6 12 ♗e3 ♕c7 13 f4 0-0 14 ♕e1 ♖fe8 15 ♖d1 ± Nunn-Tukmakov, Lugano 1986

28 11 ... Ne5 12 Be2 0-0 13 Kh1 Kh8 14 a4 Bd7 15 a5 ± Kupreichik-Radulov, Plovdiv 1980
29 15 a5 ± Sveshnikov-Vaiser, USSR 1983
30 8 ... Be6!? 9 Be3 Rc8 Larsen
31 9 Be3 a5 10 Bf3 a4 (10 ... Be6! - 9 ... Be6) 11 Nd2 a3 12 b3 Nb4 13 Nc4 Be6 14 Nb6 ±; 9 ... Be6! 10 Bf3 Na5 11 Nxa5 Qxa5 12 Qd2 Rfc8 13 Rfd1 Qb4 = Boleslavsky-Euwe, Zürich C 1953
32 9 ... ef 10 Bxf4 Ne5 ∞
33 10 Be3 a4!
34 10 ... ef 11 Bxf4 Be6!? Boleslavsky
35 Barczay-Spassov, Warsaw 1979
36 9 ... a5!? 10 a4 Nb4 11 f4 Be6 (11 ... Bd7 12 Bf3 Bc6 13 Be2 Qc7 14 fe de = Abramović-Kuzmin, Kladovo 1980) 12 f5 Bd7 13 Bg5 Bc6 14 Bxf6 Bxf6 15 Nd5 Nxd5 16 ed Bd7 = Sznapik-L.Schneider, Eksjö 1980
37 12 ... Nd7!? 13 Nxd5 Ndxe5 14 c4 Bg5 15 Qc1 (15 Bg3 Bh4) 15 ... h6 16 Bxg5 hg 17 Qd2 b5! ∞
38 15 Nxe4 de 16 Nc5 Bd5 ∞ Savon
39 7 ... Be7 8 Bg5 0-0 9 0-0 Be6 10 Bxf6

Bxf6 11 Nd5 ± Smyslov-Hort, Tilburg 1977
40 8 Bc4 Be7 9 0-0 Bg4! 10 Be3 Rc8 11 Bb3 0-0 ∓
41 8 ... Be6!? 9 b3 Be7 10 Bb2 0-0 11 a3 Rc8 12 Re1 Re8 13 h3 Bf8 14 Bd3 a6 15 Qe2 g6 ∞/= Smyslov-Speelman, Hastings 1981-82
42 9 Be3 0-0 10 Qd2 Be6 11 Rad1 Qd7 12 Qe1 Rfd8 =
   9 b3 0-0 10 Bb2 a6 11 Nd2 Nd4 12 Bd3 b5 = Smyslov-Timman, Tilburg 1977
43 10 ... Be6 11 Bf1 Rc8 (11 ... Re8 12 Nd5 Bxd5 13 ed Nb4 14 c4 a5 15 Be3 Bd7 16 a3 ± A.Sokolov-Popović, Dubai Ol 1986) 12 Nd5 Bxd5 13 ed Nb8 14 c4 Nbd7 15 b4 b6 16 Be3 ± Geller-Salov, Moscow 1986
   10 ... a6 11 Bf1 b5 12 a4 (12 a3 Bb7 13 b3 Rc8 14 Bb2 Rc7! 15 Nb1 Qa8 16 Nd2 Nd8! Khalifman, Nesis) 12 ... b4 13 Nd5 Nxd5 14 ed Nb8 (14 ... Na7 15 c3 bc 16 bc Qc7 17 Ba3 ± Sigurjonsson-Hjartarson, Reykjavik 1985) 15 a5 Bf5 16 Bd2 ± Khalifman-Piket, Groningen 1985-86
44 15 a3 Rc8 = Torre-Timman, Brussels 1986

Sicilian X (Richter-Rauzer)		1 e4 c5 2 Nf3 d6 3 d4 cd 4 Nxd4 Nf6 5 Nc3 Nc6 6 Bg5							
	6	7	8	9	10	11	12	13	14
1	...	Nb3	Bxf6[2]	Qd2[3]	0-0-0	f4	Be2	Rhf1	Kb1	±
	Qb6[1]	e6	gf	a6	Bd7	0-0-0	h5	Na5	Nxb3[4]	
2	...	Qd2	0-0-0	Qxd4	f4[6]	e5	fe	Bb5[9]	Nxd5	±
	Bd7	Rc8[5]	Nxd4	Qa5	e6[7]	de	Bc6[8]	Nd5	Bxb5[10]	

1 6 ... a6 7 Qd2 Nxd4 (7 ... e6 - 6 ... e6) 8 Qxd4 Qa5 9 f4 e6!? 10 0-0-0! ±
2 8 a4 Be7 9 a5 Qd8 10 Be2 0-0 11 0-0 h6 12 Be3 Bd7 13 f4 Nb4 14 Bf3 e5 ∞ van der Wiel-I.Ivanov, Grand Manan 1984
   8 Bd3 Be7 9 0-0 a6 10 a4 (10 Kh1 Qc7 11 f4 Bd7 12 Qe2 ± Byrne-Benjamin, US Ch 1984) 10 ... Na5 11 Be3 Qc7 12 Nxa5 Qxa5 13 h3 Bd7 14 f4 Rc8 15 Qd2 ± Grünfeld-I.Ivanov, Toronto 1984
3 9 Be2 Bd7 (9 ... a6 10 Nh5 Bd7 11 0-0 Rg8 12 Kh1 Rg7 13 f4 0-0-0 14 a4 ± Savon-Podgayets, USSR 1976) 10 0-0 h5!? 11 Bxh5 Ke7 12 a4 Na5 13 Nxa5 Qxa5 14 Bg4 Bh6 ±/∞ Shakarov-Petrienko, USSR 1981
4 15 ab Kb8 16 f5 Be7 17 Qd3 Qc5 18 Qh3 ± Belyavsky-I.Ivanov, USSR 1978
5 7 ... Nxd4 8 Qxd4 Qa5 9 Bd2 (9 f4 Rc8 - 7 ... Rc8) 9 ... e5 10 Qd3 Rc8 11 Be2 a6 12 0-0 Be6 13 Nd5 Qd8 14 Bg5 ± Tal-Radulov, Skopje Ol 1972

6 10 Bd2 e5 11 Qd3 a6 12 a3 Be6 13 Nd5 Qd8 14 Bg5 Bxd5 15 Bxf6 Qxf6 16 Qxd5 Qxf2 17 Bc4 Rc5 18 Qd3 Rc7 19 g3 ∞/= Timman-Ljubojević, Brussels 1987
7 10 ... Qc5 11 e5 ±
   10 ... Rxc3 11 bc e5 12 Qb4 ±
   10 ... h6 11 Bxf6 gf 12 f5 ±
8 12 ... Rxc3 13 Bd2 Qxa2 14 Bxc3 g6 15 b4! ± Belyavsky-Ubilava, USSR 1978
9 13 Bxf6 gf 14 Ne4 Rd8! 15 Nxf6+ Ke7 16 Qxd8+ Qxd8 17 Rxd8 Kxd8 = Dolmatov-Ruderfer, USSR 1981
   13 Nb5 Bxb5 14 ef Ba4! ∞
10 15 Qxa7 Bb4! 16 Qxb7 0-0 17 Nxb4 Qxb4 18 Rd2 Qa5 ∞ Peshina-Azmaiparashvili, USSR 1981
   15 Nc3 Bc5 (15 ... Bc6 16 Rhf1 Bb4 17 Ne4 ± Belyavsky-Yudasin, USSR Ch 1981) 16 Qg4 Bb4 17 Qxb5 Qxb5 18 Rd4! Qc6 (18 ... Qc5 19 Qe4) 19 Qe2 Bc5 20 Rg4 ± Mithrakanth-Bellin, India 1984

	6	7	8	9	10	11	12	13	14	
3	...	♕d2	0-0-0	f4	♗h4	fg	♘f3	♗g3[13]	♗e2	±
	e6	a6	♗d7	h6	g5[11]	♘g4	hg[12]	♗e7	♘ge5[14]	
4	...	...	...		♘f3	♗xf6[15]	f5[17]	♔b1	g3	±
	...	...	...	♗e7	b5	gf[16]	♕b6	0-0-0[18]	♔b8[19]	
5	...	...	...		♗xf6	♘xc6[21]	♕e1	♗d3	♔b1	±
	...	...	...	b5	gf[20]	♗xc6	♗e7[22]	♕b6	h5[23]	
6	...	...	...	♗f4[24]	♘xc6[25]	♕e1[26]	h4[28]	e5	♘e2	=
	...	...	h6	♗d7	♗xc6	♗e7[27]	♕c7	d5	♘d7[29]	
7	...	...	...	...	...	f3	♕e1	a3	♗d2[32]	±/∞
	...	...	...	...	...	d5[30]	♗b4[31]	♗a5	♕e7[33]	
8	...	...	...	♗e3	♕xd4	♗e2	f4	g4	♕d3	±
	...	...	...	♘xd4[34]	♕c7[35]	♗e7[36]	0-0[37]	e5	♗xg4[38]	
9	...	...	...	...	♗xd4	f4[39]	♗e2[41]	♘a4	♕e3	±
	...	...	...	...	b5	♗e7[40]	b4	♘xe4	♘f6[42]	
10	...	...	...	...	f4	♗d3	♖he1[44]	♗xd4	♗xf6	±/∞
	...	...	...	♗d7	b5	♕c7[43]	♘xd4[45]	b4	gf[46]	
11	...	...	...	...	f3	g4	♖g1	h4	g5[49]	±/∞
	...	...	...	...	b5	♕c7[47]	♘e5	g6[48]	hg[50]	

[11] **10 ... ♘xe4** 11 ♕e1 ♘f6 12 ♘f5 ♕a5 (12 ... ♕c7 13 ♗xf6 gf 14 ♘d5 ♕d8 15 ♕e3! ±) 13 ♘xd6+ ♗xd6 14 ♖xd6 ± *ECO*

10 ... ♖c8 11 ♘f3 ♕a5 12 ♔b1 b5 13 e5 b4 14 ef bc 15 fg ± Svensson-Schütz, Sweden 1986

[12] 12 ... ♗e7?! 13 g6! ♗xh4 14 gf+ ± Yuneyev-Mukhin, USSR 1978, and Marjanović-Popović, Yugoslavia 1980

[13] 13 ♗xg5? f6 ∓∓

[14] 15 ♔b1 f6 16 h4! gh 17 ♘xh4 ± Mokry-Banas, Trnava 1986

[15] 11 e5 b4 12 ef bc 13 ♕xc3 gf 14 ♗h4 d5 15 ♔b1 ♘a5 (15 ... ♘b4 16 ♘d4 ♖c8 17 ♕b3±) 16 f5 ♖c8 17 ♕d2 ♕c7 18 fe fe 19 ♗d3 ± Tseshkovsky-Lukin, USSR 1982

[16] 11 ... ♗xf6 12 ♘xd6 ♗e7 13 ♕d3 b4 14 ♘a4 (14 ♘e2 ♖a7 15 ♘ed4 ±) 14 ... ♖a7 15 ♕a5 16 b3 ♖b7 17 ♘d2 ♗a7 18 ♘c4 ♕c7 19 ♖xd7! ± Psakhis-Geller, Moscow 1986

[17] 12 ♗d3 ♕a5 (12 ... ♕b6 13 ♖hc1 0-0-0 14 ♔b1 ♔b8 15 ♘d5! ± Timman-Ivanović, Bugojno 1984) 13 ♔b1 0-0-0! (13 ... b4 14 ♘e2 ♕c5 15 f5 ± Fischer-Spassky, match (18) 1972) 14 f5 ♔b7 15 fe fe 16 a3 h5 ∞ Spassky-Ardiansyah, Thessaloniki Ol 1984

[18] 13 ... b4 14 ♘e2 e5 15 ♘g3 ♘a5 16 ♗d3 0-0-0 17 ♕e2 ♔b7 18 ♘f1 ♗c6 19 ♘e3 ♖d7 20 ♘c4 ± Shakarov-Akopov, USSR 1974

[19] 14 ... ♘e5 15 ♘d4 h5 16 ♗h3 ♘g4 17 fe fe 18 ♗xg4 hg 19 ♘f5! ± Bryson-Webb, corr. 1984

14 ... ♔b8 15 fe fe 16 ♗h3 ♖c8 17 ♕e1 ± Matulović-Mednis, Smederevo 1981

[20] 10 ... ♕xf6 11 e5 de 12 ♘dxb5 ♕d8 13 ♘d6+ ♗xd6 14 ♕xd6 ±

[21] 11 f5 ♗xd4 12 ♕xd4 ♗h6+ 13 ♔b1 ♗f4 14 fe fe 15 ♘e2 ♗e5 16 ♕d2 ♕b6 17 ♘f4 ♗e7 (17 ... 0-0-0 18 g3 ± Tseshkovsky-Ermenkov, Albena 1977) 18 ♘d3 ± Belyavsky-van der Wiel, Reggio Emilia 1986-87

[22] **12 ... b4** 13 ♘d5 a5 14 ♗d3 ± A.Ivanov-Ermolinsky, USSR 1981

12 ... ♕e7 13 ♗d3 ♗b7 14 ♔b1 0-0-0 15 a4! ± Spraggett-Mednis, Lugano 1985

[23] **14 ... b4** 15 ♘e2 a5 16 f5 e5 17 ♘g3 ♗c5 18 ♕e2 a4 19 ♗c4 ± Ernst-Popović, Subotica IZ 1987

14 ... h5 15 f5 ♗c5 16 ♘g3 ♗d7 17 ♕h3 ± Hellers-van der Wiel, Amsterdam 1986

[24] 9 ♗h4 ♘xe4 10 ♕f4 ♘g5 11 ♘xc6 (11 ♕g3 ∞/∓ D.Olafsson-Tal, Reykjavik 1986) 11 ... bc 12 ♕a4 ♕b6 13 f4 ♘h7 14 ♗c4 (14 f5 ♖b8 15 fe ♗xe6 16 ♗c4 ♗e7 ∓ Sax-Veingold, Tallinn 1979) 14 ... ♖b8 (14 ... ♗d7 15 ♖he1 d5 16 f5! ± Thipsay-Ravi Hedge, India

1983) 15 ♖he1 (15 ♗b3 ♗d7 $\overline{+}$) 15 ... ♕xb2+
16 ♔d2 ♕b4 17 ♕xc6+ ♗d7 18 ♕xa6 ♖c8 $\overline{+}$
Westerinen-Schüssler, Gjovik 1985
[25] 10 ♗g3 ♘xd4 11 ♕xd4 e5 12 ♕e3 ♖c8
13 ♔b1 ♗e7 14 f4 ♕c7 15 ♗d3 ef 16 ♗xf4
♗e6 = Kindermann-Dončević, Budapest 1985
[26] 11 ♕e2 ♕a5 (11 ... ♕c7 12 ♘d5 ±) 12 ♗xd6
♗xd6 13 ♖xd6 ♕b4 =
[27] 11 ... ♕c7 12 ♘d5 ± Matulović-Martinović,
Vršac 1985
     11 ... ♕a5 12 f3 (12 ♗xd6 ♗xd6 13 ♖xd6
♗xe4) 12 ... ♖d8 (12 ... 0-0-0 13 ♗c4 ♘d7
14 a3 ♕c7 15 ♗a2 ± Jansa-Csom, Sarajevo
1981, and Matanović-Csom, Indonesia 1982)
13 h4 ♗e7 14 a3 b5 15 g4 ± Ghinda-Winants,
Ostend 1985
[28] 12 e5 ♘h5 13 ♗e3 ♕c7 14 ♗e2 g6 15 ♗xh5
gh 16 ♗f4 0-0-0 ∞ Matulović-Ivanović, Stip
1979, and Chandler-Ivanović, Plovdiv 1983
     12 ♔b1 ♕c7 13 e5 de 14 ♗xe5 ♕a5 15 f3
♖d8 = Kudrin-Salov, Reykjavik 1986
[29] 15 ♘d4 ♗f6 16 ♘f3 ∞/= Jansa-Tukmakov,
Bor 1983, Arnason-Martinović, Bor 1984, and
Cuijpers-Tukmakov, Eindhoven v CSKA 1986
[30] 11 ... ♕b6 12 ♗c4 (12 ♗xd6 0-0-0 13 e5
♘e8 =) 12 ... 0-0-0 13 ♗b3 d5 (13 ... ♗e7
14 ♗e3 ♕a5 15 ♔b1 ♖he8 16 ♘d5 ±) 14 ed
♘xd5 15 ♘xd5 ♗xd5 16 ♕c3+ ♕c5 17 ♕xc5+
♗xc5 18 ♗xd5 ± Kholmov-Krementsky, USSR
1981
     11 ... e5 12 ♗e3 b5 13 ♔b1 ♗e7 14 g4 ±
Williams-Lein, Quebec 1986, and Yang-Lewis,
Dubai Ol 1986
[31] 12 ... ♗e7 13 ed ♘xd5 (13 ... ed 14 ♗d3 ±)
14 ♘xd5 ♗xd5 15 ♗e4 ± Unzicker-Radulov,
Moscow 1977
[32] 14 b4 ♗b6 15 ed ♗xd5! 16 ♗e5 0-0 17 ♕h4
a5 = Denisenko-Tukmakov, USSR 1983
     14 ed ♘xd5 15 b4 ♘xf4! 16 ♖xd8+ ♗xd8 $\overline{\infty}$
[33] 15 e5 ♘d7 16 ♔b1 ♗c7 17 f4 f6 18 ef
♕xf6 19 g3 ±/∞ Kholmov-Makarichev, USSR
1981, and Kholmov-Glek, USSR 1984
[34] 9 ... ♘g4 10 ♘xc6 bc 11 ♗c5 ± Smyslov-
Botvinnik, match (2) 1957
     9 ... ♗e7 10 f4 ♘xd4 (10 f3 ♘xd4) –
9 ... ♘xd4
     9 ... ♕c7 10 f4 ♗e7 11 ♗e2 ♗d7 (11 ...
♘a5 12 e5! ± Mikhalchishin-Csom, Copenhagen 1980; 11 ... ♘xd4 12 ♗xd4 b5 13 e5 ±
Sznapik-Martinović, Zenica 1985) 12 g4! b5
13 g5 ± Petrushin-Khasin, USSR 1985
[35] 10 ... ♘g4 11 e5! ♘xe5 (11 ... ♘xe3 12 fe
d5 13 e4 ±) 12 ♘e4 ± Klovans-Kryukov, USSR
1981
     10 ... ♕a5 11 ♗e2 ♗e7 12 f4 e5 13 fe de
14 ♕b6 ± Lanka-Goldin, USSR 1982
[36] 11 ... b5 12 f4 ♗b7 13 ♗f3 ♗e7 14 ♔b1
♖c8 15 e5 ♗xf3 16 gf de 17 fe ♖d8 18 ♕f4
♘d7 19 ♕g3 ♕xe5 20 ♖xd7 ± Klovans-

Gudimenko, USSR 1982
[37] 12 ... e5? 13 fe de 14 ♕a4+ ♗d7 15 ♖xd7! ±±
Petrushin-Vekshenkov, USSR 1985
     12 ... b5 13 e5 de 14 ♕xe5 (14 fe ♘d7
15 ♗f3 ♖b8 16 ♗f4 ±) 14 ... ♕xe5 (14 ...
♕b8 15 ♗f3 ♗b7 16 ♘xb5! ±± de Wit-
Winants, Belgium 1986) 15 fe ♘d7 16 ♗f3
♖b8 17 ♗c6! ±
[38] 14 ... ef 15 ♗xf4 ♖e8 16 g5? hg 17 ♗xg5
♘xe4! $\overline{+}$ Petrushin-Vaiser, Barnaul 1984;
16 ♖hg1 ±
     14 ... ♗xg4 15 ♗xg4 ♘xg4 16 ♘d5 ♕d7
(16 ... ♕d8 17 ♗b6 ♕d7 18 ♖hg1 ±) 17 ♘b6
♕c6 18 ♘xa8 ♘xe3 19 ♕xe3 ef 20 ♕b6 ♖xa8 ±
Vaiser
[39] 11 f3 ♗e7 12 h4 ♕a5 13 ♕f2 ♖b8 14 ♔b1
b4 15 ♘e2 e5 16 ♗a7 ♖b7 17 ♘c1 ♗e6 18 ♗e3
(18 ♘b3 ♕c7 19 ♗e3 a5 ∞) 18 ... d5 19 ♘b3
♕a4 ±/∞ Tseshkovsky-Lerner, Moscow 1985,
and Balashov-Salov, Irkutsk 1986
[40] 11 ... b4 12 ♗xf6 ♕xf6 13 ♘e2 ♖b8
14 ♘d4 ♖b6 15 ♗c4 ± Tal-Radulov, Malta Ol
1980
     11 ... ♗b7 12 ♗xf6 gf 13 ♗d3 ± Jansa-
Spassov, Sochi 1980
[41] 12 ♗d3 ♗b7 13 ♖he1 (13 ♕e2!? 0-0 14 g4)
13 ... 0-0 14 ♔b1 (14 g4 e5 15 fe ♘xg4 ∞) 14 ...
b4 15 ♘a4 ♗c6 16 ♘b6 ♖b8 17 ♘c4 ± Dvoiris-
Vekshenkov, USSR 1985
[42] 15 ♗f3 d5 16 ♔b1 (16 g4 0-0 17 h4 e5! ∞
Belyavsky-Tukmakov, Wijk aan Zee 1984) 16 ...
0-0 17 ♘b6 ♖b8 18 g4 ± Short-A.Rodriguez,
Subotica IZ 1987
[43] 11 ... ♖c8 12 ♔b1 ♘a5 13 e5 ± Hazai-
Szabo, Hungary 1983
     11 ... ♗e7 12 h3 ♘xd4 (12 ... ♕c7 13 ♗xb5!)
13 ♗xd4 ♗c6 14 ♖he1 0-0 15 ♔b1 ♕d7 16 g4 ±
Timoshchenko-Tukmakov, USSR Ch 1978
[44] 12 ♔b1 ♘a5 13 ♕e1 ♗c4 14 ♗c1 b4
15 ♘ce2 a5 $\overline{+}$ Mokry-Ivanović, Reggio Emilia
1984-85
[45] 12 ... ♗e7 13 ♗xb5 ±
[46] 15 ♘e2 ♕c5 16 ♔b1 a5 17 f5 ±/∞ Tal-
Radulov, Leningrad 1977
[47] 11 ... b4 12 ♘xc6 ♗xc6 13 ♘e2 d5
14 ♘d4 ± Matanović-Ničevski, Yugoslav Ch
1975
     11 ... ♖c8 12 h4 b4 13 ♘ce2 ♘e5 14 ♘f4 ±/±
Short-Adianto, Lugano 1986
[48] 13 ... h5 14 g5 ♘g8 15 ♗e2 ± Karpov-
van der Wiel, Amsterdam 1980
     13 ... b4 14 ♘b1 ♘c4 15 ♗xc4 ♕xc4 16 g5 ±
Arnason-Trepp, Chicago 1983
[49] 14 a3 ♖b8 15 g5 hg 16 hg ♘h5 17 f4 ♘c4
18 ♗xc4 ♕xc4 (18 ... bc 19 ♕f2 intending
f5 ± Tal-Csom, Moscow 1977) 19 ♘b3 ±/∞
Marjanović-Radulov, Bikac 1979
[50] 15 hg ♘h5 16 f4 ♘c4 17 ♗xc4 ♕xc4
18 ♔b1 ±/∞ Spraggett-Csom, Szirak 1986

307

Sicilian XI (Richter-Rauzer)
1 e4 c5 2 ♘f3 d6 3 d4 cd 4 ♘xd4 ♘f6 5 ♘c3 ♘c6 6 ♗g5 e6 7 ♕d2 ♗e7 8 0-0-0 0-0

	9	10	11	12	13	14	15	16	17	
1	f4[1]	♕xd4	♗c4[3]	e5[5]	fe	♗d2[6]	♘d5	♘xe7+	♖he1	±/∞
	♘xd4[2]	♕a5	♗d7[4]	de	♗c6	♘d7	♕d8	♕xe7	♖fd8[7]	
2	...	♗h4[8]	♘db5!	e5	♗xe7	♗xd8	♖hxf1	♘d6	♘e2[12]	±
	h6	♗d7[9]	d5[10]	♘e4[11]	♘xd2	♘xf1	♖fxd8	b6		
3	...	...	♘f5[13]	ef	♔b1[14]	♗xf6	♘xd5	♗c4[15]	♗xb5	∞
	...	e5	♗xf5	ef	d5	♗xf6	♗e5	b5[16]	♖b8[17]	
4	♘b3	a4	♗b5[19]	♘xe4	♕xd8	♗xd8	♘c5	♖d6	♖hd1	±
	a5[18]	d5	♘xe4[20]	de	♗xd8	♘xd8	f5[21]	♔f7	♔e7[22]	
5	...	...	...	♖he1[23]	♕xd8[25]	♘xe4	c4	♖xd8+	♖d1	±
	...	...	♘b4	de[24]	♖xd8[26]	♘bd5	♘c7	♗xd8	♗e7[27]	
6	...	f3	h4[29]	h5	h6[31]	♕f4	♗xe7	♕e3	♗e2[32]	±
	♕b6	a6[28]	♖d8	♕c7[30]	g6	♘e8	♕xe7	b5		
7	...	♗xf6	f4[33]	f5[34]	♘e2	♘f4	♔b1	g3	♗h3	±/∞
	a6	gf	b5	♔h8	♖g8[35]	♗f8	♗d7[36]	♕e7	♖d8[37]	

[1] **9 ♗xf6 ♗xf6 10 ♘xc6 bc 11 ♕xd6 ♕b6 12 ♕g3 ♖b8 13 e5 (13 b3 ♗xc3 14 ♕xc3 ♕xf2 ∓) 13 ... ♕xb2+ 14 ♔d2 ♗e7 15 ♖b1 ♕xc3+ 16 ♕xc3 ♖xb1 ∓ Korobov-Lisenko, USSR 1979
**9 ♘db5 ♕a5 10 ♗xf6 ♗xf6 11 ♘xd6 ♖d8 12 f4 e5 ∞

[2] 9 ... d5 10 e5 ♘d7 11 ♗xe7 ♕xe7 12 ♔b1 ♘b6 13 ♗e2 ♗d7 14 h4 ♖ac8 15 h5 h6 16 g4 ± Oll-Tal, Tallinn 1985

[3] 11 ♔b1 ♖d8 12 ♗c4 ♗d7 13 ♗b3 ♗c6 14 ♖he1 h6 15 ♗h4 ♕h5 16 ♗g3 d5 = Dvoiris-Yudasin, USSR Ch 1986

[4] 11 ... ♖d8 12 ♖hf1 ♗d7 13 f5 ±

[5] 12 ♖hf1 ♗c6 = (13 f5 b5)

[6] 14 ♗xf6?! gf ∓
**14 h4 ♖fd8 15 ♕f4 ♘h5 16 ♕g4 ♗xg5+ 17 ♕xg5 g6 = Vogt-Yudasin, Trnava 1983, Timman-Sosonko, match 1984, and Liberzon-D.Gurevich, Beer-Sheva 1984

[7] **17 ... ♕c5 18 ♕xc5 ♘xc5 19 ♗b4 b6 20 ♖e2 ±
**17 ... ♘b6 18 ♗f1 ♖fd8 19 ♕g4 ♕c5 20 ♗h6 ± Timman-Sosonko, Holland 1985-86
**17 ... ♖fe8 18 ♗f1 ♕c5 19 ♕xc5 ♘xc5 20 ♗b4 ± Gufeld-Parameswaran, New Delhi 1984
**17 ... ♖fd8 18 ♕g4 (18 ♗f1 ♘f8 19 ♕g4 ♘b6 20 ♖e3 ♖d5 ½-½ Grünfeld-Sosonko, Jerusalem 1986) 18 ... ♘c5 19 h4 ±/∞ Short-Sosonko, Wijk aan Zee 1987

[8] 10 ♗xf6 ♗xf6 11 ♘db5 (11 ♘xc6 bc 12 ♕xd6 ♕b6 13 ♕d3 ♖b8 14 b3 ♖d8 15 ♕f3 ♗d4! ∞ Wagman-Torre, Lugano 1984, and A.Rodriguez-van der Wiel, Biel IZ 1985) 11 ... e5 12 g3 a6 13 ♘xd6 ♗g4 ∞ Kupreichik-Fedorowicz, Hastings 1984-85

[9] 10 ... d5 11 e5 ♘d7 12 ♗f2 ♘b6 13 ♔b1 ♗d7 14 g4 ± Prandstetter-Kupreichik, Erevan 1984

[10] 11 ... ♘xe4 12 ♗xe7 ♘xd2 13 ♗xd8 ♘xf1 14 ♗c7 ♘e3 15 ♖d3 ♘xg2 16 ♗xd6 ♖fc8 17 ♖g1! ♘h4 18 ♘c7 ♖ab8 19 ♘e4! ± Kholmov-Kupreichik, Minsk 1985

[11] 12 ... ♘xe4 13 ♗xe7 ♕xe7 14 g3 ± Unzicker-Borik, Baden-Baden 1981

[12] van der Wiel-Ligterink, Wijk aan Zee 1981

[13] 11 ♘xc6 bc 12 fe de 13 ♕xd8 ♖xd8 14 ♖xd8+ ♗xd8 15 ♗c4 ♔f8 16 ♖f1 ♗g4 17 ♘a4 ♗e7 = Matulović-Ivanović, match 1985

[14] **13 ♗c4 ♘a5 14 ♗e2 ♖c8 ∞ Sax-Popović, Sarajevo 1985
**13 ♕xf4 d5 14 ♔b1 d4 15 ♗xf6' ♗xf6 16 ♘e4 ♗e5 (16 ... ♗g5!? Hjartarson) 17 ♕f3 ♖c8 18 ♗c4 (18 a3 b5! ∞ Ye Jiangchuan-Ma Hongding, Chinese Ch 1985) 18 ... ♘a5

19 ♗b3 (19 ♗d3?! ♘c4 20 f6 g6 21 h4 ♕b6 22 ♗xc4 ♖xc4 ∓ Sax-van der Wiel, Biel IZ 1985) 19 ... ♘xb3 20 cb (20 ab ♖c6 intending ... ♕a5; 20 ♕xb3 ♖c6! 21 ♕xb7 ♕d5! 22 ♘c3 ♕c5 van der Wiel) 20 ... ♖e8 21 g4 ± Matulović-Ivanović, match 1985; 18 ... b5 ∞ Matulović-Ivanović, match 1985, and Matulović-Damljanović, Vrnjačka Banja 1985

[15] **16 g3** fg 17 hg ♘e7! = Balashov-Salov, USSR Ch 1984

16 f6!? Korchnoi

[16] 16 ... ♕d6 17 ♖he1 (17 ♕e2!? ♖fe8 18 ♕g4 D.Olafsson-Ligterink, Reykjavik 1986) 17 ... ♖fe8 (17 ... ♖fd8 18 ♖e4 ± Barbulescu-A.Rodriguez, Havana 1986) 18 ♖e4 ♔f8 ±/∞ Horvath-Feher, Kecskemet 1985

[17] 18 c4 ♘d4 19 ♖he1 f6 20 a4 (20 ♗a4 ♘xf5 21 ♗b3 ♘e3 =) 20 ... a6! (20 ... ♖f7 21 ♘xf4 ±) 21 ♗xa6 ♖b3 22 ♗b5 ♕a8 ∞ A.Rodriguez-Popović, Dubai Ol 1986, and Marjanović-Popović, Jakarta 1986

[18] **9 ... h6** 10 ♗xf6 ♗xf6 11 ♕xd6 ♗xc3 (11 ... ♕b6 12 ♗c5 ±) 12 bc ♕h4 (12 ... ♕f6 13 ♕g3) 13 g3 ♕f6 (13 ... ♕xe4? 14 ♗d3 ♕e5 17 ♗h7+) 14 ♕c5 e5 15 ♗c4 ± Klovans-Tal, Jurmala 1983, and Chandler-Torre, London 1984

9 ... d5 10 ♗xf6 ♗xf6 11 ed ♗xc3 12 ♕xc3 ed 13 g3 ± Psakhis-Aseyev, Sevastopol 1986

[19] **11 ♗xf6** ♗xf6 12 ed ♗xc3 (12 ... ed!? 13 ♘xd5 ♗e6) 13 ♕xc3 ed 14 ♘d4 ♗d7 ∞ Psakhis-Kupreichik, USSR Ch 1985

11 ed!? ♘xd5 12 ♗xe7 ♘cxe7 13 ♗c4! Kosten-Chandler, England 1985

[20] **11 ... ♗b4** 12 ed ed 13 ♕f4 ± Anand

11 ... de 12 ♕xd8 ♗xd8 13 ♖he1 ± Tal-Korchnoi, Montpellier C 1985

[21] 15 ... b6 16 ♘xe4 ♗b7 17 ♖he1 ± Rohde-Joshi, USA 1986

[22] 18 ♗d7 ± Tal-Sisniega, Taxco IZ 1985

[23] 12 e5 ♘d7 13 ♗xe7 ♕xe7 14 f4 ± Kindermann-Felsberger, Vienna 1986, and Balashov-Khalifman, Minsk 1986

[24] 12 ... h6 13 ♗xf6 ♗xf6 14 ed ed 15 ♘xd5 ♗g4 16 f3 ♗g5 (Oll-Temirbayev, USSR 1986) 17 ♘e7+! ♕xe7 (17 ... ♗xe7 18 ♕xd8 ♖fxd8 19 ♖xd8+ ♖xd8 20 ♖xe7 ♗e6 21 ♘d2 ±± Oll)

18 ♖xe7 ♗xe7 19 ♕e2 ♗g5+ 20 ♔b1 ♗f5 21 ♘d4 ♗g6 22 ♔a1! ♗f6 23 c3 ♗xd4 24 cd ±/±± Oll-Khalifman, USSR 1987

[25] 13 ♘xe4 ♘xe4 14 ♕xd8 ♗xg5 15 ♕xg5 ♘xg5 16 h4 ± Vitolins-Inkiov, Jurmala 1985

[26] 13 ... ♗xd8 14 ♘xe4 ♘xe4 (14 ... ♗e7 15 ♘xf6+ ±) 15 ♗xd8 ♘xf2 16 ♖d2 ±

[27] 18 ♘xf6+ gf 19 ♗e3 ♘xb5 20 ab ± Anand-Inkiov, Calcutta 1986

[28] 10 ... ♖d8 and now:

11 h4 d5 12 ed ♘xd5 13 ♘xd5 ♖xd5 14 ♗d3 ± de la Villa-Gallego, Spanish Ch 1985

11 ♗e3 ♕c7 12 ♕f2 d5 (12 ... ♘d7 13 ♘b5 ± Gipslis-Tukmakov, USSR 1975) 13 ed ♘xd5 14 ♘xd5 ♖xd5 (14 ... ed 15 ♔b1 ± P.Clemance-J.Whitehead, Saint John 1988) 15 ♖xd5 ed 16 ♗b5 ± Hübner-J.Piket, Wijk aan Zee 1988

[29] 11 ♗xf6!? ♗xf6 12 ♕xd6 ± Hübner-Kasparov, match 1985

[30] 12 ... h6 13 ♗e3 ♕c7 14 ♕f2 ♘d7 15 g4 ± Hellers-Piket, Amsterdam 1985

[31] 13 g4!? b5 14 ♗e3 ♘d7 15 g5 ♘ce5 16 g6 ± Serper-Brodsky, USSR 1986

[32] Martinović-Popović, Yugoslav Ch 1986

[33] **11 h4** b5 12 g4 b4 13 ♘e2 a5 14 ♘bd4 ♘xd4 15 ♘xd4 ♗b7 16 g5 f5 ∞ Ehlvest-Yudasin, Sverdlovsk 1984, and Sax-van der Wiel, Brussels 1985

11 ♕h6 ♔h8 12 ♕h5 ♕e8 13 f4 (13 ♗d3!? ♘e5 14 f4 Chiburdanidze-Popović, match 1986) 13 ... ♖g8 14 g4 b5 15 ♗d3 ♖g7 16 h4 ±/∞ Arnason-Inkiov, Plovdiv 1986

[34] 12 ♔b1 ♘h8 (12 ... ♗d7 13 f5 ♔h8 14 ♘e2 ♖g8 15 ♘f4 ♗f8 16 g3 ♕e7 17 ♗h3 ♖d8 18 ♖hf1 ± Klovans-Tukmakov, USSR 1984) 13 ♗e2 ♕b6 14 ♖hf1 ♗d7 15 ♗h5 a5 16 ♖f3!? Marjanović-Popović, Novi Sad 1984

[35] 13 ... ef 14 ef ♘e5 15 ♘f4 ♖g8 16 g3 ♗xf5 17 ♘d4 ♗e4 18 ♗g2 ∞ Short-Popović, Subotica IZ 1987

[36] 15 ... ♗h6? 16 fe fe 17 ♘xe6! ± Hübner-Korchnoi, Tilburg 1985

[37] **17 ... a5?** 18 fe fe 19 ♘c5! ± G.Garcia-D.Gurevich, New York 1986

17 ... ♖d8 18 ♖hf1 ±/∞ Klovans-Tukmakov, USSR 1984

Sicilian XII (Sozin/Velimirović)
1 e4 c5 2 ♘f3 d6 3 d4 cd 4 ♘xd4 ♘f6 5 ♘c3 ♘c6 6 ♗c4 e6[1]

	7	8	9	10	11	12	13	14	15	
1	0-0	♗e3	♗b3[2]	f4	♗xd4	e5[5]	fe	♘e4[6]	♘d6	∞/=
	♗e7	0-0	a6[3]	♘xd4[4]	b5	de	♘d7	♗b7	♗xd6[7]	
2	♗e3	♕e2	0-0-0	♗d3	a3[10]	g4	ed	♘dxb5	♘xd5	±
	a6	♕c7[8]	♘a5	b5[9]	♗b7[11]	d5[12]	♘xd5	♕b8[13]	♗xd5[14]	
3	...	...	...	♗b3[15]	g4	g5	ab	h4[17]	♘a4	∞
	...	...	♗e7	♘a5[16]	b5	♘xb3+	♘d7	b4	♘c5[18]	
4	...	♕e2	0-0-0	♗b3[20]	♖he1[21]	♘f3	ab	ed	♔b1	∞
	♗e7	0-0	d5[19]	♘a5	e5	♘xb3+	♕a5	♗b4	♗xc3[22]	
5	...	...	...	♗b3[23]	♖hg1[24]	g4[26]	g5[27]	♖g3	♕h5	=
	...	...	a6	♕c7	♘d7[25]	♘c5	♗d7[28]	♖fc8	g6[29]	
6	...	...	...	...	...	g4	g5	ab	f4[31]	∞
	...	...	...	...	b5	♘a5[30]	♘xb3+	♘d7	b4[32]	
7	...	...	...	...	g4	♘f5!	♘d5	gf	♖hg1[36]	∞∞
	...	...	...	...	♘d7[33]	ef[34]	♕d8	♘f6[35]	♘xd5[37]	
8	...	...	...	...	...	♖xd4	g5	♖g1[38]	♖g3	∞
	...	...	...	...	♘xd4	b5	♘d7	♖b8[39]	g6[40]	

1   6 ... a6 – Najdorf

2   9 f4?! d5 10 ed ed 11 ♗e2 ♖e8 ∓

3   **9 ...** ♘a5 10 f4 b6 11 e5 ♘e8 12 ♕g4 (12 f5 ± *ECO*) 12 ... ♘xb3 13 ab ♗b7 14 ♖ad1 ± Kindermann-D.Gurevich, Beer-Sheva 1986

  9 ... ♗d7 10 ♕e2 ♘xd4 11 ♗xd4 ♗c6 12 ♖ad1 ♕a5 13 f4 e5 14 fe de 15 ♗e3 ± Nunn

  9 ... ♘xd4 10 ♗xd4 b5 11 ♘xb5 ♗a6 12 c4 ♗xb5 13 cb ♘xe4 14 ♕g4 ♘f6 15 ♕e2 ∞/±

4   10 ... ♕c7 11 f5 ± Honfi-Dončević, Budapest 1984

5   12 a3 ♗b7 13 ♕d3 a5! 14 e5 de 15 fe ♘d7 16 ♘xb5 ♘c5 ∞∞ Fischer-Spassky, match (4) 1972

6   **14 ♕f3** ♘c5! ∓

  14 ♕g4 ♘c5 15 ♖ad1 ♗b7 =

7   16 ed ♘g5 17 ♖f2 ♖ad8 (17 ... e5 18 ♗c3 e4 19 ♕f1 ♘g6 20 ♖e1 ±) 18 ♕d2 (18 ♕e2 ♗d5 19 ♖d1 ♗xb3 20 ab e5 21 ♗e3 ♕g6 22 c4 f5 ∞ Naivelt-Dvoiris, USSR 1985) 18 ... ♕xd2 19 ♖xd2 ♘f6 20 ♗xf6 gf = H.Olafsson-Mednis, New York 1977

8   8 ... ♘a5 9 ♗d3 b5 10 b4! ♘c4 (10 ... ♘b7 11 0-0 ± Mestrović-Polugayevsky, Varna 1972) 11 ♗xc4 bc 12 0-0 ± Horvath-Jasnikowski, Balatonbereny 1985

9   10 ... ♗e7 11 g4 (11 ♗g5 ♘c6! 12 ♘xc6 bc 13 f4 e5 ∞ Kupreichik-Ravikumar, Hastings 1984-85) 11 ... b5 12 g5 ♘d7 13 f4 b4 14 ♘b1 ♘c5 15 ♘d2 ± Kupreichik-Kuzmin, Moscow 1972

10   11 g4 b4 12 ♘a4!? (12 ♘b1 ♗b7 13 ♘d2 d5 14 f3 de 15 fe ♗e7 ∞ de Firmian-Kristiansen, Copenhagen 1984) 12 ... ♗b7 (12 ... ♗d7 13 g5! ♘g8 14 b3 ±) 13 ♘xe6! fe 14 ♗b6 ♕d7 15 b3 ♘c6 16 g5 ♘g8 17 f4 ∞∞ Zaichik-Kovalev, Borzomi 1984

11   **11 ... ♗e7** 12 g4 ♖b8 13 ♖he1!? ♘c4 14 g5 ♘d7 15 ♘f5! ± Nunn-Pritchett, West Germany 1985

  11 ... ♖b8 12 ♗g5 ♗e7 13 ♕e1!? (13 f4 b4 ∞ Ehlvest-Lerner, Tallinn 1986) 13 ... ♘c4 14 f4 ± A.Sokolov-Tukmakov, USSR Ch 1984

12   **12 ... ♗e7** 13 g5 ♘d7 14 f4 ♘c5 15 ♔b1 Cosulich-Ungureanu, Siegen Ol 1970, and London-D.Gurevich, New York 1985

  12 ... ♖c8 13 g5 ♘d7 14 f4 ♘c4 15 ♘dxb5 ± Hawelko-Inkiov, Warsaw Z 1987

13   14 ... ab 15 ♗xb5+ ± Nunn-Sosonko, Thessaloniki Ol 1984

14   16 ♘c3 ♗xh1 17 ♖xh1 ± Hawelko-Gaprindashvili, Polanica Zdroj 1986

15   **10 g4** ♘e5 11 ♗b3 ♘exg4 12 ♖hg1 ♖xe3 13 ♕xe3 g6 14 f4 ∞ Velimirović-Cebalo, Kavala 1985

  10 ♖hg1 ♘a5 (10 ... 0-0 11 g4 ♘xe4

ECO) 11 ♗d3 b5 12 g4 b4 13 ♘b1 ♗b7 14 ♘d2 d5 15 f3 0-0 = Dzanoyev-Kuzmin, USSR 1976

[16] **10 ... 0-0** – 7 ... ♗e7

10 ... b5? 11 ♘xc6 ♕xc6 12 ♗d4 ♗b7 (12 ... 0-0? 13 ♘d5!) 13 ♖he1 ± Hübner-Hort, Bamberg 1972

[17] 14 ♘f5 ef 15 ♘d5 ♕d8 16 ef ♗b7 17 f6 gf 18 ♖he1 ♗xd5 19 ♖xd5 ♖g8 20 gf (20 h4 ♖c8 ∓ Ehlvest-Tischbierek, Leningrad 1984) 20 ... ♘xf6 21 ♖f5 ♘d7 (21 ... ♖b8!?) 22 ♗g5 ♘e5 23 ♗xe7 ♕xe7 24 f4 ♘d3+ = Yurtayev-Korzubov, USSR 1983

[18] 16 h5 and now:

16 ... ♘xa4 17 ba ♕a5 18 g6 ♕xa4 19 ♔b1 ± Hartston Mestel, British Ch 1973

16 ... ♘xe4 17 g6 f5 (17 ... ♗d8 18 ♗f4 ±) 18 h6 ± Zaitsev-Utemov, USSR 1983

16 ... e5 17 ♘f5 ± Nunn-Murshed, London 1985.

16 ... ♗d7 17 g6 (17 ♔b1 ♗xa4 18 ba ♖c8! ∞ Hector-Cebalo, Montpellier 1985) 17 ... ♘xb3+ 18 ♘xb3 (18 ♔b1 ♘xd4 19 ♗xd4 ♗xa4 20 ♗xg7 ♖c8 ∓ Hector-A.Rodriguez, Seville 1986) 18 ... ♗xa4 19 h6 fg 20 hg ♖g8 21 ♘d4 e5 22 ♘e6 ♕c6 23 ♖xh7 ♗b3 24 ♖d5 ∞ Rehelis-Piket, Gausdal 1986

[19] 9 ... ♕a5 10 ♗b3 ♘xd4 11 ♗xd4 ♗d7 12 ♔b1 ♗c6 13 f4 ± Fischer-Geller, Skopje 1967

9 ... ♘xd4 10 ♗xd4 ♕a5 11 ♖hg1 ♗d7 12 g4 ± Wolff-Dlugy, USA 1984

9 ... ♗d7 10 ♗b3 (10 f4 ♖c8 11 e5 ♘e8 ∞) 10 ... ♖c8 (10 ... ♘xd4 11 ♖xd4 ♕a5 12 ♖hd1 ♗c6 13 f4 ± London-Dlugy, USA 1986) 11 f4 ♘a5 12 e5 ♘xb3+ 13 ab (13 ♘xb3 de 14 fe ♘d5 15 ♖xd5 ed 16 ♕xc7 ∞) 13 ... ♘e8 ∞ Yurtayev-Kochiev, USSR 1976

[20] **10 ed** ed 11 ♗b3 ♖e8 =

10 ♘f3 ♘xe4 11 ♘xe4 ♕a5 (11 ... ♕c7!?) 12 ♗d2 ♕a4 13 ♗d3 de 14 ♕xe4 ♕xe4 15 ♗xe4 f6 =

10 ♘xe6 fe 11 ed ♘a5 12 de ♕c7 13 ♗d5 ♘c6 ∞

[21] 11 e5 ♘d7 12 f4 ♘b6 13 ♔b1 ♘xb3 14 cb f6 = Hübner-Sosonko, Wijk aan Zee 1984

[22] 16 bc ♘xd5 17 ♗d2 ♘xc3+?! 18 ♗xc3 ♕xc3 19 ♕xe5 ± Wedberg-Sosonko, Amsterdam 1984; 17 ... f6 ∞

[23] 10 ♖hg1 ♘xd4 11 ♗xd4 b5 12 ♗b3 b4 13 ♘a4 ♗d7 14 g4 ♗b5 15 ♕e1 ♖b8 ∓ Tseitlin-Chernikov, USSR 1975

[24] 11 f4 ♘xd4 12 ♖xd4 b5 13 f5 ef 14 ef ♗xf5 15 g4 ∞ Karasev-Lukianov, USSR 1984

[25] 11 ... ♘xd4 12 ♗xd4 b5 13 g4 ♘d7 (13 ... b4 14 g5 ♗d7 15 ♗d5! ed 16 ♗xd5 ♗b7 17 g6 ±) 14 g5 ♘c5 15 ♗xb7 (15 ... b4 16 ♗f6! intending ♕h6!) 16 ♖g4 ±

[26] **12 ♕h5** ♘f6 13 ♕f3 ♘d7 ∞ Velimirović-Kelečević, Yugoslav Ch 1983

[12] **12 ♔b1** ♘c5 13 ♕h5 ♕a5 = Taborov-Salov, Nikolayev 1983

[27] 13 ♘f5!? b5 (13 ... ef 14 gf ∞∞) 14 ♗d5 ed (14 ... ♗b7 15 g5 ef? 16 g6 ± A.Sokolov-Salov, Nikolayev 1983; 15 ... ♖fc8 ∞∞) 15 ♘xd5 ♕b7 16 e5 ♘e6 17 ed ♗d8 18 g5 ♔h8 19 ♖g3 ♘f4! ∓ Koops-Skrodelis, corr. 1986

[28] 13 ... b5 14 ♘xc6 ♘xb3+ 15 ab ♕xc6 16 ♗d4 b4 17 ♕h5! ♗b7 (17 ... bc 18 ♕h6! e5 19 ♗xe5 ± Soltis-D.Gurevich, Lone Pine 1981; 17 ... ♖d8 18 ♖d3 bc 19 ♖f3! ± Grigorov-Spassov, Bulgarian Ch 1975) 18 ♘d5! ed 19 ♖d3 ± Howell-Wahls, Gausdal 1986

[29] 16 ♕h6 ♗f8 17 ♕h4 ♗e7 18 ♘de2?! h5 19 f4 b5 ∓; 18 ♕h6 =

[30] 12 ... b4 13 ♘xc6 ♘xc6 14 ♘d5 ed 15 g5 ♘xe4! 16 ♗xd5 ♕a4 17 ♗xe4! ♗c6 18 ♗d4 g6 19 f4!? ± Boudy-Suarez, Cuba 1972

[31] 15 ♕h5 g6 (15 ... ♖d8? 16 ♘f5 ♘f8 17 ♗b6! ±±) 16 ♕h6 ♖e8 17 ♖g3 ♗f8 18 ♕h4 b4 19 ♖h3 h5 20 ♘ce2 ∞

[32] 16 ♘a2 ♗b7 ∓ van der Wiel-Ligterink, Wijk aan Zee 1985

16 ♘f5 ef 17 ♘d5 ♕d8 18 ef ♖e8 19 g6 (19 f6 ♗f8 ∓) 19 ... fg 20 fg ♗f6 21 ♕c4 (21 ♕h5 h6 22 ♘xb4 ♗b7 ∓) 21 ... ♔h8 22 ♘c7 ♖xe3 23 ♘xa8 ♘c5 ∞ Schroeder

[33] **11 ... b5** 12 ♘xc6 ♕xc6 13 g5 ♘xe4 14 ♘d5 ♕b7 15 ♕f3 ±

11 ... ♘a5 12 g5 ♘xb3+ 13 ab ♘d7 14 h4 b5 15 g6! hg 16 h5 ±

[34] 12 ... ♘c5 13 ♘xe7+ ♕xe7 14 ♖d2 b5 15 f3 ±

[35] 14 ... ♘a5 15 ♖hg1 ♘xb3+ 16 ab ♔h8 17 ♗d4 ± Nunn-Simm, England 1977

[36] 15 ♗b6 ♕d7 16 ♖hg1 ♘xd5 17 ed ♗f6 18 dc ♕xc6 = Nunn-Liberzon, Hastings 1979-80

[37] 16 ♗xd5 ♗f6 17 ♕h5 ∞∞ ♘e7 18 ♗b3 ♕a5 19 ♖xd6 ♕e5 20 ♕xf7+ 1-0 Yakovich-Yudasin, Leipzig 1986

[38] 14 h4 ♘c5 15 h5 f5! ∞∞

14 f4 ♘c5 15 f5 (15 ♕f2 f5! ∞∞; 15 ♖f1 b4!? 16 ♖xb4 a5 ∞∞ Yuneyev-Lukin, USSR 1984) 15 ... ♘xb3+ 16 ab ef 17 ef ♗xf5 18 ♘d5 ♕d8 ∞∞ Wedberg-L.Schneider, Oslo 1980, and Iskov-Mednis, Reykjavik 1982

14 ♕h5 g6 15 ♕h6 ♖e8 16 ♖g1 ♗f8 17 ♕h4 ♖b8 18 ♖g3 ♗g7 19 ♖d1 b4 20 ♘e2 ♘f8 ∞∞ Vetemaa-Panchenko, USSR 1979

[39] **14 ...** ♘c5?! 15 e5! de 16 ♖h4 ♘xb3+ (16 ... g6 17 ♗xc5 intending ♘e4) 17 ab g6 18 ♕f3! (18 ♘e4 f5 =) 18 ... ♗b7 19 ♕h3 h5 20 ♖xh5! ±

14 ... g6 15 h4 ♘c5 16 h5 ♖e8 19 ♖h1 ±/∞∞ Dueball-Kuzmin, Nice Ol 1974

[40] 16 h4 h5 17 gh ♗xh4 18 h7+ ♔h8 19 ♖h3 ♗f6 20 ♖d1 ♘c5 ∞∞ Zuyev-Panchenko, USSR 1985

| | Sicilian XIII (Najdorf) | | 1 e4 c5 2 ♘f3 d6 3 d4 cd 4 ♘xd4 ♘f6 5 ♘c3 a6 | | | | | | |

	6	7	8	9	10	11	12	13	14	
1	h3	g4	ed	♘de2	♗g2	♗d2	♘e4	0-0	b3	=
	e6[1]	d5[2]	♘xd5	♗b4	0-0	♘b6[3]	♗e7	♘c6	f5[4]	
2	♗e3	♘b3	♕d2	f3	a4[9]	♘d5	ed	♗xb6	a5[10]	∞
	e5[5]	♗e6[6]	♘bd7[7]	b5[8]	b4	♗xd5	♘b6	♕xb6	♕b7[11]	
3	...	♘f3	a4	a5[13]	♗e2	♗b6	♘d2	ed	♘xd5	=
	...	♕c7[12]	♗e7	0-0[14]	♘c6!?[15]	♕d7	d5	♘xd5	♕xd5[16]	
4	g3	♘b3	♗g2	0-0	a4	♘d2	♘c4	♕e2	ab	∞
	e5[17]	♗e7[18]	0-0[19]	♘bd7[20]	b6	♗b7	♘c5	b5	ab[21]	
5	...	♘de2	a4[23]	♗g2	h3	g4[26]	♘g3	h4[27]	g5	∞
	...	♘bd7[22]	b6[24]	♗b7	♗e7[25]	♘c5	0-0	g6	♘fd7[28]	
6	f4	♗e2[30]	g4[31]	♘b3	ab	g5	h4[32]	♗e3	♗d4	∞/±
	♘bd7[29]	g6	♘c5	♘xb3	♗g7	♘d7	♘c5	♗d7		
7	...	♗d3[33]	0-0	♘f3[34]	♕e1	♖xf3	♔h1	♗d2	a3	∞/=
	♕c7	g6	♗g7	♗g4!?[35]	♗xf3	♘bd7	♖c8	♕c5	0-0[36]	
8	...	♘f3[37]	a4[38]	♗d3	0-0	♔h1	♕e1[42]	fe	♕g3	∞/=
	e5	♕c7	♗e7[39]	0-0	♘bd7[40]	♘c5[41]	♖e8[43]	de	♗d8[44]	

---

[1] **6 ... e5** 7 ♘de2 ♗e6 8 g4 ♗e7 9 ♗g2 ♘bd7 10 ♘g3 ±

   6 ... g6 7 g4 ♗g7 8 g5 ♘h5 9 ♗e2 e5! 10 ♘b3 ♘f4 = Fischer

   6 ... b5 7 ♘d5 ♘xe4 (7 ... e6 8 ♘xf6+ ♕xf6 9 c4? d5 10 cd ♗b4+ ∓ Sarar-Dunne, corr. 1975) 8 ♕f3 ♘c5 9 b4 e6 10 bc ed 11 ♕xd5 ♖a7 = Fischer

[2] 7 ... b5!? 8 g5 ♘fd7 9 a3 ♗b7 10 ♗e3 ♘c6 ∞ Polugayevsky

[3] 11 ... ♘xc3 12 ♘xc3 ♕c7 13 a3 ♗e7 14 ♕f3 ± Kurajica -Bukić, Yugoslavia 1972

[4] 15 gf ef ∞ Kurajica-Najdorf, Hastings 1971-72

[5] **6 ... ♘bd7** 7 g4 d5 8 ♘b3! ♘xe4 9 ♘xd5 ± Sax-Radulov, Herculana Z 1982

   6 ... ♕c7 7 ♕d2 e6 8 f3 h5 9 0-0-0 ♘bd7 10 ♗d3 b5 11 ♖he1 ♗b7 12 ♗g5 ± A.Sokolov-Karolyi, Groningen 1981-82

[6] 7 ... ♗e7 8 f3 ♗e6 9 ♕d2 0-0 10 0-0-0 b5 (10 ... a5 11 ♗b5! ± Sax-Quinteros, Moscow IZ 1982) 11 g4 b4 12 ♘a4 ♘c6 13 h4 ♖b8 ∞ Lukin-Dorfman, USSR 1983

[7] 8 ... ♗e7!? 9 f3 0-0 10 0-0-0 b5 11 g4 b4 12 ♘a4 ♘c6 13 h4 ♖b8 ∞ van der Wiel-Gutman, Wijk aan Zee 1987

[8] **9 ... ♖c8** 10 g4 h6 11 0-0-0 b5 12 h4 ♘b6 13 ♔b1 ± Tseshkovsky-Sunye, Erevan 1980

   9 ... ♕c7 10 g4 h6 11 h4 ♖c8 12 ♖g1 ♘b6 ∞ Liberzon-Brito, Hastings 1980-81

[9] 10 ♘d5 ♗xd5 11 ed ♘b6 12 ♗xb6 ♕xb6 = Peters-Browne, US Ch 1980

[10] 14 g4 g6 15 h4 ♗g7 16 h5 0-0 Hartmann-Georgadze, Hanover 1983

[11] 15 0-0-0 g6 16 ♔b1 ♗g7 17 f4 e4!? ∞ Hazai-Nunn, Lugano 1983

[12] **7 ... h6** 8 ♗c4 ♗e7 9 ♕e2 ♗e6 10 ♗xe6 fe 11 0-0-0 ± Tseshkovsky-Portisch, Las Palmas 1976

   7 ... ♗e6 8 ♘g5 ♕c7 9 ♘xe6 fe 10 a4 ♘bd7 11 g3! ± Hellers-de Firmian, Wijk aan Zee 1986

   7 ...♗e7 8 ♗c4 ♗e6 9 ♗xe6 fe 10 ♘g5 ♕d7 11 ♕f3 d5 ∞ Kudrin-de Firmian, US Ch 1986

[13] 9 ♗e2 ♘bd7!? 10 a5 ♘c5 ∞ Anand-Chandler, London 1986

[14] 9 ... ♘bd7 10 ♘d2 (10 ♖a4!? ∞ Smirin-Gelfand, USSR 1986) 10 ... ♘c5 11 ♘d5 ♘xd5 12 ed ♗f5 13 ♗e2 h6 14 0-0 ± Hübner-Portisch, match 1980

[15] 10 ... ♗e6 11 0-0 h6 12 ♘d5 ♘xd5 13 ed ♗f5 14 c4 ♘d7 ∞ Matanović

16 15 0-0 ♗e6 (15 ...♗f5!? ∞ Chandler-Portisch, London 1986) 16 ♗f3 ♛b5 17 b3 = Mestel-Chandler, British Ch 1986

17 6 ... b5 7 ♗g2 ♗b7 8 0-0 e6 9 ♖e1 ♛c7 10 a4 ±

6 ... ♗g4 7 f3 ♗d7 8 ♗e3 ♘c6 9 ♗g2 g6 10 0-0 ♗g7 11 ♘d5 ± Polugayevsky

18 7 ... ♗g4!? 8 ♛d3 ♘c6 9 ♗g2 ♖c8 10 0-0 h6 11 ♗e3 ♗e6 ∞ Popović-Ftacnik, Hastings 1980-81

19 8 ... b5 9 a4 ♗b7 10 ab ab 11 ♖xa8 ♗xa8 12 ♛d3 b4 13 ♘d5 ± Sax-R.Byrne, New York 1987

20 9 ... b5 10 a4 b4 11 ♘d5 ♘xd5 12 ♛xd5 ♖a7 13 ♗e3 ± Popović-Bachtiar, Jakarta 1986
9 ... ♗e6 10 a4 ♘c6?! (10 ... ♘bd7) 11 ♘d5 ♖c8 12 a5! ± Popović-Pinter, Dubai Ol 1986

21 15 ♖xa8 ♛xa8 ∞ Muratov-Grigorian, USSR 1977

22 7 ... b5 8 ♗g2 ♗b7 9 0-0 ♘bd7 10 h3 ♗e7 11 g4 0-0 12 ♘g3 ♘c5! 13 a3 a6 = Grigorov-Vera, Varna 1986
7 ... ♗e7 8 ♗g2 (8 ♗g5 ♘bd7 9 ♗h3 b5! ∞ Fischer) 8 ... b5 9 a4 b4 10 ♘d5 ♘xd5 11 ♛xd5 ♖a7 = Gavrikov

23 8 ♗g2 b5! 9 ♘d5 ♘xd5 10 ♛xd5 ♘b6 11 ♛d3 ♗e6 = Polugayevsky

24 8 ... ♖b8!? 9 a5 b5 10 ab ♛xb6 11 ♗g2 ♗b7 12 0-0 ♘c5 = Savon-Anikayev, USSR 1980

25 10 ... ♖c8 11 g4 g6 12 0-0 ♘c5 13 ♘g3 ♘e6 = Kholmov-Fedorov, USSR 1981

26 11 0-0 0-0 12 g4 b5! ∞ Hartston-Lukov, Plovdiv 1983

27 13 0-0 g6 14 f4 ef 15 ♗xf4 b5 16 ab ab = Kholmov-Timoshchenko, USSR 1981

28 15 ♗e3 (15 ♘d5 ♘e6 16 ♗e3 ♖c8 ∞ A.Ivanov-Chekhov, USSR 1982) ∞ A.Ivanov-Lapenis, USSR 1986

29 6 ... g6 7 e5 de 8 fe ♘d5 ± Tukmakov
6 ... ♛b6 7 ♘f3 g6 8 ♗c4 ♗g7 9 ♛e2 e6 10 f5 ±
6 ... ♘c6 7 ♘xc6 bc 8 e5 ♘d7 9 ♗c4 ♘b6 10 ♗d3 ± ECO
6 ... e6! – Scheveningen

30 7 ♘f3 g6 8 ♗d3 ♗g7 9 0-0 0-0 10 ♔h1 ♛c7 11 a4 b6 ∞ Ljubojević-Miles, Skara 1980
7 ♛f3 g6 8 ♗e3 e5 9 ♘b3 ef 10 ♗xf4 ♘e5 = Radulov-Ljubojević, Indonesia 1983

31 8 0-0 – 6 ♗e2 ♘bd7 7 f4 g6 8 0-0

32 12 ♗e3 ♖b8 13 h4 ∞/± Polugayevsky

33 7 f5 e5! 8 fe fe 9 ♗e2 ♘c6 10 ♘xc6 bc = Polovodin-Gufeld, USSR 1980
7 ♗e2 g6 8 g4 ♗g7 9 g5 ♘fd7 10 ♘d5 ♛d8 11 f5 ∞ Belyavsky-Dvoiris, USSR Ch 1986
7 a4 ♘c6! 8 ♘xc6 bc 9 ♗d3 e5 10 0-0 ♗e7

11 a5 0-0 = Nunn-Gutman, West Germany 1986

34 9 ♔h1 ♘bd7 10 ♛e1 b5 11 a4 b4 12 ♘a2 ♗b7 = A.Sokolov-Dvoiris, USSR 1981

35 9 ... 0-0 10 ♛e1 ♘bd7 11 ♔h1 e6 12 ♛h4 ♘c5 ∞
9 ... ♘bd7 10 ♛e1 ♘c5 11 ♔h1 b5 12 e5 de 13 fe ♘fd7 14 ♗f4 ♗b7 ∞ Sax-Polugayevsky, Hilversum 1973

36 15 ♛h4 ♛h5 ∞/= Ehlvest-Tal, Tallinn 1983

37 7 ♘b3 ♘bd7 8 a4 ♗e7 9 ♗e2 0-0 10 0-0 b6 11 ♗d3 ♗b7 12 ♛e2 ♖e8 = Korzubov-Novikov, USSR 1984

38 8 ♗d3 ♘bd7 9 0-0 g6 (9 ... b5 10 ♛e1 ♗b7 11 ♔h1 g6 12 fe de 13 ♛h4 h6 14 ♗d2 ±) 10 ♛e1 ♗g7 11 ♛h4 0-0 12 fe de 13 ♗h6 b5 14 ♘g5 ♗b7 15 ♖f3 ♘h5 ∞ van der Wiel-Hübner, Tilburg 1984

39 8 ... ♘bd7 9 ♗d3 g6 10 0-0 ♗g7 11 ♛e2 (11 ♔h1 0-0 12 ♛e2 ♘c5! =) 11 ... b6 12 ♗c4 ♗b7 13 f5 ± Tseshkovsky-Peshina, USSR 1984

40 10 ... b6 11 ♔h1 ♗b7 12 ♛e2 (12 ♛e1 ♘bd7 13 ♘h4 g6 14 fe de 15 ♗h6 ♖e8 16 ♘f5 ♗b4!? 17 ♛h4 ♗xc3 18 bc ♖e6 ∞) 12 ... ♘bd7 13 fe ♘xe5 (13 ... de 14 ♘h4 g6 15 ♗h6 ♖e8 16 ♗c4 ±/± Ioseliani-Sitnikova; USSR 1985) 14 ♘xe5 de 15 ♗c4 ± Sax-Groszpeter, Hungarian Ch 1984

41 11 ... ef 12 ♗xf4 ♘e5 13 ♗g5 (13 ♘h4!?) 13 ... ♗e6 14 ♘xe5 de 15 ♗xf6 ♗xf6 16 ♖xf6 gf 17 ♛h5 ∞ Glek-Maliskauskas, USSR 1986
11 ... ♖e8 12 ♘h4 ef 13 ♗xf4 ♘c5 14 ♛f3 ♗e6 15 ♗d2 (15 ♖ae1 ♛c6 16 ♘f5 ♗xf5 17 ef d5 Glek-Shnaider, USSR 1985) 15 ... ♘fd7 16 ♘f5 ♗f6 17 ♘d5 ♗xd5 18 ed ♔h8 19 ♛g3 ± Ehlvest-Neverov, USSR 1985
11 ... b6 12 ♘h4 ♘c5 13 fe de 14 ♗g5 ♛d8 15 ♘f5 ♗xf5 16 ♖xf5 ♘fd7 17 ♗xe7 ♛xe7 18 ♗c4 ± Psakhis-Ubilava, Sevastopol 1986

42 12 ♛e2 ♗d7 13 fe de 14 ♗g5 ♗e6 15 ♘h4 ♘xd3 16 cd ♔h8 17 ♖ac1 ♛d8 18 ♘f5 ± A.Sokolov-Belyavsky, Montpellier C 1985; 15 ... ♘e8!? 16 ♗xe7 ♛xe7 17 ♘f5 ♗xf5 18 ♘d5 ♛e6 19 ♖xf5 ♘xd3 20 cd ♖c8 = A.Sokolov

43 12 ... ♗e6?! 13 f5 ♗d7 14 g4! ♗c6 15 g5 ♘h5 16 f6 ♗d8 17 ♛h4 ± Nunn-Portisch, Brussels 1986
12 ... ef 13 ♗xf4 ♖e8 14 ♘d4 ♗d7 15 ♗g5 ♛d8 16 ♛f2 ♖c8 17 h3 ♗e6 = Hazai-Novikov, Camaguey 1987

44 15 ♘h4 ♔h8 16 ♘f5 ♗xf5 17 ♖xf5 ♛c6 18 ♗e3 ♛xd3 19 cd ♛d7 ∞/= Oll-Novikov, Minsk 1986

	6	7	8	9	10	11	12	13	14	
9	f4	♘f3	a4[45]	♗c4	♕e2[47]	♗a2[48]	0-0	♘xa4[50]	♔h1	=
	e5	♘bd7	♗e7	♕a5[46]	b5	ba[49]	0-0	♖b8	♕c7[51]	
10	...	...	...	♗d3	0-0	♕e1[53]	♔h1	♗xf4	♖b1	=
	...	...	...	0-0	♘c5[52]	♗e6[54]	ef	♕b6[55]	♖fe8[56]	

[45]   8 ♗d3 and now:
8 ...   ♗e7 9 0-0 0-0 10 ♕e1 b5 11 a4 b4 12 ♘e2 ♘c5 13 ♘g3 ♖e8 14 ♔h1 ± Schneider-de Firmian, Reykjavik 1984
8 ...   b5 9 0-0 g6 10 ♕e1 ♗g7 11 a4 (11 a3 0-0 12 fe de 13 ♕h4 ♗b7 ∞ van der Wiel-Ribli, Amsterdam 1986) 11 ... b4 12 ♘d1 a5 13 ♔h1 0-0 14 f5 ♗b7 15 ♕h4 ∞ Schneider-Chandler, Reykjavik 1984
8 ...   g6!? 9 0-0 ♗g7 10 ♕e1 0-0 11 fe de 12 ♕h4 ♘h5 13 ♗g5 f6 14 ♗e3 ♘f4 ∞/= Kveinis-Petrosian, Sevastopol 1986

[46]   9 ... 0-0 10 ♕e2 (10 0-0 ♕b6+ 11 ♔h1 ef 12 a5 ♕c7 13 ♗d5 ♘e5 14 ♗xf4 ♗e6 15 ♘d4 ♗xd5 16 ed ♖fe8 ∞ Gallagher-Nunn, London 1985) 10 ... ♕a5 11 ♗a2 ef 12 0-0 ♘e5 13 ♗xf4 ♗e6!? (13 ... ♘xf3+ 14 ♕xf3 ♗d7 15 ♔h1 ± Gavrikov-Portisch, Tunis IZ 1985; 13 ... ♘g6 14 ♗d2 ♕h5 15 ♖ae1 ± A.Sokolov-Portisch, Montpellier C 1985) 14 ♗xe6 fe 15 ♘g5 ♕c5+ 16 ♔h1 ♕c8 = Portisch

[47]   10 ♗d2 ef 11 ♕e2 0-0 12 ♘d5 ♕d8 13 ♗f4 ♘xd5 14 ♗xd5 ♕b6 (14 ... ♘f6 15 0-0 ♘xd5 16 ed ♗f6 17 c3 ♖e8 =) 15 c3 ♘f6 16 a5 ♕c7 17 0-0 ♘xd5 18 ed ♗f6 ∞ Popović-de Firmian, New York 1984; 11 ... ♘e5 12 ♗b3 ♘xf3+! ∞ Popovych-Tisdall, Gausdal 1985

[48]   11 ♗d3 ♗b7 12 0-0 0-0 13 fe de 14 ♗g5 ∞ Semenyuk-Polovodin, USSR 1984

[49]   11 ... b4 12 ♘d5 ♗b7 ∞ ECO

[50]   13 ♔h1 ♖b8 14 ♘d2 (14 ♗c4 ♖b4?! 15 b3! ef 16 ♗xf4 ♕c7 17 e5 ± Kindermann-Lau, Dortmund 1985) 14 ... ♗b7 15 ♘c4 ♕c7 16 fe de 17 ♗g5 ± G.Garcia-Zuckerman, New York 1986; 13 ... ♗b7! 14 ♘h4 ♖ae8 15 ♘f5 ♕b4 16 fe ♘xe5 ∞ Dolmatov-Ftacnik, Moscow 1985

[51]   Tseshkovsky-Raičević, Trnava 1986

[52]   **10 ...   b6** 11 ♔h1 ♗b7 12 ♕e2 (12 fe de 13 ♗g5 ♘c5 = Sax) 12 ... ♕c7 – 7 ... ♕c7
10 ...   ef 11 ♗xf4 (11 ♔h1 ♘e5 12 ♗xf4 ♘g6 13 ♗g3 ♘h5 ∞ Ulibin-Dvoiris, USSR 1987; 11 ... ♘c5 12 ♗xf4 ♗d7 13 ♕e2 ♖c8 14 a5 ♖e8 = Psakhis-Pigusov, Irkutsk 1986) 11 ... ♕b6+ (11 ... ♘c5 12 ♔h1 ♗d7 13 a5 ♖c8 14 ♘d4 ♘e6 15 ♗e3 ♘xd4 16 ♗xd4 ♗e6 17 ♘d5! ± Kveinis-Lapenis, USSR 1987) 12 ♔h1 ♕xb2 13 ♕e1 ♕b4 (13 ... ♘c5 14 ♖b1 ♘xd3 15 cd ♕c2 16 d4 ♖e8 17 ♖f2 ♕d3 18 ♖c1! ±) 14 ♖b1 ♕c5 15 ♘d5 ♘xd5 16 ed ♗f6! 17 ♕e4 ∞/± Korolev-Lipiridi, corr. 1984

[53]   **11 ♔h1** d5 (11 ... ♘xd3 12 cd ♕a5 13 ♕e1 ef 14 ♘d5 ♕d8 15 ♘xf4 ± Mateo-Byrne, New York 1986; 11 ... ef 12 ♗xf4 ♗g4 13 h3 ♗h5 14 ♕d2 ♗g6 15 ♖ae1 ♖ae8 16 ♕e2 d5 ∞ Grigorov-Lukov, Bulgaria 1984) 12 fe ♘fxe4 13 ♘d4 ♗e6 14 ♗b3 ♘xc3 15 bc ♘xd3 16 cd ♖c8 ∞ Prasad-de Firmian, Kolhapur 1987; 11 ... ♕c7!? – 7 ... ♕c7
11 ♕e2 ♘xd3 12 ♕xd3 (12 cd!? Khalifman) 12 ... ♕c7 13 f5 ♗d7 14 ♗g5 ♘c6 15 ♖ad1 ♖fd8 16 ♗xf6 ♗xf6 17 ♔h1 ♖ac8 = Nunn-Ribli, London 1984

[54]   11 ... ♘xd3 12 cd ef 13 ♗xf4 d5 14 e5 ♘e8 = Nunn

[55]   13 ... ♖c8 14 ♖d1 ♕b6 15 ♗e3 ♘g4 16 ♘d5 ♗xd5 17 ♗xc5 dc 18 ed ♖ce8 19 ♘e5 ½-½ de Firmian-Browne, US Ch 1984

[56]   15 ♗e3 ♕b4 16 ♗d4 = de Firmian-Byrne, US Ch 1984

Sicilian XIV (Najdorf)				1 e4 c5 2 ♘f3 d6 3 d4 cd 4 ♘xd4 ♘f6 5 ♘c3 a6					

	6	7	8	9	10	11	12	13	14	
1	♗c4	♗b3[1]	f4[3]	f5[4]	♕f3	0-0[6]	g4	♗e3	♕g3	∞
	e6	♘bd7[2]	♘c5	♗e7[5]	0-0	♔h8	♘fd7	♘e5	♗d7[7]	
2	...	...	f4[8]	f5	♘de2	♗g5	♘g3	♘h5[11]	♕xh5	=
	...	b5	♗b7[9]	e5	♘bd7[10]	♗e7	♖c8	♘xh5[12]	0-0[13]	
3	...	...	0-0	♖e1[15]	♗g5	♗h4[18]	♗g3	♗xe6!?[19]	♘xe6[20]	∞
	...	...	♗b7[14]	♘bd7[16]	h6[17]	g5!	♘e5	fe		

314

	6	7	8	9	10	11	12	13	14	
4	♗c4	♗b3	0-0	♕f3[21]	♗e3	♕g3	♘f5!?	♕xg7	♘d5	∞∞
	e6	b5	♗e7	♕b6[22]	♕b7	♘bd7[23]	ef	♖f8	♘xd5[24]	
5	...	...	...	f4	♗e3[25]	e5	ef	bc[27]	♕d2	∞
	...	...	...	♗b7	b4[26]	bc	♗xf6	0-0	♕c7[28]	
6	...	...	...	...	e5[29]	fe	♗e3	♘e4[31]	♕xd4	=
	...	...	...	0-0	de	♗c5[30]	♘fd7	♗xd4	♘c6[32]	

[1] **7 a3** ♗e7 8 ♗a2 0-0 9 0-0 b5 10 f4 ♗b7 11 ♖e1 (11 f5 e5 12 ♘de2 ♘bd7! 13 ♘g3 ♖c8 ∓ Ermenkov-Portisch, Skara 1980) 11 ... ♘bd7 12 e5 de 13 fe ♘e8 14 ♘xe6 fe 15 ♗xe6+ ♔h8 16 ♕xd7 ♗c5+ 17 ♔h1 ♕b6! = Honfi-Schneider, Hungary 1976
7 a4 ♘xe4 8 ♗xe4 d5 9 ♗d3 de 10 ♗xe4 ♘d7 11 0-0 ♗e7 12 c3 ♘c5 = Kavalek-Tarjan, US Ch 1981

[2] **7 ...** ♗e7 8 f4 0-0 (8 ... ♕c7 9 f5 e5 10 ♘de2 ±/±) 9 f5 ef 10 ef d5 11 0-0 ± Nikitin

[3] **8 ♗e3** ♘c5 9 f3 ♗d7 10 ♕d2 ♗e7 11 g4 b5 ∞

[4] **9 ♕f3** ♕d7 10 0-0 b5 11 e5 ♗b7 =

[5] **9 ...** e5 10 ♘de2 ♘xb3 11 ab d5 12 ♗g5 ±/± Sieiro-Vilela, Santa Clara 1983

[6] **11 ♗e3** ♕c7 12 0-0 b5 13 fe fe ∞ Bogdanović-Bradvarević, Yugoslav Ch 1967

[7] Honfi-Vogt, Trnava 1982

[8] **8 a3** ♗e7 9 ♗e3 0-0 10 ♕e2 ♗b7 11 f3 ♘bd7 ∞ Rajna-Barczay, Hungary 1977
8 f3 ♗e7 9 ♗e3 0-0 10 ♕d2 ♗d7 = Uitumen-Geller, Palma de Mallorca IZ 1970
8 ♗g5 ♗e7 9 ♕f3 ♕c7 10 0-0-0 0-0 11 ♖he1 ♘bd7 12 ♕g3 ♘c5 = Garcia Martinez-Pigusov, Havana 1986

[9] **8 ...** ♗e7 9 e5 de 10 fe ♘fd7 11 ♗xe6 ♘xe5 12 ♗xc8 ♕xc8 13 ♗f4 ± Sax-Nunn, London 1980
8 ... b4 9 ♘a4 ♘xe4 10 0-0 g6 11 f5 gf 12 ♘xf5 ∞/± Fischer-Tal, Yugoslavia C 1959

[10] **10 ...** ♘xe4 11 ♘xe4 ♗xe4 12 0-0 ±/± Nunn

[11] **13 0-0** h5! ∓ Byrne-Fischer, Sousse IZ 1967
13 ♗xf6 ♘xf6 14 0-0 h5! ∓

[12] **13 ...** 0-0?! 14 ♗xf6 ♘xf6 15 ♘xf6+ ♗xf6 16 ♕d3 ± Nunn

[13] **15 ♗xe6** ♘xe7 16 ♕e2 =

[14] **8 ... b4?!** 9 ♘a4 ♗b7 (9 ... ♘xe4 10 ♖e1 ♘f6 11 ♗g5 ♗e7 12 ♘f5! ±) 10 ♖e1 ♘bd7! 11 a3! ♘xe4 12 ♘xe6! fe 13 ♗xe6 ♗e7!? (13 ...♘df6 14 f3 ±/± de Firmian-Hort, Baden-Baden 1981) 14 ♕d4 ♘ef6 15 ab ∞∞ de Firmian

[15] **9 ♗xe6** fe 10 ♘xe6 ♕d7 11 ♘d5 ♔f7 12 ♘g5+ ♔g8 13 ♘b6 ♕c6 14 ♘xa8 h6! ∞ Bielczyk-Diaz, Cienfuegos 1983

[16] **9 ...** b4 10 ♘d5 ♘bd7 11 ♗g5! ± Nunn

[17] **10 ...** ♕b6!? 11 a4 b4 12 ♘d5 ed 13 ed+ ♗e5 14 f4 0-0-0 ∞ de Firmian-Kir.Georgiev, Niš 1981

[18] **11 ♗xf6** ♘xf6 (11 ... ♕xf6?! 12 a4 b4 13 ♘a2 a5 14 ♘b5 ± Yakovich-Shnaider, USSR 1987) 12 ♕f3!? Nunn

[19] **13 ♘f3** ♕c7 14 a4!? (14 ♗d5?! ed 15 ♘xe5 de 16 ♗xe5 ♕xe5! ∓ Plaskett-Tukmakov, Valletta 1980) Tukmakov

[20] M.Martinez-Alonso, Cuba 1986

[21] **9 a4** b4 10 ♘a2 0-0 11 ♘xb4 ♗b7 12 c3 a5 ∞ Kavalek-Andersson, Tilburg 1980
9 ♗e3 0-0 10 f4 ♕c7 11 f5 b4 12 ♘a4 e5 ∞ Yakovich-Novikov, USSR 1987

[22] **9 ...** ♕c7 10 ♕g3 0-0 11 ♖e1 ♘c6 12 ♘xc6 ♕xc6 13 ♗h6 ± Yurtayev-Gavrikov, USSR 1983

[23] **11 ...** ♗d7 12 ♘f5! ef 13 ♕xg7 ♖f8 14 ♗g5! ± Bielczyk-Cabarkapa, Pula 1986
11 ... 0-0!? 12 ♗h6 ♘e8 13 ♖ad1 ♗d7 ∞ Tisdall-Browne, Lone Pine 1976
11 ... g6 12 f3! ♘bd7 13 ♖ad1 ♘c5 ∞/± Zaid-Anikayev, USSR 1978

[24] **15 ♗xd5** ♕b8 16 ♖ae1 ∞∞ Azmaiparashvili-Novikov, USSR 1986

[25] **10 e5** de 11 fe ♗c5 12 ♗e3 ♗xd4 13 ♗xd4 ♘c6 14 ♖f4 ♕c7! ∓ Nunn-Kosten, London 1980

[26] **10 ...** ♘c6 11 ♘xe6 fe 12 ♗xe6 ∞ Ubilava
10 ... ♘bd7!? 11 ♗xe6 fe 12 ♘xe6 ♕c8 13 ♘xg7+ ♔f7 14 ♘f5 ♗f8 ∞ Witomski-Larsen, corr. 1986

[27] **13 f5?!** e5 14 ♘e2 cb 15 ♖b1 d5 ∓ Bielczyk-R.Bernard, Poznan 1983

[28] **15 ♖ad1** d5! (15 ... ♘d7?! 16 f5 e5 17 ♘e6! ± Velimirović-Andersson, Moscow IZ 1982) =/∞

[29] **10 ♕f3** ♕c7 11 a3 ♗b7 12 f5 e5 13 ♘de2 ♘bd7 14 ♗g5 a5 =
10 a3 ♗b7 11 f5 e5 12 ♘de2 ♘bd7 13 ♘g3 a5 = Pruner-Browne, USA 1976

[30] **11 ...** ♘fd7 12 ♗e3!? (12 ♕h5 ♗c5!? 13 ♗e3 ♗xd4 14 ♗xd4 ♘c6 Nunn) 12 ... ♘xe5 13 ♕h5 ♘c4 (13 ... ♘bd7 14 ♗xe6 g6 15 ♕e2 ♗b7 16 ♗d5 ± Nunn) 14 ♗xc4 bc 15 ♖ad1 ♕c7 16 ♖f3 g6 17 ♕h6 f5 = Inkiov-Lukov, match 1983

[31] **13 ♕h5** ♗xd4 14 ♗xd4 ♘c6 15 ♗e3!? ∞

[32] **15 ♕c3** ♗b7 16 ♘d6 b4 17 ♕e1 ♕c7 = Bouaziz-Psakhis, Las Palmas IZ 1982

Sicilian XV (Najdorf)   1 e4 c5 2 Nf3 d6 3 d4 cd 4 Nxd4 Nf6 5 Nc3 a6 6 Be2 e5[1]

	7	8	9	10	11	12	13	14	15	
1	Nb3[2]	Bg5[4]	Bxf6	Qd3[5]	0-0-0[6]	Nxd4	Nd5	ed	Qf3	∞
	Be7[3]	Be6	Bxf6	Nc6	Nd4	ed	Bxd5	0-0	Qd7[7]	
2	...	0-0	f4[8]	Kh1[9]	f5	a4	a5[11]	ab	Bg5	±/=
	...	Be6	Qc7	Nbd7[10]	Bc4	0-0	b5	Nxb6	Rfc8[12]	
3	...	...	Qd3[13]	Be3[15]	Nd5	ed	c4	Rac1	Rfd1	=
	...	0-0	Be6[14]	Nbd7	Bxd5	Re8	Bf8	g6	b6[16]	
4	...	...	Re1	Bf1	Nd5	ed	c4	Be3	Qd2	=
	...	...	Be6[17]	Nbd7[18]	Nxd5[19]	Bf5	a5[20]	Bg5	Bxe3[21]	
5	...	...	a4	Kh1[23]	f4	Bf3	Qe2	fe	Be3	=
	...	...	Nc6[22]	Nb4[24]	b6[25]	Bb7	Qc7	de	Bc8[26]	
6	...	...	Be3	Qd2[28]	a4	a5[31]	Bxc4	Rfd1	Nc1	±/=
	...	...	Be6[27]	Nbd7[29]	Nb6[30]	Nc4	Bxc4	h6[32]	Qc8[33]	
7	...	...	...	...	...	a5[34]	Rfd1[36]	Qe1[38]	Nd2	=
	...	...	...	...	Rc8	Qc7[35]	Rfd8[37]	Nc5	d5[39]	

---

1   6 ... Nbd7 and now:

7 Be3 Nc5 8 f3 e6 9 Qd2 b5 10 a3 Bb7 11 0-0-0 Be7 12 g4 ± ECO; 7 ... e5 8 Nf5 Nc5 = A.Ivanov

7 f4 g6 8 0-0 Bg7 9 a4 (9 Be3 0-0 10 Qd2 Qc7 11 a4 Nc5 = Nunn-Ljubojević, London 1982; 9 Kh1 Qc7 10 Bf3 0-0 11 Nd5 Nxd5 12 ed Nb6 ∞ Abru-Rohde, New York 1984) 9 ... 0-0 10 Nb3 (10 Kh1 Qc7 11 a5 Matanović-Mašić, Yugoslav Ch 1969) 10 ... b6 11 Bf3 Bb7 12 Be3 Rc8 13 Qe1 ∞/± Hulak-Nunn, Wijk aan Zee 1983

7 0-0 Nc5 (7 ... g6 8 a4 Bg7 9 a5 0-0 10 Nb3 Qc7 11 Be3 b5 12 ab ± ECO) 8 Bf3 e6 9 a4 Be7 10 Be3 0-0 11 a5 Qc7 12 b4 Ncd7 13 Na4 ± Geller-Quinteros, Baden-Baden 1985

2   7 Nf3 h6 (7 ... Qc7 8 Bg5 Nbd7 9 Qd2 b5 10 a4 b4 11 Na2 d5 = van der Wiel-H.Olafsson, Reykjavik 1985) 8 Bc4 Be6 9 Bxe6 fe 10 Nh4 Nc6 11 Ng6 Rg8 12 0-0 Kf7 13 Nxf8 Rxf8 14 f4 Kg8 = van der Wiel-Portisch, Tilburg 1984

3   7 ... Be6 8 f4 Qc7 9 g4! ± ef (9 ... b5 10 a3 h6 11 g5 hg 12 fg Nfd7 13 Bg4 ± ECO) 10 g5 Nfd7 11 Bxf4 Nc6 12 Qd2 Nb6 13 0-0-0 0-0-0 14 Rhg1 Ne5 15 Nd5 ±/± Vogt-Tal, Lublin 1974

4   8 a4 Qc7 9 Bg5 Nbd7! 10 0-0 h6 11 Bh4 g5 12 Bg3 Nf8 ∞ Ftacnik

8 Be3 0-0 (8 ... Be6 9 f4 ef 10 Bxf4 Nc6 11 Qd2 0-0 12 0-0-0 ± Ghinda-Chandler, Dubai Ol 1986) 9 g4 Be6 10 g5 Nfd7 11 h4 ∞ Smagin-Rashkovsky, USSR 1984

5   10 Nd5 Nd7! 11 0-0 (11 Qd3 0-0 12 Rd1 Rc8! 13 c3 Bg5 ∞ Shabalov-Kengis, USSR 1987) 11 ... 0-0 12 Bg4 Bg5 = Abramović-Savon, Erevan 1982

6   11 Nd5 Bg5 = Arnason-Kasparov, Dortmund 1980

7   16 Bd3 Rfe8 17 h4 a5 ∞ Estevez-Vilela, Santa Clara 1983

8   9 Be3 Nbd7 10 a4 Rc8 11 Qd2 Nb6 12 Rfd1 Nc4 13 Bxc4 Rxc4 14 f3 0-0 15 a5 Qc8 = Tseshkovsky-Dvoiris, USSR 1983

9 a4 Nbd7 10 Qd3 Rc8 11 Nd5 Bxd5 12 ed Nb6 13 Bf3 Qc7 14 a5 Nc4 15 c3 ± Chandler-Marjanović, Sarajevo 1985

9   10 Nd5 Bxd5 11 ed Nbd7 12 c4 0-0 13 Be3 Rfe8 14 Rc1 Bf8 ∞ Petrushin-Dvoiris, USSR 1985

10 Qd3 ef 11 Bxf4 Nc6 12 Rad1 Rd8 13 Nb3 Nxd4 14 Qxd4 0-0 =

10   10 ... b5?! 11 a4 b4 12 Nd5 Bxd5 13 ed ± ECO

11   13 Bg5 h6 14 Bh4 Rfd8 (14 ... Rfe8 15 Rf3 Rad8 16 Nd2 Bxe2 17 Qxe2 Rc8 18 a5 ± Balashov-Petrushin, USSR 1983) 15 Nd2 Bxe2 16 Qxe2 Rac8 =

12   15 ... Rfd8?! 16 Bxf6 Bxf6 17 Bxc4 Qxc4 18 Na5 Qc7 19 Qd3! ± Jansa-Lazić, Kragujevac 1984

15 ... Rfc8 16 Bxf6 Bxf6 17 Bxc4 Nxc4

18 ♘d5 ♕d8 19 ♖a2 a5 = Jansa-Szekely, Tallinn 1983; 17 ♘a5!? ±/=

[13] 9 ♔h1 b5 10 ♘d5 ♘xd5 11 ed (11 ♕xd5 ♖a7 12 ♗e3 ♗e6 13 ♕d2 ♖d7 14 a4 ba 15 ♖xa4 ♕c7 = Sznapik-Bukić, Ljubljana 1981) 11 ... ♘d7 11 a4 b4 12 ♗d2 ♖b8 =

[14] 9 ... b6 10 ♕g3 ♘bd7 11 ♗h6 ♘e8 12 ♗e3 ♗h4 13 ♕h3 ♗g5 14 ♗g4 ♗xe3 15 ♕xe3 g6 16 ♖ad1 ± Smagin-Gasanov, USSR 1985

9 ... b5 10 a4 b4 11 ♘d5 ♘xd5 12 ♕xd5 ♖a7 13 ♗e3 ♗e6 14 ♕d2 ♖b7 15 ♖fd1 (15 a5 ♕d7 16 ♖fd1 ♖c8 = Kuzmin-Gavrikov, USSR 1982) 15 ... ♕c7 16 ♖ac1 ♖c8 17 ♕e1 ♗d8 18 ♘d2 ± Tseshkovsky-Novikov, Erevan 1984

[15] 10 ♘d5 ♗xd5 11 ed ♘bd7 12 c4 a5 13 ♗e3 b6 14 f4 ♘e8 = Ye Jiangchuan-Nunn, Lucerne 1985; 12 ... ♘e8 13 ♗e3 a5 ∞ Chandler-Howell, London 1985

10 f4 ef 11 ♗xf4 ♘c6 = Dvoiris

[16] 16 ♘d2 a5 17 b3 ♗g7 = Kudrin-Ljubojević, New York 1985

[17] 9 ... ♘bd7 10 a4 b6 11 ♘d2 ♗b7 12 ♗c4 ♖c8 13 ♕e2 ♘c5 ∓; 10 ♗f1 ∞/±

[18] 10 ... h6 11 a4 a5 12 ♘d2 ♘a6 13 ♘c4 ♖c8 14 ♘d5 ♗xd5 15 ed ± Khalifman-Garcia, Moscow 1987

[19] 11 ... ♘b6 12 c4 ♖c8 13 ♘d2 ± Geller-Petrosian, Riga 1985

11 ... ♖c8 12 c4 ♘b6 13 ♘d2 ♘fxd5 14 ed ♗d7 15 b3 f5 16 ♘f3 ± Smagin-Savon, Pinsk 1986

11 ...♗xd5 12 ed ♘b6 13 c4 ♖c8 14 ♘d2 ± Tukmakov; 12 ... ♖e8 13 ♗e3 ♗f8 14 c4 g6 15 ♖c1 a5 16 ♘d2 ♗g7 17 b3 ± Jansa-Ljubojević-Biel IZ 1985

[20] 13 ... ♗g5 14 ♗xg5 ♕xg5 15 ♘a5 b6 16 ♘c6 ± Klovans-Maliskauskas, Kostroma 1985

[21] 16 ♕xe3 a4 17 ♘d2 ♕a5 = Klovans-Pigusov, USSR 1987

[22] 9 ... ♗e6!?

[23] 10 f4 ♘b4 11 ♗e3 ♗d7 12 a5 ♗c6 13 ♗d3 ♖e8 14 ♔h1 ♕c8 15 ♘d2 ± Prandstetter-Tal, Taxco IZ 1985; 10 ... b6 11 ♘d5 ♘xd5 12 ed ♘b8 13 a5 b5 14 c4 bc 15 ♗xc4 ♘d7 ∞ Morović-Portisch, Tuniz IZ 1985

[24] 10 ... ♗e6 11 f4 ♘b4 12 f5 ♗d7 13 ♗g5 ± Karpov-Bukić, Bugojno 1978

[25] 11 ... ♗d7 12 ♗e3 ♗c6 13 ♗f3 ♖c8 14 ♖f2 ♕c7 15 a5 ♖fe8 16 ♖d2 ±/± Klovans-Gavrikov, USSR 1983

[26] 16 a5 ba 17 ♖xa5 ♗e6 18 ♖fa1 ♕c4 = Klovans-Kengis, USSR 1983

[27] 9 ... b5 10 a4 ♗b7 11 ab ab 12 ♕d3 b4 13 ♘d5 ♘bd7 14 ♕b5 ♘xd5 15 ed ♕c7 16 ♗c4 ± Klovans-Vitolins, USSR 1983

9 ... ♕c7 10 a4 b6 11 ♕d2 ♖e8 12 ♗f3 ♗e6 13 ♘c1 ♘c6 14 ♘d5 ± Karpov-Georgadze, USSR 1983

9 ... ♘bd7 10 a4 b6 11 ♗c4 ♗b7 12 f3 ♕c7 13 ♕e2 ± Korzubov-Ubilava, USSR 1983

[28] 10 f4 ef (10 ... ♕c7 11 f5 ♗c4 12 ♘d2 ±) 11 ♖xf4 (11 ♗xf4 ♘c6 12 ♔h1 ♖c8 13 ♕e1 ♘e8 14 ♖d1 ♗h4 = Pritchett-Portisch, Malta Ol 1980; 12 ... d5!? 13 e5 ♘e4 14 ♗d3 f5 15 ef ♗xf6 16 ♘xe4 de = Tseshkovsky-Tukmakov, USSR Ch 1981) 11 ... ♘c6 12 ♘d5 ♗xd5 13 ed ♘e5 14 ♖b4 ♕c7 15 a4 ♘fd7 16 a5 ♖fe8 17 c3 ♗f6 18 ♗f2 ♗g5 19 ♘d2 ♘f6 ∞ Mortensen-Karpov, Plovdiv 1983

10 ♘d5 ♗xd5 11 ed ♘bd7 12 c4 a5 13 ♘d2 ♘e8 14 f3 ♗g5 ∞/=

[29] 10 ... b5 11 a4 b4 12 ♘d5 ♘xe4 13 ♘xe7+ ♕xe7 14 ♖xb4 f5 15 ♘a5 ♖c8 (15 ... ♕c7 16 f3 ♘f6 17 ♗b6 ♕d7 18 ♗c4 ±/± Abramović-de Firmian, Vrnjačka Banja 1983) 16 ♗f3 (16 ♖fd1!? I.Zaitsev) 16 ... ♘d7!? 17 ♗xe4 fe 18 ♖fd1 ♘c5 19 ♗xc5 ♖xc5 ∞ Yudasin-Gavrikov, Sverdlovsk 1984

[30] 11 ... ♕c7 12 a5 ♕c6 (12 ... ♖fc8 ∞ Gavrikov) 13 ♗f3 ♖fc8 14 ♖fc1 ♗c4 ∞ Polugayevsky

11 ... b6!? 12 ♖fd1 ♕c7 13 f3 ♖fc8 ∞

[31] 12 ♖fd1 ♗c4 13 ♗xc4 ♖xc4 14 ♗g5 ♖c8 15 ♗xf6 gf ∞ Zapata-Grünfeld, Dortmund 1984

[32] 14 ... ♖c8 15 ♘c1 ♕c7 16 ♗b6 ♕c6 17 f3 h6 18 ♘d3 ± Karpov-Ostermeyer, Hanover 1983; 14 ... ♕c8!?

[33] 15 ... ♖c8 16 ♘d3 ♗e6 17 ♗b6 ♕e8 18 f3 ± Karpov-Quinteros, Lucerne Ol 1982

15 ... ♕c8 16 ♘d3 (16 f3 ♗e6 17 ♘1e2 d5 ∞ Vasyukov-A.Petrosian, USSR 1982) 16 ... ♘g4 17 ♘b4 ♘xe3 18 ♕xe3 f5 19 ♘bd5 ± ECO

[34] 12 f3 ♕c7 (12 ... ♘b6 13 a5 ♘c4 14 ♗xc4 ♖xc4 15 ♖fd1 h6 16 ♘c1 ♕c7 17 ♗b6 ♕b8 18 ♘1a2 ± Kindermann-Nemet, Biel 1983) 13 a5!? Gavrikov

[35] 12 ... ♖e8 13 ♖fd1 h6 14 ♗f3 ♕c7 ∞ Marjanović-Fedorowicz, Paris 1986-87

[36] 13 ♖fc1 ♕c6 (13 ... ♖fe8 14 ♘d5 ♕c6 15 ♗f3 ♗xd5 16 ed ♕c4 ∞ Chandler-A.Petrosian, Jurmala 1983) 14 ♗f3 ♗c4 (14 ... h6 15 ♖a4 ♖fd8 16 ♖b4 ♕c7 17 ♘d5 ±) 15 ♖a4 ♖fe8 16 h3 h6 17 ♖b4 ♕c7 18 ♘d5 ♘xd5 19 ed f5 ∞ Filipenko-Pigusov, USSR 1985

[37] 13 ... ♕c6 14 ♗f3 ♖fe8 15 ♕e1 h6 16 ♘c1 ♖a8 17 ♘d3 b5 18 ♘b4 ♕b7 19 ♘cd5 ± Nunn-Sunye, Amsterdam 1985; 13 ... ♖fe8 14 ♕e1 ♗f8 15 ♘c1 h6 16 h3 (16 ♗f3 d5! 17 ed ♗f5 ∞) Barbulescu-de Firmian, Dubai Ol 1986) 16 ... d5 17 ed ♗f5 18 ♗d3 e4 19 ♗e2 ± Rohde-de Firmian, US Ch 1986

[38] 14 ♗f3 ♘c5 15 ♘xc5 dc 16 ♕e1 ♖xd1 17 ♕xd1 h6 ∞ Horvath-Pigusov, Sochi 1985

14 f3 d5 15 ed ♗xd5 =

[39] 16 ed ♗xd5 = I.Zaitsev

317

Sicilian XVI (Najdorf) 1 e4 c5 2 ♘f3 d6 3 d4 cd 4 ♘xd4 ♘f6 5 ♘c3 a6 6 ♗g5

	6	7	8	9	10	11	12	13	14	
1	...	f4!	♕d2	♖b1	♗xf6	♘d5	♗e2	♖b3	0-0	±
	♘bd7[1]	♕b6[2]	♕xb2	♕a3	gf[3]	♔d8[4]	e6	♕xa2[5]	ed[6]	
2	...	♕d3	0-0-0	f4	e5	fe	♕g3	♘dxb5	♗xb5	∞
	e6	♘bd7[7]	b5	♗b7	de	♘xe5	♘ed7[8]	ab	♗c8[9]	
3	...	♕f3	0-0-0	♗h4[11]	♗e2	♕e3	♗g3	h4	hg	=
	...	♘bd7	h6[10]	♕c7[12]	♗e7[13]	g5	♘e5	♖g8	hg[14]	
4	...	f4	♕f3	f5[16]	♘xc6	♗xf6	♗d3[18]	fe	♕h5+	±
	...	♕c7	b5[15]	♘c6[17]	♕xc6	gf	♗g7	fe	♔d8[19]	
5	...	...	♕e2[20]	0-0-0	a3[21]	g4	♗h4	e5[22]	♔b1	∞∞
	...	♘bd7	♕c7	b5	♗b7	h6	d5	♗xa3	♗xb2[23]	
6	...	...	♕f3	0-0-0	♗d3[24]	♖he1	a3[27]	♕f1	♘f3	=
	...	...	♕c7	b5	♗b7[25]	0-0-0[26]	♗e7	♕b6	♖he8[28]	
7	...	...	...	...	e5	♕h3	♘xe6	♕xe6+	♘xb5[29]	=
	...	...	...	...	♗b7	de	fe	♗e7	ab[30]	
8	...	...	...	...	♗xb5	♘dxb5[31]	e5	ef	♗h6	±
	...	...	...	...	ab	♕b8[32]	♖a5[33]	gf	♗xh6[34]	
9	...	...	e5	fe	ef	♗e2	0-0	♘f3	♔h1	±
	...	b5[35]	de[36]	♕c7	♕e5+	♕xg5	♕e5[37]	♗c5+	♕xf6[38]	
10	...	...	...	...	...	...	♕d3	♖f1	♖d1	±
	...	...	...	...	...	...	♕xf6!	♕e5[39]	♖a7[40]	
11	...	...	...	...	♕e2	0-0-0	♕g4	♗e2!	♘f3[43]	±/∞
	...	...	...	...	♘fd7	♗b7[41]	♕xe5	♗c5[42]	h5[44]	

---

[1] 6 ... ♘c6 7 ♕d2 – Richter-Rauzer

[2] 7 ... e6! – 6 ... e6

[3] 10 ... ♘xf6 11 e5 ±

[4] **11 ... ♕c5** 12 ♖b3 ± Klovans-Khermlin, USSR 1980

11 ... ♖b8 12 ♖b3 ♕xa2 (12 ... ♕a4 13 ♗xa6! ba 14 ♕c3 ±± Vitolins-Arakas, USSR 1978) 13 ♕b4 ± van der Wiel-Danner, Lucerne Ol 1982

[5] 13 ... ♕a4 14 ♕c3 ed 15 ♖a3 ±± Klovans-Pokhla, USSR 1981

[6] **14 ... ♘c5** 15 ♕c3 ±±

14 ... ed 15 ♕c3 de 16 ♖a1 ♕xa1+ 17 ♕xa1 b6 ±

[7] 7 ... ♗e7 8 0-0-0 h6 9 ♗h4 b5 10 f4 g5 (10 ... ♗b7? 11 ♘xe6 fe 12 e5 ±) 11 e5! ±. Romero Holmes-Kuczynski, Dubai Ol 1986

[8] 12 ... ♕b8 13 ♘dxb5! ab 14 ♗xb5+ ♘c6 (14 ... ♗c6? 15 ♕xe5!) 15 ♕f3 ± Martin Gonzalez-Magem, Spanish Ch 1986

[9] 15 ♗xf6 gf 16 ♖d3 ∞∞ Smirin-Richagov, USSR 1985

[10] 8 ... ♕c7 9 ♕g3 ♗e7 (9 ... b5?! 10 ♗xb5! ±) 10 f4 – 7 f4

[11] 9 ♗e3 ♕c7 10 ♗d3 b5 11 ♕g3 b4 12 ♘ce2 ♗b7 13 f3 0-0-0 ∞ van Riemsdyk-Tarjan, Riga IZ 1979

[12] 9 ... ♘e5 10 ♕e2 g5 11 f4 ♘g6! ∞

[13] 10 ... b5? 11 e5 ♗b7 12 ♘xe6! ± Rakowiecki-Kuligowski, Polish Ch 1981

[14] Liberzon-Portisch, Skara 1980

[15] **8 ... ♘c6** 9 0-0-0 ♘xd4 10 ♖xd4 ♗e7 11 ♗e2 0-0 12 ♕g3 ± Martin Gonzalez-Gutman, Biel IZ 1985

8 ... ♘bd7 – 7 ... ♘bd7

[16] 9 ♗xf6 gf 10 0-0-0 b4 (10 ... ♗b7 11 ♕h5 ♕c5 12 f5 ±) 11 ♘ce2 ♘d7 12 ♕h5 ♘c5 13 ♘g3 ♗b7 14 f5 ±

318

[17] 9 ... b4 10 ♘cb5! ab 11 ♗xb5+ ♗d7 12 fe ♗xb5 13 ♘xb5 ♕c5 14 ♗xf6 ♕xb5 15 ♗xg7! ± Velimirović-Gaprindashvili, Bela Crkva 1984

[18] 12 fe fe 13 ♕xf6 ♖g8 ∞

[19] 15 e5! ± Nunn-Chandler, London 1985

[20] 8 ♗d3 ♕c7 9 ♕e2 ♗e7 10 0-0-0 h6 (10 ... b5 11 ♖he1 b4 12 ♘d5! ed 13 ed 0-0 14 ♕xe7 ♖e8 15 ♕xe8+ ♘xe8 16 ♖xe8+ ♘f8 17 ♖de1 ±±) 11 ♗h4 b5 12 ♖he1 g5 ∞

[21] 10 f5 e5 11 ♘d5 ♘xd5 12 ed ♘c5 13 ♕h5 ♗e7 14 ♘c6 ♗xg5+ 15 ♕xg5 f6 16 ♕h5+ ♕f7 ∞ Tukmakov-Browne, Madrid 1973

[22] 13 ed!? ♗xa3 14 ♖d3 Vokac

[23] **15 ef** ♗xc3 16 fg ♗xd4 17 ♖xd4 ♖g8 ∓ Efimov-Vokac, Hradec Kralove 1983-84
15 ♔xb2 b4 16 ♘a2 ♘e4 ∞∞

[24] 10 ♗xf6!? ♘xf6 11 e5 ♗b7 12 ♕g3 (12 ♕h3 de 13 ♘cxb5 ♕b6! 14 fe ♘e4 ∞) 12 ... ♘d5 13 ♘xd5 ♗xd5 14 ♔b1 0-0-0 15 ♗e2 ± Strauts-Baburin, USSR 1986

[25] 10 ... b4 11 ♘d5! ed 12 ♖he1 ♗b7 13 ed+ ♔d8 14 ♘c6+ ♗xc6 15 dc ♘c5 16 ♗xf6+ gf 17 ♗c4 ± Grünfeld-Gutman, Holon 1986-87

[26] 11 ... ♕b6 12 ♘d5!? ♕xd4 (12 ... ed 13 ♘c6! ± Chiburdanidze-Dvoiris, USSR 1980) 13 ♗xf6 gf 14 ♗xb5 ♕c5 ∞ Mnatsakanian-Kr.Georgiev, Erevan Z 1982

[27] 12 f5 e5 13 ♘b3 ± Ernst-Gutman, Lugano 1987; 12 ... b4! ∞

[28] 15 h3 ♘c5 16 f5 ef 17 ef d5 = Georgadze-Shnaider, Lvov 1986

[29] 14 ♗xf6 gf 15 ♗e2 h5 16 ♘d5 ♗xd5 17 ♖xd5 ♘b6 18 ♗xh5+ ♖xh5 19 ♕g8+ =

[30] 15 ♗xb5 ♗e4! 16 ♖d2 (16 ♗xd7+ ♔f8 17 c3 ♗a3! ∓; 16 c3? 0-0-0 17 ♕e7 ♕b6 ∓) 16 ... ♔f8 17 ♗xd7 (17 ♗c4 ♗g6 18 ♗xf6 ♕xf6 19 fe ♗b4 20 ♖f2 ♗f7! ∓ Wittman-Gutman, Beer-Sheva 1985) 17 ... ♗b4 18 c3 ♗xc3 19 bc ♕xc3+ 20 ♔d1 ♖a1+ 21 ♔e2 ♕xh1 22 ♗xf6 ♕xg2+ = Vladimirov

[31] 11 e5 ♗b7 12 ♘dxb5 ♕c8! 13 ♕e2 de 14 fe ♘d5 15 ♘e4 ♖a6 ∞

[32] 11 ... ♕b6 12 e5 ♗b7 13 ♕e2 de 14 fe ♘d5 15 ♘xd5 ♗xd5 16 ♖xd5 ed 17 ♘d6+ ♗xd6 18 ed+ ♔f8 19 ♕e7+ ♔g8 20 ♕xd7 h6 21 ♗e7 ♖xa2 22 ♕c8+ ♔h7 23 ♕f5+ ♔g8 24 d7! ± Petrushin-Zilberstein, USSR 1984

[33] 12 ... ♗b7 13 ♕e2 de 14 ♕c4 ♗e7 (14 ... ♗c5 15 ♗xf6 gf 16 ♖xd7! ± Vitolins-Anikayev, USSR 1973) 15 ♗xf6 ♗xf6 16 ♘c7+ ♔f8 17 fe ± Psakhis-Anikayev, USSR 1979) 17 ♕e4 f5

(17 ... ♘f8 18 ♘c4 ♖xd1+ 19 ♖xd1 ♖c5 20 ♕d4 ♘d7 21 ♘d6 ± Petrushin-Dvoiris, USSR 1984) 18 ♕d4 ♗a6 19 ♖he1 ±

[35] Polugayevsky

[36] 8 ... h6 9 ♗h4 g5 10 fg ♘h7 11 ♕h5 hg 12 ♗g3 ♗g7 13 0-0-0 ± Kasparov-Ehlvest, USSR 1978

[37] 12 ... ♖a7 13 ♕d3 ♖d7 14 ♘e4 ♕e5 15 ♘f3 ♕xb2 (15 ... ♕c7 16 ♕e3 g6 17 c4 ±) 16 ♕e3 ♗b7 17 a4 ♕b4 18 c4 ± Diaz-Vera, Cuban Ch 1986

[38] 15 ♘e4 ♕e7 16 ♘e5 f5 (16 ... 0-0 17 ♘xf7! ♖xf7 18 ♖xf7 ♔xf7 19 ♗h5+ ♔g8 20 ♘xc5 ± Belyavsky-Polugayevsky, USSR 1979) 17 ♗h5+ g6 18 ♘xg6 hg 19 ♗xg6+ ♔f8 20 ♘xc5 ♖h6 21 ♘xe6+ ♗xe6 22 ♗xf5 ± Diaz-Vera, Havana 1986

[39] 13 ... ♕g6 14 ♕h3 ♖a7 15 ♗h5 ♕g5 16 ♘e4 ♕e5 17 0-0-0! ± Jansson-Akesson, Sweden 1981

[40] 15 ♘f3 ♕c7 16 ♘g5 f5 (16 ... ♕b6 17 ♘ce4 ± Cabral-Medeiros, corr. 1984; 16 ... ♗e7 17 ♖xf7 ♘c6 18 ♗h5! ± Lepeshkin) 17 ♕d4 ♕e7 (17 ... h5 18 ♖xf5 ef 19 ♘d5 ♕d7 20 ♖d3! ±) 18 ♗h5+ (18 ♘ge4 h5 19 ♘d6+ ♗xd6 20 ♕xa7 ♕e5! ∞ Rodriguez-Polugayevsky, Biel IZ 1985) 18 ... g6 19 ♕xh8 ♕xg5 20 ♗f3 ♗g7 21 ♖f2 ± Lepeshkin

[41] 11 ... ♘c6 12 ♘xc6 ♕xc6 13 ♕d3 and now:
13 ... h6 14 ♗h4 ♗b7 15 ♗e2 ♕c7 16 ♖hf1 (16 ♖he1 ♘c5 17 ♕d4! ± Agapov-Nepomnashy, USSR 1983) 16 ... ♘c5 (16 ... ♘xe5 17 ♕g3 g5 18 ♘xb5! ±) 17 ♕d4! ± (intending 17 ... b4 18 ♘b5!, 17 ... ♗e7 18 ♗xb5+!)
13 ... b4 14 ♘e4 ♗b7 15 ♘d6+ (15 ♗e2 ♕d5 16 ♕g3?! ♕xa2 17 ♖xd7 ♗xd7 18 ♕f3 ♗d5 19 ♕xf7+ ♘c6 ∓/∓ de Firmian-McCambridge, USA 1977) 15 ... ♘xd6 16 ed ∞
13 ... h6 14 ♗f4 ♕c5 15 ♖he1 ±±
13 ... h5 14 ♗h4 f6 15 ♗f4 g5 16 ♕xh5+ ± Balashov-Quinteros, Manila IZ 1976
13 ... ♘f6 14 ♗xf6 gf (14 ... ♕xf6 15 ♘cxb5! ±±) 15 ♖he1 ± Balinas-Tarjan, Odessa 1976, and Torre-Sigurjonsson, Geneva 1977

[43] 14 ♖hf1 ♗xd4 15 ♖xd4 f6 ∞ Timman-van der Vliet, Dutch Ch 1978

[44] **14 ... ♕c7** 15 ♗f4 ±
14 ... ♕f5 15 ♕h4 ±
14 ... ♗e3+ 15 ♔b1 h5 16 ♘xe5 hg 17 ♘xf7 ±
14 ... h5 15 ♕h4 ♗e3+ 16 ♔b1 ♗xf3 17 ♗xe3 ♗xe2 18 ♗d4 ♕f5 19 ♘xe2 0-0 20 h3 ± Bryson-Gallagher, Nottingham 1987

Sicilian XVI (Najdorf)
1 e4 c5 2 ♘f3 d6 3 d4 cd 4 ♘xd4 ♘f6 5 ♘c3 a6 6 ♗g5 *continued*

	6	7	8	9	10	11	12	13	14	
12	...	f4	e5	fe	♕e2	0-0-0	♕g4	♗e2!	♕h3[46]	∞
	e6	b5	de	♕c7	♘fd7	♗b7	♕b6	♘xe5[45]	♘bd7[47]	
13	...	...	...	...	...	...	♘xe6	♕g4[48]	♗d3	±
	...	...	...	...	...	...	fe	♕xe5[49]	♗e7[50]	

[45] **13 ... ♘c6** 14 ♘xe6! ♘cxe5 15 ♘xf8 ♘xg4 16 ♘xd7 ♕g6 17 h4 ±
13 ... ♗c5 14 ♗e3 g6 15 ♘e4 ♗xe4 16 ♕xe4 ± Polugayevsky

[46] 14 ♕g3 ♘bd7 15 ♗f4 b4 16 ♘a4 ♕a5 17 b3 (17 ♘b3 ♕xa4 18 ♗xe5 ♖c8 ∞ Balashov-Mecking, Manila IZ 1976) 17 ... g6 18 h4 ♗g7 19 h5 ∞ Alvir-Pliester, Dieren 1986

[47] 15 ♖he1 h6 (15 ... ♗c5? 16 ♘xe6!; 15 ... g6? 16 ♗g4! ±) 16 ♗h4 g6 (16 ... g5? 17 ♘xe6! ±± ECO) 17 ♗g4 h5 18 ♗xe6 ♗h6+ 19 ♔b1 fe 20 ♘xe6 ♔f7! ∞ Grünfeld-Klinger, Lugano 1984, and ECO

[48] 13 ♕h5+?! g6 14 ♕g4 ♕xe5 (14 ... ♘c5!?)

15 ♗d3 ♘c5 ∓ Shabanov-Krimerman, corr. 1986

[49] **13 ... ♕b6?** 14 ♖d6! ±±
13 ... ♘c5 14 ♖d8+ ♕xd8 15 ♗xd8 ♔xd8 16 b4 ♘cd7 17 ♗e2! (17 a3 g6! ∞) 17 ... h5 18 ♕xe6 ♗xb4 19 ♕b3 ± Winslow-Browne, USA 1976

[50] **14 ... ♘f6** 15 ♗xf6 gf 16 ♔b1! ± Browne
14 ... ♗e7 15 ♗xe7 ♔xe7 16 ♖he1 h5 (16 ... ♕f6 17 ♗e4! ±) 17 ♕b4+ ♗c5 18 ♕f4! (18 ♕h4+ ♘f6!) 18 ... g5 (18 ... ♘f6 19 ♗f5 ±) 19 ♕g3 h4 (19 ... ♖f8 20 ♗e4 ♘c6 21 ♘d5+! ± Veselovsky-Gorelov, USSR 1980) 20 ♕g4 ♔d8 21 ♖xe6 ♔c7 22 ♗e4 ± Umansky

Sicilian XVII (Najdorf)
1 e4 c5 2 ♘f3 d6 3 d4 cd 4 ♘xd4 ♘f6 5 ♘c3 a6 6 ♗g5 e6 7 f4 ♗e7 8 ♕f3

	8	9	10	11	12	13	14	15	16	
1	...	♗h4	fg	♕h5[3]	♗g3	♘f3[6]	♘xg5	♕d1	♕d4[7]	±
	h6	g5[1]	♘fd7[2]	♘e5[4]	♗xg5[5]	♘db7	♕xg5	♕e7		
2	...	...	0-0-0	♗e2!	♕g3	♖hf1[10]	fg	g6	♕h3[12]	±
	...	...	♕c7	♘bd7	♖b8[8]	♖g8[9]	g5[11]	♘e5	♖xg6	
3	...	0-0-0	♗e2	♗xf6	e5	ef[13]	♗xf3	♗xa8	♗xd5	=
	♕c7	♘bd7	b5!	♘xf6	♗b7	♗xf3	♗xf6	d5[14]	♗xd4[15]	
4	...	...	♕g3	♗h4	fg	♕e3	♔b1[19]	♗f2	♕d2	∞
	...	...	h6[16]	g5[17]	♘h5[18]	♕c5	hg	♘e5	♕c7[20]	
5	...	...	♗d3	♖he1	♕g3	♘d5	e5[23]	fe	♕h4[25]	∞/=
	...	...	b5	♗b7[21]	b4[22]	ed	de	♘h5[24]	♗xg5+[26]	
6	...	...	...	♗h4[27]	e5	ef	♖he1[30]	♖e3	♗c4	∞
	...	...	...	h6	g5	gh[28]	♘xf6[29]	♗d7	♕b6[31] 0-0-0	
7	...	...	...	...	fg	♕e2	♘f3	♗g3[33]	gf[35]	=
	...	...	...	...	♘e5	♘fg4	hg[32]	♘xf3[34]	♘e5[36]	

[1] Göteborg Variation
[2] 10 ... ♘h7 11 ♗g3 hg 12 0-0-0 ±

[3] 11 ♘xe6?! fe 12 ♕h5+ ♔f8 13 ♗b5! ♖h7! 14 0-0+ ♔g8 15 g6 ♖g7 16 ♖f7 ♗xh4 17 ♕xh6

♖xf7 (17 ... ♕f6 18 ♖f1 ±/± Nunn) 18 gf+ ♔xf7 19 ♖f1+ ♔f6 20 ♕h7+ ♔f8 (20 ... ♔e8 21 ♕g6+ ♔f8 22 e5 ±/± Nunn) 21 ♗e2 (Belyavsky) ∞ Nunn

4   11 ... ♗xg5? 12 ♘xg5 ♕xg5 13 ♘xe6 ±

5   12 ... ♕b6 13 0-0-0 ♗xg5+ 14 ♔b1 ♘bc6 (14 ... ♘g6 15 ♘xe6! ±) 15 ♘b3 ♗e7 16 ♗e2 ♗d7 17 ♖hf1 0-0-0 18 ♗f2 ♕c7 19 ♘a4 ± Rogulj-Vokac, Trencianske Teplice 1979

6   13 ♗e2 ♕b6 14 ♗xe5 (14 ♖d1!? ♕xb2 15 0-0) 14 ... de 15 ♘f3 ♕xb2 16 ♘d1 ♕b4+! 17 c3 ♕e7 18 0-0 ♖h7! 19 ♘f2 ♘d7 20 ♘g4 ♘f6 21 ♗xf6+ (Shakarov-Nasibullin, USSR 1979) 21 ... ♗xf6 ∞

7   Radulov-Inkiov, Bulgarian Ch 1976

8   11 ... g5 12 fg ♘e5 13 ♕e3! ♘h7 14 ♘f3 ♘xf3 (14 ... hg 15 ♘xg5 ♕c5 16 ♕xc5 dc 17 ♘f3 ♗xh4 18 ♘xe5 ± Levchenkov-Vitolins, USSR 1984) 15 gf hg 16 ♗g3 ±

11 ... b5 12 ♗xf6 ♘xf6 (12 ... ♗xf6 13 ♗xb5 ±) 13 e5 ♗b7 14 ♕g3 de 15 fe ♘d7 (15 ... ♘d5 16 ♘xe6 fe 17 ♕g6+ ♔d7 18 ♗g4 ±; 15 ... ♘e4 16 ♘xe6 ♕xc3 17 ♘xg7+ ♔f8 18 ♘e6+ ♔e8 19 ♕xc3 ♘xc3 20 ♘c7+ ♔f8 21 bc ±) 16 ♘xe6 fe 17 ♕g6+ ♔d8 18 ♕xe6 ♖e8! ±

9   12 ... g5 13 fg hg 14 ♗xg5 ♖g8 15 h4 ± Nunn-Nemet, Biel 1983

10   13 e5 de 14 ♘xe6 fe 15 ♕g6+ ♔f8 16 f5 e4! ∞ Garcia Martinez-Ortega, Havana 1984

11   13 ... b5 14 ♘xe6! fe 15 ♕g6+ ♔d8 16 e5 de 17 f5 ± Lombardy-Quinteros, Manila 1973, and Barczay-Ribli, Hungarian Ch 1976

12   Diaz-Ortega, Bayamo 1984

13   13 ♕g3 de 14 fe ♗d7 15 ♗f3 ♗xf3 16 gf g6 16 f4 ♕b7 ∞/= Larsen-Portisch, Manila 1974, and Morgado-Sanakoyev, corr. 1984

14   15 ... ♕c4!? 16 ♘e4 ♕xa2 17 ♘xf6+ gf ∞ Mokrishchev-Makarov, corr. 1983

15   17 ♖xd4 ed 18 ♖e1+ ♔f8 19 ♖e5 g6 = Andersson-Donner, Berlin 1971, and Richardson-V.Zagorovsky, corr. 1976

16   10 ... ♘c5 11 ♗d3 h6 12 ♗h4 0-0 13 ♘f3 b5 14 e5 de 15 fe ♘e8 16 ♗xe7 ♕xe7 17 ♘e4 ±/∞ Lanka-Pulkis, corr. 1985

10 ... b5 11 ♗xb5 (11 ♗xf6 ♘xf6!; 11 a3!?) 11 ... ab 12 ♘dxb5 ♕b8 13 e5 de 14 fe ♘xe5 15 ♖he1 ♘g6! 16 ♘c7+ ♔f8 17 ♘xa8 ♕xa8 ∞ Shirazi-Browne, US Ch 1983

17   11 ... b5 12 a3 ♗b7 13 ♗e2! ♖g8 (13 ... ♘xe4 14 ♘xe6) 14 ♗xf6 ♘xf6 15 e5 ♘d5 16 ♘xd5 ♗xd5 17 f5 ± Lanka

18   12 ... ♗g6 13 ♗g2 ♘e5 14 ♘f3 ♘xf3 15 ♕xf3 hg 16 ♗g3 ±

19   14 ♕d2 ♗xg5 15 ♘xg5 ♕xg5 =

20   17 ♘f3 b5!? (17 ... ♘xf3 18 gf ♗d7 19 h4 ± Westerinen-Petursson, Reykjavik 1976, and Shakarov-Zelinsky, corr. 1982; 17 ... g4 18 ♘xe5 de 19 ♗e2 ♘f6 20 h3 ± Sax-Tatai,

Graz 1984) 18 ♘xg5 ♗d7 19 ♗d4 (19 a3!?) 19 ... b4 20 ♗xe5 de 21 ♘d5! ed 22 ♕xd5 0-0 23 ♘xf7 ♖xf7! 24 ♕xa8+ ♔g7 25 ♕xa6 ∞ Lanka-Vitolins, USSR 1982

21   11 ... b4 12 ♘d5 ed 13 ♘f5 h6 (13 ... ♗f8 14 e5 ±) 14 ♗h4 g5 15 e5 ±

22   12 ... 0-0-0 13 ♗xb5! ab 14 ♘dxb5 ♕c5 (14 ... ♕b6 15 e5 d5 16 f5! ± Velimirović-Al Kazzaz, Nice Ol 1974) 15 e5 de 16 fe ♘d5 17 ♗xe7 ♕xe7 18 ♘d6+ ♔b8 19 ♘xd5 ±± Nunn

23   14 ed ♔d8 15 ♖xe7 ♘xe7 16 ♘f5+ ♔d8 17 ♗h4 ♕c5 18 ♕xg7 ♘c7 (∞ Nunn) 19 ♗xf6 ♖hg8 20 ♗d4 ♖xg7 21 ♗xc5 ♘xc5 22 ♘xg7 ♖g8 23 ♘h5 (23 ♘f5 ♖xg2 24 h4 ♖f2 =) 23 ... ♖xg2 24 h3 ♗xd5 = Vladimirov

24   15 ... 0-0-0? 16 ♗f5

15 ... ♘e4 16 ♗xe4 ♗xg5+ 17 ♕xg5 de 18 e6 ♘e5 19 ♘f5 ± Livshits-Kochetkov, corr. 1976

25   16 e6 ♘xg3 17 ef+ ♔xf7 18 ♖xe7+ ♔g8 19 hg ♕xg3 20 ♘e6 ♕e5 21 ♖f1 ♘f8! 22 ♗f5 ♗c8 23 ♖e8 ♔f7 24 ♖e7+ =

26   17 ♕xg5 g6 18 e6 (18 g4!?) ♕g7 19 e6) 18 ... ♘c5! 19 ef+ ♔xf7 20 ♖f1+ ♔g8 21 ♘f5 ♘e6 =

27   11 h4!? ♘c5 12 f5 hg 13 hg ♖xh1 14 ♖xh1 ♘g8 ∞ F.Larsen-Kubach, corr. 1984

11 ♕h3 ♘b6 12 f5 e5 (12 ... ♘fd5!?) 13 ♘de2 ♗d7 14 ♔b1 ♗c6 15 ♗e3 d5! = Nunn-Browne, Tilburg 1982

28   12 ... de? 13 ♘xe6 fe 14 ♗g6+ ♔d8 (14 ... ♔f8 15 fg hg 16 ♗xg5 ♔g7 17 ♘e4! ♔xg6 18 ♖xd7 ±±) 15 fg ♘e8 16 ♘e4 ♕a5 17 ♔b1 ±

29   13 ... ♗xf6 14 ♘de2 ♘c5 15 f5 ±

30   14 f5 e5 15 ♘de2 ♗d7 16 ♗e4 ♗c6 (16 ... ♖g8!?) 17 ♗xd5 ♗xd5 18 ♖xd5 ♖c8 19 ♘c3 b5 20 ♘b7 (20 ♗b3 = Nunn-Ljubojević, London 1980) 20 ... ♖b8 21 ♗xa6 0-0 22 ♗xb5 ♕c5 ∞ Smirin-Gelfand, USSR 1984

31   15 ... 0-0-0? 16 ♗xa6! ±

32   14 ... ♘xf3 15 gf (15 ♕xf3 hg 16 ♗g3 – 14 ... hg) 15 ... hg 16 fg ♖xh4 17 ♖hf1 ♖h6 18 e5 ♗d7 (18 ... de 19 ♕f3 ♖f6 20 ♕h3 ±) 19 ed ♗xd6 20 ♘d5 ♕a5 21 ♕f2 ± Geller

33   15 ♗xg5?! ♘xg5 16 ♘xg5 ♕c5 17 ♘f3 ♘f2 18 ♘xe5 ♘xd1 19 ♘xf7 ♘xc3 20 ♕f3 ♖f8 21 ♖f1 ♗d7! ∓

34   15 ... ♗d7 16 h3 ♘xf3 17 hg ♘h4 (17 ... ♖xh1 18 ♖xh1 ♘h4 19 e5 ♗c6 20 ♖f1 ± Portilho-Velloso, corr. 1983) 18 ♖h3 ♗c6 19 e5 d5 ±/∞ Grünfeld-Ljubojević, Thessaloniki Ol 1984

35   16 ♕xf3 ♘e5 17 ♗xe5 de 18 ♗e2 ♗d7 19 ♖d3 ♗c6 (19 ... f6!?) 20 ♖f1 ♖h7 21 ♕f2 f6 22 ♗g4 ♗d7 23 ♖xd7!? ∞ Matulović-Browne, Skopje Ol 1972

36   17 h4 gh 18 f4 ♘xd3+ 19 ♖xd3 ♗d7 20 ♕e1 0-0-0 21 ♖xh4 ♗c6 =

17 f4 gf 18 ♗xf4 ♗d7 19 ♖df1 ♖h7 20 h4 0-0-0 21 h5 ♗f6 =

321

Sicilian XVII (Najdorf) *continued*

1 e4 c5 2 Nf3 d6 3 d4 cd 4 Nxd4 Nf6 5 Nc3 a6 6 Bg5 e6 7 f4 Be7 8 Qf3 Qc7 9 0-0-0 Nbd7 10 g4 b5

	11	12	13	14	15	16	17	18	19	
8	Bxf6	g5[38]	a3	Bh3[39]	b4[40]	Rd3	Qg3	f5	ef	∞
	Nxf6[37]	Nd7	Rb8	Nc5	Na4	Nb6	g6	gf	e5[41]	
9	...	...	f5	h4	Nb1[43]	fe	Nd2	Nf5	Bc4+	∞
	...	...	Nc5[42]	b4	Bb7	fe	e5[44]	0-0	Kh8[45]	
10	...	...	...	f6	gf	Qh5[46]	e5[48]	ed	Qxh7[50]	∞
	...	...	...	gf	Bf8	Rg8[47]	Bd7[49]	Bxd6	0-0-0[51]	
11	...	...	...	...	...	Rg1	Nd5	ed	Rg7	∞
	...	...	...	...	...	b4[52]	ed[53]	Bd7[54]	Qa5[55]	

[37]   11 ... gf 12 f5 Ne5 13 Qh3 0-0 14 Rg1 (14 Bd3 Kh8 15 Nce2 Rg8 16 Rhg1 Qb6 17 Qh4 ± Sabitov-Gavrikov, USSR 1981) 14 ...Kh8 15 Rg3 Rg8 16 Nce2 ± Ivanović-Jacimović, Yugoslav Ch 1985

[38]   12 a3 Rb8 13 f5 0-0 (13 ... e5 14 Nde2 b4 15 ab Rxb4 16 g5 Nxe4 17 Nxe4 Bb7 18 N2c3 Bxg5+ 19 Kb1 0-0 20 Rg1 ± Szilagyi-Guizar, corr. 1979, and Pioch-Podzielny, corr. 1984) 14 g5 Ne8 15 Rg1 b4 16 ab Rxb4 ∞ Shamkovich-K.Grigorian, USSR Ch 1971, and Peres-Quinteros, Torremolinos 1975

[39]   14 h4 b4 15 ab Rxb4 16 Bh3 Qc5 17 Nb3 Qb6 18 h5 Nc5 19 Nxc5 dc 20 g6 Rxb2!? ∞ Sardini-Gaspero, corr. 1984

[40]   15 Rhg1 b4 16 ab Rxb4 17 f5 Qb7 ∞

[41]   Lhagvasuren-Danailov, Moscow 1986

[42]   13 ... Bxg5+ 14 Kb1 Ne5 15 Qh5 Qe7 16 Nxe6 Bxe6 17 fe g6 18 ef+ Kxf7 19 Qe2 Kg7 20 Nd5 Qd8 = Ervin-Gligorić, USA 1972, and Hellers-Howell, Groningen 1984-85

[43]   15 Nce2 e5 16 Nb3 Nxe4! ∓ Nunn-Browne, Gjovik 1983, and Wedberg-de Firmian, Oslo 1984

[44]   17 ... 0-0-0 18 Bh3 ±

[45]   20 g6 Nxe4! (20 ... hg 21 Qg4! ± Ljubojević-de Firmian, Wijk aan Zee 1986) 21 Nxe4 hg ∞ Ljubojević-Hodgson, Wijk aan Zee 1986

[46]   16 Bh3 Rg8! ∞
        16 a3!? intending 16 ... Bd7 17 Qh5 Olim

[47]   16 ... h4 17 Nd5 Qb7 (17 ... ed 18 ed Bd7 19 Re1+ Kd8 20 Kb1! ±) 18 Re1 Bd7 19 Bh3 0-0-0 20 Ne7+ Kb8 21 e5! ± da Costa Jr-de Almeida, corr. 1985

[48]   16 ... Bd7 17 a3 0-0-0 (17 ... Rb8 18 Rg1 b4 19 ab Rxb4 20 Rg7! ± de Firmian-Youngworth, Lone Pine 1980; 17 ... Qa5 = Matulović-de Firmian, Niš 1981, and Olim-Browne, Las Vegas 1986) 18 Kb1 Be8 ∞

[48]   17 Bh3 Rg6 18 Rhe1 Bd7 19 Nd5 Qb7 20 Kb1 (20 Nf5?! Timman-Ljubojević, Tilburg 1983) 20 ... 0-0-0 (20 ... Rh6!? 21 Qg4 Rg6 22 Qh5 = Olim) 21 Ne7+ Bxc7 22 fe Re8 ∞ da Costa Jr-Consolino, corr. 1985

[49]   17 ... de? 18 Ncxb5 ab 19 Bxb5+ Bd7 20 Nxe6 ±±

[50]   19 Bxb5!?

[51]   20 Qxf7 Rdf8 21 Qh5 b4 22 Nce2 Rxf6 ∞ Tsaturian-Makarov, corr. 1984

[52]   **16 ... Bb7** 17 Bh3 0-0-0 18 Nd5 Qa5 19 Kb1 ± Alonso-Diaz, Cuba 1986
        16 ... Bd7 17 Rg7! Bxg7 (17 ... b4 18 Nd5 ed 19 ed – 16 ... b4; 18 e5!?) 18 fg Rg8 19 e5 ± Perenyi-Browne, New York 1986, and Lobron-Chandler, West Germany 1986
        16 ... h5 17 a3 ±/± Olim

[53]   17 ... Qb7 18 Rg7 ed 19 ed Bd7 20 Nc6 ± Perenyi-Haragos, Kecskemet 1985

[54]   18 ... Nd7 19 Nc6 Bb7 20 Bh3 Ne5 21 Rge1 ± Perenyi-Deak, Eger 1986

[55]   **19 ... 0-0-0** 20 Rxf7 Nh6+ 21 Kb1 Rdf8 22 Re7 Bg5 (22 ... Qd8 23 Rxd7!! Bxd7 24 Qf5+ Kc7 25 Ne6+ Bxe6 26 de ±± Chinchilla-Hernandez, Managua 1987) 23 Rxd7 Nxd7 24 Ne6 ± Lobron
        19 ... Qa5 20 Qe3+ Kd8 21 Rxf7 Qxa2 ∞ Doghri-Hernandez, Dubai Ol 1986

　　1 e4 c5 2 ♘f3 d6 3 d4 cd 4 ♘xd4 ♘f6 5 ♘c3 a6 6 ♗g5 e6 7 f4 ♕b6

	8	9	10	11	12	13	14	15	16	
1	♘b3¹	♕f3³	0-0-0⁴	♗d3⁶	♖he1	♕h3	f5	a4	♘xa4	∞
	♗e7²	♘bd7	♕c7⁵	b5⁷	♗b7⁸	0-0-0	e5	ba	♘c5⁹	
2	♕d3	♖b1	f5	♗e2¹¹	fe	♘xc6	e5¹²	♗xf6	♗h5+	∞
	♕xb2	♕a3	♗e7¹⁰	♘c6	fe	bc	de	gf	♔f8¹³	
3	♕d2	♘b3	♗xf6	♗e2	0-0	♖f3¹⁵	♔h1	♘b1	♕e3	∓
	♕xb2	♕a3	gf	♘c6	♗d7	♗e7¹⁶	h5	♕b4	♗d8¹⁷	
4	...	♖b1	e5	fe	♗c4¹⁸	0-0	♖be1	♕f4	♘e4	∓
	...	♕a3	de	♘fd7	♕a5!	♘xe5	♗xc4¹⁹	♘d6	♕c7²⁰	
5	...	...	♗e2	0-0	e5	fe	♗xf6	♘e4	♖b3	±/∞
	...	...	♗e7²¹	♘bd7²²	de	♘xe5	gf²³	f5	♕a4²⁴	

---

¹ 8 a3 ♘c6 9 ♘b3 ♗e7 10 ♕d2 (10 ♕f3 h6 11 ♗h4 g5 12 ♗f2 ♕c7 13 g3 b5 ∞ Murei-Ftacnik, Hastings 1982-83) 10 ... 0-0 11 0-0-0 ♖d8 12 ♗xf6 ♗xf6 13 g4 ∞ Timman-Sisniega, Taxco IZ 1985

² 8 ... ♕e3+ 9 ♕e2 ♕xe2+ 10 ♗xe2 ♘bd7 11 0-0-0 b5 ±/=
8 ... ♘bd7 9 ♕e2 ♕c7 10 0-0-0 ♗e7 (10 ... b5 11 a3 ♗b7 12 g4 ±) 11 g4 h6 12 ♗h4 g5 13 fg ♘h7 14 ♗g3 hg 15 e5! ±/∞ Kupreichik-Tal, USSR Ch 1979

³ 9 ♕e2 h6! 10 ♗xf6 (10 ♗h4? ♘xe4) 10 ... ♗xf6 11 0-0-0 ♗xc3 12 bc ♘d7 13 h4 ♘f6 14 ♖h3 (14 g4 h5) 14 ... ♗d7 15 c4 e5 16 f5 ♕c7 ∓ Kozlov-Magerramov, USSR 1987

⁴ 10 ♗d3 ♕c7 11 a4 b6 12 ♗h4 ♗b7 13 0-0 0-0 = Ljubojević-Portisch, Dubai Ol 1986

⁵ 10 ... h6 11 ♗h4 ♕c7 12 ♗g3 b5 13 e5 ♗b7 14 ♕e2 ± Karpov-Quinteros, Leningrad IZ 1973

⁶ 11 g4 h6 12 ♗xf6 (12 ♗h4 g5 ∞) 12 ... ♗xf6 13 e5 de 14 f5 ∞ Dobrovolsky-Ftacnik, Czechoslovak Ch 1982

⁷ 11 ... h6 12 ♗h4 g5 13 e5! gh 14 ef ♘xf6 15 f5 ± Diaz-Ubilava, Varna 1985

⁸ 12 ... b4 13 ♘e2 ♗b7 14 g4 ♘c5 15 ♘xc5 dc 16 ♘g3 c4 17 ♗f1 c3 ∞ Yudasin-Pigusov, USSR 1982

⁹ Diaz-Pigusov, Havana 1985

¹⁰ 10 ... ♕a5? 11 ♕c4 ♔d8 12 ♗d2 ♕c5 13 fe b5 14 ♕d3 fe 15 a4 ± Nunn

¹¹ 11 fe fe 12 ♕c4 0-0 13 ♘xe6 b5 ∓

¹² 14 0-0!? ♕a5 15 ♕d2

¹³ 17 0-0 e4! ∓ van der Wiel-Gavrikov, London 1985
17 ♕d2 ♗g7 ∓ Nunn-Kasparov, Brussels 1986
17 ♕e3 ♖g8 18 ♕h6+ ♖g7 19 ♖b3 f5 ∞ Kasparov

¹⁴ 9 ... ♘c6 10 ♗d3 (10 ♗xf6 gf 11 ♘a4 ♕a3 12 ♘b6 ♖b8 13 ♘c4 ♕a4 14 ♗e2 b5 =) 10 ... ♗e7 11 0-0 ♕a3 12 ♖ae1 h6 (12 ... 0-0 13 e5 de 14 fe ♘d5 15 ♗f6! ±) 13 ♗h4 ♕b4 14 ♗f2 ♘a5 15 a3 ♘xb3 16 cb ♕a5 17 b4 ♕d8 18 e5 ∞ Belyavsky-Pinter, Lucerne Ol 1982

¹⁵ 13 f5 h5! 14 fe fe 15 ♖xf6 0-0-0 ∓ Roos-Ribli, Baden-Baden 1981
13 ♗h5 ♗g7 14 ♖f3 0-0 15 ♖d1 ♖ad8 16 ♕xd6 ♕xd6 17 ♖xd6 ♗c8 ∓
13 ♔h1 h5 14 ♘b1 ♕b4 15 ♕e3 ♘e7! 16 c4 f5 ∓ Qi-Karpov, Hanover 1983

¹⁶ 13 ... ♘a5 14 ♘d5! ed 15 ♘xa5 ± Maryasin-Savon, USSR 1980
13 ... ♖c8 14 ♔h1 ♗g7 15 ♖d1 0-0 16 ♖g3 ♔h8 17 ♖h3 ♕b4 18 ♕e3 ♘e7 ∞ Maryasin-Rashkovsky, USSR 1979

¹⁷ 17 c3 ♕b6 18 ♕d2 ♗e7 19 c4 h4 ∓ Kasparov-Magerramov, USSR 1982

¹⁸ 12 ♘e4 h6 13 ♗b5 hg 14 ♖b3 ab 15 ♖xa3 ♗xa3 16 ♕xg5 ♖a4 ∓ Quinteros-Browne, London 1981-82

¹⁹ 14 ... ♘bc6 15 ♘xc6 ♘xc6 16 ♕f4 ♗c5+ 17 ♔h1 0-0 18 ♘e4 ∞ Hellers

²⁰ 17 c4 ♘b5! (17 ... h6 18 ♘f5! ∞ Hellers-Oll, Groningen 1984-85) 18 cb ♕xf4 19 ♗xf4 ∓

²¹ 10 ... b5 11 e5 b4 12 ♖b3 bc 13 ♕xc3 ♕c5 14 ♕xc5 dc 15 ef ♘d7 16 fg ♗xg7 17 ♘c6 ± Salov-Sobolev, USSR 1980
10 ... ♘c6 11 ♘xc6 bc 12 0-0 (12 ♗xf6 - 10 ♗xf6) 12 ... d5 13 ♔h1! ± Lobron-Hulak, Indonesia 1983

²² 11 ... ♕a5 12 f5! ± Wu-Groszpeter, Lucerne 1985
11 ... h6 12 ♗h4 ♘bd7 13 ♔h1 ♕a5 14 f5 ± Lobron-Portisch, Indonesia 1983

²³ 14 ... ♗xf6 15 ♖xf6 gf 16 ♘e4 ± Tal-Ftacnik, Sochi 1982

²⁴ 17 ♘xf5! ef! (17 ... ♕xe4 18 ♘xe7 ♔xe7 19 ♖e3 ± Lobron-Ribli, Zagreb 1985) 18 ♘d6+ ♗xd6 19 ♕xd6 ♕e4 20 ♖e1 ♘c6 21 ♔f1 ♗e6 22 ♗h5 (22 ♗f3? ♖d8) 22 ... ♕c4+ 23 ♖d3 ♘d8 24 ♕d7+ ♔f8 25 ♕d6+ ♔e8 ½-½ Pogrebryak-Gik, USSR 1986; 24 ♖e2!?; 24 ♗f3!?

Sicilian XVIII (Najdorf)

1 e4 c5 2 Nf3 d6 3 d4 cd 4 Nxd4 Nf6 5 Nc3 a6 6 Bg5 e6 7 f4 Qb6 *continued*

	8	9	10	11	12	13	14	15	16	
6	Qd2	Rb1	Be2	0-0	Kh1	f5[25]	Ne6	fe	Bxf6[28]	∞
	Qxb2	Qa3	Nbd7	Bc5	Be7	e5[26]	fe	Nb6[27]	Bxf6[29]	
7	...	...	Bxf6	Be2	Nxc6	0-0	Kh1	f5	Bf3	±
	...	...	gf	Nc6	bc	Qa5[30]	Be7[31]	h5[32]	e5[33]	
8	...	...	...	...	0-0	Rfd1	ef	Nd5	c3[36]	=
	...	...	...	Bg7	f5[34]	0-0[35]	ef	Nc6	Qa5[37]	
9	...	...	f5	fe	Nxc6	Be2	0-0[39]	Rb3[41]	Be3	∞
	...	...	Nc6[38]	fe	bc	Be7	0-0[40]	Qc5+[42]	Qe5[43]	

1 e4 c5 2 Nf3 d6 3 d4 cd 4 Nxd4 Nf6 5 Nc3 a6 6 Bg5 e6 7 f4 Qb6
8 Qd2 Qxb2 9 Rb1 Qa3 10 f5 Nc6 11 fe fe 12 Nxc6 bc 13 e5

	13	14	15	16	17	18	19	20	21	
10	...	Nxd5	Be2	0-0	c4	Kh1	Bh5+	Bd1	Ba4+	∞
	Nd5[44]	cd	de	Ra7[45]	Qc5+	d4	g6	Be7	Kd8[46]	
11	...	Bxf6	Ne4	Rd1[47]	Bd3[48]	0-0	Qh6	Rf3	Rg3	=
	de	gf	Qxa2	Be7	f5	0-0[49]	Ra7[50]	Kh8	Rg8[51]	
12	...	...	Be2	Bf3	0-0	Bxe4	Rf3[55]	Kh1		∓
	...	...	Be7	h5[52]	f5[53]	fe[54]	Bd7	Qc5+	Rg8[56]	
13	...	...	...	...	Rb3	Nxf6+[57]	c4[58]	g3	0-0	∞
	...	...	...	...	Qa4	Bxf6	Bh4+[59]	Be7	h4[60]	

[25] 13 Rf3 b5 14 Re3 (14 f5 Ne5 15 Rg3 b4 16 Bxf6 Bxf6 17 Na4 Nc4 ∓ Hellers-de Wit, Groningen 1984-85) 14 ... Bb7 15 Bf3 Nb6 16 Nb3 Qb4 ∞/∓ Klovans-Gasseholm, corr. 1986

[26] 13 ... Ne5? 14 fe fe 15 Bh5+ Nf7 16 Bxf7+ Kxf7 17 Rxf6 Bxf6 18 e5 ± Ivan-Spassov, Budapest 1987

[27] 15 ... Nf8 16 Bxf6 gf (16 ... Bxf6? 17 Rxf6 gf 18 Bh5+ Kg6 19 Qh6! ±) 17 Nd5 ∞∞

[28] 16 Be3? Nc4 ∓∓
  16 Bh5+? Nxh5 17 Bxe7 Bxe6 18 Qg5 Qc7 ∓∓ Peelen-Cserna, Amsterdam 1984
  16 Rxf6? Bxf6 (16 ... gf? 17 Bh5+ Kd8 18 Be3 ±±) 17 Bh5+ (17 Bxf6 Bxe6!) 17 ... Kd8 18 e7+ Bxe7 19 Bxe7+ Kd7! ∓
  16 Qe3!? Wedberg
  16 Qd3 Bxe6 17 Be3 Bc4 18 Bxc5 Bxd3 19 Bxd3 Nbd7 20 Be3 ∞ Dobsa

[29] 17 Rxf6 gf 18 Bh5+ (18 Qh6 Qxc3 19 Qxf6 Bxe6 ∓) 18 ... Kd8 19 e7+ ∞ (19 ... Kd7! Baljon; 19 ... Kc7 20 Rxb6 Be6, Dahlgren-Moborn, corr. 1986, 21 Na4! Baljon)

[30] 13 ... h5 14 Kh1 (14 f5 Qc5+ 15 Kh1 Qe5 ∓ Grosar-Ftacnik, Vienna 1986) 14 ... Qa5 15 Qd4 Be7 16 Na4 ±

[31] 14 ... d5 15 ed cd 16 f5 ±

[32] 15 ... ef 16 ef Bf5 17 Rxa6 Qxa6 18 Rxf5 d5 19 Re1 Qb7 20 Qh6! ±

[33] 17 Qd3 ± Velimirović-Gavrikov, Vršac 1985

[34] 12 ... 0-0 13 f5 Nc6 14 Nxc6 bc 15 Kh1 Qa5 16 Rf3 ±/∞

[35] 13 ... Nc6 14 Nxc6 Bxc3 15 Qe3 bc 16 Rb3 ± Velimirović-Ftacnik, Banja Luka 1983

[36] 16 Nxc6 bc 17 Ne7+ Kh8 18 Nxc8 Rfxc8 = Parma-Fischer, Zagreb 1970

[37] 17 ♘b6 ♖b8 18 ♗f3 ♘xd4 19 cd ♕xd2 20 ♖xd2 ♖d8 = Ljubojević-Ribli, Bugojno 1984

17 ♗f3!?

[38] 10 ... e5 11 ♗xf6 gf 12 ♘d5 ±
10 ... ♗e7 11 fe fe 12 ♗c4 ±
10 ... b5 11 fe fe 12 ♖b3 ♕a5 (12 ... ♕c5? 13 ♘cxb5 ♘xe4 14 ♕a5 ± Velimirović-Marjanović, Yugoslav Ch 1979) 13 ♗xf6 gf 14 ♗e2 b4 15 ♘d1 ±/±

[39] 14 ♖b3 ♕a5 (14 ... ♕c5? 15 ♗e3 ♕e5 16 ♗d4 ♕a5 17 e5 ±) 15 0-0 ♖a7 (15 ... 0-0?! 16 ♘d5 ±) 16 ♗xf6 gf 17 ♖b8?! 0-0 ∓ Timman-Ljubojević, Tilburg 1985; 17 ♕h6 ∞ Timman

[40] 14 ... ♕a5 15 ♗f3 ♖a7 (15 ... ♗d7 16 ♖b7 ± Timman-Sunye, Thessaloniki Ol 1984) 16 e5 ± Timman-Ljubojević, Tilburg 1986

[41] 15 ♔h1 ♖a7 16 ♕e3 ♖d7 17 e5 de 18 ♗d3 (18 ♕xe5 ♕d6 ∓ Oll-Gavrikov, USSR 1983) 18 ... ♕xc3 19 ♗xh7+ ♘xh7 20 ♕xc3 ♗xg5 ∞ Oll-Ubilava, USSR 1983

[42] 15 ... ♕a5?! 16 ♘d5 ♕d8 (16 ... ♕xd2 17 ♘xe7+ ♔f7 18 ♗xd2 ♔xe7 19 e5 ±) 17 ♘xe7+ ♕xe7 18 ♖d3 ±

[43] 17 ♗f4 ♕c5+ (17 ... ♘xe4 18 ♘xe4 ♕xe4 19 ♗xd6 ± Timman-Ribli, Amsterdam 1986) 18 ♔h1 d5 19 e5 ♘d7 20 ♘a4 ♕a7 21 ♕c3 ♘c5 22 ♘xc5 ♖xc5 23 ♕h3 g6 ∞ A.Rodriguez-Ernst, Subotica IZ 1987 (24 ♖bf3! Ernst)

[44] 13 ... ♘d7 14 ed ♕xd6 15 ♗d3 ♖b8 16 ♖d1 ♕e5+ 17 ♘e4 ♗c5 18 ♗f4 ♗b4 19 c3 ♗c3 20 ♕xc3 ♗xf4 21 ♘d6+ ♔d8 22 ♗e4 ± Vitolins-Peresipkin, USSR 1974

[45] 16 ... ♗c5+ 17 ♔h1 ♖f8 18 c4 ♖xf1+ 19 ♖xf1 ♗b7 20 ♕c2 e4 21 ♖g4 ± Tal-Bogdanović, USSR v Yugoslavia 1967
16 ... ♗e7 17 c4 ♕c5+ 18 ♔h1 d4 19 ♗xe7 ♕xe7 20 ♕a5 ± Lazić-Tringov, Kragujevac 1984

[46] 22 ♗xe7+ ♖xe7!? (22 ... ♕xe7? 23 ♕a5+ ♕c7 24 ♖b6 ♖b7 25 c5 ±± Nordby-Engel, corr. 1983; 22 ... ♔xe7 23 ♕h6 ♔d8 ∞∞) 23 ♕g5 ♔c7 24 ♖fe1 ♖f8 25 ♖xe5 ♕b4 ∓ B.Jansson
22 ♖f7 h6 (22 ... e4 23 ♖xe7 ♖xe7 24 ♗f6 e5 25 ♗xh8 e3 26 ♕c2 ♖f7 27 ♕e4 ± Milovanović-Stern, corr. 1984) 23 ♗xh6 e4 24 h3 ♖b7 (24 ... e5 25 ♗g5 e3 26 ♗xe3 ♖b7 27 ♖e1 ± Timman-Sunye, Wijk aan Zee 1980) 25 ♖xb7 ♗xb7 26 ♕b2 ♔c8 27 ♗f4 e3 28 ♗d7+! ½-½ Prins-Strand, corr. 1984

[47] 16 ♘xf6+ ♔f7 17 ♖b3 ♕a1+ 18 ♔e2 ♕d4 19 ♕g5 (Matulović-Nunn, Helsinki 1981) 19 ... e4! 20 ♘g4 ♗g7 ∓ Nunn

[48] 17 ♗e2 0-0 18 0-0 f5 19 ♕h6 (19 ♖f3 fe 20 ♖g3+ ♔h8 21 ♘c3 ♖f5 22 ♕xc6 L.M.Kovacs) 19 ... ♕xc2! 20 ♖d3 ♕xe2 21 ♖g3+ ♔f7 22 ♖xf5+ = Velimirović-Ftacnik, Vršac 1981

[49] 18 ... fe? 19 ♗e2 h5 20 ♕c3 ±

[50] 19 ... fe? 20 ♗xe4 ♗c5+ 21 ♔h1 ♖a7 22 ♖d8! ±±
19 ... ♖f7 20 ♖f3 ♕a5? 21 ♗c4! ±; 20 ... ♔h8!?

[51] 22 ♖xg8+ ♔xg8 23 ♘f6+ ♗xf6 24 ♕xf6 ♖d7 ∓
22 ♗c4! ♕xc2! (22 ... ♕xc4? 23 ♘f6) 23 ♖xg8+ ♔xg8 24 ♗xe6+ ♗xe6 25 ♕xe6+ ♔g7 26 ♕xe5+ ♔g8 = Magerramov

[52] 16 ... 0-0 17 ♖b3 ♕a4 18 c4 ♔h8 19 0-0 ♖a7 20 ♕h6 ± Gipslis-Korchnoi, USSR Ch 1963

[53] 17 ... ♖a7 18 ♖b8 ♖c7 (18 ... ♔f7 19 0-0 f5 20 ♖xc8! ♖xc8 21 ♕h6 ± Ernst-Hjartarson, Gausdal 1985) 19 0-0 f5 20 ♘g3 ♕d6 21 ♗xh5+ ♔d8 ±/∞ Ernst-Hunerkopf, Gausdal 1986

[54] 18 ... ♖a7 19 ♖b8 ♔f7 - 17 ... ♖a7
18 ... ♔f7 19 c4 h4 20 ♖b3 ♕a4 21 ♕c3 ± Tisdall-H.Olafsson, Husavik 1985

[55] 20 ♖b7 ♕d6 (20 ... 0-0-0 ∞ Ribli-Barczay, Hungarian Ch 1968) 21 ♕e2 ♖b8 22 ♗g6+ ♔d8 23 ♖xd7+ ♔xd7 24 ♖d1 ♖hf8 ∓ Rogulj-Mrda, Zagreb 1977-78

[56] 22 ♖d3 ♗g4 23 ♖xd7 ♖xe4 24 ♖bb7 ♗f4! 25 ♕d1 ♖f5 26 h3, Böhmfeldt-Nunn, Dortmund 1979, 26 ... ♗f8! intending ... e4, ... ♖d5 ∓∓ Nunn; 25 ♖xe7+ ∓ Nunn

[57] 18 c4 f5 ∞

[58] 19 0-0 ♕d4+ ∓

[59] 19 ... ♖a7 20 0-0 ♖d7 21 ♕e3 (21 ♕c3 ♗g7 22 ♖a3 e4 = Timman-Ljubojević, London 1980) 21 ... ♖f7 22 ♕c5 ♗e7 23 ♕xe5 ♖xf1+ 24 ♗xf1 ♖f8 25 ♗e2 ♖f5 26 ♗xh5+ ♖xh5 27 ♕xh5+ ♔d8 = Velimirović-Musil, Maribor 1980

[60] 21 ... ♖a7 22 ♖b8 ♖c7 23 ♕d3 ♗c5+ 24 ♔h1 ♗e7 25 ♕g6 (25 ♕e4?! ♖d7!) 25 ... ♔d6 26 ♕f6 ♖e8 27 ♗xh5 ♖ce7 28 ♖d1+ ♗d4 29 ♖xd4+ = Vitolins-Gavrikov, USSR 1977

21 ... h4 22 ♕d3 ♕a5 23 ♗h5+ ♖xh5 24 ♕g6+ ♔d8 25 ♕xh5 ♕c5+ 26 ♔h1 e4 ∞ Martinez-Novikov, Mendoza 1985

	3	4	5	6	7	8	9	10	11	
1	...	♘c3	e5	♘xb5	♘g5[3]	♘e4[5]	c4	♘xc5	cb	±
	♘f6[1]	♘d4[2]	♘xb5	♘d5	f6[4]	f5	♘c7[6]	♘xb5	d6[7]	
2	...	0-0	h3	c3	♗xc6+	d4	cd	♗g5	♗xf6	±
	d6	♗g4[8]	♗h5	a6[9]	bc	cd	♘f6[10]	h6	ef[11]	
3	...	...	♖e1	c3	♗xc6[12]	d4	♗g5	♘bd2[14]	c4	∞
	...	♗d7	♘f6	a6	♗xc6	♗xe4	♗d5[13]	e6	♗xf3[15]	
4	...	0-0[16]	♘c3[17]	♘xd4[18]	♘e2	♗a4[19]	♗b3	d3	f4	±/∞
	e6	♘ge7	♘d4	cd	a6	b5	♘c6	♗e7[20]	0-0[21]	
5	...	...	...	♗xc6	d4	♘xd4	♖e1	♘xc6	♕g4	±/∞
	...	...	a6	♘xc6	cd	d6[22]	♗e7[23]	bc	g6[24]	
6	,...	0-0	♖e1	♗xc6[26]	d3	♘bd2	a3	b4	♗b2	=
	g6	♗g7	e5[25]	dc	♕e7	♘h6	0-0	♖d8	f6[27]	
7	...	...	c3	♖e1[28]	d4	cd	e5	♗xc6[29]	♘bd2	=
	...	...	♘f6	0-0	cd	d5	♘e4	bc	♗f5[30]	

[1] **3 ... a6** 4 ♗xc6 dc (4 ... bc 5 d4 cd 6 ♕xd4 ±) 5 h3 e5 6 d3 ♗d6 7 a4 a5 8 ♘bd2 ±

3 ... b6 4 0-0 ♗b7 5 ♖e1 a6 6 ♗f1 e6 7 c3 ± Glek-Gurgenidze, USSR 1984

3 ... ♕b6 4 ♘c3 e6 (4 ... a6 5 ♗xc6 ♕xc6 6 d4 ±) 5 0-0 ♘ge7 6 ♖e1 ♘d4 7 a4 ± Inkiov-Helmers, Lodz 1978

3 ... ♕c7 4 0-0 ♘f6 5 ♘c3 e6 6 ♖e1 d6 7 d4 cd 8 ♘d5 ed 9 ed+ ♗e7 10 ♘xd4 ♘xd5 11 ♘xc6 bc 12 ♕xd5 ♗b7 13 ♗g5 f6 14 ♗xf6 gf 15 ♕h5+ ∞ ECO

[2] **4 ... e6** – 3 ... e6

4 ... e5 5 ♗xc6 dc 6 ♘xe5 ♘xe4 7 ♘xe4 (7 ♕h5 ♘d6 8 ♘e4 ♕c7 9 ♘xc5 ♘f5 ∞ Veličković) 7 ... ♕d4 8 ♕e2 ♕xe5 9 f4 ♕xf4?! (9 ... ♕e6) 10 d4 ♕h4+ 11 g3 ♕e7 12 ♗g5 f6 13 0-0-0! ± Plaskett-Murei, Gausdal 1986

[3] 7 c4 ♘b4 8 d4 a6 9 ♘c3 cd 10 ♘xd4 ± Korchnoi

[4] **7 ... h6?** 8 ♘xf7! ♔xf7 9 ♕f3+ ♔e6 10 c4 ‡‡ Khalifman

7 ... f5 8 0-0 a6 9 ♘c3 ♘b4 10 a3 ♘c6 11 ♘d5! ♘xe5 12 d4 ± Khalifman-Varlamov, USSR 1985

[5] 8 ef ♗xf6 9 0-0 ± Hardicsay-Horvath, Budapest 1986

[6] **9 ... ♘b6** 10 ♘xc5 ♘xc4 11 ♕e2 ±

9 ... ♘f4 10 ♕f3 ± Tal

[7] **11 ... ♕b6** 12 d4 ♕xb5 13 ♘d3 e6 14 0-0 ± Tal-Mnatsakanian, Erevan 1986

11 ... d6 12 ed ed 13 ♕e2+ ♗f7 ±

[8] 4 ... ♘f6 5 e5 de 6 ♘xe5 ♕c7 7 d4 e6 8 ♗f4 ♗d6 9 ♘d2 0-0 10 ♗xc6 bc 11 ♘dc4 ♗a6 12 ♘xd6! ♕xd6 (12 ... ♗xf1 13 dc ♗a6 14 c4 ±) 13 ♖e1 ±

[9] **6 ... e6** 7 d4 cd 8 cd a6 – 6 ... a6

6 ... ♕b6 7 ♘a3 a6 8 ♗a4 ♕c7 9 d4 b5 10 ♘xb5 ab 11 ♗xb5 0-0-0 12 ♕a4 ♘b8 13 dc ∞ Iskov-Larsen, Copenhagen 1979

[10] 9 ... e6 10 ♖e1 (10 ♗e3 ♘f6 11 ♘bd2 ♗e7 12 ♕a4 0-0!? 13 ♗xc6 ♕b8 ∞ Hazai-Minev, Sofia 1979) 10 ... ♘f6 11 g4 ♗g6 12 d5 ± Zak

[11] 12 ♕c2 ♕d7 13 ♘h4 ± van der Wiel-Larsen, Brussels 1987

[12] 7 ♗a4 c4 8 ♗c2 ♖c8 9 ♘a3 b5 10 b3 ♗e5 ∞ Plaskett-H.Olafsson, Copenhagen 1985

7 ♗f1 ♗g4 8 d4 (8 h3 ♗xf3 9 ♕xf3 g6 10 ♖d1 d5 =; 10 ♕d1 ♗h6 =) 8 ... cd 9 cd d5 10 e5 ♘g8 11 ♗e3 e6 = Korchnoi-Portisch, Tilburg 1986

[13] **9 ... ♗xb1** 10 ♖xb1 e6 11 ♗xf6 gf 12 d5 ± Yusupov-Timoshchenko, USSR 1978, and Barle-Quinteros, Lone Pine 1979

9 ... d5 10 ♘bd2 (10 dc e6 11 b4 ♗e7 ∞ Soltis-Browne, US Ch 1983) 10 ... e6 (10 ...

♗xf3 11 ♕xf3 e6 12 ♗xf6 ± Georgadze-Tal, USSR Ch 1978) 11 ♘xe4 de 12 ♖xe4 ♗e7 13 ♗xf6 gf 14 ♕b3 ± Shabanov-Zakharov, USSR 1979

[14] 10 c4 ♗xc4 11 ♘c3 cd 12 ♕xd4 ♗e6 13 ♕h4 ♖c8 14 ♘d4 ♖c4! ∞ Korsunsky-Sher, USSR 1979

[15] 12 ♕xf3 cd 13 ♗xf6 gf 14 ♕xb7 ♗g7 15 ♕c6+ ∞ Romanishin-Sosonko, Reggio Emilia 1985-86

[16] 4 ♗xc6 bc 5 b3 d5 6 ♕e2 a5 7 ♘c3 ♘f6 8 0-0 c4!? 9 bc ♗b4 10 ♗b2 0-0 ∞ Kholmov-Sveshnikov, USSR 1984
4 ♘c3 ♘f6 (4 ... ♘d4 5 0-0 ♘e7 – 4 0-0) 5 ♗xc6 bc 6 e5 ♘d5 7 ♘e4 f5 8 ♘d6+ ♗xd6 9 ed ♗a6 (9 ... c4!? 10 b3!?) 10 d3 (Kristiansen-Pribyl, Kecskemet 1985) 10 ... ♕b8 11 c4 ♘f6 12 ♗f4 ♕xb2 13 0-0 ±

[17] 5 c3 d5 6 ed ♕xd5 = Timman-Sveshnikov, Wijk aan Zee 1981
5 b3 ♘d4 (5 ... a6 6 ♗xc6 ♘xc6 7 ♗b2 ±) 6 ♘xd4 cd 7 ♗b2 a6 (7 ... ♘c6 8 c3 ♗c5 9 ♕h5 dc 10 dc ± Plaskett-Sveshnikov, Sochi 1984) 8 ♗d3 ♘c6 9 c3 ♗c5 10 ♕h5 d6 = Benko-Christiansen, Lone Pine 1981

[18] 6 ♖e1 ♘g6 (6 ... ♘ec6 7 ♗xc6! dc 8 e5 ±) 7 ♗f1 ♘xf3+ 8 ♕xf3 ♗e7 9 ♕e3 0-0 10 d4 cd 11 ♕xd4 b6 ∞ Gurgenidze-Romanishin, Tbilisi 1986

[19] 8 ♗d3 ♘c6 9 c3 ♗c5 10 b4 ♗a7 11 cd ♘xd4? 12 ♗b2 ♘xe2+ 13 ♕xe2 0-0 14 e5 ± Tseitlin-Ionov, USSR 1984; 11 ... d5! Ionov

[20] 10 ... ♗c5 11 f4 ♘a5 12 f5 ♘xb3 13 cb ± Gurgenidze-Furman, USSR 1971

[21] 12 ♔h1 d6 13 f5 ♗e6 14 ♘f4 ef 15 ♗d5 ♗d7 16 ef ♖c8 ±/∞ Malanyuk-Georgadze, Lvov 1984

[22] 8 ... ♘xd4 9 ♕xd4 f6 10 ♗e3 ±
8 ... ♗e7 9 ♘xc6 dc (9 ... bc 10 e5 0-0 11 ♘e4 ± Dorfman-Gofstein, USSR 1976) 10 e5 (10 ♕g4!? ♗f6 11 ♕g3) 10 ... ♕xd1

11 ♖xd1 ±/= Sax-Kouatly, Brussels 1985

[23] 9 ... ♗d7 10 ♘xc6 ♗xc6 (10 ... bc 11 ♕g4 e5 12 ♕g3 ± Tal-Rantanen, Tallinn 1979) 11 ♕g4 g6?! 12 ♘d5! ± Miles-Chandler, Indonesia 1982

[24] 11 ... 0-0 12 ♗h6 ♗f6 13 e5 de 14 ♖ad1 ♕e7 15 ♘e4 ♔h8 16 ♗e3 ±
11 ... ♗f6 12 e5 de 13 ♘e4 ∞
11 ... g6 12 e5 (12 ♗h6 f6 ∞) 12 ... de 13 ♖xe5 0-0 14 ♗h6 ♖e8 15 ♖d1 ♕c7 16 ♕e2 (Andres-Arencibia, Cuba 1985) 16 ... ♗d6 (16 ... c5!?) 17 ♗f4! f6 18 ♘e4 fe 19 ♘xd6 ♖d8 20 ♗xe5 ∞ Andres

[25] 5 ... ♘f6 6 e5 ♘c3 ♘c7 (7 ... ♘xc3 8 dc 0-0 9 ♕d5 ±) 8 ♗xc6 (8 ♗c4!? 0-0 9 d3) 8 ... dc 9 h3 0-0 10 d3 b6 11 ♗f4 ♘e6 12 ♕d2 ♘d4 13 ♕h2 ♗f5 14 ♖ad1 ♕d7 15 ♘e4 ♖ad8 16 ♗h6 ± Castro-Robatsch, Rome 1980

[26] 6 c3 ♘ge7 7 d4?! cd 8 cd ed 9 ♗f4 a6 10 ♗c4 d6 + ECO
6 b4 ♗xb4 7 ♗b2 ♕c7 8 c3 ♘c6 9 d4 d6 ∞

[27] 12 ♗c3 ♗e6 (12 ... cb 13 ab ♘f7 14 ♘c4 ♗e6 = Jansa-Schneider, Skara 1980) 13 ♕b1 ♘f7 = Glek-Pigusov, USSR 1986

[28] 6 e5 ♘d5 7 d4 cd 8 cd 0-0 9 ♘c3 ♘c7 =
6 d4 ♘xe4 7 d5 ♘d6 8 a4 ♘a5 9 ♖e1 0-0 10 ♗g5 ♖e8 11 ♘a3 b6 ∞ Petrienko-Vizhmanavin, Pinsk 1986

[29] 10 ♘c3 ♘xc3 11 bc ♕a5 12 ♗xc6 (12 a4 ♗g4 13 ♖e3 ♖fc8 14 h3 ♗d7 ∞/= Levchenkov-Klovans, USSR 1978) 12 ... bc 13 ♕b3 ♗g4 14 ♕a3 ♕c7 15 ♘d2 f6 16 h3 ♗xh3!? ∞ Dvoretsky-Tseshkovsky, Frunze 1983

[30] 11 ... ♘xd2 12 ♘xd2 f6 13 ef ♗xf6 14 ♘b3 ±
11 ... c5 12 dc! ♘xc5 13 ♘b3 ±
11 ... ♗f5 12 ♘b3 (12 ♘h4 ♗e6 13 ♘b3 g5 14 ♘f3 f6 ∞ Gusev-Korsunsky, USSR 1986) 12 ... a5 13 a4 f6 14 ef ef = Korsunsky-Sturua, USSR 1978

Sicilian XX   1 e4 c5 2 Nf3 Nc6 4 d4 cd 4 Nxd4 g6

	5	6	7	8	9	10	11	12	13	
1	Nc3[1]	Nxc6	e5	Bc4	Qf3	Bf4	0-0[7]	Rad1	Rfe1	±
	Nf6[2]	bc[3]	Ng8	Bg7[4]	f5[5]	e6[6]	Nh6	Qc7	Nf7[8]	
2	...	Be3	Be2[9]	0-0	ed	Nxd5	Bf3	Nxc6	Bxc6	=
	Bg7	Nf6	0-0[10]	d5	Nxd5[11]	Qxd5	Qa5![12]	bc	Rb8[13]	

1 e4 c5 2 Nf3 Nc6 3 d4 cd 4 Nxd4 g6 5 Nc3 Bg7 6 Be3 Nf6

	7	8	9	10	11	12	13	14	15	
3	Nxc6	e5	Bd4[14]	Bc4	0-0	Re1	Bxe5	Qe2	Bb3	=
	bc	Ng8	Qa5[15]	Bxe5	Nf6	d6	de	Bf5	e4[16]	
4	...	...	Nxd5	Qxd5	Bxa7[17]	Bd4	Bd3	Qa8[18]	Qa4[19]	∞̅∞̅
	...	Nd5	cd	Rb8	Rxb2	Rxc2	e6	Rc6	Qc7[20]	
5	Bc4	0-0	Bb3[22]	h3[23]	f4[25]	Bxd4	Qd3[27]	Rad1[28]	Nd5[30]	±
	Qa5	0-0[21]	d6	Bd7[24]	Nxd4[26]	Bc6	Rad8	b5[29]	Bxd5[31]	
6	...	...	Nb3	f4[32]	Be2	Bf3[34]	Rf2	Nd5	ed	±
	...	...	Qc7	d6	Rd8[33]	Be6	Bc4	Bxd5	Na5[35]	
7	...	Bb3[36]	f3[38]	ed[39]	Nde2[40]	Nxa4	Bf2[41]	0-0	Nac3	∞/=
	0-0	a5[37]	d5	Nb4	a4	Nfxd5	Bf5[42]	b5	Nxc3[43]	

[1] **5 ♘xc6** bc 6 ♕d4 ♘f6 (6 ... f6 7 c4! ±)
7 e5 ♘d5 8 c4 ♕b6 9 ♕e4 ♘c7 ∞/∓
5 ♗e2 ♗g7 6 ♘b3 d6 7 0-0 ♗e6 8 f4
♕c8 = Torre-Miles, Biel 1977

[2] 5 ... d6 6 ♗e3 ♗g7 – 2 ... d6

[3] 6 ... dc 7 ♕xd8+ ♔xd8 8 ♗c4 ♗g7 (8 ...
♔e8 9 e5 ♘g4 10 f4 h5 11 ♗d2 ± Kapengut-
Shabanov, USSR 1977) 9 f4!? (9 ♗f4 ♘d7!?
Korchnoi) 9 ... b5 10 ♗d3 e5 11 0-0! ♘d7
12 f5 ± A.Ivanov-Shabanov, USSR 1986

[4] 8 ... ♕a5 9 ♗f4 ♗g7 10 0-0 ♗xe5 11 b4
♕c7 12 ♘d5! ±

[5] 9 ... e6 10 ♗f4 ♕a5 (Shamkovich) 11 0-0!
♗xe5 12 b4! ±

[6] 10 ... ♖b8 11 0-0 e6 12 ♖ad1 ♕c7
13 ♖fe1 ± Andersson-Bilek, Teesside 1972

[7] 11 0-0-0 ♕c7 12 ♕e3 (12 h4 ♘h6! 13 ♕g3
♘f7 14 ♖he1 ♖b8 ∞ de Firmian-Sosonko,
Wijk aan Zee 1986) 12 ... ♖b8 13 ♗b3 ♖b4
14 g3 ∞ Popović-Shamkovich, New York 1986

[8] 14 ♕g3 0-0 15 h4 ± Short-Sosonko, Wijk
aan Zee 1986

[9] 7 f4 d6 8 ♗e2 0-0 9 ♘b3 – 2 ... d6

[10] 7 ... d5?! 8 ♗b5! ♗d7 9 ed ±

[11] 9 ... ♘b4 10 d6 ♕xd6 11 ♘cb5 ♕d7 12 c4 ±

[12] 11 ... ♕d7 12 ♘xc6 bc 13 c3 ♖b8 14 ♕xd7
♗xd7 15 ♖fd1 ± Radulov

[13] Euwe

[14] 9 f4 ♘h6! 10 ♕d2 0-0 11 0-0-0 ♕a5!
12 ♗c4 ♖b8 ∞/∓

[15] 9 ... c5 10 ♗e3!? ♕c7 11 ♗c4 ♗b7 12 ♕d3
♕xe5 13 0-0-0 ♘f6 14 ♖he1 ∞∞ Tukmakov

[16] 16 ♕c4 0-0 17 ♕xc6 ♖ad8 = Tringov-Stein,
Sarajevo 1967

[17] 11 ♗c4 e6 12 ♕c5 ♗b7 13 0-0 ♖c8 =
Dückstein-Karlsson, Lucerne 1979

[18] 14 ♕b5 ♖c6 15 0-0 ♗a6 16 ♕b3 ♗xd3
17 ♕xd3 0-0 = Stein-Nei, USSR 1960

[19] 15 0-0 ♗a6 16 ♕xd8+ ♔xd8 = Boleslavsky

[20] 16 0-0 ♗xe5 17 ♗b5 ♗xd4 18 ♕xd4 e5
19 ♖fe1 ♗e6 20 ♕b4 ∞∞ Barczay

[21] 8 ... ♘g4 9 ♕xg4 ♘xd4 10 ♕h4! ♗xc2
11 ♘d5 ± Boleslavsky

[22] 9 ♘d5!? ♘xe4 10 ♘xc6 dc 11 ♘xe7+ ♔h8
12 ♘xc8 ♖axc8 13 c3 ± Adorjan

[23] 10 ♘d5!? ♕d8 11 f3 ♘a5 12 ♕d2 ♘xb3
13 ab ± Suetin-Georgadze, Lublin 1976

[24] 10 ... ♘xd4 11 ♗xd4 ♗e6 12 f4 a6 13 ♕f3 ±
Tal

[25] 11 ♖e1 ♖fe8!? (11 ... ♖ac8 12 ♕d2 ♖fe8
13 ♖ad1 a6 14 ♘f3 ± Tal-Hansen, Reykjavik
1986) 12 ♕e2 ♕h5! (12 ... ♖ad8 13 ♖ad1
♘xd4 14 ♗xd4 ♗c6 15 ♕f3 ± Popović-Renet,
Dubai Ol 1986) = Popović

[26] 11 ... ♕h5 12 ♕d3 b5 13 a3! ± Korchnoi
11 ... ♖ac8 12 ♘f3 ♖cd8 13 ♕e1 ♗c8
14 ♖d1 ± Kurajica-Kuijpers, Wijk aan Zee
1970

[27] 13 ♘d5 ♗xd5 14 ed ♘d7 15 ♗xg7 ±
Vasyukov-Ciocaltea, Bucharest 1967

[28] 14 ♕e3 ♘d7 15 ♗xg7 ♔xg7 16 ♔h2 ♕c5
17 ♕d3 b5 18 ♘d5 = Korchnoi

[29] 14 ... ♘d7 15 ♗xg7 ♔xg7 16 ♔h1 ±

[30] 15 a3?! b4 = Short-Hellers, Wijk aan Zee
1986

[31] 16 ed ± Short

[32] 10 ♗g5!? a5 11 a4 ♘b4 12 ♗e2 ♖d8
14 ♘d4 ± Kuzmin-Kapengut, USSR 1972

[33] 11 ... a6 12 ♗f3 b5 13 ♖f2 ♗b7 14 ♘d5! ±
Ghizdavu-Ribli, Bucharest 1971
11 ... a5 12 a4 ♘b4 13 ♖f2 e5 14 ♗f3 ♗d7
15 ♖d2 ± Fischer-Olafsson, Bled 1961

[34] 12 g4!? ∞/±

[35] 16 ♗d4 ± Ostojić-Musil, Yugoslav Ch 1968

[36] 8 f3 ♕b6 9 ♗b3 ♘xe4 10 ♘d5 ♕a5+
11 c3 ♘c5 12 ♘xc6 dc = Fischer-Panno,
Portorož IZ 1958
8 0-0 ♘xe4 9 ♘xe4 d5 10 ♘xc6 bc 11 ♗d3
de 12 ♗xe4 ♕c7 13 c3 ♖b8 14 ♕e2 ♕a5 ∞

[37] 8 ... ♘a5? 9 e5! ± Fischer
8 ... ♘g4 9 ♕xg4 ♘xd4 10 ♕d1 ♘xb3
11 ab b6 12 ♗d4 f6 13 ♕d3 ♗b7 14 0-0-0 ±
8 ... ♕a5 9 f3 e6 10 ♕d2 d5 11 ed ed
12 0-0-0 ±/± Korchnoi

[38] 9 a4 ♘g4 10 ♕xg4 ♘xd4 11 ♗xd4 ♗xd4
12 ♕g3 d6 13 0-0-0 ♗xc3 14 ♕xc3 ♗e6 =
Ivanović-Cebalo, Yugoslav Ch 1983

[39] 10 ♗xd5 ♘xd5 11 ed (11 ♘xd5 f5 12 ♘xc6
bc 13 ♘b6 ♖b8 = Korchnoi) 11 ... ♘b4
12 ♘de2 ♗f5 13 ♖c1 b5 = de Firmian-Forintos,
Reykjavik 1982

[40] 11 ♘db5 a4 12 ♘xa4 ♘fxd5 13 ♗f2 ♗d7
14 ♘bc3 ♗xa4 15 ♘xa4 b5 ∞/∓ Ivanović-
Wedberg, Eksjö 1980

[41] 13 ♗d2 ♗e6 14 a3 ♘a6 15 0-0 ∞

[42] 13 ... ♖xa4 14 ♗xa4 ♕a5 15 0-0 ♖d8
16 a3 ± Sax-Haik, Smederevo 1982

[43] 16 ♘xc3 ♕xd1 17 ♖fxd1 ♗xc2 18 ♗xc2
♘xc2 19 ♖ac1 ∞/= Matulović-Ristoja, Helsinki
1981

329

	6	7	8	9	10	11	12	13	14	
1	Nc2[1]	Be2[3]	ef	0-0	Nd2	Nf3	Nfd4	Bf3		=
	d6[2]	f5!?[4]	Bxf5	Nh6	0-0	Kh8	Bd7	Nf5[5]		
2	Be3	Nc3	Be2[7]	0-0	Bxd4	Qd3[10]	b3	Bxg7	f4	±
	Nf6[6]	0-0	d6[8]	Nxd4[9]	Be6	a6	Nd7	Kxg7	f6[11]	
3	...	...	...	...	Qd2[12]	Bxd4	f3	Rab1[15]	Be3	±
	...	...	...	Bd7	Nxd4[13]	Bc6	a5[14]	Nd7	Nc5[16]	
4	...	...	...	...	Rc1	Bxd4	f3[18]	b3[20]	Bxg7[21]	±
	...	...	...	...	Nxd4[17]	Bc6	a5[19]	Nd7	Kxg7[22]	
5	...	...	Qxg4	Qd1	Nb5[24]	Qd2[26]	Bd3	cd	Bxb5	±
	...	Ng4	Nxd4	e5[23]	0-0[25]	Qh4[27]	d5	Nxb5	Qxe4[28]	
6	...	...	...	...	Qd2	Rc1	Be2	0-0	Bh6	∞/=
	...	...	...	Ne6	Qa5[29]	d6[30]	Bd7	Nc5[31]	0-0[32]	
7	...	...	...	...	Rc1	b4[34]	Be2	Qd2	f3	±
	...	...	...	...	d6[33]	0-0	b6[35]	Bb7	f5[36]	
8	...	...	...	...	...	Bd3[37]	0-0	Bb1[38]	b3	±
	...	...	...	...	b6	Bb7	0-0	Rc8[39]	d6[40]	

[1] 6 Nb3 d6 7 Nc3 a5 8 Na4 Nf6 9 f3 Be6 = Ljubojević-Short, London 1980

[2] 6 ... b6 7 Be2 Ba6 8 0-0 Rc8 9 Ne3 ± Boleslavsky

6 ... Nf6 7 Nc3 0-0 8 Be2 b6 9 0-0 Bb7 10 Bg5 Rc8 11 Ne3 Nd4 12 Bd3 ±

[3] 7 Bd3 Nf6 8 Nc3 0-0 9 0-0 a6 10 b3 =

[4] 7 ... Nh6 8 g4 Qa5+ 9 Bd2 Qe5 10 Nc3 f5 11 f4 Qe6 12 ef gf 13 g5 ±

7 ... Nf6 8 Nc3 Nd7 9 Bd2 0-0 (9 ... Nc5 10 b4 Ne6 11 Rc1 0-0 12 Nd5 ± Korchnoi-Hübner, Leningrad IZ 1973) 10 0-0 (10 h4 Nc5 11 h5 f5 12 hg hg = Stean-Smejkal, Skara 1980) 10 ... Nc5 11 f3 f5 12 b4 Ne6 13 Rb1 ± Filip

[5] Botvinnik

[6] 6 ... Nh6 7 Be2 d6 8 Qd2 Ng4 9 Bxg4 Bxg4 10 Nc3 0-0 11 0-0 Qa5 12 Rac1 Rfc8 13 b3 ± Kasparov-I.Ivanov, USSR 1978

[7] 8 Nb3 d6 9 f3 Be6 10 Nd5 Nd7 11 Qd2 a5 = Korchnoi-van der Sterren, Holland 1977

8 h3 d6 9 Be2 Bd7 10 0-0 a6 11 Qd2 b5 12 cb Nxd4 13 Bxd4 ab ∞ Larsen-Kavalek, Solingen 1970

[8] 8 ... a5 9 0-0 a4 10 c5 d5 11 cd Qxd6 12 Ndb5 ± Nunn-Haik, Paris 1983

8 ... b6 9 0-0 Bb7 10 f3 d6 11 Qd2 Qd7 12 Ndb5 (12 Rfd1 Rfd8 13 Bf1 Nxd4 14 Bxd4 e6 15 a4 Ciocaltea-Forintos, Titograd 1982) 12 ... Rfc8 13 Rac1 a6 14 Na3 Qd8 15 Rfd1 ± Portisch-Garcia Gonzalez, Lucerne Ol 1982

[9] 9 ... a6 10 Qd2 Rb8 11 f3 Bd7 12 Nb3 Be6 13 Rfd1 ± Smejkal-Hébert, Lucerne Ol 1982

9 ... a5 10 f3 Bd7 11 Ndb5 ± Andersson-Larsen, Linares 1983

9 ... Nd7 10 Re1 Nc5 11 Bf1 Bd7 12 Rc1 Nxd4 13 Bxd4 ± Adorjan-Velimirović, Vrbas 1980

[10] 11 Rc1 Qa5 12 Kh1 Rfc8 13 b3 ±

11 f4 Qc8 12 b3 Rd8 13 Rc1 ± Benko-Honfi, Majdanpek 1976

[11] Vilela-Estevez, Cuba 1978

[12] 10 Nb3!? Na5 11 f3 Nxb3 12 ab a6 13 b4 Be6 14 Qd2 ± Korchnoi-Soos, Rome 1982

[13] 10 ... a5 11 Ndb5! a4 12 f4 Qa5 13 c5! Timman-Larsen, Las Palmas IZ 1982

10 ... Re8 11 f3 a6 12 Rfd1 Rb8 13 Rac1 Nxd4 14 Bxd4 Qa5 15 a3! Be6 16 b4 ± Kir.Georgiev-Smejkal, Dubai Ol 1986

[14] 12 ... Nd7 13 Bxg7 Kxg7 14 Nd5 ±

[15] 13 b3 Re8 (13 ... Nd7 14 Bc3 Nc5 15 Rab1

♕b6 16 ♘d5 ♗xd5 17 ed Mestel-Petursson, Hastings 1986-87) 14 ♖fd1 ♘d7 15 ♗e3 ♘c5 16 ♖ac1 ♕b6 17 ♘b5 ♖ec8 ∞/= Arnason-Karlsson, Helsinki 1986

13 ♔h1 ♘d7 14 ♗xg7 ♔xg7 15 f4 ± Chandler-Petursson, Chicago 1983

[16] 15 b3 e6 16 ♗d1! ± Tringov-Haik, Vrnjačka Banja 1986

[17] 10 ... a6 11 f3 ♖b8 12 ♘b3 ± Smejkal-Andersson, Sochi 1973

[18] 12 ♕d3!? ♗h6 13 ♖cd1 ♗g7 14 b4 b6 15 f4 e6 16 ♗f3 ± Smyslov-Karlsson, Las Palmas IZ 1982

[19] 12 ... ♕a5 13 a3 ♖fc8 14 ♕d2 ♘e8 15 ♗e3 ± Balashov-Panno, Lone Pine 1977

[20] 13 ♕d2 ♘d7 = Nunn-Velimirović, Dubai Ol 1986

[21] 14 ♗e3 ♘c5 15 a3 ♕b6 16 ♘b5 ♗xb5 17 cb ∞/± Marjanović-Kagan, Skara 1980

[22] 15 ♕d4+ ♔g8 16 ♖fd1 ♕b6 (16 ... ♘c5?! 17 e5! ± Andersson-Christiansen, Hastings 1978-79) 17 ♕xb6 ♘xb6 18 f4 ± Eingorn-Vaisman, USSR 1978

[23] 9 ... ♘c6 10 ♕d2 ♕a5 11 ♖c1 0-0 12 ♗e2 d6 13 0-0 ±

[24] **10 ♗e2 0-0** 11 0-0 b6 12 ♕d2 ♗b7 13 ♖ad1 ♖c8 14 ♖fe1 f5 ∞

10 ♗d3 0-0 (10 ... a6!? Botvinnik) 11 0-0 d6 12 ♕d2 f5 13 ef gf 14 f4 ± Andersson-Rogers, Malta Ol 1980

[25] 10 ... ♘xb5 11 cb d6 12 ♗c4 ♗e6 13 ♕b3 ±

[26] 11 ♗e2 ♘xb5 12 cb d6 13 ♗c4 ♗e6 14 ♖e1 ± Filip

[27] 11 ... ♕e7 12 0-0-0 ♘xb5 13 cb d5 14 ed ♗f5 15 ♗d3 ± Smyslov-Jimenez, Havana 1963

[28] 15 0-0 ♖d8 16 ♖fd1 (16 d6!?) 16 ... ♕f5

17 ♖ac1 ♗d7 18 ♗e2 ± Gufeld-Espig, Sukhumi 1972; 16 ... ♗e6? 17 f3 ± Penrose

[29] 10 ... d6 11 ♖c1 (11 ♗e2 ♗d7 12 0-0 0-0 13 ♖ad1 ♗c6 14 ♘d5 ±) 11 ... a5 (11 ... ♗d7 12 ♗d3 a5 13 0-0 ♘c5 14 ♗b1 ♗c6 15 f4 ± Polugayevsky-Kapengut, USSR Ch 1971) 12 ♗e2 ♗d7 13 0-0 ♗c6 14 f3 0-0 15 b3 ♘c5 16 ♖fd1 ± Marović-Velimirović, Osijek 1978

[30] 11 ... b6 12 ♗d3 ♗b7 13 ♗b1 (13 f3 ♗e5 14 0-0 g5 15 ♖fd1 d6 16 ♔h1 ± Polugayevsky-Kirov, Sochi 1976) 13 ... ♖c8 14 b3 f5 15 ef gf 16 ♘d5 ± Tal-Rashkovsky, USSR 1973

[31] 13 ... ♗c6!? 14 f3 f5! ∞/= Kapengut

[32] 15 ♗xg7 ♔xg7 16 b3 ♗c6 17 ♖fe1 ♖ad8 (17 ... ♘e6 18 ♗g4 ± Korchnoi-Petrosian, match 1974) 18 ♗g4 = Geller

[33] 10 ... ♕a5 11 ♗e2 (11 ♗d3 ±) 11 ... b6 12 0-0 ♗b7 13 f3 g5 14 ♕d2 ± Karpov-Larsen, Brussels 1987

[34] 11 ♗d3 0-0 (11 ... ♗d7 12 0-0 a5 13 f4 ♗c6 14 ♗b1 ±/± Portisch-Larsen, Lugano Ol 1968) 12 0-0 ♗d7 13 ♕d2 ♕a5 14 b3 ♖fc8 15 f4 ± Kudrin-Larsen, Hastings 1986-87

[35] 12 ... a5 13 a3 ab 14 ab ♗d7 15 0-0 ♗c6 16 ♕d2 ± Portisch-Pfleger, Manila 1974

[36] 15 ef gf 16 ♘d5 ± Smejkal-Radulov, Skara 1980

[37] 11 b4 ♗b7 12 ♗d3 0-0 13 0-0 ♘d4 (13 ... d6 14 ♗b1 ±) 14 ♗b1 ♘c6 15 a3 d6 16 ♕d3 ♖c8 17 f4 ± Suba-Taimanov, Bucharest 1979

[38] 13 ♖e1 ♖c8 14 b4 ± Korchnoi-Makarov, USSR 1973

[39] **13 ... a6** 14 b3 ♗c6 15 ♕d2 b5 16 c5 ±
13 ... d6 14 b4 ♗xc3 15 ♖xc3 a5 16 a3 ±

[40] 15 ♕d2 a5 16 ♘d5 ± Hübner-Hernandez, Las Palmas 1976

1 e4 c5 2 Nf3 Nc6 3 d4 cd 4 Nxd4 g6 5 c4 Nf6 6 Nc3 d6[1]

	7	8	9	10	11	12	13	14	15	
1	f3	Qxd4	Bg5	Qd2	Rc1	b3	Be2	Na4	Kxd2	±
	Nxd4	Bg7	0-0[2]	Be6	Qa5	Rfe8[3]	a6	Qxd2+	Nd7[4]	
2	...	...	Be3	Qd2	Rc1	Nd5[7]	Nxe7+	Be2[9]	Nd5	±
	...	...	0-0	Qa5[5]	Be6[6]	Qxa2[8]	Kh8	Ng8[10]	Bxd5[11]	
3	Be2	Qxd4	Bg5	Qd2[13]	Rc1[14]	f3	b3	Na4[15]	Kxd2	±
	Nxd4	Bg7	0-0[12]	Be6	Qa5	Rfc8	a6	Qxd2+	Rc6[16]	
4	...	...	Be3	Qd2	Rc1	b3[18]	f3	Na4[19]	Kxd2	±
	...	...	0-0	Be6[17]	Qa5	a6	Rfc8	Qxd2+	Nd7[20]	
5	...	...	0-0	Qd3[21]	Be3	Bd4	Bxg7	b3	f4	±
	...	...	0-0	Be6[22]	a6[23]	Nd7	Kxg7	Qa5	Qc5+[24]	

[1] 6 ... Nxd4 7 Qxd4 d6 8 c5 (8 Bg5 Bg7 9 Qd2 – 6 ... d6) 8 ... Bg7 9 Bb5 Bd7 10 cd 0-0 = Boleslavsky

[2] 9 ... h6 10 Be3 0-0 11 Qd2 Kh7 12 Rc1 Be6 13 b3 Nd7 14 Be2 ±

[3] 12 ... a6 13 Nd5 Qxd2+ 14 Kxd2 ± Byrne-Garcia Padron, Torremolinos 1977

[4] 16 h4 ± Psakhis-Pigusov, USSR 1980

[5] 10 ... Be6 11 Rc1 Rc8 12 b3 Qa5 13 Be2 a6 14 0-0 ±

[6] 11 ... Bd7 12 Be2 Rfc8 13 0-0 a6 14 b3 Bc6 (14 ... b5?! 15 c5! ± Polugayevsky-Bednarski, Siegen Ol 1970) 15 Bd4 ± Suetin-Forintos, Budapest 1970

[7] 12 b3 Rfc8 13 Bd3 a6 14 Na4 Qxd2+ 15 Kxd2 Nd7 16 f4 f5 17 Rhe1 ± Polugayevsky-Timman, Hilversum 1973

[8] 12 ... Qxd2+ 13 Kxd2 Bxd5 14 cd Rfc8 15 Rxc8+ Rxc8 16 g3 ± Polugayevsky

[9] 14 Bd4 Rfe8 15 Nd5 Bxd5 16 cd Rac8 17 Be2 Rxc1+ 18 Qxc1 ± Panchenko-Gufeld, USSR 1975

[10] 14 ... Nd7 15 Bd4 Rfe8 16 0-0 Qb3 17 Bd1 Qa2 18 Bc3 ± Andersson-Reshevsky, Palma de Mallorca 1971

[11] 16 cd Qxb2 17 Qxb2 Bxb2 18 Rc7 ± Filip

[12] 9 ... h6 10 Be3 0-0 11 Qd2 Kh7 12 0-0 Be6 13 Bd4 Rc8 14 b3 a6 15 Qe3 ± Timman-Ribli, Amsterdam 1973

[13] 10 0-0 Be6 11 Qd3 Rc8 12 b3 a6 13 Rac1 Qa5 14 Bd2 ∞/±

[14] 11 0-0 Qa5 12 Rac1 a6 13 b3 b5 14 cb ab 15 e5 b4 ∞ Psakhis-Khasin, USSR 1978

[15] 14 a4 Kf8 15 h4 h5 16 Bd1 Bd7 ∞ Kasparov-Merkulov, USSR 1976

[16] 16 Nc3 Rac8 17 Nd5 ± Karpov-Kavalek, Nice Ol 1974

[17] 10 ... Ng4 11 Bxg4 Bxg4 12 Bd4 Bxd4 13 Qxd4 Be6 14 0-0 Qa5 15 Rfe1 ± Keene-Schmid, Bath 1973

[18] 12 0-0 a6 13 f3 Rfc8 14 b3 b5 15 Nd5 (15 f5!? Bd7 16 fg hg 17 c5 ∞) 15 ... Qxd2 16 Bxd2 Nxd5 17 cd Bd7 = Filip

[19] 14 a4!? Qb4 15 Nd5 Nxd5 16 ed Qxd2+ 17 Kxd2 ± Hort-Mecking, Petropolis IZ 1973

[20] 16 g4 Rcb8 17 Nc3 ± Chekhov-Korelov, USSR 1977

[21] 10 Qe3 Be6 11 Bd2 Qb6 12 b3 (12 Qxb6 ab 13 f4 Rfc8 14 b3 b5 ∓ Matulović-Jansa, Vršac 1979) 12 ... Qxe3+ 13 Bxe3 Nd7 14 Rac1 Nc5 15 f3 a5 = Jansa

[22] 10 ... Nd7 11 Bg5 Nc5 12 Qe3 ± Smejkal-Jansa, Hradec Kralove 1981

[23] 11 ... Nd7 12 Bd4 Bxd4 13 Qxd4 Qa5 14 f4 ± Adorjan-Jansa, Luhacovice 1973

[24] 16 Kh1 ± Smejkal-Browne, Milan 1975

	5	6	7	8	9	10	11	12	13	
1	Nb5	Nd6+	Qxd6	Qc7[2]	Nc3	Bd3	0-0	Ne2	Bd2[4]	±
	a6[1]	Bxd6	Qf6	Nge7	Nb4[3]	d5	d4	0-0	Nxd3[5]	
2	...	...	...	Qd1	Nc3	h4	Bg5	ed[7]	Bxe7	±/±
	...	...	...	Qg6	Nge7	h5	d5[6]	Nb4	Kxe7[8]	
3	...	...	...	...	...	Nxd5[9]	Be3	Nc7+	Nxa8[10]	±
	...	...	...	...	d5	Qxe4+	Nd4	Ke7	Nxc2+[11]	
4	...	c4[12]	N1c3	Na3	Be2	0-0	Nc2[13]	b3	Rc1	=
	d6	Be7	a6	h6	Be6	Bg5	Nge7[14]	Bxc1	Ng6[15]	

[1] 5 ... Nf6 and now:
6 Bg5 Bc5 7 Bxf6 (7 Nd6+? Bxd6 8 Qxd6 Nxe4) 7 ... Qxf6 8 Qd2 0-0 9 Nc7 Rb8 10 Nd5 Qg6 11 N1c3 b5! 12 Bxb5 Nd4 ∞ Nunn
6 Bc4 d6 7 0-0 Be6 8 Qd2 a6 9 Nc3 Be7 = Belyavsky-Sveshnikov, Le Havre 1977
6 N5c3 h6 7 Be3 Bb4 8 a3 Qa5 9 ab Qxa1 10 Qd6 ∞ Nunn-Anthony, England 1981
6 N1c3 – 4 ... Nf6 5 Nc3 e5

[2] 8 Qxf6 Nxf6 9 Nc3 Nb4 10 Kd2 d5 11 a3 d4 12 ab dc+ 13 Ke3 ± Velimirović-Ristić, Yugoslavia 1979
8 Qa3 Nge7 (8 ... Qg6 9 Be3! Qxe4 10 Nc3 Qb4 11 Qxb4 Nxb4 12 0-0-0 ±) 9 Nc3 Rb8 10 Be3 b5 11 Nd5 Nxd5 12 ed ±

[3] 9 ... Qe6 10 Bg5! d5 (10 ... f6 11 Be3 ±) 11 Bxe7 Nxe7 12 0-0-0 d4 13 Bc4 Qc6 14 Nd5 ±

[4] 13 f4! Bg4! 14 fe Qc6 15 Qxe7 Nxd3 16 Nxd4 Qxe4 17 Nf3 Bxf3 18 cd Qd4+ = Perfors-Baumbach, East Germany 1962

[5] 14 cd Nc6 (14 ... g5 15 Qc1! ±) 15 Qb6 (15 f4?! Qd8! 16 Qxd8 Rxd8 17 fe Be6! = Shakarov-G.Georgadze, USSR 1981) 15 ... Qd8 16 Nc5 intending f4 ±

[6] 11 ... b5 12 Qd3 Bb7 13 0-0-0 Rd8 14 Qd6 ± Hazai-Csom, Warsaw Z 1987

[7] 12 Bxe7 d4 = Fischer-Tal, Curaçao C 1962

[8] 14 d6+ Kd8 15 Bd3 Nxd3+ 16 Qxd3 Qxd3 17 cd ±/±

[9] 10 ed?! Nd4 11 Bd3 Qxg2 12 Be4 Qh3 ∓ Pokojowczyk-Pytel, Poland 1980
10 Qxd5?! Be6 (10 ... Nf6 11 Qd6 Be6 ∞) 11 Qd1 Rd8 15 Bd2 Nf6 ∞

[10] 13 Qd3 Nxc2+ 14 Kd2 Qxd3+ 15 Bxd3 Nxe3 16 Nxa8 Nd5 17 Rac1 Ngf6 18 Nc7 Nb4 19 a3 Nxd3 20 Kxd3 Bd7 21 Rc5 Kd6 22 Rhc1 Bc6 (Roshchin-Gayevsky, USSR 1983) 23 Rxc6+ bc 24 Nxa6 =
13 Rc1 Rb8! (13 ... Bg4 14 Qd3 Qxd3 15 Bxd3 Rd8 16 h3 Bc8 17 f4 ± Liberzon-Franzoni, Biel 1980) 14 Qd3 Qc6 15 Qc4 Nf6 16 Bxd4 Qxc4 17 Bxc4 ed 18 Nd5 ±/= Matsukevich

[11] 14 Kd2 Nxe3 (14 ... Nxa1? 15 Rc1!) 15 fe Nf6 16 Nb3! Rd8+ 17 Ke1 Ng4 (17 ... Nd5? 18 Rd1 Bg4 19 Rd3 ±± Kopelevich-Panshin, corr. 1982) 18 Rc1 (18 Rd1!?) 18 ... Nxe3 19 Rc7+ Bd7 20 Qd3 ± Kopelevich

[12] 6 a4 Be7 7 Bc4 Be6 8 Bxe6 fe 9 Qg4 Kf7 10 0-0 Nf6 11 Qf3 a6 12 N5c3 Nd4 13 Qd3 b5 ∞ Lanka-Sveshnikov, USSR 1987
6 N1c3 Nf6 – 4 ... Nf6 5 Nc3 e5

[13] 11 Bg4 Nf6 12 Bxe6 fe 13 Bxg5 hg 14 Nc2 Kf7 15 Qd3 Qc7 16 Rfd1 Rad8 17 Ne2 Ne7 18 Ne3 Ng6 ∓ Nikolenko-Sveshnikov, Moscow Ch 1987

[14] 11 ... Nf6 12 Qd3 Qc7 13 Rd1 Rd8 14 Bxg5 hg 15 Rac1 Qb6 16 b3 Rh4 17 Rd2 Ke7 ∞ Geller-Lputian, USSR 1987

[15] 14 Bg4 0-0 15 Ne3 Nd4 = A.Kuzmin-Sveshnikov, Moscow Ch 1987

	6	7	8	9	10	11	12	13	14	
1	♘f5[1]	ed	dc	♕f3	♗g5	♗xf6	♗d3	bc	cd	∞
	d5	♗xf5	bc[2]	♕d7[3]	♗b4[4]	gf	♗xc3+	♗xd3	♕e6[5]	
2	♘db5	♘d5[7]	ed	c4[9]	♘c3	♗d3	♕xd3	0-0	♗e3	=
	d6[6]	♘xd5	♗b8[8]	a6	♗f5[10]	♗xd3	♗e7	0-0	♘d7[11]	
3	...	♗g5	♘a3[12]	♘c4	♗xf6	♗d3	♘e3[15]	0-0	fe	±
	...	a6	♗e6[13]	♖c8	gf[14]	♘e7	♗h6[16]	♗xe3	♕b6[17]	
4	...	...	...	♘d5	♗d2	c4[18]	cb	♗c4	♗e3	±
	...	...	b5	♕a5+	♕d8	♘xe4[19]	♗e6[20]	♘e7[21]	♖c8[22]	
5	...	...	...	...	♘xe7	♗d3[23]	♗xf6[25]	♕e2[26]	0-0	=
	...	...	...	♗e7	♘xe7	♗b7[24]	gf	d5	de[27]	
6	...	...	...	...	♗xf6	c3	♘xf6+	♘c2[28]	♗d3	±/∞
	...	...	...	...	♗xf6	♘e7	gf	♗b7	♕b6[29]	
7	...	...	...	...	...	...	♘c2	♗d3	0-0	±/=
	...	...	...	...	...	0-0	♖b8[30]	♗g5	a5[31]	

1 e4 c5 2 ♘f3 ♘c6 3 d4 cd 4 ♘xd4 ♘f6 5 ♘c3 e5 6 ♘db5 d6 7 ♗g5 a6 8 ♘a3 b5 9 ♗xf6 gf[32] 10 ♘d5 f5

	11	12	13	14	15	16	17	18	19	
8	♗xb5[33]	♘xb5	♘bc7+	0-0[35]	♕h5	c3[37]	♔h1	g3	♕f3	∞
	ab	♖a4[34]	♔d7	♖xe4	♘d4[36]	♘e2+	♔c6	♖g8	♕xc7[38]	
9	ef	c3[39]	♘c2	♘ce3	♗d3	♕h5	♗c2	♖d1[45]	g4[46]	±
	♗xf5	♗g7[40]	0-0	♗e6[41]	f5[42]	e4[43]	♘e7[44]	♘g6		

---

[1] 6 ♘f3 ♗b4 7 ♗c4 (7 ♗d3 d5 ∓; 7 ♗g5 h6 8 ♗xf6 ♗xc3+ ∓) 7 ... d6 (7 ... ♘xe4!?) 8 0-0 ♗e6 =

[2] 8 ... ♕xd1+ 9 ♘xd1 bc 10 ♘e3 ±

[3] 9 ... ♕c8 10 ♗a6! ♗g4! (10 ... ♕xa6? 11 ♕xf5 ♗d6 12 ♗h6! ±) 11 ♗xc8 ♗xf3 12 ♗h3 ♗h5 13 0-0 ± Shakarov

[4] 10 ... ♘d5? 11 ♘xd5 cd 12 0-0-0 ♗e6 13 ♗c4 e4 14 ♕e2 ♖b8 15 f3 ± Grünfeld-Birnboim, Jerusalem 1986
10 ... e4 11 ♕e2 ♗b4!? 12 ♗xf6 gf 13 ♕c4 ♖d8 14 ♗e2 ♕d2+ 15 ♔f1 ♗xc3 16 ♕xc6+ ♗d7 17 ♕xc3 ♕xc3 18 bc ♗a4 ∞ Shakarov-Sax-Fedorowicz, Dubai Ol 1986

[5] 6 ... ♗c5 7 ♗e3! ♗xe3 8 ♘d6+ ♔f8 9 fe ♕b6 10 ♘c4 ♕c5 11 ♕d6+ ±

[6] 6 ... h6 7 ♘d6+ ♗xd6 8 ♕xd6 ♕e7 9 ♘b5 ± Spassky-Gheorghiu, Bath 1973

[7] 7 a4 a6 8 ♘a3 ♗e7 9 ♗e3 (9 ♗c4 ♗e6 10 0-0 ♖c8 =) 9 ... ♗e6 10 ♘c4 ♘xe4 11 ♘xe4 d5 12 ♘b6 de 13 ♘xa8 ♕xa8 14 c3 0-0 15 a5 f5 ∞ Zakharov-Timoshchenko, USSR 1978, and A.Ivanov-Andrianov, Vilnius 1984

[8] 8 ... ♘e7 9 c3 (9 c4 ♘f5 10 ♗d3 ♗e7 =) 9 ... ♘f5 (9 ... f5?! 10 ♕a4 ±) 10 a4 ♗e7 11 ♗d3 0-0 12 0-0 ♘h4 ∞ Malevinsky-Lputian, USSR 1977

[9] 9 ♕f3 a6 10 ♕a3 ♗e7 11 ♗d2 0-0 12 ♗b4 ab 13 ♕xa8 ♘a6 ∞ Marković-Jokšić, Bela Crkva 1986
9 ♗e2 a6 10 ♘c3 ♗e7 11 a4 a5 12 0-0 0-0 13 f4 ef 14 ♗xf4 ♘d7 ∞ Kholmov-Gurgenidze, USSR 1981
9 ♗e3 ♗e7 10 ♕d2 a6 11 ♘a3 ♘d7 12 ♘c4 f5 13 f4 0-0 14 0-0-0 b5 15 ♘a5 ♕c7 ∞ Kholmov-Yurtayev, USSR 1982

[10] 10 ... ♗e7 11 ♗e2 0-0 12 0-0 f5 13 f4 ♗f6 ∞ Tal-Tseshkovsky, Riga IZ 1979, and Geller-Yurtayev, USSR 1979

[11] 15 b4 ♖c8 16 ♖fd1 f5 = Veselovsky-Chekhov, USSR 1978

[12] 8 ♗xf6 gf 9 ♘a3 f5?! (9 ... b5 – 8 ♘a3) 10 ♕h5 b5 (10 ... d5 11 0-0-0 ♗xa3 12 ba ± Hamilton-Davis, Australia 1975) 11 ♘axb5 ab 12 ♗xb5 ♗b7 13 ♗c4 ♘f6 14 ♘d5 ♕g6 15 ♘c7+ ♔d8 16 ♕xg6 fg 17 ♘xa8 ♗xa8 18 ♗d5 ± Tarrasch-Janowski, Vienna 1898

[13] 8 ... d5 9 ♘xd5 ♗xa3 10 ba ♕a5+ 11 ♕d2! ± Sax-Velimirović, Rio de Janeiro IZ 1979

[14] 10 ... ♕xf6 11 ♘b6! ♖b8 12 ♘cd5 ♕d8 13 c3 ♗e7 14 ♗c4 ± Karpov-Nunn, London 1982, and S.Yanovsky-Sveshnikov, Moscow Ch 1987

[15] 12 ♕e2 ♗h6 13 ♖d1 ♖c6 14 ♘e3 ♗xe3

15 ♕xe3 ♕b6 ±/∞ Tischbierek-Rovid, Budapest 1984
[16] 12 ... ♕b6 13 0-0 ♕xb2 14 ♘cd5 ♗xd5 15 ed ♕d4 16 ♕h5 ± Popović-Matulović, Vinkovci 1982
[17] 15 ♕f3 h5 16 ♘d5 ♗xd5 17 ed ♖h6 18 ♖ab1 ± Tseshkovsky-Chandler, Minsk 1982, de Firmian-Matulović, Vrnjačka Banja 1983, and Horvath-Rovid, Hungary 1983
[18] 11 ♘xf6+ ♕xf6 12 c4 ♕g6 13 f3 ♗e7 14 cb ♘d4 15 ♗e3 0-0! ∞ Anand-Hergott, Thessaloniki Ol 1984
[19] 11 ... ♘xd5 12 ed ♘d4 13 cb ±
11 ... b4 12 ♘xf6+ (12 ♕a4!? ♗d7 13 ♘b5!) 12 ... ♕xf6 13 ♘c2 ♕g6 14 f3 ♖b8 15 ♘e3 ♗e7 16 g3 ± Petrushin-Semenyuk, USSR 1976
[20] 12 ... ♘e7 13 ♗e3 ♖b8 14 ♗c4 ♕a5+ 15 b4 ♕xa3 16 ♗c1 ♘c3 17 ♕d2 ♕a4 18 ♗b3 ±± Mikhalchishin-Timoshchenko, USSR 1973
[21] 13 ... ab 14 ♘xb5 ± Belyavsky-van der Wiel, Moscow IZ 1982
[22] 14 ... ♕a5+ 15 ♔e2 ♖c8 16 ♕d3 ± Kruppa-Vizhmanavin, Irkutsk 1986
14 ... ♖c8! ± (15 ♘b6?! d5 16 ♘xc8 ♘xc8 ∞) Kasparov
[23] 11 ♗xf6 gf 12 ♕f3 (12 c4 ♗b7! 13 ♗d3 bc 14 ♘xc4 d5 = Smyslov-Sveshnikov, Lvov 1978, and Ljubojević-Tseshkovsky, Riga IZ 1979) 12 ... f5 13 ef ♗xf5 14 ♗d3 ♗e6 15 0-0 0-0 16 c4 f5 17 ♖fd1 ♔h8 (17 ... e4 18 ♕e3 ∞ Yudasin-Gorelov, USSR 1982) 18 cb d5 ∞ Lanc-Kouatly, Trnava 1986
[24] 11 ... d5 12 ed ♕xd5 13 f3 ♗f5 (13 ... e4? 14 ♗xf6) 14 ♗xf6 gf 15 ♗xf5 ♕xd1+ 16 ♖xd1 ♘xf5 17 c3 ♘e3! = Gurieli-Fatalibekova, USSR 1985
[25] 12 ♕e2 ♘d7 13 b4 f6 14 ♗d2 f5 15 c4 ♘f6 16 f3 fe 17 fe ♘c6 18 cb ♘d4 19 ♕e3 ab 20 ♘xb5 0-0 ∞ Chiburdanidze-Zaichik, USSR 1979
[26] 13 ♕f3 f5 14 0-0-0 ♖c8 ∞ Abramović-Vukić, Bela Crkva 1982
[27] 15 ♗xe4 ♗xe4 16 ♕xe4 ♕d5 17 ♕xd5 ♘xd5 = Ivanović-Vukić, Yugoslav Ch 1982
[28] 13 ♕f3 f5 14 ef ♗xf5 15 ♗d3 ♗e6 16 0-0 0-0 ∞/= Popović-Kouatly, Cannes 1986, and Popović-Kouatly, Paris 1986-87
13 ♗d3 ♗b7 14 ♕e2 d5 15 0-0-0!? Adorjan, Horvath
[29] 14 ... d5 15 ed ±
14 ... ♖g8 18 ♘e3 d5 19 ♕f3 ± Pritchett-Littlewood, England 1985
14 ... ♕b6 15 ♘e3 d5 16 ♕f3 0-0-0 17 0-0 d4 ±/∞ Grünfeld-Kouatly, Brussels 1985
[30] 12 ... ♗g5 13 a4 (13 h4 ♗h6 14 g4 ♗f4 ∞) 13 ... ba (13 ... ♖b8 14 ab ab 15 ♗d3 ±) 14 ♖xa4 a5 (14 ... ♖b8 15 ♘cb4 ♘xb4 16 cb! ±) 15 ♗c4 ♖b8 16 b3 ±/=

[31] 14 ... ♘e7 15 a4 ba 16 ♘cb4 ♗b7 17 ♕xa4 ♘xd5 18 ed ± Geller-Polgar, Baden-Baden 1985
14 ... ♗e6 15 a4 ba 16 ♘db4 ♘xb4 17 ♘xb4 ♗d7 18 ♖xa6 ♗e7 19 ♕e2 ♔h8 20 ♗c4 ± McCarthy-Belopolsky, New York 1985; 16 ... ♘e7!?
14 ... a5 15 ♕e2 b4 ±/=
[32] 9 ... ♕xf6 10 ♘d5 ♕d8 11 c4 ± (11 ... b4 12 ♕a4 ♗d7 13 ♘b5!)
[33] 11 c4 ♕a5+ 12 ♕d2 ♕xd2+ 13 ♔xd2 ♔d8 ∓
11 c3 ♗g7 (11 ... fe? 12 ♗xb5! ab 13 ♘xb5 ± A.Rodriguez-Georgadze, Tbilisi 1977, and Timoshchenko-Kishnev, Moscow Ch 1985) 12 ef ♗xf5 – 11 cf
11 ♘xb5 ab 12 ♗xb5 ♗b7 (12 ... ♗d7 13 ef ♗g7 14 a4 ♘d4 = Nunn-Adorjan, Skara 1980) 13 ef ♖a5 14 ♕d3 (14 a4 ♖b5 15 ab ♘d4 16 ♘e3 ♖g8 17 0-0 ♗h6 18 ♘g4 ♕h4 Sveshnikov) 14 ... ♗g7 15 ♕c4 ♖xb5 16 ♕xb5 ♕a5+ 17 ♕xa5 ♘xa5 ½-½ Waldmann-Hardicsay, Budapest 1982
[34] 12 ... ♕g5? 13 ♘dc7+ ♔d8 14 ♕d5! ±
12 ... ♖a7 13 ♘xa7 ♘xa7 14 ef ±/∞
12 ... ♕a5+ 13 c3 ♕a4 14 ♘bc7+ ♔d8 15 ♘xa8 ♕xa8 ∞
[35] 14 c4 ♖xc4 15 ♕h5 ♘d4 (15 ... ♖xe4+!? 16 ♔f1 ♕h4 Chiburdanidze-Maksimović, Smederevska Palanka 1983) 16 ♕xf7+ ♔c6 ∓ Christoffel-Lobron, Hastings 1977-78
[36] 15 ... ♘e7 16 ♕xf7 ♔c6 17 c4 ♕d7 18 ♘a8 ♘g6 19 ♘b4+ ♔b7 20 ♕d5+ ♔b8 21 ♘c6+ ♔xa8 22 ♕b5 ♔b7 23 ♕a5+ ♕a6 24 ♕c7 ♔b7 ½-½ Grünfeld-Fleck, Lugano 1980
[37] ♕xf7+ ♔c6 17 ♘b4+ ♔b7 18 ♘b5+ ♕d7 19 ♕d5+ ♔b6 ∓ Szabo-Horvath, Oberwart 1979
[38] 20 ♘xc7 ♔xc7 ∞ Perenyi-Horvath, Zamardi 1979
[39] 12 ♕f3 ♘d4 13 ♘c7+ ♕xc7 14 ♕xa8+ ♔e7 15 c3 ♘b4! 16 cb ♗h6! ∓ Adorjan, Horvath
12 ♗d3 e4! 13 ♕e2 ♘d4 14 ♕e3 ♗g7 ∓ ECO
[40] 12 ... ♗e6 13 ♘c2 ♗h6!? 14 a4 (14 g3!?) 14 ... 0-0! ∞/= Sigurjonsson-Sax, Ljubljana/Portorož 1977 (therefore 11 c3 ♗g7 12 ef, etc)
[41] 14 ... ♗g6 15 h4 h6 16 g4 ±
14 ... ♗e4 15 ♗d3 ±
[42] 15 ... ♘e7 16 ♘xe7+ ♕xe7 17 ♕h5 h6 18 ♗e4 ♖ac8 19 0-0 ± Garcia Martinez-Remon, Bayamo 1986
[43] 16 ... ♖a7!? intending ... ♖af7 Simić
[44] 17 ... ♗e5 18 g4 ± Donchev-Kouatly, Bulgaria v France 1985
17 ... ♘e5 18 ♘f4 ±
[45] 18 ♗b3 ♔h8 19 ♘f4 ±
18 ♘f4 ♗f7 19 ♗b3 d5 20 ♕g5 ± Honfi-Welin, Wroclaw 1984
[46] Honfi-Muse, Budapest 1986

Sicilian XXIV (Sveshnikov) 1 e4 c5 2 ♘f3 ♘c6 3 d4 cd 4 ♘xd4 ♘f6
5 ♘c3 e5 6 ♘db5 d6 7 ♗g5 a6 8 ♘a3 b5 9 ♗xf6 gf 10 ♘d5 f5 *continued*

	11	12	13	14	15	16	17	18	19	
10	ef	c3	♘c2	♘ce3[47]	g3	♘xd5	♗g2	0-0	♕e2	±/∞
	♗xf5	♗g7	♘e7	♗e6	♘xd5[48]	0-0	a5	♖b8	♕d7[49]	
11	♗d3	♕h5[50]	g3[51]	c3[53]	♗xe4	♕xh7	♕h6	♔f1	♘f6+	±
	♗e6	♖g8	♘d4[52]	fe	♗g4	♖g7	♘f3+	♖g5[54]	♔e7[55]	
12	...	...	0-0	c4	♗xc4	♖ac1	b3	♖fd1[58]	♕h4	±
	...	♗g7	f4	bc[56]	0-0	♖b8[57]	♕d7	♔h8[59]	♗xd5[60]	

[47] 14 ♘xe7 ♗xc2 15 ♕xc2 ♕xe7 16 a4 0-0 = Anka-Hardicsay, Budapest 1986

[48] 15 ... 0-0 16 ♗g2 ♖a7 17 0-0 ♘xd5 18 ♗xd5! ± Kir.Georgiev-Donchev, Bulgarian Ch 1986

[49] 20 ♖ad1 f5 21 f4 ♕f7 (21 ... ♔h8 22 ♔h1 e4 23 ♖d2 ♕f7 24 ♖fd1 ♖fc8 25 ♗h3 ± Moiseyev-Filipenko, USSR 1986) 21 ♖d2 e4 22 ♖fd1 ♖fc8 ±/∞ Yakovich-Sveshnikov, Sochi 1986

[50] 12 0-0 ♗xd5 (12 ... ♗g7 13 ♕h5 – 12 ♕h5) 13 ed ♘e7 14 ♘xb5 (14 ♕h5 e4 15 ♗e2 ♗g7 16 c3 0-0 ∞ Krasenkov-Gorelov, USSR 1982; 14 c4 ♗g7 15 ♕d2 e4 16 ♗e2 bc 17 ♘xc4 0-0 ∞ Hübner-Sax, Tilburg 1979) 14 ... ♗g7 15 ♘c3 e4 16 ♗c4 ∞ Ostos-Kouatly, Malta Ol 1980, and Short-van der Wiel, Brussels 1987

[51] 13 c3 ♗xd5 (13 ... ♖xg2 14 ♕f3 ♖g4 15 h3 ♖g8 16 ef ± Stoica-Nicolaide, Romanian Ch 1983) 14 ed ♘e7 15 g3! e4 16 ♗e2 h6 17 f4 ± Gasanov-Krasenkov, USSR 1985

[52] 13 ... h6 14 c3 ♗xd5 15 ed ♘e7 16 ♕d1 ± Sideif Zade-Dolmatov, USSR 1979

  13 ... ♗g5 14 ♕d1 ♗xd5 15 ed ♘e7 16 c3 ± Sideif Zade-Yurtayev, USSR 1980

[53] 14 0-0-0 ♖c8 ∞ Liang-Kindermann, Chicago 1983

[54] 18 ... ♖g6 19 ♕e3 ♗h6 20 ♕d3 ±

[55] 19 ... ♕xf6? 20 ♗c6+! ±± Klovans-Taborov, Kostroma 1985

  19 ... ♔e7 20 ♕h8 ♘d2+ 21 ♔g2 ♘xe4 22 ♘xe4 ± Klovans

[56] 14 ... b4 15 ♘c2 ♖b8 16 b3 0-0 17 a3 ± Prandstetter-Timoshchenko, Decin 1978

  14 ... 0-0 15 cb ♘d4 16 ♘c2! ♘xc2 17 ♗xc2 ab 18 ♗b3 ±

[57] 16 ... ♘d4 17 ♘c2 ±

  16 ... ♘e7 17 ♘c7 ♕xc7 18 ♗xe6 ♕b7 19 ♗b3 ±

[58] 18 ♕g5!? f6 (18 ... ♔h8? 19 ♘f6 ♕e7 20 ♘xh7 ♔xh7 21 ♕h5+ ♔g8 22 ♗xe6; 18 ... ♗xd5?! 19 ♗xd5 ♘b4 20 ♖fd1 ♘xa2 21 ♖c6 Lepeshkin) 19 ♕h5 ♘a5 20 ♗xa6 ♗xd5 21 ed f5 (Sax-Kindermann, Plovdiv 1983) 22 ♘c2 ± Kindermann

[59] 18 ... ♘d4 19 ♘c2 ♘xc2 20 ♖xc2 ♔h8 21 h3 f5 22 ♘c3 ♗xc4 23 bc ♖bc8 24 ♘d5 ♕e6 25 f3 ± Arseniev-Vaiser, USSR 1979

[60] 19 ... ♖g8 20 ♔h1 ♘d4 21 ♘c2 ± Dvoiris-Vaiser, Sochi 1981

  19 ... f5 20 ♗xf4 ±

  19 ... ♗xd5 20 ♗xd5 ♘d4 21 ♔f1 ± Klovans-Schaetzel, corr. 1986; 21 ♖c4 ± Sveshnikov-Vizhmanavin, Moscow 1987

Sicilian XXV   1 e4 c5 2 ♘f3 e6 3 d4 cd 3 ♘xd4

	4	5	6	7	8	9	10	11	12	
1	...	♘c3[1]	e5	♕g4	♗h6	♗xf8	♕g3	♘e2	0-0-0[4]	±
	♘f6	♗b4	♘d5[2]	0-0[3]	g6	♕xf8	♕c5	♘c6	♘xc3[5]	
2	...	...	...	♗d2	bc	♕g4	♗h6	♗d3[9]	ed	±
	...	...	...	♘xc3[6]	♗e7[7]	0-0[8]	g6	d6[10]	♕xd6[11]	
3	...	...	♘xc6[12]	e5	♘e4[13]	f4	♗d3	a3[15]	c4[16]	∞
	...	♘c6	bc	♘d5	♕c7[14]	♕b6	♗a6	♗e7	f5[17]	
4	...	...	...	...	...	...	c4	♔e2	♘f2[20]	±/∞
	...	...	...	...	...	...	♗b4+[18]	f5[19]	♗a6[21]	
5	...	...	♘db5	♗f4	♘c7+	♕f3	0-0-0[24]	bc	♘xd5	∞
	...	...	♗b4[22]	♘xe4	♔f8[23]	d5	♗xc3[25]	e5[26]	♘g5[27]	
6	...	...	...	a3	♘xc3	ed	♗d3	0-0	♘e2	±
	...	...	...	♗xc3+	d5	ed[28]	0-0[29]	d4	h6[30]	

1 5 ♗d3 ♘c6 6 ♘xc6 bc (6 ... dc 7 0-0 e5 =) 7 0-0 d5 =

2 6 ... ♘e4 7 ♕g4 ♘xc3 (7 ... ♕a5 8 ♕xe4 ♗xc3+ 9 bc ♕xc3+ 10 ♔d1 ♕xa1 11 ♘b5 d5 12 ♕b4 ♘a6 13 ♘d6+ ♔d7 14 ♗b5+! ♔c7 15 ♘e8+! ♔b6 16 ♗xa6+ ♔xa6 17 ♘c7 mate!) 8 ♕xg7 ♖f8 9 a3 ♘b5+ 10 ab ♘xd4 11 ♗g5! ♕b6 12 ♗h6 ♕xb4+ 13 c3 ± Szabo-Mikenas, Kemeri 1939

3 7 ... ♔f8 8 a3 ♗a5 9 ♗d2 ♘xc3 10 bc ♕c7 11 ♕g3 ♘c6 12 f4 ± Boleslavsky

4 12 h4!? ♗a5 (12 ... ♘xc3 13 bc ♗a5 14 f4 ±) 13 ♘h3 ♘xc3 14 ♘xc3 ♗xe5+ 15 ♕xe5 ♘xe5 16 ♗e2 ± Petrushin-Panchenko, USSR 1985

5 13 ♘xc3 ♕xe5 (13 ... ♗xc3 14 ♕xc3 ♕xc3 15 bc ♘xe5 16 ♗e2 ♔f8 17 h4 ±/± Prandstetter-Schwaninger, Oberwart 1986) 14 ♕xe5 ♘xe5 15 ♗e2 d5 16 ♘b5 ± Mestel-Hodgson, Hastings 1986-87

6 7 ... ♗xc3 8 bc 0-0 9 ♗d3 d6 10 ♕h5 g6 11 ♕e2 ±/± Vogt-Ermenkov, Berlin 1982

7 8 ... ♗a5 9 ♕g4 0-0 10 ♗d3 d6 (10 ... ♕c7 11 0-0 ♕xe5 12 ♖ae1 ±) 11 ♘f3! g6 12 h4 de 13 h5 f5 14 ♗xf5! ± Wagman-Barle, Biel 1981

8 9 ... g6 10 ♗d3 (10 h4!?) 10 ... ♘c6 11 ♘xc6 dc 12 0-0 ♕a5 13 ♖fe1 ♗d7 14 ♕f4 ± Mnatsakanian-Pavlenko, USSR 1982

9 11 h4!? ♕a5 12 ♕g3 ± Wedberg-Pokojowczyk, Copenhagen 1984

10 11 ... ♖e8 12 ♘b5 ♘c6 13 ♕g3 ♕a5 14 0-0 a6 15 ♘d6 ± Hazai-Plachetka, Kecskemet 1983

11 13 ♗xf8 ♗xf8 14 0-0 ± Popović-Barlov, Bor 1985

12 6 ♗g5 h6 7 ♗h4 ♗e7 =
6 ♗f4 ♗b4 7 ♘b5; 6 ... d6 7 ♘db5 – 6 ♘db5
6 ♗e2 ♗b4 7 0-0 ♗xc3 8 bc ♘xe4 9 ♗d3 d5 10 ♗a3 ♕a5 11 ♕c1 ♘xd4 (11 ... ♘xc3 12 ♘b3 ♕c7 13 ♕e3 ∞∞ Bielczyk-Tisdall, Gausdal 1983) 12 cd ♗d7 = Kupreichik-Taimanov, USSR 1976

6 g3 d5 7 ed ♘xd5 8 ♗g2 ♘db4 (8 ... ♗b4 9 0-0 ♘xc3 =) 9 ♘xc6 ♕xd1+ = Jansa-Sveshnikov, Sochi 1980

13 8 ♘xd5 cd 9 ♗d3 ♕c7 10 ♕e2 (10 ♗f4 ♖b8) 10 ... ♗b4+ 11 ♔f1 ♖b8 12 ♗f4 (12 h4? ♗c3!) 12 ... ♗e7 13 c3 d6 14 h4 f6 ∞/∓ Wedberg-Birnboim, Randers 1982

14 8 ... f5 9 ef ♘xf6 10 ♘d6+ ♗xd6 11 ♕xd6 ± Dolmatov-Arnason, Groningen 1977-78, and Watson-Lawton, Southampton 1986

15 11 ♗xa6!? ♕xa6 12 ♕e2 Milovanović-Vukić, Tuzla 1983

16 12 ♕e2 ♗xd3 13 ♕xd3 f5 14 ♘f2 ♗c5 15 0-0 a5 16 c4 ♘e3 17 b4 ∞ Tseshkovsky-Sveshnikov, USSR Ch 1978

17 13 ♘f2 ♘e3 14 ♕f3 ♘xc4 15 ♕e2 ♕b3 16 0-0 ♗c5 ∞∞ Schmidt-Tiagunov, corr. 1985

18 10 ... ♘e3 11 ♕d3 ♗b4+ 12 ♗d2 ♖b8 13 b3 ±/± Tringov-Hübner, Lucerne Ol 1982, and Timman-Lobron, Wijk aan Zee 1985

19 11 ... ♗a6 12 ♔f3! f5 13 ef ♘xf6 14 c5 ♕a5 15 ♘xf6+ gf 16 ♗xa6 ♕xa6 17 ♕d4 ± Panchenko-Yailian, Aktubinsk 1985

20 12 ef ♘xf6 13 ♗e3 ♕a5 (13 ... ♕d8!? 14 ♘d6+ ♗xd6 15 ♕xd6 ♕e7 ±/± Martin Gonzalez-Li Zunian, Biel IZ 1985) 14 ♘xf6+ gf 15 ♔f2 0-0 16 ♗d3 ♖f7 17 a3 ♗f8 ∞ Fernandez Garcia-Kouatly, Pontevedra 1986, and Tseshkovsky-Kouatly, Trnava 1986

21 12 ... ♗c5 13 ♘d3 ♘e3 14 ♕b3 ♘xf1 15 ♕xb6 ♗xb6 16 ♖xf1 ± Kholmov-Sveshnikov, Lvov 1983, Nunn-Kouatly, Lucerne 1985, and A.Ivanov-Gorelov, Minsk 1985
12 ... ♗a6 13 ♔f3 ♘e7 14 ♗e3 ♗c5 15 ♗xc5 ♕xc5 16 ♕d6 ♕b6 17 b3 c5 ±/∞ Chandler-Kasparov, Hamburg 1985 (simul), and Mokry-Vukić, Zenica 1986

22 6 ... d6 7 ♗f4 e5 8 ♘d5!? (8 ♗g5 – Sveshnikov Variation) 8 ... ♘xd5 9 ed ef 10 dc bc 11 ♕f3 d5 12 0-0-0! Zaitsev

23 8 ... ♔e7 9 ♕f3 d5 10 0-0-0 (10 ♘xa8? ♕a5) 10 ... ♗xc3 11 bc g5 12 ♗g3 f5 13 ♗c4 ± A.Kuzmin-Timoshchenko, USSR 1984, and Gorelov-Timoshchenko, USSR 1985

24 10 ♘xa8? e5 ∓

25 10 ... ♘xc3 11 bc ♗a3+ 12 ♔b1 e5 13 ♘xa8 ef 14 ♕xd5 ♕e7 15 ♕b3 ♗d6 16 ♗c4 ± Kapengut-Begun, USSR 1985

26 11 ... ♖b8 12 ♘xd5 ed 13 ♕xe4 de 14 ♖xd8+ ♘xd8 15 ♗xb8 a6 16 ♗c4 ♗e6 17 ♖d1 ♔e7 18 ♗d6+ ♔f6 19 ♖d4 ± Oll-Shabanov, Kostroma 1985
11 ... g5 12 ♕xe4 ♕xc7 13 ♗xc7 de 14 ♗b5 ♔e7 (14 ... ♔g7 15 h4 g4 16 ♖he1) 15 h4 g4 16 ♗d6+ ♔e8 17 ♖d4 ± Mihalko-Decsi, corr. 1985

27 13 ♕e3? ef 14 ♕c5+ ♔e8 ∓ Ernst-Hector, Swedish Ch 1985, and Gonzales-Li Zunian, Dubai Ol 1986
13 ♗xg5 ♕xg5+ 14 ♖d2 ∞

28 9 ... ♘xd5 10 ♗d2 ♕h4 (10 ... ♘xc3 11 ♗xc3 ♕xd1+ 12 ♖xd1 ± Fischer-Addison, US Ch 1962-63; 10 ... 0-0 11 ♕h5 ♘f6 12 ♕h4 ±) 11 ♕f3 0-0 12 0-0-0 ± Tal-Matulović, Kislovodsk 1966

29 10 ... d4 11 ♘e2 ♗f5 12 0-0 ♗xd3 13 ♕xd3 0-0 14 ♗g5 ± Karpov-Kuzmin, Leningrad 1977

30 12 ... ♗g4 13 f3 ♗h5 14 ♗g5 ± Petrushin-Yailian, Aktubinsk 1985
12 ... h6 13 h3 a6 14 ♖e1 ± Lobron-Gobet, Biel 1984, and Ernst-Prasad, Subotica IZ 1987

Sicilian XXV	1 e4 c5 2 ♘f3 e6 3 d4 cd 3 ♘xd4							*continued*	
	4	5	6	7	8	9	10	11	12
7	...	♘b5[31]	c4	♘1c3[33]	♘a3	cd	ed	♗e2[35]	♗e3![37]	±
	♘c6	d6[32]	♘f6	a6	d5[34]	ed	♘b4	♗c5[36]	♗xe3[38]	
8	...	...	...	...	...	♗e2	0-0	♗e3	♕b3[39]	±/∞
	...	...	...	...	♗e7	0-0	b6	♗b7	♘d7[40]	

[31] **5 c4 ♘f6 6 ♘c3 ♗b4 =**
5 ♘c3 a6 – 4 ... a6
5 g3 ♗c5 6 ♘b3 ♗e7 7 ♗g2 ♘f6 = Campora-Polugayevsky, Amsterdam 1984, and Fernandez Garcia-Kasparov, Dubai Ol 1986

[32] **5 ... ♗c5 6 ♗f4 ♕f6 7 ♕c1 ♔f8 8 ♘1c3 ±** Mokry-Plaskett, Trnava 1984
5 ... ♘f6 6 ♘1c3 – 4 ... ♘f6

[33] 7 ♘5c3 ♗e7 8 ♗e2 0-0 9 0-0 b6 10 ♗f4 ♗b7 11 ♖e1 (11 ♘d2 a6 12 a3 ♘d4 13 ♗d3 ♘d7 = Ljubojević-Karpov, Madrid 1973) 11 ... ♘e5 12 ♗f1 ♘fd7 13 ♘d2 ♗g5 = Ljubojević-Kasparov, Tilburg 1981

[34] 8 ... b6!? 9 ♗e2 ♗b7 10 0-0 ♘b8 11 f3 ♘bd7 12 ♗e3 ♕c7 13 ♖c1 ♗e7 14 ♕d2 0-0 = Barbulescu-Andonov, Dubai Ol 1986 (see also 8 ... ♗e7 9 ♗e2 0-0 10 0-0 b6 11 ♗e3 ♗b7 12 ♖c1?! ♘e5 13 f3 ♘ed7 14 ♕d2 ♕c7)

[35] **11 ♗g5 ♘bxd5 =**
11 ♕a4+ ♗d7 12 ♕b3 ♗c5 ∞∞
11 ♗c4 ♗g4 (11 ... b5? 12 0-0!) 12 ♕d4!? (12 ♗e2 ♗xe2 13 ♕xe2+ ♕e7 = Karpov-Kasparov, match (12) 1985) 12 ... b5 13 ♘cxb5! (13 ♗b3 ♗c5! 14 ♕e5+ ♔f8 ∓) 13 ... ab 14 ♗xb5+ ♗d7 15 d5! ∞∞ Jadoul-Varnusz, Budapest 1985, and Santo Roman-Kouatly, Cannes 1986

[36] 11 ... ♘bxd5 12 0-0 ♗e7 (12 ... ♗xa3? 13 ♕a4+; 12 ... ♘xc3 13 ♕xd8+ ♔xd8 14 bc ±) 13 ♘xd5 ♘xd5 14 ♗f3 ♗e6 15 ♘c2 ±

[37] 12 0-0 0-0 13 ♗f3 ♗f5 ∞∞ Karpov-Kasparov, match (16) 1985

[38] 13 ♕a4+ ♗d7 (13 ... ♘d7 14 ♕xb4 ♗c5 15 ♕e4+ ± Karpov-van der Wiel, Brussels 1986) 14 ♕xb4 ♕b6 15 ♕xb6 ♗xb6 16 0-0 ♗c5 17 ♘c4 b5 18 ♘e5 ♗d4 ±

[39] **12 f4 ♘b4 13 ♗f3 d5 =** A.Sokolov-Vasyukov, Moscow Ch 1982
12 ♖c1 ♘e5 13 f3 (13 ♕d4 ♘ed7 14 ♖fd1 ♖e8 ∞/= Tseshkovsky-Ribli, Riga IZ 1979) 13 ... ♘ed7 14 ♕d2 ♕c7 15 ♖fd1 ♖ac8 16 ♗f1 ♖fe8 (16 ... ♕b8 17 ♘ab1 ♔h8 18 a3 ♗d8 19 ♕f2 ♖g8 20 ♘d2 g5 ∞ Barbulescu-Andonov, Dubai Ol 1986) 17 ♕f2 ♕b8 18 ♔h1 ♗d8 19 ♖c2 ♗c7 20 ♖cd2 ♔h8 ∞ Yudasin-Chekhov, Lvov 1983

[40] **12 ... ♘a5** 13 ♕xb6 (13 ♕c2 ♖c8 ∞) 13 ... ♘xe4 14 ♘xe4 ♗xe4 15 ♕xd8 ♗xd8 16 ♖ad1 (Karpov-Kasparov, match (3) 1984-85) 16 ... ♘b7 ±/=
12 ... ♘d7 13 ♖fd1 (13 ♖ac1 ♘c5 14 ♕d1!? ♘b4 15 ♕d2) 13 ... ♘c5 14 ♕c2 (14 ♗xc5? bc 15 ♕xb7? ♘a5) 14 ... ♗f6 (14 ... ♕c7 15 ♖ac1 ♖ac8 16 ♘ab1 ±/∞ Jadoul-Karpov, Brussels 1986) 15 ♖ac1 (15 f3 ♗e5 ∞ Lobron-Kurajica, Indonesia 1983) 15 ... ♘b4 (15 ... ♗xc3 16 ♕xc3 ♘xe4 17 ♕b3 ♖b8 18 ♗xb6 ± Kavalek-Barczay, Wijk aan Zee 1977) 16 ♕d2 ♗xc3 17 bc ♘xe4 18 ♕b2 ♘c6 19 f3 ♘f6 20 ♗xb6 ♕e7 21 ♘c2 ♖fc8 22 ♕a3 ♘d7 23 ♗f2 ♘c5 = Mokry-Lobron, Reggio Emilia 1984-85

Sicilian XXVI (Kan)	1 e4 c5 2 ♘f3 e6 3 d4 cd 4 ♘xd4 a6								
	5	6	7	8	9	10	11	12	13
1	c4[1]	♘c3	♗d3[2]	0-0	bc	f4	fe	♘c2	♘e3	=
	♘f6	♗b4	♕c7[3]	♗xc3[4]	d6	e5	de	♗e6	♘bd7[5]	
2	♗d3	♘xc6	♘d2[8]	♕h5	♘c4	♗g5	♕e2	♗h4	0-0-0[9]	±
	♘c6[6]	dc[7]	e5	♗d6	♗c7	♘f6	h6	♕e7	♗e6[10]	
3	...	♘b3	♕e2	♗e3	♕xe3	♘c3	0-0-0	f4	♖hg1	±
	♗c5	♗a7[11]	♘c6	♗xe3	d6[12]	♘f6	0-0[13]	♕c7	b5[14]	
4	...	0-0	c4	♘c3	♗g5[16]	♕d2	♖ad1	b3	♗b1	±
	♘f6	d6[15]	g6	♗g7	0-0	♘bd7	♖e8	♕c7	b6[17]	
5	...	...	...	♘c3	♕e2[18]	f4	♘f3	f5	♕f2	±
	...	...	♗e7	0-0	♗d7[19]	♘c6	e5	♘d4	♘xf3+[20]	

	5	6	7	8	9	10	11	12	13	
6	...	...	...	♘c3	b3[21]	♗b2	♕e2	♘xc6	♖ae1!	±
	...	...	b6	♗b7	♗e7[22]	0-0	♘c6	♗xc6	♖e8[23]	
7	...	...	...	...	f4	♘xc6	♕e2	♔h1	b3	±
	...	...	...	...	♘c6[24]	♗xc6	♗e7	0-0	♕c7[25]	

[1] **5 g3 d5 =**
5 ♗e2 ♘f6 6 ♘c3 ♗b4 =

[2] **7 ♕f3 ♘c6 8 ♗c2 d5 =**
7 ♘c2 ♗xc3+ 8 bc ♕a5 9 ♕d3 ♕e5 10 f3 d5 ∞
7 ♗d2 0-0 8 e5 ♗xc3 9 ♗xc3 ♘e4 10 ♗b4 d6 =
7 e5 ♘e4 8 ♕g4 ♘xc3 9 a3 ♗f8 10 bc ♕a5 11 ♕g3 d6 12 ed ♗xd6 13 ♕xd6 ♕xc3+ 14 ♗d2 ♕xa1+ 15 ♔e2 ♕b2 16 ♔e3 ♘c6 17 ♘xc6 ♕b6+ 18 ♕d4 ♕xc6 19 ♕xg7 ♕c5+ = Berczy-Neistadt, corr. 1959

[3] **7 ... ♘c6 8 ♗xc6 (8 ♘c2 ♗xc3+ 9 bc d5 =) 8 ... dc 9 e5 ♕a5 (9 ... ♘d7 10 f4 ♘c5 11 ♗c2 ♕xd1+ 12 ♔xd1 ± ECO) 10 ef ♗xc3+ ⁻11 bc ♕xc3+ 12 ♗d2 ♕xd3 13 fg ♖g8 14 ♗h6 ♕c3+ 15 ♔f1 ∞** Karadzić-Honfi, Bajmok 1975, and Poulsen-Farago, Svendborg 1981

[4] **8 ... 0-0 9 ♗g5 ♗e7 10 ♕e2 d6 11 ♔h1 ♘c6 (11 ... b5 12 f4) 12 ♘xc6 bc 13 c5! ±** Miles-Martinović, Amsterdam 1985
8 ... ♘c6 9 ♘f3 0-0 10 ♗d2 b6 11 ♖c1 ♕b8 12 ♕e2 ± Karpov-Miles, Brussels 1986

[5] **14 ♗a3 ♘c5 =** Velimirović-Martinović, Yugoslav Ch 1986

[6] **5 ... b5 6 0-0 ♗b7 7 ♕e2 ♘e7 8 a4 ±**
5 ... ♘e7 6 0-0 ♘bc6 7 ♘xc6 ♘xc6 8 ♕g4 ♘e5 9 ♕g3 ±
5 ... g6 6 c4 ♗g7 7 ♗e3 ♘e7 (7 ... ♘f6 8 ♘c3 d6 – 5 ... ♘f6) 8 ♘c3 0-0 9 0-0 d5 10 ed (10 cd ed 11 ♖c1) 10 ... ed 11 ♖e1 h6 12 ♖c1 ± Ermenkov-Olafsson, Malta Ol 1980

[7] **6 ... bc 7 0-0 d5 (7 ... g6 8 e5 ♗g7 9 f4 ±** van der Wiel-Anand, Thessaloniki Ol 1984) **8 c4 ♘f6 9 ♘c3 ♗e7 10 ♕c2 (10 cd cd 11 ed ed 12 ♕a4+ ±** Fischer-Petrosian, match 1971) **10 ... h6 11 cd cd 12 ed ed 13 ♗e3 0-0 14 ♖fd1 ±** Zaitsev-Palacios, Havana 1983

[8] **7 f4 e5 8 f5 ♘f6 9 ♕e2 b5 10 a4 ♗b7 11 0-0 ±** Borngasser-Miles, England 1978

[9] **13 0-0 g5 14 ♗g3 h5 ∞** Ligterink-Miles, Lone Pine 1979

[10] **14 f4 ±** Tseshkovsky-Miles, Bled/Portorož 1979

[11] **6 ... ♗b6 7 ♕e2 ♘c6 8 ♗e3 ♘f6 9 ♘c3 ♗xe3 – 6 ... ♗a7**

[12] **9 ... ♘f6 10 e5 ♘g4 11 ♕g3 ±**
9 ... ♘ge7 10 ♘c3 0-0 11 0-0-0 ♕c7 12 f4 d6 13 ♕h3 ♘b4 14 ♖hf1 ± Korolev-Batakov, corr. 1984

[13] **11 ... b5 12 ♖d2 0-0 13 ♖hd1 ♕c7 14 f4 ±** Byrne-Larsen, Biel IZ 1976

[14] **11 ... e5 12 ♗e2 0-0 13 f4 ±** Psakhis-Vizhmanavin, Moscow Ch 1981
14 g4 b4 15 g5 ♘e8 16 ♘e2 ± Arnason-Suetin, Sochi 1980, and Arnason-Kirov, Plovdiv 1986

[15] **6 ... ♕c7 7 ♗e2 d6 – 6 ... d6**

[16] **9 ♗e3 0-0 10 ♗e2 (10 ♖c1 ♘bd7 11 ♕e2 d5 12 ♘b3 de 13 ♘xe4 ±** Grünfeld-Gheorghiu, Riga IZ 1979) **10 ... ♘bd7 11 ♕d2 d5 12 ed ed 13 cd ♘b6 14 ♖fd1 ♘bxd5 15 ♘xd5 ♘xd5 (15 ... ♕xd5 16 ♗f3 ±) 16 ♘b3 ±** Marjanović-Gheorghiu, Skopje 1984

[17] **14 ♘de2 ±** Tompa-Bellon, Metz 1985, and Tompa-Plachetka, Malmö 1985-86

[18] **9 b3 ♘bd7 10 ♗b2 g6!? 11 ♔h1 ♖e8 12 f4 e5 ∞** Ermenkov-Gheorghiu, Baden-Baden 1985
9 ♔h1 ♘c6 (9 ... b6 10 f4 ♗b7 – 7 ... b6) 10 ♘xc6 bc 11 b3 ♘d7 12 ♗b2 c5 13 f4 ± Chandler-Gheorghiu, Vienna 1986

[19] **9 ... b6 10 f4 ♗b7 – 7 ... b6**
9 ... ♖e8?! 10 f4 ± Sax-Fedorowicz, New York 1986
9 ... ♘bd7 10 f4 ♕c7 11 ♔h1 b6 12 ♗d2 g6 13 ♖ac1 ♗b7 14 b4 ± Commons-Peev, Plovdiv 1976

[20] **14 gf! ±** Fedorowicz-Miles, Lone Pine 1980

[21] **9 ♕e2 g6 (9 ... ♘c6 10 ♘xc6 ♗xc6 11 b3 ♗e7 – 9 b3) 10 f4 (10 b3 – 9 b3) 10 ... ♗g7 11 f5 ♕e7 12 fe fe 13 e5 de 14 ♘b3 ♘bd7 15 ♗g5 ∞∞** Short-Ionescu, Dubai Ol 1986

[22] **9 ... ♘bd7 10 f4 ♕c7 (10 ... ♗e7 11 ♗b2 0-0 12 f4 ±) 11 ♗b2 ♗e7 12 ♖ad1 0-0 13 ♗b1 (13 f4 e5 14 fe ♘xe5 ∞** Seitaj-Gheorghiu, Thessaloniki Ol 1984) **13 ... ♖e8 14 ♘f3! ♕c7 15 ♕d2 ♗f8 16 ♖fe1 ±** Fedorowicz-Ionescu, Dubai Ol 1986

[23] **14 f4 ±** Ermenkov-Gheorghiu, Prague Z 1985

[24] **9 ... ♗e7 and now:**
10 ♗e3 ♘c6 (10 ... 0-0 11 e5! de 12 fe ♘fd7 13 ♖xf7! ♖xf7 14 ♘xe6 ♕c8 18 ♕h5 ± Smagin-S.Salov, corr. 1984) **11 ♘xc6 ♗xc6 12 e5 de 13 fe ♘d7 14 ♕g4 g6 ∞** Kindermann-Gheorghiu, Zürich 1984
10 ♔h1 0-0 11 ♕e2 ♖e8?! (11 ... ♘c6 12 ♘xc6 – 9 ... ♘c6) 12 ♘f3 intending 13 e5 ± Sax-Bellon, Dubai Ol 1986

[25] **14 ♗b2 ♖ad8 15 ♖ad1 (15 ♖ae1 ♗b7 16 ♗b1 ♘d7 17 ♕h5 ±** Nunn-Gheorghiu, Biel 1983) **15 ... g6 16 ♗b1 h5 17 ♖d3 (intending 18 ♕xh5!) 17 ... e5 18 fe de 19 ♖xd8 ♖xd8 20 ♘d5 ±** Matulović-Tringov, Vrnjačka Banja 1986

Sicilian XXVII (Kan)   1 e4 c5 2 Nf3 e6 3 d4 cd 4 Nxd4 a6 5 Nc3

	5	6	7	8	9	10	11	12	13	
1	...	Nxc6!	e5	f4	ed	Ne4	Bd3	0-0	Qe2	±
	Nc6[1]	bc	Qc7[2]	d5[3]	Bxd6	Ne7[5]	Nf6	0-0	Nxe4[6]	
2	...	g3	Ne2	Bg2	0-0	h3[8]	f4	g4	a3	∞
	Qc7	Bb4	Nf6	Be7	Nc6	d6	0-0	b5[9]	Rb8[10]	
3	...	Bd3	0-0	Kh1	Nxc6	f4	e5	Qe2[13]	Bd2	∞
	...	Nf6[11]	Be7[12]	Nc6	bc	d5	Nd7	0-0	Nc5[14]	
4	...	Be2	0-0	Re1[15]	Nxc6	e5	Bd3	Qe2	Be4	±
	...	b5	Bb7	Nc6[16]	dc	Rd8[17]	c5	c4	Bb4[18]	
5	...	...	0-0	Be3	Na4	Nxc6[22]	Nb6	Nxc8	Bxa6	∞
	...	Nf6	Nc6[19]	Bb4[20]	0-0[21]	bc	Rb8	Rfxc8	Rf8![23]	
6	...	...	...	Kh1	Qxd4	Qd3	f4	e5	Qg3[26]	±
	...	...	...	Nxd4[24]	Bc5	b5	h5[25]	Ng4	Bb7[27]	
7	...	...	...	...	Nxc6[28]	f4	e5	bc		∞
	...	...	...	Bb4	bc	0-0[29]	Bxc3[30]	Nd5[31]		
8	...	...	...	...	Bg5	Bxf6	bc	Qd2	ed[34]	±
	...	...	...	...	Bxc3	gf[32]	Ne7[33]	d5	Nxd5[35]	

[1] 5 ... b5 6 Bd3 Bb7 7 0-0 Nc6 (7 ... d6 8 Re1 Nf6 9 a4 b4 10 Na2 ±) 8 Nxc6 Bxc6 9 Qe2 Nf6 10 e5 Nd5 11 Nxd5 Bxd5 12 a4 ± Tal-Ljubojević, Montreal 1979

[2] 7 ... f6 8 Bd3 ±
7 ... Ne7 8 g3 Ng6 9 Qe2 ±
7 ... Qa5 8 f4 Nh6 9 Qd3 (9 Bd3!) 9 ... Rb8 10 Bd2 ± Timman-A.Sokolov, Bugojno 1986

[3] 8 ... f5 9 Be3 Rb8 10 Be2 Rxb2 11 0-0 Ne7 12 Na4 Nd5 13 Bd4 ∞ Lukin-Taimanov, Leningrad 1984

[4] 10 Qg4!? g6 11 Bd2 Nf6 12 Qg5 ± Timman-Polugayevsky, Tilburg 1985

[5] 10 ... Bxf4 11 Bxf4 Qxf4 12 Qd4 ±

[6] 13 ... c5 14 Ng5 Bd6 15 b3 h6 16 Nge4 Nxe4 17 Qxe4 f5 18 Qc4 ± Ulibin-Kalegin, USSR 1987
13 ... Nxe4 14 Qxe4 g6 15 Be3 Bf6 16 Rab1 ± Malanyuk-Karpov, USSR Ch 1983

[7] 6 ... Nf6 7 Bg2 Be7 8 0-0 0-0 9 f4 d6 – Scheveningen
6 ... b5?! 7 Bg2 Bb7 8 0-0 Nf6 9 Re1 d6 10 Bg5 Nbd7 11 a4 ba 12 Nd5! ed 13 ed+ Kd8 (A.Ivanov-Sideif Zade, Borzomi 1984) 14 Qe2 Nc8 15 Rxa4 ±

[8] 10 Bf4 d6 11 Qd2 0-0 12 Rad1 Ne5 =
10 Be3 Ng4 11 Bf4 d6 =

[9] 12 ... d5 13 ed Rd8 14 g5 (14 f5!? Cirić-Miles, Dortmund 1976) 14 ... Nxd5 15 Nxd5 ed 16 f5 ±/∞ Inkiov-Pritchett, Dubai Ol 1986

[10] 13 ... Re8!? 14 g5 Nd7 15 f5 Bf8 Panno
13 ... Rb8 14 g5 Nd7 15 f5 (Motwani-Panno, Dubai Ol 1986) 15 ... Re8 intending
... Nde5 ∞

[11] 6 ... b5?! 7 0-0 Bb7 8 Re1 Nc6 (8 ... Bc5 9 Be3 Nf6 10 Ndxb5! ± Keres-Benko, Curaçao C 1962) 9 Nxc6 Bxc6 10 a4 b4 11 Nd5 ± Tal-Gipslis, USSR Ch 1958
6 ... Nc6 7 Nxc6 bc 8 0-0 Nf6 9 Qc2 d5 10 Bg5 Bb7 11 f4 Be7 12 e5 ± Spassky-Petrosian, Palma de Mallorca 1969

[12] 7 ... Bd6!? 8 Nf3 Nc6 9 Qe2 Bg4 10 g3 h5 ∞ Vulfson-Vizhmanavin, USSR 1981

[13] 12 Na4!? intending c4

[14] 14 Bxh7+!? Kxh7 15 Qh5+ Kg8 16 Rf3 f5 17 Rh3 ∞ Ilincić-Dizdarević, Yugoslav Ch 1986

[15] 8 Bf3 Nc6 9 Nxc6 dc 10 g3 Nf6 11 Bg2 e5 12 f4 Rd8 13 Qe2 Bc5+ 14 Kh1 Bd4 15 Bd2 0-0 16 f5 ±/∞ Arnason-Kristiansen, Vejle 1984

[16] 8 ... d6 9 Bh5 g6 10 Bf3 ±
8 ... Nf6 9 Bf3 d6 10 a4 b4 11 Na2 ±
8 ... b4 9 Nd5! ed 10 ed Kd8 (10 ... Ne7 11 Bh5 g6 12 Qf3 Bg7 13 d6! ±) 11 Bh5 Bxd5 (11 ... g6 12 Qf3 ±) 12 Bg5+ Nf6 13 Nf5 Be6 14 Qf3 ±

[17] 10 ... Nd7 11 Bd3 Qg6 12 Qh5 ±

[18] 14 a4 ± Kasparov

[19] 7 ... Bb4 8 Qd3 (8 Bg5!?) 8 ... Nc6 9 Nxc6 dc (9 ... Qxc6 10 e5 ±) 10 f4 ±

[20] 8 ... b5 9 Nxc6 dc 10 f4 ±
8 ... d6 – Scheveningen

[21] 9 ... Ne7?! 10 c4! Nxe4 11 Nb3 Bd6 12 f4 ±
9 ... Bd6 10 Nb6! Rb8 11 g3 Nxe4 12 Nxc6 Qxc6 (12 ... bc 13 Nc4 ±) 13 Bf3 ±

9 ... ♗e7 10 ♘xc6 bc 11 ♘b6 ♖b8 12 ♘xc8 ♕xc8 13 e5 ♘d5 14 ♗c1 ± Thipsay-Taimanov, New Delhi 1982, and Zapata-Taimanov, Titograd 1984

22 10 c4 ♗d6 11 ♘f3 ♘g4 12 ♗b6 ♗xh2+ 13 ♔h1 ♗f4 14 g3 ♗xg3 15 fg ♕xg3 16 ♕e1 ♕h3+ 17 ♔g1 ♘ce5 18 ♗c7 ♘e3 19 ♖f2 ♘5g4 20 ♗f1 ♗xf1 21 ♖xf1 b5 22 ♘b6 ♖a7 23 ♗d6 ♖e8 ∞ Nei-Furman, Tallinn 1971, and Kalinichenko-Tabachenkov, USSR 1986

23 14 ♕d3 ♘g4 15 g3 ♕a5 ∞ Hübner-Ribli, West Germany 1987

14 ♗d3 ♗d6 15 f4 (15 h3 ♗e5 16 c3 ♖xb2 17 ♕c1 ♕b8 18 f4 ♗c7 19 ♖b1 ±/= Stoica-Franzoni, Lucerne 1985; 15 ... ♖xb2 16 ♗d4 ♖bb8 17 ♗xf6 gf ∞ Bozek-Walendowski, Poznan 1986) 15 ... e5 16 f5 ♖xb2 17 g4 ♕a5 18 h4 (18 g5 ♘e8!) 18 ... ♗c5 19 ♗c1 ♖xa2 20 ♖xa2 ♕xa2 21 g5 ♘e8 ∞/= Hartmann-Bischoff, West Germany 1986-87

24 8 ... ♗e7 9 f4 d6 – Scheveningen

25 11 ... ♗b7 12 ♗f3 0-0 (12 ... b4 13 e5 ±; 12 ... e5 13 ♘d5 ±) 13 e5 ♘e8 14 ♘e4 ♗e7 15 a4 ± Stoica-Gavrilakis, Skopje 1984

26 13 ♕h3 ♘h6 (13 ...♘f2+ 14 ♖xf2 ♗xf2 15 ♕f3 ♕a7 16 ♘e4 ♗b6 17 a4 ± Matanović-

Matulović, Yugoslavia 1976) 14 ♘e4 ♗b7 15 ♗f3 ♗e7 16 ♘d6+ ± Marjanović-Matulović, Yugoslavia 1983

27 14 ♗f3 0-0-0 15 a4 ± Zapata-Marjanović, Titograd 1984

28 9 ♕d3 ♕d6! 10 ♘xc6 bc 11 ♘a4 ♕e5! 12 ♗f3 0-0 = Shakarov-Sideif Zade, USSR 1977

9 f4!? ♗xc3 10 bc ♘xe4 11 ♗d3 ∞ Ilincić-Matulović, Vrnjačka Banja 1986

29 10 ... ♗xc3 11 bc ♘xe4 12 ♗a3 ∞; 12 ♕d4 ∞

10 ... d5 11 e5 ♗xc3 (11 ... ♘d7 12 ♘a4 intending c4 ±) 12 bc ♘e4 13 ♗d3 c5 14 c4 ± Marjanović-Matulović, Niš 1983

30 11 ... ♘e8 12 ♘a4 ♗e7 13 b3 ± A.Sokolov-Kirov, Thessaloniki Ol 1984

31 Renet-Taimanov, Montpellier 1986

32 10 ... ♗xd4 11 ♗xd4 ♘xd4 12 ♕xd4 0-0 13 c4 ± Tseshkovsky-Sideif Zade, USSR 1982

33 11 ... b5 12 a4 ±
11 ... d6 12 f4 ♗d7 13 ♖b1 ±

34 13 ♕h6 de 14 ♕xf6 ♘g6 15 f3 e5 16 ♘f5 ♗xf5 17 ♕xf5 e3 ∞ Ivanović-Kurajica, Yugoslav Ch 1978

35 14 c4 ♘f4 15 ♗f3 0-0 16 ♘e2 ♘xe2 17 ♗xe2 ♗g7 18 ♗d3 ♗d7 19 ♖ae1 ± Torre-Belyavsky, Bugojno 1984

Sicilian XXVIII (Scheveningen)   1 e4 c5 2 ♘f3 d6 3 d4 cd 4 ♘xd4 ♘f6 5 ♘c3 e6

	6	7	8	9	10	11	12	13	14	
1	♗e3	♕d2[1]	f3	g4	♘xc6	g5	0-0-0	h4	a3!	∞
	a6	b5[2]	♗b7[3]	♘c6[4]	♗xc6	♘d7	♕c7[5]	♖c8	♗b7[6]	
2	g3	♗g2	0-0	♖e1[9]	♘xc6	a4	a5	♗e3	♘a4	=
	♘c6[7]	♗d7[8]	a6	♗e7	♗xc6	0-0[10]	♘d7	♕c7	♖ae8[11]	

[1] 7 ♕f3 ♕c7 8 0-0-0 ♘c6 9 ♗e2 ♗e7 10 ♕g3 0-0 11 f4 ♗d7 ∞ Ljubojević-Andersson, Las Palmas 1975

[2] 7 ... ♘c6 8 0-0-0 ♗e7 9 ♗e2 0-0 10 f4 ♘xd4 11 ♗xd4 ♘d7 12 ♗f3 ♕c7 13 ♕f2 ± Romero-de Wit, Groningen 1984-85

7 ... ♘bd7 8 f3 b5 (8 ... ♕c7 9 g4 h6 10 h4 ♘e5 11 ♖g1 ♘fd7 12 f4 ± Inkiov-Lukin, Plovdiv 1984) 9 g4 h6 10 0-0-0 ♗b7 11 ♗d3 b4 12 ♘ce2 d5 13 ed ♘xd5 14 ♘f4 ± Nunn-Ftacnik, Naestved 1985

[3] 8 ... b4 9 ♘ce2 d5 10 e5 ♘fd7 11 f4 ♗c5 12 ♘b3 ±

[4] 9 ... b4 10 ♘ce2 d5 11 e5 ♘fd7 12 f4 ♘c5 13 ♘g3 ♘bd7 ∞ Aseyev-Yudasin, Leningrad 1984

[5] 12 ... ♗e7 13 h4 0-0 14 h5 ♘e5 (14 ... ♖e8 15 g6! ±) 15 f4 b4 16 ♘d5! ed 17 ed ± Chandler-Howell, London 1985

[6] Short-Ribli, Montpellier C 1985

[7] 6 ... ♗e7 7 ♗g2 0-0 8 0-0 a6 9 b3 ♕c7 10 ♗b2 ♖d8! ∞ Short-Suba, Dortmund 1983

[8] 7 ... ♗e7 8 0-0 0-0 9 ♘xc6 bc 10 e5 de 11 ♕xd8 ♖xd8 12 ♗xc6 ♖b8 ∞/= Larsen-Andersson, Tilburg 1981

[9] 9 a4 ♗e7 10 ♘xc6 ♗xc6 11 a5 0-0 12 ♗e3 ♘d7 = Mestel-Liberzon, Hastings 1979-80

9 ♘de2 ♗e7 10 h3 b5 11 f4 ♖c8 ∞ van der Wiel-Suetin, Novi Sad 1982

9 ♘xc6 ♗xc6 10 ♕e2 ♕c7 11 a4 ♗e7 12 a5 0-0 = Lanka-Tal, Jurmala 1983

9 b3 ♗e7 10 ♗b2 ♖c8 11 a4 0-0 12 ♘xc6 ♗xc6 = Shamkovich-Sax, Rio de Janeiro IZ 1979

[10] 11 ... ♕c7 12 a5 b5 13 ab ♕xb6 14 ♖a3 ♕b7 = Tal-Polugayevsky, Bugojno 1980

[11] 15 ♗b6 ♘xb6 16 ♗xb6 ♕b8 17 c4 ♗d8 = Sax-Andersson, Linares 1983

15 ♘b6 f5 16 ♘xd7 ♕xd7 = Nunn-Andersson, Wijk aan Zee 1983

Sicilian XXVIII (Scheveningen)
1 e4 c5 2 ♘f3 d6 3 d4 cd 4 ♘xd4 ♘f6 5 ♘c3 e6 *continued*

	6	7	8	9	10	11	12	13	14	
3	g3	♗g2	0-0	♘ce2[12]	c4	b3	♗b2	a3	♖e1	=
	♘c6	♗d7	♗e7	♖c8[13]	0-0	a6	♕a5!?[14]	♖fd8	b5[15]	
4	...	♗g2	0-0	♖e1	♘xc6	b3[17]	e5!	♗b2	♕e2	±
	a6	♕c7	♗d7[16]	♘c6	bc	♗e7	de	0-0	♘d5[18]	
5	...	...	...	♖e1[19]	♘xc6	e5	♖xe5	♗f4	♖e1[22]	=
	...	...	♘c6	♗e7[20]	bc	de	0-0[21]	♕b7	♘d5[23]	
6	f4	♗e3[25]	♕f3[26]	♘f5	ef	0-0-0[28]	♕e2[29]	♕b5	♖g1[32]	±
	♗e7[24]	0-0	e5	♗xf5	♕a5[27]	e4	♖c8[30]	♕c7[31]	♘g4[33]	
7	...	♕f3[34]	♘b3	g4	♗d3[37]	g5	♗e3	♕h3[39]	♘e2	±
	a6	♕b6[35]	♕c7[36]	b5	♗b7[38]	♘fd7	♘c6	b4	g6[40]	
8	...	♗e3	♕f3[42]	♘xc6[44]	f5[45]	♗c4	0-0-0	♗b3	g4	∞
	♘c6	♗e7[41]	e5[43]	bc	♕a5[46]	♖b8[47]	0-0[48]	♘d7[49]	♘c5[50]	
9	...	...	...	0-0-0	♘db5[52]	g4	♘d4	♗xd4	g5	∞
	...	...	♕c7	0-0[51]	♕b8	a6	♘xd4	e5[53]	♗g4[54]	
10	...	...	...	♗d3	♘b3	0-0	♕h3[57]	♖ae1	f5	∞
	...	...	...	a6	b5[55]	♗b7[56]	g6[58]	0-0	ef[59]	
11	...	...	...	...	0-0	♔h1[60]	♖ae1[61]	a3[62]	♘xc6	=
	...	...	...	...	0-0	♗d7	b5	♖ab8!	♗xc6[63]	

---

[12] **9 ♘de2 ♕b8!?** 10 h3 b5 11 a3 a5 ∓ Geller

9 ♗e3 0-0 10 f4 a6 11 ♘b3 ♖c8 12 a4 ♘a5 = Kudrin-Shamkovich, Gausdal 1982

9 b3 0-0 10 ♗b2 ♖c8 11 ♘xc6 ♗xc6 =

9 ♘b3 a6 10 g4 h6 ∞ Popović-Razuvaev, Novi Sad 1982

9 ♖e1 0-0 10 ♘xc6 ♗xc6 11 a4 ♘d7 12 ♘d5 ♗xd5 13 ed e5 = Mestel-Tal, Lucerne Ol 1982

[13] 9 ... 0-0 10 c4 a6 11 a4 ♖b8 12 ♗d2 e5 13 ♘f5 ± Popović-Kir.Georgiev, Dubai Ol 1986

[14] 12 ... b5 13 cb ♘xd4 14 ♘xd4 ab 15 ♕d2 ♕b6 = Gligorić-Boleslavsky, Zürich C 1953

[15] Gobet-Adorjan, Biel 1983

[16] 8 ... ♗e7 and now:

9 ♗e3 ♘c6 (9 ... ♘bd7?! 10 f4 ♘b6 11 ♔h1 ♘c4 12 ♗c1 ♖b8 13 b3 ♘e5 14 ♗d2 ± Popović-Cvitan, Yugoslav Ch 1986) ∞ – 8 ... ♘c6

9 ♕d2 0-0 10 b3 ♖d8 11 ♗b2 ♗d7 12 ♖fe1 ∞/± Stehouwer-Plaskett, Hastings II 1981-82

9 ♖e1 0-0 10 ♗e3 ♘bd7 11 f4 ♘b6 12 ♔h1 ♘c4 13 ♗c1 ± Antonov-Razuvaev, Nikea 1986

[17] 11 ♘a4 e5 12 c4 c5!? Tal

[18] 15 ♘xd5 ed 16 ♗xe5 ± Fischer-Ničevski, Rovinj/Zagreb 1970

[19] **9 ♗e3 ♗e7** 10 ♕e2 0-0 11 ♘xc6 bc 12 ♘a4 c5 ∞ Matanović-Polugayevsky, 1962

9 a4 ♗e7 10 ♘b3 ♗d7 11 f4 0-0 ∞ Westerinen-Andersson, Dortmund 1973

9 b3 ♗e7 10 ♗b2 ♘xd4 11 ♕xd4 b5 12 ♖ac1 ♗b7 = Geller

[20] 9 ... ♖b8!? 10 ♘xc6 bc 11 e5 de 12 ♖xe5 ♕xe5 13 ♗f4 ♕c5 14 ♗xb8 ♗e7 15 ♕f3 ♘d5 ∞ Ivanov-Gavrikov, USSR 1980

[21] **12 ... ♘d6?** 13 ♕f3 ♗d7 14 ♖g5 ±

12 ... ♗b7 13 ♗f4 ♗d6 14 ♖xe6+ fe 15 ♗xd6 ♕d7 16 ♗c5! ± Browne-Langeweg, Amsterdam 1972

[22] 14 ♖e3 ♘d5 15 ♘xd5 ed 16 ♖b3 ♕a7 17 ♗e3 ♗c5 =

[23] 15 ♘xd5 ed – F.Garcia-Kotronias, Dubai Ol 1986

[24] 6 ... ♕b6 7 ♘b3 ♘c6 8 ♗e2 ♗e7 9 ♗f3 0-0 10 ♕e2 ±

[25] **7 ♗d3 0-0** 8 0-0 ♘c6 9 ♘f3 b6 10 ♕e1 ♘d7 11 ♕g3 ♘c5 ∞ Gutman

7 ♗b5+!? ♘fd7 8 f5 0-0 (8 ... e5? 9 ♘e6! ±)

9 fe ♘e5 10 ef+ ♖xf7 11 ♗e3 ± Ciocaltea-Cvetković, Timisoara 1983

[26] 8 ♗d3 a6 9 ♕f3 ♘bd7 10 0-0-0 ♕c7 ∞ Ghinda-Suba, match 1981

[27] 10 ... e4?! 11 ♘xe4 ♘xe4 12 ♕xe4 d5 13 ♕d3 ♘c6 14 a3! ♗f6 15 0-0-0 ± Yudasin-Lukin, USSR 1981

[28] 11 g4!? e4 12 ♕h3 ♖c8 13 ♗d2 e3 14 ♕xe3 d5 15 0-0-0 ♗c5 ∞ Kupreichik

[29] 12 ♕h3 ♖c8 13 ♗d4 ♘c6 14 ♗c4 ♕b4 ∞ Kupreichik-Sigurjonsson, Reykjavik 1980

[30] 12 ... ♕xf5 13 h3 ♕a5 14 g4 ± Kasparov

[31] 13 ... ♘c6 14 ♕xa5 ♘xa5 15 ♗d4 ± A.Ivanov-Petkevich, USSR 1982

[32] 14 h3 d5! 15 g4 d4 ∞ Hazai-W.Schmidt, Vinkovci 1986

[33] 14 ... h5?! 15 h3 h4 16 g4 hg 17 ♖xg3 ± Marjanović-Cvetković, Zemun 1983

14 ... ♘g4 15 ♗d4 d5!? 16 ♗e2 ♗f6 17 ♗xg4 ♗xd4 18 ♗xd4 ♕xf4+ 19 ♔b1 ♘c6 20 ♖xd5 ± Ehlvest-Jansa, Tallinn 1983

[34] 7 ♗d3 ♘c6 (7 ... b5 8 e5 de 9 fe ♘d5 10 ♕g4 ♘b4 11 ♗g5! ± Rantanen-Hjartarson, Dubai Ol 1986) 8 ♘f3 ♗e7 9 0-0 ♕c7 10 ♔h1 b5 =

7 ♗e3 b5 8 ♕f3 ♗b7 9 ♗d3 ♘bd7 10 g4 b4 (10 ... d5!? 11 e5 b4 12 ♘ce2 ♘e4 13 ♘g3 ♘xg3 14 hg ♗c5 ∞ Mnatsakanian-Ermenkov, Varna 1986) 11 ♘ce2 ♘c5 (11 ... e5 12 ♘b3 d5!? ∞) 12 ♘g3 ♘fd7 13 0-0-0 g6 14 h4 ♕c7 15 ♔b1 ♗g7 16 h5 e5! ∞ Mestel-Polugayevsky, London 1986

[35] 7 ... ♘bd7 8 ♗d3 (8 ♗e3 e5 9 ♘b3 ef 10 ♕xf4 ♘e5 11 0-0-0 ♗e7 = Mestel-Adorjan, Hastings 1986-87) 8 ... e5 9 ♘de2 ♗e7 10 0-0 0-0 11 a4 ♘c5 12 f5 b6 13 ♗g5 ± Large-Adorjan, Hastings 1986-87

7 ... ♕c7 8 ♗d3 (8 g4!? b5 9 g5 ♘fd7 10 a3 ♗b7 11 ♗d3 ± Balashov-Najdorf, Buenos Aires 1980) 8 ... b5 9 a3 ♗b7 10 g4 ♘c6 11 ♗e3 ♘xd4 12 ♗xd4 e5 13 ♗e3 ± Suetin-Espig, Leipzig 1986

[36] 8 ... ♘c6 9 ♗d3 ♗e7 10 ♗e3 ±

[37] 10 g5 ♘fd7 11 ♗e3 ♘b6 12 0-0-0 ♘8d7 13 h4!? ∞/± Kasparov

[38] 10 ... ♗e7 11 g5 ♘fd7 12 ♗e3 ♘c6 13 h4 ♘b4 14 0-0 0-0 15 ♘d4 ± Ligterink-van der Sterren, Holland 1981

[39] 13 0-0-0 g6!? Kasparov

[40] 15 0-0-0 ♗g7 16 ♔b1 ± Hawelko-Staniszewski, Polish Ch 1986

[41] 7 ... e5 and now:
8 ♘xc6 bc 9 ♗c4 ♘g4 10 ♗d2 ef 11 ♗xf4 ♗e7 12 ♕f3 0-0 13 0-0 ♗f6 = Hübner-Andersson, Bugojno 1982

8 ♘de2 ♗e7 9 ♕d2 a6 10 h3 b5 11 ♘g3 ♕a5 12 ♗e2 ef 13 ♗xf4 ♗e6 14 0-0 0-0 = Sibarević-Andersson, Banja Luka 1978

8 ♘f3 ♘g4 9 ♗d2 ef 10 ♗xf4 ♗e7 11 ♗c4

(11 ♕d2 ♗e6 12 0-0-0 0-0 13 h3 ♘fe5 ∞ Spassky-Larsen, Tilburg 1981) 11 ... 0-0 12 ♕d2 ♘ge5 13 ♗b3 ♗g4 14 ♖f1 ± A.Sokolev-Salov, USSR 1982

7 ... ♗d7 8 ♕f3 (8 ♘b3 a6 9 g4 h6 ∞ van der Wiel) 8 ... a6 9 0-0-0 ♕c7 10 g4 ∞

[42] 8 ♘b3 a6 9 ♗d3 b5 10 ♕e2 ♗b7 11 0-0-0 ♕c7 = Bellon-Geller, Las Palmas 1979

[43] 8 ... ♗d7 9 0-0-0 0-0 10 ♗e2 ♘xd4 11 ♗xd4 ♗c6 12 g4 ♕a5 13 g5 ♘d7 ∞

[44] 9 ♘f5 ♗xf5 10 ef ♘d4 11 ♗xd4 ed 12 ♘b5 ♕a5+ = Mariotti-Korchnoi, Rome 1981

[45] 10 fe de 11 ♗c4 0-0 12 h3 ♗e6! 13 ♗xe6 fe 14 ♕e2 ♕b8 =

[46] 10 ... h5 11 0-0-0 g6 12 ♗c4 gf 13 ef d5 14 ♗g5 ± Gufeld

[47] 11 ... ♗b7 12 0-0-0 0-0 13 g4! d5 14 g5 d4 15 gf ♗xf6 16 ♗d2 ±

[48] 12 ... ♗a6 13 ♗b3 ♘d7 14 g4 ♘b6 15 f6! ± Radulov-Cvetković, Belgrade 1982

12 ... d5 13 ed ♖xb2 14 d6! e4 15 ♘xe4 ♖xc2+ 16 ♔xc2 ♗xf5 17 ♖d4 ♗d6 18 ♖f1 ±

[49] 13 ... ♖xb3!? 14 cb d5 ∞̄

[50] 15 ♗xc5 dc 16 h4 ♖b4 17 a3 ♖d4 ∞

[51] 9 ... a6 10 g4 0-0 11 g5 ♘d7 12 ♖g1 b5 13 ♕h5 b4 14 ♘ce2 g6 15 ♕h6 ♖e8! ∞

[52] 10 ♖g1 ♘xd4 11 ♖xd4 a6 12 g4 ♘d7 13 g5 b5 14 ♕h5 b4! ∞

10 g4 ♘xd4 11 ♗xd4 (11 ♖xd4 e5 12 ♖c4 ♗g4 13 ♕g3 ef 14 ♗xf4 ♕b6 = van der Wiel-Liberzon, Baden 1980) 11 ... e5 12 fe de 13 ♕g3 ♘g4! ∞ Sax-Kasparov, Nikšić 1983

[53] 13 ... b5 14 g5 ♘d7 15 ♗d3 b4 16 ♘d5!? ed 17 ed ∞̄

[54] 15 ♕g3 ed 16 gf dc 17 fe cb+ 18 ♔b1 ♗xd1 19 ef♕+ ♕xf8 20 ♖g1 g6 ∞

[55] 10 ... ♗d7 11 0-0 ±

[56] 11 ... 0-0 12 a4 (12 ♖ae1 ♗b7 13 ♕h3 ♖ac8 14 a3 b4 15 ab ♘xb4 ∞) 12 ... b4 13 ♘b1 e5 14 a5 ♗b7 15 ♘1d2 ef ∞ Gutman

[57] 12 a3 ♖c8 13 ♕h3 h5!? 14 ♔h1 ♘g4 15 ♖g1 ♗f6 ∞

12 ♖ae1 ♖c8 13 ♕h3 ♘b4 14 a3 ♘xd3 15 cd 0-0 16 ♕g3 e5 = Gheorghiu-Stein, Moscow 1971

[58] 12 ... h5 13 a4 b4 14 ♘d1 ♘a5 15 ♘xa5 ♕xa5 16 ♘f2 ± A.Sokolov-Makarichev, Sochi 1983

[59] 15 ef ♘e5 ∞ A.Sokolov-Utasi, 1983

[60] 11 ♕g3 ♘h5 12 ♕h3 ♗xf4 13 ♖xf4 e5 14 ♘f5 ef 15 ♘d5 ♕b8 16 ♗b6 ∞

11 ♖ae1 ♘xd4 12 ♗xd4 e5 13 ♗e3!? ∞

[61] 12 ♕g3!? b5 13 e5 de 14 ♘xc6 ♗xc6 15 fe ♘d7 16 ♗f4 ♘c5 17 ♗h6 g6 ∞̄

12 a3 ♗b7 13 ♖ae1 = Miles

[62] 13 g4 ♘xd4 14 ♗xd4 e5 15 fe de 16 ♘d5! ♕d6! ∞

[63] 15 ♕h3 ♖bd8 16 ♗d4 e5! 17 fe de = Novopashin-Korchnoi, USSR Ch 1962

	6	7	8	9	10	11	12	13	14	
1	...	♗b5+[1]	♗xd7+	♘f5	gh[2]	♘d5[3]	♘g3	♕f3	h4	±
	e5	♗d7	♕xd7	h5	g6	♘xh5	♗e7	♘a6	♘c7[4]	
2	...	g5	♗e3	a3	h4[7]	h5	♖h3	g6	♕g4[9]	±
	a6	♘fd7	b5[5]	♘b6[6]	♗b7	♘8d7	♗e7[8]	♗f6		
3	...	g5	♗e3[10]	h4[12]	♗b5	ed	♕e2	0-0-0	♘b3	±
	♘c6	♘d7	♘b6[11]	d5[13]	♗d7	ed	♗e7	0-0	♗e6[14]	
4	...	g5	h4[15]	♗e3	♕d2[17]	0-0-0	♕xd4	♖g1	h5	∞
	♗e7	♘fd7	♘c6	0-0[16]	a6	♘xd4	b5	♖b8	b4[18]	
5	...	♗g2	h3	♘b3[20]	♕e2[22]	f4	♗e3	0-0-0	♕f2	∞
	h6	♘c6	a6[19]	♗e7[21]	♕c7	b5	♗b7	♖c8	♘d7[23]	
6	...	♖g1	♗e3	♕e2[26]	♗xd4	♗e3	h4	g5[28]	hg	=
	...	♘c6[24]	a6[25]	♘xd4	e5	♗e6	g6[27]	hg	♘h5[29]	
7	...	g5	♗xg5	♕d2[30]	♘b3	0-0-0	♗e3[33]	f4	♗g2	∞
	...	hg	♘c6	♕b6	a6[31]	♗d7[32]	♕c7	b5	♖c8[34]	
8	...	h4	♖g1	gh[36]	♗g5	♕d2	♘b3	0-0-0	♖g3	∞
	...	♘c6[35]	h5	♘xh5	♘f6[37]	♕b6	♗d7	a6[39]	♕c7[40]	

---

[1] 7 ♘f5 h5 8 f3 (8 g5?! ♘xe4 9 ♘xg7+ ♗xg7 10 ♘xe4 d5 11 ♘g3 h4 12 ♘h5 ♔f8! ∞) 8 ... hg 9 fg g6 10 ♘e3 ♗e7 11 ♗g2 ♘c6 12 h3 ♘d4 13 ♕d3 ± Braskett-Benjamin, USA 1977

[2] **10 f3** hg 11 fg g6 12 ♘e3 ♗e7 13 ♕f3 ♘c6 ∞

10 ♗g5 ♘h7 11 ♗d2 hg 12 ♕xg4 g6 13 ♘e3 ♕xg4 14 ♘xg4 ♘c6 =

[3] 11 ♗g5 g6 12 ♘g3 ♘c6 13 ♘d5 ♗g7 14 ♘xh5 (14 ♕d3 ♘f4! ∞) 14 ... ♖xh5 15 h4 ♖c8 16 c3 ♕e6 ∞/= A.Sokolov-Panchenko, USSR 1984

[4] 15 ♘xe7 ♕xe7 16 ♗g5 ♕d7 17 0-0-0 ± Tseshkovsky-Panchenko, Minsk 1985

[5] 8 ... ♘c6 – 6 ... ♘c6

[6] 9 ... ♗b7 10 ♕g4 ♘c6 11 0-0-0 ± Fedorowicz-Petrosian, Hastings 1977-78

9 ... ♕c7 10 h4 ♘c6 11 ♘xc6 ♕xc6 12 ♕d4 ± Ghinda-Gutman, Dortmund 1986

[7] 10 ♖g1 ♘8d7 11 f4 ♗b7 11 f5 e5 12 ♘e6! fe 13 ♕h5+ ∞ Shamkovich-Benko, US Ch 1978

[8] 12 ... ♘e5 13 g6 hg 14 hg ♖xh3 15 gf+ ♘xf7 16 ♗xh3 ± Torre-Vogt, Polanica Zdroj 1977

[9] Pokojowczyk-Sznapik, Poland 1978, and

Fernandez Garcia-D.Cramling, Barcelona 1986

[10] 8 ♘db5 ♘b6 9 ♗f4 e5 (9 ... ♘e5 10 ♕h5 ♘g6 ∞) 10 ♗e3 a6 11 ♘a3 ♗e6 ∞

[11] **8 ... ♗e7** 9 h4 – 6 ... ♗e7

8 ... ♘xd4 9 ♕xd4 ♘e5 10 ♗e2 ♘c6 11 ♕d3 ±

8 ... a6 9 h4 ♕c7 (9 ... ♘de5 10 f4 ♘xd4 11 ♗xd4 ♘c6 12 ♗e3 b5 13 ♗g2 ♗b7 14 0-0 ± Balaskas-Tringov, Istanbul 1975) 10 ♗e2 (10 ♕e2 b5 11 ♘xc6 ♕xc6 12 ♗d4 ♗b7 13 0-0-0 ± Korsunsky-Eingorn, USSR 1979) 10 ... b5 11 ♘xc6 ♕xc6 12 ♕d4 ± Ghinda-Kotronias, Sofia 1986

[12] 9 ♕d2 d5 10 ed ed 11 0-0-0 ♗e7 12 ♗b5 ♗d7 13 ♘b3 ± Kremenetsky-Andrianov, USSR 1980

[13] 9 ... ♗e7 – 6 ... ♗e7

[14] **15 ♘c5** ♗xc5 16 ♗xc5 ♖e8 17 ♕f3 a6 (17 ... ♘d7 18 ♗d4 ± Renet-Tal, Clichy v Trud 1986) 18 ♗f1 ♖c8 ∞ Guseinov-Klovsky, USSR 1979

15 f4 ± Short-Hansen, Esbjerg 1984

[15] 8 ♖g1 ♘c6 9 ♗e3 ♘b6 10 ♕h5 g6 11 ♕e2 e5 12 ♘b3 ♗e6 ∞ Kindermann-Kohlweyer, Dortmund 1986

[16] **9 ... ♘b6** 10 ♕f3 ♘e5 11 ♕g3 ♘cc4

12 0-0-0 ± Byrne-Lein, Reykjavik 1986

9 ... a6 10 ♕e2 ♘xd4 (10 ... ♕c7 11 0-0-0 b5 12 ♘xc6 ♕xc6 13 ♗d4 b4 14 ♘d5! ± Karpov-Dorfman, USSR Ch 1976) 11 ♗xd4 0-0 12 ♗g2 b5 13 e5 de 14 ♗xe5 ± Makarichev-Kalinsky, USSR 1981

[17] 10 ♕e2 a6 11 0-0-0 ♘xd4 12 ♗xd4 b5 13 a3 ♖b8 14 f4 ♖e8! ∞ Perenyi-Jansa, West Berlin 1986

[18] **15 ♘d5?!** ed 16 h6 ♘e5 17 f4 ♕c7 ∞/∓ Pokojowczyk-Timoshchenko, Polanica Zdroj 1979

15 ♘e2 e5 16 ♕d2 ♘c5 (16 ... ♕a5?! 17 ♔b1 ♘c5 18 f3 ♗e6 19 ♘c1 ± Ernst-Jansa, Gausdal 1986) 17 f3 ♗e6 18 ♔b1 ♕c7 ∞; 18 ... a5 ∞ Jansa

[19] 8 ... ♗d7 9 ♗e3 ♗e7 10 ♕e2 a6 11 f4 ♕c7 12 ♕f2 ±

[20] **9 ♗e3** ♘xd4 10 ♕xd4 e5 11 ♕d2 ♗e6 12 0-0-0 ♕a5 = Byrne-Shamkovich, USA 1981

9 ♘de2 g5!? 10 f4 gf 11 ♗xf4 ♘e5 12 ♕d4 ♕c7 ∞ Hübner-Andersson, Johannesburg 1981

[21] 9 ... ♕c7 10 a4 b6 11 0-0 ♖b8 12 ♕e2 ♗e7 13 f4 ♘d7 14 ♗e3 ± Short-Suba, Hastings 1983-84

[22] **10 f4** ♘d7! 11 ♗e3?! (11 0-0 b5 ∞) 11 ... ♗h4+ 12 ♔f1 ♗e7 ∓ Mortensen-Adorjan, Esbjerg 1985

10 ♗e3 g5!? 11 ♕e2 ♘e5 12 f4 gf 13 ♗xf4 ♘fd7 14 0-0-0 b5 ∞ Kindermann-Mokry, Polanica Zdroj 1984

[23] Mokry-Modr, Prague 1986

[24] 7 ... a6 8 ♗e3 ♗e7 (8 ... b5 9 a3 ♗b7 10 ♗d3 ♘fd7 11 ♕e2 g5 12 h4 ♖g8 13 0-0-0 ♘e5 ∞ Grünfeld-Suba, Dortmund 1984) 9 ♕e2 g5 10 0-0-0 ♘bd7 11 h4 ♖g8 ∞ Kuijf-Sax, Amsterdam 1983, and Horvath-Sax, Hungarian Ch 1984

[25] **8 ... d5** 9 ed ed 10 a3 ♗d6 11 h4 ± Korolev-Medvedev, corr. 1986

8 ... g5 9 h4 ♘d7 10 hg hg 11 ♕d2 ± Zaitsev-A.Sokolov, Moscow Ch 1983

[26] **9 h4** h5 ∞

9 ♗e2 ♕a5 10 ♘b3 (10 ♕d2 ♘xd4 11 ♗xd4 e5 =) 10 ... ♕c7 11 h4 h5 12 g5 ♘g4 13 ♗xg4 hg 14 ♕xg4 ♘e5 ∞∞ Sznapik-Suba, Prague Z 1985

9 ♕f3 g5 10 0-0-0 ♘e5 11 ♕e2 b5 ∞ Kotronias-Suba, Dubai Ol 1986

[27] 12 ... ♕a5!? 13 0-0-0 ♖c8 intending ... ♖xc3

[28] 13 0-0-0 ♖c8 14 ♘d5 ♗xd5 15 ed ♕a5

16 ♕f3 ♗g7 17 g5 ♘h5 ∞ Horvath-Stohl, Groningen 1983-84

[29] 15 0-0-0 ♘f4 16 ♗xf4 ef 17 ♘d5 ♗g7 = Karpov-Timman, Plovdiv 1983

[30] 9 ♘b3 (intending ♕e2) 9 ... ♗e7 (intending ... ♘xe4) 10 ♕f3 a6 11 h4 ♗d7 12 ♕g2 ♕c7 13 f4 (Lobron-Adorjan, Dortmund 1984) 13 ... b5 ∞

[31] 10 ... ♘e5 11 ♕e2 (11 ♗e2 ♖h3 ∞) 11 ... a6 12 0-0-0 ♗d7 13 f4 ♘g6 14 h4 ± Ljubojević-Hébert, Montreal 1984

[32] 11 ... ♕c7 12 h4 b5 13 ♗d3 (13 ♗g2 ♗b7 14 f4 ±) 13 ... ♘e5 14 ♔b1 ♘fd7 15 f4 ♘xd3 16 ♕xd3 b4 (16 ... f6? 17 e5) 17 ♘e2 a5 ∞ Alzate-Agzamov, Tunja 1984; 17 ♘d5! ed 18 ed ♘f6 19 h5 ± Alzate

[33] **12 ♗f4** ♘e5 13 ♗e3 ♕c7 14 f4 ♘c4 15 ♗xc4 ♕xc4 16 e5 de 17 fe ♘d5 ∞

12 f4 0-0-0 13 h4 ♗e7 14 ♗e2 g6 = Marjanović-Cebalo, Yugoslav Ch 1983

[34] 15 ♔b1 ♗e7 16 ♖he1 ♔f8 ∞ Kengis-A.Sokolov, USSR 1984

[35] 7 ... **e5** 8 ♘f5! ± Stanciu-Vegh, Ulan Bator 1986

7 ... **a6** 8 ♖g1 d5 (8 ... ♕a5 9 ♘b3 ♕c7 10 g5 ± Sznapik-Suba, Dortmund 1984) 9 ed ♘xd5 10 ♘xd5 ♕xd5 11 ♗g2 ♕c4 12 c3 ± Karpov-Kindermann, Vienna 1986

7 ... **♗e7!?** 8 ♕f3 (8 ♖g1 d5 9 ♗b5+ ♔f8 ∞) 8 ... h5 (8 ... ♘c6 9 ♗b5 ♗d7 10 ♗xc6 ♗xc6 11 g5 ± Ljubojević-Timman, Tilburg 1985) 9 gh ♘c6 10 ♗b5 ♗d7 11 ♗xc6 bc 12 e5 (Ljubojević-Timman, Bugojno 1986) 12 ... de 13 ♘xc6 ♗xc6 14 ♕xc6+ ♔f8 15 h6 gh 16 ♗d2 ♖b8 17 0-0-0 ♕b6 = Ljubojević

[36] 9 g5 ♘g4 10 ♗e2 d5! 11 ♘xc6 bc 12 ♗xg4 hg 13 ♕xg4 d4 ∞∞ Sznapik-Adorjan and Schmittdiel-Adorjan, Dortmund 1984

[37] 10 ... ♕b6 11 ♘b3 a6 12 ♗e2 g6 13 ♕d2 ♗e7 14 ♖g2! ♗d7 15 0-0-0 ± Lobron-Marjanović, Reggio Emilia 1985-86

[38] 11 ♗e2 a6 12 h5 ♗d7 13 ♘b3 b5 ∞ de Firmian-Suba, Tunis IZ 1985

[39] 13 ... ♘e5 14 ♗g3 ♖c8 15 ♕e1 ♘g6 16 ♘d4 (16 f4 ♘h5 ∞ Ljubojević-Suba, Thessaloniki Ol 1984) 16 ... a6 17 f4 ♘h5 18 ♖f3 ∞/± Pähtz-Ghinda, Potsdam 1985, and Stanciu-Foisor, Romanian Ch 1985

[40] **15 ♗g2** ♗e7 16 f4 0-0-0 = Karpov-Kasparov, match (1) 1984-85

15 ♕e2 b5 16 a3 ♖c8 ∞ Kindermann-A.Sokolov, Mendoza 1985

345

1 e4 c5 2 ♘f3 d6 3 d4 cd 4 ♘xd4 ♘f6 5 ♘c3 e6 6 ♗e2 a6 *(without ... ♘c6)*

	7	8	9	10	11	12	13	14	15	
1	0-0[1]	f4	♕e1[4]	♗f3	e5	♗xa8	♗e3	fe		∞
	♗e7[2]	0-0[3]	b5[5]	b4	de	♕xd4+[6]	♕c4	♘fd7[7]		
2	...	a4	f4	♗f3	♕e2	♗e3[10]	g4	♕g2	g5	±/∞
	♘bd7	b6	♗b7	♕c7[8]	♖c8[9]	♗e7[11]	♘c5	h6	hg[12]	
3	...	f4	♗f3	e5[14]	♘xf3	fe	ef[16]	fg	b3[17]	±
	...	b5[13]	♗b7	♗xf3	de[15]	b4	bc	♗xg7		
4	...	f4	♕e1	♕g3	♗e3	♗f2	e5[20]	fe	♘e4	∞
	♕c7	♗e7[18]	0-0	♕b6[19]	♕xb2	♕b4	de	♘e8	♘d7[21]	
5	...	...	♗e3	g4[22]	g5	f5	♕e1	♕g3	♖f2	∞
	...	...	0-0	♖e8[23]	♘fd7	♘e5	♘bc6	♗f8[24]	b5[25]	
6	...	...	♔h1	♕e1[26]	♗f3	e5	f5[28]	fe	ef+	∞/=
	...	...	0-0	b5	♗b7	♘e8[27]	de	♗xf3[29]	♖xf7[30]	

[1] 7 f4 ♕c7 8 g4!? b5 9 g5 ♘fd7 10 a3 ♘b6?! (10 ... ♘c6) 11 ♗f3 (11 f5!?) 11 ... ♘8d7 12 ♕e2 ♗e7 13 h4 ± Short-Ribli, Subotica IZ 1987

[2] 7 ... b5 8 ♗f3 ♖a7 (8 ... ♘fd7 9 e5 d5 10 ♘xd5! ±) 9 ♕e2 ♖c7 10 ♖d1 ♘bd7 11 a4 ± Smyslov-Kottnauer, Groningen 1946

[3] 8 ♘c6 9 ♘xc6! bc 10 e5 ± Kindermann-Ardiansyah, Dubai Ol 1986

[4] 9 ♔h1 (or 9 ♗e3, or 9 a4) ♕c7 - 7 ... ♕c7; 9 ... ♘c6 - 6 ... ♘c6

[5] **9 ... ♕b6** 10 ♗e3 ♘c6 (10 ... ♕xb2 11 ♖b1 ♕a3 12 ♖b3 ♕a5 13 ♘xe6; 12 ... ♕c5 13 ♘a4 ±) 11 ♘f5 ♕xb2 12 ♘xe7+ ♘xe7 13 ♖b1 ♕xc2 13 ♗c4 ±
   9 ... ♘c6 10 ♗e3 - 6 ... ♘c6

[6] **12 ... bc** 13 ♕xe5 ±/∞
   12 ... ed ∞

[7] **14 ... bc?** 15 ef ♗xf6 16 ♖xf6 ++
   14 ... ♘fd7 ∞ Shakarov

[8] 10 ... ♖c8 11 e5!? (11 ♕e2 ♕c7 - 10 ... ♕c7) 11 ... ♗xf3 12 ♘xf3 de 13 fe ♘g4 14 ♕e2 ♕c7 15 ♕xa6! (15 ♘g5 ♕c4!) 15 ... ♗c5+ 16 ♔h1 ♘f2+ 17 ♖xf2 ♗xf2 18 ♘b5 ±

[9] **11 ... e5** 12 ♘f5 g6 13 fe de 14 ♘h6 ±
   11 ... ♗e7 12 e5!? de 13 fe ♘c5 14 ♖d1 ♘xe5 15 ♗xb7 ♖d8 16 ♗e3 ♗fg4 (16 ... ♕xb7 17 ♘xe6) 17 ♗xa6 ♘xe3 18 ♘cb5 ♕b8 19 ♕xe3 ♘g4 20 ♕g3 ♕xg3 21 hg e5 ± Teschner-Hess, Lugano 1984

[10] 12 g4 ♕c4 13 ♕f2 h5 ∞

[11] 12 ... g6 13 ♖ad1 ± Balashov-Adorjan, Toluca IZ 1982

[12] 16 fg ♘fd7 17 g6 ±/∞

[13] 8 ... ♕c7 9 ♗f3 ♗e7 10 ♔h1 0-0 11 g4 ±

[14] 10 a3 ♕c7 11 ♕e2 (11 g4 h6 12 g5?! hg 13 fg d5 ∓; 12 ♕e2 e5 ∞) 11 ... ♖c8 12 ♔h1 ♗c4 14 ♕xc4! ♖xc4 15 ♘b3 ± Hartston-Sigurjonsson, Hastings 1975-76

[15] 11 ... ♘g4 12 ♕e2 b4 13 ♘a4! de 14 fe ♘dxe5 (14 ... ♘c5 15 ♕c4!; 14 ... ♘b6 15 ♕e4!) 15 ♘xe5 ♕d4+ 16 ♔h1 ♘xe5 17 ♗f4 ±

[16] 13 ♘a4 ♘d5 ∞

[17] Tseshkovsky-Kupreichik, USSR Ch 1981

[18] 8 ... b5 9 ♗f3 ♗b7 10 e5 de 11 fe ♘fd7 12 ♗xb7 ♕xb7 13 ♕h5 g6 14 ♕h4 ±

[19] 10 ... ♘c6 11 ♗e3 - 6 ... ♘c6; 11 ♘xc6!?

[20] 13 ♖ab1 ♕a5 14 ♘f5 ef 15 ♗b6 ♘xe4 16 ♘xe4 (Jansa-Ermenkov, Vrnjačka Banja 1978) 16 ... ♕xa2 17 ♘c3 ♕e6 18 ♗f3 ♘c6 19 ♘d5 ♗d8 ∞ Korchnoi

[21] 16 ♗d3 ♕a5 17 ♘f3 f5 (17 ... g6?! 18 ♗d4 ± Stein-Korchnoi, USSR 1964) 18 ef ♘dxf6 ∞

[22] **10 ♕e1** b5 11 ♗f3 ♗b7 12 e5 de 13 fe ♘fd7 14 ♗xb7 ♕xb7 15 ♕g3 ♔h8 16 a3 ♘c6 ∞

   10 a4 b6 (10 ... ♘c6 - 6 ... ♘c6) 11 ♗f3 ♗b7 12 f5 (12 ♕e2 ♘bd7 13 g4 ♘c5 14 ♕g2 e5 15 ♘f5 d5 16 ed e4 ∞; 13 ♗f2 ♖fe8 ∞) 12 ... e5 13 ♘b3 ♘bd7 14 g4 h6 15 ♗g2 ♖ac8 16 h4 ♘h7 ∞/= Khalifman-Psakhis, USSR Ch 1987

[23] 10 ... b5 11 g5 ♘fd7 12 f5 ♘e5 13 f6 ∞/± Prandstetter-Adorjan, Prague Z 1985
[24] 14 ... b5 15 f6 ♘xd4 16 ♗xd4 ♗f8 ∞ Prandstetter-Ftacnik, Prague Z 1985
[25] Prandstetter-Pinter, Prague Z 1985
[26] 10 a4 ♘c6 – 6 ... ♘c6
[27] 12 ... de 13 fe ♘fd7 14 ♕g3 ♔h8 15 ♗f4 ± Kudrin-Sax, Hastings 1983-84
[28] 13 ♕g3 ♘d7 14 a3 ♘b6 15 ♘e4 ♖d8 16 c3 ♘c4! ∓ Sznapik-Suba, Berlin 1979

[29] 14 ... ed 15 ♘d5 ♗xd5 16 ♗xd5 ± Jansa-Lombard, Czechoslovakia v Switzerland 1978
[30] 16 ♘xf3 ♘d7 17 ♗g5 ♗f8! 18 ♔h4 (18 a3 ♘d6 = Karpov-Kasparov, match (43) 1984-85; 18 ♖f2 ♘d6 = Sznapik-Mokry, Polanica Zdroj 1984, and Zapata-Ermenkov, Tunis IZ 1985) 18 ... ♘d6 (18 ... b4 19 ♘g5!) 19 ♖d1 h6 (19 ... ♕c4 20 ♗f2 ♖e8 21 ♘g5 ± Ermenkov-Ftacnik, Prague Z 1985) 20 ♗g3 ♖e8 = Shulman-Ionov, USSR 1986

Sicilian XXXI (Scheveningen) 1 e4 c5 2 ♘f3 d6 3 d4 cd 4 ♘xd4 ♘f6 5 ♘c3 e6 6 ♗e2 ♘c6

	7	8	9	10	11	12	13	14	15	
1	0-0[1]	♗e3[3]	f4	♕e1[5]	♗xd4	♕g3	f5[7]	♗e3	♘xe4	∞∞
	♗e7[2]	0-0	♗d7[4]	♘xd4	♗c6	g6[6]	e5	♘xe4	♗xe4[8]	
2	...	...	...	♘b3	a4	♔h1	♗f3	♖f2	f5	±
	...	...	...	a5[9]	e5	♘b4	♕c8[10]	♗g4	♗xf3[11]	
3	...	...	...	...	a4	♗f3	♕e2[13]	g4	g5	±
	...	...	...	a6	b6[12]	♕c7	♖fc8[14]	♗e8	♘d7[15]	

[1] 7 ♗e3 ♗e7 8 ♕d2 0-0 9 0-0-0 d5 (9 ... a6 10 f4 ♕c7 11 g4 ±/∞ Ghinda-Espig, Romania v East Germany 1984, and Spraggett-Pelts, Montreal 1986) 10 ed ed 11 f3 ∞ Sznapik-Ligterink, Amsterdam 1984

[2] 7 ... a6 8 ♗e3 ♗d7 9 f4 ♕c7 (9 ... ♖c8 10 ♕e1 ♕b6 11 ♖d1 ♕xb2 12 ♖b1 ♕a3 13 ♖b3 ♕a5 14 ♘xe6 ± Kuijf-Gutman, Amsterdam 1984) 10 ♕e1 b5 11 a3 ♗e7 – 7 ... ♗e7

[3] 8 ♔h1 0-0 9 f4 ♘xd4 (9 ... e5 10 ♘b3 ±; 9 ... a6 10 ♘xc6! bc 11 e5 ± Kindermann-A.Sokolov, Naleczow 1984, and van der Wiel-Jansa, Biel IZ 1985) 10 ♕xd4 b6 11 ♗f3 ♗b7 ∞

[4] 9 ... ♘xd4 10 ♗xd4 b6 11 ♕d3 ♗b7 12 ♖ad1 ± Dolmatov-Kochiev, USSR 1979
9 ... ♕c7 10 ♘db5 ♕b8 11 a4 ♖d8 12 ♗f3 ± Larsen-Korchnoi, Lone Pine 1981

[5] 10 ♔h1 ♘xd4 11 ♗xd4 (11 ♕xd4 ♗c6 12 ♖ad1 ♕b8 13 ♗f3 ♖d8 = Vogt-Bönsch, Leipzig 1981; 13 e5 de 14 fe ♘d7 = Filipović-Hulak, Banja Luka 1983) 11 ... ♗c6 12 ♕d3 ♘d7 (12 ... d5 13 e5 ♘e4 14 f5 ±) 13 ♕g3 e5 = Sznapik-Espig, Poland v East Germany 1980

[6] 12 ... ♕c7 13 ♗d3 ♖ad8 14 ♖ae1 ±

[7] 13 ♗f3 b5 14 a3 a5 =
13 ♗d3 ♘h5 intending 14 ... ♘xf4, 15 ... e5 =

[8] 16 ♗h6 ♕b6+ 17 ♔h1 ♕xb2 (17 ... ♖fc8 18 ♗d3 ♖xd3 19 cd ♗f8 20 ♕h3 ∞) 18 ♗xf8

♖xf8 19 ♗d3 ♗xd3? 20 cd ♕d4 21 ♖ac1 ± Vogt-Möhring, East German Ch 1977; 19 ... ♗d5! ∞

[9] 10 ... ♘a5 11 e5 ♘e8 12 ♘e4 ±
10 ... ♕c7 11 ♗f3 ♖fd8 12 g4 ±

[10] 13 ... ♗c6 14 fe de 15 ♕e2 ♕c7 16 ♕f2 ♘d7 17 ♖ad1 ± Geller-Polugayevsky, Portorož 1973
13 ... ♗e6 14 ♖f2 ef (14 ... ♖c8 15 ♖d2 ♘d7 16 f5 ♗xb3 17 cb ± Marjanović-Cebalo, Novi Sad 1985) 15 ♗xf4 ♕b6 16 ♘d4 ♘d7 17 ♗e3 ♕d8 18 ♘xe6 fe 19 ♗g4 ±

[11] 16 ♕xf3 ♕c4 17 g4! ± Geller-Bönsch, Sochi 1984

[12] 11 ... e5 12 ♘d5! ± Sax-Hulak, Vinkovci 1976
11 ... ♖c8 12 a5 ±
11 ... ♘a5 12 e5 ♘e8 13 ♘xa5 ♕xa5 14 ♕d2 (14 ♘e4 ±) 14 ... ♕c7 (14 ... ♖d8!? 15 b4 ♕c7) 15 ♗d4 f6 16 ef (16 ♕e3 ±) 16 ... ♘xf6 17 ♕e3 ± Karpov-Ljubojević, Tilburg 1986

[13] 13 ♔h1 ♖ab8 14 ♕e2 ♘a5 15 ♘d2 ♗c8 (15 ... b5 16 ab ab 17 e5 ± Abramović-Hulak, Yugoslav Ch 1984, and Tischbierek-Karolyi, Leipzig 1984) 16 ♗f2 ♘d7 17 ♖fc1 ♗f6 18 ♘d1 ♗b7 19 c3 ♖bc8 20 ♘e3 ± Qi Jingxuan-Schmidt, Thessaloniki Ol 1984

[14] 13 ... ♗e8 14 g4 ♘d7 15 g5 ♘c5 16 ♗g2 f6 17 h4 ± Spassky-Petrosian, USSR Ch 1973

[15] 16 ♗g2 ♘a5 17 f5 ± Tischbierek-Tseshkovsky, Rostok 1984

1 e4 c5 2 ♘f3 d6 3 d4 cd 4 ♘xd4 ♘f6 5 ♘c3 e6 6 ♗e2 ♘c6 *continued*

	7	8	9	10	11	12	13	14	15	
4	0-0	♗e3	f4	♘b3[16]	♖xf4[17]	♕d2[19]	♖ff1[20]	♖ad1	♗f4	=
	♗e7	0-0	e5	ef	♘e8[18]	♗f6	♗e5	♕h4	♘f6[21]	
5	...	...	...	fe	♘f5	♖xf5	♖f1	♔h1	♗d3	∞
	...	...	...	de	♗xf5	g6[22]	♘d4	♖c8	♔g7[23]	

1 e4 c5 2 ♘f3 d6 3 d4 cd 4 ♘xd4 ♘f6 5 ♘c3 e6 6 ♗e2 ♘c6 7 0-0 ♗e7 8 ♗e3 0-0 9 f4 a6

	10	11	12	13	14	15	16	17	18	
6	♕e1[24]	♗xd4	♖d1[25]	♗f3	e5	fe	♗xb7	♘e4	♕g3	±
	♘xd4	b5	♗b7[26]	♕c7[27]	de	♘d7	♕xb7	♕c7[28]	♖ad8[29]	
7	...	♕g3	a3[30]	♗xd4	♖ae1	♗d3	e5[31]	♗xe5	f5	±/∞
	♗d7	b5	♘xd4	♗c6	♕d7	a5	de	g6	♘h5[32]	
8	...	♕g3	♗xd4	a3[33]	♔h1[34]	f5	♗e3	ed	♘xd5	±
	♕c7	♘xd4	b5	♗b7	g6[35]	e5	d5[36]	♘xd5	♗xd5[37]	
9	...	...	♔h1[38]	a3[39]	♗xd4	♖ae1[41]	♗d3	ab	♘e2	∞
	...	♗d7	b5	♘xd4[40]	♗c6	♕b7[42]	b4	♕xb4	♕b7[43]	
10	a4	♕e1	♗xd4	♗e3[46]	♗xf4[47]	♕g3	♗h6	♔h1	♗f4	∞/=
	♕c7[44]	♘xd4[45]	e5	ef	♗e6[48]	♘d7[49]	♕c5+	♕e5	♕c5[50]	
11	...	♔h1	♗d3[52]	♕f3	♕g3	e5	♗d2[54]	cd	♘f3	∞
	...	♖e8[51]	♗d7[53]	♘b4	♗f8	♘fd5	♘xd3	♕c5	♘xc3[55]	

[16] 10 ♘f5 ♗xf5 11 ef ef 12 ♖xf4 d5 ∓ Mecking-Spassky, Nice Ol 1974

10 ♘db5 a6 11 fe ♘xe5 12 ♘d4 d5 = Marjanović-Kelečević, Sarajevo 1982

10 ♘f3 ♘g4 (10 ... ef 11 ♗xf4 ♕b6+ 12 ♔h1 ♕xb2 13 ♘d5 ∞ Psakhis-Kaidanov, Irkutsk 1983) 11 ♗c1 ef 12 ♗xf4 ♗f6! 13 ♔h1 ♖e8 14 ♗c4 ♗e6 ∞ Dolmatov-Chekhov, USSR 1983, and Tischbierek-Barbulescu, East Germany v Romania 1984

[17] 11 ♗xf4 ♗e6 12 ♔h1 d5 13 e5 ♘d7 14 ♘xd5 ♘dxe5 15 c4 ♗g5 =

[18] 11 ... ♗e6 12 ♘d5 ♘d7 (12 ... ♗xd5 13 ed ♘e5 =) 13 ♘xe7+ ♕xe7 =

[19] 12 ♘d5 ♗g5 13 ♖f2 ♗e6 = Kindermann-Barbulescu, Polanica Zdroj 1984

[20] 13 ♖f2 ♗e5 14 ♗g5 ♘f6 15 ♖af1? ♗xc3 ∞∞ Geller-Andersson, London 1982

[21] Abramović-Barbulescu, Skopje 1984

[22] 12 ... ♕a5 13 ♔h1 ♖ad8 14 ♕f1 ±/= Geller-Kasparov, Moscow IZ 1982

12 ... ♕xd1+ 13 ♖xd1 g6 14 ♖f2 (14 ♖ff1 ♘d4 15 ♗d3 ♘g4 = Ljubojević-Timman, Lucerne Ol 1982) 14 ... ♘d4 15 ♗h6 (15 ♖df1 ♖ac8 ∞ Klovans-Kovalev, USSR 1984) 15 ... ♖fd8 (15 ... ♘xc2? 16 ♗g5 ± Geller-Tal, USSR Ch 1983) 16 ♖df1 ♖ac8 ±/=

[23] 16 g4 and now:

16 ... h5 ∞ Zapata-Diaz, Bayamo 1984

16 ... ♘e6 17 ♕f3 h5 ∞ Zapata-Cvetković, Zagreb 1984

16 ... h6 ∞ Zapata-Cebalo, Titograd 1984

[24] 10 ♗f3 ♕c7 11 ♘xc6 bc 12 ♘a4 ♗b7 13 c4 c5 14 ♘c3 ♘d7 ∞ Geller-Suba, Sochi 1983, and Psakhis-Pinter, Szirak 1986

[25] 12 ♗f3 b4! 13 ♘a4 ♖b8 ∓

12 a3 ♗b7 13 ♕g3 g6 (13 ... ♕c7 – 10 ... ♕c7) 14 ♗d3 (14 ♗f3 a5! =) 14 ... ♖c8 (14 ... a5!? 15 ♖ae1 b4 16 ab ab 17 ♘d1 d5 Zapata-Winants, Brussels 1986) 15 f5 e5 16 ♗e3 ♖xc3 17 bc ♘xe4 ∞ Jansa-Hartston, Reykjavik 1975

[26] 12 ... ♕c7 13 e5 de 14 fe ♘d7 15 ♘e4 ♗b7 16 ♘f6+ ♔h8 17 ♗d3! ± A.Ivanov-Magerramov, USSR 1980

12 ... b4 13 e5 bc 14 ef ♗xf6 15 ♕xc3 ±

[27] 13 ... b4!? 14 e5 ♗xf3 15 ♖xf3 bc! (15 ... de? 16 fe ♘d5 17 ♘e4 ± Geller-Grigorian, USSR Ch 1976) 16 ef ♗xf6 17 ♕xc3 ♖c8 ∞

[28] 17 ... ♖ac8 18 c3 ♔h8 19 ♖f4 b4 20 ♕g3 ± Tseshkovsky-Petrushin, USSR 1973

17 ... ♖ad8 18 ♖d3 ± Tal-Andersson, match 1976

[29] 19 c3 f5 (19 ... ♔h8 20 ♘d6 ♔g8 21 ♕g4 ±

Lanka-Korsunsky, USSR 1979; 19 ... ♘c5!?)
20 ef ♕xg3 21 hg! gf 21 g4 ±

[30] 12 e5 de 13 fe ♘xd4 14 ♗xd4 ♗c6 ∞

[31] 16 ♔h1 b4 17 ab ab 18 ♘b1 d5 19 ♗xf6
♗xf6 20 e5 ♗e7 21 f5 ef 22 ♗xf5 ♕c7 = Hazai-
Belyavsky, Honved v Trud 1983

[32] 19 ♕h3 ef 20 ♗xf5 ♕b7 21 ♗e4 ±/∞
Kruszynski-Schmidt, Poland 1978, and Sznapik-
Ree, Amsterdam 1980

[33] 13 e5 de 14 ♗xe5 (14 fe ♗c5! ∓) 14 ... ♕c5+
15 ♔h1 ♗b7 ∓ Reshevsky-Browne, Lone Pine
1977

[34] 14 ♗d3 e5 15 fe ♘h5 16 ♕e3 de 17 ♗xe5
♕xe5 18 ♖f5 ♕e6 19 ♖xh5 g6 ∞

14 ♖ae1 d5 15 ed ♗c5 = Arnason-
Mascarinas, Malta Ol 1980

14 ♖ad1 ♖ad8 (14 ... g6 15 f5 ± Suetin-
Polugayevsky, USSR 1976; 14 ... ♗c6 – 11 ...
♗d7) 15 b4 ♖d7 16 ♔h1 ♖c8 17 ♗d3 ♘e8
18 ♕h3 h6 19 ♘e2 ♗f6 ∞ Dvoiris-Polugayevsky,
USSR 1983

[35] 14 ... ♗c6 – 11 ... ♗d7

14 ... ♖fd8 15 ♖ae1 ♘e8 16 ♗d3 ±/±

[36] 16 ... ♗xe4 17 fg ♗xg6 18 ♖xf6! ±

16 ... ♘xe4 17 ♘xe4 ♗xe4 18 f6 ±

[37] 19 ♗f3! ♗xf3 20 ♖xf3 ± Prandstetter-
Adamski, Prague 1983, and P.Cramling-Gobet,
Biel 1984

[38] 12 ♘f3 ♘b4 13 ♗d3 (13 ♖ac1 d5) 13 ...
b5 =

12 ♖ae1 b5 13 a3 (13 e5!?) 13 ... b4 14 ab
♘xb4 ∞ Tal-Kurajica, Wijk aan Zee 1976

12 ♖ad1 b5 (12 ... ♖ac8 13 ♔h1 b5 14 e5
♘e8 15 ♘e4 ± Geller-Yap, Moscow 1986)
13 e5 (13 a3 ♘xd4 14 ♗xd4 ♗c6 15 ♔h1 ♕b7
16 ♗f3 ♖ac8 =) 13 ... ♘e8 14 ♗f3 ♖d8
15 ♘e4 f5 ∞/= Tal-Andersson, match 1976

[39] 13 e5 ♘e8 (13 ... de 14 fe ♘xe5 15 ♖xf6!
♗xf6 16 ♗f4 ± Torre-Schmidt, Indonesia
1983) 14 ♗d3 f5! ∞

[40] 13 ... ♖ab8 14 e5 ♘e8 (14 ... de 15 fe
♘xe5 16 ♖xf6! ♗xf6 17 ♗f4 ± Kasparov-
Korsunsky, USSR 1978) 15 ♘e4! ± Adorjan-
Kurajica, Skopje 1976

13 ... b4!? 14 ab ♘xb4 15 e5 ♘e8

[41] 15 e5 de 16 ♗xe5 ♕b7 17 f5 ef 18 ♖xf5
♘e8 19 ♗d3 g6 20 ♕f2 ♘g7 = Barlov-Adamski,
Vrnjačka Banja 1984

[42] 15 ... ♖ae8 16 ♗d3 e5 17 fe ♘h5 18 ♕h3
de 19 ♗e3 g6 20 ♗h6 ♘g7 21 ♘d1 ± Belyavsky-
Garcia Martinez, Moscow 1975

15 ... g6 16 f5 e5 17 ♗e3 ♔h8 18 ♕h4 ±
Schmidt-Janošević, Vršac 1977

[43] 19 e5 ♘d5 20 ♕h3 g6 21 ♘g3 de 22 ♗xe5
f6!? 23 ♗xh5 fe 24 ♖xe5 ♖f7 25 ♘g3 ♖af8 ∞
Pritchett-Polugayevsky, 1981

[44] 10 ... ♗d7 11 ♘b3 – row 3

[45] 11 ... ♘a5 12 ♖d1 ♘c4 13 ♗c1 e5 14 ♘b3
ef 15 ♖xf4 ♗e6 16 ♔h1 ♖ac8 17 ♘d4 ♘e5

[18] ♘f5 ± A.Kuzmin-Avshalumov, Sevastopol
1986

[46] 13 fe de 14 ♕g3 ♗c5 15 ♗xc5 ♕xc5+
16 ♔h1 ♔h8 =

[47] 14 ♖xf4 ♗e6 15 ♕g3 ♘d7 (15 ... d5?
16 ed ♘xd5 17 ♘xd5 ♗xd5 18 ♗d4 g6 19 ♖xf7;
18... f6 19 ♖xf6) 16 ♗d4 ♘e5 17 ♗d3 (intending
♘d5 ±) 17 ... ♕a5 ∞/= Larsen-Andersson,
Manila 1974

[48] 14 ... ♕b6+ 15 ♔h1 ♕xb2 16 ♕g3 ♕b4
17 e5 de 18 ♗xe5 ±

[49] 15 ... ♔h8 16 e5 ± Balashov-Ree, Wijk aan
Zee 1982

15 ... ♖fd8 16 ♗h6 ± Dolmatov-Tal, USSR
1979, and Psakhis-Polugayevsky, USSR 1981

[50] 19 ♗e3 ♕e5 20 ♕f2 ♕a5 = Tal-Ribli,
Tilburg 1980

19 ♗g4 ♘e5 20 ♗f5 ♘g6 ∞ Oll-Averkin,
USSR 1985, and Ehlvest-Grigorian, Pinsk 1986

19 ♘d5 ♗xd5 20 ed (20 ♗h6 ♕d4
21 ed ±/∞ Tal-Ftacnik, Tallinn 1981; 20 ...
g6!? 21 ♗xf8 ♗xf8 22 ed ♕xc2 ∞) 20 ...
♖fe8 21 c4 ♗h4 22 ♕xh4 ♖xe2 ∞/= Dolmatov-
Loginov, USSR 1983

[51] 11 ... ♗d7 12 ♕e1 ♖fe8 (12 ... ♘xd4
13 ♗xd4 ♗c6 14 ♕g3 g6 15 f5! ±) 13 ♕g3 d5
14 ♘xc6 ♗xc6 15 e5 ± Sznapik-Stempin,
Poland 1985

11 ... ♘xd4 12 ♕xd4 e5 13 ♕d3 ef (13 ...
♗e6 14 f5 ±; 13 ... ♗d7 14 fe de 15 ♖xf6!
♗xf6 16 ♘d5 ±) 14 ♗xf4 ♗e6 15 ♕g3 ± (see
row 10, but with the extra move ♔h1)

11 ... ♖d8 12 ♗d3 (12 ♗g1!? ♘f8 13 ♕d3
intending ♕g3 ± Veličković-Musil, Yugoslavia
1984) 12 ... ♘xd4 (12 ... ♗d7 13 ♕f3 ♘b4
14 a5 ± Kindermann-Foisor, Lucerne Ol 1982)
13 ♗xd4 e5 14 ♗g1 ef 15 a5 ♖e8 16 ♖xf4 ±
Kindermann-Cserna, Wolfsberg 1986

[52] 12 ♕d2 ♘xd4 (12 ... ♘a5!?) 13 ♕xd4 e5
14 ♕d3 ef 15 ♗xf4 ♗e6 = Belyavsky-Portisch,
Montpellier C 1985

12 ♗g1 ♘xd4 (12 ... ♖b8 13 ♕d3 ♘xd4
14 ♗xd4 e5 15 ♗a7 ♖a8 16 ♗e3 ± Mokry-
Grünberg, Polanica Zdroj 1985) 13 ♕xd4 e5
14 ♕d2 ef 15 ♕xf4 (15 ♖xf4 ♗e6 16 ♘d5
♗xd5 17 ed ♘d7 ∞ Mäki-Schmidt, Sofia 1985)
15 ... ♗e6 16 ♗d4 ♘d7 = Geller-Andersson,
Moscow 1981

[53] 12 ... ♘xd4 13 ♗xd4 e5 14 ♗e3 ♗g4
(14 ... ef 15 ♖xf4 ♗e6 16 ♘d5 ± Tseshkovsky-
Polugayevsky, Sochi 1981) 15 ♕e1 (15 ♕d2
ef 16 ♖xf4 ♗e6 17 ♘d5 ±/∞ Morović-
Polugayevsky, Lucerne Ol 1982) 15 ... ef
16 ♗xf4 ♗e6?! 17 e5 ± Ye Jiangohuan-Liao,
Dubai Ol 1986

[54] 16 ♘xd5 ed! ∞ Sznapik-Ftacnik, Bratislava
1983

[55] 19 bc ♗c6 20 ♘d4 ♖ad8 ∞ Sigurjonsson-
Vera, Dubai Ol 1986

1 e4 c5 2 ♘f3 d6 3 d4 cd 4 ♘xd4 ♘f6 5 ♘c3 e6 6 ♗e2 ♘c6 7 0-0 ♗e7 8 ♗e3 0-0 9 f4 a6 *continued*

	10	11	12	13	14	15	16	17	18	
12	a4	♔h1	♗f3	♕d2[57]	♘b3[59]	g4[60]	g5	♕f2[61]	♗g2	∞
	♕c7	♖e8	♖b8[56]	♗d7[58]	b6	♗c8	♘d7	♗f8	♗b7[62]	

[56] **12 ... ♗d7** 13 ♘b3 ♘a5 14 e5 ± Oll-Dokhoyan, USSR 1986

12 ... ♘xd4 13 ♕xd4 e5 14 ♕d2 ef 15 ♗xf4 ♗e6 16 ♖fd1 ±

12 ... ♘a5 13 ♕d3 ♘c4 14 ♗c1 ♗f8 (14 ... e5 15 ♘de2 ef 16 ♘xf4 ♘e5 17 ♕d4 ♗e6 ∞/= Karpov-Martinović, Amsterdam 1985) 15 b3 ♘a5 ∞ Plaskett-Bellon, Hastings 1985-86

[57] 13 g4 ♗f8 (13 ... ♘xd4!? 14 ♗xd4 e5) 14 g5 ♘d7 15 ♗g2 g6 (15 ... ♘a5 16 ♗g1 b6 17 ♕h5 g6 18 ♕h3 ± A.Sokolov-Jansa, Dubai Ol 1986) 16 ♕e2 b6 17 ♖ad1 ♗b7 18 ♕f2 ♗a8 ∞ Silva-Mokry, Dubai Ol 1986

[58] 13 ... ♘xd4 14 ♗xd4 e5 15 ♗a7 ♖a8 16 ♗e3 ±/∞ Karpov-Kasparov, match (45) 1984-85, and Short-Tisdall, Westmann Islands (Iceland) 1985

[59] 14 ♕f2 ♘xd4 15 ♗xd4 e5 16 ♗e3 ef (16 ... ♗e6? 17 f5 ♘c4 18 ♗b6 ± Karpov-Kasparov, match (2) 1985) 17 ♗xf4 ♗e6 intending ... ♘d7 =

[60] 15 ♗f2 ♗c8 16 ♗g3 ♘d7 = Karpov-Kasparov, match (18) 1985

[61] 17 ♗g2 ♘a5 18 ♕f2 ♘c4 (18 ... ♗f8 19 ♖ad1 ±/∞ A.Sokolov-Ribli, Montpellier C 1985) 19 ♗c1 ♗b7 ∞

[62] **18 ... g6** 19 ♖ad1 b5 ∞ Tseshkovsky-Jansa, Calcutta 1986

18 ... ♗b7 19 ♖ad1 g6 20 ♗c1 (Karpov-Kasparov, match (24) 1985) 20 ... ♘c5! ∞

1 e4 e5
Miscellaneous

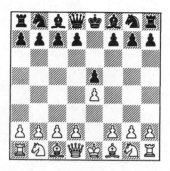

Centre Game (1 e4 e5 2 d4 ed 3 ♕xd4)   The early development of White's queen is a serious breach of the basic rules of development and not surprisingly he forfeits the initiative rather quickly. It is almost never seen in modern practice.

Bishop's Opening (2 ♗c4)   As more and more e-pawn players become frustrated by the diminishing returns of allowing the Petroff, the Bishop's Opening is bound to gain in popularity. Modern treatment steers the game into channels closely akin to the Giuoco Pianissimo or the Two Knights. Black has several paths to equality but this move order maintains positional tension while sidestepping the static formations arising from the Petroff.

Reference: *Unorthodox Openings* (Benjamin and Schiller)

					1 e4 e5				
	2	3	4	5	6	7	8	9	10
1	d4[1]	♕xd4[2]	♕a4[3]	♗g5	♘c3	♘f3	0-0-0	♕c4	♕e2	=
	ed	♘c6	♘f6	♗e7	0-0	d6	♗d7	♗e6	♘d7[4]	
2	♗c4	d3	♗b3[7]	♘f3	♘c3	♘e2	♘g3	c3	♗c2	=
	♘f6[5]	c6[6]	♗c5	d6	♕e7[8]	♗e6	g6	♗b6	h6[9]	
3	...	d4	♘f3	♕xd4	♗g5	♘c3	0-0-0	♖he1	♕h4	=
	...	ed	♘xe4[10]	♘f6	♗e7	c6![11]	d5	0-0[12]	♗e6[13]	

[1]   2 ♘e2 ♘c6 3 ♘bc3 ♗c5 4 ♘a4 ♗e7 5 d4 ♘f6 =; 2 ... ♘f6 =

[2]   3 c3 dc 4 ♗c4 cb 5 ♗xb2 d5! 6 ♗xd5 ♘f6 7 ♗xf7+ ♔xf7 8 ♕xd8 ♗b4+ 9 ♕d2 =; 3 ... ♕e7!? 4 cd ♕xe4+ 5 ♗e3 ♗b4+ 6 ♘c3 ♘f6 7 ♘f3 ♘d5 ∞/∓; 3 ... d5 – Scotch

[3]   4 ♕e3 ♘f6 5 ♘c3 ♗b4 6 ♗d2 0-0 7 0-0-0 ♖e8 8 ♗c4 d6 9 f3 (9 ♘f3 ♗e6 10 ♗xe6 ♖xe6 11 ♘g5 ♖e8 12 f4 h6 13 h4 ♕c8 ∓ Tartakower-Reshevsky, Kemeri 1937) 9 ... ♘a5! (9 ... ♘e5 10 ♗b3 ♗e6 11 ♘d5 = Larsen) 10 ♗b3 ♗e6 ∓

[4]   11 h4 ♘de5 12 ♘d5 = Milev-Chipev, Bulgaria 1961

[5]   2 ... c6 3 d4! d5 4 ed cd 5 ♗b5+ ♗d7 6 ♗xd7+ ♘xd7 7 de ±

[6]   3 ... d5 4 ed ♘xd5 5 ♘f3 ♘c6 6 0-0 ♗c5 7 ♖e1 0-0 8 ♘c3 ♘b6 9 ♗b3 h5 ∞/=
   3 ... ♗c5 – Giuoco Piano
   3 ... ♘c6 – Two Knights

[7]   4 ♘f3 d5 (4 ... d6 5 h3 ♘bd7 6 a4 ♗e7 7 0-0 0-0 8 ♘c3 ♘c5 9 ♗g5 ♘e6 10 ♗d2 ♖e8 = Vogt-Bronstein, Tallinn 1981) 5 ♗b3 ♘bd7 6 0-0 ♗d6 7 ♘c3 de 8 ♘g5 0-0 9 ♘cxe4 ♘c5 = Olafsson-Kurajica, Wijk aan Zee 1977

[8]   6 ... 0-0 7 0-0 ♘bd7 8 ♘e2 ♗b6 9 c3 ♘c5 10 ♗c2 ♗g4 = Hartston-Petrosian, Moscow 1977

[9]   11 a4 a5 12 h3 ♘bd7 = Hartston-Vasyukov, Hastings 1978-79

[10]   4 ... d5!? 5 ed ♗b4+ 6 c3 ♕e7+ 7 ♗e2 (7 ♔f1 ∞) 7 ... dc 8 bc ♗c5 9 0-0 0-0 =

[11]   7 ... ♘c6 8 ♕h4 d6 9 0-0-0 ♗e6 10 ♗d3 ♕d7 11 ♗b5 0-0 =

[12]   9 ... ♗e6 10 ♗d3 ♘bd7 11 ♕h4 ♘c5 12 ♗d4 ♗g3 13 ♗xe7 ♕xe7 14 ♕g3 g6 15 ♘ce2 ∞∞ Keres

[13]   11 ♗d3 h6 12 ♗xh6 ♘e4 13 ♕f4 ∞/= Estrin

351

King's Gambit

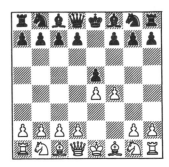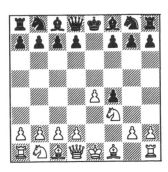

A weapon of incomparable danger in the hands of the great attacking players of the 19th century, the King's Gambit was responsible for many gems of sacrificial daring in the romantic days of chess history. But it would be only a matter of time before the elements that provided White with virulent attacks (quick development, excessive materialism) were used against him to rob the gambit of its venom. Accepting the gambit displays greater vigour than declining it, e.g. by Falkbeer's once-popular 2 ... d5, and today the defender has learned how to reach equality with the timely return of the gambit pawn in order to successfully mobilise his forces, but crucial also are his attempts to hold the pawn without going to lengths to acquire more material. Nonetheless, there is still scope here for investigation, and free spirits like Bronstein, Fischer and Spassky have been known to essay the old gambit when in an appropriately violent mood. While recent investigations have been limited due to the unfashionability of romance, the classical gambit remains lively and unrefuted.

Reference: *King's Gambit* (Korchnoi and Zak)

	King's Gambit I				1 e4 e5 2 f4					
	2	3	4	5	6	7	8	9	10	
1	... ♘f6	♘f3 d5	fe ♘xe4[1]	d3 ♘c5	d4 ♘e6[2]	c4 ♗b4+[3]	♗d2 ♗xd2+	♕xd2 c6	♘c3 0-0[4]	±
2	... ♗c5	♘f3 d6	c3 ♘f6[5]	fe de	♘xe5 ♕e7[6]	d4 ♗d6	♘f3[7] ♘xe4	♗e2 0-0	0-0 c5[8]	=
3	... ...	... ...	♘c3 ♘f6	♗c4 ♘c6	d3 ♗g4[9]	♘a4 0-0[10]	♘xc5 dc	c3 ♘a5	♗b5 a6[11]	±
4	... d5	ed c6[12]	♘c3![13] ef[14]	♘f3 ♗d6[15]	♗c4[16] ♘e7	dc ♘bxc6	d4 0-0	0-0 ♗g4	♘e2[17] ♘g6[18]	±
5	... ...	... e4	♘c3 ♘f6	♕e2[19] ♗g4	♕b5+[20] ♘bd7	h3 a6	♕c4 b5	♕c6 ♗f5	g4 ♗c5[21]	∞
6	... ...	... ...	d3 ♘f6[22]	de[23] ♘xe4	♘f3 ♗c5[24]	♕e2[25] ♗f5[26]	♘c3! ♕e7[27]	♗e3 ♗xe3	♕xe3 ♘xc3[28]	±
7	... ...	... ...	... ...	... ...	♗e3 ♕h4+[29]	g3 ♘xg3	♘f3 ♕e7[30]	hg ♕xe3+	♕e2 ♗c5[31]	±

	2	3	4	5	6	7	8	9	10	
8	...	Nc3[32]	Ke2	Nxd5	Nf3	Nxc7+	Nxa8	h3	gf	∞
	ef	Qh4+	d5	Bg4+	Nc6[33]	Kd8	Ne5	Bxf3+[34]	Qg3[35]	
9	...	Bc4	Kf1	Bxd5	Nc3	d4	Nf3	Bc4		=
	...	Qh4+[36]	d5![37]	Bd6[38]	Ne7	f6!	Qh5	Bg4![39]		
10	...	...	Nc3[40]	Bb3[41]	ed	d4	Nge2	Bxf4[42]	Nxf4	∞
	...	Nf6	c6	d5	cd	Bd6	0-0	Bxf4	Re8+[43]	

---

[1] 4 ... de 5 ef ef 6 Qxf3 Nc6 7 Bb5 Qxf6 8 Qxf6 gf 9 d4 ±

[2] 6 ... Ne4 7 Nbd2 f5 8 ef Nxf6 9 Bd3 Bd6 10 0-0 0-0 11 c4 ±

[3] 7 ... c6 8 Nc3 Be7 9 Be3 0-0 10 Qd2 b6 11 Bd3 ± Bronstein-Kholmov, USSR 1975

[4] 11 Rc1 ± Bronstein-Yusupov, Moscow 1981

[5] 4 ... Bg4 5 fe Bxf3 6 Qxf3 de 7 Qg3 ±
4 ... Nc6 5 d4 ed 6 cd Bb4+ 7 Bd2 ±
4 ... f5!? 5 fe de 6 d4 ed 7 Bc4! ∞/± Reti

[6] 6 ... 0-0 7 d4 Bd6 8 Nf3 Nxe4 9 Bd3 Re8 10 0-0 Nd7 =

[7] 8 Nc4?! Nxe4 9 Nxd6+ Bxd6+ ∓

[8] 11 d5 Bg4! =

[9] 6 ... Be6 7 Bb5 0-0 8 f5 Bd7 9 Bg5 ± *ECO*

[10] 7 ... Bb6 8 Nxb6 ab 9 c3 ±
7 ... ef 8 Nxc5 dc 9 Bxf4 Nh5 10 Be3 ±

[11] 11 Ba4 b5 12 Bc2 Nc6 13 h3 ± Tartakower

[12] 3 ... Qxd5 4 Nc3 Qe6 5 fe/±

[13] 4 dc Nxc6 5 Bb5 ef 6 Nf3 Bd6 7 d4 Ne7 8 0-0 0-0 = Ree-Short, Wijk aan Zee 1986

[14] 4 ... cd 5 fe d4 6 Ne4 Qd5 7 Bd3! ±

[15] 5 ... Nf6 6 d4 Bd6 7 Qe2+ Qe7 8 Qxe7+ Kxe7 9 Bc4 ±

[16] 6 d4 Ne7 7 dc Nbxc6 8 Bd3 0-0 9 Ne2 Bg4 10 0-0 Nd5 ∞ Day-Mercuri, Saint John 1988

[17] 10 Ne4!? Nc7 11 c3 Nd5 12 Nc5 Rb8 13 Qe1! ±/= Illescas-Nunn, Dubai Ol 1986

[18] 11 c3 ± Podgorny-Sevecek, corr. 1986

[19] 5 d3 Bb4 6 Bd2 e3! 7 Bxe3 Nxd5 8 Bd2 0-0! 9 Be2 Bxc3 10 bc Qf6 ∓∓ Gruzman-Kimmelfeld, Moscow 1966
5 Bb5+ c6 6 dc bc ∞ Estrin

[20] 6 Qe3 Bf5 7 Bb5+ c6 8 dc Nxc6 ∞

[21] 11 gf 0-0 12 b4 Ba7 ∞ Obuchovsky-Kuznetsov, Moscow 1980

[22] Qxd5 5 Nc3 Bb4 6 Bd2 Bxc3 7 Bxc3 Nge7 8 de! ±
4 ... ed 5 Qxd3 ±/± Keres

[23] 5 Nd2?! ed 6 Bxd3 Nxd5 7 Ne4 Nb4! ∓

[24] 6 ... Bf5 7 Be3 c6 8 Bc4 b5 9 Bb3 c5 10 d6! ± Alekhine-Tarrasch, St Petersburg 1914
6 ... Be7 7 Bd3 Qxd5 8 Qe2 Nc5 9 Bc4 ± Angelov-Estrin, Varna 1983

[25] 7 Bd3!? 0-0 8 Bxe4 Re8 9 Nc3! ±

[26] 7 ... Qe7 8 Be3 Na6 9 Bxc5 Nxc5 10 Nbd2 0-0 11 0-0-0 ±/± Zuckerman-Reshevsky, Netanya 1971

[27] 8 ... 0-0 9 Nxe4 Re8 10 Ne5 Bxe4 11 Qxe4 f6 12 d6! ±±

[28] 11 Qxe7+ Kxe7 12 bc ± Bronstein-Vaisman, Sandomir 1976

[29] 6 ... Bc5 7 Bxc5 Nxc5 8 Qe2+ Qe7 9 Nc3 Bg4 10 Qxe7+ Kxe7 11 h3 Bf5 12 0-0-0 ± Spassky-Limbos, Varna 1962

[30] 8 ... Qh6 9 hg! Qxh1 10 Qe2 Bg4 11 Nbd2 Nd7 12 Bd4+ ±

[31] 10 ... Qxe2+ 11 Bxe2 Bg4 12 Nc3 Bb4 13 Ng5 ± Spassky-Matanović, Belgrade 1964
10 ... Bc5 11 Nc3 Bf5 12 Qxe3+ Bxe3 13 Nh4 Bg4 14 Be2 ± *ECO*

[32] 3 Qf3 d5! 4 ed c6!? (4 ... Nf6 5 Bb5+ c6 6 dc Nxc6 ∞/∓) 5 dc Nxc6 6 Bb5 Qb6! ∓
3 Be2 d5! 4 ed Nf6 5 Nf3 Nxd5 6 Ne2 Be7 7 0-0 0-0 ∓ Littlewood-Lengyel, Hastings 1963-64
3 d4 Qh4+ 4 Ke2 d5! 5 Nf3 Bg4 6 ed Nf6 ∓

[33] 6 ... Bd6 7 d4 Nf6 8 Nxf6+ gf 9 d3 Qh5 10 Be2 ±; 7 ... Nc6 8 c3! 0-0-0 9 Kd3 Qh6 10 Kc2 Be6 11 g3 Qg6 12 Bd3! ± Sveshnikov

[34] 9 ... Bh5 10 d4! Nxf3 11 gf Bxf3+ 12 Qxf3 Qh5+ 13 Kg2 Qxd1 14 Bd3! ∞

[35] 11 d3 Qxf3+ 12 Ke1! Qxh1 13 Bxf4 Nf3+ 14 Ke2! Bc5 15 c3 ∞ Estrin

[36] 3 ... d5 4 Bxd5 Nf6 5 Nf3 Nxd5 6 ed Qxd5 7 Nc3 Qf5! =
3 ... Nf6 4 d3 d5 5 ed Nxd5 6 Nf3 Nb6 7 Bb3 Bd6 8 Qe2+! ± J.Polgar-Flear, Hastings 1988-89

[37] 4 ... b5 5 Bxb5 Nf6 6 Nf3 Qh6 7 Nc3! ±

[38] 5 ... g5 6 g3! Qh6 7 d4! Nf6 8 Qf3! ±

[39] Estrin

[40] 4 Qe2 Bc5! (4 ... d5 5 ed Be7 6 Nf3 0-0 = Gheorghiu-Portisch, Amsterdam 1969) 5 Nf3 Nc6 6 c3 0-0 7 d4 d5! ∓

[41] 5 d4 Bb4 6 Qf3 d5 7 ed 0-0 8 Nge2 cd ∓
5 Qf3 d5 6 ed Bd6 7 d3 Bg4 8 Qf2 0-0 ∓

[42] 9 0-0 g5 10 Nxd5 Nc6 11 h4! = Tartakower

[43] 11 Nfe2 Bg4 12 Nxd5 Be6 13 h3 Bxd5 14 hg = Fischer

King's Gambit II 1 e4 e5 2 f4 ef 3 ♘f3

	3	4	5	6	7	8	9	10	11	
1	... d5[1]	ed ♘f6[2]	♗b5+[3] c6[4]	dc ♘xc6[5]	d4 ♗d6	♕e2+[6] ♗e6[7]	♘g5[8] 0-0	♘xe6 fe	♗xc6 bc[9]	=/±
2	... ♘f6	e5[10] ♘h5	♕e2[11] ♗e7	d4 0-0	g4[12] fg	♘c3 d5	♕g2 ♗g4	hg ♘c6	♗e3 ♕d7[13]	∞
3	... ...	... ...	♗e2 g5[14]	0-0 ♖g8[15]	d4 d5	c4! c6	♘c3 ♗e6	cd cd	♕d3 ♖g6[16]	±
4	... ♗e7	♗c4[17] ♘f6[18]	e5[19] ♘g4	0-0[20] ♘c6	d4 d5	ed ♗xd6[21]	♕e1+[22] ♘e7[23]	h3 ♘f6[24]	♘e5 0-0[25]	±
5	... d6	d4[26] g5	h4! g4	♘g1[27] ♗h6[28]	♘c3 c6[29]	♘ge2 ♕f6	g3 f3	♘f4 ♕e7[30]	♔f2 ♘d7[31]	±
6	... h6	d4 g5	♘c3 d6[32]	g3 fg[33]	h4 g4	♘g1 g2[34]	♗xg2 ♗e7	h5 ♗h4+	♔e2 ♗g5[35]	±
7	... g5	d4[36] g4[37]	♘e5[38] ♕h4+	g3 fg	♕xg4 ♕xg4[39]	♘xg4 d5	♘e3 de	hg ♘c6	♗g2[40]	∞
8	... ...	♗c4 g4	0-0![41] gf	♕xf3 ♕f6	e5!?[42] ♕xe5	♗xf7+[43] ♔xf7	d4 ♕f5[44]	g4 ♕g6	♗xf4 ♘f6[45]	±
9	... ...	... ♗g7	0-0[46] h6	d4 d6	c3 ♘c6	h4[47] ♗g4[48]	♕b3 ♘a5	♗xf7+ ♔f8	♕a4 ♔xf7[49]	=
10	... ...	h4 g4	♘g5[50] h6[51]	♘xf7 ♔xf7	♘c3[52] f3[53]	gf ♗e7	♗c4+ d5	♘xd5 ♗xh4+	♔f1 ♔g7[54]	∞
11	... ...	... ...	♘e5 ♗g7[55]	d4 ♘f6	♘c3 d6[56]	♘d3 0-0	♗xf4 ♘xe4	♘xe4 ♖e8	♔f2 ♖xe4[57]	±
12	... ...	... ...	... ♘f6	d4[58] d6	♘d3 ♘xe4	♕e2 ♕e7	♗xf4 ♘c6[59]	c3 ♗f5	♘d2 0-0-0[60]	∞
13	... ...	... ...	... d6	♘xg4 ♗e7[61]	d4 ♗xh4+	♘f2 ♕g5	♘c3[62] ♘f6	♕f3 ♘g4!	♘fd1 ♘f2[63]	∞

[1] **3 ...** ♘e7 4 d4 d5 5 ♘c3 de 6 ♘xe4 ♘g6 7 h4! ♗e7 8 h5 ♘h4 9 ♘xf4 ♗g4 10 h6! ± Kuznetsov-Bonch Osmolovsky, Moscow 1964
3 ... f5 4 e5! d5 (4 ... g5 5 d4! d5 6 ed ♗xd6 7 ♗c4 ± Hoi) 5 h4 ♗e7 6 d4 ♘h6 7 ♗xf4 ♘g4 8 ♘c3 0-0 9 ♕d2 c6 10 0-0-0! ± Estrin

[2] **4 ...** ♗d6 5 d4! (5 ♘c3 ♘e7 6 d4 0-0 7 ♗d3 ∞/± Spassky-Bronstein, Leningrad 1960) 5 ... ♘f6 6 c4 ♗g4 7 ♗d3 0-0 8 0-0 b6 9 ♕c2 ±

[3] 5 ♘c3 ♘xd5 6 ♘xd5 ♕xd5 7 d4 ♗e7! 8 ♗d3 g5 9 ♕e2 ♗f5 10 0-0! ∞ Hund-Sternberg,

Lucerne Ol 1982

[4] **5 ...** ♗d7 6 ♗xd7+ ♘bxd7 7 0-0 ♘xd5 8 c4 ±; 6 ... ♕xd7 7 c4 ♗d6 8 0-0 0-0-0 9 d4 ±

[5] 6 ... bc 7 ♗c4 ♘d5 8 0-0 ♗d6 9 ♘c3 ♗e6 10 ♘e4 ± Tal-Haubt, 1960

[6] 8 0-0 0-0 9 c4 (9 ♘bd2 *ECO*) 9 ... ♗g4 10 ♘c3 ♖c8 ∞

[7] 8 ... ♕e7 9 ♕xe7+ ♔xe7 10 0-0 ♘d5!? 11 ♘bd2 ♘e3 12 ♖f2 ∞ Hoi

[8] 9 ♘e5?! 0-0 10 ♗xc6 bc 11 ♗xf4 ♘d5 12 ♗g3 f6 ∓/∓ Hartston-Spassky, Hastings 1965-66

[9] 12 0-0! ± Hoi-Hamilton, London 1971

[10] 4 ♘c3 d5 5 e5 ♘h5 (5 ... ♘e4 6 d3 ♘xc3 7 bc g5 8 h4 ∞) 6 ♗e2 ♖g8 7 ♘g1!? ∞

[11] 5 d4 d6 6 ♕e2 d5 7 c4!? ∞/± ECO

[12] 7 ♘c3 d6 8 ♗d2 ♘c6! 9 0-0-0 ♗g4 ∓ Keres

[13] 12 0-0-0 ∞ Estrin

[14] 5 ... d6 6 0-0 de 7 ♘xe5 ♗c5+ 8 ♔h1 ♘f6 9 c3 ±

5 ... g6 6 d4 ♗g7 7 0-0 d6 8 ♘c3 0-0 9 ed ± Chigorin

[15] 6 ... ♗g7 7 d4 d5 8 c4 c6 9 ♘c3 ± Lutikov-Kuzmin, USSR 1970

[16] 12 ♘h4 ♖h6 13 ♘f5 ± Glazkov, Estrin

[17] 4 ♘c3 ♗h4+ 5 ♔e2 c6! 6 d4 d5 7 e5 ♗g4 8 ♗xf4 f6 ∓ Prachov-Ivanov, Bulgaria 1961

[18] 4 ... ♗h4+ 5 ♔f1 d5 6 ♗xd5 ♘f6 7 ♗b3! ± Glazkov

[19] 5 ♕e2 0-0 6 0-0 d5 7 ♗xd5! =

[20] 6 ♘c3 d6 7 ed ♗xd6 8 ♕e2+ ♔f8 (8 ... ♕e7 9 ♕xe7+ ♔xe7 10 ♘d5+ ♔d8 11 d4 ±) 9 0-0 ♘c6 10 d4 ♗f5 ∞

[21] 8 ... ♕xd6? 9 ♘c3 0-0 10 ♘b5 ♕b4 11 b3 ± Yurtayev-Rozentalis, Riga 1977

[22] 9 ♕e2+ ♔f8 10 ♘c3 ♗f5 11 ♘d5 g5! 12 g3 ∞

[23] 9 ... ♔f8 10 ♘c3 g5 11 h3 ♘h6 12 ♘e4 ♗e7 13 d5 ± Bhend-Schmidt, corr. 1964

9 ... ♕e7 10 ♕xe7+ ♔xe7 11 ♘c3 ♗f5 12 ♘d5+ ±

[24] 10 ... ♘h6 11 ♘e5 ♗xe5 12 ♕xe5 0-0 13 ♕xf4 ♘g6 14 ♕f2 ±

[25] 12 ♗xf4 ♘fd5 13 ♗d2 ± Estrin

[26] 4 ♗c4 h6 5 d4 g5 6 c3! ♗g7 7 h4! – 3 ... g5

[27] 6 ♘g5 f6! 7 ♘h3 gh 8 ♕h5+ ♔d7 9 ♕f3 ♕e8! ∓

[28] 6 ... ♕f6 7 ♘c3 ♘e7 8 ♘ge2 ♗h6 9 ♕d2 ♗d7 10 g3 ♘bc6 11 gf 0-0-0 12 ♗g2 ± Planinc-Portisch, Ljubljana 1973; 7 ... c6! Estrin

6 ... f3 7 gf ♗e7 8 ♗e3! ♗h4+ 9 ♔d2 ♘c6 10 ♘c3 ♘f6 11 ♔c1 Nei

[29] 7 ... ♘c6 8 ♘ge2 f3 (Planinc-Gligorić, Ljubljana 1977) 9 ♘g3! ±

[30] 10 ... ♘d7 11 ♗e3 ♘f8 12 e5 ± Hoi

10 ... b5 11 ♗e3 b4 12 e5! de 13 ♘e4 ± Keller-Hendler, corr. 1980

[31] 12 a4! ± Estrin

[32] 5 ... ♗g7 6 g3 g4 (6 ... fg 7 h4!) 7 ♘h4 f3 8 ♗f4 ∞/±

[33] 6 ... ♗g7 7 gf g4 8 ♗e3! gf 9 ♕xf3 ∞/± Glazkov

[34] 8 ... ♗e7 9 ♗g2 ♗xh4 10 ♗f4 ♕f6 11 ♕d2 ±

[35] 12 ♗xg5 ♕xg5 13 ♕d2 (13 ♕d3!?) 13 ... ♕xd2+ 14 ♔xd2 ♘e7 15 ♘ge2 ± Zak

[36] 4 ♘c3 g4 5 ♘e5 ♕h4+ 6 g3 fg 7 ♕xg4 ♕xg4 (7 ... g2? 8 ♕xh4 gh♕ 9 ♕h5 ♗d6 10 ♕xf7+ ♔d8 11 d4 ± Keres) 8 ♘xg4 d5 9 ♗h3! de 10 ♘f6+ ♔d8 11 ♗xc8 ♔xc8 12 ♘fxe4 gh ∞ Schmidt (1884)

[37] 4 ... h6 5 ♘c3 ♗g7 6 g3 d6 7 gf g4 8 ♘g1

♕h4+ 9 ♔e2 ♘c6 10 ♗e3 ± Bhend

[38] 5 ♗xf4 gf 6 ♕xf3 d5! 7 ♘c3! ∞

[39] 7 ... g2+? 8 ♕xh4 gh♕ 9 ♘c3! d6 10 ♘xf7 ±

[40] 11 ♗b5 ♗d7! ∓ ECO

[41] 5 ♘c3 gf 6 ♕xf3 d6! 7 d4 ♗e6 ∓ Keres

5 ♗xf7+ ♔xf7 6 ♗e5+ ♔e8 7 ♕xg4 ♘f6 8 ♕xf4 d6 ∓ Schmidt (1886)

5 d4 gf 6 ♕xf3 d5! 7 ♗xd5 ♘f6 8 0-0 c6 ∓

5 ♘e5 ♕h4+ 6 ♔f1 (6 ♔e2 ♘c6) 6 ... ♘c6! ∓ Hertzfeld

[42] 7 c3!? ♘c6 8 d4 ♘xd4 9 ♗xf7+ ♕xf7 10 cd ♗h6 11 ♘c3 d6 12 ♘d5 ♗e6 = ECO1

[43] 8 d3 ♗h6 9 ♘c3 ♘e7 10 ♗d2 ♘c6 11 ♖ae1 ♕f5! 12 ♘d5 ♔d8 13 ♕e2 ♕e6! (13 ... b5? 14 ♘xe7 ♕c5+ 15 ♖f2 ♘xe7 16 ♗c3 ♖e8 17 ♗xf7 ♖f8 18 ♗d4! ±±) 14 ♕f3 ♕f5 =

[44] 9 ... ♕xd4+ 10 ♗e3 ♕f6 11 ♘c3! (11 ♗xf4 ♗e7 12 ♘c3 ♕f5 13 ♕e2 ♗e8 14 ♗e5 ± Trupan-Vanchak, corr. 1981-82) 11 ... ♘e7 12 ♘d5! ♘xd5 13 ♕xd5+ ♕e6 14 ♖xf4+ ♔g8 15 ♗g5! ♕g6 16 ♖xf8+ ♔xf8 17 ♖f1+ ±± Tsaturian; 11 ... d6 12 ♘d5! ♕f5 13 g4 ±/± Glazkov

[45] 12 ♗e5 ♘c6 13 ♗xf6 ♗xg4 14 ♕g2 ♖g8 15 ♔h1 ♗f5 16 ♕d5! ±

[46] 5 h4 h6 6 d4 d6 7 c3 ♘c6 8 ♕b3 ♕e7 9 0-0 ♘f6 ∓ Zak, Korchnoi

[47] 8 g3 ♗h3! 9 gf ♕d7! 10 f5 ♗xf1 11 ♕xf1 ♘f6 ∓ Glazkov

[48] 8 ... ♕e7 9 a4 ♗d7 10 a5 0-0-0 11 g4 ♘b8 12 b4 ∞ Anderssen (1875)

[49] 12 ♕xa5 ♗xf3 13 ♖xf3 c5 = Hoi

[50] Allgaier Gambit

[51] 5 ... ♘f6 6 e5 ♕e7 7 ♕e2 ♘h5 8 ♕xg4 ♕xe5+ 9 ♗e2 ♘g3 10 d4 ±

[52] 7 ♗c4+ d5 8 ♗xd5+ ♔g7 9 d4 f3! 10 gf ♘f6 11 ♘c3 ♗b4 ∓

[53] 7 ... ♘f6 8 d4 d5 9 ♗xf4 ∞

[54] 12 f4 ∞ Keres

[55] 5 ... h5 6 ♗c4 ♘h6 7 d4 d6 8 ♘d3 f3 9 gf gf 10 ♕xf3 ♗g4 11 ♕f2 ± Peev-Atanasov, Bulgaria 1954

5 ... d5 6 d4 ♘f6 7 ♗xf4 ♘xe4 8 ♘d2! ± Caro

[56] 7 ... d5 8 ♗xf4 ♘xe4 9 ♘xe4 de 10 ♗c4 0-0 11 c3 ± Lutikov

[57] 12 c3 ♕f6 13 g3 ± Rubinstein

[58] 6 ♗c4 d5 7 ed ♗g7 (7 ... ♗d6 =) 8 d4 ♘h5 9 0-0 =/∞ D.Byrne-Keres, USA v USSR 1955

[59] 9 ... ♗g7 10 c3 ♘c6 11 ♘d2 ♘xd2 12 ♗xd2 ♕xe2+ 13 ♗xe2 h5 14 ♖he1 ♗e6 ∞ Glazkov

[60] 12 0-0-0 ♖e8 13 d5 ♘xd2 14 ♕xd2 ∞ Estrin

[61] 6 ... ♘f6 7 ♘xf6+ ♕xf6 8 ♘c3 c6 9 ♗e2 ♖g8 10 ♗f3 ♗h6 11 d4 ± Hoi

[62] 9 ♕f3 ♘c6! 10 ♕xf4 ♗xf2+ 11 ♔xf2 ♕xf4+ 12 ♗xf4 ∞/∓

[63] Estrin

Vienna

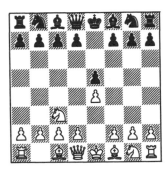

Another opening whose heyday has passed, the Vienna's original scheme was to effect a sort of delayed King's Gambit. Unfortunately, this hesitation does nothing to improve White's attacking chances and Black secures at least equality by striking out in the centre. When seen in modern tournament play, White usually opts for Smyslov's preference 3 g3. This quiet positional continuation is more in keeping with the orderly sentiments of contemporary play, but this also seems too indirect to provide White with a real advantage.

Reference: *Vienna Game* (Konstantinopolsky and Lepeshkin)

	Vienna	1 e4 e5 2 ♘c3							
	2	3	4	5	6	7	8	9	10
1	...	f4[2]	♘f3[3]	h4	♘g5	d4	♘xf7	♗c4+	♗xf4	∞
	♘c6[1]	ef	g5[4]	g4	d6[5]	h6[6]	♔xf7	♔g7	♘f6[7]	
2	...	...	...	d4	♗c4[9]	0-0	ed	♕d2!	♕xf4	±
	...	...	...	g4[8]	gf	d5[10]	♗g4	♘ce7[11]	♕d7[12]	

1 e4 e5 2 ♘c3 ♘f6

	3	4	5	6	7	8	9	10	11	
3	g3 d5	ed ♘xd5	♗g2 ♘xc3	bc ♗d6[13]	♘e2[14] 0-0	0-0 ♘d7[15]	d3 ♘f6	c4 c6	♖b1 ♕c7[16]	±
4	... ♗c5	♗g2 0-0[17]	d3[18] ♖e8	♘ge2 c6	0-0 d5	ed ♘xd5	♔h1 ♗g4[19]			=
5	♗c4 ♘xe4[20]	♕h5[21] ♕d6	♗b3[22] ♘c6[23]	♘b5 g6	♕f3 f5![24]	♕d5 ♕e7[25]	♘xc7+ ♔d8	♘xa8 b6	d3[26] ♗b7[27]	∞

[1] 2 ... ♗c5 3 ♘f3 (3 ♘a4 ♗xf2+ 4 ♔xf2 ♕h4+ 5 ♔e3 ♕f4+ 6 ♔d3 d5 7 ♔c3 ♕xe4 ∞ Hamppe-Meitner, Vienna 1870) 3 ... d6 4 d4 ed 5 ♘xd4 ♘f6 6 ♗g5 h6 7 ♗h4 ♘c6 8 ♘xc6 bc 9 ♗d3 ♕e7 10 0-0 ±

[2] 3 g3 ♗c5 (3 ... g6 4 ♗g2 ♗g7 5 ♘ge2 ♘ge7 =; 3 ... h5!? 4 ♘f3 ♗e7 5 ♘d5 ♘f6 6 d3 d6 7 ♗g2 ♗e6 8 ♘xe7 ♕xe7 9 ♗g5 0-0-0 ∞ Sommerfeld-Schön, Germany 1986) 4 ♗g2 ♘ge7 5 ♘ge2 0-0 6 0-0 a6 7 d3 d6 = Konstantinopolsky

[3] 3 ♗c4 ♗c5 4 ♕g4 g6! (4 ... ♕f6 5 ♘d5! ♕xf2+ 6 ♔d1 ± Mieses-Chigorin, Ostend 1906) 5 ♕f3 (5 ♕g3 d6 6 d3 ♘d4 7 ♗b3 ♗e6 8 ♗g5 ♕d7 = Spielmann-Tarrasch, Vienna 1922) 5 ... ♘f6 6 ♘ge2 d6 7 d3 ♗g4 8 ♕g3 h6 9 f4 ♕e7 10 ♘d5 ± Larsen-Portisch, Santa Monica 1966; 3 ... ♘f6! =

[4] 4 d4 ♕h4+ 5 ♔e2 d5 (5 ... d6 6 ♘f3 ♗g4 7 ♗xf4 0-0-0 ∞ Caldwell-Bisguier, New York 1987) 6 ed ♗g4+ (6 ... ♕e7+ 7 ♔f2 ♕h4+ 8 g3! =) 7 ♘f3 0-0-0 8 dc ♗c5 (8 ... ♘f6 =) 9 cb+ ♔b8! (9 ... ♔xb7 10 ♖e1!) 10 ♘b5 ♘f6 11 c3 ∞/=

[5] 4 ... d6 5 d4 g5 6 d5 ♘e5 7 ♗b5+ ♗d7 8 ♗xd7+ ♕xd7 9 ♕d4 ♕f6 10 ♕xf6 ♘gxf6 11 ♘g5 ± Pliester-Grünberg, Dieren 1984
6 ... h6 7 ♘xf7 ♔xf7 8 d4 f3 (8 ... d5 9 ♗xf4 ♗b4 10 ♗e2 ♗xc3+ 11 bc ♘f6 12 0-0 ±/±) 9 gf ♗e7 ∞ Estrin
6 ... d5 7 d4! h6 8 ♗xf7 ±

[6] 7 ... f6 8 ♗xf4! fg 9 hg ♗g7 10 ♗e3 ♕e7 11 ♕d2 ± Estrin, Glazkov

[7] 11 ♕d2 ♗e7 12 0-0-0 ♕e8! ∞ Hellers-Akesson, Sweden 1985

[8] 5 ... ♗g7 6 d5 ♘e5 7 d6! ± Kamber-Probst, Switzerland 1985

[9] 6 ♘e5?! ♘xe5 7 de ♕h4+ 8 ♔e2 f3+ 9 gf gf+ 10 ♔d3 ♗g7 ∓/∓

[10] 7 ... ♘xd4 8 ♗xf4! ♕f6 9 ♘d5 ♕g7 10 ♘xc7+ ♔d8 11 g3! ± Keres

[11] 9 ... ♗g7 10 ♗xf4 ♗xd4+ 11 ♔h1 ♕h4 12 dc fg+ 13 ♔xg2 0-0 14 cb+ (14 ♘d5? ♖xd5! 15 ♗xd5 ♘f6! ∓∓ Eger-Weinitschke, corr. 1985) 14 ... ♘xb7 15 ♕e4+ ♔b8 16 ♗f4! ±±

[12] 11 d6 ♗g6 12 ♕e4+ ♔d8 13 h3! ± Glazkov

[13] 6 ... ♗c5 7 ♘e2 ♘c6 8 d4!? ed 9 ♗b2 Saidy

[14] 7 ♘f3 0-0 8 0-0 (8 d3 ♗d7 9 0-0 ♘c6 10 ♖e1 ♘d7 ∞ Balashov-Kovačević, Karlovac 1979) 8 ... ♘d7 9 d3 ♖b8 10 a4 b6 11 a5 ♗b7 12 ab ab = Benko-Smyslov, Las Palmas 1972

[15] 8 ... c6 9 d3 ♘d7 10 f4 ef 11 ♗xf4 ♘e5 12 ♖b1 ♖b8 13 c4 ± Spassky-Karpov, Tilburg 1979

[16] 12 ♗g5 ♗e7 13 ♘c3 h6 14 ♗d2 ± Spassky-Timman, Montpellier C 1985

[17] 4 ... d6 5 ♘f3 ♘c6 6 d3 ♗g4 7 ♘a4 ♘d7 8 h3 ♗h5 9 c3 ♗xf2+ 10 ♔xf2 ± Averbakh-Spassky, USSR Ch 1963

[18] 5 ♘ge2 d5 6 ed c6!? 7 dc ♘xc6 ∞ Gunsberg-Pollock, Hastings 1895

[19] Portisch-Toran, Malaga 1961

[20] 3 ... ♗b4 4 ♘ge2 0-0 5 d3 c6 6 0-0 d5 7 ♗b3 de 8 ♘xe4 ♘bd7 9 ♘2g3 ♘xe4 10 de ± Honfi-Klüger, Hungary 1958
3 ... ♗c5 4 d3 d6 5 f4 ♘c6 6 ♘f3 ± – 2 f4

[21] 4 ♗xf7+ ♔xf7 5 ♘xe4 d5 6 ♕f3+ ♔g8 7 ♘g5 ♕d7 8 ♘e2 h6 9 ♘h3 ♗c5 ∓
4 ♘xe4 d5 5 ♗d3 de 6 ♗xe4 f5 ∓

[22] 5 ♕xe5+ ♕e7 6 ♕xe7+ ♗xe7 7 ♗b3 ♘f5 8 ♘f3 c6 9 0-0 d5 10 ♖e1 0-0 = Sämisch-Rubinstein, Hanover 1926

[23] 5 ... ♗e7 6 ♘f3 ♘c6 (6 ... 0-0 7 h4! ♘c6 8 ♘g5 h6 9 ♕g6 ♗xg5 10 hg ♕xg5 11 ♕xg5 hg 12 d3 =/± Gufeld-Tarve, Tallinn 1969) 7 ♘xe5 0-0 8 0-0 ± Larsen

[24] 7 ... ♘f5 8 ♕d5 ♘h6 9 d4 d6 10 ♗xh6 ♗e6 11 ♗g5 ± Estrin, Glazkov

[25] 8 ... ♕f6 9 ♘xc7+ ♔d8 10 ♘xa8 b6 11 ♘xb6 ab 12 d4! ±

[26] 11 ♘xb6 ab 12 d3 ♗b7 13 ♕f3 ♘d4 13 ♕h3 g5! ∞

[27] 12 h4 f4! 13 ♕f3 ♗h6 ∞ Wibe-Bryson, corr. 1985

	3	4	5	6	7	8	9	10	11	
6	♗c4	d3[28]	♘f3[30]	0-0	dc	♕e2	♗b3	♘h4	ab	=
	♘c6	♗b4[29]	d6	♗xc3[31]	h6	♗e6	♕c8	♗xb3	♕g4[32]	
7	f4	fe[33]	♘f3[34]	d4[36]	♗d2	♘xe4	♗xb4	♕d2	♗c3	=
	d5	♘xe4	♗e7[35]	♗b4[37]	♗g4	de	ef	♘c6	♕d5[38]	
8	...	...	d3	de	♔e2	g3[41]	♔f2	♕xg4	♗e3	=
	...	...	♗b4[39]	♕h4+	♘c6[40]	♕g4+	♗xc3	♗d4+	♗xe3+[42]	
9	...	...	...	bc	♘f3	cd	c3	♕xf3	d4	=
	...	...	♘xc3	d4[43]	♘c6[44]	♘xd4[45]	♘xf3+	c6[46]	♕h4+[47]	

[28] 4 f4 ♘xe4 5 ♘f3 ♘xc3 6 dc ♕e7! ∓
Kuundzhi-Razuvayev, USSR 1973
[29] 4 ... ♘a5 and now:
  5 ♘f3 ♘xc4 6 dc ♗b4 7 ♕d3 ♗xc3+
8 ♕xc3 d6 (8 ... ♘xe4? 9 ♕xe5+ ♕e7 10 ♕xg7
♘f6+ 11 ♔d1 ±/± Eslon-Martin Gonzalez,
Spain 1985) = Pliester
  5 ♘ge2 ♗e7 6 ♘g3 d6 7 0-0 0-0 8 h3 ±
Balashov-Rukavina, Hastings 1985-86
  4 ... ♗c5 5 ♗g5 h6 6 ♗h4 a6 7 ♘d5 g5
8 ♗g3 d6 9 h4!? ∞ Rogers-Rogulj, Mendrisio
1985
[30] 5 ♘e2 d5 6 ed ♘xd5 7 ♗xd5 ♕xd5 8 0-0
♕a5 = Spielmann-Reti, Dortmund 1928
[31] 6 ... ♘a5 7 ♗b3 ♘xb3 8 ab c6! =
[32] 12 ♕xg4 ♘xg4 = Hartston-Romanishin,
Buenos Aires Ol 1978
[33] 4 ed ef 5 d4 ♗d6 6 ♕e2+ ♔f8! ∓ Inkiov-
Pinter, Herculana Z 1982
[34] 5 ♕f3 ♘c6! 6 ♗b5 ♘xc3 7 bc ♕h4+ 8 g3
♕e4+ 9 ♕xe4 de ∓ Keres
[35] 5 ... ♘c6 6 ♗b5! ♗c5 7 d4 ♗b4 8 ♗d2
♗xc3 9 bc 0-0 10 0-0 ♗g4 11 ♕e1 f6 12 ♗e3 ±
Westerinen-Khermlin, 1965
  5 ... ♗g4 6 ♕e2 ♘g5 7 h4 ♘xf3+ 8 gf
♗e6 9 d4 ♘c6 10 ♗e3 ♗e7 = Alekhine

[36] 6 ♕e2 f5 7 d3 ♘c5 8 g3 (8 d4 ♘e4 9 ♗f4
0-0 10 h4 ♗b4! 11 ♕e3 c5 ∓ Grünfeld) 8 ...
♘e6! 9 ♗g2 0-0 ∓ Estrin
[37] 6 ... 0-0 7 ♗d3 f5 8 ef ♗xf6 9 0-0 ♘c6
10 ♘xe4 de 11 ♗xe4 ♘d4 = Spielmann-Reti,
Vienna 1922
[38] Ljubojević-Ciocaltea, Skopje Ol 1972
[39] 5 ... ♕h4+ 6 g3 ♘xg3 7 ♘f3 ♕h5 8 ♘xd5 ±
[40] 7 ... ♗xc3 8 bc ♗g4+ 9 ♘f3 de 10 ♕d4
♗h5 11 ♔d2! ♕g4 12 h3 ∞/±
[41] 8 ♘f3 ♗g4 9 ♘xd5 0-0-0 10 c3 f5 ∞
Lepeshkin
[42] 12 ♔xe3 ♗xg4 13 ed ♘xe5 = Szabo
[43] 6 ... ♗e7!? 7 d4 (7 ♘f3 0-0 8 d4 c5 9 ♗e2
♘c6 10 0-0 ∞ Horseman-Gligorić, Hastings
1956-57) 7 ... f6 8 ♗d3 ♗e6 9 ♘f3 0-0 10 h4!? ∞
Capron-Panczyk, Sofia 1985
[44] 7 ... dc!? 8 ♗e2 ♗e7 9 0-0 ♗e6 10 ♕e1
♘c6 11 ♕xc3 0-0 12 ♗e3 f6 ∞ Sax-Plaskett,
Lugano 1986
[45] 8 ... ♗b4+ 9 ♗d2 ♗xd2+ 10 ♕xd2 ♘xd4
11 c3 ♘xf3+ 12 gf ♕h4+ 13 ♕f2 ♕xf2+
14 ♔xf2 f6 = Larsen
[46] 10 ... ♗e6 11 d4 ♕d5 ∞
[47] 12 g3 ♕g4 13 ♗g2 ♕xf3 14 ♗xf3 ♗e6 =
Capron-Malevinsky, Sofia 1985

358

Latvian; Philidor; Petroff

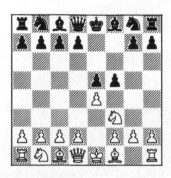 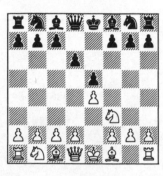 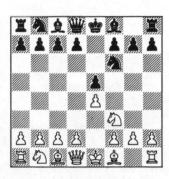

The Philidor and Latvian have never achieved a great following simply because they present the second player with difficulties in equalizing. Philidor's Defence suffers from being too passive, though it does have a few wild side variants. Larsen's variation has the most promise, an interesting attempt to inject life into an essentially inferior defence. Critical here is White's attempt to score the point by force, castling long and initiating a full scale assault against the opposing king. At present there has been insufficient testing to reach a definite conclusion regarding the viability of Larsen's plan with an early ... g6.

The Latvian Gambit (sometimes also known as the Greco Counter Gambit in honour of the Italian master who analysed it in the seventeenth century) has never been considered quite respectable. 2 ... f5, introducing a kind of King's Gambit in reverse, is a highly provocative move which at one time analysts claimed to have refuted outright. But resources have been found for Black which, although not good enough for complete equality, at least offer him a playable game. The gambit has useful surprise value since there is no simple way for White to gain an advantage and few players as White will have bothered to commit to memory an antidote to such a rare counterthrust. 3 d4, 3 ef, 3 ♘xe5 and 3 ♗c4 all offer White some advantage.

The third member of this section, Petroff's Defence, is another animal entirely. Originally envisaged by its inventors Petroff and Jaenisch (the defence bears Petroff's name, perhaps because he defeated co-author Jaenisch in a match) as a lively counterattacking alternative to 2 ... ♘c6, it has since been viewed as a colourless drawing variation. Modern ideas have injected some dynamism into the Petroff once again, though its reputation as a rock-solid choice for equality has not diminished. It is an extremely difficult nut to crack and has served Yusupov, Salov and Karpov, among others, loyally and well. In essence it remains an opening geared for static equilibrium, and in this respect it is a particularly efficient defence.

Reference: *The Open Game in Action* (Karpov)

Latvian   1 e4 e5 2 ♘f3 f5[1]

	3	4	5	6	7	8	9	10	11	
1	♘xe5[2]	♗c4[4]	♘c3	d4[6]	♗g5	♘e5	♗c4	♗xf6	♘g4	±
	♕f6[3]	fe	♕f7[5]	♘f6	♗b4	♕e6	♕f5	gf	♕g6[7]	
2	♗c4	♘xe5	♕h5+	♘xg6	♕xg6+[10]	♗xd5	♘c3	b3	♕f7	±
	fe[8]	d5[9]	g6	hg	♔d7[11]	♘f6	♕e7	♖h6!	♕xf7[12]	
3	ef	♘e5[14]	♗e2!	♗h5+	♘f7	♘c3[15]	♘d5+	♕xh5	f6	±
	e4[13]	♘f6	d6	♔e7	♕e8	♘xh5	♔d7[16]	♖g8	♘a6[17]	

[1]   2 ... **f6** 3 ♘xe5 (3 d4 ±; 3 ♗c4 ±) 5 ... ♕e7 4 ♘f3 d5 5 d3 de 6 de ♕xe4+ 7 ♗e2 ±/±

  2 ... **♕e7** 3 ♗c4 c6 4 0-0 d6 5 d4 ♗g4 6 c3 ♘f6 7 ♖e1 ± Sigurjonsson-Gonzalez, Bogotá 1978

  2 ... **d5** ("Elephant Gambit") 3 ♘xe5 ♗d6 (3 ... de 4 ♗c4 ♕g5 5 ♗xf7+ ♔e7 6 d4 ♕xg2 7 ♖f1 ♗h3 8 ♗c4 ♘f6 9 ♗f4 ± Lob-Eliskases, corr. 1932) 4 d4 de 5 ♗c4 ♗xe5 6 ♕h5 ±; 3 ed! e4 4 ♕e2 ♘f6 5 d3 ±/±

[2]   3 d4 fe 4 ♘xe5 ♘f6 5 ♗e2 d6 6 ♘g4 ♗e7 (6 ... ♘xg4?! 7 ♗xg4 ♗d7 8 ♘c3 ♘f6 9 ♗xc8 ♕xc8 10 0-0 ± Romanishin-van Riemsdyk, Riga IZ 1979) 7 ♘c3 ♘bd7 8 ♗g5 ♘xg4 9 ♗xe7 ♕xe7 10 ♗xg4 ± Kapitaniak

[3]   3 ... ♘c6 and now:

  4 **♕h5+?** g6 5 ♘xg6 ♘f6 6 ♕h3 (6 ♕h4 ♖g8? 7 e5! ± van der Sterren-van der Lijn, Apeldoorn 1977; 6 ... hg!) 7 ♕xh8 ♕e7 8 ♕h4 d5 9 d3 ♘d4 ∓ Pannullo-Ravaro, corr. 1976

  4 **♘xc6** dc 5 ♘c3 ♕e7 6 d3 ♘f6 7 ♗g5 ♗d7 8 f3 0-0-0 9 ♗e2 h6 10 ♗d2 g5 11 ef ♗xf5 ±

[4]   4 d4 d6 5 ♗c4 fe 6 ♘e3 ♘c6 7 d5 ♘e5 8 ♘c3 ♘g6 9 ♕d4 ±

[5]   5 ... **♕g6** 6 d3 ♗b4 7 ♗d2 ♗xc3 8 ♗xc3 ±

  5 ... **d6** 6 d3 ed 7 ♗xd3 ±

  5 ... **♕e6** 6 d3 ed+ 7 ♘e3 dc 8 ♕xc2 ±

[6]   6 ♘e3 c6 7 ♘xe4 d5 8 ♘g3 h5! 9 h4 g6 10 d4 ♗g7 11 c3 ♘e7 ∞ Arnlins-Anderson, corr. 1972

[7]   12 ♘e3 f5 13 ♘d5 ± Dubinsky-Chebotarev, USSR 1968

[8]   3 ... **♘f6!?** 4 d4 fe 5 ♘xe5 d5 6 ♗e2 ♗e6 7 0-0 ♗d6 8 f3 ef 9 ♗xf3 0-0 10 ♕e2 ±

[9]   4 ... **♕g5** 5 d4 ♕xg2 6 ♕h5+ g6 7 ♗f7+ ♔d8 8 ♗xg6 ♕xh1+ 9 ♔e2 c6 10 ♘c3 ♘f6 11 ♕g5! ± Pupols-Dreiburg, USA 1956

  4 ... **♘f6** 5 ♘f7 ♕e7 6 ♘xh8 d5 7 ♗e2 ♘c6 8 d3! ± Petersson-Ortiz, corr. 1974

[10]   7 ♕xh8 ♔f7 ∞

[11]   7... ♔e7? 8 d4 ♘f6 9 ♗g5 ♕d6 10 ♘c3 ± Keast-Skrastins, corr. 1976

[12]   12 ♗xf7 ♘c6 13 ♗b2 ♔e7 14 ♗c4 ♗f5 15 0-0-0 ± Kapitaniak

[13]   3 ... **♘c6** 4 ♗b5 ♗c5 5 0-0 e4 6 d4 ±

  3 ... **d6!?** 4 d4 e4 5 ♘g5 ♗xf5 6 f3 ♕e7 7 fe ♗xe4 8 ♘xe4 ♕xe4+ 9 ♗e2 ± Schmigalle-Bandick, corr. 1976

[14]   4 **♕e2** ♕e7 5 ♘d4 ♕e5 6 ♘b5 ±

  4 **♘g1!?** Bücker

[15]   8 ♘xh8 ♕xh5 (8 ... ♗xh5 9 d3 ed 10 0-0 ±) 9 ♕xh5 ♘xh5 10 g4 ♘f6 11 ♖g1 ♘c6 12 ♖g3 ± Glazkov

[16]   9 ... ♔xf7 10 ♕xh5+ g6 11 fg+ ♔g7 12 ♘xc7 ±

[17]   12 0-0 c6 13 ♘e5+ de 14 f7 ♕e6 15 fg♕ ♕xg8 16 ♘e3 ±

	Philidor	1 e4 e5 2 ♘f3 d6						

	3	4	5	6	7	8	9	10	11	
1	♗c4	d3[2]	c3	0-0	♗b3	♗c2	♖e1	♘bd2	d4	=
	♗e7[1]	♘f6	0-0	c6[3]	♗e6	h6	♘bd7	♕c7	♗g4[4]	
2	d4	♗c4	0-0	de	♘g5	♕h5	♗xg5	♕e2[7]	♗d2	±
	♘d7	c6	♗e7	de	♗xg5[5]	♕e7[6]	♘gf6	h6	0-0[8]	
3	...	♘c3[9]	♗c4	0-0[10]	a4	♖e1[11]	♗a2	♗e3	♘h4	±
	♘f6	♘bd7	♗e7	0-0	c6	♕c7[12]	b6	a6	ed[13]	
4	...	♘xd4	♘c3	♗e3	♕d2	0-0-0	f3[15]	♗xd4	g4	±
	ed	♘f6	g6	♗g7	0-0	♘c6[14]	♘xd4	♗e6	c5[16]	
5	...	...	...	♗f4[17]	♕d2	ed	0-0-0	♕xc3	♕g3	±
	...	...	♗e7	0-0	d5[18]	♗b4[19]	♗xc3	♘xd5	♘xf4[20]	

[1] **3 ... ♗e6** 4 ♗xe6 fe 5 d4 ed 6 ♘xd4 e5 7 ♘e6 ♕e7 8 ♕h5+ g6 9 ♕h3 ± Chandler-Large, Hastings 1986-87

3 ... ♕f6 4 d3 ♗g4 5 ♘bd2 ♘c6 6 c3 ♘ge7 7 h3 ♗d7 8 b4 ± Chandler-Hodgson, Hastings 1986-87

[2] 4 0-0 ♘f6 5 ♖e1 0-0 6 d4 ed 7 ♘xd4 a6 8 a4?! c5 9 ♘b3 ♗e6 10 ♕e2 ♘c6 ∓ Mestel-Georgadze, Hastings 1979-80

[3] 6 ... ♘c6 – 2 ... ♘c6

[4] **11 ...** ♖fe8 12 h3 ♘f8 13 c4 ± Kasparov-Georgadze, USSR Ch 1979

11 ... ♗g4 12 h3 ♗h5 13 ♘f1 ♘h7 = Kasparov

[5] 7 ... ♘h6 8 ♘e6! fe 9 ♗xh6 ♘b6 10 ♕h5+ g6 (10 ... ♔f8 11 f4!) 11 ♕e2 ±

[6] 8 ... g6 9 ♕xg5 ♕xg5 10 ♗xg5 ♘c5 11 ♘d2 ♗e6 12 ♗e3! ±

[7] 10 ♕h4 ♘f8! 11 ♗xf6 gf ∞

[8] 12 a4 b6 13 f3 ♗b7 14 ♗e3 ± Gipslis-Csom, Budapest 1977

[9] 4 de ♘xe4 5 ♕d5! ♘c5 6 ♗g5 ♕d7 (6 ... ♗e7 7 ed ♕xd6 8 ♘c3 ±) 7 ed ♗xd6 8 ♘c3 0-0 9 0-0-0 ±

[10] 6 ♘g5!? 0-0 7 ♗xf7+ ♖xf7 8 ♘e6 ♕e8 9 ♘xc7 ♕d8 10 ♘xa8 b5 11 de ♘xe5 12 ♗f4 ∞/± Murei-Ree, Sukhumi 1972

[11] 8 ♕e2 ed 9 ♘xd4 ♖e8 10 ♗a2 ♗f8 11 ♕f3 ♘e5 12 ♕g3 (12 ♕d1 ♘g6 13 ♖e1 a5 14 h3 h6 15 f4 ♗d7 ∞ Ivanović-Najdorf, Bugojno 1982) 12 ... ♘h5 13 ♕g5 ♕xg5 14 ♗xg5 h6 15 ♗c1 ♘f6 = Marjanović-Campora, Bor 1985

[12] 8 ... b6 9 d5 c5 10 a5 ±

[13] **12 ♕xd4** ♘c5 13 b4 ♘e6! 14 ♕d1 g6 ∞

12 ♗xd4 ♘e5 13 ♕f3 a5 14 e5 ± Vogt

[14] 8 ... ♖e8 9 f3 ♘c6 10 g4 ♘e5 11 ♗e2 a6 12 ♗h6 ♗h8 13 h4 b5 14 ♗g5 c5 15 ♗f5! gf 16 gf ♗b7 17 ♗h6 ±± Owen-Wrinn, corr. 1985

[15] 9 ♘xc6 bc 10 ♗h6 ♗e6 11 ♗xg7 ♔xg7 12 h4 h5 13 f3 ± Jansa-Castro, Malta Ol 1980

[16] 12 ♗e3 ♕a5 13 ♗h6 ± Yurtayev-Gulko, Frunze 1985, and Tseshkovsky-Vorotnikov, Aktubinsk 1985

[17] 6 ♗e2 0-0 7 0-0 a6 8 f4 c5 9 ♘b3 ♘c6 10 ♗e3 ♖e8 11 ♗f3 ♗f8 12 ♗f2 ♗e6 13 ♖e1 ± Kapengut-Kantsler, USSR 1981

[18] 7 ... a6 8 0-0-0 b5 9 f3 b4 10 ♘d5 ±

[19] 8 ... ♘xd5 9 ♗xd5 ♕xd5 10 ♘b5 ±

[20] 12 ♕xf4 ♕d5 13 ♘b3 ♕f5 14 ♕h4 ♕g4 15 g3 ♗f5 16 ♘d4 ♗d7 17 ♗d3 ± Agapov-Antoshin, USSR 1983

	3	4	5	6	7	8	9	10	11	
1	♘xe5[1]	♘xf7[3]	d4	♘c3	♗c4+	d5	0-0	♖e1	e5[6]	∞
	d6[2]	♔xf7	g6[4]	♕e8[5]	♗e6	♗c8	♗g7	♖f8	de[7]	
2	...	♘c4	d4	♘e3	♕e2[9]	c3	♘d2	g3	♗xd2	=
	...	♘xe4	d5	♕f6[8]	♗e6	♘c6	0-0-0	♘xd2	h5[10]	
3	...	♘f3	d4[11]	♗d3	0-0	c4	♘c3	♕xf3	♕h3[13]	∞
	...	♘xe4	d5[12]	♘c6	♗g4	♘f6	♗xf3	♘xd4	dc[14]	
4	...	...	...	...	...	...	cd	♕xf3	♕e2+	±
	...	...	...	...	...	...	♗xf3[15]	♕xd5	♗e7[16]	
5	...	...	...	...	0-0	c4	♘c3	bc	cd	±
	...	...	...	♗d6	0-0	c6[17]	♘xc3	♗g4[18]	cd[19]	
6	...	...	...	...	...	...	♕c2	a3[21]	♘e5[23]	±
	...	...	...	...	...	...	♘a6[20]	♗g4[22]	♗xe5[24]	
7	...	...	...	...	0-0	♖e1	c4!	♗f1	a3	±
	...	...	...	♗e7	♘c6[25]	♗f5	♘b4[26]	0-0[27]	♘c6[28]	

---

1 e4 e5 2 ♘f3 ♘f6 3 ♘xe5 d6 4 ♘f3 ♘xe4 5 d4 d5 6 ♗d3 ♗e7 7 0-0 ♘c6 8 ♖e1 ♗g4

	9	10	11	12	13	14	15	16	17	
8	c4[29]	cd	♘c3	h3	a3[31]	bc	♗f4[33]	♗e4	♘e5	±
	♘f6	♘xd5	0-0	♗e6[30]	♘xc3[32]	♗f6	g6	♘a5	c6[34]	
9	...	...	♕xf3	♕h3[35]	♘c3	♗f5[38]	♕g3	♗e3[39]	a3	∞
	...	♗xf3	♕xd5	♕xd4[36]	♖d8[37]	h5	♔f8	♕b4	♕a5[40]	

[1] **3 d3** ♘c6 intending ... d5 =
3 ♘c3 ♗b4 4 ♘xe5 0-0 5 ♗e2 ♖e8 6 ♘d3 ♗xc3 7 dc ♘xe4 =

[2] 3 ... ♘xe4 4 ♕e2 ♕e7 5 ♕xe4 d6 6 d4 de 7 de ♘c6 8 f4 ♗d7 9 ♘c3 0-0-0 10 ♗e3 f6 11 ef ♕xe4 12 ♘xe4 ♖e8 13 ♗d3 gf 14 ♔f2 ±

[3] Cochrane's Gambit

[4] **5 ... ♘xe4?** 6 ♕h5+ ±±
5 ... d5 6 e5 ♘e8 7 ♗d3 g6 8 h4 ∞
5 ... ♗e7 6 ♘c3 ♖e8 7 ♗c4+ ∞
5 ... c5 6 dc (6 ♗c4+ d5 7 ed ♗d6 8 0-0 ♖e8 ∓) 6 ... d5 7 e5 ♕e8 8 f4 ♗g4 9 ♗e2 ♗xe2 10 ♕xe2 ± Vitolins-Khalifman, Borzomi 1984; 6 ... ♘c6!? 7 ♗c4+ ♗e6 ∞

[5] 6 ... ♗g7 7 ♗c4+ ♗e6 8 ♗xe6+ ♔xe6 9 f4 ♔f7 10 e5 ♖e8 (10 ... ♘e8 11 ♕f3 c6 12 ♘e4 ± Makropoulos-Toth, Rome 1981)

11 0-0 ♘c6 12 ef ♕xf6 13 ♘b5 ♖e7 14 c3 ± O'Neill-Solomon, Australia 1985

[6] 11 f4 ♗g8 12 e5 de 13 fe ♘g4 14 d6+ ♔h8 15 e6 ♘e5 16 d7 ♘bxd7 17 ed ♕xd7 = Popov-Grodzensky, corr. 1983

[7] 12 d6+ ♗e6 13 ♖xe5 ♗xc4 14 ♖xe8 ♖xe8 15 dc ♘a6 16 ♗f4 ♖ec8 ∞ Vitolins-Anikayev, USSR 1982

[8] **6 ... g6** 7 ♘d2 ♗g7 8 c3 0-0 (8 ... ♘xd2 9 ♗xd2 0-0 10 h4 h5 11 ♕c2) 9 ♘xe4 de 10 ♗c4 ♘d7 11 0-0 ± Smagin-Mikhalchishin, USSR Ch 1985

6 ... c6 7 ♘d2 ♘xd2 8 ♗xd2 ♘d7 (8 ... ♗e6 9 ♗d3 ♗e7 10 f4! ± Smagin-Arkhipov, Moscow 1986) 9 ♕e2! ♕e7 10 0-0-0 ♘f6 11 ♗b4 ♕e6 12 ♗xf8 ♔xf8 13 f3 ± Smagin-Rozentalis, Barnaul 1984

[9] 7 Bb5+ c6 8 0-0 cb 9 Nxd5 Qd6 10 Re1 Qxd5 11 Nc3 Qd8 12 Rxe4+ Be7 13 Bg5 Nc6 14 Qe2 Bf5 15 Bxe7 Nxe7 16 Re5 0-0 17 Rxe7 ½-½ Smagin-Makarichev, Moscow Ch 1987

[10] 12 h4 g6 = Kholmov-Nikolenko, Moscow Ch 1987

[11] 5 Qe2 Qe7 6 d3 Nf6 7 Bg5 Qxe2+ 8 Bxe2 Be7 9 Nc3 c6 = Spassky-Karpov, Linares 1981 and Turin 1982
5 Nc3 Nxc3 6 dc Be7 7 Be3 0-0 8 Qd2 Nd7 9 0-0-0 Nc5 10 Nd4 (10 h4 Bg4 ∞) 10 ... Re8 11 f3 Nf6 12 h4 Bxh4 ∞ Ciocaltea-Schüssler, Bochum 1981
5 c4 Nc6 6 Nc3 (6 d4 d5 7 Nc3 Bb4 ∞ Kupreichik-Mikhalchishin, Kuibishev 1986) 6 ... Nxc3 7 dc Be7 8 Bd3 Bg4 9 Be4 Qd7 10 Be3 Bf5 = Timman-Yusupov, match 1986

[12] 5 ... Be7 6 d3 Nf6 7 0-0 0-0 8 Re1 Bg4 9 Nbd2 c5 10 h3 Bh5 11 Nf1 Nc6 12 Ng3 ± Ljubojević-Smyslov, World v USSR 1984

[13] 11 Qe3+ Ne6 12 cd Nxd5 13 Bxd5 Qxd5 14 Be4 Qb5 15 a4 Qa6 16 Rd1 Be7 17 b4! ∞ Kasparov-Karpov, match (6) 1986, and Aseyev-Ivanchuk, Irkutsk 1986

[14] 12 Bxc4 Be7 13 Bg5 0-0 14 Rad1 c5 15 Rfe1 ∞ Kupreichik-Yusupov, USSR Ch 1987

[15] 9 ... Nxd5 10 Re1+ Be7 – 6 ... Be7

[16] 12 Bb5 Qd6 13 Nc3 0-0 14 Bxc6 bc 15 Rd1! Rfe8 16 Qf3 ± Short-H.Olafsson, Reykjavik 1987

[17] 8 ... Bg4 9 cd f5 10 Nc3 Nd7 11 h3 Bh5 12 Nxe4 fe 13 Bxe4 Nf6 14 Bf5 ± Alexander-Mattison, Brighton 1938

[18] 10 ... dc 11 Bxc4 Bg4 12 Qd3 Nd7 13 Ng5 Nf6 14 h3 Bh5 15 f4 h6 16 g4 hg 17 fg Qxg4 18 hg Bd7 19 gh Qg4+ 20 Kf2 Rce8 21 Rg1 Qh4+ 22 Kg2 b5 23 Bb3 ± (Short-Hübner, Tilburg 1988) 23 ... Re4 24 Qf3 Bh2 25 Bd2! ∞

[19] 12 Rb1 Nd7 13 h3 Bh5 (13 ... Bxf3 14 Qxf3 ± Dvoiris-Yakovich, USSR Ch 1986) 14 a4 (14 Rxb7 Nb6 ∞ A.Sokolov-Rozentalis, USSR 1986) 14 ... b6 15 Rb5 ±

[20] 9 ... f5 10 Nc3 Na6 11 a3 – 9 ... Na6

[21] 10 Bxe4 de 11 Qxe4 Re8 12 Qd3 Bg4! 13 Bg5 Qd7 14 Nbd2 h6 15 Be3 f5 ∞ Kruppa-Rozentalis, USSR 1985

[22] 10 ... Re8 11 Nc3 Bg4 12 Nxe4 de 13 Bxe4 Bxf3 14 Bxf3 Qh4 15 g3 Qxd4 16 Be3 ±
10 ... f5 11 Nc3 Nc7 12 b4 Bd7 13 Bb2 Be8 14 Ne5 ±

[23] 11 c5 Bc7 12 Ne5 Bxe5 13 de Nexc5 (13 ... Naxc5?! 14 f3 Qb6 15 Be3 d4 16 Bxd4 Rfd8 17 Bxe4! Rxd4 18 Bxh7+ Kh8 19 fg Nb3 20 Kh1 Nxa1 21 Qf5 ∞ Shakarov-Rozentalis, corr. 1986) 14 Bxh7+ Kh8 ∞

[24] 12 de Nac5 13 f3 Nxd3 14 Qxd3 Nc5 15 Qd4 Nb3 16 Qxg4 Nxa1 17 Bh6 ±

[25] 7 ... 0-0 8 Re1 Bf5 9 c4 c6 10 Nc3 ±

[26] 9 ... 0-0 10 cd Qxd5 11 Nc3 Nxc3 12 bc Bxd3 13 Qxd3 b5 14 Bf4 Bd6 15 Ng5 ± Abramović-Radulov, Vrnjačka Banja 1983

[27] 10 ... dc 11 Nc3! ± Karpov-Portisch, Tilburg 1982

[28] 12 Nc3 Nxc3 13 bc dc 14 Bxc4 ± Karpov-Portisch, Turin 1982, and Ehlvest-Khalifman, USSR Ch 1987

[29] 9 c3 f5 10 Qb3! 0-0 11 Nbd2 Kh8 12 Qxb7 Rf6 13 Qb3 Rg6 ∞

[30] 12 ... Bh5? 13 Bxh7+
12 ... Bxf3 13 Qxf3 Ndb4 14 Bb1 Re8 15 d5 Bd6 16 Rxe8+ Qxe8 17 Be3 ± Dolmatov-Yusupov, USSR Ch 1981

[31] 13 Qc2 h6 14 Bf5 Ndb4 15 Qb1 Bxf5 16 Qxf5 Nf6 17 Bf4 ± Vasyukov-Andrianov, USSR 1981

[32] 13 ... Bf6 14 Ne4 Bf5 (14 ... h6 15 Nc5 ±) 15 Qb3 ± Lobron-Schissler, Reykjavik 1984

[33] 15 Qc2 g6 16 Rb1 Bd5 17 Nd2 b6 18 Nc4 ± Vasyukov-Vladimirov, USSR 1981

[34] 18 Qf3 ± Tseshkovsky-Barua, Calcutta 1986

[35] 12 Qxd5 Nxd5 13 Nc3 0-0-0! =
12 Qg3 Qxd4 13 Nc3 0-0 14 Nb5 Qg4 = Sax-Yusupov, Thessaloniki Ol 1984

[36] 12 ... Nxd4 13 Nc3 Bd7 14 Qxd7+ Kxd7 15 Be3 Ne6 16 Rad1 ∞ Kasparov-Karpov, match (28) 1984-85

[37] 13 ... 0-0 14 Nb5 ±
13 ... Ng4!?

[38] 14 Bc2!? Bg4 15 Qxg4 Nxg4 16 Ba4

[39] 16 Qxc7 Bd6 17 Qxb7 Ne7 18 Qf3 Ng4 ∞ Kurajica

[40] 18 Qf3 g6 19 Bc2 h4 ∞ Velimirović-Kurajica, Bela Crkva 1984

1 e4 e5 2 Nf3 Nf6 3 Nxe5 d6 4 Nf3 Nxe4 5 d4 d5 6 Bd3 Be7 7 0-0 Nc6 8 c4

	8	9	10	11	12	13	14	15	16	
10	...	Nc3	h3[42]	Bxc4	Bd3	Re1	a3	Bf4	Bg3	±
	Nf6[41]	0-0	dc[43]	Na5	Be6	Nc6[44]	a6[45]	Nd5[46]	Bf6[47]	
11	...	cd	Qxd3	Re1	Nc3[48]	Qxc3	Qxc7[50]	Nc2	Bd2	=
	Nb4	Nxd3	Qxd5	Bf5	Nxc3	Be6[49]	Bd6	0-0	Bf5[51]	
12	...	Be2	Nc3	Be3[53]	a3	bc	Qa4	Bd2	Rab1	±/∞
	...	0-0[52]	Be6	f5[54]	Nxc3	Nc6	f4	Kh8	Rb8[55]	

[41] 8 ... Bg4 9 cd Qxd5 10 Nc3 Nxc3 11 bc Bxf3 12 Qxf3 Qxf3 13 gf ±

[42] **10 cd** Nxd5 11 Re1 Be6 – 8 Re1 Bg4, but with an extra move (h3) for White

10 Re1 dc 11 Bxc4 Bg4 12 Be3 Bxf3 13 Qxf3 Nxd4 14 Bxd4 Qxd4 15 Rxe7 Qxc4 16 Qxb7 c6 17 Qb3 ±/= Ljubojević-Schüssler, New York 1985

[43] 10 ... Nb4 11 Be2 dc 12 Bxc4 Nbd5 13 Re1 c6 14 Bg5 Be6 15 Qb3 ± Hulak-Toth, Budva 1981

[44] 13 ... c5 14 dc Bxc5 15 Bg5 ±

[45] 14 ... Re8 15 Bb5 ± Lobron-Handoko, Zagreb 1985

[46] 15 ... Qd7 16 Ne5! ± Kasparov-Karpov, match (48) 1984-85

[47] **17 Bc2** Nce7 18 Ne4 Bf5 = Gufeld-Schüssler, Havana 1985

17 Ne4 h6 (17 ... Bxd4 18 Neg5 Nf6 19 Rxe6 ±) 18 Bc2 ±

[48] 12 Ne5 g6! = Belyavsky-Smyslov, Reggio Emilia 1986-87

[49] 13 ... c6 14 Bh6! ± Browne-Bisguier, US Ch 1974

[50] 14 Re5 Qc6! 15 Qe1?! (15 Qxc6 =) 15 ... 0-0-0 16 Bg5 Bxg5 17 Rxg5 Bd5! ∓ van der Wiel-Short, Biel IZ 1985

[51] 17 Qb3 Qxb3 18 ab f6 = Hübner-Smyslov, match 1983

[52] 9 ... dc 10 Bxc4 0-0 11 Nc3 Nd6 12 Bb3 Bf6 13 Ne5 ± A.Sokolov-Agzamov, USSR Ch 1985, and Kuznetsov-Matsukevich, corr. 1985

[53] **11 a3** Nxc3 12 bc Nc6 = Short-Seirawan, Biel IZ 1985

11 Nxe4!? de 12 Ne1

[54] 11 ... Bf6 12 Nxe4 de 13 Re1 c6 14 Qb3 ± Ljubojević-Karpov, Bugojno 1986

[55] Karpov-Seirawan, Brussels 1986, and Rohde-Seirawan, US Ch 1986

Petroff II   **1 e4 e5 2 Nf3 Nf6 3 d4**

	3	4	5	6	7	8	9	10	11	
1	...	e5	Qxd4[1]	ed	Nc3[2]	Qf4	Bd3[4]	Be3	0-0[5]	±
	ed	Ne4	d5	Nxd6	Nc6	g6[3]	Bg7	Be6	0-0[6]	
2	...	...	...	...	...	Bb5	Be3[8]	Nxb5	Qb4+[9]	±
	...	...	...	...	...	Bf5	Qe7+[7]	Nxb5		
3	...	Bd3[10]	Nxe5	Nd2	de	Nb3[13]	Qxd3	0-0	Bf4	±
	Nxe4	d5	Bd6[11]	Bxe5[12]	Nc5	Nxd3+	0-0	Nc6	Qd7[14]	
4	...	...	...	0-0	c4	de	cd[16]	Qc2	Bxe4	±
	...	...	...	0-0	Bxe5[15]	Nc6	Qxd5	Nb4	Nxc2[17]	
5	...	...	...	Nxf7[18]	Qh5+	Qxd5[21]	Qb3[22]	Qxb7	Qa6	∞
	...	...	Nd7	Kxf7[19]	Ke7[20]	Ndf6	Be6	Bd5	Kf7[23]	
6	...	...	...	Qe2	Bxe4	Qxe4	Qxe5	Be3[24]	c3	$\overline{\overline{\infty}}$
	...	...	...	Nxe5	de	Be6	Qd7	Bb4+[25]	Bd6[26]	
7	...	...	...	Nxd7	0-0	c4	c5	Nc3	Ne2	±/∞
	...	...	...	Bxd7	Qh4[27]	0-0-0[28]	g5[29]	Bg7	f5[30]	

1 5 Bb5 c6 6 Qxd4 Qa5+ 7 c3 Nxf2 8 Bc4 Nxh1! (8 ... Bc5? 9 Qf4 d5 10 ed Be6 11 b4! ± Kuijf-Hartoch, Wijk aan Zee 1984) 9 Ng5 Qb6 10 Nxf7 (10 Bxf7+ Kd8 11 Ne6+ Ke7) 10 ... Qxd4 11 cd Rg8 ∓ van der Sterren

5 Qe2 Nc5 6 Nxd4 Nc6 7 Be3 (7 Rxc6 dc 8 Nc3 Bf5 =) 7 ... Nxd4 8 Bxd4 Ne6 9 Bc3 d5 10 ed Qxd6 11 Nd2 Bd7 = Boleslavsky

2 7 Bg5 Nc6! 8 Qe3+ Be7 =
7 Bd3 Nc6 8 Qf4 g6 9 Nc3 – 7 Nc3

3 8 ... Be6 9 Bd3 g6 10 Be3 (10 Nd4 Bg7 11 Nxe6 ±; 11 Nxc6 ±) 10 ... Bg7 – 8 ... g6

4 9 Nd4 Bg7 10 Nxc6 bc 11 Be2 0-0 12 0-0 Rb8 13 Qa4 Bf5 = Khalifman-Zysk, Groningen 1985-86

5 11 0-0-0 Qf6 12 Ng5 Qxf4 13 Bxf4 ± Keres

6 12 Rad1 Qf6 13 Qxf6 Bxf6 14 Ng5 Nb4 15 Nxe6 fe 16 Bc5 Nxd3 17 Rxd3 ± Short-Murei, Hastings 1982-83

7 9 ... Nxb5 10 Nxb5 Qe7+ 11 Kf1! ± Tseshkovsky-Barua, Frunze 1983

8 10 Kf1 Be4 11 Ba4 0-0-0 12 Be3 Bxf3 13 Qxf3 Ne5 ∞ Toth

9 12 Qxb4 Bxb4+ 13 c3 Bd6 14 Nxd6+ cd 15 0-0-0 0-0-0 (15 ... Be6 16 Rxd6 Bxa2 17 Bc5! 0-0 18 Rxc6 ± Matulović-Kholmov, 1968) 16 Nd4 Be6 17 b3 a6 18 Ne2 Gurgenidze-Beim, USSR 1982

10 4 de d5 5 Nbd2 (5 Bd3 Nc6 6 0-0 Bg4 7 Nbd2 Nxd2 8 Bxd2 Nd4 = Romanishin-Makarichev, Frunze 1985) 5 ... Nxd2 6 Bxd2 Be7 7 Bf4 c5 8 c3 Nc6 9 Bd3 Be6 = Short-Seirawan, Lugano 1986

11 5 ... Be7 6 Nd2 Nd6 7 Qf3 c6 8 Nf1 Be6 9 Ng3 0-0 10 0-0 f5 11 Qe2 ± Levin-Borisov, corr. 1985

12 6 ... Nxd2 7 Bxd2 0-0 8 Qh5 ±

13 8 Nf3 Bg4 9 h3 Nxd3+ 10 Qxd3 Bxf3 11 Qxf3 0-0 = Nunn-Toth, Lugano 1984

14 12 Rfe1 Bg4 13 Bg3 Be6 14 h3 Qg6 15 Qd2 Ne7 16 Nd4 ± Gurgenidze-Dvoretsky, USSR 1978

12 Rad1 Bg4 13 Qe3 Ne7 14 f3 Qg6 15 Qc5 Qb6 16 Be3 Re8 17 Qc3 ± Grünfeld-Toth, Biel 1986

15 7 ... f6 8 cd ±
7 ... c6 8 Nc3 ±

16 9 f4 Bf5 10 Nc3 Nxc3 =
9 Bf4 Nb4 10 Na3 Bc5 (10 ... Bf5 11 Bb1 Bg6 12 Be3 Qe7 13 f4 ± van der Wiel-

Zsu.Polgar, Brussels 1985) 11 Bb1 dc! 12 Nxc4 Be6 = van der Wiel

17 12 Bxd5 Bf5 (12 ... Nxa1 13 Be4 ±) 13 g4 Bxg4 14 Be4 Nxa1 15 Bf4 f5 16 Bd5+ Kh8 17 Rc1! ± Rozentalis-Ivanchuk, USSR 1986, and van der Wiel-Mikhalchishin, Lugano 1987

18 6 Nc3 Nxe5 7 de Bb4 8 0-0 ∞ Sax-Nunn, Brussels 1985
6 0-0 Nxe5 7 de Nc5 8 Nc3 c6 9 Qf3 Qh4 = Geller-Plaskett, Sochi 1984

19 6 ... Qe7 and now:
7 Nxh8? Nc3+ 8 Nd2 Qxd1 9 Re1 Qxf2 10 Nxh7 (10 Rxe7+ Bxe7 11 Nxh7 Bg5+) 10 ... Ne5! (10 ... Ne4+?! 11 Rxe4 de 12 Bg6+ = Zaitsev-Karpov, 1966) 11 Rxe5 Be6 12 Rg8 Qh4 ∓ Tronhjem-Christensen, corr. 1984
7 Qe2! Qxf7 (7 ... Kxf7 8 Qh5+ Kf6 9 0-0 ± Gurgenidze-Bellin, Tbilisi 1977) 8 f3 Nf6 9 fe (9 0-0 Qh5 =) 9 ... Bg4 10 Qe3 de 11 Bxe4 0-0-0 ∞

20 7 ... Ke6!?
21 8 Qe2 Kf7 =
22 9 Qe5+ Kf7 10 Bxe4? Bb4+
23 Nenashev-Baikov, Moscow Ch 1985
24 10 0-0 0-0-0 11 Be3 Bb4 12 c3 (12 Nc3 f6 13 Qg3 Bxc3 14 bc h5 ∞ Karpov-Larsen, Tilburg 1980) 12 ... f6 13 Qg3 Be7 14 Nd2 h5 15 f3 g5 ∞ Kir.Georgiev-Salov, Leningrad 1987

25 10 ... 0-0-0 11 Qa5 ± Hort-Short, West Germany 1986
26 12 Qxg7 0-0-0 ∞ Oll-Khalifman, USSR 1984
12 Qa5 Nc6 13 f3 Bd5 14 Nd2 0-0 15 0-0 Rfe8 ∞; 16 Rfe1 b6 17 Qa6 Bxh2+! 18 Kxh2 Rxe3 Fedoseev-Raecky, corr. 1986

27 7 ... Nf6 8 Bg5 ± Geller-Smyslov, Moscow 1981
7 ... Qf6 8 Bxe4 de 9 Nc3 0-0-0 10 Nxe4 Qg6 11 f3 ± Klovans-Rozentalis, USSR 1985, and A.Ivanov-Kochiev, Kostroma 1985
7 ... Bd6 8 c4 c6 9 Nc3 ± Short-Hübner, Wijk aan Zee 1986

28 8 ... Bd6 9 g3 Qh3 10 Nc3 Nxc3 11 bc ±
29 9 ... g6 10 Nc3 Bg7 11 Ne2 Nf6 12 b4 ± Timman-Hübner, Tilburg 1983

30 11 ... Nf6 12 Bd2 Rhg8 13 Rc1 ± Makarichev-Kuijpers, CSKA v Eindhoven 1986
11 ... f5 12 f3 Rhf8 13 a4 Rde8 ∞ Sveshnikov-Makarichev, Moscow Ch 1987

Ponziani

Three Knights

Four Knights

Scotch

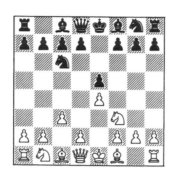
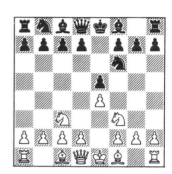
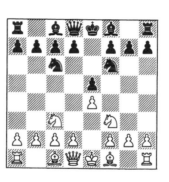
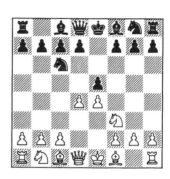

This assortment of double e-pawn openings has fallen into disuse. The Three and Four Knights are not without their pitfalls, but with a working knowledge of theory Black can work his way through to a very comfortable equality. Old-fashioned romanticism like the Belgrade Gambit of the Four Knights can be found in these quiet systems but Black has a variety of methods to defuse these volatile lines.

The Ponziani is a very old opening which fails to pose problems for the defence, despite a logical basis. Well-analysed by Ponziani in 1769, it never caught on since White's laudable intention to erect a formidable centre is simply premature. Black can equalize with straightforward developing moves or opt for the sharp and strong 3 ... d5.

The Scotch has received attention from those e-pawn players who have become dissatisfied with the well trodden paths of the Ruy Lopez, but White has yet to prove an advantage here.

References: *The Open Game in Action* (Karpov)
Open Gambits (Botterill)

	3	4	5	6	7	8	9	10	11	
1	...	d4	♗b5[3]	e5	♘xd4	0-0	♗xc6	f3[5]	fe	=
	♘f6[1]	d5[2]	ed[4]	♘e4	♗c5	0-0	bc	f6	fe[6]	
2	...	♗b5[7]	♘xe5	♕a4	♗xc6[9]	♕xc6+	♖f1	♕xa8+	♔d1[10]	=
	d5	de	♕g5![8]	♕xg2	bc	♔d8	♗h3	♔e7	♕xf1+[11]	

[1] 3 ... f5 4 d4 fe 5 ♘xe5 ♕f6 6 ♘g4 ♕g6 7 ♗f4 d6 8 ♘e3 ± Zagorovsky
3 ... ♗e7!? 4 d4 ed 5 cd d5 6 ed ♘b4 7 ♗b5+ ♗d7 = Sax-Romanishin, Tilburg 1979

[2] 4 ... ♘xe4 5 d5 ♘b8 (5 ... ♘e7 6 ♘xe5 ♘g6 7 ♘d4 ♕f6 8 ♕xe4 ♕xe5 9 ♕xe5+ ♘xe5 10 ♘d2 ± Velimirović-Smejkal, Rio de Janeiro IZ 1979) 6 ♘xe5 ♗c5 (6 ... ♕e7 7 ♕d4 d6 8 ♕xe4 ♕xe5 9 ♗d3 ♕xe4 10 ♗xe4 ♘d7 11 ♗e3 ♘f6 12 ♗f3 ± Miles-Gligorić, Bad Lauterberg 1977) 7 ♘d3! (7 ♘g4 0-0 8 ♕xe4 d6 9 ♗d3 f5 10 ♕c4 b5 11 ♕xb5 ♕e7 ∞ Szilagyi-Bezzola, corr. 1985) 7 ... ♗b6 8 ♕f3 0-0 9 ♗e2 ♖e8 10 ♘d2 ♕e7 11 ♘xe4 ♕xe4 12 ♕xe4 ♖xe4 13 d6 ± Stern-Rodin, corr. 1978
4 ... ed 5 e5 ♘e4 6 ♕e2 ♘c5 7 cd ♘e6 8 d5 ±/± Arkhipin-Natapov, Moscow 1986

[3] 5 de ♘xe4 6 ♗b5 ♗c5 7 0-0 0-0 8 b4 ♗b6 9 a4 a5 10 ba ♘xa5 ∓ Ljubojević-Filip, Nice Ol 1974

[4] 5 ... ♘xe4 6 ♘xe5 ♗d7 7 ♘xd7 ♕xd7 8 0-0 ♗e7 =

[5] 10 b4?! ♗xd4 11 cd ♗a6 12 ♖e1 ♕h4! ∓ Bator-Berkell, Sweden 1986
10 ♗e3 ♕e8! 11 f3 ♘d6 ∞ Pliester

[6] 12 ♖xf8+ ♕xf8 13 ♗e3 ed 14 cd =

[7] 4 ♕a4 and now:
4 ... ♘f6 5 ♘xe5 ♗d6 6 ♘xc6 bc 7 d3 0-0 8 ♗e2 ♖e8 9 ♗g5 h6 10 ♗xf6 ♕xf6 ∞/= Verbel-Belonogov, corr. 1984
4 ... ♗d7 5 ed ♘d4 6 ♕d1 ♘xf3+ 7 ♕xf3 f5 8 ♗c4 ♗d6 9 d3 ∞∞
4 ... ♕d6! 5 ♗b5 ♗d7 6 d4 (6 ed ♕xd5 7 0-0 ♗e7! ∓ Zagorovsky) 6 ... ♘f6 7 ed ♕xd5 8 0-0 e4 9 c4 ♕h5 10 ♖e1 ♗e7 11 ♘e5 ♘xe5 12 de ♕xe5 13 ♗xd7+ ♘xd7 ∓

[8] 5 ... ♗d7 6 ♘xd7 ♕xd7 7 d4 ed 8 ♕xd3 ♕xd3 9 ♗xd3 ± Keres
5 ... ♕d5 6 ♕a4 ♘ge7 7 f4 ef 8 ♘xf3 ±

[9] 7 ♖f1 ♗h3! 8 ♗xc6+ bc 9 ♕xc6+ ♔d8 10 ♕xa8+ ♔e7 11 ♘c6+ ♔f6! 12 ♕d8+ ♔g6 13 ♘e5+ ♔h5 ∓ Zagorovsky

[10] 11 ♘c6+? ♔d6 12 ♕xf8+ ♘e7! ∓

[11] 12 ♔c2 ♗g4!? (12 ... ♗f5 13 ♘a3 e3+ 14 d3 e2 15 ♗g5+ f6 16 ♕d5 ♗e6! 17 ♘c6+ ♔f7! =) 13 b3 ♗d1+ 14 ♔b2 f6 15 ♘c4 ♕d3 16 ♘e3 ♗f3 17 ♕xa7 ∞ Seppeur-Herbrechtsmeier, West Germany 1985-86

	3	4	5	6	7	8	9	10	11	
	Three Knights			**1 e4 e5 2 ♘f3 ♘c6 3 ♘c3**						
1	...	d4[2]	♘d5[3]	♗g5	♘xd4[5]	♗h4	♘xe7	♕d2	ed	=
	g6[1]	ed	♗g7	♘ce7[4]	h6[6]	c6	♘xe7	d5	g5[7]	

[1] 3 ... **♗b4** 4 ♘d5 ♘f6 5 ♘xb4 ♘xb4 6 ♘xe5 ♕e7 7 d4 d6 8 a3 de 9 ab ed 10 ♕xd4 ♕xe4+ 11 ♕xe4 ♘xe4 12 ♗f4 c6 13 ♗d3 ± Keres

3 ... **d6** 4 d4 ♗d7 5 ♗b5 – Ruy Lopez

3 ... **♗c5** 4 ♘xe5 ♘xe5 5 d4 ♗d6 6 de ♗xe5 7 f4 ♗xc3+ 8 bc d6 9 ♕d4 ±

[2] 4 h4 h5?! 5 d4 ed 6 ♘d5 ♗g7 7 ♗g5 ♘ce7 8 e5 d6 9 ♘f6+ ♗xf6 (9 ... ♔f8? 10 ♕xd4 ♗g4 11 0-0-0 ♘f5 12 ♕c3 ± Hector-Iskov, Malmö 1986-87) 10 ef ♘d5 11 ♕xd4 ♘dxf6 12 0-0 ∞; 4 ... ♗g7 ∞

[3] 5 ♘xd4 ♗g7 6 ♗e3 d6 – 2 ... d6; 6 ... ♘f6?! 7 ♘xc6! bc 8 e5 ♘g8 9 ♗d4 ♕e7 10 ♕e2 f6 11 ef ♘xf6 ± Keres

[4] 6 ... f6 7 ♗f4 d6 8 ♘xd4 ♘ge7 9 ♗c4 ♘e5

[5] 7 e5 h6 8 ♗xe7 ♘xe7 9 ♕xd4 ♗xd5 10 ♕xd5 d6! 11 0-0-0 0-0 = Czerniak-Sokolov, Belgrade 1962

[6] 7 ... c6 and now:

8 ♘c3 h6 9 ♗f4 (9 ♗e3?! ♘f6 10 ♕e2 0-0 11 0-0-0 b5! ∓ Utasi-Westerinen, Havana 1985) 9 ... d5 10 ♕d2 ♘f6 11 0-0-0 ♘xe4 12 ♘xe4 de 13 ♗c4 ∞ Lehmann-Keres, Hamburg 1960

8 ♘xe7! ♗xe7 9 ♕d2 h6 10 ♗h4 d5 11 0-0-0 g5 12 ♗g3 de 13 ♕e3 ♕b6 =/± Fernandez-Pigusov, Jurmala 1983

[7] 12 ♗g3 ♕xd5 13 c3 0-0 = Karlsson-Geller, Reykjavik 1986

Four Knights 1 e4 e5 2 ♘f3 ♘c6 3 ♘c3 ♘f6

	4	5	6	7	8	9	10	11	12	
1	♗b5	♗a4[2]	♘xe5	♘d3	e5[4]	0-0	ed	d7	♗xd7	=
	♘d4[1]	♗c5[3]	0-0	♗b6	♘e8	d6	♘f6[5]	♗xd7	♕xd7[6]	
2	...	0-0	d3[7]	♗g5[9]	bc	♖e1[11]	d4	h3	g4	∞/=
	♗b4	0-0	d6[8]	♗xc3	♕e7[10]	♘d8	♗g4[12]	♗h5	♗g6[13]	
3	d4	♘xe5[14]	♕g4	♕xg7	a3	ab	♔d2	♔xc3		∞
	♗b4	♘xe4[15]	♘xc3	♖f8	♘xd4![16]	♘xc2+	♘xa1	a5![17]		
4	...	♘xd4[18]	♘xc6	♗d3	ed	0-0	♗g5	♘b5	a3	=
	ed	♗b4	bc[19]	d5[20]	cd[21]	0-0	♗e6[22]	c5	♗a5[23]	

---

[1] 4 ... ♗c5 5 ♘xe5 ♘xe5 6 d4 ♗b4 7 de ♘xe4 8 ♕d4 ♘xc3 9 bc ♗e7 10 ♕g4 g6 11 ♕f3 0-0 12 ♗h6 ♖e8 13 0-0 ± Motwani-Hawksworth, Southampton 1986

  4 ... a6!? 5 ♗xc6 dc 6 d3 ♗d6 7 ♕e2 ♕e7 8 ♗d2 ♗d7 9 ♘d1 ♘h5 = Smagin-Ivanchuk, USSR 1986

[2] 5 ♗c4 ♗c5 6 0-0 d6 7 ♘xd4 ♗xd4 8 d3 ♗e6 9 ♘d5 c6 = Campora-Seirawan, Dubai Ol 1986

  5 ♘xd4 ed 6 e5 dc 7 ef ♕xf6 8 dc ♕e5+ (8 .... c6 9 ♗d3 ♕e5+ 10 ♗e3 d5 11 ♕f3 ♗c5 12 0-0 ± Imanaliev-Thipsay, Frunze 1985) 9 ♗e2 ♗c5 10 0-0 0-0 11 ♗d3 d5 12 ♕f3 ♗d6 ∞ Imanaliev-Chiburdanidze, Frunze 1985

[3] 5 ... ♘xf3+ 6 gf!? ♗c5 7 f4 ♕e7 8 d3 c6 9 ♕e2 d6 10 h3 ♗d7 11 ♗b3 ± Dubinin-Maseyev, corr. 1960

[4] 8 ♘f4 d5 9 d3 c6 10 h3 ♖e8 11 0-0 de 12 de ♘xe4 13 ♘xe4 ♖xe4 = Spielmann

[5] 10 ... ♘xd6 11 ♘e1 h5!? 12 ♕xh5 g6 ∞ Franzoni-Bhend, Berne 1987

[6] 13 ♘e1 ♖ae8 14 d3 ♘g4 = Estrin

[7] 6 ♗xc6 dc and now:

  7 ♘xe5 ♖e8 8 ♘d3 ♗xc3 9 dc ♘xe4 10 ♕f3 ♕f6 = Spassky-Ljubojević, Linares 1985

  7 d3 ♗g4 (7 ... ♗d6 8 h3 c5 9 ♘h2 ♗e6 10 b3 ♘d7 11 ♗e3 ♖e8 = Wittman-Unzicker, Graz 1984) 8 h3 ♗h5 9 ♕e2 ♗xc3 10 bc ♘d7 = Hug-Spassky, Zürich 1984

[8] 6 ... ♗xc3 7 bc d6 8 ♗xc6 bc 9 ♖b1 h6 10 c4 c5 11 ♘e1 ♗g4 12 f3 ♗e6 = Spassky-Hort, Reggio Emilia 1986-87; 8 ♖e1 ♘e7 9 d4 ± Kristjansson-Halldarsson, Reykjavik 1984

[9] 7 ♘e2 ♘e7 8 c3 ♗a5 9 ♘g3 c6 10 ♗a4 ♗g6 11 d4 ♖e8 = Sveshnikov-Yusupov, USSR Ch 1979

[10] 8 ... ♗d7!? 9 ♖b1 h6 10 ♗h4 a6 11 ♗xc6 ♗xc6 12 ♖e1 ♖e8 13 ♘d2 b5 = Spassky-Portisch, Bugojno 1986

[11] 9 ♗xc6 bc 10 h3 h6 11 ♗d2 ♘h7 12 ♕e2 f5 13 ef ♗xf5 ∞ Martin-Yusupov, Dubai Ol 1986

[12] 10 ... ♘e6 11 ♖c1 (11 ♗c1 c5 12 ♗f1 ♕c7 13 g3 ♖e8 14 d5 ♘f8 15 c4 ± Hodgson-Spassky, Brussels 1985) 11 ... ♖d8 12 a4 c5 13 ♗f1 ♘f8 14 d5 ♘g6 15 ♘d2 ♖f8 16 ♘c4 ± Spassky-Yusupov, Bugojno 1986

[13] 13 d5 c6 14 ♗d3 cd 15 ed ∞/= Spassky-Gligorić, Sarajevo 1986

[14] 5 d5 ♘e7 6 ♘xe5 d6 7 ♗b5+ ♔f8 8 ♘d3 ♗xc3+ 9 bc ♘xe4 10 ♕f3 ♘f6 ∞

[15] 5 ... ♕e7 6 ♕d3 ♘xe5 7 de ♕xe5 8 ♗d2 0-0 9 0-0-0 ±

[16] 8 ... ♗a5 9 ♘xc6 dc 10 ♕e5+ ♕e7 11 ♕xe7+ ♔xe7 12 ♗d2 ±

[17] Angantysson-Polgar, Dresden 1969

[18] 5 ♘d5 (Belgrade Gambit) 5 ... ♘b4!? 6 ♗c4 ♘bxd5 7 ed ♗b4+ 8 ♔f1 0-0 9 ♕xd4 h6 10 h4 d6 11 ♗g5 ♗c5 ∞/= Hector-Karolyi, Copenhagen 1985

[19] 6 ... ♗xc3+!? 7 bc dc 8 ♕xd8+ ♔xd8 9 ♗g5 h6 10 0-0-0+ ♔e7 11 ♗h4 g5 12 ♗g3 ♗e6 13 f3 ♘e8 14 h4 ♘d6 = Rigo-Mira, Vienna 1986

[20] 7 ... 0-0 8 ♗g5 d5 9 ed ♖e8+ 10 ♔f1 ♗xc3 11 bc cd 12 ♕f3 ♘e4!? = Thorhallsson-Howell, Groningen 1986-87; 8 0-0 ♖e8 9 ♗g5 h6 10 ♗h4 g5 11 ♗g3 ± Pomar-Ljubojević, Las Palmas 1979

[21] 8 ... ♕e7+ 9 ♕e2 ♘xd5 10 ♕xe7+ ♔xe7 11 a3 ♗xc3+ 12 bc ♖e8 13 ♗d2 ± Braga-Weemaes, Dubai Ol 1986

[22] 10 ... c6 11 ♕f3 h6 12 ♗xf6 ♕xf6 13 ♕xf6 gf 14 ♘e2 ♗d6 = Sveshnikov-Yudasin, USSR 1986

[23] 13 b4 ♗b6 (13 ... cb 14 ab ♗xb4 15 ♖a7 ♖xa7 16 ♘xa7 ± Salazar-Sanchez Guirado, Vigo 1985) 14 bc ♗xc5 15 ♕f3 h6 16 ♗xf6 ♕xf6 17 ♕xf6 gf = Gheorghiu-Suba, Prague Z 1985

	Scotch I			1 e4 e5 2 ♘f3 ♘c6 3 d4 ed				

	4	5	6	7	8	9	10	11	12	
1	c3[1]	ed[3]	cd	♗e2	♘c3	♗xf3	♕b3[6]	ab	0-0	=
	d5[2]	♕xd5	♗g4[4]	♗b4+[5]	♗xf3	♕c4!	♕xb3	♘ge7	a6[7]	
2	...	♗c4	♗xb2	0-0[9]	♗xe6	♕b3	♘g5	f4	f5[11]	⩱/∓
	dc	cb!	d6![8]	♗e6	fe	♕d7[10]	♘d8	♘f6	e5[12]	
3	...	♘xc3	♗c4[14]	♘g5[15]	bc	0-0	f4	♗e2	f5	∞
	...	♗b4[13]	d6	♗xc3	♘h6[16]	0-0	♘a5	♔h8	f6[17]	

[1] 4 ♗c4 ♗c5 (4 ... ♘f6! – Scotch Variation of the Two Knights Defence) 5 c3 ♘f6! (5 ... d3?! 6 0-0 d6 7 b4 ♗b6 8 a4 a6 9 a5 ♗a7 10 ♕b3 ♕f6 11 b5! ♘e5 12 ♘xe5 de 13 ba ba 14 ♕a4+! ± Sveshnikov-A.Petrosian, USSR 1974) – Giuoco Piano

[2] 4 ... d3 5 ♗xd3 d6 6 ♗f4! (6 h3 g6! 7 ♗g5 ♘f6 8 ♘bd2 ♗g7 9 ♘d4 0-0 10 ♘xc6 bc 11 f4 ♖b8 12 0-0 ♕e8! = Raaste-Westerinen, Helsinki 1979) 6 ... ♗e7 7 h3 ♘f6 8 ♘bd2 ♗d7 9 ♕c2 ±

[3] 5 ♗d3!? de 6 ♗xe4 ♘f6 7 ♗xc6+ bc 8 ♗d2 = Smit

[4] 6 ... ♘f6 7 ♗e2 ♗g4 8 ♘c3 ♕a5 9 0-0 ♗d6 (9 ... 0-0-0 10 ♗e3 ♗c5?! 11 ♘g5! ± Striković-D'Amore, Biel II 1985) 10 ♗e3 0-0

[5] 7 ... 0-0-0 8 ♗e3 ♗b4+ 9 ♘c3 ♘ge7 10 0-0 ♕d7 11 ♖c1 = Pellegrino-Morrison, corr. 1979

[6] 10 ♗e3? ♗xc3+ 11 bc ♕xc3+ 12 ♔f1 ♕c4+ 13 ♔g1 ♘ge7 14 ♖c1 ♕xa2 15 ♖a1 ♕c4 16 ♖c1 (½-½ Marshall-Capablanca, Lake Hopatcong 1926) 16 ... ♕a2 17 ♖a1 ♕c4 18 ♖c1 ♕b4! ∓ Bryson-Flear, Edinburgh 1985
10 ♗xc6+ bc 11 ♕e2+ ♕xe2+ 12 ♔xe2 0-0-0 13 ♗e3 ♘e7 = Emma-Vogt, Skopje Ol 1972

[7] 13 ♖a4 ♗d6 14 ♗g5 f6 15 ♗h5+ ♘g6 16 ♖e1+ ♘ce7 17 ♗d2 0-0-0 = Ljubojević-Ree, Amsterdam 1972

[8] 6 ... ♗b4+ 7 ♘c3 ♘f6 8 ♕c2 d6 9 0-0-0 0-0 10 e5 ± Keres

[9] 7 ♕b3 ♕d7! 8 ♗c3 ♘f6! ∓ Smit
7 ♘c3 ♗e7 8 ♕b3 ♘h6 9 ♘d5 f6 10 0-0 ♘a5 ∓ Csom-Barczay, Hungary 1967

[10] 9 ... ♕c8 10 ♘g5 ♘d8 11 f4 ±

[11] 12 e5 de 13 fe ♘d5 14 ♘d2 (Krantz-Sellberg, corr. 1974) 14 ... ♗e7! ∓

[12] 13 ♘c3 h6 14 ♘e6 c6 15 ♖ad1 ♘xe6 16 fe ♕c7 17 ♔h1 ♗e7 ∓ E.Szabo-Kocsis, corr. 1979

[13] 5 ... d6 6 ♗c4 and now:
6 ... ♗e7 8 ♕b3 ♘a5 9 ♗xf7+ ♔f8 9 ♕a4 ♔xf7 10 ♕xa5 c6 11 ♕xd8 ♗xd8 12 ♗f4 ♗e7 13 0-0-0 ± Bryson-Thipsay, Edinburgh 1985
6 ... ♘f6 7 ♕b3 ♕d7 8 ♘g5 ♘e5 9 ♗b5 c6 10 f4 cb (10 ... ♘g6 11 e5 h6 12 ef hg ∞ B.Andersson-Overas, corr. 1984) 11 fe de 12 ♗e3 a5! 13 0-0-0 a4! ∞ Dubini-Chiesa, corr. 1985

[14] 6 ♗g5 ♘ge7 7 ♕c2 d6 8 0-0-0 ♗xc3 9 ♕xc3 0-0 10 h4 ♗e6 11 h5 h6 ⩲ Gufeld-Stein, USSR 1959

[15] 7 0-0 ♗xc3 8 bc ♕e7 (8 ... ♗g4 9 ♕b3 ♗xf3 10 ♗xf7+ ♔f8 11 gf ♘e5 12 ♗xg8 ♖xg8 13 f4 ♘f3+ 14 ♔g2 ♘h4+ 15 ♔h1 ♕d7 16 f5 ♖e8 17 ♕xb7 ♕a4 18 f3 ♕c2 19 ♕b2 ±/± Milukas-Sutkus, corr. 1976) 9 e5 ♘xe5 10 ♘xe5 de 11 ♕b3 ♘f6 12 ♗a3 c5 ⩲/∓ Jokšić-Medančić, Catanzaro 1979

[16] 8 ... ♘e5 9 ♗b3 h6 10 f4 ♗g4 ∞ Thiele-Brilla Banfalvi, corr. 1983

[17] 13 ♘xh7 ♔xh7 14 ♗h5 ∞ Thiele-van Perlo, corr. 1984

	Scotch II			1 e4 e5 2 ♘f3 ♘c6 3 d4 ed 4 ♘xd4				

	4	5	6	7	8	9	10	11	12	
1	...	♘b5[2]	♗d2[4]	♗e2	0-0	♘xd2	g3	♘c4	♗f3![7]	±
	♕h4[1]	♗b4+[3]	♕xe4+	♔d8	♗xd2[5]	♕f4[6]	♕h6	♘ge7		

1 e4 e5 2 ♘f3 ♘c6 3 d4 ed 4 ♘xd4 ♘f6 5 ♘xc6 bc

	6	7	8	9	10	11	12	13	14	
2	♗d3[8]	e5[9]	0-0	♕e2	h3	♘d2	♘f3	b4	c4	∞
	d5	♘g4	♗c5	♕h4	h5	♕g3	h4[10]	♗b6	dc[11]	
3	e5	♗e3[13]	ed	♗d3	0-0	c4	♘c3	♖e1	cd	±
	♘e4[12]	d5	cd	♘f6	♗e7	0-0	♗e6	d5	♘xd5[14]	
4	...	♕e2	c4	♘c3[16]	♕e4[17]	♗d2	♗d3	ef	0-0-0	±
	♕e7	♘d5	♘b6[15]	♕e6	♗b4[18]	0-0	f5	♖xf6	♕xe4[19]	
5	...	...	...	♕e4[20]	♕e2	♘d2	♕e4[23]	a4[24]	cd	=/∓
	...	...	♗a6	♘f6[21]	♘d5	0-0-0[22]	♘b6	d5![25]	♗xf1[26]	

---

[1] **4 ... ♕f6 5 ♘b5** (5 ♗e3 ♗c5 – 4 ... ♗c5) 5 ... ♗c5 6 ♕e2 ♘b6 7 ♘1c3 ♘ge7 8 ♗e3 ± Kupreichik-Nei, USSR 1975
4 ... g6 5 c4 (5 ♘c3 ♗g7 6 ♗e3 – 3 ♘c3 g6) ± Evans
4 ... ♗b4+ 5 c3 ♗e7 6 ♗c4 (6 ♗f4 d6 7 ♘d2 ♘f6 8 ♗e2 ± Harding, Botterill) 6 ... ♘e5 7 ♗b3 d6 8 f4 ♘g6 9 ♘f5 ± Mesing-Planinc, Yugoslav Ch 1968

[2] **5 ♘c3 ♗b4 6 ♘b5 ♗a5 7 ♗d3 a6 8 ♗a3** b5 9 ♗d2 ♘f6 10 0-0 ♗xc3 11 bc d6 ∓ Zhuravlev-Bronstein, USSR 1980
5 ♘f3 ♕xe4+ 6 ♗e2 ♕e7! ∓ Evans

[3] **5 ... ♕xe4+ 6 ♗e2 ♔d8 7 0-0 a6 8 ♘1c3** ♕e8 9 ♘d4 ∞/± Staunton
5 ... ♗c5 6 ♕e2 ♘d4 7 ♘xd4 ♗xd4 8 c3 ♗b6 9 g3 ♕e7 10 ♗g2 ±/± Harding, Botterill

[4] **6 c3 ♗a5 7 ♘d2 a6 8 ♘a3 ♗b6 9 ♕e2 d6** 10 g3 ♘g4 11 f3 ♕e6 12 ♘dc4 ± Radulov-G.Garcia, Torremolinos 1975

[5] **8 ... ♘f6 9 ♘1c3 ♕h4 10 g3 ♕h3 11 ♘d5!** ±

[6] **9 ... ♕g6 10 ♘c4 intending 11 ♗f3** ±

[7] Botterill-Staples, Manchester 1974

[8] **6 ♘d2 d5 7 ♗d3 ♗d6 8 0-0 0-0 9 h3 ♖e8 10 ed cd** = Botterill-Dilworth, Manchester 1975

[9] **7 ♕e2 ♗e7 8 0-0 0-0 9 ♗f4 ♖b8 10 ♘d2 ♖e8 11 e5 ♗f8** =

[10] **12 ... a5 13 e6! ♗xe6 14 hg hg 15 ♕e5** ± Mascarinas-O'Kelly, Penang 1978

[11] **15 ♗xc4 ♖h5** ∞ Zdanov-Baturinsky, corr. 1957

[12] **6 ... ♘d5 7 c4 ♘b6 8 ♗d3** (8 ♘c3 ♕e7 9 ♕e2 ♗a6 10 ♕e4 ♕e6 11 b3 ♗b4 ∞ Ljubojević-Spassky, Montreal 1979) 8 ... ♗a6 9 0-0 ♗xc4 10 ♗xc4 ♘xc4 11 ♕g4 ♘b6 12 ♘c3 ♘d5 13 ♘xd5 cd 14 ♗g5 ± Padevsky-Witkowski, Laibach 1955

[13] **7 ♘f3 ♕h4 8 g3 ♘g5 9 ♕e2! ♕e4 10 ♗xg5!** ♕xh1 11 ♘c3 h6 (11 ... ♗b4 12 0-0-0 ♗xc3 13 bc ♕xh2? 14 ♕f3! ± Hünerkopf-Klundt, West Germany 1983-84) 12 ♗f4 ♕xh2 13 ♘e4 ♗e7 ∞

[14] **15 ♘xd5 ♗xd5 16 ♕c2** ± Timman-Korchnoi, Sarajevo 1984

[15] **8 ... ♕b4+ 9 ♘d2 ♘f4 10 ♕e4 ♘e6 11 ♗e2** ♗b7 (11 ... a5 12 0-0 a4 13 ♗g4 ±) 12 a3 ♕b6 13 ♘f3 c5 14 ♕c2 ♗e7 15 0-0 ±/= Sveshnikov-Geller, Sochi 1984

[16] **.9 b3 g6! 10 ♗b2 ♗g7 11 ♘d2 0-0 12 0-0-0** d5 ∞ Zhuravlev-Christiansen, corr. 1983
9 ♗f4 ♕b4+ 10 ♘d2!? ♕xb2 11 ♖b1 ♕xa2 12 ♕e4 ∞; 10 ♔d1 ♗a6 11 b3 0-0-0 12 g3 d5 13 ♗h3+ ♔b7 ∞ Yousser-Kiprov, corr. 1983

[17] **10 b3 ♗b4 11 ♗b2 0-0 12 0-0-0 ♖e8 13 ♕c2** ♕xe5 ∞/= Botterill-Corden, Birmingham 1975
10 ♗d2 ♗a6 11 b3 0-0-0 12 ♕e4 f5! ∞ Kember-Samarian, corr. 1981

[18] **10 ... ♗a6!? 11 b3 ♗b4 12 ♗d2 ♗xc3 13 ♗xc3 d5** ∞/±

[19] **15 ♘xe4 ♗xd2+ 16 ♖xd2** ± Oll-Rozhdestvensky, Pärnu 1982

[20] **9 b3 0-0-0 10 ♗b2 f6!** (10 ... ♕g5 11 ♘d2 f6 12 h4! ♕h6 13 0-0-0 ± Hort-Unzicker, West Germany 1983-84) = Hort

[21] **9 ... ♘b6 10 ♘c3!** (10 ♘d2 0-0-0 11 c5 ♗xf1 12 cb ♗a6! ∞/∓ Timman-Karpov, London 1984) 10 ... f5 11 ♕xf5 ♗xc4 12 ♗xc4 ♘xc4 13 0-0 g6 14 ♕e4 ± Sveshnikov-Zaitsev, USSR 1975

[22] **11 ... ♘b4 12 ♘f3 c5!** (12 ... d5 13 a3! ♗xc4 14 ♕d1 ♗xf1 15 ♔xf1 ♘a6 16 ♕a4 ±) 13 a3 ♘c6 ∞/=

[23] **12 b3 ♖e8 13 ♗b2 f6! 14 ♕e4 ♘b6 15 f4** fe 16 fe ♗b7 17 0-0 g6 18 ♗d3 ± Prandstetter-Kovacz, Tetschen 1978; 18 ... ♗h6!?

[24] **13 c5 ♗xf1 14 cb ♗a6** =

[25] **13 ... ♔b7? 14 a5 ♘c8 15 b4! ♔b8 16 ♗e2** f6 17 f4 ± Handoko-Kovačević, Agram 1985

[26] **15 d6 ♖xd6 16 ♘xf1 ♖e6!** Timman-Karpov, Amsterdam 1985

Scotch III   1 e4 e5 2 ♘f3 ♘c6 3 d4 ed 4 ♘xd4 ♗c5

	5	6	7	8	9	10	11	12	13	
1	♗e3[1]	c3[2]	g3[3]	♗g2	♘b5	♘xc7+	0-0[5]	fe	♕b3	∞
	♕f6	♘ge7	d5!	de[4]	♗xe3	♔f8	♖b8	♕e5	f5[6]	
2	♘f5!?	♘xg7+[8]	♘h5	♘g3	♗e2	b4![10]	c3	♗a3	♗xc5	∞
	d6[7]	♔f8	♕h4	♘f6	♘e5	♗xb4+	♗c5	♘xe4	♘xc5[11]	
3	♘b3	a4[12]	♕e2	a5	♘xd4	c3	g3[15]	♗g2	0-0	±
	♗b6	♕f6	♘ge7[13]	♘d4	♗xd4	♗c5![14]	0-0	a6	d6[16]	
4	...	...	♘c3	♗g5[18]	♕e2[19]	♗h4	♘xd4	♕d2	♗d3	±
	...	a6	♘f6[17]	d6	h6	♘d4	♗xd4	♗e5[20]	♗e6[21]	
5	...	c3[22]	f4[23]	♗d3	g3	♗e3	h3	♕d2	gf	∞
	♗b4+	♗e7	d6	♗h4+[24]	♗f6	h5	g5!?	gf	♘ge7[25]	

---

[1] 5 ♘xc6 ♕f6! 6 ♕e2 (6 f4!? = Larsen-Brinck Claussen, Copenhagen 1979) 6 ... bc 7 ♘c3 ♘e7 =

[2] 6 ♘b5 ♗xe3 7 fe (Blumenfeld Attack) 7 ... ♕h4+ 8 g3 ♕d8 9 ♕g4 ♔f8 10 ♕f4 d6 ∓ Mieses-Scheffhout, Amsterdam 1946

[3] 7 ♗c4 ♘e5! 8 ♗b3 d6 =
7 ♘c2 ♗xe3 8 ♘xe3 ♕e5! 9 ♘d2 d5 10 ed ♘xd5 11 ♘dc4 ∞/= Sveshnikov-Korchnoi, USSR Ch 1973
7 f4 ♗xd4 8 cd d5 9 ♘c3 0-0! = Botterill, Harding

[4] 8 ... ♗xd4!? 9 cd de (Parma) 10 ♘c3 ♗f5 11 ♘xe4 ♗xe4 12 ♗xe4 ♕e6 13 ♗g2 ♕c4 14 ♖c1 ♕a6 ∞ Gheorghiu-Romanishin, Leningrad 1977

[5] 11 fe ♖b8 12 ♘d5 ♕g5 = Klovans-Romanishin, Odessa 1974

[6] Sveshnikov-Geller, Sochi 1976

[7] 5 ... d5 6 ♘c3 (6 ♘xg7+ ♔f8 7 ♘h5 ♕h4 8 ♘g3 ♘f6 ∓) 6 ... ♗xf5!? (6 ... de 7 ♘xg7+ ♔f8 8 ♕xd8+ ♘xd8 9 ♘xe4 ±) 7 ef d4 8 ♘e4 ∞
5 ... ♕f6 6 ♘c3 ♘ge7 7 ♘e3 0-0 8 g3 ♘e5 9 f4 ♘g6 10 ♗g2 ± Ljubojević-Karpov, Montreal 1979
5 ... g6 6 ♗e3 ♘f6 7 ♘c3 0-0 8 ♗d3 ♖e8 9 0-0 d6 10 ♔h1 ♘e5 11 ♗e2 ♘ed7! (11 ... ♘c6 12 f3 ♘d4 13 ♗c4! ± Timman-Smyslov, Bugojno 1984) 12 f3 a6 ∞ Handoko-Smejkal, Agram 1985

[8] 6 ♗e3 ♕f6 7 ♘c3 ♗e6 8 ♗e2 ♘ge7 9 0-0 0-0 10 ♔h1 ♕d4 ∞ Schulz-Herbrechtsmeier, West Germany 1984-85

[9] 9 f3 ♖g8!

[10] 10 f3 ♖g8! (10 ... ♘eg4? 11 fg ♘xe4 12 ♕d5! ± Handoko-Timman, Agram 1985) ∞

[11] 14 0-0 ♖g8 15 ♘d2 ♗d7 16 ♘f3 ∞ Timman-Borm, Dutch Ch 1985

[12] 6 ♘c3 ♘f6 (6 ... ♘ge7 7 ♗g5 f6 8 ♗h4 0-0 9 ♕d2 d6 ∞ Radulov-Kolarov, Sofia 1979) 7 ♗g5 h6 8 ♗h4 d6 9 ♕e2 (Costro-Parma, Rome 1980) 9 ... g5 10 ♗g3 ♘d4 11 ♘xd4 ♗xd4 ∞

[13] 7 ... a5 8 ♘c3 ♘ge7 9 ♗e3! ♘b4! (9 ... ♗xe3 10 ♕xe3 0-0 11 0-0-0 d6 12 ♗e2 ♗e6 13 f4 ± Prandstetter-Hernandez, Cienfuegos 1983) =

[14] 10 ... ♗e5?! 11 g3 c6 12 ♗g2 0-0 13 0-0 ± Barczay

[15] 11 e5!? ♕c6 12 ♘d2 a6 (Damjanović-Barczay, Tallinn 1969) 13 ♘b3 ♗a7 14 ♗e3 ± Harding, Botterill

[16] 14 b4 ♗a7 15 ♗b2 ♘c6 ∞ ECO

[17] 7 ... ♘ge7 8 ♕e2 0-0 9 ♗g5 d6 10 ♘d5 ♗a7 11 0-0-0 ± Pasman-Unzicker, Beer-Sheva 1984
7 ... ♕f6 8 ♕e2 ♘ge7 9 ♘d5 ♘xd5 10 ed ♘e7 11 a5 ♗a7 12 h4 ±
7 ... d6 8 ♕e2 ♗e6 9 ♘d5 ♗a7 10 g3 ♕e7 11 ♗e3 ± Botterill, Harding

[18] 8 g3 d6 9 ♗g2 ♗g4! 10 f3 (10 ♗f3?! ♘e5! ∓ Prandstetter-Hort, Czechoslovak Ch 1984) 10 ... ♗d7 11 ♕e2 ∞

[19] 9 a5!? ♗a7 10 ♗e2 ♗e6 10 0-0 h6 11 ♗h4 g5 12 ♗g3 h5 13 h3 ∞/± Agzamov-Ivanov, USSR 1974

[20] 12 ... ♗a7?! 13 ♘d5 ±

[21] 14 f4!? ♗xc3 15 ♕xc3 ♗xe4 16 ♗xd8 ♘xc3 17 ♗xc7 ♘d5 18 ♗xd6 ♖d8 19 ♗e5 f6 20 f5 ±/= Botterill, Harding
14 ♗g3! ±

[22] 6 ♗d2 a5! 7 a3 ♗xd2+ 8 ♕xd2 ♘f6 9 ♘c3 0-0 10 0-0-0 d6 11 ♗e2 ♗d7 = Radulov-Smejkal, Vrbas 1977

[23] 7 ♘d4 ♗f6 8 g3 ♘ge7 9 ♗g2 0-0 10 0-0 d6 = Radulov-Keres, Budapest 1970
7 c4 ♘f6 8 ♘c3 ♗b4 (8 ... 0-0 9 ♗e2 ♖e8 10 0-0 a5 11 a4 d6 12 ♗e3 ♘d7 13 ♘b5 ± Ljubojević-Gligorić, Nikšić 1978) 9 f3 a5! ∞

[24] 8 ... d5!? 9 e5 h5 = Urzica-Romanishin, Groningen 1972

[25] Hübner-Spassky, Linares 1985

Giuoco Piano (Italian) and Two Knights

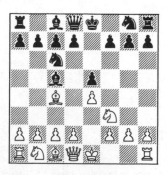

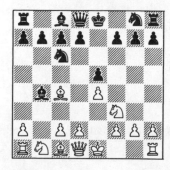

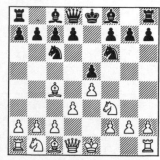

The Giuoco Piano eyes the sensitive f7 square and simply continues development. It is schizophrenic in character, ranging in mood from the exceedingly quiet (Giuoco Pianissimo) 4 d3 to the untamed pyrotechnics of the Evans Gambit. One of the oldest of openings, it has been analysed in detail and there appear to be few surprises left in several lines, particularly those beginning 4 c3, 5 d4. A perusal of the Giuoco's large and long standing body of theory will unearth several paths to equality for Black.

For the more daring, Black can liven the play with 3 ... ♘f6, initiating a much sharper struggle in the shape of the Two Knights' Defence. White may head back to the calm of the Giuoco with 4 d3 (but see the comments below) or plunge into a maelstrom of complications with 4 ♘g5, when he must be ready to cope with the main lines stemming from 4 ... d5 as well as the obscurities of 4 ... ♗c5!?, the Wilkes Barre Variation. At present, these discussions are usually conducted in correspondence rather than over-the-board circles due to the intensely confusing positions that result. Theory (and there is a great deal of it available) has yet to reach a definite conclusion concerning these hair-raising lines.

The position after 1 e4 e5 2 ♘f3 ♘c6 3 ♗c4 ♘f6 4 d3, or 1 e4 e5 2 ♗c4 ♘f6 3 d3 ♘c6 4 ♘f3, commanded little attention from theorists and practical players until quite recently, when it began to appear in the repertoire of Nunn and several young Soviet players. Frequently play transposes into the Giuoco Piano if Black responds with 4 ... ♗c5, but many original variations have been developed. The game often takes on characteristics of the Ruy Lopez, especially when White plays c3 and brings the bishop back to c2 via b3. Less complex than the Ruy Lopez, these systems have the practical advantage of being less mapped as well.

References: *The Two Knights Defence* (Estrin)
The Open Game in Action (Karpov)
Open Gambits (Botterill)

	3	4	5	6	7	8	9	10	11	
Giuoco Piano I			**1 e4 e5 2 ♘f3 ♘c6 3 ♗c4**							
1	...	d4	de[3]	♗d5[4]	♘g5	c3	♗b3	g3	h3	±
	♗e7[1]	d6[2]	de	♗d6	♘h6	♘e7	♘g6	♕e7	♗d7[5]	
2	...	d3	♘c3[6]	♗g5[8]	♗xf6	♘d5	c3	d4	cd	=
	♗c5	♘f6	d6[7]	h6[9]	♕xf6	♕d8	♘e7![10]	ed	♗b6[11]	
3	...	c3	d3	♘bd2[12]	♗b3[13]	0-0	♖e1[14]	♖e2	h3[16]	∞/=
	...	♘f6	d6	a6	♗a7	0-0	♘g4[15]	♔h8	♘h6[17]	
4	...	...	...	0-0	♗b3[19]	♗g5	♘bd2	h4	♗g3	∞
	...	...	a6	♗a7[18]	0-0	d6	h6[20]	g5	♗g4[21]	

[1]   3 ... d6 4 c3 (4 d4 ♗g4 5 h3! ±) 4 ... ♗g4 5 d4 ♕e7 6 ♗e3 ♘f6 7 ♕b3 ♗d8 8 ♘bd2 ± Levenfish-Tolush, Leningrad 1939
[2]   4 ... ed 5 ♘xd4 d6 6 0-0 ♘f6 7 ♘c3 0-0 8 h3 ♖e8 9 ♖e1 ♗f8 10 ♗g5 h6 (Estrin-Chaplinsky, Moscow 1970) 11 ♗xc6 bc 12 ♘h4 ♗e6 13 ♗d3 ± Harding, Botterill
[3]   5 ♘c3 ♘f6 6 h3 0-0 7 0-0 ± Tal-Filip, Miskolc 1963
[4]   6 ♕xd8+ ♗xd8 7 ♘c3 a6 8 ♗e3 ♗e6 9 ♗xe6 fe 10 0-0-0 h6 11 ♖d2 ± Vasyukov-Tseshkovsky, USSR 1975
[5]   12 ♕e2 0-0-0 13 ♘f3 ± Bronstein-Reshevsky, Petropolis IZ 1973
[6]   5 ♗g5 h6 6 ♗h4 d6 7 c3 a6 (7 ... g5 8 ♗g3 ♗g4 9 ♘bd2 a6 = van der Wiel) 8 ♘bd2 ♗a7 9 b4 ♕e7 = Barua-Chiburdanidze, London 1985
[7]   **5 ... 0-0** 6 ♗g5 ♗b4 7 0-0 ♗xc3 8 bc h6 9 ♗h4 d6 10 ♖e1 ± Larsen-Kuzmin, Reykjavik 1978
5 ... h6 6 0-0 0-0 7 h3 d6 8 ♘a4 ♗b6 9 c3

♖e8 10 ♗b3 ♗e6 11 ♗c2 d5 12 d4 ± Malanyuk-Short, Erevan 1984
[8]   **6 ♗e3** ♗b6 7 ♕d2 ♗e6 8 ♗b5 0-0 9 ♗xc6 bc =
6 ♘a4 ♗b6 7 ♘xb6 ab 8 a3 ♗e6 9 ♕e2 h6 10 h3 ♕e7 = Ivanović-Kovačević, Yugoslavia 1985; 7 c3 ♗e6 8 ♗b5 0-0 9 ♗xc6 bc 10 ♗g5 ♕e7 11 0-0 h6 12 ♗h4 ♗c8! 13 h3 ♕e6! = Rantanen-Razuvayev, Helsinki 1984
[9]   **6 ... ♘a5** 7 ♗b3 h6 8 ♗xf6 ♕xf6 9 ♘d5 ♕d8 10 0-0 0-0 11 d4 ed 12 ♘xd4 c6 13 ♘c3 ♕f6 14 ♘de2 ♗g4 = Horvath-Lukacs, Hungarian Ch 1984
[10]   **9 ... a6** 10 d4 ed 11 cd ♗a7 12 ♖c1 (12 h3 ♘e7 13 ♖c1 ♘xd5 14 ♗xd5 c6 15 ♗b3 0-0 16 0-0 ♕f6 = Ivanović-Timman, Agram ∞/±
[11]   12 ♘xb6 ab 13 0-0 d5 14 ed ♘xd5 15 ♖e1+ ♗e6 ∞/= Timman-Nunn, Amsterdam 1985
[12]   **6 0-0** ♗b6 (6 ... 0-0 7 b4 ♗b6 8 ♘bd2 a5 9 b5 ♘e7 10 ♗b2 ∞ Rachels-Polgar, New York 1987; 10 a4 – 6 ... b4) 7 ♗g5!? h6 8 ♗h4 ♕e7

9 ⨍bd2 g5! 10 ⨍g3 ⨍g4 ∞ Barua-Korchnoi, London 1982

6 h3 a6 7 0-0 ⨍a7 8 ⧮e1 0-0 9 ⨍b3 ⨍e7 10 ⨍bd2 ⨍e6 11 ⨍f1 ⧮ad8 = Dzindzihashvili-Korchnoi, Chicago 1982

6 b4 ⨍b6 7 a4 a6 (7 ... a5 8 b5 ⨍e7 9 0-0 0-0 10 ⨍bd2 ⨍g6 11 ⨍a2 ∞/± Mestel-Pinter, Las Palmas IZ 1982; 11 ⨍b3 ⨍g4 12 h3 ⨍h5 13 ⨍h2 Torre-Tukmakov, Leningrad 1987; 11 ⨍b3 d5?! 12 ⨍a3 Ljubojević-Korchnoi, Brussels 1987) 8 0-0 0-0 (8 ... h6 9 ⨍bd2 0-0 10 ⨍a2 ⨍a7 11 b5 ⨍a5 12 ⨍a3 ± Miles-Sanz, Montilla 1978) 9 ⨍bd2 ⨍e7 10 ⨍a2 ⨍e6 11 ⨍c4 ⨍a7 12 ⨍g5 ⧮ae8 ∞ Durao-De Eccher, Rome 1980

[13] 7 a4 0-0 8 0-0 ⨍a7 9 ⧮e1 ⨍h8 10 ⨍f1 ⨍g4 = Castro-Campora, Montevideo 1985

[14] 9 h3 ⨍e6 10 ⨍c2 d5 11 ⧮e1 de 12 de = Karpov-Korchnoi, match (8) 1981

[15] 9 ... ⨍e6 and now:
10 ⨍c4 h6 11 a4 ⧮e8 12 a5 ⨍e7! 13 ⨍e3 ⨍g6 14 ⨍xa7 ⧮xa7 15 d4 ½-½ Nunn-Kavalek, Wijk aan Zee 1982
10 ⨍f1 ⨍d7 11 ⨍g5 ⨍h5 12 ⨍e3 ⨍xe3 13 ⨍xe3 ⨍f6 14 ⨍c2 ⨍g4 15 d4 ⨍xe3

16 ⧮xe3 ± Nunn-Smejkal-Lucerne Ol 1982

[16] 11 ⨍f1 f5 12 ef ⨍xf5 13 ⨍g3 ⨍d7 14 d4 ed 15 ⨍g5 ⨍f6 16 ⨍xd4 ⨍xd4 17 cd h6! ∞ Vujačić-Lukacs, Belgrade 1984

[17] 12 ⨍f1 f5 13 ⨍xh6 gh 14 ef ⨍xf5 15 ⨍d5 ⨍e7! ∞/= Gipslis-Podgayets, USSR 1985

[18] 6 ... d6 7 ⨍b3 0-0 (7 ... h6 8 ⧮e1 ⨍g4!? 9 ⨍bd2 ⨍d7 10 ⨍f1 ⨍e7 11 h3 ⨍f3 12 ⨍xf3 ⨍g6 = Gavrikov-Korzubov, Minsk 1983) and now:
8 ⧮e1 ⨍e6 9 ⨍g5 (9 ⨍bd2 ⧮e8 10 ⨍f1 ⨍xb3 11 ⨍xb3 h6 12 ⨍e3 ⨍xe3 13 ⨍xe3 ⨍d7 = Torre-van der Sterren, Wijk aan Zee 1984) 9 ... h6 10 ⨍h4 g5 11 ⨍g3 ⨍a7 12 ⨍a3 ⨍d7 = van der Wiel-Hübner, Wijk aan Zee 1986
8 ⨍g5!? h6 9 ⨍h4 g5 10 ⨍g3 ⨍g4 11 ⨍bd2 ⨍h5 12 ⨑h1 Nunn-Pinter, Helsinki 1983

[19] 7 ⧮e1 0-0 8 ⨍bd2 ⧮e8 9 ⨍b3 d5! 10 ed ⨍xd5 11 ⨍c4 ⨍g4 = Kudrin-Korchnoi, Wijk aan Zee 1985

[20] 9 ... ⨍e7!? ∞ Nunn-Karpov, Hamburg 1982

[21] 12 ⨑h1 ⨍h5 13 ⨍e1 ⨑g7 14 ⨍d1 ⨍g6 ∞ Chandler-Karpov, Bath 1983

	Giuoco Piano II		**1 e4 e5 2 ⨍f3 ⨍c6 3 ⨍c4 ⨍c5**					
	4	5	6	7	8	9	10	11	12
1	c3[1]	d4[3]	⨍g5[4]	d5	d6!	⨍a3	⨍c2	⨑e2	⨍h4	±/±
	⨍e7[2]	⨍b6	⨍f6	⨍d8[5]	cd6[6]	a6	⨍xf2+[7]	⨍c5	⨍e6[8]	
2	...	d4[9]	0-0[10]	cd	dc	⨍e2[11]	⧮e1	⨍bd2	⨍xe4	=
	⨍f6	ed	⨍xe4	d5	dc	⨍d3!	f5	0-0	fe[12]	

---

[1] 4 0-0 d6 5 h3 (5 c3 ⨍f6 6 d3 h6 ∞ Yusupov) 5 ... ⨍f6 6 d3 h6 7 c3 ⨍b6 8 d4 ed 9 cd d5 10 ed ⨍xd5 11 ⨍xd5 ⨍xd5 = Basagić-Djurić, Yugoslav Ch 1984

[2] 4 ... d6 5 d4 ed 6 cd ⨍b6 (6 ... ⨍b4+ 7 ⨍c3 ⨍f6 8 ⨍g5 ±) 7 ⨍c3 ⨍f6 8 ⨍e3 ⨍g4 9 ⨍b3 0-0 10 ⨍d3 ⧮e8 11 0-0 ±/± Leonhardt-Teichmann London 1904
4 ... ⨍f6 5 d4 ⨍b6 6 0-0 h6 7 a4 a6 8 de ⨍xe5 9 ⨍xe5 ⨍xe5 10 ⨍f3 ±/± Keres

[3] 5 b4 ⨍b6 6 a4 a6 7 d3 d6 8 ⨍g5 ⨍f6 9 ⨍bd2 h6 (9 ... ⨍d8 10 0-0 ⨍e6 11 a5 ⨍a7 12 ⨍e3 ± Sveshnikov-Ivanović, Sarajevo 1983) =

[4] **6 d5** ⨍d8 7 de ⨍xd6 8 ⨍xd6 cd6 cd 9 0-0 ⨍f6 ∞
6 0-0 d6 7 h3 ⨍f6 8 ⧮e1 h6! (8 ... 0-0 9 ⨍a3 ⨍d7 10 ⨍f1 ed 11 ⨍xd4 ± Dür-Haik, Amsterdam 1980) 9 a4 a6 10 ⨍e3 g5 ∞ Unzicker

[5] 7 ... ⨍b8 8 d6! cd 9 0-0 d5 10 ⨍xd5 h6

[6] 8 ... ⨍xd6 9 ⨍xd6 cd 10 ⨍xf6 gf 11 ⨍h4 ± Mestel

[7] 10 ... h6 11 ⨍xf6 ⨍xf6 12 ⨍b4 ± Harding, Botterill

[8] 13 ⨍f5 ±/± Mestel-Doyle, Dublin 1975

[9] 5 d3 – Giuoco Piano I

[10] 6 e5 d5 7 ⨍b5 ⨍e4 8 cd (8 ⨍xd4 ⨍d7 9 ⨍xc6 bc 10 0-0 f6! ∓ Boutteville-Larsen, Le Havre 1966) 8 ... ⨍b6 9 ⨍c3 0-0 10 0-0 ⨍g4 11 ⨍e3 f5 12 ef ⨍xc3 13 bc ⨍xf6 = Unzicker

[11] 9 ⨍xd8+ ⨑xd8 (9 ... ⨍xd8 10 ⧮e1 f5 11 ⨍c3 0-0 12 ⨍xe4 fe 13 ⧮xe4 ± Popov-Schneider, corr. Ol 1972-74) 10 ⧮d1+ ⨍d7 11 ⨍e3 ⨑e7 =

[12] 13 ⨍xe4 ⨍f5 14 ⨍f4 ⧮ae8 = Popov

375

1 e4 e5 2 Nf3 Nc6 3 Bc4 Bc5 4 c3 Nf6 5 d4 ed 6 cd Bb4+

	7	8	9	10	11	12	13	14	15	
3	Nc3[13]	0-0	d5	Re1	Rxe4	Bg5	Nxg5	Qh5[19]	Rae1	∞/∓
	Nxe4[14]	Bxc3[15]	Bf6![16]	Ne7[17]	d6	Bxg5	h6[18]	0-0	Nf5[20]	
4	Bd2	Nbxd2	ed	Qb3	0-0	Ne5![22]	Ne4	Rad1	Bxb3	±
	Bxd2+[21]	d5	Nxd5	Nce7	0-0	c6	Qb6	Qxb3	Rd8[23]	
5	...	...	...	...	Qa4+	Qb3[25]	Qa4+			=
	...	...	...	Na5	Nc6[24]	Na5	Nc6[26]			

[13] Greco's Attack

[14] 7 ... d5 8 ed Nxd5 9 0-0 Be6 (9 ... Nxc3 10 bc Bxc3 11 Qb3! Bxa1 12 Bxf7+ Kf8 13 Ba3+ ± Bilguer's *Handbuch*) 10 Bg5 Be7 11 Bxd5 Bxd5 12 Nxd5 Qxd5 13 Bxe7 Nxe7 (13 ... Kxe7 14 Re1+ Kd7 15 Qa4 Rae8 16 Ne5+! ±) 14 Re1 f6 15 Qa4+ Kf7 16 Rac1 ± I.Zaitsev

[15] 8 ... Nxc3 9 bc d5 (9 ... Bxc3 10 Ba3! d6 11 Rc1 ± Aitken 1937) 10 cb dc 11 Re1+ Ne7 12 Bg5 f6 13 Qe2! ± Sakharov

[16] 9 ... Ne5 10 bc Nxc4 11 Qd4 f5 12 Qxc4 d6 13 Nd4 0-0 14 f3 Nc5 15 Re1 Kh8 16 Ba3 ± Romanov-Kotkov, corr. 1964

9 ... Ba5 10 dc bc 11 Ne5! d6 12 Qg4 Qf6 13 b4! Bxb4 (13 ... Qxe5 14 Bf4 Qf6 15 Rae1+ Kf8 16 Bg5 ±) 14 Bb2 ∞ Harding, Botterill

[17] 10 ... 0-0 11 Rxe4 Ne7 12 d6! cd 13 Qxd6 Nf5 13 Qd5 Ne7 15 Qd6 =

[18] 13 ... 0-0 14 Nxh7! Bf5 (14 ... Kxh7 =) 15 Rxe7 (15 Rh4 Re8 16 Qh5 Ng6 17 Rd4 Re5 Thorhallsson-Schüssler, Reykjavik 1986) 15 ... Qxe7 16 Nxf8 Rxf8 17 Rc1 c5 = Tyroler-Bottlik, Budapest 1973

[19] 14 Bb5+ Bd7 15 Qe2 Bxb5 16 Qxb5+ Qd7 =/∓ Levin-Idema, corr. 1979, and Barczay-Portisch, Hungarian Ch 1968-69

[14] Qe2 hg 15 Bb5+ Bd7 16 Re1 Bxb5 17 Rxe7+ Kf8 18 Qxb5 Qxe7 19 Rxe7 Kxe7 ∓ Girod-Multala, corr. 1984

[20] 16 Ne6!? (16 Nxf7 Qf6! ∓ Zak) 16 ... fe 17 de Ne7! (17 ... Ne7? 18 Rf4! ± Bateman-Boisvert, corr. 1984) ∞/∓

[21] 7 ... Nxe4!? 8 Bxb4 Nxb4 9 Bxf7+ Kxf7 10 Qb3+ Kf8! (10 ... d5 11 Ne5+ Ke6 12 Qxb4 c5 13 Qa3 cd 14 Nf3 Qb6 15 0-0 Kf7 16 Rd1 d3 17 Ne5+ Kf6 18 Nxd3 ±/± Botterill, Harding

[22] 12 Rfe1 c6 (12 ... Nb6 13 Bd3 Bf5 14 Rxc7 Bxd3 15 Rae1 ± Bastian-Eng, Bad Neuenahr 1984) 13 Ne4 Qb6 (13 ... h6 14 Ne5! ± van der Wiel-Karpov, Amsterdam 1980) 14 Nc3! (14 Qa3 Bg4! 15 Ne5 Qxd4! ∞/= Sveshnikov-Chekhov, Sochi 1983) 14 ... Qxb3 15 Bxb3 Bg4 16 Nxd5 Nxd5 17 Bxd5 cd 18 Re7! ± Makarichev

[23] 16 Rfe1 ± Miles-Korchnoi, South Africa 1979

[24] 11 ... c6 12 Bxd5 Qxd5 13 0-0 0-0-0 14 Rfe1 ± Tarrasch

[25] 12 Ne5 0-0 13 Nxc6 Qe8+! ∓

12 Bb5 Bd7 13 0-0 (13 Qb3?! Qe7+ 14 Kf1 Be6 15 Bxc6 bc 16 Qc2 0-0 =/∓ Sveshnikov-Mortensen, Leningrad 1984

[26] Miles-Korchnoi, South Africa 1979

	Evans Gambit		1 e4 e5 2 Nf3 Nc6 3 Bc4 Bc5 4 b4 Bxb4[1]						

	5	6	7	8	9	10	11	12	13	
1	c3	d4[3]	Nxe5[4]	Nxc4	ed	Ne3	0-0	c4		=
	Be7[2]	Na5	Nxc4	d5	Qxd5	Qd7[5]	Nf6	b5![6]		
2	...	d4	0-0[7]	cd	Nc3[9]	Bg5	Bxf7+	Nd5	Bxe7	=
	Bc5	ed	d6[8]	Bb6	Na5	Ne7[10]	Kxf7	Re8!	Rxe7[11]	
3	...	d4[12]	0-0[13]	de	Qb3[15]	Bg5	Bd5	Bxe7	Bxc6	∞
	Ba5	d6	Bb6[14]	de	Qf6	Qg6	Nge7	Kxe7	Qxc6[16]	
4	...	...	Qb3	de!	Bb5[18]	Ba4	Bxc6+	0-0	Qxe6	±
	...	...	Qd7	Bb6	a6	Qe6	bc	Rb8	fe[19]	
5	...	...	...	...	0-0	Rd1[20]	a4	Ba3[22]	a5	∞
	...	...	...	de	Bb6	Qe7	a6[21]	Qf6	Bxa5[23]	
6	...	...	0-0	cd[24]	ed	Ba3![25]	Bb5	Bxc6+	Bxb4	∞
	...	ed	Nge7!	d5	Nxd5	Be6	Bb4[26]	bc	Nxb4[27]	

[1] 4 ... Bb6 5 a4 a6 6 Nc3 d6 (6 ... Nf6 7 Nd5! Nxd5 8 ed e4 9 dc ef 10 Qxf3 Qe7+ 11 Kd1 dc 12 Re1 Be6 13 Bb2 ±/± Estrin) 7 Nd5 Ba7 8 d3 h6 9 Be3 ± Panov, Estrin

[2] 5... Bd6?! 6 d4 Qe7 7 0-0 Nf6 8 Nbd2 ∞/±

[3] 6 Qb3 Qh6 7 d4 Na5 8 Qb5! (8 Qa4?! Nxc4 9 Qxc4 Bg4 ∓) 8 ... Nxc4 9 Qxh6 gh 10 Qxc4 ∞ Harding-J.H.Hodgson, corr. 1974-75

[4] 7 Bd3 d6 8 de Bg4 9 ed cd 10 0-0 Nf6 = Estrin

[5] 10 ... Qd8 11 0-0 Nf6 12 c4 0-0 13 Nc3 ± Tartakower-Trifunović, Paris 1950
10 ... Qa5 11 0-0 Nf6 12 c4 0-0 13 d5 ± Timman-Tatai, Amsterdam 1977

[6] Nunn
12 ... 0-0 13 Nc3 c6 14 d5 cd 15 Ncxd5 Nxd5 16 Nxd5 ± Nunn-Larsen, London 1980

[7] 7 cd Bb6! 8 0-0 d6 – 7 0-0

[8] 7 ... d3 8 Bg5! Nh6 9 Nxf7! ±

[9] 9 d5 Na5! 10 Bb2 Ne7 11 Bd3 0-0 12 Nc3 Ng6 (12 ... c6!? 13 Ne2 cd 14 ed Bf5) 13 Ne2 c5 ∓ W.Paulsen-Anderssen, Barmen 1869
9 h3 Nf6 10 Re1 h6 11 Ba3 0-0 12 Nc3 Re8 ∞ Mariotti-Gligorić, Venice 1971

[10] 10 ... Qd7 11 Bd3 ∞ (∞)
10 ... f6!? 11 Bf4 Ne7! 12 h3 c6 ∞ Asharin-Chigorin, Riga 1892

[11] 14 Ng5+ Kg8 15 Qh5 h6 16 Qg6! hg 17 Nf6+ Kf8 18 Nh7+ Kg8 19 Nf6+ = Chigorin

[12] 6 Qb3 Qf6 7 0-0 Bb6 8 d4 d6 9 de Nxe5 10 Nxe5 de 11 a4 a6 12 Kh1 Ne7 ∞ Nunn-Hübner, Johannesburg 1981; 12 a5!? Botterill

[13] 7 Bg5 Nge7 8 Bxe7 Kxe7 = Estrin

[14] Lasker's Defence
7 ... Bg4 8 Qa4 Bxf3 9 gf cd 10 cd Qf6! Chigorin
7 ... Bd7 8 Bg5 Nh6 9 f4!? Botterill

[15] 9 Qxd8+ Kxd8 10 Nxe5 Nf6! Lasker; 10 ... Be6 =Estrin

[16] 14 Nxe5 Be6 (Chigorin) 15 Nc4 ∞ Keres; 15 ... Rd8! Botterill

[17] 8 0-0 Bb6 9 de!? (9 Bb5?! a6 10 Bxc6 Qxc6 11 de Be6 12 Qc2 0-0-0 ∓ Keres) ∞/=

[18] 9 Nbd2 Na5! 10 Qc2 Nxc4 11 Nxc4 de 12 Nfxe5 Qe6 13 Ba3! ± Harding, Botterill; 11 ... d5 12 Nxb6 ab 13 0-0 de 14 Qxe4 Qg4 Estrin-Palciauskas, 10th World corr. Ch

[19] 14 ed cd 15 Ba3! ± Estrin

[20] 10 Ba3 Na5 11 Nxe5 Nxb3 12 ab Qe6! 13 Bxe6 Bxe6 ∓ Sokolsky

[21] 11 ... a5 12 Bd5 Bg4 13 Rd3 Be6 14 Ba3 ± Shaposhnikov-Veltmander, USSR 1958

[22] 12 a5 Bc5 13 Ba3 Bxa3 14 Nxa3 Nf6 15 Bd5 0-0 16 Nc4 Bd7 ∞/=

[23] 13 ... Ba7 14 Nbd2 Nge7 15 Bd5 0-0 16 Nc4 Bg4 17 Bxe7 Qxe7 18 Rd3 ∞
13 ... Bxa5 14 Bd5 Bb6 15 Nbd2 Nge7 16 Nc4 Ba7 17 Rd2! ∞ Estrin

[24] 8 Ng5 d5! 9 Bxd5? Nxd5 10 Qh5 g6 11 Qh6 Be6! ∓ Estrin-Kondali, corr. 1971

[25] 10 Qb3 Be6 11 Qxb7 (11 Ba3 Qd7! 12 Nbd2 ∞/∓) 11 ... Ndb4 12 Bb5 Bd5! Botterill

[26] 11 ... f6!? intending ... Kf7 Botterill

[27] 14 Qa4 Rb8!? 15 a3 Nd5 16 Qxc6+ Qd7 17 Qa6 ∞ Botterill

	4	5	6	7	8	9	10	11	12	
1	d4[1]	e5[2]	♗b5	♘xd4	♗xc6	0-0	f3	♗e3	♔h1	∞
	ed	d5[3]	♘e4[4]	♗d7[5]	bc	♗c5[6]	♘g5	0-0	♗b6[7]	
2	...	0-0	e5	ef	♖e1+	♗g5	♗h6+	♘c3	♘xd4[11]	=
	...	♗c5[8]	d5[9]	dc	♔f8[10]	gf	♔g8	♗f8	♗xh6![12]	
3		...	♖e1[13]	♘c3	♖xe4+	♘xd4	♖f4	♘xc6	♘xd1	=
		♘xe4	d5[14]	dc4[15]	♗e7[16]	f5	0-0	♕xd1+	bc[17]	
4				♗xd5	♘c3	♘xe4[19]	♗d2[20]	♗g5	♗f6[22]	=
				♕xd5	♕a5[18]	♗e6	♕d5[21]	♗d6	0-0[23]	
5	♘g5	♘xf7	♔f1![25]	♘xh8	ed	d6![27]	c3	♕a4+	♘f7	∞∞
	♗c5!?[24]	♗xf2+	♕e7	d5!	♘d4[26]	cd[28]	♗g4	♘d7[29]	♕f6[30]	
6		♗xf7+	♗d5[31]	♘f3[33]	c3	♗xc6	d4	♕d3	cd	±
		♔e7	♖f8[32]	d6	♗g4[34]	bc	♗b6	ed	♔d7[35]	
7		ed	♗xb5[37]	♘c3![38]	♕f3	♘xf3	0-0	♗xc6	♘xe5	=/±
	d5	b5[36]	♕xd5	♕xg2	♕xf3	♗d7	♗d6	♗xc6	♘xe5[39]	
8			c3[40]	♗f1	♘e4[41]	♘g3	f3	cd	♗xb5+	=
		♘d4	b5	♘xd5	♕h4![42]	♗g4[43]	e4[44]	♗d6	♔d8[45]	
9			♗b5+[46]	dc	♕f3	♗d3[49]	♘e4	b3[50]	♗b2	∞
		♘a5	c6[47]	bc	♖b8[48]	h6	♘d5	g6	♗g7[51]	
10			...	...	♗e2	♘f3	♘e5	d4[52]	♗d2	=
			...	...	h6	e4	♗d6	♕c7[53]	0-0[54]	
11			...	...		♘h3	0-0	♔h1	♘g1	∞
			...	...		♗c5[55]	g5!?[56]	g4	♘e4[57]	

---

[1] **4 0-0** ♘xe4 5 ♘c3 ♘xc3 6 dc f6 7 ♘h4 g6
8 f4 f5 9 ♘f3 e4 10 ♘g5 ♗c5+ ∞/=
    4 ... ♗c5 – 3 ... ♗c5

[2] **5 ♘g5** ♘e5 (5 ... d5 6 ed ♕e7+ 7 ♔f1
♘e5 8 ♕xd4 ♘xc4 ♕xc4 h6 = Keres) 6 ♗b3
(6 ♕xd4!?) 6 ... h6 7 f4 hg 8 fe ♘xe4 9 ♕xd4
♘c5 = Pfleger-Spassky, Hastings 1965-66
    5 ♘xd4 ♘xe4! 6 ♕h5! ♕f6 7 ♘f3 (7 ♘b5
♗b4+! 8 c3 ♗a5) 7 ... ♗b4+ 8 c3 ♕e7 9 0-0
♗c5 = Estrin

[3] 5 ... ♘g4 6 ♕e2 ♕e7 7 ♗f4 ± Estrin-Buj,
corr. 1981

[4] 6 ... ♘d7 7 0-0 ♗e7 8 ♗xc6 bc 9 ♘xd4
♘b8 10 f4 c5 11 ♘e2 ±

[5] 7 ... ♗c5 8 ♗e3 ♗d7 9 ♗xc6 bc 10 0-0
♕e7 11 ♖e1 0-0 12 f3 ♘g5 13 ♕d2 ∞

[6] 9 ... ♗e7 10 f3 ♗c5 11 f4 ♘e4 12 f5 ±
    9 ... c5 10 ♘b3! c6 11 c4 dc 12 ♘3d2
♘xd2 13 ♘xd2 ±

[7] 13 c4! ∞ Estrin

[8] 5 ... d6 7 ♘xd4 ♗e7 8 ♘c3 0-0 9 h3 ♖e8

10 ♖e1 ♗f8 11 ♗g5 h6 12 ♗h4 ♘e5 12 ♗f1 ±
Estrin-Chaplinsky, Moscow 1970

[9] 6 ... ♘g4 (Steinitz Variation) 7 ♗f4 (7 c3!?
d5 8 ♗b3 ± Estrin) 7 ... d6 8 ed ♗xd6 9 ♖e1+
♔f8 10 ♗xd6+ ♕xd6 11 c3 ± Harding, Botterill

[10] 8 ... ♗e6 9 ♘g5 ♕d5 10 ♘c3 ♕f5 11 ♘ce4
0-0-0 12 g4 ♕e5 13 ♘e6 fe 14 fg (14 ♗g5
g6! = Kliesch-Teblis, East Germany v Romania
corr. 1972) 14 ... ♖hg8 15 ♗h6! d3 16 c3
d2 17 ♖e2 ♖d3 (Marshall-Leonhardt, San
Sebastian 1911) 18 ♕f1 ♕d5 19 ♖d1 ♘e5
20 ♕g2! ±/∓ Martinek-Vajs, corr. 1985

[11] 12 ♗xf8 ♔xf8 13 ♘e4 f5! ∓

[12] 13 ♘xc6 ♕xd1 14 ♘e7+ ♔g7 15 ♖axd1
♗e6 = Harding, Botterill

[13] 6 ♘c3 ♘xc3! 7 bc d5 8 ♗b5 ♗e7 ∓
Novopashin-Nezhmetdinov, Kislovodsk 1966

[14] 6 ... ♗e7 7 ♖xe4 d5 8 ♖xe7+ ♘xe7 9 ♗f1
c5 10 b4 ± Estrin

[15] 7 ... dc3 8 ♗xd5 ♗f5 9 ♗xe4 ♗xe4
10 ♖xe4+ ♗e7 = Gligorić

16 8 ... Be6 9 Nxd4 Nxd4 10 Rxd4 Qf6! ∞ Estrin

17 13 Rxc4 Bd6 14 Nc3 = Botvinnik

18 8 ... Qd8 9 Rxe4+ Be6 10 Nxd4 Nxd4 11 Rxd4 ± Tringov-Rossetto, Amsterdam 1964
8 ... Qh5 9 Nxe4 Be6 10 Bg5 Bb4! 11 Nxd4 Qxd1 12 Rexd1 Nxd4 13 Rxd4 Be7 14 Re1 ±

19 9 Rxe4+ Be6 10 Nxd4 0-0-0 11 Be3 Nxd4 12 Rxd4 Bc5 ∓ Estrin

20 10 Neg5 0-0-0 11 Nxe6 fe 12 Rxe6 Qf5 13 Qe2 h6 14 Bd2 Qxc2 = Bogoljubow

21 10 ... Bb4 11 Nxd4 Nxd4 12 c3 Be7! 13 cd Qd5 =

22 12 c3 0-0 = Littlewood-Medina, Hastings 1969-70

23 13 Nxd4 Nxd4 14 Qxd4 Qxd4 15 Bxd4 = Marić-Djurasević, Yugoslav Ch 1956

24 Wilkes-Barre Variation or Traxler Counter-attack

25 6 Kxf2 Nxe4+ 7 Kg1 Qh4 8 g3 Nxg3 9 Nxh8 (9 d4 Ne4! 10 Be3 ed 11 Nxh8 de ∓; 9 hg? Qxg3+ 10 Kf1 Rf8 11 Qh5 d5! 12 Bxd5 Nb4 13 Bc4 b5! ∓ Klem-Hentsgen, corr. 1969) 9 ... d5 10 Qe1 Qd4+ 11 Qe3 Nxh1 12 Bb5 Qg4+ 13 Kxh1 Bf5! (13 ... d4, Krc-Sapundzhiev, corr. 1965-66, 14 Qe2! ± Lepeshkin) 14 d3 Kf8 15 Bxc6 bc 16 Bd2 Qd1+ 17 Kg2 Qg4+ 18 Kg3 Qe2+ = Estrin

26 8 ... Bg4 9 Qe2 Bxe2+ 10 Qxe2 Nd4 11 Qxf2 0-0 12 b3! Ne4 13 Ba3! ± Muravyev

27 9 Kxf2 Bg4 10 Qf1 Ne4+ 11 Kg1 Ne2+ ∓∓ Brančić-Marić, corr. 1963
9 c3 Bg4 10 Qa4+ Nd7 11 Qxf2 Qh4+ 12 Ke3 Qg5+ 13 Kf2 Qf5+ 14 Kg1 0-0-0 ∓∓ Mikishka-Traxler, corr. 1896

28 9 ... Qxd6 10 c3 Bg4 11 Qa4+ Nd7 12 Kxf2 Qf6+ 13 Ke1 0-0-0 14 Rf1 ± Radchenko

29 11 ... Bd7 12 Qd1 (12 Qb4 Nc6!) 12 ... Bg4 = Estrin

30 Estrin

31 6 Bb3 Rf8 7 0-0 h6 8 Nf3 d6 9 h3 Nxe4 ∞

32 6 ... d6 7 c3! Qe8 (7 ... Rf8 8 d4 ed 9 Bxc6 bc 10 0-0 h6 11 cd Bb6 12 e5! ±/± Estrin) 8 d4 ed 9 cd Nxd4 10 Nc3 Qh5 11 Qd3 Rf8 (Karpov-Belyavsky, Moscow 1983) 12 e5! de 13 0-0 ± Estrin

33 7 0-0 d6 8 h3 Qe8 9 c3 Qg6 10 d4 Bb6 11 f4 ef 12 Bxf4 Nxd5 13 ed Rxf4 14 Rxf4 Qg5 15 Re4 Ne5 16 Kh1 Bf5 17 Re2! Rf8 18 de Bg4 19 ed+ Kxd6 20 Nd2 f4! 21 Qc1 Kd7 = Minte-Wanke, corr. 1985

34 8 ... Qe8 9 d4 ed 10 cd Bb4+ 11 Nc3 ±

35 13 Be3 ± Belov-Matsukevich, USSR 1962

36 5 ... Nxd5 and now:
6 Nxf7!? Kxf7 7 Qf3+ Ke6 8 Nc3 Nb4! 9 a3! Nxc2+ 10 Kd1 Nd4 11 Bxd5+ Kd6 12 Qf7 Qe7 13 Ne4+ Kd7 14 Nc5+ Kd6 15 Nxb7+ Bxb7 16 Qxe7+ Bxe7 17 Bxb7 Rab8 18 Be4 Nb3 19 Rb1 ±

6 d4! ed 7 0-0 Be6 8 Re1 ± Euwe

37 6 Bf1! Nd4 7 c3 – 5 ... Nd4

38 7 Bxc6+ Qxc6 8 Qf3 e4 9 Qb3 Bc5! ∓

39 13 Re1 =/± Turmurbator-Hemmansy, Singapore 1969

40 6 Nc3 h6 7 Nf3 Bg4 8 Be2 Bxf3 9 Bxf3 Bb4 10 0-0 0-0 11 Re1 Re8

41 8 cd Qxg5 9 Nc3! (9 Bxb5+ Kd8 10 Qf3 ed 11 Bc6 Nb4! ∓ Rothman-Schiller, New York 1981) 9 ... ed 10 Bxb5+ Bd7 11 Bxd7+ Kxd7 12 0-0! = van der Wiel-Timman, Amsterdam 1980

8 Nxf7 Kxf7 9 cd ed! 10 Bxb5 (10 Qf3+ Nf6 11 Rxa8 Bc5 12 d3? Qe7+ 13 Kd2 Bb4+ ∓∓ Salgado-Bademian, Mar del Plata 1985; 12 Bxb5 Re8+! ∞) 10 ... Qe7+ 11 Qe2 Qxe2+ 12 Bxe2 Nb4 13 Bc4+ Be6 Suetin-Ravinsky, USSR 1949

42 8 ... Ne6 9 Bxb5+ Bd7 10 Bxd7+ Qxd7 11 0-0 Be7 12 d4 ed 13 cd 0-0 14 Nbc3 ± Spassky-Shamkovich, USSR 1960

43 9 ... Bb7!? 10 cd 0-0-0 11 Be2 Nf4 12 0-0 Rd4 ∞ Estrin

44 10 ... Nf5 11 Bxb5+ Kd8 12 0-0! Bc5+ 13 d4 ed 14 Ne4! ± Kopilov

45 13 0-0 ef 14 Rxf3 (14 Qb3 Nb4! 15 Rxf3 c6! 16 Be2 Bxf3 17 Qxf3 Qxd4+ 18 Kh1 Bc5 ∓∓ Berliner) 14 ... Rb8 15 a4 a6 16 Bxa6 Re8 17 Nc3 Nb4 18 Bf1 ∞/=
13 Qb3 Bxg3+ 14 Kd1 Be6 15 Bc6 ef 16 Bxd5 fg 17 Qxg3 Qxg3 18 hg Bxd5 19 Rg1 Re8! ∞ Berliner

46 6 d3 h6 7 Nf3 e4 8 Qe2 Nxc4 9 dc Bc5 = Kopilov-Kondratiev, USSR 1955

47 6 ... Bd7 7 Qe2 Be7 8 Nc3 (8 d4 ed 9 b4 0-0 10 ba Bb4+ 11 Kd1 Re8 ∞ Kurkin-Mantevfel, corr. 1966-67) 8 ... 0-0 9 0-0 c6 10 dc Nxc6 ∞ Estrin

48 Colman's Defence

49 9 Be2 Bd6 10 Nc3 0-0 11 a3 Bb7 12 Qh3 c5 ∞ Kaufman-Nordström, corr. 1985

50 11 Ng3 g6 ∞

51 13 Qg3 ∞ Carlier-Condie, London 1985

52 11 f4 ef 12 Nxf3 0-0 ∞ Estrin-Strand, corr. 1966

53 11 ... ed 12 Nxd3 Qc7 13 b3 0-0 (13 ... c5?! 14 Na3 Bd7 15 h3 0-0 16 0-0 Rab8 17 Bd2 ± Herbrechtsmeier-Spassky, West Germany 1985-86) 14 Bb2 Nd5 15 Nc3 Nf4 ∞ Honfi-Tal, Sarajevo 1966

54 13 0-0 Nb7 14 Na3 Bxe5 15 de Qxe5 16 Qe7 17 Qc1 Re8 = Nunn-Nikolić, Naestved 1985

55 9 ... Be7 10 0-0 0-0 11 d3 Rb8 12 Kh1 c5 13 Kg1 Nc6 ∞ Klaman-Faibisovich, USSR 1979

56 10 ... 0-0 11 d3 Nb7 12 Nc3 Bb6 13 Kh1 Nc5 ∞ Hamann-Geller, Kislovodsk 1966

57 13 Bxg4 Nxf2+ 14 Rxf2 Bxf2 ∞ Herbrechtsmeier-Raty, corr. 1984

| | Two Knights II | 1 e4 e5 2 ♘f3 ♘c6 3 ♗c4 ♘f6 4 d3 | | | | | | | |

	4	5	6	7	8	9	10	11	12	
1	...	♘c3[1]	a3	h3	♗e3	♕d2	g4	♖g1		=
	h6!?	d6	g6[2]	♗g7	0-0	♔h7	♘d7	♘b6[3]		
2	...	0-0[4]	c3[5]	ed	♖e1	h3	♘bd2	♗b5	a4	±
	♗e7	0-0	d5[6]	♘xd5	♗g4	♗h5	♘b6	♗d6	a6[7]	
3	...	♗b3	0-0	c3	♘bd2	♕xb3	♖e1	♘f1	♕c2	=
	...	0-0	d6[8]	♗e6[9]	♗xb3	♖b8	♘d7	♘c5	d5[10]	

[1] **5 ♗b3** d6 6 c3 g6 7 ♘bd2 ♗g7 8 ♘f1 d5 9 ♕e2 ♗e6 10 ♘g3 ♕e7 11 h4 0-0-0 = Gipslis-Eingorn, Tallinn 1980
5 0-0 d6 6 c3 g6 7 d4 ♕e7 8 ♘bd2 ♗g7 9 ♖e1 0-0 10 h3 ♗d7 11 ♘f1 ♖ae8 = Nunn-Spassky, London 1982

[2] 6 ... ♗e7 7 ♗e3 0-0 8 h3 ♗e6 9 ♘d5 ♗xd5 10 ed ♘b8 11 ♘h4 c6 12 dc bc 13 ♘f3 d5 ∞ Herzog-Hazai, Keszthely 1981

[3] Spassky-Belyavsky, USSR 1981

[4] **5 ♘c3** d6 6 h3 0-0 7 0-0 ♘a5 8 ♗b3 ♘xb3 9 ab c5 10 ♗e3 ♗e6 11 ♘d2 d5 = Zita-Smyslov, Prague v Moscow 1946
5 ♘bd2 0-0 6 c3 d6 7 ♗b3 ♘d7 8 ♘f1 ♘c5 9 ♗d5 ♗f6 10 ♗e3 ♘e7 11 ♗c4 ♗e6 = Bronstein-Nei, Tallinn 1973

[5] 6 ♖e1 d6 7 c3 ♘a5 8 ♗b5 ♗d7 9 ♗xd7 ♕xd7 10 d4 ed 11 cd d5 12 e5 ♘e4 =

[6] 6 ... a6 7 ♗b3 d6 8 ♘bd2 ♘a5 9 ♗c2 c5 10 ♖e1 ♖e8 11 ♘f1 ± Sax-Gligorić, Vrbas 1980

6 ... d6! = − 5 ♗b3

[7] 13 ♗xc6 bc 14 ♘e4 ± Dolmatov-Yandemirov-Kostroma 1985

[8] 6 ... d5 7 ed ♘xd5 8 ♖e1 ♗g4 9 h3 ♗h5 10 g4 ♗g6 11 ♘xe5 ♘xe5 12 ♖xe5 c6 13 ♕f3 (13 ♗xd5 cd 14 ♕f3 d4 15 ♗d2 ♗d6 ∞/± Kudrin-Psakhis, Graz 1981) 13 ... ♗d6 14 ♖e2 ♔h8 15 ♘c3 ♗xc3 16 bc ± Gipslis-F.Garcia, Jurmala 1983; 12 ... ♘b6! = Dolmatov-Chekhov, USSR 1981

[9] **7 ... ♗d7** 8 ♗e3 ♘c5 9 ♗c2 ♗g4 10 b4 ♘e6 11 ♗b3 ♗g5 = Dounia-Geller, Malta Ol 1980
7 ... ♘a5 8 ♗c2 c5 9 ♘bd2 ♘c6 10 ♖e1 ♕c7 11 ♘f1 ♗e6 = Dolmatov-Timman, Amsterdam 1980
7 ... ♗g4 8 h3 ♗h5 9 ♘bd2 ♘d7 10 ♗c2 ♗g6 11 d4 ed 12 ♘xd4 ♘xd4 13 cd Djurić-Bronstein, Tallinn 1981

[10] 13 ♘e3 de 14 de ♕d3 = Dolmatov-Klovans, USSR 1981

380

Ruy Lopez (Spanish)

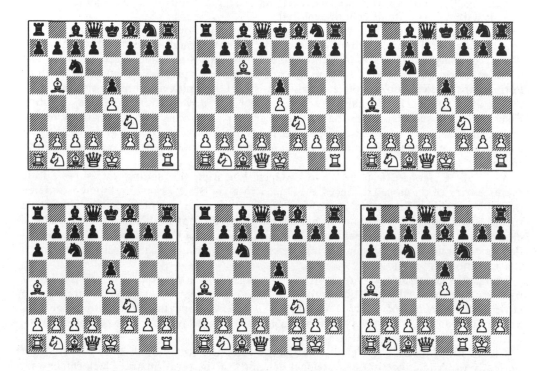

Analysed by the Spanish priest Ruy Lopez in 1561, this opening, with its idea of direct pressure on the Black e-pawn, has been continuously popular with players and theoreticians. Clearly the Lopez has weathered the test of time and despite long scrutiny by generations of chess thinkers it retains its strategical complexity. Mastery of either side of the opening requires the positional virtuosity of a truly mature player and it is no accident that the Lopez has figured in the repertoire of nearly every major figure in chess history, and ex-champion Karpov's ease in handling both sides is testimony to its continuing vitality.

It is more common that one specializes in the White side of the Lopez, because of the lasting pull it affords to players versed in its mysteries. Defending the Lopez can take a wide variety of forms, from the stolid classicism of the Closed Defence to the violent aggression of the Schliemann or the Marshall. Although 3 ... a6 is the automatic choice in modern practice, the older defences which omit this swipe at the Lopez bishop are not without merit.

3 ... ♘d4 Bird's Defence conceals a multiplicity of tricks to spring on the unwary Lopez player, but theory claims a small edge for White if he can steer clear of the pitfalls. An obscure and probably underestimated defence which is enjoying a recent rush of enthusiasm.

3 ... ♗c5 Classical Defence. The oldest of Black's options against the Lopez, it offers the second player reasonable chances and leads to an early skirmish of complications.

3 ... f5!? Theoretically doubtful but often successful in practice, the **Schliemann Defence** enjoys sporadic revivals before returning to hibernation. Perhaps this is because the element of surprise is a helpful addition to its arcane complications. A sharp variation offering great risk to both players.

3 ... d6 **Steinitz Defence**. Fully playable but more than a little passive and cramped. Only recommended for those willing to suffer a few indignities for the prospect of eventually exploiting the indiscretions of an overzealous attacker.

3 ... ♘ge7. The **Cozio Defence** has never enjoyed a real following, although Larsen has used it with success. Relatively unexplored.

3 ... ♘f6 **Berlin Defence**. Another neglected but solid defence – Black's chances for equality are fairly promising but White enjoys a small though lingering advantage.

3 ... g6 **Smyslov Defence**. A solid and resilient variation which received attention when ex-world champion Vasily Smyslov scored some surprisingly good results with it. Perhaps insufficient for complete equality, it is both complex and uninvestigated.

3 ... a6 4 ♗xc6. The **Exchange Variation** was a feared weapon in the hands of Bobby Fischer but his success was probably due in greater part to his own powerful technique rather than the advantages of the opening. It has now fallen into disuse and is once again regarded as safe and uninspired, though Timman has demonstrated the variation still has some bite.

3 ... a6 4 ♗a4 ♘f6 5 0-0 ♘xe4 **Open Variation**. Foregoing the slow, subtle manoeuvring of the closed defences, the Open Ruy gives Black rapid development and free piece play in return for a static pawn formation. A large body of theory has coalesced as a result of the World Championship matches between Karpov and Korchnoi, where both combatants unveiled new ideas for their respective sides of the opening. The theoretical debate continues, with White enjoying preference, though there can hardly be a threat to the variation's soundness.

Marshall Counterattack. Frank Marshall's ingenious attempt to overrun the Lopez by force has attracted theoreticians for years and now one must be very well prepared to cope with the reams of analysis available to Black. It appears White can emerge with advantage but this is a nerve-wracking business and an examination of one of the Anti-Marshall systems may appeal to the practical player.

Closed Ruy Lopez. The classical battleground of the Ruy Lopez, both players must be ready to handle the subtle strategical demands of the position and Black can choose from a wide assortment of different systems. His position is resilient and has survived over a hundred years of protracted struggle. Current darlings are the Breyer and Zaitsev Variations, though the Chigorin has lasting appeal.

References: *Spanish (Ruy Lopez): Chigorin* (Bikhovsky)
Spanish: Schliemann (Jaenisch) (Shamkovich and Schiller)
Spanish Without ... a6 (Yudovich)
Spanish Gambits (Shamkovich and Schiller)
How to Play the Ruy Lopez (Taulbut)
The Open Game in Action (Karpov)

	Ruy Lopez I		1 e4 e5 2 ♘f3 ♘c6 3 ♗b5							
	3	4	5	6	7	8	9	10	11	
1	...	0-0	c3[3]	d4	cd	ed	♖e1+[5]	♗g5[6]	♘c3	±
	♘ge7[1]	g6[2]	♗g7	ed[4]	d5	♘xd5	♗e6	♕d6	0-0[7]	
2	...	d4	♘c3	0-0	♖e1	♘xd4	♗xc6	♗f4	♘f3	±
	d6	♗d7	♘f6[8]	♗e7[9]	ed[10]	0-0	bc	c5[11]	♗g4[12]	

	3	4	5	6	7	8	9	10	11	
3	...	♘c3[13]	♗c4[15]	0-0	ef	♘xd4	♖e1+	♘e2	♘f4[18]	±
	f5	♘d4[14]	d6[16]	♘f6	♗xf5[17]	ed	♗e7	c5		
4	...	...	♘xe4	♘xe5	♘xc6	♕e2	f4	♘e5+[21]	d4	±
	...	fe	d5	de	♕g5[19]	♘f6	♕xf4[20]	c6	♕h4+[22]	

---

[1] 3 ... ♗b4 4 0-0 ♘ge7 5 c3 ♗a5 6 ♗xc6 ♘xc6 7 b4 ♗b6 8 b5 ♘a5 9 ♘xe5 0-0 10 d4 ♕e8 11 ♘d2 d6 12 ♘d3 ♕xb5 13 c4! ♕d7 14 ♗b2 ± C.Hansen-Dreyev, Kiljava 1984

[2] 4 ... a6 5 ♗c4! ♘g6 6 d4 ed 7 ♘xd4 ± Byrne-Böhm, Wijk aan Zee 1980

[3] 5 d4 ed 6 ♘xd4 ♗g7 7 ♗e3 0-0 8 ♘c3 d5!? (8 ... d6 9 f4 f5 ±/∞) 9 ed ♘xd5 10 ♘xc6 bc 11 ♗xc6 ♘xe3 12 fe ♖b8 ∞ Kuznetsov-Vul, USSR 1985

[4] 6 ... 0-0 7 d5 a6 8 ♗e2 ♘a7 9 c4 d6 10 ♘c3 f5 11 b4 ± Grünfeld-Sanz, Buenos Aires Ol 1978

[5] 9 ♗g5 ♕d6 10 ♕e2+ ♗e6 11 ♘bd2 0-0 12 ♘e4 ♕b4 13 a3 ♕a5 14 ♗xc6 bc ∞ Timman-Spassky, Bugojno 1986

[6] 10 ♘e5 0-0 11 ♗xc6 (11 ♘xc6 bc 12 ♗xc6 ♖b8 ∞∞) 11 ... bc 12 ♘xc6 ♕d6 13 ♘e5 ♖fd8 (13 ... c5!?) 14 ♘d2 ♗b4 ∞∞/= Oll-Serper, USSR 1987

[7] 12 ♕d2 a6 (12 ... ♘xc3 13 bc ♗d5 14 ♗f4 ♕d8 15 ♕e2 a6 16 ♗c4 ±) 13 ♘e4 ♕b4 14 ♗xc6 bc 15 ♖ac1 ± Chandler-Wedberg, Amsterdam 1984

[8] 5 ... ed 6 ♘xd4 g6 7 ♗e3 ♗g7 8 ♕d2 ♘f6 9 ♗xc6 bc 10 ♗h6 ± Psakhis-Haik, Sochi 1985

[9] 6 ... ed 7 ♘xd4 ♗e7 (7 ... ♘xd4 8 ♗xd7+ ♕xd7 9 ♕xd4 ♗e7 10 ♖d1 0-0 11 e5 ♘e8 12 ♗f4 ±) 8 ♗xc6 bc (8 ... ♗xc6 9 ♘f5 0-0 10 ♗g5 ±) 9 ♗f4 0-0 10 e5 ±

[10] 7 ... 0-0? 8 ♗xc6 ♗xc6 9 de de 10 ♕xd8 ♖axd8 (10 ... ♖fxd8 11 ♘xe5 ♗xe4 12 ♘xe4 ♘xe4 13 ♘d3 f5 14 f3 ♗c5+ 15 ♔f1 ±±) 11 ♘xe5 ♗xe4 12 ♘xe4 ♘xe4 13 ♘d3 f5 14 f3 ♗c5+ 15 ♔xc5 ♘xc5 16 ♗g5 ±± Tarrasch-Marco, Dresden 1892

[11] 10 ... ♖b8 11 b3 d5 12 ed ♗b4 13 ♕d3 ♘xd5 14 ♘xd5 cd 15 c3 ♗a5 16 ♖e5 c6 17 ♖ae1 ± Klovans-Buturin, USSR 1983

[12] 12 e5 ♘h5 13 ♗e3 ± Geller-Welling, CSKA v Eindhoven 1986

[13] 4 ef e4 5 ♕e2 ♕e7 6 ♗xc6 dc 7 ♘d4 ♕e5 = 4 d4 fe 5 ♘xe5?! (5 ♗xc6 dc 6 ♘xe5 ♕h4 =) 5 ... ♘xe5 6 de c6 7 ♘c3 (7 ♗c4 ♕a5+ ∓) 7 ... cb 8 ♘xe4 d5 9 ed ♘f6 10 ♗g5 (10 ♕d4 ♕d7! ∓ Hansen-Briem, Aarhus 1965) 10 ... ♕a5+ 11 ♘c3 b4 12 ♗xf6 gf 13 ♘d5 b3+ 14 c3 ♗e6! 15 ♘c7+ ♔d7 16 0-0 ♗xd6 = Piskov-Yandemirov, USSR 1984

[14] 4 ... ♘f6 5 ef ♗c5 6 0-0-0-0 7 ♘xe5 ±

[15] 5 ♘xd4!? ed 6 ♘d5 c6 7 ef cd 8 ♕h5+ ♔e7 9 0-0 ±/∞ Kostakiev-Kolev, Bulgaria 1986

5 ef c6 6 ♗e2 ♘f6 7 ♘xe5 ♕e7 8 ♘d3 d5 9 0-0 ♗xf5 10 ♘e1 0-0-0 11 d3 ± Sax-Romero, Rome 1986; 6 ... ♘xf3+! intending 7 ... d5 = Shamkovich, Schiller; 6 ♘xd4! ed 7 ♕h5+ ♔e7 8 0-0 d5!? ∞

[16] 5 ... c6 6 0-0 (6 ♘xg8!? ♖xg8 7 0-0 Sax-O.Rodriguez, Las Palmas 1978) 6 ... ♘f6 7 ♘xe5 fe 8 ♘f7 ♕e7 (8 ... ♕c7!?) 9 ♘xh8 d5 10 ♗e2 ± Geller-O.Rodriguez, Las Palmas 1976

[17] 7 ... ♘xf5 8 d4 e4 9 ♗g5! c6 (9 ... ef 10 ♖e1+) 10 ♗xf6 gf 11 ♘e5! ±± Latash-Anzans, corr. 1986

[18] 11 ... d5? 12 ♘xd5 ±± Euwe

[19] 7 ... bc 8 ♗xc6+ ♗d7 9 ♕h5+ ♔e7 10 ♕e5+ ♗e6 11 ♗xa8 ±

7 ... ♕d5 8 c4 ♕d6 9 ♗xa7+ ♗d7 10 ♗xd7+ ♕xd7 11 ♕h5+ g6 (11 ... ♔d8 12 ♘b5 ♘f6 13 ♕e2 ±) 12 ♕e5+ ♔f7 13 ♘b5 c6 14 ♕d4! ♕xd4 (14 ... ♕e7 15 ♕xh8 ♘f6 16 b3 ♖d8 17 ♗b2 ♗g7 18 ♗a3! ± Chandler; 14 ... ♕g4 15 0-0 cb 16 f3 ±) 15 ♘xd4 ♗g7 16 ♘e2 ♖a4 16 b3! ± Jansa-Vera, Bratislava 1983

[20] 9 ... ♕h4+ 10 g3 ♕h3 11 ♘e5+ c6 12 ♗c4 ♗c5 13 d3 ♘g4 (13 ... ed 14 ♘xd3+ ♗e7 15 ♘e5 ±) 14 ♕xe4 (14 ♘f7! ♗f2+ 15 ♔d1 e3!? 16 ♕f3 ± Nunn-Rumens, London 1978) 14 ... ♘f2 15 ♕e2 (15 ♗f7+ ♔d8 16 ♕c4 ±) 15 ... ♘xh1 16 ♘g6+ ♔d8 17 ♘xh8 ♗g4 18 ♘f7+ ♔c7 19 ♕e5+ ♔b6 20 ♕xc5+! ♔xc5 21 ♗e3+ ♔b4 22 a3+ ♔a5 23 b4+ ♔a4 24 ♘d6 ♗e6 25 ♘e4 1-0 V.Nikitin-Kazantsev, USSR 1978

[21] 10 ♘xa7+ ♗d7 11 ♗xd7+ ♔xd7 12 ♘b5 ♖e8 13 b3 ♗b4 14 c3 ♗c5 15 ♗a3 ± Lukov-Inkiov, Bulgarian Ch 1984

[22] 12 g3 ♕h3 13 ♗c4 ♗e6 14 ♗g5 ♗d6 15 0-0-0 0-0-0 16 ♕f1! ± Sax-Inkiov, Rome 1984

	3	4	5	6	7	8	9	10	11	
5	...	♘c3	♘xe4	♘xf6+[23]	♕e2[25]	♗xc6	♘xe5	d3	0-0	±
	f5	fe	♘f6	♕xf6[24]	♗e7	dc	♗f5	0-0[26]	♗d6[27]	
6	...	d4	♗g5	♗xe7[29]	♘xd4	♘c3	♗xc6+	♘xc6	♖xd1	=
	g6	ed	♗e7[28]	♘gxe7[30]	d5	de	♘xc6	♕xd1+	bc[31]	
7	...	c3	d4	0-0	♕b3[33]	♕a4	♕xb5+	♕e2	de	±
	...	d6[32]	♗d7	♗g7	♘a5	♗xb5[34]	c6	b6	de[35]	
8	...	♘xd4	0-0	♗c4	c3[38]	cd	♕a4+	♗d5	♗xc6+	±
	♘d4	ed	♗c5[36]	d6[37]	♘e7[39]	♗xd4	♘c6	♗b6	bc[40]	
9	...	...	...	d3	♗a4[41]	f4[42]	f5	de	♗b3[43]	±
	...	...	...	c6	♘e7	d5	de	0-0		
10	...	0-0	♘xd4[44]	c3	d4	♗a4	♘a3	cd	d5[47]	±
	♗c5	♘d4	♗xd4	♗b6	c6	d6	ed[45]	♘e7[46]	0-0[48]	
11	...	...	♘xe5[49]	d4	♗a4[52]	♕e2	♕xe4	f4	♗b3[53]	±
	...	♘f6	♘xe5[50]	a6[51]	♘xe4	♗e7	♘g6	0-0		
12	...	c3	d4[55]	♗xc6[56]	♘xe5[57]	♕h5+	♕e2	♗f4	♘d2	±
	...	f5[54]	fe	dc	♗d6[58]	g6	♗f5[59]	♘f6	0-0[60]	
13	...	0-0	d4[61]	♗xc6	de	♕xd8+	♘c3[63]	b3[65]	h3	±
	♘f6	♘xe4	♘d6	dc	♘f5[62]	♔xd8	♔e8[64]	h6	♗e6[66]	

[23] 6 ♕e2 d5 7 ♘xf6+ (7 ♘xe5? de 8 ♕c4 ♕d6! 9 ♘xc6 a6 ∓) 7 ... gf 8 d4 ♗g7 9 de 0-0 10 ♗xc6 (10 e6 ♘e5 ∞ Popović-Kurajica, Sarajevo 1985; 10 ef ♕xf6 ∞ Klovans-Arbakov, USSR 1984) 10 ... bc 11 e6 ♖e8 12 0-0 a5 ∞ Nenashev-Arbakov, Moscow Ch 1986

[24] 6 ... gf 7 d4 ±

[25] 7 0-0 ♘d4 8 ♘xd4 ed 9 ♖e1+ (9 b3 c6 10 ♗d3 d5 11 c4 ♗e6 ∞) 9 ... ♗e7 10 ♕e2 c6 11 ♗d3 d5 12 b3 0-0! 13 ♕xe7 ♕xf2+ 14 ♔h1 ♗h3 15 ♖g1?! (15 gh =) 15 ... ♖ae8 16 ♕xf8+ ♕xf8 17 ♖f1 ♗xg2+ 18 ♔xg2 ♕d6 ∓ Kalegin-Mikh.Tseitlin, USSR 1986; 7 ... ♗e7!? 8 ♗xc6 dc 9 ♕e1 e4!? Schiller

[26] 10 ... 0-0-0 11 0-0 ♖he8 12 f4 ♗d6 13 ♕f2! ± Glek-Arbakov, corr. 1985, and Glek-Yandemirov, USSR 1985

[27] 12 f4 ♖ac8 13 d4 ♗xe5 14 de ♕g6 15 ♖f2 ± Unzicker-Mikh.Tseitlin, Moscow 1982
12 ♘c4 ♖hf8 13 ♗e3!? Shamkovich, Schiller

[28] 5 ... f6 6 ♗h4 ♗g7 (6 ... ♗b4+ 7 c3 dc 8 ♘xc3 d6 9 ♕b3 ♗d7 10 0-0-0 ♗xc3 11 ♕xc3 ± Klinger-Zúñiga Granda, Gausdal 1986) 7 0-0 ♘ge7 8 ♗c4 ♘a5 9 ♕xd4 ♘ec6 10 ♕d5 ♘xc4 11 ♕xc4 ± van der Wiel-Ree,

Dutch Ch 1983, and Klinger-Armas, Havana 1986

[29] 6 ♗f4 ♘f6 7 e5 ♘d5 8 ♗h6 a6 9 ♗c4 (9 ♗xc6!?) 9 ... ♘b6 10 ♗b3 d5 ∓ Sax-Radulov, Warsaw Z 1987

[30] 6 ... ♕xe7 7 ♗xc6 dc 8 ♕xd4 ♘f6 9 ♘c3 0-0 10 0-0-0 ± Sax-Smyslov, New York 1987

[31] 12 ♘xe4 ♗f5 13 ♖d4 ♖d8 14 ♖a4 0-0 = Kupreichik-Malanyuk, USSR Ch 1987

[32] 4 ... a6! and now:
5 ♗c4 ♗g7 6 d4 d6 7 ♗g5 ♘ge7 8 de de 9 ♕e2 h6 10 ♗h4 b5 11 ♗b3 ♘a5 ∞ Timman-Smyslov, Tilburg 1982
5 ♗xc6 dc 6 0-0 ♗g7 7 d4 ed 8 cd ♘e7 9 ♘c3 ♗g4 10 ♗e3 0-0 = Chandler-Spassky, Vienna 1986
5 ♗a4! d6 – 3 ... a6

[33] 7 ♖e1 ♗ge7 8 de ♘xe5 9 ♘xd7+ ♕xd7 10 ♘xe5 de 11 ♕b3 c6 12 ♘a3 ± Maliskauskas-Kholmov, Norilsk 1987

[34] 8 ... c6 9 ♕e2 b5 10 ♕c2 ♘e7 11 ♗e3 0-0 12 de de 13 a4 ± Kupreichik-Smyslov, USSR Ch 1976

[35] 12 ♘bd2 ♕c7 13 a4 ♘e7 14 b4 ♘b7 15 ♘c4 ± Stern-Smit, corr. 1985

[36] 5 ... c6 6 ♗c4 ♘f6 (6 ... g6 7 c3 ♗g7 8 ♕f3

♕e7 9 d3 ± Ljubojević-Spassky, London 1982)
7 ♖e1 d6 8 d3 ♗e7 9 ♘d2 0-0 10 ♘f3 c5 11 h3
(11 e5 ♘e8 12 ed ♘xd6 13 ♗b3 ♗g4 14 h3 ±)
11 ... ♖b8 12 c3 ± Liberzon-Henley, Lone Pine 1980

[37] 6 ... ♘e7? 7 ♗xf7+
6 ... ♕h4 7 d3 ♘e7 8 ♘d2 0-0 9 c3 ±

[38] 7 d3 ♘e7 (7 ... ♘f6 8 ♗g5 ± Ghinda-Kotronias, Athens 1986) 8 ♗g5 0-0 9 ♕h5 ♗e6 = Dolmatov-Tukmakov, USSR Ch 1987

[39] 7 ... ♕f6 8 ♘a3! ♖xa3 9 ♕a4+ ♗d7 10 ♕xa3 ± Khalifman-Kupreichik, Minsk 1986, and Ehlvest-Kupreichik, Kuibishev 1986
7 ... ♘f6 8 cd ♗xd4 9 ♕a4+ ♔f8 ±/± Romanishin-Balashov, Erevan 1986
7 ... c6!?

[40] 12 d4 ± Romanishin

[41] 7 ♗c4 d5! 8 ed cd 9 ♗b5+ (9 ♗b3 ♘e7 = Dvoiris-Balashov, USSR Ch 1986, and Belyavsky-Tseshkovsky, USSR Ch 1986) 9 ... ♗d7 (9 ... ♔f8!? Sigurjonsson-Kupreichik, Winnipeg 1986) 10 ♗xd7+ ♕xd7 = Lanc-Tseshkovsky, Trnava 1986, and Rohde-Christiansen, US Ch 1986

[42] 8 c3 d5 9 ♘d2 ♗b6 10 cd ♗xd4 11 ♔h1 0-0 12 f4 f5 13 e5 ± Hübner-Nunn, Brussels 1986

[43] Spassky-Barua, New York 1987

[44] 5 b4!? ♗xb4 (5 ... ♘xf3+ 6 ♕xf3 ♗xb4 7 ♗b2 ♕e7 8 ♕g3 f6 9 d4 ♗d6 10 ♘d2 ∞ Karafiath-Kalmar, corr. 1985) 6 ♘xd4 ed 7 ♗b2 ∞ Plaskett-Kupreichik, Hastings 1984-85, and Ghinda-Hector, Budapest 1986

[45] 9 ... ♗c7 10 d5 ♗d7 11 dc bc 12 ♘c4 ± Ljubojević-Durao, Orense 1974
9 ... ♘f6 10 ♗g5 h6 11 ♗xf6 ♕xf6 12 d5 ♗d7 13 ♘c4 ♗c7 14 dc bc 15 ♕d3 ±

[46] 10 ... ♕h4 11 g3 ♕h3 12 ♘c4 ♗c7 13 ♗f4 b5 14 ♗xd6 ♕d7 15 d5 ba 16 dc ♕d8 17 ♕xa4 ± Bator-Hector, Swedish Ch 1986

[47] 11 ♗g5 f6 12 ♗h4 (12 ♗f4 0-0 13 d5 ♗c5? 14 dc bc 15 b4! ±±; 13 ... ♗c7 ±) 12 ... 0-0 13 ♘c4 d5 14 ed ♘xd5 15 ♖e1 ♗f5 16 ♗b3 ♕d7 17 ♗g3 ± Jansa-Pedersen, Svendborg 1981

[48] 12 ♘c4 ♗c7 (12 ... ♗c5 13 dc bc 14 ♗e3 ±) 13 dc bc 14 ♖e1 ± Campora-Wedberg, Amsterdam 1984

[49] 5 c3 0-0 6 d4 ♗b6 7 ♗g5 h6 8 ♗h4 d6 9 a4 a5 10 ♖e1 ed (10 ... ♗g4 11 ♗xc6 bc 12 de de 13 ♘bd2 g5 14 ♗g3 ♖e8 ∞ A.Ivanov-Gulko, USSR 1983) 11 ♗xc6 bc 12 ♘xd4 ♖e8 13 ♘d2 c5 14 ♘4f3 ♗b7 = Thorsteins-Spassky, Reykjavik 1985

[50] 5 ... ♘xe4 6 ♕e2 ♘xe5 7 ♕xe4 ♕e7 8 ♘c3 ♕xe7+ ♗xe7 10 ♘d5 ♗d6 11 ♖e1+ ±/± Adorjan-Kirov, Sochi 1976, and Hulak-Knežević, Yugoslav Ch 1978

[51] 6 ... c6 7 de ♘xe4 8 ♗d3 d5 9 ed ♘f6 (9 ... ♘xd6? 10 ♖e1+ ♗e6 11 ♖xe6+) 10 ♕e2+ ♗e6 11 ♗g5 ♕xd6 12 ♗xf6 gf 13 ♘d2 0-0-0

14 ♘e4 ♕e5 15 ♘xc5 ♕xc5 16 ♕e3 ± Tseshkovsky-Vasyukov, USSR 1983

[52] 7 ♗e2 ♗a7 8 de ♘xe4 9 ♗f3 ♘g5 10 ♗d5 0-0 11 ♕h5 ♘e6 12 ♘c3 d6 = Popović-Flear, Clichy 1986-87

[53] 11 f5 d5 12 ♕d3 ♘h4 ∞ Plaskett-Donchev, Plovdiv 1984
11 ♗b3 ± Plaskett

[54] 4 ... ♘f6 5 d4 ed (5 ... ♗b6 6 ♕e2 ed 7 e5 0-0 8 cd ±) 6 e5 ♘e4 7 0-0 d5 (7 ... dc 8 ♕d5) 8 ♘xd4 ± ECO
4 ... ♕f6 5 d4 ed 6 e5 ♕g6 7 cd ♗b4+ 8 ♘c3 ♘ge7 9 0-0 d5 10 ♕b3 ♗xc3 11 bc ± Blackburne-Pillsbury and Steinitz-Schiffers, Nuremberg 1896, and A.Sokolov-Kharitonov, USSR Ch 1984(!)

[55] 5 ef e4 6 d4 ef 7 dc ♕e7+ 8 ♗e3 fg 9 ♖g1 ♘f6 10 ♖xg2 0-0 11 ♘d2 d5 12 cd cd 13 ♕c2 ± Unzicker-Campora, Berne 1987

[56] 6 dc ef 7 ♕xf3 ♘f6 8 ♗g5 0-0 9 ♘d2 ♕e8 10 ♗xf6 ♖xf6 11 ♕e3 ♕h5 12 ♘e4 ♖f4 13 0-0 ± Matulović-Crepan, Vrnjačka Banja 1986

[57] 7 ♘fd2 ♕g5?! (7 ... ♗d6 8 de e3 9 fe ♗xe5 ±) 8 dc ♘f6 9 ♕e2! (9 0-0 ♗h3 10 g3 0-0-0 ∞; 9 ♖g1 ♕h4 10 ♘f1 ♗g4 ∞ Wedberg-Rantanen, Helsinki 1983) 9 ... ♕xg2 10 ♕f1 ♕g4 11 ♘c4 ± de Firmian-Rogers, Philadelphia 1986

[58] 7 ... ♕d5 8 ♗f4 ♗d6 9 c4 ♕e6 10 ♕h5+ g6 11 ♕e2 ± Arnason-Rantanen, Helsinki 1986

[59] 9 ... ♕h4 10 0-0 ♗xe5 11 de ♗f5 12 ♘d2 0-0-0 13 f3 ef 14 ♘xf3 ♕h5 15 ♕f2 ± Anand-Pulkkinen, Oakham 1986

[60] 12 0-0 ♕e7 13 f3 ef 14 ♘dxf3 ± Mestel-Plaskett, Brighton Z 1984

[61] 5 ♖e1 ♘d6 6 ♘xe5 ♘xe5 7 ♖xe5+ ♗e7 8 ♘c3 0-0 (8 ... ♘xb5? 9 d5) 9 ♗d3 ♗f6 10 ♖e3 g6 = Kasparov-Vasilenko, USSR 1976

[62] 7 ... ♘e4 8 ♕e2 ♗f5 (8 ... ♘c5 9 ♗g4 10 ♘c3 ♕e7 11 ♖fe1 ± Gulko-Reshevsky, Vilnius 1978) 9 ♖d1 ♕c8 10 ♖d4 ♘c5 11 ♘c3 ± Lobron-Lombardy, New York 1987

[63] 9 c4 ♗e6 10 b3 h6 11 ♘c3 ♔c8 12 h3 a5 13 g4 ♘e7 14 ♘d4 ± Watson-Sturua, Frunze 1985
9 b3 h6 10 ♗b2 ♗e6 11 ♘bd2 a5 12 h3 c5 13 a4 ♔e8 14 ♖ad1 ♖d8 15 ♘c4 ± Sax-Torre, Biel IZ 1985

[64] 9 ... h6 10 ♘e2 g5 11 h3 ♗g7 12 ♖d1+ ♗d7 13 g4 ♘e7 14 ♘g3 ± Psakhis-Romanishin, Erevan Z 1982

[65] 10 ♘e2 ♘e7 (10 ... ♗e6 11 ♘f4 ♗d5 12 ♘xd5 cd 13 g4 ±) 11 h3 ♗e6 12 ♘f4 ♗d5 13 ♘xd5 cd 14 ♗f4 ± Kavalek-Karaklajić, Manila 1975

[66] 12 ♗b2 ♗b4 13 ♘e2 ♖d8 14 ♘f4 ♗d5 15 ♘xd5 cd 16 g4 ± Ljubojević-Kavalek, Reggio Emilia 1985-86

	3	4	5	6	7	8	9	10	11	
14	...	0-0	d4	♕e2[67]	♗xc6	de	♘c3	♖e1	♗f4[69]	±
	♘f6	♘xe4	♗e7	♘d6	bc	♘b7[68]	0-0	♘c5	♘e6[70]	

[67] 6 de 0-0 7 ♕d5 ♘c5 8 ♗e3 ♘e6 9 ♘c3 a6 10 ♗a4 f6! 11 ♗b3 ♔h8 12 ♖ad1 fe 13 ♘xe5 ♘xe5 14 ♕xe5 d6 = Ernst-Hartman, Swedish Ch 1986

[68] 8 ... ♘f5 9 ♕e4 g6 10 b3 0-0 11 ♗b2 ♗b7 12 ♖e1 d5 13 ed cd 14 ♘bd2 d5 15 ♕f4 f6 16 c4 ± Popović-Kavalek, Subotica IZ 1987

[69] 11 ♗e3 ♘e6 12 ♖ad1 ♖b8 (12 ... d5 13 ed cd 14 ♘d4 ± Karpov-Korchnoi, match (2) 1981) 13 b3 ♗b4 14 ♗d2 d5 ∞ Kindermann-Zsu.Polgar, Dortmund 1985

[70] 12 ♗g3 ♖b8 13 b3 f5 14 ef ♗xf6 15 ♘e5 ± Geller-Bastian, Baden-Baden 1985

	5	6	7	8	9	10	11	12	13	
1	♘c3[2]	d4	♘xd4	♘de2	♕xd1	♗f4	♘e3	h4	♖d1	±/=
	f6	ed	c5[3]	♕xd1+	♗e6[4]	0-0-0	♘e7	h5	♖xd1+[5]	
2	0-0	♘xe5[7]	♕h5	♘f3[8]	♕a5	d3	♘bd2	a3![10]		±
	♘e7[6]	♕d4	g6	♕xe4	♕f4[9]	♕d6	♘d5			
3	...	♘a3[11]	♘g5	♘xe6	b3	♘c4	d3	♕e2	♖b1	±
	♕d6	♗e6[12]	h6[13]	♕xe6	♗c5	♘e7	0-0	♗d4	a5[14]	
4	...	h3	d3[16]	♘bd2	♖e1	d4	hg	♘h2	♕xg4	±
	♗g4	h5[15]	♕f6	♘e7	♘g6	♗d6[17]	hg	♖xh2	♕h4[18]	
5	...	d4	de	♖xd1	♖d3	♘bd2	b3	♗b2	g3	=
	f6	♗g4	♕xd1	fe	♗d6[19]	b5[20]	♘e7	♘g6	0-0[21]	
6	...	...	c3	♗e3	♘bd2	de	h3[24]	♘g5	♕h5+	±
	...	...	♗d6	♘e7[22]	♕d7[23]	fe	♗e6	♗g8	♘g6[25]	
7	...	...	...	cd	♗e3[27]	♘bd2	♕c2	b4	♖fc1[28]	±/∞
	...	...	ed	♕d7[26]	0-0-0	g5	♘e7	♘g6		
8	...	...	♘xd4	♘b3[30]	♖xd1	♗f4[32]	♘c3	♖xd8+	♖d1+	±
	...	ed	c5[29]	♕xd1	♗d7[31]	0-0-0	♗e6	♔xd8	♔c8[33]	
9	...	...	...	...	...	f3	♗f4[34]	♘d4	♘c3	±/=
	...	...	...	...	♗g4	♗e6	c4	0-0-0	♗f7[35]	

[1] 4 ... bc 5 ♘c3 (5 d4 ed 6 ♕xd4 ♕f6! 7 ♕d3! ±) 5 ... d6 6 d4 f6 7 ♗e3 ♘e7 (7 ... ♖b8 8 ♕d3! ♖xb2 9 de fe 10 ♘xe5 ±) 8 ♕d3 ♗e6 9 0-0-0 ♘g6 10 h4 h5 11 ♘d2 a5 12 g3 ± Padevsky-Daskalov, Bulgarian Ch 1972

[2] 5 d4 ed 6 ♕xd4 ♕xd4 7 ♘xd4 ♗d7 8 ♗e3 0-0-0 9 ♘d2 (9 ♘c3 ♖e8 10 0-0-0 ♗b4 11 ♘de2 f5 = Smyslov-Keres, USSR Ch 1940)

[3] 7 ... ♗b4 8 ♕d3 c5 9 ♘e2 ♕xd3 10 cd ♗e6 11 ♗e3 0-0-0 12 0-0-0 ♘e7 13 a3 ♗xc3 14 bc ± Chudinovsky-A.Kuzmin, USSR 1986

[4] 9 ... ♗d7 10 ♗f4 0-0-0 11 ♘e3 ♗c6 12 f3 ♗e7 13 ♖d1 ♖e8 14 h4 h5 15 ♔f2 ♘g6 16 ♗g3 ♘e5 17 ♗xe5 fe 18 ♘c3 ± Yanovsky-

9 ... c5 10 ♘e2 b6 11 0-0-0 ♘e7 12 ♖he1 ♘c6 = Ljubojević-Belyavsky, Tilburg 1986

Muratov, USSR 1985

[5] 14 Kxd1 Nc6 15 Bg3 b5 16 Nd5 Ne5 17 Kc1 Bxd5 18 ed Ng6 19 Nf4 Nxf4 20 Bxf4 Bd6 ±/= Yanovsky-Nikolenko, USSR 1986

[6] 5 ... Qf6 6 d4 ed 7 Bg5 Qg6 8 Qxd4 Bd6 9 Nbd2 Be6 10 Rfe1 Ne7 11 Nc4 Rd8 12 Nxd6+ cd 13 e5 ± Gipslis

5 ... Qe7 6 d4 ed 7 Qxd4 Bg4 8 Bf4 Bxf3 9 gf Nf6 10 Nc3 Nh5 11 Bg3 Rd8 12 Qe3 ± Dvoretsky-Smyslov, Odessa 1974

5 ... Be7 6 Nxe5 Qd4 7 Nf3 Qxe4 8 Re1 Qf5 9 b3 ± Fischer

5 ... Bd6 6 d4 ed 7 Qxd4 f6 8 Be3 Ne7 9 Nbd2 Be6 10 Qc3! 0-0 11 Nd4 Bf7 12 Rad1 ± Shakarov-Hölscher, corr. 1987

[7] 6 d4 ed 7 Nxd4 c5 8 Nb3 Qxd1 9 Rxd1 Ng6 =

[8] 8 Qg5 Bg7 9 Nd3 (9 Nf3 Qxe4 10 Re1 Qb4 =) 9 ... f5 10 e5 c5 ∞∞ ECO

[9] 9 ... Bg4!?

[10] 12 Re1+ Be7 13 Ne4 Qb4 ∞ Lein-Biyiasas, New York 1977

12 a3! ±

[11] 6 d4 ed 7 Nxd4 Bd7 8 Be3 c5! (8 ... 0-0-0 9 Nd2 Nh6 10 f3 ±) 9 Nb3 Qxd1 10 Rxd1 b6 = Hecht-Grün, West Germany 1984-85

6 d3 f6 (6 ... Ne7 7 Be3 c5 8 Nfd2 Ng6 9 Nc4 Qu8 10 Qh5 Bd6 11 Nc3 Be6 = Gobet-Hübner, Biel 1984) 7 Be3 c5 8 Nfd2 Be6 9 Nc3 Ne7 10 Nc4 Bxc4 11 dc Qxd1 12 Rfxd1 Nc6 = Timman-Torre, Hamburg 1982

[12] 6 ... b5 7 Nb1 (7 d3 Ne7 8 Be3 Ng6 9 Nb1 ±) 7 ... Ne7 8 a3 Ng6 9 d4 ±

[13] 7 ... f6 8 Nxe6 Qxe6 9 d3 (9 b3 ±) 9 ... Bxa3 10 ba Ne7 11 f4 ± Arkhipov-Romanishin, Moscow 1986

[14] 14 Be3 Rfd8 15 Bxd4 Rxd4 16 Qh5 f6 17 f4 ± Rozentalis-Yakovich, USSR 1987

[15] 6 ... Bxf3 7 Qxf3 Qd7 8 d3 Bd6 9 Nd2 Ne7 10 Nc4 0-0 11 Be3 f5 12 ef Rxf5 13 Qe2 ± Nunn-Korchnoi, Wijk aan Zee 1985

[16] 7 c3 Qd3 8 Re1 (8 hg hg 9 Nxe5 Bd6 =) 8 ... Bxf3 9 Qxf3 Qxf3 10 gf 0-0-0 11 Kf1 Be7 (11 ... Ne7 12 Ke2 Ng6 13 d3 Be7 14 Be3 c5 15 Na3 ±) 12 Ke2 Bg5 13 Na3 Ne7 14 Rg1 Bh6 15 Nc4 f6 (15 ... Ng6 16 Rxg6!) 16 h4 c5 17 d3 ± de Wit-van der Sterren, Amsterdam 1985

[17] 10 ... Nf4 11 de (11 hg hg 12 g3 gf 13 Qxf3 Ne6 14 de Qh6! ∞ Povah-Corden, Birmingham 1977) 11 ... Qg6 12 Nh4 ±

[18] 14 Qxh4 Rxh4 15 Nf3 Rh5 16 c3! (16 de Nxe5 17 Nxe5 Bxe5 18 c3 g5! 19 Be3 g4 =) 16 ... f6 17 Be3 ± Pinter-Perenyi, Budapest 1972

[19] 9 ... Bxf3 10 gf! Bd6 11 Be3 intending Nd2 ±

[20] 10 ... Nf6 11 Nc4 0-0 12 Nfxe5 Be2 13 Re3 Bxc4 14 Nxc4 Bc5 15 Re1 Rae8 16 Be3 Bxe3 17 Rxe3 Rxe4 +/=

[21] Nunn-Portisch, Wijk aan Zee 1985, and Timman-Kasparov, match 1985

[22] 8 ... Qd7 9 h3! ed 10 Qxd4 Be6 11 e5 ±

8 ... Nh6 9 h3 (9 Bxh6 gh 10 Nbd2 ±) 9 ... Bh5 10 Nbd2 Nf7 11 Qb3 b6 12 Nh4 0-0 13 Nc4 Kh8 14 Nf5 ± Rozentalis-Klovans, USSR 1983

8 ... Qe7 9 Nbd2 0-0-0 10 Qc2 ed 11 cd (11 Nxd4 ±) 11 ... Re8 12 e5 Bb4 (Smyslov-Geller, USSR Ch 1973) 13 Bf4! ±

[23] 9 ... ed 10 cd f5 11 ef! Bxf5 12 Bg5 ± Petrushin-Rabinovich, USSR 1982

[24] 11 Nc4 Ng6 12 h3 Be6 13 Qe2 b5! (13 ... 0-0 14 Ng5 ±) 14 Nxd6+ cd =

[25] 14 Rfd1 0-0-0 15 Nf1 ± Kagan-Harandi, Rio de Janeiro IZ 1979

[26] 8 ... Bxf3 9 Qxf3 Qxd4 10 Rd1 Qc4 11 Bf4 Qf7 12 Qg3 Bd6 13 Bxd6 0-0-0 14 e5 fe? 15 Qg4+ Qd7 16 Be7! 1-0 Volchok-Kreslavsky, USSR 1970

8 ... c5 9 Qb3! Bxf3 10 Qxf3 cd 11 e5 c6 12 Re1 Be7 13 Nd2 ± Shakarov-Badzarani, USSR 1982

[27] 9 h3 Be6 10 Nc3 0-0-0 11 Bf4 g5 (11 ... Ne7 12 Rc1 Ng6 13 Bg3 Bd6 14 Na4 ± Fischer-Gligorić, Havana Ol 1966) 12 Bg3 g4 ∞ Petrushin-Yudasin, USSR 1981

[28] Gipslis-Shulman, USSR 1983

[29] 7 ... Bd6 8 Qh5+ g6 9 Qf3 ± ECO

7 ... Ne7 8 Be3 Ng6 9 Nd2 (9 Qh5 Bd6 10 Nf5 ±) 9 ... Bd6 10 Nc4 0-0 11 Qd3 ± Fischer-Unzicker, Siegen Ol 1970

[30] 8 Ne2 Qxd1 9 Rxd1 Bd7 10 Bf4 0-0-0 11 c4 Ne7 12 Nbc3 Ng6 13 Bg3 Ne5 14 b3 ±/= Hort-Nunn, Zürich 1984

[31] 9 ... Bd6 10 Na5! b5 11 c4 ± Fischer-Portisch, Havana Ol 1966

[32] 10 a4!? b6 (10 ... 0-0-0 11 a5) 11 Bf4 0-0 12 Nc3 c4 (12 ... Ne7 13 a5 c4 14 ab! cb3 15 bc ±) 13 Nd4 ±

[33] 14 Nd5 Nxd5 15 Rxd5 b6 16 Nd2 Ne7 17 Rd3 Nc6 18 c3 ± Browne-Hübner, Wijk aan Zee 1975, and Kuporosov-Kantsler, USSR 1980

[34] 11 Be3 b6 12 a4 Bd6 (12 ... Kf7 13 Nc3 Bd6 14 a5 c4 15 Nd4 b5 16 f4 Ne7 17 e5! fe 18 fe Bxe5 19 Rf1+ Bf6 20 Rae1 ±/∞ Kosikov-Bezman, USSR 1986) 13 a5 0-0-0 14 Nc3 Bb7 15 ab cb 16 e5! ±/∞ Rozentalis-Muhamedzanov, USSR 1983, and Janssen-Pachman, Baden-Baden 1985

[35] 13 ... Rxd4 14 Rxd4 Bc5 15 Ne2 Bxd4+ 16 Nxd4 Bd7 17 Re1 ± Rozentalis-Psakhis, Sverdlovsk 1984

13 ... Bc5 14 Ne2 Ne7 15 Be3 Bf7 16 Nf5 Bxe3+ 17 Nxe3 ± Rozentalis-Korzubov, USSR 1985

13 ... Bf7 14 Nf5 Rxd1+ 15 Rxd1 Ne7 16 Be3 Ng6 17 Bg3 Bc5 18 Kf2 Rd8 ±/= Vitolins-Romanishin, USSR 1984

	Ruy Lopez III			1 e4 e5 2 ♘f3 ♘c6 3 ♗b5 a6 4 ♗a4					
	4	5	6	7	8	9	10	11	12	
1	… b5[1]	♗b3 ♘a5	0-0[2] d6	d4 ed[3]	♘xd4 ♗b7[4]	♗d2[5] ♘xb3[6]	♘xb3 ♘f6[7]	♖e1 ♗e7	♘a5 ♖b8[8]	±
2	… f5	d4[9] ed[10]	e5 ♗c5[11]	0-0 ♘ge7	♗b3[12] d5	ed ♕xd6	♖e1 ♗d7[13]	♘g5 ♘d8	♘d2 h6[14]	±
3	… d6	c4[15] ♗d7[16]	♘c3[17] ♘f6[18]	d3[19] ♗e7	0-0 0-0	h3[20] ♘d4	♗xd7 ♘xf3+	♕xf3 ♘xd7	♗e3 ♗g5[21]	=
4	… …	0-0 ♗d7	d4 b5	♗b3 ed[22]	c3 d3[23]	♕xd3 ♘f6	♗f4[24] ♗e7	h3 0-0	♘bd2 ♘a5[25]	±
5	… …	… ♗g4	h3 h5[26]	d4[27] b5[28]	♗b3 ♘xd4	hg hg	♘g5[29] ♘h6	♗d5[30] c6	c3 cd[31]	∞/±
6	… …	♗xc6+ bc	d4 f6[32]	♗e3[33] ♘e7	♘c3 ♘g6	♕e2 a5[34]	h4 ♗a6	♕d2 h5	0-0-0 ♕c8[35]	±
7	… …	c3 f5	ef ♗xf5	0-0[36] ♗d3	♖e1[37] ♗e7	♗c2[38] ♗xc2[39]	♕xc2 ♘f6	d4 ed[40]	cd 0-0[41]	±

[1] **4 … ♗e7** 5 0-0 (5 d4 ed 6 ♘xd4 ♘xd4 7 ♕xd4 c5 8 ♕xg7 ♗f6 9 ♕g3 b5 10 e5 ♕e7 11 0-0 ♗e5 12 f4 ♗d4+! ⩱ Pantaleoni-Buccardini, corr. 1987) 5 … d6 6 c3 b5 7 ♗c2 ±

4 … ♕f6 5 c3! b5 6 ♗c2 d6 7 a4 ♖b8 8 ab ab 9 d4 ♗g4 10 d5 ± Veličković-Klarić, Yugoslavia 1986

4 … g6 5 d4 ed 6 ♘xd4 (6 c3?! dc! 7 ♘xc3 ♗g7 8 ♗g5 f6 9 ♗f4 ♘ge7 10 h4 h5 11 e5 fe 12 ♗g5 d5! ⩱ Littlewood-Levitt, England 1986) 6 … ♗g7 7 ♘xc6! bc 8 0-0 ♗b7 (8 … ♘e7 9 ♘c3 0-0 10 ♗f4 d6 11 ♕d2 ± Tal) 9 ♘c3 d6 10 ♘d5 ♔f8 11 ♘f4 ♘f6 12 ♖e1 ♘d7 13 c3 ± de Firmian-Smyslov, Copenhagen 1985

4 … ♘ge7 5 ♘c3 d6 6 d4 ed 7 ♘xd4 ♗d7 8 ♗b3 ±

[2] **6 ♗xf7+?!** ♔xf7 7 ♘xe5+ ♔e7 8 d4 (8 ♘c3 ♕e8! Shamkovich, Schiller) 8 … ♘f6 9 0-0!? (9 ♕f3 ♗b7 10 ♘c3 ♕e8 ⩱ Spassky-Taimanov, USSR 1954) 9 … ♕e8 10 ♘c3 ♔d8 11 ♘d5 ∞/∞̄ Vitolins-Zhuravlev, USSR 1980

6 d4 ed 7 ♕xd4 ♘xb3!? 8 ab ♗b7 ±

[3] **7 … f6** 8 ♗e3 ♗b7 (8 … ♘xb3 9 ab ♘e7 10 c4 ♗b7 11 ♘c3 b4 12 ♘d5 a5 Suetin) 9 ♘c3 ♘xb3 10 ab ♘e7 11 de de 12 ♕e2 ±

7 … ♘xb3 8 ab f6 (8 … ed 9 ♕xd4 ♗g4 10 ♕d3 ♘e7 11 ♘c3 ♘c6 12 ♘d5 ♗d7 13 ♕c3 ± Serper-Akopian, Leningrad 1985) 9 ♘h4!? (9 c4 b4 10 ♘h4 ♘e7 11 ♗e3 g6 12 ♕d2 ed 13 ♗xd4 ♗g7 14 ♗e3 ± Ernst-Agdestein, Gausdal Z 1987) 9 … ♘e7 10 f4 ♗b7 11 d5 c6 12 c4 ± Arnason-Agdestein, Gausdal Z 1987

[4] 8 … ♗d7 9 ♕e1 ♘xb3 10 ab ♗e7 (10 … ♘e7 11 ♘c3 ♘c6 12 ♘xc6 ♗xc6 13 ♘d5 ♗b7 16 ♕c3 ± Kozlov-Shabanov, USSR 1985) 11 e5! c5 12 ed cd 13 ♕e5! ♕b8 14 ♗f4 ± Yudasin-Shabanov, USSR 1985

[5] 9 c4 c5 10 ♘f5 (10 ♘c2 ♘f6 11 ♘c3 ♗e7 12 ♘e3 ±) 10 … g6 11 ♘g3 ♗g7 12 ♘c3 b4 13 ♘d5 ± Tseshkovsky-Kupreichik, Minsk 1985

[6] 9 … c5 10 ♕e1 (10 ♗d5 ±) 10 … ♘xb3 11 ♘xb3 b4 12 ♗f4 ±

[7] 10 … ♘e7 11 ♘a5 ♗c8 12 ♖e1 c5 13 b4 ± *ECO*

[8] 13 ♘xb7 ♖xb7 14 ♕f3 ± Smagin-Kupreichik, Minsk 1985

[9] 5 ♘c3 b5 6 ♗b3 b4 7 ♘d5 fe 8 d4 ef 9 ♕xf3 ♗e7 ∞ Tiller-Cramling, Groningen 1978-79

[10] 5 … fe 6 ♘xe5 ♕h4 7 0-0 ♘f6 8 ♘c3 ♘d8 9 f3 b5 10 ♗b3 ±/±

[11] 6 … ♗b4+?! 7 c3! dc 8 ♘xc3 ♘ge7 9 0-0 ♗xc3 10 bc 0-0 11 ♗b3+ ♔h8 12 ♖e1 ± Lobron-Bialas, West Germany 1987

[12] 8 c3 dc 9 ♘xc3 (9 ♗b3 d5 10 ♘xc3 ♘a5 11 ♗xd5 c6 12 ♗b3 ♕xd1 13 ♗xd1 = Romanishin-Pytel, Jurmala 1983) 9 … 0-0 (9 … d5 10 ♗b3 = *ECO*; 10 ♗g5! ♔f8 11 ♖c1 ♗a7 12 ♗xc6 bc 13 ♘e2 c5 14 ♘f4 ± Watson-

Nunn, London 1984) 10 ♗b3+ ♔h8 11 ♘g5 ♕e8 ±

[13] 10 ... h6 11 ♘bd2 b5 12 a4 ♖b8 13 ab ab 14 ♘f1 ♗d7 15 c3 dc 16 ♕c2! ± Brzozka-Angelov, corr. 1985

[14] 13 ♘c4 ♕f6 14 ♘f3 ♘c6 15 ♘ce5 ♘xe5 16 ♘xe5 g6 17 ♗f4 ± Vukčević, Diaconescu, corr. 1985

[15] 5 d4 b5 6 ♗b3 ♘xd4 7 ♘xd4 ed 8 ♗d5 (8 c3 dc 9 ♕d5 ♗e6 =) 8 ... ♖b8 9 ♗c6+ ♗d7 10 ♗xd7+ ♕xd7 11 ♕xd4 ♘f6 12 0-0 ♗e7 = Medina-Keres, Wijk aan Zee 1969

[16] 5 ... ♗g4 6 h3 (6 ♘c3 ♘f6 7 h3 ♗xf3 8 ♕xf3 ♗e7 9 d3 ♘d7 = Ivanović-Mestrović, Yugoslav Ch 1978) 6 ... ♗xf3 7 ♕xf3 g6 8 ♘c3 ♗g7 = Wedberg-Plachetka, Skara 1980

[17] 6 0-0 g6 7 d4 ♗g7 8 ♗e3 ed 9 ♘xd4 ♘e5! 10 ♗xd7+ ♕xd7 11 ♕b3 ♘f6 12 ♘c3 0-0 ∞ Wedberg-Mortensen, Helsinki 1983

[18] 6 ... g6 7 d4 ed 8 ♘xd4 ♗g7 9 ♘xc6 bc 10 0-0 ♘f6 =

[19] 7 d4 ♗e7 8 0-0 ed 9 ♘xd4 0-0 10 ♗c2 ♘xd4 11 ♕xd4 b5 = Cirić-Keres, Wijk aan Zee 1970

[20] 9 ♘d5 ♗g4 10 ♗xc6 bc 11 ♘e3 ♗xf3 12 ♕xf3 g6 = Janošević-Bobotsov, Wijk aan Zee 1970

[21] Ljubojević-Ivkov, Hilversum 1973

[22] 7 ... ♘xd4 8 ♗xd4 ed 9 c3 d3 (9 ... dc 10 ♕h5 ± ECO) 10 ♕xd3 ♘f6 11 ♗g5 ♗e7 12 ♘d2 0-0 13 ♖ae1 ± Geller-Suetin, USSR 1980

[23] 8 ... dc 9 ♕d5 ♕e7 10 ♘xc3 ± Tseitlin-Klovans, USSR 1978

[24] 10 ♗g5 ♗e7 11 a4 ♘a5 12 ♗c2 ♘c4 13 ♖a2 ± ECO

[25] 13 ♗c2 ± Matanović-Ciocaltea, Havana Ol 1966

[26] 6 ... ♗h5 7 c4 ♘f6 8 ♘c3 ♘d7 9 g4 ♗g6 10 d4 f6 11 ♗e3 h5 12 ♕e2 ± Kapengut-Sakharov, USSR 1971

[27] 7 d3 ♕f6 8 ♗e3 ♗e7 9 ♘bd2 ♕g6 10 ♔h1 f5 ∞

[28] 7 ... ♕f6 8 ♗xc6+ bc 9 ♘bd2 ♗e6 10 ♘b3 ♕g6 11 ♘g5 ♗c8 12 de ± Kozlov-Vorotnikov, USSR 1979

[29] 10 ♗xf7+ ♕xf7 11 ♘g5+ ♔e8 12 c3 ∞

[30] 11 g3 ♘c6 12 f4 ♕e7 (12 ... c6 13 ♗e3 ♘xb3 14 cb d5 15 ♗c5 ∞/± Kapengut-Vorotnikov, USSR 1977) 13 fe ∞

[31] 13 cd ♗e7 14 de ♗xg5 15 ♕xd5 ♖c8 16 ♘c3 ♗xc1 17 ♖fxc1 (17 ♖axc1 g3! 18 ♕xd6 ♘g4 19 ♕xd8+ ♖xd8 20 ♘d1 gf+ 22 ♔xf2 ♘xe5 = Schutze-Kampfenkel, corr. 1983) ∞/± Mestel-Dawson, Brighton 1984

[32] 6 ... ♗g4 7 de (7 ♗e3 ♘f6 8 ♘c3 ♘d7 9 h3 ♗xf3 10 ♕xf3 ♗e7 11 ♕e2 ± Iskov-Lein, Copenhagen 1983-84) 7 ... de 8 ♘bd2 f6 9 ♕e2 ♘e7 10 ♘b3 ♘g6 11 ♕c4 ♕d7 12 ♗e3 ±/±

Zapata-Zysk, Dortmund 1984
6 ... ed and now:

[—] 7 ♘xd4 c5 8 ♗e2 (8 ♘c6 ♕h4 9 0-0 ♘e7 10 ♘a5 ♕xe4 11 c4 ∞ Gufeld-Knaak, Leipzig 1980) 8 ... ♘f6 9 ♘bc3 ♗b7 10 f3 ♖b8 11 0-0 g6 12 ♗e3 ♗g7 13 ♕d2 0-0 ∞ Chiburdanidze-Hort, Dortmund 1983

[—] 7 ♕xd4 c5 8 ♕d3 g6 (8 ... ♗b7 9 ♘c3 ♘e7 10 ♗g5! ♕d7 11 0-0-0 f6 12 ♗e3 0-0-0 13 ♕c4 ♕e8 14 ♖he1 ± Timman-Mortensen, Plovdiv 1983) 9 ♘c3 ♗g7 10 ♗g5 (10 ♗f4 ♘e7 11 0-0-0 0-0 12 ♕d2 ♖e8! ∞ Timman-Spassky, Linares 1983) 10 ... f6 11 ♗f4 (11 ♗h4?! ♘e7 12 0-0-0 ♗e6! 13 h3 0-0 14 g4 ♘c6 ∓ Timman-Spraggett, Taxco IZ 1985) ± Spraggett

[33] 7 ♘c3 ♗g4 (7 ... ♘e7 8 ♕d3 ♗e6 9 ♗e3 ♕b8 10 b3 ♕b4 11 ♗d2 ♕b7 12 0-0 ♘g6 13 de de 14 ♘a4 ± Cladouras-Nikolac, West Germany 1984-85) 8 ♗e3 ♕b8 9 b3 ♘e7 10 ♕d3 ♘g6 ∞/=

7 ♕d3 ♘e7 8 h4!? ± ECO

[34] 9 ... ♗e6 10 0-0-0 ♕b8 11 ♔b1 ♕b7 12 ♗c1! ♗e7 13 g3 ± Spassky-Lutikov, USSR 1979

9 ... ♗d7 10 h4 h5 11 de fe 12 ♘g5 ♗e7 13 ♕c4 ± Lutikov-Ciocaltea, Bucharest 1975

[35] 13 g3 ± Short-Smyslov, Subotica IZ 1987

[36] 7 d4 e4 8 ♘g5 d5 9 f3 h6 10 fe hg 11 ef ♗d6 12 ♘d2 ♕f6 (12 ... g4?! 13 ♕xg4 ♘f6 14 ♕e2+ ♔f8 15 ♘f3 ±/± Mehner-Hanich, corr. 1983) 13 ♗c2 0-0-0 14 ♘f3 ♖e8+ 15 ♔f2 g4 16 ♗g5 ♕f7 17 ♘h4 ♕h5 = Sarink-Toothill, corr. 1984

[37] 8 ♕b3 ♖b8 (8 ... b5 9 ♕d5 ♘d4 10 cd ♘e7 11 ♕e6 ♗xf1 12 ♗b3 ♗c4 13 ♗xc4 bc 14 de de 15 ♘c3 ♕d6 16 ♕xc4 ± Lanka-Bankieres, corr. 1983) 9 ♖e1 ♗e7 10 ♕d5 e4 11 ♘d4 ♘f6 12 ♕g5 ♘d7 13 ♕h5+ g6 14 ♕h3 ∞ Cole-Jacobs, corr. 1985

[38] 9 ♖e3 e4 10 ♘e1 ♗g5 11 ♖h3 ♘h6!? (11 ... ♘f6 12 ♗xd3 ed 13 ♖xd3 0-0 14 ♖h3 ± Kurtenkov-Angelov, corr. 1985) 12 ♘xd3 ed 13 ♖xd3 0-0 14 ♖h3 ♕e7 15 ♘a3 ♖ae8 16 ♘c2 ♕e2 ∞ Fodor-Bubenko, corr. 1981

[39] 9 ... e4 10 ♗xd3 ed 11 ♖e3 ♘h6 12 ♖xd3 0-0 13 ♖e3 ± Timoshchenko-Trapl, Decin 1978

[40] 11 ... ♕d7 12 de de 13 ♘bd2 0-0-0 14 ♘f1 ♗d6 15 ♗g5 ± Rittner-Condali, corr. 1984

11 ... 0-0 12 de ♘xe5 13 ♘xe5 de 14 ♘d2 ♗c5 15 ♘b3 ♗b6 16 ♗e3 ± Steffan-Kampfenkel, corr. 1983

[41] 13 ♘c3 ♔h8 (13 ... d5 14 ♗g5 ♕d7 15 ♘e5 ♘xe5 16 de ♘g4 17 ♗xe7 ♕xe7 18 ♘xd5 ♕h4 19 h3 ♗xf2 20 ♕b3 ♕h8 21 e6! ± Dvoiris-Vorotnikov, USSR 1985) 14 ♘g5 ♘xd4 15 ♕d3 h6 16 ♕xd4 hg 17 ♗xg5 ♕d7 18 ♘d5! ± Glek-Vorotnikov, USSR 1986

	4	5	6	7	8	9	10	11	12	
8	...	c3	d4	♗b3[43]	♘bd2[44]	♘c4	♘e3[45]	♘xg5!	g3	±
	d6	♗d7	♘ge7[42]	h6	♘g6	♗e7	♗g5	hg	♘ce7[46]	
9	...	...	...	0-0[47]	de[48]	♗e3	♘bd2	♗c5	♗b3	∞
	...	...	g6	♗g7	de[49]	♘f6[50]	0-0[51]	♖e8	h6[52]	
10	...	...	...	...	♖e1	♗e3[54]	♘bd2[55]	♗b3	de	±
	...	...	...	...	♘ge7[53]	0-0	♕e8	b6	de[56]	

[42] 6 ... ♘f6 7 0-0 ♕e7 (7 ... g6 8 ♗xc6 ♗xc6 9 de ± *ECO*) 8 ♖e1 (8 ♗b3 h6 9 ♖e1 g6 10 ♗d5 ♗g7 11 de de 12 b3 ♘h5 13 a4 ♕f6 ∞ de Firmian-Ivkov, Baden-Baden 1981) 8 ... g6 9 ♘bd2 ♗g7 10 ♘f1 0-0 11 ♗g5 h6 12 ♗h4 ♕e8 (12 ... b5?! 13 ♗b3 ♖fe8 14 ♘e3 ♕f8 15 de ♘xe5 16 ♘xe5 ♖xe5 17 f4 ± Klundt-Hort, Berlin 1984) 13 ♗c2 ♘h5 14 ♘e3 ∞ Jansa-Psakhis, Bor 1985; 10 de de 11 ♘f1 0-0 12 ♗g5 ± *ECO*

[43] 7 0-0 ♘g6 8 ♘bd2 (8 c4 ed 9 ♗xc6 bc 10 ♕xd4 f6 11 c5 dc 12 ♘c3 ∞ Murei-Rodriguez, Moscow IZ 1982) 8 ... ♗e7 9 ♖e1 0-0 10 h3 ♗f6 11 ♘f1 ♖e8 12 ♘g3 ♘h4 ∞

7 ♗g5 f6 8 ♗e3 ♘g6 9 ♘bd2 ♗e7 10 ♗b3 ♘a5 11 ♗c2 c5 12 d5 ♖c8 13 b3 0-0 14 0-0 b5 ∞ Marjanović-Pliester, Amsterdam 1986

[44] 8 ♕e2 ♘g6 9 ♘c4 ♕f6 10 d5 b5 11 ♕e2 ♘a5 12 ♗d1 c6! 13 a4 ♕d8! ∓ Donchev-Ciocaltea, Lucerne Ol 1982

8 h4!? ed 9 ♘xd4 ♘g6 10 h5 ♘ge5 11 f4 ♘g4 12 ♘e6! ♗xe6 13 ♗xe6 ♘f6 14 ♗f5 ♘e7 15 ♗g4 ± Ciocaltea-Rantanen, Bourgoin-Jallieu 1982

8 ♘a3!? ♘g6 9 ♘c4 ♗e7 10 ♘e3 0-0 11 0-0 ♖e8 12 ♖e1 ♗f6 13 ♘d5 ed 14 ♘xd4 ± Short-Hort, Wijk aan Zee 1986

[45] 10 0-0 ♗g5 11 ♘xg5 (11 ♘e3 ♗xe3 12 ♗xe3 0-0 13 ♘d2 ♘a5 =) 11 ... hg 12 g3 ♕f6 13 de de 14 f3 0-0-0 ∞ Formanek-Norman, London 1979

[46] **13 ♕f3!** ± Balashov-Ye Rongguang, Hangzoi 1983

13 ♗d2 f6 14 ♕e2 ♗b5 15 c4 ± *ECO*

[47] 7 de ♘xe5 8 ♕xe5 de 9 0-0 ♘f6 (9 ... ♗g7 – 7 0-0 ♗g7 8 de) 10 ♗g5 ♗e7 11 ♘d2 ± Ambroz-Mikh.Tseitlin, Prague Z 1985

7 ♗g5 f6 8 ♗e3 ♘h6 9 h3 (9 b4 ♗g7 10 ♗b3 ♕e7 11 0-0 ♘f7 12 ♗d5 ed 13 ♘xd4 0-0 14 ♘d2 ♔h8 ∞/= Kindermann-Mokry, Trnava 1987) 9 ... ♗g7 10 0-0 ♘f7 11 ♘bd2

(11 de fe 12 c4 0-0 13 ♘c3 b6 ∞ Grünfeld-Spassky, Brussels 1985) 11 ... 0-0 12 ♖e1 ♕e7 13 ♗c2 ♘cd8 14 ♘f1 ♘e6 = Sokolov-Salov, Leningrad 1987

[48] **8 h3** ♘f6 9 ♖e1 0-0 10 ♘bd2 ♕e8 11 ♗c2 ♗h6 12 ♘c4 ♗xc1 13 ♖xc1 ±/= Ljubojević-Salov, Szirak IZ 1987

8 d5 ♘b8 (8 ... ♘ce7 9 ♗xd7+ ♕xd7 10 c4 h6 11 ♘c3 f5 12 ef ♘xf5 13 ♘e4 ♘f6 14 ♘xf6+ ♗xf6 15 ♘d2 ± Short-Spassky, London 1986; 12 ♘d2 ♘f6 13 f3 0-0 14 b4 ± Sax-Smyslov, Subotica IZ 1987) 9 ♗c2 a5 10 c4 ♘a6 11 ♘c3 ♗h6 ∞ Tringov-Rukavina, Vrnjačka Banja 1986

[49] 8 ... ♘xe5 9 ♘xe5 de 10 f4 ♗xa4!? (10 ... ♘e7 11 f5! ±/± Geller-Savon, Moscow 1987) 11 ♕xa4+ b5 12 ♕b3 ef ∞ Geller-Smyslov, Sochi 1986

[50] 9 ... ♘ge7 ± *ECO*

[51] 10 ... ♕e7 11 b4 b6 12 ♗b3 0-0 13 ♖e1 (13 ♕c2 ± *ECO*) 13 ... h6 14 ♕c2 ♘h5 15 ♗d5 ♖ab8 16 ♘f1 ♔h8 17 ♕e2 a5 18 a3 ♕e8 = Tseshkovsky-Malanyuk, USSR Ch 1986

[52] 13 ♖e1 ♘a5 14 ♗c2 b6 15 ♗a3 ♕c8 ∞ Qi-Spassky, Lucerne 1985

[53] 8 ... ♕e7 9 d5 ♘b8 10 c4 ♘f6 11 ♘c3 0-0 12 b4 ± Ghinda-Gavrilakis, Dubai Ol 1986; 9 h3 ♘f6 10 ♘bd2 ± Sax-Xu, Subotica IZ 1987

[54] 9 de de (9 ... ♘xe5 10 ♘xe5 ♗xe5 11 ♗b3 ♘c6 12 ♘d2 ♗g7 13 ♘f3 ± Short-Spraggett, Montpellier C 1985) 10 ♗g5 f6 11 ♗e3 b6 12 h3 0-0 13 b4 ♔h8 14 ♗b3 ♕e8 15 ♖e2 ♖d8 16 ♖d2 ± Hansen-Bjarnason, Gausdal 1987

[55] 10 de ♘xe5 11 ♘xe5 ♗xa4 (11 ... ♗xe5 12 ♗b3 ♘c6 13 ♘d2 ♗g7 14 ♘f3 h6 15 ♘d4 ± *ECO*) 12 ♕xa4 de 13 ♘d2 ♘c6 14 ♖ad1 ♕e7 15 ♕b3 b6 16 ♘f3 ± Jansa-Dominguez, Dubai Ol 1986

[56] 13 ♘c4 ♔h8 14 ♕c1 ♗g4 15 ♘g5 ± Karpov-Spassky, Bugojno 1986

	5	6	7	8	9	10	11	12	13	
1	d4[1]	e5[3]	0-0[4]	♗g5	♗xe7	♗xc6	♘xd4			=
	ed[2]	♘e4	♘c5	♗e7	♕xe7	dc	0-0			
2	♕e2	♗xc6[6]	♘c3[7]	d4	♘xd4	♘f5[8]	♗d2	0-0-0[9]	ef	=
	♗e7[5]	dc	♘d7	ed	0-0	♗f6	♘c5	♗xf5		
3	d3	c3	♘bd2[11]	♘f1	♘g3	0-0	h3	♗e3	b4[13]	∞
	d6	g6[10]	♗g7	0-0	♗d7[12]	♖e8	h6	d5		

[1] **5 ♗xc6** dc 6 d3 (6 ♘c3 ♗d6 7 d4?! ♗b4 ∓ Kurajica-Karpov, Skopje 1976; 7 d3 c5 =) 6 ... ♗d6 7 ♘bd2 c5 8 ♘c4 ♘d7 9 a4 b6 =
  5 ♘c3 b5 6 ♗b3 ♗e7 7 d3 (7 a4 b4 8 ♘d5 ♘xe4 ∓; 7 ♗d5 b4 =) 7 ... d68 ♗d5 ♘a5 =

[2] **5 ... ♘xe4** 6 ♕e2 ±
  5 ... ♘xd4 6 ♘xd4 ed 7 e5 ♘e4 8 ♕xd4 ♘c5 9 ♘c3 ♗e7 10 ♕g4 ± Short-Korchnoi, London 1980

[3] 6 0-0 ♗e7 – 5 0-0 ♗e7 6 d4

[4] 7 ♘xd4 ♘xf2 8 ♔xf2 ♕h4+ 9 ♔e3 ♕xd4+ 10 ♕xd4 ♘xd4 11 ♖xd4 c5+ intending 12 ... b5 ∓

[5] **5 ... b5** 6 ♗b3 ♗c5 7 c3 0-0 8 d3 d6 9 ♗g5 ∞; 7 a4 ♖b8! 8 ab ab 9 ♘c3 0-0! =
  5 ... ♕e7 6 0-0 g6 7 d4 (7 c3 ♗g7 8 ♖e1 0-0 9 d4 d6 =) 7 ... ♘xd4 8 ♘xd4 ed 9 e5 ♘d5 10 ♗b3 ♘b6 11 c3 ∞ Gurgenidze-Mikhalchishin, Tbilisi 1980

[6] 6 c3 b5 7 ♗c2 0-0 8 d4 d6 =

[7] 7 b3 ♗d6 8 ♗b2 ♕e7 9 d3 0-0 (9 ... ♗g4!? intending ... 0-0-0) 10 ♘bd2 b5 11 ♘h4 ♖e8

[8] 10 ♗e3 ♗b4 11 0-0 ♗xc3 ∓ Gurgenidze-A.Petrosian, USSR Ch 1985
  10 ♗d2 ♗f6 11 ♘f3 ♖e8 12 0-0-0 ♕e7 13 ♖he1 b5 ∞/∓ Gurgenidze-Yakovich, Kharkov 1985

[9] 12 ♘g3 b5 13 f4 b4 14 ♘d1 a5 ∓ Gurgenidze-Agzamov, USSR Ch 1985

[10] 6 ... ♗e7 7 ♘bd2 0-0 8 ♘f1 b5 9 ♗b3 (9 ♗c2 d5 10 ♕e2 ♖e8 =) 9 ... d5 (9 ... ♘a5 10 ♗c2 c5 =) 10 ♕e2 de (10 ... ♗e6!?) 11 de ♗e6 12 ♗xe6 fe = Fischer-Smyslov, Havana 1965

[11] **7 d4** ed! 8 cd (8 e5!? de 9 ♘xe5 ♗d7 = Dorfman) 8 ... b5 9 ♗b3 ♗g7 10 0-0 0-0 11 h3 ♘a5 12 ♗c2 ♖e8 13 ♖e1 c5 ∞/∓ Romanishin-Dorfman, Lvov 1984
  7 0-0 ♗g7 8 ♖e1 0-0 =

[12] 9 ... h6 10 0-0 b5 11 ♗c2 a5 (11 ... d5!?) 12 h3 ♗d7 13 d4 a4 14 ♗e3 ♕e7 ∞/= Smyslov-Ciocaltea, Havana 1965

[13] Hort-Torre, Malta Ol 1980

391

Ruy Lopez V   1 e4 e5 2 ♘f3 ♘c6 3 ♗b5 a6 4 ♗a4 ♘f6 5 0-0

	5	6	7	8	9	10	11	12	13	
1	...	c3[1]	d4	♖e1[4]	♘bd2	♘xe4	♖xe4	♗g5	de	±/±
	♗c5	♘xe4[2]	♗b6[3]	f5	0-0	fe	d6	♕e8	♗f5[5]	
2	...	♗b3	d4[7]	♘xd4[8]	e5[9]	c3[10]	♕f3	ed	d7+[11]	=
	b5	♗b7[6]	♘xd4	ed	♘e4	dc	d5	♕f6!	♔d8![12]	
3	...	...	c3	d4	♗c2	b4[15]	♗xe4	♖e1	♘xd4	∞
	...	...	♘xe4[13]	♘a5[14]	ed	♘c4	♗xe4	d5[16]	♗d6[17]	

1 e4 e5 2 ♘f3 ♘c6 3 ♗b5 a6 4 ♗a4 ♘f6 5 0-0 b5 6 ♗b3 ♗b7 7 ♖e1 ♗c5

	8	9	10	11	12	13	14	15	16	
4	c3	d4	a4[19]	♘h4[20]	♕d3	h3	ab	♘a3[21]	♘f5	∞
	d6[18]	♗b6	h6	♘e7	♕d7	0-0-0	ab	g5	c6	
5	...	...	♗g5	♗h4	a4	ab	♗xf6[24]	♗d5	♔h1	±
	...	...	h6[22]	♕d7[23]	0-0-0	ab	gf	♖hg8[25]	♕g4[26]	
6	...	...	...	...	a4	ab	♖xa8	cd	♘c3[28]	∞
	...	...	...	0-0	ed[27]	ab	♗xa8	♖e8	g5[29]	
7	...	...	...	...	♕d3	♘bd2	♗c2	d5	♕e2	±
	...	...	...	...	♖e8[30]	♘a5	c5	c4	♔h7[31]	

---

[1] 6 d3 b5 7 ♗b3 d6 8 ♘c3 ♗g4 = Jansa-Nogueiras, Novi Sad 1978

6 ♘xe5 ♘xe5 (6 ... ♘xe4 7 ♘xc6 dc 8 ♕e2 ±) 7 d4 ♘xe4 8 ♖e1 ♗e7 9 de (9 ♖xe4 ♘g6 10 c4 0-0 11 ♘c3 ±) 9 ... ♘c5 10 ♘c3 0-0 11 ♗f4 ♘xa4 12 ♘xa4 f6 13 ♕d5+ ♔h8 14 ♖ad1 fe 15 ♕xe5 ± Klompus-Jaroš, corr. 1965-66

[2] 6 ... 0-0 7 d4 ed 8 cd ♗b6 9 ♘c3 d6 10 h3 ±

6 ... ♗b6 7 d4 (7 ♖e1 d6 8 d4 ±) 7 ... ♘xe4 – 6 ... ♘xe4

6 ... ♗a7 7 d4 ♘xe4 (7 ... b5 8 ♗b3 ♕e7 9 ♗d5 ±) – 6 ... ♘xe4

[3] 7 ... ♗a7 and now:

8 ♕e2 f5 9 ♘bd2 0-0 10 ♘xe4 fe 11 ♕xe4 d5 12 ♗b3 ♗e6 13 ♕e3 ♖f5 14 ♘g5 ♕d7 (14 ... ♕e8 15 ♗c2 e4 16 f3 h6 17 ♘xe6 ♕xe6 18 ♗d2 ± Rauzer-Ragozin, USSR 1936) 15 ♗c2 e4 16 ♕g3 ♖af8 17 ♗e3 ± Rauzer-Budo, USSR 1936

8 ♖e1 f5 9 ♘bd2 (9 ♖xe4!? e6 10 ♗g5 ♘e7 11 ♘xe5 0-0 12 ♕g4 c6 13 ♕h4 ♖e8 14 ♘d2 d5 15 ♘xe4 ♗b8 16 ♘f6+ gf 17 ♗xf6 ±/± Aleksandrov-Tanin, corr. 1984) 9 ... 0-0 10 ♘xe4 fe 11 ♖xe4 d6 12 ♗g5 ♕e8 13 de ♗f5 14 ♖f4! ± ECO

[4] 8 ♕e2 f5 9 ♘bd2 0-0 10 ♘xe4 fe 11 ♕xe4 d5 12 ♗b3 ♗e6 13 ♕e3 ♖f5 14 ♘g5 ♗f7 15 ♕g3 ♕f6 16 ♗c2 ± Kuzmin-Kirov, Sochi 1976

[5] 14 ♖e1?! ♕g6 15 ♗xc6 bc 16 ♗e3 ♗g4 17 ♕b3+ d5! ∞/∓ Lyubomirov-Grozhdensky, corr. 1976

14 ♕d5+! ♗e6 15 ♕d2 ♕g6 16 ♗c2 ±/± Radchenko

[6] 6 ... ♘xe4 7 a4 (7 ♖e1 d5 8 ♘c3 ♘xc3 9 dc ♗e6 10 a4 ±/±) 7 ... ♗b7 8 d4 ed 9 ♖e1 d5 10 ♗xd5 ♕xd5 11 ♘c3 ♕d8 12 ♘xe4 ± Keres

6 ... d6 7 c3 ♗g4 (7 ... ♗e7 8 d4 ±) 8 d3 ±; 8 ♖e1 ±

[7] 7 ♘c3 ♗e7 – 5 ... ♗e7

7 d3 ♗e7! (7 ... ♗c5 8 a4 d6 9 ab ab 10 ♖xa8 ♗xa8 11 ♘c3 ± Lechtynsky-Belyavsky, Vilnius 1978) – 5 ... ♗e7

[8] 8 ♗xf7+ ♔xf7 9 ♘xe5+ ♔g8 10 ♕xd4 c5 and now:

11 ♗e3 ♕c7 12 ♕g3 ♘xe4 13 ♕f4 d5 ∓ Hecht-Malanyuk, Moscow 1985

11 ♕d1 ♕e8 12 ♘f3 (12 ♘g4 ♘xg4 13 ♕xg4 ♕xe4 14 ♕h3 ♗c6 15 c3 ♖e8 ∓ Gurgenidze-Mikhalchishin, USSR 1976) 12 ... ♕xe4 13 ♗g5!? ♘c6 14 ♘c3 ♗g4 15 ♖e1 b4 16 ♕e2 c4 ∞ Vitolins-Chandler, Jurmala 1983

[9] 9 c3 ♘xe4 10 ♖e1 ♗e7 11 ♕g4 0-0 12 ♖xe4 ♗xe4 13 ♕xe4 ♗f6 = Byrne-Smejkal, Leningrad 1973

[10] 10 ♕f3 ♕e7 11 ♘d2 ♘c5 12 ♗d5 c6 13 ♘e4 ♘xe4 14 ♗xe4 0-0-0 15 a4 b4 ∞ G.Garcia-A.Rodriguez, Havana 1983

[11] 13 ♖e1 0-0-0 14 dc ♔xc7 15 ♕xf6 ♘xf6 16 ♘xc3 ♗c5 = Vitolins-Mikhalchishin, USSR 1978

[12] 14 ♕xf6+ ♘xf6 15 ♘xc3 ♔xd7 16 ♗f4 = Hort

[13] 7 ... h6 8 d4 d6 9 ♕e2! g6 (9 ... ♗e7 10 ♖d1 ♘d7 11 ♘bd2 0-0 12 ♘f1 ♖e8 13 ♘g3 ♗f8 ± Petrushin-Malanyuk, Tallinn 1983) 10 a4 ♗g7 11 de de 12 ab ab 13 ♖xa8 ♕xa8 14 ♘a3 0-0 15 ♘xb5 ± Popović-Tal, Subotica IZ 1987

[14] 8 ... d5 9 de ♘a5 10 ♗c2 ♕d7 11 ♘d4! c5 12 ♘b3 ♘xb3 13 ab ♗e7 14 ♕e2 ± Plaskett-Flear, Hastings 1984-85
8 ... ♗e7!? 9 ♖e1 d5 10 de ♘a5 11 ♗c2 0-0 ∞/=

[15] 10 ♗xe4 ♗xe4 11 ♖e1 d5 12 ♘xd4 c5 13 f3 cd 14 fe de 15 ♕g4 ♕d5 = Hellers-Mortensen, Gausdal Z 1987

[16] 12 ... f5?! 13 ♕xd4! ± Larsen

[17] 14 ♗3 ♕h4 15 h3 ♕g3 16 ♘f5 ♕h2+ 17 ♔f2 0-0-0 18 fe de! 19 ♕g4 (19 ♘xd6+ ♖xd6 20 ♕g4+ ♔b8 21 ♗f4 ♖f6 = Chandler-Jacobs, London 1986) 19 ... ♔b8 (19 ... ♘e5 20 ♕xe4 ♖he8 21 ♗g5! ± Abramović-Flear, Brussels 1986) 20 ♕xe4 ♖he8 21 ♕xe8 ♖xe8 22 ♖xe8+ ♔b7 ∞ Ornstein

[18] 8 ...♗b6 9 a4 0-0 10 d3 h6 11 ab ab 12 ♖xa8 ♕xa8 13 ♘a3 ♕a7 14 ♖e2 ♘g4 15 d4 ∞/± Karpov-F.Garcia, Bilbao 1987; 9 d4 ±
8 ... 0-0 9 d4 ♗b6 10 ♗e3 d6 – 8 ... d6

[19] 10 ♘h4 ♘e7 11 ♕f3 h6 12 ♘d2 ♕d7 13 ♘f1 ♕g4 14 ♕xg4 ♘xg4 15 f3 ed (15 ... ♘f6 16 ♗e3 ed 17 ♗xd4 ± Kapengut-Kupreichik, USSR 1973) 15 fg dc+ ∞; 10 ... ♕d7!? 11 ♗g5 0-0-0 12 d5 ♘e7 ∞
10 ♗e3 0-0 11 ♘bd2 ♕d7 12 ♘f1 ♔h8 13 ♘g3 f6 14 ♗e3 ± Khalifman-Mikhalchishin, USSR 1986; 11 ... h6 12 h3 ed 13 cd ♘b4 14 ♕b1 c5 15 a3 ♘c6 16 e5 de ∞ Khalifman-Malanyuk, Minsk 1985

[20] 11 ab ab 12 ♖xa8 ♕xa8 13 ♘a3 ed 14 ♘xb5 0-0 =
11 ♗c2 0-0 12 ab ab 13 ♖xa8 ♕xa8 14 d5 ♘e7 15 h3 ♘g6 ∞

[21] 15 ♗xf7 ♖hf8 16 ♗b3 d5 ∓ Arnason-Timman, Reykjavik 1987; 16 ♗g6 ♘xg6 17 ♘xg6 ♖f7 ∞

[22] 10 ... ♕d7 11 a4 0-0-0 12 ab ab 13 ♘a3 ♖de8 14 ♘xb5 ed 15 ♗xf6 gf 16 ♘bxd4 ±/± Pankov-Fadeyev, USSR 1986

[23] 11 ... ♕e7 12 a4 g5 13 ♗g3 h5 (13 ... 0-0-0 14 ab ab 15 ♘a3 ♘a7 16 ♕d3 ± Arseniev-

Baikov, USSR 1979) 14 ab ab 15 ♖xa8+ ♗xa8 16 h4 g4 17 ♘g5 ♘d8 18 ♕d3 ±; 12 ♗d5!? g5 13 ♗g3 0-0-0 14 a4 h5 15 ab ab 16 h4 g4 17 ♘fd2 ± Fomin-Guseinov, Moscow 1972

[24] 14 ♘a3 g5 15 ♗g3 h5 and now:
16 de?! h4 17 ef hg 18 hg g4 19 ♘d4 ♖h7 20 ♗d5 ♖dh8 ∓
16 h4 gh 17 ♗xh4 ♖h6 18 ♘c2!? (18 ♗xb5 ♖g8 19 ♕d3 ed 20 cd ♘b4 ∞ Marjanović-Chandler, Minsk 1982) 18 ... ♖g8 19 ♘g5 ♖hg6 20 ♗xf7 ♖xg5 21 ♗xg8 ♖xg8 22 ♗xf6 ♕h3 ∞ Chepurnoi-Tsaturian, corr. 1984

[25] 15 ... ♖dg8 16 ♔h1! ♖h7 17 ♖g1 ± Klovans-Kozlov, USSR 1982
15 ... f5 16 ♕d3! ±/± Rogers-Flear, Szirak 1986

[26] 16 ... ♘e7?! 17 ♗xb7+ ♔xb7 18 ♘bd2 ± Klovans-Malanyuk, Lvov 1984
16 ... ♕g4 17 ♖g1 ed 18 cd f5 19 ♘c3 fe 20 ♗xe4 (20 ♘xe4 ♕f5 21 ♘c3 ♗b4 22 ♗xb7+ ♔xb7 = Klovans-Shirov, Riga 1987) 20 ... ♖de8 21 ♗d5 ± Ulibin-Shirov, USSR 1987

[27] 12 ... g5!? 13 ♘xg5 hg 14 ♗xg5 ∞ Dias-Rodriguez, Cienfuegos 1983
12 ... ♖e8 13 ab ab 14 ♖xa8 ♗xa8 15 d5 ♘a7 16 ♘a3 g5 17 ♗g3 c6 ∞ Ehlvest-Yakovich, Tallinn 1986

[28] 16 ♕d3 ♘a5 17 ♗c2 (17 ♗xf6 ♕xf6 18 ♗c2 g5! ∓ Tukmakov-Dorfman, USSR 1975) 17 ... g5 18 ♘xg5 hg 19 ♗xg5 ♖e6 20 ♖e2 ♔f8 21 ♘d2 ♘e4 ∓ Toothill-Kosenkov, corr. 1984
16 d5 ♘e5 17 ♘xe5 ♖xe5 18 ♗c2 c6 19 ♗g3 ♖e8 20 dc ♗xc6 ∓

[29] 17 ♗xg5 hg 18 ♘xg5 d5! (18 ... ♖e7 19 ♘d5 ♖xd4 ∞ Korolev-Kosenkov, corr. 1986) 19 ♘xd5 ♖xd5 20 ♕h5 ♕f6 ∓/∓ Janocha-Krosny, corr. 1984
17 ♗g3 ♘a5 18 e5 ♘xb3 19 ♕xb3 ♗xf3 20 gf ♗xd4 ∞ Kuper-Iskov, Zürich 1976
17 ♕d2! ♘a5 18 ♗c2 ♘c4 (18 ... b4? 19 ♘xg5 bc 20 ♕f4! ± Penrose-Vukčević, corr. 1984) 19 ♕c1 ∞

[30] 12 ... ♘a5 13 ♗c2 c5 14 de (14 d5 c4 15 ♕e2 g5?! 16 ♗g3 ♘h5 17 ♘bd2 ♘f4 18 ♗xf4 gf 19 ♔h1 ± Oll-Yakovich, USSR 1986; 15 ... g6 ∞ Mecking-Planinc, Mar del Plata 1971) 14 ... de 15 ♘xe5 ± Hort

[31] 16 ... g6 17 ♘f1 ♔g7 18 ♕d2 ♖h8 19 h3 ♕c7 20 ♘g3 ± Belyavsky-Dorfman, USSR Ch 1975
16 ... ♖c8 17 ♘f1 ♗h7 18 ♕d2 ♖g8 19 ♘e3 g5 20 ♗g3 ♘h5 21 ♘f5 ± Belyavsky-Vasyukov, USSR 1977
16 ... ♔h7 17 ♘f1 ♗c8 18 ♘e3 ♗d7 19 ♘d2 (19 ♘f5!?) 19 ... ♖c8! 20 ♔h1 ♘b7 ∞ Klovans-Malanyuk, Tbilisi 1985; 17 b4 cb 18 ab g5 19 ♗g3 ♖c8 20 c4 ± Savon-Gipslis, USSR 1970

Ruy Lopez VI   1 e4 e5 2 ♘f3 ♘c6 3 ♗b5 a6
4 ♗a4 ♘f6 5 0-0 ♘xe4 6 d4[1] b5[2] 7 ♗b3[3] d5[4] 8 de[5] ♗e6

	9	10	11	12	13	14	15	16	17	
1	a4	a5	♗e3[7]	cb	♕c2	♗c5	♕c1	♗xf8	♘bd2	∞
	b4[6]	♘c5	♘xb3[8]	♕d7	♘d8	♗f5[9]	♘e6	♖xf8	0-0-0[10]	
2	♗e3	c3	♗c2[13]	♘bd2	♕b1	♗f5[15]	♘b3[16]	♕xf5	♖ad1[17]	±
	♗e7[11]	♘c5[12]	♗g4	♘e6[14]	♗h5	♗g6	♗xf5	♕d7		
3	...	...	...	♖e1[18]	♘xe5	♗d4	♗xg7	♗d4	cd	∞
	...	...	♘d7	♘dxe5	♘xe5	♘c6[19]	♖g8	♘xd4	♗d6[20]	
4	♕e2	♗e3	♖d1[23]	♕xe3	♘bd2	♕e2	♕xd2	a4	ab	±/=
	♗c5[21]	0-0[22]	♗xe3	♘e7	♘f5	♘xd2	c6	♕b6	ab[24]	
5	...	♖d1	♗xd5[25]	♘c3	♖xd8+	♕e3	b3	♘e4	♗e1	±
	♗e7	♘c5	♗xd5	♗c4	♖xd8	b4	♗e6[26]	♖d1+	♘d4[27]	
6	...	...	c4	♗xc4	♗e3	♕xe3	♗b3	♘bd2[29]	♘d4[30]	=
	...	0-0	bc	♗c5[28]	♗xe3	♕b8	♘a5	♕a7	♘xd2[31]	
7	♘bd2	c3	♗xe6[34]	cd	♘e4[35]	♗e3	♕c2	♖ad1[38]	fe	∞/=
	♘c5[32]	d4[33]	♘xe6	♘cxd4	♗e7[36]	♘f5[37]	0-0	♘xe3	♕c8[39]	
8	...	...	♘g5	♘xe6	bc	♘f3[42]	♗xd1	♗e3	♗b3	±/=
	...	...	dc[40]	fe	♕d3[41]	♕xd1	♗e7	♘d3	♔f7[43]	

[1] **6 ♕e2 ♘c5 7 ♗xc6 dc 8 d4 ♘e6 9 de ♘d4! =**
   6 ♖e1 ♘c5 7 ♘xe5 ♗e7 8 ♗xc6 dc 9 d4 ♘e6 10 ♗e3 0-0 =

[2] **6 ... ed 7 ♖e1 d5 8 ♘xd4 ♗d6 9 ♘xc6 ♗xh2+ 10 ♔h1! ♕h4 11 ♖xe4+ de 12 ♕d8+ ♕xd8 13 ♘xd8+ ♔xd8 14 ♔xh2 ± Capablanca-Ed.Lasker, New York 1915**
   6 ... ♗e7 7 ♖e1 f5 8 de 0-0 9 ♘c3 (9 ♗b3+ ♔h8 10 ♘c3 ± Shamkovich, Schiller) 9 ... ♘xc3 10 bc ♔h8 11 c4 ± Kristiansen-Smyslov, Copenhagen 1985; 7 ... b5 8 ♖xe4 d5! 9 ♘xe5 ♘xe5 10 ♗xb5+! ab 11 ♖xe5 0-0 ∞ Hellsten-Hawkes, corr. 1983

[3] **7 d5 ba! 8 dc d6 9 ♖e1 ♘f6! 10 c4 ♗e6 =**

[4] **7 ... ed 8 ♖e1 d5 9 ♘c3 ♗e6 10 ♘xe4 de 11 ♖xe4 ±**

[5] **8 ♘xe5 ♘xe5 9 de c6 10 ♗e3 (10 c3 ♗c5 =) 10 ... ♗e7 11 c3 0-0 12 f3 ♘c5 13 ♗c2 f5 14 ef ♖xf6 = Barle-Tukmakov, Yugoslavia v USSR 1976**

[6] **9 ... ♖b8 10 ab ab 11 c3 ±**
   9 ... ♘a5 10 ab ab (10 ... ♘xb3 11 cb ab 12 ♖xa8 ♕xa8 13 ♘d4 ±) 11 ♘d4 ♗c5 12 c3 0-0 13 ♗c2 ± Grigorov-Stoica, Bucharest 1980

[7] **11 ♗g5 ♕d7 12 ♘bd2 h6 13 ♗h4 ♗e7 14 ♗xe7 ♘xe7 15 ♘d4 0-0 = Kristiansen-Yusupov, Esbjerg 1980**

[8] **11 ... d4 12 ♗g5! ∞**

[9] 14 ... ♕c6 15 ♖c1 ♗xc5 16 ♕xc5 ♕xc5 17 ♖xc5 ♔d7 18 ♘d4 ♘b7 19 ♖c6 =

[10] L.Bronstein-Yusupov, Lucerne Ol 1982

[11] 9 ... ♗c5 10 ♕e2 – 9 ♕e2 (row 4)

[12] 10 ... 0-0 11 ♘bd2 ♗g4 12 ♘xe4 de 13 ♕d5! ± Alekhine-Teichmann, match 1921, and Kasparov-Yusupov, USSR Ch 1979
   10 ... ♕d7 11 ♘bd2 ♖d8 (11 ... ♘xd2 12 ♕xd2 ♘a5 13 ♗g5 c5 14 ♗xe7 ♕xe7 15 ♘g5 ± A.Sokolov-Yusupov, Montpellier C 1985) 12 ♘xe4 de 13 ♕xd7+ ♗xd7 14 ♘g5 ♘xe5 15 ♗d4 ♗xg5 16 ♗xe5 0-0 17 ♗xc7 ±/= Timman-Korchnoi, Reykjavik 1987

[13] 11 ♘bd2?! ♘d3

[14] 12 ... ♕d7 13 ♕b1 h5 (13 ... h6 14 ♘d4! ♘xe5 15 f4 ± Hulak-Hort, Wijk aan Zee 1983) 14 ♗xc5! ♗xc5 15 ♖e1 ♕e7 (15 ... ♗g6 16 e6) 16 b4 ♗b6 17 a4 ± Horvath-Karsa, Hungarian Ch 1982

[15] 14 a4 b4 15 a5 ♗g6 16 ♘b3 (16 c4 d4 17 ♗xg6 hg 18 ♕e4 0-0! 19 ♕xc6 de 20 fe ♕d3 =) 16 ... bc 17 bc ♖b8 18 ♗xg6 fg 19 ♕a2 ♕d7 20 ♖fd1 0-0 21 c4 ♖xf3 ∞ Lanka-Chekhov, USSR 1980
   14 b4 ♗g6 15 ♘b3 0-0 16 a4 ♕d7 ∞/=

[16] 15 ♖d1 0-0 16 a4 ♕d7 17 ab ab 18 ♖xa8 ♖xa8 19 ♘f1 ♖d8 20 ♘g3 b4 21 h4 ±/∞ Jansa-Bernal, Thessaloniki Ol 1984

[17] Klinger-Opl, Vienna 1984

[18] 12 ♗f4?! g5!
   12 ♘d4 ♘dxe5 13 f4 ♘c4! = Tal-Timman, match 1985

[19] 14 ... ♘g6 15 ♗xg7 ♖g8 16 ♗xg6 ♖xg7

17 ♗h5 (17 ♖xe6!?) 17 ... ♔f8 18 ♘d2 ♗d6 ∞
Kapengut-Kaidanov, USSR 1983
20 Watson-Kaidanov, Moscow 1985
21 9 ... ♘c5 10 ♖d1 ♗xb3?! (10 ... ♗e7 –
9 ... ♗e7) 11 ab ♕c8 12 c4! ± Smyslov-Euwe,
The Hague/Moscow 1948
22 10 ... ♕e7 11 ♖d1 ♖d8 12 ♘bd2 ♖xd2
13 ♕xd2 h6 14 ♖ad1 ± Parma-Korchnoi,
Rome 1981
23 11 ♘bd2 ♘xd2 12 ♕xd2 d4 13 ♗g5 ♕d7
14 h3 ♖fe8 15 ♖fe1 ♗b4 = Schmid-Korchnoi,
Lucerne Ol 1982
24 Balashov-Smyslov, Tilburg 1977
25 11 c4 d4 12 cb ♘xb3 (12 ... d3 13 ♕f1 ±)
13 ab ab 14 ♖xa8 ♕xa8 15 ♗g5 ♗xb3 16 ♖c1
♗xg5 17 ♘xg5 h6 18 ♘d2! hg 19 ♘xb3 ±
A.Rodriguez-Agzamov, Cienfuegos 1984
26 15 ... bc? 16 ♗a3 ±±
27 18 ♗b2 ♘xc2 19 ♕e2 ♖xa1 20 ♗xa1
♘xa1 21 ♘xc5 ♗xc5 22 ♘d3 ♗b6 (22 ... ♗e7
23 ♘f4 ±) 23 ♘xb4 0-0 24 ♘c6 ± Timman-
Yusupov, Montpellier C 1985
28 12 ... ♕d7 13 ♘c3 ♘xc3 14 bc f6 15 ef
♗xf6 16 ♘g5 (16 ♕xe6+ ♕xe6 17 ♗xd5
♕xd5 18 ♖xd5 ♘b4 19 ♖c5 ♘c2 20 ♖b1
♖ab8 = Larsen; 16 ♗g5 ♔h8! = Sigurjonsson-
Olafsson, Geneva 1977) 16 ... ♗xg5 17 ♗xg5 h6
18 ♗e3 ♕d6 19 ♗b3 ♘e5 ∞ Korchnoi
29 16 ♘e1 ♕b6 (16 ... ♘xb3!? 17 ab f5)
17 ♕xb6 cb = Karpov-Korchnoi, match (12)
1978
30 17 ♕xa7 ♖xa7 18 ♖ac1 c5 19 ♘xe4 ♘xb3
20 ab de = Matanović-Korchnoi, Yugoslavia v
USSR 1966
31 18 ♕xd2 ♕b6 19 ♗c2 c5 = Kavalek-Karpov,
Montreal 1979, and Jansa-Stean, Vršac 1979
32 9 ... ♗c5 10 ♘xe4 de 11 ♘g5 ±
9 ... ♗e7 10 c3 – 9 c3
33 10 ... ♘xb3 11 ♘xb3 ♗e7 12 ♘fd4! ±

Kuzmin-Belyavsky, USSR 1977
10 ... ♗g4 11 h3 ♗h5 12 ♗c2 d4 (12 ...
♗e7 or 12 ... ♕d7 – 9 c3 ♘c5) 13 ♘b3 d3
14 ♗b1 ♘xb3 15 ab ♗g6 16 ♗e3 ±
34 11 cd ♘xd4 12 ♘xd4 ♕xd4 13 ♗xe6 ♘xe6
14 ♕f3 ♖d8 15 a4 (Capablanca-Lasker, St
Petersburg 1914) 15 ... ♗b4! =
35 13 a4 ♗e7 14 ♘xd4 (14 ab ♗xb5 = Sax-
Yusupov, Sofia 1984) 14 ... ♕xd4 (14 ... ♘xd4
15 ♘e4 ♘e6?! 16 ♗e3 ± Karpov-Korchnoi,
match (18) 1981) 15 ab ♕xe5 16 ba 0-0 17 ♘f3
♕b5 = Psakhis-Dolmatov, USSR Ch 1981
36 13 ... ♕d5 14 ♘xd4 ♘xd4 15 ♘c3 ♕d7
16 ♗e3 ♗c5 17 ♕h5 ± Romanishin-Yusupov,
USSR Ch 1981
37 14 ... ♘xf3+ 15 ♕xf3 0-0 16 ♖fd1 ±
Karpov-Korchnoi, match (14) 1981
14 ... c5 15 b4! ♘xf3+ 16 ♕xf3 c4 17 ♖fd1 ±
Pisarev-Sobol, USSR 1978
38 16 ♘eg5 ♗xg5 17 ♘xg5 (Karpov-Korchnoi,
match (16) 1981) 17 ... h6 =
16 ♘f6+ ♗xf6 17 ♕xf5 ♗e7 18 ♖ad1
♕c8 = van der Wiel-Korchnoi, Sarajevo 1984
39 18 ♘d4 ♘xd4 19 ed ♕e6 = Chandler-
Yusupov, Minsk 1982, Short-Yusupov, Montpellier C 1985, and Hübner-Ljubojević, Tilburg
1985
18 h3 ♖d8 =/∞ Karpov-Yusupov, Linares
1983, and Tal-Korchnoi, Reykjavik 1987
40 11 ... ♕xg5 12 ♕f3 0-0-0! (12 ... ♔d7?!
13 ♗d5; 12 ... ♗d7?! 13 ♗xf7+) 13 ♗xe6+
(13 ♕xc6 ♘xe5 14 ♕f3 ♕d5! =) 13 ... fe
14 ♕xc6 ♕xe5 15 b4! ± Timman-Smyslov,
West Germany 1979
41 13 ... ♘xb3 14 ab ♕d3 15 ♕h5+ g6 16 ♕g4
♕f5 17 ♕e2 intending ♘e4 ±
42 14 ♗c2?! ♕xc3 15 ♖b1 0-0-0 ∓
14 c4 ♘d4 15 ♕g4 0-0-0 ∞
43 Karpov-Korchnoi, match (10) 1978

	Ruy Lopez VII	1 e4 e5 2 ♘f3 ♘c6 3 ♗b5 a6						
	4 ♗a4 ♘f6 5 0-0 ♘xe4 6 d4 b5 7 ♗b3 d5 8 de ♗e6 9 c3							

	9	10	11	12	13	14	15	16	17
1	...	♗c2[1]	♖e1	h3	♘bd2	♘b3	♗xe4[5]	♕xd8	♖xe4	∞∞
	♘c5	♗g4	♗e7[2]	♗h5	0-0[3]	♘e4[4]	de	♖axd8	♖d1+[6]	

1 10 ♘d4!? ♘xe5 11 f4 ♘ed3 12 f5 ♗c8
13 ♗c2 ♘xc1 14 ♖e1+ ♘e4 15 ♘d2! ±
Rusakov-Shakhzadov, corr. 1983; 10 ... ♘xd4
11 cd ♘xb3 12 ♕xb3 c5 13 dc ♗xc5 14 ♕g3 ±
Ivkov-Lehmann, Yugoslavia v West Germany
1954
2 11 ... d4 12 h3 ♗h5 13 e6! fe (13 ... ♘xe6
14 ♗e4 ♕d7 15 cd ±) 14 cd ♗xf3 15 ♕xf3
♘xd4 16 ♕h5+ ±

3 13 ... d4 14 ♘b3 d3 15 ♗b1 ♘xb3 16 ab
♗g6 17 ♗e3 0-0 18 ♗d4 ♘xd4 19 cd ♗b4
20 ♖e3 ± Liberzon-Radashkovich, Israel 1974,
and Klovans-Numan, corr. 1986
13 ... ♕d7 14 ♘b3 ♘e6 – row 3
4 14 ... ♘e6 15 ♗f5 ♕d7 – row 3
5 15 ♗f4 ♗g6 =
6 18 ♔h2 f6 ∞ Mikhalchishin-Kaidanov,
Kuibishev 1986

Ruy Lopez VII   1 e4 e5 2 Nf3 Nc6 3 Bb5 a6
4 Ba4 Nf6 5 0-0 Nxe4 6 d4 b5 7 Bb3 d5 8 de Be6 9 c3   *continued*

	9	10	11	12	13	14	15	16	17	
2	...	Bc2	Re1	Nbd2	Nf1	Ne3	Qxf3	Qh5	Nf5[9]	∞
	Nc5	Bg4	Be7	Qd7[7]	0-0[8]	Bxf3	Nxe5	Ncd3	g6[10]	
3	...	...	...	...	Nb3	h3[11]	Bf5	Qd3[13]	Be3	±
	...	...	...	...	Ne6	Bh5	0-0[12]	Bg6	Ncd8[14]	
4	...	Nbd2[15]	Bc2	Nd4	cd	Bxd2	dc	Bb3	Qf3	±
	Be7	0-0[16]	f5[17]	Nxd4	Nxd2	c5	Bxc5	Qb6	Rad8[18]	
5	...	...	...	Nb3	Nfd4	Nxd4[19]	Nxe6	f3	a4	±
	...	...	...	Qd7	Nxd4	c5	Qxe6	Ng5	g6[20]	
6	...	Nbd2[21]	Bc2	Rxf2	ef	Kxf2	Nf1[23]	Be3[25]	Bd4[26]	±
	Bc5	0-0	Nxf2	f6	Bxf2+[22]	Qxf6	Ne5[24]	Rae8	Qh4+[27]	
7	...	...	...	Nb3	Nfd4	Nxd4	Qxd4[29]	Qd1	f3	±
	...	...	f5	Bb6	Nxd4	Bxd4[28]	c5	f4	Ng5[30]	
8	...	...	...	Nb3	Nfd4	cd[32]	Be3	Nd2[33]	Nxe4	±/=
	...	...	Bf5	Ng6[31]	Bxd4	a5	a4	a3	ab[34]	

[7]   **12 ... 0-0** 13 Nb3 Ne6 (13 ... Ne4 14 Bf4 f5 15 ef Bxf6 16 Qd3 ± Alekhine-Nimzowitsch, St Petersburg 1914) 14 Qd3 g6 15 Nbd4 ±
12 ... Bh5 13 Nf1 0-0 14 Ng3 Bg6 15 Be3 ± Short-Torre and Ljubojević-Torre, Brussels 1987

[8]   **13 ... Bh5** 14 Ng3 Bg6 15 h4! ± Mokry-Yusupov, Dubai Ol 1986, and A.Rodriguez-Xu Jun, Subotica IZ 1987
13 ... Rd8 14 Ne3 Bh5 (14 ... Bxf3 15 Qxf3 Nxe5 16 Qg3 Ng6 17 Nf5 ±) 15 Nf5 0-0 (15 ... Ne6 16 a4 ±) 16 Nxe7+ Nxe7 17 Be3 ± Geller-Hazai, Sochi 1982

[9]   17 Rd1 g6

[10]   18 Nh6+ Kg7 19 Qe2 Nxe1 20 Qxe5+ f6 21 Qxe1 Rae8 22 Qd1 f5 ∞ E.Vitolins-Lutovinov, corr. 1986

[11]   14 Qd3 Bh5 15 Nfd4 Bg6 = Schmid-Korchnoi, London 1979

[12]   15 ... Bg6 16 Nfd4 0-0 17 Bg4! ± Nunn-Tal, Naestved 1985

[13]   16 g4 Bg6 17 Be3 Ncd8 intending ... Nb7, ... c5 ∞ Tseshkovsky-Agzamov, USSR Ch 1981

[14]   18 Rad1 Bxf5 19 Qxf5 Nb7 20 Ng5 ± Korolev-Gott, corr. 1984

[15]   10 Be3 – 9 Be3

[16]   10 ... Nxd2 11 Qxd2 Qd7 12 Rd1 Rd8 13 Qf4 0-0 14 Qg3 ±

[17]   **11 ... Bf5** 12 Nd4 ±
11 ... Nxd2 12 Qxd2 f6 13 ef Bxf6 14 Ng5 ±
11 ... Nc5 12 Nb3 ±

[18]   18 Rac1 ± Short-Prasad, Subotica IZ 1987

[19]   14 cd a5 15 f3 a4 16 fe ab 17 Bxb3 fe 18 Be3 ±/= Grünfeld-Tal, Riga IZ 1979

[20]   **17 ... Rad8** 18 ab ab 19 Qe2 c4 20 Be3 ± Belyavsky-Tarjan, Bogotá 1979
17 ... g6 18 Qe2! (A.Rodriguez-Passerotti, Malta Ol 1980) 18 ... b4 19 cb c4 ± A.Rodriguez

[21]   10 Qd3 0-0 11 Nbd2 f5 12 ef Bxf6 13 a4 (13 Ng5 Ne5 14 Qg3 Qd6 15 Bc2 Bd7 ∞ Khalifman-Kaidanov, Kuibishev 1986) 13 ... Bf7 14 Ng5 (14 ab Bg6) 14 ... Ne5 15 Qg3 Qd6 16 Bc2 Bg6 (16 ... h6?! 17 Nxf7 ± A.Sokolov-Yusupov, match 1986) 17 Bxg6 Nxg6 =

[22]   13 ... Qxf6 14 Nf1 (14 Qf1 Rae8! ∞) 14 ... Bxf2+ – 13 ... Bxf2+

[23]   15 Kg1 Rae8 16 Qf1 Bf5 17 Bxf5 Qxf5 18 Nb3 Ne5 = Medina-Mocete, corr. 1974; 16 Nf1 Ne5 17 Be3 Nxf3+ 18 gf Qxf3 19 Qxf3 Rxf3 =

[24]   15 ... d4! 16 Qd3 (16 Be4 dc ∞; 16 cd? Nxd4 17 Be4 Rad8 ∓ Selke-Roth, corr. 1986) 16 ... g6 ∞ Monsalvo-Roth, corr. 1977

[25]   16 Kg1!? Nxf3+ 17 gf Qxf3 18 Qxf3 Rxf3 (Morović-Yusupov, Tunis IZ 1985) 19 Be3! Bh3 20 Bd4 ± Shamkovich

[26]   17 Bc5 Nxf3 18 gf Rf7 19 Kg2 d4! 20 Bxd4 Qg5+ 21 Ng3 c5 22 Bf2 Rxf3! 23 Kxf3 Bg4+ ±/= Kupreichik-Mikhalevsky, USSR 1981

[27]   18 Kg1 Nxf3+ 19 gf Qg5+ 20 Ng3 Bh3 21 a4 ± Tseshkovsky-Chekhov, Rostock 1984, and Enders-Chekhov, Dresden 1985

[28]   14 ... Qd7 15 f3 Nc5 16 Kh1 ±

[29]   15 cd f4 16 f3 Ng3 ∞ *ECO*

[30]   18 a4 ± Haag-Estrin, corr. 1979, and Rantanen-Ornstein, Reykjavik 1981

[31]   **12 ... Bxf2+** 13 Rxf2 Nxf2 14 Kxf2 Bxc2 15 Qxc2 f6 16 e6 Qd6 17 Be3 ± Morović-

Murei, Thessaloniki Ol 1984

12 ... ♗g4 13 h3 ♗h5 (13 ... ♗xf3 14 gf)
14 g4! ♗g6 15 ♗xe4 de 16 ♘xc5 ef 17 ♗f4 ±
Karpov-Korchnoi, match (14) 1978
[32] 14 ♘xd4 ♕d7! = Klovans-Dorfman, USSR
1981, and Korchnoi-Karl, Swiss Ch 1982

[33] 16 ♘c1 a3 17 ba ♖xa3 18 ♗b3 ♘c3
19 ♕d2 b4 20 ♘d3 ±/∞ Ljubojević-Timman,
Bugojno 1984
[34] 18 ♖b1 ♗xe4 19 ♖xb2 ♕d7 20 ♗d3 ♗xd3
21 ♕xd3 ±/= Karpov-Yusupov, USSR Ch
1983, and Popović-Timman, Sarajevo 1984

	Ruy Lopez VIII		1 e4 e5 2 ♘f3 ♘c6 3 ♗b5 a6 4 ♗a4 ♘f6 5 0-0 ♗e7						
	6	**7**	**8**	**9**	**10**	**11**	**12**	**13**	**14**	
1	♗xc6	d3[1]	♘bd2	♘c4[4]	b3[6]	♗b2	a4	h3	♘h2	±
	dc	♘d7[2]	0-0[3]	♗f6[5]	♖e8	c5	b6	♖e6[7]	♕e8[8]	
2	...	...	...	...	♘h4	♘f5[10]	ef	♕g4[13]	♖e1	=
	...	...	...	f6	♘c5[9]	♗xf5[11]	♕d5[12]	♖ad8[14]	♖fe8[15]	

---

[1] **7 ♕e2** ♗g4 8 h3 ♗xf3?! 9 ♕xf3 0-0 10 d3
♘d7 11 ♘c3 ♘c5 12 ♕g3 ♗d6 13 f4 ± Wolff-
Christiansen, US Ch 1985; 8 ... ♗h5 =
    7 ♖e1 ♘d7 8 d4 cd 9 ♕xd4 0-0 10 ♗f4
♘c5 11 ♕xd8 ♗xd8 12 ♘c3 h6 13 ♘d4 ♘e6 =
Ermenkov-Romanishin, Plovdiv 1983; 7 ...
♗g4 ∞ *ECO*
    7 ♕e1 ♘d7 8 d4 ed 9 ♘xd4 ♘c5! =
    7 ♘c3 ♗g4 8 h3 ♗h5 9 g4 (9 ♕e2 ♕c8
10 ♕e3 ♘d7 11 g4 ♗g6 12 d4 f6 13 ♘e2
h5 ∞/∓ Wolff-Kavalek, US Ch 1985) 9 ...
♗g6 (9 ... ♘xg4 10 hg ♗xg4 11 ♔g2 ♗c5
12 ♖g1 ♕f6 13 d3 h5 ∞ Large-Littlewood,
London 1983; 12 ♕e1!?) 10 ♘xe5 ♘xe4
11 ♖e1 ♘xc3 12 bc 0-0 = Boey-Miclot, corr.
1986
[2] **7 ...** ♗d6 8 d4 ♘xe4 9 ♕d3 f5 10 de ♗c5
11 ♗e3 ♗e6 12 ♘d4 ♕d5 ∞ Sax-Hresc,
Amsterdam 1983; 9 ♘bd2 ± *ECO*
    7 ... ♕d6 8 ♗g5 c5 9 ♘bd2 ♗e6 10 ♕e2
♘d7 11 ♗g4 ± ½-½ Martinović-Karpov,
Amsterdam "OHRA" 1985
[3] 8 ... f6!? 9 ♘h4 g6 10 ♘c4 ♘c5 11 ♗e3
(11 ♗h6 ♗e6 12 ♘a5 ♖b8 13 a4 ♗f7! ∞
Donchev-Lukacs, Wroclaw 1980) 11 ... 0-0
(11 ... ♗e6?! 12 ♘a5 ♗c8 13 f4 ef 14 ♖xf4
0-0 15 ♖f1 ± Wedberg-Pinter, Helsinki 1983)
12 g3 Lukacs, Hazai
[4] 9 b3 c5!? (9 ... f6 10 ♗b2 c5 11 ♘h4 ♘b8
12 ♘f5 ♗xf5 13 ef ♘c6 14 ♘e4 ♕d5 15 ♖e1 ±
Richardson-Sarink, corr. 1980) 10 ♗b2 ♗d6
11 ♘c4 ♖e8 12 a4 b6 13 ♖e1 f6 = Sarink-Bang,
corr. 1985
[5] 9 ... ♗d6 10 ♗d2 ♖e8 11 ♗e3 c5 12 a4
b6 =; 10 b3 c5 - 9 ... c5
[6] 10 b4!? ♖e8 11 ♗b2 g6 (11 ... b6 12 ♘c3
g6 13 ♘fd2 c5 14 a3 ± Timman-Najdorf, Mar
del Plata 1982) 12 ♗c3 ♗g7 13 ♕b1 ♕e7
14 a3 f6 15 ♘fd2 ± Malanyuk-Romanishin,

Lvov 1984
[7] 13 ... ♖b8 14 ♘h2 b5 15 ab ab 16 ♘e3 ±
Kholmov-Belyavsky, USSR 1982; 14 ♖a2!?
intending ♕a1 ± Kholmov
[8] 15 ♕d2 ♖b8 16 f4 ± Kholmov-Vasyukov,
Moscow Ch 1987
[9] 10 ... ♖e8 11 ♕f3 ♘f8 12 ♘f5 ♗d6 13 ♗e3
♗e6 14 ♖ad1 c5 15 ♔h1 b5 16 ♘d2 ∞/±
Pinal-Rivas Pastor, Havana 1983
[10] 11 ♕f3 ♘e6 12 ♘f5 (12 ♗e3 g6 13 ♕g3
♘g7 14 ♗h6 ♖f7 15 ♕e3 ♗e6 = Wedberg-
Hjartarson, Reykjavik 1984) 12 ... ♘d4
13 ♘xd4 ♕xd4 (13 ... ed!? 14 ♕g3 ♗e6
15 ♗f4 ♖c8 ∞ Wedberg-Geller, Reykjavik
1984) 14 ♗e3 ♕d8 15 ♘a5 ♗b4 = Hort-
Spassky, match 1977
[11] 11 ... g6 12 ♘xe7+ ♕xe7 13 ♗h6 (13 f4
ECO) 13 ... ♖f7 14 f4 ♗e6 15 ♘e3 ♔h8 16 fe
fe 17 ♖xf7 ♕xf7 18 ♕e1 ± West-Eltaher,
Dubai Ol 1986
[12] **12 ...** ♖e8 13 ♖e1 ♕d5 14 ♘d2 ♖ad8
15 ♕g4 – 12 ... ♕d5
    12 ... ♕d7 13 ♕g4 ♔h8 (13 ... ♖fe8 = *ECO*)
14 ♗d2 b5 15 ♘e3 ♖fe8 16 ♖ad1 ♗f8 17 b3
a5 18 ♗c3 ½-½ Tal-Balashov, Jurmala 1985
[13] 13 b3 ♖ad8 (13 ... e4! Sax) 14 ♗b2 ♖fe8
15 ♕g4 ♘d7 = Matanović-Geller, Monte Carlo
1967
[14] **13 ...** a5 14 b3 ♕d4 15 ♕xd4 ed 16 ♖e1
♔f7 17 ♗a3 b6 18 ♖e2 ♖fd8 19 ♖ae1 ±
Horvath-Psakhis, Sochi 1985
    13 ... ♖fe8 14 ♖e1 e4 15 ♘e3 ± Wedberg-
Karpov, Oslo 1984; 14 b3 e4 15 d4! ♕xd4
16 ♗h6 ♗f8 17 ♖fd1 ♕c3 18 ♖ac1 ±
Horvath-Barbero, Kecskemet 1986
[15] 15 ♘d2 ♗f8 (15 ... ♕f7 16 b3 a5 17 ♗b2
a4 ∞ Tal-Dorfman, Lvov 1984) 16 h3 ♕f7
17 b3 ♖d4 18 ♕e2 ♖ed8 = Kurajica-Gligorić,
Sarajevo 1983; 16 ♘e4!? Sax

397

	6	7	8	9	10	11	12	13	14	
3	d4	e5	♘xd4	♘f5	♗xc6	♘xe7+	♖e1	f3	b3[19]	∞/=
	ed[16]	♘e4	0-0[17]	d5	bc	♕xe7	♖e8[18]	♘d6	f6[20]	
4	...	♖e1	e5	♗f4[22]	♗b3	c3	h3	g4	cd	∞/=
	...	0-0[21]	♘e8	b5[23]	d5	♗g4[24]	♗h5	♗g6	♘b4[25]	
5	...	...	e5[26]	♖xe5[28]	♖e1	♘xd4	♕f3	♘c6	♕xc6	=
	...	b5	♘xe5[27]	d6	ba	♗d7	0-0	♗xc6	d5[29]	
6	♕e2	♗b3	c3[31]	h3[32]	♗c2	d4	d5	♔h1	♖g1	=
	b5	d6[30]	0-0	♘a5[33]	c5	♕c7[34]	c4[35]	♘b7	♘c5[36]	

[16] 6 ... ♘xe4 – 5 ... ♘xe4

[17] 8 ... ♘xd4 9 ♕xd4 ♗c5 10 ♘c3 0-0 (10 ... ♘xa4 11 ♕xa4 0-0 12 ♗f4! b5 13 ♕d4 ♗b7 14 ♖ad1 ♗c6 15 ♘d5 ♖e8 16 ♖d3 ± Marjanovic-Yilmaz, Pucarevo Z 1987) 11 ♗g5 (11 ♗e3 ♘xa4 12 ♕xa4 d5 13 ed ♗xd6 14 ♖fd1 ♕f6 = Wittman-Mokry, Frunze 1983) 11 ... ♗xg5 12 ♕xc5 d6 13 ed cd 14 ♕d5 ♗f6 = Marjanovic-Muco, Kavala 1985

[18] 12 ... f5 13 f3 ♗g5 14 b3 ♖e8 15 ♗a3 ♕f7 ∞ Marjanović-Yusupov, Minsk 1982

[19] 14 ♗f4!? ♘f5 15 ♕d2 ♖b8 ∞ Milos-Smejkal, Dubai Ol 1986

[20] 15 ♗b2 ♘f7 16 f4 fe 17 fe ♗f5 ∞/= Hjartarson-H.Olafsson, Reykjavik 1984

[21] 7 ... d6 8 ♘xd4 ♗d7 9 ♗xc6 bc 10 ♕f3 0-0 11 ♘c3 ♖e8 12 ♗f4 c5 13 ♘b3 ♗g4 ∞ Meyer-Hort, West Germany 1982-83

[22] 9 c3 b5?! 10 ♗b3 d5 11 cd ♗g4 12 ♘c3 ♗b4 13 a3 ♗a5 14 ♗e3 ± Berkovich-Zaitsev, Moscow 1983; 9 ... dc 10 ♘xc3 d6 11 ed (11 ♘d5?! ♘xe5 12 ♘xe5 de 13 ♖xe5 ♗d6 14 ♗g5 f6 ∓ Zapata-Karpov, Brussels 1986) 11 ... ♘xd6 (11 ... ♗xd6 12 ♗g5 ♘f6 13 ♗xc6 bc 14 ♕a4 h6 = Short-Bellin, British Ch 1979) 12 ♘d5 (12 ♗f4 ♗e6!? Nunn) 12 ... ♖e8 13 ♗f4 ♗d7 14 ♖c1 ♖c8 = Sathe-Durao, London 1986
9 ♘xd4 ♘xd4 10 ♕xd4 d6 11 ♘c3 c5 12 ♕e4 ♘c7 13 ♗b3 de ∞ Bjarnason-Halldorson, Reykjavik 1984

[23] 9 ... f6 10 ♗xc6 dc 11 ♕xd4 ♕xd4 12 ♘xd4 f5 13 ♘f3 g6 14 ♗g5 ♗xg5 15 ♘xg5 h6 16 ♘f3 ♗e6 = Lanka-Schneider, Jurmala 1978

[24] 11 ... dc 12 ♘xc3 d4 13 ♘d5 ♗e6 14 ♘xe7+ ♕xe7 15 ♘xd4 ♘xd4 16 ♕xd4 ♗xb3 17 ab c5 ∞ Meyer-Unzicker, West Germany 1982-83

[25] 15 ♖e3 a5 16 a3 a4 ∞ Cuijpers-Lau, Ramsgate 1982
15 ♗g3 c5 16 dc ♘c7 = Cuijpers-Fucak, Bela Crkva 1983

[26] 8 ♗b3 d6 9 ♗d5 ♘xd5 (9 ... ♗b7 10 ♘xd4 ♘xd5 11 ♘xc6 ♗xc6 12 ed ♗b7 13 a4 0-0

14 ab ab 15 ♖xa8 ♗xa8 16 ♕e2 ♗f6 17 ♕xb5 c6 18 dc ♕c8 ∞ Nicholson-Hawksworth, Southampton 1986; 9 ... ♗d7 10 ed ♘e5 11 ♘xd4 0-0 12 a4 (12 ♘c3 ♗d7! 13 a4 ba 14 f4 c5! ∓ Kosanović-Gligorić, Budva 1986) 12 ... ♗g4 13 ♕d2 ♗d7 14 ♘c3 ba 15 ♘xa4 ♖e8 16 b3 ♕b8 17 ♘c3 ♕b7 + Chevallier-Thipsay, London 1985

[27] 8 ... ♘g4?! 9 ♗b3 h5 10 ♗d5 ♖b8 11 h3 ♘h6 12 ♘xd4 ±/± Petursson-Bjarnason, Reykjavik 1984

[28] 9 ♘xe5 ba 10 ♕xd4 0-0 11 ♕xa4 ♖b8 12 a3 ♖b6 13 ♘c3 ♖e6 14 ♗g5 c6 = Chiburdanidze-Romanishin, Frunze 1985

[29] **14 ... ♖e8** 15 ♘c3 ♘g4 ∞ Franco-Lengyel, Amsterdam 1983
14 ... d5 15 ♗f4 ♗d6 16 ♗xd6 ♕xd6 = Nicholson-Hjartarson, London 1986

[30] 7 ... 0-0 8 d4 d6 9 de ♘xe5 10 ♘xe5 de 11 ♖d1 ♕e8 12 a4 ♗b7 13 ♘c3 c6 14 ♕f3 ♖d8 = Braga-Frey, Havana 1983; 8 c3 d5!? 9 d3 ♖e8 10 ♖e1 ♗f8 ∞/=

[31] 8 a4!? ♗g4 9 c3 0-0 10 h3 ♘a5 11 ♗c2 ♗e6 ∞ Unzicker-Greenfeld, Beer-Sheva 1984

[32] **9 d4** ♗g4 10 ♖d1 ed 11 cd d5 12 ed ♘a5 13 ♗c2 ♖e8 14 ♘c3 ♗b4 15 ♕d3 ♗h5! Lukin-Lerner, USSR 1982
9 ♖d1 ♗e6 (9 ... ♘a5 10 ♗c2 c5 11 d3 ♘c6 12 ♘bd2 ♖c8 13 ♘f1 ♗f8 14 a4! ♗b7 15 ♗g5 ± Barlov-Agzamov, Sochi 1984) 10 ♗c2 d5 =

[33] 9 ... h6 10 ♖d1 ♘a5 11 ♗c2 c5 12 d4 ♕c7 13 d5 c4 14 ♔h1 ♘h7 15 ♘bd2 f5 16 ef ♗xf5 17 ♗xf5 ♖xf5 18 ♘e4 ± Marjanović-Pavlović, Bor 1983

[34] 11 ... cd 12 cd ♕c7 13 ♖d1 ♗d7 14 ♘c3 ± Marjanović-Hon, Subotica 1984

[35] 12 ... ♗d7 13 ♔h1 ♘c4 14 ♖g1 ♘b6 15 g4 ♘e8 16 ♘bd2 g6 17 ♘f1 f6 18 ♗h6 ♖f7 19 ♘3d2 ± Marjanović-Gligorić, Subotica 1984

[36] 15 g4 a5 16 ♘bd2 ♗a6! ∞ Marjanović-Lengyel, Sarajevo 1980

	7	8	9	10	11	12	13	14	15	
1	...	d4[1]	♘xd4[2]	e5	♕g4	♕xg7	♕xh7	♖xe4	ab	±
	♗b7	♘xd4	ed	♘e4[3]	c5	♖f8	c4[4]	cb	♗xe4[5]	
2	...	d4	♗xf7+[7]	♘xe5	♕xd4	♕d1[9]	♘c3	♘g4	♕xg4	∞∞
	0-0	♘xd4[6]	♖xf7	♖f8[8]	c5	♗b7[10]	♕c7	♘xg4	♗d6[11]	
3	...	a4	d4[12]	de	♘xe5	♗g5[14]	♗d5	♗e3	♗b3	±
	...	b4	d6	♘xe5[13]	de	♘d7	♖b8	♘b6	a5[15]	
4	...	...	d3	♘c3[16]	♗a2[17]	♘e2	c3	♘g3[19]	♕xd3	=
	...	♗b7	d6	♘a5	b4	c5	c4[18]	cd	b3[20]	
5	...	...	...	...	...	...	♘g3	h3[22]	♘d2	=
	...	...	...	...	...	...	♗c8[21]	♖b8[23]	♗e6[24]	

[1] 8 c3 d5 9 ed ♘xd5 10 ♘xe5 ♘xe5 11 ♖xe5 ♘f4 ∞/± *ECO*

[2] 9 ♗xf7+ ♔f8 10 ♗b3 (10 ♘xe5?! d6; 10 ♗h5?! ♘c6 ∓) 10 ... ♘xb3 11 ab d6 =

[3] 10 ... ♘d5 11 ♕f3 (11 ♕g4!?) 11 ... c6 12 ♕g4 ♕b6 (12 ... g6 13 ♗xd5 cd 14 ♕xd4 ±) 13 ♕xg7 0-0-0 14 ♕h6! ♖hg8 15 ♗xd5 ♖g6 16 ♕xh7 cd 17 ♘d2 ± Kindermann-Yilmaz, Dubai Ol 1986

[4] 13 ... ♗g5 14 ♗xg5 ♗xg5 15 e6 ± Bondarevsky-Trajković, corr. 1962

[5] 16 ♕xe4 ♕c8 (16 ... ♗c5 17 ♗h6 ±) 17 ♕xd4 ♕xc2 18 ♘c3 ♖c8 19 ♗e3 ♗c5 20 ♕d5 ± Kindermann

[6] 8 ... ed 9 e5 ♘e8 10 ♗d5 ♖b8 11 ♗f4 ± 8 ... d6 9 c3 – 7 ... d6

[7] 9 ♘xd4 ed 10 e5 ♘e8 11 c3 (11 ♕xd4 ♗b7 12 c3 d6 =) 11 ... dc 12 ♘xc3 d6 13 ♕f3 ∞∞ Vogt-Goldberg, East German Ch 1986, and Tseshkovsky-Malanyuk, USSR Ch 1987

[8] 10 ... ♘c6!? 11 ♘xf7 ♔xf7 12 e5 ♘g8 Matanović

[9] 12 ♕d2 ♕c7 13 ♘f3 ♗b7 14 ♘c3 ♖ae8 15 e5 b4 16 ef bc 17 bc ♗xf6 ∓ Vogt-Goldberg, East Germany 1986

[10] 12 ... ♕c7 13 ♘g4 ♘xg4 14 ♕xg4 d5 15 ♕h5 de 16 ♘c3 ♖f5 17 ♕e8+ ♖f8 18 ♕h5 ♖f5 ½-½ Smejkal-Zaitsev, USSR 1970

[11] 16 ♕h3 ♖ae8 14 ♗g5 ♗e5 18 ♖ad1 d6 ∞∞ Rantanen-Pinter, Helsinki 1983

[12] 9 c3 d5!? (9 ... d6 – 7 ... d6) 10 ed ♘xd5 11 ♘xe5 ♘xe5 12 ♖xe5 ♘f6 13 d4 ♗d6 14 ♖e2 ♖b8 ∞∞ Kremenetsky-Zaitsev, USSR 1983

9 a5 d6 (9 ... d5!? 10 ed e4 Suetin-Zaitsev, USSR 1983) 10 d4 ♘xd4 11 ♘xd4 ed 12 ♕xd4 ♖b8! 13 ♗g5 h6 14 ♗h4 ♘g4 = Klinger-Hort, Biel 1986

[13] 10 ... de 11 ♕xd8 (11 ♘bd2 ♗c5 12 ♕e2 ♕e7 13 a5 ♖d8 ±/∞ Ivanović-Spassky, Bugojno 1982) 11 ... ♖xd8 12 ♗g5 ♗b7 13 ♘bd2 h6 14 ♗xf6 ♗xf6 15 ♗d5 ± Sax-A.Rodriguez, Lucerne Ol 1982

[14] 12 ♕f3 ♗b7 13 ♘d2 ♔h8 14 g4 ♗c5 15 ♘c4 ♘xe4!? 16 ♖xe4 f5 17 gf ♖xf5 18 ♕xf5 ♕d1+ 19 ♔g2 ♖f8 ∞ Ehlvest-Kupreichik, USSR Ch 1987

[15] 16 ♘d2 ♗a6 17 ♕h5 ± Kupreichik-Tseshkovsky, USSR Ch 1987

[16] 10 ♗d2 b4 11 c3 bc (11 ... d5 12 cb ♖e8 13 ♘c3 ♘xb4 14 ♘xe5 ♗d6 15 d4 c5 16 ♘xf7! ± Hobusch-van der Heijden, corr. 1986) 12 ♘xc3 ♘a5 =

[17] 11 ab ♘xb3 12 cb ab 13 ♖xa8 ♕xa8 14 ♖xb5 ♖b8 ∞∞

[18] 13 ... bc 14 bc c4 15 ♘g3 ♘d7 (15 ... cd 16 ♕xd3 ± Ljubojević-Karpov, London 1982) 16 ♗a3 g6 17 d4 ♕c7 ∞ Kupreichik-A.Rodriguez, Minsk 1982

[19] 14 dc b3 15 ♗xb3 ♘xb3 16 ♕xb3 ♗xe4 ∞∞ Karpov-Nunn, London 1984

14 cb cd 15 ♘c3 ♘c6 16 ♗d5 ♖b8 ∞ Kupreichik-Psakhis, USSR Ch 1987

[20] 16 ♗b1 g6 = A.Rodriguez-Tseshkovsky, Erevan 1984

[21] 13 ... b3 14 ♗xb3 ♘xb3 15 cb a5 ½-½ Karpov-Tukmakov, USSR Ch 1983

13 ... ♖b8 14 ♘f5 (14 ♘d2 ♗c8 15 ♘c4 ♘xc4 16 ♗xc4 ♘e8 = Tal-Kuzmin, Tallinn 1985) 14 ... ♗c8 15 ♘3h4 (15 ♘xe7+ ♕xe7 16 ♘d2 ♗e6 = Short-Kholmov, Erevan 1984) 15 ... ♘e8 16 ♘xe7+ ♕xe7 17 g3 b3 18 cb ♘c6 19 ♔g2 ♘b4 = Kupreichik-Razuvayev, Minsk 1985

[22] 14 ♘d2 ♗g4 15 f3 ♗e6 16 ♘c4 ♘c6 17 f4 ef 18 ♗xf4 d5 = Matulović-Balashov, USSR 1979

[23] 14 ... ♗e6 15 ♗xe6 fe 16 c3 ± Chandler-Tal, World v USSR 1984, and Watson-Tseshkovsky, Moscow 1985

[24] 15 ... ♘e8 16 ♘c4 ♘xc4 17 ♗xc4 ♗g5 = Chandler-Tal, Naestved 1985

15 ... ♗e6 16 ♘c4 ♘xc4 (16 ... ♘c6 17 f4 ef 18 ♗xf4 ♖c8 ∞ Yudasin-Kuporosov, USSR 1985) 17 ♗xc4 ♘xc4 18 dc ♘e8 19 ♘f5 ♗f6 = Thipsay-Tseshkovsky, Calcutta 1986

Ruy Lopez X (Marshall)

1 e4 e5 2 Nf3 Nc6 3 Bb5 a6 4 Ba4 Nf6 5 0-0 Be7 6 Re1 b5 7 Bb3 0-0 8 c3 d5 9 ed Nxd5[1] 10 Nxe5 Nxe5 11 Rxe5

	11	12	13	14	15	16	17	18	19	
1	... / Nf6	d4 / Bd6	Re1[2] / Ng4	h3 / Qh4	Qf3 / Nxf2[3]	Bd2[4] / Bb7[5]	Qxb7 / Nd3	Re2 / Qg3	Kf1 / Nf4[6]	±
2	... / Bb7	d4[7] / Qd7[8]	Nd2[9] / c5[10]	Nf3 / cd	cd / Bf6	Re1 / Rfe8	Rxe8+ / Rxe8	Bd2 / Qd6	h3 / Nf4[11]	±
3	... / c6	Bxd5[12] / cd	d4 / Bd6	Re3 / Qh4[13]	h3 / Qf4[14]	Re5 / Qf6	Re1 / Qg6	Qf3[15] / Be6	Bf4 / Bxf4[16]	=
4	... / ...	Re1 / Bd6	g3[17] / Qd7	d3 / Qh3[18]	Re4 / Qf5	Nd2 / Qg6[19]	Re1[20] / f5[21]	c4[22] / f4	Ne4 / fg[23]	∞
5	... / ...	d4 / Bd6	Re2 / Qh4[24]	g3 / Qh5	Nd2 / Bh3[25]	f3[26] / Bc7[27]	Ne4! / Qxf3[28]	Ng5 / Qh5	Nxh3 / Qxh3[29]	±
6	... / ...	... / ...	... / ...	... / Qh3	Nd2 / Bf5	Bc2[30] / Bxc2	Qxc2 / f5	c4 / Qg4	Re1[31] / f4[32]	∞

1 e4 e5 2 Nf3 Nc6 3 Bb5 a6 4 Ba4 Nf6 5 0-0 Be7 6 Re1 b5 7 Bb3 0-0 8 c3 d5 9 ed Nxd5 10 Nxe5 Nxe5 11 Rxe5 c6 12 d4 Bd6 13 Re1 Qh4 14 g3 Qh3

	15	16	17	18	19	20	21	22	23	
7	Be3[33] / Bg4	Qd3 / Rae8	Nd2 / f5	f4 / Kh8[34]	Bxd5 / cd	Qf1 / Qh5	a4 / ba[35]	Rxa4 / g5	Raa1[36] / a5[37]	∞
8	... / ...	... / ...	... / Re6	a4[38] / f5[39]	Qf1 / Qh5	f4 / ba[40]	Rxa4[41] / Rb8[42]	Bxd5[43] / cd	Rxa6[44] / Rbe8[45]	±

---

[1] 9 ... e4 10 dc ef 11 d4! fg (11 ... Bd6 12 Qxf3 Re8 13 Bd2 ±; 12 Bg5 Bxh2+ 13 Kxh2 Ng4+ 14 Kg1 Qxg5 15 Qxf3 ±) 12 Qf3 Be6 (12 ... Re8 13 Bg5 ±; 12 ... Ng4 13 Bf4 ±) 13 Bf4 ± *ECO*

[2] 13 Re2 Bb7 (13 ... Nh5 14 Be3 Bb7 15 Nd2 Kh8 16 Re1! Qh4 17 Nf1 intending f3, Bf2 ± Hazai) 14 Nd2 Qd7 15 f3 Rae8 16 Nf1 ± Hazai-Nikolac, Maribor 1985

[3] 15 ... h5!? (Shamkovich) 16 Be3 Nxe3 17 Rxe3 Qf4 ±

[4] **16 Qxf2?** Bh2+! 17 Kf1 Bg3 18 Qe2 Bxh3 19 gh Rae8 ∓∓
16 Re8? Nxh3+ 17 gh Bb7! 18 Rxf8+ Rxf8 19 Qe3 Bf4 20 Qxf4 Qe1+ ∓∓
16 Re2 Ng4! = Tartakower

[5] **16 ... Ng4?** 17 Re8 ±±
16 ... Nxh3+? 17 gh Bxh3 18 Re4 ±±
16 ... Bxh3 17 gh Nxh3+ 18 Kf1 ±

[6] **20 Bxf4?** Qxf4+ 21 Qf3 Qc1+ 22 Kf2 Bh2! ∓ Hansson-Westerinen, Esbjerg 1983
20 Rf2 Qd3+ 21 Kg1 Ne2+ 22 Rxe2 Qxe2 23 Qf3 ± Wedberg

[7] 12 Qf3 Bd6 13 Bxd5 c6 14 Re2 cd 15 d4 Qc7 16 g3 Rae8 ∞ A.Sokolov-Kharitonov, USSR 1984, and A.Sokolov-Ermolinsky, USSR 1984

[8] 12 ... Bf6 13 Re1 Qd7 14 Nd2 Rfe8

15 Rxe8+ Rxe8 16 Nf3 ± Aseyev-Tseitlin, USSR 1984

[9] 13 Bxd5 Bxd5 14 Nf4 Bb7 15 Re1 c5 16 dc (16 Nd2!? cd 17 Nb3) 16 ... Nc6 17 Qg4 Bxc5 18 Nd2 Rae8 ∞ Dvoiris-Ermolinsky, USSR 1984

[10] 13 ... Nf4 14 Ne4! (14 Nf3 Nxg2!) 14 ... Ng6 (14 ... Nxg2 15 Kxg2 Bf6 16 f3 Bxe5 17 de ±) 15 Nc5 ±

[11] 20 Ne5 Bxe5 21 de Qc6 22 Qg4 ± Klovans-Tseitlin, USSR 1986

[12] **12 Qf1** Bd6 13 Re1 Qh4 14 g3 Qh5 ∞ Kapengut-Malanyuk, USSR 1985
12 g3 Nf6 13 Re1 c5 14 d4 Bb7! ∞ Braga-Geller, Amsterdam 1986

[13] 14 ... f5 15 Nd2 f4 16 Re1 ± *ECO*

[14] **15 ... g5** 16 Qf3 Be6 17 Qf6 Qh5 18 Nd2 g4 19 Rxe6 ± Tal
15 ... f5 16 Nd2 f4 17 Re1 Ra7 (17 ... Bxh3? 18 Qf3 ±±) 18 Qf3 Qg5 19 a4 ±

[15] 18 Kh1 Be6 (18 ... Bf5 19 Be3 Rae8 20 Nd2 Bb8 ∞) 19 Nd2 (19 Be3?! f5) ∞

[16] 20 Qxf4 Bxh3 21 Qg3 Qc2 22 c4 Be6 = Kholmov-Tal, Kislovodsk 1966

[17] 13 d3 Bf5 (13 ... Qh4 14 g3 Qh3 – 13 g3) 14 Nd2 Nf4! (14 ... Bxd3 15 Nf3 ±) 15 Ne4 (15 d4 Nxg2!) 15 ... Nxd3 16 Bg5 Qd7 17 Re3 Bxe4 18 Rxe4 Rae8 = Kir.Georgiev-Nunn,

Dubai Ol 1986
[18] 14 ... ♕f5 15 ♘d2! ♕g6 16 ♘e4 ♗c7
17 ♕f3 ± Byrne-Hebden, New York 1983
[19] 16 ... ♘f6 17 ♖e1 ♖xd3 18 ♘e4 ±
[20] 17 ♘f1 f5 (17 ... h5!? 18 a4 ♗g4 ∞
A.Kuzmin-Shulman, USSR 1986) 18 ♖d4 f4
19 ♖xd5 cd 20 ♗xd5+ ♗e6 21 ♗xa8 ♖xa8
22 ♕f3 ♖f8 ∞ Timman-Hübner, Tilburg
1985
[21] 17 ... ♗c7 18 ♘f3 ♗g4 19 ♘h4 ♕h5
20 f3 ♗h3 21 ♕e2 ± Smagin-Malanyuk, USSR
Ch 1986
17 ... ♗b7 18 ♘f3 ♖fe8 19 ♖xe8+ ♖xe8
20 ♘h4 ± Hjartarson-Hebden, London 1986
[22] 18 ♘e4? fe 19 de ♗g4 20 ♕d4 ♕h5
21 ed c5 ∓
18 ♕f3 ♗h8 19 ♗xd5 cd 20 ♕xd5 ♖a7 ∞
[23] 20 fg ♗g4 21 ♕c2 bc 22 dc ∞ A.Ivanov-
Agapov, USSR 1984, and Smagin-Hebden,
Moscow 1986
[24] 13 ... ♗g4 14 f3 ♗h5 15 ♗xd5 (15 ♘d2
♘f4) 15 ... cd 16 ♘d2 b4 (16 ... ♕c7!? 17 ♘f1
♖fe8 van der Sterren-Pein, Brussels 1984)
17 cb ♕b8 18 ♘f1 ♕xb4 19 ♗d2!? ♕xd4+
20 ♗e3 ♕c4 21 b3 ♕b5 22 ♖d2 ♖fd8 23 ♘g3 ±
Kosten-Hebden, Gausdal 1987
[25] 15 ... ♗f5 16 ♖e1 ♕g6 17 ♘f3 ♗g4
18 ♘h4 ± Sax-Pinter, Hungarian Ch 1981
15 ... ♗g4 16 f3 ♗xf3 17 ♘xf3 ♕xf3
18 ♖f2 ± Sax-Nikolić, Plovdiv 1983
[26] 16 ♖e1? ♖ae8! ∓ Psakhis-Geller, Sochi
1982
16 ♖e4 ♕g6 (16 ... ♕xd1+!? 17 ♗xd1
f5) 17 ♖e1 ∞
[27] 16 ... f5 17 c4 bc 18 ♘xc4 ♗c7 19 ♘e5 ±
Rodriguez-Malanyuk, Erevan 1984
16 ... ♖ae8 17 ♖xe8 ♖xe8 18 ♘e4 ♗c7
19 ♗d2 ± Garcia Martinez-Pinter, Lucerne
Ol 1982
16 ... ♖ad8 17 ♘e4 (17 ♕e1!? intending
♕f2) 17 ... ♕xf3 18 ♘g5 ♕h5 19 ♘xh3 ♕xh3
20 ♕f1 ♕g4 21 ♗d2 ± Aseyev-Taborov, USSR
1985
[28] 17 ... ♖ae8 18 ♕d3 ♖e6 19 ♗d2 ±
Belyavsky-Malanyuk, USSR Ch 1987
[29] 20 ♗d2 ♖ae8 21 ♕f1 ± Ehlvest-Nikolić,
Zagreb IZ 1987
[30] 16 ♗xd5 cd 17 f3 ♖ae8 ∞ Grünfeld-
Pinter, Zagreb IZ 1987
[31] 19 ♖e6? ♘f4! 20 ♖xd6 ♖ae8 21 cb ♖e2 ∓
Ljubojević-Nunn, Szirak IZ 1987
[32] 20 f3 ♕h3 21 cd fg 22 ♘f1 gh+ 23 ♔h1
♖f6 ∞ Mokry-Panczyk, Polanica Zdroj 1984
[33] 15 ♖e4 g5 (15 ... ♗b7!?) 16 ♕f1 (16 ♕f3?!
♗f5) 16 ... ♕h6 (16 ... ♕xf1+!? 17 ♔xf1 f5)
17 f3 ♗h8 18 ♘d2 ♗h3 19 ♕e1 ♘f4 ∞
Kr.Georgiev-Tseshkovsky, Moscow 1985
15 ♗xd5 cd 16 ♕f3 ♗f5 17 ♕xd5 ♖ae8
18 ♗d2 ♖e6 (18 ... ♗d3 19 ♘a3 ♗xa3 20 ba ±
Chandler-Nikolić, Leningrad 1987) 19 ♖xe6

(19 ♘a3!?) 19 ... fe 20 ♕g2 ♕h5 ∞ Marshall
[34] 18 ... ♖e6 19 ♕f1 ♕h5 20 ♕g2 ±
18 ... g5 19 ♕f1 ♕h5 20 ♕g2 ± ECO
[35] 24 ... g5 25 ab ab (25 ... a5 26 fg ± Varadi-
Papai, corr. 1984) 23 fg (23 ♖a6!?) 23 ... ♖xe3
24 ♖xe3 f4 25 gf ♗xf4 26 ♖g3 ♕xg5 27 ♔h1
♗d6 28 ♕e1! ♕xg3 29 hg ± van der Heijden
[36] 23 fg ♖xe3 24 ♖xe3 f4 25 gf ♗xf4 26 ♖g3
♕e8! ∓ Ulmanis-van der Heijden, corr. 1986
[37] 24 fg f4 25 ♗xf4 ½-½ Schlosser-Nunn,
Krefeld 1986
[38] 18 c4? ♗f4! 19 ♕f1 (19 cd? ♖h6 20 ♕e4
♕xh2+ 21 ♔f1 f5 22 dc+ ♔h8 23 ♕d5 ♖e6!
24 gf ♖e4 ∓∓) 19 ... ♘xe3 20 ♕xh3 ♗xh3
21 cb ♘c2 22 ♖xe6 fe 23 gf ♘xa1 24 ♖xa1
♖xf4 25 f3 cb 26 ♘e4 ♗f5! ∓ Feldmus-
Vitomsky, corr. 1983
[39] 18 ... ♖fe8 19 ♗xd5 (19 ab? ♘xe3 intending
... ♗xg3) 19 ... cd 20 ab f5 21 ♕f1 f4 22 ♕xh3
♗xh3 23 ba fe 24 ♖xe3 ♖a8 25 b4 ½-½ Lanka-
Tseitlin, USSR 1985
18 ... ba 19 ♖xa4 f5 20 ♕f1 ♕h5 (20 ...
f4 21 ♕xh3 ♗xh3 22 ♖xa6 fe 23 ♖xe3 ± ECO)
21 c4 (21 f4 – 18 ... f5) 21 ... ♘xe3 (21 ... f4
22 cd ♖xe3 23 fe fg 24 dc+ ♔h8 25 hg ♖xf1+
26 ♖xf1 ♕g5 27 ♖f4 ♗xf4 28 ef ♕e7 29 ♘f1
h5 30 ♖xa6 ♕e2 ∞ Kayumov-Sternberg, USSR
1979) 22 fe c5 23 ♖aa1 ♔h8 intending ... f4,
... ♖h6, ... cd ∞ Harding
[40] 20 ... g5? 21 ab ab 22 fg ♖xe3 23 ♖xe3 f4
24 ♖f3 ±
20 ... ♖fe8? 21 ab ♖xe3 22 ♖xe3 ♖xe3
23 bc ♖e2 24 ♗xd5+ ♔f8 25 h3! ♗xh3
26 ♖f3 ±±
[41] 21 ♗xd5 cd 22 ♕g2 ♖fe8 23 ♕xd5 ♔h8
24 ♗f2 ♗e2 (24 ... ♖xe1+ 25 ♖xe1 ♖xe1+
26 ♗xe1 ♕e8 27 ♗f2 h6! 28 ♕xd6 ♕e2 =
Matsukevich) 25 ♔g2 (25 ♘c4? ♗c7 26 ♘e5
♗xe5 intending ... ♗f3 ∓; 25 ♖xa4 ♗xf4!
26 gf ♗c4 =) 25 ... h6 26 ♘f3 ♗xf4 27 ♘g1
♗d2 = Matsukevich-Filippov, corr. 1983
[42] 21 ... ♖fe8 22 ♕f2 ♔f8 (22 ... g5 23 ♖a6
gf 24 gf ±) 23 ♗xd5 cd 24 c4! dc 25 ♖xa6 ±
21 ... g5 22 ♖xa6 gf (22 ... ♕e8 23 ♖xc6)
23 ♗xf4 ♗xf4 24 ♖xe6! ♗d2 25 ♗xd5 cd
26 ♕g2 ±
[43] 22 ♗f2 ♗e2 23 ♗xd5 (23 ♕g2 ♖xb3
24 ♘xb3 ♗xf4) 23 ... cd 24 ♕g2 ♕f7 25 ♘f3
(25 ♕xd5 ♗xf4) 25 ... ♕e8 26 ♖aa1 ♕b5
27 ♘e5 ♗xe5 28 de ♗d3 = Usachy-Gabrans,
corr. 1977
[44] 23 ♕g2 ♕e8 24 ♗xd5 ♔h8 25 ♗f2 (25 ♘f1?
♗xf4! 26 gf ♕g6 ∓; 25 ♘c4 ♗xf4 26 gf ♖g6
27 ♘d6! =) 25 ... ♖xb2 (25 ... g5?! 26 ♖xa6
♖xb2 27 ♖a8'♖b8 28 ♕c6 ♕h5 29 h3! ♕xh3
30 ♕g2 ±) 26 ♖a2 ♖xa2 27 ♕xa2 g5 ∞
Chiburdanidze-Tseshkovsky, USSR 1980
[45] 23 ... ♖be8 24 ♕b5! ♕f7 25 h3! ±± Short-
Pinter, Rotterdam 1988
23 ... ♖xb2 24 ♕g2 ♖b5 25 c4 dc 26 ♕c6 ±

	8	9	10	11	12	13	14	15	16	
1	a4	c3	♗c2	d4	cd	♘bd2[4]	ab	d5	b4	=
	♗b7[1]	♘a5[2]	c5	cd[3]	0-0	♕c7[5]	ab	♘d7	♘c4[6]	
2	c3	a4	a5[8]	♗c4[10]	ed	♘xe5	♖xe5	d4	♖e1	∞
	0-0	b4[7]	♖b8[9]	d5[11]	♘xd5	♘xe5	♘xe5	♗b7	♗f6 c5[12]	
3	...	...	h3[13]	d3[15]	♗c2	♘bd2	g4	♘f1[17]	♘e3	∞
	...	♗g4	♗h5[14]	♘a5	b4	c5[16]	♗g6	♖b8	b3[18]	
4	...	...	d4	♗c2	de[20]	♘xe5[21]	ab	♘d7	♗xe4	=
	...	♗b7	♘a5[19]	c5	de	♘xe4[22]	ab	♖e8	♗xe4[23]	
5	...	d4	d5[24]	♗c2	h3[26]	♕xf3	ed	♘d2[29]	♘f1	∞
	...	♗g4	♘a5	c6[25]	♗xf3[27]	cd	♘c4[28]	♘b6	♕c7[30]	
6	...	...	...	...	...	dc	♘bd2[31]	♘f1	♘g3	∞/=
	...	...	...	...	♗c8	♕c7	♕xc6	♗b7[32]	g6[33]	
7	...	...	♗e3	cd	e5	h3[35]	♘c3[36]	bc	♗c2	±
	...	...	ed[34]	d5	♘e4	♗h5	♘xc3	♘a5	♘c4[37]	
8	...	...	...	...	♗c2	dc[39]	♘bd2[40]	♕b1[41]	e5	∞
	...	...	...	♘a5	c5[38]	dc	♘d7	♖e8	♘f8[42]	

---

[1]   **8 ...**   **♗g4** 9 c3 0-0 – 8 c3

    8 ...   **♗d7** 9 c3 ♘a5 10 ♗c2 c5 11 d4 ± Nunn-Romanishin, Wijk aan Zee 1985

    8 ...   **♘a5** 9 ab! ♘xb3 10 cb ♗b7 11 ba ♗xe4 (11 ... ♗xa6 12 d4 ±) 12 d4 ± Nunn-Torre, London 1984

    8 ...   **b4** 9 d4 ♗g4 (9 ... 0-0 – 7 ... 0-0 8 a4) 10 de ♘xe5 11 ♘bd2 0-0 12 h3 ± Kupreichik-Zaitsev, Minsk 1983

[2]   9 ... 0-0 – 8 c3

[3]   11 ... ♕c7 12 ab ab 13 ♘a3! ± Kupreichik-Kholmov, USSR 1984

[4]   **13 ♗d2** ♘c4 14 ♗c3 b4! 15 ♗xb4 ♘xb2 16 ♕c1 ♘c4 = Kupreichik-Tal, USSR 1981

    13 d5 b4 14 ♘bd2 ♕b8 intending ... ♗d8-b6 = Kupreichik-Timoshchenko, USSR Ch 1981

[5]   13 ... ♘c6 14 ♘b3 d5 15 ab ab 16 ♖xa8 ♗xa8 17 de ♘xe4 18 ♘fd4 ±/∞ Kupreichik-Hjartarson, Winnipeg 1986

[6]   Balashov-Vasyukov, USSR Ch 1980-81

[7]   9 ... ♗d7 10 d4 h6 11 ♘bd2 ♖e8 12 ♘f1 ♗f8 13 ♘g3 ♘a5 14 ♗c2 c5 ±/= Mestel-Belyavsky, Lucerne 1985

[8]   10 d4 bc (10 ... ed 11 ♘xd4 ♗d7 =) 11 bc ♗g4 =

[9]   **10 ...** ♗g4 11 h3 ♗h5 12 ♗a4! ♘xa5 13 cb ♘b7 14 d4 ±

    10 ... bc 11 dc ♗e6 12 ♘bd2 ± Tal-Spassky, match 1965

[10]   **11 d4** bc 12 bc ed 13 cd d5 ∓

    11 h3 ♗e6 ±

[11]   **11 ...** bc 12 dc ± Spraggett-Nunn, Wijk aan Zee 1985, and Nunn-Karpov, Amsterdam 1985

    11 ... ♗b7 12 d3 h6 13 ♘bd2 ±/∞ Mestel-Rubinetti, Lucerne 1985

[12]   A.Ivanov-Klovans, Kostroma 1985

[13]   10 d3 ♘a5 11 ♗c2 b4 12 ♘bd2 ♖b8 13 h3 ♗xf3! (13 ... ♗h5 – 10 h3) 14 ♘xf3 c5 ∓ Klinger-Nunn, Vienna 1986

[14]   10 ... ♗xf3 11 ♕xf3 ♘a5 12 ♗a2! ± Ljubojević-Portisch, Tilburg 1986, Ljubojević-

Karpov, Dubai Ol 1986, and Ljubojević-Smejkal, Dubai Ol 1986

[15] 11 ab ab 12 ♖xa8 ♕xa8 13 d3 ♖d8 14 ♘bd2 (Chandler-Nikolić, Sochi 1982) 14 ... d5 15 g4 ♗g6 16 g5 ♘h5 17 ♗xd5 ♘f4 ∞ Nikolić

[16] 13 ... ♖b8 ,14 g4 ♗g6 15 d4 ± Short-Torre, Biel IZ 1985

[17] 15 d4!?

[18] 17 ♗b1 ♖e8 ∞ Zapata-Sanchez, Bogotá 1977

[19] **10 ... h6** 11 ♘bd2 ♖e8 12 ♕e2 ♕b8 13 ♗c2 ♗f8 14 d5 ± Kupreichik-Kakageldiev, USSR 1978

10 ... ♘d7 11 ♘bd2 ♗f6 12 ♘f1 ♘a5 13 ♗c2 c5 14 ♘e3! ± Kupreichik-Gomez, Barcelona 1984

[20] 12 ♘bd2 cd 13 cd – row 1

[21] 13 ♕e2 ♘c4 14 b3 (14 ♘bd2 ♘xd2 15 ♗xd2 ♕b8) 14 ... ♘d6 15 ♘bd2 ♘d7 = Torre

[22] 13 ... ♘d6!? 14 ♘g4 ♘xe4 Torre

[23] 17 ♖xe4 ♖a7 = van der Wiel-Torre, Biel IZ 1985

[24] **10 ♗d5** ♘xd5 11 ed ♘a5 12 de de 13 ♖xe5 ♘c4 14 ♖e1 ♘b6 ∓ Yates-Alekhine, Scheveningen 1913

10 h3 ♗xf3 11 gf ♘a5 12 ♗c2 ♘h5 ∓

10 a4 ♕d7 11 ab (11 d5 ♘a5 12 ♗c2 c6 =) 11 ... ab 12 ♖xa8 (12 ♗xf7+? ♔xf7 13 ♕b3+ d5!) 12 ... ♖xa8 13 ♘a3 ♖b8 =

[25] 11 ... c5?! 12 ♘bd2 g6 13 b4 ± Yudasin-Balashov, USSR Ch 1986

[26] 12 dc ♕c7 13 ♘bd2 ♕xc6 14 ♘f1 ♘c4 15 h3 ♗e6 =

[27] **12 ...** ♗d7?! 13 ♘xe5 de 14 d6 ±

12 ... ♗h5 13 dc ♕c7 (13 ... ♘xc6 14 ♘bd2 ♖c8 15 ♘f1 ±) 14 ♘bd2 ♕xc6 15 ♘f1 ♘c4 16 ♘g3 ♗g6 17 ♘h4 ±

[28] 14 ... ♕c7 15 ♘d2 b4 16 ♘e4! ± Belyavsky-Razuvayev, Frunze 1979

[29] 15 a4 g6 (15 ... ♘b6!?) 16 ♗d3 ♕d7 17 ♕e2 ♕b7 ∞ Benjamin-Short, match 1983

[30] **16 ...** ♘bxd5 17 ♘g3 ♕c7 18 ♘f5 ♘e6 19 a4 ± Stean-Janatschek, Haifa Ol 1976, and Gufeld-Govashelishvili, USSR 1977

16 ... ♕c7 17 ♘g3 g6 18 ♗h6 ♖fc8 ∞ Timman-Hübner, Wijk aan Zee 1979

[31] 14 a4 ♕xc6 15 ♘a3 ♗e6 16 ♘g5 ♗d7 17 b4 ♘c4 = Lobron-Hort, Biel 1982

[32] **15 ...** ♗e6 16 ♘g3 g6 = Ligterink-Timman, Amsterdam 1978, and Sax-Byrne, Buenos Aires Ol 1978

15 ... ♘c4 16 ♘g3 g6 17 ♗h6 ♘xb2!? 18 ♕c1 ♘c4 19 ♗xf8 ♗xf8 20 a4 ♖b8 ∞ Tseitlin-Sturua, USSR 1983

[33] 17 ♗g5 ♘c4 18 b3 ♘b6 19 ♖c1 ♘bd7 20 c4 ♕b6 ∞/= Vogt-Smagin, Dresden 1985

[34] **10 ...** ♘a5 11 de ♗xf3 12 ♕xf3 de 13 ♗c2 ♘c4 14 ♗c1 ± Kasparov-Litvinov, USSR 1978

10 ... ♖e8 11 ♘bd2 ♗f8 (11 ... d5 12 h3! ♗h5 13 g4 ♗g6 ECO) 12 h3 ♗h5 13 g4 ♗g6 14 ♗g5 ± van der Wiel-F.Olafsson, Wijk aan Zee 1983

10 ... d5 11 ed ed 12 ♗xd4 ♘xd4 13 cd ♗b4 14 ♘c3 ♗xc3 (14 ... a5 15 ♕d3 ±) 15 bc ♘xd5 16 ♕d3 ± van der Wiel-Nikolić, Novi Sad 1982

[35] 13 ♘bd2 ♘xd2 14 ♕xd2 ♗xf3 15 gf ♗b4 16 ♕c2 ♘a5! ∓ Arnason-Torre, Sochi 1980

[36] 14 g4 ♗g6 15 ♘h2 ♗b4 (15 ... a5!? Khalifman-Aseyev, USSR 1983, and Tseshkovsky-Aseyev, USSR 1985) 16 f3 (16 ♖e2 f5 ∞ Yudasin-Tseshkovsky, USSR Ch 1981) 16 ... ♘g5 (16 ... ♗xe1 17 ♕xe1 ♘g5 18 ♘c3 ♘e6! ∞ van der Wiel-Timman, Tilburg 1983) 17 ♖f1 ♘e6 ∞ Lobron-Greenfeld, Beer-Sheva 1985

[37] 17 g4 ♗g6 18 ♗f5! ± Sznapik-van der Wiel, Copenhagen 1984

[38] 12 ... ♘c4 13 ♗c1 c5 14 b3 ♘b6 (14 ... ♘a5 15 d5 ±) 15 ♗b2 ♖c8 16 ♘bd2 ± Sznapik-Kuzmin, Polanica Zdroj 1984, and Tseshkovsky, Short, Erevan 1984

[39] **13 ♘bd2** cd 14 ♗xd4 ♘c6 15 ♗e3 d5 =

13 h3 ♗h5 (13 ... ♗xf3 14 ♕xf3 ♘c4 ∞ Marjanović-Smejkal, Sarajevo 1982) 14 dc dc 15 ♕e2 ♘c4 ∞ Marjanović-Abramović, Yugoslavia 1982

[40] 14 ♕e2 ♘c4 15 ♘c3 ♘d7! ∓ Rantanen-Keres, Tallinn 1975, and Hartmann-Kavalek, West Germany 1983

[41] **15 ♗f4** ♕b6 16 e5 ♖ad8 ∞ Gulko-Geller, USSR Ch 1985

15 h3 ♗h5 16 ♖c1 ♖e8 17 b3 ♖c8 ,∞ Tseshkovsky-Dorfman, Moscow 1985

[42] 17 ♗f5 ♗xf5 18 ♕xf5 ♕d5 ∞ Marjanović-Smejkal, Novi Sad 1984, and Barle-Nikolić, Yugoslavia 1985

Ruy Lopez XII   1 e4 e5 2 Nf3 Nc6 3 Bb5 a6
4 Ba4 Nf6 5 0-0 Be7 6 Re1 b5 7 Bb3 d6 8 c3 0-0 9 h3

	9	10	11	12	13	14	15	16	17	
1	...	d4	a4[2]	ab	Be3	d5[4]	Na3	Qe2[5]	Nd2	±
	Nd7	Bf6[1]	Rb8[3]	ab	Ne7	g6	Bg7	Nf6	Bd7[6]	
2	...	d4	ab	cd	e5	Nc3	ef	Ne5[9]	Na2	=
	Be6	Bxb3	ed[7]	d5	Ne4	f5	Nxf6[8]	Nb4	Qe8[10]	
3	...	...	Qxb3	ed	Qc2	cd[12]	Nc3	Qxc3	Bf4[14]	±
	...	...	d5[11]	Na5	ed	Nxd5	Nxc3[13]	Nc4		
4	...	d4	Nbd2	Nf1[15]	Ng3	Bc2	b3	d5	Be3[18]	±
	h6	Re8	Bf8	Bd7	Na5	c5[16]	Nc6[17]	Ne7		
5	...	...	...	...	Ng3	Bc2	b3	a4	de	±
	...	...	...	Bb7	Na5	Nc4[19]	Nb6	g6[20]	de[21]	

[1]   10 ... Nb6 11 Nbd2 ed (11 ... Bf6 12 d5 Na5 13 Bc2 c6 14 dc Qc7 15 Nf1 Qxc6 16 Ne3 ± Vasyukov-Smyslov, USSR Ch 1966) 12 cd d5 (12 ... Nb4 13 Nf1 c5 14 a3 Nc6 15 Be3 ± Karpov-Ivkov, Bugojno 1980) 13 ed Nxd5 14 Ne4 Bf5 15 Bd2 Ndb4 16 Rc1 ± Jansa-Miličević, Kragujevac 1984
10 ... Bb7 11 Nbd2 Bf6 12 Nf1 Re8 13 Ng3 g6 14 Bh6 Na5 15 Bc2 c5 16 d5 ± Ljubojević-Karpov, Turin 1982
[2]   11 Be3 Na5 12 Bc2 Nc4 13 Bc1 ed 14 cd c5 15 Nc3 Bb7 16 b3 cd 17 Nxd4 Qa5 18 Nce2 ± Tolnai-Nickoloff, Saint John 1988
[3]   11 ... Na5 12 Nc2 Nb6 13 ab ab 14 b4 ± Torre-Ivkov, Geneva 1977
11 ... Bb7 12 ab ab 13 Rxa8 Bxa8 14 d5 ± Tal-Torre, Bugojno 1984
[4]   14 Nbd2 c5 = Spassky-Smyslov, Bugojno 1984
14 Ng5 h6 15 Bxf7+ Rxf7 16 Ne6 Qe8 17 Nxc7 Qd8 18 Ne6 Qe8 = Arnason
[5]   16 c4 bc 17 Nxc4 Nf6 18 Bd2 Bd7 = Ljubojević-Smyslov, Bugojno 1984
[6]   18 Nc2 c6 19 dc Nxc6 20 Bg5 ± Arnason-Hecht, Thessaloniki Ol 1984
[7]   11 ... Qd7 12 d5 Nd8 13 c4 ±
11 ... Re8 12 d5 Nb8 13 c4 ±
[8]   15 ... Bxf6 16 Nxe4 de 17 Rxe4 Qd5 18 Rg4 Ne7 (18 ... Rad8 19 Be3 Nb4 20 Qd2 h5 21 Rg6 c5 22 Bg5! ± Dorfman, Nikitin) 19 Qc2 Nf5 (Velimirović-Kurajica, Kavala 1985) 20 Qe4 ± Kurajica
[9]   16 Ng5 Qd7 =
16 Qe2 Bd6 17 Bg5 Nb4 = Dvoiris-Smagin, Barnaul 1984
16 Bf4 Bd6 17 Be5 Nb4 = Jansa-Abramović, Zenica 1986
[10]   Suetin-Smagin, Moscow Ch 1983, and Geller-Smagin, USSR Ch 1985

[11]   11 ... Qb8 12 Bg5 ± Romanishin-Nei, Tallinn 1977
11 ... Re8 12 Nbd2 Bf8 13 d5 ± Yudasin-Vasyukov, USSR 1982
11 ... Qd7 12 Nbd2 Rfb8 13 Qc2! Bf8 14 b3 ± Yudasin-Vasyukov, USSR 1982
[12]   14 Nxd4 Re8 15 Bg5 Nxd5 16 Bxe7 Nxe7 17 Nd2 ±/= Short-Sharif, Lucerne 1985
[13]   15 ... Bb4!? 16 Bd2 Bxc3 17 Bxc3 Nc4 18 b3 Nd6 19 Ba5 or 19 Bd2 ± Dorfman, Nikitin
[14]   Short-van der Sterren, Wijk aan Zee 1986, and Arnason-Dorfman, Helsinki 1986
[15]   12 a4 Bd7 (12 ... Bb7 – 9 ... Bb7) 13 Bc2 Qc8 (13 ... b4!? Geller) 14 Nf1 Bb7 15 Ng3 Rad8 16 ab ab 17 Be3 ± Sznapik-Djurić, Vrnjačka Banja 1981
12 Bc2 Bb7 (12 ... Bd7 13 Bd3 Qb8 14 b3 g6 15 Bb2 Bg7 16 d5 ± Savon-Geller, Lvov 1978) 13 d5 Nb8 14 b3 c6 15 c4 ± Karpov-Balashov, Munich 1979
[16]   14 ... Nc4 15 b3 Nb6 16 Nh2 c5 17 f4 ± ECO
[17]   15 ... g6 16 Be3 Qc7 17 Qd2 Kh7 18 Rad1 ±
15 ... cd 16 cd Nc6 17 Bb2 ± Fischer-Spassky, Havana Ol 1966, and Gufeld-Savon, Vilnius 1975
[18]   Smejkal-Timman, Amsterdam 1976
[19]   14 ... g6 15 Nh2 Bg7 16 f4 ±
14 ... c5 15 d5 Bc8 16 b3 ±
[20]   16 ... c5 17 d5 c4 18 b4 ± Fischer-Gligorić, Zagreb 1970
16 ... d5 17 Nxe5 de 18 Nxe4 Nxe4 19 Bxe4 Bxe4 20 Rxe4 f6 21 Nc6 Qd5 22 Rxe8 Rxe8 23 ab ab ± Gligorić
16 ... ba!? 17 ba a5
[21]   18 Qe2 c6 19 Be3 ± Matulović-Rukavina, Vršac 1985

Ruy Lopez XIII 1 e4 e5 2 ♘f3 ♘c6 3 ♗b5 a6 4 ♗a4 ♘f6
5 0-0 ♗e7 6 ♖e1 b5 7 ♗b3 d6 8 c3 0-0 9 h3 ♗b7 10 d4 ♖e8[1]

	11	12	13	14	15	16	17	18	19	
1	♘g5	f4[2]	♗xf4	♗c2[3]	ed	♕h5	♘d2[4]	♘e4	♕f5	=
	♖f8	ef	♘a5	♘d5	♗xg5	h6	♗xd5	♗xf4	g6[5]	
2	a4	♘bd2[7]	cd	♕e2[9]	e5	de	♕xd3	♖e3	♖xc1	∞∞
	h6[6]	ed[8]	♘b4	♗f8	de[10]	♕d3	♘xd3	♖xc1	♘d5[11]	
3	♘bd2	♗c2[12]	b3[14]	de	♘xe5	f4[16]	♔h2	♘xe4	♗e3	=
	♗f8	g6[13]	d5[15]	♘xe5	♖xe5	♗c5+	♖xe4	de	♗xe3[17]	

[1] **10 ...** ♘a5 11 ♗c2 ♘c4 12 b3 ♘b6 13 ♘bd2 ♖e8 (13 ... ♘bd7 14 b4 ± Fischer-Stein, Sousse IZ 1967) 14 ♗b2 (14 de de 15 ♘xe5 ♗c5 ∞∞) 14 ... ♗f8 15 c4 bc 16 de ± Timoshchenko-Klovans, USSR 1974

10 ... ♕d7 11 ♘bd2 ♖ae8 (11 ... ♖ad8 12 ♗c2 ♖fe8 13 d5 ♘b8 14 b3 ± Lanka-Litvinov, USSR 1979) 12 ♗c2 ♗d8 13 a3 ♘b8 14 b4 ± Kuzmin-Glauser, Bath 1973

[2] 12 de ♘xe5 13 f4 ♘c4 14 ♗c2 d5! ∓ Sax-Lukacz, Hungarian Ch 1981

[3] 14 ♘d2 ♘xb3 15 ab c5 (15 ... ♘d5 16 ed ♗xg5 17 ♗xg5 ♕xg5 18 c4 ± Yurtayev-Podgayets, USSR 1981) 16 dc dc 17 ♕c2 h6 18 ♘gf3 ♘h7! ∓ Gutman

[4] 17 ♗g3 g6 18 ♕f3 ♘c4 ∓ Ljubojević-Gligorić, match 1979

[5] **19 ...** ♗xe4 20 ♗xe4 ♗h2+ 21 ♔xh2 g6 22 ♕f4 d5 23 ♗f3 ♔h7 24 b3 ∞∞ Gutman

19 ... g6 20 ♘f6+ ♗g7 21 ♘h5+ gh (21 ... ♔h8 22 ♕xf4 ♕g5 23 ♕xg5 hg 24 ♘f6 ♗e6 25 g4 ∞∞) 22 ♕h7+ ♔f6 23 ♕f5+ =

[6] **11 ...** ♗f8 12 ♗g5 h6 (12 ... ♘a5 13 ♗c2 h6 14 ♗xf6 ♕xf6 15 ♘a3 c6 16 ♕d3 ±) 13 ♗xf6 ♕xf6 14 ♗d5 ± Murei-Kudrin, New York 1982

11 ... ♕d7 12 ♘bd2 ♗f8 – 11 ♘bd2

[7] 12 d5 ♘a5 13 ♗a2 c6 14 ♘a3 ♕c7 15 ♘h4 (15 b4 ♘c4 ∓ A.Ivanov-Belyavsky, USSR 1980) 15 ... cd 16 ed ♘c4! ∞ Ljubojević-Karpov, Lucerne Ol 1982, and Ivanović-Smejkal-Sarajevo 1983

[8] 12 ... ♗f8 – 11 ♘bd2

[9] **14 d5** c5 15 dc ♘xc6 ∞ Tseshkovsky-A.Ivanov, USSR 1984

14 ab ab 15 ♖xa8 ♗xa8 (15 ... ♕xa8? 16 e5 ± de Firmian-Nikolić, Tunis IZ 1985) 16 e5 (16 ♕e2!?) 16 ... de 17 de ♘fd5 ∞

[10] 15 ... ♗c6?! 16 ab ♗xb5 17 ♕d1 ♘fd5 18 ♘e4 ± Kasparov-Karpov, match (44) 1984-85

[11] 20 ♗xd5 ♗xd5 21 ab ab 22 ♖xc7 ♖a1+ 23 ♔h2 ♖a2 ∞∞/= Aseyev-A.Ivanov, Kostroma 1985

[12] **12 ♘g5** ♖e7 13 d5 (13 f4?! h6 14 ♘df3 ♕e8! Arnason-Geller, Reykjavik 1986) 13 ... ♘a5 14 ♗c2 c6 = Liberzon-Greenfeld, Israel 1983

12 d5 ♘b8 (12 ... ♘a5 13 ♗c2 c6 14 b4 ± Kindermann-Smejkal, Baden-Baden 1985; 12 ... ♘e7 13 c4 ± Ermenkov-Lukacs, Albena 1985) 13 ♗c2 ♘bd7 14 b3 c6 – 9 ... ♘b8 (row 2)

[13] 12 ... ♘b8 13 a4 c5?! (13 ... ♘bd7 – 9 ... ♘b8, rows 4-5) 14 d5 ♘bd7 15 b4 ± A.Sokolov-Karpov, Bugojno 1986

[14] **13 ♘b3** ed 14 cd ♘b4 ∓ Geller-Belyavsky, USSR Ch 1978, and Tseshkovsky-Psakhis, USSR Ch 1987

13 a4 ed 14 ♕xd4 (14 cd ♗g7 ∞ Marjanović-Nikolić, Kavala 1985) 14 ... ♘xd4 15 cd ♗h5 = Timoshchenko-Podgayets, USSR 1979

13 d5 ♘e7 14 ♘f1 (14 b3!?) 14 ... ♗g7 15 b3 ♘xe4! 16 ♗xe4 f5 17 ♗c2 e4 18 ♘d4 ♘xd5 ∞∞ Geller-Eingorn, USSR Ch 1985

[15] **13 ... b4** 14 d5 bc 15 ♘c4 ± Hübner-Hort, Biel 1986

13 ... ♘b8 14 a4 ♘bd7 or 14 d5 c6 15 c4 ♕c7 16 ♘f1 ♘bd7 – 9 ... ♘b8 (rows 2-3)

[16] 16 ♘f3 ♖xe4 17 ♗xe4 ♘xe4 18 ♗b2 ♗g7 19 ♕c2 ♕f6 ∞∞ A.Rodriguez-Belyavsky, Bogotá 1979, and Tseshkovsky-Belyavsky, USSR 1980

[17] 20 ♖xe3 ♘d5 21 ♗xe4 ♘xe3 22 ♕xd8+ ♖xd8 23 ♗xb7 a5 = Hübner-Belyavsky, Tilburg 1986

1 e4 e5 2 ♘f3 ♘c6 3 ♗b5 a6 4 ♗a4 ♘f6
5 0-0 ♗e7 6 ♖e1 b5 7 ♗b3 d6 8 c3 0-0 9 h3 ♗b7 10 d4 ♖e8 11 ♘bd2 ♗f8 12 a3

	12	13	14	15	16	17	18	19	20	
1	...	♗a2[2]	d5	b4	♘b3[4]	cb	♘a5	dc	♕b3	±
	♕d7[1]	g6[3]	♘e7	a5	ab	♗g7	c6	♗xc6	♖f8[5]	
2	...	♗a2[6]	d5[7]	b4	c4	♗b2	dc	♗xc4		±
	g6	♗g7	♘b8[8]	c6	♖a7[9]	bc[10]	♗xc6			
3	...	♗c2[11]	b4[13]	♗b2	c4[15]	cb	♘xd4	a4[16]	♗xa4	∞
	h6	♘b8[12]	♘bd7	g6[14]	ed	ab	c6	ba	♕b6[17]	

[1] 12 ... ♘b8?! 13 de! de 14 ♘g5 (14 ♗xf7+!?) 14 ... ♖e7 15 ♘xf7!? ♖xf7 16 ♘f3 ♕xd1 17 ♖xd1 c5 18 ♗e6! ± Kuporosov-Zhukovitsky, USSR 1986

[2] 13 ♗c2 ♖ad8 14 ♘b3 h6 15 d5 ♘e7 16 ♘a5 c6 17 c4 ± Psakhis-Balashov, USSR Ch 1980-81

[3] 13 ... a5 14 d5 ♘e7 15 c4 c6 16 dc ♕xc6 17 b4! ab 18 ♘g5! ± Gutman
   13 ... ♖ad8 14 ♘g5! ♖e7 15 d5 ±
   13 ... ♘d8 14 d5 c6 15 c4 ♘h5 16 b4 ♘f4 17 ♘f1 bc 18 ♗xf4 ef 19 ♗xc4 ± Gufeld-Veingold, USSR 1981

[4] 16 ba c6 17 c4 cd! 18 cd ♖xa5 19 ♘b1 ♘c8 20 ♗d2 ♖a8 ∞ Gutman

[5] 21 ♗g5 ± Gutman

[6] 13 ♗c2 ♗g7 (13 ... ♘b8 14 b4 ♘bd7 15 ♗b2 ♗g7 16 ♕b1 d5 17 ed ed 18 c4 bc = Smagin-Psakhis, Moscow 1986) 14 d5 ♘e7 (14 ... ♘b8 15 c4 c6 16 b4! ♕c7 17 ♗b2 bc 18 dc ♘xc6 19 ♘xc4 ± Sax-Short, Biel IZ 1985) 15 c4 c6 16 dc ♘xc6 17 b4 ♘d4! ∞ Hall-Littlewood, England 1981

[7] 14 b4 a5 15 d5 ♘e7 16 ba (16 ♘b3 ab 17 cb ♘xe4! 18 ♖xe4 ♗xd5 19 ♖e1 e4 20 ♘fd4 c5 ⩲̄ Chiburdanidze-A.Ivanov, USSR 1980) 16 ... c6! 17 dc ♗xc6 18 c4 bc 19 ♗xc4 ♕xa5 ∞ Gutman

[8] 14 ... ♘e7 15 c4! c6 16 b4 bc 17 dc ± Gutman

[9] 16 ... bc 17 dc! ♗xc6 18 ♘xc4 ♘d4 19 ♗g5!
   16 ... cd 17 cd a5 18 ♘b3 ab 19 ab ± Gutman

[10] 17 ... ♘bd7 18 ♖c1 ♕a8 19 dc! ♗xc6 20 ♕c2! ± Gufeld-Aseyev, USSR 1986

[11] 13 ♗a2 ♘b8 (13 ... ♘a7!?) 14 b4 ed (14 ... ♘bd7 15 ♗b2 g6 16 ♕b1 ♗g7 17 c4 ½-½ Dobrovolsky-Plachetka, Trnava 1983) 15 cd ♘xe4 16 ♕b3 ♕f6 17 ♕c2 ♘xd2 18 ♖xe8 ♘xf3+ 19 gf ♘c6 ⩲̄ Mortensen-Hjartarson, 1985

[12] 13 ... a5 14 ♗d3 b4 15 ♗b5 ♖e7 16 d5 ♘a7 17 ♗f1 bc 18 bc c6 19 c4 ± Psakhis-Belyavsky, USSR Ch 1981
   13 ... d5 14 ed (14 de!? ±) 14 ... ♕xd5 15 ♘e4 ed 16 ♘xf6+ gf 17 ♗f4! ± Smyslov
   13 ... g6!? 14 ♘f1 ♘a5 15 ♘g3 ♘c4 16 b3 ♘b6 17 ♗d3 ♗g7 ∞ Aseyev-Timoshchenko, Irkutsk 1986

[13] 14 b3 ♘bd7 15 ♗b2 (15 d5 c6 16 c4 ♕c7 17 ♗b2 ♖eb8 18 dc ♗xc6 19 cb ab ½-½ Smyslov-Gligorić, Sochi 1986) 15 ... g6 16 a4 (16 ♖b1 c5 17 d5 ♗g7 18 ♗d4 ♗g7 19 b4 ♕c7 20 c5 dc 21 bc ♘h5 ∞ Romanishin-van der Sterren, Tallinn 1987) 16 ... c6 17 ♕b1 ♗g7 18 ab cb 19 d5 h5 20 b4 ± Short-Hjartarson, Reykjavik 1987; 16 ... ♘h5!? Hjartarson

[14] 15 ... a5 16 ba! c5 (16 ... ♖xa5 17 ♗d3 ± A.Rodriguez) 17 de ♘xe5 18 ♘xe5 de 19 c4 ♕xa5 20 ♕e2 ± Kovalov-Klovans, USSR 1986
   15 ... c5 16 bc dc 17 ♘xe5 ♘xe5 18 de ♘h5 19 c4 ♘f4 20 ♗e3 ♘g6 21 a4 ± A.Rodriguez-Frey, Medina del Campo 1986
   15 ... ♖b8!? 16 c4 ed 17 cb ab 18 ♘xd4 c5 ½-½ Byrne-Geller, Reykjavik 1986

[15] 16 ♕b1 ♗g7 17 ♘b3 ♖c8! 18 ♘a5 ♗a8 19 d5 ♘b6 20 a4 ♕d7 21 ab ab 22 ♗d3 ∞ Psakhis-Portisch, Sarajevo 1986; 16 ... ♘h5!? 17 g3 c5 ∞

[16] 19 ♖c1 ♕b6 20 ♗d3 ♗g7 21 ♘2b3 ∞ Sokolov-Izeta, Bilbao 1987
   19 ♘2b3 ♖c8 20 ♘a5 ♗a8 21 ♕d2 ♕b6 22 ♘db3 c5 ∞ Klovans-Goldin, USSR 1987

[17] 21 b5?! cb 22 ♖xb5 d5! 23 ♖xa8 ♗xa8 ∞/=̄ Timman-Kasparov, match 1985
   21 ♘c2 ♕c7 22 ♗b3 ♖xa1 (22 ... ♗a6 23 ♖c1 ♗g7 ∞ Timman-Kasparov, match 1985) 23 ♗xa1 (23 ♕xa1 ♗g7 24 ♗c3 ♘e5 = Hübner-Portisch, Tilburg 1986) 23 ... ♗g7 24 ♘e3 c5 25 bc ♘xc5 26 ♗xf6 ♗xf6 ∞ ½-½ Timman-Karpov, Bugojno 1986

Ruy Lopez XV   1 e4 e5 2 Nf3 Nc6 3 Bb5 a6 4 Ba4 Nf6 5 0-0 Be7
6 Re1 b5 7 Bb3 d6 8 c3 0-0 9 h3 Bb7 10 d4 Re8 11 Nbd2 Bf8 12 a4

	12	13	14	15	16	17	18	19	20	
1	...	ab[1]	Rxa8	d5	Ba2	b4	Nf1[4]	ed	Bg5[5]	∞
	Qd7	ab	Bxa8	Na5[2]	c6	Nb7[3]	cd	Rc8		
2	...	d5	c4	ab	Rxa8	dc	Ba4	Nf1	g4[9]	∞
	h6	Nb8[6]	c6[7]	ab	Bxa8	b4[8]	Nxc6	Qb8	Rc8[10]	
3	...	Bc2	cd	Bb1	d5[13]	Ra3[15]	Nd4[16]	Nf3	Bxd3[19]	∞
	...	ed[11]	Nb4	c5[12]	Nd7[14]	c4!	Qf6[17]	Nd3[18]	b4[20]	

[1] 13 d5 Ne7?! 14 c4 ± Hübner-Portisch, Brussels 1986; 13 ... Na5!? ∞

[2] 15 ... Nd8 16 Nf1 h6 17 N3h2 ± Kasparov-Karpov, match (46) 1984-85

15 ... Nb8 16 Nf1 Na6 17 Bg5 Be7 18 Ng3 ± Kasparov-Smejkal, Dubai Ol 1986

15 ... Ne7 16 c4 (16 Nf1!?) 16 ... Rb8 ∞ Popović-Smejkal, Zagreb 1985

[3] 17 ... Nc4? 18 Nxc4 bc 19 Bxc4 (19 Bg5!?) 19 ... cd 20 ed Rc8 21 Qb3 ±

[4] 18 c4 Rc8! 19 dc Qxc6 = Kasparov-Karpov, match (5) 1985

[5] 20 ... Rxc3?! 21 Bxf6 gf 22 Nh4 ∞∞

20 ... Be7 21 Nd2 ∞ Kasparov

[6] 13 ... Ne7 14 c4 ± Sznapik-Panczyk, Polish Ch 1981, and Jansa-Nikolić, Esbjerg 1982

13 ... Na7 14 Nf1 c6 15 N3h2 ± Nunn-Smejkal, Dubai Ol 1986

[7] 14 ... bc 15 Nxc4 ± Kindermann-Greenfeld, Beer-Sheva 1984

[8] 17 ... bc 18 Nxc4 Bxc6 (18 ... Nxc6 19 Ba4 =) 19 Ba4 =

[9] 20 Ng3 g6 intending ... Rc8 =∓

[10] 21 Ng3 Nd8 22 g5 hg 23 Nxg5 ∞ Kasparov-Dorfman, USSR Ch 1978

[11] 13 ... Qd7 14 d5 Ne7 15 b3 ± Spassky-Balashov, Toluca IZ 1982

13 ... Nb8 14 Bd3 c6 15 Nf1 ± Kasparov-Karpov, match (9) 1985

13 ... Rb8 14 ab ab 15 Bd3 Bc8 16 Nf1 ± Timman-Karpov, Tilburg 1986, and Hjartarson-Karpov, Dubai Ol 1986

[12] 15 ... g6 16 e5! ± Matulović-Lukacs, Vrnjačka Banja 1985

15 ... ba 16 Rxa4 a5 17 Ra3 Ra6 (17 ... g6 18 Rae3 ± Sax-Belyavsky, Moscow IZ 1982; 17 ... Qd7 18 Nh4 ± Ehlvest-Belyavsky, USSR Ch 1984) 18 Nh2 ± Sax-Banas, Balatonbereny 1984

15 ... Qd7 16 Ra3 ba 17 Rxa4 a5 18 Ra3 Qb5 19 Nh2 ± Dvoiris-Lerner, Kharkov 1985

[13] 16 dc dc 17 e5 Nd7 = Kasparov-Balashov, USSR 1982

16 b3 cd 17 Nxd4 ba 18 Rxa4 a5 = Tseshkovsky-Balashov, Minsk 1982

[14] 16 ... g6 17 Nf1 Bg7 18 Ra3 ba 19 Rxa4 a5 20 Ra3 Ba6 21 Ng3 ± Aseyev-Dorfman, USSR Ch 1984

[15] 17 Nf1 f5! ∞/∓ de Firmian-Belyavsky, Tunis IZ 1985

[16] 18 ab ab 19 Nd4 Rxa3 20 ba Nd3 21 Bxd3 cd ∞ Kasparov-Karpov, match (14) 1986

[17] 18 ... Ne5?! 19 ab Qb6 20 Nf5 (20 Nxc4!? Nxc4 21 Rg3 ∞∞ Sax-Short, Subotica IZ 1987) 20 ... Nbd3 21 Bxd3 Nxd3 22 Re3 ab 23 Nxh6+ gh 24 Rg3+ Bg7 25 Rxd3 cd 26 Nb3 ∞∞ Oll-Kruppa, Uzgorod 1987

18 ... Qb6?! 19 Nf5 ± Sax-Nikolić, Lugano 1987

[18] 19 ... Nc5 20 ab ab 21 Nxb5 Rxa3 22 Nxa3 Ba6 ∞∞ Kasparov-Karpov, match (16) 1986

[19] 20 Rxd3!? cd 21 ab ∞

[20] 21 Ra1 cd 22 Qxd3 Nc5 23 Qc4 a5! 24 Nb5 Rac8 ∓

21 Bxc4 ba 22 b3 ∞ Kasparov

Ruy Lopez XVI 1 e4 e5 2 ♘f3 ♘c6 3 ♗b5 a6 4 ♗a4 ♘f6
5 0-0 ♗e7 6 ♖e1 b5 7 ♗b3 d6 8 c3 0-0 9 h3 ♘b8 10 d4¹ ♘bd7

	11	12	13	14	15	16	17	18	19	
1	♗g5²	♘bd2	♗h4	♗g3⁴	♘h4	de	♗c2	♘hf3	♕xf3	∞
	♗b7	h6	♖e8³	♗f8	c5	♘xe5⁵	g6	♘xf3+	♖e6⁶	
2	♘bd2	♗c2	b3	d5	c4	♘f1⁸	♘e3	♗d2	♘g4	=
	♗b7	♖e8⁷	♗f8	c6	♕c7	♖ec8⁹	g6¹⁰	♘c5¹¹	♘xg4¹²	
3	...	...	...	♗b2	a4	♗d3	♕c2¹⁴	♖ad1¹⁶	♕b1	=
	...	...	...	g6	♗g7¹³	c6	♖c8¹⁵	♕b6	♘h5¹⁷	
4	...	...	a4	♗d3	♘f1	♘g3	♘xe4	♘xf6+	♖xe8	=
	...	...	♗f8	c6¹⁸	d5¹⁹	de	ed	♘xf6	♕xe8²⁰	
5	...	...	...	b4	a5²²	♗b2	♖b1²⁴	♗a1	c4	=
	...	...	...	♘b6²¹	♘bd7	♖b8²³	♗a8	g6	bc²⁵	
6	...	...	♘f1	♘g3	a4	d5	♗g5²⁹	♗c3	♕d2	±/∞
	...	...	♗f8²⁶	g6	c5²⁷	c4²⁸	h6	♘c5	h5³⁰	

1 10 d3 ♘bd7 11 ♘bd2 ♗b7 12 ♘f1 ♘c5
13 ♗c2 ♖e8 14 ♘g3 ♗f8 15 b4 (15 ♘h2 d5 =)
15 ... ♘cd7 16 d4 (16 ♗b3 d5 =) 16 ... a5!?
(16 ... g6 17 a4 ♗g7 18 ♗d3 ba 19 de ♘xe5
20 ♘xe5 ♖xe5 =) 17 ♗d2 ab 18 cb ed 19 ♘xd4
d5! = Tal-Timman, Nikšić 1983
2 11 ♘h4 ed (11 ... ♘xe4 12 ♘f5 ∞) 12 cd
♘b6 13 ♘f3 (13 ♘d2 c5 = Byrne-Spassky,
Moscow 1971) 13 ... c5 14 ♗f4 ♗b7 15 dc dc
16 ♕xd8 ♗xd8 17 ♗d6 ♖e8 18 ♗xc5 ♘bd7 =
Fischer-Robatsch, Vinkovci 1968
   11 c4 c6 12 c5 ♕c7 13 cd ♗xd6 14 ♗g5
ed! 15 ♗xf6 gf 16 ♕xd4 (16 ♘xd4 ♘c5 ∞/=
Gligorić-Petrosian, Los Angeles 1963) 16 ...
♘e5 17 ♘bd2 ♖d8 18 ♕e3 ♘d3 ∞ Fischer-
Portisch, Santa Monica 1966
3 13 ... ♘h7 14 ♗xe7 (14 ♗g3!?) 14 ... ♕xe7
15 ♘f1 ♘g5 16 ♘g3 g6 = Tal-Psakhis, Sochi
1984
4 14 ♖e3?! c5 Zapata-A.Rodriguez, Cienfuegos 1983
   14 a4 ed 15 ♘xd4 c5 16 ♘f5 ♗f8 intending
... g6 =
5 16 ... de 17 c4! ♘b8 18 ♘f5 intending ♘e3
Ljubojević
6 Ljubojević-Portisch, Manila 1974
7 12 ... d5?! 13 de ♘xe4 14 ♘xe4 de 15 ♗xe4
♗xe4 16 ♖xe4 ♘xe5 17 ♖d4 ± Hjartarson-
Reshevsky, Reykjavik 1984
   12 ... c5 13 ♘f1 ♖e8 14 ♘g3 ♗f8 15 d5
g6 16 a4 – 12 ... ♖e8 (row 6)
8 16 a4 ♖ec8 17 ♖a2 bc 18 bc a5 = Karpov-
Romanishin, USSR 1979
9 16 ... g6 17 ♗d2 bc 18 bc a5 19 ♘3h2 h5
20 ♖e3 ± Ljubojević-Reshevsky, New York 1984
10 17 ... a5 18 ♗d2 bc 19 bc ♘c5 20 ♘f5 ±
Geller-Lukacs, Sochi 1984
   17 ... cd 18 cd a5 19 ♗d2 b4 20 a3 ± Geller-
Belyavsky, Sochi 1986
11 18 ... a5 19 ♖c1 ♗a6 ∞ Tseshkovsky-
Belyavsky, USSR Ch 1980-81
12 20 hg cd 21 cd ♘a4 22 ♗d3 ♘b2 =
Ljubojević-Portisch, Tilburg 1983, and Psakhis-
Smejkal, Szirak 1986
13 15 ... ♖b8 16 ♗d3 c6 17 ♕c2 ♘h5 ∞/=
Ljubojević-Karpov, Tilburg 1986
14 17 ♖b1!? ♕b6 18 b4 ♘h5 19 ♘b3

Ljubojević-Smejkal, Reggio Emilia 1985-86
15 17 ... ♕b6 18 b4 c5!? ∞ Ljubojević-Spassky,
Tilburg 1983
16 18 de?! de 19 b4 ♗f8 20 ♖ed1 ♕b6 21 ♕b3
c5 ∓ Korchnoi-Portisch, Belgrade 1970
17 Spassky-Smejkal, Thessaloniki Ol 1984
18 14 ... d5?! Ljubojević-Portisch, Bugojno
1986
19 15 ... g6 16 ♘g3 ♗g7 17 ♗d2 ♕c7 18 ♕c1
d5! = Smagin-Klovans, Pinsk 1986
20 20 cd c5 = Spraggett-Smejkal, Szirak 1986
21 14 ... a5 15 ba ♖xa5 16 ♖b1 ± ECO
22 15 ab ab 16 ♖xa8 ♕xa8 = Timman-
Kasparov, World v USSR 1984
23 16 ... g6 17 ♖b1 ♗g7 18 c4 c6 19 cb cb
20 d5 ± Timman-Torre, Bugojno 1984
24 17 ♕b1 ♘h5 18 c4?! bc 19 ♘xc4 ed
20 ♗xd4 c5 ∓ Ljubojević-Karpov, Manila 1976
25 20 de ♘xe5 21 ♘xe5 de 22 ♗c3 ♗c6
23 ♕e2 ♗b5 24 ♘xc4 c5 25 bc ♖c8 = Browne-
Karpov, Amsterdam 1976
26 13 ... d5?! 14 ♗xe5! ♘xe5 (14 ... ♘xe4
15 ♘xf7! ♔xf7 16 ♖xe4 ±) 15 de ♘xe4 16 f3!
♘c5 (16 ... ♘g5 17 ♘g3 ± Chandler-Spassky,
West Germany 1985, and Lobron-Portisch,
Wijk aan Zee 1985) 17 b4 ♘d7 18 f4 c5 (18 ...
a5 19 ♕d3 ± Kindermann-Spassky, West
Germany 1984) 19 ♕d3 ± Greenfeld-Shvidler,
Israel 1984
27 15 ... c6 16 ♗g5 h6 17 ♗e3 ♕c7 18 ♕d2
♔h7 19 ♗d3 ♗g7 20 de de 21 c4 ± Kruppa-
Agzamov, Sevastopol 1986
28 16 ... ♘b6 17 ♕e2 ♖xa4 18 ♗xa4 ba
19 ♖xa4 ± Karpov-Gligorić, Milan 1975, and
Geller-Romanishin, USSR 1978
29 17 ♗e3 ♘c5 (17 ... ♗g7 18 ♕d2 ♕e7
19 ♖a3 ±/= Ljubojević-Hort, Lucerne Ol 1982)
18 ♕e2 ♘fd7 19 ♘d2 ♕c7 20 ♖a3 ♘b6 =
Karpov-Portisch, Milan 1975
30 19 ... ♔h7 20 ♘h2 ♗g7 21 ♖f1 ± Spassky-
Portisch, match 1977, and Timman-Portisch,
Reggio Emilia 1984-85
   19 ... h5 20 ♘g5 (20 ♗g5!? Kavalek-Spassky,
Turin 1982) 20 ... ♗g7 (20 ... ♘h7 21 ♘xh7
♔xh7 22 ♖f1 intending 23 f4 ±) 21 ab ab
22 ♖xa8 ♗xa8 23 f4 ±/∞ Short-Spassky,
Montpellier C 1985

	11	12	13	14	15	16	17	18	19	
1	...	cd	♘bd2[2]	♘f1[3]	de[5]	♘1d2[6]	♘b3			±
	cd[1]	♗b7	♖c8	d5[4]	♘xe4	f5				
2	...	d5[7]	b3[9]	a4	ab	♗e3	♘bd2	b4	cb	±/∞
	♘c6	♘a5[8]	♘e8[10]	♗d7	ab	g6	♘g7	cb	♘c4[11]	
3	...	dc[12]	♘bd2	♘h4	♕e2[14]	♘f1	♘g3	♘hf5[15]		∞
	♘d7	dc	f6[13]	♘b6	♗e6	♖a7	♖f7	♗f8		
4	...	♘bd2	cd	♘b3[16]	♗e3[17]	♘bd2	d5[19]	♖c1	♗b1	±
	...	cd	♘c6	a5	a4	♗f6[18]	♘d4	♗b7[20]	♕b6[21]	
5	...	♘bd2	d5[23]	a4	ab	b4	♘f1	♘g3[26]	♘h2	±
	♕c7	♘c6[22]	♘d8[24]	♖b8	ab	c4[25]	♘e8	g6	♘g7[27]	
6	...	...	♘f1	d5[29]	g4	gh!	♘3h2	♘xf1	♘g3	±
	...	♗d7	♘c4[28]	♘b6	h5	♗xh3	♗xf1![30]	♕d7	♕h3[31]	
7	...	...	cd	♘b3[32]	♗e3	♘bd2	♖c1	♕e2	♗d3	±
	...	cd	♘c6	a5	a4	♗d7[33]	♕b8[34]	♖e8	♘b4[35]	
8	...	...	...	d5[36]	♗d3[38]	♘f1	♗g5[40]	ef	♗xe7	±
	...	...	♗b7	♖ac8[37]	♘d7	f5[39]	♘c5	♗xd5[41]	♗xf3[42]	
9	...	...	...	♘f1	♘e3[43]	d5[45]	♗b1	a3	b4!	±/∞
	...	...	♗d7	♖ac8	♘c6[44]	♘b4	a5	♘a6	♖a8[46]	

[1]   11 ... ♗b7 12 d5 ♗c8 – 11 ... ♘c6
[2]   13 d5 ♗c8 (13 ... ♕c7 14 ♗d3 ♗c8 15 ♗e3 ♗d7 16 ♘bd2 ± Romanishin-Lukacs, Sochi 1984) 14 ♘bd2 g6 15 b4 ♘b7 16 a4 ♗d7 17 ab (Fischer-Weinstein, US Ch 1963) 17 ... ♗xb5 =
[3]   14 d5 ±
[4]   14 ... ♕c7 – 11 ... ♕c7
[5]   15 ed ed 16 ♗g5 (16 ♘xd4 ♘xd5 17 ♘g3 ♗f6 ∓ Large-Littlewood, British Ch 1983) 16 ... h6 17 ♗h4 ♘xd5 = Matulović-Hennings, Sarajevo 1969
[6]   16 ♘g3 f5 17 ef ♗xf6 18 ♘xe4 de 19 ♕xd8 ♖fxd8 20 ♘xe4 ♗xe4 21 ♖xe4 ♖c2 ∓
[7]   12 a4 ♗d7 13 d5 ♘a5 14 b4 ♘b7 15 ♗e3 ♕c7 16 ♘bd2 ♖fc8 17 ♖a2 a5 = Ljubojević-Romanishin, Tilburg 1985
     12 ♘bd2 cd 13 cd ♘d7 – 11 ... ♘d7; 13 ... ♕c7 – 11 ... ♕c7
[8]   12 ... ♘a7 13 ♘bd2 ♗d7 14 ♘f1 ♘c8 15 b3 ♕c7 (15 ... ♘b6 16 ♘xe5 ±) 16 ♘e3 ♘b6 17 c4 ± Vitolins-Klovans, Jurmala 1978
[9]   13 ♘bd2 g6 14 b4 ♘b7 15 a4 ♗d7 16 ♘f1

♕c7 = Psakhis-Romanishin, Sochi 1984, and Geller-Romanishin, Moscow 1985
[10]   13 ... ♗d7 14 ♘bd2 (14 ♘xe5 ±) 14 ... g6 15 ♘f1 ♘h5 16 ♗h6 ♖e8 17 ♕d2 ♗f8 18 ♗g5 ♗e7 19 ♗e3 ♗f6 20 ♖ac1 c4 21 b4 ± Psakhis-Romanishin, Erevan 1986
[11]   20 ♘xc4 bc 21 ♕d2 f5 ±/∞ Psakhis-Romanishin, Moscow 1986
[12]   12 b3 ed 13 cd ♘c6 14 ♘c3 (14 d5 ♘b4 =) 14 ... ♗f6 =
     12 d5 ♘b6 13 b3 (13 g4 h5! 14 ♘h2 hg 15 hg ♗g5 ∞/∓ Fischer-Keres, Curaçao C 1962) 13 ... f5 ∞
[13]   13 ... ♗b7 14 ♘f1 ♘c4 15 ♘g3 g6 16 b3 ♘d6 ∞ Tal-Romanishin, Jurmala 1983
[14]   15 ♘f5!? ♖f7 16 ♕g4 ♔h8 17 h4 Fischer
[15]   18 f4?! ef 19 ♘gf5 ♗f8 ∞/∓ A.Sokolov-A.Rodriguez, Biel IZ 1985
[16]   14 d5 ♘b4 15 ♗b1 a5 16 ♘f1 g6 =
     14 ♘f1 ed 15 ♘xd4 ♘xd4 16 ♕xd4 ♘e5 17 ♖d1 ♗b7 (17 ... ♗xh3? 18 ♕xe5 ±±; 17 ... ♕c7 18 ♘e3 ♗xh3 19 ♘d5! ♕d8 20 ♘xe7+

410

♕xe7 21 ♕xd6 ± Ljubojević-Portisch, Tilburg 1984) 18 ♘g3 ♗f6!? (18 ... ♕c7 19 ♗b3 ± Timman-Romanishin, Wijk aan Zee 1985) 19 ♕xd6 ♕c8 20 ♕d2 ♖d8 21 ♕e2 ♕c4! ∞ Spraggett-Romanishin, Wijk aan Zee 1985

[17] 15 ♗d3 ♗a6 16 d5 ♘b4 17 ♗f1 a4 18 a3 ♘xd5 19 ♕xd5 ♘b6 20 ♕d1 ab 21 ♕xb3 ♕d7 ∞/= Hellers-Timman, Amsterdam 1986

[18] **16 ... ed** 17 ♘xd4 ♘xd4 18 ♗xd4 ♘e5 19 ♘f1 ♗e6 20 ♘e3 ±

16 ... ♗a6 17 ♖c1 ♖c8 18 ♗b1 ♕a5 19 ♘f1 ♗f6 20 d5 ± Ostojić-Romanishin, Erevan 1976

[19] 17 ♘f1 ♘b6 18 b3 ♘b4 19 ♗b1 ♗e6 20 ♕d2 (20 d5 ♗d7 =) 20 ... ab! 21 ♕xb4 ♖a4 ∓ Watson-Rogers, Belgrade 1986

[20] 18 ... ♘xc2 19 ♕xc2 intending ♕c6, ♕c7 ±

[21] 20 ♘f1 ♖fc8 21 ♕d2 ± Gufeld-Romanishin, Vilnius 1975

[22] **12 ... ♗b7** 13 d5 ♗c8 – 12 ... ♘c6

12 ... ♖e8 13 ♘f1 ♗f8 (13 ... ♗d7 – 12 ... ♗d7) 14 ♗g5 ♘d7 15 b3 ±

12 ... ♖d8 13 ♘f1 cd (13 .. d5 14 de de 15 ♘1d2 ef 16 ef ♗xf6 17 ♕xf3 ±) 14 cd ed 15 ♘g3! (15 ♘xd4 d5 16 e5 ♘e4 ∞ Sigurjonsson-Torre, Reykjavik 1980, and Chiburdanidze-Torre, Baku 1980) 15 ... d5 16 e5 ♘e4 17 ♘xe4 de 18 ♗xe4 ♗b7 19 ♗g5 ± Rajna-Damljanović, Titovo Uzice 1981

[23] 13 dc?! dc 14 ♘f1 ♗e6 15 ♘e3 ♖ad8 16 ♕e2 c4 17 ♘f5 (17 ♘g5 h6 18 ♘xe6 fe 19 b4? ♘d4! ∓ Fischer-Kholmov, Havana 1965; 19 b3 ♗c5 ∞/= Suetin-Nei, USSR 1966) 17 ... ♖fe8! = ECO

[24] 13 ... ♘a5 14 b3 ♗d7 15 ♘f1 ± Karpov-Andersson, Stockholm 1969, and Geller-Mecking, Palma de Mallorca IZ 1970

[25] 16 ... ♘b7 17 ♘f1 ♗d7 18 ♗e3 ♖a8 19 ♕d2 ± Karpov-Unzicker, Nice Ol 1974

[26] 18 ♘3h2 f6 19 f4 ♘f7 20 ♘f3 ± Karpov-Spassky, USSR Ch 1973

[27] 20 ♖f1 ± Nunn-Short, Brussels 1986

[28] 13 ... ♖fe8 14 b3 cd (14 ... g6 15 ♗g5 ♘h5 16 ♗xe7 ♖xe7 17 ♘e3 ± Stein-Matanović, Tel Aviv Ol 1964) 15 cd ♖ac8 16 ♘e3 ♘c6 17 ♗b2 ± Matanović-Bisguier, Zagreb 1965

[29] 14 ♘e3 ♘xe3 15 ♗xe3 ± Tal-Petrosian, USSR Ch 1958, and Karpov-Petrosian, Milan 1975

[30] 17 ... g6 18 ♘g3 ♔g7 19 ♕f3 ♖h8 20 h6+ ♔g8 21 ♘f5 ±

[31] 20 ♕f3 g6 21 ♗d1! ± Kasparov-Petrosian, Banja Luka 1979

[32] **14 d5** ♘b4 15 ♗b1 a5 16 ♘f1 ♗d7 =

14 a3 ♗d7 15 ♘b3 (15 d5 ♘a5) 15 ... ♖fc8 = Smyslov-Dorfman, USSR Ch 1977

[33] **16 ... ♗e6** 17 a3 ♘a5 18 ♗d3 ♕b8 19 ♕e2 b4 (19 ... ♗d7 – 16 ... ♘b4) 20 ab ♕xb4 21 ♖eb1 ± Byrne-F.Olafsson, Reykjavik 1984

16 ... ♘b4 17 ♗b1 ♗d7 18 a3 ♘c6 19 ♗d3 (19 ♗a2!?) 19 ... ♕b8 20 ♕e2 ♘a5 21 ♖ec1! ± Hazai-Barle, Maribor 1985, and Byrne-Beelby, Hollywood 1985

[34] 17 ... ♕b7 18 ♕e2 ♖fe8 19 ♗d3 ♖ab8 20 a3 h6 21 de de 22 ♗c5 ± Spassky-Torre, Hamburg 1982

[35] 20 ♗b1 h6 21 ♘f1 ♗d8 22 ♘g3 ♘c6 23 ♖ed1 ± Timman-Torre, Indonesia 1983

[36] 14 ♘f1 ♖ac8 15 ♖e2 (15 ♗b1 ed! 16 ♘xd4 ♖fe8 = Kindermann-Honfi, Budapest 1986; 15 ♗d3 d5 16 ed e4 ∞; 16 de ♘xe4 17 ♘g3 f5 18 ef ♗xf6 ∞ ECO) 15 ... ♘h5 16 d5 (16 ♗d3 f5!? ∞ Ivanović-Kovačević, Zagreb 1985) 16 ... ♘c4 17 b3 ♘b6 intending ... ♗d7, ... ♘f4 ± Kovačević

[37] 14 ... ♖c8 15 b4 ♘c4 16 ♘xc4 bc (16 ... ♕xc4 17 ♖b1 ± Tseshkovsky-van Riemsdijk, Riga IZ 1979) 17 ♖e3 ♗d7 18 a4 ± Kremenetsky-Donchenko, Moscow Ch 1983

[38] 15 ♗b1 ♘h5 16 ♘f1 ♘f4 17 ♗h2! ± Thipsay-Littlewood, Commonwealth Ch 1985

[39] **16 ... ♘c5** 17 ♘g3 ♘xd3 18 ♕xd3 ♕c2 19 ♕xc2 ♖xc2 20 ♘f5 ♖e8 21 b3 ± Aseyev-Sturua, USSR 1985

16 ... ♘c4 17 b3 ♘cb6 (Short-Nunn, Naestved 1985) 18 ♗d2 ±

[40] 17 ef ♘c5 (17 ... ♗xd5 18 ♘g5) 18 ♗c2 ♘c4 19 ♘e3 (Sznapik-Pinter, Herculana Z 1982) 19 ... ♘b6! intending ... ♕b8-a8 ∞ Sznapik; 18 ♗g5 – 17 ♗g5

[41] 18 ... ♘c4 19 ♗xc4 bc 20 ♗xe7 ♕xe7 21 ♘e3 ♗d3 22 ♖e2 e4 23 ♘d2 ± Akopian-Guseinov, USSR 1986

[42] **19 ... ♕xe7** 20 ♗e2! ♗xf3 21 ♗xf3 b4 22 ♘e3 ±

19 ... ♗xf3 20 ♕xf3 ♕xe7 21 ♖ad1 ± Akopian

[43] 15 ♗d3 ♘c6 16 ♗e3 ed 17 ♘xd4 ♘e5 18 ♗c2 d5 = Byrne-Nikolić, Reykjavik 1986

15 ♖e2 ♖fe8 16 b3 (16 ♘g3 ♘c6 17 ♗e3 ed 18 ♘xd4 d5 = de Firmian-Hjartarson, New York 1984) 16 ... ♘c6 17 ♗b2 ♗f8 18 d5 (Anand-Thipsay, Indian Ch 1986) 18 ... ♘b4 19 ♗b1 a5 =

[44] 15 ... ♖fe8 16 b3 ± Popović-Smyslov, Portorož/Ljubljana 1985

[45] **16 a3** ♘xd4 17 ♘xd4 ed 18 ♕xd4 d5! ∓ Jansa-Pytel, Metz 1985, and Gavrikov-Hort, Tunis IZ 1985

16 ♗b3 ♘a5! = Geller-Hjartarson, Reykjavik 1984

16 ♗b1 ♘xd4 17 ♘xd4 ed 18 ♕xd4 ♗e6 = Sax-Hjartarson, Thessaloniki Ol 1984

[46] **19 ... g6** 20 ♗d2 ab 21 ab ♕b7 22 ♘h2! ± Jansa-Prasad, Calcutta 1986

19 ... ♖a8 20 ♗d2 ab 21 ab ♕b7 22 ♗d3 ♖fc8 ±/∞ Sax-Hardicsay, Hungary 1986

411

Index of Main Variations